McDougal Littell
CLASSZONE

Visit classzone.com and get connected.

ClassZone resources provide instruction, practice and learning support for students and parents.

Help with the Math

- @Home Tutor enables students to focus on the math and be more prepared for class, using animated examples and instruction.
- Extra examples similar to those in the book provide additional support.
- Hints and Homework Help offers assistance solving select homework exercises.

Games and Activities

- Crossword puzzles, memory games, and other activities help students connect to essential math concepts.
- Math Vocabulary Flipcards are a fun way to learn math terminology.

Practice, Practice, Practice

- eWorkbook includes interactive worksheets with additional practice problems.
- Problem of the Week features a new problem to solve every week.

Animated Math

- Engaging activities with animated problem-solving graphics support each lesson.

Access the online version of your textbook at classzone.com

Your complete text is available for immediate use!

McDougal Littell
Where Great Lessons Begin

Algebra 2

Concepts and Skills

Ron Larson • Laurie Boswell
Timothy D. Kanold • Lee Stiff

McDougal Littell

A DIVISION OF HOUGHTON MIFFLIN COMPANY

Evanston, Illinois • Boston • Dallas

About Algebra 2: Concepts and Skills

This book has been written so that all students can succeed in Algebra 2. The course focuses on the key topics that provide a strong foundation in algebra. Lesson concepts are presented in a clear, straightforward manner, supported by frequent worked-out examples. The page format makes it easy for students to follow the flow of a lesson, and the vocabulary and visual tips in the margins help students learn how to read the text and diagrams. Checkpoint questions within lessons give students a way to check their understanding as they go along. The exercises for each lesson provide many opportunities to practice and maintain skills, as well as to apply concepts to real-world problems.

Cover, Title page, Copyright page: McDougal Littell/Houghton Mifflin Company

Photography: iii *top* Meridian Creative Group; *top center* Jenks Studio, *bottom center* McDougal Littell/Houghton Mifflin Company, *bottom* Jerry Head Jr.; **vi** © Arnuif Husmo/Stone/Getty Images; **vii** NOAA/NESDIS; **viii** © Paul J. Sutton/Duomo/Corbis; **ix** © Purestock/Getty Images; **x** Henny Wiggers/AP Images; **xi** © Thinkstock/Alamy; **xii** © TAOLMOR/Shutterstock; **xiii** © Paola Kathuria/Alamy; **xiv** © Jim Reed/Corbis; **xv** © Bonnie Kamin/PhotoEdit; **xvi** © Lester Lefkowitz/The Image Bank/Getty Images; **xvii** © Hermann Erber/LOOK/Getty Images; **xviii** © Owaki/Kulla/Corbis; **xxvii** © Arnuif Husmo/Stone/Getty Images.

Illustration: xxi Steve Cowden

ISBN-13: 978-0-618-55210-8

ISBN-10: 0-618-55210-3

2 3 4 5 6 7 8 9 – DWO – 12 11 10 09 08

Internet Web Site: http://www.mcdougallittell.com

About the Authors

Ron Larson is a professor of mathematics at Penn State University at Erie, where he has taught since receiving his Ph.D. in mathematics from the University of Colorado. Dr. Larson is well known as the author of a comprehensive program for mathematics that spans middle school, high school, and college courses. Dr. Larson's numerous professional activities keep him in constant touch with the needs of teachers and supervisors. He closely follows developments in mathematics standards and assessment.

Laurie Boswell is a mathematics teacher at The Riverside School in Lyndonville, Vermont, and has taught mathematics at all levels, elementary through college. A recipient of the Presidential Award for Excellence in Mathematics Teaching, she was also a Tandy Technology Scholar. She served on the NCTM Board of Directors (2002–2005), and she speaks frequently at regional and national conferences on topics related to instructional strategies and course content.

Timothy D. Kanold is the superintendent of Adlai E. Stevenson High School District 125 in Lincolnshire, Illinois. Dr. Kanold served as a teacher and director of mathematics for 17 years prior to becoming superintendent. He is the recipient of the Presidential Award for Excellence in Mathematics and Science Teaching, and a past president of the Council for Presidential Awardees in Mathematics. Dr. Kanold is a frequent speaker at national and international mathematics meetings.

Lee Stiff is a professor of mathematics education in the College of Education and Psychology of North Carolina State University at Raleigh and has taught mathematics at the high school and middle school levels. He served on the NCTM Board of Directors and was elected President of NCTM for the years 2000–2002. He is a recipient of the W. W. Rankin Award for Excellence in Mathematics Education presented by the North Carolina Council of Teachers of Mathematics.

Teacher Reviewers and Advisers

Carol Armour
Math Department Chair
Central High School
Providence, RI

Craig Auten
Mathematics Teacher
Walled Lake Central
    High School
Walled Lake, MI

Kelly Berg
Math Department Chair
Dobson High School
Mesa, AZ

Doug Bloom
Mathematics Teacher
Elk River High School
Elk River, MN

David Boucher
Mathematics Teacher
Brunswick High School
Brunswick, ME

Jeffrey Bradley
Supervisor of Mathematics
Hempfield High School
Landisville, PA

Barbara Brooks
Mathematics Teacher
Mumford High School
Detroit, MI

Veronica Carlson
Mathematics Teacher
Moon Valley High School
Phoenix, AZ

Ronnee Sue Carpenter
Mathematics Teacher
Flint Southwestern Academy
Flint, MI

Gene De Costa
Mathematics Teacher
Henry Snyder High School
Jersey City, NJ

Diana Faoro
Mathematics Teacher
Romeo High School
Romeo, MI

John Gianotti
Math Department Chair
Argo Community High School
Summit, IL

Deborah Gomola
Mathematics Teacher
Sterling Heights High School
Sterling Heights, MI

Judy Hicks
Mathematics Teacher
Ralston Valley High School
Arvada, CO

Marjorie A. Hill
District Coordinating Teacher
    for Mathematics K–12
Blue Valley District School
Overland Park, KS

Robert Hose
Mathematics Teacher
Williamsport High School
Williamsport, MD

Judy Howell
Mathematics Teacher
La Plata High School
La Plata, MD

Kristen Karbon
Mathematics Teacher
Troy High School
Troy, MI

David Kaynor
Mathematics Teacher
East Detroit High School
Detroit, MI

Mary Ellen Kelly

Math Department Chair
St. John Neumann and Maria
  Goretti High School
Philadelphia, PA

Greg Kembitzky

Mathematics Teacher
Hilliard Davidson
  High School
Hilliard, OH

Andrea Kopco

Curriculum Leader
Midpark High School
Cleveland, OH

Kathy Lackow

Mathematics Teacher
Sabino High School
Tucson, AZ

Richard McGuinness

Math Coordinator
  K–12
Lynn Public Schools
Lynn, MA

Joseph Pawloski

Mathematics Teacher
Brighton High School
Brighton, MI

Donald Pratt

Mathematics Teacher
Huron High School
Ann Arbor, MI

Wayne Rumple

Mathematics Teacher
Monroe Senior High School
Monroe, MI

Ken Rundquist

Mathematics Teacher
Elk Grove High School
Elk Grove, IL

Michael Schulte

Mathematics Teacher
Warren Mott High School
Warren, MI

Brenda J. Taylor

Mathematics Teacher
Fenger Academy
Chicago, IL

Annemarie Tuffner

Mathematics Teacher
Neshaminy School District
Langhorne, PA

Vicalyn S. Tyson

Mathematics Teacher
Pickerington High School North
Pickerington, OH

Nancy Vander Tuuk

Math Department Chair
Mother McAuley Liberal Arts
  High School
Chicago, IL

Zen M. Villafuerte

Math Department Chair
Savanna High School
Anaheim, CA

Real Numbers, p. 4
$-117 < -113$

CHAPTER 1

Tools of Algebra

Student Help

Take Notes 2
Vocabulary *3, 9, 46, 47, 53*
Avoid Errors *7, 12, 17, 27, 29, 40, 41*
Help Notes *5, 22, 28, 32, 35, 41, 47*
Geometry *8, 15, 21, 31, 33, 39, 45, 51, 56*

Applications and Careers

Meteorologists *4*
Golf *7*
Bar Codes *8*
Mountain Biking *13*
Cell Phones *20*
Veterinary Technician *30*
Yearbook *35*
Skyscrapers *41*
Railroads *42*
Music *44*
High School Coach *48*
Space Missions *55*

ASSESSMENT

Chapter Summary
 and Review *57*
Chapter Test *61*
Chapter Standardized
 Test *62*

CHAPTER 2

Correlation, p. 111
$(0, 11), (1, 9), (2, 3), (3, 10)$

Linear Equations and Functions

Systems of Linear Equations

CHAPTER 4

Inequalities, p. 173
$1.5t + 9 \leq 45$

Inequalities and Absolute Value

Quadratic Equations, p. 257
$$h = -16t^2 + 6000$$

Quadratic Functions and Factoring

CHAPTER 6

Polynomial Models, p. 311
$$-3t^2 + 258t + 11,281$$

Polynomials and Polynomial Equations

Square Root Functions, p. 393

$$d = \sqrt{\frac{r}{30\sqrt{P}}}$$

Powers, Roots, and Radicals

Exponential Growth, p. 416
$$\frac{1}{7} \cdot 8^x - \frac{1}{7}$$

Exponential and Logarithmic Functions

Rational Functions, p. 477
$$s = \frac{1000}{0.6T^2 + 331}$$

Rational Equations and Functions

CHAPTER 10

Combinations, p. 549
$_9C_4$

Data Analysis and Probability

Sequences, p. 612
$33,000 + 2400n$

Discrete Mathematics

Trigonometric Ratios, p. 647
$$\csc 15° = \frac{x}{800}$$

Introduction to Trigonometry

Parabolic Models, p. 699
$$x^2 = 4py$$

Conic Sections

Contents of Student Resources

Help Right in Your Textbook

The Study Guide will help you prepare for each chapter

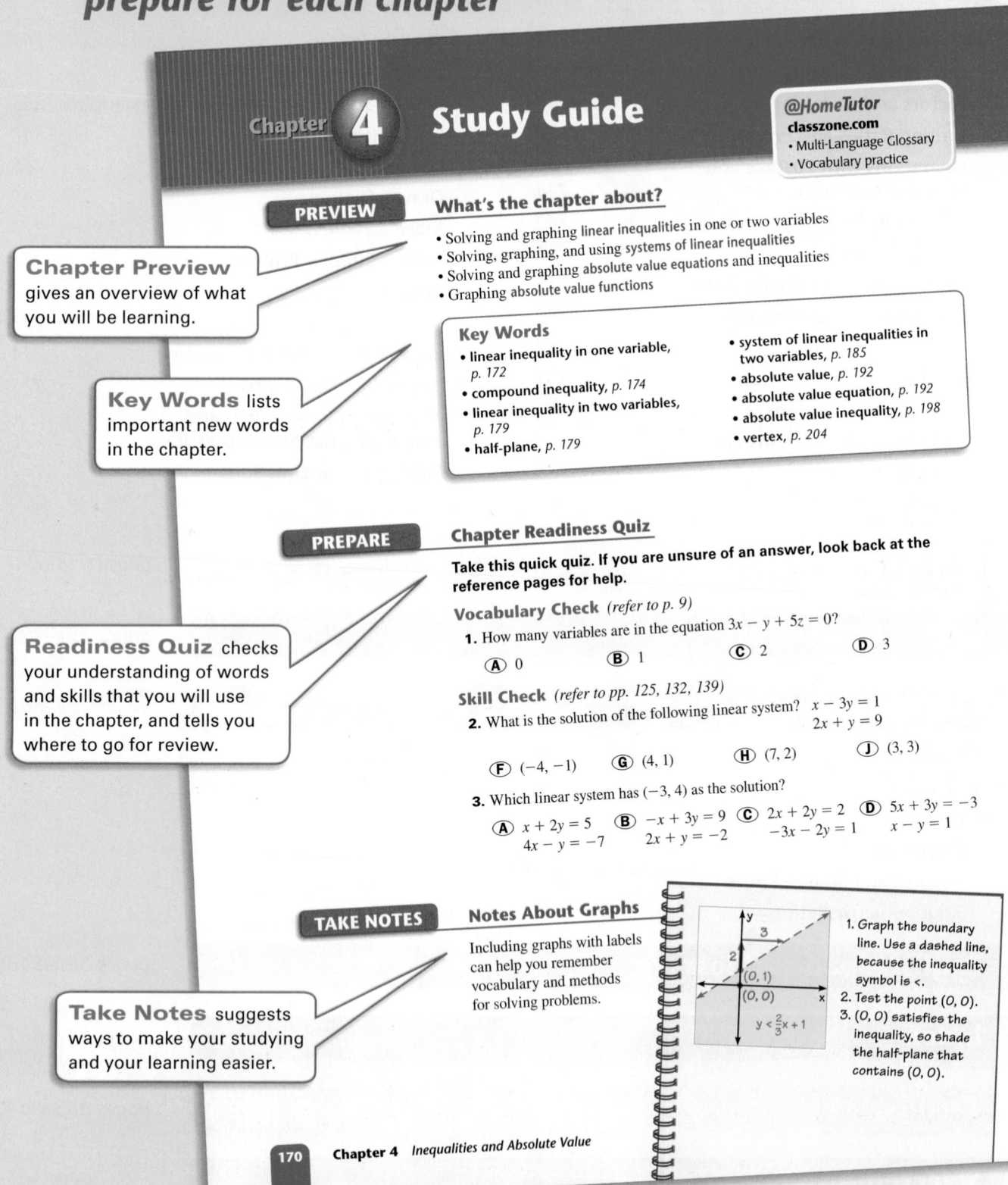

Chapter **4** **Study Guide**

@HomeTutor
classzone.com
• Multi-Language Glossary
• Vocabulary practice

PREVIEW **What's the chapter about?**

• Solving and graphing linear inequalities in one or two variables
• Solving, graphing, and using systems of linear inequalities
• Solving and graphing absolute value equations and inequalities
• Graphing absolute value functions

Chapter Preview gives an overview of what you will be learning.

Key Words
• linear inequality in one variable, *p. 172*
• compound inequality, *p. 174*
• linear inequality in two variables, *p. 179*
• half-plane, *p. 179*

• system of linear inequalities in two variables, *p. 185*
• absolute value, *p. 192*
• absolute value equation, *p. 192*
• absolute value inequality, *p. 198*
• vertex, *p. 204*

Key Words lists important new words in the chapter.

PREPARE **Chapter Readiness Quiz**

Take this quick quiz. If you are unsure of an answer, look back at the reference pages for help.

Vocabulary Check *(refer to p. 9)*
1. How many variables are in the equation $3x - y + 5z = 0$?

   Ⓐ 0   Ⓑ 1   Ⓒ 2   Ⓓ 3

Skill Check *(refer to pp. 125, 132, 139)*
2. What is the solution of the following linear system? $\begin{array}{l} x - 3y = 1 \\ 2x + y = 9 \end{array}$

   Ⓕ $(-4, -1)$ Ⓖ $(4, 1)$ Ⓗ $(7, 2)$ Ⓙ $(3, 3)$

Readiness Quiz checks your understanding of words and skills that you will use in the chapter, and tells you where to go for review.

3. Which linear system has $(-3, 4)$ as the solution?

   Ⓐ $\begin{array}{l} x + 2y = 5 \\ 4x - y = -7 \end{array}$ Ⓑ $\begin{array}{l} -x + 3y = 9 \\ 2x + y = -2 \end{array}$ Ⓒ $\begin{array}{l} 2x + 2y = 2 \\ -3x - 2y = 1 \end{array}$ Ⓓ $\begin{array}{l} 5x + 3y = -3 \\ x - y = 1 \end{array}$

TAKE NOTES **Notes About Graphs**

Including graphs with labels can help you remember vocabulary and methods for solving problems.

1. Graph the boundary line. Use a dashed line, because the inequality symbol is <.
2. Test the point $(0, 0)$.
3. $(0, 0)$ satisfies the inequality, so shade the half-plane that contains $(0, 0)$.

$y < \frac{2}{3}x + 1$

Take Notes suggests ways to make your studying and your learning easier.

Use Student Help notes as your guide on the side

Reading Notes help you with learning vocabulary, understanding notation, and getting information from graphs.

Avoid Errors point out ways to avoid the more common errors.

STUDENT HELP

HOMEWORK HELP
Example 1: Exs. 16–23
Example 2: Exs. 24–31
Example 3: Exs. 32–43
Example 4: Exs. 44–55

▲ **Other Student Help notes** will help you by providing *solving notes, homework help, another way* to solve problems, and where to *look back* for review of previous skills.

STUDENT HELP

READING GRAPHS
A dashed line indicates that the points on the line are *not* solutions. A solid line indicates that the points on the line are solutions.

STUDENT HELP

AVOID ERRORS
Because your test point cannot be on the boundary line, you may not always be able to use (0, 0). In that case, test another convenient point, such as (0, 1), (1, 0), or (1, 1).

EXAMPLE 2 **Graph Linear Inequalities in One Variable**

Graph (a) $y < -2$ and (b) $x \le 3$ in a coordinate plane.

Solution

a. **Graph** the boundary line $y = -2$. Use a dashed line because $y < -2$.

Test the point (0, 0). It is *not* a solution, so shade the half-plane that does not contain (0, 0).

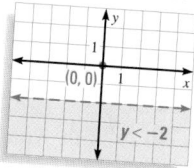

b. **Graph** the boundary line $x = 3$. Use a solid line because $x \le 3$.

Test the point (0, 0). It *is* a solution, so shade the half-plane that contains (0, 0).

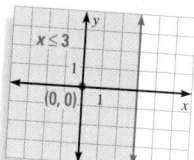

Checkpoint ✓ **Graph Linear Inequalities in One Variable**

Graph the inequality in a coordinate plane.

5. $x > -1$ **6.** $y \ge 1$ **7.** $y \le -3$ **8.** $x < 4$

EXAMPLE 3 **Graph Linear Inequalities in Two Variables**

Graph (a) $y < 2x$ and (b) $3x - 2y \ge 8$ in a coordinate plane.

Solution

a. **Graph** the boundary line $y = 2x$. Use a dashed line because $y < 2x$.

Test the point (1, 1). Because (1, 1) *is* a solution, shade the half-plane that contains (1, 1).

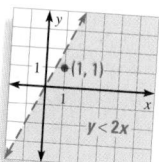

b. **Graph** the boundary line $3x - 2y = 8$. Use a solid line because $3x - 2y \ge 8$.

Test the point (0, 0). Because (0, 0) is *not* a solution, shade the half-plane that does not contain (0, 0).

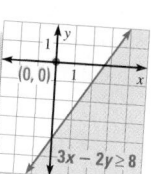

Checkpoint ✓ **Graph Linear Inequalities in Two Variables**

Graph the inequality in a coordinate plane.

9. $y \ge x$ **10.** $y \le -3x$ **11.** $x + 2y < 6$ **12.** $x - 3y > 1$

Use the diagrams and art to help you understand real-world problems.

Pre-Course Test

FRACTIONS, DECIMALS, AND PERCENTS

Skills Review Handbook
pp. 743–746

Write the percent as a decimal.

1. 4% **2.** 6.5% **3.** 0.92% **4.** 108%

Write the fraction as a decimal and as a percent. Round the percent to the nearest whole number.

5. $\dfrac{24}{25}$ **6.** $\dfrac{17}{40}$ **7.** $\dfrac{18}{54}$ **8.** $\dfrac{49}{28}$

Answer the question.

9. What is 33% of 66? **10.** 52% of what number is 104? **11.** What percent of 78 is 26?

Find the least common denominator.

12. $\dfrac{3}{4}, \dfrac{1}{3}$ **13.** $\dfrac{5}{6}, \dfrac{1}{18}$ **14.** $\dfrac{1}{4}, \dfrac{1}{6}, \dfrac{3}{8}$ **15.** $\dfrac{1}{2}, \dfrac{2}{5}, \dfrac{7}{10}$

Perform the indicated operation(s). Simplify the result.

16. $\dfrac{5}{8} + \dfrac{9}{10}$ **17.** $\dfrac{2}{9} - \dfrac{1}{8}$ **18.** $\dfrac{12}{15} + \dfrac{2}{3} + \dfrac{3}{5}$ **19.** $\dfrac{5}{6} - \dfrac{7}{9} + \dfrac{1}{3}$

WRITING RATIOS AND PROPORTIONS

Skills Review Handbook
p. 747

Solve the proportion.

20. $\dfrac{7}{x} = \dfrac{21}{15}$ **21.** $\dfrac{x}{11} = \dfrac{36}{66}$ **22.** $\dfrac{3}{4} = \dfrac{x}{50}$ **23.** $\dfrac{20}{4} = \dfrac{16}{x}$

INTEGERS AND SCIENTIFIC NOTATION

Skills Review Handbook
pp. 748–751

Perform the indicated operation.

24. $-7 + 19$ **25.** $-25 + (-5)$ **26.** $-10 - 14$ **27.** $-18 - (-9)$

28. $(-4)(5)$ **29.** $(-7)(-6)$ **30.** $-18 \div 3$ **31.** $-56 \div (-8)$

Write the number in scientific notation.

32. 1581 **33.** 0.0004 **34.** 97,000,000,000 **35.** 0.00000205

THE COORDINATE PLANE

Skills Review Handbook
p. 752

Plot and label the ordered pairs in a coordinate plane.

36. $A(-4, -4)$ **37.** $B(-1, 5)$ **38.** $C(0, -3)$ **39.** $D(4, 2)$

Find the perimeter or circumference of the figure.

40. a rectangle with length 4 ft and width 7 ft

41. a circle with radius 3 in.

42. a triangle with sides 2 m, 5 m, and 6 m

43. a circle with diameter 8 cm

Find the area of the figure.

44. a parallelogram with height 2 yd and base 9 yd

45. a circle with diameter 18 cm

46. a triangle with base 4 in. and height 7 in.

47. a square with sides 12 m

Find the volume of the solid.

48. a box with length 12 cm, width 8 cm, and height 6 cm

49. a cylinder with diameter 3.8 m and height 2 m

50. a box with length 4 in., width 4 in., and height 3 in.

51. a cube with sides of length 2.3 in.

Can a triangle have the given angle measures? Explain.

52. $12°, 23°, 145°$

53. $10°, 95°, 100°$

54. $40°, 50°, 88°$

55. $3°, 15°, 162°$

Can the given side lengths form a triangle? Explain.

56. 2, 4, 6

57. 3, 5, 12

58. 4, 7, 9

59. 12, 14, 22

Find the value of *x*. Give your answer in simplest radical form.

60.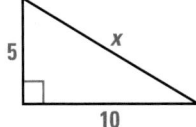

61.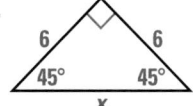

62.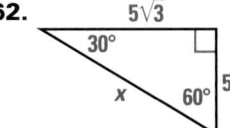

Give the coordinates of *P*(3, 2) and *Q*(−1, 4) after the transformation. For rotations, rotate about the origin.

63. Translate 2 units up.

64. Rotate 90° counterclockwise.

65. Translate 4 units right.

Write the phrase as an algebraic expression.

66. 32 less than a number

67. 8 more than twice a number

68. 5 times a number

69. 7 less than 3 times a number

70. 6 times a number divided by 7

71. 3 more than a number

Solve the equation.

72. $1 = 21 - 4x$

73. $10 = 9 - 0.5x$

74. $3(2x - 3) = -7x$

75. $2(x + 11) = 5$

Pre-Course Practice

FRACTIONS, DECIMALS, AND PERCENTS

Skills Review Handbook pp. 743–746

Write the percent as a decimal.

1. 55%   **2.** 34%   **3.** 120%   **4.** 0.25%

Write the fraction as a decimal and as a percent. Round the percent to the nearest whole number.

5. $\dfrac{9}{40}$ **6.** $\dfrac{19}{55}$ **7.** $\dfrac{84}{90}$ **8.** $\dfrac{43}{50}$

Write the decimal as a percent and as a fraction in simplest form.

9. 0.6   **10.** 2.78   **11.** 0.875   **12.** 1.375

Answer the question.

13. What is 23% of 70?   **14.** 130% of what number is 85?   **15.** What percent of 34 is 9?

Perform the indicated operation(s). Simplify the result.

16. $\dfrac{7}{15} + \dfrac{3}{10}$ **17.** $\dfrac{5}{7} - \dfrac{1}{4}$ **18.** $\dfrac{2}{5} + \dfrac{2}{3} + \dfrac{3}{5}$ **19.** $\dfrac{1}{3} + \dfrac{3}{4} - \dfrac{1}{6}$

WRITING RATIOS AND PROPORTIONS

Skills Review Handbook p. 747

Write the ratio in simplest form. Express the answer in three ways.

1. 12 to 8   **2.** 28 : 200   **3.** $\dfrac{21}{36}$ **4.** $\dfrac{15}{45}$

Solve the proportion.

5. $\dfrac{36}{x} = \dfrac{9}{17}$ **6.** $\dfrac{x}{8} = \dfrac{15}{24}$ **7.** $\dfrac{7}{10} = \dfrac{x}{44}$ **8.** $\dfrac{25}{32} = \dfrac{3}{x}$

INTEGERS, SIGNIFICANT DIGITS, AND SCIENTIFIC NOTATION

Skills Review Handbook pp. 748–751

Perform the indicated operation.

1. $-2 + 15$ **2.** $-21 + (-4)$ **3.** $-8 - 5$ **4.** $-11 - (-11)$

5. $3(-14)$ **6.** $-18(-9)$ **7.** $27 \div (-3)$ **8.** $-16 \div (-4)$

Simplify the expression. Write your answer with the appropriate number of significant digits.

9. $145 + 15$ **10.** $18.08 - 0.9$ **11.** $0.005 \cdot 1000$ **12.** $0.027 \div 300$

Write the number in scientific notation.

13. 631   **14.** 0.00045   **15.** 52,000,000   **16.** 0.000079

THE COORDINATE PLANE

Give the coordinates of the point on the graph.

1. A **2.** B

3. C **4.** D

5. E **6.** F

7. G **8.** H

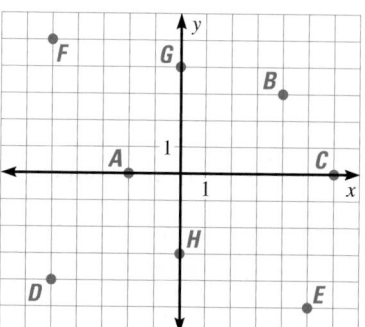

Plot and label the ordered pairs in a coordinate plane.

9. $A(3, 4)$, $B(-1, 5)$, $C(0, 6)$ **10.** $A(-7, 5)$, $B(-4, 0)$, $C(-3, -5)$

PERIMETER, CIRCUMFERENCE, AREA, AND VOLUME

Find the perimeter or circumference of the figure.

1. a triangle with sides 4 m, 7 m, and 12 m

2. a square with sides of 4.2 in.

3. a circle with diameter 3.8 cm

4. a semicircle with diameter 4 ft

Find the area of the figure.

5.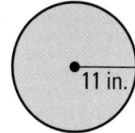

6.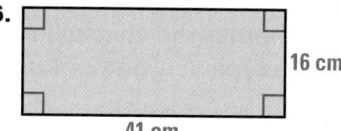

7.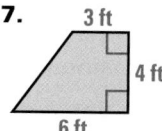

Find the volume of the solid.

8.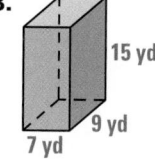

9.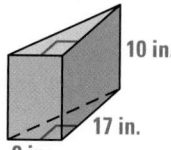

10.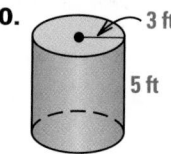

TRIANGLE RELATIONSHIPS

Can a triangle have the given angle measures? Explain.

1. 24°, 62°, 94°   **2.** 32°, 90°, 95°   **3.** 60°, 60°, 60°   **4.** 8°, 48°, 80°

Can the given side lengths form a triangle? Explain.

5. 5, 12, 13   **6.** 18, 14, 32   **7.** 7, 9, 11   **8.** 20, 32, 48

Find the value of *x*. Give your answer in simplest radical form.

9.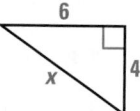

10.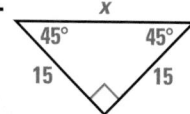

11.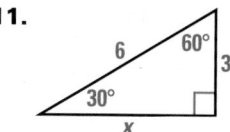

Identify any lines of symmetry.

1.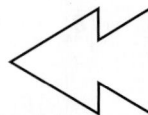

2.

3.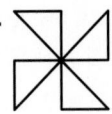

Give the coordinates of $A(-3, -5)$ and $B(0, 4)$ after the transformation. For rotations, rotate about the origin.

4. Translate 4 units up.

5. Translate 3 units down.

6. Rotate 90° clockwise.

The two polygons are similar. Find the value of x.

7.

8.

9.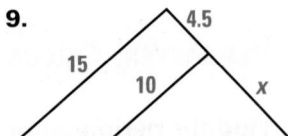

Use logical reasoning to decide whether the conclusion is *valid* or *invalid*. If the conclusion is valid, name the type of argument used.

1. If $ABCD$ is a square, then $ABCD$ is a rhombus.
$ABCD$ is a rhombus.
Therefore, $ABCD$ is a square.

2. If $x = 4$, then $2x - 7 = 1$.
If $2x - 7 = 1$, then $2x = 8$.
Therefore, if $x = 4$, then $2x = 8$

Determine whether the statement is *true* or *false*. If it is false, give a counterexample.

1. If an integer is not negative, then it is positive.

2. If a triangle has 3 equal angle measures, then it is an equilateral triangle.

3. If B is 7 inches from A and 4 inches from C, then A is 11 inches from C.

Name the property that justifies the statement.

4. If $3x - 4 = 17$, then $3x = 21$.

5. If $4x = 2.4$, then $x = 0.6$.

6. If $8(2x - 3) = 5$, then $16x - 24 = 5$.

7. If $7x + 8 = 15$, then $7x = 7$.

8. If $12x + 9 = 18$, then $4x + 3 = 6$

9. If $\dfrac{x + 13}{2} = 10$, then $x + 13 = 20$.

Solve the equation for x. Justify each step.

10. $2x = 32$

11. $x + 4 = 12$

12. $x - 18 = 2$

13. $-x + 3 = 7$

14. $4x - 5 = 15$

15. $\dfrac{x}{2} = -7$

16. $-3(x - 6) = 9$

17. $\dfrac{1}{3}(12 - 3x) = 5$

PROBLEM SOLVING STRATEGIES

Skills Review Handbook
pp. 768–773

Use an equation, formula, diagram, table, or list to solve the problem.

1. A teacher must choose 2 students from a group of 5 to participate in a spelling bee. How many different possibilities are there?

2. A triangle with an area of 15 square feet has a base length of $2x$ feet and a height of 5 feet. How long is the base of the triangle?

3. John is driving from his home to the store. He drives the car 4.5 miles due east and 6 miles due south. How far is the store from John's home?

Solve the problem by first solving simpler problems.

4. What is the area of the figure at the right?

5. Without using a calculator, compute $(2000)^5$.

6. What is the last digit of $(547,348)^6$?

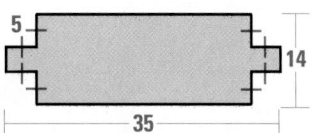

Use the strategy *guess*, *check*, and *revise* to solve the problem.

7. You have $100 to buy 1 pair of jeans and some t-shirts. The jeans cost $25 and the t-shirts cost $8. How many t-shirts can you buy?

8. The sum of 4 consecutive integers is 50. What are the integers?

TRANSLATING WORDS INTO SYMBOLS

Skills Review Handbook
p. 774

Write the phrase as an algebraic expression.

1. 15 less than a number

2. 11 minus twice a number

3. 2 times a number

4. the quotient of a number and 4

5. 1 more than half a number

6. the cube of a number

COMBINING LIKE TERMS AND MULTIPLYING POLYNOMIALS

Skills Review Handbook
pp. 775–776

Simplify the expression by combining like terms.

1. $5a - 3 + 2a - 6$

2. $3n^2 + n - 4 + n^2 - 8n$

3. $5x(x - 1) - x^2 + x$

4. $y^2 + xy - 2y^2$

Find the product.

5. $(x + 2)(x - 2)$

6. $(x + 3)(x - 9)$

7. $(4 + x)(x - 6)$

8. $(x - 3)(x - 8)$

SOLVING LINEAR EQUATIONS

Skills Review Handbook
p. 777

Solve the equation.

1. $3x - 5 = 14$

2. $\frac{2}{3}t + 8 = 6$

3. $-0.25m + 7 = 4$

4. $-6x - 9 = 45$

5. $c + 12 = 4c - 6$

6. $2y - 5 = 10 - 8y$

7. $0.8k = -0.2k - 3$

8. $-(x + 9) = 10$

9. $6(x - 3) = -6$

10. $3(c - 12) = 4 - c$

11. $4(n - 3) = -6(2n + 1)$

12. $5(3x + 7) = 15$

Tools of Algebra

▶ How can you compare temperatures recorded in the Arctic?

APPLICATION: Arctic

Scientists collect data about the environment to track and analyze conditions. The environment in the Arctic is known for its extremely cold temperatures. In Lesson 1.1 you will learn how using a number line can help you compare and order temperatures.

Think & Discuss

The table shows the record low temperatures for five months in Barrow, Alaska.

Month	Low temperature
August	21°F
September	1°F
October	−32°F
November	−38°F
December	−51°F

1. Is the record low temperature colder in September or October?

2. Is the record low temperature warmer in October or November?

3. Name a temperature that would set a new record low temperature in December in Barrow, Alaska.

Learn More About It

You will use a number line to order temperatures at the South Pole in Example 3 on page 4.

@HomeTutor
classzone.com
• Multi-Language Glossary
• Vocabulary practice

PREVIEW | **What's the chapter about?**

• Evaluating and simplifying algebraic expressions
• Solving linear equations and rewriting formulas
• Using verbal and algebraic models to solve real-life problems
• Analyzing and representing data

Key Words

• origin, graph, coordinate, *p. 3*
• opposite, reciprocal, *p. 5*
• base, exponent, power, *p. 9*
• numerical expression, *p. 9*
• variable, *p. 10*
• algebraic expression, *p. 10*
• term, coefficient, *p. 16*
• like terms, constant term, *p. 16*
• simplified expression, *p. 17*

• equation, linear equation, *p. 26*
• solution, *p. 26*
• mean, median, mode, *p. 46*
• range, *p. 47*
• box-and-whisker plot, *p. 47*
• lower quartile, *p. 47*
• upper quartile, *p. 47*
• histogram, *p. 52*
• frequency distribution, *p. 52*

PREPARE | **Chapter Readiness Quiz**

Take this quick quiz. If you are unsure of an answer, look at the reference pages for help.

Vocabulary Check *(refer to pp. 3, 9)*

1. Which of the following is *not* a rational number?

Ⓐ -4 Ⓑ 2 Ⓒ $\frac{7}{3}$ Ⓓ π

2. Which part of the expression 3^5 is the exponent?

Ⓕ 3 Ⓖ 5 Ⓗ 3^5 Ⓙ 243

Skill Check *(refer to p. 4)*

3. Choose the value that forms a true statement: $-0.5 < \underline{\ ?\ }$.

Ⓐ $-\frac{1}{4}$ Ⓑ $-\frac{1}{2}$ Ⓒ $-\frac{3}{4}$ Ⓓ $-\frac{3}{2}$

TAKE NOTES | **Keep a Notebook**

Keep a notebook that includes new vocabulary, properties, and worked-out examples. You can keep your homework in a separate section.

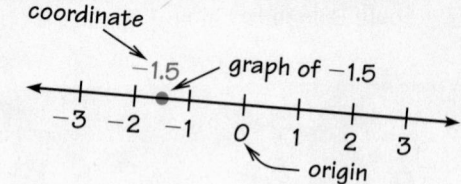

Vocabulary related to Number Lines

coordinate

-1.5 ⟶ graph of -1.5

-3 -2 -1 0 1 2 3

origin

1.1 Real Numbers and Number Operations

Key Words
- origin
- graph
- coordinate
- opposite
- reciprocal

Prerequisite Skills

Order the numbers from least to greatest.

1. $0.95, 0.09, 0.192, 0.7\overline{9}$

2. $3.55, 3.\overline{3}, 0.3, 3.13$

3. $\frac{1}{2}, \frac{3}{5}, \frac{1}{4}, \frac{5}{16}$

4. $\frac{4}{3}, \frac{5}{8}, \frac{3}{4}, \frac{3}{2}$

STUDENT HELP

READING ALGEBRA
The three dots at the end of a number show that the digits continue without end.
The symbol $\approx$ means *is approximately equal to.*

GOAL Graph, order, and use real numbers.

How cold does it get at the South Pole?

In Example 3, you will list five of the lowest recorded monthly temperatures at the South Pole from least to greatest. You will use this list to find the lowest temperature.

The numbers that are used most often in algebra are the *real numbers.* Every real number is either a *rational number* or an *irrational number.*

Integers and whole numbers are subsets of the rational numbers.

REAL NUMBERS

Rational Numbers	Irrational Numbers
$\frac{3}{4} = 0.75 \quad -\frac{1}{3} = -0.333...$ $-4 \quad$ **Integers** $\quad -1 \quad -27$ $0 \quad 5 \quad$ **Whole Numbers** $\quad 16$	$\sqrt{2} \approx 1.414213...$ $-\sqrt{14} \approx -3.74165...$ $\pi \approx 3.14159...$

Rational numbers
- can be written as the ratios of integers
- can be written as decimals that terminate or repeat

Irrational numbers
- cannot be written as the ratios of integers
- cannot be written as decimals that terminate or repeat

Real numbers can be pictured as points on a line called a *real number line.* The numbers increase from left to right, and the point labeled 0 is the **origin**.

origin

$-5 \quad -4 \quad -3 \quad -2 \quad -1 \quad 0 \quad 1 \quad 2 \quad 3 \quad 4 \quad 5$

The point on a number line that corresponds to a real number is the **graph** of the number. Drawing the point is called *graphing* the number or *plotting* the point. The number that corresponds to a point on a number line is the **coordinate** of the point.

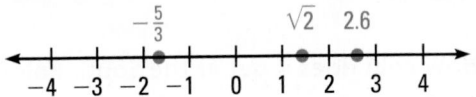

EXAMPLE 1 Graph Numbers on a Number Line

Graph the real numbers $-\frac{5}{3}$, $\sqrt{2}$, and 2.6.

Solution

First, recall that $-\frac{5}{3} = -1\frac{2}{3}$, so $-\frac{5}{3}$ is between -2 and -1. Then, approximate $\sqrt{2}$ as a decimal to the nearest tenth: $\sqrt{2} \approx 1.4$. Finally, graph the numbers.

Inequality Symbols A number line can be used to order real numbers. The *inequality symbols* $<$, $\leq$, $>$, and $\geq$ can be used to compare two numbers.

EXAMPLE 2 Compare Real Numbers

Graph the numbers -1 and -4. Then compare them using the symbol $<$ or $>$.

Solution

Begin by graphing both numbers on a real number line.

Because -4 is to the left of -1, it follows that -4 is *less than* -1, or $-4 < -1$. You can also say that -1 is *greater than* -4, or $-1 > -4$.

Link to
CAREERS

METEOROLOGISTS working at the South Pole provide information for scientists and researchers who study global weather.

EXAMPLE 3 Order Temperatures

Science The table shows the record low temperatures for five months at the South Pole. Use a number line to order the temperatures from lowest to highest.

Month	May	June	July	Aug.	Sept.
Record low temp.	$-109°F$	$-117°F$	$-113°F$	$-108°F$	$-111°F$

Solution

ANSWER ▶ From lowest to highest, the temperatures are $-117°F$, $-113°F$, $-111°F$, $-109°F$, and $-108°F$.

Checkpoint ✓ Graph and Order Real Numbers

Graph the numbers on a number line. Then write the numbers in order from least to greatest.

1. 5, -2, -3 **2.** -6, -3, -10 **3.** $-\frac{3}{2}$, $\sqrt{2}$, -0.5

STUDENT HELP

SOLVING NOTE
- If *a* is positive, then its opposite is negative.
- The opposite of 0 is 0.
- If *a* is negative, then its opposite is positive.

Opposite and Reciprocal The **opposite**, or *additive inverse*, of any number a is $-a$. The **reciprocal**, or *multiplicative inverse*, of any nonzero number a is $\frac{1}{a}$. When you add or multiply real numbers, several properties can help you.

Properties of Addition and Multiplication

Let a, b, and c be real numbers.

PROPERTY	ADDITION	MULTIPLICATION
Commutative	$a + b = b + a$	$ab = ba$
Associative	$(a + b) + c = a + (b + c)$	$(ab)c = a(bc)$
Identity	$a + 0 = a, 0 + a = a$	$a \cdot 1 = a, 1 \cdot a = a$
Inverse	$a + (-a) = 0$	$a \cdot \frac{1}{a} = 1, a \neq 0$

The following property involves both addition and multiplication.

Distributive	$a(b + c) = ab + ac$

EXAMPLE 4 Use Properties of Real Numbers

Show how you can use the distributive property to evaluate $5 \cdot 203$.

Solution

$$5 \cdot 203 = 5(200 + 3) \qquad \text{Rewrite 203 as } 200 + 3.$$
$$= 5(200) + 5(3) \qquad \text{Distributive property}$$
$$= 1000 + 15 = 1015 \qquad \text{Simplify.}$$

Subtraction and Division Subtraction is defined as *adding the opposite*. Division is defined as *multiplying by the reciprocal*.

Subtraction: $a - b = a + (-b)$ **Division:** $\frac{a}{b} = a \cdot \frac{1}{b}, b \neq 0$

EXAMPLE 5 Operations with Real Numbers

a. Find the difference of 4 and -9.

$$4 - (-9) = 4 + 9 \qquad \text{Add 9, the opposite of } -9.$$
$$= 13 \qquad \text{Simplify.}$$

b. Find the quotient of -15 and $\frac{1}{3}$.

$$-15 \div \frac{1}{3} = -15 \cdot 3 \qquad \text{Multiply by 3, the reciprocal of } \frac{1}{3}.$$
$$= -45 \qquad \text{Simplify.}$$

Checkpoint ✓ *Operations with Real Numbers*

Select and perform an operation to answer the question.

4. What is the quotient of -16 and $-\frac{1}{2}$?   **5.** What is the product of -5 and 8?

1.1 Exercises

Guided Practice

Vocabulary Check

1. List two ways that a rational number is different from an irrational number.

2. What is the opposite of 2.8?

3. Explain how you could use the distributive property to find the product $4 \cdot 298$.

Tell whether the statement is *always*, *sometimes*, or *never* true. Explain your reasoning.

4. An integer is an irrational number.

5. An integer is a rational number.

6. A whole number is an integer.

7. A rational number is an integer.

Skill Check

Graph the numbers on a number line. Then decide which number is greater.

8. 3 and -5 9. 8 and 13   10. -4 and -7

Identify the property shown.

11. $3 + (-3) = 0$ 12. $8 + 3 = 3 + 8$

13. $7 \cdot 11 = 11 \cdot 7$ 14. $13 \cdot 1 = 13$

Practice and Applications

STUDENT HELP

HOMEWORK HELP
Example 1: Exs. 15–23,
         36–41
Example 2: Exs. 24–29
Example 3: Exs. 30–41
Example 4: Exs. 42–49
Example 5: Exs. 50–58

Using a Number Line **Graph the numbers on a number line.**

15. -2 and 3   16. -9 and -11 17. -6 and 0.2

18. -3.3 and -3.9 19. $\frac{1}{2}$ and -5 20. $-\frac{1}{2}$ and $-\frac{1}{3}$

21. 0.6 and $\frac{2}{3}$ 22. $-\frac{7}{4}$ and -1.7 23. $-\frac{7}{2}$ and $\sqrt{7}$

Comparing Numbers **Graph the numbers on a number line. Then compare the numbers using the symbol < or >.**

24. -53 and -78 25. -2.36 and -1.04 26. $-\sqrt{4}$ and -2.1

27. $\frac{2}{5}$ and $\frac{1}{6}$ 28. $-\frac{3}{2}$ and $-\frac{2}{3}$ 29. $-\frac{7}{12}$ and $-\frac{9}{14}$

Ordering Numbers **Graph the numbers on a number line. Then write the numbers in order from least to greatest.**

30. $-3, 5, -6, 0, -10$ 31. $5, 3, -5, 6, -1$

32. $1, -\frac{5}{2}, 4.5, -0.5, 6$ 33. $3.2, \frac{3}{2}, -2, 8, -3.6$

34. $\sqrt{5}, 3, -5, -\frac{5}{2}, -1$ 35. $-4.2, -5, -\sqrt{8}, 4.8, 4.5$

GOLF Michelle Wie won the 2003 U.S. Women's Amateur Public Links Championship at age 13. She was the youngest winner ever of a USGA adult event.

Golf Scores Use the information to complete the following.

The table shows the final scores of several competitors in a masters golf tournament. The lowest golf score indicates the best position in the tournament.

36. Graph the golf scores on a number line. Label each point with the name of the player.

37. List the players in order from lowest score to highest score.

38. Which player has the lowest score?

Player	Score
Se Ri Pak	−12
Angela Standford	+2
Michelle Wie	−15
Annika Sorenstam	−9
Karrie Webb	−16
Meg Mallon	+6

Geography Use the information to complete the following.

The table shows the elevations, in feet, of five locations in Imperial Valley, California.

39. Graph the elevations on a number line. Label each point with the name of the location.

40. List the locations in increasing order based on their elevation.

41. Which locations have elevations below −100 feet?

Location	Elevation (ft)
Alamorio	−135
Curlew	−93
Gieselmann Lake	−162
Moss	−100
Orita	−92

Naming Properties Identify the property shown.

42. $2 \cdot 8 = 8 \cdot 2$

43. $(3 + 5) + 7 = 3 + (5 + 7)$

44. $(6 \cdot 3) \cdot 8 = 6 \cdot (3 \cdot 8)$

45. $4(9 + 2) = 4 \cdot 9 + 4 \cdot 2$

Distributive Property Use the distributive property to evaluate the expression.

46. $8(302)$

47. $11(190)$

48. $-6(0.95)$

Error Analysis Describe and correct the error.

49.
$$9(603) = 9(600 + 3)$$
$$= 9 \cdot 600 + 3$$
$$= 5400 + 3$$
$$= 5403$$
✗

50.
$$6 \div \left(-\frac{3}{2}\right) = 6 \cdot \left(-\frac{3}{2}\right)$$
$$= -\frac{18}{2}$$
$$= -9$$
✗

Operations Select and perform an operation to answer the question.

51. What is the sum of −8 and 25?

52. What is the product of −12 and −3?

53. What is the quotient of −15 and $-\frac{5}{3}$?

54. What is the difference of 3 and −4?

55. What is the product of −6 and 0?

56. What is the sum of −7 and −5?

57. What is the difference of −10 and −1?

58. What is the quotient of 7 and $-\frac{1}{2}$?

0 25215 04658 2

first digit   check digit

BAR CODES Using the operations on this bar code produces $(0 + 5 + 1 + 0 + 6 + 8)(3) + (2 + 2 + 5 + 4 + 5) = 78$. The next greatest multiple of 10 is 80, and $80 - 78 = 2$, which is the check digit.

Bar Codes In Exercises 59 and 60, use the following information.

Almost all products sold in the United States have a Universal Product Code (UPC), or bar code. The last digit of the UPC code is called the *check digit*. This digit allows a scanner to quickly determine whether an item was scanned correctly or not. The following operations are performed on the first eleven digits. The result should equal the check digit.

- Add the six digits in the odd-numbered positions. Multiply by 3.

- Add the five digits in the even-numbered positions. Do *not* add the check digit.

- Add the results of the first two steps.

- Subtract the result of the previous step from the next highest multiple of 10.

59. Does a UPC of 0 45674 05326 6 check? Explain.

60. Does a UPC of 0 28835 71293 5 check? Explain.

Challenge In Exercises 61 and 62, tell whether the statement is *true* or *not true* for all real numbers *a*, *b*, and *c*. Explain your reasoning.

61. $(a - b) + c = a - (b + c)$ **62.** $(-a) \cdot (-b) = (-b) \cdot (-a)$

Standardized Test Practice

63. Multiple Choice What is the quotient of 12 and $-\frac{1}{4}$?

   A -48 **B** -3 **C** 3   **D** 48

64. Multiple Choice Which set of numbers is in increasing order?

   F $-5.2, 5, -7, 7.1, \frac{7}{2}$ **G** $-7, -5.2, 5, \frac{7}{2}, 7.1$

   H $-5.2, -7, \frac{7}{2}, 5, 7.1$ **J** $-7, -5.2, \frac{7}{2}, 5, 7.1$

Mixed Review

Operations with Signed Numbers **Perform the operation.** (Skills Review Handbook, p. 748)

65. $7 - (-2)$ **66.** $-6 + 8$ **67.** $(-7)(-7)$ **68.** $-21 \div 3$

Fractions and Decimals **Write the decimal as a fraction in simplest form.** (Skills Review Handbook, p. 743)

69. 0.25 **70.** 0.3 **71.** 0.8

Algebraic Expressions **Write the given phrase as an algebraic expression.** (Skills Review Handbook, p. 774)

72. 6 more than a number *n*   **73.** 14 times a number *n*

74. 4 less than a number *n*   **75.** $\frac{1}{5}$ of a number *n*

Geometry Skills

Find the perimeter and the area of the geometric figure.

76.

14 ft

7 ft   7 ft

14 ft

77.

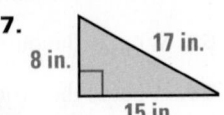

8 in.   17 in.

15 in.

78.

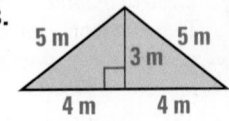

5 m   3 m   5 m

4 m   4 m

1.2 Algebraic Expressions and Models

Key Words
- base
- exponent
- power
- numerical expression
- variable
- algebraic expression

Prerequisite Skills

Simplify.

1. $2 \cdot 2 \cdot 2 \cdot 2$

2. $(-4)(-4)(-4)$

3. $-(7 - 9)$

4. $-(5 \cdot 5 \cdot 5)$

GOAL Define and use algebraic expressions.

In Lesson 1.1, you worked with addition, subtraction, multiplication, and division. In this lesson you will work with exponents. The figures below show how exponents are used to represent repeated factors in multiplication.

 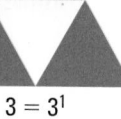  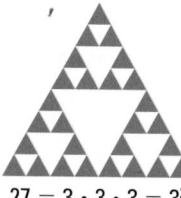 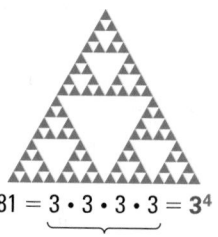

$3 = 3^1$ $9 = 3 \cdot 3 = 3^2$ $27 = 3 \cdot 3 \cdot 3 = 3^3$ $81 = \underbrace{3 \cdot 3 \cdot 3 \cdot 3}_{4 \text{ factors of } 3} = 3^4$

The **exponent** in a **power** tells the number of times the **base** is used as a factor.

$$\overset{\text{exponent}}{\underset{\underset{\text{power}}{\text{base}}}{7^3}} = 7 \cdot 7 \cdot 7$$

EXAMPLE 1 Evaluate Powers

a. $-2^4 = -(2 \cdot 2 \cdot 2 \cdot 2)$
   $= -16$

b. $(-2)^4 = (-2) \cdot (-2) \cdot (-2) \cdot (-2)$
   $= 16$

Checkpoint ✓ *Evaluate Powers*

Evaluate the power.

1. 4^3

2. $(-3)^2$

3. -3^3

4. 2^1

In Example 1, notice how parentheses are used in part (b) to show that the base is -2. In the expression -2^4, however, the base is 2, not -2. An *order of operations* helps avoid confusion when evaluating numerical expressions. A **numerical expression** consists of numbers, operations, and grouping symbols.

STUDENT HELP

READING ALGEBRA
The expression 3^4 is read *three to the fourth power.* Two commonly used powers have special names.
3^2 three squared
5^3 five cubed

Order of Operations

STEP ❶ Perform operations that occur within grouping symbols.

STEP ❷ Evaluate powers.

STEP ❸ Perform multiplications and divisions from left to right.

STEP ❹ Perform additions and subtractions from left to right.

EXAMPLE **2** **Use Order of Operations**

$$36 \div 4 \cdot (-1 + 4)^2 = 36 \div 4 \cdot 3^2 \qquad \text{Add within parentheses.}$$
$$= 36 \div 4 \cdot 9 \qquad \text{Evaluate power.}$$
$$= 9 \cdot 9 \qquad \text{Divide.}$$
$$= 81 \qquad \text{Multiply.}$$

Algebraic Expressions A **variable** is a letter that is used to represent one or more numbers. Any number used to replace a variable is a *value of the variable*. An expression involving variables is called an **algebraic expression**.

When you replace the variables in an algebraic expression with numbers, you are *evaluating* the expression, and the result is called the *value of the expression*. To evaluate an algebraic expression, substitute values for the variables and then simplify using the order of operations.

EXAMPLE **3** **Evaluate an Algebraic Expression**

Evaluate $2(x + 5) - 7x$ when $x = 4$.

Solution

$$2(x + 5) - 7x = 2(4 + 5) - 7(4) \qquad \text{Substitute 4 for } x.$$
$$= 2(9) - 7(4) \qquad \text{Add within parentheses.}$$
$$= 18 - 28 \qquad \text{Multiply.}$$
$$= -10 \qquad \text{Subtract.}$$

EXAMPLE **4** **Evaluate an Algebraic Expression**

Evaluate $4p^2 - (2p - 9)$ when $p = -3$.

Solution

$$4p^2 - (2p - 9) = 4(-3)^2 - [2(-3) - 9] \qquad \text{Substitute } -3 \text{ for } p.$$
$$= 4(9) - [2(-3) - 9] \qquad \text{Evaluate power.}$$
$$= 36 - [-6 - 9] \qquad \text{Multiply.}$$
$$= 36 - (-15) \qquad \text{Subtract within parentheses.}$$
$$= 51 \qquad \text{Add the opposite.}$$

Checkpoint ✓ *Evaluate Expressions*

Evaluate the expression.

5. $8 - 3 + 7$ **6.** $-2 \div 2 + 6 \cdot 4$ **7.** $4 - 3(7 - 5)^2$

Evaluate the expression for the given value of the variable.

8. $-3 + 6(y + 1)$ when $y = 2$ **9.** $-2w^2 + 8w + 11$ when $w = -5$

An expression that represents a real-life situation is a *mathematical model*.

EXAMPLE 5 **Write and Evaluate a Mathematical Model**

Shopping You have $40 and are buying some DVDs that cost $12 each. Write an expression that shows how much money you have left after buying *d* DVDs. Evaluate the expression when *d* = 2 and *d* = 3.

Solution

VERBAL MODEL		Original amount	−	Price per DVD	·	Number of DVDs bought

LABELS   Original amount = 40   (dollars)

Price per DVD = 12   (dollars per DVD)

Number of DVDs bought = *d*   (DVDs)

ALGEBRAIC MODEL $40 - 12d$

ANSWER ▶ If you buy 2 DVDs, you will have $40 - 12(2) = \$16$ left.
If you buy 3 DVDs, you will have $40 - 12(3) = \$4$ left.

Unit Analysis In Example 5, you can use *unit analysis* to check that your units make sense. Notice how units within a term can be canceled.

$$\text{dollars} - \left(\frac{\text{dollars}}{\text{DVD}}\right)(\text{DVDs}) = \text{dollars} - \text{dollars} = \text{dollars}$$

Link to
GEOGRAPHY

MEXICO Each year, about 10,000 students from the United States spend the year studying in Mexico.

EXAMPLE 6 **Write and Evaluate a Mathematical Model**

Mexico For a trip to Mexico you need to exchange some U.S. dollars for Mexican pesos. The exchange rate is 11 pesos per dollar. You already have 110 pesos left from a previous trip. Write an expression that shows how many pesos you will have after exchanging *d* dollars. Evaluate the expression for *d* = 250.

Solution

VERBAL MODEL	Pesos per dollar	·	Dollars exchanged	+	Pesos you already have

LABELS   Number of pesos per dollar = 11   (pesos per dollar)

Number of dollars being exchanged = *d*   (dollars)

Number of pesos you already have = 110   (pesos)

ALGEBRAIC MODEL $11d + 110$

ANSWER ▶ When you exchange $250, you will have $11(250) + 110 = 2860$ pesos.

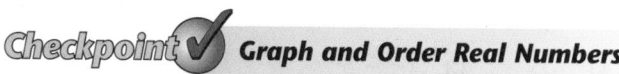

Checkpoint ✓ *Graph and Order Real Numbers*

10. Repeat Example 5 if you have $60 to spend and each DVD costs $16.

1.2 Exercises

Guided Practice

Vocabulary Check

1. Copy 7^5 and label the base and exponent. What does each number represent?

2. What do you call an expression that involves only numbers and operation symbols?

3. When you substitute 3 for n to evaluate the algebraic expression $2n + 1$, what is the value of the variable? What is the value of the expression?

4. An algebraic model is an algebraic expression that represents a real-life situation. Compare this meaning of *model* to other English meanings.

Skill Check **Evaluate the power.**

5. 2^3 6. 3^4 7. $(-6)^2$ 8. -6^2

Evaluate the expression for the given value of x.

9. $x - 6$ when $x = 9$ 10. $4(2 + x)$ when $x = 3$

11. $x(x + 5)$ when $x = -3$ 12. $(x - 2)^3$ when $x = 1$

Error Analysis Describe and correct the error.

13.
$$3 + (2 \cdot 5)^2 = 3 + 2 \cdot 25$$
$$= 3 + 50$$
$$= 53$$

14.
$$3(5) + 2(5) = 3(5 + 2)$$
$$= 3(7)$$
$$= 21$$

Practice and Applications

STUDENT HELP

HOMEWORK HELP
Example 1: Exs. 15–32
Example 2: Exs. 33–44
Example 3: Exs. 45–64
Example 4: Exs. 45–64
Example 5: Exs. 65–73
Example 6: Exs. 65–73

Writing Powers Write the expression using exponents.

15. nine to the fourth power 16. 3 to the fourth power

17. n to the sixth power 18. 4 to the nth power

19. $7 \cdot 7 \cdot 7 \cdot 7 \cdot 7 \cdot 7$ 20. $y \cdot y \cdot y \cdot y \cdot y$

Evaluating Powers Evaluate the power.

21. 2^5 22. 5^2 23. 4^4 24. 9^2

25. $(-3)^4$ 26. -3^4 27. -7^2 28. $(-7)^1$

29. $(-4)^3$ 30. -4^1 31. $(-1)^7$ 32. $(-1)^8$

Using Order of Operations Evaluate the expression.

33. $20 - 10 + 8$ 34. $8 \cdot 4 \div 2$ 35. $8 + (3 \cdot 4) - 3$

36. $5 + 3 \cdot 4 \div 6$ 37. $16 \div (6 - 2) \cdot 5$ 38. $3(-6 + 5)^5 + 10$

39. $3^3 - (7 - 4)^2$ 40. $(7 - 5) \cdot (8 + 6) \div 7$ 41. $(18 - 12) \cdot (-3^2)$

42. $(5 - 8 + 2 \cdot 4)^2$ 43. $20^2 - 5^2$ 44. $(20 - 5)^2$

Evaluating Expressions **Evaluate the expression when $x = 3$.**

45. $x + 7$ **46.** $5x$ **47.** x^2 **48.** $x^3 + x$

Evaluating Expressions **Evaluate the expression for the given value.**

49. $x + 9$ when $x = 8$ **50.** $28 + 4x$ when $x = -6$

51. $16(x - 21)$ when $x = 23$ **52.** $4x(6 - 3x)$ when $x = 3$

53. $2x^2 + 4x + 8$ when $x = -4$ **54.** $2x^2 - 4x + 12$ when $x = 5$

Evaluating Expressions **Evaluate the expression for the given values of x and y.**

55. $x + 8y$ when $x = 4$ and $y = 2$ **56.** $6y - x$ when $x = -6$ and $y = 4$

57. $5x + 4y$ when $x = 5$ and $y = -3$ **58.** $9y - 6x$ when $x = 0.7$ and $y = 0.5$

59. $y(x - 5)^2$ when $x = 3$ and $y = 3$ **60.** $x(4 + y)^2$ when $x = 4$ and $y = -7$

61. $x - \dfrac{y}{x}$ when $x = 8$ and $y = -8$ **62.** $x + \dfrac{y}{x} - y$ when $x = 14$ and $y = 10$

63. *Statistics Link* The population of Florida (in thousands) from 1995 through 2005 can be modeled by $316t + 14{,}194$ where t is the number of years since 1995. For 1995, where $t = 0$, the model approximates Florida's population as $316(0) + 14{,}194 = 14{,}194$ *thousands*, or 14,194,000. Substitute 10 for t in the expression to approximate Florida's population in 2005.

64. **Mountain Biking** You ride a bicycle through the mountains. You average 6 miles per hour riding uphill and 22 miles per hour riding downhill. You can model your total distance by $6u + 22d$ where u is your total hours riding uphill and d is your total hours riding downhill. Use the model to find your distance if you ride uphill for 4 hours and downhill for 1 hour.

Exercise **In Exercises 65 and 66, use the following information.**

In 1992, the number of people in the United States who walked for exercise was about 67.8 million. From 1992 through 2005, the number of people walking for exercise increased by an average of about 1.42 million people per year.

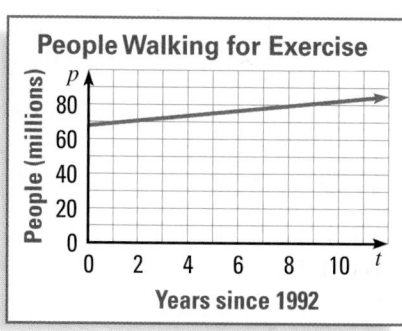

People Walking for Exercise

| VERBAL MODEL | Average increase of people per year | · | Years since 1992 | + | Number of people in 1992 |

LABELS   Number of people in 1992 = 67.8   (millions of people)

Average increase per year = 1.42   (millions of people per year)

Years since 1992 = t (years)

65. Use the verbal model and labels to write an algebraic expression for the number of people who walked for exercise t years after 1992.

66. Evaluate the expression when $t = 5$, $t = 8$, and $t = 10$. Explain what these results mean in the context of the problem.

CAR WASH Many nonprofit organizations hold car washes to raise money. *Free* car washes work by finding sponsors who pay a small amount for every car that is washed.

Car Wash In Exercises 67–69, use the following information.

Your class holds a car wash to raise money for a local charity. You pay $35 for cleaning supplies. You charge $5.50 for each vehicle you wash.

VERBAL MODEL		Charge per car	$\cdot$	Number of cars	$-$	Amount paid for cleaning supplies

LABELS	Charge per car $= 5.50$	(dollars per car)
	Number of cars $= n$	(cars)
	Amount paid for cleaning supplies $= 35$	(dollars)

67. Use the verbal model and labels to write an algebraic expression for the amount of money you raise by washing n cars.

68. Evaluate the expression when $n = 70$ and $n = 100$.

69. Explain what each result from Exercise 68 means in the context of the problem.

70. Movie Rentals You buy a DVD player for $57. You rent movies for $4.28 each. Write an expression to represent the total amount that you spend for the DVD player and renting x movies during the first year. Evaluate the expression if you rent a total of 65 movies during the year.

71. Used Cars You buy a used car with 67,150 miles on the odometer. You expect to drive the car 12,500 miles each year. Write an expression for the expected number of miles on the odometer after t years. Evaluate the expression to find the expected number of miles on the odometer on the day you have owned the car for 4 years.

72. Shopping Centers There were about 40,000 shopping centers in the United States in 1993. From 1993 through 2005, the number of shopping centers increased by an average of about 740 per year. Write an expression that models the number of shopping centers n years after 1993. Use the model to approximate the number of shopping centers in 2003.

73. Challenge You earn $40 per week delivering newspapers. You also earn $6.50 per hour pet-sitting for your neighbors on the weekend. Write an expression that shows your total weekly earnings. Evaluate the expression if you spent 6 hours pet-sitting last weekend.

Standardized Test Practice

74. Multiple Choice Evaluate the power -3^4.

 (**A**) -81 (**B**) -64 (**C**) 64 (**D**) 81

75. Multiple Choice What is the value of the expression below?

$$6 \cdot 3 + (9 - 7) \cdot 2$$

 (**F**) 13 (**G**) 22 (**H**) 30 (**J**) 40

76. Multiple Choice What is the value of the expression $x^3 + x^2$ when $x = 4$?

 (**A**) 20 (**B**) 80 (**C**) 96 (**D**) 1024

77. Multiple Choice Which expression has a value of 22?

 (**F**) $(5 + 3) \cdot 3 - 2$ (**G**) $5 + 3 + 3 \cdot 2$

 (**H**) $(4 + 5)^2 - 7$ (**J**) $3 \cdot 2^2 - (8 + 6)$

Using a Number Line Graph the numbers on a number line. Then compare the numbers using the symbol < or >. *(Lesson 1.1)*

78. -4 and 7

79. -4 and -5

80. -5.1 and -5.8

81. $\frac{1}{4}$ and $\frac{2}{3}$

82. $-\frac{4}{5}$ and -0.6

83. $\sqrt{5}$ and 2.2

Identifying Properties Identify the property shown. *(Lesson 1.1)*

84. $6 \cdot 8 = 8 \cdot 6$

85. $9 + 0 = 9$

86. $(3 \cdot 5) \cdot 2 = 3 \cdot (5 \cdot 2)$

87. $5 \cdot \frac{1}{5} = 1$

Distributive Property Use the distributive property to evaluate the expression. *(Lesson 1.1)*

88. $4(89)$

89. $40(19)$

90. $8(403)$

Geometry Skills

Area Write an expression for the area of the figure. Then evaluate the expression for the given value(s) of the variable(s).

91. $n = 30$

92. $r = 5, s = 3$

93. $a = 9, b = 3$

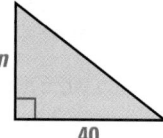
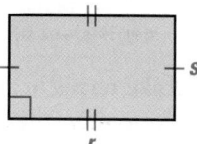
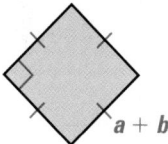

Quiz 1

Lesson 1.1   Graph the numbers on a number line. Then write the numbers in order from least to greatest.

1. $-7, 7, -4, 3, 1$

2. $-4, -\frac{7}{2}, -3.8, -\frac{13}{3}$

3. $1, -2.5, 4.5, -0.5, 6$

4. $3.2, -0.7, \frac{3}{4}, -\frac{3}{2}, 0$

Lesson 1.1   Identify the property shown.

5. $4 + 5 = 5 + 4$

6. $\frac{1}{9} \cdot 9 = 1$

7. $8 + 12 + (-12) = 8 + 0$

8. $(11 \cdot 7) \cdot 2 = 11 \cdot (7 \cdot 2)$

Lesson 1.2   Evaluate the power.

9. 2^5

10. -10^4

Lesson 1.2   Evaluate the expression when $x = -2$.

11. $(7x + 4) + 3(x - 1)$

12. $2(3x^2 + 5)$

Lesson 1.2   **13. Savings** You have $155 in a savings account. You decide to add $20 to the account every week. Write an expression that shows your savings after n weeks. Evaluate the expression to find your savings after 6 weeks.

1.3 Simplifying Algebraic Expressions

Key Words
- terms
- coefficient
- like terms
- constant terms
- simplified expression

Prerequisite Skills

Simplify.

1. $(3 + 1 + 6)p$

2. $(-24 - 11)y$

3. $(-5 - (-8))x$

4. $(4 + 7 - 10)q$

GOAL Simplify algebraic expressions.

How much does it cost to rent a rowboat?

In Example 5, you will use an *algebraic expression* to help answer this question.

For an expression such as $2x + 1$, the parts that are added together, $2x$ and 1, are called **terms**. In a term with a variable, such as $2x$ or $5x^2$, the number is the **coefficient** of the term.

$$-x^2 + 4x$$

−1 is the coefficient of x^2.   4 is the coefficient of *x*.

Like terms in an expression have the same variable with matching exponents. For example, $4x^2$ and $2x^2$ are like terms. The terms x^2 and x are *not* like terms. They have the same variable but not the same exponent. **Constant terms** such as -3 and 2 are also considered like terms.

EXAMPLE 1 Identify Terms in an Expression

Identify the terms in the expression $-11 - 7x - 2x^2$.

Solution

Write the expression as a sum. $-11 - 7x - 2x^2 = -11 + (-7x) + (-2x^2)$

ANSWER ▶ The terms of the expression are -11, $-7x$, and $-2x^2$.

EXAMPLE 2 Identify Coefficients and Like Terms

Identify the coefficients and like terms in the expression $x^2 - 7x + 5 - 3x^2 - 10$.

Solution

Begin by writing the expression as a sum in order to identify the terms.

$$x^2 - 7x + 5 - 3x^2 - 10 = x^2 + (-7x) + 5 + (-3x^2) + (-10)$$

ANSWER ▶ The coefficients of the expression are 1, -7, and -3. The terms x^2 and $-3x^2$ are like terms. The terms 5 and -10 are also like terms.

 **Identify Terms, Coefficients, and Like Terms**

1. Identify the terms, coefficients, and like terms in the expression $4x^3 - 5x^2 + x^2 - 9x - 9x^3 + 7x$.

Simplified Expressions The distributive property lets you *combine like terms* by adding the coefficients. An expression is **simplified** if it has no grouping symbols and if all the like terms have been combined.

Two algebraic expressions are *equivalent* if, when you substitute the same value for the variable in each expression, you always get the same result. For example, the expressions $5x^2 + 2x^2$ and $7x^2$ are equivalent.

EXAMPLE 3 Simplify by Combining Like Terms

Simplify the expression.

   a. $5x + 9x$ **b.** $2x^2 + 3x - x^2 + 6x$ **c.** $4y - 7x - 12y + 3x$

Solution

  a. $5x + 9x = (5 + 9)x$ Distributive property

            $= 14x$ Add.

  b. $2x^2 + 3x - x^2 + 6x = (2x^2 - x^2) + (3x + 6x)$ Group like terms.

                  $= (2 - 1)x^2 + (3 + 6)x$ Distributive property

                  $= x^2 + 9x$ Add or subtract.

  c. $4y - 7x - 12y + 3x = (4y - 12y) + (-7x + 3x)$ Group like terms.

                  $= (4 - 12)y + (-7 + 3)x$ Distributive property

                  $= -8y - 4x$ Add or subtract.

EXAMPLE 4 Simplify Expressions with Grouping Symbols

Simplify the expression.

   a. $12 - 5(x - 1)$ **b.** $4(6 - x) + 3(x - 8)$

Solution

  a. $12 - 5(x - 1) = 12 - 5x + 5$ Distributive property

               $= -5x + (12 + 5)$ Group like terms.

               $= -5x + 17$ Add.

  b. $4(6 - x) + 3(x - 8) = 24 - 4x + 3x - 24$ Distributive property

                  $= (-4x + 3x) + (24 - 24)$ Group like terms.

                  $= (-4 + 3)x + (24 - 24)$ Distributive property

                  $= -x$ Add or subtract.

STUDENT HELP

AVOID ERRORS
Be extra careful when the expression involves subtractions or negative signs. In part (a) of Example 4, you need to multiply each term in the parentheses by -5.

Checkpoint ✓ *Simplify Expressions*

Simplify the expression.

  2. $7x - 3x$ **3.** $1 + x + 10x - 8$ **4.** $x + x^2 - 4x^2 - 5x$

  5. $3 + 2(x + 4)$ **6.** $x - 6(x - 2)$ **7.** $3(x - 1) - (x - 9)$

EXAMPLE **5** **Use a Real-Life Model**

Rowboat Rentals A boat rental company charges customers for rowboats as shown in the advertisement. There is a 1 hour minimum rental time.

a. Write and simplify an expression that gives the total cost to rent a rowboat for h hours, where $h \geq 1$.

b. Find the total cost of renting a rowboat for 8 hours.

Solution

a.

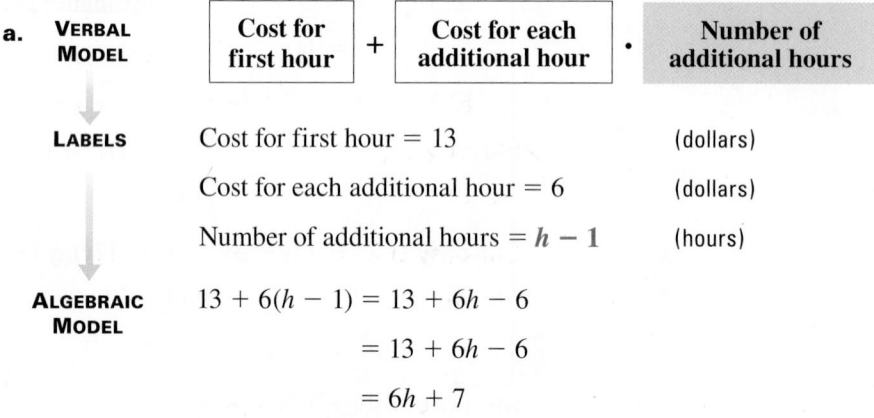

| **VERBAL MODEL** | Cost for first hour | + | Cost for each additional hour | · | Number of additional hours |

LABELS   Cost for first hour = 13   (dollars)

Cost for each additional hour = 6   (dollars)

Number of additional hours = $h - 1$ (hours)

ALGEBRAIC MODEL

$$13 + 6(h - 1) = 13 + 6h - 6$$
$$= 13 + 6h - 6$$
$$= 6h + 7$$

ANSWER ▶ The total cost of renting a rowboat for 1 hour or longer is given by the expression $6h + 7$.

b. To find the total cost of renting a rowboat for 8 hours, evaluate the expression for $h = 8$.

$6h + 7 = 6(8) + 7$ Substitute 8 for h.

$= 48 + 7$ Multiply.

$= 55$ Add.

ANSWER ▶ Renting a rowboat for 8 hours will cost $55.

 **Use a Real-Life Model**

A calling card charges $1 for all phone calls up to 15 minutes and $.25 for each additional minute.

8. Write and simplify an expression that gives the total cost of a phone call that lasts m minutes, where m is at least 15.

9. Use your answer from Exercise 8 to find the total cost of a phone call that lasts for 28 minutes.

10. Use your answer from Exercise 8 to find the total cost of a phone call that lasts for 1 hour 10 minutes.

Guided Practice

Vocabulary Check

1. Is $3x$ a term in the expression $14 - 3x$? Explain.

2. In the expression $3x^2 - 7x + 2$, what is the coefficient of the x^2-term? What is the coefficient of the x-term?

Copy and complete the statement.

3. The terms in an expression that have the same variable with matching exponents are __?__.

4. An expression that has no grouping symbols and has all like terms combined is called __?__.

5. Two algebraic expressions that have the same value for all values of their variable(s) are called __?__.

Skill Check

Identify the terms in the expression.

6. $12 - 4x$
7. $-5y + 3$
8. $w^2 - 2w + 8$

Simplify the expression by combining like terms.

9. $9p + 4p$
10. $7d^2 - 3 - d^2 + 7$

11. $5s^2 + 5s + s^2 - 7s$
12. $3x - 4x^2 - 8x^2 - 6x$

Simplify the expression.

13. $4(x + 1) - 2x$
14. $6 + 12(n - 3)$

15. $5(2 - r) + 3r$
16. $7(a + 4) - 5(a - 6)$

$7a + 28 - 5a - 30$

17. Jobs There were about 155,000 physical therapy jobs in the United States in 2004. The expected number of physical therapy jobs in the following years can be modeled by the expression $163{,}370 + 4185(t - 2)$, where t represents the number of years after 2004. Simplify the expression. Then find the expected number of physical therapy jobs in the United States in 2008.

Practice and Applications

STUDENT HELP

HOMEWORK HELP
Example 1: Exs. 18–23
Example 2: Exs. 24–29
Example 3: Exs. 30–38
Example 4: Exs. 39–50
Example 5: Exs. 51–56

Identifying Terms Identify the terms in the expression.

18. $5t + 9$
19. $11f - 3$

20. $-14x + 3y$
21. $8m - 12n$

22. $4k - k^2 + 5k - 2$
23. $9 - 3w + 2w^2 + 12$

Identifying Coefficients and Like Terms Identify the coefficients and like terms in the expression.

24. $7a + 2a$
25. $5b^2 - 10b^2$

26. $s + 5 + 6s$
27. $2m + 1 + 3m + 3$

28. $-4w + 9 + w - 3w^2$
29. $13x^2 - 5x + 6x - 2x^2$

Combining Like Terms Simplify the expression by combining like terms.

30. $-2c + 7c$

31. $3y - 4y$

32. $5d - 2 - d$

33. $-7h + 6h + 8$

34. $9z + 15 - 2z$

35. $10 - 4n - 7 - 6n$

36. $6r - 2t + 5r + t$

37. $4p + 2p^2 - 2p + p^2$

38. $7x^2 + 2x - x^2 - x$

Simplifying Expressions Simplify the expression.

39. $-2(m - 2) + 3m$
$-2m - 4$

40. $7 + 5(f + 2)$

41. $-(z + 2) + 3z$

42. $2(a + 1) - 5(a - 1)$
$2a + 2 \quad 5a - 5$

43. $-4(b + 2) - (9 - b)$
$-4b + 8$

44. $-3(4 - 2k) + 5$
$-12 + 6k + 5$

45. $5(h^2 + h) - 3(h^2 - 2h)$

46. $5(x + y) - 3(x - y)$

47. $4(2g - 1) - 6g$

48. $12(n - 3) + 3(n + 13)$

49. $3 - 2(1.5w + 7)$

50. $x(x - 3) + 2(x - 4)$

Cable TV Rates In Exercises 51–53, use the following information.

You subscribe to a digital cable TV service that also provides access to pay-per-view movies. The monthly fee for the service is $43.49, which includes 3 pay-per-view movies. Each additional pay-per-view movie costs $3.99.

VERBAL MODEL	Monthly fee	+	Cost for each additional movie	·	Number of additional movies

LABELS   Monthly fee = 43.49   (dollars)

Cost for each additional movie = 3.99   (dollars per movie)

Number of additional movies = $m - 3$ (movies)

51. Use the verbal model and labels to write an expression that gives the total cost for a month in which you ordered m pay-per-view movies. Assume that you order at least 3 movies.

52. Simplify the expression.

53. Find the total cost for your cable service last month when you ordered 8 pay-per-view movies.

Cell Phones In Exercises 54–56, use the following information.

A cell phone company charges you a monthly fee of $35.00 for up to 400 minutes of cell phone usage and $.35 for each additional minute.

VERBAL MODEL	Monthly fee	+	Cost for each additional minute	·	Number of additional minutes

LABELS   Monthly fee = 35.00   (dollars)

Cost for each additional minute = 0.35   (dollars per minute)

Number of additional minutes = $m - 400$ (minutes)

54. Use the verbal model and labels to write an expression that gives the total cost of your monthly cell phone bill when you use m minutes. Assume that you use at least 400 minutes.

55. Simplify the expression.

56. Use your expression to find the total cost of your cell phone bill when you use 450 minutes.

57. Multiple Choice Which expression is *not* a term in the expression $3x - 7y + z - 12$?

    (A) $3x$ **(B)** $7y$ **(C)** z **(D)** -12

58. Multiple Choice Which expression is simplified?

    (F) $7 + 3x - 2$ **(G)** $2x + 7x$

    (H) $6 + 4x - 5x^2$ **(J)** $2x + 3x^2 - 7x$

59. Multiple Choice Simplify the expression $6y + 2y^2 - 3y^2 - y$.

    (A) $5y - y^2$ **(B)** $6y - 2y^2$ **(C)** $7y + y^2$ **(D)** $8y - 4y^2$

60. Multiple Choice Simplify the expression $-(z - 2) + 4z$.

    (F) $3z - 2$ **(G)** $3z + 2$ **(H)** $5z - 2$ **(J)** $5z + 2$

Least Common Denominator **Find the least common denominator.** *(Skills Review Handbook, p. 745)*

61. $\dfrac{2}{3}, \dfrac{3}{5}$ **62.** $\dfrac{1}{10}, \dfrac{3}{40}$ **63.** $\dfrac{5}{8}, \dfrac{7}{36}$

64. $\dfrac{1}{2}, \dfrac{3}{4}, \dfrac{4}{5}$ **65.** $\dfrac{1}{2}, \dfrac{1}{4}, \dfrac{5}{6}$ **66.** $\dfrac{1}{4}, \dfrac{3}{8}, \dfrac{3}{10}$

67. $\dfrac{1}{3}, \dfrac{2}{5}, \dfrac{3}{7}$ **68.** $\dfrac{2}{3}, \dfrac{1}{6}, \dfrac{5}{9}$ **69.** $\dfrac{1}{2}, \dfrac{3}{4}, \dfrac{5}{16}$

70. The table shows the lowest recorded temperatures for five months in Detroit, Michigan.

Months	Dec.	Jan.	Feb.	Mar.	Apr.
Temperature (°F)	-10	-21	-15	-4	10

List the months in increasing order based on these temperatures. Which months have a record low temperature below $-12°F$? *(Lesson 1.1)*

Finding Reciprocals **Give the reciprocal of the number.** *(Lesson 1.1)*

71. -11 **72.** 5 **73.** $\dfrac{5}{8}$ **74.** $-\dfrac{5}{4}$

75. $\dfrac{7}{15}$ **76.** $-\dfrac{1}{8}$ **77.** 42 **78.** -33

Order of Operations **Evaluate the expression.** *(Lesson 1.2)*

79. $15 - 7 + 8$ **80.** $6 \div 2 \cdot 3$ **81.** $8 + 3 \cdot 5 - 1$

82. $1 + 2 \cdot 6 \div 3$ **83.** $-2(1 + 3) - 1$ **84.** $6 - 4(5 - 3)$

85. $9 \cdot 4 - 2(5^2 - 10)$ **86.** $-7(8 - 3^2)$ **87.** $(6 - 2^2)^3$

Perimeter **Write an expression for the perimeter of the figure. Then simplify the expression.**

88.

$3x$

$2(x - 1)$ $2(x - 1)$

$3x$

89.

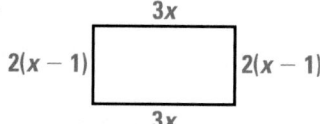

$8(x - 1)$

$x + 7$

$2(x + 4)$

USING A GRAPHING CALCULATOR *(For use with Lesson 1.3)*
Evaluating Expressions

You can use a scientific calculator or a graphing calculator to evaluate expressions. Keystrokes for evaluating several expressions are shown below. Because the keystrokes shown may not be the same keystrokes for your calculator, make sure you know how to evaluate the expressions using your calculator.

On a scientific calculator, notice the difference between the change sign key, [+/−], and the subtraction key, [−]. Likewise, on a graphing calculator, the negation key, [(−)], and the subtraction key, [−], do not perform the same operation.

STUDENT HELP

KEYSTROKE HELP
See keystrokes for several models of calculators at www.classzone.com.

EXAMPLE 1

	Expression	Calculator	Keystrokes	Result
a.	$-3^2 + 5$	Scientific	3 [x^2] [+/−] [+] 5 [=]	-4
	$-3^2 + 5$	Graphing	[(−)] 3 [x^2] [+] 5 [ENTER]	-4
b.	$(-3)^2 + 5$	Scientific	3 [+/−] [x^2] [+] 5 [=]	14
	$(-3)^2 + 5$	Graphing	[(] [(−)] 3 [)] [x^2] [+] 5 [ENTER]	14

EXERCISES

Write an expression that corresponds to the calculator keystrokes. Then evaluate the expression.

1. Scientific: 4 [+/−] [x^2] [−] 3 [=]

2. Graphing: 87 [−] 4 [^] 3 [+] 6 [x^2] [ENTER]

Use a calculator to evaluate the expression. Round the result to three decimal places, if necessary.

3. $21 + 5^3$	**4.** $17 - 2^6$	**5.** $2(9 - 3)^2$
6. $11^2 \div 4^3$	**7.** $6^3 \div (-3)^4$	**8.** $12 \div 2^2 + 5^2 - 4$

Grouping Symbols When evaluating some expressions using a calculator, parentheses must be used even if they do not appear in the expression. For example, fraction bars and square root symbols are grouping symbols. Expressions involving these symbols often require you to use the parentheses keys on your calculator.

STUDENT HELP

WRITING ALGEBRA
The symbol ^ is commonly used on calculators and when typing to indicate that the following number is an exponent.

EXAMPLE 2

	Expression	Calculator	Keystrokes	Result
a.	$(48 \div 6)^4$	Scientific	[(] 48 [÷] 6 [)] [x^2] 4 [=]	4096
	$(48 \div 6)^4$	Graphing	[(] 48 [÷] 6 [)] [^] 4 [ENTER]	4096
b.	$\dfrac{5}{4 + 3 \cdot 2}$	Scientific	5 [÷] [(] 4 [+] 3 [×] 2 [)] [=]	0.5
	$\dfrac{5}{4 + 3 \cdot 2}$	Graphing	5 [÷] [(] 4 [+] 3 [×] 2 [)] [ENTER]	0.5

EXERCISES

Write an expression that corresponds to the calculator keystrokes. Then evaluate the expression.

9. Scientific: 5 ÷ (3 +⁄− − 7) =

10. Graphing: (2 + 1) ^ 8 ENTER

Use a calculator to evaluate the expression. Round the result to three decimal places, if necessary.

11. $2(9 - 3)^2$

12. $(-6 - 5)^4$

13. $1024(1 + 0.42)^5$

14. $3(-6)^2 - (4 - 7)^2$

15. $(2 + 3)^2 - (-9 + 8)^5$

16. $(1.2)^6 - (5.3 + 7)^2$

17. $\dfrac{7}{-3 - 5}$

18. $\dfrac{1 + 3 \cdot 4^2}{6}$

19. $\dfrac{2^3 + 1}{2 \cdot 5^2}$

Square Roots Expressions may involve square roots. The square root key on a scientific calculator works differently than the square root key on a graphing calculator. Be sure you know how your calculator works.

EXAMPLE 3

Expression	Calculator	Keystrokes	Result
a. $\sqrt{63 + 37}$	Scientific	(63 + 37) √ =	10
$\sqrt{63 + 37}$	Graphing	2nd √ (63 + 37) ENTER	10
b. $\dfrac{\sqrt{484}}{11}$	Scientific	484 √ ÷ 11 =	2
$\dfrac{\sqrt{484}}{11}$	Graphing	2nd √ 484) ÷ 11 ENTER	2

EXERCISES

Write an expression that corresponds to the calculator keystrokes. Then evaluate the expression.

20. Scientific: 5 × (32 + 49) √ =

21. Graphing: (4 + 2nd √ 289)) × 3 ENTER

Use a calculator to evaluate the expression. Round the result to three decimal places, if necessary.

22. $2\sqrt{36} - 17$

23. $5\sqrt{579} + 7^2$

24. $3\sqrt{137} + 4^3$

25. $4\sqrt{6756} - 987$

26. $-\sqrt{57846} + 3^4$

27. $-\sqrt{26811} - 4^2$

28. $\dfrac{3\sqrt{225}}{5}$

29. $\dfrac{5\sqrt{1764}}{17 - 4}$

30. $\dfrac{4\sqrt{1296}}{6^2}$

DEVELOPING CONCEPTS *(For use with Lesson 1.4)*
Variables on Both Sides

Goal
Use algebra tiles to solve equations with variables on both sides.

Materials
• algebra tiles

An *equation* is a statement in which two expressions are equal. The steps for solving an equation can be modeled using algebra tiles.

Each **+** represents 1, and each **–** represents -1. Each **+** represents x, and each **–** represents $-x$.

QUESTION

How can you use algebra tiles to solve an equation with a variable on both the left and right sides of the equation?

EXPLORE

1 Use algebra tiles to model the equation $4x + 2 = 2x + 6$.

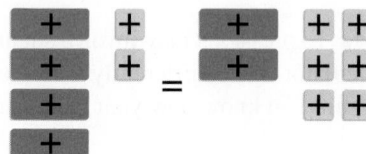

2 You want to have x-tiles on only one side of the equation. Remove two x-tiles from each side. Write the new equation $\underline{?} + 2 = \underline{?}$.

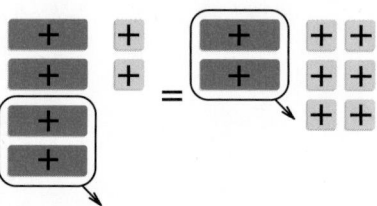

3 You want to have only x-tiles on one side of the equation. Remove two 1-tiles from each side. Write the new equation.

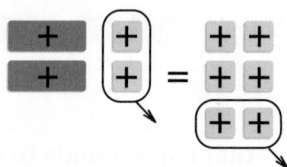

4 You know the value of $2x$. To find the value of x, split the tiles on each side of the equation in half. You get $x = \underline{?}$.

THINK ABOUT IT

1. The model at the right shows the steps in solving an equation. Sketch the result of the last step. Write an equation and an explanation for each of the steps.

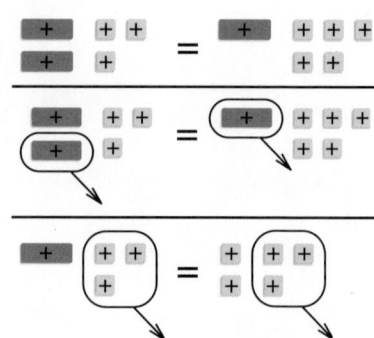

Use algebra tiles to solve the equation.

2. $2x + 4 = 3x + 3$　　**3.** $5x + 2 = 3x + 6$

4. $3x + 3 = x + 11$　　**5.** $4x + 5 = 3x + 5$

6. $7x + 1 = 13 + 4x$　　**7.** $10 + 2x = 1 + 5x$

An equation that involves subtraction or negative coefficients can be solved by using algebra tiles to create *zero pairs*.

QUESTION

How can you use algebra tiles to solve a subtraction equation with a variable on both the left and right sides of the equation?

EXPLORE

1 Use algebra tiles to model the equation $3x - 2 = -x + 6$.

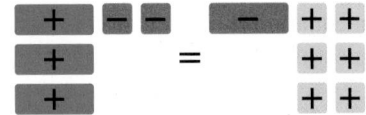

2 You want to have *x*-tiles on only one side of the equation. Add one positive *x*-tile to each side. Remove the zero pair on the right side. Write the new equation. $\underline{?} - 2 = \underline{?}$.

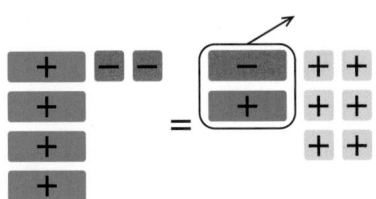

3 To isolate the *x*-tiles, add two 1-tiles to each side. Remove the two zero pairs on the left side. Write the new equation. $4x = \underline{?}$.

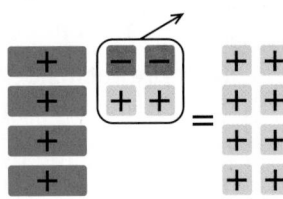

4 You know the value of $4x$. To find the value of *x*, split the tiles on each side of the equation into fourths. You get $x = \underline{?}$.

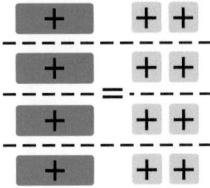

THINK ABOUT IT

8. The model at the right shows the steps in solving an equation. Sketch the result of the last step. Write an equation and an explanation for each of the steps.

Use algebra tiles to solve the equation.

9. $5x - 2 = 3x + 6$ **10.** $4x - 1 = x - 7$

11. $6 - 3x = 2x - 4$ **12.** $-3x + 1 = -x + 9$

13. $-6x + 13 = 1 - 2x$ **14.** $8 - 2x = 12 - x$

1.4 Solving Linear Equations

Key Words

- equation
- linear equation
- solution

GOAL Solve linear equations.

As you climb a mountain, how can you estimate your altitude?

In Example 6, you will use an *equation* to find a climber's altitude based on the temperature.

An **equation** is a statement in which two expressions are equal. A **linear equation** in one variable is an equation that can be written in the form $ax = b$ where a and b are constants and $a \neq 0$. A number is a **solution** of an equation if the equation is true when the number is substituted for the variable.

Two equations are *equivalent* if they have the same solutions. For example, the equations $x - 2 = 1$ and $x = 3$ are equivalent because both have the number 3 as their only solution. You can use *properties of equality* to solve an equation.

Properties of Equality

To write an equivalent equation, you can use:

ADDITION PROPERTY	**Add** the same number to each side: If $a = b$, then $a + c = b + c$.
SUBTRACTION PROPERTY	**Subtract** the same number from each side: If $a = b$, then $a - c = b - c$.
MULTIPLICATION PROPERTY	**Multiply** each side by the same nonzero number: If $a = b$ and $c \neq 0$, then $a \cdot c = b \cdot c$.
DIVISION PROPERTY	**Divide** each side by the same nonzero number: If $a = b$ and $c \neq 0$, then $a \div c = b \div c$.

EXAMPLE 1 Solve a One-Step Equation

Solve $x - 8 = 12$.

Solution

Isolate the variable on one side of the equation.

$x - 8 = 12$	Write original equation.
$x - 8 + 8 = 12 + 8$	Add 8 to each side.
$x = 20$	Simplify.

CHECK Substitute 20 for x in the original equation.

$20 - 8 \overset{?}{=} 12$	Substitute 20 for x.
$12 = 12 \checkmark$	Solution checks.

EXAMPLE 2 Solve a Multi-Step Equation

Solve $-3x + 6 = -12$.

Solution

$$-3x + 6 = -12 \quad \text{Write original equation.}$$

$$-3x = -18 \quad \text{Subtract 6 from each side to isolate the variable.}$$

$$\frac{-3x}{-3} = \frac{-18}{-3} \quad \text{Divide each side by } -3.$$

$$x = 6 \quad \text{Simplify.}$$

ANSWER ▶ The solution is 6. Check $x = 6$ in the original equation.

EXAMPLE 3 Solve an Equation with Variables on Both Sides

Solve $3p + 7 = 5p - 1$.

STUDENT HELP

AVOID ERRORS
You may want to keep the variable on the side of the equation that makes its coefficient positive.

Solution

$$3p + 7 = 5p - 1 \quad \text{Write original equation.}$$

$$7 = 2p - 1 \quad \text{Subtract } 3p \text{ from each side.}$$

$$8 = 2p \quad \text{Add 1 to each side.}$$

$$4 = p \quad \text{Divide each side by 2.}$$

ANSWER ▶ The solution is 4. Check $p = 4$ in the original equation.

 **Checkpoint** ✓ **Solve Equations**

Solve the equation. Check your solution.

1. $\frac{t}{4} = -7$ **2.** $5n - 1 = 9$

3. $2m - 5 = m + 3$ **4.** $-6 + 7r = 2r - 9$

EXAMPLE 4 Use the Distributive Property

Solve $2(5x - 6) = -4(x - 3) + 4$.

Solution

$$2(5x - 6) = -4(x - 3) + 4 \quad \text{Write original equation.}$$

$$10x - 12 = -4x + 12 + 4 \quad \text{Distributive property}$$

$$10x - 12 = -4x + 16 \quad \text{Combine like terms.}$$

$$14x - 12 = 16 \quad \text{Add } 4x \text{ to each side.}$$

$$14x = 28 \quad \text{Add 12 to each side.}$$

$$x = 2 \quad \text{Divide each side by 14.}$$

ANSWER ▶ The solution is 2. Check $x = 2$ in the original equation.

EXAMPLE 5 **Solve an Equation with Fractions**

Solve $\frac{1}{2}z - \frac{3}{4} = z - \frac{5}{8}$.

Solution

Multiply each side of the equation by the least common denominator of the fractions.

$\frac{1}{2}z - \frac{3}{4} = z - \frac{5}{8}$	Write original equation.
$8\left(\frac{1}{2}z - \frac{3}{4}\right) = 8\left(z - \frac{5}{8}\right)$	Multiply each side by the LCD, 8.
$4z - 6 = 8z - 5$	Distributive property
$-6 = 4z - 5$	Subtract $4z$ from each side.
$-1 = 4z$	Add 5 to each side.
$-\frac{1}{4} = z$	Divide each side by 4.

ANSWER ▶ The solution is $-\frac{1}{4}$. Check $z = -\frac{1}{4}$ in the original equation.

 **Solve Equations**

Solve the equation. Check your solution.

5. $5(2x - 1) = 3(x - 4)$ **6.** $2 - \frac{1}{4}y = \frac{1}{12}y + \frac{2}{3}$

EXAMPLE 6 **Use a Verbal Model**

Mountain Climbing You are with a group of climbers at the base of a mountain where the temperature is 59°F and the altitude is 7000 feet. A climber in another group radios down to tell you the temperature at their altitude is 47°F. You know that the temperature drops about 3°F for every 1000 feet of increased altitude. Write and solve an equation to estimate the altitude of the other group.

Solution

VERBAL MODEL	Temp. on mountain	=	Temp. at base	+	Rate of change	·	Increase in altitude

LABELS
Temperature on the mountain = 47   (degrees Fahrenheit)

Temperature at the base = 59   (degrees Fahrenheit)

Rate of temperature change = -0.003 (degrees per foot)

Increase in altitude = a (feet)

ALGEBRAIC MODEL
$47 = 59 + (-0.003)a$	Write equation.
$-12 = -0.003a$	Subtract 59 from each side.
$4000 = a$	Divide each side by -0.003.

ANSWER ▶ The other group of climbers is at $7000 + 4000$, or 11,000 feet.

1.4 Exercises

Guided Practice

Vocabulary Check

1. What is an equation?

2. How do you know that the equations $3x - 2 = 1$ and $3x = 3$ are equivalent?

3. Why is the equation $2x = 6$ a linear equation?

Skill Check

Solve the equation. Check your solution.

4. $x + 2 = 6$ 5. $x - 5 = 8$ 6. $3x = 9$

7. $\frac{x}{5} = 15$ 8. $2x - 3 = 9$ 9. $\frac{x}{2} + 4 = 3$

10. $2x = x + 3$ 11. $5x - 6 = x + 2$ 12. $3(x - 3) = x + 3$

Error Analysis Describe and correct the error.

13.
$$3x + 5 = 2x$$
$$5x + 5 = 0$$
$$5x = -5$$
$$x = -1 \quad \times$$

14.
$$\frac{1}{6}x + \frac{1}{3} = 3$$
$$\left(\frac{1}{6}x + \frac{1}{3}\right) = 3$$
$$x + 2 = 3$$
$$x = 1 \quad \times$$

15. **T-Shirts** You are ordering T-shirts with your school's mascot printed on the back. The T-shirt company charges $25 for the mascot design, plus an additional cost per T-shirt. If the total charge for 40 shirts is $345, what is the additional cost per T-shirt?

Practice and Applications

STUDENT HELP

HOMEWORK HELP
Example 1: Exs. 16–33
Example 2: Exs. 16–33,
      47
Example 3: Exs. 37–42
Example 4: Exs. 43–46
Example 5: Exs. 34–36,
      48–56
Example 6: Exs. 57–61

Naming Properties Name the property or properties you would use to solve the equation.

16. $x - 14 = 5$ 17. $x + 54 = -23$ 18. $5x = -20$

19. $\frac{x}{4} = 4$ 20. $3x + 11 = 20$ 21. $\frac{x}{3} - 4 = 11$

Solving Equations Solve the equation. Check your solution.

22. $y + 13 = 0$ 23. $a - 12 = 19$ 24. $x + 6 = -12$

25. $b - 9 = 19$ 26. $8s = 24$ 27. $-9g = 36$

28. $\frac{b}{4} = 7$ 29. $\frac{y}{3} = -21$ 30. $5n - 4 = 26$

31. $16 - z = -14$ 32. $2x + 4 = 18$ 33. $6 - 5q = 21$

34. $\frac{c}{6} + 3 = 5$ 35. $\frac{d}{4} - 11 = -16$ 36. $\frac{1}{3}x + \frac{1}{2} = 2$

Solving Equations Solve the equation. Check your solution.

37. $7x = x - 18$

38. $8r - 36 = -r$

39. $7s - 9 = 4s$

40. $6t - 4 = 5t + 8$

41. $5u + 10 = 3u + 26$

42. $2n - 8 = 5n + 10$

43. $4(3x + 2) = 44$

44. $7(r + 2) = 4(9 - r)$

45. $6(y - 5) = 0$

46. $3(w - 6) = -7(w + 4)$

47. *History Link* Abraham Lincoln's Gettysburg Address begins with the phrase "Four score and seven years ago." He was referring to a period of time that was 87 years long. How many years are represented by a *score*?

Equations with Fractions Solve the equation. Check your solution.

48. $\frac{1}{3}y + 4 = y - 2$

49. $\frac{1}{2}(x - 8) = 5$

50. $\frac{1}{7}(p - 35) = 4$

51. $\frac{3}{4}(b + 4) = \frac{2}{3}(b - 4)$

52. $2d - 6 = \frac{1}{4}d + 1$

53. $\frac{1}{4}x + \frac{5}{8} = x - \frac{1}{8}$

54. $\frac{3}{4}z + 5 = \frac{1}{4}z - 1$

55. $\frac{2}{3}a - \frac{2}{9} = \frac{1}{3}a + \frac{7}{9}$

56. $\frac{3}{5} - \frac{2}{5}b = \frac{4}{5}b$

57. **Testing** You took a standardized test on which all of the questions had to be answered. You received 2 points for each correct answer but lost $\frac{1}{2}$ point for each incorrect answer. Your score on the test was 132 points and you answered 68 questions correctly. How many incorrect answers did you have?

58. **Car Repair** A car repair bill was $210. The cost for parts was $75. The cost for labor was $45 per hour. How many hours did the repair work take?

59. **Summer Jobs** You have two summer jobs. For one of the jobs, you work 18 hours per week and earn $9 per hour. For the other job, you earn $8 per hour and can work as many hours as you want. Suppose you want to earn $250 one week. How many hours do you need to work at your second job?

In Exercises 60 and 61, use the following formula.

$$\text{degrees Fahrenheit} = \frac{9}{5} \cdot (\text{degrees Celsius}) + 32$$

60. **Dry Ice** Dry ice is solid carbon dioxide. Instead of melting, dry ice changes directly from a solid to a gas. Dry ice changes to a gas at $-109°F$. What is this temperature in degrees Celsius, to the nearest degree?

61. **Veterinary Medicine** The normal body temperature of a dog is $39°C$. A veterinary technician finds that a dog's temperature is $102°F$. Does the dog have a fever? Explain.

62. **Challenge** You are roping off a border around a sidewalk art piece. The art piece is 15 feet long and 11 feet wide. You want the border to have a uniform width and you have 80 feet of rope. What is the maximum width of the border?

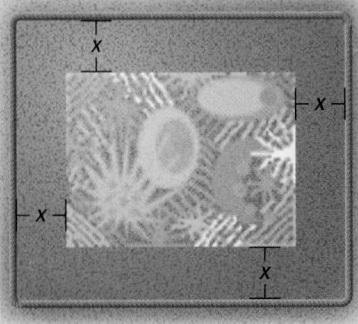

63. Multi-Step Problem You are constructing a fence around the running track at a high school. The distance between the outside edge of the track and the fence is uniform all the way around.

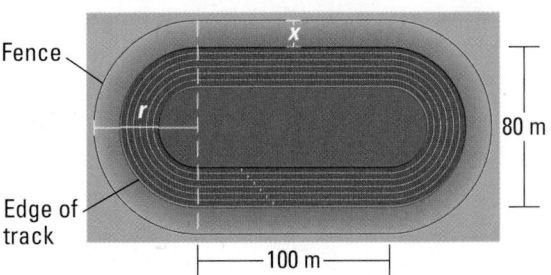

a. 🖩 Each curved end of the track is a semicircle with a radius of 40 meters. Find the total distance around both curved parts of the track. (*Hint:* Remember that the circumference of a circle is given by $C = 2\pi r$.)

b. Find the total distance around the entire track by adding your answer from part (a) to the lengths of the straight edges of the track.

c. The curved edges of the fence are also semicircles. Write an expression for the total distance around both curved parts of the fence in terms of x.

d. Write an expression for the total distance around the entire fence in terms of x. You have 500 meters of fencing. How far away from the track can you build the fence? Round your answer to two decimal places.

Mixed Review

Evaluating Powers Evaluate the power. *(Lesson 1.2)*

64. 3^4 **65.** 4^3 **66.** $(-2)^6$ **67.** -2^6

68. -4^3 **69.** $(-4)^3$ **70.** -1^4 **71.** $(-1)^9$

Using Order of Operations Evaluate the expression. *(Lesson 1.2)*

72. $12 - 6 + 3$ **73.** $1 + 4 \div 2 \cdot 5$ **74.** $7 - 3 \cdot 2 + 3$

75. $(2 + 2^3)^2$ **76.** $12 \div (6 - 2) \cdot 3$ **77.** $(7 - 4) \cdot (3 + 6)$

Evaluating Expressions Evaluate the expression for the given value. *(Lesson 1.2)*

78. $x + 6$ when $x = 3$ **79.** $18 + 4x$ when $x = -5$

80. $5(x - 4)$ when $x = 11$ **81.** $3x(10 - 2x)$ when $x = 3$

Simplifying Expressions Simplify the expression by combining like terms. *(Lesson 1.3)*

82. $8s + 4s$ **83.** $4x - 8x$

84. $6z^2 + 5z - 3z^2 + 6z$ **85.** $4t^2 + 5t + 6t^2 - 8t$

Geometry Skills

Using Formulas Find the dimensions of the figure.

86. Area = 32 square units **87.** Perimeter = 32 units

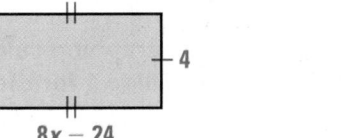

USING A GRAPHING CALCULATOR *(For use with Lesson 1.4)*
Using Tables to Solve Equations

You can use the *Table* feature of a graphing calculator to solve linear equations.

STUDENT HELP

KEYSTROKE HELP
See keystrokes for several models of calculators at www.classzone.com.

EXAMPLE

Use the *Table* feature of a graphing calculator to solve the equation
$5x - 2 = 2x + 16$.

SOLUTION

① Let y_1 equal the left side of the equation, and let y_2 equal the right side of the equation, as shown.

```
Y1 = 5X-2
Y2 = 2X+16
Y3 =
Y4 =
Y5 =
Y6 =
Y7 =
```

② Set the starting value of the table at 0 and the step value (the value by which the *x*-values increase) to 1.

```
TABLE SETUP
TblStart=0
ΔTbl=1
Indpnt: Auto  Ask
Depend: Auto  Ask
```

③ Scroll down in the table, comparing the values for y_1 and y_2 in each row. Look for a row where $y_1 = y_2$. Where this occurs, the *x*-value in this row is the solution of the equation. For the equation $5x - 2 = 2x + 16$, the solution is $x = 6$.

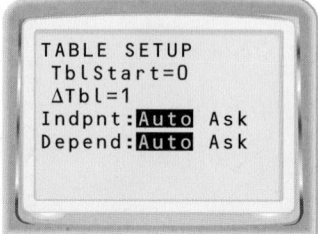

```
X     Y1     Y2
2     8      20
3     13     22
4     18     24
5     23     26
6     28     28
X=6
```

STUDENT HELP

REASONING
If no row in the table shows $y_1 = y_2$, look for the two rows with the least difference between y_1 and y_2. The solution is a value between the *x*-values in these two rows. You can scroll up to check negative values of *x*.

EXERCISES

Use the table shown to decide whether the statement is *true* or *false*. Explain your reasoning.

1. The solution of
$4 - 3x = 12 + 5x$ is 1.

```
X     Y1     Y2
-3    13     -3
-2    10      2
-1     7      7
 0     4     12
 1     1     17
 2    -2     22
 3    -5     27
```

2. The solution of
$7x + 19 = -2x + 55$ is 4.

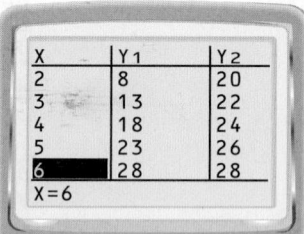

```
X     Y1     Y2
0     19     55
1     26     53
2     33     51
3     40     49
4     47     47
5     54     45
6     61     43
```

Use the *Table* feature of a graphing calculator to solve the equation. Set *TblStart* to −10 and *ΔTbl* to 1 for these exercises.

3. $8x + 1 = 6x + 5$ **4.** $2x - 11 = 19 - 4x$ **5.** $5x + 2 = 2x - 1$

6. $-10 + 7x = 11x + 18$ **7.** $-3x + 10 = 59 + 4x$ **8.** $-13x + 8 = -9x - 4$

1.5 Rewriting Equations and Formulas

Key Words
- interest
- principal
- perimeter
- area
- circumference

GOAL Rewrite common formulas and equations that have more than one variable.

When an equation involves more than one variable, you can solve for one of its variables. Several common formulas are listed below.

Common Formulas

	FORMULA	VARIABLES
Distance	$d = rt$	d = distance, r = rate, t = time
Simple Interest	$I = Prt$	I = interest, P = principal, r = rate, t = time
Temperature	$F = \frac{9}{5}C + 32$	F = degrees Fahrenheit, C = degrees Celsius

Geometry Formulas

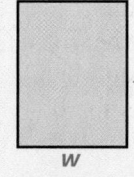

RECTANGLE

Perimeter
$P = 2\ell + 2w$

Area
$A = \ell w$

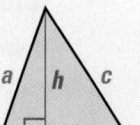

TRIANGLE

Perimeter
$P = a + b + c$

Area
$A = \frac{1}{2}bh$

TRAPEZOID

Area
$A = \frac{1}{2}(b_1 + b_2)h$

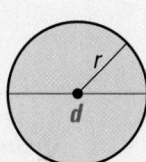

CIRCLE

Circumference
$C = \pi d$ or $C = 2\pi r$

Area
$A = \pi r^2$

EXAMPLE 1 Rewrite a Common Formula

A formula for the circumference of a circle is $C = \pi d$. Solve for d.

Solution

$C = \pi d$	Write circumference formula.
$\dfrac{C}{\pi} = \dfrac{\pi d}{\pi}$	Divide each side by π.
$\dfrac{C}{\pi} = d$	Simplify.

EXAMPLE 2 Use a Rewritten Formula

Plumbing A plumber needs to replace a pipe but cannot measure the diameter of the pipe directly. Instead, the plumber measures the circumference. It is $3\frac{1}{8}$ inches. What is the diameter of the pipe, to the nearest $\frac{1}{8}$ inch?

Solution

$d = \dfrac{C}{\pi}$ Use the rewritten formula from Example 1.

$= \dfrac{3.125}{\pi}$ $3\frac{1}{8} = 3.125$; substitute 3.125 for C.

≈ 0.995 Divide. Use the π key on a calculator.

ANSWER ▶ To the nearest $\frac{1}{8}$ inch, the diameter of the pipe is 1 inch.

Equations with Two Variables Given an equation in two variables, x and y, you can use either of two methods to find the value of y for a given value of x.

Method 1: First substitute for x. Solve the resulting equation for y.

Method 2: First solve for y. Then substitute for x.

EXAMPLE 3 Calculate the Value of a Variable

Find the value of y in the equation $2x + 3y = 9$ when $x = -6$ and when $x = 9$.

Solution

Method 1: First substitute for x. Then solve for y.

When $x = -6$ **When $x = 9$**

$2x + 3y = 9$ $2x + 3y = 9$

$2(-6) + 3y = 9$ $2(9) + 3y = 9$

$-12 + 3y = 9$ $18 + 3y = 9$

$3y = 21$ $3y = -9$

$y = 7$ $y = -3$

Method 2: First solve for y. Then substitute for x.

$2x + 3y = 9$ Write original equation.

$3y = -2x + 9$ Subtract $2x$ from each side.

$y = -\dfrac{2}{3}x + 3$ Divide each side by 3.

When $x = -6$: $y = -\dfrac{2}{3}(-6) + 3 = 7$ **When $x = 9$:** $y = -\dfrac{2}{3}(9) + 3 = -3$

Checkpoint ✓ *Calculate the Value of a Variable*

1. Find the value of y in the equation $2y + x = 5x + 6$ when $x = -3$ and when $x = 6$.

EXAMPLE **4** **Write an Equation with Two Variables**

Yearbook Ads in your school's yearbook sell for $150 per half page and $250 per full page. Write an equation with more than one variable to represent the total revenue from the sale of the ads.

VERBAL MODEL	**Total revenue**	=	**Price of half-page ads**	·	**Number of half-page ads**	+	**Price of full page ads**	·	**Number of full-page ads**

LABELS

Total revenue = R (dollars)

Price of half-page ad = 150   (dollars)

Number of half-page ads = h (ads)

Price of full-page ad = 250   (dollars)

Number of full-page ads = f (ads)

ALGEBRAIC MODEL

$R = 150h + 250f$

EXAMPLE **5** **Use an Equation with Two Variables**

Yearbook The yearbook staff needs to raise an additional $3500 through the sale of ads before printing the yearbook. What are some combinations of full-page ads and half-page ads that will meet this objective?

Solution

Use the algebraic model from Example 4. Substitute 3500 for R and solve for f.

$$R = 150h + 250f \qquad \text{Algebraic model}$$

$$3500 = 150h + 250f \qquad \text{Substitute 3500 for } R.$$

$$3500 - 150h = 250f \qquad \text{Subtract } 150h \text{ from each side.}$$

$$\frac{3500 - 150h}{250} = f \qquad \text{Divide each side by 250.}$$

$$\frac{50(70 - 3h)}{250} = f \qquad \text{Distributive property}$$

$$\frac{70 - 3h}{5} = f \qquad \text{Divide numerator and denominator by 50.}$$

Make a table showing some values that solve the problem.

h	5	10	15	20
$f = \dfrac{70 - 3h}{5}$	11	8	5	2

ANSWER ▶ One solution is 10 half-page ads and 8 full-page ads.

Checkpoint ✓ **Use an Equation with Several Variables**

2. Refer to Example 5. Suppose the goal was to sell $6000 worth of ads. What is one combination of full-page and half-page ads that meets this objective?

1.5 Exercises

Guided Practice

Vocabulary Check

1. Copy and complete the statement: $A = \pi r^2$ is an example of a(n) __?__.

2. Describe the two methods you could use to find the value of y in the equation $2x + 5y = 4$ when $x = -1$.

Skill Check

Solve the equation for y. Then find the value of y when $x = 3$.

3. $2x + 3y = 9$

4. $-x + 3y = -6$

5. $5y - 3x = 1$

6. $-2y + 7x = 9$

7. $4y + x = 15$

8. $\frac{1}{5}x - y = 2$

Parks In Exercises 9–11, use the following information.

A park employee is enclosing two rectangular gardens with fencing. The gardens are exactly the same size and share one common side as shown in the diagram.

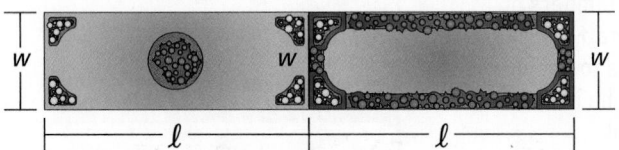

9. The equation for the total amount of fencing to be used for the garden is $P = 3w + 4\ell$. Solve the equation for w.

10. Write an equation for the combined area of the two gardens.

11. The park employee uses 100 feet of fencing. Express the combined area of the gardens in terms of the length only.

Practice and Applications

STUDENT HELP

HOMEWORK HELP
Example 1: Exs. 12–17
Example 2: Exs. 19–21
Example 3: Exs. 18–33
Example 4: Exs. 34–43
Example 5: Exs. 34–43

Rewriting Formulas Solve the formula for the indicated variable.

12. Distance formula $D = rt$ for t.

13. Energy formula $E = mc^2$ for m.

14. Interest formula $I = Prt$ for t.

15. Volume formula $V = \ell wh$ for h.

16. The height of a falling object $h = -16t^2 + h_0$ for h_0.

17. The height of a launched object $h = -16t^2 + v_0 t + h_0$ for v_0.

18. Critical Thinking The solution steps below show the equation $x + 2y - z = 1$ solved for the variable y. Write an explanation for each step.

Solution Step	Explanation
$x + 2y - z = 1$	Original Equation
$x + 2y = 1 + z$	__a.__
$2y = 1 + z - x$	__b.__
$y = \dfrac{1 + z - x}{2}$	__c.__

In Exercises 19–21, use the formula for simple interest, $I = Prt$.

19. Solve the formula for the rate r.

20. After one quarter $\left(\frac{1}{4}\text{ year}\right)$, the interest on a principal of $1000 is $8.75. Find the rate. Write your answer as a percent.

21. You deposit $1000 in an account that earns interest at a rate of 3.5%. After one full year, how much interest will you earn? How much money will be in the account?

Exploring Methods Find the value of y for the given value of x using Method 1 on page 34. (Substitute for x. Then solve for y.)

22. $x + y = 7; x = 2$ **23.** $-x + 2y = 6; x = 2$

24. $3x - 8y = -3; x = -1$ **25.** $-x - 5y = 14; x = -4$

26. $\frac{1}{2}x = -\frac{2}{3}y + 10; x = 12$ **27.** $-2(y - 1) - 2x = -8; x = 4$

Exploring Methods Find the value of y for the given value of x using Method 2 on page 34. (Solve for y. Then substitute for x.)

28. $x - y = 8; x = 5$ **29.** $-y + 3x = 6; x = 4$

30. $4x - 2y = 18; x = 8$ **31.** $-2x - 9y = 63; x = 0$

32. $\frac{3}{4}x + \frac{7}{8}y = 5; x = 2$ **33.** $6x - 5(y + 1) = 39; x = 4$

Link to
BIOLOGY

HONEYBEES A honeybee has 5 functional eyes. Three simple eyes are located on the top of the bee's forehead and see polarized light. They help a bee to navigate when the sun is not shining. The other two eyes see objects.

Biology Link  **In Exercises 34–37, use the following information.**

A forager honeybee spends the first three weeks of its life becoming accustomed to the immediate surroundings of its hive. Then the bee leaves the hive and spends the rest of its life collecting pollen and nectar. The verbal model below shows the total number of miles a forager honeybee flies during its lifetime.

VERBAL MODEL

$$\boxed{\text{Distance flown in a lifetime}} = \boxed{\text{Average distance flown daily}} \left(\boxed{\text{Life span}} - \boxed{\text{Time spent in the hive}} \right)$$

LABELS

Distance flown in a lifetime = D	(miles)
Average distance flown daily = m	(miles per day)
Life span = L	(days)
Time spent in the hive = 21	(days)

34. Use the verbal model and labels to write an equation with more than one variable for the total number of miles a forager honeybee flies in its lifetime.

35. Solve the equation for L.

36. A forager honeybee flies 360 miles over a lifetime, flying about 30 miles each day. Approximately how many days does this bee live?

37. **Critical Thinking** In Exercise 35, you solved the equation for L. Explain why this was helpful when finding the answer to Exercise 36. Then write an exercise similar to Exercise 36 for which solving the equation for m would be helpful.

Phone Charges In Exercises 38–40, use the following information.

A cell phone company charges a monthly fee of $17.50 for up to 250 minutes of long distance calls. After 250 minutes, the company charges $.10 per additional minute.

38. Write an equation that represents the total long distance phone charge T for one month if you talked for m minutes and m is greater than 250.

39. Solve the equation you wrote in Exercise 38 for m.

40. Your long distance phone charge last month was $24.30. How many minutes of long distance calls did you make during that month?

Challenge In Exercises 41–43, your baseball team is raising money by selling baseball caps and T-shirts.

41. Write an equation with more than one variable that represents the total amount of money you raise.

42. How many variables are in the equation you wrote in Exercise 41? Describe what each variable represents.

43. The price of a baseball cap is $8 and the price of a T-shirt is $12. Your team raises a total of $4500 and sells 132 baseball caps. How many T-shirts did your team sell?

Standardized Test Practice

44. Multi-Step Problem The formula for the height h of an equilateral triangle is $h = \frac{b}{2}\sqrt{3}$ where b is the length of a side.

   a. Write and simplify a formula for the area of an equilateral triangle in terms of the length of a side.

   b. Find the area of the triangle when $b = 5$ and when $b = 15$. Round to the nearest tenth.

45. Multi-Step Problem The surface area S of a rectangular solid with a square base is given by the formula $S = 2\ell^2 + 4h\ell$. In the solid shown, the length ℓ of each side of the base is one third of the height h.

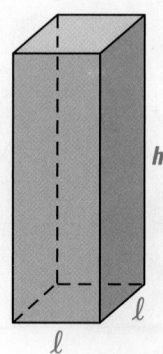

   a. Write a formula for the surface area of the solid in terms of the length of its base.

   b. Find the surface area of the solid when $\ell = 1$ and $\ell = 4$.

Mixed Review

Writing Expressions Write an expression to answer the question. (*Skills Review Handbook, p. 774*)

46. You buy n birthday cards for $1.95 each. How much do you spend?

47. You have $30 and spend x dollars. How much money do you have left?

48. You drive 55 miles per hour for h hours. How many miles do you drive?

49. You have $250 in your bank account and you deposit x dollars. How much money do you now have in your account?

50. A ball bearing weighs 2 ounces. A box contains b ball bearings. What is the total weight of the ball bearings in the box?

Solving Equations Solve the equation. Check your solution.
(Lesson 1.4)

51. $y + 13 = 0$

52. $b - 9 = 19$

53. $-9g = 36$

54. $\dfrac{c}{6} + 3 = 5$

55. $2x + 3 = x + 5$

56. $\dfrac{1}{2}(x - 8) = 5$

Geometry Skills **Solving Formulas** Solve the formula for the indicated variable. Then evaluate the rewritten formula for the given values. Use 3.14 for π.

57. Area: $A = \dfrac{1}{2}bh$

Solve for b. Find the value of b when $A = 160$ and $h = 20$.

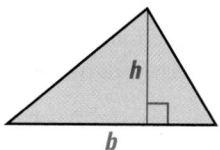

58. Volume: $V = \dfrac{1}{3}\pi r^2 h$

Solve for h. Find the value of h when $V = 84$ and $r = 4$.

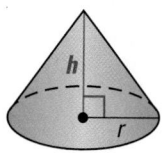

59. Volume: $V = \pi r^2 h$

Solve for h. Find the value of h when $V = 790$ and $r = 5$.

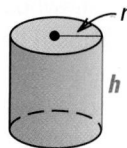

60. Area: $A = \dfrac{1}{2}(b_1 + b_2)h$

Solve for b_1. Find the value of b_1 when $A = 30$, $b_2 = 8$, and $h = 5$.

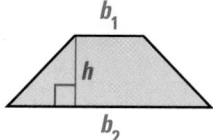

Quiz 2

Lesson 1.3 **Simplify the expression.**

1. $-8x + 3x$

2. $3x + 2y - x$

3. $-x + 7y - 9y - x$

4. $-2(x + 1) + 4x$

5. $6 + 3(x - 1)$

6. $5x - 7(x + 1)$

Lesson 1.4 **Solve the equation. Check your solution.**

7. $x + 4 = 9$

8. $3x - 5 = 1$

9. $\dfrac{x}{4} + 2 = 5$

10. $5(x - 6) = -40$

11. $-(x + 3) = 3(x - 5)$

12. $\dfrac{1}{6}x + \dfrac{2}{3} = \dfrac{1}{3}x - 1$

Lesson 1.5 **Solve the formula for the indicated variable.**

13. Perimeter of a triangle
Solve for b: $P = a + b + c$.

14. Surface area of a cone
Solve for ℓ: $S = \pi r^2 + \pi r \ell$.

15. Surface area of a prism
Solve for h: $S = 2\ell w + 2\ell h + 2wh$.

16. Celsius to Fahrenheit
Solve for C: $F = \dfrac{9}{5}C + 32$.

Lesson 1.5 **17. Fitness** Each day you exercise at a fitness center for 1 hour. You lift weights and do aerobics during each visit. Today you spent 25 minutes doing aerobics. If you spent 7 minutes at each weight-lifting machine, how many machines did you use?

1.6 Problem Solving Using Algebraic Models

Key Words
- verbal model
- algebraic model

Prerequisite Skills

Solve the formula or equation for the indicated variable.

1. $I = Prt$ for P

2. $A = \frac{1}{3}bh$ for h

3. $10 = 3x + 7$ for x

4. $7w - 3(w - 4) = 4$ for w

GOAL Use problem solving strategies to solve real-life problems.

In previous lessons, you have seen how to solve real-life problems by writing an equation in words *before* writing the equation using mathematical symbols. The equation written in words is called a **verbal model**. The verbal model is used to write a mathematical statement, called an **algebraic model**. The key steps in this problem solving plan are shown in the flow chart below.

Write a verbal model. → Assign labels. → Write an algebraic model. → Solve the algebraic model. → Answer the question.

EXAMPLE 1 Write and Use a Formula

Chairlifts Chairlifts transport snowboarders and skiers to the tops of the ski runs. The Iron Horse Quad Chairlift in Montana carries skiers a distance of 3250 feet. The chairlift moves at a speed of 450 feet per minute. Find the time it takes the chairlift to travel the entire distance.

Solution
You can use the formula $d = rt$ to write a verbal model.

VERBAL MODEL

| Distance | = | Rate | · | Time |

LABELS

Distance = 3250   (feet)

Rate = 450   (feet per minute)

Time = t (minutes)

ALGEBRAIC MODEL

$3250 = 450t$ Write algebraic model.

$\dfrac{3250}{450} = t$ Divide each side by 450.

$7.2 \approx t$ Use a calculator.

ANSWER ▶ It takes the chairlift about 7 minutes to travel the entire distance.

STUDENT HELP

AVOID ERRORS
Use unit analysis to confirm that your answer is in the correct units.
$\text{feet} = \dfrac{\text{feet}}{\text{minute}} \times \text{minutes}$

 ✓ **Write and Use a Formula**

1. Find the time it takes the chairlift in Example 1 to travel 1800 feet.

40 **Chapter 1** *Tools of Algebra*

EXAMPLE **2** Write and Use an Algebraic Model

Conservation Low-flow faucets help conserve water. They have a flow rate of at most 2.5 gallons per minute. To test whether a faucet meets this standard, you time how long the faucet takes to fill a 1-gallon container. The result is 0.3 minute. Find the flow rate for the faucet. Is it a low-flow faucet?

Solution

VERBAL MODEL					
	Volume of container	=	Flow rate of faucet	·	Time needed fill container

LABELS

Volume of container = 1   (gallon)

Flow rate of faucet = r (gallons per minute)

Time needed to fill container = 0.3   (minute)

ALGEBRAIC MODEL

$1 = r(0.3)$ Write algebraic model.

$3.3 \approx r$ Divide each side by 0.3; use a calculator.

ANSWER ▶ The flow rate is about 3.3 gallons per minute, which is greater than the standard for low-flow faucets. This is not a low-flow faucet.

STUDENT HELP

AVOID ERRORS
The solution of the equation in Example 2 is about 3.3, but this is not the answer to the question. You must next compare 3.3 to 2.5.

EXAMPLE **3** Look for a Pattern

Skyscrapers The table below gives the heights from the ground to the top of the first few stories of the Republic Plaza in Denver, Colorado. Determine the height from the ground to the top of the 9th story.

Story	Lobby	2	3	4	5
Height to top of story (ft)	36	48.5	61	73.5	86

Solution

Look at the difference in the heights given in the table. After the lobby, the height increases by 12.5 feet per story. You can use the observed pattern to write a model for the height.

VERBAL MODEL							
	Height to top of a story	=	Height of lobby	+	Height of story	·	Number of stories above lobby

LABELS

Height to top of a story = h (feet)

Height of lobby = 36   (feet)

Height of story = 12.5   (feet per story)

Number of stories above lobby = n (stories)

ALGEBRAIC MODEL

$h = 36 + 12.5n$ Write algebraic model.

$h = 36 + 12.5(8)$ Substitute $9 - 1 = 8$ for n.

$h = 136$ Simplify.

ANSWER ▶ The height to the top of the 9th story is about 136 feet.

STUDENT HELP

SOLVING NOTE
The lobby of the Republic Plaza is the first floor of the building. So, the ninth floor of the building is 8 stories above the lobby.

Link to
HISTORY

RAILROADS In 1862, two companies were given the rights to build a railroad from Omaha, Nebraska, to Sacramento, California. The Central Pacific Railroad began from Sacramento in late 1863. Twenty months later, the Union Pacific Railroad began from Omaha.

EXAMPLE **4** **Draw a Diagram**

Railroads Use the information under the illustration at the left. The Central Pacific Railroad averaged 10.5 miles of track per month. The Union Pacific Railroad averaged 23.6 miles of track per month. The illustration shows the two companies meeting in Promontory Summit, Utah, as the 1780 miles of track were completed. When did the companies meet? How many miles of track did each company build?

Solution

Begin by drawing and labeling a diagram, as shown.

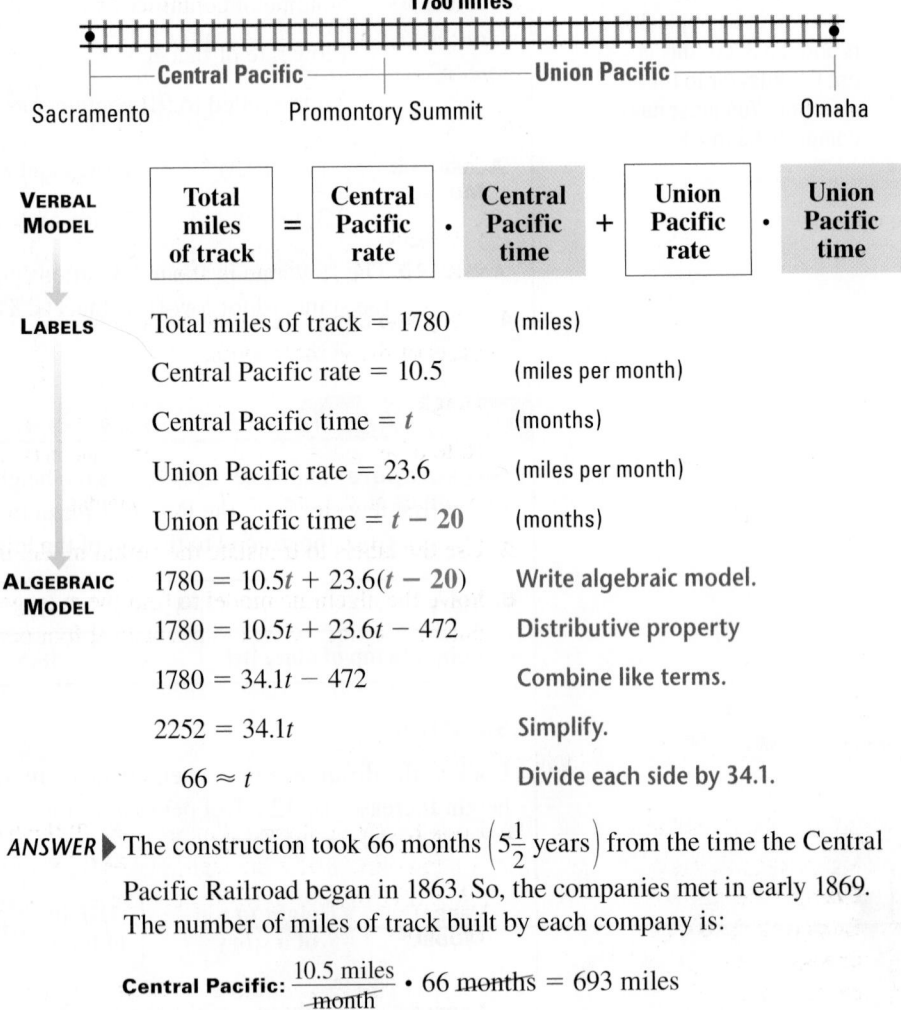

VERBAL MODEL

| Total miles of track | = | Central Pacific rate | · | Central Pacific time | + | Union Pacific rate | · | Union Pacific time |

LABELS

Total miles of track = 1780   (miles)

Central Pacific rate = 10.5   (miles per month)

Central Pacific time = t (months)

Union Pacific rate = 23.6   (miles per month)

Union Pacific time = $t - 20$ (months)

ALGEBRAIC MODEL

$1780 = 10.5t + 23.6(t - 20)$ Write algebraic model.

$1780 = 10.5t + 23.6t - 472$ Distributive property

$1780 = 34.1t - 472$ Combine like terms.

$2252 = 34.1t$ Simplify.

$66 \approx t$ Divide each side by 34.1.

ANSWER ▸ The construction took 66 months $\left(5\frac{1}{2} \text{ years}\right)$ from the time the Central Pacific Railroad began in 1863. So, the companies met in early 1869. The number of miles of track built by each company is:

Central Pacific: $\dfrac{10.5 \text{ miles}}{\text{month}} \cdot 66 \text{ months} = 693 \text{ miles}$

Union Pacific: $\dfrac{23.6 \text{ miles}}{\text{month}} \cdot (66 - 20) \text{ months} \approx 1086 \text{ miles}$

Checkpoint ✓ **Write and Use a Simple Model**

2. You borrow $195 from your aunt. Your aunt is not charging you any interest, but you want to repay her as soon as possible. You can afford to pay her $15 per week. Use the problem solving plan to find how long it will take you to repay your aunt.

Guided Practice

Vocabulary Check

1. What is a verbal model?

2. What is an algebraic model?

Skill Check

Science Link In Exercises 3–6, use the following information.

While at a park, you take a ride in a hot-air balloon. The balloon takes about 3.8 minutes to rise to its maximum height of 400 feet.

3. Copy and complete the verbal model for the height of the balloon.

Height	=	Rate of ascent	·	?

4. Copy and complete the labels for the parts of the verbal model.

Height = __?__   (feet)

Rate of ascent = __?__   (feet per minute)

Number of minutes = __?__   (minutes)

5. Use the labels to translate the verbal model into an algebraic model.

6. Solve the algebraic model to find the average rate at which the balloon rises during the ride. Round to the nearest foot per minute.

Practice and Applications

STUDENT HELP

HOMEWORK HELP
Example 1: Exs. 7–23
Example 2: Exs. 7–23
Example 3: Exs. 24–26
Example 4: Ex. 27

7. Look back at Example 2 on page 41. Tell whether each of the following faucets is a low-flow faucet. Faucet A takes 0.25 minute to fill the container. Faucet B takes 0.41 minute to fill the container. Faucet C takes 0.0075 hour to fill the container.

Steamboat In Exercises 8–11, use the following information.

You are taking a steamboat cruise on the Mississippi River from New Orleans to Baton Rouge, a distance of 108 nautical miles. The steamboat will travel at a steady rate of 8 nautical miles per hour. Use the following verbal model.

Distance	=	Rate	·	Time

8. Assign labels to the parts of the verbal model.

9. Use the labels to translate the verbal model into an algebraic model.

10. Solve the algebraic model.

11. How long will the cruise last?

Music **In Exercises 12–14, use the following information.**

Musicians use a *metronome* to keep the desired tempo while practicing musical pieces. Suppose a violinist is practicing a musical piece that is 160 measures long, with each measure having 4 beats. The instructor has a metronome set for a tempo of 80 beats per minute. Use the following verbal model.

| Metronome tempo | · | Length of musical piece | = | Number of measures in musical piece | · | Number of beats per measure |

12. Assign labels to the parts of the verbal model.

13. Use the labels to translate the verbal model into an algebraic model.

14. How long does it take to perform the piece? Use unit analysis to check your answer.

Owning a Car **In Exercises 15–18, use the following information.**

You just bought a used car and are determining your monthly costs. Your monthly car payment will be $252. Your car insurance costs $684 every 6 months.

15. Write a verbal model for the monthly car expenses.

16. Assign labels to the parts of the verbal model.

17. Write an algebraic model.

18. If you have budgeted $450 each month for car expenses, how much money will you have available for buying gasoline each month?

Science Link **In Exercises 19–22, use the following information.**

The table shows the number of calories in three food nutrients. You can determine the number of calories in a food item by adding the numbers of calories it provides from its fat, protein, and carbohydrate content.

19. Write a verbal model that gives the number of calories in a food item in terms of the grams of fat, protein, and carbohydrate in the item.

20. Assign labels to the parts of the verbal model.

21. Use the labels to translate the verbal model into an algebraic model.

Nutrient	Calories per Gram
protein	4 C
carbohydrate	4 C
fat	9 C

22. A peanut butter sandwich provides 253 calories. It has 17 grams of fat and 15 grams of carbohydrates. How many grams of protein are in the peanut butter sandwich?

23. Borrowing Money You have borrowed $529 from your parents to buy a computer. Your parents expect you to pay back the money at a steady weekly rate. Write an algebraic model for the situation. Use it to determine how many weeks it will take to pay back your parents at $20 per week.

Pets In Exercises 24–26, use the table, which shows the weight of a German shepherd puppy at weekly intervals from 3 to 8 weeks of age.

Age (months)	3	4	5	6	7	8
Weight (pounds)	5.5	8	10.5	13	15.5	18

24. Use the pattern of the weights to write a verbal model for the puppy's weight.

25. Assign labels to the parts of the verbal model. Use the labels to translate the verbal model into an algebraic model.

26. Use the algebraic model to predict the puppy's weight at 12 weeks of age.

27. **Woodshop** You are working on a project in woodshop. You have a wooden rod that is 72 inches long. You need to cut the rod so that one piece is 6 inches longer than the other piece. Copy and complete the diagram. Write an algebraic model to find how long each piece should be.

28. **Challenge** You need to cut a wooden rod into four pieces. The rod is 64 inches long. You need one piece of one length, two pieces twice that length, and one piece that is three times the smallest length. Use a diagram and algebraic model to find the length of each piece.

Standardized Test Practice

29. **Multi-Step Problem** You and three friends are ordering sunglasses from a catalog. The cost of the first pair is one and one half times the cost of each additional pair. Shipping is free for orders over $99.

   a. Write a verbal model for the total cost of the sunglasses.

   b. Assign labels to the parts of the verbal model. Use the labels to translate the verbal model into an algebraic model.

   c. If the total cost for the four pairs of sunglasses is $144, what was the charge for the first pair?

Mixed Review

Naming Properties Name the property or properties you would use to solve the equation. *(Lesson 1.4)*

30. $x + 11 = 7$ **31.** $3x = -24$ **32.** $x - (-7) = -17$

33. $\frac{x}{3} = -12$ **34.** $\frac{x}{3} + 6 = 15$ **35.** $8x - 20 = 44$

Evaluating Equations Find the value of *y* for the given value of *x*. *(Lesson 1.5)*

36. $3x - 4y = 7; x = 5$ **37.** $-2x + y = -3; x = -1$

38. $-x + 3y = -3; x = 6$ **39.** $6x - 5y = 44; x = 4$

Geometry Review

Bisectors An angle bisector is a ray that divides an angle into two angles that have equal measure. In the diagram, $\overrightarrow{BD}$ bisects $\angle ABC$. Find the value of *x*.

40. **41.** **42.**

1.7 Analyzing and Displaying Data

GOAL Use statistical measures and data displays to represent data.

Key Words
- mean, median, mode
- range
- box-and-whisker plot
- lower quartile
- upper quartile

Prerequisite Skills

Evaluate the expression.

1. $\dfrac{12 + 14 + 13}{3}$

2. $\dfrac{4 + 7 + 5 + 4 + 10}{5}$

3. $\dfrac{85 + 93 + 97 + 89}{4}$

How many points per game do professional basketball teams normally score?

In Example 4 you will use a *box-and-whisker* plot to help answer this question.

The two data sets below show the average number of points per game scored by the teams in the National Basketball Association during the 2005–2006 season.

National Basketball Association Team Points Per Game	
Eastern Conference	94, 94, 95, 96, 97, 97, 97, 98, 98, 98, 98, 99, 100, 101, 102
Western Conference	89, 90, 92, 92, 92, 93, 96, 97, 99, 99, 99, 99, 100, 103, 108

The following *measures of central tendency* are three commonly used statistics.

The **mean**, or average, of n numbers is the sum of the numbers divided by n.

For the data $x_1, x_2, \ldots, x_n$, the mean is : $\dfrac{x_1 + x_2 + \cdots + x_n}{n}$.

The **median** of n numbers is the middle number when the numbers are written in order. If n is even, the median is the mean of the two middle numbers.

The **mode** of n numbers is the number or numbers that occur most frequently. There may be one mode, no mode, or more than one mode.

STUDENT HELP

READING ALGEBRA
The notation x_1 is read as "x sub one." The subscript numbers indicate which value in a set of values for *x* is meant.

EXAMPLE 1 Find Measures of Central Tendency

Find the mean, median, and mode(s) of the 30 team scores.

Solution

Mean: $\dfrac{89 + 90 + \ldots + 108}{30} = \dfrac{2912}{20} \approx 97.1$

Median: Write the scores in numerical order.
89, 90, 92, 92, 92, 93, 94, 94, 95, 96, 96, 97, 97, 97, 97,
98, 98, 98, 98, 99, 99, 99, 99, 99, 100, 100, 101, 102, 103, 108

The median is between the 15th and 16th numbers. Median $= \dfrac{97 + 98}{2} = 97.5$.

Mode: The number that occurs most frequently is 99.

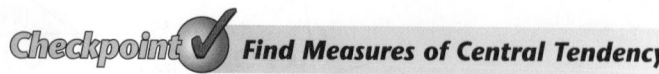 **Find Measures of Central Tendency**

1. Find the mean, median, and mode of the 15 Eastern Conference scores.

Measures of Dispersion Measures of central tendency tell you what the center of the data is. Other commonly used statistics are called *measures of dispersion*. They tell you how spread out the data are. One measure of dispersion is the **range**. It is the difference between the greatest and least data values.

STUDENT HELP

SOLVING NOTE
The points for Western Conference teams show a greater range. So, the numbers of points per game for these teams are more spread out.

EXAMPLE 2 Find Ranges of Data Sets

Find the range of the two data sets on the previous page.

Solution

The ranges of the points per game in the two data sets are:

Eastern Conference: Range = 102 − 94 = 8

Western Conference: Range = 108 − 89 = 19

Box-and-Whisker Plots Although statistics are useful in describing a data set, sometimes a graph of the data can be more informative. One type of statistical graph is a **box-and-whisker plot**.

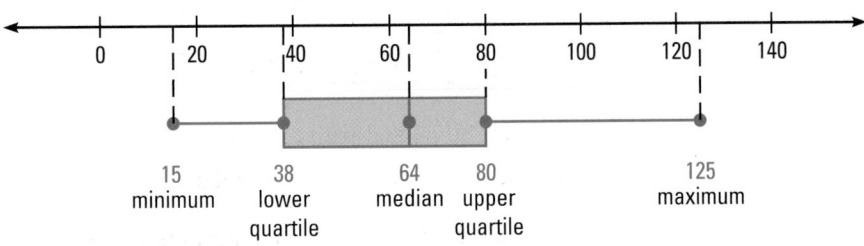

STUDENT HELP

VOCABULARY
The minimum value and the maximum value of a data set are sometimes called the *extremes*.

The "box" encloses the middle half of the data set and the "whiskers" extend to the minimum and maximum values. The median divides the data set in half. The **lower quartile** is the median of the lower half, and the **upper quartile** is the median of the upper half.

EXAMPLE 3 Find Lower and Upper Quartiles

Find the lower and upper quartile of each set of data.

a. 10, 15, 17, 18, 20, 21   **b.** 31, 33, 33, 35, 36, 39, 40, 41, 41

Solution

a. The values are already in order. The median is between 17 and 18. Each half of the data has three items.

Lower quartile: The median of 10, 15, and 17 is 15.

Upper quartile: The median of 18, 20, and 21 is 20.

b. The values are already in order. The median is 36. This value does not belong to either the upper half or the lower half of the data set. So, each half of the data has four items.

Lower quartile: The median of 31, 33, 33, and 35 is 33.

Upper quartile: The median of 39, 40, 41, and 41 is 40.5.

Find the range, median, lower quartile, and upper quartile of the data set.

2. 11, 15, 16, 16, 17, 20, 24, 24, 24, 27, 29

3. 47, 50, 51, 55, 55, 55, 57, 63, 66, 68, 68, 75

Drawing Box-and-Whisker Plots You can use the following steps in order to draw a box-and-whisker plot.

Drawing a Box-and-Whisker Plot

STEP ❶ *Order* the data from least to greatest.

STEP ❷ *Find* the minimum and maximum values, the median, and the lower and upper quartiles.

STEP ❸ *Plot* the five numbers below a number line.

STEP ❹ *Draw* the box, the whiskers, and a line segment through the median.

Link to
CAREER

HIGH SCHOOL COACH
A high school coach conducts practice sessions that improve the abilities of the members of the team. A coach also manages the team during games.

EXAMPLE 4 Draw a Box-and-Whisker Plot

Draw a box-and-whisker plot of the Eastern Conference data set on page 46. How many points per game did Eastern Conference teams normally score in the 2005–2006 season?

Solution

❶ The 15 values are already in order.

❷ *Find* the significant values for this data set. The minimum is 94 and the maximum is 102. The median is 98. The lower quartile is 96 and the upper quartile is 99.

❸ *Plot* these five numbers below a number line.

❹ *Draw* the box, the whiskers, and a line segment through the median.

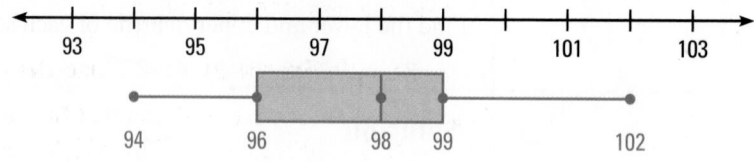

4. Use your answers to Checkpoint Exercises 2 and 3 to draw box-and-whisker plots of each data set.

5. Draw a box-and-whisker plot of the Western Conference data on page 46. How do the scores for the Western Conference teams compare to those for the Eastern Conference teams?

1.7 Exercises

Guided Practice

Vocabulary Check

1. Define mean, median, mode, and range of a set of *n* numbers.

2. When you read a box-and-whisker plot, can you determine the *mean* of the data? Can you determine the *median*? Can you determine the *mode*?

Skill Check

In Exercises 3–9, use the following data set which gives the lengths of calls in minutes by a cellular telephone user.

$$1, 2, 2, 4, 5, 5, 8, 12, 15$$

3. Find the mean.

4. Find the median.

5. Find the mode(s).

6. Find the range.

7. Find the lower quartile.

8. Find the upper quartile.

9. Draw a box-and-whisker plot of the data set.

Practice and Applications

STUDENT HELP

HOMEWORK HELP
Example 1: Exs. 10–17, 25–27
Example 2: Exs. 18–24
Example 3: Exs. 29–36
Example 4: Exs. 37–46

Measures of Central Tendency **Find the mean, median, and mode(s) of the data set.**

10. 2, 2, 3, 5, 6, 8, 9

11. 6, 7, 9, 9, 9, 10

12. 12, 18, 28, 32, 34, 35, 37, 44

13. 60, 75, 75, 75, 80, 85, 85, 90, 95

14. 10, 12, 9, 6, 11, 9, 15, 12

15. 16, 33, 31, 9, 37, 32, 33, 29, 24, 36

16. 373, 364, 360, 380, 372, 379

17. 350, 80, 880, 1040, 290, 500, 710

Finding Range **Find the range of the data set.**

18. 77, 80, 81, 81, 81, 83, 84, 84

19. 33, 56, 59, 62, 76, 89, 90

20. 78, 54, 24, 46, 98, 27, 66, 61

21. 52, 114, 102, 34, 158, 85

22. 158, 137, 144, 129, 165, 181, 130

23. 24.5, 22.7, 26.8, 28.1, 25.3. 23.9

Car Prices **In Exercises 24–28, use the following information.**

At a car lot, you find six used cars that fit your needs. The prices of these cars are $9460, $10,400, $7500, $9720, $10,400, and $9800.

24. Find the range of the prices.

25. Find the mean, median, and mode(s) of the prices.

26. You are also interested in a new car on the lot. The sticker price is $20,250. Find the mean, median, and mode of the prices of the seven cars.

27. Describe how the price of the seventh car changes the mean. Describe how this price changes the median.

28. **Critical Thinking** Does the mean or median better represent the prices of the seven cars you are considering? Explain.

Quartiles Find the lower quartile and upper quartile of the data set.

29. 2, 4, 6, 8, 10, 12

30. 1, 3, 3, 5, 5, 6, 7, 8

31. 44, 48, 49, 51, 52, 52, 52, 54

32. 121, 124, 133, 134, 148, 148

33. 228, 335, 442, 192, 267, 211

34. 62, 9, 23, 54, 48, 33, 17, 11, 28, 41

35. 10.3, 10.5, 10.1, 9.9, 10.7, 11.0, 10.8

36. 3.4, 1.2, 5.1, 1.8, 1.7, 2.3, 3.1

Drawing Box-and-Whisker Plots Draw a box-and-whisker plot of the data set.

37. 1, 2, 2, 4, 5, 7

38. 20, 30, 30, 40, 60, 80, 90, 100

39. 44, 22, 32, 48, 52, 18, 30, 42

40. 56, 42, 51, 54, 40, 59, 48, 47

41. 40, 90, 20, 40, 100, 70, 90

42. 47, 88, 89, 61, 70, 71, 79

Travel Time In Exercises 43–46, use the following box-and-whisker plots representing the numbers of minutes that the students at two schools spend traveling to school.

A.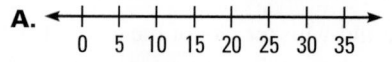

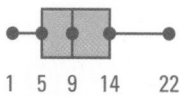

1 5 9 14 22

B.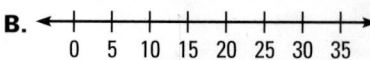

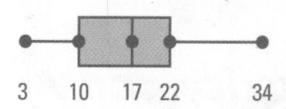

3 10 17 22 34

43. About half of the students at school A take fewer than how many minutes to get to school?

44. About three quarters of the students at school B take fewer than how many minutes to get to school?

45. At which school is the range of travel times greater?

46. What fraction of the students at school B take longer to get to school than any of the students at school A?

EXAMPLE **Find the Interquartile Range of a Data Set**

The difference between the upper quartile and the lower quartile is called the *interquartile range*. Find the interquartile range of the following data set.

$$12, 17, 25, 28, 36, 45, 46, 51, 59, 62, 66, 70, 77$$

Solution

1. **Find** the upper and lower quartiles.

   The values are already in order. The median is the seventh value, 46.

   The lower quartile is $\dfrac{25 + 28}{2} = 26.5$. The upper quartile is $\dfrac{62 + 66}{2} = 64$.

2. **Subtract** the lower quartile from the upper quartile.

   The interquartile range is $64 - 26.5 = 37.5$.

---

47. Find the interquartile range of the data set in Exercise 34.

48. Find the interquartile range of the data set in Exercise 42.

49. Multiple Choice What is the mean of 2, 2, 4, 5, and 6?

(A) 2   (B) 3.4   (C) 3.8   (D) 4

50. Multiple Choice What is the median of 1, 3, 4, 6, 11, and 11?

(F) 5   (G) 6   (H) 8.5   (J) 11

51. Multiple Choice What is the lower quartile of 5, 2, 1, 5, 3, 8, and 6?

(A) 1   (B) 2   (C) 3   (D) 4

52. Multiple Choice What is the upper quartile of 26, 14, 11, 22, 15, and 30?

(F) 22   (G) 26   (H) 28   (J) 30

53. Multiple Choice For the data set 5, 3, 7, 5, 4, 1, which measure has a value of 5?

(A) mean   (B) median   (C) mode   (D) range

54. Multiple Choice What is the range of the data set represented by the box-and-whisker plot below?

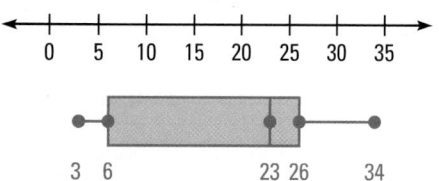

(F) 20   (G) 23   (H) 31   (J) 34

Mixed Review

Solving Equations Solve the equation. Check your solution.
(Lesson 1.4)

55. $d + 7 = 0$ **56.** $b - 20 = 10$ **57.** $\frac{x}{5} = 35$

58. $9s = 45$ **59.** $3c + 3 = 12$ **60.** $13 - 4n = -3$

61. $7x = 3x + 24$ **62.** $x - 9 = -x + 3$ **63.** $6x - 5 = 2x + 11$

Two Variable Equations Find the value of *y* for the given value of *x*.
(Lesson 1.5)

64. $2x + 3y = 15; x = 6$ **65.** $x - 5y = -7; x = 3$

66. $4x = 6y + 2; x = -4$ **67.** $6y - 11 = 5x + 1; x = 6$

68. Petition Signatures You are collecting signatures on a petition. If you collect an average of 22 signatures per hour, write an algebraic model for the total number T you collect in x hours. *(Lesson 1.6)*

Geometry Skills

Finding Angle Measures The measure of a straight angle is 180°. Find the value of *x* for the given value of *y*.

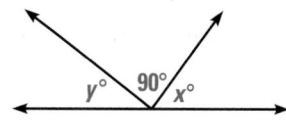

69. $y = 40$ **70.** $y = 37$ **71.** $y = 34$

1.8 Frequency Distributions and Histograms

Key Words
- histogram
- frequency distribution

GOAL Display data in frequency distributions and histograms.

Prerequisite Skills

Find the mean, median, and mode(s) of the data.

1. 21, 40, 56, 83, 90
2. 3, 4, 4, 7, 7, 7, 9, 10
3. 48, 26, 34, 80, 61, 48
4. 6, 1, 5, 4, 3, 3, 2, 5, 1

How much money does a popular film earn during its opening weekend?

The data below shows the money earned on opening weekend for the top 20 films in a recent year. Displaying this data using either a *frequency distribution* or a *histogram* can help you see what is typical of the data.

Opening Weekend Earnings (millions of dollars)
108, 103, 77, 66, 61, 59, 56, 56, 50, 50, 49, 43, 40, 36, 35, 34, 34, 32, 31, 31

A **histogram** is a special type of bar graph. Data values in a histogram are grouped into intervals of the same size. The number of data values in each interval is the *frequency* of the interval.

Before you draw a histogram, you need to determine the intervals and make a *frequency distribution*. A **frequency distribution** shows how many times the numbers in each interval occur in the data.

EXAMPLE 1 Make a Frequency Distribution

Make a frequency distribution of the film data above. Use eight intervals beginning with the interval 31–40.

Solution

Use these steps to make a frequency distribution.

1. **Write** the six intervals. The second interval extends from 41 to 50.
2. **Tally** the data values by interval.
3. **Count** the tally marks to obtain the frequencies.

Opening Weekend Earnings (millions of dollars)		
Interval	Tally	Frequency
31–40	Ⱶℍℐ Ⅲ	8
41–50	Ⅲ	4
51–60	Ⅲ	3
61–70	Ⅱ	2
71–80	Ⅰ	1
81–90		0
91–100		0
101–110	Ⅱ	2

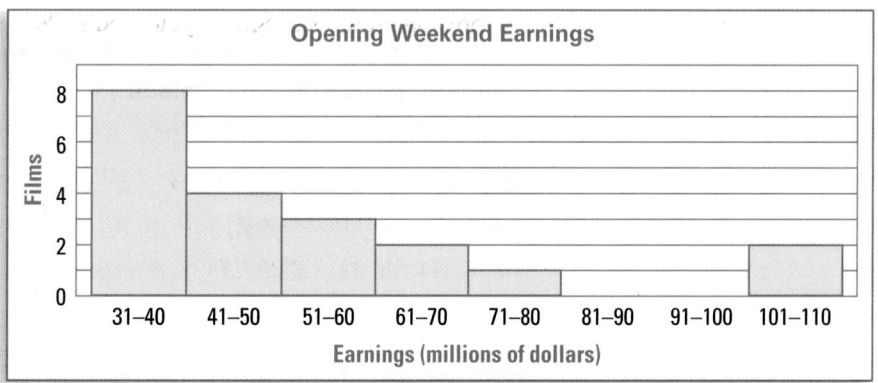

Checkpoint ✓ Make a Frequency Distribution

In Exercises 1 and 2, use the following table, which shows the test scores for 16 students on a recent Algebra 2 test.

Algebra 2 Test Scores
67, 68, 72, 73, 77, 81, 83, 83, 86, 88, 91, 95, 95, 98, 98, 100

1. List seven intervals you would use for a frequency distribution of the data. Make the first interval 66–70.

2. Make a frequency distribution of the test scores. Use the intervals you found in Exercise 1.

EXAMPLE 2 Draw a Histogram

Draw a histogram of the film data on the previous page. What can you conclude about how much money is earned during opening weekend by a popular film?

Solution

Use the frequency distribution in Example 1. Follow these steps.

1. Divide the horizontal axis into eight equal sections. Label the sections with the intervals shown in the frequency distribution.

2. Draw a scale on the vertical axis to measure the frequencies.

3. Draw bars of the appropriate heights to represent the frequencies of the intervals. Label the axes, and include a title.

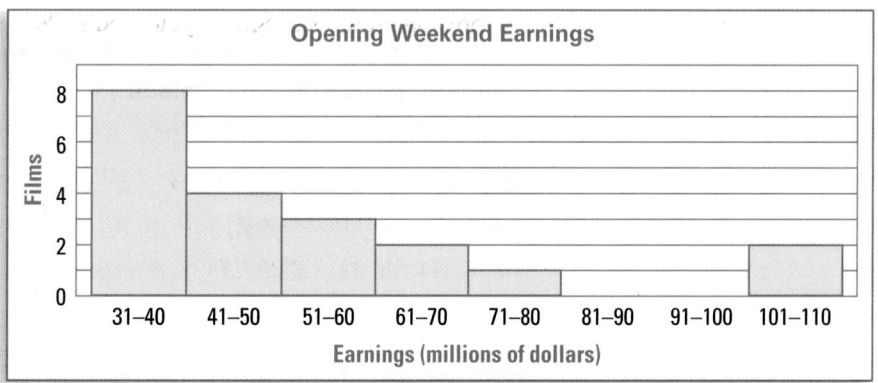

From the histogram you can see that popular films will usually earn between $30 and $60 million dollars on their opening weekends. A few very popular films earn over $100 million on their opening weekend.

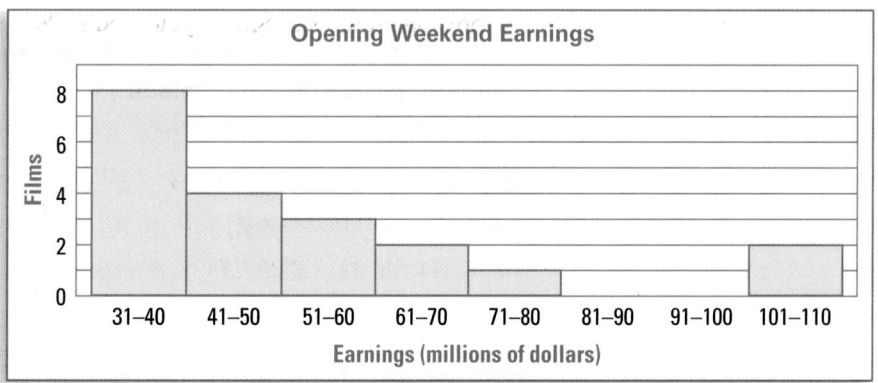

STUDENT HELP

READING GRAPHS
Notice that a histogram does not have space between the vertical bars. The spaces at 81–90 and 91–100 are because the frequency for those intervals is 0.

Checkpoint ✓ Draw a Histogram

3. Make a histogram of the test scores in the Checkpoint at the top of the page. Use the same intervals as the frequency distribution. Most of the test scores are between which values?

1.8 Exercises

Guided Practice

Vocabulary Check

1. What are two differences between a bar graph and a histogram?

2. How is a frequency distribution used to draw a histogram?

Skill Check

In Exercises 3–5, use the following data, which show the lengths of songs (in seconds) on a CD.

190, 235, 230, 256, 227, 227, 242, 219, 288, 244, 178, 257, 291, 174

3. List five intervals for a frequency distribution if the first interval is 150–179.

4. Make a frequency distribution of the data. Use the intervals from Exercise 3.

5. Draw a histogram of the data. Use the frequency distribution from Exercise 4.

Practice and Applications

Listing Intervals **List the intervals needed to make a frequency distribution of the data. Start with the given interval.**

6. 1, 2, 3, 3, 4, 5, 5, 6, 6, 7, 8, 8, 10, 12; first interval: 1–3

7. 44, 48, 49, 51, 52, 52, 52, 54, 55, 57, 60, 61; first interval: 42–44

8. 95, 84, 88, 100, 89, 91, 79, 81, 96, 94, 84, 91, 99, 86, 99; first interval: 76–80

9. 133, 121, 124, 144, 134, 148, 148, 141, 157, 160, 129; first interval: 121–125

Frequency Distributions **Make a frequency distribution of the data. Start with the given interval.**

10. The data in Exercise 6

11. The data in Exercise 7

12. The data in Exercise 8

13. The data in Exercise 9

14. 11, 14, 18, 22, 23, 25, 27, 28, 30, 36, 38, 39, 42, 45; first interval: 11–15

15. 46, 55, 57, 63, 66, 67, 68, 74, 77, 82, 83, 84, 86, 88, 91; first interval: 46–55

Histograms **Make a frequency distribution of the data set. Then draw a histogram of the data set.**

16. Use five intervals beginning with 1–2.

    Numbers of chin-ups done in 20 seconds:
    1, 1, 1, 2, 2, 2, 3, 3, 4, 4, 4, 4, 5, 6, 6, 7, 7, 7, 7, 8, 8, 8, 8, 9, 9

17. Use five intervals beginning with 10–19.

    Numbers of minutes spent on math homework:
    10, 12, 14, 15, 15, 23, 26, 26, 27, 28, 37, 37, 37, 37, 38, 39, 39, 40, 48, 58

18. Use four intervals beginning with 69–76.

    Student test scores:
    78, 87, 92, 70, 94, 99, 76, 70, 81, 95, 82, 71, 78, 79, 88, 98, 77, 84, 72, 75

Space Missions In Exercises 19–21, use the histogram. It shows flight duration information for the missions of one space shuttle.

19. How many missions were 4–5.99 days long?

20. In which interval were the greatest number of missions?

21. How many more missions were 8–9.99 days long than were 6–7.99 days long?

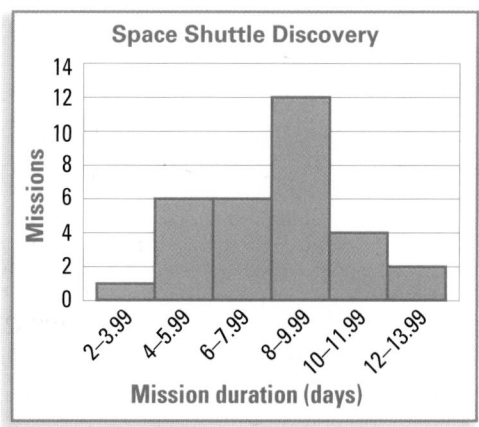

History Link In Exercises 22–24, use the table below. It gives the ages at inauguration of the Presidents of the United States.

Ages at Inauguration of the First 43 U.S. Presidents
42, 43, 46, 46, 47, 48, 49, 49, 50, 51, 51, 51, 51, 51, 52, 52, 54, 54, 54, 54, 54, 55, 55, 55, 55, 56, 56, 56, 57, 57, 57, 57, 58, 60, 61, 61, 61, 62, 64, 64, 65, 68, 69

22. Make a frequency distribution of the data set using six intervals beginning with 40–44.

23. Draw a histogram of the data set.

24. **Visual Thinking** What is one conclusion you can make about the ages of the presidents based on your histogram?

25. **Multiple Choice** A frequency distribution has six intervals beginning with 6–10. What is the fourth interval?

    (A) 18–22   (B) 19–23   (C) 20–24   (D) 21–25

26. **Multiple Choice** Use the histogram shown below. How many students have a grade point average (GPA) greater than 3.4?

    (F) 6   (G) 9   (H) 14   (J) 15

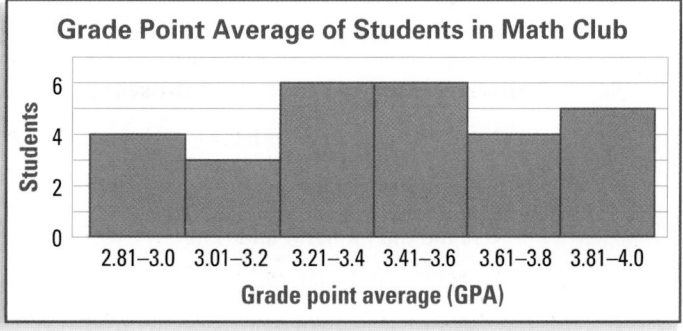

27. **Multiple Choice** What is the highest GPA shown in the histogram above?

    (A) 3.81   (B) 3.9

    (C) 4.0   (D) Cannot determine

Mixed Review

Simplifying Expressions **Simplify the expression.** *(Lesson 1.3)*

28. $7a + 3 - 5a$ **29.** $9w - (4w + 7)$ **30.** $-10 + 8(2 - 3b)$

31. $6(x + 4) - 4x$ **32.** $-3(n + 2) - (5n + 1)$ **33.** $3p - 5(2 - p)$

Mean, Median, and Mode **Find the mean, median, and mode(s) of the data set.** *(Lesson 1.7)*

34. 14, 23, 30, 37, 44, 49, 53, 54, 65 **35.** 3, 3, 4, 5, 6, 8, 8, 8, 10, 12, 12, 14

36. 142, 121, 175, 155, 109, 162 **37.** 4.6, 3.3, 1.8, 2.2, 5.7, 1.8, 6.3, 3.3

38. Quartiles Find the lower and upper quartiles of this data set: 6, 12, 15, 10, 8, 5, 21, 16, 11, 22, 9, 15, 20, 18, 24. *(Lesson 1.7)*

Geometry Review

Finding Midpoints **Give the coordinates of the midpoint of the line segment.**

39.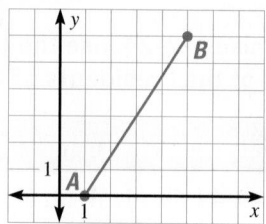

40.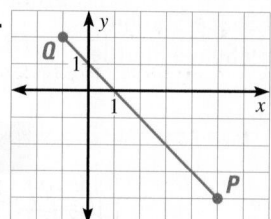

Quiz 3

Lesson 1.6

In Exercises 1–4, use the following information.

You are taking flying lessons to get a private pilot's license. The cost of the introductory lesson is $\frac{5}{8}$ of the cost of each additional lesson, which is $80. So far, you have spent $450 on the lessons. How many lessons have you taken?

1. Write a verbal model for the cost of the lessons.

2. Assign labels to the parts of the verbal model.

3. Use the labels to translate the verbal model into an algebraic model.

4. Solve the algebraic model. Answer the question.

Lesson 1.7

In Exercises 5–7, use the following data set.

1, 2, 3, 4, 6, 8, 10, 10

5. Find the mean.

6. Find the mode(s) and range.

7. Draw a box-and-whisker plot of the data set.

Lesson 1.8

In Exercises 8–9, use the following data set.

0, 0, 0, 1, 1, 1, 1, 2, 2, 2, 3, 3, 3, 6, 8

8. Make a frequency distribution using five intervals beginning with 0–1.

9. Make a histogram of the data set. Use five intervals beginning with 0–1.

Chapter Summary and Review

@HomeTutor
classzone.com
• Multi-Language Glossary
• Vocabulary practice

VOCABULARY

- origin, *p. 3*
- graph, coordinate, *p. 3*
- opposite, *p. 5*
- reciprocal, *p. 5*
- base, exponent, power, *p. 9*
- numerical expression, *p. 9*
- variable, *p. 10*
- algebraic expression, *p. 10*

- term, coefficient, *p. 16*
- like terms, constant term, *p. 16*
- simplified expression, *p. 17*
- equation, linear equation, *p. 26*
- solution, *p. 26*
- verbal model *p. 40*
- algebraic model *p. 40*

- mean, median, mode *p. 46*
- range, *p. 47*
- box-and-whisker plot, *p. 47*
- lower quartile, upper quartile, *p. 47*
- histogram, *p. 52*
- frequency distribution, *p. 52*

VOCABULARY EXERCISES

1. Give an example of each of the following: a whole number, an integer, a rational number, and an irrational number.

2. State the order of operations.

3. What does it mean for an algebraic expression to be simplified? Give two examples of simplified algebraic expressions.

4. What is the relationship between a verbal model and an algebraic model?

1.1 REAL NUMBERS AND NUMBER OPERATIONS

Examples on pp. 3–5

EXAMPLE Graph the numbers $-\frac{8}{3}$, 1.5, $-\frac{3}{2}$, 3.6, and $\sqrt{3}$ on a number line. Then write the numbers in order from least to greatest.

Graph the numbers on a number line.

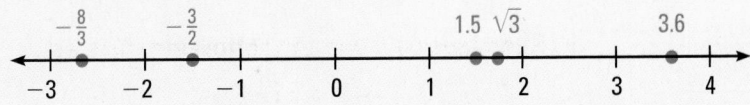

REVIEW HELP

Exercises	Examples
5–7	**3**, p. 4
8–10	**4**, p. 5

From the number line, you can see that the numbers in increasing order are $-\frac{8}{3}$, $-\frac{3}{2}$, 1.5, $\sqrt{3}$, and 3.6.

Graph the numbers on a number line. Then write the numbers in order from least to greatest.

5. 3, −7, −4, 5, 1, −1   **6.** 2, −4.1, −3, 5.2, 3.5, −1   **7.** $-1.6, \frac{11}{4}, -0.5, 0.8, \frac{5}{3}, -5, 4$

Use the distributive property to evaluate the expression.

8. 7(405)   **9.** 12(198)   **10.** 9(330)

1.2 ALGEBRAIC EXPRESSIONS AND MODELS

Examples on pp. 9–11

EXAMPLES Evaluate the expression.

a. Evaluate $5 + 3(4 - 2)^3$.

$$5 + 3(4 - 2)^3 = 5 + 3(2)^3 \quad \text{Subtract within the parentheses.}$$
$$= 5 + 3(8) \quad \text{Evaluate power.}$$
$$= 5 + 24 \quad \text{Multiply.}$$
$$= 29 \quad \text{Add.}$$

b. Evaluate $2(x - 3) + 4x$ when $x = -3$.

$$2(x - 3) + 4x = 2(-3 - 3) + 4(-3) \quad \text{Substitute } -3 \text{ for } x.$$
$$= 2(-6) + 4(-3) \quad \text{Subtract within the parentheses.}$$
$$= -12 + (-12) \quad \text{Multiply.}$$
$$= -24 \quad \text{Add.}$$

REVIEW HELP

Exercises	Examples
11–16	**2**, p. 10
17–19	**3**, p. 10
20–22	**4**, p. 10

Evaluate the expression.

11. $6 - 4 + 8$

12. $4 + 16 \div 4$

13. $10 \div 2 - 3 \cdot 4$

14. $24 \div (7 - 5) \cdot -3$

15. $4 - (-6 + 2)^2$

16. $(4 \cdot 5)^2 \div (12 - 2)$

Evaluate the expression for the given value of x.

17. $x + 5$ when $x = 3$

18. $10 - 2x$ when $x = 5$

19. $3x(x - 14)$ when $x = -1$

20. $6(2 - x)^2$ when $x = 6$

21. $x^2 - 25$ when $x = -7$

22. $-x^2 + 5x - 4$ when $x = 2$

1.3 SIMPLIFYING ALGEBRAIC EXPRESSIONS

Examples on pp. 16–18

EXAMPLES Simplify the expression.

a. $5 + 2x - 3x - 8 = (2x - 3x) + (5 - 8) \quad \text{Group like terms.}$
$$= -x - 3 \quad \text{Combine like terms.}$$

b. $4(x + 1) - 2(x - 2) = 4x + 4 - 2x + 4 \quad \text{Distributive property}$
$$= (4x - 2x) + (4 + 4) \quad \text{Group like terms.}$$
$$= 2x + 8 \quad \text{Combine like terms.}$$

REVIEW HELP

Exercises	Examples
23–25	**3**, p. 17
26–28	**4**, p. 17
29	**5**, p. 18

Simplify the expression.

23. $-5x + 7x$

24. $8 - 5x + 7x - 2$

25. $x + 9x^2 + 3x^2 - 11x$

26. $6 - 4(x - 1)$

27. $15 + 2(3x - 7)$

28. $3(x + 4) - 5(x - 2)$

29. A restaurant charges $9.95 for a large pizza with two toppings, and $1.25 for each additional topping. Write an algebraic model for the total cost C of a pizza with t toppings. Find the cost of a pizza with three toppings and the cost of a pizza with five toppings.

58 **Chapter 1** *Tools of Algebra*

1.4 SOLVING LINEAR EQUATIONS

EXAMPLES Solve the linear equation $-15x = 4(x - 3) - 7$.

To solve, isolate the variable on one side of the equation.

$-15x = 4(x - 3) - 7$	Write original equation.
$-15x = 4x - 12 - 7$	Distributive property
$-15x = 4x - 19$	Combine like terms.
$0 = 19x - 19$	Add 15x to each side.
$19 = 19x$	Add 19 to each side.
$1 = x$	Divide each side by 19.

CHECK $-15(1) \stackrel{?}{=} 4(1 - 3) - 7$

$-15 \stackrel{?}{=} 4(-2) - 7$

$-15 \stackrel{?}{=} -8 - 7$

$-15 = -15$ ✓

REVIEW HELP

Exercises	Examples
30–31	**2**, p. 27
32–33	**3**, p. 27
34–36	**4**, p. 27
37–38	**5**, p. 28

Solve the equation. Check your solution.

30. $2x + 5 = -3$

31. $18 - 7x = 4$

32. $2x + 3 = 4x - 15$

33. $7x - 3 = 5x + 17$

34. $-(x + 2) = -8$

35. $6(x - 6) = -2x - 4$

36. $3(x - 1) = x + 7$

37. $\frac{x}{5} + 2 = -4$

38. $\frac{4}{9}x - \frac{1}{3} = \frac{3}{9}x + \frac{4}{3}$

1.5 REWRITING EQUATIONS AND FORMULAS

EXAMPLES Solve the equation for the given variable.

a. Solve the equation $3x - 4y = 12$ for y.

$3x - 4y = 12$	Write original equation.
$-4y = -3x + 12$	Subtract 3x from each side.
$y = \frac{3}{4}x - 3$	Divide each side by −4.

b. Solve for h in the formula for the area of a triangle, $A = \frac{1}{2}bh$.

$A = \frac{1}{2}bh$	Write original formula.
$2A = bh$	Multiply each side by 2.
$\frac{2A}{b} = h$	Divide each side by b.

REVIEW HELP

Exercises	Examples
39–40	**1**, p. 33
41–46	**3**, p. 34

39. Solve the formula for the perimeter of a triangle, $P = a + b + c$, for a.

40. Solve the distance formula, $D = rt$, for r.

Solve the equation for y.

41. $3x + 2y = 6$

42. $-6x + 4y = -44$

43. $3x - 5y = 15$

Find the value of y for the given value of x.

44. $x - 2y = 5; x = 11$

45. $2x + 5y = 18; x = 9$

46. $-y + 3x = 4; x = -5$

EXAMPLE A new snowboard costs $405. How many weeks must you save to buy the snowboard if you can save $15 each week?

VERBAL MODEL	Amount saved per week	·	Number of weeks	=	Cost of snowboard

LABELS   Amount saved per week = 15   (dollars per week)

Number of weeks = w   (weeks)

Cost of snowboard = 405   (dollars)

<table>
<tr><td>ALGEBRAIC MODEL</td><td>15w = 405</td><td>Write algebraic model.</td></tr>
<tr><td></td><td>w = 27</td><td>Divide each side by 15.</td></tr>
</table>

REVIEW HELP
Exercises Example
47–48   **3**, p. 42

ANSWER ▶ You must save for 27 weeks.

47. A taxi charges $3.50 plus $1.75 per mile. Your ride in the taxi costs $21.00. Write and solve an algebraic model to find the length (in miles) of your ride.

48. Tulip bulbs cost $7 per pack. Crocus bulbs cost $4 per pack. You buy *n* packs of each type of flower bulb and pay $48. How many packs of each do you buy?

1.7–1.8 **BOX-AND-WHISKER PLOTS AND HISTOGRAMS**

EXAMPLE The following data set shows the ages of the players on a baseball team. Display the data using a box-and-whisker plot.

33, 29, 38, 23, 29, 25, 26, 22, 31, 27, 31, 32, 25, 30, 37, 31, 35

Write the numbers in increasing order and locate the **minimum value**, **maximum value**, and **median**. Then find the lower and upper quartiles.

22, 23, 25, 25, 26, 27, 29, 29, **30**, 31, 31, 31, 32, 33, 35, 37, **38**

REVIEW HELP
Exercises Examples
49, 52   **2**, p. 53
50   **1**, p. 46
51   **4**, p. 48

Lower quartile: $\dfrac{25 + 26}{2} = 25.5$

Upper quartile: $\dfrac{32 + 33}{2} = 32.5$

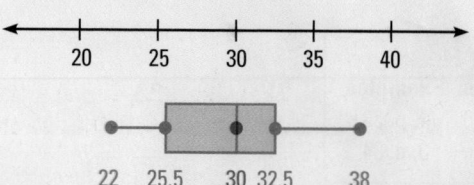

49. Display the data in the Example using a histogram. Begin with the interval 21–23.

In Exercises 50–52, use the data set of test scores below.

95, 65, 90, 55, 88, 70, 88, 100, 80, 88

50. Find the mean, median, mode(s), and range of the data set.

51. Draw a box-and-whisker plot of the data.

52. Draw a histogram of the data. Use five intervals beginning with 51–60.

Graph the numbers on a number line. Then write the numbers in order from least to greatest.

1. $-4, 5, -2, 0, -5, 6$

2. $\sqrt{3}, -2, 3, -\dfrac{3}{2}, -1$

3. $-2.25, -1, -\sqrt{15}, 3.8, 1.6$

Identify the property shown.

4. $6 + 0 = 6$

5. $8 + (-1) = (-1) + 8$

6. $7(2 + 3) = 7 \cdot 2 + 7 \cdot 3$

Evaluate the expression.

7. $12 - 9 \div 3$

8. $6 + 5 \cdot 2 - 4$

9. $20 \div (8 - 3) \cdot 7$

Simplify the expression.

10. $-3(x - 2) + 5x$

11. $2(y^2 + 2y) - (y^2 - y)$

12. $6z(z - 4) + 4(z - 7)$

Solve the equation.

13. $y + 15 = 8$

14. $5s = 35$

15. $7u + 12 = 3u - 12$

Solve the equation for y. Then find the value of y when $x = -2$.

16. $3x + 4y = 0$

17. $-x + 3y = 5x + 24$

18. $\dfrac{y}{5} - x = 4$

Road Trip In Exercises 19–21, use the following information.

You are driving from Los Angeles to San Francisco, California. The total distance of the trip is about 340 miles. You drive at a steady rate of 60 miles per hour. Use the following verbal model.

$$\boxed{\text{Distance}} = \boxed{\text{Rate}} \cdot \boxed{\text{Time}}$$

19. Assign labels to the parts of the verbal model.

20. Use the labels to translate the verbal model into an algebraic model.

21. Solve the algebraic model. How long (in hours) is your car ride?

Football In Exercises 22–25, use the table. It gives the ages of the Most Valuable Player (MVP) in each Super Bowl from 1984 to 2006.

Ages of Super Bowl MVPs
26, 25, 24, 25, 28, 38, 25, 26, 26, 33, 24, 26, 29, 34, 33, 26, 32, 31, 25, 28, 23, 25, 29

22. Draw a box-and-whisker plot of the data set.

23. Make a frequency distribution of the data using four intervals, starting with 20–24.

24. Draw a histogram of the data set.

25. Critical Thinking What is one conclusion you can draw about the ages of the Most Valuable Players in Super Bowls based on your displays?

Chapter Standardized Test

Test Tip  **Work backward from the answer choices.**

Ⓐ Ⓑ Ⓒ Ⓓ

EXAMPLE Which value is the solution of the equation $-5x = 2x + 14$?

Ⓐ $-\dfrac{14}{3}$ Ⓑ -2

Ⓒ 2 Ⓓ $\dfrac{14}{3}$

Solution

Choice A: $-5\left(-\dfrac{14}{3}\right) \stackrel{?}{=} 2\left(-\dfrac{14}{3}\right) + 14$ $\dfrac{70}{3} \ne \dfrac{14}{5}$ ✗

Choice B: $-5(-2) \stackrel{?}{=} 2(-2) + 14$ $10 = 10$ ✓

Choice B is the correct answer. You do not have to solve the equation directly to choose the correct answer.

Multiple Choice

1. Which set of numbers is in order from least to greatest?

Ⓐ $-2.5, \sqrt{6}, -3, 2.5, \dfrac{7}{3}, 5$

Ⓑ $-2.5, -3, \sqrt{6}, 2.5, \dfrac{7}{3}, 5$

Ⓒ $-3, -2.5, \dfrac{7}{3}, \sqrt{6}, 2.5, 5$

Ⓓ $-3, -2.5, \sqrt{6}, 2.5, 5, \dfrac{7}{3}$

2. Which property is illustrated by the statement $3(9 + 2) = 3(2 + 9)$?

Ⓕ Associative property of addition

Ⓖ Commutative property of addition

Ⓗ Distributive property

Ⓙ Inverse property of addition

3. What is the value of $-4 + 6 \cdot 2 - 7$?

Ⓐ -10 Ⓑ -3

Ⓒ 1 Ⓓ 9

4. Evaluate $-2x^2 + 5x + 3$ when $x = 4$.

Ⓕ -49 Ⓖ -9

Ⓗ 49 Ⓙ 55

5. Which expression is simplified?

Ⓐ $5 + 2x - 11$ Ⓑ $2x + 3x^2 - 1$

Ⓒ $5x + x^2 + x$ Ⓓ $-3x + 2x$

6. Simplify the expression $-(x + 1) - 4x$.

Ⓕ $-5x - 1$ Ⓖ $-5x + 1$

Ⓗ $-3x - 1$ Ⓙ $-3x + 1$

7. Which property would you use to solve the equation $6x = 42$?

Ⓐ Addition property of equality

Ⓑ Subtraction property of equality

Ⓒ Multiplication property of equality

Ⓓ Division property of equality

8. What is the solution of $\frac{1}{2}(x - 4) = 1$?

   (**F**) −3.5   (**G**) −2

   (**H**) 4.5   (**J**) 6

9. Solve $5x + 2y = 4$ for y.

   (**A**) $y = \frac{5}{2}x - 2$ (**B**) $y = -\frac{5}{2}x + 2$

   (**C**) $2y = -5x + 4$ (**D**) $y = -5x + 2$

10. A plane is flying from New York City, New York, to Philadelphia, Pennsylvania, at a speed of 300 miles per hour. The distance between the two cities is about 86 miles. Which equation can be used to find the time t in hours that it takes to make the trip?

   (**F**) $86 = 300t$ (**G**) $t = \dfrac{300}{86}$

   (**H**) $86t = 300$ (**J**) $t = 86(300)$

11. You mow lawns to earn extra money. You charge $14 per lawn. How many lawns do you have to mow to earn $70?

   (**A**) 4   (**B**) 5

   (**C**) 6   (**D**) 7

12. What is the median of 4, 7, 9, 7, 6, 8, 7, 3?

   (**F**) 6   (**G**) 6.375

   (**H**) 6.5   (**J**) 7

13. Which data set matches the box-and-whisker plot shown?

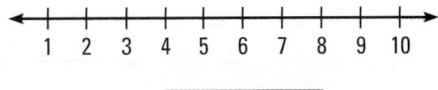
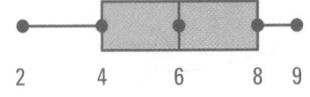

   (**A**) 2, 4, 5, 6, 7, 8, 8   (**B**) 2, 4, 6, 6, 8, 8, 9

   (**C**) 2, 4, 4, 5, 7, 8, 9   (**D**) 1, 3, 3, 6, 7, 7, 9

Gridded Response

14. What is the opposite of −3.2?

15. What is the quotient of −15 and $-\frac{1}{5}$?

16. What is the value of the expression $5x^2 - x + 3$ when $x = 3$?

17. A video store charges $4 to rent a DVD for one night and $6.50 to rent a DVD for five nights. How much would it cost in dollars to rent one DVD for one night and two DVDs for five nights?

In Exercises 18–21, use the data, which show the prices of several used cars.

   $5500, $8000, $9500, $8000, $8500, $3900, $9600, $7000, $7500, $6700

18. What is the mean of the data?

19. What is the mode of the data?

20. What is the median of the data?

21. What is the range of the data?

Extended Response

22. You are saving money to buy a new computer. So far you have saved $152. Each week you save $11.

   a. Use a verbal model to write an equation for your savings s after w weeks.

   b. Solve the equation for w.

   c. The computer costs $592. How long does it take to save enough money to buy it? How long would it take if you could save $20 each week?

Back to School SALE! $592⁰⁰

2

Linear Equations and Functions

▷ How can you predict the wind speed of a hurricane?

APPLICATION: Hurricanes

Hurricanes can cause great destruction with their strong winds and heavy rain. Weather forecasters use many factors and tools to make predictions about hurricanes.

Think & Discuss

The graph below compares wind speed (in miles per hour) and pressure (in millibars) for tropical storms and huricanes in 2005.

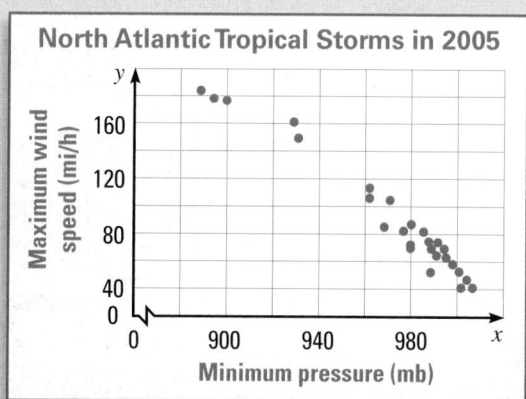

North Atlantic Tropical Storms in 2005

1. As minimum pressure decreases, what happens to the maximum wind speed of a hurricane?

2. Predict the maximum wind speed of a hurricane with a minimum pressure of 940 millibars. Explain.

Learn More About It

You will make a scatter plot of the number of hurricanes per year in Exercises 16 and 17 on page 111.

@HomeTutor
classzone.com
• Multi-Language Glossary
• Vocabulary practice

PREVIEW   **What's the chapter about?**

- Graphing and using relations and functions
- Writing and graphing equations of lines using points, slopes, and intercepts
- Writing and graphing direct variation equations
- Using scatter plots to identify correlation and find best-fitting lines

Key Words

- relation, function, *p. 67*
- domain, range, *p. 67*
- equation in two variables, *p. 68*
- independent variable, *p. 69*
- dependent variable, *p. 69*
- linear function, *p. 73*
- function notation, *p. 73*
- slope, *p. 79*
- *y*-intercept, *p. 87*

- slope-intercept form, *p. 87*
- *x*-intercept, *p. 88*
- standard form of a linear equation, *p. 88*
- direct variation, *p. 101*
- constant of variation, *p. 101*
- scatter plot, *p. 107*
- correlation, *p. 107*
- best-fitting line, *p. 108*

PREPARE   **Chapter Readiness Quiz**

Take this quick quiz. If you are unsure of an answer, look back at the reference pages for help.

Vocabulary Check *(refer to p. 9)*

1. What is the variable in the expression $3x^2 - 4x + 2$?

Ⓐ $3x^2$ Ⓑ $-4x$ Ⓒ 2   Ⓓ x

Skill Check *(refer to p. 33)*

2. What is the result of solving $6x - 2y = 10$ for y?

Ⓕ $y = 3x + 5$ Ⓖ $y = -3x - 5$ Ⓗ $y = 3x - 5$ Ⓙ $y = -3x + 5$

3. What is the value of y when $x = 2$ for the equation $6x - 2y = 10$?

Ⓐ -11 Ⓑ -1 Ⓒ 1   Ⓓ 11

TAKE NOTES   **Vocabulary**

To understand and remember a new vocabulary term, you need more than just a definition. Also include in your notebook properties, examples, and non-examples of the term.

Definition	Properties
set of output values	*y*-values in y = f(x)

range of a relation

Example	Non-example

x	0	1	2	3
y	7	8	9	10

range is 7, 8, 9, 10

Non-example
range of data:
max − min = range
10 − 7 = 3

2.1 Functions and Their Graphs

Key Words
- relation
- domain
- range
- function
- equation in two variables
- independent variable
- dependent variable

Prerequisite Skills

Evaluate the expression when *x* = −2.

1. $3x + 5$
2. $250 - 8x$
3. $\frac{1}{2}x + 6$
4. $5x - 2$

GOAL Identify and graph functions.

How is a hang glider's height related to the time descending?

In Example 4, you will use an equation and graph to model a hang glider's height when the glider descends at a constant rate.

A **relation** is a *mapping*, or pairing, of input values with output values. The set of input values is the **domain**, and the set of output values is the **range**.

A relation is a **function** if each input has exactly one output. A relation is *not* a function if any input has more than one output. Relations and functions may be represented by mapping diagrams, tables, ordered pairs, graphs, equations, or verbal descriptions.

EXAMPLE 1 Identify Functions

Identify the domain and range. Then tell whether the relation is a function. Explain.

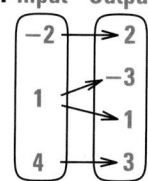

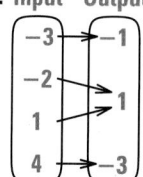

Solution

a. The domain consists of the inputs: −2, 1, and 4. The range consists of the outputs: −3, 1, 2, and 3. The relation is *not* a function because the input 1 is mapped onto both −3 and 1.

b. The domain consists of the inputs: −3, −2, 1, and 4. The range consists of the outputs: −3, −1, and 1. The relation is a function because each input is mapped onto exactly one output.

Checkpoint ✓ *Identify Functions*

Identify the domain and range. Then tell whether the relation is a function. Explain.

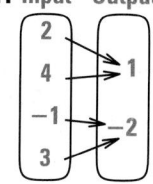

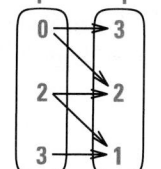

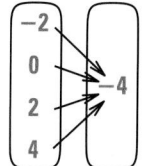

Vertical Line Test You can tell whether a relation is a function from its graph in the coordinate plane by applying the *vertical line test*.

STUDENT HELP

SKILLS REVIEW
A if and only if B means if *A* then *B* and if *B* then *A*. For help with if and only if statements, see page 765.

Vertical Line Test for Functions

A relation is a function if and only if no vertical line intersects the graph of the relation at more than one point.

Function

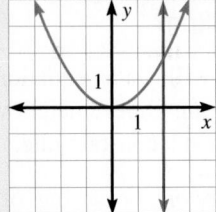

Not a function

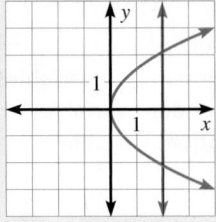

STUDENT HELP

SKILLS REVIEW
For help with ordered pairs and graphing points in the coordinate plane, see page 752.

EXAMPLE 2 Apply the Vertical Line Test

Graph the relations from Example 1. Use the vertical line test to tell whether the relations are functions.

a. First, write the relation as a set of ordered pairs.

$(-2, 2), (1, -3), (1, 1), (4, 3)$

Then plot the points.

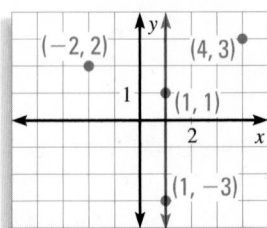

The vertical line at $x = 1$ contains two different points in the relation. So, the relation is not a function.

b. First, write the relation as a set of ordered pairs.

$(-3, -1), (-2, 1), (1, 1), (4, -3)$

Then plot the points.

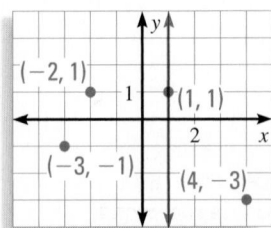

No vertical line contains more than one point in the relation. So, the relation is a function.

Checkpoint ✓ Apply the Vertical Line Test

4. Graph the relation shown in the diagram.

5. Explain how to use the vertical line test to show whether the relation is a function.

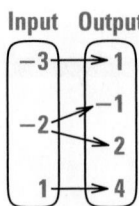

Equations You can represent many functions using an **equation in two variables**, such as $y = 2x - 5$. An ordered pair (x, y) is a *solution* of such an equation if substituting the values of x and y into the equation makes a true statement. For example, $(3, 1)$ is a solution of $y = 2x - 5$ because $1 = 2(3) - 5$.

The input variable in an equation is the **independent variable**. The output variable is the **dependent variable**. In $y = 2x - 5$, x is the independent variable and y is the dependent variable. The *graph* of an equation in two variables is all points (x, y) whose coordinates are solutions of the equation.

Graphing Equations in Two Variables

STEP ❶ *Make* a table of values, and write the ordered pairs.

STEP ❷ *Plot* enough solutions to recognize a pattern.

STEP ❸ *Connect* the points with a line or a curve.

EXAMPLE 3 Graph an Equation

Graph $y = x + 1$.

Solution

❶ *Make* a table of values, and write the ordered pairs.

Choose *x*	−2	−1	0	1	2
Evaluate *y*	−1	0	1	2	3

(x, y): $(-2, -1)$, $(-1, 0)$, $(0, 1)$, $(1, 2)$, $(2, 3)$

❷ *Plot* the points. Notice that all the points lie on a line.

❸ *Connect* the points with a line. Observe that the graph represents a function.

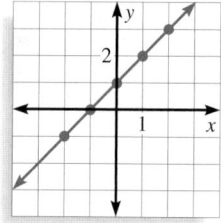

EXAMPLE 4 Graph a Real-World Equation

Hang Gliding A hang glider at a height of 450 feet begins descending at a rate of 10 feet per second. The height *h* in feet after descending for *t* seconds is given by:

$$h = 450 - 10t$$

Graph the equation. Use input values of $t = 0, 10, 20,$ and 30 seconds.

Solution

❶ *Make* a table of values, and write the ordered pairs.

t	0	10	20	30
h	450	350	250	150

(t, h): $(0, 450)$, $(10, 350)$, $(20, 250)$, $(30, 150)$

❷ *Plot* the ordered pairs.

❸ *Connect* the points with a line.

 **Checkpoint ✓** *Graph an Equation*

Graph the equation.

6. $y = x - 3$ **7.** $y = -x + 4$ **8.** $y = 2x + 3$

Guided Practice

Vocabulary Check

1. Copy and complete the statement: A mapping of input values with output values is called a __?__.

2. What are the domain and range of a relation?

Skill Check

Identify the domain and range of the relation. Then tell whether the relation is a function.

3. Input Output

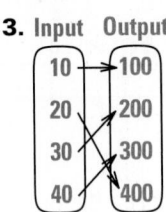

4.

x	y
−4	5
−3	1
−2	5
−1	1

5. (−10, 0)
(−6, 2)
(−6, −2)
(−1, 3)
(−1, −3)
(6, 4)
(6, −4)

Graph the equation.

6. $y = x - 1$

7. $y = x + 2$

8. $y = 2x$

9. $y = -3x$

10. $y = 2x + 1$

11. $y = 3x - 4$

Concerts In Exercises 12 and 13, use the following information.

A radio station gives away 16 pairs of concert tickets at a rate of 2 pairs of tickets each hour. The number of pairs of tickets p remaining can be modeled by $p = 16 - 2t$ where t is the time in hours after the giveaway begins.

12. Copy and complete the table of values.

t	0	1	2	3	4	5	6	7	8
p	?	?	?	?	?	?	?	?	?

13. Use the table of values to graph the equation.

Practice and Applications

STUDENT HELP

HOMEWORK HELP
Example 1: Exs. 14–20,
30–34
Example 2: Exs. 21–35
Example 3: Exs. 36–47
Example 4: Exs. 48–51

Identify Functions Identify the domain and the range. Then tell whether the relation is a function. Explain.

14. Input Output

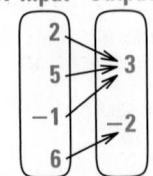

15. Input Output

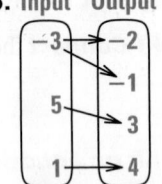

16. Input Output

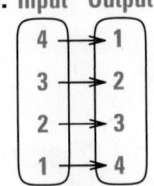

17. (8, 0), (7, 4), (6, 8), (5, 12)

18. (5, 4), (3, 1), (5, 0), (2, 7)

19. (4, 4), (2, 2), (0, 0), (2, −2), (4, −4)

20. (−3, 2), (−1, 6), (1, 6), (3, 2)

Vertical Line Test Use the vertical line test to determine whether the graph represents a function. Explain.

21.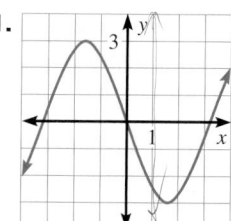

22.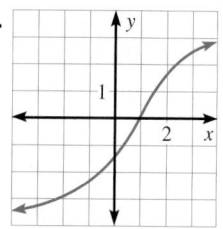

23.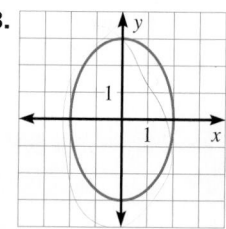

Ordered Pairs Write the relation as a set of ordered pairs. Then graph the relation.

24.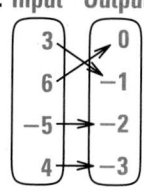

25.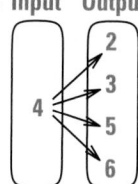

26.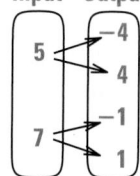

Graphing Relations Graph the relation. Then tell whether the relation is a function.

27.

x	0	0	2	2	4	4
y	−4	4	−3	3	−1	1

28.

x	−5	−4	−3	0	3	4
y	−6	−4	−2	−1	−2	−4

29.

x	0	3	6	9	12	15
y	1	1	1	1	1	1

Logical Reasoning In Exercises 30–34, copy and complete the statement with *always*, *sometimes*, or *never*.

30. A function is __?__ a relation.

31. A relation is __?__ a function.

32. The graph of a vertical line __?__ represents a function.

33. The first coordinate of an ordered pair is __?__ a number in the domain.

34. For each input value of a function, there is __?__ more than one output value.

35. Critical Thinking Explain why the vertical line test works to distinguish functions from relations that are not functions.

Graphing Equations Graph the equation.

36. $y = x$

37. $y = x - 3$

38. $y = -x + 9$

39. $y = -x + 6$

40. $y = -2x$

41. $y = 2x + 7$

42. $y = -5x + 1$

43. $y = -2x - 3$

44. $y = 4x + 2$

45. $y = 3x - 1$

46. $y = \frac{1}{2}x - 1$

47. $y = -\frac{2}{3}x + 4$

SCUBA DIVING Basic scuba diving certification requires about 30 hours of instruction. Half a million Americans become certified to scuba dive each year.

Recreation In Exercises 48 and 49, use the following information.

The pressure on a scuba diver at the ocean's surface is 1 *atmosphere*. The pressure increases by 1 atmosphere for every 33 feet the diver descends. For a recreational diver, the maximum recommended depth is 130 feet. The pressure p in atmospheres a recreational diver experiences at a depth d in feet is given by the equation below.

$$p = \frac{1}{33}d + 1 \text{ where } 0 \le d \le 130$$

48. Make a table of values. Round values of p to one decimal place.

49. Use the table of values to graph the equation.

Hot Air Balloons In Exercises 50 and 51, use the following information.

You are 250 feet above the ground in a hot air balloon when you fire the balloon's burner and begin rising at a rate of 6 feet per second. Your height h in feet t seconds after firing the burner is given by the equation below.

$$h = 250 + 6t$$

50. Make a table of values where $0 \le t \le 60$.

51. Use the table of values to graph the equation.

Standardized Test Practice

52. Multiple Choice What is the domain of the relation shown below?

$$(3, 5), (2, -2), (1, 5), (0, -2), (1, 2)$$

   Ⓐ 0, 1, 2, 3   **Ⓑ** −2, 2, 5   **Ⓒ** 0, 2, 3   **Ⓓ** −2, 0, 1, 2, 3, 5

53. Multiple Choice Which point lies on the graph of $y = 8x - 2$?

   Ⓕ (8, 2)   **Ⓖ** (8, 6)   **Ⓗ** (2, 14)   **Ⓙ** (2, 18)

54. Multiple Choice Which ordered pair is included in the function represented by the diagram?

   Ⓐ (−5, 0)   **Ⓑ** (0, 3)

   Ⓒ (5, 3)   **Ⓓ** (5, 5)

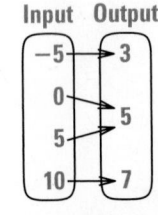

Mixed Review

Evaluating Expressions Evaluate the expression for the given values of *x* and *y*. *(Lesson 1.2)*

55. $x - \dfrac{y}{x}$ when $x = 3$ and $y = 7$

56. $3x - 4y$ when $x = -5$ and $y = -4$

57. $\dfrac{y - 5}{x - 2}$ when $x = 9$ and $y = -9$

58. $\dfrac{x - (-1)}{y + 4}$ when $x = 11$ and $y = 5$

Solve the equation. *(Lesson 1.4)*

59. $2x = -7$ **60.** $3x + 8 = -4$ **61.** $3(x + 1) + 2 = 2x$

Geometry Skills

Vertical Angles Vertical angles have equal measures. Find the value of *x*.

62.
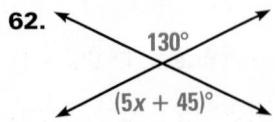

63.
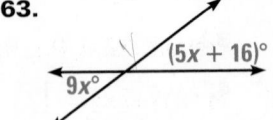

64.
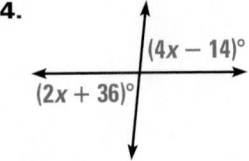

2.2 Linear Functions and Function Notation

Key Words
- linear function
- function notation

GOAL Identify, evaluate, and graph linear functions.

Prerequisite Skills

Evaluate the expression.

1. $-4(5) + 7$

2. $11 - 2(-1)$

3. $7^2 - 5(7) + 10$

4. $(-3)^2 + 6(-3) + 11$

How much does it cost to join a fitness club for one year?

Fitness clubs frequently charge a monthly fee in addition to a one-time membership fee. In Example 4, you will write a *linear function* to model the cost of a fitness club membership.

A function of the form $y = mx + b$ where m and b are constants, such as $y = 2x + 1$, is a **linear function**. The graph of a linear function is a line. By naming a function "f" you can write it using **function notation**.

$$f(x) = mx + b \longleftarrow \text{Function notation}$$

Read as "the value of f at x" or simply as "f of x."

Note that in function notation $f(x)$ is used in the place of y. The domain of a function f consists of all values of x for which f is defined. The range consists of all values of $f(x)$ where x is in the domain of f.

A function does not have to be named by the letter f. You can also use other letters such as g or h, as in the following example.

STUDENT HELP

AVOID ERRORS
Notice that $f(x)$ does *not* mean "f times x."

EXAMPLE 1 **Identify a Linear Function**

Tell whether the function is linear. Explain.

    a. $f(x) = x^2 + 2x + 1$ **b.** $g(x) = \dfrac{x}{x + 1}$ **c.** $h(x) = -4$

Solution

    a. f is *not* a linear function because it has an x^2-term.

    b. g *is not* a linear function because it has a variable term in the denominator.

    c. h is a linear function because it can be rewritten as $h(x) = 0x + (-4)$, so $m = 0$ and $b = -4$.

 **Identify a Linear Function**

Tell whether the function is linear. Explain.

  1. $f(x) = 4x - 1$ **2.** $g(x) = 5 - x^3$ **3.** $h(x) = \dfrac{9}{x}$ **4.** $r(x) = \dfrac{x}{9}$

EXAMPLE 2 Evaluate a Function

Evaluate the function when $x = -2$.

a. $f(x) = -3x + 7$ **b.** $g(x) = x^2 + 2x - 10$

Solution

a. $f(x) = -3x + 7$ Write original function.

     $f(-2) = -3(-2) + 7$ Substitute -2 for x.

            $= 6 + 7$ Multiply.

            $= 13$ Simplify.

b. $g(x) = x^2 + 2x - 10$ Write original function.

     $g(-2) = (-2)^2 + 2(-2) - 10$ Substitute -2 for x.

            $= 4 - 4 - 10$ Multiply.

            $= -10$ Simplify.

 **Checkpoint** ✓ **Evaluate a Function**

Evaluate the function when $x = 3$.

5. $f(x) = 4x - 1$ **6.** $g(x) = -2x^2 + 5$ **7.** $p(x) = x^2 + 3x + 8$

Graphing Linear Functions In Lesson 2.1, you graphed functions by first making a table of values. Because the graph of a linear function is a line, you need only two points to graph a linear function.

EXAMPLE 3 Graph a Linear Function

Graph $f(x) = 2x - 1$.

Solution

Rewrite the function as $y = 2x - 1$. Find a point on the graph by substituting a convenient value for x.

STUDENT HELP

AVOID ERRORS
To check your work, substitute to find a third point. If your work is correct, the third point will lie on the line.

$y = 2x - 1$ Write equation.

$y = 2(0) - 1$ Substitute 0 for x.

$y = -1$ Simplify.

One point is $(0, -1)$. Find a second point.

$y = 2(1) - 1$ Substitute 1 for x.

$y = 1$ Simplify.

A second point is $(1, 1)$. Draw a line through the two points.

Reasonable Domains In a real-world situation, a function model may not make sense for all mathematically possible values of the independent variable. For example, a function relating the circumference of a circle to its radius makes sense only for positive radius values. In cases like this, you can restrict the domain of the model.

EXAMPLE 4 **Write and Use a Linear Function**

Fitness Clubs You are joining a fitness club that charges a one-time membership fee of $60 and a monthly fee of $50.

a. Write a function that models your total membership cost.

b. Graph your function from part (a).

c. Use your function model to find the cost of membership for the first year.

Solution

a. Use a verbal model to write an algebraic model for the situation.

VERBAL MODEL	$\boxed{\text{Total cost}}$ =	$\boxed{\text{Monthly fee}}$ ·	$\boxed{\text{Number of months}}$ +	$\boxed{\text{One-time fee}}$

LABELS	Total cost = $f(t)$	(dollars)
	Monthly fee = 50	(dollars)
	Number of months = t	(months)
	One-time fee = 60	(dollars)
ALGEBRAIC MODEL	$f(t) = 50t + 60$	(dollars)

b. Note that $f(t)$ is a linear function. To graph $f(t)$, first rewrite it as $y = 50t + 60$. Then find two points by substituting convenient values for t.

$y = 50t + 60$ **Write equation.**

$y = 50(0) + 60$ **Substitute 0 for t.**

$y = 60$ **Simplify.**

One point is (0, 60). Find a second point.

$y = 50(2) + 60$ **Substitute 2 for t.**

$y = 160$ **Simplify.**

A second point is (2, 160). Because neither time nor cost can be negative, draw the graph in the first quadrant as shown.

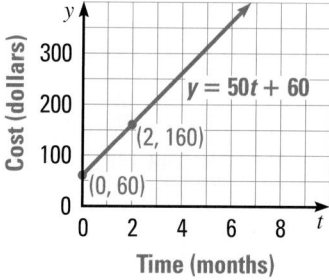

c. Since there are 12 months in a year, substitute 12 for t to find the total cost for the first year.

$f(t) = 50t + 60$ **Write function model.**

$f(12) = 600 + 60$ **Substitute 12 for t.**

$= 660$ **Simplify.**

ANSWER ▶ The cost of membership for the first year is $660.

Checkpoint ✓ **Graph a Linear Function**

Graph the function.

8. $h(x) = 4x - 1$ **9.** $p(t) = -t - 2$ **10.** $s(x) = -2x + 5$

11. For the club in Example 4, find the cost of membership for the first two years.

Guided Practice

Vocabulary Check

1. What is a linear function?

2. Write $y = 2x + 5$ in function notation.

Skill Check

Tell whether the function is linear.

3. $f(x) = x^2 + 2$ 4. $h(x) = 1 - 2x$ 5. $g(x) = -0.2x + 4$

Evaluate the function when $x = 4$.

6. $h(x) = -2x + 3$ 7. $f(x) = x^2 - x - 1$ 8. $g(x) = \frac{3}{4}x + 6$

Graph the function.

9. $h(x) = x - 1$ 10. $f(x) = 2x + 1$ 11. $g(x) = -x - 3$

Gardening In Exercises 12 and 13, suppose that a garden center sells hosta plants for $8 each.

12. Write a linear function $f(p)$ that models the cost of p plants.

13. Use your function from Exercise 12 to find the cost of 15 plants.

$8.00

Practice and Applications

STUDENT HELP

HOMEWORK HELP
Example 1: Exs. 14–19
Example 2: Exs. 20–27
Example 3: Exs. 28–36
Example 4: Exs. 38–46

Identifying Linear Functions **Tell whether the function is linear.**

14. $f(x) = -3$ 15. $h(x) = x - 1$ 16. $d(x) = -\frac{4}{x} + 1$

17. $g(x) = x^2 + 1$ 18. $p(x) = -x^4 + x + \frac{1}{5}$ 19. $v(x) = -\frac{1}{3}x - 2$

Evaluating Functions **Evaluate the function for the given value of x.**

20. $h(x) = -2x; x = 2$ 21. $f(x) = 3x - 4; x = 1$

22. $g(x) = x^2 + 1; x = -3$ 23. $b(x) = -x^2 + 3; x = 2$

24. $r(x) = \frac{1}{4}x^2 - x - 2; x = 2$ 25. $w(x) = \frac{1}{3}x + 4; x = -9$

26. $r(x) = 6x^3 - 4x^2 - 3; x = -1$ 27. $w(x) = \frac{x^2 - 1}{x - 1}; x = -6$

Graphing Linear Functions **Graph the function.**

28. $f(x) = -x$ 29. $q(x) = 3x$ 30. $v(x) = x + 3$

31. $h(x) = 2x + 2$ 32. $g(x) = 4x - 3$ 33. $p(x) = -3x + 2$

34. $g(x) = -2x - 4$ 35. $f(x) = -\frac{1}{2}x - 3$ 36. $h(x) = \frac{1}{2}x + \frac{1}{2}$

37. **Critical Thinking** The equation $y = 1$ represents a linear function, but the equation $x = 1$ does not. Explain why this is true.

Flying **In Exercises 38 and 39, use the following information.**

An airplane on a flight from Chicago, Illinois, to Amsterdam, the Netherlands, flies 4100 miles in about 8 hours. The function $d(t) = 510t$ models the distance d in miles that the plane flies in t hours.

38. Graph $d(t)$.

39. How far does the plane fly in 5 hours?

Sports Link **In Exercises 40–42, use the following information.**

In 2004, British swimmer Lewis Gordon Pugh swam 100 kilometers around the Cape Peninsula in South Africa from Cape Town to Muizenberg in water temperatures as cold as 52°F. Because of the cold, he swam in stages over a 13-day period. His total swimming time was 37 hours.

The function $d(t) = 2.7t$ models the total distance d in kilometers that Pugh traveled in t hours of swimming.

40. Writing Explain how you can choose reasonable domain and range values for $d(t)$.

41. Graph $d(t)$.

42. Use the model to predict how far Pugh swam in 12 hours.

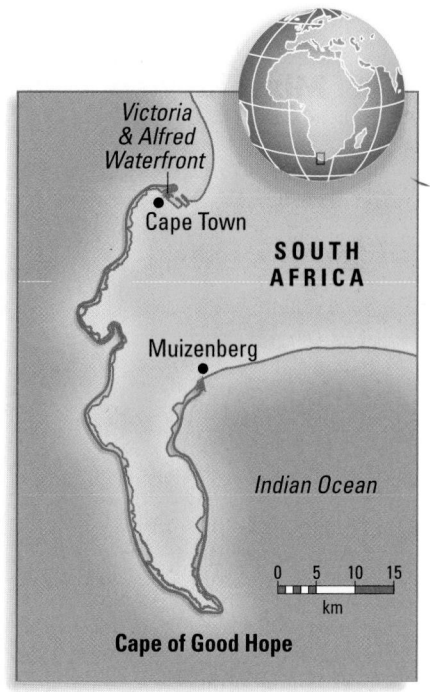

Car Payments **In Exercises 43–46, use the following information.**

You buy a used car from a local dealership. You pay $1600 and agree to make payments of $200 per month for the next 3 years, at which time the car will be paid off. The function $p(t) = 200t + 1600$ models the total amount p that you have paid for the car after making payments for t months.

43. What is a reasonable domain for $p(t)$? Explain.

44. Graph $p(t)$.

45. How much have you paid for the car after you have been making payments for 16 months?

46. What is the total amount that you pay for the car? Explain.

47. Critical Thinking You graph a linear function using two input values. Your friend graphs the same function using two different input values. Will you *sometimes*, *always*, or *never* obtain the same graph? Explain.

48. Multiple Choice Which of the following is a linear function?

Ⓐ $f(x) = x^2 + 1$ Ⓑ $h(x) = x^2 + x$

Ⓒ $g(x) = \dfrac{x}{4}$ Ⓓ $p(x) = -\dfrac{3}{x} - 1$

49. Multiple Choice What is the value of $f(x) = x^2 + 2x - 3$ when $x = -3$?

Ⓕ -3 Ⓖ -1 Ⓗ 0 Ⓙ 3

50. Multiple Choice What function is shown in the graph?

(A) $g(x) = 3x + 1$ (B) $g(x) = 2x - 1$

(C) $g(x) = 2x + 1$ (D) $g(x) = 3x - 1$

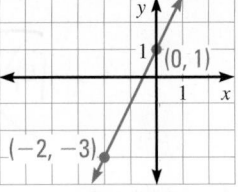

51. Multiple Choice The function $d(t) = 0.125t$ models the distance in miles a jogger runs in t minutes. How many miles does the jogger run in half an hour?

(F) 0.0625 mi   (G) 3.75 mi   (H) 6.25 mi   (J) 7.5 mi

Mixed Review

Combining Like Terms Simplify the expression by combining like terms. (Lesson 1.3)

52. $4x - 3x$

53. $y + 7y$

54. $5s - 7s + 2$

55. $9 - 6z + 8z - 8$

56. $4b + 3b^2 - 7b + 2b^2$

57. $a^2 - a + 3a^2$

Basketball In Exercises 58–61, use the histogram. It shows the margin of victory for games played by the U.S. Men's Basketball team in the 2000 Summer Olympics. (Lesson 1.8)

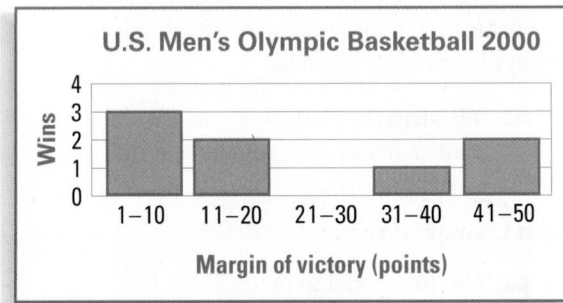

58. How many games were won by 11–20 points?

59. How many more games were won by 1–10 points than by 31–40 points?

60. What percent of the wins were by more than 30 points?

61. What is the smallest possible total margin of victory for all the games? Explain.

Identify the domain and the range. Then tell whether the relation is a function. Explain. (Lesson 2.1)

62.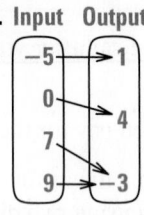

63.

x	y
−3	1
−1	2
0	2

64.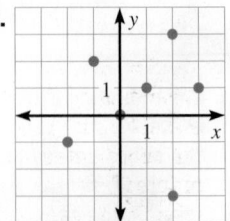

Geometry Skills

Finding Angles The sum of the measures of the angles of a triangle is 180°. Write and solve an equation to find the value of x. Then give the measure of each angle.

65.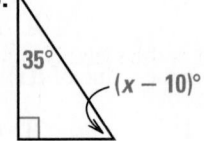

66.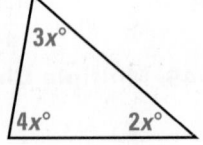

67.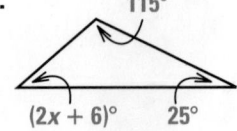

2.3 Slope and Rate of Change

GOAL Find and use the slope of a line.

Key Words
- slope

Prerequisite Skills

Evaluate the expression.

1. $\dfrac{4-2}{1-3}$

2. $\dfrac{3-5}{2-1}$

3. $\dfrac{0-(-3)}{5-(-1)}$

4. $\dfrac{2-6}{-2-(-3)}$

How can you describe the steepness of a skateboard ramp?

The **slope** of a nonvertical line is the ratio of the line's vertical change, or *rise*, to its horizontal change, or *run*. Slope gives a measure of steepness. To find the slope of the skateboard ramp shown, write the ratio of the ramp's rise to its run.

$$\text{slope} = \frac{\text{rise}}{\text{run}} = \frac{3}{7}$$

Just as two points determine a line, two points are needed to find a line's slope. The slope of a line is the same regardless of which two points on the line are used to find the slope.

3 ft

7 ft

The Slope of a Line

The slope m of the nonvertical line passing through the points (x_1, y_1) and (x_2, y_2) is given by the formula below.

$$m = \frac{y_2 - y_1}{x_2 - x_1} = \frac{\text{rise}}{\text{run}}$$

slope

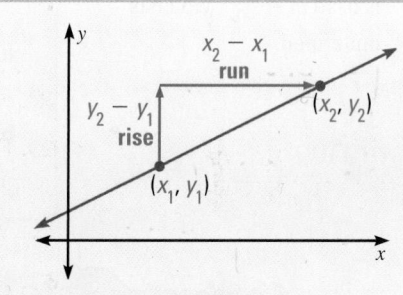

EXAMPLE 1 Find the Slope of a Line

Find the slope of the line passing through $(-1, 5)$ and $(3, 2)$.

Solution

Let $(x_1, y_1) = (-1, 5)$ and $(x_2, y_2) = (3, 2)$.

$m = \dfrac{y_2 - y_1}{x_2 - x_1}$ ⟵ Rise: Difference of y-values
⟵ Run: Difference of x-values

$\quad = \dfrac{2-5}{3-(-1)}$ Substitute values.

$\quad = \dfrac{-3}{4}$, or $-\dfrac{3}{4}$ Simplify.

You can check that the result is the same if you let $(x_1, y_1) = (3, 2)$ and $(x_2, y_2) = (-1, 5)$.

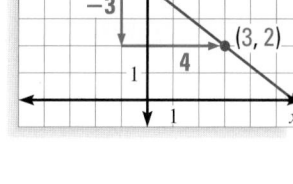

STUDENT HELP

AVOID ERRORS
When finding the slope of a line, be sure to subtract the coordinates of one ordered pair from the other in the same order.

Positive and Negative Slope In Example 1, the graphed line *falls* from left to right, and the line's slope is *negative*. This relationship is true in general. The box below details the relationship between the slope of a line and its graph.

Classifying Lines by Slope

Positive slope $m > 0$	Negative slope $m < 0$	Zero slope $m = 0$	Undefined slope m is undefined.

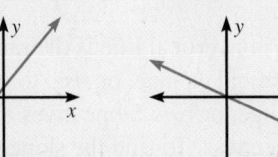 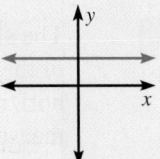 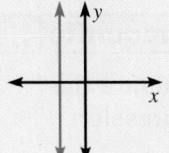

Line rises from left to right.	Line falls from left to right.	Line is horizontal.	Line is vertical.

EXAMPLE 2 Classify Lines Using Slope

STUDENT HELP

AVOID ERRORS
For horizontal lines, the *rise* is 0, so $m = \frac{0}{\text{run}} = 0$. For vertical lines, the *run* is 0, so $m = \frac{\text{rise}}{0}$, which is undefined.

Without graphing, tell whether the line through the given points *rises*, *falls*, *is horizontal*, or *is vertical*.

a. $(-4, 1), (-1, -2)$ **b.** $(3, 2), (3, 5)$

Solution

a. $m = \dfrac{-2 - 1}{-1 - (-4)} = \dfrac{-3}{3} = -1$. Because $m < 0$, the line falls.

b. $m = \dfrac{5 - 2}{3 - 3} = \dfrac{3}{0}$, which is undefined. Because m is undefined, the line is vertical.

Checkpoint ✓ Find and Use Slope

Find the slope of the line passing through the given points. Then tell whether the line *rises*, *falls*, *is horizontal*, or *is vertical*.

1. $(3, 2), (-2, -3)$ **2.** $(-1, 8), (-1, -1)$ **3.** $(-5, 4), (-1, 4)$

Steepness of Lines The slope of a line tells you not only if the line rises, falls, is horizontal, or is vertical, but also how steep the line is. For two lines with *positive slope*, the line with the greater slope is steeper. For two lines with *negative slope*, the line whose slope has the greater absolute value is steeper.

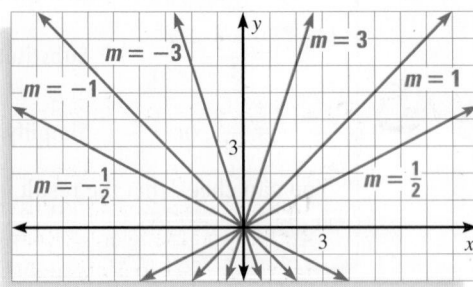

EXAMPLE 3 Compare Steepness of Lines

Tell which line is steeper.

Line 1: through $(2, 5)$ and $(4, -1)$ Line 2: through $(-1, 6)$ and $(4, 2)$

Solution

Line 1 and Line 2 pass through the given points.

Slope of **line 1**: $m_1 = \dfrac{-1 - 5}{4 - 2} = \dfrac{-6}{2} = -3$

Slope of **line 2**: $m_2 = \dfrac{2 - 6}{4 - (-1)} = -\dfrac{4}{5}$

Both lines have negative slope. Because $|m_1| > |m_2|$, line 1 is steeper than line 2.

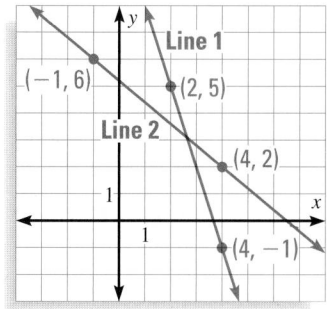

Checkpoint ✓ *Compare Steepness of Lines*

Tell which line is steeper.

4. Line 1: through $(-3, 0)$ and $(1, 5)$
Line 2: through $(-2, -6)$ and $(4, -1)$

5. Line 1: through $(21, 2)$ and $(2, 27)$
Line 2: through $(2, 3)$ and $(5, -5)$

Rate of Change In real-world situations, the slope of a line often represents an *average rate of change*, or how much a quantity changes, on average, compared to a given change in another quantity. A slope representing a rate of change will involve units of measure such as miles per hour or dollars per month.

Link to
CAREERS

VOLCANOLOGISTS
are scientists who study volcanoes. One goal of volcanologists is to predict accurately when eruptions may occur.

EXAMPLE 4 Slope as a Rate of Change

Volcanoes A volcanologist measures the temperature of a lava sample to be 2100°F. Thirty minutes later, the lava sample has cooled to a temperature of 1800°F. Find the average rate of change in the temperature of the sample.

Solution

Let $(x_1, y_1) = (0, 2100)$ and $(x_2, y_2) = (30, 1800)$.

$$\text{Average rate of change} = \frac{\text{Change in temperature}}{\text{Change in time}}$$

$$= \frac{1800°\text{F} - 2100°\text{F}}{30\ \text{min} - 0\ \text{min}} = \frac{-300°\text{F}}{30\ \text{min}} = -10°\text{F/min}$$

ANSWER ▶ The average rate of change is $-10°$F per minute. On average, the lava cools 10 degrees Fahrenheit each minute.

Checkpoint ✓ *Slope as a Rate of Change*

6. Cellular Phones The estimated number of cellular phone subscribers in the United States was 13 million in 1993, 61 million in 1998, and 219 million in 2006. Find the average yearly rate of change in the number of subscribers (a) from 1993 to 1998 and (b) from 1998 to 2006.

Guided Practice

Vocabulary Check   **Copy and complete the statement.**

1. The ratio of vertical change (rise) to horizontal change (run) of a nonvertical line is the __?__ of the line.

2. A(n) __?__ line has a slope of 0.

3. A(n) __?__ line has a slope that is undefined.

Skill Check   **Find the slope of the line passing through the given points. Then tell whether the line *rises*, *falls*, *is horizontal*, or *is vertical*.**

4. $(0, 0)$, $(1, 3)$ 5. $(2, 5)$, $(4, 3)$ 6. $(1, 1)$, $(1, -2)$

7. $(3, 2)$, $(-1, 2)$ 8. $(2, -2)$, $(-7, 1)$ 9. $(6, -3)$, $(-4, -8)$

Tell which line is steeper.

10. Line 1: through $(2, -2)$ and $(4, 6)$
   Line 2: through $(1, 0)$ and $(2, 3)$

11. Line 1: through $(-3, -5)$ and $(1, 0)$
   Line 2: through $(-2, 7)$ and $(-1, 9)$

12. **Snowfall** At 8:00 A.M., you measure the depth of snow in your backyard to be 4 inches. At 6:00 P.M., you measure the snow depth to be 19 inches. What is the average rate of change in the snow depth?

13. **Reading** You read a 210 page novel for an American Literature class. It takes you 8 hours to read the novel. What is the average rate of change per hour in the number of pages you have read?

Practice and Applications

STUDENT HELP

HOMEWORK HELP
Example 1: Exs. 14–17, 21–30, 48–50
Example 2: Exs. 18–30
Example 3: Exs. 31–38
Example 4: Exs. 39–47, 51–53

Finding Slope   **Find the slope of the line.**

14.
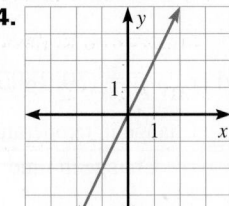

15.

16.

17. **Slope of a Road** A road rises 50 feet over a horizontal distance of 600 feet. What is the slope of the road?

Classifying Slope   **Tell whether the slope of each segment in the figure is *positive*, *negative*, *zero*, or *undefined*.**

18.
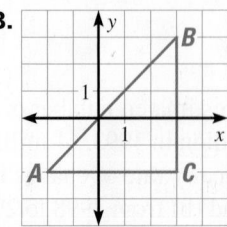

19.
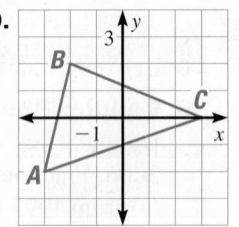

20.
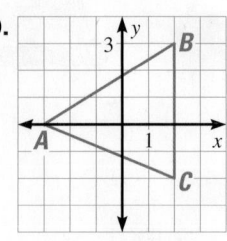

Finding Slope **Find the slope of the line passing through the given points. Then tell whether the line *rises*, *falls*, *is horizontal*, or *is vertical*.**

21. $(3, 1), (2, 6)$

22. $(-2, 5), (-2, 4)$

23. $(0, 8), (2, 10)$

24. $(-3, -3), (3, 1)$

25. $(5, 0), (6, -2)$

26. $(-2, -8), (5, -8)$

27. $(-1, 2), (5, 3)$

28. $\left(\frac{1}{2}, 4\right), (-1, 4)$

29. $\left(4, \frac{1}{2}\right), \left(5, \frac{1}{4}\right)$

30. Graphing and Slope Graph the line through the points $(-1, -3)$ and $(7, -8)$. From the graph, tell whether the slope of the line is *positive*, *negative*, *zero*, or *undefined*. Then calculate the slope to verify your answer.

Matching **Match the slope with the correct line.**

31. -2

32. $-\frac{1}{3}$

33. 0

34. 1

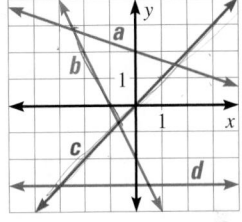

Comparing Steepness **Tell which line is steeper.**

35. Line 1: through $(3, 4)$ and $(1, 2)$
Line 2: through $(3, -2)$ and $(7, 5)$

36. Line 1: through $(1, 9)$ and $(5, 3)$
Line 2: through $(-1, 3)$ and $(1, -1)$

37. Line 1: through $(3, -8)$ and $(5, 6)$
Line 2: through $(-4, 1)$ and $(-2, 11)$

38. Line 1: through $\left(2, \frac{1}{3}\right)$ and $(1, 0)$
Line 2: through $(-4, 3)$ and $(3, 10)$

Average Rate of Change **In Exercises 39–43, find the average rate of change in *y* relative to *x* for the ordered pairs. Include the units of measure for the rate of change.**

39. $(2, 8)$ and $(6, 16)$, where x is measured in hours and y is measured in miles.

40. $(1, 10)$ and $(4, 25)$, where x is measured in seconds and y is measured in meters.

41. $(3, 5)$ and $(5, 11)$, where x is measured in days and y is measured in inches.

42. $(8, 3)$ and $(5, 15)$, where x is measured in weeks and y is measured in feet.

43. $(4, 0)$ and $(2, 4)$, where x is measured in hours and y is measured in degrees Fahrenheit ($^\circ$F).

Visual Thinking **The graph represents the distance *d* traveled by a vehicle in time *t*.**

44. During what interval was the average speed greatest?

45. During what interval was the average speed least?

46. Between which two intervals did the average speed decrease?

47. Between which two intervals did the average speed increase?

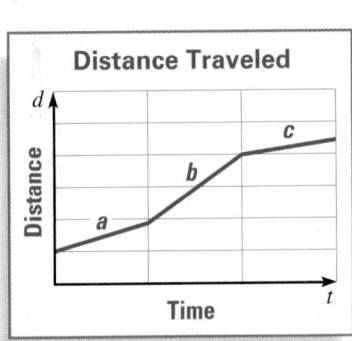

48. Rome The ancient Romans built aqueducts to carry water from rivers to towns using gravity. In a common design, an aqueduct fell 3 meters for each kilometer in length. What is the slope of an aqueduct built using this design?

49. Pitch of a Roof A town's building codes require the roof of a house to have a minimum slope, or *pitch*. To comply, a roof must rise at least 1 foot for every 3 horizontal feet. Does the roof of the house shown in the diagram comply with the code? Explain.

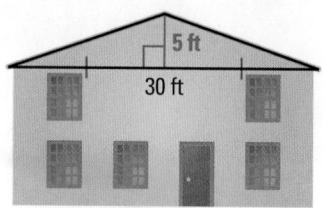

50. Volcanoes Cone-shaped Shishaldin Volcano in Alaska rises to a height of 9372 feet. One mile in elevation below the top of the volcano, its diameter is about $3\frac{1}{2}$ miles. What is the slope of the sides of Shishaldin Volcano?

51. Grand Canyon You are camping on the North Rim of the Grand Canyon at an elevation of 8200 feet. When it is 75°F at your camp, it is 104°F along the Colorado River at the canyon's bottom at an elevation of 2400 feet. What is the average rate of change in temperature with rising elevation?

52. Gas Stations A storage tank at a 24-hour gas station contains 25,000 gallons of gasoline at 8:00 A.M. on Monday. At 8:00 A.M. on Friday of the following week, the amount of gasoline in the tank has decreased to 7000 gallons. What is the average hourly rate of change of gasoline in the tank?

53. Downloads You begin downloading a 1400 megabyte (MB) movie, then go do homework. Fifty minutes later, you find that 825 MB remain to be downloaded. What is the average rate of change per minute in the amount downloaded?

Challenge In Exercises 54–57, find the value of *k* so that the line through the given points has the given slope.

54. $(k, 2)$ and $(0, 0)$, $m = 2$

55. $(1, 0)$ and $(3, k)$, $m = 3$

56. $(k, 4)$ and $(3, 2k)$, $m = -1$

57. $(1, -k)$ and $(3k, 5)$, $m = \frac{1}{2}$

58. Multi-Step Problem You are in charge of building a handicapped-access ramp for a school. To meet federal regulations, the ramp will extend 12 inches for every inch of rise. The ramp needs to rise 18 inches.

a. What is the slope of the ramp?

b. How far must the ramp extend horizontally?

c. How does shortening or lengthening a ramp of a given height affect the slope of the ramp? Explain.

59. Multiple Choice The line passing through which pair of points has a slope of −3?

A $(-2, 2)$ and $(0, 8)$ **B** $(-3, 7)$ and $(1, 1)$

C $(-1, 6)$ and $(2, -3)$ **D** $(2, 3)$ and $(3, -1)$

Mixed Review

Evaluating Evaluate the expression for the given value of *x*. *(Lesson 1.2)*

60. $x - 3$ when $x = 4$

61. $7 + 5x$ when $x = 2$

62. $2(8 + x)$ when $x = -11$

63. $3x(2x - 6)$ when $x = 4$

Evaluating Find the value of *y* for the given value of *x*. *(Lesson 1.5)*

64. $y - x = 7; x = 4$

65. $3x + 2y = -8; x = -2$

66. $9 - 5y = 7x + 1; x = -1$

67. $3(x - 4) - 6y = 22; x = 3$

Measures of Central Tendency Find the mean, median, and mode(s) of the data set. *(Lesson 1.7)*

68. 1, 2, 2, 2, 3, 3, 4, 5, 7, 8

69. 8, 12, 7, 11, 3, 17, 12

Geometry Skills

Similar Triangles Triangles *RTQ* and *QSP* are similar. Find the coordinates of *P*. Compare the slopes of $\overline{PQ}$, $\overline{QR}$, and $\overline{PR}$.

70.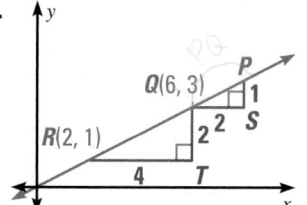

71.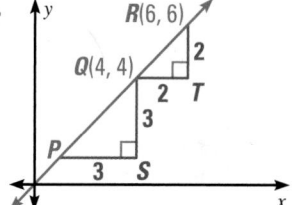

Quiz 1

Lesson 2.1

Identify the domain and the range. Then tell whether the relation is a function. Explain.

1.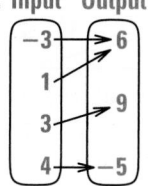

2.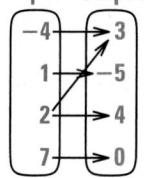

Lesson 2.1

Graph the equation.

3. $y = x + 5$

4. $y = x - 2$

5. $y = 3x + 2$

6. $y = -3x - 3$

Lesson 2.2

Tell whether the function is linear. Then evaluate the function when $x = -2$.

7. $y = x^2 - 1$

8. $y = 4x + 7$

9. $y = -2x - \frac{2}{3}$

10. $y = \frac{1}{2}x - 3$

Lesson 2.3

In Exercises 11–13, find the slope of the line passing through the given points.

11. $(6, -1), (0, -1)$

12. $(-3, -1), (5, 3)$

13. $(-2, 1), (9, -1)$

Lesson 2.3

14. Rent The amount your family pays for rent increases from $1125 per month to $1395 per month over a 6 year period. What is the average annual rate of change in the rent that your family pays?

DEVELOPING CONCEPTS *(For use with Lesson 2.4)*
Slope-Intercept Form

Goal

Determine how the constants *m* and *b* affect the graph of $y = mx + b$.

Materials

- graph paper
- protractor
- straightedge

QUESTION

How do the values of *m* and *b* affect the graph of $y = mx + b$?

EXPLORE

1 Copy the graph of $y = \frac{1}{3}x$ shown below on a coordinate grid. Then graph each given equation on the same grid. Describe any patterns you see.

  a. $y = \frac{1}{3}x - 1$

  b. $y = \frac{1}{3}x + 2$

  c. $y = \frac{1}{3}x + 3$

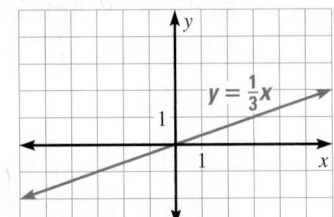

2 For each equation in Step 1, give the slope of the line and the coordinates of the point where the graph crosses the *y*-axis.

3 On another grid, copy the graph of $y = -\frac{1}{4}x$ shown below. Then graph each equation given on the same grid. Use a protractor to measure the angles formed by all pairs of intersecting lines. Which pairs of lines are perpendicular?

  a. $y = 4x$

  b. $y = 4x - 2$

  c. $y = -4x + 4$

  d. $y = -4x - 2$

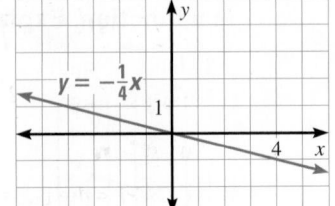

4 For each equation in Step 3, give the slope of the line and the coordinates of the point where the graph crosses the *y*-axis.

STUDENT HELP

LOOK BACK
Lines that intersect at a right angle (or 90°) are *perpendicular*.

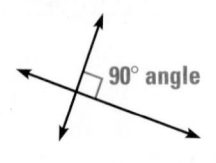
90° angle

THINK ABOUT IT

1. Predict the slope and the coordinates of the point where the graph crosses the *y*-axis for the equation $y = 3x + 5$.

2. Graph the line $y = 3x + 5$ to test your predictions from Exercise 1. Were your predictions correct?

3. Based on your observations, predict the relationship between the graphs of $y = 2x$ and $y = 2x - 4$. Explain your reasoning.

4. Based on your observations, predict the relationship between the graphs of $y = \frac{2}{5}x$ and $y = -\frac{5}{2}x$. Explain your reasoning.

5. What information do you think the values of *m* and *b* give you about the graph of an equation of the form $y = mx + b$? How can you use *m* or *b* to determine whether two lines are parallel or perpendicular?

2.4 Quick Graphs of Linear Equations

Key Words
- *y*-intercept
- slope-intercept form
- *x*-intercept
- standard form of a linear equation

Prerequisite Skills

Solve for *y*.

1. $4x + 2y = 8$

2. $x + 5y = 10$

3. $3x - 6y = 12$

4. $-2y - 7x = 42$

GOAL Use slope-intercept form and standard form to graph equations.

In Activity 2.4, you saw that the graph of $y = mx + b$ has slope *m* and intersects the *y*-axis at $(0, b)$. The *y*-coordinate of a point where a graph intersects the *y*-axis is a **y-intercept**. So, the graph of $y = mx + b$ has *y*-intercept *b*. A linear equation $y = mx + b$ is in **slope-intercept form**.

slope ⟶   ⟵ *y*-intercept
$$y = mx + b$$

Graphing Equations in Slope-Intercept Form

STEP ❶ *Write* the equation in slope-intercept form by solving for *y*.

STEP ❷ *Find* the *y*-intercept and plot the corresponding point.

STEP ❸ *Find* the slope and use it to plot a second point on the line.

STEP ❹ *Draw* a line through the two points.

EXAMPLE 1 Use Slope-Intercept Form to Graph a Line

Graph $y - \frac{3}{4}x = 2$.

Solution

❶ *Write* the equation in slope-intercept form by adding $\frac{3}{4}x$ to each side: $y = \frac{3}{4}x + 2$.

❷ *Find* the *y*-intercept. Comparing $y = \frac{3}{4}x + 2$ to $y = mx + b$, you can see that $b = 2$. Plot a point at $(0, 2)$.

❸ *Find* the slope. The slope is $m = \frac{3}{4}$, so $\frac{\text{rise}}{\text{run}} = \frac{3}{4}$. From $(0, 2)$, move up 3 units and right 4 units. Plot a second point at $(4, 5)$.

❹ *Draw* a line through the two points.

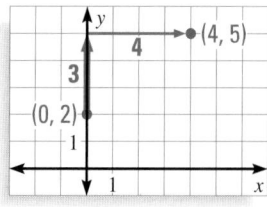

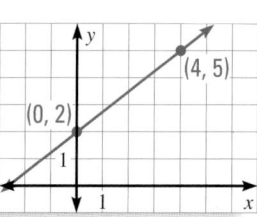

 **Use Slope-Intercept Form to Graph a Line**

Graph the equation.

1. $y = \frac{1}{2}x$

2. $y = -x - 2$

3. $y - 3 = \frac{2}{3}x$

2.4 *Quick Graphs of Linear Equations* **87**

Standard Form In Example 1, you found a y-intercept. An **x-intercept** is the x-coordinate of a point where a graph intersects the x-axis. Every linear equation can be written in the **standard form** $Ax + By = C$ where A and B are not both zero. Using the standard form of a linear equation, you can easily find x- and y-intercepts and then draw a graph.

Graphing Equations in Standard Form

STEP ❶ **Write** the equation in standard form.

STEP ❷ **Find** the x-intercept by letting $y = 0$ and solving for x. Plot the corresponding point.

STEP ❸ **Find** the y-intercept by letting $x = 0$ and solving for y. Plot the corresponding point.

STEP ❹ **Draw** a line through the two points.

EXAMPLE 2 Draw Quick Graphs

Graph $3x + 2y = 12$.

Solution

Method 1 Use Standard Form

❶ The equation is already written in standard form.

❷ **Find** the x-intercept.

$$3x + 2(0) = 12 \qquad \text{Let } y = 0.$$
$$x = 4 \qquad \text{Solve for } x.$$

The x-intercept is 4, so plot the point $(4, 0)$.

❸ **Find** the y-intercept.

$$3(0) + 2y = 12 \qquad \text{Let } x = 0.$$
$$y = 6 \qquad \text{Solve for } y.$$

The y-intercept is 6, so plot the point $(0, 6)$.

❹ **Draw** a line through the intercepts.

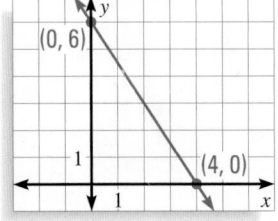

Method 2 Use Slope-Intercept Form

Solve for y to rewrite the equation.

$$3x + 2y = 12 \qquad \text{Standard form}$$
$$2y = -3x + 12 \qquad \text{Solve for } y.$$
$$y = -\frac{3}{2}x + 6 \qquad \text{Slope-intercept form}$$

Now graph using the method of Example 1.

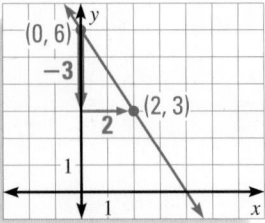

> **STUDENT HELP**
>
> **SOLVING NOTE**
>
> To find the x-intercept, let $y = 0$.
>
> To find the y-intercept, let $x = 0$.

Checkpoint ✔ Draw Quick Graphs

Graph the equation. Choose either method.

4. $x + y = 7$ **5.** $y = -\frac{1}{2}x + 3$ **6.** $5x + 2y = 10$

Parallel and Perpendicular Lines Two lines are *parallel* if they lie in the same plane and never intersect. Two lines are *perpendicular* if they intersect to form a right angle. You can use slope to determine whether two different nonvertical lines are parallel or perpendicular.

Slopes of Parallel and Perpendicular Lines

Consider two different nonvertical lines ℓ_1 and ℓ_2 with slopes m_1 and m_2.

The lines are parallel if and only if they have the same slope.

$$m_1 = m_2$$

The lines are perpendicular if and only if their slopes are negative reciprocals of each other.

$$m_1 = -\frac{1}{m_2} \quad \text{or} \quad m_1 \cdot m_2 = -1$$

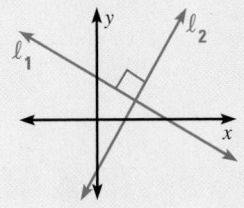

EXAMPLE 3 **Graph Parallel and Perpendicular Lines**

a. Draw the graph of $y = 3x + 4$.

b. Graph the line that passes through $(0, -1)$ and is parallel to the graph of $y = 3x + 4$.

c. Graph the line that is perpendicular to the graph of $y = 3x + 4$ at its *y*-intercept.

Solution

a. Draw the graph of $y = 3x + 4$ using the *y*-intercept 4 and slope 3.

b. Graph the point $(0, -1)$. Any line parallel to the graph of $y = 3x + 4$ has the same slope, 3. From $(0, -1)$, move up 3 units and right 1 unit. Plot a second point at $(1, 2)$. Draw a line through the two points.

c. The slope of any line perpendicular to the graph of $y = 3x + 4$ is the negative reciprocal of 3, or $-\frac{1}{3}$. So, from $(0, 4)$, move down 1 unit and right 3 units.

Plot a second point at $(3, 3)$. Draw the line.

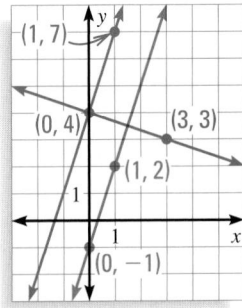

Checkpoint ✓ **Graph Parallel and Perpendicular Lines**

Graph the line. On the same grid, graph (a) the line passing through the origin that is parallel to the original line, and (b) the line perpendicular to the original line at its *y*-intercept.

7. $y = 2x - 1$ **8.** $y = \frac{3}{4}x + 2$ **9.** $y = -\frac{1}{5}x + 1$

2.4 Exercises

Guided Practice

Vocabulary Check

1. What are the slope-intercept form and the standard form of a linear equation?

2. What is the slope of any line perpendicular to the line $y = 7x + 3$? Explain.

3. What is the slope of any line parallel to the line $y = 7x + 3$? Explain.

Skill Check

Find the slope and *y*-intercept of the line.

4. $y = x + 10$

5. $y = -2x - 7$

6. $y = \frac{2}{3}x - 2$

In Exercises 7–9, find the *x*- and *y*-intercepts of the line.

7. $x + y = 9$

8. $2x - y = 12$

9. $3x - 2y = 18$

10. Movies The average cost y in dollars of a movie ticket in the United States can be modeled by $y = 0.22t + 4$ where t represents the number of years since 1994. Identify the slope and the *y*-intercept. Then graph the equation.

Practice and Applications

STUDENT HELP

HOMEWORK HELP
Example 1: Exs. 14–28
Example 2: Exs. 29–37,
    57–66
Example 3: Exs. 38–49,
    67–68

Graph of a Line **Use the graph to find the indicated value.**

11. slope of the line

12. *x*-intercept of the line

13. *y*-intercept of the line

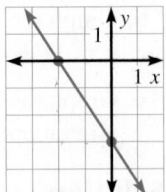

Matching Graphs **Match the equation with its graph.**

14. $y = -5x + 10$

15. $y = -\frac{1}{2}x - 5$

16. $y = 4x - 12$

A.
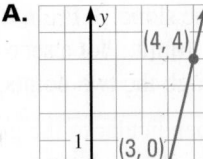

B.
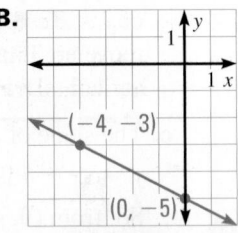

C.
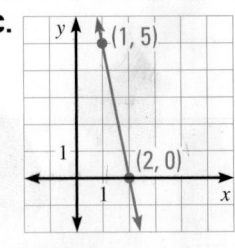

Using Slope and *y*-Intercept **Draw the line with the given slope and *y*-intercept.**

17. $m = 3, b = -2$

18. $m = -2, b = 0$

19. $m = 1, b = 1$

20. $m = -1, b = 0$

21. $m = \frac{1}{2}, b = 5$

22. $m = \frac{1}{2}, b = -1$

Slope-Intercept Form **Graph the equation.**

23. $y = -x + 5$

24. $y = 4x + 1$

25. $y = x - 9$

26. $y = -3x - 6$

27. $y = \frac{1}{2}x + 4$

28. $y = \frac{2}{3}x - 1$

Matching Graphs Match the equation with its graph.

29. $x - 4y = -8$ **30.** $3x + 6y = -9$ **31.** $2x - 3y = -12$

A. 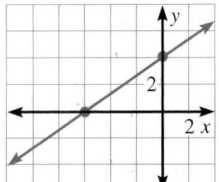   **B.** 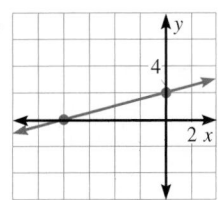   **C.**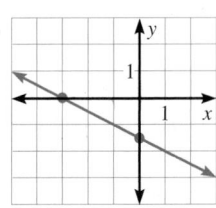

Standard Form Graph the equation. Label the intercepts.

32. $2x + y = 8$ **33.** $x + 2y = -8$ **34.** $3x + 4y = -10$

35. $3x - y = 3$ **36.** $x - 6y = -1$ **37.** $-9x + 6y = 12$

Parallel and Perpendicular Lines Tell whether the lines are *parallel*, *perpendicular*, or *neither*.

38. $y = 6x + 2$ and $y = -\frac{1}{6}x + 4$ **39.** $y = 3x + 6$ and $y = 6x + 3$

40. $y = -2x + 2$ and $y = -2x - 2$ **41.** $x + y = 3$ and $x - y = 3$

42. $2x + y = 5$ and $4x + 2y = 1$ **43.** $3x - 2y = 0$ and $4x + 6y = 5$

Graphing Related Lines Graph the line. On the same grid, graph (a) the line passing through (1, 1) that is parallel to the original line, and (b) the line perpendicular to the original line at its *y*-intercept.

44. $y = -x$ **45.** $y = 7x + 2$ **46.** $y = 3x + 10$

47. $y = \frac{5}{3}x$ **48.** $x + 2y = 8$ **49.** $-x + 4y = -4$

EXAMPLE Horizontal and Vertical Lines

Graph the equation.

   a. $y = 4$ **b.** $x = -1$

Solution

  a. The *y*-coordinate is 4 no matter what the value of *x* is. So, the graph of $y = 4$ is the horizontal line that passes through (0, 4). The *y*-intercept is 4.

  b. The *x*-coordinate is -1 no matter what the value of *y* is. So, the graph of $x = -1$ is the vertical line that passes through $(-1, 0)$. The *x*-intercept is -1.

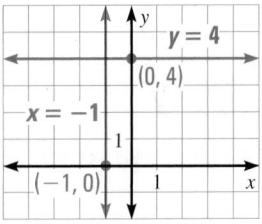

Horizontal and Vertical Lines Graph the equation.

50. $x = 0$ **51.** $x = 1.5$ **52.** $y = 3$

53. $y = -1$ **54.** $y = 4.5$ **55.** $x = -3$

56. Critical Thinking Can a line have no *x*-intercept? no *y*-intercept? no *x*-intercept *and* no *y*-intercept? If so, describe the lines that satisfy each condition.

Quick Graphs Graph the equation using any method.

57. $y = 3x + 7$ **58.** $y = -6$ **59.** $-7y = -2x + 14$

60. $-x + 8y = 18$ **61.** $x = 15$ **62.** $x = -2y + 6$

63.  **Taxes** The amount a (in billions of dollars) in taxes collected from 1980 to 2005 by the Internal Revenue Service can be modeled by $a = 72.2t + 396$ where t represents the number of years since 1980. Graph the equation.

64. Sales The numbers of individual memberships x and family memberships y a zoo employee must sell to meet a weekly sales goal of $4000 is modeled by $50x + 80y = 4000$. Graph the equation.

Backpacking In Exercises 65 and 66, use the following information.

The weight W (in pounds) of a backpack a hiker carries on a multi-day hike can be modeled by $W = 2.5d + 35$ where d represents the length of the trip (in days).

65. Identify the slope and the y-intercept. Then graph the equation.

66. Writing Describe what the slope and the y-intercept represent in this situation.

Challenge Find the value of h that makes the line through the given points perpendicular to the graph of $y = \frac{1}{3}x + 14$.

67. $(0, h)$ and $(2h, 5)$ **68.** $(h + 1, 5)$ and $(4, h)$

69. Multiple Choice What is the slope-intercept form of $x - 3y = 4$?

    Ⓐ $x = 3y + 4$ **Ⓑ** $-3y = -x + 4$

    Ⓒ $-y = -\frac{1}{3}x + \frac{4}{3}$ **Ⓓ** $y = \frac{1}{3}x - \frac{4}{3}$

70. Multiple Choice Which equation represents the graph shown?

    Ⓕ $y = \frac{1}{2}x + 1$ **Ⓖ** $y = \frac{1}{2}x - 2$

    Ⓗ $y = 2x + 1$ **Ⓙ** $y = 2x - 2$

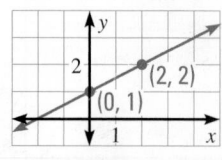

Mixed Review

Box-and-Whisker Plots Draw a box-and-whisker plot of the data set. *(Lesson 1.7)*

71. 14, 15, 19, 15, 12, 14, 16, 10, 14   **72.** 32, 24, 23, 39, 29, 21, 38, 23

Finding Slope Find the slope of the line passing through the given points. *(Lesson 2.3)*

73. $(5, 5), (2, 4)$ **74.** $(4, 3), (0, 0)$ **75.** $(3, -3), (7, -7)$

Geometry Skills

76. Right Triangles In a right triangle, two sides are perpendicular to one another. Find the slope of each side of the triangle shown. Is the triangle a right triangle? Explain.

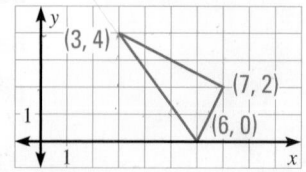

You can use a graphing calculator to graph linear equations.

EXAMPLE

Use a graphing calculator to graph $2x + 5y = 30$.

SOLUTION

① Solve the equation for y to change it
from standard form to slope-intercept
form, which is the form required by
most calculators.

$$2x + 5y = 30$$
$$5y = -2x + 30$$
$$y = -\frac{2}{5}x + 6$$

② Enter the equation into the
calculator, using parentheses for
the fractional coefficient. So, enter
$y = -(2/5)x + 6$.

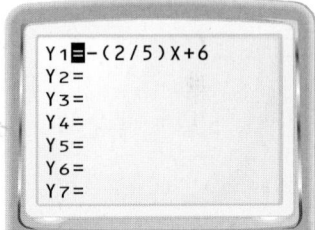

③ Set a viewing window for the graph. To do this, enter the least and greatest
x- and y-values and the x- and y-scales as shown. Then graph the equation.

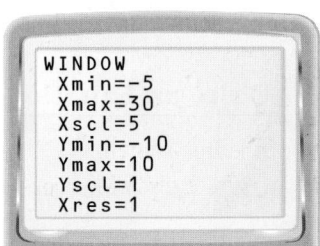

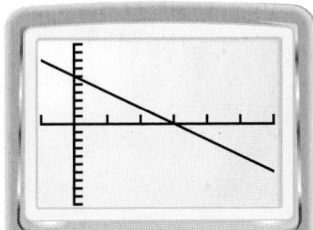

EXERCISES

**Use a graphing calculator to graph the equation in the standard
viewing window.**

1. $2x + y = -3$ **2.** $-5x + y = 1$ **3.** $x - 4y = 3$

**Use a graphing calculator to graph the equation in the indicated
viewing window.**

4. $-4x + 2y = -34$ Xmin $= -2$, Xmax $= 12$, Xscl $= 2$,
                         Ymin $= -20$, Ymax $= 2$, Yscl $= 5$

5. $100x - y = 2200$ Xmin $= -10$, Xmax $= 30$, Xscl $= 10$,
                         Ymin $= -3000$, Ymax $= 1000$, Yscl $= 1000$

**Use a graphing calculator to graph the equation. Choose a viewing
window that shows the x- and y-intercepts.**

6. $7x = 3y + 40$ **7.** $-x - 2y = -24$ **8.** $150x - y = 3000$

2.5 Writing Equations of Lines

Key Words

• point-slope form

Prerequisite Skills

Find the slope and y-intercept of the line.

1. $y = 4x - 7$

2. $y = -\dfrac{2}{5}x + 8$

3. $-x - y = 6$

4. $5x + 2y =$

GOAL Write linear equations.

How many California condors live in the wild?

In 1987, the last wild California condor was captured as part of an effort to breed condors in captivity. In 1992, the first condors were released back into the wild. In Example 5, you will write a linear model to represent the number of California condors in the wild.

If you know the slope and y-intercept of a line, you can write its equation using slope-intercept form. If you know the slope and any point on a line, you can write its equation using **point-slope form**.

Writing an Equation of a Line

SLOPE-INTERCEPT FORM	Given the slope m and the y-intercept b, use slope-intercept form: $y = mx + b$.
POINT-SLOPE FORM	Given the slope m and a point (x_1, y_1), use point-slope form: $y - y_1 = m(x - x_1)$.

EXAMPLE 1 Write an Equation Given Slope and y-Intercept

Write an equation of the line shown.

Solution

From the graph, you can see that the slope is $m = \dfrac{3}{5}$.

Because the line intersects the y-axis at $(0, -2)$, the y-intercept is $b = -2$.

Use slope-intercept form to write an equation of the line.

$y = mx + b$ Use slope-intercept form.

$y = \dfrac{3}{5}x + (-2)$ Substitute $\dfrac{3}{5}$ for m and -2 for b.

$y = \dfrac{3}{5}x - 2$ Simplify.

Checkpoint  **Write an Equation Given Slope and y-Intercept**

Write an equation of the line that has the given slope and y-intercept.

1. $m = 3, b = 1$ **2.** $m = -2, b = -4$ **3.** $m = \dfrac{1}{2}, b = -5$

EXAMPLE 2 **Write an Equation Given Slope and a Point**

Write an equation of the line that passes through (4, 2) and has a slope of $-\frac{1}{4}$.

Solution

Because you know the slope and a point on the line, use point-slope form with $(x_1, y_1) = (4, 2)$ and $m = -\frac{1}{4}$.

$y - y_1 = m(x - x_1)$	Use point-slope form.
$y - 2 = -\frac{1}{4}(x - 4)$	Substitute 2 for y_1, $-\frac{1}{4}$ for m, and 4 for x_1.

Rewrite the equation in slope-intercept form.

$y - 2 = -\frac{1}{4}(x - 4)$	Point-slope form
$y - 2 = -\frac{1}{4}x + 1$	Distributive property
$y = -\frac{1}{4}x + 3$	Slope-intercept form

STUDENT HELP

AVOID ERRORS
Watch out for negatives when you use the distributive property. Here you must multiply $-\frac{1}{4}$ by each term inside the parentheses.

CHECK You can check the result by graphing the equation. Draw a line that passes through (4, 2) and has a slope of $-\frac{1}{4}$. Notice that the line has a y-intercept of 3, which agrees with the slope-intercept form found above. ✓

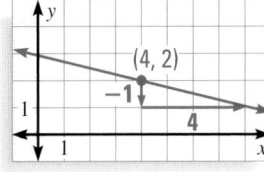

Checkpoint ✓ **Write an Equation Given Slope and a Point**

Write an equation of the line that passes through the given point and has the given slope. Write your equation in slope-intercept form.

4. $(-1, 3)$, $m = 2$ **5.** $(4, -5)$, $m = -3$ **6.** $(-2, 4)$, $m = 5$

7. $(-3, -3)$, $m = \frac{2}{3}$ **8.** $(8, 0)$, $m = -\frac{1}{4}$ **9.** $(10, -8)$, $m = \frac{3}{5}$

EXAMPLE 3 **Write Equations of Parallel Lines**

Write an equation of the line that passes through $(-1, 4)$ and is parallel to the line $y = -2x + 5$.

Solution

The given line has a slope of -2. Any line parallel to this line will also have a slope of -2. Use point-slope form with $(x_1, y_1) = (-1, 4)$ and $m = -2$ to write an equation of the line.

$y - y_1 = m(x - x_1)$	Use point-slope form.
$y - 4 = -2[x - (-1)]$	Substitute 4 for y_1, -2 for m, and -1 for x_1.
$y - 4 = -2x - 2$	Distributive property
$y = -2x + 2$	Slope-intercept form

EXAMPLE **4** Write Equations of Perpendicular Lines

Write an equation of the line that passes through $(-1, 4)$ and is perpendicular to the line $y = -2x + 5$.

Solution

The given line has a slope of -2. The slope of any line perpendicular to this line will be the negative reciprocal of -2, which is $\frac{1}{2}$. Use point-slope form with $(x_1, y_1) = (-1, 4)$ and $m = \frac{1}{2}$ to write an equation of the line.

$y - y_1 = m(x - x_1)$	Use point-slope form.
$y - 4 = \frac{1}{2}[x - (-1)]$	Substitute 4 for y_1, $\frac{1}{2}$ for m, and -1 for x_1.
$y - 4 = \frac{1}{2}x + \frac{1}{2}$	Distributive property
$y = \frac{1}{2}x + \frac{9}{2}$	Slope-intercept form

Checkpoint ✔ *Writing Equations of Parallel and Perpendicular Lines*

Write an equation of the line described.

10. passes through $(-6, -5)$; parallel to $y = -x + 2$

11. passes through $(-6, -5)$; perpendicular to $y = -x + 2$

12. passes through $(-2, 3)$; parallel to $y = 4x - 1$

13. passes through $(-2, 3)$; perpendicular to $y = 4x - 1$

Link to
WILDLIFE

CONDORS The California condor is North America's largest bird, with a wingspan that can reach over 9 feet. Introducing condors into the wild in multiple locations increases the chances that the species will survive.

EXAMPLE **5** Write a Linear Model

Condors In 1995 there were only 6 California condors living in the wild (all in California). In 2006 there were 138 California condors living in the wild (in California, Arizona, and Mexico). Write a linear model that represents the number of California condors living in the wild between 1995 and 2006.

Solution

The average rate of change in the wild population is $m = \dfrac{138 - 6}{2006 - 1995} = 12$.

The average rate of change is the slope in a linear model.

VERBAL MODEL	Number of condors	=	Number in 1995	+	Average rate of change	·	Years since 1995

LABELS	Number of condors = y	(condors)
	Number in 1995 = 6	(condors)
	Average rate of change = 12	(condors per year)
	Years since 1995 = t	(years)

ALGEBRAIC MODEL	$y = 6 + 12t$

ANSWER ▶ A linear model for the number of condors is $y = 6 + 12t$.

Guided Practice

Vocabulary Check

1. An equation written in the form $y - y_1 = m(x - x_1)$ is in __?__ form. Describe the meaning of m, x_1, and y_1 in this equation.

2. Compare writing an equation of a line using the slope and y-intercept with writing an equation of a line using the slope and any point on the line.

Skill Check   **Write an equation of the line that has the given slope and y-intercept.**

3. $m = 2$, $b = -3$

4. $m = -5$, $b = 7$

5. $m = \dfrac{2}{5}$, $b = 1$

In Exercises 6–8, write an equation of the line that passes through the given point and has the given slope.

6. $(0, 3)$, $m = -3$

7. $(-4, -1)$, $m = 2$

8. $(-3, 5)$, $m = -4$

9. **Parallel Lines** Write an equation of the line that passes through $(6, -2)$ and is parallel to the line $y = 2x - 1$.

10. **Perpendicular Lines** Write an equation of the line that passes through $(-1, 1)$ and is perpendicular to the line $y = -x + 2$.

11. **Car Value** A car that cost \$19,000 in 2003 was sold for \$10,200 in 2007. Find the average rate of change in the car's value. Write a linear model for the value V of the car from 2003 to 2007 where t represents the number of years since 2003.

Practice and Applications

STUDENT HELP

HOMEWORK HELP
Example 1: Exs. 12–23
Example 2: Exs. 24–36
Example 3: Exs. 37–39, 43
Example 4: Exs. 40–42, 55
Example 5: Exs. 53–54

Slope and Intercept **Identify the slope and y-intercept of the line shown in the graph.**

12.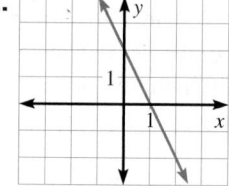

13.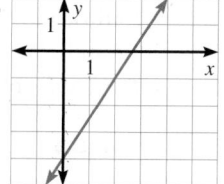

14.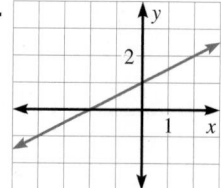

Slope-Intercept Form **Write an equation of the line that has the given slope m and y-intercept b.**

15. $m = 1$, $b = 3$

16. $m = -3$, $b = -1$

17. $m = 0$, $b = 5$

18. $m = -7$, $b = 0$

19. $m = \dfrac{3}{2}$, $b = -3$

20. $m = -\dfrac{1}{6}$, $b = 4$

Graphical Reasoning **Write an equation in slope-intercept form of the line shown in the graph.**

21.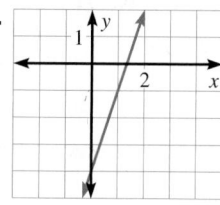

22.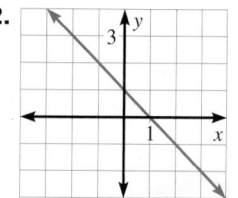

23.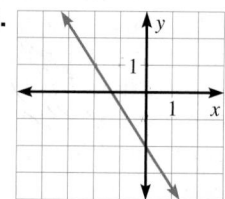

24. Error Analysis Describe and correct the error in writing an equation of the line that passes through $(-5, 3)$ and has slope 4.

$$y - y_1 = m(x - x_1)$$
$$y - 3 = 4(x - 5)$$
$$y - 3 = 4x - 20$$
$$y = 4x - 17$$

Point-Slope Form Write an equation of the line that passes through the given point and has the given slope.

25. $(0, 2)$, $m = 3$ **26.** $(-1, 0)$, $m = 2$ **27.** $(-5, -2)$, $m = 0$

28. $(3, -1)$, $m = -2$ **29.** $(-3, -5)$, $m = -5$ **30.** $(4, 1)$, $m = -\frac{1}{2}$

31. $(6, 4)$, $m = -\frac{2}{3}$ **32.** $(-2, 8)$, $m = \frac{4}{5}$ **33.** $(-13, 0)$, $m = \frac{6}{7}$

Graphical Reasoning Write an equation of the line shown in the graph.

34. 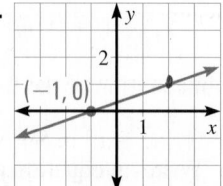   **35.** 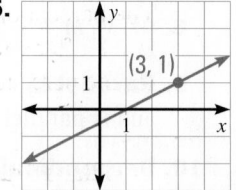   **36.**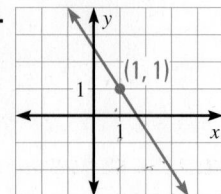

Parallel Lines Write an equation of the line that passes through the given point and is parallel to the given line.

37. $(2, 5)$, $y = 2x - 1$ **38.** $(1, -1)$, $y = -3x + 7$ **39.** $(-6, 3)$, $y = \frac{1}{2}x + 4$

Perpendicular Lines Write an equation of the line that passes through the given point and is perpendicular to the given line.

40. $(-2, 0)$, $y = \frac{1}{4}x - 2$ **41.** $(4, -1)$, $y = -\frac{4}{3}x - 3$ **42.** $(1, 1)$, $y = -2x + 5$

43. Fundraising You and a friend spend a day selling candy bars to raise money for the school choir. The number of candy bars c you have remaining h hours after you begin selling is modeled by $c = 60 - 8h$. A graph of your friend's sales is parallel to a graph of yours and passes through $(h, c) = (2, 60)$. Write a model for your friend's sales. How many candy bars does your friend start the day with?

EXAMPLE   **Write an Equation Given Two Points**

Write an equation of the line that passes through $(-1, -2)$ and $(1, 4)$.

Solution

First find the slope. Let $(x_1, y_1) = (-1, -2)$ and $(x_2, y_2) = (1, 4)$.

$$m = \frac{y_2 - y_1}{x_2 - x_1} = \frac{4 - (-2)}{1 - (-1)} = \frac{6}{2}, \text{ or } 3$$

Use point-slope form to write an equation and then simplify.

$y - y_1 = m(x - x_1)$	Use point-slope form.
$y - (-2) = 3[x - (-1)]$	Substitute -2 for y_1, 3 for m, and -1 for x_1.
$y + 2 = 3(x + 1)$	Simplify.
$y = 3x + 1$	Slope-intercept form

STUDENT HELP

ANOTHER WAY
After you find the slope, you can substitute the slope for m and the coordinates of one of the points for x and y in slope-intercept form. Then solve for b.

Writing Equations In Exercises 44–52, write an equation of the line that passes through the given points.

44. $(4, 7), (3, 4)$ **45.** $(-2, 3), (2, -5)$ **46.** $(-5, -4), (-7, 6)$

47. $(0, 2), (-2, -1)$ **48.** $(4, -1), (2, -2)$ **49.** $(6, -9), (-4, -9)$

50. $(-6, -4), (8, 4)$ **51.** $(6, 5), (6, -4)$ **52.** $(-8, 10), (-2, 17)$

53. Grizzly Bears In 1979, 13 female grizzly bears with first-year cubs were observed in the Greater Yellowstone Ecosystem (GYE). In 2004, the number observed was 49. Use the verbal model shown to write a linear model for the observed number of females with first-year cubs in the GYE from 1979 to 2004.

Number of bears	=	Number in 1979	+	Average rate of change	·	Years since 1979

54. Politics In 1971, 4.5% of the state legislators in the United States were women. The percent of state legislators who were women had increased to 22.5% by 2000, after which the percent leveled off for several years. Write a linear model for the percent of state legislators who were women from 1971 to 2000.

55. Nature Trails The new Link Trail in Spruce Creek Park will run from the Woodland Trail to the Lake Trail in a straight line as shown in the diagram. Write an equation of the line that contains the Link Trail.

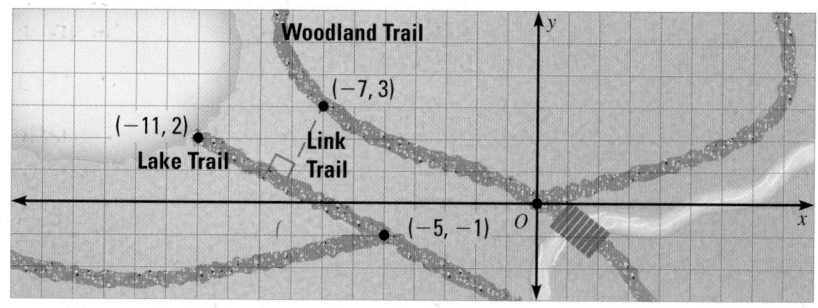

56. Challenge Show that an equation of the line that has x-intercept a and y-intercept b is the following:

$$\frac{x}{a} + \frac{y}{b} = 1$$

Standardized Test Practice

57. Multiple Choice What is an equation of the line with a slope of $\frac{5}{4}$ and a y-intercept of -3?

   A $y = 3x - \frac{5}{4}$ **B** $y = \frac{5}{4}x - 3$ **C** $y = \frac{5}{4}x + 3$ **D** $y = 3x + \frac{5}{4}$

58. Multiple Choice What is an equation of the line that passes through $(3, -2)$ and has a slope of -1?

   F $y = 3x - 2$ **G** $y = -x - 1$ **H** $y = x + 1$ **J** $y = -x + 1$

59. Multiple Choice The graph of which equation is a line perpendicular to the line $y = -3x + 4$?

   A $y = 3x + 2$ **B** $y = -3x + 2$ **C** $y = \frac{1}{3}x + 4$ **D** $y = -\frac{1}{3}x$

60. Multiple Choice What is an equation of the line that passes through $(-2, 5)$ and has a slope of -2?

   F $y = -\frac{1}{2}x + 1$ **G** $y = -2x + 1$ **H** $y = 2x + 9$ **J** $y = -2x - 1$

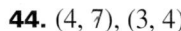

Link to
HABITAT

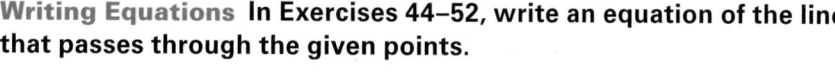

GRIZZLY BEARS once ranged from Texas to North Dakota and westward to Washington and California. Hunting and habitat loss eliminated grizzlies from 98% of their original U.S. range outside of Alaska by the 1970s.

Identifying Coefficients and Like Terms Identify the coefficients and like terms in the expression. *(Lesson 1.3)*

61. $4c - 3c$

62. $5y^2 - 11y^2 + y$

63. $7x - 2 + 5x - 8x^2 + 1$

64. $6n + 2n^2 - 1 + 5n + 2.5 - 6n^2$

Graphing Functions Graph the equation. *(Lesson 2.4)*

65. $y = 2x$

66. $y = 3x$

67. $y = x - 2$

68. $y = 2x + 1$

69. $y = -4x + 1$

70. $y = -3x - 4$

Geometry Skills

Triangle Proportionality If a line segment divides two sides of a triangle proportionally, then it is parallel to the third side. Determine whether $\overline{WY}$ is parallel to $\overline{VZ}$ in the diagram.

71.

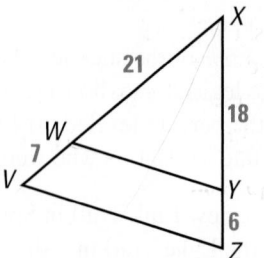

72.

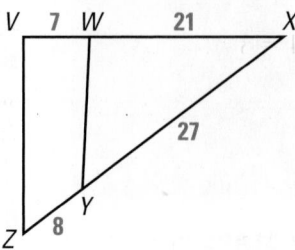

73.

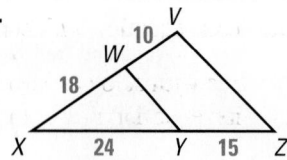

74.

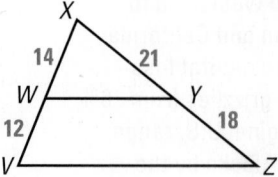

Quiz 2

Lesson 2.4

Graph the equation.

1. $y = 3x + 4$

2. $y = \frac{1}{2}x - 2$

3. $y = -7$

4. $3x - 2y = 10$

Lesson 2.4

Graph the line that is perpendicular to the graph of the equation at its *y*-intercept.

5. $y = -2x + 5$

6. $y = x$

7. $y = \frac{3}{5}x - 3$

Lesson 2.5

Write an equation of the line that has the given slope and *y*-intercept.

8. $m = 3, b = -3$

9. $m = -4, b = 9$

10. $m = \frac{1}{2}, b = \frac{4}{3}$

Lesson 2.5

Write an equation of the line with the given characteristics.

11. passes through $(-4, 3)$; slope $m = -\frac{1}{2}$

12. passes through $(4, -1)$; perpendicular to $y = 5x + 4$

13. passes through $(6, 0)$; parallel to $y = 3x - 2$

Lesson 2.5

14. House Value In 1991 a house was valued at \$125,000. The same house was valued at \$225,000 in 2007. Write a linear model for the value v of the house for the period 1991 to 2007 where t represents the number of years since 1991.

2.6 Direct Variation

Key Words
- direct variation
- constant of variation

Prerequisite Skills

Solve the equation.

1. $2.5x = 35$

2. $44 = 8y$

3. $\frac{z}{4} = 1.4$

4. $\frac{2}{3}w = 36$

GOAL Write and graph direct variation equations.

How can you adjust this salsa recipe to serve more people?

By the recipe, 2 tomatoes make 4 servings. So, 4 tomatoes make 8 servings, 6 tomatoes make 12 servings, and, if t represents the number of tomatoes and s the number of servings, $s = 2t$.

Two variables x and y show **direct variation**, or *vary directly*, if $y = kx$ where k is a nonzero constant called the **constant of variation**.

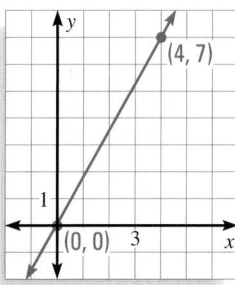

SALSA (serves 4)
2 tomatoes, diced
3 Tbsp. onion, diced
1 Tbsp. cilantro, chopped
1 Tbsp. lime juice
1 clove garlic, chopped
salt, pepper, chilis to taste

Direct variation equation

$$y = kx$$

└── constant of variation

So, $s = 2t$ is a direct variation equation with constant of variation $k = 2$.

The graph of $y = kx$ is a line with slope k. Also, the y-intercept is 0, so the graph of any direct variation equation passes through the origin.

EXAMPLE 1 Graph a Direct Variation Equation

Graph $y = \frac{7}{4}x$.

Solution

Plot a point at the origin.

Find a second point by substituting a convenient value for x.

$y = \frac{7}{4}x$	Write equation.
$y = \frac{7}{4}(4)$	Substitute 4 for x.
$y = 7$	Simplify.

A second point is $(4, 7)$.

Plot the second point. Then draw a line through the two points as shown.

Checkpoint ✓ **Graph a Direct Variation Equation**

Graph the equation.

1. $y = -x$ **2.** $y = 2x$ **3.** $y = -4x$ **4.** $y = \frac{2}{3}x$

CHEFS create dishes and menus that will appeal to their customers. Executive chefs supervise kitchen operations and food service staff.

EXAMPLE 2 Write a Direct Variation Equation

Recipes To make mango salsa, replace the tomatoes in the recipe on the previous page with mangoes, using 3 mangoes for 2 recipes. Write an equation relating the number of servings y to the number of mangoes x given so that y varies directly with x. How many servings of salsa can you make if you have 5 mangoes?

Solution

In 2 recipes there are $2(4) = 8$ servings, so 3 mangoes make 8 servings. This means $y = 8$ when $x = 3$. Write an equation using these values of y and x to solve for k.

$y = kx$ Write a direct variation equation.

$8 = k(3)$ Substitute 8 for y and 3 for x.

$\dfrac{8}{3} = k$ Simplify.

An equation is $y = \dfrac{8}{3}x$. To find how many servings of salsa you can make using 5 mangoes, substitute 5 for x.

$$y = \frac{8}{3}x = \frac{8}{3}(5) = \frac{40}{3} = 13\frac{1}{3}$$

ANSWER ▶ Five mangoes will make about 13 servings.

Checkpoint ✓ Write a Direct Variation Equation

The variables x and y vary directly. Write an equation that relates x and y.

5. $x = 3$, $y = -9$ **6.** $x = 10$, $y = 2$

Identify Direct Variation You can rewrite $y = kx$ as $\dfrac{y}{x} = k$. So, a set of data pairs (x, y) shows direct variation if the ratio of y to x is constant.

STUDENT HELP

SOLVING NOTE
In a real-world data set, the ratio of the variables in each data pair does not always have to be *exactly* the same to assume direct variation, but the ratio should vary only by a small amount.

EXAMPLE 3 Identify Direct Variation

Tell whether the data, the numbers of words y in the first x lines of the Declaration of Independence, show direct variation. If so, write an equation relating x and y.

Lines, x	5	10	15	20	25
Words, y	153	305	454	602	757

Solution

Find the ratio of y to x for each data pair.

$$\frac{153}{5} = 30.6 \qquad \frac{305}{10} = 30.5 \qquad \frac{454}{15} \approx 30.27 \qquad \frac{602}{20} = 30.1 \qquad \frac{757}{25} = 30.28$$

The ratio of y to x in each pair is nearly the same, so the data show direct variation. Substituting 30.3 for k in $y = kx$ gives the direct variation equation $y = 30.3x$.

Checkpoint ✓ Identify Direct Variation

7. Tell whether the data $(1, 2)$, $(2, 4)$, $(3, 8)$, $(4, 14)$, $(5, 22)$ show direct variation. If so, write an equation relating x and y.

2.6 Exercises

Guided Practice

Vocabulary Check

Copy and complete the statement.

1. If $y = kx$ and $k \neq 0$, then the equation is a(n) __?__ equation.

2. If $y = kx$ is a direct variation equation, then k is called the __?__.

Skill Check

Graph the direct variation equation.

3. $y = 3x$

4. $y = -2x$

5. $y = \frac{1}{4}x$

The variables x and y vary directly. Write an equation that relates x and y.

6. $x = 3, y = -6$

7. $x = -6, y = -24$

8. $x = 22, y = -2$

9. The variables x and y vary directly, and $y = 3$ when $x = 4$. Write and graph an equation relating x and y. Then find y when $x = 2$.

Practice and Applications

STUDENT HELP

HOMEWORK HELP
Example 1: Exs. 10–21
Example 2: Exs. 22–40
Example 3: Exs. 41–48

Recognizing Direct Variation Graphs **Tell whether the graph represents direct variation. Explain.**

10.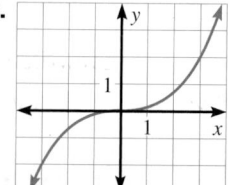

11.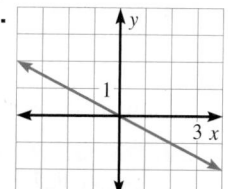

12.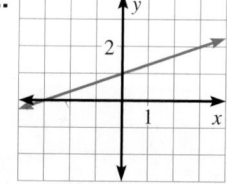

Graphing Direct Variation Equations **Graph the equation.**

13. $y = -3x$

14. $y = 4x$

15. $y = 7x$

16. $y = -5x$

17. $y = -\frac{1}{2}x$

18. $y = \frac{1}{3}x$

Logical Reasoning **Tell whether the statement is *sometimes*, *always*, or *never* true.**

19. The origin is a point on the graph of a direct variation equation.

20. The graph of a direct variation equation has a positive slope.

21. The constant of variation in a direct variation equation is the opposite of the slope of the graph of the equation.

Finding a Constant of Variation **Find the constant of variation.**

22. y varies directly with x, and $y = 14$ when $x = 2$.

23. d varies directly with t, and $d = 36$ when $t = -4$.

24. P varies directly with x, and $P = -3$ when $x = -15$.

25. z varies directly with w, and $z = -8$ when $w = 84$.

26. Geometry Link The circumference C of a circle varies directly with its diameter d. The constant of variation is the number π, which is about 3.14. What is the circumference of a circle whose diameter is 5 inches?

Writing Equations The variables x and y vary directly. Write an equation that relates x and y. Then find the value of y when $x = 9$.

27. $x = 2, y = 16$ **28.** $x = 3, y = 27$ **29.** $x = -8, y = 64$

30. $x = -18, y = -54$ **31.** $x = 12, y = 6$ **32.** $x = -21, y = 7$

33. $x = 54, y = -6$ **34.** $x = -2, y = \dfrac{1}{3}$ **35.** $x = \dfrac{7}{2}, y = 14$

36. Waves A wave's length is the distance from its crest to the crest of the next wave. The height h at which a wave breaks varies directly with its length L. A wave that breaks at a height of 3 feet has a length of 21 feet. Write an equation that relates h and L. Then predict the height of a wave with a length of 35 feet.

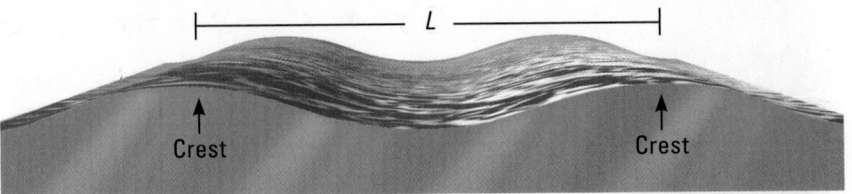

A wave's length L is the distance between one crest and the next.

37. Sales Tax The sales tax t on an item varies directly with the price p of the item. Write an equation that relates t and p for a state that has a sales tax rate of 6%. What is the sales tax on a $250 digital camera?

38. Tipping In general, the tip t on a restaurant meal varies directly with the total amount of the bill b. Write an equation that relates t and b for a meal if you wish to tip the server 15% of the amount of your bill. How much should you tip if the total bill is $18?

39. Discount For a percent discount, the amount d of the discount on an item varies directly with the price p of the item. Write an equation that relates d and p for winter coats that are discounted by 60%. What is the amount of the discount on a coat that regularly costs $180? What is the discounted price?

40. Science Link Weight varies directly with the force of gravity. An object that weighs 6 pounds on Earth weighs only 1 pound on the moon, where the gravitational force is weaker. The rocks gathered from the moon during the Apollo 11 mission weighed 46 pounds on Earth. How much, to the nearest pound, did the rocks weigh on the moon?

41. Challenge If y varies directly with x, does x vary directly with y? Explain.

Identifying Direct Variation Tell whether the data show direct variation. If so, write an equation that relates x and y.

42.

x	−4	−3	−2	−1
y	16	17	8	4

43.

x	3	6	9	12
y	12	21	30	39

44.

File size, x (Mb)	5.4	12.2	19.5	22.4	36.8
Download time, y (sec)	4	9	14	17	27

Link to
SCIENCE

APOLLO 11 On July 20, 1969, the Apollo 11 mission landed the first two humans, Neil Armstrong and Buzz Aldrin, on the moon. Armstrong was on the lunar surface for about 2.5 hours, and Aldrin for about 2 hours.

Measurement Conversions Write and use a direct variation equation to perform the conversion. Use the given variables.

45. Convert 7.5 inches to centimeters. 1 inch (n) = 2.54 centimeters (c)

46. Convert 8.3 ounces to grams. 1 ounce (z) = 28.4 grams (g)

47. Convert 5 kilometers to miles. 1 mile (m) = 1.61 kilometers (k)

48. Convert 3 liters to quarts. 1 quart (q) = 1.1 liters (L)

Standardized Test Practice

49. Multiple Choice The variables x and y vary directly. When $x = -4$, $y = 16$. What is the constant of variation?

(**A**) -4 (**B**) $-\frac{1}{4}$ (**C**) $\frac{1}{4}$ (**D**) 4

50. Multiple Choice The variables x and y vary directly. When $x = 3$, $y = 15$. Which equation correctly relates x and y?

(**F**) $y = 5x$ (**G**) $x = 5y$ (**H**) $y = 6x$ (**J**) $x = 6y$

51. Multiple Choice The variables t and p vary directly. When $t = -12$, $p = -4$. What is the value of p when $t = 9$?

(**A**) -27 (**B**) -3 (**C**) 3 (**D**) 27

Mixed Review

Solving Equations Solve the equation. *(Lesson 1.4)*

52. $6 - x = -3$ **53.** $2m + 11 = 7$ **54.** $10 - 5p = 65$

Identifying Linear Functions Tell whether the function is linear. Then evaluate the function when *x* = 3. *(Lesson 2.2)*

55. $f(x) = 2x - 7$ **56.** $f(x) = x^2 - 3x + 1$ **57.** $f(x) = \frac{4}{3}x + 2$

Standard Form Graph the equation. Label the intercepts. *(Lesson 2.4)*

58. $2x + y = 2$ **59.** $-2x + 5y = 10$ **60.** $6x + y = -2$

Point-Slope Form Write an equation of the line that passes through the given point and has the given slope. *(Lesson 2.5)*

61. $(0, -1), m = 2$ **62.** $(4, 0), m = -1$ **63.** $(-3, -4), m = 0$

64. $(-2, 5), m = 3$ **65.** $(-8, 3), m = -\frac{1}{4}$ **66.** $(2, -3), m = \frac{1}{2}$

Geometry Skills

67. Volume of a Prism Write an equation relating the volume V of a rectangular prism to its height h if the area of the base of the prism is held constant at 16 square units.

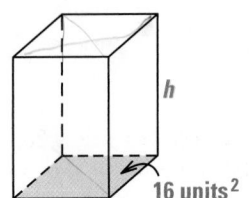

16 units²

68. Volume of a Pyramid Write an equation relating the volume V of a rectangular pyramid to its height h if the area of the base of the pyramid is held constant at 9 square units.

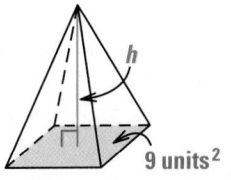

9 units²

DEVELOPING CONCEPTS *(For use with Lesson 2.7)*
Fitting a Line to Data

Goal
Find a linear model for a set of data.

Materials
- overhead projector
- overhead transparency and marker
- metric ruler
- meter stick
- graph paper

QUESTION

How can you approximate the *best-fitting line* for a set of data?

EXPLORE

1 Draw a line segment 15 centimeters long on a transparency, and place the transparency on an overhead projector. Position the projector a convenient distance from the screen, and measure this distance in centimeters. Then measure the length of the segment projected on the screen.

2 Record your Step 1 data in a table like the one below. (Sample projector-to-screen distances are given.) Move the projector a little farther from the screen several times, each time measuring and recording the projector-to-screen distance and the length of the projected segment.

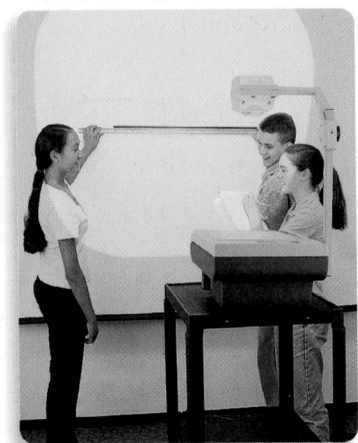

Distance from projector to screen (cm), *x*	200	220	240	260	280	300
Length of line segment on screen (cm), *y*	?	?	?	?	?	?

3 Write the data recorded in your table as ordered pairs (x, y). Then graph the ordered pairs on a coordinate grid. Describe any pattern you see.

4 Use a ruler to draw a line on your graph lying as close as possible to as many of the plotted points as possible. Your line approximates the *best-fitting line* for the data.

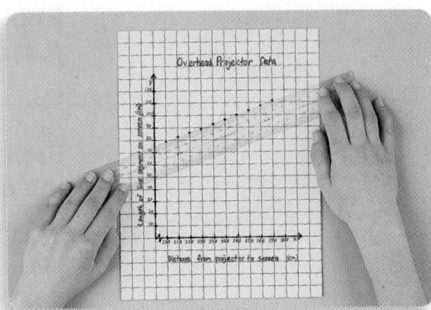

STUDENT HELP

READING GRAPHS
Your line does not have to contain any of the actual data points, but it should model the overall trend of the data as closely as possible.

THINK ABOUT IT

1. Find the slope of your line. To do this, you may first need to estimate the coordinates of two points on your line. What does the slope represent?

2. Estimate the *y*-intercept of your line. What does the *y*-intercept represent?

3. Use the slope and *y*-intercept to write an equation of your line.

4. Using your equation from Exercise 3, predict the length of the projected segment for a particular projector-to-screen distance greater than those in your table.

5. Test your prediction from Exercise 4. How accurate was your prediction?

2.7 Scatter Plots and Correlation

Key Words
- scatter plot
- positive correlation
- negative correlation
- relatively no correlation
- best-fitting line

Prerequisite Skills

Find the slope of the line passing through the given points.

1. $(-3, 1), (2, 6)$

2. $(-2, 8), (1, -4)$

3. $(5, 2), (-3, 6)$

4. $(0, 7), (4, 0)$

GOAL See correlation in a scatter plot and find a best-fitting line.

A **scatter plot** is a graph of a set of data pairs (x, y). A scatter plot can help you identify the type of relationship, or *correlation*, between two variables.

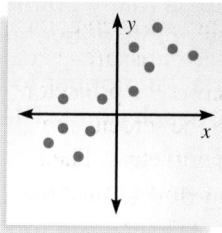
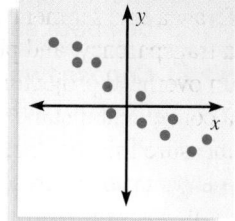
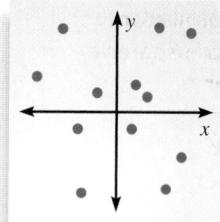

Positive correlation
As x increases, y tends to increase.

Negative correlation
As x increases, y tends to decrease.

Relatively no correlation
There is no obvious pattern between x and y.

EXAMPLE 1 Identify Correlation

Televisions The scatter plots compare unit sales of plasma television sets with those of LCD television sets and with those of analog direct-view color television sets (older-style "picture-tube" sets). Describe the correlation shown by each plot.

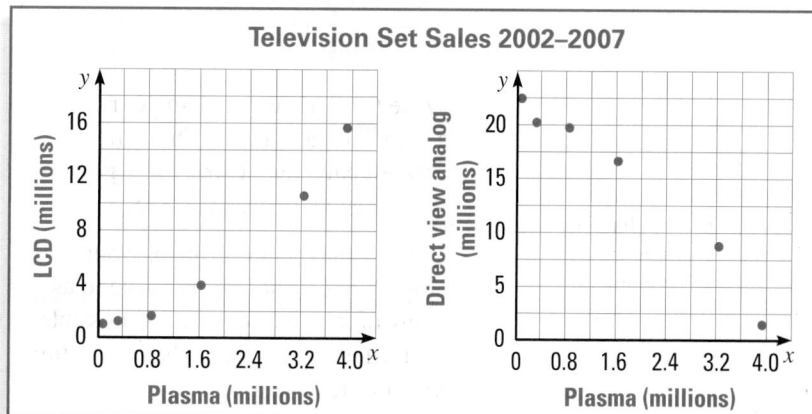

Solution

The first scatter plot shows a positive correlation: as sales of plasma sets increased, sales of LCD sets increased. The second plot shows a negative correlation: as sales of plasma sets increased, sales of analog direct-view color sets decreased.

Checkpoint ✓ *Identify Correlation*

1. Draw a scatter plot of the data. Then tell whether the data show a *positive correlation*, a *negative correlation*, or *relatively no correlation*.

$(1, 7), (1, 5), (2, 3), (3, 2), (3, 6), (5, 5), (6, 4), (6, 8), (7, 6), (8, 2)$

Lines of Fit If the points in a scatter plot appear to lie close to some line with a positive or negative slope, then the correlation is *strong*, and you can reasonably model the data with a line. The line that most closely models the data is called the **best-fitting line**. You can approximate a best-fitting line by graphing.

STUDENT HELP

SOLVING NOTE
To learn how to use a graphing calculator to find a best-fitting line, see page 114.

Approximating a Best-Fitting Line

STEP ❶ *Draw* a scatter plot of the data.

STEP ❷ *Sketch* a line that follows the trend of the data points. The line should be close to as many points as possible. There should be about as many points above the line as below it.

STEP ❸ *Choose* two points that appear to lie on the line, and estimate the coordinates of each point. These points do not have to be original data points.

STEP ❹ *Write* an equation of the line that passes through the two points from Step 3. This equation gives a model for the data.

EXAMPLE 2 **Find a Best-Fitting Line**

Movies The table gives the total number y (in billions) of U.S. movie admissions x years after 1993. Approximate the best-fitting line for the data.

Year, x	0	1	2	3	4	5
Admissions, y	1.24	1.29	1.26	1.34	1.39	1.48
Year, x	6	7	8	9	10	11
Admissions, y	1.47	1.42	1.49	1.63	1.57	1.53

Solution

❶ *Draw* a scatter plot of the data.

❷ *Sketch* the line that appears to best fit the data. A possibility is shown.

❸ *Choose* two points. The line shown appears to pass through the data point (3, 1.34) and through (11, 1.6), which is not a data point.

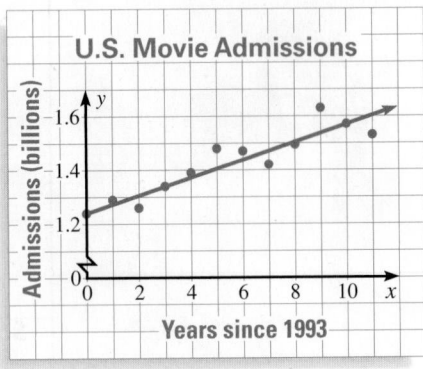

❹ *Write* an equation of the line. First find the slope using the two points:

$$m = \frac{1.6 - 1.34}{11 - 3} = \frac{0.26}{8} = 0.0325$$

Now use point-slope form to write an equation. Choose $(x_1, y_1) = (11, 1.6)$.

$y - y_1 = m(x - x_1)$	Point-slope form
$y - 1.6 = 0.0325(x - 11)$	Substitute for y_1, m, and x_1.
$y - 1.6 = 0.0325x - 0.3575$	Distributive property
$y = 0.0325x + 1.2425$	Solve for y.

ANSWER ▶ An approximation of the best-fitting line is $y = 0.0325x + 1.24$.

PHYSICAL FITNESS

WALKING On a walk in the woods, you might travel approximately 1 or 1.5 yards per second (about 2–3 mi/h). A race walker might reach a speed of 4 yards per second (over 8 mi/h) or more.

EXAMPLE 3 Use a Best-Fitting Line

Walking In a class experiment, students walked a given distance at various paces, from normal to as fast as possible ("race walking"). By measuring the time required and the number of steps, the class calculated the speed and the stride, or step length, for each trial. The table shows the data recorded.

Speed (yd/sec)	0.8	0.85	0.9	1.3	1.4	1.6	1.75	1.9
Stride (yd)	0.5	0.6	0.6	0.7	0.7	0.8	0.8	0.9
Speed (yd/sec)	2.15	2.5	2.8	3.0	3.1	3.3	3.35	3.4
Stride (yd)	0.9	1.0	1.05	1.15	1.25	1.15	1.2	1.2

a. Approximate the best-fitting line for the data.

b. Predict the stride length for a class member walking at 2 yards per second.

Solution

a. *Draw* a scatter plot of the data.

Sketch the line that appears to best fit the data. A possibility is shown.

Choose two points on the line. It appears to pass through (0.9, 0.6) and (2.5, 1).

Write an equation of the line. First find the slope using the two points:

$$m = \frac{1 - 0.6}{2.5 - 0.9} = \frac{0.4}{1.6} = 0.25$$

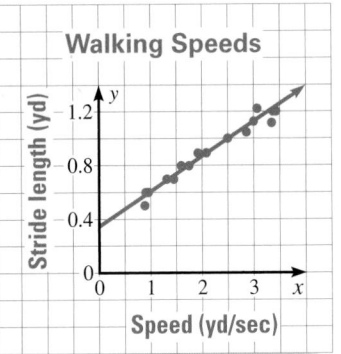

Use point-slope form as in Example 2 to write an equation.

ANSWER ▶ An approximation of the best-fitting line is $y = 0.25x + 0.38$.

b. To predict the stride length for a class member walking at 2 yards per second, use the equation from part (a), substituting 2 for x.

$y = 0.25x + 0.38$	Write the linear model.
$y = 0.25(2) + 0.38$	Substitute 2 for x.
$y = 0.88$	Simplify.

ANSWER ▶ A class member walking at 2 yards per second will have a stride length of about 0.88 yard.

Checkpoint ✓ **Find and Use a Best-Fitting Line**

2. Employment The table shows the percent p of the U.S. work force made up of civilian federal government employees t years after 1970. Approximate the best-fitting line for the data. What does your model predict for the percent of the work force made up of civilian federal government employees in 2015?

Years, t	0	5	10	15	20	25	30	35
Percent, p	3.81	3.35	3.01	2.80	2.72	2.36	2.10	1.91

Guided Practice

Vocabulary Check

1. Explain the meaning of *positive correlation*, *negative correlation*, and *relatively no correlation* between two variables *x* and *y*.

2. Copy and complete the statement: The line that most closely models the data on a scatter plot is called the ___?___.

Skill Check

3. Does the scatter plot at the right show a *positive correlation*, a *negative correlation*, or *relatively no correlation*? Explain.

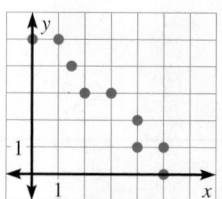

Internet Use **The table shows estimates of the U.S. annual average total hours of consumer Internet use per person (ages 12 and over) since the year 2000.**

Years since 2000, *x*	0	1	2	3	4	5	6
Hours, *y*	104	131	147	164	176	183	190

4. Draw a scatter plot of the data.

5. Approximate the best-fitting line for the data.

6. Use your best-fitting line to predict the hours of Internet use in 2010.

Practice and Applications

STUDENT HELP

HOMEWORK HELP
Example 1: Exs. 7–17
Example 2: Exs. 18–26
Example 3: Exs. 27, 28

Describing Correlations Tell whether *x* and *y* show a *positive correlation*, a *negative correlation*, or *relatively no correlation*.

7.

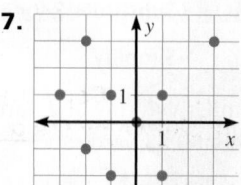

8.

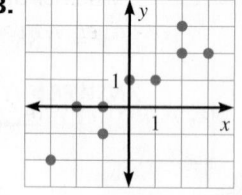

9.

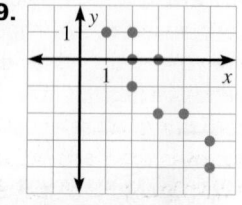

Drawing Scatter Plots Draw a scatter plot of the data. Then tell whether the data show a *positive correlation*, a *negative correlation*, or *relatively no correlation*.

10.

x	1	1	2	2	3	5	5	7	7	8
y	6	5	5	4	3	2	1	1	0	0

11.

x	1	2	2	4	5	6	6	7	8	8
y	0	1	2	3	4	4	5	5	5	6

Stars In Exercises 12–15, use the scatter plot, which represents stars of various types. The plot compares the magnitude, or brightness, of a star with its surface temperature, which influences the star's color.

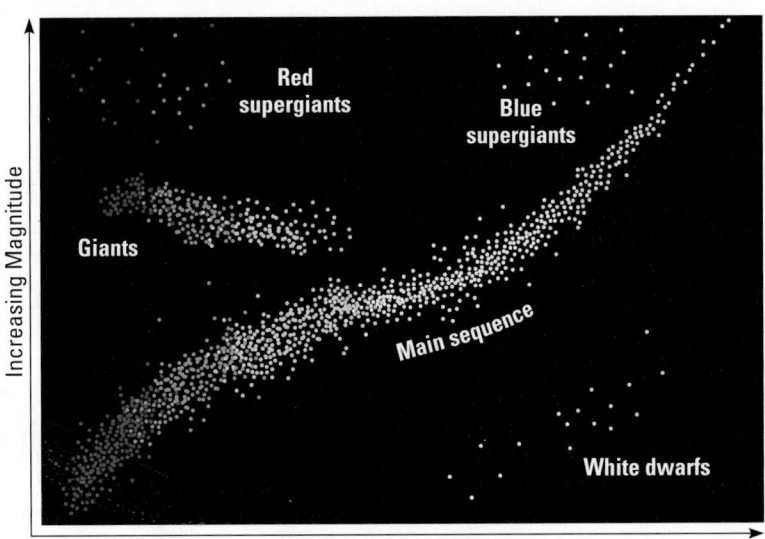

Tell whether the stars plotted for the given class show a *positive correlation*, a *negative correlation*, or *relatively no correlation*.

12. blue supergiants

13. giants

14. main sequence

15. white dwarfs

Hurricanes For Exercises 16 and 17, use the table. It shows the number of hurricanes *y* that have formed in the North Atlantic Ocean during the annual hurricane season *x* years after 1995.

x	0	1	2	3	4	5	6	7	8	9	10	11
y	11	9	3	10	8	8	9	4	7	9	15	5

16. Draw a scatter plot of the data.

17. Tell whether the data show a *positive correlation*, a *negative correlation*, or *relatively no correlation*.

Approximating Best-Fitting Lines Copy the graph. Then approximate the best-fitting line for the data shown by the graph.

18.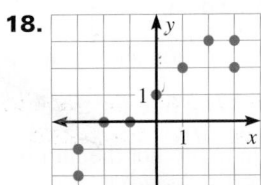

19.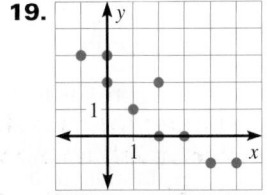

20.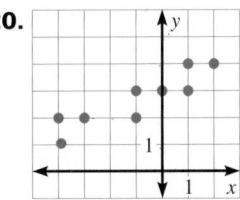

For Exercises 21 and 22, use the graph shown.

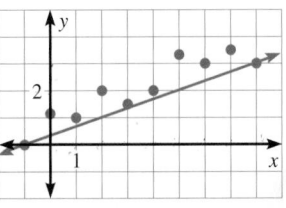

21. Critical Thinking Explain why the line shown is not a good fit for the data.

22. Copy the graph and draw an approximation of the best-fitting line. Then find an equation of your line.

Fitting a Line to Data In Exercises 23–26, (a) draw a scatter plot of the data, (b) approximate the best-fitting line, and (c) predict the value of *y* when *x* = 9.

23.

x	2	2	3	3.5	4	4.5	5	6	7	7.5
y	2	4	6	5	1	3.5	6	1.5	3.5	6

24.

x	2	3	3	3.5	4	4.5	5.5	6	7	7.5
y	6.5	6	5	5	4	3	2.5	1.5	1	0

25.

x	−1	−0.5	0	0	1	1	1.5	2	3
y	−2	−3	−0.5	−1	0	1	3	3	4

26.

x	−2	−1	−1	0	1	2	2	3	4	5
y	3	3	2.5	2.5	2	2	2.5	2	1.5	1

Biology Link In Exercises 27 and 28, use the table below. It shows the average life expectancy at birth (in years) for a person born in the United States in the indicated year.

Years after 1950	0	10	20	30	40	50
Life expectancy	68.2	69.7	70.8	73.7	75.4	77.0

27. Approximate the best-fitting line for the data.

28. Use your equation to predict the life expectancy at birth of a person born in the United States in 2010.

29. **Logical Reasoning** Explain how you can use a table to determine the type of correlation that a data set shows without drawing a scatter plot.

30. **Multi-Step Problem** The table below shows the number of commercial television stations in the United States beginning in the year 2000.

Years since 2000, x	0	1	2	3	4	5
Stations, y	1288	1309	1333	1349	1366	1370

   a. Draw a scatter plot of the data.

   b. Describe the type of correlation shown by the data.

   c. Approximate the best-fitting line for the data.

   d. Use the best-fitting line to predict the number of commercial television stations in the United States in 2011.

31. **Multiple Choice** Which equation best models the data shown in the scatter plot?

   A $y = 15$ **B** $y = x + 30$

   C $y = -x + 30$ **D** $y = -\frac{4}{5}x + 33$

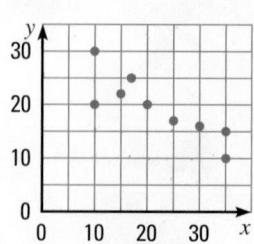

Rewriting Formulas Solve the formula for the indicated variable. *(Lesson 1.5)*

32. Area of an ellipse formula $A = \pi ab$ for a.

33. Kinetic energy and momentum formula $K = \dfrac{p^2}{2m}$ for m.

34. Surface area of a right cylinder cone formula $S = \pi r \ell + \pi r^2$ for ℓ.

Evaluating Functions Evaluate the function for the given value of x. *(Lesson 2.2)*

35. $f(x) = 1.8x + 32;\ x = 100$

36. $g(x) = -16x^2 + 80;\ x = 2$

37. $h(x) = x^4 - x^3 + x^2 - x;\ x = -2$

38. $k(x) = \dfrac{2 - 4x^3}{x - 5};\ x = 3$

Finding Slope Find the slope of the line passing through the given points. *(Lesson 2.3)*

39. $(0, -3), (4, 1)$

40. $(-2, 7), (-2, 4)$

41. $(12, 1), (4, 9)$

42. $(3, -3), (-1, 2)$

43. $(1, -6), (-4, -6)$

44. $(14, 6), (7, -5)$

Geometry Skills

Lines of Symmetry Tell whether the line indicated in the photograph is a line of symmetry.

45.

46.

47.

Quiz 3

Lesson 2.6

In Exercises 1–6, the variables x and y vary directly. Write an equation that relates x and y.

1. $x = -4, y = -4$

2. $x = 20, y = 5$

3. $x = 3, y = -30$

4. $x = -17, y = -51$

5. $x = -6, y = 15$

6. $x = -27, y = -18$

Lesson 2.6

7. Business A company's market value v varies directly with the price per share p of its stock. A company has a market value of \$1.2 billion when its price per share is \$39. What is the market value if the price per share drops to \$32?

Lesson 2.7

In Exercises 8–10, tell whether x and y show a *positive correlation*, a *negative correlation*, or *relatively no correlation*.

8.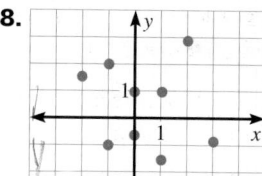

9.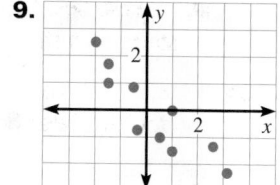

10.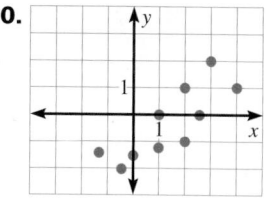

Lesson 2.7

11. Baseball In his first six seasons, a baseball player hits 7, 5, 9, 11, 16, and 14 home runs. Draw a scatter plot of the data where x represents the season and y the number of home runs. Then approximate a best-fitting line for the data.

STUDENT HELP

KEYSTROKE HELP
See keystrokes for
several models of
calculators at
www.classzone.com.

You can use a graphing calculator to find the best-fitting line for a set of data.

EXAMPLE

The table gives the price p (in cents) of a first-class stamp over time where t is the number of years since 1975. Use the linear regression feature of a graphing calculator. Find an equation of the best-fitting line for the data.

t	0	3	6	6	10	13	16	20	24	26	27	31
p	13	15	18	20	22	25	29	32	33	34	37	39

SOLUTION

1 Use the *Stat Edit* feature to enter the data into two *lists*. Enter years since 1975 in L_1 and prices in L_2.

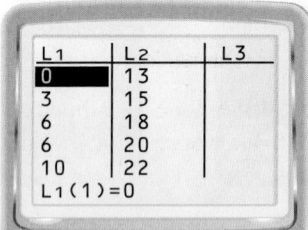

2 Use the *Stat Calc* feature to find an equation of the best-fitting ("linear regression") line. Rounding, $p = 0.840t + 13.7$.

3 Now graph the data pairs and the best-fitting line in the same viewing window to see how the line fits the data. To make a scatter plot, you can use the *Stat Plot* and *ZoomStat* features. Then you can add the best-fitting line to your plot.

STUDENT HELP

ANOTHER WAY
ZoomStat chooses a
graphing window, but
you can also choose a
window by observing the
data. For example,
$0 \le x \le 35$, $0 \le y \le 45$ is
an appropriate window.

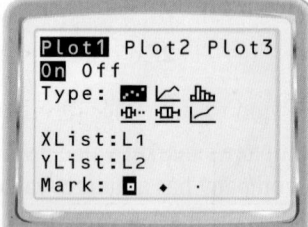

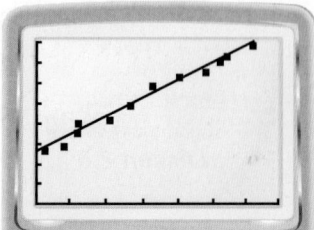

EXERCISES

Use a graphing calculator to find and graph an equation of the best-fitting line.

1.

x	50	75	80	100	150	175	210	250	260
y	0.3	0.5	0.6	0.7	0.75	0.85	1.05	0.9	1.1

2.

x	4	7	8.5	10	11	14	15	16	18
y	150	450	600	600	900	1100	1250	1400	1400

@HomeTutor
classzone.com
• Multi-Language Glossary
• Vocabulary practice

VOCABULARY

- relation, *p. 67*
- domain, range, *p. 67*
- function, *p. 67*
- equation in two variables, *p. 68*
- independent variable, *p. 69*
- dependent variable, *p. 69*
- linear function, *p. 73*

- function notation, *p. 73*
- slope, *p. 79*
- *y*-intercept, *p. 87*
- slope-intercept form, *p. 87*
- *x*-intercept, *p. 88*
- standard form of a linear equation, *p. 88*
- point-slope form, *p. 94*

- direct variation, *p. 101*
- constant of variation, *p. 101*
- scatter plot, *p. 107*
- positive correlation, *p. 107*
- negative correlation, *p. 107*
- relatively no correlation, *p. 107*
- best-fitting line, *p. 108*

VOCABULARY EXERCISES

1. Explain how to identify the domain and range of a relation. How can you tell whether a relation is a function?

2. In an equation, what does the value of the dependent variable depend on?

3. Sketch and label one line that has a positive slope, one that has a negative slope, one that has a slope of zero, and one whose slope is undefined. Which line is not the graph of a function?

4. You create a scatter plot using solutions of a direct variation equation. The equation has a positive constant of variation. What type of correlation does the graph show?

2.1 FUNCTIONS AND THEIR GRAPHS

Examples on pp. 67–69

EXAMPLE You can represent a relation with a table of values or a graph.

x	−3	−2	0	1	1	3
y	3	−1	2	1	−1	1

REVIEW HELP
Exercises Example
5, 6   **1,** p. 67

The domain consists of −3, −2, 0, 1, and 3. The range consists of −1, 1, 2, and 3. The relation is *not* a function because *x* = 1 is paired with both *y* = 1 and *y* = −1.

Identify the domain and range. Tell whether the relation is a function.

5.

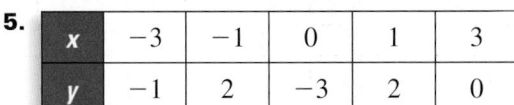

x	−3	−1	0	1	3
y	−1	2	−3	2	0

6.

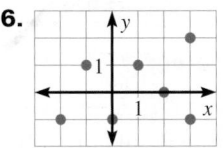

2.2 LINEAR FUNCTIONS AND FUNCTION NOTATION

Examples on pp. 73–75

EXAMPLE You can (a) identify, (b) evaluate, and (c) graph linear functions.

a. $f(x) = 2x - 3$ is a linear function because it has the form $f(x) = mx + b$.

b. Evaluate $f(x) = 2x - 3$ when $x = 2$.

$$f(x) = 2x - 3$$
$$f(2) = 2(2) - 3 = \mathbf{1}$$

c. From part (b), you know that one point on the graph of $f(x) = 2x - 3$ is $(\mathbf{2, 1})$. Rewrite $f(x) = 2x - 3$ as $y = 2x - 3$.

Find a second point on the line by substituting an x-value, such as $x = 0$.

$$y = 2x - 3$$
$$y = 2(\mathbf{0}) - 3$$
$$y = -3$$

A second point is $(0, -3)$.

The graph of $y = 2x - 3$ is the line passing through $(2, 1)$ and $(0, -3)$.

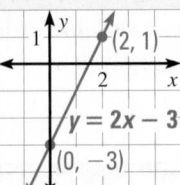

REVIEW HELP

Exercises	Examples
7–10	**1**, p. 73
7–10	**2**, p. 74
11–14	**3**, p. 74

Tell whether the function is linear. Then evaluate the function when $x = 2$.

7. $f(x) = 5x - 4$ **8.** $h(x) = 2x^2$ **9.** $p(x) = -x^3 - 3$ **10.** $g(x) = -\dfrac{6}{x} - 7$

Graph the function.

11. $h(x) = x - 2$ **12.** $f(x) = -2x + 4$ **13.** $g(x) = -\dfrac{1}{2}x + 5$ **14.** $p(x) = 3x - 1$

2.3 SLOPE AND RATE OF CHANGE

Examples on pp. 79–81

EXAMPLE You can find the slope of a line passing through two points. Then you can tell whether the line *rises, falls, is horizontal*, or *is vertical*.

POINTS $(1, -2)$ and $(5, 6)$ **SLOPE** $m = \dfrac{y_2 - y_1}{x_2 - x_1} = \dfrac{6 - (-2)}{5 - 1} = \dfrac{8}{4} = 2$

Because $m > 0$, the line passing through the points rises from left to right.

REVIEW HELP

Exercises	Examples
15–20	**1**, p. 79
21, 22	**3**, p. 81

POINTS $(-3, 5)$ and $(-3, -4)$ **SLOPE** $m = \dfrac{y_2 - y_1}{x_2 - x_1} = \dfrac{-4 - 5}{-3 - (-3)} = \dfrac{-9}{0}$

Because m is undefined, the line passing through the points is vertical.

Find the slope of the line passing through the given points. Then tell whether the line *rises, falls, is horizontal*, or *is vertical*.

15. $(5, 2), (1, -2)$ **16.** $(0, -6), (0, 2)$ **17.** $(-6, 3), (-5, 1)$

18. $(-6, -2), (-3, -2)$ **19.** $(-4, 1), (2, -1)$ **20.** $(3, -4), (3, 4)$

Tell which line is steeper.

21. Line 1: through $(-3, 7)$ and $(4, 3)$
Line 2: through $(5, -3)$ and $(4, -2)$

22. Line 1: through $(-8, -5)$ and $(2, 0)$
Line 2: through $(-4, 6)$ and $(5, 9)$

2.4 QUICK GRAPHS OF LINEAR EQUATIONS

EXAMPLE You can graph a linear equation in slope-intercept form or in standard form.

EQUATION $y = -3x + 4$

slope $= -3$; y-intercept $= 4$

EQUATION $5x + 2y = -10$

x-intercept: $5x + 2y = -10$

$5x + 2(0) = -10$

$x = -2$

y-intercept: $5x + 2y = -10$

$5(0) + 2y = -10$

$y = -5$

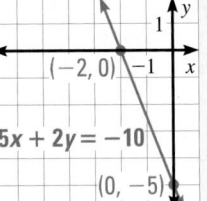

REVIEW HELP

Exercises	Examples
23, 24	**1**, p. 87
25, 26	**2**, p. 88
27–30	**3**, p. 89

Graph the equation.

23. $y = x - 7$ **24.** $y = 2x + 5$ **25.** $6x + 3y = 18$ **26.** $x - 2y = 8$

Graph the line that is perpendicular to the given line at its *y*-intercept.

27. $y = x + 3$ **28.** $y = -x - 4$ **29.** $y = -2x + 2$ **30.** $y = \frac{1}{2}x - 5$

2.5 WRITING EQUATIONS OF LINES

EXAMPLE There are several approaches to writing equations of lines. In the graph at the right, the lines are parallel.

a. Solid line: Use slope-intercept form with $m = -\frac{1}{4}$ and $b = 1$.

$y = -\frac{1}{4}x + 1$

b. Solid line: Use point-slope form with $m = -\frac{1}{4}$ and $(x_1, y_1) = (-4, 2)$.

$y - 2 = -\frac{1}{4}[x - (-4)]$

$y = -\frac{1}{4}x + 1$

c. Dashed line: Any line parallel to $y = -\frac{1}{4}x + 1$ also has a slope of $-\frac{1}{4}$. Substitute values using $(x, y) = (-3, -1)$ to find the value of b.

REVIEW HELP

Exercises	Examples
31, 32	**1**, p. 94
33, 34	**2**, p. 95
35	**3**, p. 95
36	**4**, p. 96

$y = -\frac{1}{4}x + b$

$-1 = -\frac{1}{4}(-3) + b$

$-\frac{7}{4} = b$ An equation of the line is $y = -\frac{1}{4}x - \frac{7}{4}$.

Write an equation of the line with the given characteristics.

31. slope: -2; y-intercept: 8 **32.** slope: 6; y-intercept: -3

33. slope: -3; point: $(1, -4)$ **34.** slope: $\frac{1}{4}$; point: $(-8, 0)$

35. point: $(2, -3)$; parallel to $y = 3x - 11$ **36.** point: $(0, 8)$; perpendicular to $y = \frac{1}{3}x + 5$

2.6 DIRECT VARIATION

Examples on
pp. 101–102

EXAMPLE You can write and graph a direct variation equation $y = kx$ given any point on the line.

The variables x and y vary directly, and $y = 35$ when $x = 7$.

$$y = kx$$
$$35 = k(7)$$
$$5 = k$$

An equation that relates x and y is $y = 5x$.

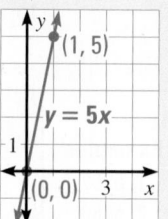

REVIEW HELP
Exercises	Examples
37–40	**2**, p. 102
41, 42	**3**, p. 102

The variables *x* and *y* vary directly. Write an equation that relates *x* and *y*.

37. $x = 6$, $y = 12$ **38.** $x = -6$, $y = -27$ **39.** $x = -100$, $y = 20$ **40.** $x = 30$, $y = 12$

Tell whether the data show direct variation. If so, write an equation that relates *x* and *y*.

41.

x	−2	−1	0	1
y	6	3	0	−3

42.

x	−4	−2	0	2	4
y	−2	−1	1	1	2

2.7 SCATTER PLOTS AND CORRELATION

Examples on
pp. 107–109

EXAMPLE You can graph a set of data pairs to see what relationship, if any, exists.

The table shows the number of millions of barrels b of crude oil produced in Alaska where t is the number of years since 1995.

t	0	1	2	3	4	5
b	542	508	473	429	383	354

The scatter plot shows a negative correlation. Approximate the best-fitting line. Use (1, 508) and (3, 429).

$$m = \frac{508 - 429}{1 - 3} = -\frac{79}{2} = -39.5$$

$$y - 508 = -39.5(x - 1) \quad \text{Point-slope form}$$

$$y = -39.5x + 547.5 \quad \text{Best-fitting line}$$

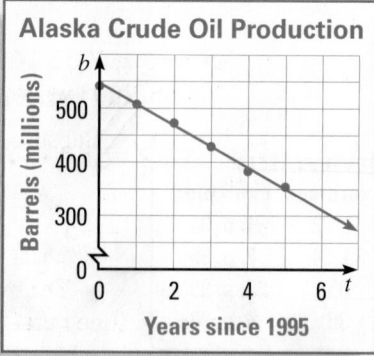

REVIEW HELP
Exercises	Example
43	**1**, p. 107

43. Draw a scatter plot of the data. Then tell whether the data show a *positive correlation*, a *negative correlation*, or *relatively no correlation*.

x	−4	−2	−1	0	0	1	2	3	4
y	3	−2	1	3	−2	−3	2	1	−2

Identify the domain and range. Tell whether the relation is a function.

1. Input Output
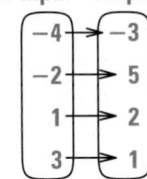

2. Input Output
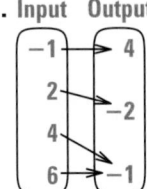

3. Input Output
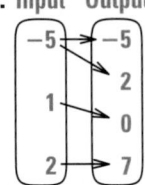

Tell whether the function is linear. Then evaluate the function when $x = -3$.

4. $h(x) = x^2 - 2$ **5.** $f(x) = -3x + 6$ **6.** $g(x) = \frac{1}{3}x - 4$

Find the slope of the line passing through the given points. Then tell whether the line *rises*, *falls*, *is horizontal*, or *is vertical*.

7. $(1, 3), (3, 5)$ **8.** $(-2, 1), (-2, -4)$ **9.** $(2, 7), (-4, 7)$

10. Skiing Section A of a ski trail at a ski resort falls 45 feet over a horizontal distance of 75 feet. Section B falls 80 feet over a horizontal distance of 125 feet. Which section is steeper?

11. Graph $y = -2x + 3$.

12. Graph the line that is perpendicular to $y = -x + 7$ at its y-intercept.

Write an equation of the line with the given characteristics.

13. slope: -3; y-intercept: 5   **14.** slope: 3; point: $(-1, -3)$

15. point $(1, -4)$; parallel to $y = -2x + 9$ **16.** point $(3, 5)$; perpendicular to $y = 3x + 1$

17. Credit Unions In 1995 there were 4358 credit unions. The number decreased to 3735 in 2002. Write a linear model for the number of credit unions n from 1995 to 2002 where t represents the number of years since 1995.

The variables *x* and *y* vary directly. Write an equation that relates *x* and *y*.

18. $x = 1, y = -5$ **19.** $x = -4, y = -20$ **20.** $x = -33, y = 11$

21. Machinery The number of parts p that a machine can make varies directly with the time t that the machine is operating. The machine can make 36 parts in 6 hours. How many parts can it make in 72 hours?

22. Draw a scatter plot of the data in the table. Then tell whether the data show a *positive correlation*, a *negative correlation*, or *relatively no correlation*. If the correlation is positive or negative, approximate the best-fitting line.

x	0	1	2	3	4	5	6
y	2.3	2.4	2.6	2.6	2.9	3.0	3.2

Chapter Standardized Test

> **EXAMPLE** What is an equation of the line perpendicular to $y = -\frac{1}{4}x + 1$ that passes through $(0, 1)$?
>
> Ⓐ $y = -4x + 1$ Ⓑ $y = -4x - 1$ Ⓒ $y = 4x + 1$ Ⓓ $y = 4x - 1$
>
> **Solution**
>
> Sometimes you can quickly eliminate answer choices. The slope of the perpendicular line must be the negative reciprocal of $-\frac{1}{4}$, which is 4. This eliminates choices A and B. When the point $(0, 1)$ is substituted into C and D, only choice C is correct.

Multiple Choice

1. Which relation is *not* a function?

Ⓐ
x	1	2	3
y	3	4	4

Ⓑ
x	0	2	4
y	0	2	4

Ⓒ
x	1	3	3
y	1	1	0

Ⓓ
x	1	5	9
y	0	0	3

2. Which of the equations does *not* represent a function?

Ⓕ $y = 2x - 5$ Ⓖ $x = 7$

Ⓗ $x - y = 1$ Ⓙ $y = -3$

3. Which of the functions below is *not* a linear function?

Ⓐ $f(x) = 2$ Ⓑ $f(x) = -\frac{1}{2}x + 2$

Ⓒ $f(x) = 5x^2 + 1$ Ⓓ $f(x) = 1.1 - 2.3x$

4. What is the value of $f(x) = 2x^2 - x$ when $x = -1$?

Ⓕ -3 Ⓖ -1 Ⓗ 1 Ⓙ 3

5. What is the slope of the line $y = -x + 2$?

Ⓐ -1 Ⓑ 0 Ⓒ 1 Ⓓ 2

6. The line passing through which two points is parallel to $y = 3x + 1$?

Ⓕ $(2, -2), (1, 1)$ Ⓖ $(1, 2), (2, -1)$

Ⓗ $(-3, 4), (-4, 1)$ Ⓙ $(3, -5), (2, -2)$

7. Which function does the graph represent?

Ⓐ $y = -2x - 1$

Ⓑ $y = -2x + 1$

Ⓒ $y = 2x - 1$

Ⓓ $y = 2x + 1$

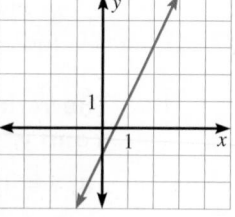

8. Which table shows direct variation?

Ⓕ
x	1	2	3
y	3	6	8

Ⓖ
x	1	2	3
y	2	4	6

Ⓗ
x	2	4	6
y	1	2	4

Ⓙ
x	2	3	4
y	1	6	8

9. What is an equation of the line that has a slope of 3 and passes through (2, 2)?

   (A) $y = 3x + 4$ **(B)** $y = 3x + 8$

   (C) $y = 3x - 4$ **(D)** $y = 3x - 8$

10. What is an equation of the line that is perpendicular to $y = -x + 3$ and passes through $(-1, -2)$?

   (F) $y = x - 1$ **(G)** $y = -x - 1$

   (H) $y = -x + 1$ **(J)** $y = x + 1$

11. The variables x and y vary directly, and $x = 5$ when $y = -10$. Which equation relates x and y?

   (A) $y = x - 15$ **(B)** $y = -\frac{1}{2}x$

   (C) $y = -2x$ **(D)** $y = 2x$

12. The variables x and y vary directly, and $y = 2$ when $x = 4$. What is the value of y when $x = 10$?

   (F) 20   **(G)** 10

   (H) 5   **(J)** 4

Gridded Response

In Exercises 13 and 14, use the table below. It gives the price p (in dollars) of x items.

x	2	4	6	8	10
p	26	42	58	74	90

13. The ordered pairs (x, p) all lie on a line. What is the slope of this line?

14. What is the y-intercept of the line that contains all of the data pairs?

15. What is the value of $h(x) = \frac{1}{2}x^2 - x + 3$ when $x = -8$?

16. Two variables x and y vary directly, and $y = 4$ when $x = 5$. What is the constant of variation in the direct variation equation that relates x and y?

17. What is the slope of a line that is perpendicular to $y = -\frac{2}{3}x + 2$?

Extended Response

18. The table shows the U.S. average annual consumption of bottled water g (in gallons) per person from 1996 to 2004 where t represents the number of years since 1996.

t	0	1	2	3	4	5	6	7	8
g	12.4	13.4	14.4	15.8	16.7	18.2	20.1	21.6	23.2

   a. Draw a scatter plot of the data.

   b. Describe the correlation shown by the data.

   c. Approximate the best-fitting line for the data. Explain your steps.

   d. Using your equation in part (c), find the average rate of change in consumption.

   e. Predict the average amount of bottled water consumed per person in 2012.

Systems of Linear Equations

▶ How many calories do you use when swimming?

APPLICATION: Swimming

The calories you use while exercising varies depending on the type of exercise. You use about 12 Calories per minute swimming.

Think & Discuss

1. Suppose you want to use a total of 180 Calories while swimming. Write and solve a linear equation to find the number of minutes you should swim.

2. The graphs of the equations $y = 180$ and $y = 12x$ are shown below. What are the coordinates of the point of intersection?

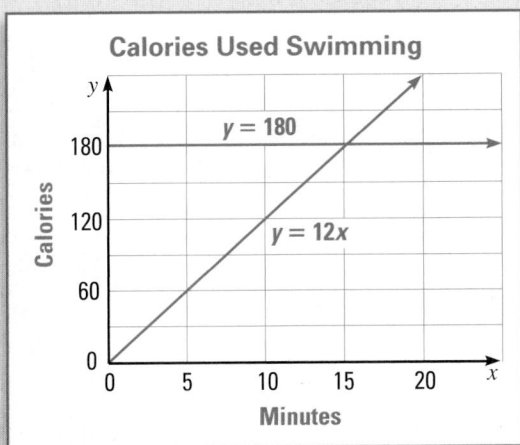

Calories Used Swimming

3. Explain the significance of the point of intersection in terms of the situation.

Learn More About It

You will solve a system of linear equations to determine the time you should spend swimming.

@HomeTutor
classzone.com
• Multi-Language Glossary
• Vocabulary practice

PREVIEW

What's the chapter about?

• Graphing a system of linear equations in two variables
• Solving a system of linear equations in two variables
• Graphing linear equations in three variables
• Solving a system of linear equations in three variables

Key Words

• system of two linear equations, *p. 125*
• solution of a system of two linear equations, *p. 125*
• substitution method, *p. 132*
• linear combination method, *p. 139*
• three-dimensional coordinate system, *p. 147*

• z-axis, *p. 147*
• ordered triple, *p. 147*
• octants, *p. 147*
• linear equation in three variables, *p. 148*
• system of three linear equations, *p. 153*

PREPARE

Chapter Readiness Quiz

Take this quick quiz. If you are unsure of an answer, look back at the reference pages for help.

Vocabulary Check *(refer to p. 87)*

1. What is the slope of the equation $y = \frac{3}{4}x + 6$?

    A -6 **B** $-\frac{3}{4}$ **C** $\frac{3}{4}$ **D** 6

Skill Check *(refer to p. 26)*

2. What is the solution of $3x + 4 = -4x - 10$?

    F -14 **G** -6 **H** -2 **J** 2

3. What is the solution of $2(x - 13) = -4x - 14$?

    A 20 **B** 2 **C** $-\frac{1}{6}$ **D** -2

TAKE NOTES

Using Your Notebook

Use your notes and homework exercises to study for tests.

NOTES
Review the vocabulary and examples from your notes. These are the important concepts you need to know.

HOMEWORK
Re-solve a few exercises from each assignment. These are the important skills you need to know. Pay special attention to exercises that gave you trouble.

3.1 Solving Linear Systems by Graphing

Key Words

- system of two linear equations
- solution of a system of two linear equations

Prerequisite Skills

1. Graph the equations $x + y = 3$ and $x - y = 2$ in the same coordinate plane.

Tell whether the point is a solution of the equation.

2. $(1, 2)$, $2x + y = 3$

3. $(2, -1)$, $x - 3y = 5$

4. $(-3, 5)$, $2x + y = 1$

GOAL Solve a system of linear equations in two variables by graphing.

How can a system of linear equations be used to help you plan a vacation?

In Example 3, you will use a system of linear equations to budget for a trip to two California cities, Anaheim and San Diego (shown).

A **system of two linear equations** in two variables x and y consists of two equations. The coefficients of the terms in the equations can be any real numbers.

$$3x - y = 3 \quad \text{Equation 1}$$
$$x + 2y = 8 \quad \text{Equation 2}$$

A **solution** of a system of two linear equations in two variables is an ordered pair (x, y) that satisfies both equations. When you graph the system, the solution is represented by the point (or points) of intersection of the two lines.

EXAMPLE 1 Solve a System by Graphing

Solve the system by graphing. Then check your solution algebraically.

$$3x - y = 3 \quad \text{Equation 1}$$
$$x + 2y = 8 \quad \text{Equation 2}$$

Solution

Graph both equations, as shown. From the graph, you can see the lines appear to intersect at $(2, 3)$.

You can check the solution by substituting 2 for x and 3 for y into the original equations.

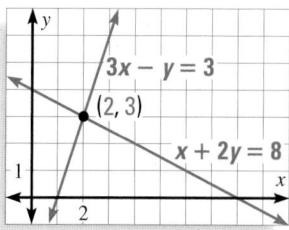

Equation 1	Equation 2
$3x - y = 3$	$x + 2y = 8$
$3(2) - 3 \stackrel{?}{=} 3$	$2 + 2(3) \stackrel{?}{=} 8$
$6 - 3 \stackrel{?}{=} 3$	$2 + 6 \stackrel{?}{=} 8$
$3 = 3$ ✓	$8 = 8$ ✓

ANSWER ▶ The solution of the system is $(2, 3)$.

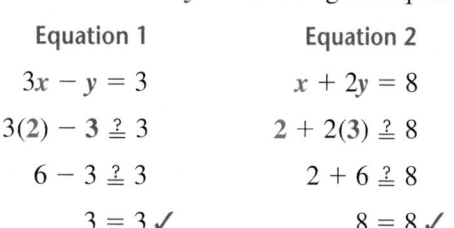

Checkpoint ✓ **Solve a System by Graphing**

Solve the system by graphing. Then check your solution.

1. $y = -x + 3$
$\ y = 2x + 9$

2. $x - 3y = 1$
$\ -x + y = -1$

3. $-x + 4y = 2$
$\ 2x - 3y = 6$

Solutions of Systems The system in Example 1 has exactly one solution. It is also possible for a system to have infinitely many solutions or no solution.

EXAMPLE 2 Systems with Many or No Solutions

Tell how many solutions the linear system has.

a. $2x - y = 1$
$-4x + 2y = -2$

b. $x + 2y = 4$
$x + 2y = 1$

Solution

a. Because the graph of each equation is the same, each point on the line is a solution. So, the system has infinitely many solutions.

b. Because the graphs of the equations are two parallel lines, the two lines have no point of intersection. So, the system has no solution.

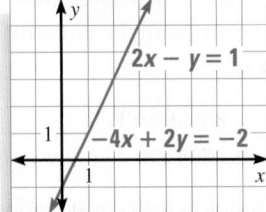

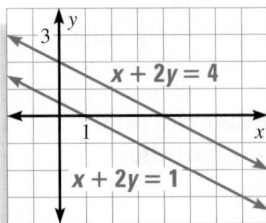

Finding the Number of Solutions You can find out how many solutions a linear system has by graphing each equation and analyzing the graphs.

Number of Solutions of a Linear System

EXACTLY ONE SOLUTION

The graph of the system is a pair of lines that intersect in one point.

The lines have different slopes.

The system has exactly one solution.

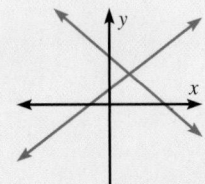

INFINITELY MANY SOLUTIONS

The graph of the system is a pair of identical lines.

The lines have the same slope and the same y-intercept.

The system has infinitely many solutions.

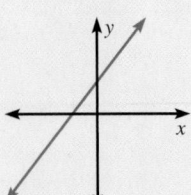

NO SOLUTION

The graph of the system is a pair of parallel lines, which do not intersect.

The lines have the same slope and different y-intercepts.

The system has no solution.

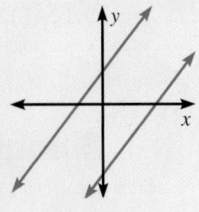

EXAMPLE 3 Write and Use a Linear System

Vacation You are planning a 7-day trip to California. You estimate that it will cost $300 per day in San Diego and $400 per day in Anaheim. Your total budget for the trip is $2400. How many days should you spend in each city?

Solution

You can use a verbal model to write a system of linear equations.

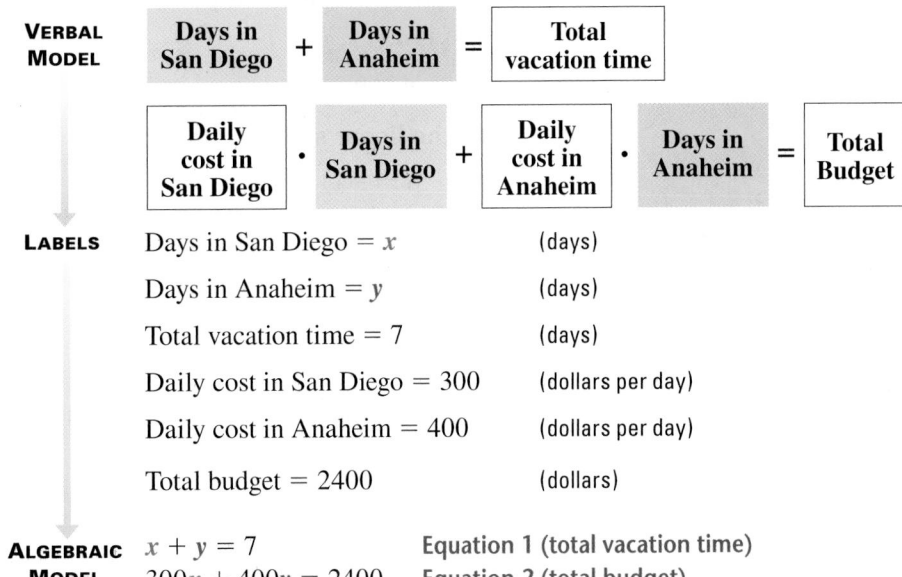

VERBAL MODEL

| Days in San Diego | + | Days in Anaheim | = | Total vacation time |

| Daily cost in San Diego | · | Days in San Diego | + | Daily cost in Anaheim | · | Days in Anaheim | = | Total Budget |

LABELS

Days in San Diego = x (days)

Days in Anaheim = y (days)

Total vacation time = 7   (days)

Daily cost in San Diego = 300   (dollars per day)

Daily cost in Anaheim = 400   (dollars per day)

Total budget = 2400   (dollars)

ALGEBRAIC MODEL

$x + y = 7$ Equation 1 (total vacation time)

$300x + 400y = 2400$ Equation 2 (total budget)

Graph both equations only in the first quadrant because the only values that make sense in this situation are positive values of x and y.

The lines appear to intersect at $(4, 3)$.

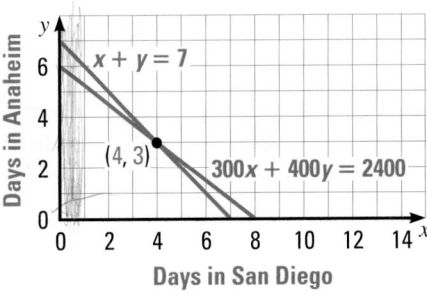

CHECK Substitute 4 for x and 3 for y in the original equations.

Equation 1 $x + y = 4 + 3 = 7$ ✓

Equation 2 $300x + 400y = 300(4) + 400(3) = 2400$ ✓

ANSWER ▶ The solution is $(4, 3)$. You should plan to spend 4 days in San Diego and 3 days in Anaheim.

Checkpoint ✓ **Write and Use Linear Systems**

Tell how many solutions the linear system has.

4. $2x + 3y = 1$
$4x + 6y = 3$

5. $x - 4y = 5$
$-x + 4y = -5$

6. $x - 5y = 5$
$x + 5y = 5$

7. Vacation Your family is planning a 6-day trip to Florida. You estimate that it will cost $450 per day in Tampa and $600 per day in Orlando. Your total budget is $3000. How many days should you spend in each city?

Guided Practice

Vocabulary Check

1. Copy and complete the statement: An ordered pair (x, y) that satisfies both equations in a system of linear equations is called a(n) __?__ of the system.

Skill Check

Tell whether the ordered pair (3, 4) is a solution of the system.

2. $-2x + y = -2$
$4x - 2y = 3$

3. $x + 2y = 11$
$2x - y = 2$

4. $x + y = 7$
$x - y = -1$

Graph the linear system. How many solutions does it have?

5. $2x + 3y = -1$
$x - 2y = 3$

6. $2x - y = 4$
$-6x + 3y = -18$

7. $9x - 3y = 3$
$-3x + y = -1$

Practice and Applications

STUDENT HELP

HOMEWORK HELP
Example 1: Exs. 8–22
Example 2: Exs. 23–34
Example 3: Exs. 35–40

Identifying Solutions **Tell whether the ordered pair is a solution of the system.**

8. $(2, 0)$;
$2x + y = 4$
$x - y = 1$

9. $(3, -1)$;
$x + 2y = 1$
$-2x + y = -7$

10. $(-4, 3)$;
$x + y = -1$
$-x - 3y = -5$

11. $(-2, -2)$;
$2x - 3y = -10$
$-4x + y = 6$

12. $(4, -5)$;
$3x + 2y = 2$
$-2x + y = -13$

13. $(0, 3)$;
$-4x + 3y = 9$
$2x - 5y = -16$

Graphing Systems **Solve the system by graphing. Then check your solution.**

14. $y = -\frac{1}{2}x - 1$
$y = \frac{1}{2}x - 3$
$y = -3x+16$

15. $y = -x - 1$
$y = -3x + 5$

16. $y = \frac{1}{3}x + \frac{5}{3}$
$y = \frac{2}{3}x + \frac{7}{3}$

17. $3x + y = 16$
$-x + 2y = 11$

18. $3x - 2y = 9$
$2x + 5y = 25$

19. $3x + 4y = 9$
$x - 2y = -7$

20. $2x + 5y = 2$
$-x + 2y = -10$

21. $-2x + 3y = -11$
$2x - 5y = 9$

22. $5x - 3y = -14$
$-2x + 7y = -6$

Matching Graphs **Match the linear system with its graph. Tell how many solutions the system has.**

23. $2x - y = 5$
$-4x + 2y = -10$

24. $-x + 5y = 8$
$2x - 10y = 6$

25. $4x - 7y = 27$
$-6x - 9y = -21$

A.

B.
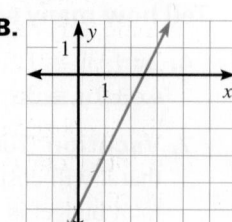

C.
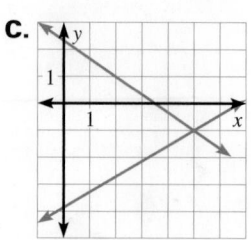

Finding Solutions Graph the linear system and tell how many solutions it has. If it has exactly one solution, find and check the solution.

26. $2x + 3y = 2$
$-x + 4y = 21$

27. $3x - 4y = 6$
$-9x + 12y = -18$

28. $-5x + y = 17$
$3x + 2y = 8$

29. $y = 2x + 4$
$y = 2x - 1$

30. $-4x + y = 3$
$8x - 2y = -6$

31. $5x - 6y = 12$
$x + 2y = 12$

32. $2x - y = 2$
$x + 2y = -14$

33. $x - 3y = 6$
$2x - 6y = 8$

34. $3x - 5y = 15$
$3x - 10y = 30$

35. Basketball You played in a basketball game in which you scored a total of 21 points. In the game, you made twice as many two-point shots as three-point shots. Use the verbal model to write and solve a system of linear equations. How many of each type of shot did you make?

Number of two-point shots	$= 2 \cdot$	Number of three-point shots

2 points per shot	$\cdot$	Number of two-point shots	$+$	3 points per shot	$\cdot$	Number of three-point shots	$=$	Total points

36. Theater You attend a play with a group of people. Each adult ticket costs $15, and each student ticket costs $10. There are 15 people in your group, and the total price of the tickets is $175. Use the verbal model to write and solve a system of linear equations. How many adults and students are there in your group?

Number of adults	$+$	Number of students	$=$	Number of people in group

Cost of adult ticket	$\cdot$	Number of adults	$+$	Cost of student ticket	$\cdot$	Number of students	$=$	Total cost of tickets

37. Decoration Costs You decorate the community center with balloons and paper lanterns. You can spend $75 on decorations. Balloons cost $1, and paper lanterns cost $4. You want to have 25 more balloons than lanterns. Use a verbal model to write and solve a system of linear equations. How many of each decoration can you buy?

38. Math Club You purchased T-shirts and sweatshirts for the math club at your school. T-shirts cost $12 each, and sweatshirts cost $20 each. You ordered 6 more T-shirts than sweatshirts. The total cost is $296. Use a verbal model to write and solve a system of linear equations. How many T-shirts did you order? How many sweatshirts did you order?

39. Commuting You take a bus from the center of town to your street. You have two payment options. Option A is to buy a monthly pass and pay $1 per ride. A monthly pass costs $30. Option B is to pay $2.50 per ride. Use a verbal model to write and solve a system of linear equations. After how many rides will the total costs of the two options be equal?

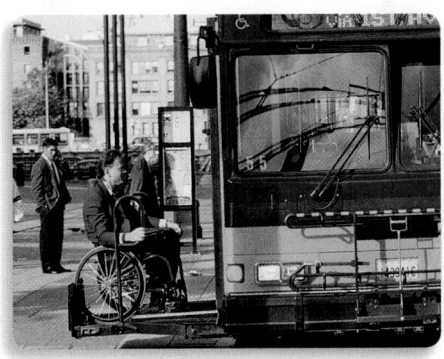

40. Weekend Jobs You and a friend mow lawns and wash cars on the weekends. Last month, your friend mowed four lawns and washed five cars. You mowed five lawns and washed three cars. Your friend earned $155, and you earned $145. Use a verbal model to write and solve a system of linear equations. How much do you earn for washing one car? How much do you earn for mowing one lawn?

41. Critical Thinking You graph a system of linear equations. The coefficients of the second equation (including the constant terms) are each twice the corresponding coefficients of the first equation. What can you conclude about the graph of the system? Explain.

Standardized Test Practice

42. Multiple Choice Which ordered pair is a solution of the system of linear equations?

$$5x + 2y = 5$$
$$-x + 3y = -18$$

A $(-3, 5)$ **B** $(-5, 3)$ **C** $(3, -5)$ **D** $(5, -3)$

43. Multiple Choice Which system of linear equations has no solution?

F $7x + y = 10$
  $3x - 2y = -3$

G $2x - y = 7$
  $2x - y = -7$

H $6x - 2y = 8$
  $-3x + y = -4$

J $x + y = -5$
  $x + 2y = -9$

44. Multiple Choice Which system of linear equations has infinitely many solutions?

A $3x - y = -1$
  $2x + 5y = 22$

B $x - 2y = 5$
  $-3x + 6y = 10$

C $7x + 3y = -6$
  $-x + 2y = 13$

D $-2x + 3y = 5$
  $6x - 9y = -15$

Mixed Review

Solving Equations Solve the equation. *(Lesson 1.4)*

45. $3x + 5 = -7$
46. $y - 7 = -4$
47. $2a - 5 = 1$

48. $4n + 2 = -10$
49. $-x + 3 = -3$
50. $-2y - 7 = 9$

51. $-3n + 12 = -42$
52. $-10x - 13 = -3$
53. $-2b - 13 = 10$

Rewriting Equations Solve the equation for *y*. *(Lesson 1.5)*

54. $x + 3y = 5$
55. $4y - x = -10$
56. $2x - 3y = 8$

57. $-6y + 3x = 2$
58. $3y - x = 5$
59. $x + 7y = -12$

60. $-12y + 36x = 24$
61. $-6y - x = 54$
62. $2x + y = -21$

63. $-4x - 14y = -16$
64. $15y + 5x = 45$
65. $-x + 3y = -9$

Geometry Skills

Finding Angle Measures Find the value of the variable.

66.

67.

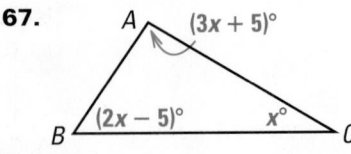

USING A GRAPHING CALCULATOR *(For use with Lesson 3.1)*
Graphing Systems

You can solve a system of linear equations by graphing the equations using a graphing calculator. A graphing calculator provides an answer that is either very close to or *exactly* equal to the actual answer.

STUDENT HELP

KEYSTROKE HELP
See keystrokes for several models of calculators at www.classzone.com.

EXAMPLE

Solve the linear system using a graphing calculator.

$$x + 2y = -16 \quad \text{Equation 1}$$
$$6x + 3y = 12 \quad \text{Equation 2}$$

SOLUTION

1 Solve each equation for y.

$$x + 2y = -16 \quad \text{Equation 1}$$
$$2y = -x - 16$$
$$y = -\frac{1}{2}x - 8$$

$$6x + 3y = 12 \quad \text{Equation 2}$$
$$3y = -6x + 12$$
$$y = -2x + 4$$

2 Enter each rewritten equation into a graphing calculator. Use parentheses to enter any fractions.

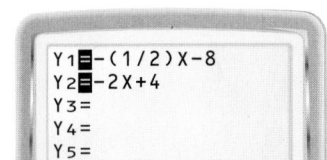

3 Graph the equations in the standard viewing window of the graphing calculator.

If the graphs do not intersect on the screen, set a different viewing window.

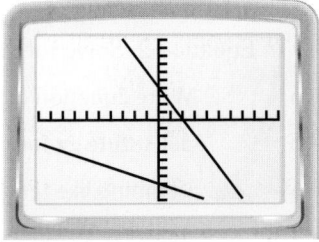

4 Use the *Intersect* feature to find the point where the graphs intersect. The solution is $(8, -12)$.

Remember to check your solution to be sure that you entered the equations correctly.

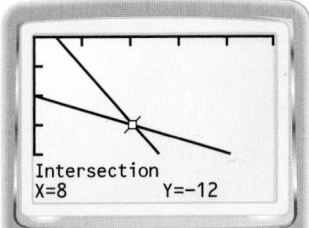

EXERCISES

Use a graphing calculator to solve the linear system.

1. $y = x + 4$
$y = 2x + 5$

2. $y = -x + 8$
$y = 4x - 12$

3. $y = 2x - 6$
$y = -3x + 4$

4. $2x - y = 9$
$6x - 3y = 27$

5. $-4x + 2y = 4$
$3x + y = -13$

6. $y = -3x + 30$
$5x - y = -40$

3.2 Solving Linear Systems by Substitution

Key Words
• substitution method

GOAL Solve a system of linear equations in two variables by substitution.

How many people visited the Henry Ford Museum during one day?

In Example 3, you will write and solve a system of linear equations to determine how many students and adults visited the museum based on the amount of ticket sales.

One way to solve a linear system without using graphs is the **substitution method**.

Rosa Parks exhibit

Solving a Linear System by Substitution

STEP ❶ Solve one equation for one of its variables.

STEP ❷ Substitute the expression from Step 1 into the other equation and solve for the other variable.

STEP ❸ Substitute the value from Step 2 into the revised equation from Step 1 and solve.

STEP ❹ Check the solution in each of the original equations.

EXAMPLE 1 Use Substitution

Solve the system using substitution.

$$y = 2x \qquad \text{Equation 1}$$
$$4x - y = 6 \qquad \text{Equation 2}$$

Solution

Substitute $2x$ for y in Equation 2. Solve for x.

$4x - y = 6$	Write Equation 2.
$4x - 2x = 6$	Substitute $2x$ for y.
$2x = 6$	Combine like terms.
$x = 3$	Solve for x.

Substitute 3 for x in Equation 1. Solve for y.

$y = 2x$	Write Equation 1.
$y = 2(3)$	Substitute 3 for x.
$y = 6$	Solve for y.

You can check your answer by substituting 3 for x and 6 for y in both equations.

ANSWER ▶ The solution is $(3, 6)$.

EXAMPLE 2 Use Substitution

Solve the system using substitution.

$$3x + 2y = 7 \quad \text{Equation 1}$$
$$x - 2y = -3 \quad \text{Equation 2}$$

Solution

STUDENT HELP

SOLVING NOTE
When using substitution, you will get the same solution whether you solve for y first or x first. You should begin by solving for the variable that is easier to use.

❶ **Solve** Equation 2 for x.

$x - 2y = -3$	Choose Equation 2 because the coefficient of x is 1.
$x = 2y - 3$	Solve for x to get revised Equation 2.

❷ **Substitute** $2y - 3$ for x in Equation 1. Solve for y.

$3x + 2y = 7$	Write Equation 1.
$3(2y - 3) + 2y = 7$	Substitute $2y - 3$ for x.
$6y - 9 + 2y = 7$	Use the distributive property.
$8y - 9 = 7$	Combine like terms.
$8y = 16$	Add 9 to each side.
$y = 2$	Solve for y.

❸ **Substitute** 2 for y in revised Equation 2. Solve for x.

$x = 2y - 3$	Write revised Equation 2.
$x = 2(2) - 3$	Substitute 2 for y.
$x = 1$	Simplify.

❹ **Check** by substituting **1** for x and **2** for y in the original equations.

Equation 1		Equation 2
$3x + 2y = 7$	Write original equations.	$x - 2y = -3$
$3(1) + 2(2) \stackrel{?}{=} 7$	Substitute for x and y.	$1 - 2(2) \stackrel{?}{=} -3$
$3 + 4 \stackrel{?}{=} 7$	Simplify.	$1 - 4 \stackrel{?}{=} -3$
$7 = 7 \checkmark$	Solution checks.	$-3 = -3 \checkmark$

ANSWER ▶ The solution is (1, 2).

Use a Graph to Check After you use substitution to solve a system of linear equations, you can use a graph to check the reasonableness of your solution. For example, you can see the graphs of the equations in Example 2 appear to intersect at (1, 2).

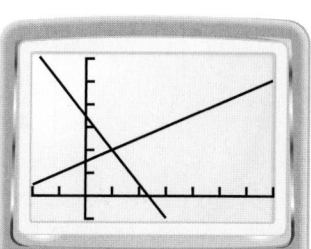

 **Use Substitution**

Solve the system using substitution. Tell which equation you chose to solve and use for the substitution. Explain.

1. $2x + y = 3$
$3x + y = 0$

2. $2x + 3y = 4$
$x + 2y = 1$

3. $3x - y = 5$
$4x + 2y = 10$

MUSEUM CURATOR
Curators are responsible
for obtaining artifacts and
specimens for display at
museums, zoos, nature
centers, or historic sites.
They also study, document,
and help preserve the items
they acquire.

EXAMPLE 3 Write and Use a Linear System

Museum Admissions On one day, the Henry Ford Museum in Dearborn, Michigan, admitted 4400 adults and students and collected $57,200 in ticket sales. The price of admission is $14 for an adult and $10 for a student. How many adults and how many students were admitted to the museum that day?

Solution

VERBAL MODEL

| Number of adults | + | Number of students | = | Total number admitted |

| Adult price | · | Number of adults | + | Student price | · | Number of students | = | Total amount collected |

LABELS

Number of adults $= x$ (adults)

Number of students $= y$ (students)

Total number admitted $= 4400$ (people)

Price for one adult $= 14$ (dollars)

Price for one student $= 10$ (dollars)

Total amount collected $= 57,200$ (dollars)

ALGEBRAIC MODEL

$x + y = 4400$ Equation 1 (number admitted)

$14x + 10y = 57,200$ Equation 2 (amount collected)

Use substitution to solve the linear system.

$x = \mathbf{4400} - y$	Solve Equation 1 for x; revised Equation 1.
$14(\mathbf{4400} - y) + 10y = 57,200$	Substitute $4400 - y$ for x in Equation 2.
$61,600 - 14y + 10y = 57,200$	Use the distributive property.
$61,600 - 4y = 57,200$	Combine like terms.
$-4y = -4400$	Subtract 61,600 from each side.
$y = \mathbf{1100}$	Divide each side by -4.
$x = 4400 - y$	Write revised Equation 1.
$x = 4400 - \mathbf{1100}$	Substitute 1100 for y.
$x = 3300$	Simplify.

ANSWER ▶ There were 3300 adults and 1100 students admitted to the Henry Ford Museum that day.

Checkpoint ✓ Write and Use a Linear System

4. On another day, the Henry Ford Museum admitted 1300 more adults than students and collected $56,000. How many adults and how many students were admitted to the museum that day?

5. Solve the system of equations in Example 3 by solving Equation 1 for y instead of x. Compare your solution to the solution in Example 3. What conclusion can you make?

Guided Practice

Vocabulary Check

1. Describe how to solve a system of two linear equations using the substitution method.

2. After solving a system of equations using the substitution method, describe two ways you can check your solution.

Skill Check **In Exercises 3–6, use the following system of linear equations.**

$$4x + 7y = -3 \quad \text{Equation 1}$$
$$3x - y = 4 \quad \text{Equation 2}$$

3. Which equation would you choose to solve and use for the substitution? Explain.

4. Solve the equation you chose in Exercise 3 for one of its variables.

5. Substitute the expression from Exercise 4 into the other equation and solve for the remaining variable.

6. Substitute the value of the solved variable into the equation from Exercise 4. What is the solution of the linear system? Check your solution.

Solve the system using substitution. Justify each step.

7. $2x - y = 1$
$\ x = -y + 5$

8. $4x + 2y = 16$
$\ -2x + y = 4$

9. $2x + 2y = 6$
$\ -2x - 3y = -9$

10. Parks The perimeter of a rectangular park is 2000 feet. The length is three times the width. What are the dimensions of the park?

Practice and Applications

STUDENT HELP

HOMEWORK HELP
Example 1: Exs. 11–28
Example 2: Exs. 11–29
Example 3: Exs. 30–34

Critical Thinking **Tell which equation you would choose to solve and use for the substitution. Explain.**

11. $y = 2x$
$\ 4x - y = 2$

12. $m - 5n = 0$
$\ 2m + n = 11$

13. $5c + 7d = 15$
$\ 10c - d = 0$

14. $3x + 4y = 12$
$\ x + y = 3$

15. $7a - 5b = 21$
$\ a - b = 3$

16. $3r + 2s = 19$
$\ 2r - 4s = 12$

Solving Linear Systems **Solve the system using substitution.**

17. $y = 3x$
$\ -2x + y = 7$

18. $2m - 4n = 16$
$\ m = 6n$

19. $5x + 3y = 8$
$\ y = -5x + 16$

20. $-3x + 4y = 11$
$\ 2x + y = 0$

21. $x - y = 2$
$\ 5x - 2y = 7$

22. $2x + 3y = 5$
$\ 2x + y = 4$

23. $2x - 3y = 2$
$\ 3x - y = -4$

24. $3x + y = 4$
$\ 5x - 2y = 3$

25. $5x + y = 5$
$\ 9x - 4y = -20$

26. $2a + b = 0$
$\ 6a + b = 10$

27. $3x - y = 4$
$\ 5x + 3y = 9$

28. $\frac{1}{2}x + y = 9$
$\ 7x + 4y = 26$

29. Error Analysis Describe and correct the error in solving the system.

$$2x - y = 7 \qquad \text{Equation 1}$$
$$x - 5y = -1 \qquad \text{Equation 2}$$

$x = 5y - 1$	Solve Equation 2 for x.
$5y - 1 - y = 7$	Substitute in Equation 1.
$4y - 1 = 7$	Combine like terms.
$4y = 8$	Add 1 to each side.
$y = 2$	Divide each side by 2.
$x = 5(2) - 1$	Substitute 2 for y in revised Equation 2.
$x = 9$	Solve for x.

30. Museum Admissions On one day, the Rock and Roll Hall of Fame and Museum in Cleveland, Ohio, admitted 541 adults and children and collected $9020 in ticket sales. The price of admission is $20 for an adult and $11 for a child. Use the following verbal model to find how many adults and children were admitted to the museum that day.

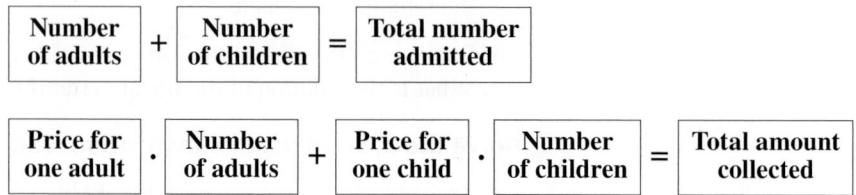

31. Investing An investor decides to buy two different types of stock in a company, Class-A and Class-B. The investor buys a total of 800 shares worth $3200. One Class-A share of the stock costs $4.75, and one Class-B share of the stock costs $2.25. How many shares of each type of stock did the investor buy?

Renting an Apartment In Exercises 32 and 33, use the following information.

Two friends rent a two-bedroom apartment for $1040 per month. One of the bedrooms has 50 square feet more floor space than the other. They decide to split the rent based on bedroom sizes. They will each pay $3.25 per square foot of bedroom floor area.

32. Assign labels to the verbal model below. Then write an algebraic model.

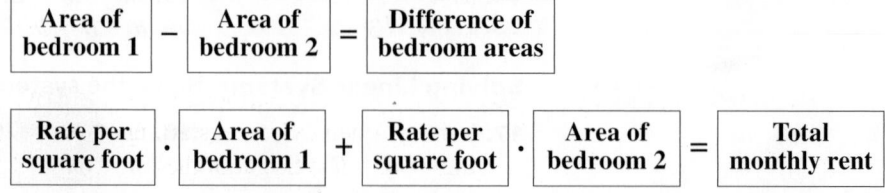

33. Find the area of each bedroom.

34. Food Your friend bought a total of 8 pounds of sliced turkey and sliced ham for a party. The total cost was $28.50. How much of each type of meat did your friend buy? Use the data from the sign to help you write the equations.

35. Challenge Find values of v and t that will make the solution of the system below be $(3, 3)$.

$$vx - y = 3 \quad \text{Equation 1}$$
$$x + ty = 12 \quad \text{Equation 2}$$

Standardized Test Practice

36. Multiple Choice Which linear system has a solution of $(6, -2)$?

(A) $-3x + y = 0$
$4x + 3y = 15$

(B) $x - 2y = 10$
$-3x + 7y = 4$

(C) $2x - 11y = 34$
$x + 4y = -2$

(D) $8x + 4y = 12$
$x - y = 20$

37. Multiple Choice The total number of points you can earn on a math test is 200 points. Your grade is 85% and you answered 42 problems correctly. Each problem is worth either 3 points or 5 points. How many 5-point problems did you answer correctly?

(F) 7   **(G)** 22   **(H)** 29   **(J)** 30

Mixed Review

Distributive Property Simplify the expression. *(Lesson 1.3)*

38. $2(x + 3y)$ **39.** $-(2x - 3y)$ **40.** $-2(-4x + y)$

41. $-3(2x + y)$ **42.** $\frac{3}{2}(-6x + 8y)$ **43.** $-6\left(\frac{4}{3}x + \frac{1}{3}y\right)$

44. $3(-2x + 3y) + 4x$ **45.** $-4(x - 5y) + 12y$ **46.** $3(4x + 2y) - 15x$

Matching Graphs Match the equation with its graph. *(Lesson 2.4)*

47. $y = -4x + 5$ **48.** $y = 3x - 4$ **49.** $y = \frac{1}{3}x + 9$

A. 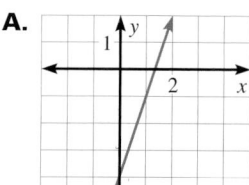   **B.** 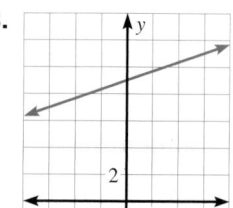   **C.**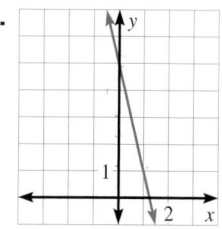

Slope-Intercept Form Write an equation of the line that has the given slope *m* and *y*-intercept *b*. *(Lesson 2.5)*

50. $m = 3, b = -2$ **51.** $m = -4, b = 0$ **52.** $m = 0, b = 4$

53. $m = \frac{1}{3}, b = 5$ **54.** $m = 2\frac{2}{3}, b = 1$ **55.** $m = \frac{3}{2}, b = -3$

Geometry Skills

56. Perimeter The Parthenon was built in Athens, Greece, starting in 447 B.C. The height of the Parthenon is shown. The ratio of the length to the height of the rectangle shown is $9 : 4$. To the nearest tenth of a meter, what is the length of the rectangle?

30.9 m

Goal

Discover a relationship between the graph of a linear system and the graph of the line whose equation is the sum of the equations in the system.

Materials

- graph paper
- ruler

QUESTION

A system of two linear equations in two variables may have exactly one solution. How is the graph of the sum of the equations in such a system related to the graph of the system?

EXPLORE

1 Graph the system of linear equations. Label the point of intersection.

$$2x + y = 4 \quad \text{Equation 1}$$
$$4x - y = 2 \quad \text{Equation 2}$$

2 Find the sum of the two equations in the system. Solve the resulting equation. Then graph the equation in the same coordinate plane you used in Step 1.

$$2x + y = 4$$
$$\underline{4x - y = 2}$$
$$6x = 6$$
$$x = 1$$

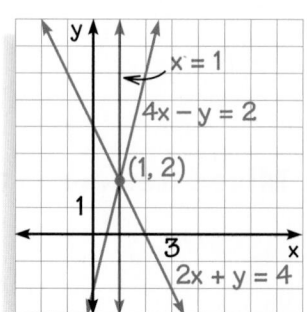

3 How is the graph of the sum of the equations from Step 2 related to the graph of the system from Step 1?

THINK ABOUT IT

In Exercises 1–9, repeat the steps above for the system of linear equations.

1. $3x + y = 1$
  $-3x + y = 7$

2. $x + 2y = 2$
  $x - 2y = 6$

3. $x - 3y = 0$
  $2x + 3y = 3$

4. $2x + y = -1$
  $x - 3y = -11$

5. $2x - 2y = -3$
  $x + 2y = 6$

6. $2x + y = 3$
  $-2x - 5y = -6$

7. $3x + 2y = 9$
  $-3x + y = 5$

8. $2x + y = 3$
  $x - 4y = 7$

9. $x - 4y = -8$
  $3x - 2y = 6$

10. What seems to be true about the graph of the sum of the equations in a system of linear equations that has exactly one solution?

Reasoning Use your observations to complete the following exercises.

11. When will the graph of the sum of the equations in a system of equations be a vertical line? How is this vertical line related to the solution of the system?

12. When will the graph of the sum of the equations in a system of equations be a horizontal line? How is this horizontal line related to the solution of the system?

13. When will the graph of the sum of the equations in a system of equations be neither a vertical nor a horizontal line?

3.3 Solving Linear Systems by Linear Combinations

Key Words

- linear combination method

GOAL Solve a system of linear equations in two variables by the linear combination method.

Sometimes you obtain an equation with fractions when you solve for one variable in a linear system. These systems may be easier to solve using the **linear combination method**. A linear combination of two equations is an equation obtained by (1) multiplying one or both equations by a constant, if necessary, and (2) adding the resulting equations.

Prerequisite Skills

Simplify the expression.

1. $3(x - 2y)$

2. $-4(-4x + y)$

3. $-6(3x + y)$

4. $5(4x - 3y)$

Using the Linear Combination Method

STEP ❶ Multiply, if necessary, one or both equations by a constant so that the coefficients of one of the variables differ only in sign.

STEP ❷ Add the revised equations from Step 1. Combining like terms will eliminate one variable. Solve for the remaining variable.

STEP ❸ Substitute the value obtained in Step 2 into either of the original equations and solve for the other variable.

STEP ❹ Check the solution in each of the original equations.

EXAMPLE 1 Multiply One Equation

Solve the linear system using the linear combination method.

$$2x - 3y = 6 \qquad \text{Equation 1}$$
$$4x - 5y = 8 \qquad \text{Equation 2}$$

Solution

❶ **Multiply** the first equation by **−2** so that the coefficients of x differ only in sign.

$$2x - 3y = 6 \qquad \times (-2) \qquad -4x + 6y = -12$$
$$4x - 5y = 8 \qquad \longrightarrow \qquad \underline{4x - 5y = 8}$$

❷ **Add** the revised equations and solve for y. $y = -4$

❸ **Substitute** −4 for y in one of the original equations and solve for x.

$2x - 3y = 6$	Write Equation 1.
$2x - 3(-4) = 6$	Substitute −4 for y.
$2x + 12 = 6$	Simplify.
$2x = -6$	Subtract 12 from each side.
$x = -3$	Solve for x.

❹ **Check** by substituting −3 for x and −4 for y in the original equations.

ANSWER The solution is $(-3, -4)$.

EXAMPLE 2 **Multiply Both Equations**

Solve the system using the linear combination method.

$$7x - 12y = -22 \quad \text{Equation 1}$$
$$-5x + 8y = 14 \quad \text{Equation 2}$$

Solution

❶ **Multiply** the first equation by **2** and the second equation by **3**.

$7x - 12y = -22$	**× 2**	$14x - 24y = -44$
$-5x + 8y = 14$	**× 3**	$-15x + 24y = 42$

❷ **Add** the revised equations and solve for x. $\quad -x \qquad = -2$

$$x = 2$$

❸ **Substitute** 2 for x in one of the original equations and solve for y.

$-5x + 8y = 14$	Write Equation 2.
$-5(2) + 8y = 14$	Substitute 2 for x.
$-10 + 8y = 14$	Multiply.
$y = 3$	Solve for y.

❹ **Check** by substituting 2 for x and 3 for y in the original equations.

ANSWER ▶ The solution is $(2, 3)$.

Solutions of Linear Systems When Step 2 of the linear combinations method yields a coefficient of 0 for both variables, the system has no unique solution. If you get the true equation $0 = 0$, the system has infinitely many solutions. If you get a false statement, such as $0 = 6$, the system has no solution.

EXAMPLE 3 **A Linear System with No Solution**

Solve the system using the linear combination method.

$$-4x + 8y = -12 \quad \text{Equation 1}$$
$$2x - 4y = 7 \quad \text{Equation 2}$$

Solution

Multiply the second equation by **2** so that the coefficients of y differ only in sign.

$-4x + 8y = -12$	⟶	$-4x + 8y = -12$
$2x - 4y = 7$	**× 2**	$4x - 8y = 14$

Add the revised equations. $\qquad\qquad\qquad\qquad 0 = 2$

ANSWER ▶ Because the statement $0 = 2$ is false, there is no solution.

Checkpoint ✓ **Solve a Linear System**

Solve the system using the linear combination method.

1. $x - 4y = 5$
$\quad 2x + y = 1$

2. $2x - y = 4$
$\quad 4x - 2y = 8$

3. $3x - 2y = 2$
$\quad 4x - 3y = 1$

4. How can you tell when a system has no solution? infinitely many solutions?

EXAMPLE 4 Use a Linear System as a Model

Catering A customer hires a caterer to prepare food for a party of 30 people. The customer has $80 to spend on food and would like there to be a choice of sandwiches and pasta. A $40 pan of pasta contains 10 servings, and a $10 sandwich tray contains 5 servings. The caterer must prepare enough food so that each person receives one serving of either food. How many pans of pasta and how many sandwich trays should the caterer prepare?

Solution

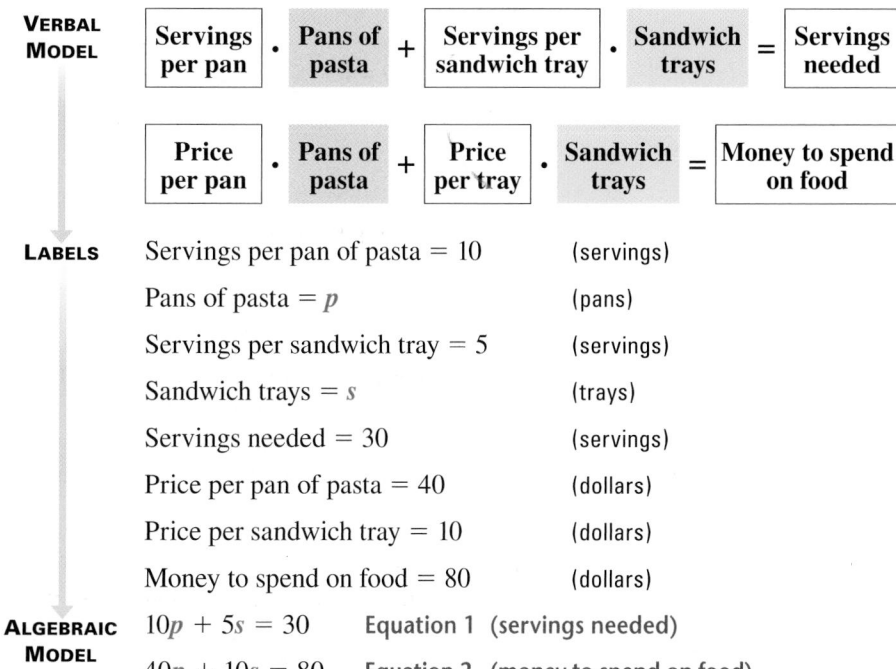

VERBAL MODEL

| Servings per pan | · | Pans of pasta | + | Servings per sandwich tray | · | Sandwich trays | = | Servings needed |

| Price per pan | · | Pans of pasta | + | Price per tray | · | Sandwich trays | = | Money to spend on food |

LABELS

Servings per pan of pasta = 10 (servings)

Pans of pasta = p (pans)

Servings per sandwich tray = 5 (servings)

Sandwich trays = s (trays)

Servings needed = 30 (servings)

Price per pan of pasta = 40 (dollars)

Price per sandwich tray = 10 (dollars)

Money to spend on food = 80 (dollars)

ALGEBRAIC MODEL

$10p + 5s = 30$ Equation 1 (servings needed)

$40p + 10s = 80$ Equation 2 (money to spend on food)

Multiply Equation 1 by **−2** so that the coefficients of s differ only in sign.

$$10p + 5s = 30 \quad \times -2 \quad -20p - 10s = -60$$
$$40p + 10s = 80 \quad\quad\quad 40p + 10s = 80$$

Add the revised equations and solve for p.

$$20p \quad = 20$$
$$p = 1$$

Substitute **1** for p in one of the original equations and solve for s.

$10p + 5s = 30$ Write Equation 1.

$10(1) + 5s = 30$ Substitute 1 for p.

$5s = 20$ Subtract 10 from each side.

$s = 4$ Solve for s.

ANSWER ▶ The caterer should make 1 pan of pasta and 4 sandwich trays.

Checkpoint ✓ **Solve a Linear System**

5. Another customer asks the caterer in Example 4 to plan a party for 40 people. This customer also wants both sandwiches and pasta and has $120 to spend. How many pans of pasta and how many sandwich trays should the caterer prepare?

3.3 Exercises

Guided Practice

Vocabulary Check

1. When you use the linear combination method to solve a linear system, why do you add the revised equations in Step 2?

Skill Check **Error Analysis** In Exercises 2 and 3, describe and correct the error.

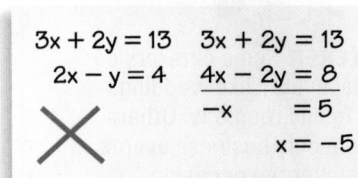

2.
$$2x - y = 7 \qquad 4x - 2y = 7$$
$$3x + 2y = 14 \qquad 3x + 2y = 14$$
$$\qquad\qquad\qquad\quad 7x \quad\quad = 21$$
$$\qquad\qquad\qquad\qquad x = 3$$

3.
$$3x + 2y = 13 \qquad 3x + 2y = 13$$
$$2x - y = 4 \qquad 4x - 2y = 8$$
$$\qquad\qquad\qquad -x \quad\quad = 5$$
$$\qquad\qquad\qquad\qquad x = -5$$

Solve the system. Explain each step.

4. $2x + 3y = 1$
   $x - 3y = -13$

5. $4x - 3y = 2$
   $x + 2y = 6$

6. $2x + 3y = 7$
   $3x + 5y = 10$

7. **Counting Change** You have a jar with quarters and dimes in it. There are a total of 47 coins worth $7.70. Use a verbal model to write a system of linear equations. Use the linear combination method to solve the system. How many quarters are in the jar? How many dimes are in the jar?

Practice and Applications

STUDENT HELP

HOMEWORK HELP
Example 1: Exs. 8–25
Example 2: Exs. 14–25
Example 3: Exs. 27–32
Example 4: Exs. 26, 33–37

Using Addition Solve the system using the linear combination method. Then check your solution.

8. $x + y = -1$
   $x - y = 9$

9. $x - y = 7$
   $2x + y = 5$

10. $x + 2y = -11$
    $3x - 2y = -1$

11. $3x - 2y = 17$
    $-3x + 5y = -11$

12. $3x - y = -3$
    $x + y = 3$

13. $x + 2y = 14$
    $-x + y = -5$

Using Multiplication and Addition Solve the system using the linear combination method. Then check your solution.

14. $3x - y = 4$
    $2x + 3y = 32$

15. $4x - 3y = 10$
    $x + 2y = -14$

16. $2x + 2y = -16$
    $2x + 3y = -3$

17. $x - 3y = 2$
    $2x + 5y = 15$

18. $3x + 2y = -2$
    $x - y = 11$

19. $4x - y = 3$
    $-2x + 3y = 21$

20. $-2x - 2y = 30$
    $5x + 3y = 7$

21. $4x + 5y = -6$
    $3x + 2y = 27$

22. $3x + 7y = -4$
    $2x + 5y = -2$

23. $4x + 3y = 33$
    $5x - 4y = -13$

24. $5x - 7y = -2$
    $3x + 2y = 36$

25. $3x + 2y = 27$
    $-4x + 5y = -36$

26. **Fundraiser** You are selling sandwiches for a school fundraiser. You are selling vegetarian sandwiches for $3 each and turkey sandwiches for $4 each. You sell 25 sandwiches for a total of $85. Use a verbal model to write a system of linear equations. Use the linear combination method to solve the system. How many of each type did you sell?

Number of Solutions Tell whether the system has *one solution*, *no solution*, or *infinitely many solutions*.

27. $4x - 14y = 12$
$-2x + 7y = -6$

28. $2x + 5y = 0$
$4x + 6y = 24$

29. $5x - 3y = 15$
$-10x + 6 = -15$

30. $3x + 2y = 3$
$-6x + 3y = 43$

31. $3x - 4y = -4$
$-5x + 2y = 2$

32. $4x + 6y = -10$
$6x + 9y = -15$

Using Linear Combinations In Exercises 33–37, use a verbal model to write a linear system. Use the linear combination method to solve.

33. Cross-Training You want to burn 580 Calories during 60 minutes of exercise. You burn about 8 Calories per minute in-line skating and 12 Calories per minute swimming. How long should you spend doing each activity?

34. Concert Your school band is performing a concert. Tickets for the concert cost $3 for students and $5 for adults. A total of 125 people attend the concert. Ticket sales total $475. How many students are at the concert? How many adults are at the concert?

35. Birdhouses You are selling handmade birdhouses and bird feeders. You sell birdhouses for $12.50 and bird feeders for $15. You earned $245 from selling a total of 17 items. How many birdhouses and bird feeders did you sell?

36. Compact Discs A store sells recordable compact discs in packs of 5 for $5 and packs of 10 for $8. You buy 45 discs for $37. How many of each type of pack did you buy?

37. Supplies A supply clerk for a company is ordering two kinds of light bulbs. One kind comes in a pack of 24 for $12, and the other comes in a pack of 12 for $18. The clerk ordered a total of 108 light bulbs at a cost of $66. How many of each kind of light bulb did the clerk order?

Standardized Test Practice

38. Multiple Choice Which ordered pair is a solution of the system of equations?
$$3x + 2y = 2$$
$$6x + 5y = -1$$

A $(4, -5)$ **B** $(-5, 4)$ **C** $(-4, 5)$ **D** $(5, -4)$

39. Multiple Choice Which ordered pair is a solution of the system of equations?
$$5x + 6y = 1$$
$$2x + 5y = 16$$

F $(7, 6)$ **G** $(-7, 6)$ **H** $(6, -7)$ **J** no solution

40. Multiple Choice Which system of equations has a solution where $y = 3$?

A $x + 2y = 14$
$2x - 5y = 1$

B $4x + y = -4$
$3x + y = -1$

C $2x + 5y = -1$
$2x + 2y = 14$

D $-2x + y = 2$
$3x - y = 1$

41. Multiple Choice Which system has a solution of the form $(0, y)$?

F $3x - 4y = -20$
$25x + 2y = 10$

G $5x + 3y = -2$
$7x - 2y = -9$

H $4x + 6y = 8$
$2x + 3y = -4$

J $7x + 5y = -1$
$9x + 8y = -6$

Finding Quartiles Find the median, the upper quartile, and the lower quartile of the data set. *(Lesson 1.7)*

42. 13, 26, 19, 8, 16, 17, 22

43. 71, 44, 92, 37, 65, 54, 80, 28

44. 10.1, 22.8, 15.7, 13.4, 19.2, 9.3

45. 2, 1, 6, 4, 6, 5, 5, 3, 1, 8, 7

Finding Slope Find the slope of the line passing through the given points. *(Lesson 2.3)*

46. $(3, -1)$, $(7, 7)$

47. $(-2, -2)$, $(5, 3)$

48. $(-4, 1)$, $(-1, -5)$

49. $(4, 3)$, $(-7, 3)$

50. $(-3, 4)$, $(-1, 6)$

51. $(2, 7)$, $(5, 2)$

Graphing Equations Graph the equation. *(Lesson 2.4)*

52. $2x + 3y = 6$

53. $x - 3y = 8$

54. $5x - 2y = 4$

Solving Linear Systems Solve the system by graphing. Then check your solution. *(Lesson 3.1)*

55. $3x - y = 5$
$x + y = 3$

56. $x + y = 0$
$2x + 2y = 9$

57. $2x - y = 6$
$x - y = 2$

Geometry Skills

Area Find the area of the circle. Round to the nearest tenth.

58. $r = 2.25$ in.

59. $d = 1.5$ ft

60. $d = 5.1$ cm

Quiz 1

Lesson 3.1 **Solve the system by graphing. Then check your solution.**

1. $3x + y = 4$
$6x + y = 10$

2. $5x + 2y = 3$
$-4x + y = 8$

3. $2x - y = 1$
$x + 2y = 13$

Lesson 3.2 **Solve the system using substitution.**

4. $x - 2y = 13$
$2x + 3y = 5$

5. $3x + 2y = 16$
$4x - y = 14$

6. $2x + 7y = -3$
$x + 3y = -2$

Lesson 3.3 **Solve the system using the linear combination method.**

7. $2x + 5y = 9$
$-4x + 2y = 42$

8. $5x - 2y = -2$
$3x + 5y = 36$

9. $4x - 5y = 8$
$3x + 2y = -17$

Lesson 3.3 **10. Books** The manager of a bookstore at a mall placed some hardcover books and some paperback books on a table for the mall's "Sidewalk Sale." Hardcover books cost $14.95, and paperback books cost $4.95. Mary bought 6 books for $49.70. Use a verbal model to write a linear system of equations. Solve the system using the linear combination method. How many hardcover books did she buy? How many paperback books did she buy?

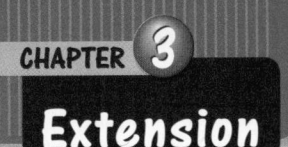

CHAPTER 3 Extension

Key Words

- substitution method, p. 132
- linear combination method, p. 139

STUDENT HELP

SOLVING NOTE
To avoid working with fractions you may want to use the linear combination method. To avoid working with large numbers you may want to use the substitution method.

Choosing a Method

GOAL Choose a method to solve a system of linear equations.

To solve a linear system algebraically, you can use either the substitution method or the linear combination method. You must decide which method is more convenient.

- If one of the variables has a coefficient of 1 or -1, the *substitution method* is convenient. In general, you should solve for that variable.

- If neither variable has a coefficient of 1 or -1, the *linear combination method* is often more convenient, although you can still use substitution.

EXAMPLE 1 Choose a Method to Solve a Linear System

Choose a method to solve the linear system. Explain your choice. Then solve the system.

$$-3x + y = -5 \quad \text{Equation 1}$$
$$5x - 3y = 3 \quad \text{Equation 2}$$

Solution

The coefficient of y is 1 in Equation 1. So, you should use the substitution method.

❶ Solve for y in Equation 1.

$-3x + y = -5$	Write Equation 1.
$y = 3x - 5$	Solve for y to get revised Equation 1.

❷ Substitute $3x - 5$ for y in Equation 2 and solve for x.

$5x - 3y = 3$	Write Equation 2.
$5x - 3(3x - 5) = 3$	Substitute $3x - 5$ for y.
$5x - 9x + 15 = 3$	Use the distributive property.
$-4x + 15 = 3$	Combine like terms.
$-4x = -12$	Subtract 15 from each side.
$x = 3$	Solve for x.

❸ Substitute 3 for x in revised Equation 1 and solve for y.

$y = 3x - 5$	Write revised Equation 1.
$y = 3(3) - 5$	Substitute 3 for x.
$y = 4$	Simplify.

❹ Check by substituting 3 for x and 4 for y in the original equations.

ANSWER ▸ The solution is $(3, 4)$.

 **Choose a Method to Solve a Linear System**

Choose a method to solve the system. Explain your choice. Then solve the system.

1. $2x + y = 7$
$3x + 4y = 8$

2. $3x + 5y = -1$
$6x + 7y = -5$

3. $2x - y = 7$
$x + 3y = 14$

EXAMPLE 2 Choose a Method to Solve a Linear System

Choose a method to solve the linear system. Explain your choice. Then solve the system.

$2x - 5y = -1$ **Equation 1**
$4x + 3y = 11$ **Equation 2**

Solution

Neither variable has a coefficient of 1 or -1. So, it is more convenient to use the linear combination method.

❶ *Multiply* the first equation by -2 so that the coefficients of x differ only in sign.

$2x - 5y = -1$ **× (−2)** $-4x + 10y = 2$

$4x + 3y = 11$ $\underline{4x + 3y = 11}$

❷ *Add* the revised equations and solve for y. $13y = 13$

$y = 1$

❸ *Substitute* 1 for y in one of the original equations and solve for x.

$2x - 5y = -1$ Write Equation 1.

$2x - 5(1) = -1$ Substitute 1 for y.

$2x = 4$ Add 5 to each side.

$x = 2$ Solve for x.

❹ *Check* by substituting 2 for x and 1 for y in the original equations.

ANSWER ▶ The solution is $(2, 1)$.

Exercises

Choose a Method Tell which method you would use to solve the system. Explain your choice.

1. $-x + 2y = -4$
    $3x - 5y = 7$

2. $2x - 5y = 12$
    $x + 5y = -24$

3. $3x + 5y = 2$
    $6x + 7y = -8$

Solve Linear Systems Choose a method to solve the linear system. Then solve the system.

4. $-x + 2y = -2$
    $x + 4y = -10$

5. $2x + 5y = 17$
    $3x - 5y = -12$

6. $3x - 4y = 12$
    $5x - 2y = -8$

7. $2x + y = -1$
    $3x - y = 16$

8. $4x + 3y = 2$
    $-2x + 5y = -14$

9. $x - 4y = -6$
    $2x + 3y = 21$

10. $3x - 2y = 14$
    $x + 3y = 23$

11. $4x + 3y = -1$
    $5x + 6y = 10$

12. $2x + 3y = 9$
    $5x - y = -3$

13. Sports Cards At a yard sale, you buy a box of 240 football and baseball cards. The seller says there are three times as many baseball cards in the box as there are football cards. How many baseball cards are in the box?

14. Movies Tickets at a local movie theater are $4 for students and $7 for adults. One night, the theater sells 578 tickets and collects $3365 in ticket sales. How many student tickets were sold? How many adult tickets were sold?

3.4 Graphing Linear Equations in Three Variables

Key Words
- three-dimensional coordinate system
- *z*-axis
- ordered triple
- octants
- linear equation in three variables

Prerequisite Skills

Find the *x*- and *y*-intercepts of the graph of the equation.

1. $3x + 2y = 6$

2. $2x - 5y = 10$

3. $-4x + y = 8$

4. $5x + 4y = 20$

GOAL Graph linear equations in three variables.

Solutions of equations in three variables can be pictured with a **three-dimensional coordinate system**. To construct such a system, begin with the *xy*-coordinate plane in a horizontal position. Then draw the **z-axis** as a vertical line through the origin, as shown.

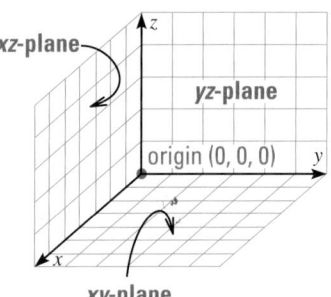

Points in a two-dimensional coordinate system are represented by ordered pairs. Each point in space can be represented by an **ordered triple** (x, y, z), such as $(1, -2, 3)$.

The three axes, taken two at a time, determine three coordinate planes. These planes divide space into eight **octants**. The first octant is the one for which all three coordinates are positive.

EXAMPLE 1 Plot Points in Three Dimensions

Plot the ordered triple in a three-dimensional coordinate system.

a. $(-5, 3, 4)$ **b.** $(3, -4, -2)$

Solution

a. To plot $(-5, 3, 4)$, first find the point $(-5, 3)$ in the *xy*-plane. The point $(-5, 3, 4)$ lies 4 units above it.

b. To plot $(3, -4, -2)$, find the point $(3, -4)$ in the *xy*-plane. The point $(3, -4, -2)$ lies 2 units below it.

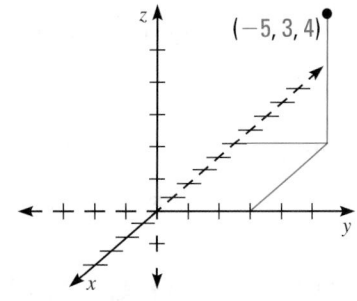
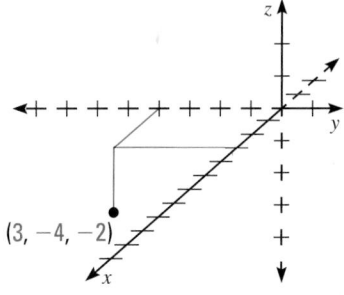

Checkpoint ✓ *Plot Points in Three Dimensions*

Plot the ordered triple in a three-dimensional coordinate system.

1. $(1, 2, 4)$ 2. $(-2, 1, 3)$ 3. $(-4, -1, -5)$ 4. $(3, -2, -4)$

A **linear equation in three variables** x, y, and z is an equation of the form

$$ax + by + cz = d$$

where the constants a, b, and c are not all zero. An ordered triple (x, y, z) is a solution of a linear equation in three variables if the values of x, y, and z make the equation true. The graph of a *linear* equation in three variables is a *plane*. In a three-dimensional coordinate system, the graphs of equations in one or two variables are also planes.

STUDENT HELP

READING GRAPHS
Recall that a plane has two dimensions and that it extends without end, even though the drawing of a plane appears to have edges.

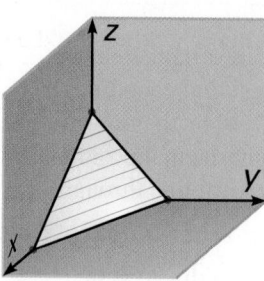

Plane $ax + by + cz = d$ intersects all three axes.

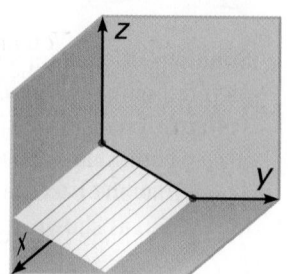

Plane $by + cz = d$ intersects the y-axis and z-axis and is parallel to the x-axis.

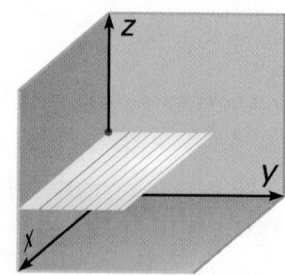

Plane $cz = d$ intersects the z-axis and is parallel to the xy-plane.

EXAMPLE 2 Graph a Linear Equation in Three Variables

Sketch the graph of $3x + 2y + 4z = 12$. Label the points where the graph crosses the x-, y-, and z-axes.

Solution

Find the points where the graph intersects the axes.
First let $x = 0$ and $y = 0$, and then solve for z.

$$3(0) + 2(0) + 4z = 12 \qquad \text{Substitute 0 for } x \text{ and for } y.$$
$$4z = 12 \qquad \text{Simplify.}$$
$$z = 3 \qquad \text{Solve for } z.$$

The z-intercept is 3, so plot the point $(0, 0, 3)$.
Next, let $y = 0$ and $z = 0$, and then solve for x.

$$3x + 2(0) + 4(0) = 12 \qquad \text{Substitute 0 for } y \text{ and for } z.$$
$$3x = 12 \qquad \text{Simplify.}$$
$$x = 4 \qquad \text{Solve for } x.$$

The x-intercept is 4, so plot the point $(4, 0, 0)$.
Finally, let $x = 0$ and $z = 0$, and then solve for y.

$$3(0) + 2y + 4(0) = 12 \qquad \text{Substitute 0 for } x \text{ and for } z.$$
$$2y = 12 \qquad \text{Simplify.}$$
$$y = 6 \qquad \text{Solve for } y.$$

STUDENT HELP

SOLVING NOTE
To find other solutions of the equation, solve for one of its variables, such as $z = -\frac{3}{4}x - \frac{1}{2}y + 3$. Substitute any real numbers for x and y and simplify to find the corresponding value of z.

The y-intercept is 6, so plot $(0, 6, 0)$.

Connect the points with lines. The lines form the triangular region of the plane that lies in the first octant.

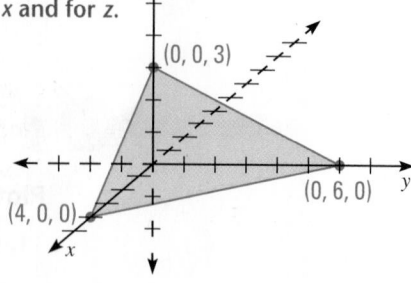

Sketch the graph of the equation. Label the points where the graph crosses the *x*-, *y*-, and *z*-axes.

5. $x + 3y + 2z = 6$　　　**6.** $5x + y + 2z = 10$　　　**7.** $x + y = 4$

Link to
SCIENCE

GARDENING Tulips come in a variety of sizes, shapes, and colors. The bulbs must be planted in late fall or early winter in order to bloom the following spring.

EXAMPLE 3 **Model a Real-Life Situation**

Gardening You are planting tulip bulbs and daffodil bulbs in a community garden. Tulip bulbs cost $6 per dozen, and daffodil bulbs cost $5 per dozen. Fertilizer for the bulbs costs $10.

a. Write a linear model for the total cost you will spend for both the bulbs and the fertilizer.

b. Evaluate the model for several different numbers of tulip bulbs and daffodil bulbs. Organize your results in a table.

Solution

a. Your total cost involves two variable costs (for the two types of bulbs) and one fixed cost (for the fertilizer).

VERBAL MODEL	**Total cost**	=	**Cost of tulip bulbs (per dozen)**	·	**Dozens of tulip bulbs**	+	**Cost of daffodil bulbs (per dozen)**	·	**Dozens of daffodil bulbs**	+	**Cost of fertilizer**

LABELS　　Total cost = C　　　　　　　　　　(dollars)

　　　　　　Cost of tulip bulbs (per dozen) = 6　　(dollars)

　　　　　　Dozens of tulip bulbs = t　　　　　(dozens of bulbs)

　　　　　　Cost of daffodil bulbs (per dozen) = 5　(dollars)

　　　　　　Dozens of daffodil bulbs = d　　　(dozens of bulbs)

　　　　　　Cost of fertilizer = 10　　　　　　(dollars)

ALGEBRAIC MODEL　$C = 6t + 5d + 10$

b. To evaluate the model, substitute values for *t* and *d*. For example, substitute **4** for *t* and **3** for *d*.

　　$C = 6t + 5d + 10$　　　Write algebraic model.

　　$C = 6(4) + 5(3) + 10$　　Substitute 4 for *t* and 3 for *d*.

　　$C = 49$　　　　　　　Simplify.

The total cost is $49 for 4 dozen tulip bulbs and 3 dozen daffodil bulbs.

The table shows the total cost for several more values of *t* and *d*.

		t (dozens of tulip bulbs)		
		2	**4**	**6**
d (dozens of daffodil bulbs)	**1**	$27	$39	$51
	2	$32	$44	$56
	3	$37	$49	$61

Guided Practice

Vocabulary Check

1. Copy and complete the statement: Each point in space can be represented by a(n) __?__ of the form (x, y, z).

2. Copy and complete the statement: The three axes, taken two at a time, determine three coordinate planes that divide space into eight __?__.

3. Write the general form of a linear equation in three variables.

4. Copy and complete the statement: The graph of a linear equation in three variables is represented by a(n) __?__ in three-dimensional space.

Skill Check

Plot the ordered triple in a three-dimensional coordinate system.

5. $(2, 1, 3)$ **6.** $(3, -2, -5)$ **7.** $(-1, -3, 4)$

Sketch the graph of the equation. Label the points where the graph crosses the x-, y-, and z-axes.

8. $3x + 2y + 6z = 6$ **9.** $4x + 8y + 2z = 16$ **10.** $5x + 10y = 20$

11. $3x + 4y + 6z = 12$ **12.** $6x + 9y + 12z = 36$ **13.** $6y = 18$

Practice and Applications

STUDENT HELP

HOMEWORK HELP
Example 1: Exs. 14–21
Example 2: Exs. 22–33
Example 3: Exs. 38–44

Plotting Points **Plot the ordered triple in a three-dimensional coordinate system.**

14. $(3, 5, 0)$ **15.** $(4, 1, 3)$ **16.** $(0, -3, -1)$ **17.** $(2, 5, 2)$

18. $(3, 5, -2)$ **19.** $(2, -1, 1)$ **20.** $(1, -2, -3)$ **21.** $(-3, -1, -5)$

Sketching Graphs **Sketch the graph of the equation. Label the points where the graph crosses the x-, y-, and z-axes.**

22. $x + y + z = 3$ **23.** $x + 2z = 6$ **24.** $3x + 5y + 15z = 15$

25. $12x + 8y + 6z = 24$ **26.** $8x + 12y + 16z = 48$ **27.** $4x + 2y + 8z = 16$

28. $3y - 7z = 21$ **29.** $6x + 9y + 4z = 36$ **30.** $8x = 32$

31. $4x + 14y - 7z = 28$ **32.** $-5x - 15y + 9z = 45$ **33.** $4x + 2y + 8z = -8$

Geometry Link **Use the given coordinates to find the coordinates of the vertices J, K, L, and M of the rectangular prism.**

34.

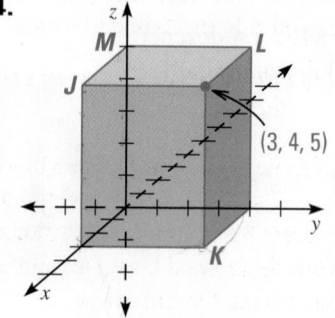

$(3, 4, 5)$

35.

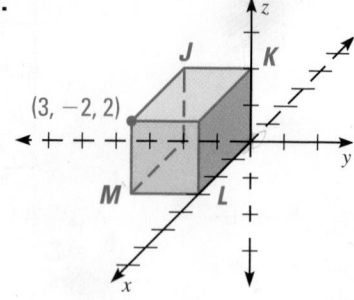

$(3, -2, 2)$

Geometry Link Use the given point to find the volume of the rectangular prism.

36.

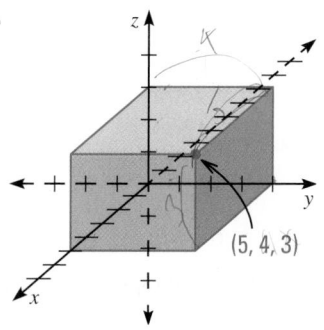

(5, 4, 3)

37.

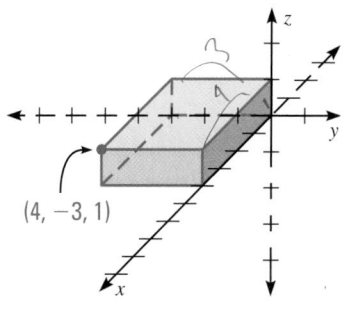

(4, −3, 1)

38. Family Vacation A family of four is planning a camping trip. The family spends $300 on new camping equipment. The campsite costs $17 per night, and the family budgets $6 per meal for each person. Use the verbal model below to write an algebraic model for the total cost C of the camping trip. Let x be the number of nights, and let y be the number of meals. Evaluate the model for several values of x and y. Organize your results in a table.

Total cost	=	Campsite cost per night	·	Number of nights	+	Budgeted cost per meal	·	Total number of meals	+	Cost of new equipment

After-School Jobs In Exercises 39 and 40, use the following information.

After school you work as a cashier at a grocery store for $6 per hour. On weekends, you work as a lifeguard for $8 per hour. You also receive a weekly allowance of $15 for doing chores.

39. Write a verbal model for your total weekly earnings. Then write an algebraic model. Let c be the number of hours you work as a cashier, and let ℓ be the number of hours you work as a lifeguard.

40. Evaluate the model for several values. Organize your results in a table.

Transportation In Exercises 41 and 42, use the following information.

Every month you buy a bus pass for $30. The pass allows you to ride the bus for free and get discounts on the express bus and the subway. The discounted cost for the express bus is $.75. The discounted cost for the subway is $.50.

41. Write a model for the total cost of transportation for the month. Let b be the number of times you ride the express bus and s be the number of subway rides.

42. Evaluate the model for several numbers of express bus and subway rides. Organize your results in a table.

43. Uniforms A summer basketball league buys a T-shirt for each member of each team in the league. The league pays $30 to have artwork designed for the shirts. A medium shirt costs $10 and a large shirt costs $13. Write a model for the total cost of the artwork design and both medium and large T-shirts. Evaluate the model for several orders. Organize your results in a table.

44. Home Aquarium You want to buy an aquarium starter kit for $180 and stock the aquarium with rainbow fish, tetras, and angelfish. A pet store sells rainbow fish for $4.50 each, tetras for $2 each, and angelfish for $9 each. Using a verbal model, write an algebraic model for the amount you will spend given the number of rainbow fish, tetras, and angelfish you buy. Evaluate the model for several numbers of rainbow fish, tetras, and angelfish. Organize your results in a table.

Standardized Test Practice

45. Multiple Choice At which point does the graph of the equation $4x + 7y + 28z = 56$ cross the y-axis?

    A $(0, 7, 0)$ **B** $(0, 8, 0)$ **C** $(0, 14, 0)$ **D** $(0, 2, 0)$

46. Multiple Choice Which equation is represented by the graph?

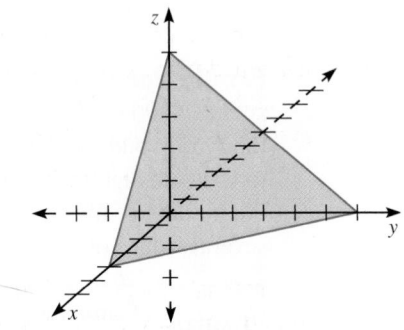

    F $3x + 6y + 5z = 30$ **G** $15x + 10y + 12z = 60$

    H $x + y + z = 6$ **J** $10x + 5y + 6z = 30$

Mixed Review

Identifying Direct Variation **Tell whether the data show direct variation. If so, write an equation relating x and y.** *(Lesson 2.6)*

47.

x	2	4	6	8	10
y	10	20	30	40	50

48.

x	1	3	4	5	6
y	3	6	8	15	16

Graphing Linear Systems **Graph the linear system and tell how many solutions it has. If it has exactly one solution, find and check the solution.** *(Lesson 3.1)*

49. $2x + 4y = 8$ **50.** $x + 5y = 18$ **51.** $x - 2y = 10$
      $x + 2y = 4$ $2x + 3y = 8$ $x - 2y = -3$

Solving Linear Systems **Solve the system using substitution.** *(Lesson 3.2)*

52. $y = 4x$ **53.** $4m - 5n = 21$ **54.** $2a + 3b = -2$
      $-3x + 2y = 5$ $m - 2n = 0$ $6a + b = 10$

55. $-3x + 4y = -9$ **56.** $x - 2y = 2$ **57.** $-x + 3y = 5$
      $2x + y = 6$ $5x - 2y = -6$ $2x + y = 4$

Geometry Skills

Parallel Lines and Angles **Find the values of x and y.**

58.

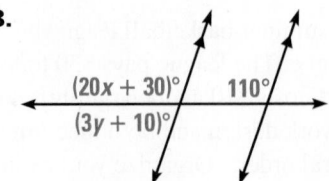

59.

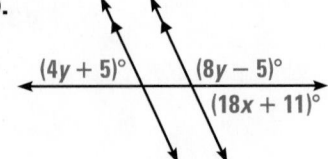

3.5 Solving Systems of Linear Equations in Three Variables

Key Words

- system of three linear equations
- solution of a system of three linear equations

Prerequisite Skills

Solve the linear system.

1. $-2x + y = 2$
$x - 3y = -1$

2. $4x + 8y = -2$
$-x - 2y = 1$

3. $3x + 4y = 5$
$-6x - 8y = -10$

GOAL Solve systems of linear equations in three variables.

How many adults, students, and children attended a band concert?

A system of equations in three variables is needed when a situation involves three variable quantities. You will use such a system in Exercise 32 to determine the number of adults, students, and children who attended a band concert.

In Lessons 3.1–3.3, you learned how to solve a system of two linear equations in two variables. In this lesson, you will learn how to solve a **system of three linear equations** in three variables, such as the one shown below.

$$x + 3y - 4z = -16 \quad \text{Equation 1}$$
$$-x - 2y + 3z = 11 \quad \text{Equation 2}$$
$$4x - y - 6z = -5 \quad \text{Equation 3}$$

A **solution** of such a system is an ordered triple (x, y, z) that is a solution of all three equations. For example, $(1, -3, 2)$ is the solution of the system above.

$$1 + 3(-3) - 4(2) = 1 - 9 - 8 = -16 \checkmark$$
$$-1 - 2(-3) + 3(2) = -1 + 6 + 6 = 11 \checkmark$$
$$4(1) - (-3) - 6(2) = 4 + 3 - 12 = -5 \checkmark$$

In Lesson 3.4, you learned that the graph of a linear equation in three variables is a plane. The graphs of three such equations that form a system are three planes whose intersection determines the number of solutions of the system.

Exactly one solution

If the planes intersect in a single point, the system has exactly one solution.

Infinitely many solutions

If the planes intersect in a line or a plane, the system has infinitely many solutions.

No solution

If the three planes do not intersect, the system has no solution.

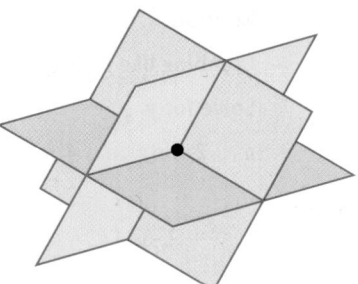

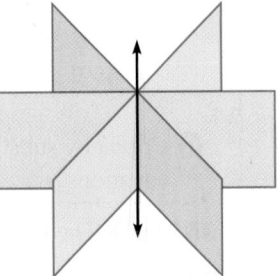

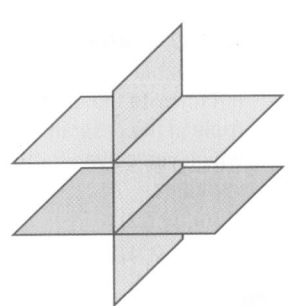

The Linear Combination Method (3-Variable Systems)

STEP ① *Rewrite* the linear system in three variables as a linear system in two variables using the linear combination method.

STEP ② *Solve* the new linear system for both of its variables.

STEP ③ *Substitute* the values found in Step 2 into one of the original equations and solve for the remaining variable.

STEP ④ *Check* the solution in each of the original equations.

EXAMPLE ① Use the Linear Combination Method

Solve the system.

$$3x + 2y + 4z = 11 \quad \text{Equation 1}$$
$$2x - y + 3z = 4 \quad \text{Equation 2}$$
$$5x - 3y + 5z = -1 \quad \text{Equation 3}$$

Solution

STUDENT HELP

ANOTHER WAY
In Step 1, you could also eliminate x to get two equations in y and z, or you could eliminate z to get two equations in x and y.

① *Rewrite* the system as a system in two variables. First, add 2 times Equation 2 to Equation 1 to eliminate y.

$$3x + 2y + 4z = 11 \quad\Rightarrow\quad 3x + 2y + 4z = 11$$
$$2x - y + 3z = 4 \quad \times 2 \quad\Rightarrow\quad \underline{4x - 2y + 6z = 8}$$
$$7x \qquad + 10z = 19 \quad \text{New Equation 1}$$

Now add -3 times Equation 2 to Equation 3 to eliminate y.

$$5x - 3y + 5z = -1 \quad\Rightarrow\quad 5x - 3y + 5z = -1$$
$$2x - y + 3z = 4 \quad \times (-3) \quad \underline{-6x + 3y - 9z = -12}$$
$$-x \qquad - 4z = -13 \quad \text{New Equation 2}$$

② *Solve* the new system of linear equations in two variables. First, add 7 times new Equation 2 to new Equation 1 to eliminate x.

$$7x + 10z = 19 \quad\Rightarrow\quad 7x + 10z = 19$$
$$-x - 4z = -13 \quad \times 7 \quad \underline{-7x - 28z = -91}$$
$$-18z = -72$$
$$z = 4 \qquad \text{Solve for } z.$$

Substitute 4 for z in new Equation 1 or 2 and solve for x to get $x = -3$.

③ *Substitute* -3 for x and 4 for z in one of the original equations and solve for y.

$$2x - y + 3z = 4 \qquad \text{Equation 2}$$
$$2(-3) - y + 3(4) = 4 \qquad \text{Substitute } -3 \text{ for } x \text{ and 4 for } z.$$
$$-6 - y + 12 = 4 \qquad \text{Multiply.}$$
$$-y + 6 = 4 \qquad \text{Combine like terms.}$$
$$y = 2 \qquad \text{Solve for } y.$$

STUDENT HELP

AVOID ERRORS
In Example 1, be careful not to write the ordered triple in the order in which you solved for the variables.
$(4, -3, 2)$ ✗
$(-3, 2, 4)$ ✓

④ *Check* by substituting -3 for x, 2 for y, and 4 for z in each of the original equations.

ANSWER ▶ The solution is $x = -3$, $y = 2$, and $z = 4$, or the ordered triple $(-3, 2, 4)$.

Systems Without Unique Solutions Recall that it is possible to obtain a numerical statement in any of the steps using the linear combination method.

EXAMPLE 2 Solve a System with No Solution

STUDENT HELP

SOLVING NOTE
In Example 2, a numeric statement is obtained in the first step. Depending on how you start, you may not obtain a numeric statement until the third step.

Solve the system.

$$x + y + z = 2 \qquad \text{Equation 1}$$
$$3x + 3y + 3z = 14 \qquad \text{Equation 2}$$
$$x - 2y + z = 4 \qquad \text{Equation 3}$$

Solution

Multiply Equation 1 by -3 and add the result to Equation 2.

$$
\begin{array}{ll}
-3x - 3y - 3z = -6 & \text{Add } -3 \text{ times Equation 1} \\
\underline{3x + 3y + 3z = 14} & \text{to Equation 2.} \\
\qquad\qquad\quad 0 = 8 & \text{False statement}
\end{array}
$$

ANSWER ▸ Because solving the system resulted in the false statement $0 = 8$, the original system of equations has no solution.

EXAMPLE 3 Solve a System with Infinitely Many Solutions

Solve the system.

$$x + y + z = 4 \qquad \text{Equation 1}$$
$$x + y - z = 4 \qquad \text{Equation 2}$$
$$3x + 3y + z = 12 \qquad \text{Equation 3}$$

Solution

❶ *Rewrite* the system as a system in two variables.

$$
\begin{array}{ll}
x + y + z = 4 & \text{Add Equation 1} \\
\underline{x + y - z = 4} & \text{to Equation 2.} \\
\quad 2x + 2y = 8 & \text{New Equation 1}
\end{array}
$$

$$
\begin{array}{ll}
x + y - z = 4 & \text{Add Equation 2} \\
\underline{3x + 3y + z = 12} & \text{to Equation 3.} \\
\quad 4x + 4y = 16 & \text{New Equation 2}
\end{array}
$$

❷ *Solve* the new system of linear equations in two variables.

STUDENT HELP

SOLVING NOTE
When a system of linear equations in three variables has infinitely many solutions there are two possibilities: The planes intersect in a line or the planes are coplanar.

$$
\begin{array}{ll}
-4x - 4y = -16 & \text{Add } -2 \text{ times new Equation 1} \\
\underline{4x + 4y = 16} & \text{to new Equation 2.} \\
\qquad\quad 0 = 0 &
\end{array}
$$

ANSWER ▸ Because solving the system resulted in the true statement $0 = 0$, the original system of equations has infinitely many solutions. The three planes intersect in a line.

 **Solve Systems**

Tell how many solutions the linear system has. If the system has one solution, solve the system. Then check your solution.

3. $x + y + 3z = 1$
$\quad\ x + y - z = 1$
$\ -x - 3y + 4z = -1$

5. $x - y + z = 4$
$\quad 3x + y - 2z = -2$
$\quad 2x - 2y + 2z = 5$

6. $x + y + 2z = 10$
$\ -x + 2y + z = 5$
$\ -x + 4y + 3z = 15$

3.5 Exercises

Guided Practice

Vocabulary Check

1. Give an example of a system of three linear equations in three variables.

Copy and complete the statement.

2. If the graphs of three linear equations in three variables intersect in a(n) __?__, then the system of equations has exactly one solution.

3. If the graphs of three linear equations in three variables are parallel planes, then the system has __?__ solution(s).

Skill Check

Tell whether the ordered triple is a solution of the system of linear equations.

4. $(1, -4, 2)$;
$-2x - y + 5z = 12$
$3x + 2y - z = -7$
$-5x + 4y + 2z = -17$

5. $(7, -1, 0)$;
$-3x + 4y - 2z = -25$
$-4x - 9y + 8z = -19$
$-x - 10y + 3z = 3$

6. $(0, -3, 2)$;
$7x - 2y + 3z = -12$
$-x + 6y - 4z = 19$
$-5x + y + 3z = 12$

Solve the system using the linear combination method.

7. $x + 2y - 3z = -13$
$3x - y + 2z = 15$
$x + 3y = -7$

8. $\frac{1}{2}x + y - 2z = -5$
$-\frac{1}{2}x - 3y + z = 4$
$2x + 4y + 3z = 13$

9. $x - 3y + z = -2$
$2x - 5y + 4z = 9$
$3x - 2y + z = 5$

Tell how many solutions the linear system has.

10. $x + y + z = -9$
$x - 2y = 3$
$-x + 3y = -6$

11. $2x + 3y - 4z = 6$
$x + 4y + 5z = 12$
$-2x - 3y + 4z = -10$

12. $2x + y - 3z = 5$
$x - y + 2z = 6$
$-x + y - 2z = -6$

Practice and Applications

STUDENT HELP

HOMEWORK HELP
Example 1: Exs. 13–24, 31–33
Example 2: Exs. 22–24
Example 3: Exs. 22–24

Checking Solutions Tell whether the ordered triple is a solution of the system of linear equations.

13. $(-6, 1, 2)$;
$x + 2y - 2z = -8$
$-2x + 3y + z = 17$
$-x + 5y - 3z = 11$

14. $(3, 1, -2)$;
$2x + y + 5z = -3$
$4y + 3z = -2$
$-2x + 3y + z = -5$

15. $(5, 0, 4)$;
$2x - 3z = -2$
$4x + 6y - 5z = 0$
$-x + 3y + 2z = 3$

Linear Combination Method Solve the system using the linear combination method.

16. $x + 2y = -1$
$-x - 3y + 2z = -4$
$-x + y - 4z = 10$

17. $2x - y - 3z = 6$
$x + y + 4z = -1$
$3x - 2z = 8$

18. $x + 2y - 3z = 5$
$-y + 4z = 1$
$3x - 4y + 3z = -3$

19. $2x - 2y + z = 5$
$-2x + 3y + 2z = -1$
$x - 4y + 5z = 4$

20. $-4x + 3y + 2z = -1$
$x - 2y + z = 11$
$2x - y - 2z = 2$

21. $2x + y - z = 7$
$2x - y + 3z = 3$
$3x + 2y - z = 17$

Number of Solutions Tell whether the linear system has *no solution*, *exactly one solution*, or *infinitely many solutions*.

22. $x - y + z = 6$
$-3x + 3y - 3z = 10$
$x + 2y - 4z = 1$

23. $x + y - 2z = 5$
$x + 2y + z = 8$
$2x + 3y - z = 13$

24. $2x - y - 2z = 3$
$-x + 2y + 5z = 7$
$3x + y + z = 8$

EXAMPLE **Use the Substitution Method**

Solve the system.

$$x - y - z = 3 \qquad \text{Equation 1}$$
$$-x + 2y + 5z = -1 \qquad \text{Equation 2}$$
$$x + y + 4z = 4 \qquad \text{Equation 3}$$

Solution

❶ Solve for one of the variables in any of the equations.

$$x - y - z = 3 \qquad \text{Write Equation 1.}$$
$$x = 3 + y + z \qquad \text{Solve for } x.$$

STUDENT HELP

AVOID ERRORS
In Steps 2 and 3, be careful that you don't substitute into the equation you solved for a variable.

❷ Substitute $3 + y + z$ for x in another equation.

$$-x + 2y + 5z = -1 \qquad \text{Write Equation 2.}$$
$$-(3 + y + z) + 2y + 5z = -1 \qquad \text{Substitute } 3 + y + z \text{ for } x.$$
$$-3 - y - z + 2y + 5z = -1 \qquad \text{Use distributive property.}$$
$$-3 + y + 4z = -1 \qquad \text{Combine like terms.}$$
$$y + 4z = 2 \qquad \text{New Equation 2}$$

❸ Substitute $3 + y + z$ for x in the third equation.

$$x + y + 4z = 4 \qquad \text{Write Equation 3.}$$
$$(3 + y + z) + y + 4z = 4 \qquad \text{Substitute } 3 + y + z \text{ for } x \text{ and simplify.}$$
$$2y + 5z = 1 \qquad \text{New Equation 3}$$

❹ You now have a system of two equations in two variables. Use your preferred method to solve the system.

$$y + 4z = 2 \qquad \text{New Equation 2}$$
$$2y + 5z = 1 \qquad \text{New Equation 3}$$

❺ When you solve this system you get $y = -2$ and $z = 1$. Substitute these values into original Equation 1, and you get $x = 2$.

ANSWER ▶ The solution is $x = 2$, $y = -2$, and $z = 1$, or $(2, -2, 1)$.

Substitution Method Solve the system using substitution.

25. $2x - 3y + z = 4$
$x - 2z = 1$
$y + z = 2$

26. $2x - z = -5$
$x + 3y + 2z = 5$
$3x + y = -7$

27. $-y - 3z = -4$
$x + 2z = 1$
$3x - y - 2z = 9$

28. $-x + z = 2$
$x + 2y - 3z = 2$
$3x + 4y - 2z = -3$

29. $2x - 3y + z = -1$
$3y - z = 3$
$x + 4y + 3z = -8$

30. $2x - y + 3z = 2$
$x + 2y - 2z = -3$
$3x - y + 3z = 7$

31. Sale Prices Joe, Stacy, and Rob are shopping during a sale at a local department store. The sale items are jeans, shorts, and shirts. The purchases made by the three people are as follows.

- Joe buys one pair of jeans, four pairs of shorts, and two shirts for $84.
- Stacy buys two pairs of jeans, one pair of shorts, and three shirts for $76.
- Rob buys one pair of jeans, two pairs of shorts, and one shirt for $52.

What is the sale price of each piece of clothing?

32. Band A high school band performed a spring concert for a crowd of 600 people. The tickets for students sold for $3 each, the tickets for adults sold for $7 each, and tickets for children sold for $2 each. The revenue for the concert was $3150. There were 150 more adults at the concert than students. Use the verbal models to write a system of three linear equations. Solve the system to determine how many of each type of ticket were sold.

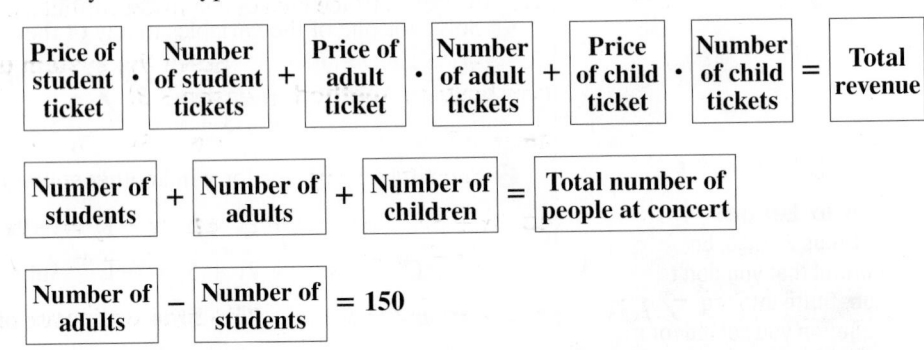

| Price of student ticket | • | Number of student tickets | + | Price of adult ticket | • | Number of adult tickets | + | Price of child ticket | • | Number of child tickets | = | Total revenue |

| Number of students | + | Number of adults | + | Number of children | = | Total number of people at concert |

| Number of adults | − | Number of students | = 150 |

33. Geometry Link The sum of the measures of angle B and angle C of triangle ABC is twice the measure of angle A. The measure of angle B is 32° less than the measure of angle C. Find the measures of the three angles.

Challenge In Exercises 34–36, use the system of equations.

$$x + y - 2z = 5 \quad \text{Equation 1}$$
$$x + 2y + z = 8 \quad \text{Equation 2}$$
$$2x + 3y - z = 13 \quad \text{Equation 3}$$

34. Verify that $(-3, 6, -1)$ and $(7, 0, 1)$ are solutions of the system of equations.

35. Explain how it is possible for both ordered triples to be solutions of the system of equations.

36. Find another solution of the system of equations.

Standardized Test Practice

37. Multiple Choice What is the value of z in the solution of this system?

$$x + 3y + 2z = 1$$
$$-2x + 4y + 5z = 5$$
$$2x + y = 0$$

(A) −1   (B) 1   (C) 2   (D) 3

38. Multiple Choice Which ordered triple is a solution of the system?

$$3x - y + 4z = -10$$
$$-x + y + 2z = 6$$
$$2x - y + z = -8$$

(F) $(1, 1, -3)$ (G) $(-2, 4, 0)$ (H) $(0, -3, 10)$ (J) $(-3, 0, -2)$

39. Multiple Choice How many solutions does the linear system have?

$$x + 3y - 2z = 0$$
$$-x + y - 4z = 4$$
$$x + 5y + 5z = 2$$

Ⓐ none　　Ⓑ exactly one　　Ⓒ exactly two　　Ⓓ infinitely many

Mixed Review

Solving Equations Solve the equation. *(Lesson 1.4)*

40. $-2n + 4 = -12 + 8n$　　**41.** $3x + 4 = -4x - 10$　　**42.** $3(-2m + 4) = 4m$

Rewriting Formulas **Solve the formula for the indicated variable.** *(Lesson 1.5)*

43. Solve the area of a trapezoid formula, $A = \frac{1}{2}(b_1 + b_2)h$, for h.

44. Solve the surface area of a cylinder formula, $S = 2\pi rh + 2\pi r^2$, for h.

Solving Linear Systems **Solve the system using the linear combination method.** *(Lesson 3.3)*

45. $x + 3y = 4$
$\quad\, -2x - 4y = -10$

46. $-3x + 5y = -30$
$\quad\,\, 2x - 3y = 19$

47. $4x + y = 5$
$\quad\,\, -2x - y = 3$

48. $3x + 5y = 10$
$\quad\, -2x - 4y = -10$

49. $2x - 3y = -15$
$\quad\, -5x + 4y = 27$

50. $-x + y = -8$
$\quad\,\,\, x + 6y = -6$

Geometry Skills

Pythagorean Theorem **Find the unknown length.**

51.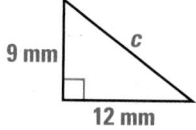

52.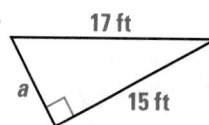

53.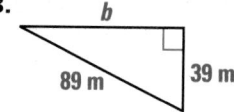

Quiz 2

Lesson 3.4

Sketch the graph of the equation. Label the points where the graph crosses the x-, y-, and z-axes.

1. $3x + 4y + 8z = 24$　　**2.** $5x + 15y + 9z = 45$　　**3.** $2x + 4y + 3z = -12$

4. $15x + 12y - 10z = -60$　　**5.** $6x - 18y + 27z = 54$　　**6.** $20x + 5y + 4z = 40$

Lesson 3.5

7. Copy and complete the statement: If the graphs of three linear equations in three variables intersect in a line, then the system of equations has __?__ solution(s).

Lesson 3.5

Solve the system using any method.

8. $-x + 2y + z = -1$
$\quad\,\,\, x + y + 3z = 3$
$\quad -4x - 5y + z = 16$

9. $3x + 2y - z = -1$
$\quad -3x - y + 4z = 3$
$\quad\,\,\, x - 3y - 5z = 5$

10. $2x + 3y + z = -7$
$\quad\quad\,\, -y + 2z = 12$
$\quad\,\,\, x + 2y + 6z = 10$

Lesson 3.5

11. Car Wash A car wash company offers three types of car washes. The ultimate car wash costs $12, the premium car wash costs $10, and the regular car wash costs $7. In one week, the total revenue for 500 car washes was $5450. The car wash company sold twice as many ultimate car washes as premium car washes that week. How many car washes of each type were sold that week?

@HomeTutor
classzone.com
• Multi-Language Glossary
• Vocabulary practice

VOCABULARY

- system of two linear equations, *p. 125*
- solution of a system of two linear equations, *p. 125*
- substitution method, *p. 132*
- linear combination method, *p. 139*
- three-dimensional coordinate system, *p. 147*
- *z*-axis, *p. 147*

- ordered triple, *p. 147*
- octants, *p. 147*
- linear equation in three variables, *p. 148*
- system of three linear equations, *p. 153*
- solution of a system of three linear equations, *p. 153*

VOCABULARY EXERCISES

1. Explain how to solve a system of two linear equations by graphing. How do you know that a linear system of equations has no solution by looking at its graph?

2. Explain how to solve a system of two linear equations by using substitution.

3. The solution of a particular system of three linear equations in three variables is one ordered triple. What can you say about the graphs of the equations?

3.1 SOLVING LINEAR SYSTEMS BY GRAPHING

Examples on pp. 125–127

EXAMPLE Solve the system by graphing. $2x - y = -5$ Equation 1
$3x + 2y = 3$ Equation 2

Graph both equations as shown on the right.

From the graph, you can see that the lines appear to intersect at $(-1, 3)$.

You can check the solution by substituting -1 for x and 3 for y into the original equations.

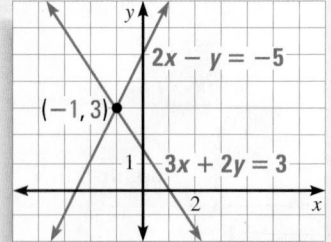

$$2(-1) - (3) = -2 - 3 = -5 \checkmark$$
$$3(-1) + 2(3) = -3 + 6 = 3 \checkmark$$

ANSWER The solution is $(-1, 3)$.

REVIEW HELP
Exercises Example
4–7   **1,** p. 125

Solve the system by graphing. Then check your solution.

4. $2x + y = -2$
$x - y = 5$

5. $3x + y = 3$
$-3x + 2y = -12$

6. $2x + 4y = 12$
$-x + 3y = 9$

7. $2x + 3y = 13$
$4x - y = 5$

3.2 SOLVING LINEAR SYSTEMS BY SUBSTITUTION

Examples on pp. 132–134

EXAMPLE Solve the system using substitution.

$$2x - y = 1 \quad \text{Equation 1}$$
$$-3x + 4y = 11 \quad \text{Equation 2}$$

Solve Equation 1 for y.

$2x - y = 1$	Write Equation 1.
$y = 2x - 1$	Solve for y to get revised Equation 1.

Substitute $2x - 1$ for y in Equation 2 and solve for x.

$-3x + 4y = 11$	Write Equation 2.
$-3x + 4(2x - 1) = 11$	Substitute $2x - 1$ for y.
$-3x + 8x - 4 = 11$	Use the distributive property.
$x = 3$	Combine like terms and solve for x.

Substitute 3 for x in revised Equation 1 and solve for y.

$y = 2x - 1$	Write revised Equation 1.
$y = 2(3) - 1$	Substitute 3 for x.
$y = 5$	Simplify.

ANSWER ▶ The solution is $(3, 5)$. Check by substituting in the original equations.

REVIEW HELP
Exercises | Example
8–11 | 1, p. 132

Solve the system using substitution.

8. $y = -5x$
$4x + 2y = 6$

9. $-2x + y = 7$
$3x + y = -8$

10. $-5x + 2y = 12$
$x + 3y = 1$

11. $2x + 3y = -27$
$2x + 5y = -41$

3.3 SOLVING LINEAR SYSTEMS BY LINEAR COMBINATIONS

Examples on pp. 139–141

EXAMPLE Solve the system using the linear combinations method.

$$4x + 3y = -5 \quad \text{Equation 1}$$
$$2x + 5y = 1 \quad \text{Equation 2}$$

Multiply the second equation by -2 to eliminate the variable x.

$4x + 3y = -5$		$4x + 3y = -5$	Rewrite Equation 1.
$2x + 5y = 1$	× (−2)	$-4x - 10y = -2$	Multiply Equation 2 by −2.
		$-7y = -7$	Add Equation 1 to Equation 2.
		$y = 1$	Solve for y.

$4x + 3y = -5$	Write Equation 1.
$4x + 3(1) = -5$	Substitute 1 for y.
$x = -2$	Solve for x.

REVIEW HELP
Exercises | Examples
12, 13 | 1, p. 139
14, 15 | 2, p. 140

ANSWER ▶ The solution is $(-2, 1)$. Check by substituting in the original equations.

Solve the system using the linear combination method.

12. $x - 3y = 8$
$-2x + y = 9$

13. $3x - y = 4$
$2x + 3y = 32$

14. $4x - 3y = 10$
$3x + 2y = -18$

15. $5x + 4y = 10$
$2x + 3y = -3$

Chapter Summary and Review **161**

3.4 GRAPHING LINEAR EQUATIONS IN THREE VARIABLES

Examples on pp. 147–149

EXAMPLE Sketch the graph of $6x + 12y + 9z = 36$.

To graph $6x + 12y + 9z = 36$, find the intercepts.

When $y = 0$ and $z = 0$, then $x = 6$. Plot $(6, 0, 0)$.

When $x = 0$ and $z = 0$, then $y = 3$. Plot $(0, 3, 0)$.

When $x = 0$ and $y = 0$, then $z = 4$. Plot $(0, 0, 4)$.

Connect the points to form the plane.

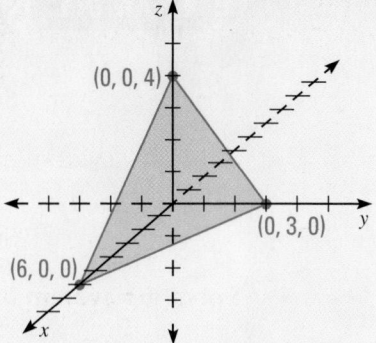

REVIEW HELP

Exercises	Example
16–18	**2**, p. 148

Sketch the graph of the equation. Label the points where the graph crosses the *x*-, *y*-, and *z*-axes.

16. $2x + 3y + 6z = 6$ **17.** $6x + 3y + 9z = 18$ **18.** $16x + 8y + 12z = 48$

3.5 SOLVING SYSTEMS OF LINEAR EQUATIONS IN THREE VARIABLES

Examples on pp. 153–155

EXAMPLE Solve the system.

$$x - y + 2z = -4 \quad \text{Equation 1}$$
$$3x + y - 4z = -6 \quad \text{Equation 2}$$
$$2x + 3z = -1 \quad \text{Equation 3}$$

Rewrite the system as a system in two variables. First add Equation 1 and Equation 2 to eliminate *y*.

$$x - y + 2z = -4$$
$$3x + y - 4z = -6$$
$$\overline{4x - 2z = -10} \quad \text{New Equation 1}$$

Solve the new system of linear equations in two variables. First, add -2 times Equation 3 to new Equation 1 to eliminate *x*.

$$4x - 2z = -10$$
$$-4x - 6z = 2$$
$$\overline{ -8z = -8}$$
$$z = 1 \quad \text{Solve for } z.$$

Solve Equation 3 for *x*.

$$2x + 3(1) = -1 \quad \text{Substitute 1 for } z \text{ in original Equation 3.}$$
$$x = -2 \quad \text{Solve for } x.$$

Solve Equation 2 for *y*.

$$3(-2) + y - 4(1) = -6 \quad \text{Substitute } -2 \text{ for } x \text{ and 1 for } z \text{ in original Equation 2.}$$
$$y = 4 \quad \text{Combine like terms and solve for } y.$$

REVIEW HELP

Exercises	Example
19–21	**1**, p. 154

ANSWER ▶ The solution is $x = -2$, $y = 4$, and $z = 1$, or $(-2, 4, 1)$.

Solve the system using the linear combination method.

19. $2x + 2y + 6z = 8$
$x + y - 2z = -6$
$x - 4y - 2z = 9$

20. $x + y + z = -1$
$4x + y - 3z = -3$
$2x - 3y + 2z = -12$

21. $3x - y - 2z = 15$
$2x + 2y + 3z = -2$
$6x - 3y + z = 8$

Solve the system by graphing. Then check your solution.

1. $2x + y = 7$
$-x + y = 1$

2. $x + 2y = 7$
$-3x - y = -1$

3. $4x + 2y = 12$
$x - 2y = 8$

Solve the system using substitution.

4. $3x + 2y = 4$
$2x + y = 1$

5. $x - 4y = 7$
$3x + 5y = 4$

6. $3x + y = 4$
$4x + 3y = 17$

7. Football Tickets A total of 1025 student and general admission tickets were sold at the gate for a high school football game. The cost for students was $3 per ticket and the cost for general admission was $4 per ticket. The school collected $3525 selling tickets for the game. How many student tickets were sold?

Solve the system using the linear combination method.

8. $4x + 3y = -11$
$x - 3y = -14$

9. $-3x - 2y = -4$
$5x + 6y = 4$

10. $5x + y = -4$
$3x + 4y = 18$

11. Carnival On the first night of a carnival, 300 children and 175 adults bought tickets. The total revenue from ticket sales was $1150. On the second night, 520 children and 350 adults bought tickets. The total revenue that night was $2180. What are the admission prices to the carnival for a child and for an adult?

Sketch the graph of the equation. Label the points where the graph crosses the *x*-, *y*-, and *z*-axes.

12. $x + 2y + 3z = 6$

13. $2x + y - 2z = 8$

14. $2x - 3y + 4z = 12$

Solve the system using any algebraic method.

15. $x + 3y + 2z = 3$
$3x - 3y + z = -10$
$2x + 3y - 4z = 8$

16. $4x - y + 2z = 3$
$y - 3z = 6$
$x + 2y - 5z = 13$

17. $3x + y - 2z = 7$
$2x + 5y - 4z = -5$
$x - 3z = -2$

18. Geometry The figure shown has both vertical and horizontal symmetry. Find the values of *x*, *y*, and *z*. (*Hint:* The sum of the angle measures of any pentagon is 540°.)

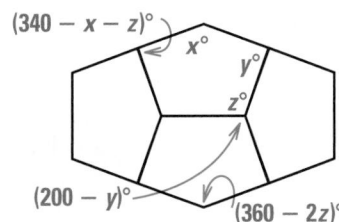

19. School Store A school store sells jackets for $50, hooded sweatshirts for $30, and T-shirts for $15. Last month, the total revenue from the school clothing was $7800, from the sale of 360 pieces of clothing. The school store sold eight times as many T-shirts as jackets. How many of each type of clothing were sold?

Chapter Standardized Test

Test Tip   Check your answers using a different method.
ⓐ ⓑ ⓒ ⓓ

EXAMPLE Solve the system.

$$2x + y = -1 \quad \text{Equation 1}$$
$$3x + 3y = 3 \quad \text{Equation 2}$$

Ⓐ $(-1, 1)$ Ⓑ $(-2, 3)$ Ⓒ $(1, 1)$ Ⓓ $(0, -1)$

Solution

On standardized tests, it can be more efficient to check each given ordered pair in the system of equations until you find the correct one.

Choice A: $2(-1) + 1 \overset{?}{=} -1 \longrightarrow -2 + 1 = -1$ ✓

           $3(-1) + 3(1) \overset{?}{=} 3 \longrightarrow -3 + 3 \neq 3$ ✗

Choice B: $2(-2) + 3 \overset{?}{=} -1 \longrightarrow -4 + 3 = -1$ ✓

           $3(-2) + 3(3) \overset{?}{=} 3 \longrightarrow -6 + 9 = 3$ ✓

Choice B is the solution of the system.

You can check your answer by graphing. The graph of the system of equations is shown.

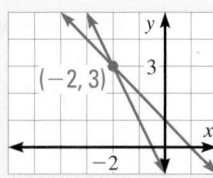

Multiple Choice

1. Which ordered pair is the solution of the system?

$$3x - y = -4$$
$$-2x - 4y = -2$$

Ⓐ $(-2, -2)$ Ⓑ $(1, 0)$

Ⓒ $(-1, 1)$ Ⓓ $(3, -2)$

2. The perimeter of a rectangular backyard is 130 feet. The length is 5 feet longer than three times the width. What is the length of the backyard?

Ⓕ 100 feet   Ⓖ 50 feet

Ⓗ 20 feet   Ⓙ 15 feet

3. How many solutions does the system have?

$$3x - y = 9$$
$$-6x + 2y = -14$$

Ⓐ 0   Ⓑ 1

Ⓒ 2   Ⓓ infinitely many

4. A construction company placed two orders with a building supply store. The first order was for 12 cases of nails and 5 cases of screws, and it totaled $695. The second order was for 4 cases of nails and 3 cases of screws, and it totaled $305. What is the cost of one case of nails?

Ⓕ $17   Ⓖ $25

Ⓗ $35   Ⓙ $50

5. Which ordered triple is the solution of the system?

$$-x - 2y - 3z = 6$$
$$x - 3y + z = -10$$
$$2x + y - 4z = 12$$

(A) $(-1, 2, -3)$ **(B)** $(3, -1, 2)$

(C) $(0, 3, -4)$ **(D)** no solution

6. How many solutions does the system have?

$$x - y + 4z = -1$$
$$x - y + z = 0$$
$$-2x + 2y - 8z = 2$$

(F) 0   **(H)** 1

(G) 2   **(J)** infinitely many

7. Which ordered triple describes where the graph of $6x + 10y - 15z = 60$ crosses the x-axis?

(A) $(0, 6, 0)$ **(B)** $(-10, 0, 0)$

(C) $(10, 0, 0)$ **(D)** $(0, 0, -4)$

8. A sports stadium has 10,000 seats, divided into box seats, lower-deck seats, and upper-deck seats. Box seats sell for $10, lower-deck seats sell for $8, and upper-deck seats sell for $5. If all the seats are sold, the total revenue for a game is $70,000. The stadium has four times as many upper-deck seats as box seats. How many lower-deck seats are in the stadium?

(F) 1000 seats   **(G)** 5000 seats

(H) 6000 seats   **(J)** 8000 seats

Gridded Response

9. What is the value of x in the solution of the system of equations?

$$3x + 2y = 4$$
$$-x + 4y = -6$$

10. What is the value of y in the solution of the system of equations?

$$4x + y = -7$$
$$2x + 5y = 1$$

11. What is the y-coordinate of the point where the graph of $8x + 12y - 18z = 72$ crosses the y-axis?

12. What is the value of z in the solution of the system of equations?

$$-x + 3y + z = -2$$
$$2x - y + 2z = 11$$
$$4y + z = -1$$

13. You are making bags of trail mix with mixed nuts and raisins for a camping trip. The mixed nuts cost $6.75 per pound and the raisins cost $2 per pound. The package of bags for the trail mix costs $5. Find the total cost (in dollars) of the trail mix for 4 pounds of mixed nuts and 3 pounds of raisins.

Extended Response

14. You want to paint your bedroom, living room, and kitchen. The new painting equipment you need for this project costs $100. The paint you decide to use costs $12 per gallon and the primer costs $15 per gallon.

a. Write a model for the total cost C of the project where x is the number of gallons of paint needed and y is the number of gallons of primer needed.

b. Evaluate the model for several different values of x and y, and organize your results in a table.

c. You use a total of 15 gallons of paint and primer to complete the project. You spend $195 on paint and primer. How many gallons of each do you use?

Graph the numbers on a number line. Then write the numbers in order from least to greatest. *(Lesson 1.1)*

1. $2, -1, -2, 5, -3$
2. $2.5, 1, -0.5, 0, -1.5$
3. $80, 10, -50, -40, -10$

Evaluate the expression for the given value of *x*. *(Lesson 1.2)*

4. $x^2 - 2x + 4$ when $x = 4$
5. $x^3 - x$ when $x = -3$
6. $x^2 - 5x + 7$ when $x = -4$

Simplify the expression. *(Lesson 1.3)*

7. $-4x + 3(x + 1)$
8. $3x + 5y + 2x - 3y$
9. $-3(-x)^2$

10. $2x + 4(x + y)$
11. $6 - 5x + 4(2x + 1)$
12. $2(-x)^3$

Solve the equation. Check your solution. *(Lesson 1.4)*

13. $y - 17 = -13$
14. $9x = 45$
15. $\frac{x}{3} = 12$

16. $2x + 5 = -1$
17. $3t + 7 = 5t - 9$
18. $3(y - 5) = 6$

19. Phone Company A long distance phone company charges \$.03 a minute for each call. The company also charges a \$.10 connection charge. Write a verbal model for the price of a phone call. How much will a 25-minute phone call cost? *(Lesson 1.4)*

Find the value of *y* for the given value of *x*. *(Lesson 1.5)*

20. $3y + 2x = 13; x = 2$
21. $4x - 3y = -1; x = 5$
22. $2x - 7 = -3y; x = -4$

23. $-3x = -y - 5; x = 7$
24. $\frac{1}{2}x + \frac{1}{3}y = 0; x = 6$
25. $3(y - 1) + 4x = 1; x = -2$

In Exercises 26–29, use the following information. *(Lesson 1.6)*

You have 160 feet of fencing to enclose an area for a swimming pool. You want the length of the pool area to be 40 feet greater than the width.

26. Write a verbal model for the perimeter of the pool area.

27. Assign labels to the parts of the verbal model.

28. Write an algebraic model.

29. What dimensions should you make the pool area?

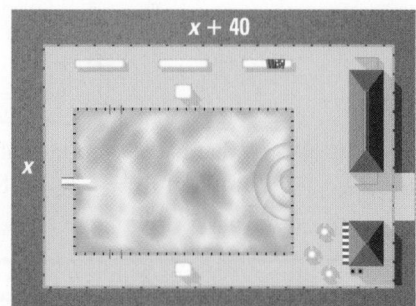

Find the mean, median, and mode(s) of the data set. *(Lesson 1.7)*

30. 33, 35, 15, 27, 18, 29, 30, 23, 20, 10
31. 95, 100, 75, 83, 87, 90, 90, 100, 85, 90

32. 19, 12, 16, 10, 15, 10, 20, 16, 17
33. 112, 127, 140, 112, 135, 124, 139

Graph the linear function. *(Lessons 2.1, 2.2, 2.4)*

34. $y = x - 1$
35. $y = 2x$
36. $y = -x + 3$
37. $y = 3x - 4$

Find the slope of the line passing through the given points. *(Lesson 2.3)*

38. $(3, 5), (-1, 7)$
39. $(-2, 1), (0, 3)$
40. $(5, -4), (2, -3)$
41. $(-4, 8), (-5, -6)$

Write an equation of the line that passes through the given point and has the given slope. *(Lesson 2.5)*

42. $(2, 3)$, $m = -2$ **43.** $(-6, -2)$, $m = 3$ **44.** $(5, -3)$, $m = -1$

45. $(4, 1)$, $m = \dfrac{1}{2}$ **46.** $(3, -4)$, $m = -\dfrac{3}{2}$ **47.** $(1, 5)$, $m = \dfrac{3}{5}$

The variables *x* and *y* vary directly. Write an equation that relates the variables. *(Lesson 2.6)*

48. $x = 5$, $y = 20$ **49.** $x = 4$, $y = 3$ **50.** $x = 2$, $y = -6$ **51.** $x = -3$, $y = 5$

Draw a scatter plot of the data. Then tell whether the data have a *positive correlation*, a *negative correlation*, or *relatively no correlation*. *(Lesson 2.7)*

52.

x	1	1	2	2	3	4	4	5	6	6	7
y	8	7	7	6	6	6	5	3	3	2	2

53.

x	1	1	2	3	3	4	4	6	6	7	8
y	8	2	8	4	1	5	9	3	2	7	4

54.

x	1	2	2	3	3	4	5	5	6	8	8
y	0	2	1	2	3	5	5	6	6	7	8

Solve the system. *(Lessons 3.1, 3.2, 3.3)*

55. $x + y = 4$
$\quad\; 2x - y = 5$

56. $3x - y = 4$
$\quad\; -3x + 2y = -8$

57. $4x + y = 3$
$\quad\; -x + 2y = 15$

58. $2x + 7y = -4$
$\quad\; 3x - 2y = 19$

59. $x + y = -9$
$\quad\; -2x + 3y = -7$

60. $2x - 5y = -3$
$\quad\; 3x - 4y = 6$

61. $3x + 5y = -2$
$\quad\; x - 2y = -8$

62. $4x + y = 6$
$\quad\; -x + 2y = -15$

63. $5x + 6y = 10$
$\quad\; 3x - 2y = 34$

64. Fundraiser The football team at your school is selling T-shirts and hats for a fundraiser. The team sells T-shirts for $10 and hats for $15. The team sells 95 items for $1140. How many T-shirts were sold? How many hats were sold? *(Lesson 3.3)*

Sketch the graph of the equation. Label the points where the graph crosses the *x*-, *y*-, and *z*-axes. *(Lesson 3.4)*

65. $x + 2y - z = 2$ **66.** $x - 2y + 4z = 8$ **67.** $4x + 6y + 3z = 12$

68. $6x - 3y + 2z = 12$ **69.** $-x + 8y - z = 8$ **70.** $5x + 6y - 3z = 30$

Solve the system using any algebraic method. *(Lesson 3.5)*

71. $x + y + z = 0$
$\quad\; 4x - 2y + 3z = 15$
$\quad\; x - 3y + 4z = -1$

72. $2x - y - 3z = 6$
$\quad\; 3x + 3y + z = -13$
$\quad\; x + 2y - z = 1$

73. $x - 4y - z = 1$
$\quad\; 2x + 5y + z = 21$
$\quad\; -x + 2y - 3z = -11$

Inequalities and Absolute Value

▶ How many ride tickets can you buy at an amusement park?

Some amusement parks charge for admission and for each ride ticket. If you have a limited amount of money you can spend, a graph can help you determine the possible numbers of ride tickets you can purchase.

Think & Discuss

The graph below shows the amount *A* in dollars spent at an amusement park as a function of *t* ride tickets.

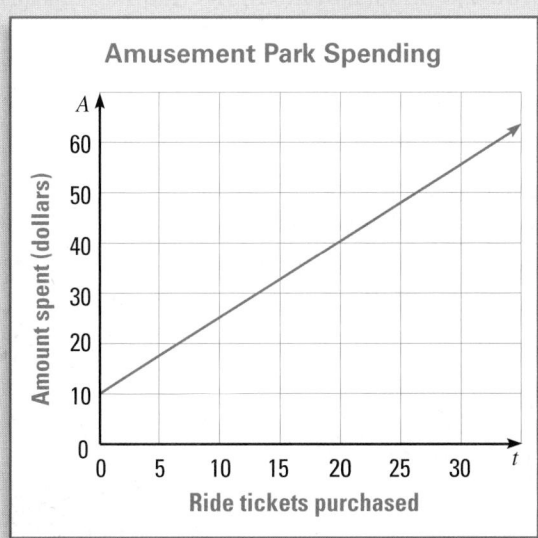

Amusement Park Spending

1. About how much will it cost for 15 rides?

2. If you have $45 to spend, can you buy 10 ride tickets? 20 ride tickets? 30 ride tickets? Explain.

Learn More About It

You will use a linear inequality to describe the number of ride tickets you can buy in Example 3 on page 173.

PREVIEW

What's the chapter about?

• Solving and graphing linear inequalities in one or two variables
• Solving, graphing, and using systems of linear inequalities
• Solving and graphing absolute value equations and inequalities
• Graphing absolute value functions

> **Key Words**
>
> • linear inequality in one variable, *p. 172*
> • compound inequality, *p. 174*
> • linear inequality in two variables, *p. 179*
> • half-plane, *p. 179*
>
> • system of linear inequalities in two variables, *p. 185*
> • absolute value, *p. 192*
> • absolute value equation, *p. 192*
> • absolute value inequality, *p. 198*
> • vertex, *p. 204*

PREPARE

Chapter Readiness Quiz

Take this quick quiz. If you are unsure of an answer, look back at the reference pages for help.

Vocabulary Check (*refer to p. 9*)

1. How many variables are in the equation $3x - y + 5z = 0$?

   A 0   **B** 1   **C** 2   **D** 3

Skill Check (*refer to pp. 125, 132, 139*)

2. What is the solution of the following linear system? $x - 3y = 1$
                                                      $2x + y = 9$

   F $(-4, -1)$ **G** $(4, 1)$ **H** $(7, 2)$ **J** $(3, 3)$

3. Which linear system has $(-3, 4)$ as the solution?

   A $x + 2y = 5$ **B** $-x + 3y = 9$ **C** $2x + 2y = 2$ **D** $5x + 3y = -3$
         $4x - y = -7$ $2x + y = -2$ $-3x - 2y = 1$ $x - y = 1$

TAKE NOTES

Notes About Graphs

Including graphs with labels can help you remember vocabulary and methods for solving problems.

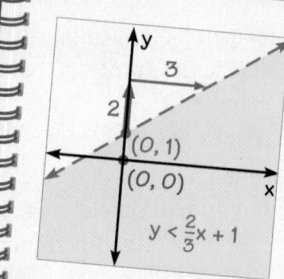

1. Graph the boundary line. Use a dashed line, because the inequality symbol is <.
2. Test the point (0, 0).
3. (0, 0) satisfies the inequality, so shade the half-plane that contains (0, 0).

DEVELOPING CONCEPTS *(For use with Lesson 4.1)*
Investigating Inequalities

Goal

Discover which arithmetic operations change the direction of an inequality symbol.

Materials

- pencil
- paper

QUESTION

How do arithmetic operations affect an inequality?

EXPLORE

1 Apply the operations below to each side of the inequality $4 > -2$. Write the correct inequality symbol between the resulting values. Two samples are shown below.

a. Add 2. **b.** Subtract 2.

$$
\begin{aligned}
a. \quad & 4 > -2 \\
& 4 + 2 \ \underline{\ ?\ } \ -2 + 2 \\
& 6 > 0
\end{aligned}
$$

$$
\begin{aligned}
b. \quad & 4 > -2 \\
& 4 - 2 \ \underline{\ ?\ } \ -2 - 2 \\
& 2 > -4
\end{aligned}
$$

c. Add -2. **d.** Subtract -2.

e. Multiply by 2. **f.** Divide by 2.

g. Multiply by -2. **h.** Divide by -2.

2 When did you have to change the direction of the inequality symbol?

3 Repeat Steps 1 and 2 using the inequality $2 < 6$.

THINK ABOUT IT

Predict whether the direction of the inequality symbol will change when you apply the given operation. Check your prediction.

1. $3 < 7$; add 4. **2.** $5 > -3$; add -1. **3.** $3 < 5$; subtract -2.

4. $6 > 1$; multiply by 7. **5.** $2 > -5$; multiply by -3. **6.** $0 < 8$; divide by -4.

Reasoning **Copy and complete the statement with *stays the same* or *reverses direction*.**

7. When you add the same positive or negative number to each side of an inequality, the direction of the inequality symbol __?__.

8. When you subtract the same positive or negative number from each side of an inequality, the direction of the inequality symbol __?__.

9. When you multiply each side of an inequality by the same positive number, the direction of the inequality symbol __?__.

10. When you multiply each side of an inequality by the same negative number, the direction of the inequality symbol __?__.

11. When you divide each side of an inequality by the same positive number, the direction of the inequality symbol __?__.

12. When you divide each side of an inequality by the same negative number, the direction of the inequality symbol __?__.

4.1 Solving Linear Inequalities

GOAL Solve and graph simple and compound inequalities in one variable.

Key Words

- linear inequality in one variable
- solution of an inequality in one variable
- graph of an inequality in one variable
- compound inequality

Prerequisite Skills

Solve the equation.

1. $8x + 5 = 4x - 3$

2. $12 - 3t = -t + 6$

3. $\frac{1}{2}y + 1 = y - 4$

4. $\frac{3}{4}n + \frac{1}{3} = \frac{1}{4}n - 4$

How many amusement park ride tickets can you buy for a given amount?

In Example 3, you will solve a *linear inequality* to find the maximum number of ride tickets you can buy.

Inequalities such as $x \le 1$ and $p - 3 > 7$ are **linear inequalities** in one variable. A **solution of an inequality** in one variable is a value of the variable that makes the inequality true. For example, -4, 0.7, and 1 are solutions of $x \le 1$.

Two inequalities are *equivalent* if they have the same solutions. The following properties can be used to solve inequalities, because they create equivalent inequalities.

Properties of Inequalities

To write an equivalent inequality:

Add the same number to each side.

Subtract the same number from each side.

Multiply or *divide* each side by the same *positive* number.

Multiply or *divide* each side by the same *negative* number and *reverse* the inequality symbol.

EXAMPLE 1 Inequality with a Variable on One Side

Solve the inequality.

   a. $x - 4 > -6$ **b.** $-5y + 2 \ge -13$

Solution

   a. $x - 4 > -6$ Write original inequality.

         $x > -2$ Add 4 to each side.

   ANSWER ▶ The solution is all real numbers greater than -2.

   b. $-5y + 2 \ge -13$ Write original inequality.

        $-5y \ge -15$ Subtract 2 from each side.

          $y \le 3$ Divide each side by -5 and reverse the inequality.

   ANSWER ▶ The solution is all real numbers less than or equal to 3.

Graphing Inequalities The **graph of an inequality** in one variable consists of all points on a real number line that are solutions of the inequality. To graph an inequality in one variable, use an open dot for $<$ or $>$ and a solid dot for $\leq$ or $\geq$. For example, the graphs of $x < 2$ and $x \geq -1$ are shown below.

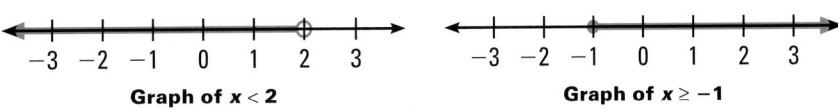

Graph of $x < 2$ Graph of $x \geq -1$

EXAMPLE 2 Inequality with a Variable on Both Sides

STUDENT HELP

AVOID ERRORS
To check the solution, try several numbers greater than 3 in the original inequality. Also, try some numbers that are less than or equal to 3 to see that they are not solutions.

Solve $7 - 4x < 1 - 2x$. Graph the solution.

Solution

$7 - 4x < 1 - 2x$	Write original inequality.
$7 - 2x < 1$	Add $2x$ to each side.
$-2x < -6$	Subtract 7 from each side.
$x > 3$	Divide each side by -2 and reverse the inequality.

ANSWER ▶ The solution is all real numbers greater than 3. The graph is shown at the right.

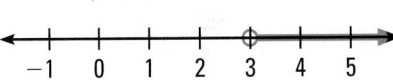

Checkpoint ✓ Solve an Inequality

Solve the inequality. Then graph your solution.

1. $x + 3 < 8$ **2.** $4 - x \leq 5$ **3.** $2x - 1 > 2$ **4.** $2x - 3 > x$

EXAMPLE 3 Use a Simple Inequality

Amusement Park Admission to an amusement park costs $9 and each ride ticket costs $1.50. The total amount A in dollars spent is given by $A = 1.5t + 9$ where t is the number of ride tickets. Use an inequality to describe the number of ride tickets you can buy if you have at most $45 to spend at the park.

Solution

$A \leq 45$	The most money you can spend is $45.
$1.5t + 9 \leq 45$	Substitute $1.5t + 9$ for A.
$1.5t \leq 36$	Subtract 9 from each side.
$t \leq 24$	Divide each side by 1.5.

ANSWER ▶ You can buy up to 24 ride tickets.

Checkpoint ✓ Use a Simple Inequality

5. Admission to an amusement park costs $5 and each ride ticket costs $1.25. You have at most $45 to spend. Write and solve an inequality to describe the number of tickets you can buy.

A **compound inequality** is two simple inequalities joined by the word "and" or the word "or." Here are two examples.

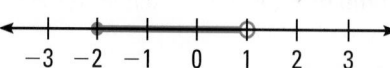

AND

All real numbers greater than or equal to -2 *and* less than 1 can be written as $-2 \leq x < 1$.

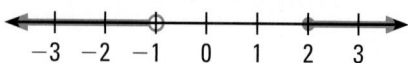

OR

All real numbers less than -1 *or* greater than or equal to 2 can be written as $x < -1$ or $x \geq 2$.

EXAMPLE **4** **Solve an "And" Compound Inequality**

Music The B-flat trumpet plays tones that range from 607 hertz greater than concert A (440 hertz) to 255 hertz less than concert A. Solve the inequality $-255 \leq x - 440 \leq 607$ to find the range of the B-flat trumpet (in hertz).

Solution

To solve, isolate the variable between the two inequality symbols.

$-255 \leq x - 440 \leq 607$	Write original inequality.
$-255 + 440 \leq x - 440 + 440 \leq 607 + 440$	Add 440 to each expression.
$185 \leq x \leq 1047$	Simplify.

ANSWER ▸ The range of the B-flat trumpet is from 185 hertz to 1047 hertz.

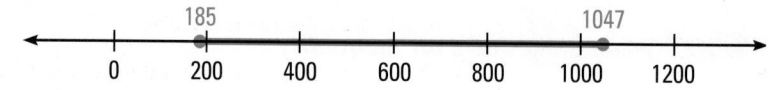

EXAMPLE **5** **Solve an "Or" Compound Inequality**

Solve $3x + 2 < 8$ or $2x - 9 > 3$.

Solution

Solve each part separately.

FIRST INEQUALITY		**SECOND INEQUALITY**	
$3x + 2 < 8$	Write first inequality.	$2x - 9 > 3$	Write second inequality.
$3x < 6$	Subtract 2 from each side.	$2x > 12$	Add 9 to each side.
$x < 2$	Divide each side by 3.	$x > 6$	Divide each side by 2.

ANSWER ▸ The solution is all real numbers less than 2 or greater than 6.

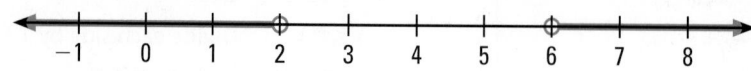

 **Solve Compound Inequalities**

Solve the inequality. Then graph your solution.

6. $4 < x + 5 < 7$

7. $-1 \leq 3x + 8 \leq 8$

8. $x + 3 \leq 4$ or $x - 6 \geq -1$

9. $-x > 4$ or $-2x - 6 < 0$

4.1 Exercises

Guided Practice

Vocabulary Check

1. How does the solution of the inequality $3x - 2 < 1$ differ from the solution of the equation $3x - 2 = 1$?

2. Explain the difference between the graphs of the inequalities $x < 2$ and $x \le 2$.

3. Explain the difference between the graph of the "and" compound inequality $-6 < x < 7$ and the graph of the "or" compound inequality $x < -6$ or $x > 7$.

Skill Check

Solve the inequality. Then graph your solution.

4. $x + 3 < 1$ **5.** $x - 2 \ge -1$ **6.** $3x > 9$

7. $\frac{1}{3}x \le 2$ **8.** $-x - 5 \ge -4$ **9.** $-x + 2 < -3$

Graph the inequality.

10. $x < -2$ or $x \ge 3$ **11.** $x \le -2$ or $x > 3$ **12.** $-2 < x \le 3$

13. The sum of the lengths of two sides of a triangle is greater than the length of the third side.

   a. For the triangle shown, write three inequalities using the information above.

   b. Describe the possible lengths s using a compound inequality.

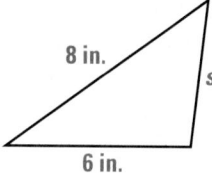

8 in.

6 in.

s

Practice and Applications

STUDENT HELP

HOMEWORK HELP
Example 1: Exs. 14–22, 29–34
Example 2: Exs. 23–28, 35–37
Example 3: Exs. 38, 39
Example 4: Exs. 23–28, 40–56
Example 5: Exs. 23–28, 40–56

Checking Solutions Decide whether the given number is a solution of the inequality.

14. $x > -2$; 0   **15.** $x \ge 8$; 5   **16.** $x - 2 \le 1$; 4

17. $x + 3 < 0$; -6 **18.** $4x + 2 > 6$; 1   **19.** $-2x - 3 < 5$; -3

20. $-3 \le x + 1 < 3$; 1   **21.** $-1 < x - 2 < 2$; 5   **22.** $-3 \le -3x \le 9$; 1

Matching Inequalities Match the inequality with the graph.

23. $x < 2$ **24.** $x \ge -2$ **25.** $-2 \le x \le 2$

26. $-2 \le x < 2$ **27.** $x \le -2$ or $x > 2$ **28.** $x < -2$ or $x \ge 2$

A.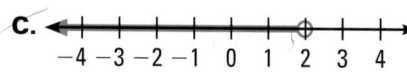

B.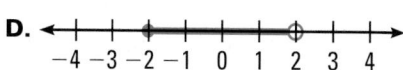

C.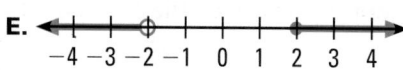

D.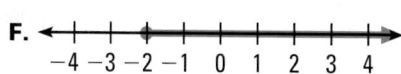

E.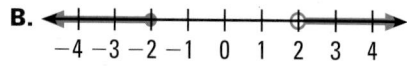

F.

Simple Inequalities Solve the inequality. Then graph your solution.

29. $x - 2 \le -6$

30. $4x \ge 12$

31. $6 - x > 1$

32. $2x - 3 < 3$

33. $5x + 3 \ge 13$

34. $2 - 3x < 17$

35. $x + 2 \ge -x - 2$

36. $5x \le 2x + 18$

37. $6 - 2x > 5x - 1$

38. **Bowling** The total amount A in dollars you spend in a visit to a bowling alley is given by $A = 2.5x + 10$ where x is the number of games you bowl, $2.50 is the cost of a game, and $10 is the cost of food. Write and solve an inequality to describe the number of games you bowl if you can spend at most $25.

39. **Postage** The total weight W of a letter is given by $W = 0.16s + 0.2$ where s is the number of sheets of paper, the weight of a sheet is 0.16 ounce, and the weight of the envelope is 0.2 ounce. Write and solve an inequality to describe the number of sheets you can include if the total weight cannot exceed 4 ounces.

Writing Inequalities **In Exercises 40–42, write a compound inequality that represents the statement.**

40. x is greater than or equal to 2 and less than or equal to 5.

41. x is less than -7 or greater than 4.

42. x is less than 0 or greater than or equal to 6.

43. **Tornados** The Enhanced Fujita scale for tornados designates an F3 tornado as having estimated maximum wind speeds of 158–206 miles per hour. Write a compound inequality representing the estimated maximum wind speeds s of an F3 tornado.

Geography Link **In Exercises 44 and 45, use the following information.**

The highest point in California is 14,494 feet above sea level on Mount Whitney. The lowest point is 282 feet below sea level in Death Valley.

44. Write a compound inequality describing the range of elevations h in California.

45. **Critical Thinking** A friend tells you that the average elevation in California is the mean of 14,494 and -282, or 7106 feet above sea level. Explain why your friend is probably wrong.

Botany **In Exercises 46–48, use the following information.**

A map of *hardiness zones* identifies regions where different plants can tolerate the winter temperatures. The zones are defined by the average lowest temperature in winter. The hardiness zones for New York are shown. Assume each range includes the lower temperature but not the higher temperature.

46. Write an inequality for the average lowest winter temperature in Zones 5A and 5B combined.

47. Write an inequality for the average lowest winter temperature in all of the hardiness zones found in New York.

48. Write an inequality for the average lowest winter temperature for the hardiness zones colder than Zone 3A and warmer than Zone 7B.

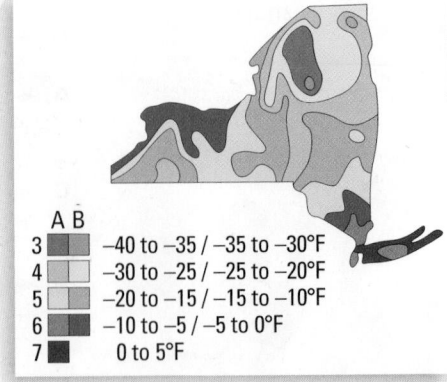

	A B	
3		−40 to −35 / −35 to −30°F
4		−30 to −25 / −25 to −20°F
5		−20 to −15 / −15 to −10°F
6		−10 to −5 / −5 to 0°F
7		0 to 5°F

TORNADOS are categorized by using damage reports to estimate wind speed. The Enhanced Fujita scale ranges from F0 for the weakest tornados up to F5 for "incredible" tornados.

Compound Inequalities Solve the inequality. Then graph your solution.

49. $-4 < x + 3 < 7$

50. $-8 < x - 10 < -2$

51. $-1 \leq 2x - 1 < 5$

52. $-1 < -x + 2 \leq 3$

53. $4x \leq -12$ or $x - 3 > -2$

54. $2x - 5 \leq -3$ or $3x - 8 > 7$

55. $-2x + 6 \leq 10$ or $-x - 9 \geq -4$

56. $-2x - 3 < -7$ or $-x + 2 > 3$

57. Challenge Write a compound inequality that has no solution. Show why it has no solution.

58. Challenge Write a compound inequality whose solution is all real numbers. Show why the solution is all real numbers.

59. Multiple Choice What is the solution of $8 - 5x > 3x - 16$?

ⓐ $x > -3$　　　ⓑ $x > 3$　　　ⓒ $x < 3$　　　ⓓ $x < -3$

60. Multiple Choice Which number is *not* a solution of $3x > 12$ or $2x < -6$?

Ⓕ -12　　　Ⓖ 0　　　Ⓗ 6　　　Ⓙ 12

61. Multiple Choice The graph below represents which inequality?

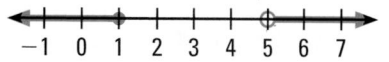

ⓐ $x < 1$ or $x > 5$　　　　ⓑ $x < 1$ or $x \geq 5$

ⓒ $x \leq 1$ or $x \geq 5$　　　　ⓓ $x \leq 1$ or $x > 5$

Mixed Review

Determining Steepness Tell which line is steeper. *(Lesson 2.3)*

62. Line 1: through $(-2, -3)$ and $(-5, 6)$
Line 2: through $(7, -1)$ and $(-3, -1)$

63. Line 1: through $(5, 9)$ and $(3, 5)$
Line 2: through $(4, 5)$ and $(-2, -1)$

Slope-Intercept Form Graph the equation. *(Lesson 2.4)*

64. $y = -2x$

65. $y = 3x + 2$

66. $y = 2x - 1$

67. $y = -2x + 1$

68. $y = -4x - 3$

69. $y = \frac{1}{2}x + 3$

Correlation Tell whether *x* and *y* have a *positive correlation*, a *negative correlation*, or *relatively no correlation*. *(Lesson 2.7)*

70.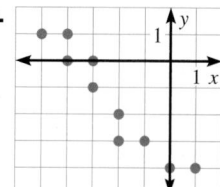

71.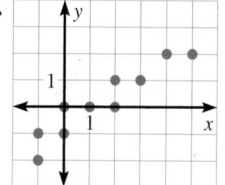

72.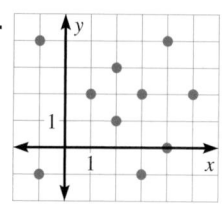

Geometry Skills

Triangles and Inequalities In triangles, longer sides are opposite larger angles. Complete the statement with < or >.

73. $m\angle A$ __?__ $m\angle C$

74. $m\angle D$ __?__ $m\angle F$

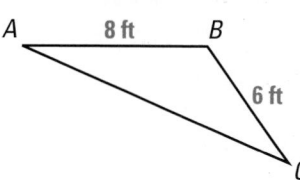

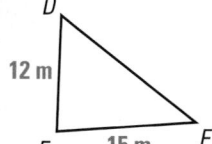

One way to solve a linear inequality is to use the *Test* feature of a graphing calculator. The *Test* feature evaluates whether a statement is true or false. If a statement is true, the calculator returns a 1. If a statement is false, the calculator returns a 0.

In this Activity, you will use this feature to determine which values of x make an inequality true.

EXAMPLE

Solve the inequality $2x + 3 > -5$.

SOLUTION

1 Enter the inequality $y = (2x + 3 > -5)$ on your calculator as shown at the right. To enter the inequality symbol, press [2nd] [MATH] and choose it from a list.

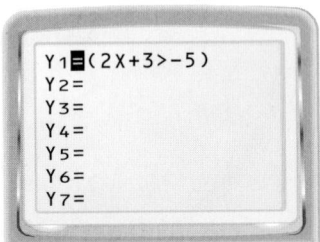

2 Press [GRAPH]. The y-values are 1 for all x-values greater than -4. So, the inequality is true for all real numbers greater than -4.

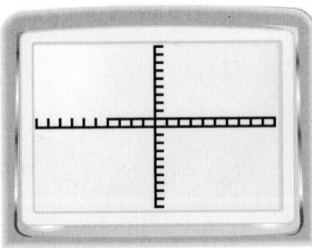

EXERCISES

The *Test* feature of a graphing calculator was used to create the graph shown. Use the graph to solve the inequality.

1. $y = (4x - 5 \le 11)$

2. $y = (5x + 6 \ge -4)$

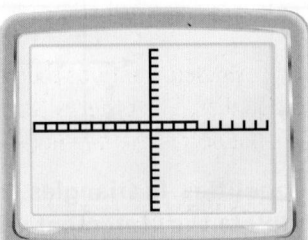

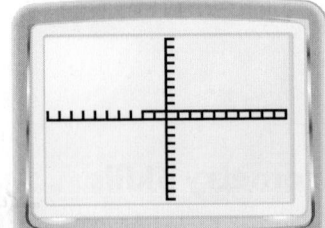

Use a graphing calculator to solve the inequality. Check several solutions in the original inequality.

3. $2x - 7 > -1$ **4.** $4x + 2 < 18$ **5.** $0.5x + 2 \le -1$

6. $-x + 5 \ge -3$ **7.** $-6x - 3 > -9$ **8.** $-0.5x - 1.5 \le 3$

9. $5x < 4x + 6$ **10.** $3x - 4 \le 2x + 5$ **11.** $x - 8 > 4x + 1$

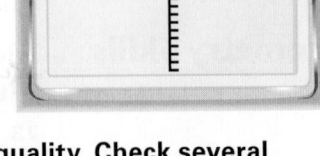

4.2 Linear Inequalities in Two Variables

Key Words
- linear inequality in two variables
- half-plane

GOAL Solve and graph linear inequalities in two variables.

A **linear inequality in two variables** is an inequality that can be written in one of these forms, where A, B, and C are constants:

$$Ax + By < C \quad Ax + By \leq C \quad Ax + By > C \quad Ax + By \geq C$$

An ordered pair (x, y) is a *solution* of a linear inequality if the inequality is true when the values of x and y are substituted into the inequality. For example, $(4, -1)$ is one solution of $2x + y > 5$ because $2(4) + (-1) > 5$ is a true statement.

Prerequisite Skills

Graph the equation.

1. $y = -5x + 1$
2. $x + 4y = 8$

EXAMPLE 1 Check Solutions of Inequalities

Check whether the given ordered pair is a solution of $2x + y < 5$.

a. $(1, 4)$ **b.** $(2, -1)$

Solution

ORDERED PAIR	SUBSTITUTE	CONCLUSION
a. $(1, 4)$	$2(1) + 4 = 6 < 5$ ✗	$(1, 4)$ is *not* a solution.
b. $(2, -1)$	$2(2) + (-1) = 3 < 5$ ✓	$(2, -1)$ is a solution.

 **Check Solutions of Inequalities**

Check whether the given ordered pair is a solution of $x - 3y > 4$.

1. $(0, 0)$ **2.** $(4, -1)$ **3.** $(-2, -2)$ **4.** $(3, -5)$

Graphs of Linear Inequalities The graph of a linear inequality in two variables is the graph of all solutions of the inequality. The boundary line of the inequality divides the coordinate plane into two **half-planes**.

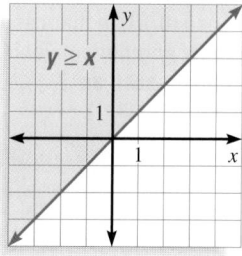

One half-plane, which is shaded, contains the points that are solutions of the inequality. The other half-plane, which is not shaded, contains the points that are not solutions

---

Graphing a Linear Inequality

STEP ❶ Graph the boundary line of the inequality. Use a dashed line for $<$ or $>$. Use a solid line for $\leq$ or $\geq$.

STEP ❷ Test a point that is *not* on the boundary line to see whether it is a solution of the inequality. Then shade the appropriate half-plane.

EXAMPLE 2 Graph Linear Inequalities in One Variable

Graph (a) $y < -2$ and (b) $x \leq 3$ in a coordinate plane.

Solution

a. **Graph** the boundary line $y = -2$. Use a dashed line because $y < -2$.

Test the point $(0, 0)$. It is *not* a solution, so shade the half-plane that does not contain $(0, 0)$.

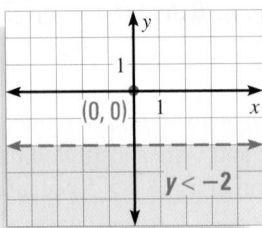

b. **Graph** the boundary line $x = 3$. Use a solid line because $x \leq 3$.

Test the point $(0, 0)$. It *is* a solution, so shade the half-plane that contains $(0, 0)$.

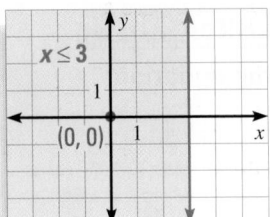

> **STUDENT HELP**
>
> **READING GRAPHS**
> A dashed line indicates that the points on the line are *not* solutions. A solid line indicates that the points on the line are solutions.

Checkpoint ✔ **Graph Linear Inequalities in One Variable**

Graph the inequality in a coordinate plane.

5. $x > -1$ **6.** $y \geq 1$ **7.** $y \leq -3$ **8.** $x < 4$

EXAMPLE 3 Graph Linear Inequalities in Two Variables

Graph (a) $y < 2x$ and (b) $3x - 2y \geq 8$ in a coordinate plane.

Solution

a. **Graph** the boundary line $y = 2x$. Use a dashed line because $y < 2x$.

Test the point $(1, 1)$. Because $(1, 1)$ *is* a solution, shade the half-plane that contains $(1, 1)$.

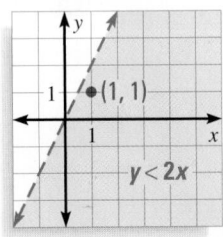

b. **Graph** the boundary line $3x - 2y = 8$. Use a solid line because $3x - 2y \geq 8$.

Test the point $(0, 0)$. Because $(0, 0)$ is *not* a solution, shade the half-plane that does not contain $(0, 0)$.

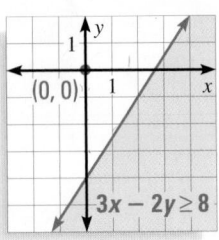

> **STUDENT HELP**
>
> **AVOID ERRORS**
> Because your test point cannot be on the boundary line, you may not always be able to use $(0, 0)$. In that case, test another convenient point, such as $(0, 1)$, $(1, 0)$, or $(1, 1)$.

Checkpoint ✔ **Graph Linear Inequalities in Two Variables**

Graph the inequality in a coordinate plane.

9. $y \geq x$ **10.** $y \leq -3x$ **11.** $x + 2y < 6$ **12.** $x - 3y > 1$

EXAMPLE 4 Write and Use a Linear Inequality

Fish Tank You receive a $50 gift certificate to stock your fish tank with moonfish and minnows. Moonfish cost $2.00 each, and minnows cost $3.30 each.

a. Write a linear inequality in two variables to represent the numbers of moonfish and minnows you can buy.

b. Graph the inequality. Then give three possible combinations of moonfish and minnows you can buy.

Solution

a. **VERBAL MODEL**

Moonfish price	·	Number of moonfish	+	Minnow price	·	Number of minnows	≤	Value of gift

LABELS

Moonfish price = 2.00 (dollars)

Number of moonfish = x (moonfish)

Minnow price = 3.30 (dollars)

Number of minnows = y (minnows)

Value of gift = 50 (dollars)

ALGEBRAIC MODEL

$2x + 3.3y \leq 50$

b. Use these steps to graph the inequality.

1. ***Graph*** the boundary line $2x + 3.3y = 50$. Use a solid line because the boundary line is included in the solution.

2. ***Test*** the point $(0, 0)$. Because $(0, 0)$ is a solution of the inequality, shade the half-plane that contains $(0, 0)$. Finally, because x and y cannot be negative, restrict the graph to points in the first quadrant.

Possible solutions are points within the shaded region shown. Only points with whole number coordinates are reasonable in this situation.

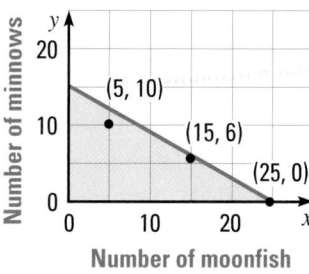

One solution is (5, 10). So, you can buy 5 moonfish and 10 minnows. The total amount spent is $43.

Another solution is (15, 6). So, you can buy 15 moonfish and 6 minnows. The total amount spent is $49.80.

Another solution is (25, 0). So, you can buy 25 moonfish and no minnows. The total amount spent is $50.

Checkpoint ✓ Write and Use a Linear Inequality

13. Give three more possible combinations of moonfish and minnows you can buy in Example 4.

14. Redo Example 4 if you receive a $30 gift certificate, moonfish are $1.50 each, and minnows are $3.50 each.

Guided Practice

Vocabulary Check   **Tell whether the statement is *true* or *false*. Explain your reasoning.**

1. Any point that lies on the line $x + y = 4$ is a solution of the inequality $x + y > 4$.

2. The graph of $y < 3x + 5$ is the half-plane below the line $y = 3x + 5$.

3. The graph of the inequality $x - y \geq 7$ contains the points on its boundary line.

Skill Check   **Check whether (0, 0) is a solution of the inequality.**

4. $y > 5$ **5.** $-2 < x$ **6.** $y \leq -4x + 1$

7. $y \leq 14x$ **8.** $2x + 5y \geq -2$ **9.** $-4x + y < 13$

Tell whether you would use a *dashed line* or a *solid line* to graph the inequality.

10. $x < -7$ **11.** $y \geq 8x + 1$ **12.** $x - y > 14$

Matching Graphs   **Match the inequality with its graph.**

13. $y > 3$ **14.** $x < 3$ **15.** $y \geq 3$

A. 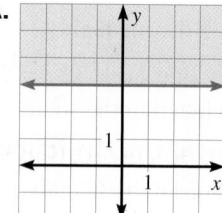   **B.** 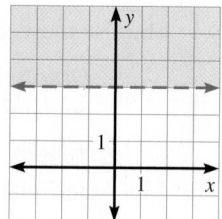   **C.**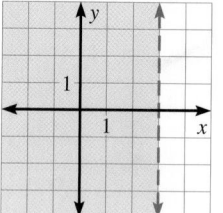

Practice and Applications

STUDENT HELP

HOMEWORK HELP
Example 1: Exs. 16–23
Example 2: Exs. 24–31
Example 3: Exs. 32–43
Example 4: Exs. 44–55

Checking Solutions   **Check whether each given ordered pair is a solution of the inequality.**

16. $x < -5$; $(0, 2)$, $(-5, 1)$ **17.** $y \leq 4$; $(10, 2)$, $(-4, 4)$

18. $2y > 7$; $(1, -6)$, $(0, 4)$ **19.** $-x \geq 3$; $(1, -3)$, $(-5, 5)$

20. $y \leq -9x + 7$; $(-2, 2)$, $(3, -8)$ **21.** $y > 4x - 6$; $(-2, 1)$, $(0, 3)$

22. $19x + y \geq -0.5$; $(2, 3)$, $(-1, 0)$ **23.** $x - 2y < 5$; $(4, 4)$, $(-2, 3)$

Inequalities in One Variable   **Graph the inequality in a coordinate plane.**

24. $x > 5$ **25.** $y < -4$ **26.** $-x \geq 20$

27. $3x \leq 1$ **28.** $8y > -4$ **29.** $\dfrac{y}{4} > 3$

30. Logical Reasoning   Describe the graph of an inequality of the form $x \geq c$ where c is any real number.

31. Logical Reasoning   Describe the graph of an inequality of the form $y < c$ where c is any real number.

Matching Graphs Match the inequality with its graph.

32. $x + y > 2$

33. $y < -x + 2$

34. $x + y \leq 2$

A.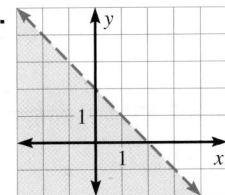

B.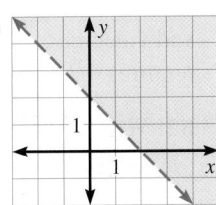

C.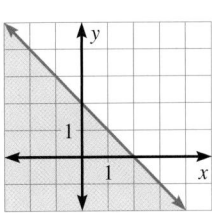

Inequalities in Two Variables Graph the inequality.

35. $y \geq -x + 7$

36. $y > \dfrac{2}{3}x - 1$

37. $y > -4 - x$

38. $y < 5 - 2x$

39. $2x - 3y \geq 6$

40. $9x - 9y > -36$

41. $y < \dfrac{3}{4}x - 5$

42. $7x + 3y < 21$

43. $3x - 8y \leq -14$

Baseball Equipment In Exercises 44–46, use the following information.

A baseball coach will spend at most $600 of the budget to buy new baseballs and batting helmets. Baseballs are $4 each and helmets are $30 each.

44. Write a linear inequality in two variables to represent the numbers of baseballs and helmets the coach can purchase.

45. Graph the inequality.

46. Give three possible combinations of the numbers of baseballs and helmets that can be purchased.

Nutrition In Exercises 47–49, use the following information about calcium requirements.

Teenagers should consume at least 1300 milligrams of calcium per day. One cup of skim milk contains 300 milligrams of calcium and one cup of plain yogurt contains 275 milligrams of calcium.

47. Write an inequality to represent the amounts of skim milk and yogurt you could consume to meet your daily requirements of calcium.

48. Graph the inequality.

49. Give three possible combinations of yogurt and skim milk you could consume to meet your daily requirements of calcium.

Science Link In Exercises 50–52, use the following information.

When a hot day is also humid, it feels even hotter. The Heat Stress Index measures this apparent temperature. You should be careful when exercising or working outside if the apparent temperature is above 90°F, which happens when the sum of 10 times the relative humidity r (where $0.4 \leq r \leq 1$) and 0.6 times the temperature is greater than 58.

50. Write a linear inequality in two variables to represent the relative humidity and temperature conditions that give an apparent temperature above 90°F.

51. Graph the inequality.

52. Give three possible combinations of relative humidity and temperature conditions that give an apparent temperature above 90°F.

HEAT STRESS When it's humid outside, your body is less able to cool itself than when the air is dry. Too much exercise in hot, humid conditions can put you at risk for heat exhaustion and even heat stroke.

Web Sites In Exercises 53–55, use the following information.

Your Internet service provider allows you to create your own World Wide Web site. Suppose you have 100 megabytes (MB) of storage space for photographs and video clips. A photograph requires 1.4 MB of space and a video clip requires 6.2 MB of space.

53. Write an inequality to represent the numbers of photographs and video clips you can offer on your site.

54. Graph the inequality.

55. Give three possible combinations of numbers of photographs and video clips you can offer on your site.

56. Challenge Write an inequality for the graph shown at the right. Explain how you determined the inequality.

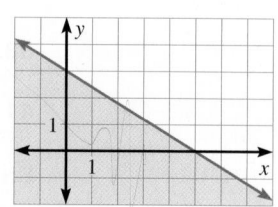

57. Multi-Step Problem You plan to open your own truck rental company. You find that the majority of truck rental companies in your area charge a flat fee of $30, plus $.99 for every mile driven. You want to charge less so that you can advertise your lower rate and get more business.

  a. Write and graph an equation for the cost of renting a truck from other truck rental companies.

  b. Shade the region of the coordinate plane where the amount you will charge must fall.

  c. Write an equation for the cost of renting a truck from your company. Then graph the equation in the same coordinate plane used in part (b).

Mixed Review

Choose a Method Graph the linear equation. *(Lesson 2.4)*

58. $y = -8$

59. $x = \dfrac{5}{2}$

60. $y = -\dfrac{4}{3}x + 1$

61. $y = \dfrac{1}{2}x - 3$

62. $x - 4y = 8$

63. $5x + 2y = 12$

Graph and Check Solve the linear system graphically. Then check your solution algebraically. *(Lesson 3.1)*

64. $x + y = 2$
  $5x - y = 4$

65. $4x - y = 12$
  $2x + 3y = -8$

66. $2x - y = -7$
  $x + 2y = 9$

Geometry Skills

Drawing Translated Figures Draw the image of the figure after the given translation.

67. $(x, y) \rightarrow (x - 1, y + 3)$

68. $(x, y) \rightarrow (x + 2, y + 2)$

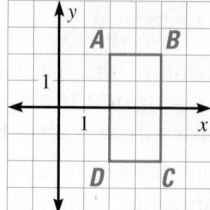

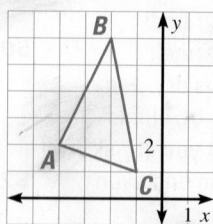

4.3 Systems of Linear Inequalities

GOAL Graph, write, and use a system of linear inequalities.

Key Words

- system of linear inequalities in two variables
- solution of a system of linear inequalities
- graph of a system of linear inequalities

A **system of linear inequalities** in two variables consists of two or more linear inequalities in the same variables. An example is shown below.

$$x + y \leq 2 \qquad \text{Inequality 1}$$
$$4x - y > 3 \qquad \text{Inequality 2}$$

A **solution of a system** of linear inequalities is any ordered pair that is a solution of each inequality in the system. The system above has $(3, -2)$ as one solution.

Prerequisite Skills

Graph the inequality.

1. $y < -4x$

2. $x + 3y \geq 3$

EXAMPLE 1 Check Solutions of Inequalities

Check whether (4, 2) is a solution of the system of inequalities.

a. $x + y > -2$
$x - y \geq 4$

b. $x - 3y \leq 4$
$x > 1$

Solution

ORDERED PAIR	SUBSTITUTE	CONCLUSION
a. $(4, 2)$	$4 + 2 = 6 > -2$ ✓ $\quad$ $4 - 2 = 2 \geq 4$ ✗	$(4, 2)$ is *not* a solution.
b. $(4, 2)$	$4 - 3(2) = -2 \leq 4$ ✓ $\quad$ $4 > 1$ ✓	$(4, 2)$ is a solution.

Checkpoint ✓ Solutions of Inequalities

Check whether (3, −1) is a solution of the system of inequalities.

1. $x + y > 1$
$y < 2$

2. $-2x + y \leq -4$
$x - 2y > 6$

3. $x - y \geq 4$
$3x + 4y > 8$

Graphing a System The **graph of a system** of linear inequalities shows all solutions of the system. Use the following method to graph a system.

Graphing a System of Linear Inequalities

STEP ❶ Graph the boundary lines of the inequalities. Use a dashed line for an inequality with < or >. Use a solid line for an inequality with ≤ or ≥.

STEP ❷ Shade the half-planes for the inequalities. The graph of the system is the region common to all the half-planes.

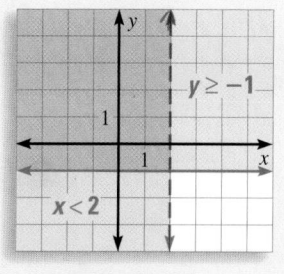

The purple region shown above is the graph of $x < 2$ and $y \geq -1$.

STUDENT HELP

AVOID ERRORS
The solution is the region shaded with *every* color. If there is no such region, a system has *no solution*.

EXAMPLE **2** **Graph a System of Two Inequalities**

Graph the system.

$y < 2x - 3$ Inequality 1
$y \geq -x - 1$ Inequality 2

Solution

1 *Graph* the boundary line of each inequality.
Use a dashed line for Inequality 1.
Use a solid line for Inequality 2.

2 *Shade* the half-plane below $y = 2x - 3$
red to represent **Inequality 1**.

Shade the half-plane on and above $y = -x - 1$
blue to represent **Inequality 2**.

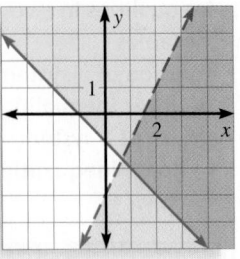

The graph of the system is the overlap, or intersection, of the red and blue regions.

Checkpoint ✓ Graph a System of Two Inequalities

Graph the system.

4. $y < 2$
    $y \geq -1$

5. $x > -3$
    $x + 2y \leq 4$

6. $x + y > 4$
    $2x - y \geq 3$

EXAMPLE **3** **Graph a System of Three Inequalities**

Graph the system.

$x \geq 2$ Inequality 1
$y \geq -2$ Inequality 2
$3x + 2y \leq 12$ Inequality 3

Solution

The inequality $x \geq 2$ implies that the region is on
and to the right of the line $x = 2$.

The inequality $y \geq -2$ implies that the region is
on and above the line $y = -2$.

The inequality $3x + 2y \leq 12$ implies that the
region is on and below the line $3x + 2y = 12$.

The graph of the system is the shaded triangular
region shown at the right.

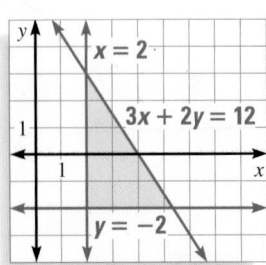

Checkpoint ✓ Graph a System of Three Inequalities

Graph the system.

7. $x \geq 0$
    $y \geq 0$
    $x + y < 5$

8. $x \geq 0$
    $y > 2$
    $y < 2x + 6$

9. $y \leq 5$
    $x < 2$
    $3x + y \geq 5$

You can use a system of linear inequalities to describe a real-life situation, as shown in the following example.

Link to SPORTS

CROSS COUNTRY RUNNING is an aerobic activity. It improves the efficiency of a runner's heart and lungs, helps control weight, and increases flexibility.

EXAMPLE 4 Write and Use a System of Inequalities

Target Heart Rate To get the most benefit to your health during exercising, you should increase your heart rate so that it is within your target heart rate range. Your target heart rate is from 50% to 75% of your maximum heart rate. Your maximum heart rate is 220 minus your age for people aged 20 to 70.

a. Write and graph a system of linear inequalities that shows the target heart rate for people from the ages of 20 to 70 as a function of their age.

b. What is the range of target heart rates for a person at age 20?

Solution

a. Use verbal models to write a system of linear inequalities.

VERBAL MODEL

$20 \le$ Age ≤ 70

Target heart rate $\ge 0.50 \cdot$ Maximum heart rate

Target heart rate $\le 0.75 \cdot$ Maximum heart rate

LABELS

Age $= x$ (years)

Target heart rate $= y$ (beats per minute)

Maximum heart rate $= 220 - x$ (beats per minute)

ALGEBRAIC MODEL

$20 \le x \le 70$ Inequality 1

$y \ge 0.50(220 - x)$ Inequality 2

$y \le 0.75(220 - x)$ Inequality 3

Write Inequalities 2 and 3 in slope-intercept form for easy graphing.

$y \ge 110 - 0.5x = -0.5x + 110$
$y \le 165 - 0.75x = -0.75x + 165$

b. From the graph, you can see that the range for a 20-year-old is from 100 to 150 beats per minute.

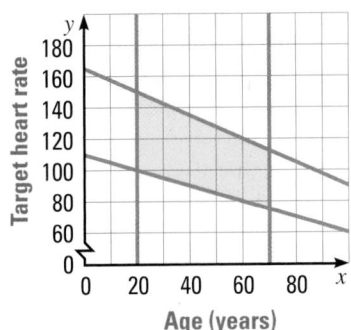

Age (years)

Use a System of Inequalities

Use the information in Example 4.

10. What is the range of target heart rates for a person at age 30? at age 40?

11. For what ages is a heart rate of 120 beats per minute within the range of target heart rates?

Guided Practice

Vocabulary Check

1. What term is used to describe two or more linear inequalities in the same variables?

2. What must be true for an ordered pair to be a solution of a system of linear inequalities?

Skill Check

Tell whether (1, −2) is a solution of the system of linear inequalities.

3. $x + y < 2$
  $y \geq -3$

4. $2x + y > 24$
  $x - y \leq 3$

5. $2x - 2y < 6$
  $3x + y > -1$

Graph the system of linear inequalities.

6. $y < x + 1$
  $x > 2$

7. $x + y \geq -2$
  $y \leq 4$

8. $y > -1$
  $2x + y \geq 1$

9. Fishing You are fishing for trout. Regulations permit you to keep a fish that you catch only if its length ℓ is between 12 and 16 inches (inclusive). You also decide to keep a fish only if its weight w is at least 2.25 pounds. Write a system of linear inequalities describing fish that meet both requirements.

Practice and Applications

STUDENT HELP

HOMEWORK HELP
Example 1: Exs. 10–21
Example 2: Exs. 22–25,
  29–40
Example 3: Exs. 26–28,
  41–50
Example 4: Exs. 51–59

Check Solutions Use the graph to tell whether (0, 1) is a solution of the system of linear inequalities.

10.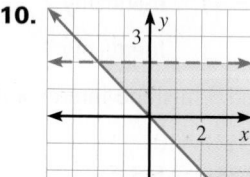

11.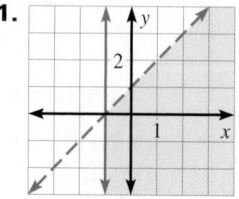

12.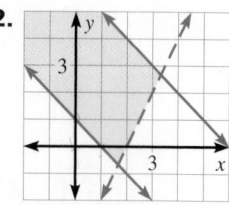

Check Solutions Tell whether (−3, 1) is a solution of the system of linear inequalities.

13. $x \leq 0$
  $x - y < -1$

14. $2x + 3y \geq 1$
  $2x - y \leq -7$

15. $4x + 7y > -5$
  $2x + 3y < 1$

Finding a Solution Give an ordered pair that is a solution of the system of linear inequalities.

16. $x < 7$
  $x + y \geq -2$

17. $y < 2$
  $2x - y > 1$

18. $x > 2y$
  $y \leq -1$

19. $y > 3$
  $x < 2$
  $x - y \leq -2$

20. $y < 0$
  $x > 3$
  $x + 2y \geq -3$

21. $x \leq -2$
  $y > x$
  $x + y \geq 5$

22. Writing Inequalities Write a system of inequalities representing all points in the coordinate plane that lie on or above the x-axis, on or to the right of the y-axis, and below the line $x + y = 10$.

Matching Match the system of linear inequalities with the graph that shows its solution.

23. $x \le 3$
$y > -2$

24. $y < 3$
$y - x > 2$

25. $x + y \le 1$
$-x + 2y \ge 2$

26. $y < 3$
$x \le 3$
$x > -2$

27. $y \le 3$
$x \ge -2$
$y - x > 2$

28. $y > 1$
$x > -3$
$y + 2x \ge -3$

A.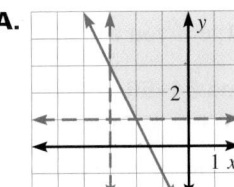

B.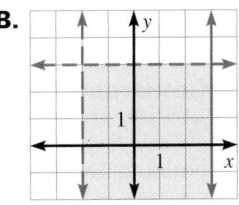

C.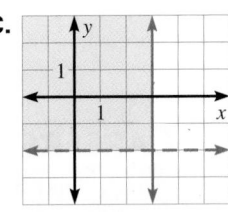

D.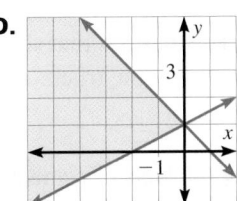

E.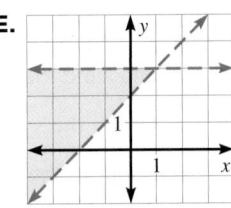

F.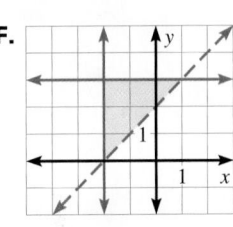

Systems of Two Inequalities Graph the system of linear inequalities.

29. $x > -2$
$x \le 4$

30. $y \le 0$
$y \ge -2$

31. $x > 5$
$y > 2$

32. $x \ge -1$
$y < 2x + 2$

33. $y \le 1$
$y \ge x - 3$

34. $y \le 2x$
$x + y < 3$

35. $y < 2x + 1$
$y \ge x - 2$

36. $x + y < -1$
$5x + y \le 1$

37. $2x + 2y \le 4$
$3y \le -3$

38. $2y < x - 4$
$y < 3x + 1$

39. $2x + y > 3$
$4x - 2y \le -2$

40. $4x - 2y \ge 8$
$2x + 3y < 6$

STUDENT HELP

AVOID ERRORS
You may find it helpful to rewrite the equations of boundary lines in slope-intercept form if they are given in standard form.

Systems of Three Inequalities Graph the system of linear inequalities.

41. $x \ge 0$
$x \le 4$
$y \ge 0$

42. $y < -1$
$y > -5$
$y \le x$

43. $x \ge -2$
$y \le 3$
$y > x - 3$

44. $x < 5$
$y < 2x$
$y > -2$

45. $x + y \ge 2$
$y > x$
$y \ge 4$

46. $y < 3 + x$
$2x + y \le -1$
$y \le 0$

47. $2x - y \le 3$
$y < 2x + 5$
$x > 1$

48. $2x - 3y \le 12$
$3x - y > 1$
$y < x$

49. $x + y \le 5$
$2x + y < 2$
$x - 3y \le 3$

50. Error Analysis Describe and correct the error in the graph of the following system of linear inequalities.

$y \le 3$
$y > 1$
$y - 2x \le 0$

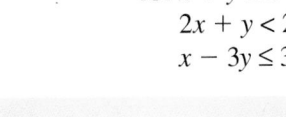
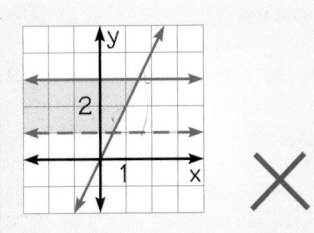

Shopping In Exercises 51–53, use the following information.

You are buying movie passes and gift certificates as prizes for an event. You need at least 5 movie passes and 2 gift certificates. A movie pass costs $6 and a gift certificate costs $10. The most you can spend is $70.

51. Write a system of linear inequalities that shows the number of movie passes x and gift certificates y that can be purchased.

52. Graph the system.

53. Use the graph to determine if you can buy 6 movie passes and 3 gift certificates.

Construction In Exercises 54–56, use the following information.

A team of masons needs at least 10 bags of cement and 30 bags of sand to complete building a wall. Each bag of cement weighs 70 pounds and each bag of sand weighs 50 pounds. The maximum weight their truck can carry is 3500 pounds.

54. Write a system of linear inequalities that shows the number of bags of cement and sand that can be carried by the truck.

55. Graph the system.

56. Suppose the masons need 15 bags of cement and 40 bags of sand. Can their truck carry the materials in one trip?

Volunteering In Exercises 57–59, use the following information.

To raise money for a charity, you participate in a 12 mile walk-a-thon and sell $15 tickets to a benefit concert. The amount you raise is $12x + 15y$ where x is the dollar amount in pledges per mile walked and y is the number of tickets you sell. You have 12 tickets available to sell. Your goal is to raise at least $300.

57. Write a system of linear inequalities that shows the amount in pledges per mile and tickets sold that will meet your goal.

58. Graph the system.

59. Use the graph to determine whether $16 in pledges per mile and 9 tickets sold allow you to meet your goal.

Challenge Write a system of linear inequalities that defines the triangle connecting the points.

60. $(0, -2), (4, 6), (4, -2)$

61. $(0, 0), (1, 3), (4, 0)$

Link to
CAREERS

MASONS work in a wide variety of environments, most of them outdoors. The work is physically demanding and the work environment often contains many dangers so a strict respect for safety regulations is vital.

Standardized Test Practice

62. Multiple Choice Which system of inequalities is shown in the graph?

A $y > 1$
$\quad y < 2x$

B $y > 1$
$\quad y \le 2x$

C $y > 1$
$\quad y > 2x$

D $y > 1$
$\quad y \ge 2x$

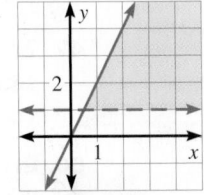

63. Multiple Choice Which ordered pair is a solution of the following system of linear inequalities?

$$3x - 2y < -1$$
$$-2x + 3y > 5$$

F $(4, -5)$ **G** $(-4, 5)$ **H** $(-4, -5)$ **J** $(4, 5)$

Standard Form **Graph the equation.** *(Lesson 2.4)*

64. $3x + y = 3$ **65.** $x + 2y = 12$ **66.** $3x + 2y = -6$

67. $4x - y = -4$ **68.** $-3x + 3y = 9$ **69.** $-4x - 2y = 5$

Checking Solutions **Check whether the ordered pair is a solution of the system.** *(Lesson 3.1)*

70. $(0, 0)$
   $x + y = 0$
   $x - y = -3$

71. $(4, -1)$
   $2x - y = 9$
   $2x + 2y = -6$

72. $(-2, -5)$
   $4x - 3y = 7$
   $-2x - y = 9$

Linear Combination Method **Solve the system using the linear combination method.** *(Lesson 3.5)*

73. $x + 2y - 4z = 3$
   $2x - 2y + 5z = 14$
   $x + y - 5z = -2$

74. $-3x + y + 2z = -14$
   $2x - y - 3z = 11$
   $2x + 2y + z = 7$

75. $-3x + 2y - z = 8$
   $x - 4y + z = -10$
   $3x + y + 3z = 9$

Geometry Skills

Area **Find the area of the shaded region in the coordinate plane.**

76.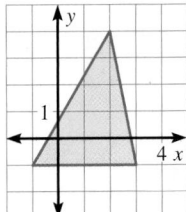

77.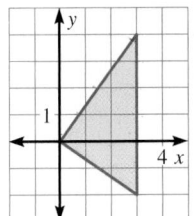

Quiz 1

Lesson 4.1 **Solve the inequality. Then graph your solution.**

1. $x + 3 > -1$ **2.** $5 - 2x > 3$

3. $1 \leq 2x - 1 < 5$ **4.** $-7 \leq -3x - 7 \leq 2$

5. $x - 1 < -4$ or $x + 2 \geq 4$ **6.** $2x - 1 \leq -5$ or $x + 4 > 9$

Lesson 4.2 **Graph the inequality in a coordinate plane.**

7. $x < -2$ **8.** $y \geq -3$ **9.** $-2x \geq 8$

10. $y \leq x - 4$ **11.** $y \leq 2x + 3$ **12.** $3x - y > -1$

13. You have $5 to spend on stamps and envelopes. Each stamp is $.39 and each envelope is $.05. Write a linear inequality in two variables to represent the situation.

Lesson 4.3 **Tell whether (3, 1) is a solution of the system of linear inequalities.**

14. $y \geq 0$
   $x \leq -2$
   $y < 2x$

15. $x - y < -6$
   $y > -2$
   $x \leq 7$

16. $x - y < 3$
   $y < 2x - 3$

Lesson 4.3 **Graph the system of linear inequalities.**

17. $x > 2$
   $y \leq -1$

18. $y \geq 3x$
   $y + x < 6$

19. $y + x \geq 2$
   $y - x > -1$
   $y \geq 2$

4.4 Solving Absolute Value Equations

Key Words
- absolute value
- absolute value equation

GOAL Solve and write absolute value equations in one variable.

Prerequisite Skills

Solve the equation.

1. $x - 8 = -12$

2. $10 + x = -7$

3. $3x + 7 = 16$

4. $4x - 3 = -1$

How can you describe the range of frequencies of a radio station?

In Example 4, you will write an absolute value equation to describe the lowest and highest frequencies for an FM station.

The **absolute value** of a number x, written $|x|$, is the distance the number is from 0 on a number line. Because distances are always positive or zero, the absolute value of a number cannot be negative.

The distance between −4 and 0 is 4. So, $|-4| = 4$.

The distance between 4 and 0 is 4. So, $|4| = 4$.

4 units   4 units

The distance between 0 and 0 is 0. So, $|0| = 0$.

STUDENT HELP

AVOID ERRORS
The expression $-x$ represents the opposite of x. When x is negative, $-x$ is positive.

The absolute value of x can be defined algebraically as follows:

- If x is a positive number, then $|x| = x$.
- If x is zero, then $|x| = 0$.
- If x is a negative number, then $|x| = -x$.

An **absolute value equation** of the form $|x| = c$ where $c > 0$ can have two possible values for x that make the statement true: a positive value c and a negative value $-c$.

For example, if $|x| = 4$, then the solutions are 4 and -4, because $|4| = 4$ and $|-4| = 4$.

Solving an Absolute Value Equation

The absolute value equation $|ax + b| = c$ where $c > 0$ is equivalent to the compound statement $ax + b = c$ or $ax + b = -c$.

EXAMPLE	EQUIVALENT FORM	SOLUTIONS
$|x + 4| = 7$	$x + 4 = 7$ or $x + 4 = -7$	$3, -11$

So, the solutions of $|x + 4| = 7$ are 3 and -11.

EXAMPLE 1 Solve an Absolute Value Equation

Solve $|5 - 2x| = 9$.

Solution

Rewrite the absolute value equation as two linear equations.
Then solve each equation.

$\|5 - 2x\| = 9$			Write original equation.
$5 - 2x = 9$	or	$5 - 2x = -9$	Expression can equal 9 or -9.
$-2x = 4$	or	$-2x = -14$	Subtract 5 from each side.
$x = -2$	or	$x = 7$	Divide each side by -2.

ANSWER ▶ The equation has two solutions: -2 and 7. Check the solutions.

$$\text{CHECK} \quad |5 - 2(-2)| \stackrel{?}{=} 9 \qquad |5 - 2(7)| \stackrel{?}{=} 9$$
$$|5 - (-4)| \stackrel{?}{=} 9 \qquad |5 - 14| \stackrel{?}{=} 9$$
$$|9| \stackrel{?}{=} 9 \qquad |-9| \stackrel{?}{=} 9$$
$$9 = 9 \checkmark \qquad 9 = 9 \checkmark$$

EXAMPLE 2 Solve an Absolute Value Equation

Solve $|3x - 9| - 10 = 14$.

Solution

First isolate the absolute value expression on one side of the equation.

$\|3x - 9\| - 10 = 14$	Write original equation.
$\|3x - 9\| = 24$	Add 10 to each side.

Rewrite $|3x - 9| = 24$ as two linear equations. Then solve each equation.

$\|3x - 9\| = 24$			Write equation.
$3x - 9 = 24$	or	$3x - 9 = -24$	Expression can equal 24 or -24.
$3x = 33$	or	$3x = -15$	Add 9 to each side.
$x = 11$	or	$x = -5$	Divide each side by 3.

ANSWER ▶ The equation has two solutions: 11 and -5. Check the solutions.

$$\text{CHECK} \quad |3(11) - 9| - 10 \stackrel{?}{=} 14 \qquad |3(-5) - 9| - 10 \stackrel{?}{=} 14$$
$$|24| - 10 \stackrel{?}{=} 14 \qquad |-24| - 10 \stackrel{?}{=} 14$$
$$24 - 10 \stackrel{?}{=} 14 \qquad 24 - 10 \stackrel{?}{=} 14$$
$$14 = 14 \checkmark \qquad 14 = 14 \checkmark$$

Checkpoint ✓ *Solve an Absolute Value Equation*

Solve the absolute value equation and check your solutions.

1. $|x + 2| = 5$ **2.** $|x - 6| = 7$ **3.** $|2x - 7| = 15$

4. $|1 - 2x| = 9$ **5.** $|3x + 6| + 4 = 4$ **6.** $|4x - 3| - 1 = 2$

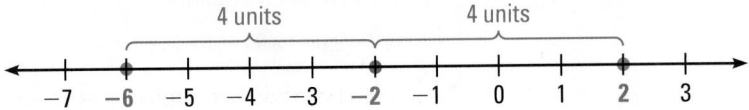

EXAMPLE **3** **Write an Absolute Value Equation**

Write an absolute value equation that has −6 and 2 as its solutions.

Solution

Graph the numbers on a number line. Then locate the midpoint of the graphs.

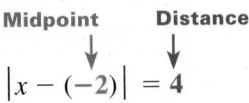

The graph of each solution is 4 units from the midpoint, −2. The distance between a number x and −2 on a number line is $\left|x - (-2)\right|$. You can use the midpoint and the distance to write an absolute value equation.

Midpoint   **Distance**

$$\left|x - (-2)\right| = 4$$

ANSWER ▶ An equation that has −6 and 2 as its solutions is $\left|x - (-2)\right| = 4$, or $\left|x + 2\right| = 4$.

CHECK $\left|-6 + 2\right| = \left|-4\right| = 4 \checkmark$ $\left|2 + 2\right| = \left|4\right| = 4 \checkmark$

EXAMPLE **4** **Write an Absolute Value Equation**

Radio Claire's favorite FM radio station broadcasts using the frequency range from 91.425 megahertz to 91.575 megahertz. Write an absolute value equation that has the lowest and highest frequencies as its solutions.

Solution

Graph the numbers on a number line. Then locate the midpoint of the graphs. Then use the method of Example 3 to write the equation.

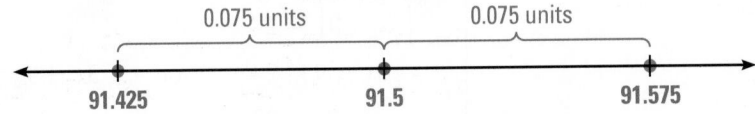

The midpoint is 91.5. Each solution is 0.075 units from 91.5.

Midpoint   **Distance**

$$\left|x - 91.5\right| = 0.075$$

ANSWER ▶ An absolute value equation that has 91.425 and 91.575 as its solutions is $\left|x - 91.5\right| = 0.075$.

CHECK $\left|91.425 - 91.5\right| = \left|-0.075\right| = 0.075 \checkmark$

$\left|91.575 - 91.5\right| = \left|0.075\right| = 0.075 \checkmark$

STUDENT HELP

ANOTHER WAY

You can calculate the midpoint by finding the mean of the endpoints' coordinates.

$$\frac{91.425 + 91.575}{2} = 91.5$$

Checkpoint ✓ **Write an Absolute Value Equation**

7. Write an absolute value equation that has 3 and 7 as its solutions.

8. Write an absolute value equation that has −4 and 10 as its solutions.

4.4 Exercises

Guided Practice

Vocabulary Check

1. Write the definition of the absolute value of a number x.

2. How many solutions does $|ax + b| = c$ have if $c > 0$? if $c = 0$?

Skill Check

Rewrite the absolute value equation as two linear equations.

3. $|x - 9| = 5$ **4.** $|1 - x| = 3$ **5.** $|2x + 2| = 4$

6. $|5 - 2x| = 7$ **7.** $|x - 3| + 3 = 8$ **8.** $|4 - x| - 4 = 1$

Write an absolute value equation that has the given solutions.

9. 1 and 5   **10.** 5 and 11   **11.** -2 and 8

12. Packaging To meet a company's standards, a bag of salt that is labeled as 25 pounds can have a minimum weight of 24.5 pounds and a maximum weight of 25.5 pounds. Write an absolute value equality that has the minimum and maximum weights as its solutions.

Practice and Applications

STUDENT HELP

HOMEWORK HELP
Example 1: Exs. 13–33, 37, 38
Example 2: Exs. 34–36
Example 3: Exs. 39–47
Example 4: Exs. 48–52

Checking Solutions Decide whether the given number is a solution of the equation.

13. $|x + 2| = 7; 5$ **14.** $|x - 3| = 2; 1$ **15.** $|x - 6| = 8; -3$

16. $|3 + 2x| = 1; -1$ **17.** $|1 - 4x| = 16; 4$ **18.** $|5 - 3x| = 2; -1$

Rewriting Equations Rewrite the absolute value equation as two linear equations.

19. $|x + 3| = 2$ **20.** $|x - 5| = 5$ **21.** $|4x - 2| = 1$

22. $|3 - x| = 4$ **23.** $|3 + 2x| = 1$ **24.** $|7 - 5x| = 2$

Solving Equations Solve the absolute value equation and check your solutions.

25. $|x - 2| = 7$ **26.** $|x + 4| = 6$ **27.** $|2 + x| = 1$

28. $|3 - x| = 8$ **29.** $|6x + 3| = 0$ **30.** $|2x + 1| = 3$

31. $|4x - 2| = 6$ **32.** $|1 + 9x| = 10$ **33.** $|3 - 2x| = 5$

34. $|3x + 1| - 7 = 10$ **35.** $|1 - 4x| + 2 = 11$ **36.** $|5 + 4x| - 9 = 8$

37. Record Temperatures The solutions of $|x - 50| = 55$ give the record low and high temperatures in degrees Fahrenheit in Washington D.C. Solve the equation to determine the record low and high temperatures.

38. Daylight Hours The solutions of $|x - 12 \text{ h } 24.5 \text{ min}| = 6 \text{ h } 56.5 \text{ min}$ give the number of hours and minutes of daylight in Anchorage, Alaska, on the longest and shortest days of the year. Solve the equation to determine the lengths of the longest and shortest days.

Matching Absolute Value Equations **Match the absolute value equation with its graph.**

39. $|x - 3| = 4$ **40.** $|x + 3| = 4$ **41.** $|x - 4| = 3$

A.

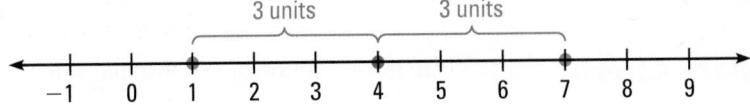

B.

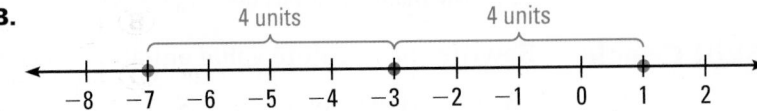

C.

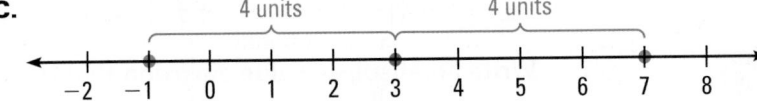

Writing Absolute Value Equations **Write an absolute value equation that has the given solutions.**

42. 2 and 4   **43.** 0 and 8   **44.** −4 and 6

45. −7 and 5   **46.** −20 and 0   **47.** −9 and −3

48. Manufacturing Specifications for a product require that its length be within 3 millimeters of 125 millimeters. Write an absolute value equation that has the upper and lower allowable lengths as its solutions.

49. Baseball The oldest ever World Series player, Jack Quinn, was 47 when he played in 1930. The youngest ever player, Freddie Lindstrom, was 18 when he played in 1924. Write an absolute value equation that has the greatest and least ages as its solutions.

50. Currency Values In 2002, Europeans in 12 countries began using a new currency called the euro. During a 5 year period, the value of 1 euro in U.S. dollars ranged from $.86 to $1.37. Write an absolute value equation that has the least and greatest values of 1 euro in this time period as its solutions.

Science Link **In Exercises 51 and 52, use the following information.**

The minimum distance between planets Earth and Venus is about 38.2 million kilometers. The maximum distance is about 261 million kilometers.

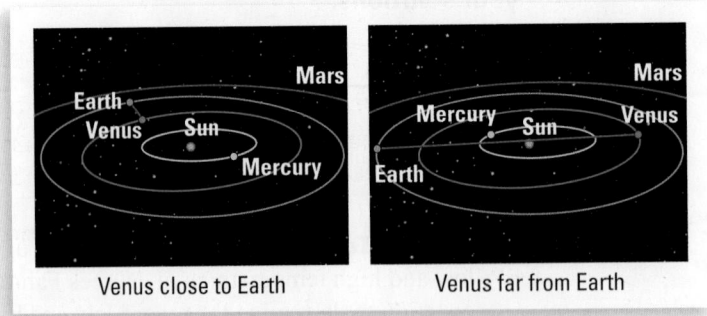

Venus close to Earth   Venus far from Earth

51. Calculate the mean of the minimum and maximum distances. Then find the difference between the maximum distance and the mean.

52. Write an absolute value equation that has the minimum and maximum distances between Earth and Venus as its solutions.

Critical Thinking Decide whether the statement is *true* or *false*.

53. $|-4| \cdot |3| = |4 \cdot 3|$

54. $|2| + |-3| = |2 + (-3)|$

55. $|-5| - |2| = |-5 - 2|$

56. $|5 - 4| = |4 - 5|$

57. Logical Reasoning Does the absolute value equation $|x + 2| = -3$ have a solution? Explain your reasoning.

58. Writing Explain the difference between the graphs of $|x - 8| = 2$ and $|x + 8| = 2$.

59. Multi-Step Problem The solutions of the equation $|x - 17| = 8$ correspond to the number of gold medals and total medals won by the United States in a recent Winter Olympic Games.

   a. Rewrite the absolute value equation as two linear equations. Then solve each linear equation.

   b. How many gold medals did the United States win? How many total medals did the United States win?

   c. There are 3 types of medals (gold, silver, and bronze). The United States won 9 silver medals. How many bronze medals did the U.S. win?

   d. Error Analysis Explain what is wrong with the following graph of $|x - 17| = 8$.

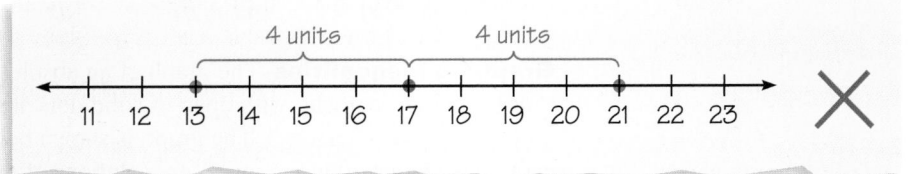

Perpendicular Lines Write an equation of the line that passes through the given point and is perpendicular to the given line. *(Lesson 2.5)*

60. $(-3, 0)$, $y = -\frac{1}{3}x + 1$

61. $(-2, 1)$, $y = \frac{2}{3}x - 2$

62. $(4, -1)$, $y = -2x - 3$

63. $(8, 5)$, $y = 4x + 3$

Compound Inequalities Solve the inequality. Then graph your solution. *(Lesson 4.1)*

64. $-13 < x - 8 \le -5$

65. $-5 < 3x - 2 < 7$

66. $x - 3 < -5$ or $x + 8 \ge 9$

67. $-x + 3 < -5$ or $-3x + 2 \ge 17$

68. Stock The cost C of buying shares of a stock is given by $C = 3.5x + 7$ where x is the number of shares you buy. Use an inequality to describe the number of shares you can buy if you spend at most $1000. *(Lesson 4.1)*

Congruence Determine if the line segments shown are congruent.

69.

70.

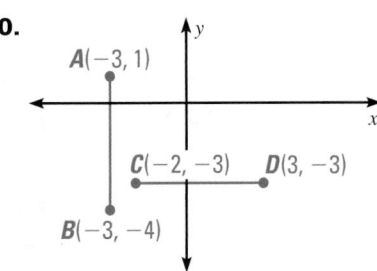

4.5 Solving Absolute Value Inequalities

Key Words

- absolute value inequality

GOAL Solve and graph absolute value inequalities.

Prerequisite Skills

Solve the inequality. Then graph your solution.

1. $4x - 3 > 13$

2. $2x + 6 \leq -7$

3. $5 - x < 2x + 11$

What wavelengths of electromagnetic radiation are visible to the human eye?

The electromagnetic spectrum includes radio waves, microwaves, infrared, visible light, ultraviolet radiation, X-rays, and gamma rays.

In Exercises 46 and 47, you will solve an inequality to find the frequency range of visible light waves.

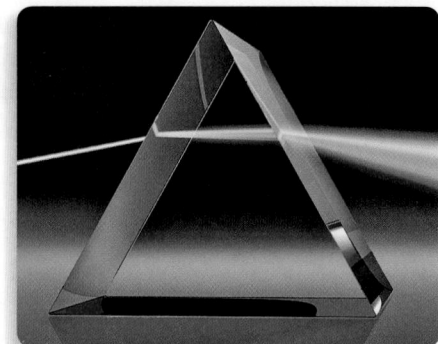

An **absolute value inequality** has one of these forms:

$$|ax + b| < c \qquad |ax + b| \leq c \qquad |ax + b| > c \qquad |ax + b| \geq c$$

Graphing Inequalities The graph of an absolute value inequality involving < or ≤ is a line segment, with open or solid dots at the endpoints. For example, $|x| \leq 3$ means $-3 \leq x \leq 3$. The graph is shown below. The solid dots at the endpoints indicate that -3 and 3 *are* solutions of the inequality.

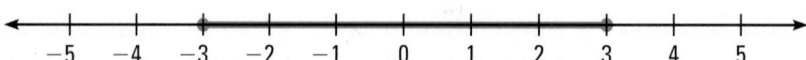

The graph of an absolute value inequality involving > or ≥ is two rays pointing in opposite directions, with open or solid dots at the endpoints. For example, $|x| > 4$ means $x < -4$ or $x > 4$. The graph is shown below. The open dots at the endpoints indicate that -4 and 4 *are not* solutions of the inequality.

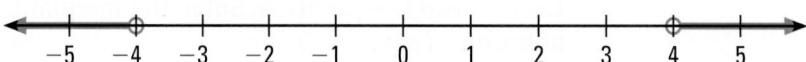

To solve and graph more complex absolute value inequalities, you write and solve an equivalent compound inequality that does not use absolute value, as shown in the table below.

Solving Absolute Value Inequalities

INEQUALITY	EQUIVALENT FORM	GRAPH
$\lvert ax + b \rvert < c$	$-c < ax + b < c$	
$\lvert ax + b \rvert \leq c$	$-c \leq ax + b \leq c$	
$\lvert ax + b \rvert > c$	$ax + b < -c$ or $ax + b > c$	
$\lvert ax + b \rvert \geq c$	$ax + b \leq -c$ or $ax + b \geq c$	

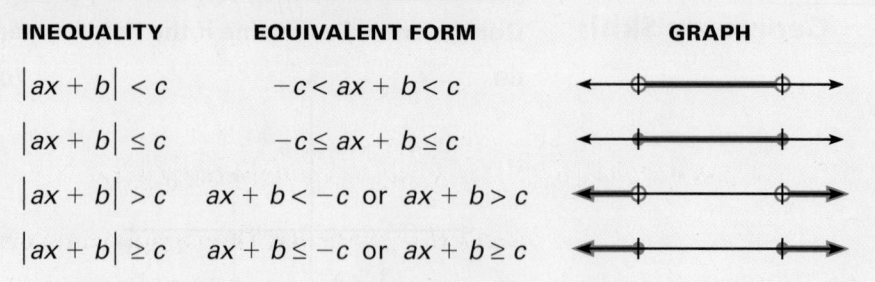

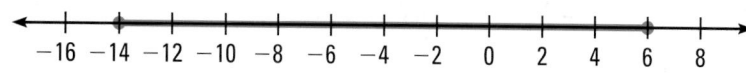

EXAMPLE 1 Solve an Inequality of the Form $|x + b| \leq c$

Solve $|x + 4| \leq 10$. Then graph the solution.

Solution

$$|x + 4| \leq 10 \qquad \text{Write original inequality.}$$

$$-10 \leq x + 4 \leq 10 \qquad \text{Write equivalent compound inequality.}$$

$$-14 \leq x \leq 6 \qquad \text{Subtract 4 from each expression.}$$

STUDENT HELP

AVOID ERRORS

When you check your solution, choose values that make computation simple.

ANSWER ▶ The solution is all real numbers greater than or equal to -14 and less than or equal to 6. The graph is shown below.

<image: number line from -16 to 8 with filled dots at -14 and 6, line shaded between>

CHECK Test one value from each region of the graph.

$$|-16 + 4| \leq 10 \qquad |0 + 4| \leq 10 \qquad |8 + 4| \leq 10$$

$$12 \leq 10 \; ✗ \qquad\qquad 4 \leq 10 \; ✓ \qquad\qquad 12 \leq 10 \; ✗$$

Checkpoint ✓ Solve an Absolute Value Inequality

Solve the inequality. Then graph your solution.

1. $|x + 1| \leq 4$ **2.** $|x - 3| \leq 5$ **3.** $|x - 8| < 1$

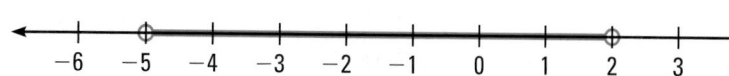

EXAMPLE 2 Solve an Inequality of the Form $|ax + b| < c$

Solve $|2x + 3| < 7$. Then graph the solution.

Solution

$$|2x + 3| < 7 \qquad \text{Write original inequality.}$$

$$-7 < 2x + 3 < 7 \qquad \text{Write equivalent compound inequality.}$$

$$-10 < 2x < 4 \qquad \text{Subtract 3 from each expression.}$$

$$-5 < x < 2 \qquad \text{Divide each expression by 2.}$$

ANSWER ▶ The solutions are all real numbers greater than -5 and less than 2. The graph is shown below.

<image: number line from -6 to 3 with open dots at -5 and 2, line shaded between>

CHECK Test one value from each region of the graph.

$$|2(-6) + 3| < 7 \qquad |2(0) + 3| < 7 \qquad |2(3) + 3| < 7$$

$$9 < 7 \; ✗ \qquad\qquad 3 < 7 \; ✓ \qquad\qquad 9 < 7 \; ✗$$

Checkpoint ✓ Solve an Absolute Value Inequality

Solve the inequality. Then graph your solution.

4. $|2x - 1| < 9$ **5.** $|1 + 4x| < 3$ **6.** $|3x + 6| \leq 12$

EXAMPLE 3 Solve an Inequality of the Form $|ax + b| \geq c$

Solve $\left| \frac{1}{2}x - 1 \right| \geq 3$. Then graph the solution.

Solution

The absolute value inequality is equivalent to $\frac{1}{2}x - 1 \leq -3$ or $\frac{1}{2}x - 1 \geq 3$.

FIRST INEQUALITY

$\frac{1}{2}x - 1 \leq -3$ Write inequalities.

$\frac{1}{2}x \leq -2$ Add 1 to each side.

$x \leq -4$ Multiply each side by 2.

SECOND INEQUALITY

$\frac{1}{2}x - 1 \geq 3$

$\frac{1}{2}x \geq 4$

$x \geq 8$

ANSWER ▸ The solution is all real numbers less than or equal to -4 or greater than or equal to 8. The graph is shown below.

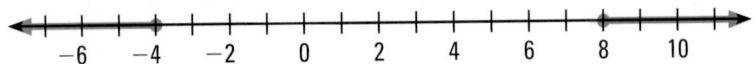

 **Solve an Absolute Value Inequality**

Solve the inequality. Then graph your solution.

7. $|2x + 3| > 7$ **8.** $|4x + 1| \geq 5$ **9.** $\left| \frac{1}{4}x - 2 \right| \geq 1$

EXAMPLE 4 Write a Model for Tolerance

Link to
INDUSTRY

TOLERANCES In industrial manufacturing, the maximum acceptable deviation of a product from some ideal or average measurement is called the *tolerance*.

Industrial Design A bicycle manufacturer uses a tolerance of 0.05 millimeters for a bicycle crank assembly pin that is 8.5 millimeters wide. Write and solve an absolute value inequality that describes the acceptable widths for the pins.

Solution

VERBAL MODEL

$$\left| \boxed{\text{Actual width}} - \boxed{\text{Ideal width}} \right| \leq \boxed{\text{Tolerance}}$$

LABELS

Actual width $= x$ (millimeters)

Ideal width $= 8.5$ (millimeters)

Tolerance $= 0.05$ (millimeters)

ALGEBRAIC MODEL

$|x - 8.5| \leq 0.05$ Write algebraic model.

$-0.05 \leq x - 8.5 \leq 0.05$ Write equivalent compound inequality.

$8.45 \leq x \leq 8.55$ Add 8.5 to each side.

ANSWER ▸ The acceptable widths for the pins is between 8.45 millimeters and 8.55 millimeters, inclusive.

Checkpoint ✔ **Write a Model for Tolerance**

10. Suppose the bicycle manufacturer uses a tolerance of 0.07 millimeters for the pins. How does the absolute value inequality change?

4.5 Exercises

Guided Practice

Vocabulary Check

Skill Check

1. Explain how to solve the absolute value inequality $|x + 2| < 2$.

2. How is the graph of the absolute value inequality $|x - 7| \leq 5$ related to the graph of the absolute value equality $|x - 7| = 5$?

3. Describe the graph of the inequality $|x - b| > c$ when $c > 0$.

4. Choose the compound inequality you would use to solve the absolute value inequality $|x + 5| > 4$. Explain your reasoning.

   A. $-4 < x + 5 < 4$ **B.** $-4 < x + 5 > 4$

   C. $x + 5 < -4$ or $x + 5 > 4$ **D.** $x + 5 > -4$ or $x + 5 < 4$

Tell whether the given number is a solution of the inequality.

5. $|x + 7| < 2; 0$ 6. $|x - 3| > 1; 2$ 7. $|x + 4| \geq -5; 3$

Solve the inequality. Then graph and check the solution.

8. $|x + 9| > 5$ 9. $|2x + 1| \leq 5$ 10. $|2x - 4| < 17$

Practice and Applications

STUDENT HELP

HOMEWORK HELP
Example 1: Exs. 11–45
Example 2: Exs. 11–45
Example 3: Exs. 11–45
Example 4: Exs. 46–57

Rewriting Inequalities Write the equivalent compound inequality you would use to solve the absolute value inequality.

11. $|x - 7| < 9$ 12. $|x + 10| \geq 15$ 13. $|x + 8| < 10$

14. $|x - 3| \geq 18$ 15. $|2x + 7| \geq 11$ 16. $|4x - 5| \leq 15$

Matching Match the absolute value inequality with the graph of its solution.

17. $|x + 4| < 2$

18. $|x + 4| > 2$

19. $|x + 4| \leq 2$

20. $|x + 4| \geq 2$

A.

B.

C.

D.

Solving Absolute Value Inequalities Solve the inequality. Then graph and check the solution.

21. $|x| < 3$ 22. $|x| \geq 6$ 23. $|x + 3| > 9$

24. $|x - 6| < 6$ 25. $|5x| < 5$ 26. $|3x| > 1$

27. $\left|\dfrac{x}{4}\right| \geq 7$ 28. $|-2 + x| \leq 18$ 29. $|5 + x| > 1$

Logical Reasoning Copy and complete the statement with *always*, *sometimes*, or *never*.

30. If $c < 0$, then $|x| > c$ is __?__ a true statement.

31. A solution of the inequality $|x + 7| < 3$ will __?__ be positive.

32. A solution of the inequality $|x - 5| > 1$ will __?__ be negative.

33. A solution of the inequality $|x + 2| \le 5$ will __?__ be negative.

Solving Inequalities Solve the inequality. Then graph and check the solution.

34. $|2x + 5| \le 7$

35. $|3x + 3| \le 9$

36. $|4x - 3| < 5$

37. $|2x - 6| \le 12$

38. $\left|\frac{1}{4}x + 1\right| < 4$

39. $\left|3x + \frac{1}{2}\right| < \frac{3}{2}$

40. $|5x + 10| > 5$

41. $|2x - 3| > 9$

42. $|3x - 6| \ge 15$

43. $|3x + 5| \ge 11$

44. $\left|\frac{1}{7}x - 1\right| > 1$

45. $\left|2x + \frac{5}{3}\right| \ge \frac{1}{3}$

Light Spectrum In Exercises 46 and 47, use the following information about wavelengths of visible light.

Electromagnetic waves are measured in nanometers (10^9 nanometers = 1 meter). The range of wavelengths of light visible to a typical human eye can be modeled by this inequality:

$$|x - 550| \le 150$$

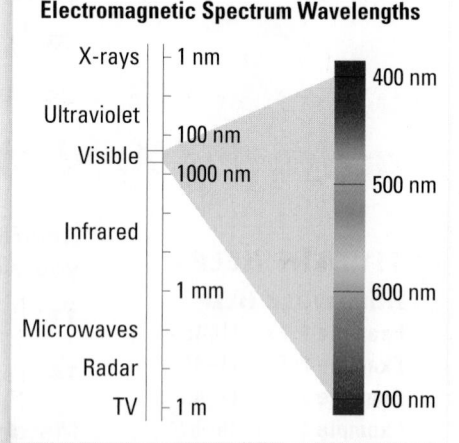

Electromagnetic Spectrum Wavelengths

46. Solve the inequality describing the values of x for visible light. Graph and check your solution.

47. Some people can see visible light with wavelengths from 380 nanometers to 780 nanometers. Write an absolute value inequality for this range.

Science Link In Exercises 48–50, use the following information.

The absolute value inequality $|t - 98.4| \le 0.6$ is one model for normal body temperatures of an adult where t is measured in degrees Fahrenheit.

48. Solve the inequality. Then graph your solution.

49. Describe the range of normal body temperatures.

50. Is a temperature of 99.5°F considered normal according to this model?

Tolerance In Exercises 51 and 52, use the following information.

A quality control inspector for a paper cup manufacturer must make sure that consecutive paper cups are able to be stacked. So, a paper cup that is supposed to have a 6.35 centimeter diameter has a tolerance of 0.1 centimeter.

51. Use a verbal model to write an absolute value inequality that describes the acceptable diameters for cups with a 6.35 centimeter diameter.

52. Solve the inequality. Then graph your solution.

Wrestling In Exercises 53–57, use the following information.

According to international wrestling rules, a senior Olympic wrestler must weigh in prior to his wrestling match. Then he must wrestle in his weight class or the next higher weight class, except for category 7. The senior Olympic weight categories are shown in the table.

53. The inequality $|w - 62| \le 2$ describes a wrestler's weight w on the day of the official weigh-in. Solve and graph the inequality.

54. In what categories could the wrestler in Exercise 53 wrestle?

55. The inequality $|w - 52.5| < 2.5$ describes another wrestler's weight w on the day of the official weigh-in. Solve and graph the inequality.

56. In what categories could the wrestler in Exercise 55 wrestle?

57. Can any of the weight ranges be expressed as an absolute value inequality? Explain.

Wrestler category	Weight, w (in kilograms)
1	$50 \le w < 55$
2	$55 \le w < 60$
3	$60 \le w < 66$
4	$66 \le w < 74$
5	$74 \le w < 84$
6	$84 \le w < 96$
7	$96 \le w < 120$

Challenge Solve the inequality. Then graph and check the solution.

58. $|5x + 1| > x + 5$

59. $|2x - 5| > x + 1$

60. **Multiple Choice** What is the graph of $|2x - 3| < 5$?

Ⓐ 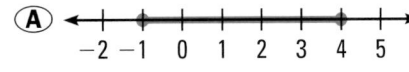   Ⓑ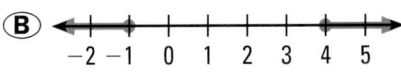

Ⓒ 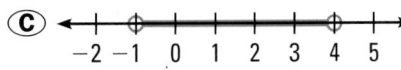   Ⓓ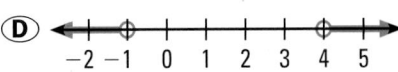

61. **Multiple Choice** What is the solution of the absolute value inequality $|x + 3| \ge 10$?

Ⓕ $-13 \le x \le 7$

Ⓖ $x \ge 7$

Ⓗ $x \le -13$ or $x \ge 7$

Ⓙ $x \le 7$ or $x \ge -13$

Evaluating Functions Evaluate the function for the given value of x. (Lesson 2.2)

62. $h(x) = -6x; x = 3$

63. $f(x) = 5x - 7; x = 2$

64. $g(x) = x^2 + 4; x = -2$

65. $b(x) = -x^2 + 9; x = 0$

Systems of Two Inequalities Graph the system of linear inequalities. (Lesson 4.3)

66. $x \le -4$
    $y > 3$

67. $y < 2$
    $x - y < 3$

68. $x + 2y \le 10$
    $-2x + y \ge -1$

Area Find the area of the parallelogram.

69.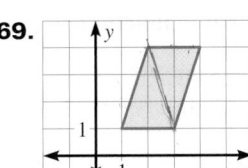

70.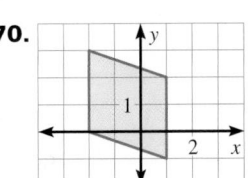

4.6 Absolute Value Functions

GOAL Evaluate, graph, and use simple absolute value functions.

Key Word
- vertex

The absolute value of x can be defined algebraically as

$$|x| = \begin{cases} x, & \text{if } x \text{ is positive} \\ 0, & \text{if } x = 0 \\ -x, & \text{if } x \text{ is negative} \end{cases}$$

Evaluate the expression.

1. $|6 - 4|$

2. $|-3 - 1|$

3. $|2 - 10|$

4. $|-5 + 12|$

The graph of the absolute value function $y = |x|$ is V-shaped and consists of two rays that have a common endpoint at the origin. The common endpoint is called the **vertex** of the graph.

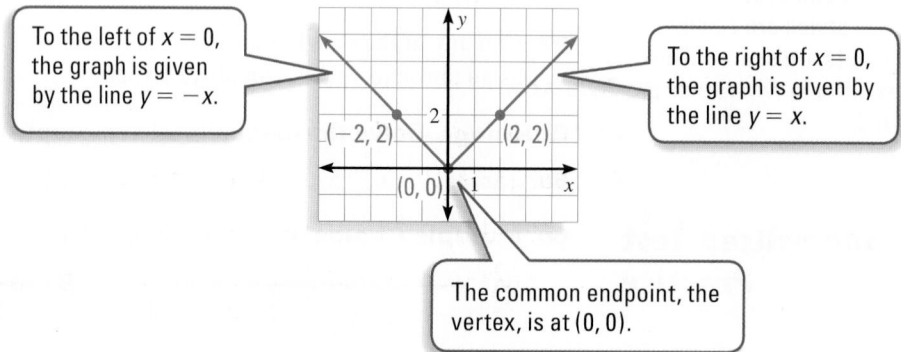

To the left of $x = 0$, the graph is given by the line $y = -x$.

To the right of $x = 0$, the graph is given by the line $y = x$.

$(-2, 2)$ $(2, 2)$ $(0, 0)$

The common endpoint, the vertex, is at $(0, 0)$.

Note that the graph of $y = |x|$ is symmetric in the y-axis because each half is a reflection of the other over the y-axis. For every point (x, y) on the graph, the point $(-x, y)$ is also on the graph.

EXAMPLE 1 Evaluate Absolute Value Functions

Evaluate the function when $x = 2$ and $x = -3$.

a. $f(x) = |x - 5|$
b. $g(x) = |x| + 8$

Solution

a. When $x = 2$:

$f(x) = |x - 5|$	Write function.
$f(2) = |2 - 5|$	Substitute 2 for x.
$= |-3|$	Simplify.
$= 3$	

When $x = -3$:

$f(x) = |x - 5|$	Write function.
$f(-3) = |-3 - 5|$	Substitute -3 for x.
$= |-8|$	Simplify.
$= 8$	

b. When $x = 2$:

$g(x) = |x| + 8$
$g(2) = |2| + 8$
$= 2 + 8$
$= 10$

When $x = -3$:

$g(x) = |x| + 8$
$g(-3) = |-3| + 8$
$= 3 + 8$
$= 11$

Evaluate the function when $x = 1$ and when $x = -4$.

1. $f(x) = |x + 3|$ **2.** $g(x) = |x| - 8$ **3.** $h(x) = |2x + 9|$

Graphs of Absolute Value The graph of $y = |x|$ is symmetric in the y-axis. This fact can help you graph absolute value functions of the form $y = a|x|$. When graphing such functions, use this information:

- If $a > 0$, the graph opens *up*.

- If $a < 0$, the graph opens *down*.

- If $|a| > 1$, the V-shape will be *narrower* than the graph of $y = |x|$.

- If $|a| < 1$, the V-shape will be *wider* than the graph of $y = |x|$.

EXAMPLE 2 **Graph an Absolute Value Function**

Graph $y = 2|x|$.

Solution

❶ *Plot* the vertex at the origin.

❷ *Find* a second point by substituting an x-value.

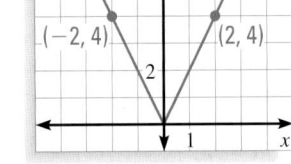

$$y = 2|x| \qquad \text{Write original equation.}$$
$$= 2|2| \qquad \text{Substitute 2 for } x.$$
$$= 2(2) \qquad \text{Evaluate } |2|.$$
$$= 4 \qquad \text{Multiply.}$$

A second point is $(2, 4)$.

❸ *Plot* the second point and use symmetry to plot a third point at $(-2, 4)$.

❹ *Connect* these three points with a V-shaped graph, as shown.

EXAMPLE 3 **Graph an Absolute Value Function**

Graph $y = -4|x|$.

Solution

❶ *Plot* the vertex at the origin.

❷ *Find* a second point by substituting an x-value.

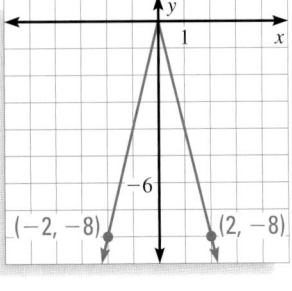

$$y = -4|x| \qquad \text{Write original equation.}$$
$$= -4|2| \qquad \text{Substitute 2 for } x.$$
$$= -4(2) \qquad \text{Evaluate } |2|.$$
$$= -8 \qquad \text{Multiply.}$$

A second point is $(2, -8)$.

❸ *Plot* the second point and use symmetry to plot a third point at $(-2, -8)$.

❹ *Connect* these three points with a V-shaped graph, as shown.

Graph the function.

4. $y = 3|x|$

5. $y = \frac{1}{2}|x|$

6. $y = 1.5|x|$

7. $y = -\frac{1}{2}|x|$

8. $y = -2|x|$

9. $y = -5|x|$

EXAMPLE 4 **Graph and Use an Absolute Value Function**

Transportation You are in an airplane traveling at 500 miles per hour. The captain announces that the plane will be passing over Hoover Dam in 2 hours.

a. Draw a graph that shows the airplane's distance from Hoover Dam as a function of time. Use $t = 0$ when the plane passes over the dam.

b. Write an equation for the function.

c. The plane begins its descent 3 hours after flying over Hoover Dam. How far is the plane from the dam?

Solution

a. Let t represent the hours before and after flying over Hoover Dam. Let d represent the number of miles the plane is from Hoover Dam.

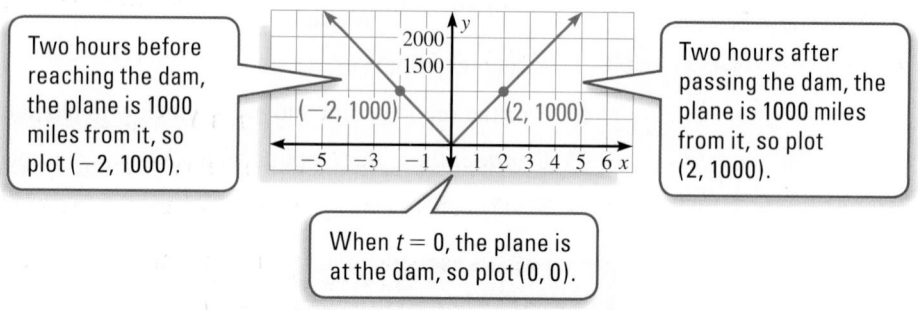

Two hours before reaching the dam, the plane is 1000 miles from it, so plot $(-2, 1000)$.

Two hours after passing the dam, the plane is 1000 miles from it, so plot $(2, 1000)$.

When $t = 0$, the plane is at the dam, so plot $(0, 0)$.

Connect the three points with a V-shaped graph, as shown.

b. An equation for the function is $d = 500|t|$.

c. From the graph, you can see that 3 hours after flying over Hoover Dam, the plane is 1500 miles from the dam.

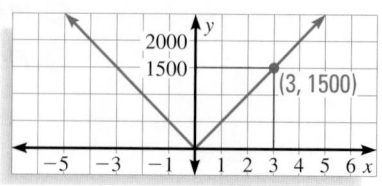

---

10. An airplane traveling at 525 miles per hour will pass over the Grand Canyon in 1 hour. Graph the distance from the canyon as a function of time. Use the graph to find how far past the canyon the plane will be 2 hours after flying over it.

4.6 Exercises

Guided Practice

Vocabulary Check

1. What is the vertex of an absolute value graph?

2. How can you tell if the graph of $y = a|x|$ opens up or down?

Skill Check

Evaluate the function when $x = -2$.

3. $f(x) = |x| + 1$

4. $g(x) = |x + 2|$

5. $h(x) = -2|x|$

Graph the function.

6. $f(x) = \frac{2}{3}|x|$

7. $h(x) = -3|x|$

8. $k(x) = \frac{1}{5}|x|$

9. **Car Travel** You are in a car traveling at 60 miles per hour. You see a sign that says you are 180 miles from Gardena. Draw a graph that shows your distance from Gardena as a function of time. Use $t = 0$ when you are in Gardena.

Practice and Applications

STUDENT HELP

HOMEWORK HELP
Example 1: Exs. 10–20
Example 2: Exs. 21–44
Example 3: Exs. 21–44
Example 4: Exs. 45–50

Evaluating Absolute Value Functions **Evaluate the function when $x = -1$ and $x = 3$.**

10. $f(x) = |x|$

11. $g(x) = -5|x|$

12. $h(x) = |x| - 2$

13. $p(x) = |x - 2|$

14. $c(x) = |x + 3| + 4$

15. $r(x) = |x - 5| - 2$

16. $v(x) = 3|x + 1|$

17. $w(x) = 2|x - 3| + 2$

18. $n(x) = \frac{1}{2}|x + 1|$

Temperature **In Exercises 19 and 20, use the following information.**

The temperature in degrees Fahrenheit during a summer day can be modeled by the function $y = -2|x| + 84$ where x is the number of hours after 3 P.M.

19. What is the temperature at 7 P.M.?

20. What is the temperature at 11 A.M.?

Identifying Characteristics **Tell whether the graph of the function opens *up* or *down*. Then tell whether the graph is *wider* or *narrower* than the graph of $y = |x|$.**

21. $y = 2|x|$

22. $y = -7|x|$

23. $y = 4|x|$

24. $y = \frac{2}{3}|x|$

25. $y = -\frac{3}{4}|x|$

26. $y = \frac{5}{4}|x|$

Matching **Match the function with its graph.**

27. $y = -2|x|$

28. $y = -\frac{1}{2}|x|$

29. $y = 2|x|$

A.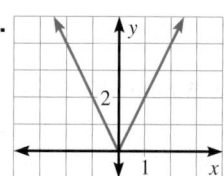

B.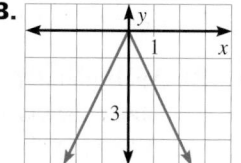

C.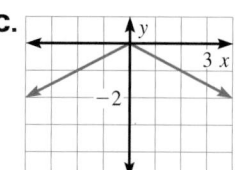

Symmetry Find the point on the graph that is symmetric to the given point in the *y*-axis.

30. $y = 8|x|$; $(1, 8)$　　　　　　**31.** $y = 10|x|$; $(-2, 20)$

32. $y = -5|x|$; $(-1, -5)$　　　　**33.** $y = -3|x|$; $(3, -9)$

34. $y = \frac{5}{4}|x|$; $(-4, 5)$　　　　　**35.** $y = \frac{3}{2}|x|$; $(6, 9)$

Graphing Absolute Value Functions Graph the function.

36. $y = |x|$　　　　　**37.** $y = 4|x|$　　　　　**38.** $y = -2.5|x|$

39. $y = \frac{1}{4}|x|$　　　　**40.** $y = \frac{8}{5}|x|$　　　　**41.** $y = -\frac{2}{3}|x|$

42. $y = -\frac{3}{4}|x|$　　　**43.** $y = -\frac{1}{2}|x|$　　　**44.** $y = -\frac{1}{3}|x|$

45. Miniature Golf You are playing on the miniature golf green shown. Imagine that a coordinate plane is placed over the green so that the ball is at $(-3, -6)$ and the hole is at $(3, -6)$. You bounce the ball off the side wall at $(0, 0)$. Do you make your shot? Explain.

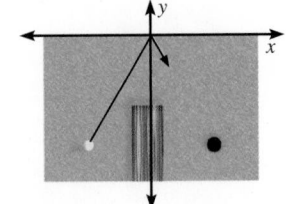

Fountain In Exercises 46–48, use the following information.

A fountain is being drained at a rate of 3 inches per minute and then refilled at the same rate. Before being drained, the water is 3 feet deep.

46. Draw a graph that shows the depth of the water as a function of time. Use $t = 0$ for the moment the fountain is completely empty.

47. Write an equation for the function you graphed in Exercise 46.

48. Use the graph or the equation to find the depth of the water at three different times.

Pool Table In Exercises 49–51, use the following information.

Imagine that a coordinate plane is placed over a pool table as shown, so that the five-ball is at $(-1, -2)$.

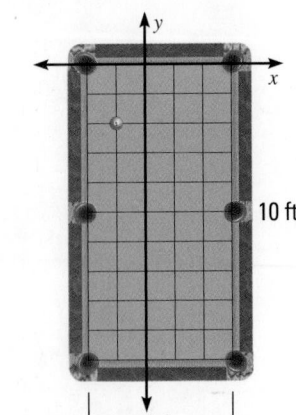

10 ft

5 ft

49. Suppose your cue ball hits the five-ball so that it bounces against the top cushion at $(0, 0)$. What is an absolute value equation for the path of the ball?

50. If the five-ball bounces against the top cushion at $(0, 0)$, will it go into any of the pockets? Explain.

51. Challenge Write an absolute value equation for the path the five-ball must take to bounce against the top cushion and land in the bottom right corner pocket.

52. Critical Thinking In the same coordinate plane, graph $y = |x| + k$ for several values of k. What is the effect of k on the graphs?

53. Critical Thinking In the same coordinate plane, graph $y = |x - h|$ for several values of h. What is the effect of h on the graphs?

Challenge The functions below have graphs that are translated absolute value graphs. Match the function with its graph.

54. $y = 2|x + 2| + 1$

55. $y = 2|x - 2| + 1$

56. $y = 2|x + 1| - 2$

A.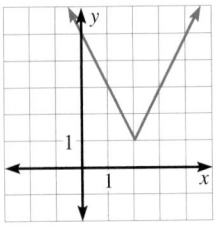

B.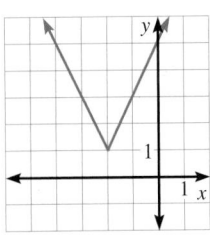

C.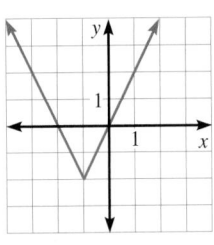

57. Multiple Choice What is the value of $h(x) = |x - 3| - 1$ when $x = -2$?

Ⓐ -6　　　Ⓑ -4　　　Ⓒ 0　　　Ⓓ 4

58. Multiple Choice The graph of which function opens down?

Ⓕ $y = 8|x|$　　Ⓖ $y = 4|x|$　　Ⓗ $y = \frac{1}{4}|x|$　　Ⓙ $y = -8|x|$

59. Multiple Choice What is an equation for this graph?

Ⓐ $y = \frac{1}{3}|x|$　　Ⓑ $y = 3x$

Ⓒ $y = -3x$　　Ⓓ $y = \frac{1}{4}|x|$

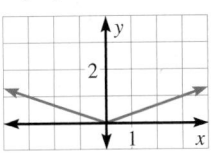

Mixed Review

Graphing Linear Functions Graph the linear function. *(Lesson 2.2)*

60. $f(x) = 2x$

61. $h(x) = -3x$

62. $g(x) = x - 5$

63. $p(x) = -2x + 3$

64. $r(x) = -3x - 1$

65. $q(x) = \frac{1}{3}x + 2$

Systems of Equations Solve each system of equations. *(Lesson 3.5)*

66. $x + y - z = 4$
$x - y + z = 0$
$2x + y + z = -2$

67. $-2x - y + 2z = 0$
$x - 3y + z = -11$
$x + y - 2z = 3$

68. $3x + 2y + z = 11$
$2x - 2y + z = -9$
$x + 5y - 2z = 23$

Checking Solutions Check whether the given ordered pairs are solutions of the inequality. *(Lesson 4.2)*

69. $x \geq -2; (0, 2), (-3, 1)$

70. $y < 1; (3, 2), (-2, 0)$

71. $-3y > 9; (2, -3), (0, -5)$

72. $2x \leq 1; (-1, 3), (-2, 3)$

73. $y < x - 4; (-2, -5), (5, 0)$

74. $y > 2x + 3; (-2, 6), (0, 3)$

Checking Solutions Use the graph to check whether the ordered pair is a solution of the system of linear inequalities. *(Lesson 4.3)*

75. $(2, 2)$

76. $(1, -1)$

77. $(1, 2)$

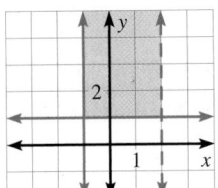

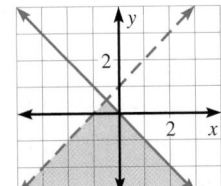

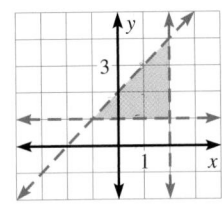

Reflections Use the graph to answer Exercises 78–80.

78. Which triangle is a reflection of △*ABC* in the *y*-axis?

79. Which triangle is a reflection of △*ABC* in the *x*-axis?

80. Is △*PQR* a reflection of △*XYZ* in the *x*-axis? Explain.

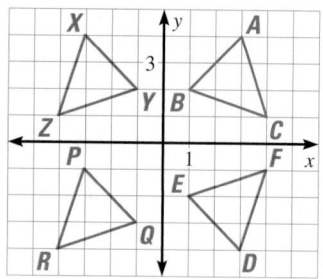

Classifying Triangles Tell whether a triangle with the given side lengths is *equilateral*, *isosceles*, or *scalene*.

81. Side lengths: 20 cm, 40 cm, 30 cm

82. Side lengths: 55 in., 20 in., 55 in.

83. Side lengths: 12 ft, 12 ft, 12 ft

Quiz 2

Lesson 4.4   **Rewrite the absolute value equation as two linear equations.**

1. $|x - 7| = 11$ **2.** $|x + 4| = 2$ **3.** $|3x - 6| = 9$

Lesson 4.4   **Solve the absolute value equation and check your solutions.**

4. $|x - 4| = 5$ **5.** $\left|x + \frac{1}{5}\right| = \frac{4}{5}$ **6.** $|2x + 3| = 7$

7. $|8 - 2x| = 9$ **8.** $|3 - x| + 5 = 11$ **9.** $|5 + 3x| - 6 = 14$

Lesson 4.4   **Write an absolute value equation that has the given solutions.**

10. 0 and 6   **11.** 2 and 8   **12.** −5 and 5

Lesson 4.5   **Write the equivalent compound inequality you would use to solve the absolute value inequality.**

13. $|5x + 2| \le 8$ **14.** $|4x - 9| > 3$ **15.** $|3 - 8x| \ge 11$

Lesson 4.5   **Solve the inequality. Then graph the solution.**

16. $|x| \ge 5$ **17.** $|x| < 11$ **18.** $|x + 2| > 7$

19. $|5 + x| \le 16$ **20.** $|4x| > 4$ **21.** $\left|\frac{x}{5}\right| \ge 10$

22. $|3x + 12| \ge 15$ **23.** $|5x + 5| \le 10$ **24.** $|2x - 3| < 7$

25. Manufacturing A bicycle manufacturer has a tolerance of 0.05 millimeters for a bicycle crank assembly shaft that is 4.5 millimeters wide. Write and solve an absolute value inequality that describes the acceptable widths for these shafts.

Lesson 4.6   **Identifying Characteristics** Tell whether the graph of the function opens *up* or *down*. Then tell whether the graph is *wider* or *narrower* than the graph of *y* = |*x*|.

26. $y = 9|x|$ **27.** $y = \frac{1}{4}|x|$ **28.** $y = -\frac{5}{4}|x|$

USING A GRAPHING CALCULATOR *(For use with Lesson 4.6)*
Transforming Functions

In Lesson 4.6, you saw how the value of a affects the graph of $y = a|x|$.

You can use a graphing calculator to see how the values of b and c affect the graph of $y = |x - b| + c$.

EXAMPLE

Use a graphing calculator to graph $y = |x + 3| - 4$.

SOLUTION

1 Enter $y = |x + 3| - 4$ using the *abs* function.

Press **Y=** **MATH** and choose the NUM menu to find the *abs* function.

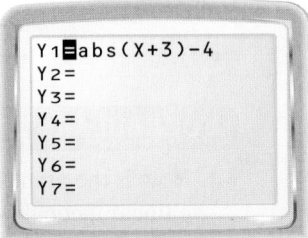

2 Press **GRAPH** to view the absolute value function. The V-shape may look distorted if the scales on the axes are different.

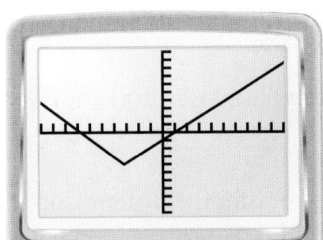

3 Press **ZOOM** and choose the *ZSquare* zoom option so the display uses the same scale on both axes.

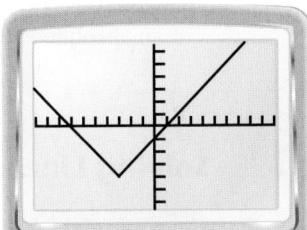

EXERCISES

1. Graph $y = |x| - 4$, $y = |x|$, and $y = |x| + 4$ on a coordinate plane. Name the coordinates of the vertex of each graph.

2. Describe how changing the value of c changes the graph of $y = |x| + c$.

3. Graph $y = |x - 5|$, $y = |x|$, and $y = |x + 5|$ on a coordinate plane. Name the coordinates of the vertex of each graph.

4. Describe how changing the value of b changes the graph of $y = |x - b|$.

Predict the coordinates of the vertex of the graph of the function. Then graph the function to test your prediction.

5. $y = |x - 5| + 4$ 　　　　**6.** $y = |x - 5| - 4$

7. $y = |x + 5| + 4$ 　　　　**8.** $y = |x + 5| - 4$

9. Reasoning Describe the graph of $y = |x - b| + c$ and name the coordinates of its vertex.

Chapter Summary and Review

@HomeTutor
classzone.com
• Multi-Language Glossary
• Vocabulary practice

VOCABULARY

- linear inequality in one variable, *p. 172*
- solution of an inequality in one variable, *p. 172*
- graph of an inequality in one variable, *p. 173*
- compound inequality, *p. 174*

- linear inequality in two variables, *p. 179*
- half-plane, *p. 179*
- system of linear inequalities in two variables, *p. 185*
- solution of a system of linear inequalities, *p. 185*

- graph of a system of linear inequalities, *p. 185*
- absolute value, *p. 192*
- absolute value equation, *p. 192*
- absolute value inequality, *p. 198*
- vertex, *p. 204*

VOCABULARY EXERCISES

1. How is the graph of a linear inequality in one variable different from the graph of a linear inequality in two variables?

2. Explain how to determine which half-plane to shade when graphing a linear inequality in two variables.

3. You are at point $(p, 0)$ and your friend is at point $(q, 0)$. Write an absolute value expression representing the distance between you and your friend.

4. The word *vertex* comes from a root which means "to turn." Explain why the graph of an absolute value function has a vertex.

4.1 Solving Linear Inequalities

Examples on pp. 172–174

EXAMPLES Use properties of inequalities to solve simple and compound inequalities. Reverse the inequality symbol when you multiply or divide each side by a negative number.

REVIEW HELP	
Exercises	**Examples**
5, 6	**1**, p. 172
7, 8	**4**, p. 174
9, 10	**5**, p. 174

SIMPLE INEQUALITY

$$-2x + 3 > 11$$
$$-2x > 8$$
$$x < -4$$

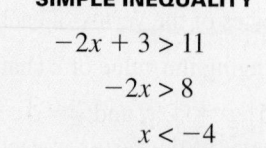

COMPOUND INEQUALITY

$$-7 \le 2x - 7 \le 1$$
$$0 \le 2x \le 8$$
$$0 \le x \le 4$$

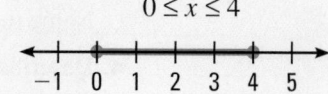

Solve the inequality. Then graph your solution.

5. $x - 3 > 2$

6. $2x + 1 \ge -1$

7. $-6 < x - 5 \le -1$

8. $-3 < 2x + 3 < 7$

9. $4x + 3 \le -5$ or $x + 6 \ge 8$

10. $2x + 3 \le 1$ or $3x - 2 > 7$

4.2   Linear Inequalities in Two Variables

Examples on pp. 179–181

EXAMPLE   Graph a linear inequality in two variables.

To graph $y > x + 1$, first graph the boundary line: $y = x + 1$. Use a dashed line because the inequality symbol is $>$.

Test the point $(0, 0)$. It is not a solution, so shade the half-plane above the line.

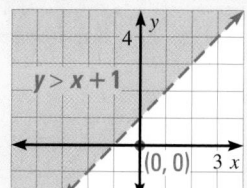

$y > x + 1$

$(0, 0)$ $3\ x$

REVIEW HELP
Exercises	Example
11–14	**3**, p. 180

Graph the inequality in a coordinate plane.

11. $y > x - 3$ **12.** $y \le \frac{1}{2}x + 3$ **13.** $x - 2y > 6$ **14.** $2x + y \ge 5$

4.3   Systems of Linear Inequalities

Examples on pp. 185–187

EXAMPLE   Graph the solutions of a system of linear inequalities.

$$x \ge 0$$
$$y \ge 0$$
$$2x + y < 4$$

The graph of $x \ge 0$ is the half-plane on and to the right of the line $x = 0$.

$y = 0$

$2x + y = 4$

$x = 0$

The graph of $y \ge 0$ is the half-plane on and above the line $y = 0$.

The graph of $2x + y < 4$ is the half-plane below the line $2x + y = 4$.

The graph of the system is the shaded region common to all the half-planes.

REVIEW HELP
Exercises	Examples
15, 16	**2**, p. 186
17, 18	**3**, p. 186

Graph the system of linear inequalities.

15. $x \ge -2$ **16.** $y < x$ **17.** $y \ge 0$ **18.** $y > 2$
   $y < 5$ $2x - y \le 1$ $x \ge 0$ $y \ge x$
                                        $x + y > 3$ $y - x < 4$

4.4   Solving Absolute Value Equations

Examples on pp. 192–194

EXAMPLES   Solve an absolute value equation by rewriting it as two linear equations.

$$|x - 3| = 8 \qquad\qquad |1 - 2x| = 5$$

$x - 3 = 8$ or $x - 3 = -8$ $1 - 2x = 5$ or $1 - 2x = -5$
$\quad x = 11$ or $\quad x = -5$ $-2x = 4$ or $-2x = -6$
                                            $x = -2$ or $x = 3$

REVIEW HELP
Exercises	Examples
19–21	**1**, p. 193
22	**2**, p. 193

The solutions are 11 and -5.   The solutions are -2 and 3.

Solve the equation.

19. $|x - 4| = 2$ **20.** $|x - 9| = 11$ **21.** $|2x - 6| = 4$ **22.** $|2x + 1| + 3 = 6$

4.5 Solving Absolute Value Inequalities

Examples on pp. 198–200

EXAMPLES Solve an absolute value inequality by rewriting it as a compound inequality.

$$|x + 4| < 3$$
$$-3 < x + 4 < 3$$
$$-7 < x < -1$$

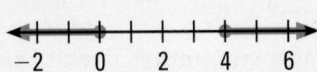

CHECK Test one value from each region of the graph.

Test −8: $|-8 + 4| \overset{?}{<} 3$
$$4 < 3 \ \text{✗}$$

Test −4: $|-4 + 4| \overset{?}{<} 3$
$$0 < 3 \ \text{✓}$$

Test 0: $|0 + 4| \overset{?}{<} 3$
$$4 < 3 \ \text{✗}$$

$$|x - 2| \geq 2$$
$$x - 2 \geq 2 \quad \text{or} \quad x - 2 \leq -2$$
$$x \geq 4 \quad \text{or} \quad x \leq 0$$

CHECK Test one value from each region of the graph.

Test −2: $|-2 - 2| \overset{?}{\geq} 2$
$$4 \geq 2 \ \text{✓}$$

Test 1: $|1 - 2| \overset{?}{\geq} 2$
$$1 \geq 2 \ \text{✗}$$

Test 5: $|5 - 2| \overset{?}{\geq} 2$
$$3 \geq 2 \ \text{✓}$$

REVIEW HELP

Exercises	Examples
23, 24	**1**, p. 199
25, 26	**2**, p. 199
27, 28	**3**, p. 200

Solve the inequality. Then graph and check the solution.

23. $|x - 7| < 12$

24. $|x + 2| \leq 6$

25. $|2x - 5| \leq 9$

26. $|7x + 7| < 14$

27. $|x + 3| > 5$

28. $|2x + 1| \geq 3$

4.6 Absolute Value Functions

Examples on pp. 204–206

EXAMPLE Graph the absolute value function $y = -3|x|$.

The graph of $y = -3|x|$ has vertex $(0, 0)$. Find and plot a second point on the graph.

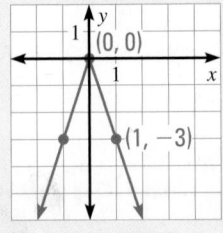

$y = -3|x|$ Write original equation.

$y = -3|1|$ Substitute 1 for x.

$y = -3$ Evaluate. The point is $(1, -3)$.

REVIEW HELP

Exercises	Examples
29–31	**1**, p. 204
32	**2**, p. 205
33, 34	**3**, p. 205

The graph is symmetric in the y-axis. Use this symmetry to plot a third point, $(-1, -3)$. Connect the points with a V-shaped graph, as shown.

Evaluate the function when $x = -3$.

29. $f(x) = |x| + 3$

30. $g(x) = |x - 5| + 2$

31. $h(x) = \frac{1}{3}|x + 3| - 2$

Graph the function.

32. $y = \frac{3}{5}|x|$

33. $y = -7|x|$

34. $y = -\frac{1}{4}|x|$

Decide whether the given number is a solution of the inequality.

1. $x \geq -5; -7$ **2.** $x + 3 \leq 12; 9$ **3.** $-10 \leq -5x \leq 30; 5$

Solve the inequality. Then graph your solution.

4. $x + 5 \geq 8$ **5.** $3x < -15$

6. $7 \leq x + 3 < 12$ **7.** $-1 < 2x - 1 \leq 7$

8. $3x + 4 < -8$ or $x - 7 \geq -5$ **9.** $2x + 6 > 8$ or $\frac{1}{2}x + 13 < 9$

Graph the inequality in a coordinate plane.

10. $y \geq -x + 5$ **11.** $y < \frac{3}{2}x - 4$ **12.** $4x - y \geq 1$

Use the graph to tell whether (4, 4) is a solution of the system of linear inequalities.

13. 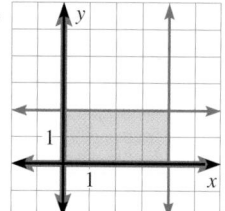   **14.** 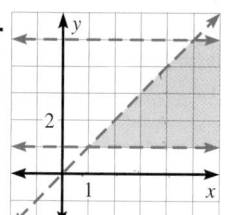   **15.**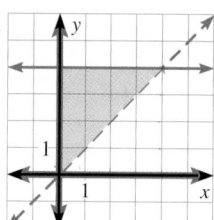

Graph the system of linear inequalities.

16. $x > 3$
$\quad\ y \leq -2$

17. $y < 2x$
$\quad\ x - y \leq 5$

18. $x + y < 7$
$\quad\ y < 3x - 2$
$\quad\ y > 3$

Solve the absolute value equation and check your solutions.

19. $|x + 6| = 3$ **20.** $|6x - 5| = 7$ **21.** $|2x + 1| - 4 = 3$

Write an absolute value equation that has the given solutions.

22. -17 and 17 **23.** -10 and 20 **24.** 0 and 24

Solve the inequality. Then graph the solution.

25. $|3x| < 27$ **26.** $\left|\frac{x}{2} + 1\right| > 8$ **27.** $|3x - 6| \leq 15$

Evaluate the function when $x = -5$ and $x = -7$.

28. $h(x) = |x| - 4$ **29.** $c(x) = |x + 2| + 5$ **30.** $w(x) = |x - 7| + 2$

Graph the function.

31. $y = 5|x|$ **32.** $y = -\frac{3}{2}|x|$ **33.** $y = \frac{2}{5}|x|$

Ⓐ Ⓑ Ⓒ Ⓓ

Test Tip Choose the easiest method that you can use accurately.

EXAMPLE Which ordered pair is a solution of the system? $x + y < 5$
$x - 2y < -4$

Ⓐ $(3, 5)$ **Ⓑ** $(6, -1)$ **Ⓒ** $(1, 3)$ **Ⓓ** $(2, -1)$

Solution

METHOD 1 *Graph the system* of inequalities, as shown at the right. Only $(1, 3)$ lies in the solution region.

METHOD 2 *Substitute* the coordinates of each answer into the inequalities. Choice C is correct because $1 + 3 < 5$ and $1 - 2(3) < -4$.

METHOD 3 *Eliminate choices* B and D because $x - 2y$ is positive when x is positive and y is negative. Eliminate choice A because $x + y$ is not less than 5. This leaves only choice C.

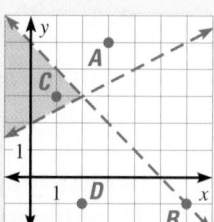

Multiple Choice

1. What is a solution of $2x - 3 > 11$?

Ⓐ 10   **Ⓑ** 7

Ⓒ 5   **Ⓓ** 0

2. What is the solution of $-5 \le -2x + 3 \le 7$?

Ⓕ $x \ge 4$ or $x \le -2$ **Ⓖ** $-2 \le x \le 4$

Ⓗ $-4 \le x \le -2$ **Ⓙ** $-4 \le x \le 2$

3. What ordered pair is a solution of $4x + y \le 3$?

Ⓐ $(2, -1)$ **Ⓑ** $(0, 5)$

Ⓒ $(-1, 8)$ **Ⓓ** $(1, -1)$

4. What is an equation of the graph shown?

Ⓕ $y < -2x$

Ⓖ $y \le -2x$

Ⓗ $y \ge -2x$

Ⓙ $y \le 2x$

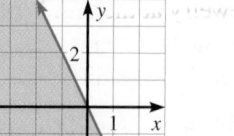

5. Which ordered pair is $x - 2y < 3$
a solution of the system? $y < 3$

Ⓐ $(-2, 4)$ **Ⓑ** $(0, 0)$

Ⓒ $(-4, -4)$ **Ⓓ** $(5, 3)$

6. The graph of what system is shown?

Ⓕ $x < -1$
$y > -x$

Ⓖ $x \le -1$
$y \ge -x$

Ⓗ $x < -1$
$y \ge -x$

Ⓙ $x \le -1$
$y > -x$

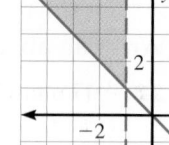

7. What are the solutions of $|2x - 3| - 8 = -5$?

Ⓐ $x = 0, x = -2$ **Ⓑ** $x = 0, x = 2$

Ⓒ $x = -2, x = 2$ **Ⓓ** $x = 0, x = 3$

8. What is the solution of $|3x + 1| < 5$?

   (F) $x > 2$ or $x < \frac{4}{3}$ **(G)** $-2 < x < \frac{4}{3}$

   (H) $x > \frac{4}{3}$ or $x < 2$ **(J)** $-\frac{4}{3} < x < 2$

9. What is the solution of $|2x - 1| \geq 9$?

   (A) $x \geq 5$ or $x \leq -4$ **(B)** $-5 \leq x \leq 4$

   (C) $x \geq 4$ or $x \leq -5$ **(D)** $-4 \leq x \leq 5$

10. What is the value of $f(x) = 5|x - 7|$ when $x = -3$?

   (F) -50 **(G)** -20

   (H) 20 **(J)** 50

11. Which absolute value function has a graph that contains $(-2, -1)$, $(0, 0)$, and $(2, -1)$?

   (A) $y = 2|x|$ **(B)** $y = \frac{1}{2}|x|$

   (C) $y = -\frac{1}{2}|x|$ **(D)** $y = -2|x|$

Gridded Response

12. The amount of time t (in minutes) that you can use a car wash is given by $0.5t + 2 \leq A$ where A is the amount of money you have to spend. You have \$6.50 to spend. At most, how many minutes can you spend in the car wash?

13. What is the y-value of the only solution of the following system of linear inequalities?

$$x \leq 0$$
$$y \leq 10$$
$$y \geq -x + 10$$

14. An equation of the form $|x + b| = c$ has solutions -3 and 9. What is the value of c?

Use the following information to answer Exercises 15–17.

The solutions of the equation $|x - 4.45| = 0.3$ give the fastest and slowest 40-yard dash times (in seconds) for a football player in today's practice.

15. How many seconds did the football player's fastest run take?

16. What is the difference between the player's fastest and slowest runs, in seconds?

17. What is the mean of the player's fastest and slowest times, in seconds?

Extended Response

18. You are selling necklaces x and bracelets y at a craft fair. You need to sell at least 20 necklaces and at least 15 bracelets to pay for your entrance fee.

   a. Write and graph a system of linear inequalities representing the number of necklaces and bracelets sold that satisfy your goal.

   b. You will sell at most 50 pieces of jewelry at the fair. Write and graph a new system of linear inequalities with this new restriction. Explain the meaning of each inequality.

   c. You sell 36 necklaces and 14 bracelets at the fair. Did this meet your goal? Explain. Give three combinations of necklaces and bracelets sold that meet your goal.

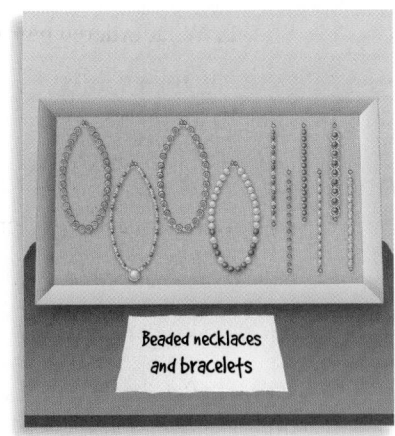

Beaded necklaces and bracelets

Quadratic Functions and Factoring

▷ How are freefall time and the altitude of a skydiver related?

APPLICATION: Skydiving

Several seconds of freefall are experienced by a skydiver before a parachute is opened. As the time since jumping from the plane increases, the height of the skydiver above the ground decreases.

Think & Discuss

1. The table gives data for a skydiver jumping from a height of 6000 feet. Draw a scatter plot of the data. Then draw a smooth curve through the points.

Time x (seconds)	Height y above the ground (feet)
0	6000
4	5744
8	4976
12	3696

2. Does the skydiver's height above the ground decrease by the same amount every 4 seconds?

3. Estimate the skydiver's height above the ground after 10 seconds.

Learn More About It

You will use a quadratic model that relates time since jumping and height above the ground in Example 4 on page 257.

PREVIEW

What's the chapter about?

• Graphing quadratic functions written in standard form, vertex form, and intercept form
• Solving quadratic equations by factoring
• Solving quadratic equations by taking square roots, completing the square, and using the quadratic formula

> **Key Words**
> • **quadratic function,** *p. 222*
> • **parabola,** *p. 222*
> • **vertex,** *p. 222*
> • **axis of symmetry,** *p. 222*
> • **trinomial,** *p. 234*
> • **quadratic equation,** *p. 235*
> • **zeros of a function,** *p. 242*
>
> • **square root,** *p. 255*
> • **imaginary unit *i*,** *p. 261*
> • **complex number,** *p. 262*
> • **imaginary number,** *p. 262*
> • **completing the square,** *p. 268*
> • **quadratic formula,** *p. 274*
> • **discriminant,** *p. 276*

PREPARE

Chapter Readiness Quiz

Take this quick quiz. If you are unsure of an answer, look back at the reference pages for help.

Vocabulary Check *(refer to p. 87)*

1. What is the *y*-intercept of $x + 2y = -10$?

   A -10 **B** -5 **C** 5 **D** 10

Skill Check *(refer to p. 9)*

2. Evaluate the expression $-x^2 + 3x - 10$ when $x = 5$.

   F -20 **G** 0 **H** 23 **J** 30

3. Evaluate the expression $5x^2 + 2x + 4$ when $x = 7$.

   A 53 **B** 67 **C** 263 **D** 347

TAKE NOTES

Preview the Chapter

When you begin a new chapter, list a few things you think you will learn. When you study each topic, write the date on the list. Then you can use the list as a table of contents for your notes.

Chapter 5
How to graph quadratic functions   12/10
How to solve quadratic equations   12/13
                                      12/14
How to use square roots
How to use complex numbers
The quadratic formula

DEVELOPING CONCEPTS *(For use with Lesson 5.1)*

Graphing $y = ax^2$

Goal

Decide how the value of a affects the graph of $y = ax^2$.

Materials

• graph paper

QUESTION

What does the graph of $y = ax^2$ look like?

EXPLORE

❶ Copy the table. Use the equation $y = x^2$ to complete the table.

x	−3	−2	−1	0	1	2	3
$y = x^2$	?	?	?	?	?	?	?

❷ Plot the points in the completed table from Step 1. Connect the points with a smooth curve. The curve is the graph of $y = x^2$. Label the curve with the equation. You will use the same coordinate plane to graph equations in Steps 4 and 6.

❸ Copy the table. Use the equation $y = -x^2$ to complete the table.

x	−3	−2	−1	0	1	2	3
$y = -x^2$	?	?	?	?	?	?	?

❹ Use the same coordinate plane that you used in Step 2. Plot the points in the completed table from Step 3. Connect the points with a smooth curve. Label the curve with the equation $y = -x^2$.

❺ Copy the table. Use the equation $y = 2x^2$ to complete the table.

x	−3	−2	−1	0	1	2	3
$y = 2x^2$	?	?	?	?	?	?	?

❻ Use the same coordinate plane that you used in Step 4. Plot the points in the completed table from Step 5. Connect the points with a smooth curve. Label the curve with the equation $y = 2x^2$.

THINK ABOUT IT

1. Each equation below has the form $y = ax^2$. Identify the value of a in each equation.

   a. $y = x^2$ **b.** $y = -x^2$ **c.** $y = 2x^2$

2. Describe the shape of the graph of $y = x^2$. Does the graph open up or open down? Identify its lowest point or highest point.

3. **Reasoning** Compare the graph of $y = x^2$ to the graph of $y = -x^2$. Describe the similarities and differences. How does the value of a affect the graphs?

4. **Reasoning** Compare the graph of $y = x^2$ to the graph of $y = 2x^2$. Describe the similarities and differences. How does the value of a affect the graphs?

5.1 Graphing Quadratic Functions in Standard Form

Key Words
- quadratic function
- parabola
- vertex
- axis of symmetry
- monomial
- binomial

GOAL Graph quadratic functions in the form $y = ax^2 + bx + c$.

A **quadratic function** is a function that can be written in the standard form $y = ax^2 + bx + c$ where $a \neq 0$. The graph of a quadratic function is a **parabola**. The graph of $y = x^2$ is shown below.

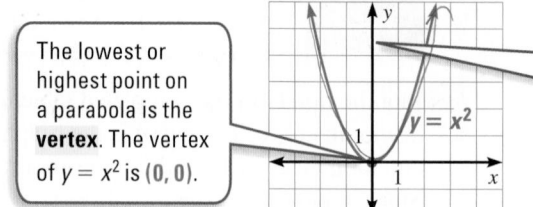

The lowest or highest point on a parabola is the **vertex**. The vertex of $y = x^2$ is $(0, 0)$.

The **axis of symmetry** divides the parabola into mirror images and passes through the vertex. The axis of symmetry of $y = x^2$ is $x = 0$.

Prerequisite Skills

Find the value of y when $x = -1, 0,$ and 2.

1. $y = x^2 + 3x - 2$
2. $y = 2x^2 + 2x - 24$
3. $y = -x^2 + 2x + 2$

For any function $y = ax^2 + bx + c$ where $a \neq 0$ and $b = 0$, the vertex of its graph lies on the y-axis, and the axis of symmetry is the y-axis.

EXAMPLE 1 Graph a Quadratic Function Using a Table

Graph $y = \frac{1}{2}x^2 - 1$.

Solution

The function $y = \frac{1}{2}x^2 - 1$ is in standard form $y = ax^2 + c$. Because $b = 0$, you know that the axis of symmetry is $x = 0$.

❶ **Make** a table of values for $y = \frac{1}{2}x^2 - 1$. Choose values of x on both sides of the axis of symmetry $x = 0$.

x	−4	−2	0	2	4
y	7	1	−1	1	7

❷ **Plot** the points from the table.

❸ **Draw** a smooth curve through the points.

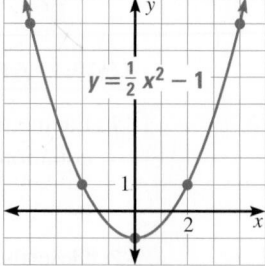

$y = \frac{1}{2}x^2 - 1$

Checkpoint ✓ Graph a Quadratic Function Using a Table

Graph the function using a table of values.

1. $y = -3x^2$

2. $y = -x^2 - 2$

3. $y = \frac{1}{4}x^2 + 3$

Graphing a Parabola You can use the steps below to graph any quadratic function of the form $y = ax^2 + bx + c$ where $a \neq 0$. When $a > 0$, the parabola opens up. When $a < 0$, the parabola opens down.

Standard Form of a Quadratic Function

STEPS FOR GRAPHING $y = ax^2 + bx + c$

STEP ❶ *Draw* the axis of symmetry. It is the line $x = -\dfrac{b}{2a}$.

STEP ❷ *Find* and plot the vertex. The x-coordinate of the vertex is $-\dfrac{b}{2a}$. Substitute this value for x in the function and evaluate to find the y-coordinate of the vertex.

STEP ❸ *Plot* two points on one side of the axis of symmetry. Use symmetry to plot two more points on the opposite side.

STEP ❹ *Draw* a parabola through the points.

EXAMPLE 2 Graph a Quadratic Function in Standard Form

Graph $y = x^2 - 6x + 5$.

Solution

The function is in standard form $y = ax^2 + bx + c$ where $a = 1$, $b = -6$, and $c = 5$. Because $a > 0$, the parabola opens up.

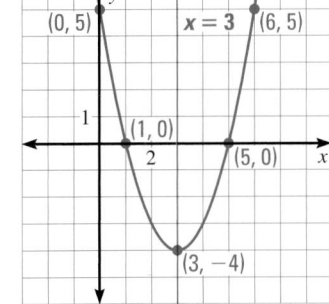

❶ *Draw* the axis of symmetry.

$$x = -\frac{b}{2a} = -\frac{-6}{2(1)} = 3$$

❷ *Find* and plot the vertex. The x-coordinate of the vertex is 3. Find the y-coordinate.

$$y = x^2 - 6x + 5$$
$$= (3)^2 - 6(3) + 5 = -4$$

The vertex is $(3, -4)$.

❸ *Plot* two points to the left of the axis of symmetry. Evaluate the function for two x-values that are less than 3, such as 0 and 1.

$$y = x^2 - 6x + 5 \qquad\qquad y = x^2 - 6x + 5$$
$$= (0)^2 - 6(0) + 5 = 5 \qquad = (1)^2 - 6(1) + 5 = 0$$

Plot the points $(0, 5)$ and $(1, 0)$. Plot their mirror images by counting the distance to the axis of symmetry then counting the same distance beyond the axis of symmetry.

❹ *Draw* a parabola through the points.

STUDENT HELP

AVOID ERRORS
Be sure to include the negative sign before the fraction when calculating the axis of symmetry.

 **Graph a Quadratic Function in Standard Form**

Graph the function. Label the vertex and the axis of symmetry.

4. $y = x^2 + 6x - 2$ **5.** $y = -x^2 - 2x + 1$ **6.** $y = 2x^2 + x - 1$

Multiplying Binomials A **monomial** is a number, a variable, or the product of a number and one or more variables with whole number exponents. A **binomial** is the sum of two monomials.

$$\text{Monomials:} \quad x \qquad y^3 \qquad 3 \qquad -5x \qquad 9xy$$

$$\text{Binomials:} \quad x - 4 \qquad 2 + x^2 \qquad x - 3y \qquad n - 1$$

You can multiply two binomials using the **FOIL** method. The letters of the word FOIL remind you to multiply the **F**irst terms, the **O**uter terms, the **I**nner terms, and the **L**ast terms. For example:

$$\text{F} \quad \text{O} \quad \text{I} \quad \text{L}$$
$$(x + 3)(x + 5) = x^2 + 5x + 3x + 15 = x^2 + 8x + 15$$

STUDENT HELP

SOLVING NOTE
You can check your answer by substituting easy values for x in the original expression and in your result. The values of the expressions should be the same.

EXAMPLE **3** **Multiply Binomials**

Find the product $(2x + 3)(x - 7)$.

Solution

$$(2x + 3)(x - 7) = 2x(x) + 2x(-7) + 3x + 3(-7) \qquad \text{Write products of terms.}$$
$$= 2x^2 - 14x + 3x - 21 \qquad \text{Multiply.}$$
$$= 2x^2 - 11x - 21 \qquad \text{Combine like terms.}$$

Checkpoint ✔ **Multiply Binomials**

Find the product.

7. $(x - 4)(x + 6)$ **8.** $(3x + 1)(x - 1)$ **9.** $(2x - 5)(x - 2)$

EXAMPLE **4** **Write a Quadratic Function in Standard Form**

Write the function $y = 2(x - 2)^2 + 5$ in standard form.

Solution

$$y = 2(x - 2)^2 + 5 \qquad \text{Write original function.}$$
$$= 2(x - 2)(x - 2) + 5 \qquad \text{Rewrite } (x - 2)^2 \text{ as } (x - 2)(x - 2).$$
$$= 2(x^2 - 2x - 2x + 4) + 5 \qquad \text{Multiply using FOIL.}$$
$$= 2(x^2 - 4x + 4) + 5 \qquad \text{Combine like terms.}$$
$$= 2x^2 - 8x + 8 + 5 \qquad \text{Use the distributive property.}$$
$$= 2x^2 - 8x + 13 \qquad \text{Combine like terms.}$$

Checkpoint ✔ **Write a Quadratic Function in Standard Form**

Write the function in standard form.

10. $y = 2(x + 1)(x - 3)$ **11.** $y = 3(x - 4)(x - 6)$ **12.** $y = -(x - 1)^2 - 3$

5.1 Exercises

Guided Practice

Vocabulary Check   **Copy and complete the statement.**

   1. The graph of a quadratic function is called a(n) __?__.

   2. The __?__ divides the graph of a quadratic function into mirror images.

Skill Check   **Graph the function. Label the vertex and the axis of symmetry.**

   3. $y = -x^2 - 1$ **4.** $y = x^2 + 3$ **5.** $y = 2x^2 + 4$

   6. $y = x^2 + 5x - 1$ **7.** $y = 2x^2 - 8x + 4$ **8.** $y = x^2 + 4x + 3$

   9. Error Analysis Describe and correct the error in finding the product.

$$(x - 4)(x - 3)$$
$$x^2 - 3x - 4x - 7$$
$$x^2 - 7x - 7$$

Write the function in standard form.

   10. $y = (x + 4)(x + 1)$ **11.** $y = -3(x - 4)(x + 2)$ **12.** $y = 2(x + 1)^2 - 6$

   13. $y = -(x - 5)^2 + 3$ **14.** $y = -\frac{1}{3}(x + 3)^2 - 1$ **15.** $y = \frac{3}{4}(x + 4)(x - 2)$

Practice and Applications

STUDENT HELP

HOMEWORK HELP
Example 1: Exs. 16–19
Example 2: Exs. 20–44, 67–69
Example 3: Exs. 45–56
Example 4: Exs. 57–65

Using a Table   **Copy and complete the table of values for the function.**

   16. $y = -2x^2$

x	−2	−1	0	1	2
y	?	?	?	?	?

   17. $y = 4x^2 + 1$

x	−2	−1	0	1	2
y	?	?	?	?	?

   18. $y = \frac{1}{3}x^2$

x	−6	−3	0	3	6
y	?	?	?	?	?

   19. $y = \frac{1}{2}x^2 + 2$

x	−4	−2	0	2	4
y	?	?	?	?	?

Identifying Coefficients   **Identify the values of _a_, _b_, and _c_ for the function in standard form.**

   20. $y = 5x^2 + x - 1$ **21.** $y = x^2 + 3x$ **22.** $y = 2x^2 - 4$

Finding the Vertex   **Find the vertex of the graph of the function.**

   23. $y = -x^2$ **24.** $y = -2x^2 + 1$ **25.** $y = x^2 + 2x + 1$

   26. $y = 3x^2 - 4x - 2$ **27.** $y = -\frac{1}{2}x^2 - 4x - 1$ **28.** $y = \frac{1}{4}x^2 - 1$

29. Error Analysis Describe and correct the error in finding the axis of symmetry of the graph of $y = 4x^2 + 16x + 3$.

$$y = 4x^2 + 16x + 3$$

$$x = \frac{b}{2a} = \frac{16}{2(4)} = \frac{16}{8} = 2 \quad \times$$

Matching Graphs Match the function with its graph.

30. $y = -\frac{1}{2}x^2 + x - 1$ **31.** $y = 3x^2 + 9x + 4$ **32.** $y = x^2 + 2x - 3$

A.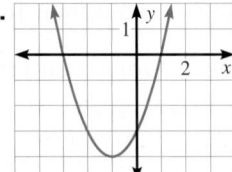

B.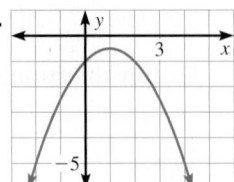

C.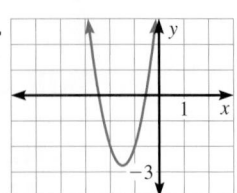

Graphing with Standard Form Graph the function. Label the vertex and the axis of symmetry.

33. $y = x^2 + 2x - 2$ **34.** $y = -x^2 - 8x - 13$ **35.** $y = 2x^2 - 12x + 14$

36. $y = -x^2 - 12x + 31$ **37.** $y = \frac{1}{2}x^2 + 3x - 5$ **38.** $y = 3x^2 - 12x - 5$

39. $y = -\frac{1}{2}x^2 - 4x + 1$ **40.** $y = -7x^2 - 14x + 2$ **41.** $y = 2x^2 - 10x - 3$

42. $y = \frac{1}{2}x^2 - 2x + 3$ **43.** $y = -\frac{1}{3}x^2 - 2x - 2$ **44.** $y = 3x^2 - 6x + 4$

Multiplying Binomials Find the product.

45. $(x + 1)(x + 2)$ **46.** $(x + 3)(x + 2)$ **47.** $(n - 1)(n - 5)$

48. $(x - 5)(x + 5)$ **49.** $(a - 4)(a - 6)$ **50.** $(2x - 1)(3x + 1)$

51. $(2x - 3)(x - 4)$ **52.** $(x + 6)(3x - 2)$ **53.** $(5y + 1)(2y - 3)$

54. $(3h - 2)(h - 5)$ **55.** $(x + 7)(4x + 3)$ **56.** $(8x + 5)(5x - 1)$

Writing in Standard Form Write the function in standard form.

57. $y = (x + 3)(x - 2)$ **58.** $y = -(x + 3)(x + 7)$ **59.** $y = 2(x - 5)(x + 2)$

60. $y = -3(x - 1)(x - 6)$ **61.** $y = -(x + 2)^2 + 5$ **62.** $y = (2x + 1)(x - 4)$

63. $y = 2(x - 4)^2 - 1$ **64.** $y = \frac{1}{4}(x + 2)(x - 4)$ **65.** $y = \frac{2}{3}(x - 3)^2 + 6$

66. Critical Thinking Without graphing the function, decide if the vertex of the graph of $y = 0.2304x^2 + 5.123x - 1.236$ is its *highest point* or its *lowest point*. Explain how you know.

Biology Link In Exercises 67 and 68, use the following information.

A flea can jump very long distances. The path of the jump of a flea can be modeled by the graph of the function $y = -\frac{1}{6}x(x - 13)$ where x and y are measured in inches.

67. Find the vertex and the axis of symmetry of the graph of the function.

68. Graph the function. Label the vertex and the axis of symmetry.

69. Juggling You throw a ball into the air with your right hand and catch it in your left hand. The path of the ball can be modeled by the graph of the function $y = -24x^2 + 24x + 4$, for values of x from 0 to 1, where x and y are measured in feet. Graph the function. Label the vertex.

70. Challenge A function has the form $y = ax^2 + bx + c$ where $a = 0$. What does the graph of the function look like? Explain your reasoning.

Standardized Test Practice

71. Multiple Choice What is the vertex of the graph of the function $y = -2x^2 - 16x - 29$?

(A) $(-8, -29)$ (B) $(-4, -16)$

(C) $(-4, 3)$ (D) $(4, 3)$

72. Multiple Choice What is the axis of symmetry of the graph of the function $y = x^2 - 12x + 32$?

(F) $x = -12$ (G) $x = -6$ (H) $x = 6$ (J) $x = 32$

73. Multiple Choice What is the product $(x - 8)(x - 9)$?

(A) $x^2 + 17x - 72$ (B) $x^2 - 17x + 72$

(C) $x^2 - 17x - 72$ (D) $x^2 + 17x + 72$

74. Multiple Choice What is the product $(x - 5)(x + 3)$?

(F) $x^2 + 8x - 15$ (G) $x^2 - 8x - 15$

(H) $x^2 - 2x + 15$ (J) $x^2 - 2x - 15$

Mixed Review

Solving Equations Solve the equation. *(Lesson 1.4)*

75. $-x + 4 = 7$ **76.** $3x + 5 = 8$ **77.** $5x + 2 = 1$

78. $-2x + 7 = -3$ **79.** $4 - 2y = 7$ **80.** $7 - 4x = 8$

Solving Systems Solve the system using the linear combination method. *(Lesson 3.3)*

81. $4x + 3y = 9$
$2x - y = -3$

82. $4x - 6y = 10$
$-2x + 5y = -3$

83. $3x + 5y = 10$
$-2x + 3y = -13$

84. $2x - 3y = 0$
$5x + 2y = -38$

85. $2x + 5y = 11$
$3x - 2y = -31$

86. $5x + 7y = 1$
$2x - 5y = 16$

Geometry Skills

Quadrilaterals The sum of the measure of the angles in a quadrilateral is 360°. Find the value of x.

87.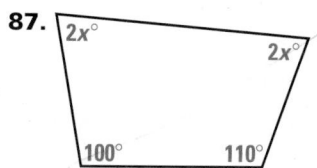

88.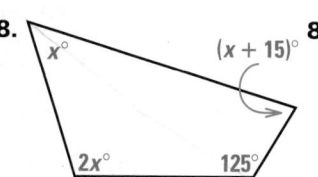

89.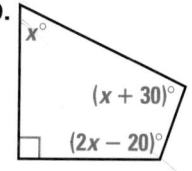

5.2 Graphing Quadratic Functions in Vertex or Intercept Form

Key Words

- vertex form
- intercept form
- minimum value
- maximum value

Prerequisite Skills

Find the vertex of the graph of the function.

1. $y = x^2 - 10x + 5$

2. $y = x^2 + 2x - 1$

3. $y = 3x^2 + 12x + 1$

GOAL Graph quadratic functions in different forms.

How far does a football travel?

You will use a quadratic function in Exercises 71–73 to model the path of a football and to find out how far it travels.

A quadratic function can be written in **vertex form**, $y = a(x - h)^2 + k$. When $a > 0$, the parabola opens up. When $a < 0$, the parabola opens down.

Vertex Form of a Quadratic Function

STEPS FOR GRAPHING $y = a(x - h)^2 + k$

STEP ❶ *Draw* the axis of symmetry. It is the line $x = h$.

STEP ❷ *Plot* the vertex, (h, k).

STEP ❸ *Plot* two points on one side of the axis of symmetry. Use symmetry to plot two more points on the opposite side of the axis of symmetry.

STEP ❹ *Draw* a parabola through the points.

EXAMPLE 1 Graph a Quadratic Function in Vertex Form

Graph $y = -2(x - 2)^2 + 1$.

Solution

The function is in vertex form $y = a(x - h)^2 + k$ where $a = -2$, $h = 2$, and $k = 1$. Because $a < 0$, the parabola opens down.

❶ *Draw* the axis of symmetry, $x = h = 2$.

❷ *Plot* the vertex, $(h, k) = (2, 1)$.

❸ *Plot* points. The x-values 3 and 4 are to the right of the axis of symmetry.

$$y = -2(3 - 2)^2 + 1 = -1$$

One point on the parabola is $(3, -1)$.

$$y = -2(4 - 2)^2 + 1 = -7$$

Another point on the parabola is $(4, -7)$.

Plot the points $(3, -1)$ and $(4, -7)$. Then plot their mirror images across the axis of symmetry.

❹ *Draw* a parabola through the points.

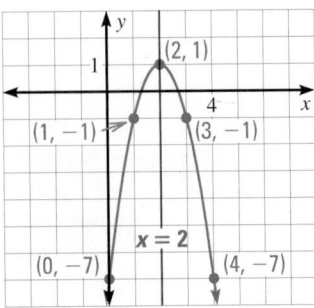

Graphing with Intercept Form If the graph of a quadratic function has at least one x-intercept, the function can be written in **intercept form**, $y = a(x - p)(x - q)$. When $a > 0$, the parabola opens up. When $a < 0$, the parabola opens down. The graph will contain $(p, 0)$ and $(q, 0)$.

Intercept Form of a Quadratic Function

STEPS FOR GRAPHING $y = a(x - p)(x - q)$

STEP ❶ *Draw* the axis of symmetry. It is the line $x = \dfrac{p + q}{2}$.

STEP ❷ *Find* and plot the vertex. The x-coordinate of the vertex is $\dfrac{p + q}{2}$. Substitute the x-coordinate for x in the function to find the y-coordinate of the vertex.

STEP ❸ *Plot* the points where the x-intercepts, p and q, occur.

STEP ❹ *Draw* a parabola through the points.

EXAMPLE 2 **Graph a Quadratic Function in Intercept Form**

Graph $y = (x + 1)(x - 3)$.

Solution

The function is in intercept form $y = a(x - p)(x - q)$ where $a = 1$, $p = -1$, and $q = 3$. Because $a > 0$, the parabola opens up.

❶ *Draw* the axis of symmetry.
The axis of symmetry is:
$$x = \frac{p + q}{2} = \frac{-1 + 3}{2} = 1$$

❷ *Find* and plot the vertex.
The x-coordinate of the vertex is $x = 1$.
Calculate the y-coordinate of the vertex.
$$y = (x + 1)(x - 3)$$
$$= (1 + 1)(1 - 3) = -4$$
Plot the vertex $(1, -4)$.

❸ *Plot* the points where the x-intercepts occur.
The x-intercepts are $p = -1$ and $q = 3$.
Plot the points $(-1, 0)$ and $(3, 0)$.

❹ *Draw* a parabola through the points.

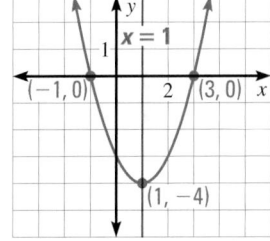

Checkpoint ✔ *Graph a Quadratic Function*

Graph the function. Label the vertex and the axis of symmetry.

1. $y = (x - 3)^2 - 1$　　　**2.** $y = -(x - 2)^2 + 3$　　　**3.** $y = 2(x + 1)^2 + 4$

Graph the function. Label the vertex and the x-intercepts.

4. $y = (x - 3)(x - 7)$　　　**5.** $y = -(x - 2)(x - 5)$　　　**6.** $y = 2(x + 1)(x - 3)$

Minimum and Maximum Values For the standard form, vertex form, and intercept form of a quadratic function, a tells you whether the parabola opens up or down. When $a > 0$, the y-coordinate of the vertex is the **minimum value** of the function. When $a < 0$, the y-coordinate of the vertex is the **maximum value** of the function.

EXAMPLE 3 Find the Minimum or Maximum Value

Tell whether the function $y = -4(x + 6)(x - 4)$ has a minimum value or a maximum value. Then find the minimum or maximum value.

Solution

The function is in intercept form $y = a(x - p)(x - q)$ where $a = -4$, $p = -6$, and $q = 4$. Because $a < 0$, it has a maximum value. Find the y-coordinate of the vertex.

$$x = \frac{p + q}{2} = \frac{-6 + 4}{2} = -1$$

$$y = -4(x + 6)(x - 4) = -4(-1 + 6)(-1 - 4) = 100$$

ANSWER ▶ The maximum value of the function is 100.

EXAMPLE 4 Using a Quadratic Function

Civil Engineering The Golden Gate Bridge in San Francisco, CA, has two towers. The top of each tower is 500 feet above the road. The towers are connected by suspension cables. Each cable forms a parabola with the equation $y = \frac{1}{8690}(x - 2100)^2 + 8$ where x and y are measured in feet.

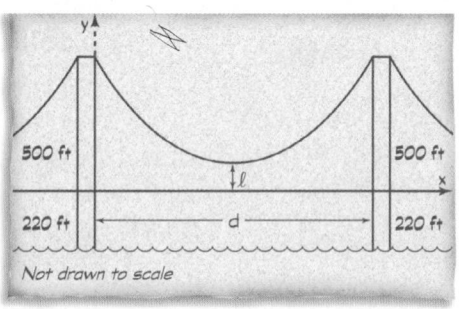

Not drawn to scale

a. Find the height ℓ of the cable above the road, when the cable is at the lowest point. The road is represented by $y = 0$.

b. What is the distance d between the towers?

Solution

The function is in vertex form where $a = \frac{1}{8690}$, $h = 2100$, and $k = 8$.

a. The vertex is $(h, k) = (2100, 8)$. The height of the cable at its lowest point is the y-coordinate of the vertex. So, the cable is 8 feet above the road.

b. The vertex is 2100 feet from the left tower. The axis of symmetry passes through the vertex. So, the vertex is also 2100 feet from the right tower. The distance between the towers is $2100 + 2100 = 4200$ feet.

Checkpoint ✓ **Find the Minimum or Maximum Value**

Tell whether the function has a minimum or maximum value. Then find the minimum or maximum value.

7. $y = \frac{1}{2}(x + 8)^2 - 12$ **8.** $y = 3(x - 4)(x - 7)$ **9.** $y = x(x + 4)$

Guided Practice

Vocabulary Check

1. Tell whether the statement is *true* or *false*: A quadratic function in vertex form where $a < 0$ has a minimum value.

2. Is $y = 2(x - 3)^2 + 1$ in *standard form*, *vertex form*, or *intercept form*?

3. Is $y = -(x + 3)(x - 5)$ in *standard form*, *vertex form*, or *intercept form*?

Skill Check

Graph the function. Label the vertex and the axis of symmetry.

4. $y = -(x - 1)^2 + 3$ **5.** $y = \frac{1}{2}(x + 4)^2 - 5$ **6.** $y = 4(x - 3)^2 + 5$

Graph the function. Label the vertex and the *x*-intercepts.

7. $y = \frac{2}{3}(x - 1)(x - 3)$ **8.** $y = -6(x + 1)(x + 3)$ **9.** $y = 7(x + 1)(x - 1)$

Tell whether the function has a minimum value or a maximum value. Then find the minimum or maximum value.

10. $y = (x - 2)(x - 3)$ **11.** $y = -(x - 2)^2 - 1$ **12.** $y = -3x^2 + x - 1$

Practice and Applications

STUDENT HELP

HOMEWORK HELP
Example 1: Exs. 13–27,
   34–43, 54
Example 2: Exs. 28–33,
   44–53, 55
Example 3: Exs. 56–64
Example 4: Exs. 65–73

Describing Functions Tell whether the quadratic function is in *standard form*, *vertex form*, or *intercept form*. Identify the axis of symmetry.

13. $y = -2(x + 4)(x - 6)$ **14.** $y = x^2 - 2x - 35$ **15.** $y = 3(x - 1)^2 + 3$

16. $y = -(x + 3)^2 - 1$ **17.** $y = 2(x + 4)(x + 2)$ **18.** $y = \frac{1}{2}x^2 + 2x - 2$

19. $y = -2x^2 + 16x - 24$ **20.** $y = -(x - 3)(x + 2)$ **21.** $y = \frac{2}{3}(x - 4)^2 + 7$

Identifying the Vertex Identify the vertex of the graph of the function.

22. $y = 3(x - 7)^2 - 1$ **23.** $y = 3(x + 2)^2 - 5$ **24.** $y = (x - 3)^2$

25. $y = -4(x - 2)^2 + 4$ **26.** $y = 2(x + 1)^2 - 3$ **27.** $y = (x + 4)^2$

Identifying Intercepts Identify the *x*-intercepts of the graph of the function.

28. $y = 3(x + 1)(x - 3)$ **29.** $y = -(x + 6)(x - 4)$ **30.** $y = (x + 3)(x - 3)$

Matching Graphs Match the function with its graph.

31. $y = (x - 4)(x + 1)$ **32.** $y = -(x + 3)^2 - 1$ **33.** $y = 2x(x + 1)$

A. 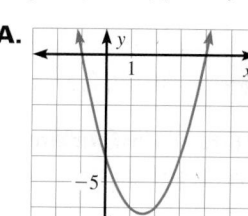   **B.** 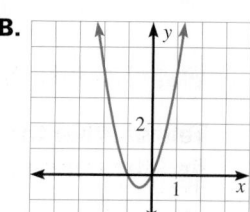   **C.**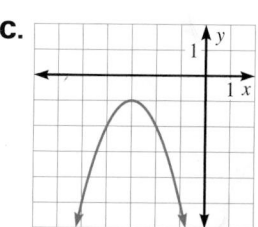

34. Error Analysis Describe and correct the error in finding the vertex of the graph of the function $y = -(x + 3)^2 + 5$.

$y = -(x + 3)^2 + 5$
vertex: $(3, 5)$

Graphing with Vertex Form Graph the function. Label the vertex and the axis of symmetry.

35. $y = (x - 3)^2 + 2$ **36.** $y = -2(x + 2)^2 + 4$ **37.** $y = -(x - 1)^2 - 3$

38. $y = 4(x + 3)^2 - 1$ **39.** $y = -\frac{1}{5}(x - 5)^2 - 2$ **40.** $y = \frac{3}{4}(x + 4)^2 + 2$

41. $y = -2(x + 3)^2 - 4$ **42.** $y = \frac{5}{4}(x - 3)^2$ **43.** $y = (x - 2)^2$

Graphing with Intercept Form Graph the function. Label the vertex and the *x*-intercepts.

44. $y = (x - 3)(x - 5)$ **45.** $y = -(x + 2)(x - 2)$ **46.** $y = (x + 1)(x + 2)$

47. $y = -2(x - 1)(x - 2)$ **48.** $y = \frac{1}{2}(x + 4)(x - 2)$ **49.** $y = \frac{1}{3}(x - 3)(x - 6)$

50. $y = 3(x + 3)(x - 1)$ **51.** $y = 4(x - 7)(x + 2)$ **52.** $y = x(x - 5)$

53. Error Analysis Describe and correct the error in finding the *x*-intercepts of the function $y = -3x(x - 2)$.

$y = -3x(x - 2)$
x-intercepts: $-3, 2$

Graphing Functions Find the vertex of the graph of the function. Use a graphing calculator to graph the function.

54. $y = -0.25(x - 5.2)^2 + 8.5$ **55.** $y = \frac{5}{2}\left(x - \frac{4}{3}\right)\left(x - \frac{2}{5}\right)$

Minimum and Maximum Values Tell whether the function has a *minimum value* or a *maximum value*. Then find the minimum or maximum value.

56. $y = -4(x + 6)^2 - 12$ **57.** $y = (x - 1)^2 + 2$ **58.** $y = 3(x - 3)^2 - 4$

59. $y = -(x + 3)(x + 5)$ **60.** $y = -5(x + 9)(x - 4)$ **61.** $y = 4(x + 1)(x - 1)$

62. $y = 2(x - 3)(x - 6)$ **63.** $y = 9x^2 + 7$ **64.** $y = 2x^2 + 8x + 7$

Biology Link In Exercises 65–67, use the following information.

The jump of a red kangaroo can be modeled by the graph of the function

$$y = -0.03(x - 14)^2 + 6$$

where x is the horizontal distance (in feet) and y is the height (in feet).

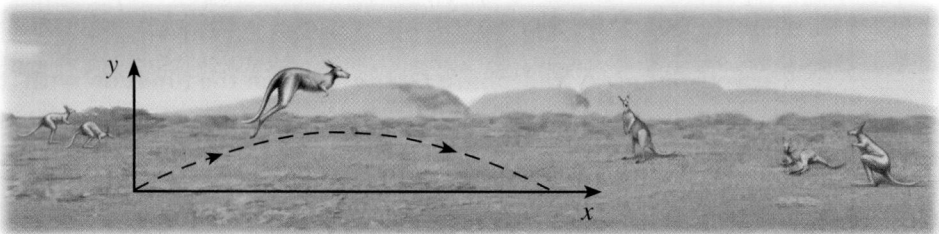

65. Find the vertex of the graph of the function.

66. What is the horizontal distance that the kangaroo travels?

67. What is the maximum height of the kangaroo's jump?

Biology Link In Exercises 68–70, use the following information.

The hop of a woodland jumping mouse can be modeled by the graph of the function $y = -\frac{2}{9}x(x - 6)$ where x and y are measured in feet.

68. Is the function in *standard form*, *vertex form*, or *intercept form*?

69. What is the horizontal distance of the hop?

70. What is the maximum height of the hop?

Football In Exercises 71–73, use the following information.

You kick a football. The path the football travels can be modeled by the graph of the function $y = -0.026x(x - 46)$ where x is the horizontal distance (in feet) and y is the height of the football (in feet).

71. Is the function in *standard form*, *vertex form*, or *intercept form*?

72. What is the horizontal distance that the football travels?

73. What is the maximum height of the football?

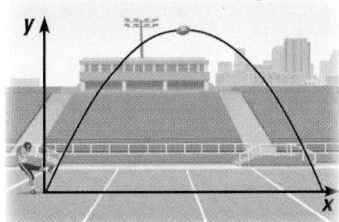

74. Multiple Choice What is the vertex of the graph of $y = 2(x + 1)^2 - 3$?

   Ⓐ $(-1, -3)$ Ⓑ $(-1, 3)$ Ⓒ $(1, -3)$ Ⓓ $(1, 3)$

75. Multiple Choice What is the vertex of the graph of $y = -(x - 6)(x + 4)$?

   Ⓕ $(-5, -11)$ Ⓖ $(-1, 21)$ Ⓗ $(1, 25)$ Ⓙ $(5, 9)$

76. Multiple Choice What is the axis of symmetry of the graph of $y = 4(x - 1)^2 + 9$?

   Ⓐ $x = -9$ Ⓑ $x = -1$ Ⓒ $x = 1$ Ⓓ $x = 9$

77. Multiple Choice What is the axis of symmetry of the graph of $y = (x - 4)(x + 8)$?

   Ⓕ $x = -2$ Ⓖ $x = 4$ Ⓗ $x = -8$ Ⓙ $x = -4$

Mixed Review

Solving Equations Solve the equation. *(Lesson 1.4)*

78. $x - 3 = 9$ **79.** $6 - 3y = 4$ **80.** $4x + 5 = 9$

81. $-5x + 11 = -4$ **82.** $4x + 1 = 2$ **83.** $11 - 6x = 8$

Multiplying Binomials Find the product. *(Lesson 5.1)*

84. $(x + 4)(x - 11)$ **85.** $(x - 7)(x + 9)$ **86.** $(x + 6)(x + 1)$

87. $(2x + 1)(3x - 2)$ **88.** $(5x - 2)(4x + 1)$ **89.** $(x + 6)(3x + 5)$

90. $(7x - 1)(6x + 3)$ **91.** $(4x - 1)(-2x + 1)$ **92.** $(-x + 7)(4x + 3)$

Geometry Skills

Triangles **The sum of the measures of the angles in a triangle is 180°. Find the value of x.**

93.
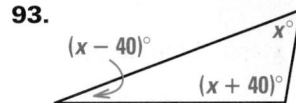

94.
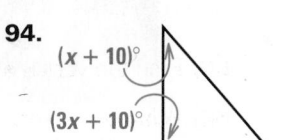

95.
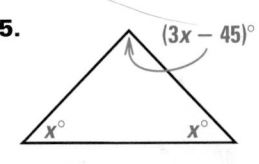

Factoring $x^2 + bx + c$

Key Words
- trinomial
- quadratic equation

GOAL Factor trinomials of the form $x^2 + bx + c$.

How many feet should a patio be extended?

The owner of a café wants to increase the area of the outdoor patio. You can use factoring in Exercise 54 to find the width of the additional patio space.

Prerequisite Skills

Write all the factors of the number.

1. 15
2. 24
3. 28
4. 35

You know how to write $(x + 3)(x + 5)$ as $x^2 + 8x + 15$. The expressions $x + 3$ and $x + 5$ are binomials. A **trinomial** is the sum of three monomials. So $x^2 + 8x + 15$ is a trinomial.

You can use factoring to write a trinomial as the product of two binomial factors. To write $x^2 + bx + c$ as the product $(x + m)(x + n)$, notice the pattern below.

$$(x + m)(x + n) = x^2 + nx + mx + mn = x^2 + (m + n)x + mn$$

So, to factor $x^2 + bx + c$, you must find integers m and n such that $m + n = b$ and $mn = c$.

EXAMPLE 1 Factor $x^2 + bx + c$ when c is Positive

Factor the expression.

    a. $x^2 + 5x + 6$ **b.** $y^2 - 6y + 8$

Solution

STUDENT HELP

AVOID ERRORS
Remember that the product of two negative numbers is positive, so be sure to check the negative factors of b.

a. You want $x^2 + 5x + 6 = (x + m)(x + n)$ where $mn = 6$ and $m + n = 5$. Because mn is positive, m and n must have the same sign. Since $mn = 6$, find factors of 6 that have a sum of 5.

Factors of 6: m, n	1, 6	−1, −6	2, 3 ✓	−2, −3
Sum of factors: $m + n$	7	−7	5	−5

ANSWER ▶ $x^2 + 5x + 6 = (x + 2)(x + 3)$. Check your answer by multiplying.

CHECK $(x + 2)(x + 3) = x^2 + 2x + 3x + 6 = x^2 + 5x + 6$ ✓

b. You want $y^2 - 6y + 8 = (y + m)(y + n)$ where $mn = 8$ and $m + n = -6$. Because mn is positive, m and n must have the same sign.

Factors of 8: m, n	1, 8	−1, −8	2, 4	−2, −4 ✓
Sum of factors: $m + n$	9	−9	6	−6

ANSWER ▶ $y^2 - 6y + 8 = (y - 2)(y - 4)$. Check your answer by multiplying.

EXAMPLE **2** **Factor $x^2 + bx + c$ when c is Negative**

Factor the expression.

a. $x^2 + 8x - 9$

b. $z^2 - 14z - 15$

Solution

a. You want $x^2 + 8x - 9 = (x + m)(x + n)$ where $mn = -9$ and $m + n = 8$. Because mn is negative, m and n must have different signs.

Factors of −9: *m*, *n*	1, −9	−1, 9 ✓	3, −3
Sum of factors: *m* + *n*	−8	8	0

ANSWER ▶ $x^2 + 8x - 9 = (x - 1)(x + 9)$.

CHECK Check your answer by multiplying.

$(x - 1)(x + 9) = x^2 + 9x - x - 9$ Multiply using FOIL.

$\qquad\qquad\qquad = x^2 + 8x - 9$ Combine like terms.

When you multiply the binomial factors, you obtain the original expression, so the answer is correct. ✓

b. You want $z^2 - 14z - 15 = (z + m)(z + n)$ where $mn = -15$ and $m + n = -14$. Because mn is negative, m and n must have different signs.

Factors of −15: *m*, *n*	1, −15 ✓	−1, 15	3, −5	−3, 5
Sum of factors: *m* + *n*	−14	14	−2	2

ANSWER ▶ $z^2 - 14z - 15 = (z + 1)(z - 15)$. Check your answer by multiplying.

 **Checkpoint** ✓ **Factor $x^2 + bx + c$**

Factor the expression.

1. $x^2 + 6x + 5$ **2.** $b^2 + 7b + 12$ **3.** $s^2 - 5s + 4$

4. $y^2 + 11y - 12$ **5.** $x^2 + x - 6$ **6.** $x^2 - 15x - 16$

Solving a Quadratic Equation by Factoring You can use factoring to solve certain *quadratic equations*. A **quadratic equation** in one variable can be written in the form $ax^2 + bx + c = 0$ where $a \neq 0$. This is called the standard form of the equation. If you can factor the left side of $ax^2 + bx + c = 0$, then you can solve the equation using the *zero product property*.

Zero Product Property

WORDS	When the product of two expressions is zero, then at least one of the expressions must equal zero.
ALGEBRA	Let A and B be expressions. If $AB = 0$, then $A = 0$ or $B = 0$.
EXAMPLE	If $(x + 5)(x + 2) = 0$, then $x + 5 = 0$ or $x + 2 = 0$.

EXAMPLE 3 Solve a Quadratic Equation by Factoring

Solve the equation $x^2 + 2x = 15$.

Solution

$x^2 + 2x = 15$	Write original equation.
$x^2 + 2x - 15 = 0$	Write in standard form.
$(x - 3)(x + 5) = 0$	Factor.
$x - 3 = 0$ or $x + 5 = 0$	Use the zero product property.
$x = 3$ $x = -5$	Solve for x.

ANSWER ▸ The solutions are 3 and -5.

EXAMPLE 4 Use a Quadratic Equation as a Model

Community Service A group of students from your school volunteers to build a neighborhood playground. The playground will have a mulch border along two sides. The mulch border will have the same width on both sides. The playground is a rectangle, as shown. The length of the playground is 20 yards. The width of the playground is 10 yards. There is enough mulch to cover 64 square yards for the border. How wide should the border be?

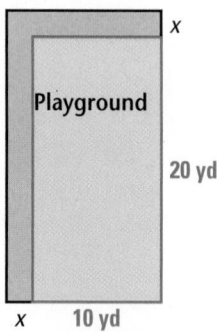

Solution

Use the formula for the area of a rectangle, Area = length • width. The area of the playground is 20 • 10 = 200 square yards. The area of the border will be 64 square yards. So, the total area of the border and the playground will be 264 square yards.

$A = \ell \cdot w$	Formula for area of a rectangle
$264 = (x + 20)(x + 10)$	Substitute $x + 20$ for ℓ and $x + 10$ for w.
$264 = x^2 + 10x + 20x + 200$	Multiply using FOIL.
$264 = x^2 + 30x + 200$	Combine like terms.
$0 = x^2 + 30x - 64$	Write in standard form.
$0 = (x + 32)(x - 2)$	Factor.
$x + 32 = 0$ or $x - 2 = 0$	Use the zero product property.
$x = -32$ $x = 2$	Solve for x.

Reject -32 as a solution, because a negative width does not make sense.

ANSWER ▸ The border should be 2 yards wide.

STUDENT HELP

AVOID ERRORS
To solve a quadratic equation by factoring, one side of the equation must be equal to 0. Before solving, make sure the equation is in standard form.

 **Solve a Quadratic Equation by Factoring**

Solve the equation.

7. $x^2 - 10x + 9 = 0$ **8.** $y^2 + 5y = 14$ **9.** $x^2 - 5 = -4x$

5.3 Exercises

Guided Practice

Vocabulary Check

1. Copy and complete the statement: The sum of three monomials is called a(n) __?__ .

2. Define the zero product property.

Skill Check

Match the expression with its factored form.

3. $x^2 - 14x + 48$　　　**4.** $x^2 + 2x - 48$　　　**5.** $x^2 - 2x - 48$

A. $(x + 8)(x - 6)$　　**B.** $(x - 8)(x + 6)$　　**C.** $(x - 8)(x - 6)$

Factor the expression.

6. $x^2 + 3x + 2$　　　**7.** $y^2 + 11y + 18$　　　**8.** $x^2 - 12x + 27$

9. $x^2 - 9x + 14$　　　**10.** $x^2 - 3x - 10$　　　**11.** $t^2 - 10t - 24$

Solve the equation.

12. $w^2 + 7w + 6 = 0$　　**13.** $x^2 + 3x - 28 = 0$　　**14.** $x^2 - 4x - 12 = 0$

Practice and Applications

STUDENT HELP

HOMEWORK HELP
Example 1: Exs. 15–33
Example 2: Exs. 15–33
Example 3: Exs. 34–46
Example 4: Exs. 47–54

Factoring **Choose the correct factorization.**

15. $x^2 + 11x + 24$　　　**16.** $s^2 + 8s - 48$　　　**17.** $z^2 - 12z + 32$

A. $(x + 6)(x + 4)$　　**A.** $(s + 12)(s - 4)$　　**A.** $(z - 16)(z + 2)$

B. $(x + 8)(x + 3)$　　**B.** $(s + 8)(s - 6)$　　**B.** $(z - 4)(z - 8)$

C. $(x + 2)(x + 12)$　　**C.** $(s - 6)(s - 8)$　　**C.** $(z + 8)(z - 4)$

Factoring **Factor the expression.**

18. $x^2 + 7x + 10$　　　**19.** $x^2 + 14x + 24$　　　**20.** $r^2 + 10r + 25$

21. $x^2 + 15x + 56$　　　**22.** $b^2 - b - 12$　　　**23.** $x^2 - 9x + 18$

24. $h^2 - 12h + 36$　　　**25.** $x^2 + 9x - 10$　　　**26.** $x^2 - 18x + 81$

27. $x^2 - 6x - 16$　　　**28.** $x^2 - 8x + 15$　　　**29.** $v^2 + 6v - 27$

30. $x^2 - 3x - 28$　　　**31.** $y^2 + 4y - 96$　　　**32.** $x^2 - 9x - 52$

33. Error Analysis Describe and correct the error in factoring $x^2 - 2x - 8$.

$$x^2 - 2x - 8$$
$$(x + 4)(x - 2) \quad \times$$

Solving Quadratic Equations **Solve the equation.**

34. $(b + 2)(b + 4) = 0$　　**35.** $(x - 5)(x + 1) = 0$　　**36.** $x^2 - 16x + 63 = 0$

37. $x^2 + 6x + 9 = 0$　　**38.** $y^2 + 5y - 14 = 0$　　**39.** $x^2 + 9x - 22 = 0$

40. $x^2 - 13x = -42$　　**41.** $x^2 + 4x = 45$　　**42.** $t^2 - 14t = -48$

43. $x^2 - 33 = 8x$　　**44.** $z^2 + 10z = -16$　　**45.** $x^2 - 72 = -6x$

46. Error Analysis Describe and correct the error in solving the equation $x^2 - 3x - 4 = 0$.

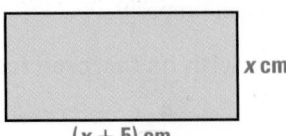

Geometry Link **Find the value of x.**

47. Area of rectangle = 36 cm²

x cm

$(x + 5)$ cm

48. Area of rectangle = 40 ft²

x ft

$(x + 3)$ ft

Parking Lot In Exercises 49–52, use the following information.

Your school plans to increase the area of the parking lot by 1000 square yards. The original parking lot is a rectangle, as shown. The length and width of the parking lot will each increase by x yards. The width of the original parking lot is 40 yards, and the length of the original parking lot is 50 yards.

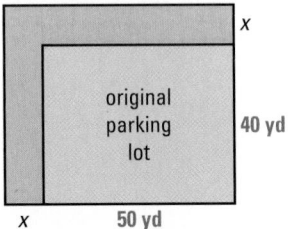

49. Find the area of the original parking lot.

50. Find the total area of the parking lot with the new space.

51. Write an equation that you can use to find the value of x.

52. Solve the equation from Exercise 51. By how many yards should the length and width of the parking lot increase?

Café Patio A café has an outdoor patio. The patio is a rectangle. The café owner wants to add 464 square feet to the area of the patio by expanding the existing patio as shown.

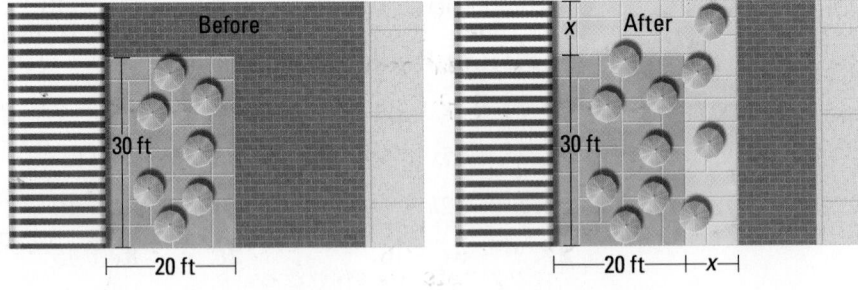

53. Write an equation that you can use to find the value of x.

54. Solve the equation from Exercise 53. By how many feet should the length and width of the patio be extended?

Critical Thinking In Exercises 55–57, use the diagram shown.

55. Write a quadratic trinomial that represents the area of the diagram.

56. Factor the expression you wrote in Exercise 55. Explain how the diagram models the factorization.

57. Draw a diagram like the one shown. Your diagram should show that $x^2 + 7x + 12 = (x + 3)(x + 4)$.

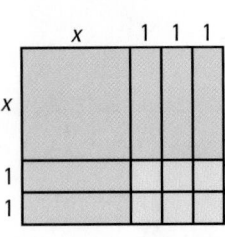

58. Challenge Suppose $x^2 + bx + 7$ can be factored into two binomials. What are the possible integer values of b? Explain your reasoning.

59. Multiple Choice What is the correct factorization of $x^2 - 7x - 18$?

(A) $(x - 9)(x - 2)$ (B) $(x - 9)(x + 2)$

(C) $(x + 9)(x - 2)$ (D) $(x + 9)(x + 2)$

60. Multiple Choice What is the correct factorization of $x^2 - 18x + 65$?

(F) $(x + 5)(x + 13)$ (G) $(x - 5)(x + 13)$

(H) $(x + 5)(x - 13)$ (J) $(x - 5)(x - 13)$

61. Multiple Choice What are the solutions of $y^2 - 18y + 80 = 0$?

(A) -8 and -10 (B) -4 and 20

(C) -4 and -20 (D) 8 and 10

62. Multiple Choice What are the solutions of $x^2 - 14x - 72 = 0$?

(F) -24 and 3 (G) -18 and -4

(H) -4 and -4 (J) -12 and 6

Mixed Review

Matching Inequalities Match the inequality with its graph. *(Lesson 4.1)*

63. $x \geq 3$ **64.** $-2 \leq x \leq 2$

65. $-3 \leq x < 4$ **66.** $x > -1$ or $x < -4$

A.   **B.**

C.   **D.**

Rewriting Equations Rewrite the absolute value equation as two linear equations. *(Lesson 4.4)*

67. $|x + 5| = 11$ **68.** $|x - 3| = 5$ **69.** $|2x + 6| = 10$

70. $|12 + 3x| = 6$ **71.** $\left|\frac{1}{2}x + 4\right| = 8$ **72.** $\left|\frac{3}{4}x - 6\right| = 3$

Graphing Parabolas Graph the function. Label the vertex and the x-intercepts. *(Lesson 5.2)*

73. $y = (x - 3)(x + 2)$ **74.** $y = -(x + 4)(x - 9)$ **75.** $y = 3(x + 1)(x - 4)$

76. $y = (x - 3)(x + 9)$ **77.** $y = -(x + 3)(x + 5)$ **78.** $y = 2(x - 1)(x - 3)$

Geometry Skills

SSS Similarity Theorem Tell whether the two triangles are similar. If they are similar, find the scale factor of Triangle B to Triangle A.

79.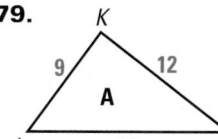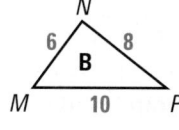

80.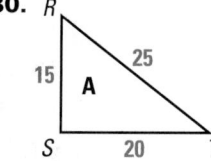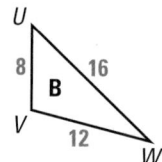

5.4 Factoring $ax^2 + bx + c$

Key Word

- zero of a function

Prerequisite Skills

Find the product.

1. $(2x + 1)(x + 1)$

2. $(x + 3)(2x - 1)$

3. $3(2x - 1)(x - 2)$

GOAL Factor trinomials of the form $ax^2 + bx + c$.

How much should a shop charge for a surfboard?

The owner of a surfboard shop wants to maximize the amount of money earned selling surfboards. You can use factoring in Example 5 to find how much the shop should charge for a surfboard.

To factor a trinomial of the form $ax^2 + bx + c$, write the trinomial as the product of two binomials.

You can factor $ax^2 + bx + c$ by finding numbers k and j whose product is a and numbers m and n whose product is c.

$$kj = a$$

$$ax^2 + bx + c = (kx + m)(jx + n) = kjx^2 + (kn + jm)x + mn$$

$$mn = c$$

EXAMPLE 1 Factor $ax^2 + bx + c$ when c is Positive

Factor $3x^2 + 7x + 2$.

Solution

You want $3x^2 + 7x + 2 = (kx + m)(jx + n)$ where $kj = 3$ and $mn = 2$. Because mn is positive, m and n have the same sign.

Factors of 3: k, j	Factors of 2: m, n	$(kx + m)(jx + n)$	$ax^2 + bx + c$
1, 3	1, 2	$(x + 1)(3x + 2)$	$3x^2 + 5x + 2$
1, 3	**2, 1**	$(x + 2)(3x + 1)$	$3x^2 + 7x + 2$ ✓
1, 3	−1, −2	$(x - 1)(3x - 2)$	$3x^2 - 5x + 2$
1, 3	−2, −1	$(x - 2)(3x - 1)$	$3x^2 - 7x + 2$

ANSWER ▶ $3x^2 + 7x + 2 = (x + 2)(3x + 1)$

Checkpoint ✓ *Factor $ax^2 + bx + c$ when c is Positive*

Factor the expression.

1. $2x^2 + 11x + 5$

2. $2y^2 + 9y + 7$

3. $3r^2 + 8r + 5$

EXAMPLE **2** Factor $ax^2 + bx + c$ when c is Negative

Factor $4x^2 - 16x - 9$.

Solution

You want $4x^2 - 16x - 9 = (kx + m)(jx + n)$ where $kj = 4$ and $mn = -9$. Because mn is negative, m and n have different signs.

Factors of 4: k, j	Factors of -9: m, n	$(kx + m)(jx + n)$	$ax^2 + bx + c$
1, 4	1, −9	$(x + 1)(4x - 9)$	$4x^2 - 5x - 9$
1, 4	−1, 9	$(x - 1)(4x + 9)$	$4x^2 + 5x - 9$
1, 4	9, −1	$(x + 9)(4x - 1)$	$4x^2 + 35x - 9$
1, 4	−9, 1	$(x - 9)(4x + 1)$	$4x^2 - 35x - 9$
1, 4	3, −3	$(x + 3)(4x - 3)$	$4x^2 + 9x - 9$
1, 4	−3, 3	$(x - 3)(4x + 3)$	$4x^2 - 9x - 9$
2, 2	1, −9	$(2x + 1)(2x - 9)$	$4x^2 - 16x - 9$ ✓
2, 2	−1, 9	$(2x - 1)(2x + 9)$	$4x^2 + 16x - 9$
2, 2	3, −3	$(2x + 3)(2x - 3)$	$4x^2 - 9$

ANSWER ▶ $4x^2 - 16x - 9 = (2x + 1)(2x - 9)$

Factoring Out a Constant When you factor a trinomial $ax^2 + bx + c$, first check whether the terms have a common constant factor.

EXAMPLE **3** **Factor Out a Common Constant**

Factor $6x^2 + 27x - 15$.

Solution

The coefficients of $6x^2 + 27x - 15$ have a common factor of 3. Factor out 3.

$$6x^2 + 27x - 15 = 3(2x^2 + 9x - 5)$$

Now, factor $2x^2 + 9x - 5$. You want $2x^2 + 9x - 5 = (kx + m)(jx + n)$ where $kj = 2$ and $mn = -5$. Because mn is negative, m and n have different signs.

STUDENT HELP
AVOID ERRORS
Make sure you factor out the common constant from all terms of the expression, not just the first term.

Factors of 2: k, j	Factors of -5: m, n	$(kx + m)(jx + n)$	$ax^2 + bx + c$
1, 2	1, −5	$(x + 1)(2x - 5)$	$2x^2 - 3x - 5$
1, 2	−1, 5	$(x - 1)(2x + 5)$	$2x^2 + 3x - 5$
1, 2	−5, 1	$(x - 5)(2x + 1)$	$2x^2 - 9x - 5$
1, 2	5, −1	$(x + 5)(2x - 1)$	$2x^2 + 9x - 5$ ✓

ANSWER ▶ $6x^2 + 27x - 15 = 3(x + 5)(2x - 1)$

Factor the expression.

4. $6z^2 + z - 12$ **5.** $11x^2 + 17x + 6$ **6.** $4w^2 - 6w + 2$

Finding Zeros of a Function The **zeros of a function** are the x-values for which the function's value is zero. The zeros of a function are also the x-intercepts of the function's graph. You may be able to find the zeros of a function $y = ax^2 + bx + c$ by letting $y = 0$, factoring, and using the zero product property.

EXAMPLE 4 **Find the Zeros of a Quadratic Function**

Find the zeros of $y = 3x^2 - x - 4$.

Solution

To find the zeros of the function, let $y = 0$. Then solve for x.

$y = 3x^2 - x - 4$	Write original function.
$0 = 3x^2 - x - 4$	Let $y = 0$.
$0 = (3x - 4)(x + 1)$	Factor the right side.
$3x - 4 = 0$ or $x + 1 = 0$	Use the zero product property.
$x = \dfrac{4}{3}$ $x = -1$	Solve for x.

ANSWER ▶ The zeros of the function are $\dfrac{4}{3}$ and -1.

CHECK The zeros of a function are also the x-intercepts of the graph of the function. So, the answer can be checked by graphing $y = 3x^2 - x - 4$. The x-intercepts of the graph are $\dfrac{4}{3}$ and -1, so the answer is correct. ✓

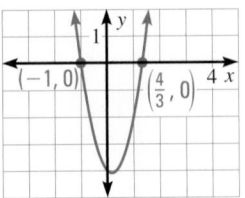

Find the zeros of the function.

7. $y = 3x^2 - 2x - 1$ **8.** $y = 2x^2 - 7x + 3$ **9.** $y = 4x^2 - 18x + 8$

Minimum or Maximum Values In Lesson 5.2, you learned that the minimum or maximum value of a quadratic function is the y-value of the vertex. The vertex lies on the axis of symmetry. The axis of symmetry is halfway between the x-intercepts, or zeros, of the function. So, the function has a minimum or maximum value when x equals the *average* of the zeros.

For a function in intercept form, $y = a(x - p)(x - q)$, the maximum or minimum value occurs at $x = \dfrac{p + q}{2}$.

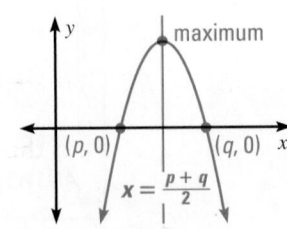

EXAMPLE **5** **Find a Maximum Value**

Surfboard Shop A surfboard shop sells 40 surfboards per month when it charges $500 per surfboard. Each time the shop decreases the price by $10 it sells 1 additional surfboard per month. How much should the shop charge per surfboard in order to maximize the amount of money earned? What is the maximum amount the shop can earn per month?

Solution

❶ *Write* a function for the amount of money earned per month. The amount of money earned per month, y, is the product of the price per surfboard and the number of surfboards sold.

Price per surfboard $= 500 - 10x$

Number of surfboards sold $= 40 + x$

$y = (500 - 10x)(40 + x)$

❷ *Identify* the zeros of the function.

$y = (500 - 10x)(40 + x)$	Write the function from Step 1.
$y = -10(-50 + x)(40 + x)$	Factor out a common constant.
$0 = -10(x - 50)(x + 40)$	Let $y = 0$.
$x - 50 = 0$ or $x + 40 = 0$	Use the zero product property.
$x = 50 \qquad x = -40$	Solve for x.

The zeros of the function are 50 and -40.

❸ *Find* how much the shop should charge per surfboard. The maximum value of the function occurs when x equals the average of the zeros.

$$x = \frac{50 + (-40)}{2} = 5 \qquad \text{Average of the zeros}$$

Substitute 5 for x in the expression for the price per surfboard. Then evaluate.

$$500 - 10(5) = 450$$

The shop should charge $450 per surfboard.

❹ *Find* the maximum amount of money earned. Substitute 5 for x in the function for the amount of money earned.

$y = (500 - 10x)(40 + x)$

$y = (500 - 10 \cdot 5)(40 + 5) = 20{,}250$

ANSWER ▶ The shop should charge $450 per surfboard. The maximum amount of money the shop can earn per month is $20,250.

 **Find the Minimum or Maximum Value of a Function**

Find the minimum or maximum value of the function.

10. $y = (x + 2)(x + 4)$ **11.** $y = (x + 4)(x - 8)$ **12.** $y = (2x + 3)(x - 4)$

Guided Practice

Vocabulary Check

1. Describe how to find the zeros of the function $y = 3x^2 + x - 2$.

2. How can you use the zeros of a function to find the maximum or minimum value of the function?

Skill Check

Match the expression with its factors.

3. $4x^2 - 11x - 3$

4. $4x^2 - 4x - 3$

5. $4x^2 + 11x - 3$

A. $(2x + 1)(2x - 3)$

B. $(4x - 1)(x + 3)$

C. $(4x + 1)(x - 3)$

Factor the expression.

6. $2x^2 + 3x - 5$

7. $3w^2 + 22w + 7$

8. $4x^2 - 8x + 3$

9. $6x^2 - x - 12$

10. $6x^2 + 28x - 10$

11. $18y^2 + 33y + 9$

Find the zeros of the function.

12. $y = 4x^2 + 9x - 9$

13. $y = 6x^2 + 23x + 7$

14. $y = 2x^2 - 7x - 4$

15. $y = 10x^2 - 31x + 15$

16. $y = 10x^2 - 11x + 3$

17. $y = 20x^2 - 7x - 3$

Practice and Applications

STUDENT HELP

HOMEWORK HELP
Example 1: Exs. 18–45
Example 2: Exs. 18–45
Example 3: Exs. 18–45
Example 4: Exs. 46–68,
81–85
Example 5: Exs. 69–80,
86–91

Factoring Choose the correct factorization.

18. $9x^2 + 9x - 10$

19. $8b^2 - 6b - 9$

20. $5x^2 - 13x + 8$

A. $(3x - 5)(3x + 2)$

A. $(4b + 3)(2b - 3)$

A. $(5x - 8)(x - 1)$

B. $(3x + 5)(3x - 2)$

B. $(4b + 9)(2b - 1)$

B. $(5x - 4)(x - 2)$

Factoring Factor the expression.

21. $5y^2 + 8y + 3$

22. $2x^2 - 13x - 7$

23. $3x^2 - 16x + 5$

24. $2x^2 + x - 1$

25. $7h^2 + 10h + 3$

26. $5x^2 - 11x + 2$

27. $3x^2 + 9x + 6$

28. $2x^2 + 14x + 24$

29. $5z^2 + 25z - 70$

30. $2x^2 - 30x + 112$

31. $3b^2 - 4b - 4$

32. $6x^2 - 29x - 5$

33. $4x^2 - 15x + 9$

34. $5x^2 + 13x + 6$

35. $18t^2 - 45t + 25$

36. $6x^2 - 25x - 9$

37. $12x^2 - 12x - 9$

38. $20x^2 + 66x - 14$

39. $12r^2 + 44r + 24$

40. $8x^2 + 14x - 15$

41. $18s^2 - 54s + 28$

42. $8x^2 - 14x - 9$

43. $-6s^2 + 36s - 30$

44. $-4x^2 - 4x + 24$

45. **Error Analysis** Describe and correct the error in factoring $12x^2 - 14x - 6$.

$$12x^2 - 14x - 6$$
$$2(6x^2 - 7x - 3)$$
$$2(2x - 1)(x - 3) \quad \times$$

Finding Zeros Find the zeros of the function.

46. $y = x^2 - 5x - 14$ **47.** $y = 2x^2 + 11x - 21$ **48.** $y = 5x^2 + 21x + 4$

49. $y = 9x^2 - 9x + 2$ **50.** $y = 4x^2 - 16x + 15$ **51.** $y = 2x^2 + 3x - 27$

52. $y = 4x^2 + 21x + 5$ **53.** $y = 7x^2 + 11x - 6$ **54.** $y = 8x^2 - 10x - 3$

Error Analysis Describe and correct the error in finding the zeros of the function.

55.

$$y = 16x^2 - 2x - 5$$
$$0 = 16x^2 - 2x - 5$$
$$0 = (4x + 1)(4x - 5)$$
Zeros are $-\dfrac{1}{4}$ and $\dfrac{5}{4}$.

   ✗

56.

$$y = 5x^2 + 17x - 12$$
$$0 = 5x^2 + 17x - 12$$
$$0 = (5x - 3)(x - 4)$$
Zeros are $\dfrac{3}{5}$ and 4.

   ✗

Solving Equations Solve the equation.

57. $9x^2 + 38x + 8 = 0$ **58.** $10b^2 - 3b - 4 = 0$ **59.** $9x^2 - 27x + 20 = 0$

60. $8z^2 + 10z = 12$ **61.** $4x - 11 = -7x^2$ **62.** $6x^2 + 20 = 23x$

63. $42x^2 + 22x = 4$ **64.** $16u^2 - 32u = 9$ **65.** $6x^2 + 29x = -28$

66. $18x^2 = -9x + 14$ **67.** $10x^2 = 39x + 27$ **68.** $12t^2 = -62t + 22$

Finding Maximum Values Find the maximum value of the function.

69. $y = -2(x - 4)(x + 2)$ **70.** $y = -3(x + 7)(x + 1)$ **71.** $y = -x(x - 5)$

72. $y = -(x - 36)(x + 18)$ **73.** $y = -5(x + 8)(x - 4)$ **74.** $y = -12x(x - 9)$

Finding Minimum Values Find the minimum value of the function.

75. $y = 2(x + 3)(x - 7)$ **76.** $y = (x - 4)(x - 6)$ **77.** $y = 3(x + 4)(x - 2)$

78. $y = 3(x + 10)(x - 8)$ **79.** $y = 2(x - 3)(x - 6)$ **80.** $y = 8x(x + 15)$

Geometry Link Find the value of *x*.

81. Area of rectangle $= 30$ in.^{2}

x in.
$(3x + 1)$ in.

82. Area of trapezoid $= 114$ cm^2

$(2x + 1)$ cm
x cm
$(4x + 1)$ cm

83. Gardening You planted an urban vegetable garden that is a rectangle. The width of the garden is 8 feet. The length of the garden is 12 feet. You want to plant a border of flowers around the garden. The border will have the same width on every side of the garden. The border will have the same area as the garden. What should the width of the border be?

84. Swimming Pool A rectangular swimming pool has a width of 18 feet and a length of 32 feet. You have 1400 square feet of material to build a deck around the swimming pool. The deck will have the same width on every side of the swimming pool. What can the width of the deck be?

85. Quilting You make a quilt that is a rectangle. The length of the quilt is 5 feet. The width of the quilt is 4 feet. You want to add a border to the quilt. You have 10 square feet of fabric for the border. The border will have the same width on every side. What should the width of the border be?

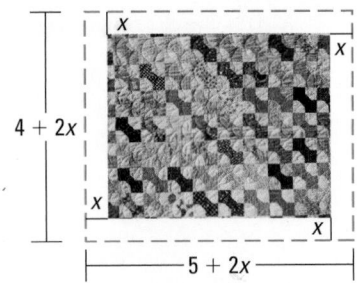

Sporting Goods **In Exercises 86–89, use the following information.**

An athletic store sells about 200 pairs of basketball shoes per month when it charges $120 per pair. Each time the shop increases the price by $2 it sells 2 fewer pairs of basketball shoes per month.

86. Write a function for the amount of money the store earns per month from the sale of basketball shoes.

87. Identify the zeros of the function.

88. The store wants to maximize the amount of money earned per month. How much should the store charge for each pair of basketball shoes?

89. What is the maximum amount of money the store can earn per month from the sale of the basketball shoes?

90. Electronics An electronics store sells about 60 DVD players per month when it charges $80 per DVD player. Each time the store decreases the price by $5, the store sells about 5 additional DVD players per month. How much should the store charge for a DVD player in order to maximize the amount of money earned? What is the maximum amount the store can earn in a month from the sale of DVD players?

91. Restaurant A restaurant sells about 330 sandwiches each day when it charges $6 per sandwich. Each time the restaurant decreases the price by $.25, the restaurant sells 15 more sandwiches per day. How much should the restaurant charge per sandwich in order to maximize the amount of money earned per day? What is the maximum amount the restaurant can earn in a day from the sale of sandwiches?

Standardized Test Practice

92. Multiple Choice What is the correct factorization of $4x^2 + 17x - 15$?

(A) $(2x - 3)(2x + 5)$ (B) $(4x + 3)(x - 5)$

(C) $(4x - 3)(x + 5)$ (D) $(2x + 3)(x - 5)$

93. Multiple Choice What is the correct factorization of $6s^2 - s - 15$?

(F) $(3s - 5)(2s + 3)$ (G) $(3s + 5)(2s - 3)$

(H) $(6s - 5)(s + 3)$ (J) $(6s + 5)(s - 3)$

94. Multiple Choice What are the solutions of $3x^2 - x - 14 = 0$?

(A) $-\frac{7}{3}$ and -2 (B) $\frac{3}{7}$ and -2 (C) $\frac{7}{3}$ and -2 (D) $\frac{7}{3}$ and 2

95. Multiple Choice What are the solutions of $8x^2 - 2x - 1 = 0$?

(F) $-\frac{1}{2}$ and $-\frac{1}{4}$ (G) $-\frac{1}{2}$ and $\frac{1}{4}$ (H) $\frac{1}{2}$ and $-\frac{1}{4}$ (J) $\frac{1}{2}$ and $\frac{1}{4}$

Mixed Review

Solving Inequalities Solve the inequality. Then graph your solution.
(Lesson 4.1)

96. $3x > 15$

97. $2x + 5 \le -7$

98. $3a - 4 \ge 8$

99. $7y + 4 < 11$

100. $4 - 5x \ge -1$

101. $-4x + 11 > 3$

102. $15 - 3x > 3$

103. $11 + 8r \ge 7$

104. $4 + \frac{3}{2}x \le 13$

Solving Absolute Value Equations Solve the equation. *(Lesson 4.4)*

105. $|x + 9| = 3$

106. $|s - 4| = 10$

107. $|2x + 4| = 12$

108. $|5k - 4| = 11$

109. $|3x + 2| = 8$

110. $|4x - 3| = 7$

111. $|2x - 5| = 13$

112. $|3x + 14| = 7$

113. $|7h - 10| = 4$

Solving Absolute Value Inequalities Solve the inequality. Then graph your solution. *(Lesson 4.5)*

114. $|z - 1| \le 5$

115. $|x + 8| > 5$

116. $|11 - x| < 10$

117. $|2x + 4| \ge 8$

118. $|3x - 5| < 10$

119. $|4g - 7| \ge 13$

120. $|3x - 15| < 30$

121. $|2x + 6| \ge 10$

122. $|4x - 9| \le 7$

Geometry Skills

Using Area Find the value of *x*.

123. Area of rectangle $= 88$ ft^2

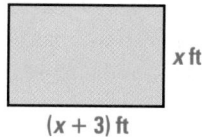

x ft

$(x + 3)$ ft

124. Area of rectangle $= 45$ in.^{2}

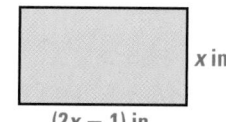

x in.

$(2x - 1)$ in.

Quiz 1

Lessons 5.1 and 5.2

Graph the quadratic function. Label the vertex and axis of symmetry.

1. $y = (x - 5)^2 + 7$

2. $y = x^2 - x + 12$

3. $y = -x^2 + 4x + 21$

4. $y = -2(x - 6)(x + 4)$

5. $y = 3(x + 2)(x + 1)$

6. $y = (x + 3)^2 - 2$

Lessons 5.3 and 5.4

Factor the expression.

7. $x^2 + 2x - 15$

8. $x^2 + 8x + 12$

9. $x^2 - 9x + 20$

10. $2x^2 + 3x - 20$

11. $3x^2 - 22x + 24$

12. $4x^2 + 4x - 35$

Lessons 5.3 and 5.4

Solve the equation by factoring.

13. $x^2 + x - 20 = 0$

14. $x^2 - 12x + 27 = 0$

15. $x^2 + 10x + 24 = 0$

16. $x^2 - 6x = 27$

17. $x^2 + 18x = -81$

18. $x^2 + 12x = 45$

19. $2x^2 + 13x - 7 = 0$

20. $2x^2 - 13x + 15 = 0$

21. $3x^2 + 5x = 12$

Lesson 5.3

22. Poster You buy a poster that is a rectangle. The width of the poster is x inches. The length of the poster is $(x + 6)$ inches. The area of the poster is 187 square inches. Find the length and width of the poster.

USING A GRAPHING CALCULATOR *(For use with Lesson 5.4)*
Finding Zeros of Functions

You can use the *zero* feature on a graphing calculator to approximate the zeros of a quadratic function.

EXAMPLE

Find the zeros of the function $y = 3(x - 2)^2 - 7$ to the nearest hundredth.

SOLUTION

① Graph the function. Go to the CALCULATE screen. Select *zero*.

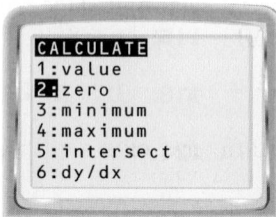

② Move the cursor to the left of the smaller zero. Press **ENTER**.

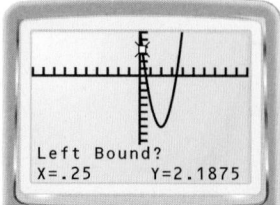

③ Move the cursor to the right of the smaller zero. Press **ENTER**.

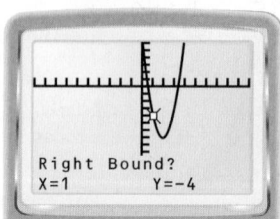

④ Move the cursor as close to the smaller zero as possible. Press **ENTER**.

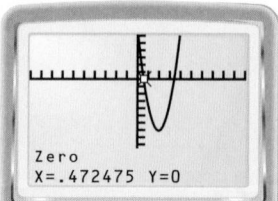

⑤ Repeat steps 1–4 to find the larger of the zeros.

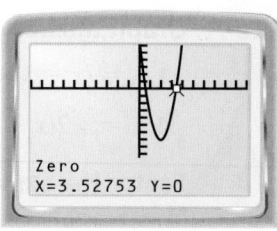

ANSWER ▶ The zeros of the function are about 0.47 and 3.53.

EXERCISES

Use a graphing calculator to find the zeros of the function to the nearest hundredth.

1. $y = 3x^2 - 7$ **2.** $y = -x^2 + 5$ **3.** $y = 2x^2 + x - 8$

4. $y = x^2 - 4x - 11$ **5.** $y = 4(x - 1)^2 - 6$ **6.** $y = 5(x + 2)^2 - 5$

7. Use the minimum function and Steps 2–4 above to find the minimum value of $y = 3x^2 + 6x - 2$.

5.5 Factoring Using Special Patterns

Key Words
- trinomial, p. 234

GOAL Factor using special patterns.

Prerequisite Skills

Solve the equation.

1. $x - 4 = 0$

2. $x + 4 = 0$

3. $2x - 5 = 0$

4. $2x + 5 = 0$

What size rope do you need to lift an object safely?

You need to lift an object using a rope. You can use factoring in Example 5 to find the diameter of the rope that you need to lift an object safely.

Some quadratic expressions can be factored using special patterns. To see one special pattern, find the product $(x - n)(x + n)$ using FOIL.

$$(x - n)(x + n) = x^2 + nx - nx - n^2 = x^2 - n^2$$

This result leads to the difference of two squares pattern.

Differences of Two Squares Pattern

ALGEBRA $a^2 - b^2 = (a + b)(a - b)$

EXAMPLE $x^2 - 4 = (x + 2)(x - 2)$

EXAMPLE 1 Factor a Difference of Two Squares

Factor the expression.

  a. $m^2 - 25$ **b.** $q^2 - 625$ **c.** $9y^2 - 16$

Solution

  a. $m^2 - 25 = m^2 - 5^2$ Write as $a^2 - b^2$.

            $= (m + 5)(m - 5)$ Difference of two squares pattern

  b. $q^2 - 625 = q^2 - 25^2$ Write as $a^2 - b^2$.

             $= (q + 25)(q - 25)$ Difference of two squares pattern

  c. $9y^2 - 16 = (3y)^2 - 4^2$ Write as $a^2 - b^2$.

             $= (3y + 4)(3y - 4)$ Difference of two squares pattern

---

Checkpoint ✓ **Factor Using the Difference of Two Squares Pattern**

Factor the expression.

  1. $x^2 - 36$ **2.** $r^2 - 100$ **3.** $9m^2 - 64$ **4.** $\frac{1}{4}p^2 - 81$

Perfect Square Trinomials To see another special pattern, find the product $(x + n)^2$ using FOIL.

$$(x + n)^2 = (x + n)(x + n) = x^2 + nx + nx + n^2 = x^2 + 2nx + n^2$$

$$(x - n)^2 = (x - n)(x - n) = x^2 - nx - nx + n^2 = x^2 - 2nx + n^2$$

This result leads to the perfect square trinomial patterns.

Perfect Square Trinomial Patterns

ALGEBRA

$a^2 + 2ab + b^2 = (a + b)^2$

$a^2 - 2ab + b^2 = (a - b)^2$

EXAMPLE

$x^2 + 14x + 49 = (x + 7)^2$

$x^2 - 10x + 25 = (x - 5)^2$

EXAMPLE 2 Factor a Perfect Square Trinomial

Factor the expression.

a. $m^2 + 16m + 64$ **b.** $9p^2 + 30p + 25$ **c.** $16r^2 - 56r + 49$

Solution

a. $m^2 + 16m + 64 = m^2 + 2(m)(8) + 8^2$ Write as $a^2 + 2ab + b^2$.

$\qquad\qquad\qquad\quad = (m + 8)^2$ Perfect square trinomial pattern

b. $9p^2 + 30p + 25 = (3p)^2 + 2(3p)(5) + 5^2$ Write as $a^2 + 2ab + b^2$.

$\qquad\qquad\qquad\quad = (3p + 5)^2$ Perfect square trinomial pattern

c. $16r^2 - 56r + 49 = (4r)^2 - 2(4r)(7) + 7^2$ Write as $a^2 - 2ab + b^2$.

$\qquad\qquad\qquad\quad = (4r - 7)^2$ Perfect square trinomial pattern

---

EXAMPLE 3 Factor Out a Common Constant

Factor $5u^2 - 40u + 80$.

Solution

$5u^2 - 40u + 80 = 5(u^2 - 8u + 16)$ Factor out 5.

$\qquad\qquad\qquad = 5[u^2 - 2(u)(4) + 4^2]$ Write as $a^2 - 2ab + b^2$.

$\qquad\qquad\qquad = 5(u - 4)^2$ Perfect square trinomial pattern

CHECK Check your answer by multiplying.

$5(u - 4)^2 = 5(u - 4)(u - 4) = 5(u^2 - 8u + 16) = 5u^2 - 40u + 80$ ✓

Checkpoint ✓ *Factor the Expression*

Factor the expression.

5. $x^2 + 10x + 25$ **6.** $4x^2 + 12x + 9$ **7.** $9p^2 - 24p + 16$

8. $5x^2 + 10x + 5$ **9.** $8y^2 - 18$ **10.** $12u^2 - 36u + 27$

EXAMPLE 4 Solve a Quadratic Equation

Solve $9p^2 + 30p = -25$.

Solution

$$9p^2 + 30p = -25 \qquad \text{Write original equation.}$$
$$9p^2 + 30p + 25 = 0 \qquad \text{Write in standard form.}$$
$$(3p)^2 + 2(3p)(5) + 5^2 = 0 \qquad \text{Write as } a^2 + 2ab + b^2.$$
$$(3p + 5)^2 = 0 \qquad \text{Perfect square trinomial pattern}$$
$$3p + 5 = 0 \qquad \text{Use the zero product property.}$$
$$p = -\frac{5}{3} \qquad \text{Solve for } p.$$

ANSWER ▸ The solution is $-\frac{5}{3}$.

STUDENT HELP

SOLVING NOTE
If the square of an expression is zero, then the expression is zero.

EXAMPLE 5 Use a Quadratic Equation as a Model

Rope Strength Every rope has a safe working load. A rope should not be used to lift a weight greater than its safe working load. The safe working load (in pounds) for a rope can be found using the function $S = 180C^2$ where C is the circumference (in inches) of the rope. Find the diameter of rope needed to lift an object that weighs 720 pounds.

Solution

❶ *Find* the circumference of a rope that can be used to lift 720 pounds.

$$S = 180C^2 \qquad \text{Function for safe working load}$$
$$720 = 180C^2 \qquad \text{Substitute 720 for } S.$$
$$0 = 180C^2 - 720 \qquad \text{Write in standard form.}$$
$$0 = 180(C^2 - 4) \qquad \text{Factor out 180.}$$
$$0 = 180(C + 2)(C - 2) \qquad \text{Difference of two squares pattern}$$
$$C + 2 = 0 \quad \text{or} \quad C - 2 = 0 \qquad \text{Use the zero product property.}$$
$$C = -2 \qquad\qquad C = 2 \qquad \text{Solve for } C.$$

Reject the negative value of C. The rope must have a circumference of 2 inches.

❷ *Find* the diameter of the rope. Use the formula for circumference, $C = \pi d$.

$$2 = \pi d \qquad \text{Substitute 2 for } C \text{ in } C = \pi d.$$
$$d = \frac{2}{\pi} \approx 0.637 \qquad \text{Solve for } d.$$

ANSWER ▸ The rope must have a diameter of $\frac{2}{\pi}$ or about 0.637 inch.

 *Checkpoint* ✓ *Solve a Quadratic Equation*

Solve the equation.

11. $x^2 - 6x = -9$ **12.** $a^2 - 4 = 12$ **13.** $2y^2 = 40y - 200$

Guided Practice

Vocabulary Check

1. Name two special factoring patterns. Give an example of each pattern.

2. How can you tell whether the factors of a perfect square trinomial are sums or differences?

Skill Check

Factor the expression.

3. $x^2 - 16$

4. $x^2 - 144$

5. $z^2 - 49$

6. $4x^2 - 1$

7. $x^2 + 22x + 121$

8. $y^2 - 4y + 4$

9. $81x^2 - 18x + 1$

10. $2r^2 - 18$

11. $3s^2 - 75$

12. **Error Analysis** Describe and correct the error in factoring $x^2 - 6x + 9$.

$$x^2 - 6x + 9$$
$$(x - 3)(x + 3) \quad \times$$

Solve the equation.

13. $n^2 - 121 = 0$

14. $x^2 + 2x + 1 = 0$

15. $p^2 - 14p + 49 = 0$

16. $-36 + x^2 = 0$

17. $3y^2 - 18y + 27 = 0$

18. $5x^2 - 125 = 0$

Practice and Applications

STUDENT HELP

HOMEWORK HELP
Example 1: Exs. 19–36
Example 2: Exs. 19–36
Example 3: Exs. 37–49
Example 4: Exs. 50–64
Example 5: Exs. 65–77

Factoring Factor the expression.

19. $x^2 - 4$

20. $t^2 - 81$

21. $x^2 + 8x + 16$

22. $9x^2 - 30x + 25$

23. $m^2 + 12m + 36$

24. $x^2 + 28x + 196$

25. $4k^2 - 49$

26. $100x^2 - 1$

27. $w^2 - 30w + 225$

28. $x^2 - 26x + 169$

29. $x^2 - 225$

30. $x^2 + 32x + 256$

31. $\frac{1}{9}x^2 - 64$

32. $121 - \frac{1}{4}x^2$

33. $16x^2 - 8x + 1$

34. $36y^2 - 84y + 49$

35. $49x^2 - 81$

36. $4q^2 - 36q + 81$

37. **Error Analysis** Describe and correct the error in factoring $24x^2 - 72x + 54$.

$$-24x^2 + 72x - 54$$
$$-6(4x^2 + 12x + 9)$$
$$-6(2x + 3)(2x + 3) \quad \times$$

Factoring Factor the expression.

38. $3x^2 - 27$

39. $2n^2 - 128$

40. $4x^2 - 64$

41. $5r^2 + 50r + 125$

42. $48x^2 + 24x + 3$

43. $32x^2 - 48x + 18$

44. $28x^2 - 84x + 63$

45. $99z^2 - 44$

46. $8x^2 + 120x + 450$

47. $72x^2 - \frac{8}{9}x$

48. $12x^2 - 36x + 27$

49. $11y^2 - 44$

Solving Equations Solve the equation.

50. $16x^2 - 4 = 0$ **51.** $81y^2 + 54y + 9 = 0$

52. $2x^2 - 32x + 128 = 0$ **53.** $-72 + 2x^2 = 0$

54. $49b^2 = 256$ **55.** $-9x^2 = 42x + 49$

56. $3x^2 - 72x = -432$ **57.** $160t^2 = 480t - 360$

58. Error Analysis Describe and correct the error in solving $4x^2 - 4x = -1$.

$$4x^2 - 4x = -1$$
$$4x(x - 1) = -1$$
$$4x = -1 \quad \text{or} \quad x - 1 = -1$$
$$x = -\frac{1}{4} \qquad\qquad x = 0 \qquad \times$$

Finding Zeros Find the zeros of the function.

59. $y = x^2 - 25$ **60.** $y = x^2 - 22x + 121$

61. $y = x^2 - 81$ **62.** $y = 9x^2 - 64$

63. $y = 4x^2 + 20x + 25$ **64.** $y = 36x^2 + 84x + 49$

Geometry Link Find the value of *x*.

65. Area of square $= 36$ yd^2 **66.** Area of square $= 64$ mm^2

2x yd

3x mm

67. Rope Strength The safe working load (in pounds) for a rope can be found using the function $S = 450C^2$ where C is the circumference (in inches) of the rope. Find the diameter of rope needed to lift an object that weighs 4050 pounds.

68. Rope Strength The safe working load (in pounds) for a rope can be found using the function $S = 880C^2$ where C is the circumference (in inches) of the rope. Find the diameter of rope needed to lift an object that weighs 3520 pounds.

Landscaping In Exercises 69–73, use the following information.

You want to build a fence around a piece of land for a garden. The garden will be a rectangle. You have material for 32 feet of fence.

69. Use the formula for the perimeter of a rectangle to write a linear equation for the length ℓ (in feet) of the garden where w is the width (in feet).

70. Use the equation from Exercise 69 to write a quadratic function for the area (in square feet) of the garden.

71. Find the zeros of the function from Exercise 70.

72. What length and width give the garden the maximum possible area?

73. What is the maximum area of the garden?

Geometry Link Find the length and width of the rectangle with the given area and perimeter.

74. Area = 20 square feet
Perimeter = 18 feet

75. Area = 108 square feet
Perimeter = 42 feet

76. Area = 90 square inches
Perimeter = 42 inches

77. Area = 216 square meters
Perimeter = 66 meters

78. Multiple Choice What is the correct factorization of $45x^2 - 125$?

A $5(3x - 5)^2$

B $5(x + 5)(x - 5)$

C $5(3x + 5)(3x - 5)$

D $5(3x^2 + 5)^2$

79. Multiple Choice What is the correct factorization of $147y^2 - 84y + 12$?

F $3(7y + 2)(7y - 2)$

G $3(7y + 2)^2$

H $3(7y - 2)^2$

J $-3(7y + 2)^2$

80. Multiple Choice What is a solution of $3x^2 - 72x + 432 = 0$?

A -12 **B** -4 **C** 3 **D** 12

81. Multiple Choice What is a solution of $4x^2 + 12x + 9 = 0$?

F $-\dfrac{3}{2}$ **G** $-\dfrac{2}{3}$ **H** $\dfrac{2}{3}$ **J** $\dfrac{3}{2}$

Mixed Review

Sketching Graphs Sketch the graph of the equation. Label the points where the graph crosses the *x*-, *y*-, and *z*-axes. *(Lesson 3.4)*

82. $x + y + z = 5$

83. $3x + 6y + 2z = 12$

84. $6x + 9y + 3z = 18$

85. $7x + 4y + 14z = 28$

86. $9x + 6y + 12z = 36$

87. $18x + 9y + 27z = 54$

Factoring Factor the expression. *(Lesson 5.3)*

88. $z^2 + 5z + 6$

89. $x^2 + 11x + 28$

90. $x^2 - 4x - 32$

91. $x^2 - 18x + 32$

92. $t^2 - 8t + 15$

93. $x^2 - 9x + 18$

Solving Equations Solve the equation. *(Lesson 5.4)*

94. $16x^2 - 8x + 1 = 0$

95. $2w^2 + 5w + 3 = 0$

96. $7x^2 + 16x - 15 = 0$

97. $3s^2 - 3s - 18 = 0$

98. $6x^2 - 5x - 14 = 0$

99. $30b^2 - 24 = 16b$

Geometry Skills

Proportions and Similar Triangles Find the value of *x*. Use the fact that corresponding sides of similar triangles are proportional.

100.

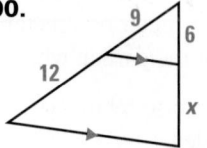

101.

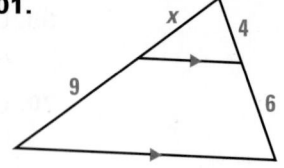

102.

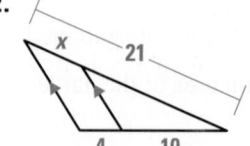

103.

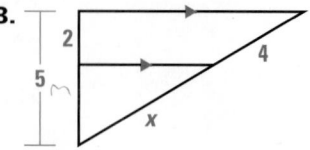

5.6 Solving Quadratic Equations by Finding Square Roots

Key Words

- square root
- radical
- radicand
- rationalizing the denominator

Prerequisite Skills

Solve the equation.

1. $5x - 3 = 17$
2. $-2x + 3 = 11$
3. $-4x - 5 = -13$

GOAL Solve quadratic equations by finding square roots.

How long does a skydiver fall before opening her parachute?

In Example 4, you will use a quadratic equation and square roots to find the number of seconds a skydiver falls through the air before opening her parachute.

A number b is a **square root** of a number a if $b^2 = a$. A positive number a has two square roots written $\sqrt{a}$ and $-\sqrt{a}$. For example, because $2^2 = 4$ and $(-2)^2 = 4$, the two square roots of 4 are $\sqrt{4} = 2$ and $-\sqrt{4} = -2$.

The expression $\sqrt{a}$ is a **radical**. The symbol $\sqrt{}$ is a *radical sign*. The number a beneath the radical symbol is the **radicand**.

Properties of Square Roots ($a > 0$, $b > 0$)

PRODUCT PROPERTY $\sqrt{ab} = \sqrt{a} \cdot \sqrt{b}$ **EXAMPLE** $\sqrt{8} = \sqrt{4} \cdot \sqrt{2} = 2\sqrt{2}$

QUOTIENT PROPERTY $\sqrt{\dfrac{a}{b}} = \dfrac{\sqrt{a}}{\sqrt{b}}$ **EXAMPLE** $\sqrt{\dfrac{15}{16}} = \dfrac{\sqrt{15}}{\sqrt{16}} = \dfrac{\sqrt{15}}{4}$

Simplifying Square Roots You can use the properties above to simplify expressions containing square roots. A square root expression is simplified if:

- no radicand has a perfect-square factor other than 1, and

- there is no radical in a denominator

EXAMPLE 1 Use Properties of Square Roots

Simplify the expression.

   a. $\sqrt{18}$ **b.** $\sqrt{2} \cdot \sqrt{10}$ **c.** $\sqrt{\dfrac{5}{9}}$

Solution

   a. $\sqrt{18} = \sqrt{9} \cdot \sqrt{2} = 3\sqrt{2}$

   b. $\sqrt{2} \cdot \sqrt{10} = \sqrt{20} = \sqrt{4} \cdot \sqrt{5} = 2\sqrt{5}$

   c. $\sqrt{\dfrac{5}{9}} = \dfrac{\sqrt{5}}{\sqrt{9}} = \dfrac{\sqrt{5}}{3}$

Rationalizing the Denominator To simplify an expression, you must eliminate any radical from the denominator. This is called **rationalizing the denominator**.

EXAMPLE **2** **Rationalize the Denominator of a Fraction**

Simplify $\sqrt{\dfrac{5}{2}}$.

Solution

$$\sqrt{\frac{5}{2}} = \frac{\sqrt{5}}{\sqrt{2}} \qquad \text{Quotient property of square roots}$$

$$= \frac{\sqrt{5}}{\sqrt{2}} \cdot \frac{\sqrt{2}}{\sqrt{2}} \qquad \text{Multiply by } \frac{\sqrt{2}}{\sqrt{2}}.$$

$$= \frac{\sqrt{10}}{2} \qquad \text{Simplify.}$$

Checkpoint ✓ **Use Properties of Square Roots**

Simplify the expression.

1. $\sqrt{12}$ **2.** $\sqrt{15} \cdot \sqrt{3}$ **3.** $\sqrt{\dfrac{7}{3}}$

Solving Quadratic Equations You can use square roots to solve some quadratic equations. For example, if $a > 0$, then the quadratic equation $x^2 = a$ has two real-number solutions: $x = \sqrt{a}$ and $x = -\sqrt{a}$. These solutions can be written $x = \pm\sqrt{a}$, which is read "plus or minus the square root of a."

EXAMPLE **3** **Solve a Quadratic Equation**

Solve $x^2 + 1 = 13$.

Solution

$$x^2 + 1 = 13 \qquad \text{Write original equation.}$$

$$x^2 = 12 \qquad \text{Subtract 1 from each side.}$$

$$x = \pm\sqrt{12} \qquad \text{Take the square root of each side.}$$

$$x = \pm\sqrt{4} \cdot \sqrt{3} \qquad \text{Product property of square roots}$$

$$x = \pm 2\sqrt{3} \qquad \text{Simplify.}$$

ANSWER ▶ The solutions are $2\sqrt{3}$ and $-2\sqrt{3}$.

CHECK Substitute $2\sqrt{3}$ and $-2\sqrt{3}$ into the original equation.

$$x^2 + 1 = 13 \qquad\qquad x^2 + 1 = 13$$

$$(2\sqrt{3})^2 + 1 \stackrel{?}{=} 13 \qquad\qquad (-2\sqrt{3})^2 + 1 \stackrel{?}{=} 13$$

$$4 \cdot 3 + 1 \stackrel{?}{=} 13 \qquad\qquad 4 \cdot 3 + 1 \stackrel{?}{=} 13$$

$$12 + 1 = 13 \checkmark \qquad\qquad 12 + 1 = 13 \checkmark$$

Solve the equation.

4. $x^2 - 4 = 14$ **5.** $x^2 + 3 = 13$ **6.** $3y^2 = 24$

Falling Objects When an object falls, its height h (in feet) above the ground after t seconds can be modeled by the function below where h_0 is the initial height (in feet) of the object. The model assumes that the force of air resistance on the object does not greatly influence the fall.

Falling Object Model $h = -16t^2 + h_0$

Link to

CAREERS

SMOKEJUMPER
A smokejumper is a specially trained firefighter who parachutes from a plane to fight a forest fire.

EXAMPLE **4** **Use a Quadratic Equation as a Model**

Skydiving A skydiver jumps from an airplane that is 6000 feet above the ground. The skydiver opens her parachute when she is 2500 feet above the ground.

a. Write an equation that gives the height (in feet) of the skydiver above the ground as a function of time (in seconds).

b. For how many seconds does the skydiver fall before opening her parachute?

Solution

a. The initial height of the skydiver is $h_0 = 6000$.

$$h = -16t^2 + h_0$$ Write falling object model.

$$h = -16t^2 + 6000$$ Substitute 6000 for h_0.

b. The height of the skydiver when she opens her parachute is $h = 2500$. Substitute 2500 for h in the model from part (a). Solve for t.

$$h = -16t^2 + 6000$$ Write model from part (a).

$$2500 = -16t^2 + 6000$$ Substitute 2500 for h.

$$-3500 = -16t^2$$ Subtract 6000 from each side.

$$\frac{-3500}{-16} = t^2$$ Divide each side by -16.

$$\pm\sqrt{\frac{-3500}{-16}} = t$$ Take the square root of each side.

$$\pm 15 \approx t$$ Use a calculator.

ANSWER ▶ Reject the solution -15, because time must be positive. The skydiver falls for about 15 seconds before opening her parachute.

Checkpoint ✓ *Use a Quadratic Equation*

7. Skydiving A skydiver jumps from a plane that is 5000 feet above the ground. The skydiver opens his parachute when he is 2000 feet above the ground.

a. Write an equation that gives the height (in feet) of the skydiver above the ground as a function of time (in seconds).

b. For how many seconds does the skydiver fall before opening his parachute?

5.6 Exercises

Guided Practice

Vocabulary Check

1. In the expression $\sqrt{10}$ what is 10 called?

2. Explain what it means to *rationalize the denominator* of a fraction.

Skill Check

Simplify the expression.

3. $\sqrt{36}$ **4.** $\sqrt{28}$ **5.** $\sqrt{63}$ **6.** $\sqrt{5} \cdot \sqrt{20}$

7. $\sqrt{\dfrac{9}{16}}$ **8.** $\sqrt{\dfrac{3}{25}}$ **9.** $\dfrac{2}{\sqrt{5}}$ **10.** $\sqrt{\dfrac{11}{3}}$

11. Error Analysis Describe and correct the error in simplifying the expression.

$$\sqrt{27} = \sqrt{9 \cdot 3}$$
$$= 9\sqrt{3} \quad \times$$

Solve the equation.

12. $x^2 = 49$ **13.** $b^2 - 11 = 25$ **14.** $3x^2 + 2 = 14$

15. $2x^2 + 7 = 31$ **16.** $3x^2 - 1 = 14$ **17.** $\dfrac{1}{3}y^2 + 1 = 7$

Practice and Applications

STUDENT HELP

HOMEWORK HELP
Example 1: Exs. 18–37
Example 2: Exs. 38–45
Example 3: Exs. 46–59
Example 4: Exs. 69–73

Using the Product Property **Simplify the expression.**

18. $\sqrt{45}$ **19.** $\sqrt{32}$ **20.** $\sqrt{48}$ **21.** $\sqrt{75}$

22. $\sqrt{147}$ **23.** $\sqrt{99}$ **24.** $3\sqrt{5} \cdot \sqrt{5}$ **25.** $\sqrt{5} \cdot \sqrt{20}$

26. $\sqrt{27} \cdot \sqrt{3}$ **27.** $2\sqrt{12} \cdot \sqrt{3}$ **28.** $\sqrt{12} \cdot \sqrt{50}$ **29.** $5\sqrt{10} \cdot \sqrt{30}$

Using the Quotient Property **Simplify the expression.**

30. $\sqrt{\dfrac{1}{16}}$ **31.** $\sqrt{\dfrac{9}{64}}$ **32.** $\sqrt{\dfrac{81}{49}}$ **33.** $\sqrt{\dfrac{36}{25}}$

34. $\sqrt{\dfrac{3}{4}}$ **35.** $\sqrt{\dfrac{13}{25}}$ **36.** $\sqrt{\dfrac{11}{16}}$ **37.** $\sqrt{\dfrac{7}{36}}$

Rationalizing a Denominator **Simplify the expression.**

38. $\dfrac{4}{\sqrt{5}}$ **39.** $\dfrac{7}{\sqrt{13}}$ **40.** $\sqrt{\dfrac{7}{11}}$ **41.** $\sqrt{\dfrac{7}{6}}$

42. $\sqrt{\dfrac{18}{15}}$ **43.** $\sqrt{\dfrac{13}{28}}$ **44.** $\sqrt{\dfrac{5}{8}}$ **45.** $\sqrt{\dfrac{24}{63}}$

Checking Solutions **Tell whether the given value of x is a solution of the equation.**

46. $4x^2 = 108; x = 3\sqrt{2}$ **47.** $3x^2 = 150; x = 5\sqrt{2}$

48. $3x^2 - 5 = 55; x = 2\sqrt{5}$ **49.** $2x^2 + 3 = 15; x = 2\sqrt{3}$

Solving Equations Solve the equation.

50. $x^2 = 81$

51. $2x^2 = 32$

52. $t^2 = 60$

53. $x^2 = 54$

54. $w^2 - 11 = 16$

55. $7x^2 - 10 = 25$

56. $3h^2 + 7 = 55$

57. $-2x^2 + 13 = -43$

58. $5 + \dfrac{x^2}{4} = 23$

EXAMPLE **Solve a Quadratic Equation**

Solve $2(x - 5)^2 = 12$.

Solution

$2(x - 5)^2 = 12$	Write original equation.
$(x - 5)^2 = 6$	Divide each side by 2.
$x - 5 = \pm\sqrt{6}$	Take the square root of each side.
$x = 5 \pm \sqrt{6}$	Add 5 to each side.

ANSWER ▶ The solutions are $5 + \sqrt{6}$ and $5 - \sqrt{6}$.

Solving Equations Solve the equation.

59. $(y - 5)^2 = 9$

60. $(x + 3)^2 = 5$

61. $3(b - 4)^2 = 27$

62. $2(x + 5)^2 = 32$

63. $-4(z - 7)^2 = -72$

64. $4(x - 2)^2 = 7$

65. $9(x - 4)^2 = 8$

66. $\dfrac{1}{2}(p + 4)^2 = 22$

67. $\dfrac{1}{7}(x + 6)^2 = 8$

68. *Geometry Link* The side length of a square is $(x + 3)$ feet. The area of the square is 16 square feet. What is the length (in feet) of a side of the square?

Golden Gate Bridge **In Exercises 69 and 70, use the following information.**

The Golden Gate Bridge in San Francisco, California, was under construction from 1933 to 1937. Suppose a construction worker dropped a tool from a point on the bridge that is 220 feet above the water.

69. Write an equation that gives the height (in feet) of the tool above the water as a function of time (in seconds).

70. How many seconds would the tool take to hit the water?

71. Falling Object A rock falls from a height of 80 feet. Write an equation that gives the height (in feet) of the rock above the ground as a function of time (in seconds). How many seconds will the rock take to hit the ground?

72. Ribbon Falls Ribbon Falls is in Yosemite National Park in California. The height of the falls is about 1612 feet. A rock falls from the top of Ribbon Falls. How many seconds will the rock take to reach the bottom of the falls?

73. Niagara Falls Niagara Falls is made up of three waterfalls. One of the falls is Horseshoe Falls, in Canada. The height of Horseshoe Falls is 167 feet. A log falls from the top of Horseshoe Falls. How many seconds will the log take to reach the bottom of the falls?

74. Challenge The side lengths of a quadrilateral are shown. The quadrilateral is divided into two right triangles. Use the Pythagorean theorem to find the value of x. What is the length (in feet) of each side of the quadrilateral?

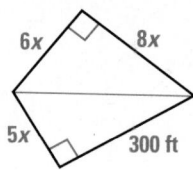

75. Multiple Choice What is a completely simplified expression for $\sqrt{108}$?

  A $2\sqrt{27}$ **B** $3\sqrt{12}$ **C** $6\sqrt{3}$ **D** $18\sqrt{3}$

76. Multiple Choice What is a completely simplified expression for $\sqrt{\dfrac{18}{11}}$?

  F $\dfrac{3\sqrt{2}}{11}$ **G** $\dfrac{3\sqrt{22}}{11}$ **H** $\dfrac{\sqrt{198}}{11}$ **J** $3\sqrt{2}$

77. Multiple Choice What are the solutions of $\dfrac{1}{2}x^2 - 11 = 25$?

  A $\sqrt{72}$ and $-\sqrt{72}$ **B** 6 and -6

  C $6\sqrt{2}$ and $-6\sqrt{2}$ **D** $36\sqrt{2}$ and $-36\sqrt{2}$

78. Multiple Choice What are the solutions of $5y^2 + 4 = 14$?

  F $\sqrt{2}$ and $-\sqrt{2}$ **G** $\sqrt{\dfrac{18}{5}}$ and $-\sqrt{\dfrac{18}{5}}$

  H 2 and -2 **J** $\sqrt{5}$ and $-\sqrt{5}$

Systems of Inequalities **Graph the system of linear inequalities.** *(Lesson 4.3)*

79. $x \le 5$
$\quad y < 0$

80. $y \ge x$
$\quad y > 3$

81. $y > 2x + 1$
$\quad y < x + 3$

82. $x + 2y \le 5$
$\quad 2x - y \ge 1$

83. $y > -5$
$\quad x - y \ge 3$
$\quad x + y \le 3$

84. $2y - x < 6$
$\quad x \le y$
$\quad x + y > 5$

Writing in Standard Form **Write the function in standard form.** *(Lesson 5.1)*

85. $y = (x - 7)(x + 2)$ **86.** $y = (x + 5)(x + 8)$ **87.** $y = (2x - 1)(x - 4)$

88. $y = (3x - 2)(x + 5)$ **89.** $y = (x - 4)^2 + 6$ **90.** $y = (x + 3)^2 - 4$

Factoring **Factor the expression.** *(Lesson 5.4)*

91. $8x^2 - 6x - 9$ **92.** $3y^2 - 17y + 10$ **93.** $6x^2 - 19x - 20$

94. $10z^2 + 31z + 15$ **95.** $12x^2 + 19x - 21$ **96.** $9x^2 - 36x + 32$

Radius of a Circle **Use the area A of the circle to find the radius r. Round your answer to the nearest whole number.**

97. $A = 201$ ft^2 **98.** $A = 707$ m^2 **99.** $A = 154$ in.^{2}

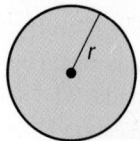   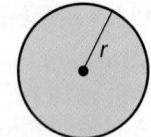   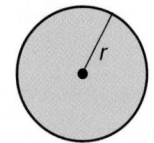

5.7 Complex Numbers

GOAL Understand and use complex numbers.

Key Words
- imaginary unit i
- complex number
- imaginary number
- complex conjugates

The square of any real number x is never negative, so the equation $x^2 = -1$ has no real number solution.

To solve this equation, mathematicians created an expanded system of numbers using the **imaginary unit i**, defined as a number such that $i^2 = -1$. Note that $i = \sqrt{-1}$. The imaginary unit i can be used to write the square root of *any* negative number

---

Prerequisite Skills

Simplify.

1. $\sqrt{8}$

2. $\sqrt{20}$

Find the product.

3. $(x + 2)(x - 2)$

4. $2x(3 - x)$

The Square Root of a Negative Number

PROPERTY	EXAMPLE
1. If r is a positive real number, then $\sqrt{-r} = i\sqrt{r}$.	$\sqrt{-5} = i\sqrt{5}$
2. By Property (1), it follows that $(i\sqrt{r})^2 = -r$.	$(i\sqrt{5})^2 = i^2 \cdot 5 = -5$

EXAMPLE 1 Solve a Quadratic Equation

Solve the equation.

a. $7x^2 = -49$ 　　　　　 **b.** $3x^2 - 5 = -29$

Solution

a. $7x^2 = -49$	Write original equation.
$x^2 = -7$	Divide each side by 7.
$x = \pm\sqrt{-7}$	Take the square root of each side.
$x = \pm i\sqrt{7}$	Write in terms of i.

b. $3x^2 - 5 = -29$	Write original equation.
$3x^2 = -24$	Add 5 to each side.
$x^2 = -8$	Divide each side by 3.
$x = \pm\sqrt{-8}$	Take the square root of each side.
$x = \pm i\sqrt{8}$	Write in terms of i.
$x = \pm 2i\sqrt{2}$	Simplify the radical.

STUDENT HELP

READING ALGEBRA
The letter i represents a number. It is a constant, not a variable. Writing i instead of $\sqrt{-1}$ makes writing complex numbers simpler.

Checkpoint ✓ *Solve a Quadratic Equation*

Solve the equation.

1. $x^2 = -3$ 　　　　 **2.** $x^2 = -7$ 　　　　 **3.** $x^2 = -20$

4. $x^2 + 3 = -2$ 　　　 **5.** $y^2 - 4 = -12$ 　　　 **6.** $2x^2 + 7 = -17$

Complex Numbers A **complex number** written in standard form is a number $a + bi$ where a and b are real numbers. The number a is the *real part* of the complex number. The number bi is the *imaginary part*. The diagram below shows the different types of complex numbers.

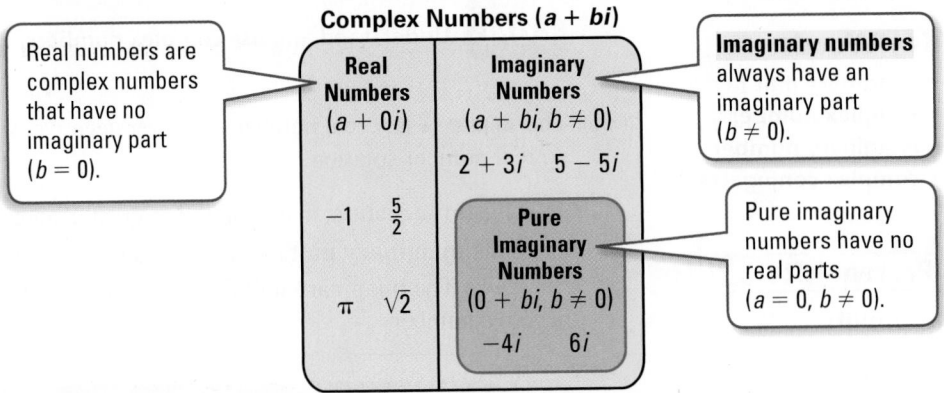

Complex Numbers ($a + bi$)

Real numbers are complex numbers that have no imaginary part ($b = 0$).

Real Numbers ($a + 0i$)
-1 $\frac{5}{2}$
π $\sqrt{2}$

Imaginary Numbers ($a + bi$, $b \neq 0$)
$2 + 3i$ $5 - 5i$

Imaginary numbers always have an imaginary part ($b \neq 0$).

Pure Imaginary Numbers ($0 + bi$, $b \neq 0$)
$-4i$ $6i$

Pure imaginary numbers have no real parts ($a = 0$, $b \neq 0$).

Add Complex Numbers To add complex numbers, add their real parts and their imaginary parts separately.

EXAMPLE 2 **Add Complex Numbers**

Write $(3 + 2i) + (1 - i)$ as a complex number in standard form.

Solution

$(3 + 2i) + (1 - i) = (3 + 1) + (2 - 1)i$ Group real and imaginary terms.

$\qquad\qquad\qquad\quad = 4 + i$ Write in standard form.

Subtract Complex Numbers To subtract complex numbers, subtract their real parts and their imaginary parts separately.

EXAMPLE 3 **Subtract Complex Numbers**

Write $(6 - 2i) - (1 - 2i)$ as a complex number in standard form.

Solution

$(6 - 2i) - (1 - 2i) = (6 - 1) + (-2 + 2)i$ Group real and imaginary terms.

$\qquad\qquad\qquad\quad = 5 + 0i$ Simplify.

$\qquad\qquad\qquad\quad = 5$ Write in standard form.

Checkpoint ✓ *Add and Subtract Complex Numbers*

Write the expression as a complex number in standard form.

7. $(4 - 2i) + (1 + 3i)$

8. $(3 - i) + (2 + 4i)$

9. $(4 + 6i) - (2 + 3i)$

10. $(-2 + 4i) - (2 + 7i)$

11. $(1 - 2i) + (4 + 5i)$

12. $(2 - i) - (-1 - 4i)$

Multiply Complex Numbers To multiply two complex numbers, use the distributive property or the FOIL method.

EXAMPLE 4 **Multiply Complex Numbers**

Write the expression as a complex number in standard form.

　a. $2i(-1 + 3i)$ 　　　　　　　　　　　**b.** $(6 + 3i)(4 - 3i)$

Solution

　a. $2i(-1 + 3i) = -2i + 6i^2$ 　　　Multiply using distributive property.

　　　　　　　　$= -2i + 6(-1)$ 　　Use $i^2 = -1$.

　　　　　　　　$= -6 - 2i$ 　　　　Write in standard form.

　b. $(6 + 3i)(4 - 3i) = 24 - 18i + 12i - 9i^2$ 　　　Multiply using FOIL.

　　　　　　　　　　　$= 24 - 6i - 9i^2$ 　　　　Simplify.

　　　　　　　　　　　$= 24 - 6i - 9(-1)$ 　　Use $i^2 = -1$.

　　　　　　　　　　　$= 33 - 6i$ 　　　　　　Write in standard form.

Complex Conjugates Two complex numbers of the form $a + bi$ and $a - bi$ are called **complex conjugates**. The product of complex conjugates is always a real number. You can use complex conjugates to write the quotient of two complex numbers in standard form.

EXAMPLE 5 **Divide Complex Numbers**

Write $\dfrac{3 + 2i}{1 - 2i}$ as a complex number in standard form.

Solution

$\dfrac{3 + 2i}{1 - 2i} = \dfrac{3 + 2i}{1 - 2i} \cdot \dfrac{1 + 2i}{1 + 2i}$　　Multiply the numerator and the denominator by $1 + 2i$, the complex conjugate of $1 - 2i$.

$= \dfrac{3 + 6i + 2i + 4i^2}{1 + 2i - 2i - 4i^2}$　　Multiply using FOIL.

$= \dfrac{3 + 8i + 4(-1)}{1 - 4(-1)}$　　Simplify and use $i^2 = -1$.

$= \dfrac{-1 + 8i}{5}$　　Simplify.

$= -\dfrac{1}{5} + \dfrac{8}{5}i$　　Write in standard form.

STUDENT HELP

SOLVING NOTE
Notice that the result of multiplying a complex number by its complex conjugate is very similar to the difference of two squares pattern used to multiply binomials.

 **Multiply and Divide Complex Numbers**

Write the expression as a complex number in standard form.

13. $3i(2 - i)$ 　　　　**14.** $(1 + 2i)(2 - i)$ 　　　　**15.** $\dfrac{2 + i}{1 - i}$

Guided Practice

Vocabulary Check

1. Identify the *real* part and the *imaginary* part of the complex number $4 - 7i$.

2. What is the complex conjugate of the number $2 - 5i$?

Skill Check

Solve the equation.

3. $x^2 = -14$ **4.** $x^2 = -4$ **5.** $t^2 + 20 = -4$

6. $r^2 - 3 = -9$ **7.** $3x^2 + 7 = -29$ **8.** $2x^2 + 31 = 9$

Write the expression as a complex number in standard form.

9. $(2 + 3i) + (5 + 4i)$ **10.** $(3 + 2i) + (-6 + 5i)$

11. $(10 - 6i) - (5 + 8i)$ **12.** $3i(1 + 5i)$

13. $(-3 + 4i)(2 - i)$ **14.** $\dfrac{5 - 3i}{1 + i}$

Practice and Applications

STUDENT HELP

HOMEWORK HELP
Example 1: Exs. 15–26
Example 2: Exs. 27–32
Example 3: Exs. 33–38
Example 4: Exs. 39–50
Example 5: Exs. 51–58

Solving Equations **Solve the equation.**

15. $x^2 = -36$ **16.** $x^2 = -7$ **17.** $5w^2 = -65$

18. $4n^2 = -48$ **19.** $x^2 + 7 = -11$ **20.** $x^2 - 5 = -13$

21. $x^2 - 6 = 4$ **22.** $3y^2 + 9 = -30$ **23.** $4x^2 + 8 = -48$

24. $4x^2 + 5 = -31$ **25.** $3x^2 + 6 = -60$ **26.** $(k - 6)^2 = -9$

Adding **Write the expression as a complex number in standard form.**

27. $(3 + 2i) + (4 + 5i)$ **28.** $(2 - 6i) + (-7 + 3i)$

29. $(3 + i) + (-5 - 6i)$ **30.** $(10 + i) + (-3 - i)$

31. $(6 - 2i) + (2 - 3i)$ **32.** $(12 - 8i) + (6 + 5i)$

Subtracting **Write the expression as a complex number in standard form.**

33. $(5 + 6i) - (7 + 3i)$ **34.** $(-4 + 9i) - (-5 + 3i)$

35. $(-2 + 4i) - (-4 - 3i)$ **36.** $(8 - 3i) - (10 - 6i)$

37. $(5 - 10i) - (8 - 11i)$ **38.** $(30 + 13i) - (-30 + 7i)$

Multiplying **Write the expression as a complex number in standard form.**

39. $5(6i)$ **40.** $(3i)(4i)$ **41.** $(-2i)(10i)$

42. $i(2 + 5i)$ **43.** $2i(3 - 7i)$ **44.** $-12i(5 + 6i)$

45. $(4 + i)(7 + i)$ **46.** $(6 + 2i)(-3 - 5i)$ **47.** $(4 + 8i)(1 - 3i)$

48. $(5 - 7i)(-4 - 3i)$ **49.** $(9 + 2i)(9 - 2i)$ **50.** $(7 - 6i)^2$

Dividing Write the expression as a complex number in standard form.

51. $\dfrac{4}{i}$

52. $\dfrac{6}{5+i}$

53. $\dfrac{6+i}{4-i}$

54. $\dfrac{3+2i}{2+5i}$

55. $\dfrac{1+5i}{6-3i}$

56. $\dfrac{-7+4i}{2+8i}$

57. $\dfrac{-2-5i}{3i}$

58. $\dfrac{-1-6i}{5+9i}$

Logical Reasoning Copy and complete the statement with *always*, *sometimes*, or *never*.

59. A real number can __?__ be written as a complex number.

60. A rational number can __?__ be written as a complex number.

61. The sum of two imaginary numbers is __?__ an imaginary number.

62. The product of complex conjugates is __?__ an imaginary number.

63. A complex number is __?__ a real number.

Challenge In Exercises 64–71, use the following information.

Every complex number corresponds to a point in the complex plane. The complex plane has a horizontal axis called the *real axis* and a vertical axis called the *imaginary axis*. To plot the point $3 - 2i$ on the complex plane, start at the origin, move 3 units to the right, and then move 2 units down, as shown in the figure.

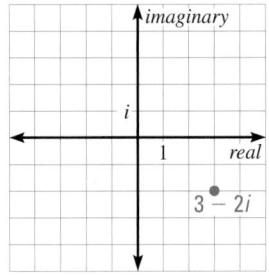

Name the complex number represented by the point in the complex plane.

64. A

65. B

66. C

67. D

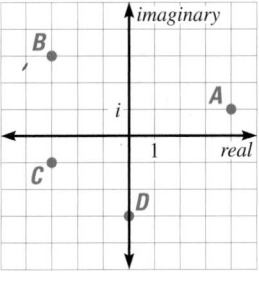

Plot the complex number in the complex plane.

68. $2 + 3i$

69. $-4 + i$

70. $5 - 4i$

71. $-1 - 2i$

72. Multiple Choice What are the solutions of $4x^2 + 5 = -67$?

   (A) $6\sqrt{2}$ and $-6\sqrt{2}$ **(B)** $3i\sqrt{2}$ and $-3i\sqrt{2}$

   (C) $3i\sqrt{7}$ and $-3i\sqrt{7}$ **(D)** $3\sqrt{2}$ and $-3\sqrt{2}$

73. Multiple Choice What are the solutions of $3x^2 + 7 = -29$?

   (F) $i\sqrt{12}$ and $-i\sqrt{12}$ **(G)** $2i\sqrt{3}$ and $-2i\sqrt{3}$

   (H) $4i\sqrt{3}$ and $-4i\sqrt{3}$ **(J)** $4\sqrt{3}$ and $-4\sqrt{3}$

74. Multiple Choice What is the standard form of the expression $\dfrac{2+3i}{3-4i}$?

   (A) $\dfrac{18}{25} + \dfrac{2}{25}i$ **(B)** $-\dfrac{6}{25} + \dfrac{17}{25}i$ **(C)** $-2\dfrac{4}{7} - \dfrac{2}{7}i$ **(D)** $\dfrac{6}{7} + i$

Inequalities in Two Variables Graph the inequality in a coordinate plane. *(Lesson 4.2)*

75. $y > x + 7$

76. $y < 3x + 11$

77. $y > \frac{3}{4}x - 1$

78. $y < -5 - x$

79. $y < \frac{1}{4}x - 5$

80. $y > 5 - 2x$

Evaluating Absolute Value Functions Evaluate the function when $x = 2$ and when $x = -4$. *(Lesson 4.6)*

81. $f(x) = |x|$

82. $f(x) = -3|x|$

83. $f(x) = \frac{1}{2}|x|$

84. $f(x) = |x - 6|$

85. $f(x) = |x + 2| + 7$

86. $f(x) = |x - 10| - 1$

Using the Product Property Simplify the expression. *(Lesson 5.6)*

87. $\sqrt{40}$

88. $\sqrt{63}$

89. $\sqrt{125}$

90. $\sqrt{147}$

91. $\sqrt{80}$

92. $\sqrt{60}$

93. $4\sqrt{6} \cdot \sqrt{6}$

94. $3\sqrt{8} \cdot \sqrt{24}$

95. $\sqrt{5} \cdot 5\sqrt{45}$

96. $\sqrt{7} \cdot \sqrt{56}$

97. $\sqrt{6} \cdot \sqrt{21}$

98. $\sqrt{8} \cdot \sqrt{28}$

Geometry Skills

The Distance Formula Find the distance between the points. Use the distance formula $d = \sqrt{(x_2 - x_1)^2 + (y_2 - y_1)^2}$.

99. $A(1, 4)$, $B(3, -2)$

100. $A(4, 2)$, $B(-4, -2)$

101. $A(-1, 6)$, $B(2, -7)$

102. $A(5, 1)$, $B(-8, -4)$

103. $A(2, -3)$, $B(-4, 1)$

104. $A(-2, 0)$, $B(5, 1)$

Quiz 2

Lesson 5.5

Factor the expression.

1. $36x^2 - 100$

2. $9x^2 - 48x + 64$

3. $y^2 + 30y + 225$

4. $12x^2 - 36x + 27$

5. $4v^2 - 28v + 49$

6. $x^2 - 169$

7. $5x^2 + 50x + 125$

8. $25x^2 + 30x + 9$

9. $4t^2 - 121$

Lesson 5.6

Simplify the expression.

10. $\sqrt{180}$

11. $\sqrt{5} \cdot \sqrt{60}$

12. $4\sqrt{3} \cdot \sqrt{18}$

13. $\sqrt{\frac{75}{49}}$

14. $\sqrt{\frac{54}{5}}$

15. $\sqrt{\frac{16}{80}}$

Lesson 5.6

Solve the equation.

16. $x^2 - 3 = 77$

17. $x^2 - 7 = 29$

18. $5x^2 = 80$

19. $7x^2 - 5 = 9$

20. $2x^2 + 5 = 19$

21. $3x^2 + 5 = 41$

Lesson 5.7

Write the expression as a complex number in standard form.

22. $(6 + 7i) + (4 - 5i)$

23. $(5 + 10i) - (5 + 15i)$

24. $(3 - 3i) - (7 + 8i)$

25. $(26 + 9i) - (14 + i)$

26. $(5 - 2i)(6 + 7i)$

27. $(-2 + 3i)(-2 - 3i)$

28. $(2 + 9i)(3 - 4i)$

29. $\dfrac{-6 + 7i}{10 - 4i}$

30. $\dfrac{-7 + 4i}{2 + 8i}$

DEVELOPING CONCEPTS *(For use with Lesson 5.8)*
Completing the Square

Goal
Complete the square using algebra tiles.

Materials
- algebra tiles

QUESTION

How can you use algebra tiles to complete the square?

You can add a constant c to an expression of the form $x^2 + bx$ so that $x^2 + bx + c$ is a perfect square trinomial. This is called *completing the square*.

EXPLORE

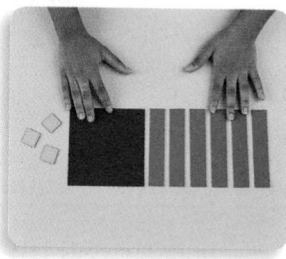 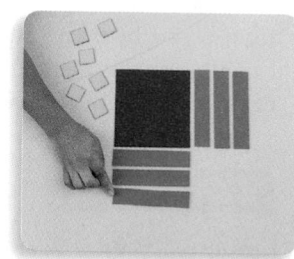 

1 Use algebra tiles to model the expression $x^2 + 6x$. You will need one x^2-tile and six x-tiles.

2 Arrange the x^2-tile and the x-tiles to form part of a square. You want the length and width of the square to be equal.

3 Fill the incomplete corner with 1-tiles. You need to add nine 1-tiles to complete the square.

4 Your model shows that $x^2 + 6x + 9 = (x + 3)^2$.

THINK ABOUT IT

1. Copy and complete the table by following the steps above.

Expression	Number of 1-tiles to complete the square	Expression written as a square
$x^2 + 2x + \underline{?}$	?	$(x + \underline{?})^2$
$x^2 + 4x + \underline{?}$	?	$(x + \underline{?})^2$
$x^2 + 6x + \underline{?}$	?	$(x + \underline{?})^2$

2. Reasoning Look for patterns in the table you completed in Exercise 1.

   a. For each expression, how are the red values in the third column related to the blue values in the first column?

   b. For each expression, how are the green values in the second column related to the red values in the third column?

3. Consider your answers to Exercises 1 and 2. Explain how you could obtain the green values in the second column of the table directly from the blue values in the first column.

5.8 Completing the Square

GOAL Solve quadratic equations by completing the square.

Key Word
• completing the square

Prerequisite Skills

Solve the equation.

1. $x^2 = 9$

2. $2x^2 = 32$

3. $x^2 = 12$

What are the dimensions of a deck?

In Example 5, you will determine what the length and width of a new deck can be by writing a perfect square trinomial.

In Lesson 5.6, you solved equations of the form $x^2 = k$ by taking square roots. You can also use this method if one side of an equation is a perfect square trinomial.

EXAMPLE 1 Solve a Quadratic Equation

Solve $x^2 + 6x + 9 = 36$.

Solution

$x^2 + 6x + 9 = 36$	Write original equation.
$(x + 3)^2 = 36$	Factor perfect square trinomial on left side.
$x + 3 = \pm 6$	Take the square root of each side.
$x = -3 \pm 6$	Solve for x.

ANSWER ▶ The solutions are $-3 + 6 = 3$ and $-3 - 6 = -9$.

Perfect Squares Sometimes you can add a constant c to the expression $x^2 + bx$ to make it a perfect square trinomial. This process is called **completing the square**.

In each diagram below, the total area of the shaded regions is $x^2 + bx$. To complete the square in the second diagram, add $\left(\dfrac{b}{2}\right)^2$.

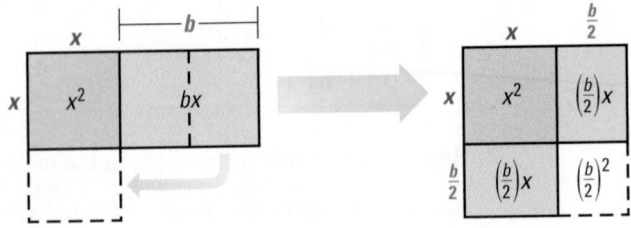

Completing the Square

To complete the square for $x^2 + bx$, add $\left(\dfrac{b}{2}\right)^2$.

ALGEBRA $x^2 + bx + \left(\dfrac{b}{2}\right)^2 = \left(x + \dfrac{b}{2}\right)^2$ **EXAMPLE** $x^2 + 6x + 3^2 = (x + 3)^2$

EXAMPLE 2 Complete the Square

Find the value of c that makes $x^2 - 6x + c$ a perfect square trinomial. Then write the expression as the square of a binomial.

Solution

To find the value of c, complete the square using $b = -6$.

❶ **Find** half the coefficient of x. $\qquad$ $\frac{1}{2}(-6) = -3$

❷ **Square** the result of Step 1. $\qquad$ $(-3)^2 = 9$

❸ **Replace** c with the result of Step 2. $\qquad$ $x^2 - 6x + 9$

ANSWER ▸ The trinomial $x^2 - 6x + c$ is a perfect square when $c = 9$.
Then $x^2 - 6x + 9 = (x - 3)^2$.

Checkpoint ✓ **Perfect Square Trinomials**

1. Solve $x^2 - 2x + 1 = 9$ by finding square roots.

2. Find the value of c that makes $x^2 - 12x + c$ a perfect square trinomial. Then write the expression as the square of a binomial.

Solving Equations Many quadratic equations, such as $x^2 + 6x - 5 = 0$, cannot be solved by factoring. You can solve any quadratic equation by completing the square.

EXAMPLE 3 Solve a Quadratic Equation

Solve $2x^2 - 4x + 6 = 0$ by completing the square.

Solution

$2x^2 - 4x + 6 = 0$	Write original equation.
$x^2 - 2x + 3 = 0$	Divide each side by the coefficient of x^2.
$x^2 - 2x = -3$	Write the left side in the form $x^2 + bx$.
▸ $x^2 - 2x + 1 = -3 + 1$	Add $\left(\frac{-2}{2}\right)^2 = (-1)^2 = 1$ to each side.
$(x - 1)^2 = -2$	Write the left side as the square of a binomial.
$x - 1 = \pm\sqrt{-2}$	Take the square root of each side.
$x = 1 \pm \sqrt{-2}$	Add 1 to each side.
$x = 1 \pm i\sqrt{2}$	Write in terms of i.

ANSWER ▸ The solutions are $1 + i\sqrt{2}$ and $1 - i\sqrt{2}$.

STUDENT HELP

AVOID ERRORS
When completing the square to solve an equation, you must always add the same number to *both sides* of the equation.

Checkpoint ✓ **Solve a Quadratic Equation by Completing the Square**

Solve the equation by completing the square.

3. $x^2 + 4x - 2 = 0$ $\qquad\qquad$ **4.** $x^2 + 8x + 3 = 0$

5. $3w^2 - 6w + 12 = 0$ $\qquad\qquad$ **6.** $w^2 - 12w + 4 = 0$

Vertex Form The vertex form of a quadratic function is $y = a(x - h)^2 + k$ where (h, k) is the vertex. Use completing the square to write a quadratic function in vertex form.

EXAMPLE 4 **Write a Quadratic Function in Vertex Form**

Write $y = x^2 - 10x + 22$ in vertex form. Then identify the vertex.

Solution

$y = x^2 - 10x + 22$	Write original equation.
$y + ? = (x^2 - 10x + ?) + 22$	Prepare to complete the square.
$y + 25 = (x^2 - 10x + 25) + 22$	Add $\left(\dfrac{-10}{2}\right)^2 = (-5)^2 = 25$ to each side.
$y + 25 = (x - 5)^2 + 22$	Write $x^2 - 10x + 25$ as $(x - 5)^2$.
$y = (x - 5)^2 - 3$	Solve for y.

ANSWER ▶ The vertex form is $y = (x - 5)^2 - 3$. The vertex is $(5, -3)$.

You can check your answer by graphing the original equation.

Link to

CAREERS

CONTRACTOR Building and construction contractors work on projects as small as building decks and as large as building skyscrapers.

EXAMPLE 5 **Use a Quadratic Equation to Model Area**

Construction A contractor is building a deck onto the side of a house. The deck will be a rectangle with an area of 120 square feet. The contractor has 32 feet of railing to use along 3 sides of the deck. Each side will be at least 8 feet long. What should the length and width of the deck be?

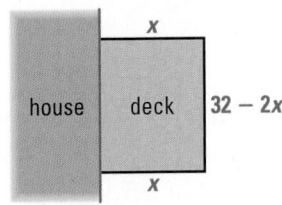

Solution

$x(32 - 2x) = 120$	length $\cdot$ width = area
$32x - 2x^2 = 120$	Use the distributive property.
$x^2 - 16x = -60$	Divide each side by -2.
$x^2 - 16x + 64 = -60 + 64$	Add $\left(\dfrac{-16}{2}\right)^2 = 64$ to each side.
$(x - 8)^2 = 4$	Write left side as the square of a binomial.
$x - 8 = \pm 2$	Take the square root of each side.
$x = 10 \text{ or } 6$	Solve for x.

Reject the solution $x = 6$ because the sides of the deck are at least 8 feet long.

ANSWER ▶ The width is 10 feet. The length is $32 - 2(10) = 12$ feet.

Checkpoint ✓ **Use Completing the Square**

7. Write $y = x^2 - 8x + 19$ in vertex form. Then identify the vertex.

8. Geometry A rectangle has a length of $3x$ and a width of $x + 2$. The area of the rectangle is 72 square units. Find the length and width of the rectangle.

5.8 Exercises

Guided Practice

Vocabulary Check

1. Explain how to complete the square for the expression $x^2 + bx$.

2. Give an example of a quadratic function in vertex form.

Skill Check

Solve the equation by finding square roots.

3. $x^2 - 10x + 25 = 16$ 4. $x^2 + 4x + 4 = 100$ 5. $x^2 - 6x + 9 = 25$

6. $x^2 + 16x + 64 = 36$ 7. $x^2 + 14x + 49 = 1$ 8. $x^2 - 2x + 1 = 144$

Find the value of c that makes the expression a perfect square trinomial. Then write the expression as the square of a binomial.

9. $x^2 + 8x + c$ 10. $x^2 - 10x + c$ 11. $v^2 - 14v + c$

12. $h^2 + 18h + c$ 13. $x^2 - 7x + c$ 14. $a^2 + 3a + c$

Write the quadratic function in vertex form. Then identify the vertex.

15. $y = x^2 - 4x + 7$ 16. $y = x^2 + 8x + 10$ 17. $y = x^2 + 12x + 25$

18. $y = x^2 - 6x - 1$ 19. $y = x^2 + 10x + 30$ 20. $y = x^2 - 8x + 13$

Practice and Applications

STUDENT HELP

HOMEWORK HELP
Example 1: Exs. 21–28
Example 2: Exs. 29–38
Example 3: Exs. 39–57
Example 4: Exs. 58–66
Example 5: Exs. 67–72

Solving Equations **Solve the equation by finding square roots.**

21. $x^2 - 8x + 16 = 25$ 22. $r^2 - 10r + 25 = 1$

23. $y^2 - 24y + 144 = 100$ 24. $x^2 - 22x + 121 = 13$

25. $x^2 - 18x + 81 = 5$ 26. $m^2 + 8m + 16 = 45$

27. $4w^2 + 4w + 1 = 75$ 28. $x^2 - 4x + 4 = 1$

Completing the Square **Find the value of c that makes the expression a perfect square trinomial. Then write the expression as the square of a binomial.**

29. $x^2 + 10x + c$ 30. $y^2 - 12y + c$ 31. $x^2 + 20x + c$

32. $t^2 - 22t + c$ 33. $x^2 - 6x + c$ 34. $x^2 + 24x + c$

35. $z^2 - 5z + c$ 36. $x^2 + 9x + c$ 37. $w^2 + 13w + c$

38. **Error Analysis** Describe and correct the error in finding the value of c that makes $x^2 + 30x + c$ a perfect square trinomial.

$$x^2 + 30x + \left(\frac{900}{2}\right)$$
$$x^2 + 30x + 450$$ ✗

Solving Equations **Solve the equation by completing the square.**

39. $x^2 + 6x = -3$ 40. $x^2 - 10x = 4$ 41. $x^2 + 6x - 6 = 0$

42. $y^2 - 10y - 15 = 0$ 43. $z^2 + 9z = 1$ 44. $x^2 + 8x + 20 = 0$

45. $x^2 + 18x + 100 = 0$ 46. $s^2 - 3s = -5$ 47. $x^2 + 11x = 6$

Solving Equations Solve the equation by completing the square.

48. $2x^2 + 8x = 4$ **49.** $2b^2 - 16b - 10 = 0$ **50.** $3x^2 + 6x = 18$

51. $3x^2 - 12x = -27$ **52.** $5x^2 + 30x = -50$ **53.** $4w^2 - 12w = 24$

54. $2v^2 + 10v + 8 = 0$ **55.** $3x^2 + 15x - 18 = 0$ **56.** $2u^2 + 14u = 10$

57. Error Analysis Describe and correct the error in solving $4x^2 + 24x - 16 = 0$.

$$4x^2 + 24x - 16 = 0$$
$$x^2 + 6x - 4 = 0 \quad \times$$
$$x^2 + 6x = 4$$
$$x^2 + 6x + 9 = 4 + 9$$
$$(x + 3)^2 = 13$$
$$x = -3 + \sqrt{13} \approx 0.61$$

Writing in Vertex Form Write the quadratic function in vertex form. Then identify the vertex.

58. $y = x^2 - 2x + 5$ **59.** $y = x^2 + 10x + 28$ **60.** $y = x^2 - 6x + 4$

61. $y = x^2 - 6x - 2$ **62.** $y = x^2 + 12x + 38$ **63.** $y = x^2 + 8x + 4$

64. $y = x^2 + x + 6$ **65.** $y = x^2 + 3x - 1$ **66.** $y = x^2 - 11x + 5$

Geometry Link Find the value of x.

67. Area of parallelogram $= 48$ ft^2

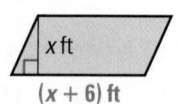

x ft

$(x + 6)$ ft

68. Area of rectangle $= 50$ m^2

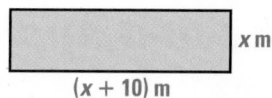

x m

$(x + 10)$ m

Gardening In Exercises 69 and 70, use the following information.

You are planting a garden. The garden will be a rectangle with an area of 80 square feet. You have 40 feet of fencing to use along 3 sides of the garden. The fourth side of the garden is formed by the side of a shed. You want every side of the garden to be more than 3 feet long.

69. Write expressions for the length and width of the garden. Then write an equation for the area of the garden.

70. Use the equation from Exercise 69 to find the length and width of the garden. Explain how you decided which solution of the equation to use in your answer.

Farming In Exercises 71 and 72, use the following information.

A farmer is building a pen for animals beside a barn. The pen will be a rectangle with an area of 1512 square feet. The barn will serve as one side of the pen. The farmer has 120 feet of fencing to use on the other three sides. Each side of the pen will be at least 20 feet long.

71. Write an equation for the area of the pen.

72. Use the equation from Exercise 71 to find the length and width of the pen. Explain how you decided which solution of the equation to use in your answer.

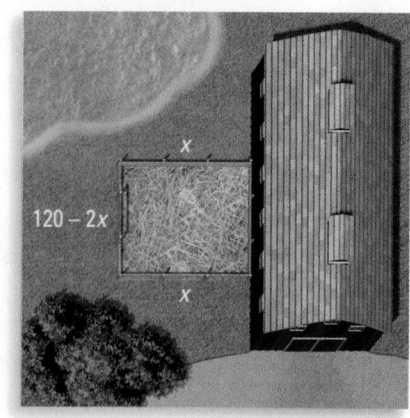

Challenge In Exercises 73–75, use the following information.

While marching, a drum major tosses a baton into the air and catches it. The height h (in feet) of the baton after t seconds can be modeled by the function $h = -16t^2 + 32t + 6$.

73. Write the function in vertex form. If you add a multiple of a number to one side of the function, remember that you must add the same multiple of the number to the other side of the function.

74. What is the maximum height of the baton? Explain how you know.

75. For how many seconds is the baton in the air? Explain how you know.

Standardized Test Practice

76. Multiple Choice Which value of c makes the expression $x^2 - 11x + c$ a perfect square trinomial?

   Ⓐ $\frac{11}{2}$ Ⓑ 22   Ⓒ $\frac{121}{4}$ Ⓓ 121

77. Multiple Choice What are the solutions of $x^2 + 6x - 18 = 0$?

   Ⓕ $3 + 3\sqrt{2}$ and $3 - 3\sqrt{2}$ Ⓖ $3 + 3\sqrt{3}$ and $3 - 3\sqrt{3}$

   Ⓗ $-3 + 3\sqrt{2}$ and $-3 - 3\sqrt{2}$ Ⓙ $-3 + 3\sqrt{3}$ and $-3 - 3\sqrt{3}$

78. Multiple Choice What are the solutions of $x^2 + 4x = 6$?

   Ⓐ $-2 + \sqrt{10}$ and $-2 - \sqrt{10}$ Ⓑ $-\sqrt{10}$ and $\sqrt{10}$

   Ⓒ $-\sqrt{6}$ and $\sqrt{6}$ Ⓓ $2 + \sqrt{10}$ and $2 - \sqrt{10}$

Mixed Review

Solving Equations Solve the equation by factoring. *(Lessons 5.3–5.4)*

79. $x^2 - x - 12 = 0$ **80.** $x^2 + 8x + 15 = 0$ **81.** $t^2 - 13t + 42 = 0$

82. $x^2 + 8x + 7 = 0$ **83.** $x^2 - 4x - 21 = 0$ **84.** $x^2 - 12x + 20 = 0$

85. $4y^2 + 19y - 5 = 0$ **86.** $10x^2 + 27x + 5 = 0$ **87.** $3x^2 - 17x - 6 = 0$

88. $4x^2 - 3x - 10 = 0$ **89.** $12w^2 + 4w - 5 = 0$ **90.** $6s^2 - 29s + 35 = 0$

Adding and Subtracting Write the expression as a complex number in standard form. *(Lesson 5.7)*

91. $(3 + i) + (1 + 4i)$ **92.** $(2 + 3i) - (3 - i)$ **93.** $(5 - 2i) - (7 + 3i)$

94. $(3 + 2i) + (1 - 2i)$ **95.** $(4 + 5i) - (4 + i)$ **96.** $(6 + i) + (-2 - 3i)$

Geometry Skills

Area of Trapezoid Find the value of x.

97. Area $= 48$ ft^2

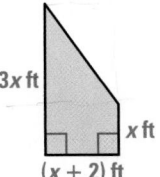

3x ft x ft
$(x + 2)$ ft

98. Area $= 120$ in.^{2}

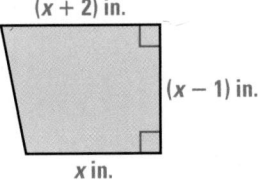

$(x + 2)$ in.
$(x - 1)$ in.
x in.

99. Area $= 12$ cm^2

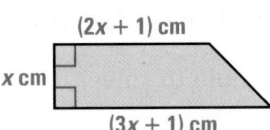

$(2x + 1)$ cm
x cm
$(3x + 1)$ cm

100. Area $= 30$ m^2

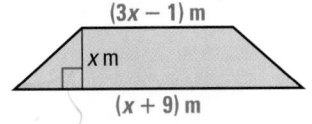

$(3x - 1)$ m
x m
$(x + 9)$ m

5.9 The Quadratic Formula and the Discriminant

Key Words
- quadratic formula
- discriminant

GOAL Solve quadratic equations using the quadratic formula.

Prerequisite Skills

Simplify the expression.

1. $\dfrac{2 + \sqrt{2^2 - 4(1)(-2)}}{2(1)}$

2. $\dfrac{-3 - \sqrt{(-3)^2 - 4(3)(-1)}}{2(3)}$

How long is a volleyball in the air?

In Exercise 67, you will use the quadratic formula to find the amount of time a volleyball is in the air.

In Lesson 5.8, you solved quadratic equations by completing the square for *each equation separately*. By completing the square *once* for the equation $ax^2 + bx + c = 0$, you can develop a formula that gives the solutions of *any* quadratic equation. The formula for the solutions is called the **quadratic formula**.

STUDENT HELP

READING ALGEBRA
The quadratic formula is read as "*x* equals the opposite of *b*, plus or minus the square root of *b* squared minus 4*ac*, all divided by 2*a*."

The Quadratic Formula

Let *a*, *b*, and *c* be real numbers with $a \neq 0$. The solutions of the quadratic equation $ax^2 + bx + c = 0$ are:

$$x = \dfrac{-b \pm \sqrt{b^2 - 4ac}}{2a}$$

EXAMPLE 1 Solve an Equation with Two Real Solutions

Solve $x^2 + 3x - 5 = 0$.

Solution

$x^2 + 3x - 5 = 0$	Write original equation.
$x = \dfrac{-b \pm \sqrt{b^2 - 4ac}}{2a}$	Quadratic formula
$x = \dfrac{-3 \pm \sqrt{3^2 - 4(1)(-5)}}{2(1)}$	Substitute values in the quadratic formula: $a = 1$, $b = 3$, and $c = -5$.
$x = \dfrac{-3 \pm \sqrt{29}}{2}$	Simplify.

ANSWER The solutions are $\dfrac{-3 + \sqrt{29}}{2} \approx 1.19$ and $\dfrac{-3 - \sqrt{29}}{2} \approx -4.19$.

Checkpoint ✓ *Solve an Equation with Two Real Solutions*

Use the quadratic formula to solve the equation.

1. $x^2 + 2x - 3 = 0$ **2.** $2x^2 + 4x - 1 = 0$ **3.** $3x^2 - 2x - 6 = 0$

Write in Standard Form The quadratic formula can be used to solve any quadratic equation that is in standard form. To use the quadratic formula to solve a quadratic equation, you must first write the equation in standard form, $ax^2 + bx + c = 0$.

EXAMPLE 2 Solve an Equation with One Real Solution

Solve $x^2 - 6x = -9$.

Solution

$x^2 - 6x = -9$	Write original equation.
$x^2 - 6x + 9 = 0$	Write equation in standard form.
$x = \dfrac{-b \pm \sqrt{b^2 - 4ac}}{2a}$	Quadratic formula
$x = \dfrac{-(-6) \pm \sqrt{(-6)^2 - 4(1)(9)}}{2(1)}$	Substitute values in the quadratic formula: $a = 1$, $b = -6$, and $c = 9$.
$x = \dfrac{6 \pm \sqrt{0}}{2}$	Simplify.
$x = 3$	Simplify.

ANSWER ▶ The solution is 3.

EXAMPLE 3 Solve an Equation with Imaginary Solutions

Solve $x^2 + 2x + 2 = 0$.

Solution

$x^2 + 2x + 2 = 0$	Write original equation.
$x = \dfrac{-b \pm \sqrt{b^2 - 4ac}}{2a}$	Quadratic formula
$x = \dfrac{-2 \pm \sqrt{2^2 - 4(1)(2)}}{2(1)}$	Substitute values in the quadratic formula: $a = 1$, $b = 2$, and $c = 2$.
$x = \dfrac{-2 \pm \sqrt{-4}}{2}$	Simplify.
$x = \dfrac{-2 \pm 2i}{2}$	Simplify and rewrite using the imaginary unit i.
$x = -1 \pm i$	Simplify.

ANSWER ▶ The solutions are $-1 + i$ and $-1 - i$.

Checkpoint ✓ *Use the Quadratic Formula*

Use the quadratic formula to solve the equation.

4. $x^2 - 2x - 4 = 0$ **5.** $-x^2 - 1 = -3x$ **6.** $2x^2 = -5x + 7$

7. $x^2 + 4x + 5 = 0$ **8.** $-x^2 + 2x - 3 = 0$ **9.** $-2x^2 + x = 4$

Using the Discriminant In the quadratic formula, the expression $b^2 - 4ac$ is called the **discriminant** of the equation $ax^2 + bx + c = 0$.

$$x = \frac{-b \pm \sqrt{b^2 - 4ac}}{2a} \longleftarrow \text{discriminant}$$

You can use the discriminant of a quadratic equation to determine the number of solutions and the type of solutions of the equation.

Discriminant of a Quadratic Equation

The discriminant determines the number and type of solutions.

$b^2 - 4ac > 0$	2 real solutions
$b^2 - 4ac = 0$	1 real solution
$b^2 - 4ac < 0$	2 imaginary solutions

EXAMPLE 4 Use the Discriminant

Find the discriminant of the quadratic equation and give the number and type of solutions of the equation.

a. $x^2 - 6x + 8 = 0$ **b.** $x^2 - 6x + 9 = 0$ **c.** $x^2 - 6x + 10 = 0$

Solution

EQUATION	DISCRIMINANT	TYPE OF SOLUTION(S)
$ax^2 + bx + c = 0$	$b^2 - 4ac$	$x = \dfrac{-b \pm \sqrt{b^2 - 4ac}}{2a}$
a. $x^2 - 6x + 8 = 0$	$(-6)^2 - 4(1)(8) = 4$	Two real
b. $x^2 - 6x + 9 = 0$	$(-6)^2 - 4(1)(9) = 0$	One real
c. $x^2 - 6x + 10 = 0$	$(-6)^2 - 4(1)(10) = -4$	Two imaginary

 **Checkpoint** **Use the Discriminant**

Find the discriminant of the quadratic equation and give the number and type of solutions of the equation.

10. $x^2 + 2x + 3 = 0$ **11.** $-x^2 + 3x + 4 = 0$ **12.** $x^2 - 4x + 4 = 0$

Vertical Motion In Lesson 5.6, you used $h = -16t^2 + h_0$ to model the height of a falling object after t seconds. For an object that is *launched or thrown*, the term $v_0 t$ is used to account for the initial vertical velocity v_0 (in feet per second).

Vertical Motion Models

Dropped or falling object: $h = -16t^2 + h_0$

Launched or thrown object: $h = -16t^2 + v_0 t + h_0$

h = height of object (feet) t = time in motion (seconds)

h_0 = initial height (feet) v_0 = initial vertical velocity (feet per second)

Initial Vertical Velocity In the vertical motion model for a launched object, the value of v_0 can be positive, negative, or zero. The sign of v_0 depends on whether the object is launched upward, downward, or parallel to the ground.

$v_0 > 0$

$v_0 < 0$

$v_0 = 0$

EXAMPLE 5 | Model Vertical Motion

Baton Twirling A baton twirler tosses a baton into the air. The baton leaves her hand when it is 6 feet above the ground. The initial vertical velocity of the baton is 30 feet per second. The baton twirler catches the baton when it falls back to a height of 5 feet.

a. Write an equation that gives the height (in feet) of the baton as a function of time (in seconds).

b. For how many seconds is the baton in the air?

Solution

a. The baton is thrown, so use the model $h = -16t^2 + v_0t + h_0$ with $v_0 = 30$ and $h_0 = 6$.

$h = -16t^2 + v_0t + h_0$ Write vertical motion model for a thrown object.

$h = -16t^2 + 30t + 6$ Substitute 30 for v_0 and 6 for h_0.

b. To find the number of seconds the baton is in the air, find the number of seconds that have passed when the height of the baton is 5 feet. Find the value of t when $h = 5$.

$h = -16t^2 + 30t + 6$ Write model from part (a).

$5 = -16t^2 + 30t + 6$ Substitute 5 for h.

$0 = -16t^2 + 30t + 1$ Write in standard form.

$t = \dfrac{-30 \pm \sqrt{30^2 - 4(-16)(1)}}{2(-16)}$ Substitute values in the quadratic formula: $a = -16$, $b = 30$, and $c = 1$.

$t \approx 1.9$ or $t \approx -0.03$ Use a calculator.

ANSWER ▶ The solution -0.03 doesn't make sense, because time cannot be negative. The baton is in the air for about 1.9 seconds.

CHECK You can check your results by graphing $y = -16x^2 + 30x + 1$ and finding when $y = 0$. Because the graph crosses the x-axis at about $x = 1.9$, your answer is correct. ✓

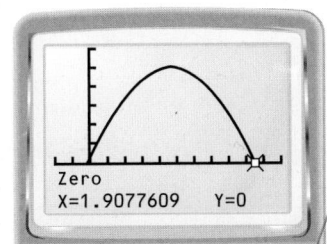

Guided Practice

Vocabulary Check

1. In the quadratic formula, what is the expression $b^2 - 4ac$ called?

2. In the vertical motion model for a launched object, what does v_0 represent?

Skill Check **Use the quadratic formula to solve the equation.**

3. $x^2 - 7x + 10 = 0$ **4.** $x^2 + 3x - 7 = 0$ **5.** $x^2 + 4x + 9 = 0$

6. $3x^2 + 7x + 3 = 0$ **7.** $2x^2 - 6x + 1 = 0$ **8.** $x^2 - 2x + 7 = 0$

Find the discriminant of the quadratic equation and give the number and type of solutions of the equation.

9. $x^2 - 4x + 4 = 0$ **10.** $x^2 - x - 3 = 0$ **11.** $3x^2 - 7x + 10 = 0$

12. $2x^2 + 8x - 1 = 0$ **13.** $2x^2 + 12x + 18 = 0$ **14.** $2x^2 + 5x + 9 = 0$

15. Error Analysis Describe and correct the error in finding the discriminant.

$$x^2 - 8x + 16 = 0$$
$$(-8)^2 - 4(-8)(16) = 576 \quad \times$$

Practice and Applications

STUDENT HELP

HOMEWORK HELP
Example 1: Exs. 25–50
Example 2: Exs. 16–50
Example 3: Exs. 25–50
Example 4: Exs. 51–62
Example 5: Exs. 63–74

Standard Form Write the equation in standard form. Identify the values of *a*, *b*, and *c*.

16. $2x^2 = -3x + 4$ **17.** $3 - 4x^2 = x$ **18.** $5x = x^2$

19. $3x^2 - 4x = -1$ **20.** $x^2 = 7$ **21.** $-3x + 7 = -2x^2$

22. $5x^2 + 7 = 2x$ **23.** $3x^2 = -x$ **24.** $2 = -x + 2x^2$

Solving Equations in Standard Form Use the quadratic formula to solve the equation.

25. $x^2 - x + 12 = 0$ **26.** $x^2 - 5x + 2 = 0$ **27.** $2x^2 + 4x - 5 = 0$

28. $3x^2 - 6x - 1 = 0$ **29.** $5x^2 + 7x + 1 = 0$ **30.** $2x^2 - 5x + 5 = 0$

31. $x^2 + 2x + 6 = 0$ **32.** $-2x^2 + 3x - 5 = 0$ **33.** $4x^2 - 4x - 1 = 0$

34. $-3x^2 + x - 2 = 0$ **35.** $2x^2 + 9x + 6 = 0$ **36.** $-x^2 + 3x - 9 = 0$

Solving Equations Not in Standard Form Use the quadratic formula to solve the equation.

37. $x^2 + 11 = -10x$ **38.** $4x + 2 = -x^2$ **39.** $2x^2 + 3x = 6$

40. $5x - x^2 = -7$ **41.** $3x^2 + 7 = 7x$ **42.** $2x^2 = 15x + 9$

43. $11x = 2x^2 + 20$ **44.** $x^2 - 7x = -20$ **45.** $20x - 16x^2 = -5$

46. $14x + 11 = -5x^2$ **47.** $x^2 + 16x = -65$ **48.** $2x^2 + 75 = 20x$

Error Analysis Describe and correct the error in solving the equation.

49.
$$x^2 - 3x - 2 = 0$$
$$x = \frac{3 \pm \sqrt{(-3)^2 - 4(1)(-2)}}{2(1)}$$
$$x = \frac{3 \pm \sqrt{9 - 8}}{2}$$
$$x = \frac{3 \pm 1}{2}$$
$$x = 2 \text{ and } x = 1$$
$\times$

50.
$$2x^2 + 4x - 7 = 0$$
$$x = \frac{4 \pm \sqrt{4^2 - 4(2)(-7)}}{2(2)}$$
$$x = \frac{4 \pm \sqrt{16 + 56}}{4}$$
$$x = \frac{4 \pm 6\sqrt{2}}{4}$$
$$x = 1 \pm \frac{3\sqrt{2}}{2}$$
$\times$

Using the Discriminant Find the discriminant of the quadratic equation and give the number and type of solutions of the equation.

51. $2x^2 - 5x + 2 = 0$

52. $9x^2 - 24x + 16 = 0$

53. $x^2 + 14x + 49 = 0$

54. $5x^2 - 11x + 9 = 0$

55. $-2x^2 + 12x - 21 = 0$

56. $-x^2 + 10x + 10 = 0$

57. $3x^2 - 9x = -14$

58. $2x^2 + 11x = 15$

59. $3x^2 + 5 = 5x$

60. $4x^2 + 64 = 32x$

61. $4x^2 + 12x + 9 = 0$

62. $2x^2 + x = 7$

Olympic Platform Diving In Exercises 63–65, use the following information.

In Olympic platform diving, the athletes dive from a platform that is 32.8 feet above the water. A diver leaves the platform with an initial vertical velocity of 4 feet per second.

63. Which vertical motion model can you use to represent this situation? Explain your reasoning.

64. Use the model from Exercise 63 to write an equation that gives the height (in feet) of the diver above the water as a function of time (in seconds).

65. For how many seconds is the diver in the air before reaching the water?

Volleyball In Exercises 66 and 67, use the following information.

You are playing volleyball. You hit the volleyball with an initial vertical velocity of -30 feet per second when it is 7 feet above the ground. The volleyball lands on the ground after you hit it.

66. Write an equation that gives the height (in feet) of the volleyball above the ground as a function of time (in seconds).

67. For how many seconds is the volleyball in the air before it lands on the ground?

Baseball In Exercises 68 and 69, use the following information.

A player hits a baseball with an initial vertical velocity of 90 feet per second when it is 3 feet above the ground. No player in the field catches the baseball.

68. Write an equation that gives the height (in feet) of the baseball above the ground as a function of the time (in seconds) after it is hit.

69. Find the number of seconds that the baseball is in the air.

70. Golf After a golfer hits a golf ball, the ball leaves the ground with an initial vertical velocity of 100 feet per second. Make a sketch to model the situation. For how many seconds is the golf ball in the air before landing on the ground?

71.  **Football** You and a friend are playing catch with a football. The football leaves your hand with an initial vertical velocity of 40 feet per second when it is 6 feet above the ground. Your friend catches the ball when it is 3 feet above the ground. Make a sketch to model the situation. For how many seconds is the ball in the air before your friend catches it?

Rock Climbing In Exercises 72–74, use the following information.

A rock climber stands on a cliff and drops a coil of rope from a height of 75 feet above the ground below.

72. Which vertical motion model can you use to represent this situation? Explain your reasoning.

73. Use the model from Exercise 72 to write an equation that gives the height (in feet) of the rope as a function of time (in seconds).

74. For how many seconds is the rope in the air before it hits the ground?

75. Critical Thinking Explain the differences between the vertical motion model for launched objects and the model for falling objects.

Challenge Use the discriminant to find all values of *c* for which the equation has (a) two real solutions, (b) one real solution, and (c) two imaginary solutions.

76. $x^2 - 10x + c = 0$ **77.** $x^2 + 16x + c = 0$ **78.** $x^2 - 18x + c = 0$

79. Multiple Choice What are the solutions of $2x^2 + 8x + 7 = 0$?

Ⓐ $2 + \dfrac{\sqrt{2}}{2}$ and $2 - \dfrac{\sqrt{2}}{2}$ Ⓑ $-2 + \dfrac{\sqrt{2}}{2}$ and $-2 - \dfrac{\sqrt{2}}{2}$

Ⓒ $-4 + \sqrt{2}$ and $-4 - \sqrt{2}$ Ⓓ $-2 + \dfrac{i\sqrt{2}}{2}$ and $-2 - \dfrac{i\sqrt{2}}{2}$

80. Multiple Choice What are the solutions of $x^2 + 4x + 8 = 0$?

Ⓕ 0 and -4 Ⓖ $-4 + 4i$ and $-4 - 4i$

Ⓗ $-2 + 2i$ and $-2 - 2i$ Ⓙ $2 + 2i$ and $2 - 2i$

81. Multiple Choice What are the solutions of $3x^2 - 5x = -2$?

Ⓐ $\dfrac{5 + i}{6}$ and $\dfrac{5 - i}{6}$ Ⓑ 1 and $\dfrac{2}{3}$

Ⓒ -1 and $-\dfrac{2}{3}$ Ⓓ $\dfrac{-5 + i}{6}$ and $\dfrac{-5 - i}{6}$

82. Multiple Choice How many real solutions does $x^2 + 8x + 17 = 0$ have?

  (F) No real solutions   **(G)** One real solution

  (H) Two real solutions   **(J)** Many real solutions

Mixed Review

Parallel Lines **Write an equation of the line that passes through the given point and is parallel to the given line.** *(Lesson 2.5)*

83. $(1, -1)$, $y = 2x - 5$ **84.** $(2, 4)$, $y = -x + 8$ **85.** $(-4, -3)$, $y = \frac{1}{2}x + 4$

Solving Linear Systems **Use the substitution method to solve the linear system.** *(Lesson 3.2)*

86. $2x + y = 5$
  $x - 2y = 10$

87. $x - 2y = 8$
  $3x - y = -1$

88. $5x - 3y = -11$
  $3x + y = 13$

89. $3x + y = 3$
  $5x + 2y = 7$

90. $4x + 3y = 12$
  $-x + 2y = -3$

91. $3x + 4y = 0$
  $2x + y = 10$

Solving Quadratic Equations **Solve the equation.** *(Lesson 5.5)*

92. $3x^2 - 11 = 64$ **93.** $2x^2 + 12 = 108$ **94.** $-2x^2 + 5 = -35$

95. $4x^2 - 16x = 24$ **96.** $3x^2 + 90x + 75 = 81$ **97.** $x^2 + 2x - 9 = 0$

Geometry Skills

Area of Triangle **Find the value of x.**

98. Area $= 54$ in.^{2} **99.** Area $= 72$ ft^2 **100.** Area $= 20$ m^2

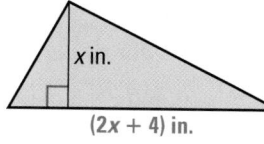
x in.
$(2x + 4)$ in.

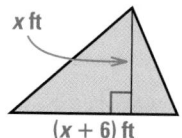
x ft
$(x + 6)$ ft

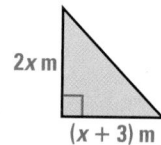
2*x* m
$(x + 3)$ m

Quiz 3

Lesson 5.8

Solve the equation by completing the square.

1. $x^2 - 10x = -21$ **2.** $w^2 + 16w = -20$ **3.** $x^2 + 12x = -30$

4. $x^2 - 18x + 100 = 0$ **5.** $x^2 + 7x - 3 = 0$ **6.** $t^2 - 5t + 15 = 0$

Lesson 5.8

Write the quadratic function in vertex form. Then identify the vertex.

7. $y = x^2 + 8x + 15$ **8.** $y = x^2 - 12x + 21$ **9.** $y = x^2 - 6x - 5$

10. $y = x^2 + 16x + 69$ **11.** $y = x^2 + 11x - 1$ **12.** $y = x^2 - 7x + 3$

Lesson 5.9

Use the quadratic formula to solve the equation.

13. $2x^2 - 5x + 7 = 0$ **14.** $3x^2 + 10x - 4 = 0$ **15.** $x^2 + 12x - 6 = 0$

16. $5x^2 + 10x = -12$ **17.** $4x^2 - 5x = 11$ **18.** $2x^2 + 8x = -13$

Lesson 5.9

Find the discriminant of the quadratic equation and give the number and type of solutions of the equation.

19. $2x^2 + 5x + 15 = 0$ **20.** $2x^2 + 12x + 18 = 0$ **21.** $3x^2 + x - 7 = 0$

22. $3x^2 - 12x + 12 = 0$ **23.** $4x^2 + 7x + 5 = 0$ **24.** $x^2 - 12x - 9 = 0$

Writing Quadratic Functions

Key Words

- best-fitting quadratic model

GOAL Write a quadratic function using given information.

In Lessons 5.1 and 5.2, you graphed quadratic functions. You can also write a quadratic function when you know information about its graph.

EXAMPLE 1 Write a Quadratic Function in Vertex Form

Write a quadratic function for the parabola shown.

Solution

You know the vertex of the parabola is $(1, -2)$. You can use vertex form to write the function.

$y = a(x - h)^2 + k$ Vertex form

$y = a(x - 1)^2 - 2$ Substitute 1 for h and -2 for k.

Use the other given point, $(3, 2)$, to find a.

$2 = a(3 - 1)^2 - 2$ Substitute 3 for x and 2 for y.

$2 = 4a - 2$ Simplify.

$1 = a$ Solve for a.

ANSWER ▶ A quadratic function for the parabola is $y = (x - 1)^2 - 2$.

EXAMPLE 2 Write a Quadratic Function in Intercept Form

Write a quadratic function for the parabola shown.

Solution

You know the x-intercepts of the graph are -2 and 3. You can use intercept form to write the function.

$y = a(x - p)(x - q)$ Intercept form

$y = a(x + 2)(x - 3)$ Substitute -2 for p and 3 for q.

Use the other given point, $(0, 6)$, to find a.

$6 = a(0 + 2)(0 - 3)$ Substitute 0 for x and 6 for y.

$6 = -6a$ Simplify.

$-1 = a$ Solve for a.

ANSWER ▶ A quadratic function for the parabola is $y = -(x + 2)(x - 3)$.

 **Write a Quadratic Function**

Write a quadratic function for the parabola.

   1. vertex: $(4, -3)$; point: $(2, -1)$ **2.** x-intercepts: $-2, 5$; point: $(6, 2)$

Quadratic Regression In Chapter 2, you used a graphing calculator to perform linear regression on a data set. This gave you a linear model for the data. You can also perform *quadratic regression* on a data set to find the **best-fitting quadratic model**.

EXAMPLE **3** **Use Quadratic Regression to Find a Model**

Temperature The table shows the mean temperature (in degrees Fahrenheit) in Chicago, Illinois, for each month (January = 1, February = 2, . . .) of 2005. Use a graphing calculator to find the best-fitting quadratic model for the data.

Month	1	2	3	4	5	6
Temperature	24.5	32.4	35.0	51.6	57.1	74.2
Month	7	8	9	10	11	12
Temperature	75.6	74.3	69.4	55.2	42.0	23.3

Solution

① ***Enter*** the data into two lists on a graphing calculator.

② ***Make*** a scatter plot of the data.

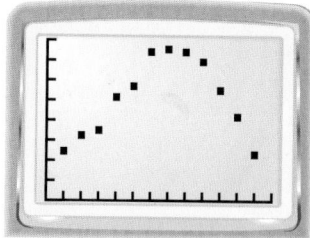

STUDENT HELP

READING GRAPHS
You can use the graph of your model and the data points to see how well the model fits the data.

③ ***Use*** the quadratic regression feature to find the best-fitting model for the data.

④ ***Graph*** the model and the data in the same viewing window.

```
QuadReg
y=ax²+bx+c
a=-1.631218781
b=22.4526973
c=-6.368181818
```

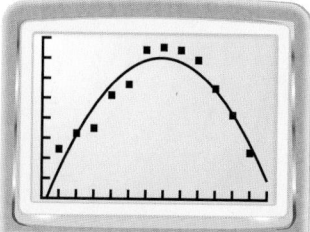

ANSWER ▶ The best-fitting quadratic model is $y = -1.63x^2 + 22.4x - 6.37$.

Checkpoint ✓ **Use Quadratic Regression**

3. Sound Velocity The table shows the velocity (in feet per second) of sound in water of various temperatures (in degrees Fahrenheit). Use a graphing calculator to find the best-fitting quadratic model for the data.

Water temperature	250	300	350	400	450	500
Sound velocity	4974	4806	4587	4331	4010	3650

Exercises

STUDENT HELP

HOMEWORK HELP
Example 1: Exs. 1–6
Example 2: Exs. 7–12
Example 3: Exs. 13, 14

Writing in Vertex Form Write a quadratic function in vertex form for the parabola shown.

1.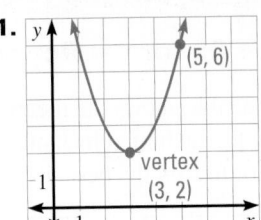

2.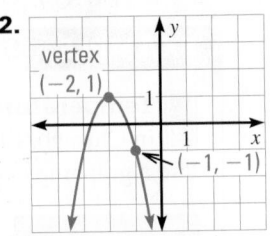

3.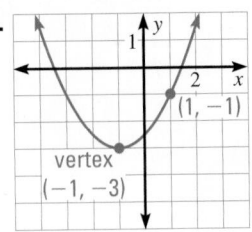

Writing in Vertex Form Write a quadratic function in vertex form whose graph has the given vertex and passes through the given point.

4. vertex: $(2, -1)$
point: $(4, 3)$

5. vertex: $(-4, 6)$
point: $(-1, 9)$

6. vertex: $(4, 5)$
point: $(8, -3)$

Writing in Intercept Form Write a quadratic function in intercept form for the parabola shown.

7.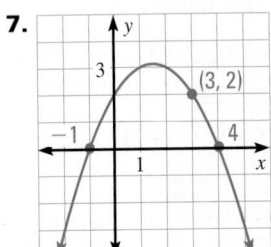

8.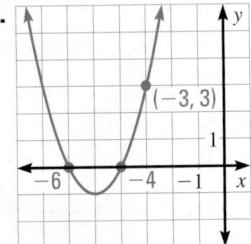

9.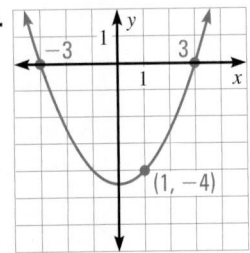

Writing in Intercept Form Write a quadratic function in intercept form whose graph has the given x-intercepts and passes through the given point.

10. x-intercepts: 1, 4
point: $(3, 2)$

11. x-intercepts: -2, 2
point: $(-4, 8)$

12. x-intercepts: -1, 6
point: $(1, -20)$

13. Television Prices The table shows the prices of some popular brands of one type of television for various sizes (in inches). Use a graphing calculator to find the best-fitting quadratic model for the data.

Size	14	20	24	27	32	36
Price	86.99	122.99	159.99	269.99	494.99	899.99

14. Touchdown Record In 2007, Jerry Rice held the record for scoring the most touchdowns in the history of the National Football League. The table shows the total number of touchdowns Rice scored in his career after certain numbers of years since 1985 (0 represents 1985, 1 represents 1986, . . .). Use a graphing calculator to find the best-fitting quadratic model for the data.

Years since 1985	0	3	6	9	12	15	18
Career touchdowns	4	53	97	138	164	185	203

VOCABULARY

• quadratic function, *p. 222*
• parabola, *p. 222*
• vertex, *p. 222*
• axis of symmetry, *p. 222*
• monomial, *p. 224*
• binomial, *p. 224*
• vertex form, *p. 228*
• intercept form, *p. 229*

• minimum value, *p. 230*
• maximum value, *p. 230*
• trinomial, *p. 234*
• quadratic equation, *p. 235*
• zero of a function, *p. 242*
• square root, *p. 255*
• radical, *p. 255*
• radicand, *p. 255*

• rationalizing the denominator, *p. 256*
• imaginary unit *i*, *p. 261*
• complex number, *p. 262*
• imaginary number, *p. 262*
• complex conjugates, *p. 263*
• completing the square, *p. 268*
• quadratic formula, *p. 274*
• discriminant, *p. 276*

VOCABULARY EXERCISES

1. Copy and complete: The quadratic function $y = -2(x - 8)^2 + 3$ is written in __?__ form.

2. A quadratic function is written in standard form. How do you know if the function has a maximum value or a minimum value?

3. How can the discriminant be used to determine the number and type of solutions of a quadratic equation?

5.1 GRAPHING QUADRATIC FUNCTIONS IN STANDARD FORM

Examples on pp. 222–224

> **EXAMPLE** To graph a quadratic function in standard form, find the axis of symmetry and the vertex. Graph the function $y = x^2 - 4x + 3$.
>
> The function is in standard form $y = ax^2 + bx + c$ where $a = 1$, $b = -4$, and $c = 3$.
>
> **Axis of symmetry** $x = -\dfrac{b}{2a} = -\dfrac{(-4)}{2(1)} = 2$
>
> **Vertex** The *x*-coordinate of the vertex is 2. Find the *y*-coordinate.
> $y = (2)^2 - 4(2) + 3 = -1.$
> The vertex is $(2, -1)$.
>
> Evaluate the function for *x*-values less than 3, such as 0 and 1, to find points to the left of the axis of symmetry. Plot the points and their mirror images.
> $(1, 0), (3, 0), (0, 3), (4, 3)$
> Draw a parabola through the points.

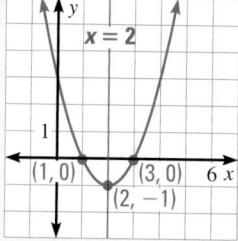

REVIEW HELP
Exercises	Example
4–6	**2**, p. 223

Graph the function. Label the vertex and the axis of symmetry.

4. $y = x^2 - 2x - 8$

5. $y = x^2 + 4x - 3$

6. $y = x^2 + 2x - 5$

EXAMPLE   To graph a quadratic function in intercept form, plot the x-intercepts and the vertex. Graph the function $y = (x - 4)(x + 2)$.

The function is in intercept form $y = a(x - p)(x - q)$ where $a = 1$, $p = 4$, and $q = -2$.

The axis of symmetry is $x = \dfrac{p + q}{2} = \dfrac{4 + (-2)}{2} = 1$.

The x-coordinate of the vertex is 1. The y-coordinate is:

$$y = (1 - 4)(1 + 2) = -9$$

Plot the vertex $(1, -9)$.

The x-intercepts are 4 and -2. Plot $(4, 0)$ and $(-2, 0)$.

Draw a parabola through the points.

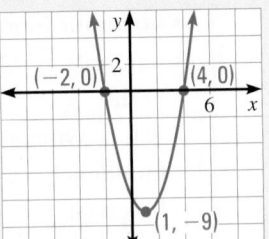

REVIEW HELP

Exercises	Examples
7, 8	**1**, p. 228
9	**2**, p. 229

Graph the function. Label the vertex and the axis of symmetry.

7. $y = (x - 4)^2 + 2$ **8.** $y = (x - 3)(x + 5)$ **9.** $y = (x + 7)(x + 6)$

EXAMPLE   You can sometimes factor to solve equations of the form $x^2 + bx + c = 0$.

$x^2 - 4x = 21$	Write original equation.
$x^2 - 4x - 21 = 0$	Write in standard form.
$(x - 7)(x + 3) = 0$	Factor.
$x - 7 = 0$ or $x + 3 = 0$	Use the zero product property.
$x = 7$ or $x = -3$	Solve for x.

REVIEW HELP

Exercises	Example
10–12	**3**, p. 236

Solve the equation by factoring.

10. $x^2 - 11x + 28 = 0$ **11.** $n^2 + n = 30$ **12.** $x^2 + 6x = 16$

EXAMPLE   You can sometimes factor to solve equations of the form $ax^2 + bx + c = 0$.

$6x^2 - 7x - 20 = 0$	Write original equation.
$(2x - 5)(3x + 4) = 0$	Factor.
$2x - 5 = 0$ or $3x + 4 = 0$	Use the zero product property.
$x = \dfrac{5}{2}$ or $x = -\dfrac{4}{3}$	Solve for x.

REVIEW HELP

Exercises	Example
13–15	**4**, p. 242
13–15	**5**, p. 243

Solve the equation by factoring.

13. $2x^2 - 3x - 5 = 0$ **14.** $6x^2 - 17x + 5 = 0$ **15.** $28y^2 - y - 15 = 0$

5.5 FACTORING SPECIAL PRODUCTS

Examples on pp. 249–251

EXAMPLE You can factor some quadratic expressions using special patterns.

a. $x^2 - 36 = x^2 - 6^2$ Write as $a^2 - b^2$.

          $= (x + 6)(x - 6)$ Difference of two squares pattern

b. $x^2 + 8x + 16 = x^2 + 2(x)(4) + 4^2$ Write as $a^2 + 2ab + b^2$.

          $= (x + 4)^2$ Perfect square trinomial pattern

REVIEW HELP

Exercises	Examples
16, 17	**1**, p. 249
18, 19	**2**, p. 250

Factor the expression.

16. $x^2 - 81$ **17.** $4x^2 - 49$ **18.** $x^2 + 12x + 36$ **19.** $x^2 - 20x + 100$

5.6 SOLVING QUADRATIC EQUATIONS BY FINDING SQUARE ROOTS

Examples on pp. 255–257

EXAMPLE You can use square roots to solve some quadratic equations that have no x-terms.

$4x^2 - 37 = 251$ Write original equation.

$4x^2 = 288$ Add 37 to each side.

$x^2 = 72$ Divide each side by 4.

$x = \pm\sqrt{72}$ Take the square root of each side.

$x = \pm\sqrt{36} \cdot \sqrt{2}$ Product property of square roots

$x = \pm 6\sqrt{2}$ Simplify.

REVIEW HELP

Exercises	Example
20–23	**3**, p. 256

Solve the equation.

20. $2x^2 = 62$ **21.** $x^2 + 9 = 90$ **22.** $5x^2 - 21 = 99$ **23.** $\frac{1}{2}x^2 + 12 = 45$

5.7 COMPLEX NUMBERS

Examples on pp. 261–263

EXAMPLE You can perform operations with complex numbers.

a. $(6 - 3i) + (4 + 5i) = (6 + 4) + (-3 + 5)i$ Group real and imaginary terms.

          $= 3 + 8i$ Write in standard form.

b. $(3 - 5i)(1 + 3i) = 3 + 9i - 5i - 15i^2$ Multiply using FOIL.

          $= 3 + 4i - 15(-1)$ Use $i^2 = -1$.

          $= 18 + 4i$ Write in standard form.

REVIEW HELP

Exercises	Examples
24	**2**, p. 262
25	**3**, p. 262
26, 27	**4**, p. 263
28, 29	**5**, p. 263

Write the expression as a complex number in standard form.

24. $(4 + 2i) + (3 - i)$ **25.** $(3 - 2i) - (6 - 3i)$ **26.** $(1 - 7i)(3 + 2i)$

27. $(4 - 5i)(2 - 6i)$ **28.** $\dfrac{5 + 2i}{2 - 4i}$ **29.** $\dfrac{6 - 5i}{2 + i}$

5.8 COMPLETING THE SQUARE

Examples on pp. 268–270

EXAMPLE You can use completing the square to solve quadratic equations.

$x^2 - 6x - 8 = 0$	Write original equation.
$x^2 - 6x = 8$	Write the left side in the form $x^2 + bx$.
$x^2 - 6x + 9 = 8 + 9$	Add $\left(\dfrac{-6}{2}\right)^2 = (-3)^2 = 9$ to each side.
$(x - 3)^2 = 17$	Write the left side as the square of a binomial.
$x - 3 = \pm\sqrt{17}$	Take the square root of each side.
$x = 3 \pm \sqrt{17}$	Add 3 to each side.

REVIEW HELP
Exercises Example
28–30   **3**, p. 269

Solve the equation by completing the square.

30. $x^2 + 10x = -17$ **31.** $x^2 - 6x = 2$ **32.** $x^2 - 8x + 21 = 0$

5.9 THE QUADRATIC FORMULA AND THE DISCRIMINANT

Examples on pp. 274–277

EXAMPLE You can use the quadratic formula to solve any quadratic equation.

Solve $x^2 + 7x + 11 = 0$.

$x = \dfrac{-b \pm \sqrt{b^2 - 4ac}}{2a}$	Quadratic formula
$x = -7 \pm \dfrac{\sqrt{7^2 - 4(1)(11)}}{2(1)}$	Substitute values in the quadratic formula: $a = 1$, $b = 7$, and $c = 11$.
$x = \dfrac{-7 \pm \sqrt{5}}{2}$	Simplify.

REVIEW HELP
Exercises Example
31–33   **1**, p. 274

EXAMPLE You can use the discriminant to determine the number and type of solutions of a quadratic equation.

$b^2 - 4ac > 0$ 2 real solutions
$b^2 - 4ac = 0$ 1 real solution
$b^2 - 4ac < 0$ 2 imaginary solutions

Find the discriminant of the quadratic equation $x^2 + 8x + 12 = 0$ and give the number and type of solutions of the equation.

REVIEW HELP
Exercises Example
34–36   **4**, p. 276

The discriminant is $b^2 - 4ac = 8^2 - 4(1)(12) = 16$.

Because $16 > 0$, the equation has two real solutions.

Use the quadratic formula to solve the equation.

33. $x^2 - 12x + 20 = 0$ **34.** $x^2 + 10x - 7 = 0$ **35.** $5x^2 - 2x = -3$

Find the discriminant of the quadratic equation and give the number and type of solutions of the equation.

36. $x^2 + 12x + 12 = 0$ **37.** $2x^2 + 10x - 15 = 0$ **38.** $2x^2 - 3x - 5 = 0$

Graph the function. Label the vertex and the axis of symmetry.

1. $y = x^2 - 10x + 8$

2. $y = (x - 7)^2 + 2$

3. $y = -(x + 5)(x + 3)$

Factor the expression.

4. $x^2 - 2x - 3$

5. $y^2 - 8y + 15$

6. $6x^2 - 11x + 5$

7. $8h^2 - 10h - 7$

8. $x^2 - 25$

9. $9t^2 + 6t + 1$

Solve the equation by factoring.

10. $x^2 - 10x + 21 = 0$

11. $12x^2 - 31x + 7 = 0$

12. $25w^2 - 16 = 0$

13. $x^2 + 8x = -16$

14. $6x^2 + 11x = 10$

15. $z^2 + 13z = -42$

Solve the equation by finding square roots.

16. $3s^2 = 27$

17. $3x^2 - 15 = 66$

18. $4x^2 + 13 = 125$

19. $x^2 = -16$

20. $v^2 = -54$

21. $3x^2 = -63$

Write the expression as a complex number in standard form.

22. $(5 - 2i) + (-7 + 6i)$

23. $(4 + 2i) - (3 + 4i)$

24. $(3i)(6i)$

25. $(2 + 5i)(1 + 3i)$

26. $(2 - 5i)(2 + 2i)$

27. $\dfrac{5}{3 - i}$

Solve the equation by completing the square.

28. $x^2 + 18x = -5$

29. $n^2 - 10n - 13 = 0$

30. $x^2 + 8x + 20 = 0$

Use the quadratic formula to solve the equation.

31. $x^2 - 7x + 4 = 0$

32. $x^2 + 10x - 12 = 0$

33. $4x^2 + 2x = -5$

Find the discriminant of the quadratic equation and give the number and type of solutions of the equation.

34. $x^2 - 4x + 7 = 0$

35. $x^2 + 10x + 25 = 0$

36. $2x^2 + 5x - 6 = 0$

Geometry **The area of the rectangle is given. Find the length and width of the rectangle.**

37. Area = 96 square yards

x yd

$(x + 4)$ yd

38. Area = 70 square feet

$(x - 3)$ ft

x ft

39. Baseball You throw a baseball into the air. The baseball leaves your hand with an initial vertical velocity of 60 feet per second when it is 5 feet above the ground. You catch the baseball when it falls back to a height of 4 feet. For how many seconds is the baseball in the air?

Chapter Standardized Test

Test Tip   **Read the question carefully.**

> **EXAMPLE**   You are planting a garden. The garden will be a rectangle with a width of x feet and a length of $(10 + x)$ feet. You have enough seeds to plant a garden with an area of 200 square feet. What should the length (in feet) of the garden be?
>
>   **A** -20 feet   **B** 10 feet   **C** 20 feet   **D** 40 feet
>
> **Solution**
>
> Use the formula for the area of a rectangle to write an equation. Then solve the equation for x.
>
> $$\text{Area} = \text{length} \cdot \text{width}$$
>
> $$200 = (10 + x) \cdot x$$
>
> $$0 = x^2 + 10x - 200$$
>
> $$0 = (x + 20)(x - 10)$$
>
> $$x = -20 \text{ or } x = 10$$
>
> The width x of the garden must be 10, because a width cannot be negative. However, the question asks for the length of the garden, not the width. The length $(x + 10)$ of the garden is $10 + 10 = 20$. Choice **C** is the correct answer.

Multiple Choice

1. What is the vertex of the graph of $y = x^2 - 10x + 27$?

   A $(-10, -7)$ **B** $(5, 2)$

   C $(-5, 2)$ **D** $(5, -7)$

2. What is the correct factorization of $x^2 - 6x - 27$?

   F $(x + 3)(x - 9)$ **G** $(x - 3)(x + 9)$

   H $(x - 3)(x - 9)$ **J** $(x + 3)(x + 9)$

3. What is the correct factorization of $12x^2 - 8x - 15$?

   A $(6x + 5)(2x - 3)$ **B** $(6x - 5)(2x + 3)$

   C $(4x + 3)(3x - 5)$ **D** $(4x - 3)(3x + 5)$

4. What are the solutions of the equation $y^2 - 11y + 30 = 0$?

   F $-5, 6$ **G** $-6, -5$

   H $-6, 5$ **J** $5, 6$

5. What are the solutions of the equation $10x^2 + x - 2 = 0$?

   A $-5, -2$ **B** $-\dfrac{1}{2}, \dfrac{2}{5}$

   C $-\dfrac{2}{5}, \dfrac{1}{2}$ **D** $2, 5$

6. What are the solutions of the equation $x^2 + 5 = 32$?

   F $\pm 9\sqrt{6}$ **G** $\pm 3\sqrt{3}$

   H $\pm\sqrt{32}$ **J** $\pm 3\sqrt{6}$

7. What are the solutions of $x^2 - 14x + 49 = 48$?

Ⓐ $-7 \pm 4\sqrt{3}$ Ⓑ $-7 \pm 16\sqrt{3}$

Ⓒ $7 \pm 4\sqrt{3}$ Ⓓ $7 \pm 16\sqrt{3}$

8. Write $(3 + 2i) - (4 - 3i)$ in standard form.

Ⓕ $-1 + 5i$ Ⓖ $-1 - i$

Ⓗ $7 - i$ Ⓙ $7 + 5i$

9. Write $(2 - i)(4 + 5i)$ in standard form.

Ⓐ $13 - 6i$ Ⓑ $8 + i$

Ⓒ $3 + 6i$ Ⓓ $13 + 6i$

10. What is the vertex form of $y = x^2 + 8x + 10$?

Ⓕ $y = (x + 4)^2 + 10$ Ⓖ $y = (x + 4)^2 - 6$

Ⓗ $y = (x + 4)^2 + 26$ Ⓙ $y = (x + 4)^2 - 6$

11. What are the solutions of $x^2 + 6x + 10$?

Ⓐ $-4, -22$ Ⓑ $2, 4$

Ⓒ $-3 \pm i$ Ⓓ $3 \pm i$

12. How many real solutions does the equation $4x^2 + 4x + 1 = 0$ have?

Ⓕ 0 Ⓖ 1

Ⓗ 2 Ⓙ more than 2

Gridded Response

13. Find the value of c that makes $x^2 + 11x + c$ a perfect square trinomial.

14. The area of the rectangle is 126 square feet. Find the value of x.

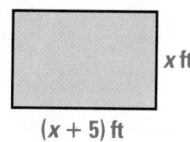

$(x + 5)$ ft

15. What is the x-coordinate of the vertex of the graph of $y = x^2 - 6x + 14$?

16. Find the minimum value of $y = x^2 - 6x + 30$.

17. The area of the triangle is 42 square inches. Find the value of x.

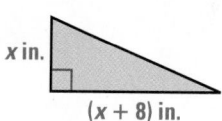

x in.

$(x + 8)$ in.

18. Find the discriminant of $2x^2 - 9x + 7 = 0$.

19. How many real solutions does the equation $2x^2 + 16x + 31 = 0$ have?

Extended Response

20. You are playing volleyball. Your friend hits the ball into the air with an initial vertical velocity of 30 feet per second when it is 2 feet above the ground.

  a. Which vertical motion model can you use to represent this situation? Explain your reasoning.

  b. Use the model from part (a) to write an equation that gives the height (in feet) of the volleyball as a function of the time (in seconds) after it is hit.

  c. You hit the ball when it is falling towards the ground and reaches a height of 9 feet. How many seconds after your friend hits the ball do you hit the ball? Explain how you found your answer.

CHAPTER 6

Polynomials and Polynomial Functions

▶ How has the enrollment of students in public high schools changed?

APPLICATION: School Enrollment

A graph can show how a quantity changes over time. The graph below shows the number of students enrolled in public high schools in the United States from 1990 to 2002. This graph is an example of a kind of function that you will study in Chapter 6.

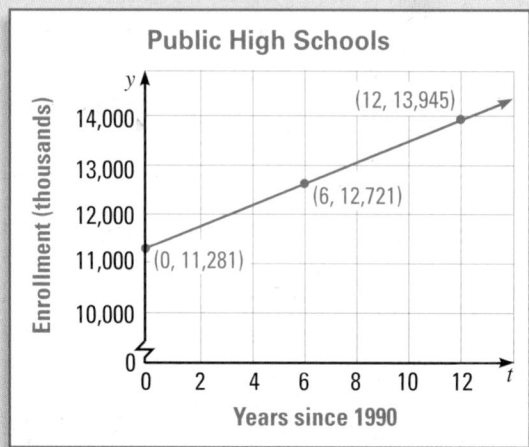

Public High Schools

Think & Discuss

Use the graph to answer the following questions.

1. Describe the change in enrollment from 1990 to 2002.

2. Use the graph to estimate the number of students enrolled in public high schools in 2000.

Learn More About It

You will use polynomial functions to find the total enrollment of students in high school in Example 4 on page 311.

PREVIEW What's the chapter about?

- Using properties of exponents to evaluate and simplify expressions
- Defining, graphing, and using polynomial functions
- Adding, subtracting, multiplying, and dividing polynomials
- Factoring polynomial expressions and solving polynomial equations

Key Words

- scientific notation, *p. 298*
- polynomial, *p. 302*
- standard form of a polynomial function, *p. 302*
- leading coefficient, *p. 302*
- degree of a polynomial, *p. 302*
- constant term, *p. 302*

- end behavior, *p. 303*
- polynomial long division, *p. 317*
- factor by grouping, *p. 324*
- quadratic form, *p. 329*
- repeated solution, *p. 331*
- local maximum, *p. 335*
- local minimum, *p. 335*

PREPARE Chapter Readiness Quiz

Take this quick quiz. If you are unsure of an answer, look back at the reference pages for help.

Vocabulary Check *(refer to p. 16)*

1. Complete the statement: The coefficient of the term $4x^3$ is __?__.

  A 4   **B** 3   **C** x **D** x^3

Skill Check *(refer to pp. 228, 249)*

2. What is the value of the function $f(x) = x^2 + 3x - 2$ when $x = -4$?

  F 0   **G** 2   **H** 3   **J** 4

3. Factor the expression $49x^2 - 14x + 1$.

  A $(x - 7)^2$ **B** $(7x + 1)^2$ **C** $(7x - 1)^2$ **D** $(7x - 1)(7x + 1)$

TAKE NOTES Compare Topics

Look for similarities and differences between math topics. For example: How is working with polynomials similar to working with monomials and binomials? How is it different?

> ### Polynomials vs. Binomials
>
> **Similarities**
> Standard form uses descending order of exponents.
>
> **Differences**
> Polynomials may have more than two terms. Need to graph more points of a polynomial function to get an accurate graph.

DEVELOPING CONCEPTS *(For use with Lesson 6.1)*
Products and Quotients of Powers

Goal

Discover patterns for multiplying or dividing powers with the same base.

Materials

- pencil
- paper

QUESTION

How do you multiply or divide powers with the same base?

EXPLORE

1 To multiply powers with the same base, write the product in expanded form. Then count the number of factors and write the result as a single power. Copy and complete the table.

Product of powers	Expanded form	Single power	Sum of exponents
$4^1 \cdot 4^1$	$4 \cdot 4$	4^2	$1 + 1 = 2$
$4^2 \cdot 4^2$	$(4 \cdot 4)(4 \cdot 4)$	?	?
$4^2 \cdot 4^3$	?	?	?
$4^2 \cdot 4^4$	?	?	?

2 To divide powers with the same base, write both the numerator and denominator in expanded form. Then divide out all common factors. Write the result as a single power. Copy and complete the table.

Quotient of powers	Expanded form	Single power	Difference of exponents
$\dfrac{2^2}{2^1}$	$\dfrac{2 \cdot 2}{2}$	2^1	$2 - 1 = 1$
$\dfrac{2^4}{2^2}$	$\dfrac{2 \cdot 2 \cdot 2 \cdot 2}{2 \cdot 2}$	?	?
$\dfrac{2^5}{2^2}$	?	?	?
$\dfrac{2^6}{2^2}$	?	?	?

THINK ABOUT IT

1. Use your observations from the table in Step 1 to complete the statement: For any real number a and any positive integers m and n, $a^m \cdot a^n = \underline{\quad ? \quad}$.

Write the product as a single power.

2. $6^2 \cdot 6^3$ **3.** $2^5 \cdot 2$ **4.** $x^2 \cdot x^5$ **5.** $y^4 \cdot y^4$

6. Use your observations from the table in Step 2 to complete the statement: For any nonzero real number a and any positive integers m and n, $\dfrac{a^m}{a^n} = \underline{\quad ? \quad}$.

Write the quotient as a single power.

7. $\dfrac{2^3}{2}$ **8.** $\dfrac{4^8}{4^3}$ **9.** $\dfrac{x^7}{x^3}$ **10.** $\dfrac{y^6}{y^3}$

Properties of Exponents

Key Words

• scientific notation

GOAL Use properties of exponents to evaluate and simplify expressions involving powers.

Prerequisite Skills

Evaluate the expression.

1. 2^3

2. 4^4

3. $(-7)^2$

4. $(-3)^5$

In the activity on the previous page, you may have seen that when multiplying two powers with the same base, you can add their exponents. This is also true for powers with zero exponents negative integer exponents. Here is how you can find what these exponents mean.

ZERO EXPONENT		NEGATIVE INTEGER EXPONENT
$3^n \cdot 3^0 = 3^{n+0}$	Property of exponents	$3^n \cdot 3^{-n} = 3^{n-n}$
$3^n \cdot 3^0 = 3^n$	Simplify exponents.	$3^n \cdot 3^{-n} = 3^0$
$\dfrac{3^n \cdot 3^0}{3^n} = \dfrac{3^n}{3^n}$	Divide each side by 3^n.	$\dfrac{3^n \cdot 3^{-n}}{3^n} = \dfrac{3^0}{3^n}$
$3^0 = 1$	Simplify.	$3^{-n} = \dfrac{1}{3^n}$

The properties of exponents are summarized below. Throughout this book, it is assumed that any base with a zero or negative exponent is nonzero.

Properties of Exponents

Let a and b be real numbers and let m and n be integers.

	ALGEBRA	**EXAMPLE**
Product of Powers	$a^m \cdot a^n = a^{m+n}$	$3^2 \cdot 3^5 = 3^{2+5}$
Power of a Power	$(a^m)^n = a^{mn}$	$(2^3)^2 = 2^{3 \cdot 2}$
Power of a Product	$(ab)^m = a^m b^m$	$(4 \cdot 3)^3 = 4^3 \cdot 3^3$
Negative Exponent	$a^{-m} = \dfrac{1}{a^m},\ a \neq 0$	$5^{-2} = \dfrac{1}{5^2}$
Zero Exponent	$a^0 = 1,\ a \neq 0$	$100^0 = 1$
Quotient of Powers	$\dfrac{a^m}{a^n} = a^{m-n},\ a \neq 0$	$\dfrac{3^5}{3^2} = 3^{5-2}$
Power of a Quotient	$\left(\dfrac{a}{b}\right)^m = \dfrac{a^m}{b^m},\ b \neq 0$	$\left(\dfrac{3}{5}\right)^4 = \dfrac{3^4}{5^4}$

STUDENT HELP

LOOK BACK
For help with evaluating powers, see page 9.

EXAMPLE 1 Evaluate Expressions with Negative Exponents

$(-2)^{-8}(-2)^4 = (-2)^{-8+4}$	Product of powers property
$= (-2)^{-4}$	Simplify exponent.
$= \dfrac{1}{(-2)^4}$	Negative exponent property
$= \dfrac{1}{16}$	Evaluate power.

EXAMPLE 2 Evaluate Quotients with Exponents

Evaluate $\left(\dfrac{3^5}{3^3}\right)^2$.

$$\left(\dfrac{3^5}{3^3}\right)^2 = (3^2)^2 \qquad \text{Quotient of powers property}$$

$$= 3^4 \qquad \text{Power of a power property}$$

$$= 81 \qquad \text{Evaluate power.}$$

 **Evaluate Numerical Expressions**

Evaluate the expression.

1. $(2^4)^3$ **2.** $(5^0)^3$ **3.** $(-3)^2(-3)^{-7}$ **4.** $\left(\dfrac{2}{7}\right)^3$

Simplifying Expressions A *simplified* algebraic expression contains only positive exponents.

EXAMPLE 3 Simplify Algebraic Expressions

a. $\left(\dfrac{x}{y^{-3}}\right)^2 = \dfrac{x^2}{(y^{-3})^2} \qquad \text{Power of a quotient property}$

$$= \dfrac{x^2}{y^{-3\cdot 2}} \qquad \text{Power of a power property}$$

$$= \dfrac{x^2}{y^{-6}} \qquad \text{Simplify exponent.}$$

$$= x^2 y^6 \qquad \text{Negative exponent property}$$

b. $(5y^{-3})^2 y^5 y = 5^2(y^{-3})^2 y^5 y \qquad \text{Power of a product property}$

$$= 25 y^{-3\cdot 2} y^5 y \qquad \text{Power of a power property}$$

$$= 25 y^{-6} y^5 y \qquad \text{Simplify exponent.}$$

$$= 25 y^{-6+5+1} \qquad \text{Product of powers property}$$

$$= 25 y^0 \qquad \text{Simplify exponent.}$$

$$= 25 \qquad \text{Zero exponent property}$$

c. $\dfrac{x^3 y^6}{x^5 y^{-2}} = x^{3-5} y^{6-(-2)} \qquad \text{Quotient of powers property}$

$$= x^{-2} y^8 \qquad \text{Simplify exponents.}$$

$$= \dfrac{y^8}{x^2} \qquad \text{Negative exponent property}$$

STUDENT HELP

SOLVING NOTE
Remember that $y = y^1$.

 **Simplify Algebraic Expressions**

Simplify the expression. Tell which properties of exponents you used.

5. $(2p)^3 p^4$ **6.** $\dfrac{x^5 y^3}{xy^{-4}}$ **7.** $(3b^{-2})^3 b^8$ **8.** $\left(\dfrac{r^2}{s^{-4}}\right)^{-3}$

DRUMS The two heads of a bass drum are hit using mallets to produce a low pitch. The bass drum used by Purdue Universtiy's marching band has a diameter of about 8 feet and a depth of about 4 feet.

EXAMPLE 4 Compare Areas

Drums The head of the bass drum used by Purdue University's marching band has a radius about 4 times greater than a common bass drum. How many times greater is the area of Purdue's bass drum's head than a common bass drum's head? Let r represent the radius of a common bass drum's head.

Solution

Divide the area of Purdue's drum head by the area of a common drum head.

$$\frac{\text{Area of Purdue's drum head}}{\text{Area of common drum head}} = \frac{\pi(4r)^2}{\pi r^2} \qquad \text{The area of a circle is } A = \pi r^2.$$

$$= \frac{\pi \cdot 4^2 \cdot r^2}{\pi r^2} \qquad \text{Power of a product property}$$

$$= \pi^{1-1} \cdot 4^2 \cdot r^{2-2} \qquad \text{Quotient of powers property}$$

$$= \pi^0 \cdot 4^2 \cdot r^0 \qquad \text{Simplify exponents.}$$

$$= 1 \cdot 16 \cdot 1 = 16 \qquad \text{Zero exponent property}$$

ANSWER ▶ The area of Purdue's bass drum's head is about 16 times greater.

Scientific Notation A number is written in **scientific notation** if it is in the form $c \times 10^n$ where $1 \le c < 10$ and n is an integer. When you use numbers in scientific notation, the properties of exponents help make calculations easier.

EXAMPLE 5 Use Scientific Notation

Transportation In 2003 the population of the United States was 2.91×10^8. In that same year, the total motor fuel usage was 1.70×10^{11} gallons. Estimate the average number of gallons used per person in the United States in 2003.

Solution

Divide the total motor fuel usage by the population.

$$\frac{\text{Total fuel usage}}{\text{Population}} = \frac{1.70 \times 10^{11}}{2.91 \times 10^8} \qquad \text{Divide fuel used by population.}$$

$$= \frac{1.70}{2.91} \times 10^{11-8} \qquad \text{Quotient of powers property}$$

$$= \frac{1.70}{2.91} \times 10^3 \qquad \text{Simplify exponent.}$$

$$\approx 0.584 \times 10^3 \qquad \text{Use a calculator.}$$

$$= 584 \qquad \text{Simplify.}$$

ANSWER ▶ The average number of gallons used per person was about 584.

Checkpoint ✓ *Use Scientific Notation*

9. In 2003, about 4.25×10^{11} local phone calls were made in the United States. Use the population in Example 5 to estimate the average number of local calls made per person.

6.1 Exercises

Guided Practice

Vocabulary Check

1. State the name of the following property: $a^m \cdot a^n = a^{m+n}$.

2. Write the power of a power property and the power of a product property.

Skill Check

Evaluate the expression.

3. $(3^2)^2$

4. $(4^{-3})^{-1}$

5. $\left(\dfrac{3}{4}\right)^{-2}$

6. $5^8 \cdot 5^0 \cdot 5^{-5}$

Simplify the expression.

7. $x^2 \cdot \dfrac{1}{x}$

8. $(2x^4)^5$

9. $\dfrac{x^3}{x^{-2}}$

10. $(xy^5)^{-3}$

11. Windows The radius of a circular window is about 5 times as great as the radius of a smaller circular window. How many times greater is the area of the large window than the area of the smaller window? Let r be the radius of the smaller window.

Practice and Applications

STUDENT HELP

HOMEWORK HELP
Example 1: Exs. 12–23
Example 2: Exs. 12–23
Example 3: Exs. 24–35
Example 4: Exs. 40–44
Example 5: Exs. 45–49

Evaluating Expressions Evaluate the expression. Tell which properties of exponents you used.

12. $3^3 \cdot 3^{-3}$

13. $(2^3)^2$

14. $(4 \cdot 5)^2$

15. $(-3)^4 \cdot (-3)^2$

16. $(2)^{-3} \cdot (2)^{-2}$

17. $(5)^{-1} \cdot (5)^{-3}$

18. $(3^{-5})^{-1}$

19. $\left(\dfrac{2}{5}\right)^3$

20. $\dfrac{6^2}{6^5}$

21. $\dfrac{8^{-5}}{8^{-6}}$

22. $(-6)^{-5} \cdot (-6)^5$

23. $9^0 \cdot 9^5 \cdot 9^{-7}$

Simplifying Expressions Simplify the expression. Tell which properties of exponents you used.

24. $x^7 \cdot \dfrac{2}{x^5}$

25. $(3x^3)^{-2}$

26. $(2x^5 \cdot x)^{-2}$

27. $\dfrac{x^{-5}}{x^2}$

28. $(x^7y)^{-2}$

29. $(x^4y^{-2})^{-5}$

30. $\dfrac{x^6 y^3}{x^3 y}$

31. $\dfrac{xy^5}{x^4 y^{-2}}$

32. $(5x^2y^{-3})^{-4}$

33. $(3x^{-4}y^{-6})^{-5}$

34. $\dfrac{x^2 y^{-2}}{x^{-1}y}$

35. $\dfrac{8x^3y}{2x^{-2}y}$

Evaluating Expressions Evaluate the expression. Write your answer in scientific notation.

36. $(4 \times 10^3) \times (2 \times 10^{-4})$

37. $(8.7 \times 10^{-8}) \times (7.9 \times 10^{-6})$

38. $\dfrac{6 \times 10^{12}}{3 \times 10^{-3}}$

39. $\dfrac{9.8 \times 10^{-9}}{4.3 \times 10^3}$

Geometry Link Write an expression in simplified form for the volume of the figure in terms of x.

40. $V = s^3$

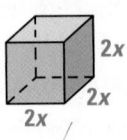

2x
2x
2x

41. $V = \pi r^2 h$

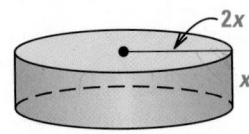

2x
x

42. $V = \frac{4}{3}\pi r^3$

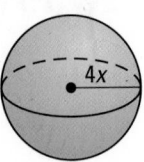

4x

43. Packaging You buy a gift for a gift exchange and wrap it in a box whose length and width are each equal to twice the height. The gift you receive is in a box that has a length and width equal to half the height. The two boxes have the same height. Sketch and label the boxes. How many times larger is the volume of the box you give than the volume of the box you receive?

44. Machine Parts Technical specifications for the design of a machine require two sizes of steel cylinder rods. The larger rod should have a radius that is 7 times greater than the smaller rod. The height of each rod is twice as long as the radius. Sketch and label the rods. How many times greater is the volume of the large rod than the volume of the small rod?

45. Lake Volume The volume of the Caspian Sea is about 7.82×10^4 cubic kilometers. The volume of Lake Baikal is about 2.30×10^4 cubic kilometers. How many times larger is the volume of the Caspian Sea than the volume of Lake Baikal?

Country Area and Population In Exercises 46–50, use the information in the table. It shows the mid-year population and the area of four countries in 2004. Estimate the population per square mile for each country.

Country	Population	Area (square miles)
Luxembourg	4.63×10^5	9.98×10^2
Madagascar	1.75×10^7	2.25×10^5
Russia	1.44×10^8	6.59×10^6
United States	2.93×10^8	3.54×10^6

46. Luxembourg

47. Madagascar

48. Russia

49. United States

50. Population Density The population per square mile is a measure of *population density*. Write the four countries in the table in order from greatest to least population density.

51. Sand Some spherical sand grains have a radius of about 5×10^{-4} meter. How many grains of sand could fit across the blade of a shovel that is 0.25 meter wide?

Speed of Light In Exercises 52 and 53, use the fact that the speed of light through air is about 3.00×10^5 kilometers per second.

52. It takes about 499 seconds on average for light to travel from the sun to Earth. Find the approximate distance between Earth and the sun. Write the result in scientific notation.

53. Challenge The mean distance between the sun and Mars is about 2.28×10^8 kilometers. How long, in seconds, does light from the sun take to reach Mars?

Standardized Test Practice

54. Multiple Choice What is the value of the expression $(3)^{-1}(3)^2$?

(A) $\frac{1}{9}$ (B) $\frac{1}{3}$ (C) 3   (D) 9

55. Multiple Choice Which expression is equivalent to $\frac{x^{-5}y^6}{xy}$?

(F) $\frac{y^5}{x^6}$ (G) $\frac{y^7}{x^4}$ (H) $\frac{x^5}{y^6}$ (J) x^6y^5

56. Multiple Choice What is the value of the expression $\frac{2.4 \times 10^5}{6.0 \times 10^2}$?

(A) 0.4   (B) 4   (C) 40   (D) 400

Mixed Review

Perfect Squares Factor the expression. *(Lesson 5.4)*

57. $x^2 + 6x + 9$ **58.** $x^2 - 14x + 49$ **59.** $x^2 - 22x + 121$

60. $x^2 + 2x + 1$ **61.** $x^2 + 20x + 100$ **62.** $x^2 - 24x + 144$

63. $4x^2 - 4x + 1$ **64.** $9x^2 + 24x + 16$ **65.** $16x^2 + 48x + 36$

Completing the Square Find the value of *c* that makes the expression a perfect square trinomial. *(Lesson 5.8)*

66. $x^2 + 6x$ **67.** $x^2 - 10x$ **68.** $x^2 + 14x$

69. $x^2 - 26x$ **70.** $x^2 - 0.4x$ **71.** $x^2 + 1.6x$

Geometry Skills

Finding Volume of Solids Find the volume of the solid.

72.
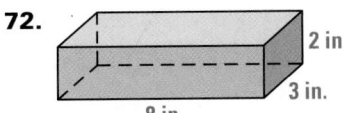
2 in.   3 in.   8 in.

73.
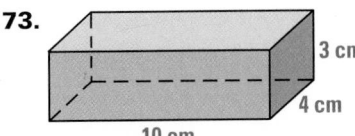
3 cm   4 cm   10 cm

74.
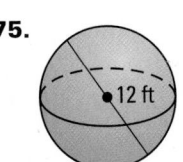
4 m

75.
12 ft

76.
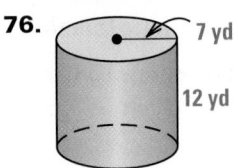
7 yd   12 yd

77.
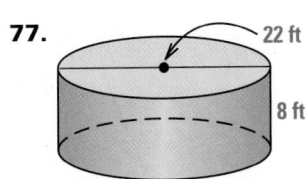
22 ft   8 ft

6.2 Polynomial Functions and Their Graphs

Key Words
- polynomial
- standard form of a polynomial function
- leading coefficient
- degree of a polynomial
- constant term
- end behavior

GOAL Define, graph, and use polynomial functions.

A **polynomial** is a monomial or a sum of monomials with real number coefficients. A polynomial is in **standard form** if its terms are written in descending order of exponents from left to right, such as

$$9x^5 - x^3 + 4x + 7$$

When a polynomial is written in standard form, the coefficient of the first term is the **leading coefficient**, and the exponent of the first term is the **degree** of the polynomial. A term that has no variable is a **constant term**.

Linear functions and quadratic functions are simple forms of *polynomial functions*. A summary of common types of polynomial functions is shown below.

Prerequisite Skills

Evaluate the function when $x = -3$.

1. $f(x) = 7x + 2$

2. $f(x) = x^2 + 3x - 4$

3. $f(x) = 2x^3 - 9$

4. $f(x) = x^3 - x^2 - x - 3$

Degree	Type	Standard form	Example(s)
0	Constant	$f(x) = k$	$f(x) = 8, g(x) = -3$
1	Linear	$f(x) = ax + b$	$f(x) = 2x + 7$
2	Quadratic	$f(x) = ax^2 + bx + c$	$f(x) = 4x^2 + x - 5$
3	Cubic	$f(x) = ax^3 + bx^2 + cx + d$	$f(x) = 2x^3 - 5x^2 - 1$
4	Quartic	$f(x) = ax^4 + bx^3 + cx^2 + dx + e$	$f(x) = 3x^4 + x^3 - x + 4$

EXAMPLE 1 Identify Polynomial Functions

Tell whether the function is a polynomial function. If it is, write the function in standard form. Then state its degree, type, and leading coefficient.

a. $f(x) = 2x^2 - 1 + 7x^3$ **b.** $f(x) = x^4 - 3x^{-2} - 5x$

c. $f(x) = \pi x - 4x^2 + \sqrt{5}$ **d.** $f(x) = 6x^3 - 3x^2 + 2x + 3^x$

Solution

a. This is a polynomial function. Its standard form is $f(x) = 7x^3 + 2x^2 - 1$. It has degree 3, so it is a cubic function. The leading coefficient is 7.

b. This is not a polynomial function. The term $3x^{-2}$ has an exponent that is not a whole number.

c. This is a polynomial function. Its standard form is $f(x) = -4x^2 + \pi x + \sqrt{5}$. It has degree 2, so it is a quadratic function. The leading coefficient is -4.

d. This is not a polynomial function. The term 3^x has an exponent that is not a whole number.

Tell whether the function is a polynomial function. If it is, write the function in standard form. Then state its degree, type, and leading coefficient.

1. $f(x) = 5x^4 + 2x^3 - x^2 + \sqrt{x}$

2. $f(x) = \frac{1}{4}x - \frac{1}{2}x^3 + \frac{5}{8}$

3. $f(x) = 2 - x$

4. $f(x) = x^2 - \frac{5}{x} + 7$

Graphing Polynomial Functions When you graph a polynomial, you have to look at where the graph turns. You also need to know the **end behavior**, which is what happens to $f(x)$ as x gets very large or very small. The end behavior depends on the degree and leading coefficient of the function.

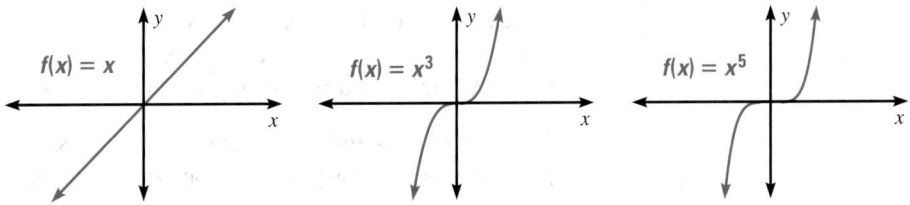

Notice that for each graph above, the leading coefficient is positive and the degree is odd. In these cases, $f(x)$ approaches positive infinity $(+\infty)$ as x gets very large.

End Behavior of Polynomial Functions

The graph of a polynomial function has the following end behavior.

Degree: even
Leading coefficient: positive

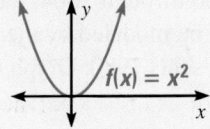

$f(x)$ approaches $+\infty$ as
x approaches $+\infty$ or $-\infty$.

Degree: even
Leading coefficient: negative

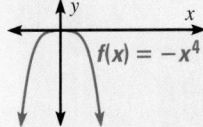

$f(x)$ approaches $-\infty$ as
x approaches $+\infty$ or $-\infty$.

Degree: odd
Leading coefficient: positive

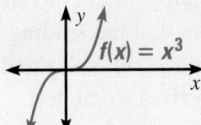

$f(x)$ approaches $-\infty$ as
x approaches $-\infty$ and
$f(x)$ approaches $+\infty$ as
x approaches $+\infty$.

Degree: odd
Leading coefficient: negative

$f(x)$ approaches $+\infty$ as
x approaches $-\infty$ and
$f(x)$ approaches $-\infty$ as
x approaches $+\infty$.

EXAMPLE 2 Graph Polynomial Functions

Graph the polynomial function. Use the domain $x = -3, -2, -1, 0, 1, 2, 3$. Then describe the end behavior of the graph.

a. $f(x) = -x^3 - x^2 + 2x$ **b.** $f(x) = x^4 - 4x - 1$

STUDENT HELP

LOOK BACK
For help with evaluating functions, see page 73.

Solution

a. First, make a table of values. Plot the corresponding points. Then connect the points with a smooth curve.

x	−3	−2	−1	0	1	2	3
f(x)	12	0	−2	0	0	−8	−30

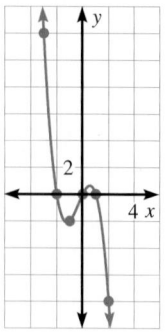

The degree is odd, and the leading coefficient is negative. So, $f(x)$ approaches $+\infty$ as x approaches $-\infty$ and $f(x)$ approaches $-\infty$ as x approaches $+\infty$.

b. First, make a table of values. Plot the corresponding points. Then connect the points with a smooth curve.

x	−3	−2	−1	0	1	2	3
f(x)	92	23	4	−1	−4	7	68

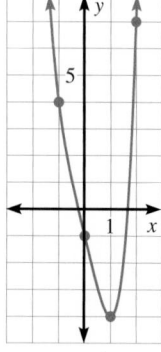

The degree is even, and the leading coefficient is positive. So, $f(x)$ approaches $+\infty$ as x approaches $-\infty$ and $f(x)$ approaches $+\infty$ as x approaches $+\infty$.

Link to
INDUSTRY

EXPORTS are goods that are shipped out of a country. The United States exported 348 million cubic feet of lumber in 2004.

EXAMPLE 3 Graph a Real-World Function

Exports For 1980 through 2004, the total exports E (in billions of dollars) of the United States can be modeled by the function $E = -0.12x^3 + 5x^2 - 28x + 244$ where $x = 0$ represents 1980. Graph the function.

Solution

Make a table of values.

x	0	5	10	15	20
E	244	214	344	544	724

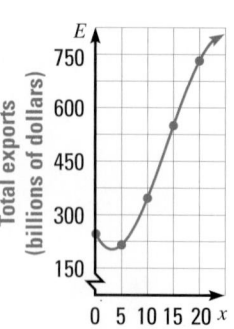

lot the points. Then connect the points with a smooth curve. Note that the leading coefficient of the function is negative, and the degree is odd. So, the graph rises to the left.

Checkpoint ✓ *Graph Polynomial Functions*

Graph the function using the domain $x = -3, -2, -1, 0, 1, 2, 3$.

5. $f(x) = -x^3 + 4x^2$ **6.** $f(x) = x^3 + 2x^2 - x + 1$ **7.** $f(x) = -x^4 + x + 2$

6.2 Exercises

Guided Practice

Vocabulary Check

1. Copy and complete the statement: If the terms of a polynomial function are written in descending order of exponents from left to right, it is in __?__.

2. Is the degree of $f(x) = 7x^2 - 4x + 3x^3 - 9$ equal to 2? Explain.

Skill Check

Identify the degree and the leading coefficient of the polynomial function. Then describe the end behavior of its graph.

3. $f(x) = 2 - x + x^2 - x^3$ **4.** $f(x) = -x^5$ **5.** $f(x) = x^4 - x^2$

6. The graph of which function is shown? Explain your reasoning.

A. $f(x) = x^2 + 3$

B. $f(x) = -x^3 + 3$

C. $f(x) = -x^4 + 3$

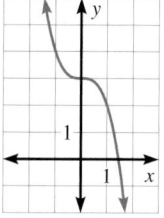

Practice and Applications

STUDENT HELP

HOMEWORK HELP
Example 1: Exs. 7–22
Example 2: Exs. 23–49
Example 3: Exs. 50–53

Identifying Polynomials Tell whether the function is a polynomial function. Explain your reasoning.

7. $f(x) = 4x^3 - \sqrt{6} + x^2$

8. $f(x) = 5^x + 4x + 3x^2 - 2x^3$

9. $f(x) = x^2 + 3x - x^{-2}$

10. $f(x) = -x^5 + 13x^3 - 1.33x$

11. $f(x) = \frac{2}{3}x^2 + \frac{3}{4}x - \frac{1}{3}$

12. $f(x) = x^3 + \frac{5}{x^2} + x$

Matching Match the polynomial function with its description.

13. $f(x) = -2 + 2x$

A. a quadratic function with a leading coefficient of -2

14. $f(x) = 2 + x - 2x^2 + 2x^3$

B. a quartic function with a leading coefficient of -2

15. $f(x) = -2x^2 - 2x^4 + 1$

C. a cubic function with a leading coefficient of 2

16. $f(x) = -2x^2 + 2x + 1$

D. a linear function with a leading coefficient of 2

Classifying Polynomials Write the polynomial function in standard form. Then state its degree, type, and leading coefficient.

17. $f(x) = 8 - x^3$

18. $f(x) = x^4 - x^2 + 9$

19. $f(x) = x^2 - x^4 + 4$

20. $f(x) = x^2 - x^3 + 4x - 7$

21. $f(x) = -6x^4 + x^3 - 6x$

22. $f(x) = 6x^2 + 2x^4 + x^3 + 1$

Evaluating Polynomials Evaluate the polynomial function for the given value of *x*.

23. $f(x) = -2x^2 + 4x + 1; x = -2$ **24.** $f(x) = 2x^2 - 15x + 27; x = 3$

25. $f(x) = 2x^3 - x + 5x^2 - 5; x = 1$ **26.** $f(x) = 10x - x^3 + 25; x = 4$

27. $f(x) = x^2 - x^5 + 4; x = -1$ **28.** $f(x) = -2x^5 - 6x^4 - x; x = -3$

Describing End Behavior Identify the degree and the leading coefficient of the polynomial function. Then describe the end behavior of its graph.

29. $f(x) = x^3$ **30.** $f(x) = -2x^5$ **31.** $f(x) = 3x$

32. $f(x) = x^2 - 11$ **33.** $f(x) = -3x^2 - x + 8$ **34.** $f(x) = -x^4 - 5$

35. $f(x) = x^5 - x^2 + 3$ **36.** $f(x) = -2x^6 + x^3 + 2$ **37.** $f(x) = 7x^3 - x^2 + 4$

Matching Use what you know about end behavior to match the function with its graph.

38. $f(x) = -x^4 - 5x + 5$ **39.** $f(x) = x^4 + x - 7$ **40.** $f(x) = x^3 - 4x$

A. 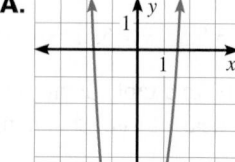 **B.** 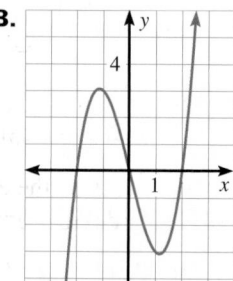 **C.**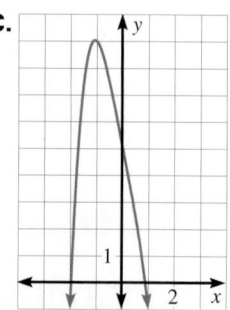

Graphing Polynomials Graph the polynomial function using the domain *x* = −3, −2, −1, 0, 1, 2, 3.

41. $f(x) = -x^2$ **42.** $f(x) = -x^3$

43. $f(x) = x^2 + 5$ **44.** $f(x) = x^4 + 1$

45. $f(x) = x^5 - 10$ **46.** $f(x) = -x^4 + x + 3$

47. $f(x) = x^3 - x^2 + 3$ **48.** $f(x) = -x^5 + 3x^4 - 3x^3$

49. Roller Coasters The diagram shows a section of track for a roller coaster. Use what you know about end behavior to determine which equation best models the section of track that is shown below.

A. $f(x) = \frac{1}{10,000}x^3 - \frac{1}{50}x^2 + \frac{3}{5}x + 85$

B. $f(x) = -\frac{1}{10,000}x^3 - \frac{1}{50}x^2 + \frac{3}{5}x + 85$

Postal Service In Exercises 50 and 51, use the following information.

From 1990 through 2004, the average annual salary S for a postal employee can be modeled by the following function. The variable t is the number of years since 1990.

$$S(t) = 14.96t^3 - 268.1t^2 + 2446t + 37,575$$

50. Copy and complete the table using a calculator. Round values to the nearest integer.

t	0	1	2	3	4	5	6
S(t)	?	?	?	?	?	?	?

51. Graph the polynomial function by plotting the points in the table and connecting them with a smooth curve.

College Fees In Exercises 52 and 53, use the following information.

The average tuition fee for two-year public colleges in the United States from 1985 to 2004 can be modeled by the following polynomial function. The variable C is the yearly cost of tuition in dollars and t is the number of years since 1985.

$$C = 0.098t^4 - 3.82t^3 + 46.0t^2 - 114t + 585$$

52. Use a calculator to make a table using t-values of 0, 3, 6, 9, 12, 15, and 17. Round values to the nearest integer. Then graph the function.

53. Describe the end behavior of the polynomial. Does it make sense to use this model to predict tuition in 2050? Explain.

54. Challenge Give an example of a polynomial function f that has the following end behaviors. Explain how you found your answer.

    a. The graph of the function rises to the left and falls to the right.

    b. The graph of the function rises to the left and rises to the right.

55. Critical Thinking Suppose the graph of a polynomial function $f(x)$ rises to the left and falls to the right. Describe the end behavior of $-f(x)$. Explain.

Standardized Test Practice

56. Multiple Choice Which polynomial function is *not* in standard form?

    A $f(x) = 8x^2 - 13x + 58$

    B $f(x) = -x^4 + 2x^2 - 6$

    C $f(x) = 2x^3 - 4x^2 + 6x - 8$

    D $f(x) = 7 + 3x + 6x^2 - x^3$

57. Multiple Choice What is the degree of $f(x) = -6x^4 + 5x^2 - 3$?

    F -6 **G** -4 **H** 4   **J** 6

58. Multiple Choice What function is shown in the graph?

    A $f(x) = x^3 - 3x^2 - x + 2$

    B $f(x) = -x^3 - 3x^2 - x + 2$

    C $f(x) = x^4 - 3x^2 + 2$

    D $f(x) = -x^4 - 3x^2 + 2$

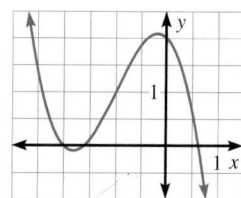

Mixed Review

Simplifying Expressions Simplify the expression. *(Lesson 1.3)*

59. $-5x + 4y - 6x - y$

60. $x - 9y - 3x + 13y$

61. $-15x - 24y - 11y + 6x$

62. $-3(x - 2) + 3x$

63. $8 + 4(y + 1)$

64. $-(z + 5) + 6z$

Writing in Vertex Form Write the quadratic function in vertex form $y = a(x - h)^2 + k$ and identify the vertex. *(Lesson 5.8)*

65. $y = x^2 + 6x + 2$

66. $y = x^2 + 2x + 2$

67. $y = x^2 - 8x + 12$

68. $y = x^2 - 2x + 10$

69. $y = x^2 - 10x + 26$

70. $y = x^2 + 14x + 38$

71. Astronomy Saturn is the second largest planet in our solar system. It has a radius of about 5.8×10^4 kilometers. Use the formula for the volume of a sphere, $V = \frac{4}{3}\pi r^3$, to estimate Saturn's volume. *(Lesson 6.1)*

Geometry Skills

Area of a Parallelogram Find the value(s) of x. The formula for the area of a parallelogram is $A = bh$.

72. $A = 10$ ft^2

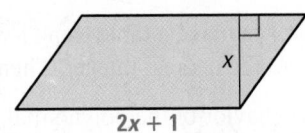

x

$2x + 1$

73. $A = 36$ in.^{2}

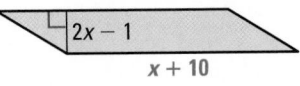

$2x - 1$

$x + 10$

Quiz 1

Lesson 6.1 **Evaluate the expression. Tell which properties of exponents you used.**

1. $4^3 \cdot 4^2$

2. $8^0 \cdot 8^9 \cdot 8^{-7}$

3. $\left(\frac{3}{7}\right)^{-2}$

4. $\dfrac{5^2}{5^{-11}}$

5. $\dfrac{4^4}{4^{-1}}$

6. $(2^3)^{-3}$

7. $(2 \cdot 5)^2$

8. $\dfrac{9^3}{9^5}$

Lesson 6.1 **Simplify the expression. Tell which properties of exponents you used.**

9. $x^6 \cdot \dfrac{5}{x^3}$

10. $(7x^3 \cdot x^2)^{-2}$

11. $\dfrac{x^5 y^2}{x^4 y}$

12. $\dfrac{3x^3 y}{9x^{-2} y^3}$

13. $(4x^5)^{-2}$

14. $(2x^{-3}y^4)^5$

15. $\dfrac{x^7 y^9}{x^{12} y^{-3}}$

16. $\dfrac{12x^{-6} y^7}{3x^4 y}$

Lesson 6.2 **Write the polynomial function in standard form. Then state its degree, type, and leading coefficient.**

17. $f(x) = x^2 - x^4 + 11$

18. $f(x) = 2x^2 - 3x - 15$

19. $f(x) = 2x^3 - 6 + x^2 - 4x$

20. $f(x) = 22 + 15x$

Lesson 6.2 **Graph the polynomial function using the domain $x = -3, -2, -1, 0, 1, 2, 3$.**

21. $f(x) = -x^3 - 2$

22. $f(x) = x^4 - 3x^3 - 2x^2$

23. $f(x) = -x^5 + 6x$

You want to graph a polynomial function using a graphing calculator. What viewing window should you use to display the important characteristics of the graph? You can use what you know about end behavior to find an appropriate viewing window.

EXAMPLE

Graph $f(x) = -0.3x^3 + 10x - 8$.

SOLUTION

1 Enter the function into the graphing calculator. Then graph the function using the standard viewing window.

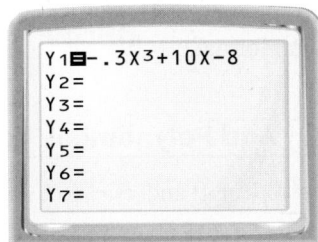 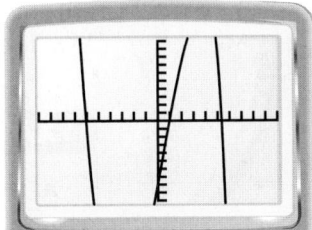

Because the polynomial function has an odd degree and a negative leading coefficient, the graph should rise to the left and fall to the right.

2 Adjust the viewing window so you can see the end behavior and all *turning points* on the graph. A good viewing window for this graph is shown below.

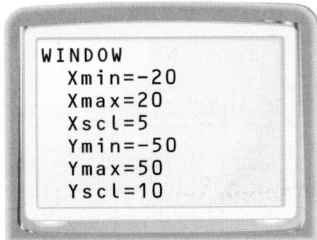 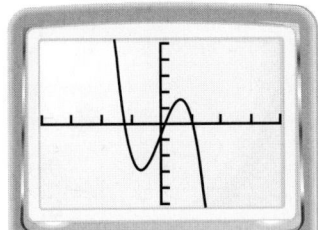

STUDENT HELP

KEYSTROKE HELP
See keystrokes for several models of calculators at www.classzone.com.

STUDENT HELP

READING GRAPHS
A *turning point* is a point on a graph where the graph changes direction. The graph at the right has two turning points.

EXERCISES

1. Graph the polynomial function $f(x) = -x^3 + 10x^2 + 8$ using the viewing window $-10 \le x \le 20$ and $-50 \le y \le 175$. Describe the end behavior of the graph.

2. Graph the polynomial function $f(x) = -x^4 + 8x^2 + 5$ using the viewing window $-10 \le x \le 20$ and $-50 \le y \le 175$. Describe the end behavior of the graph.

Use a graphing calculator to graph the polynomial function. Describe a good viewing window for the graph.

3. $f(x) = 0.2x^3 - 5x + 12$

4. $f(x) = -x^3 + 6x^2 - x + 4$

5. $f(x) = x^4 - 2x^2 + x - 9$

6. $f(x) = x^4 - 9x^3 + 0.1x^2 + 9x$

7. $f(x) = -\frac{1}{10}x^5 + 3x^3$

8. $f(x) = x^5 + 4x^4 - 8x^3 - 16x + 20$

6.3 Adding and Subtracting Polynomials

Key Words
- polynomial, p. 302

Prerequisite Skills

Simplify the expression.

1. $-3(x^2 + 4x - 1)$

2. $8 + 5(x - 3)$

3. $7x^2 - 11x^2 + x^2$

4. $2 - 7x^3 + 10 - x^3$

GOAL Add and subtract polynomials.

How can you model the number of high school students?

In Example 4, you will write a model that represents the total number of high school students in the United States from 1990 to 2002. From this model you can estimate the high school enrollment in 2000.

To add polynomials, add the coefficients of like terms. To subtract polynomials, add the opposite of each term of the polynomial being subtracted. You can use a vertical or horizontal format.

EXAMPLE 1 Add Polynomials Vertically and Horizontally

a. Add $2x^3 + 4x^2 - x + 9$ and $x^3 - 6x^2 + 5x - 1$ in a vertical format.

b. Add $5x^2 + 2x$ and $4x^2 - 7x + 3$ in a horizontal format.

Solution

STUDENT HELP

LOOK BACK
For help with combining like terms, see page 16.

a.
$$\begin{array}{r} 2x^3 + 4x^2 - x + 9 \\ + \quad x^3 - 6x^2 + 5x - 1 \\ \hline 3x^3 - 2x^2 + 4x + 8 \end{array}$$

b. $(5x^2 + 2x) + (4x^2 - 7x + 3)$
$$= (5x^2 + 4x^2) + (2x - 7x) + 3$$
$$= 9x^2 - 5x + 3$$

EXAMPLE 2 Subtract Polynomials Vertically and Horizontally

a. Subtract $3x^3 + 4x^2 + 9x$ from $6x^3 - x^2 + 7x - 12$ in a vertical format.

b. Subtract $9x^3 - x + 11$ from $2x^3 - 5x^2 - 10x$ in a horizontal format.

Solution

a. Align like terms, then add the opposite of the subtracted polynomial.

$$\begin{array}{r} 6x^3 - \ x^2 + 7x - 12 \\ -(3x^3 + 4x^2 + 9x) \\ \hline \end{array}$$

Add the opposite.

$$\begin{array}{r} 6x^3 - \ x^2 + 7x - 12 \\ + \ -3x^3 - 4x^2 - 9x \\ \hline 3x^3 - 5x^2 - 2x - 12 \end{array}$$

b. Write the opposite of the subtracted polynomial, then add like terms.

$$(2x^3 - 5x^2 - 10x) - (9x^3 - x + 11)$$
$$= 2x^3 - 5x^2 - 10x - 9x^3 + x - 11 \qquad \text{Distributive property}$$
$$= (2x^3 - 9x^3) + (-5x^2) + (-10x + x) - 11 \qquad \text{Group like terms.}$$
$$= -7x^3 - 5x^2 - 9x - 11 \qquad \text{Combine like terms.}$$

EXAMPLE 3 Use the Distributive Property

Simplify the expression.

a. $4(2x^2 - x + 5) + 2(x^2 + 3x - 7)$

$= 8x^2 - 4x + 20 + 2x^2 + 6x - 14$ Use distributive property.

$= (8x^2 + 2x^2) + (-4x + 6x) + (20 - 14)$ Group like terms.

$= 10x^2 + 2x + 6$ Combine like terms.

b. $x(x^3 + x^2 + x + 1) - (x^3 + x^2 - x + 1)$

$= x^4 + x^3 + x^2 + x - x^3 - x^2 + x - 1$ Use distributive property.

$= x^4 + (x^3 - x^3) + (x^2 - x^2) + (x + x) - 1$ Group like terms.

$= x^4 + 2x - 1$ Combine like terms.

EXAMPLE 4 Find a Polynomial Model

High School Enrollment The number of students (in thousands) enrolled in high schools in the United States from 1990 to 2002 can be approximated by the models shown, where t is the number of years since 1990.

Public: $-3t^2 + 258t + 11{,}281$ **Private:** $2t^2 - t + 1149$

a. Write a model for the total number of high school students E from 1990 to 2002.

b. Use the model to estimate the high school enrollment in 2000.

Solution

a. To write a model for the total number, add the polynomials.

$E = (-3t^2 + 258t + 11{,}281) + (2t^2 - t + 1149)$

$= (-3t^2 + 2t^2) + (258t - t) + (11{,}281 + 1149)$ Group like terms.

$= -t^2 + 257t + 12{,}430$ Combine like terms.

ANSWER ▶ A model for the total number of students is $-t^2 + 257t + 12{,}430$.

b. In this model, $t = 10$ represents 2000. So, substitute 10 for t in the model.

$E = -t^2 + 257t + 12{,}430$

$= -(10)^2 + 257(10) + 12{,}430$ Substitute 10 for t.

$= 14{,}900$ Simplify.

ANSWER ▶ The high school enrollment in 2000 was about 14.9 million.

Checkpoint ✓ Simplify Polynomial Expressions

Perform the indicated operation. Write the answer in standard form.

1. $(x^2 - 4x + 9) + (3x^2 + 5x + 5)$ **2.** $(x^3 + 4x^2 + 8x - 5) - (3x^2 + 2x + 7)$

Simplify the expression.

3. $2(3x^2 - 1) - 4(x^2 + 3)$ **4.** $5(x^2 + x + 2) + 2(x^2 - x - 4)$

6.3 Exercises

Guided Practice

Vocabulary Check

1. Copy and complete the statement: To add polynomials, you add the __?__ of like terms.

2. Copy and complete the statement: To subtract polynomials, multiply each term in the subtracted polynomial by __?__ and add.

Skill Check

Perform the indicated operation. Write the answer in standard form.

3. $(x^2 + x - 1) + (x^2 - 2x + 1)$

4. $(x^2 - 2x + 3) - (x^2 + x + 2)$

5. $(3x^3 - x - 5) - (2x^3 + 2x - 7)$

6. $(5x^4 + x^3 - x) + (-3x^4 - x^3 + x)$

7. $(x^5 - 4x^2 - 3) + (-2x^5 + 2x^3 - 5)$

8. $(7x^4 + 2x^3 - 1) - (x^3 + 6x - 4)$

Simplify the expression.

9. $2(2x^2 - 5) - (x^2 - 7)$

10. $3(x^3 + x - 2) + 2(x^3 - 2x + 1)$

11. Surface Area The formula for the surface area of a rectangular prism is $S = 2\ell w + 2hw + 2\ell h$. Write the surface area of the prism as a polynomial in standard form.

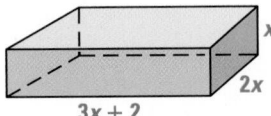

Practice and Applications

STUDENT HELP

HOMEWORK HELP
Example 1: Exs. 12–21
Example 2: Exs. 22–27
Example 3: Exs. 28–33, 36
Example 4: Exs. 34–35, 37–41

Identify Like Terms **Identify the like terms in the expression.**

12. $5xy + 3x - 2y + x - 4xy - 3$

13. $6x^2 + 11xy - 1 + x^2 - 3xy - 4$

14. $10xy^2 + 6y - 5x + 2xy^2 - 4y$

15. $5xy^2 - 6x + 2 - 8 + 4x^2y - 3x$

Adding Polynomials **Find the sum. Write the answer in standard form.**

16. $(3x^2 - 4) + (x^2 + 3)$

17. $(8x + 9) + (2x^5 + x^4 - 7x - 12)$

18. $(8x^3 + 3x^2 - x + 4) + (x^3 - 2x^2 + 5x)$

19. $(5x^2 + 2x - 15) + (3x^2 + 7x - 10)$

20. $(x^4 + x^3 + 11x + 3) + (2x^2 - 8x - 3)$

21. $(xy^2 + 4x^2y - x) + (9 - x^2y - 4x)$

Subtracting Polynomials **Find the difference. Write the answer in standard form.**

22. $(5x^4 + 3) - (7 - 2x^4)$

23. $(x^2 + x - 1) - (x^2 - 2x + 1)$

24. $(x^4 + x^2 - 3x) - (x^3 + 3x^2 + 1)$

25. $(2x^3 - x + 7) - (2x^3 + 6x - 7)$

26. $(2x^3 - 4x - 1) - (x^3 + 5x + 7)$

27. $(x^2 + 4xy + y) - (x + 3xy + 2y)$

Using the Distributive Property **Simplify the expression.**

28. $5(x^2 - x - 2) + 3(-2x^2 + 2x - 1)$

29. $(x^3 - 2x - 6) + 4(x^2 + x - 3)$

30. $2(3x^3 - x^2 + 5x) + x(-4x^2 + x - 7)$

31. $2x(x^5 + 3x^3) + x(-x^5 - 8x^3 + x)$

32. $3(y^2 + 3xy - 2y) - y(2x + 4y - 7)$

33. $x(x^2 + x + 1) - (x^3 + 2x^2 + 1)$

Write the surface area of the figure as a polynomial in standard form.

34. $S = \pi r^2 + \pi r \ell$

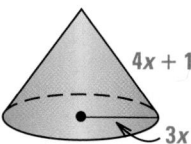
4x + 1
3x

35. $S = 2\pi r^2 + 2\pi rh$

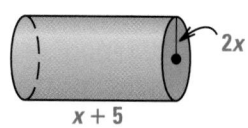
2x
x + 5

36. Error Analysis Describe and correct the error.

$2(y^2 - 5x^2y) + y(-2xy - y)$
$= (2y^2 - 10x^2y) + (-2xy^2 - y^2)$
$= (2y^2 - y^2) + (-10x^2y - 2xy^2)$
$= y^2 - 12x^2y^2$ ✗

37. Carpets A carpet has a floral border around a contrasting center area. The dimensions of these areas are shown below.

a. Write an expression for the area of the border on the carpet.

b. Write an expression for the perimeter of the carpet.

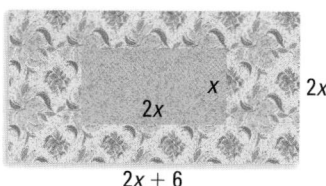
x
2x
2x
2x + 6

Link to
BIOLOGY

BALD EAGLES can be found throughout most of North America. They were listed as an endangered species until 1995 when their status was upgraded to threatened.

Biology Link In Exercises 38 and 39, use the following information.

Let the number of bald eagle nesting pairs from 1996 to 2005 in Yellowstone National Park be E and the number of peregrine falcon nesting pairs be P. These numbers can be modeled by the following equations where t is the number of years since 1996.

$$E = -0.023t^3 + 0.21t^2 + 1.5t + 20$$
$$P = 0.22t^2 + 0.23t + 12$$

38. Write a model that represents the total number of bald eagle and peregrine falcon nesting pairs from 1996 to 2005.

39. Use the model to estimate the total number of bald eagle and peregrine falcon nesting pairs in 2002.

Vehicle Sales In Exercises 40 and 41, use the following information.

Let T be the number of new-truck sales (in thousands). Let C be the number of new-car sales (in thousands). From 2000 through 2005, T and C can be modeled by the following equations where t is the number of years since 2000.

$$T = -20.9t^4 + 186t^3 - 453t^2 + 372t + 8955$$
$$C = 3.58t^4 - 13.2t^3 + 8.33t^2 - 394t + 8846$$

40. Find a new model D by subtracting C from T. Explain the meaning of the model.

41. Evaluate D for the year 2003. Interpret the meaning of this value.

42. Multi-Step Problem From 1998 through 2004, the number (in thousands) of male U.S. residents M and female U.S. residents F can be modeled by the equations below. The variable t is the number of years since 1998.

$$M = -7.7t^3 + 64t^2 + 1454t + 135{,}161$$

$$F = -5.2t^3 + 41t^2 + 1336t + 140{,}751$$

a. Find a model that represents the total number of residents from 1998 through 2004.

b. Use the model to estimate the total number of residents in 2001.

c. Find a model that represents how many more female residents than male residents there were from 1998 through 2004.

d. Use the model to estimate how many more female residents than male residents there were in 2000.

e. Critical Thinking Graph the function from part (c). Determine whether the number of female residents grew or declined with respect to the number of male residents.

Mixed Review

Average Rate of Change Find the average rate of change in y relative to x for the ordered pairs. Include the units of measure for the rate of change. *(Lesson 2.3)*

43. $(5, 12)$ and $(9, 28)$, x is measured in seconds and y is measured in meters.

44. $(2, 7)$ and $(5, 16)$, x is measured in hours and y is measured in miles.

45. $(9, 20)$ and $(14, -5)$, x is measured in hours and y is measured in degrees.

Writing in Standard Form Write the quadratic function in standard form. *(Lesson 5.1)*

46. $y = (x + 3)(x - 5)$ **47.** $y = -(x + 1)(x - 2)$ **48.** $y = 3(x - 4)(x - 1)$

49. $y = -2(x + 3)(x + 4)$ **50.** $y = (2x - 3)(x + 5)$ **51.** $y = -(x + 3)^2 - 7$

Solving Quadratic Equations Use the quadratic formula to solve the equation. *(Lesson 5.9)*

52. $x^2 - 8x + 12 = 0$ **53.** $x^2 - 6x + 7 = 0$ **54.** $x^2 - 4x + 1 = 0$

55. $2x^2 - 5x - 3 = 0$ **56.** $-11x^2 + x + 1 = 0$ **57.** $5x^2 - 5x - 1 = 0$

58. $x^2 - 2x + 5 = 0$ **59.** $-4x^2 + 4x - 5 = 0$ **60.** $x^2 + 4x + 9 = 0$

Geometry Skills

Perimeter Use the figure and the given value of the perimeter P to write an equation for P in terms of x. Then find the value of x.

61. $P = 40$

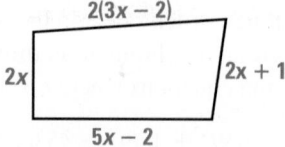

62. $P = 57$

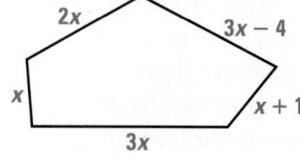

63. $P = 48$

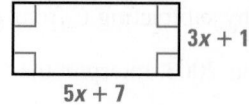

64. $P = 26$

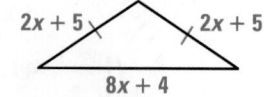

6.4 Multiplying and Dividing Polynomials

Key Words
- polynomial long division

GOAL Multiply and divide polynomials.

Prerequisite Skills

Simplify the expression.

1. $8(3x - 4)$

2. $3(x^2 + 7x + 5)$

3. $-5(x^2 - 2x - 10)$

4. $x^2(4x^3 + x^2 + 1)$

To multiply two polynomials, you multiply each term of the first polynomial by each term of the second polynomial. You can use a vertical or a horizontal format.

EXAMPLE 1 Multiply Polynomials Vertically

Find the product $(x^2 + 4x - 7)(x - 2)$.

Solution

Line up like terms vertically. Then multiply as shown below.

$$
\begin{array}{r}
x^2 + 4x - 7 \\
\times \qquad x - 2 \\
\hline
-2x^2 - 8x + 14 \\
x^3 + 4x^2 - 7x \\
\hline
x^3 + 2x^2 - 15x + 14
\end{array}
$$

Multiply $x^2 + 4x - 7$ by -2.
Multiply $x^2 + 4x - 7$ by x.
Combine like terms.

EXAMPLE 2 Multiply Polynomials Horizontally

Find the product.

a. $(3x + 4)(5x^2 + x - 6)$ **b.** $(x - 2)(x - 1)(x + 3)$

Solution

a. $(3x + 4)(5x^2 + x - 6)$

$= 3x(5x^2 + x - 6) + 4(5x^2 + x - 6)$ Use distributive property.

$= 15x^3 + 3x^2 - 18x + 20x^2 + 4x - 24$ Use distributive property.

$= 15x^3 + (3x^2 + 20x^2) + (-18x + 4x) - 24$ Group like terms.

$= 15x^3 + 23x^2 - 14x - 24$ Combine like terms.

b. To multiply three polynomials, first multiply two of the polynomials. Then multiply the result by the third polynomial.

$(x - 2)(x - 1)(x + 3)$

$= (x - 2)(x^2 + 2x - 3)$ Multiply $(x - 1)(x + 3)$.

$= x(x^2 + 2x - 3) - 2(x^2 + 2x - 3)$ Use distributive property.

$= x^3 + 2x^2 - 3x - 2x^2 - 4x + 6$ Use distributive property.

$= x^3 + (2x^2 - 2x^2) + (-3x - 4x) + 6$ Group like terms.

$= x^3 - 7x + 6$ Combine like terms.

STUDENT HELP

AVOID ERRORS
Pay careful attention to negative terms when you use the distributive property.

Find the product. Use either a horizontal or vertical format.

1. $(x^2 + x + 2)(x + 1)$

2. $(2x^2 - x + 4)(x - 3)$

3. $(3x^2 + x - 1)(2x + 1)$

4. $(x - 1)(x + 4)(x - 2)$

Special Products Some products occur so frequently that it is worth memorizing their *special product patterns*. You can verify these products by multiplying.

Special Product Patterns

SUM AND DIFFERENCE

$(a + b)(a - b) = a^2 - b^2$

EXAMPLE

$(x + 4)(x - 4) = x^2 - 16$

SQUARE OF A BINOMIAL

$(a + b)^2 = a^2 + 2ab + b^2$

$(a - b)^2 = a^2 - 2ab + b^2$

EXAMPLE

$(x + 3)^2 = x^2 + 6x + 9$

$(3x - 4)^2 = 9x^2 - 24x + 16$

CUBE OF A BINOMIAL

$(a + b)^3 = a^3 + 3a^2b + 3ab^2 + b^3$

$(a - b)^3 = a^3 - 3a^2b + 3ab^2 - b^3$

EXAMPLE

$(x + 2)^3 = x^3 + 6x^2 + 12x + 8$

$(x - 2)^3 = x^3 - 6x^2 + 12x - 8$

EXAMPLE **3** **Use Special Product Patterns**

STUDENT HELP

AVOID ERRORS
You can check your answer by substituting 1 for *x* in the answer and in the original expression. The result should be the same.

$(1 + 9)(1 - 9) = -80$

$1^2 - 81 = -80$ ✓

Find the product.

a. $(x + 9)(x - 9)$

b. $(7x - 3)^2$

c. $(2x + 1)^3$

Solution

a. $(a + b)(a - b) = a^2 - b^2$ Write sum and difference pattern.

    $(x + 9)(x - 9) = (x)^2 - 9^2$ Substitute for *a* and *b*.

       ▶ $= x^2 - 81$ Simplify.

b. $(a - b)^2 = a^2 - 2ab + b^2$ Write square of a binomial pattern.

    $(7x - 3)^2 = (7x)^2 - 2(7x)(3) + 3^2$ Substitute for *a* and *b*.

         $= 49x^2 - 42x + 9$ Simplify.

c. $(a + b)^3 = a^3 + 3a^2b + 3ab^2 + b^3$ Write cube pattern.

    $(2x + 1)^3 = (2x)^3 + 3(2x)^2(1) + 3(2x)(1)^2 + 1^3$ Substitute for *a* and *b*.

         $= 8x^3 + 12x^2 + 6x + 1$ Simplify.

Find the product.

5. $(z + 7)(z - 7)$

6. $(3y + 2)^2$

7. $(4x - 1)^3$

Dividing Polynomials You can divide polynomials using **polynomial long division**. You follow the same steps to divide polynomials as you do to divide whole numbers: divide, multiply, subtract, and bring down. Before dividing polynomials, make sure the dividend and divisor are in standard form.

EXAMPLE 4 Use Long Division

Find the quotient $985 \div 23$.

$$
\begin{array}{r}
42 \\
23\overline{)985} \\
\end{array}
$$

$$
\begin{array}{r}
92 \\
\hline
65 \\
46 \\
\hline
19 \\
\end{array}
$$

Divide 98 by 23.

Subtract the product $4(23) = 92$.

Simplify and bring down 5.

Subtract the product $2(23) = 46$.

Remainder

ANSWER ▶ The result is written as $42\frac{19}{23}$.

EXAMPLE 5 Use Polynomial Long Division

Find the quotient $(x^3 - 6x - 4 + 3x^2) \div (x + 4)$.

Rewrite the dividend in standard form.

$$(x^3 - 6x - 4 + 3x^2) \div (x + 4) = (x^3 + 3x^2 - 6x - 4) \div (x + 4)$$

Write division in the same format you use to divide whole numbers.

$$
\begin{array}{r}
x^2 - x - 2 \\
x + 4 \overline{)x^3 + 3x^2 - 6x - 4} \\
\underline{x^3 + 4x^2} \\
-x^2 - 6x \\
\underline{-x^2 - 4x} \\
-2x - 4 \\
\underline{-2x - 8} \\
4 \\
\end{array}
$$

$x^3 \div x = x^2$

Subtract the product $x^2(x + 4) = x^3 + 4x^2$.

Simplify and bring down $-6x$.

Subtract the product $-x(x + 4) = -x^2 - 4x$.

Simplify and bring down -4.

Subtract the product $-2(x + 4) = -2x - 8$.

Remainder

ANSWER ▶ The result is written as $x^2 - x - 2 + \frac{4}{x + 4}$.

CHECK You can check the result of a division problem by multiplying the divisor by the quotient and adding the remainder. The result should be the dividend.

$$
\begin{aligned}
(x^2 - x - 2)(x + 4) + 4 &= x^2(x + 4) - x(x + 4) - 2(x + 4) + 4 \\
&= x^3 + 4x^2 - x^2 - 4x - 2x - 8 + 4 \\
&= x^3 + 3x^2 - 6x - 4 \checkmark
\end{aligned}
$$

Checkpoint ✓ *Use Long Division*

Use long division to find the quotient.

8. $4900 \div 27$

9. $(4x^3 + 5x + 1) \div (x + 1)$

6.4 Exercises

Guided Practice

Vocabulary Check

1. Identify the divisor, the quotient, and the remainder in the long division problem shown.

$$
\begin{array}{r}
x + 4 \\
x + 2 \overline{)\, x^2 + 6x - 3} \\
x^2 + 2x \\
\hline
4x - 3 \\
4x + 8 \\
\hline
-11
\end{array}
$$

2. Which special product pattern could you use to find the product $(3x + 2)(3x - 2)$?

Skill Check

Find the product of the polynomials.

3. $x(5x - 3)$

4. $4x^2(2x^2 + x - 2)$

5. $(4x^2 - 3x + 1)(x - 2)$

6. $(x - 1)(x + 3)(x - 2)$

7. $(x + 11y)(x - 11y)$

8. $(2x - 9)^2$

Use long division to find the quotient.

9. $(x^2 - 5x - 6) \div (x + 4)$

10. $(-3x^2 + x - 2) \div (x - 3)$

11. $(8x^3 - 6x^2 - 5x + 3) \div (x - 1)$

12. $(x^3 - 8x + 32) \div (x + 5)$

Practice and Applications

STUDENT HELP

HOMEWORK HELP
Example 1: Exs. 13–18, 57–64
Example 2: Exs. 19–30, 57–64
Example 3: Exs. 31–51, 57–64
Example 4: Exs. 72–77
Example 5: Exs. 78–85

Multiplying Polynomials Use a vertical format to find the product.

13. $x(3x + 5)$

14. $2x^2(x^2 - 3x + 7)$

15. $(x + 1)(-x^2 + 11x + 1)$

16. $(x + 3)(9x^2 + x + 1)$

17. $(2x - 1)(x^2 - 5x - 4)$

18. $(5x^2 + 2x - 1)(3x - 2)$

Multiplying Polynomials Use a horizontal format to find the product.

19. $2x(6x - 1)$

20. $5x^2(4x + 1)$

21. $(x^2 + 3x - 1)(x + 2)$

22. $(3x^2 + x - 4)(2x + 1)$

23. $(x + 4)(x^2 - x + 3)$

24. $(-2x^2 + x + 3)(5x - 6)$

25. $(3x - 2)(4x^3 - x)$

26. $(6x^3 - 4x^2 + 1)(x + 3)$

Multiplying Three Binomials Find the product of the binomials.

27. $(x + 2)(x + 6)(x + 3)$

28. $(x - 1)(x - 2)(x - 3)$

29. $(x - 6)(x + 2)(x + 6)$

30. $(x + 2)(x + 3)(x - 4)$

Special Products Find the product.

31. $(x + 6)^2$

32. $(x + 7)^2$

33. $(3x + 4)^2$

34. $(2x + 1)^2$

35. $(x + 10)^3$

36. $(x + 1)^3$

37. $(x + 4)^3$

38. $(4x + 2)^3$

39. $(3x + 5)^3$

Special Products Find the product.

40. $(x + 6)(x - 6)$ **41.** $(x + 3)(x - 3)$ **42.** $(x + 7)(x - 7)$

43. $(2x + 4)(2x - 4)$ **44.** $(5x + 3)(5x - 3)$ **45.** $(6x + 8)(6x - 8)$

46. $(x - 2)^2$ **47.** $(y - 3)^2$ **48.** $(x - y)^3$

49. $(3x - 4)^3$ **50.** $(6x - 1)^3$ **51.** $(4x - y)^2$

Logical Reasoning Complete the statement with *always*, *sometimes*, or *never*.

52. If a and b are whole numbers, then $(a + b)^2$ is __?__ equal to $a^2 + b^2$.

53. If a and b are whole numbers, then $(a - b)^2$ is __?__ equal to $a^2 - b^2$.

54. If $x - k$ is a factor of a polynomial $f(x)$, then the remainder __?__ equals zero when $f(x)$ is divided by $x - k$.

Geometry Link The formula for the volume of a rectangular solid is $V = \ell wh$. Write the volume of the figure as a polynomial in standard form.

55.
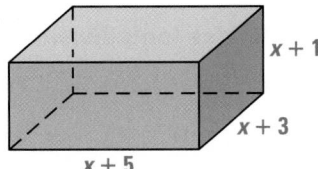

56.
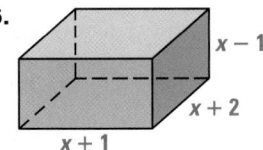

Choosing a Method Find the product of the polynomials.

57. $(-x^2 + 6x - 2)(x + 5)$ **58.** $(x + 12)(x - 12)$

59. $(x + 8)^3$ **60.** $(5x + 7)^2$

61. $(4x - 3)^3$ **62.** $(x - 5)(x - 4)(x + 3)$

63. $(2x + 5y)(2x - 5y)$ **64.** $(x - 5y)^2$

65. Soccer Fields The soccer field shown has a width of $(4x + 10)$ meters and a length of $(9x - 20)$ meters. Write the area of the soccer field as a polynomial expression in standard form.

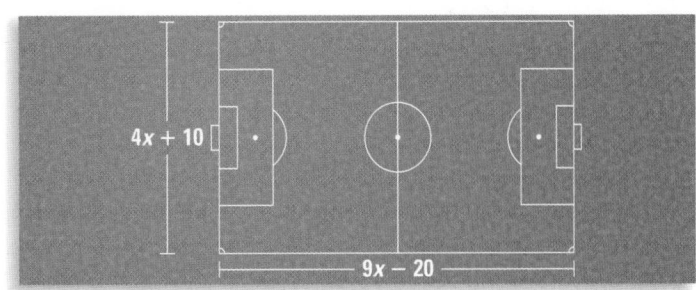

66. Error Analysis Describe and correct the error.

$(x + 9)(x^2 - 7x + 3)$
$= x^3 - 7x^2 + 3x + 9x^2 - 7x + 3$
$= x^3 + 2x^2 - 4x + 3$ ✗

67. Critical Thinking Explain why $(x + 3)^2 \neq x^2 + 9$ if $x \neq 0$.

Swimming Pools In Exercises 68–71, use the following information.

The swimming pool in the diagram has a length of $(x + 10)$ feet, a width of $(x + 5)$ feet, and a depth of $(x - 5)$ feet.

68. You are trying to find a cover to just fit on top of the pool. Write a polynomial expression in standard form for the area of the cover.

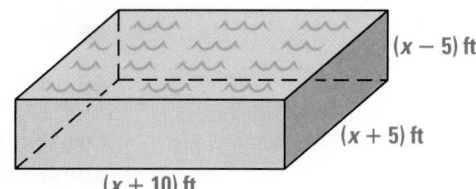

69. What is the area of the pool cover when $x = 10$?

70. You are filling the pool with water. Write the volume of the swimming pool as a polynomial expression in standard form.

71. What is the volume of the pool when $x = 10$?

Dividing Use long division to find the quotient.

72. $640 \div 25$ **73.** $460 \div 30$ **74.** $872 \div 45$

75. $7542 \div 21$ **76.** $5673 \div 15$ **77.** $9346 \div 52$

Dividing Polynomials Use long division to find the quotient.

78. $(x^2 - 7x + 10) \div (x - 2)$ **79.** $(4x^2 - x - 1) \div (x + 2)$

80. $(2x^2 + 7x - 10) \div (2x - 3)$ **81.** $(3x^2 + 2x - 66) \div (3x + 11)$

82. $(6x^3 - x^2 + 7) \div (x + 1)$ **83.** $(-x^3 + 8x^2 + 38x + 15) \div (x + 3)$

Geometry Link The formula for the area of a parallelogram is $A = bh$. Find an expression for the missing dimension.

84. $A = 6x^2 - 5x - 4$

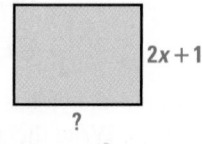

85. $A = 8x^2 + 30x + 28$

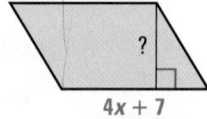

86. Challenge Look at the following quotients of polynomials.

$$(x^2 - 1) \div (x - 1) = x + 1$$
$$(x^3 - 1) \div (x - 1) = x^2 + x + 1$$
$$(x^4 - 1) \div (x - 1) = x^3 + x^2 + x + 1$$

a. Describe a pattern.

b. Extend the pattern to find the quotient when $(x^5 - 1)$ and $(x^6 - 1)$ are divided by $(x - 1)$.

c. Check your answers to part (b) by multiplying.

87. Multiple Choice For what value of k is the equation below true?

$$(2x + 3)^2 = 4x^2 + kx + 9$$

   (A) 5   **(B)** 6   **(C)** 10   **(D)** 12

88. Multiple Choice Find the product $(x - 5)(2x^2 - x + 4)$.

   (F) $2x^3 - 11x^2 + 9x - 20$ **(G)** $2x^3 + 9x^2 - 11x + 20$

   (H) $2x^3 + 11x^2 - 9x + 20$ **(J)** $2x^3 - 11x^2 - 9x - 20$

89. Multiple Choice Find the product $(3x - 1)^3$.

    (A) $9x^2 - 6x + 1$ **(B)** $3x^3 - 27x^2 + 9x - 1$

    (C) $27x^3 - 9x^2 + 3x - 1$ **(D)** $27x^3 - 27x^2 + 9x - 1$

90. Multiple Choice Find the product $(4x + 7)(4x - 7)$.

    (F) $4x^2 - 49$ **(G)** $16x^2 + 28x - 49$

    (H) $16x^2 - 49$ **(J)** $16x^2 + 49$

Mixed Review

Factoring Special Products Factor the expression. *(Lesson 5.4)*

91. $x^2 - 25$ **92.** $x^2 - 81$ **93.** $x^2 - 36$

94. $x^2 + 12x + 36$ **95.** $2x^2 + 12x + 18$ **96.** $2x^2 - 98$

Adding Complex Numbers Write the expression as a complex number in standard form. *(Lesson 5.7)*

97. $(5 + 2i) + (6 - 7i)$ **98.** $(4 - 3i) + (8 - i)$

99. $(-9 + 5i) + (2 + 6i)$ **100.** $(11 - 8i) + (7 + 10i)$

Using the Distributive Property Simplify the expression. *(Lesson 6.3)*

101. $4(3x^3 + 1) - 2(x^3 - 1)$ **102.** $3(x^2 - 6x - 9) + 5(-x^2 + 2x - 4)$

103. $2(x^2 + 7x - 2) - (6x^2 + 8x - 14)$ **104.** $(x^3 - 3x - 8) + 4(x^2 + 10x - 5)$

Geometry Skills

Surface Area Find the surface area of the rectangular solid.

105.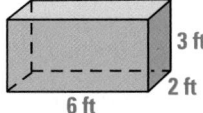
3 ft   2 ft   6 ft

106.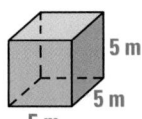
5 m   5 m   5 m

Quiz 2

Lesson 6.3   **Find the sum or difference. Write the answer in standard form.**

    1. $(x^2 + 4x - 3) + (x^2 - 2x + 5)$ **2.** $(x^2 - 8x + 8) - (x^2 + 7x + 1)$

    3. $(9x^3 - 3x - 4) - (2x^3 + x - 10)$ **4.** $(6x^4 + x^3 - 5x) + (-7x^4 - x^3 + 12x)$

    5. $(5x^4 + 3x^2 - 9) + (8x^3 - 7x^2 + 1)$ **6.** $(6x^3 - 2x^2 - x) - (3x^3 + 4x^2 - 7x)$

Lesson 6.4   **Find the product of the polynomials.**

    7. $x(2x + 7)$ **8.** $5x^2(x^3 - 8x + 4)$

    9. $(x^2 + 6x + 4)(x - 7)$ **10.** $(x + 13)(x - 13)$

    11. $(x + 11)^2$ **12.** $(x + 2)(x - 6)(x + 2)$

Lesson 6.4   **Use long division to find the quotient.**

    13. $890 \div 42$ **14.** $3748 \div 31$

    15. $(x^2 + 5x + 1) \div (x + 3)$ **16.** $(4x^2 - 11x - 25) \div (x - 6)$

    17. $(6x^2 + x - 8) \div (2x - 3)$ **18.** $(3x^3 - 4) \div (x + 1)$

Goal

Use three-dimensional models to factor the sum or difference of two cubes.

Materials

- pencil
- paper

QUESTION

How can you use a three-dimensional model to factor the sum of two cubes?

EXPLORE

The sum of two cubes can be modeled as shown.

The volume of the model is $a^3 + b^3$, which is equal to the sum of the volumes of the three rectangular solids.

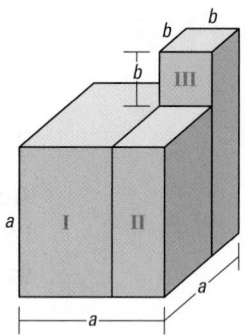

1 Write an equation for the model.

$$a^3 + b^3 = \boxed{\text{Volume of Solid I}} + \boxed{\text{Volume of Solid II}} + \boxed{\text{Volume of Solid III}}$$

2 Write an algebraic expression in factored form for the volume of Solid I, Solid II, and Solid III.

Volume of Solid I $= a \cdot a \cdot (a - b) = a^2(a - b)$

Volume of Solid II $= a \cdot b \cdot (a - b) = ab(a - b)$

Volume of Solid III $= b \cdot b \cdot (a + b) = b^2(a + b)$

3 Substitute the expressions from Step 2 into the equation from Step 1. Then factor the resulting expression.

$$a^3 + b^3 = a^2(a - b) + ab(a - b) + b^2(a + b)$$
$$= a \cdot a(a - b) + b \cdot a(a - b) + b^2(a + b)$$
$$= a(a - b)(a + b) + b^2(a + b) \quad \longleftarrow$$
$$= [a(a - b) + b^2](a + b) \quad \longleftarrow$$
$$= (a^2 - ab + b^2)(a + b)$$

Factor out the common factor $a(a - b)$ from the first two terms.

Factor out the common factor $(a + b)$.

THINK ABOUT IT

1. The difference of two cubes can be modeled as shown. The volume of the model is $a^3 - b^3$. Follow the steps above to factor the expression $a^3 - b^3$. (*Hint:* In Step 3, factor out the common factor $(a - b)$ from all three terms.)

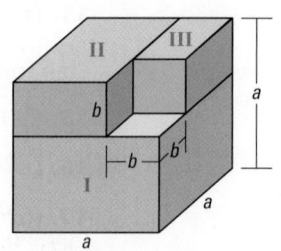

Factoring Cubic Polynomials

Key Words

- factor by grouping

Factor the expression.

1. $60 + 18x^2$

2. $4x^2 + 4x - 24$

3. $3x^2 - 13x - 10$

4. $6x^2 - 7x - 5$

GOAL Factor cubic polynomials and solve cubic equations.

How can you factor the expression for the volume of a shipping container?

A container ship transports large containers of goods by sea. Once the ship reaches its destination, the containers can be transferred to trucks or trains. In Example 3, you will factor an expression for the volume of a container.

In the activity on page 322, you may have found how to factor the difference of two cubes. In this lesson, you will learn how to factor some types of cubic polynomials.

Special Product Patterns

SUM OF TWO CUBES

$a^3 + b^3 = (a + b)(a^2 - ab + b^2)$

EXAMPLE

$x^3 + 8 = (x + 2)(x^2 - 2x + 4)$

DIFFERENCE OF TWO CUBES

$a^3 - b^3 = (a - b)(a^2 + ab + b^2)$

EXAMPLE

$27x^3 - 1 = (3x - 1)(9x^2 + 3x + 1)$

EXAMPLE 1 Factor the Sum or Difference of Two Cubes

a. Factor $x^3 + 64$.

b. Factor $8p^3 - q^3$.

Solution

a. $x^3 + 64 = x^3 + 4^3$ Write as sum of two cubes.

$= (x + 4)(x^2 - 4x + 4^2)$ Use special product pattern.

$= (x + 4)(x^2 - 4x + 16)$ Simplify.

b. $8p^3 - q^3 = (2p)^3 - q^3$ Write as difference of two cubes.

$= (2p - q)[(2p)^2 + 2pq + q^2]$ Use special product pattern.

$= (2p - q)(4p^2 + 2pq + q^2)$ Simplify.

Checkpoint ✓ *Factor the Sum or Difference of Two Cubes*

Factor the polynomial.

1. $x^3 + 1$

2. $125x^3 + 8$

3. $x^3 - 216$

4. $27x^3 - y^3$

Common Monomials Sometimes you can factor out a monomial common to all the terms in a polynomial. You may be able to factor the resulting polynomial.

EXAMPLE 2 Factor Polynomials

a. Factor $x^3 - 5x^2 + 6x$.   **b.** Factor $16x^4 - 2x$.

Solution

a. $x^3 - 5x^2 + 6x = x(x^2 - 5x + 6)$ Factor common monomial.

$\qquad\qquad\qquad\ \ = x(x - 3)(x - 2)$ Factor trinomial.

b. $16x^4 - 2x = 2x(8x^3 - 1)$ Factor common monomial.

$\qquad\qquad\quad = 2x(2x - 1)(4x^2 + 2x + 1)$ Use special product pattern.

EXAMPLE 3 Factor a Polynomial in Real Life

Ships The volume of a container carried on a container ship can be modeled by the expression $36h^3 - 288h^2 + 320h$ where h is the height of the container. Factor the expression for the volume of the container.

Solution

$36h^3 - 288h^2 + 320h = 4h(9h^2 - 72h + 80)$ Factor common monomial.

$\qquad\qquad\qquad\qquad\ = 4h(3h - 4)(3h - 20)$ Factor trinomial.

ANSWER ▶ The factored form is $4h(3h - 4)(3h - 20)$.

Link to
INDUSTRY

CONTAINER SHIPS began being used in 1956 when Malcom McClean shipped 58 truck trailers on a converted oil tanker from New Jersey to Texas.

 *Checkpoint* ✓ *Factor Polynomials*

Factor the polynomial.

5. $x^3 + 2x^2 - 3x$ **6.** $2x^3 - 10x^2 + 8x$ **7.** $3x^4 + 24x$ **8.** $54x^4 - 16x$

Factor by Grouping For some polynomials, you can **factor by grouping** pairs of terms that have a common monomial factor. The pattern is shown below.

$$ra + rb + sa + sb = r(a + b) + s(a + b)$$
$$= (r + s)(a + b)$$

EXAMPLE 4 Factor by Grouping

Factor the polynomial.

a. $x^2(x - 1) - 9(x - 1)$ **b.** $x^3 - 2x^2 - 16x + 32$

STUDENT HELP

AVOID ERRORS
Make sure you factor each polynomial as much as possible.

Solution

a. $x^2(x - 1) - 9(x - 1) = (x^2 - 9)(x - 1)$ Use distributive property.

$\qquad\qquad\qquad\qquad\quad = (x - 3)(x + 3)(x - 1)$ Difference of two squares

b. $x^3 - 2x^2 - 16x + 32 = (x^3 - 2x^2) + (-16x + 32)$ Group terms.

$\qquad\qquad\qquad\qquad\quad = x^2(x - 2) + (-16)(x - 2)$ Factor each group.

$\qquad\qquad\qquad\qquad\quad = (x^2 - 16)(x - 2)$ Use distributive property.

$\qquad\qquad\qquad\qquad\quad = (x - 4)(x + 4)(x - 2)$ Difference of two squares

Factor the polynomial by grouping.

9. $x^2(x + 6) - 4(x + 6)$

10. $x^3 - 4x^2 - 25x + 100$

11. $x^3 + 3x^2 + 4x + 12$

12. $4x^3 - 5x^2 + 8x - 10$

Solving Cubic Equations In Lesson 5.3, you found the zeros of some quadratic functions by setting the functions equal to 0, factoring, and then solving each factor for x. You can use this method when solving certain cubic equations, as shown in Example 5.

EXAMPLE **5** **Solve a Cubic Equation by Factoring**

Solve $2x^3 - 14x^2 = -24x$.

Solution

$2x^3 - 14x^2 = -24x$	Write original equation.
$2x^3 - 14x^2 + 24x = 0$	Rewrite in standard form.
$2x(x^2 - 7x + 12) = 0$	Factor common monomial.
$2x(x - 4)(x - 3) = 0$	Factor trinomial.
$2x = 0$ or $x - 4 = 0$ or $x - 3 = 0$	Use zero product property.
$x = 0, x = 4, x = 3$	Solve for x.

ANSWER ▶ The solutions are 0, 4, and 3. Check these in the original equation.

EXAMPLE **6** **Solve a Cubic Equation by Factoring**

Solve $x^3 - 6x^2 + 12 = 2x$.

Solution

$x^3 - 6x^2 + 12 = 2x$	Write original equation.
$x^3 - 6x^2 - 2x + 12 = 0$	Rewrite in standard form.
$(x^3 - 6x^2) + (-2x + 12) = 0$	Group terms.
$x^2(x - 6) + (-2)(x - 6) = 0$	Factor each group.
$(x^2 - 2)(x - 6) = 0$	Use distributive property.
$x - 6 = 0$ or $x^2 - 2 = 0$	Use zero product property.
$x = 6, x = \sqrt{2}, x = -\sqrt{2}$	Solve for x.

ANSWER ▶ The solutions are 6, $\sqrt{2}$, and $-\sqrt{2}$. Check these in the original equation.

Solve the equation by factoring.

13. $x^3 + 3x^2 = 4x$

14. $3x^3 - 30x = 9x$

15. $x^3 + 2x^2 - 3x = 6$

16. $x^3 - 7x^2 = 5x - 35$

Guided Practice

Vocabulary Check

1. Explain what it means to factor the common monomial from a polynomial.

2. Explain how to factor an expression by grouping.

Skill Check

Factor the polynomial.

3. $x^3 - 8$

4. $x^3 + 27$

5. $x^3 + 7x^2 - 8x$

6. $x^4 + x$

7. $x(x + 5) - 7(x + 5)$

8. $x^3 + x^2 - 9x - 9$

Solve the equation by factoring.

9. $x^3 - 2x^2 - 25x = -50$

10. $x^3 + 3x^2 - x - 7 = -4x^2$

11. $x^3 - 3x^2 - x = -3$

12. $x^3 - 4x^2 = 4x - 16$

13. **Error Analysis** Describe and correct the error in solving $2x^3 + 2x^2 - 12x = 0$.

$$2x^3 + 2x^2 - 12x = 0$$
$$2x(x^2 + x - 6) = 0$$
$$2x(x + 3)(x - 2) = 0$$
$$x + 3 = 0 \text{ or } x - 2 = 0$$
$$x = -3 \qquad x = 2$$

Practice and Applications

STUDENT HELP

HOMEWORK HELP
Example 1: Exs. 25–32
Example 2: Exs. 14–24
Example 3: Exs. 52–56
Example 4: Exs. 33–38
Example 5: Exs. 39–44
Example 6: Exs. 39–44

Monomial Factors **Find the greatest common factor of the terms in the polynomial.**

14. $x^3 + x^2$

15. $3x^3 - 18$

16. $2x^3 + 8x^2 - 12x$

17. $21x^3 + 14x^2 + 49x$

18. $8x^3 - 16x^2 + 12x - 20$

19. $9x^3 - 15x^2 + 12x$

Matching **Match the polynomial with its factorization.**

20. $3x^3 - 9x$

21. $x^3 - 9x$

22. $24x^3 - 54x$

23. $x^3 + 6x^2 + 9x$

24. $x^3 + 9x$

A. $x(x^2 + 9)$

B. $6x(2x + 3)(2x - 3)$

C. $x(x + 3)(x - 3)$

D. $x(x + 3)(x + 3)$

E. $3x(x^2 - 3)$

Sum or Difference of Two Cubes **Factor the polynomial.**

25. $x^3 - 1$

26. $x^3 + 125$

27. $27x^3 + 1$

28. $216x^3 - 1$

29. $8x^3 + 27$

30. $125x^3 - 64$

31. $x^3 - y^3$

32. $x^3 + 64y^3$

Grouping **Factor the polynomial by grouping.**

33. $x(x - 2) + 3(x - 2)$

34. $x^2(x + 8) - 4(x + 8)$

35. $x^3 - x^2 + x - 1$

36. $3x^3 + x^2 + 9x + 3$

37. $2x^3 - 8x^2 + x - 4$

38. $2x^3 + 3x^2 - 4x - 6$

Solving Cubic Equations Solve the equation by factoring.

39. $2x^3 - 12x^2 = 14x$

40. $x^3 + 8x^2 = -15x$

41. $16x^3 = 4x$

42. $x^3 - 2x^2 + 8 = 4x$

43. $x^3 - 6x^2 = 3x - 18$

44. $4x^3 + 8x^2 - 9x - 8 = 10$

EXAMPLE **Solve a Cubic Equation by Graphing**

Use a graphing calculator to solve the equation $x^3 - 6x - 4 = 0$.

Solution

You can see that the polynomial has three zeros or x-intercepts. Using the *Zero* (or *Root*) feature of a graphing calculator, you can determine that two of the zeros are -2 and -0.7320508 as shown. Similarly, the third zero is 2.7320508.

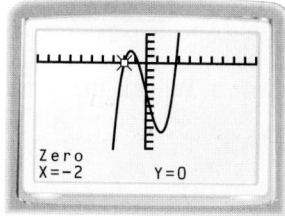
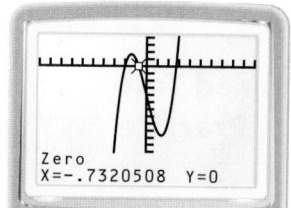

Matching Match the equation with its graph.

45. $y = x^2(x + 3)$

46. $y = x(x - 2)(x + 1)$

47. $y = (x^2 - 1)(x - 2)$

A.
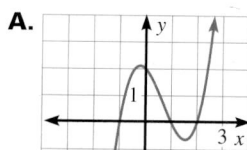

B.
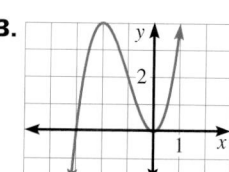

C.
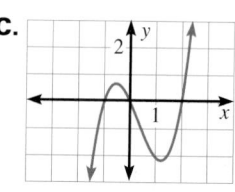

Solving Cubic Equations by Graphing Use a graphing calculator to solve the equation. Round answers to two decimal places.

48. $x^3 - 5x - 1 = 0$

49. $x^3 + 3x^2 + x - 1 = 0$

50. $x^3 - 3x + 1 = 0$

51. $-x^3 - 2x^2 + 3x - 2 = 0$

Sears Tower In Exercises 52–54, use the following information.

The Sears Tower is made up of nine rectangular prisms with square bases and varying heights. A scale model of one of the two tallest prisms has base side lengths of x inches and a height of $(x + 55)$ inches.

52. The volume of the scale model is 522 cubic inches. Write an equation for the volume of the scale model in terms of x.

53. Use a graphing calculator to solve the equation. What are the dimensions of the model?

54. **Challenge** The height of the actual rectangular prism is 1450 feet. Approximate the volume of the actual prism.

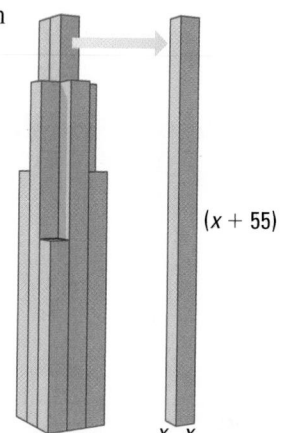

$(x + 55)$

x x

55. Packaging A package has a height of x inches, a width of $3x - 2$ inches, and a length of $3x - 7$ inches. The volume of the package is 42 cubic inches.

    a. Use the formula for the volume of a prism to write an equation for the volume of the package.

    b. Solve the equation from part (a). Use your solution to calculate the dimensions of the package.

56. Geometry Link The figures below have equal volumes. Write an equation relating the volumes. Solve the equation to find the value of x.

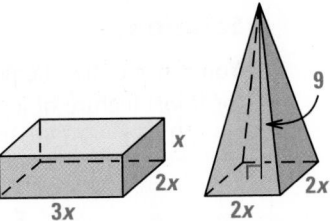

Standardized Test Practice

57. Multiple Choice What is the factored form of $4x^3 - 12x^2 - 16x$?

    (A) $4(x^2 + 4)(x - 1)$ **(B)** $4x(x + 4)(x - 1)$

    (C) $4(x + 4)(x^2 - 1)$ **(D)** $4x(x - 4)(x + 1)$

58. Multiple Choice Which expressions is a factor of $4x^3 - 6x^2 - 10x + 15$?

    (F) $2x^2 + 5$ **(G)** $2x^2 - 3$

    (H) $2x^2 - 5$ **(J)** $2x^2 + 3$

59. Multiple Choice What are the solutions of $x^3 - 7x^2 - x + 28 = 3x$?

    (A) $0, 7$ **(B)** $-2, 2, -7$

    (C) $-2, 2, 7$ **(D)** $-2, 7$

Mixed Review   **Solving Quadratic Equations Solve the equation by factoring.** *(Lesson 5.4)*

60. $x^2 - 10x + 9 = 0$ **61.** $6x^2 + 7x - 3 = 0$ **62.** $2x^2 - 98 = 0$

63. $4x^2 - 9 = 0$ **64.** $4x^2 - 12x + 9 = 0$ **65.** $16x^2 + 8x + 1 = 0$

Solving Equations Solve the equation. *(Lesson 5.7)*

66. $x^2 = -25$ **67.** $2x^2 = -72$ **68.** $3x^2 = -36$

69. $x^2 + 5 = -15$ **70.** $x^2 + 6 = -44$ **71.** $x^2 + 3 = -24$

72. $4x^2 + 6 = -38$ **73.** $3x^2 + 7 = -47$ **74.** $2x^2 + 17 = -31$

Geometry Skills   **Similar Solids Decide whether the two solids are similar. If so, compare the volumes of the solids.**

75.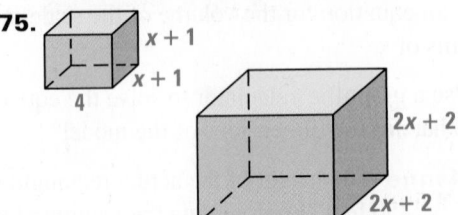

76.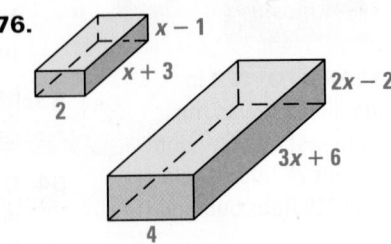

6.6 Polynomials of Greater Degree

Key Words
- quadratic form
- repeated solution

GOAL Factor polynomials and solve polynomial equations of degree greater than three.

How many pilots have airline transport licenses?

In Exercise 58, you will use the graph of a fourth degree polynomial to model the number of active pilots with airline transport licenses. You will use the graph to find values.

Prerequisite Skills

Factor each polynomial.

1. $125x^3 + 1$
2. $64x^3 - y^3$
3. $x^3 - 4x^2 + 3$
4. $3x^4 - 9x^3 - 30x^2$

EXAMPLE 1 Factor a Common Monomial

Factor $16x^5 - 54x^2$.

Solution

$$16x^5 - 54x^2 = 2x^2(8x^3 - 27)$$
Factor common monomial.

$$= 2x^2[(2x)^3 - 3^3]$$
Write as difference of two cubes.

$$= 2x^2(2x - 3)(4x^2 + 6x + 9)$$
Use special product pattern.

Quadratic Form An expression of the form $au^2 + bu + c$ where u is an expression in terms of x is said to be in **quadratic form**. The factoring techniques you studied in Chapter 5 can sometimes be used to factor such expressions.

EXAMPLE 2 Factor Polynomials in Quadratic Form

Factor the polynomial.

a. $16x^4 - 81$

b. $6x^6 - 6x^4 - 12x^2$

Solution

a. $16x^4 - 81 = (4x^2)^2 - 9^2$
Write as difference of two squares; $u = 4x^2$.

$$= (4x^2 + 9)(4x^2 - 9)$$
Factor difference of two squares.

$$= (4x^2 + 9)(2x + 3)(2x - 3)$$
Factor difference of two squares.

b. $6x^6 - 6x^4 - 12x^2 = 6x^2(x^4 - x^2 - 2)$
Factor common monomial; $u = x^2$.

$$= 6x^2(x^2 - 2)(x^2 + 1)$$
Factor trinomial.

STUDENT HELP

VOCABULARY
The expression $16x^4 - 81$ is in *quadratic form* because it can be written as $u^2 - 81$, where $u = 4x^2$.

Checkpoint ✓ *Factor Polynomials*

Factor the polynomial.

1. $27x^5 - x^2$

2. $x^4 - 16$

3. $2x^5 - 4x^3 - 6x$

EXAMPLE 3 Factor a Polynomial

Factor $8x^6 - 32x^4 + 24x^2$.

Solution

$$8x^6 - 32x^4 + 24x^2 = 8x^2(x^4 - 4x^2 + 3)$$ Factor common monomial.

$$= 8x^2(x^2 - 3)(x^2 - 1)$$ Factor trinomial.

$$= 8x^2(x^2 - 3)(x - 1)(x + 1)$$ Factor difference of two squares.

Solve Polynomial Equations You have solved quadratic and cubic equations. You can use the same techniques to solve polynomial equations of greater degree.

EXAMPLE 4 Solve a Polynomial Equation

Solve the polynomial equation.

a. $2x^5 + 4x = 6x^3$ **b.** $x^4 - 3x^3 + 4x^2 = 0$

Solution

a.

$$2x^5 + 4x = 6x^3$$ Write original equation.

$$2x^5 - 6x^3 + 4x = 0$$ Rewrite in standard form.

$$2x(x^4 - 3x^2 + 2) = 0$$ Factor common monomial.

$$2x(x^2 - 2)(x^2 - 1) = 0$$ Factor trinomial.

$$2x(x^2 - 2)(x + 1)(x - 1) = 0$$ Factor difference of two squares.

$$x = 0, x = \sqrt{2}, x = -\sqrt{2}, x = -1, x = 1$$ Use the zero product property.

ANSWER ▸ The solutions are 0, $\sqrt{2}$, $-\sqrt{2}$, -1, and 1.

b.

$$x^4 - 3x^3 + 4x^2 = 0$$ Original equation is in standard form.

$$x^2(x^2 - 3x + 4) = 0$$ Factor common monomial.

$$x^2 = 0 \text{ or } x^2 - 3x + 4 = 0$$ Use zero product property.

$$x = \frac{3 \pm \sqrt{(-3)^2 - 4(1)(4)}}{2(1)}$$ Substitute values in the quadratic formula: $a = 1$, $b = -3$, and $c = 4$.

$$x = \frac{3 \pm \sqrt{-7}}{2}$$ Simplify.

$$x = \frac{3 \pm i\sqrt{7}}{2}$$ Write using the imaginary unit i.

ANSWER ▸ The solutions are 0, $\dfrac{3 + i\sqrt{7}}{2}$, and $\dfrac{3 - i\sqrt{7}}{2}$.

STUDENT HELP

AVOID ERRORS
Note that the solution 0 is listed only once even though $x^2 = 0$ yields the solution $x = 0$ twice.

Checkpoint ✓ *Factor and Solve Polynomial Equations*

4. Factor $x^6 + 2x^4 - 24x^2$.

5. Factor $4x^5 - 20x + 16x^3$.

6. Solve $4x^5 - 28x^3 + 48x = 0$.

7. Solve $x^4 + 2x^3 + 2x^2 = 0$.

Fundamental Theorem of Algebra A polynomial function of degree n has exactly n solutions. A polynomial function may have a **repeated solution** which appears more than once.

$$f(x) = x^4 + x^3 - 2x^2 = x^2(x - 1)(x + 2)$$

Solutions: $x = 0 \quad x = 0 \quad x = 1 \quad x = -2$

$x = 0$ appears twice and is a repeated solution

The function $f(x) = x^4 + x^3 - 2x^2$ has degree 4 and has 4 real solutions. As you can see in part (b) of Example 4, some solutions may be complex numbers.

This result was first proved by the German mathematician Carl Friedrich Gauss (1777–1855) and is stated formally in the box below.

The Fundamental Theorem of Algebra

THEOREM If $f(x)$ is a polynomial of degree n where $n > 0$, then the equation $f(x) = 0$ has at least one root in the set of complex numbers.

COROLLARY If $f(x)$ is a polynomial of degree n where $n > 0$, then the equation $f(x) = 0$ has exactly n solutions provided each repeated solution is counted individually.

EXAMPLE 5 Approximate Real Zeros

Use a graphing calculator to approximate the real zeros of the function.
$$f(x) = x^4 - x^3 - 2x^2 - x + 1$$

Solution

One way to approximate real zeros is to use the *Zero* (or *Root*) feature of a graphing calculator as shown below.

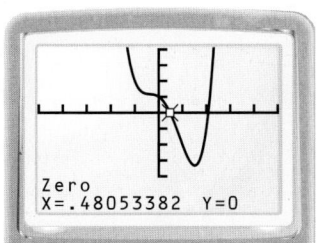
```
Zero
X=.48053382  Y=0
```

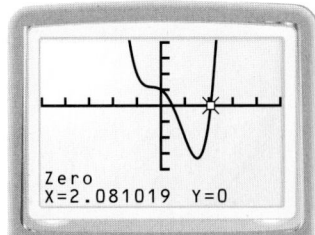
```
Zero
X=2.081019  Y=0
```

ANSWER ▶ From these screens, you can see that the real zeros are about 0.48 and 2.08. By the corollary to the fundamental theorem of algebra, this function also has two imaginary roots.

 *Approximate Real Zeros*

Use a graphing calculator to approximate the real zeros of the function.

8. $f(x) = x^4 - 4x^2 - x - 2$

9. $f(x) = -x^4 - 2x^3 + x^2 + 3$

Guided Practice

Vocabulary Check

1. An expression of the form $au^2 + bu + c$ where u is any expression in terms of x is said to be in what form?

2. Explain what it means for a function to have a *repeated solution*.

Skill Check **Find the greatest common factor of the terms in the polynomial.**

3. $x^5 + 6x^2$

4. $7x^6 - 49x^3$

5. $6x^4 + 18x^2 - 14x$

Factor the polynomial.

6. $x^4 - 100$

7. $4x^4 - 9$

8. $x^4 + 5x^2 - 6$

Solve the polynomial equation.

9. $x^4 - 144 = 0$

10. $x^4 - 7x^2 = 18$

11. $x^5 + 5x^3 + 4x = 0$

Practice and Applications

STUDENT HELP

HOMEWORK HELP
Example 1: Exs. 12–26
Example 2: Exs. 21–35
Example 3: Exs. 31–35
Example 4: Exs. 36–44
Example 5: Exs. 49–56

Monomial Factors **Find the greatest common factor of the terms in the polynomial.**

12. $x^4 - 21x^3$

13. $3x^5 + 16x^2$

14. $5x^4 - 15x^3$

15. $8x^4 - 20x^2 + 16x$

16. $9x^4 + 12x^3 + 6$

17. $7x^9 + 13x^3 + 21x^2$

18. $6x^8 - 3x^4 + 5x^3$

19. $4x^6 - 20x^5 + 14x^2$

20. $12x^7 - 48x^3 + 24x$

Matching **Match the polynomial with its factorization.**

21. $2x^6 - 32x^2$

A. $3(x^2 + 1)(x^2 + 3)$

22. $2x^6 + 16x^4 + 32x^2$

B. $x^3(x - 10)$

23. $x^4 - 10x^3$

C. $2x^2(x + 2)(x - 2)(x^2 + 4)$

24. $x^5 - 12x^3 + 27x$

D. $2x^2(x^2 + 4)^2$

25. $3x^4 + 6x^2 - 9$

E. $3(x - 1)(x + 1)(x^2 + 3)$

26. $3x^4 + 12x^2 + 9$

F. $x(x^2 - 3)(x + 3)(x - 3)$

Quadratic Form **Factor the polynomial.**

27. $x^4 - 49$

28. $\frac{1}{81}x^4 - 1$

29. $x^4 - 4x^2 + 3$

30. $x^4 - 27x$

31. $3x^5 - 48x$

32. $x^4 + 8x^2 + 12$

33. $2x^4 - 5x^2 + 3$

34. $\frac{1}{3}x^6 - \frac{1}{27}x^2$

35. $4x^5 + 12x^3 - 40x$

Solving Equations **Solve the polynomial equation.**

36. $x^4 - 8x^2 + 16 = 0$

37. $x^4 - 5x^2 = -6$

38. $x^4 - 4 = 0$

39. $4x^4 = 25$

40. $x^5 - 6x^3 + 8x = 0$

41. $x^4 + 3x^2 - 28 = 0$

42. $2x^6 + 60x^2 = -2x^4$

43. $6x^4 - 45x^3 = 24x^2$

44. $3x^4 - 5 = 2x^2$

Matching Match the equation with its graph.

45. $y = \frac{1}{2}(x^2 - 2)(x^2 - 5)$

46. $y = (x + 2)(x - 2)(x^2 + 1)$

47. $y = (x^2 + 2)(x^2 + 1)$

48. $y = (x + 2)^2(x^2 + 1)$

A.

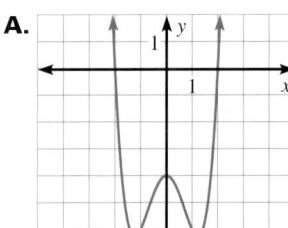

B.

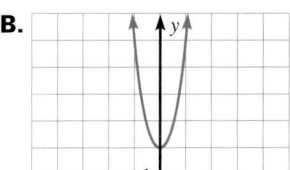

C.

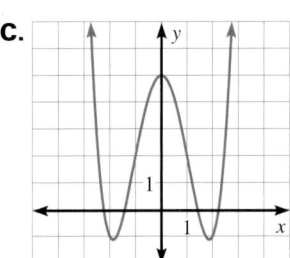

D.

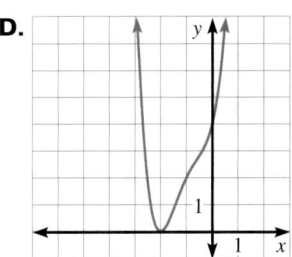

Finding Zeros Use a graphing calculator to graph the polynomial function. Then use the *Zero* (or *Root*) feature of the calculator to approximate the real zeros of the function to two decimal places.

49. $f(x) = x^4 - 3x^2 - 3$

50. $f(x) = x^4 - 5x^2 + 3$

51. $f(x) = x^4 - x^3 - 5x^2 + 2$

52. $f(x) = -x^4 + 3x^3 + x^2 - x - 5$

53. $f(x) = x^5 - 8x + 1$

54. $f(x) = x^5 - 9x^3 + 14x$

55. $f(x) = -x^5 + x^4 - 3x^3 + 3x^2 - x + 2$

56. $f(x) = x^6 - 7x^4 - 2x^3 + 14x$

57. **Temperature** The normal daily minimum temperature T (in degrees Fahrenheit) for each month ($0 \le x \le 11$) in Barrow, Alaska, can be modeled by the equation $T = 0.075x^4 - 2.18x^3 + 19.6x^2 - 53.9x + 18.7$. Approximate the zeros of the function to one decimal place. Explain what information about the temperatures in Barrow the zeros represent.

58. **Aviation** The number of active pilots (in thousands) with airline transport licenses in the United States for the years 1997 to 2004 can be modeled by the equation below where t is the number of years since 1997.

$$p = 0.0369t^4 - 0.530t^3 + 1.94t^2 + 1.65t + 131$$

a. Write a function in standard form for the year there were 140 active pilots with airline transport licenses. ($p = 140$)

b. Use a graphing calculator to determine during what year there were 140,000 active pilots with transport licenses.

59. **Visual Thinking** The graph of $y = \frac{1}{4}(x^4 + x^3 - 5x^2 + x - 6)$ is shown at the right. How many real zeros does the function have? How many imaginary zeros does the function have? Explain your reasoning.

60. ▣ **Challenge** Graph each polynomial function on a graphing calculator. Then make a conjecture about polynomial functions with repeated real solutions and their corresponding graphs.

a. $f(x) = (x - 3)^2(x - 1)$ **b.** $f(x) = (x - 3)^3(x - 1)$

c. $f(x) = (x - 3)^4(x - 1)$ **d.** $f(x) = (x - 3)^5(x - 1)$

e. $f(x) = (x - 3)^6(x - 1)$ **f.** $f(x) = (x - 3)^7(x - 1)$

Standardized Test Practice

61. Multiple Choice What is the greatest common factor of the terms of $16x^8 + 36x^4 + 24x^3$?

Ⓐ $8x^3$ Ⓑ $4x^3$ Ⓒ $8x$ Ⓓ $4x$

62. Multiple Choice What is the factorization of $2x^5 - 28x^3 - 64x$?

Ⓕ $x(x + 4)(x - 4)(x^2 + 2)$ Ⓖ $2x(x + 4)(x - 4)(x^2 - 2)$

Ⓗ $x(x^2 - 2)(x^2 + 16)$ Ⓙ $2x(x + 4)(x - 4)(x^2 + 2)$

63. Multiple Choice What are the solutions of $x^4 = 625$?

Ⓐ $-5, 5, -\sqrt{5}, \sqrt{5}$ Ⓑ $-5, 5, -i\sqrt{5}, i\sqrt{5}$

Ⓒ $-5, 5, -5i, 5i$ Ⓓ $-5i, 5i, -i\sqrt{5}, i\sqrt{5}$

64. ▦ **Multiple Choice** Use a calculator to approximate the real zeros of $f(x) = x^4 - x^3 - 3x + 2$.

Ⓕ $0.64, 1.65$ Ⓖ $0.63, 1.65$ Ⓗ $0.64, 1.66$ Ⓙ $0.64, 1.24$

Mixed Review

Classifying Polynomials Identify the degree and leading coefficient of the polynomial function. *(Lesson 6.2)*

65. $f(x) = x$ **66.** $f(x) = -x^3$

67. $f(x) = x^3 - 4x^2 - 3$ **68.** $f(x) = 3x^4 + 8x^2 + 9$

69. $f(x) = -8x^8 - 12x + 1$ **70.** $f(x) = 5 - 4x^2 + x$

Graphing Polynomials Graph the function using the domain $x = -3, -2, -1, 0, 1, 2, 3$. *(Lesson 6.2)*

71. $f(x) = x^3$ **72.** $f(x) = -x^2 + 3$

73. $f(x) = x^4 - 6x + 1$ **74.** $f(x) = x^4 - 2$

Multiplying Polynomials Find the product. *(Lesson 6.4)*

75. $(2x - 3)(5x + 2)$ **76.** $(x - 3)(x^2 + x + 2)$

77. $(x - 2)(x + 2)(x + 4)$ **78.** $(3x + 5)(x + 1)(x + 2)$

Geometry Skills

Volume of Solids Write an equation for the volume of the figure. Then solve the equation.

79. $V = 16 \text{ cm}^3$ **80.** $V = 27 \text{ in.}^3$

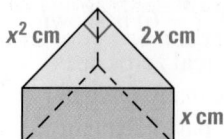

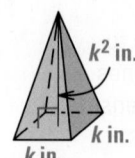

6.7 Modeling with Polynomial Functions

GOAL Use polynomial functions to model finding a maximum or minimum value in real-life situations.

Key Words
- local maximum
- local minimum

Prerequisite Skills

Graph each function.

1. $f(x) = x^3 + 3x^2$

2. $f(x) = x^4 - x^3 - x^2 + 1$

How can you design a box with the greatest volume possible?

In Example 3, you will use a polynomial model to find the maximum volume of a box made from a rectangular sheet of cardboard.

Graphs of polynomial functions have *turning points*.

- The *y*-coordinate of a turning point is a **local maximum** of the function if the point is higher than all nearby points.

- The *y*-coordinate of a turning point is a **local minimum** of the function if the point is lower than all nearby points.

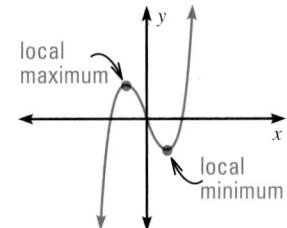

Turning Points of Polynomial Functions

- The graph of every polynomial function of degree *n* has at most *n* − 1 turning points.

- If a polynomial function of degree *n* has *n* distinct real zeros, then its graph has exactly *n* − 1 turning points.

EXAMPLE 1 Find the Number of Turning Points

Find the number of turning points for the function $f(x) = x(x + 4)(x - 2)$.

Solution

Rewrite the function $f(x) = x(x + 4)(x - 2)$ as $f(x) = x^3 + 2x^2 - 8x$.

The function has degree 3, so it can have at most $3 - 1 = 2$ turning points.

The factored form of the function shows that it has three distinct real zeros.

So, the function has exactly $3 - 1 = 2$ turning points.

Checkpoint ✓ Find the Number of Turning Points

Find the exact or maximum number of turning points for the function. Label each number as *exact* or *maximum*.

1. $f(x) = x(x - 1)(x + 3)$

2. $g(x) = x^2(x + 2)(x + 5)$

3. $f(x) = (x^2 - 7)(x + 9)$

4. $g(x) = (x - 6)^2(x + 8)$

EXAMPLE 2 Find Turning Points

 Graph each function. Identify the *x*-intercepts and the coordinates where the local maximums and local minimums occur.

a. $f(x) = x^3 - 2x^2 + 4$ **b.** $f(x) = x^4 - 3x^3 - x^2 + 6x - 4$

Solution

a. Use a graphing calculator to graph the function. Notice that the graph has one *x*-intercept and two turning points. Use the graphing calculator's *Zero*, *Maximum*, and *Minimum* features to approximate the *x*-intercept and the coordinates of the local maximum and local minimum.

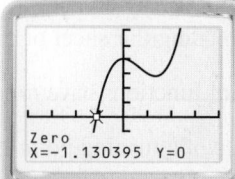 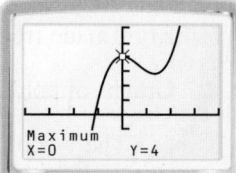 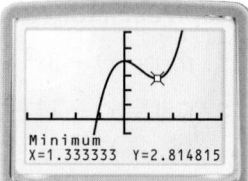

ANSWER ▶ The *x*-intercept is $x \approx -1.13$. The function has a local maximum at $(0, 4)$ and a local minimum at about $(1.33, 2.81)$.

b. Use a graphing calculator to graph the function. Notice that the graph has two *x*-intercepts and three turning points. Use the graphing calculator's *Zero*, *Maximum*, and *Minimum* features to approximate the *x*-intercepts and the coordinates of the local maximum and local minimums.

x-intercepts

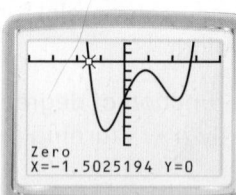 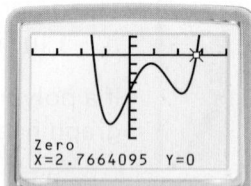

turning points

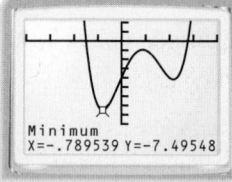 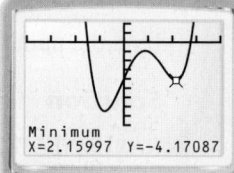 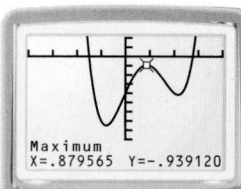

ANSWER ▶ The *x*-intercepts are $x \approx -1.50$ and $x \approx 2.77$. The function has local minimums at about $(-0.79, -7.5)$ and $(2.16, -4.17)$, and a local maximum at about $(0.88, -0.94)$.

Checkpoint ✓ **Find Turning Points**

Graph the function. Identify the *x*-intercepts and the coordinates where the local maximums and local minimums occur.

5. $f(x) = 2x^3 - 4x^2 - 1$ **6.** $f(x) = x^4 + 3x^2 - 4$

7. $f(x) = x^4 - 2x^3 - x^2 + x - 2$ **8.** $f(x) = x^3 + 2x^2 - 3x + 3$

Polynomial Models In a real-world model, a local maximum on the graph often indicates a value that maximizes the quantity being modeled.

EXAMPLE 3 Maximize a Polynomial Model

Manufacturing You are designing an open box. It will be made from a piece of cardboard that is 16 inches by 20 inches. You want it to have the greatest possible volume. You will form the box by cutting and folding the four square corners. Then you will fold up the sides.

How long should you make the cuts? What are the dimensions of the finished box?

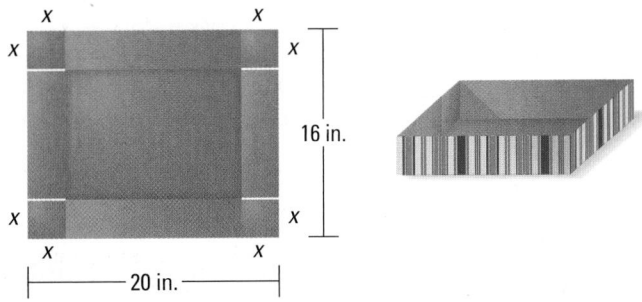

Solution

VERBAL MODEL	Volume	=	Length	·	Width	·	Height

LABELS

Volume = V (cubic inches)

Length = $20 - 2x$ (inches)

Width = $16 - 2x$ (inches)

Height = x (inches)

ALGEBRAIC MODEL

$$V = (20 - 2x)(16 - 2x)x$$
$$= (4x^2 - 72x + 320)x$$
$$= 4x^3 - 72x^2 + 320x$$

To find the maximum volume, graph the volume function on a graphing calculator as shown.

Next use the *Maximum* feature. Look at only the interval $0 < x < 8$, because 8 inches is the longest possible length for a corner square.

From the graph, you can see that the maximum volume is about 420 cubic inches. It occurs when $x \approx 2.94$

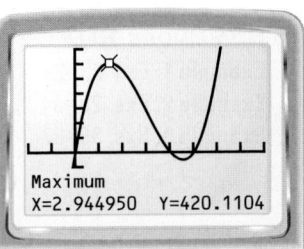

Maximum
X=2.944950   Y=420.1104

ANSWER ▶ You should make the cuts approximately 3 inches long. The dimensions of the finished box will be $x = 3$ inches by $16 - 2x = 16 - 2(3) = 10$ inches by $20 - 2x = 20 - 2(3) = 14$ inches.

Checkpoint ✓ *Maximize a Polynomial Model*

9. In Example 3, suppose you use a piece of cardboard that is 12 inches by 16 inches. What are the dimensions of the box with the greatest volume?

Guided Practice

Vocabulary Check 1. Explain the difference between the terms *local minimum* and *local maximum*.

Skill Check **Tell whether you can find the exact number of turning points. Explain.**

2. $f(x) = (x - 3)^2(x + 4)$

3. $f(x) = (x - 7)(x^2 + 3x + 2)$

4. $f(x) = (x + 2)(x + 5)(x - 4)$

5. $f(x) = x^2(x + 6)(x - 8)$

Find the exact or maximum number of turning points for the function. Label the number as *exact* or *maximum*.

6. $f(x) = (x - 1)(x - 5)(x + 7)$

7. $f(x) = x^2(x^2 - x - 3)$

8. $f(x) = x^2(x + 2)$

9. $f(x) = x(x + 3)(x^2 + 4)$

Graph the function. Identify the local minimums and local maximums.

10. $f(x) = x^3 - 3x^2 + 3$

11. $f(x) = -x^3 + 4x^2 - 3$

12. $f(x) = -x^4 + 8x^2 + 1$

13. $f(x) = x^4 - x^3 - 3x^2 + x - 1$

14. **Profit** The profit P (in thousands of dollars) that a small company made each year from 2000 to 2005 can be modeled by

$$P = -t^4 + 13t^3 - 51t^2 + 63t + 10$$

where t is the number of years since 2000. Use a graphing calculator to find the year with the least profit in the interval $0 \le t \le 5$. What is this profit?

Practice and Applications

STUDENT HELP

HOMEWORK HELP
Example 1: Exs. 23–25
Example 2: Exs. 23–34
Example 3: Exs. 35–37

Turning Points Find the exact or maximum number of turning points for the function. Label the number as *exact* or *maximum*.

15. $f(x) = x(x - 4)(x - 1)$

16. $f(x) = x(x + 9)(x^2 - 2)$

17. $f(x) = x^2(x + 1)(x - 8)$

18. $f(x) = x^2(x^2 - 3)$

19. $f(x) = (x^2 - 5)(x^2 - x - 1)$

20. $f(x) = 2(x^2 - 3)(x^2 + x + 2)$

21. $f(x) = -(x^2 + x + 1)(x - 3)^2$

22. $f(x) = x(x^4 - 16)$

Matching Use what you know about turning points and end behavior to match the equation with its graph.

23. $y = -x^2(x - 3)$

24. $y = x(x^2 - 3)(x + 1)$

25. $y = x(x^2 - 2)$

A.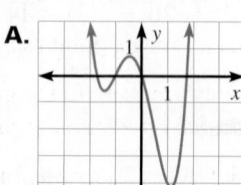

B.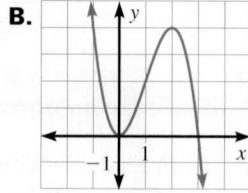

C.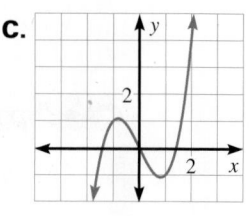

Analyzing Graphs Estimate the coordinates of each turning point. State whether each is a local maximum or a local minimum. Then list all the real zeros and find the least degree that the function can have.

26.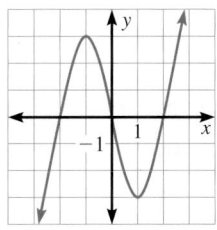

27.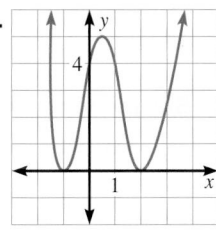

28.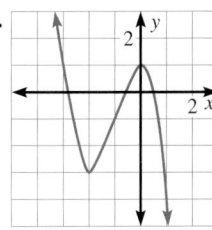

Using Graphs Use a graphing calculator to graph the polynomial function. Identify the x-intercepts and the coordinates where the local maximums and local minimums occur.

29. $f(x) = x^3 - 3x + 2$

30. $f(x) = 2x^3 - 6x - 1$

31. $f(x) = x^4 - 2x^2 + 1$

32. $f(x) = x^4 - 3x^3 - x^2 + 3x$

33. $f(x) = -x^5 + 5x^3 - 4x$

34. $f(x) = 3x^5 - 5x^3$

35. Precipitation The average number of days y per month x with precipitation of 0.01 inch or more in Cincinnati, Ohio, can be modeled by

$$y = 0.053x^3 - 1.03x^2 + 5.46x + 4.$$

The variable $x = 2$ corresponds to February. Use the interval $2 \le x \le 12$. Graph the function and interpret the turning points in the context of the problem.

36. Manufacturing You are designing an open box to be made of cardboard that is 10 inches by 10 inches. The box will be made like the one in Example 3. The volume of the box can be modeled by the following function.

$$V = 4x^3 - 40x^2 + 100x.$$

Use a graphing calculator to graph the function. Find the height that maximizes the volume of the box. What is the maximum volume?

37. Consumer Prices The annual percent change p from the previous year in consumer prices for the United States from 1997 to 2001 can be modeled by

$$p = -0.26x^3 + 1.61x^2 - 2.17x + 2.32.$$

The variable x is the number of years since 1997. Graph the function and identify any turning points on the interval $0 \le x \le 4$.

Standardized Test Practice

38. Multi-Step Problem A portion of the path that a hummingbird flew while feeding can be modeled by the equation below.

$$y = -\frac{1}{5}x(x - 4)^2(x - 7) \qquad 0 \le x \le 7$$

The variable x is the horizontal distance (in meters) and y is the height (in meters). The hummingbird feeds each time it is at ground level.

a. Writing Explain what a turning point represents in this problem.

b. How many turning points are there in the graph of the function? What is the maximum height reached by the hummingbird?

c. How many times did it feed as it crossed 7 meters of ground?

Writing Equations Write an equation of the line that has the given slope *m* and *y*-intercept *b*. (Lesson 2.5)

39. $m = 3, b = 2$ **40.** $m = -4, b = 6$ **41.** $m = 8, b = 1$

42. $m = \frac{3}{4}, b = -3$ **43.** $m = \frac{5}{2}, b = 4$ **44.** $m = -\frac{2}{3}, b = 7$

Simplifying Radical Expressions Simplify the expression. (Lesson 5.6)

45. $\sqrt{63}$ **46.** $\sqrt{32}$ **47.** $\sqrt{7} \cdot \sqrt{7}$

48. $\sqrt{3} \cdot \sqrt{12}$ **49.** $\sqrt{\frac{1}{4}}$ **50.** $\sqrt{\frac{49}{81}}$

Solving Quadratic Equations Solve the equation. (Lesson 5.6)

51. $3x^2 = 120$ **52.** $2x^2 = 48$ **53.** $4x^2 - 25 = 47$

54. $3(x - 5)^2 = 108$ **55.** $-(x + 1)^2 = -27$ **56.** $2(x - 4)^2 = 24$

Geometry Skills

Volume Write an expression for the volume of the solid.

57.
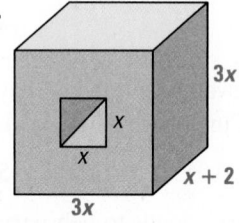

58.
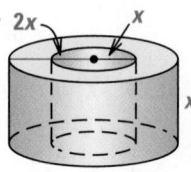

Quiz 3

Lesson 6.5

Factor the polynomial.

1. $x^3 + 8$ **2.** $27x^3 - 64$ **3.** $343x^3 + 1$

4. $x^3 + 8y^3$ **5.** $x^3 - 3x^2 - 9x + 27$ **6.** $x^3 + 5x^2 - 4x - 20$

Lesson 6.5

Solve the equation by factoring.

7. $x^3 + 4x^2 - 9x - 36 = 0$ **8.** $x^3 - 6x^2 + 30 = 5x$ **9.** $4x^3 + 20x^2 = x + 5$

Lesson 6.6

Factor the polynomial.

10. $8x^5 + x^2$ **11.** $3x^4 - 24x$ **12.** $x^4 - 81$

13. $x^4 - 6x^2 + 8$ **14.** $3x^5 + 9x^3 - 12x$ **15.** $x^6 - 2x^4 - 15x^2$

Lesson 6.6

Use a graphing calculator to approximate to two decimal places the real zeros of the function.

16. $f(x) = x^4 - 2x^3 + x - 3$ **17.** $f(x) = 2x^5 - 3x^3 - 4x$

Lesson 6.7

Find the number of turning points for the function.

18. $f(x) = (x + 6)(x - 4)(x - 3)$ **19.** $f(x) = (x + 4)(x^2 - 5x + 3)$

20. $f(x) = x^2(x^2 - 12)$ **21.** $f(x) = x(x - 5)^2(x^2 - 2x + 3)$

22. Plant Growth The growth y of a plant from the previous year (in inches) can be modeled by $y = x^3 - 12x^2 + 36x + 25$, for $1 \le x \le 7$. Graph the function and identify the turning points. In which year did the plant grow the most? In which year did it grow the least?

VOCABULARY

- scientific notation, *p. 298*
- polynomial, *p. 302*
- standard form of a polynomial function, *p. 302*
- leading coefficient, *p. 302*

- degree of a polynomial, *p. 302*
- constant term, *p. 302*
- end behavior, *p. 303*
- polynomial long division, *p. 317*

- factor by grouping, *p. 324*
- quadratic form, *p. 329*
- repeated solution, *p. 331*
- local maximum, *p. 335*
- local minimum, *p. 335*

VOCABULARY EXERCISES

1. Tell why 45.37×10^3 is not written in scientific notation. Then write the expression in scientific notation.

2. When does a repeated solution occur?

3. Explain how the end behavior of a polynomial function depends on the function's degree and leading coefficient.

4. A cubic function $P(t)$ gives the price of a product for several years t. The function has a local maximum and a local minimum. Explain the meaning of the turning points in the given context.

6.1 PROPERTIES OF EXPONENTS

Examples on
pp. 296–298

EXAMPLE You can use properties of exponents to evaluate numerical expressions and to simplify algebraic expressions.

$$\left(\frac{2y^2}{x^{-5}}\right)^2 = \frac{2^2(y^2)^2}{(x^{-5})^2} \quad \text{Power of a quotient property, power of a product property}$$

$$= \frac{2^2 y^{2 \cdot 2}}{x^{-5 \cdot 2}} \quad \text{Power of a power property}$$

$$= \frac{4y^4}{x^{-10}} \quad \text{Simplify exponents.}$$

$$= 4x^{10}y^4 \quad \text{Negative exponent property}$$

REVIEW HELP

Exercises	Examples
5, 6	**1**, p. 296
7, 8	**2**, p. 297
9–12	**3**, p. 297

Simplify the expression. Tell which properties of exponents you used.

5. $(-2)^9(-2)^{-4}$ **6.** $8^3 \cdot 8^{-5} \cdot 8^{-7}$ **7.** $\left(\frac{4^5}{4^2}\right)^3$ **8.** $\left(\frac{3}{5}\right)^3$

9. $(8y^{-4})^2 y^8$ **10.** $\left(\frac{2u^4}{y^{-3}}\right)^3$ **11.** $(4x^2)^3 x^5$ **12.** $\frac{x^6 y^3}{x^{-2} y^4}$

EXAMPLE You can make a table of values and plot points to graph a polynomial function.

The function $f(x) = 1 + x^3 + 3x^2$ is a polynomial function. Its standard form is $f(x) = x^3 + 3x^2 + 1$. The degree is 3, so it is a cubic function. The leading coefficient is 1.

Make a table of values to graph $f(x) = x^3 + 3x^2 + 1$.

x	−3	−2	−1	0	1
f(x)	1	5	3	1	5

Plot the corresponding points. Then connect the points with a smooth curve.

The degree is odd and the leading coefficient is positive, so $f(x)$ approaches $-\infty$ as x approaches $-\infty$ and $f(x)$ approaches $+\infty$ as x approaches $+\infty$.

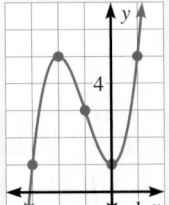

REVIEW HELP

Exercises	Examples
13, 14	**1**, p. 302
15–17	**2**, p. 304

Tell whether the function is a polynomial function. If it is, write the function in standard form. Then state its degree, type, and leading coefficient.

13. $f(x) = 3x^3 - x^4 - 4 + \sqrt{x}$ **14.** $f(x) = \frac{1}{2}x^3 - 2x^2 - 1.1$

Graph the function using the domain $x = -3, -2, -1, 0, 1, 2, 3$.

15. $f(x) = -2x^3 + 6x + 4$ **16.** $f(x) = -x^4 + 5x + 4$ **17.** $f(x) = x^4 - 3x^2 - 1$

EXAMPLES You can add and subtract polynomial expressions. You can also use the distributive property to simplify expressions.

ADDITION

$$\begin{array}{r} 5x^3 - 2x^2 + x + 3 \\ +\quad 3x^2 - x - 2 \\ \hline 5x^3 + \quad x^2 \quad + 1 \end{array}$$

SUBTRACTION

$$2x^3 - x^2 + 3x - 2$$
$$-(3x^3 - 3x^2 + x)$$

$$\Longrightarrow \quad \begin{array}{r} 2x^3 - x^2 + 3x - 2 \\ + -3x^3 + 3x^2 - x \\ \hline -x^3 + 2x^2 + 2x - 2 \end{array}$$

DISTRIBUTIVE PROPERTY

$$3(x^4 - x^2 + 3x) + x(x^3 + x - 2) = 3x^4 - 3x^2 + 9x + x^4 + x^2 - 2x$$
$$= (3x^4 + x^4) + (-3x^2 + x^2) + (9x - 2x)$$
$$= 4x^4 - 2x^2 + 7x$$

REVIEW HELP

Exercises	Examples
18	**1**, p. 310
19	**2**, p. 310
20, 21	**3**, p. 311

Find the sum or difference. Write the answer in standard form.

18. $(4x^4 - 5x^2 + 1) + (-3x^4 + 2x^2 - 2)$ **19.** $(2x^4 - 3x^3 + x - 4) - (x^4 + x^2 - 3x + 1)$

Simplify the expression.

20. $3(x^3 - x - 1) - 2(-2x^2 + x - 3)$ **21.** $2(x^3 + 3x^2 - x) + x(-3x^2 - 5x + 9)$

6.4 MULTIPLYING AND DIVIDING POLYNOMIALS

Examples on pp. 315–317

EXAMPLES You can multiply and divide polynomials.

Find $(x - 1)(x + 2)(x - 4)$.

$(x - 1)(x + 2)(x - 4)$

$= (x^2 + x - 2)(x - 4)$

$= x^2(x - 4) + x(x - 4) - 2(x - 4)$

$= x^3 - 4x^2 + x^2 - 4x - 2x + 8$

$= x^3 + (-4x^2 + x^2) + (-4x - 2x) + 8$

$= x^3 - 3x^2 - 6x + 8$

Find $(x^3 + 3x^2 - 4x - 13) \div (x - 2)$.

$$
\begin{array}{r}
x^2 + 5x + 6 \\
x - 2 \overline{)x^3 + 3x^2 - 4x - 13} \\
\underline{x^3 - 2x^2} \\
5x^2 - 4x \\
\underline{5x^2 - 10x} \\
6x - 13 \\
\underline{6x - 12} \\
-1
\end{array}
$$

The quotient is $x^2 + 5x + 6 - \dfrac{1}{x - 2}$.

REVIEW HELP

Exercises	Examples
22–24	**1–2**, p. 315
25–27	**3**, p. 316
28–30	**5**, p. 317

Find the product.

22. $(x + 3)(2x^3 - x + 1)$ **23.** $(x^2 + 2)(x^2 + 3x - 5)$ **24.** $(x + 2)(x - 3)(x + 5)$

25. $(4x - 3)(4x + 3)$ **26.** $(5x - 1)^2$ **27.** $(2x + 3)^3$

Use polynomial long division to find the quotient.

28. $(x^2 - 5x + 6) \div (x - 3)$ **29.** $(x^3 + 5x^2 - 5) \div (x + 2)$ **30.** $(x^3 - 8) \div (x - 2)$

6.5 FACTORING CUBIC POLYNOMIALS

Examples on pp. 323–325

EXAMPLES You can factor cubic polynomials and you can use actoring to solve some cubic polynomial equations.

Factor $64x^3 + 27$.

$64x^3 + 27 = (4x)^3 + 3^3$

$\quad = (4x + 3)(16x^2 - 12x + 9)$

Factor $x^3 + 6x^2 - 16x$.

$x^3 + 6x^2 - 16x = x(x^2 + 6x - 16)$

$\quad = x(x + 8)(x - 2)$

Solve $2x^3 - 5x^2 - 6x = -15$.

$2x^3 - 5x^2 - 6x + 15 = 0$

$(2x^3 - 5x^2) + (-6x + 15) = 0$

$x^2(2x - 5) + (-3)(2x - 5) = 0$

$(x^2 - 3)(2x - 5) = 0$

$x^2 - 3 = 0 \quad \text{or} \quad 2x - 5 = 0$

$x = \sqrt{3}, x = -\sqrt{3}, x = \dfrac{5}{2}$

The solutions are $\sqrt{3}$, $-\sqrt{3}$, and $\dfrac{5}{2}$.

REVIEW HELP

Exercises	Examples
31, 32	**1**, p. 323
33, 34	**2**, p. 324
35, 36	**4**, p. 324
37–39	**5–6**, p. 325

Factor the polynomial.

31. $x^3 - 125$ **32.** $64x^3 + 1$ **33.** $x^3 - 3x^2 - 10x$

34. $2x^3 - 2x^2 - 40x$ **37.** $x^3 - 4x^2 - 7x + 28$ **36.** $x^3 - 2x^2 + 11x - 22$

Solve the equation by factoring.

37. $x^3 + 7x^2 + 6x = 0$ **38.** $x^2(x + 5) = x + 5$ **39.** $x^3 + 11x^2 - 4x = 44$

EXAMPLES You can factor polynomials of greater degree and you can use factoring to solve some polynomial equations of greater degree.

Factor $x^4 - 81$.

$x^4 - 81 = (x^2)^2 - 9^2$

$= (x^2 + 9)(x^2 - 9)$

$= (x^2 + 9)(x - 3)(x + 3)$

Factor $3x^6 + 9x^4 + 6x^2$.

$3x^6 + 9x^4 + 6x^2 = 3x^2(x^4 + 3x^2 + 2)$

$= 3x^2(x^2 + 2)(x^2 + 1)$

Solve $12x^3 = x^5 + 27x$.

$12x^3 = x^5 + 27x$

$0 = x^5 - 12x^3 + 27x$

$0 = x(x^4 - 12x^2 + 27)$

$0 = x(x^2 - 3)(x^2 - 9)$

$0 = x(x^2 - 3)(x - 3)(x + 3)$

$x = 0, x = \sqrt{3}, x = -\sqrt{3}, x = 3, x = -3$

The solutions are 0, $\sqrt{3}$, $-\sqrt{3}$, 3, and -3.

REVIEW HELP

Exercises	Examples
40	**1**, p. 329
41, 42	**2**, p. 329
43–45	**3**, p. 330
46–48	**4**, p. 330

Factor the polynomial.

40. $5x^5 - 40x^2$ **41.** $16x^4 - 1$ **42.** $81x^4 - 16$

43. $2x^5 - 16x^3 + 30x$ **44.** $5x^6 - 30x^4 + 25x^2$ **45.** $x^5 - 17x^3 + 16x$

Solve the equation by factoring.

46. $2x^5 - 18x^3 = -28x$ **47.** $x^4 - 4x^3 - 6x^2 = 0$ **48.** $3x^6 - 12x^2 = 0$

EXAMPLE Use a graphing calculator to graph $f(x) = x^3 - 3x + 4$.

Notice that the graph has one x-intercept and two turning points. You can use the graphing calculator's *Zero*, *Maximum*, and *Minimum* features to approximate the x-intercept and the coordinates of the turning points.

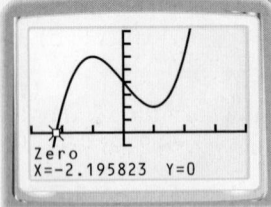 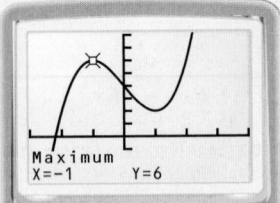 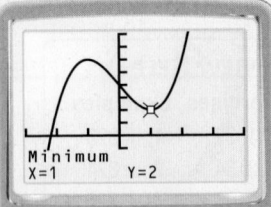

REVIEW HELP

Exercises	Example
49–54	**2**, p. 336

The x-intercept is about -2.20. The function has a local maximum at $(-1, 6)$ and a local minimum at $(1, 2)$.

Graph the function. Identify the x-intercepts and the coordinates where the local maximums and local minimums occur.

49. $f(x) = x^3 - 2x^2 - 4x$ **50.** $f(x) = -x^3 + 5x - 9$ **51.** $f(x) = -2x^4 + 3x^3 + 4x^2 - 5$

52. $f(x) = x^4 - 4x^2 - 2$ **53.** $f(x) = x^5 - 6x^4 + 8x^2$ **54.** $f(x) = -x^5 + 6x^3 - 5x$

Simplify the expression. Tell which properties of exponents you used.

1. $x^3 \cdot x^7$

2. $(2y^2)^{-3}$

3. $(x^5 y^{-3})^{-2}$

4. $\dfrac{z^4}{z^{-3}}$

5. $\left(\dfrac{a^3}{b^2}\right)^4$

6. $(4b^{-5})^2 b^{10}$

Graph the function using the domain $x = -3, -2, -1, 0, 1, 2, 3$.

7. $f(x) = 2x^3 - 6x + 1$

8. $f(x) = -2x^4 + 5x^2 + 3$

9. $f(x) = -x^4 + 3x^3 - 5$

Find the sum or difference. Write the answer in standard form.

10. $(4x^3 - 3x^2 + x - 4) + (7x^2 - x + 1)$

11. $(x^4 + 6x^3 - x - 8) - (4x^4 + 5x^3 - 2x - 7)$

Find the product.

12. $(x + 3)(x^2 + 3x - 7)$

13. $(x + 2)(x - 3)(x - 6)$

14. $(4x - 5)(4x + 5)$

15. $(5x - 3)^3$

Use long division to find the quotient.

16. $(x^3 - 2x^2 - 13x - 10) \div (x - 5)$

17. $(2x^3 + 3x^2 - 3x - 2) \div (2x + 1)$

Factor the polynomial.

18. $27x^3 - 1$

19. $2x^3 - 18x^2 - 72x$

20. $24x^5 - 3x^2$

21. $81x^4 - 1$

22. $4x^3 - 32x^2 - 80x$

23. $36x^2 - 25$

Solve the equation by factoring.

24. $x^3 + 3x^2 = 13x + 39$

25. $x^5 - 8x^3 = -7x$

26. $2x^3 - 4x^2 - 6x = 0$

Graph the function. Identify the x-intercepts and the coordinates where the local maximums and local minimums occur.

27. $f(x) = -x^3 + 2x^2 + 2x + 1$

28. $f(x) = x^3 - 6x + 4$

29. $f(x) = -2x^4 - 7x^3 - x^2 + 10x$

30. $f(x) = x^4 - x^3 - 3x^2 + x - 5$

31. Ant Strength An ant of mass 3.0×10^{-6} kilogram can lift a leaf of mass 1.5×10^{-4} kilogram. How many times its own mass can the ant lift?

32. Aquarium An aquarium has a length of $(x + 6)$ feet, a width of $(x - 1)$ feet, and a height of $(x - 2)$ feet. The volume of the aquarium is 60 cubic feet. Write and solve an equation to find the dimensions of the aquarium.

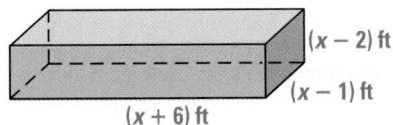

$(x - 2)$ ft
$(x - 1)$ ft
$(x + 6)$ ft

33. Basketball The number of points p your school's basketball team has scored in the last seven games can be modeled by $p = x^3 - 12x^2 + 36x + 48$ where x is the game number from 1 to 7. Use a graphing calculator to graph the function. Identify the local minimum and local maximum on the interval $1 \le x \le 7$ and explain the meaning of each in the context of the problem.

Chapter Standardized Test

EXAMPLE Which of the following is a true statement?

Ⓐ $a^3 + b^3 = (a + b)^3$

Ⓑ $(a - b)^2 = a^2 - b^2$

Ⓒ $\sqrt{a^2 + b^2} = a + b$

Ⓓ $\frac{1}{2}(a - b) = \frac{1}{2}a - \frac{1}{2}b$

Solution

Choice A does not follow the sum of two cubes pattern and Choice B does not follow the square of a binomial pattern. So, choices A and B are false.

$\sqrt{a^2 + b^2} \neq \sqrt{a^2} + \sqrt{b^2} = a + b$, so choice C is false.

Choice D is a true statement of the distributive property.

Multiple Choice

1. What is the simplified form of $(3x^3y^{-4})^{-2}$?

Ⓐ $\dfrac{y^8}{6x^{-6}}$

Ⓑ $\dfrac{9y^8}{x^6}$

Ⓒ $\dfrac{y^8}{9x^6}$

Ⓓ $\dfrac{y^8}{9x^{-6}}$

2. Which cubic function has a leading coefficient of 1?

Ⓕ $f(x) = x^3 + x^2 - x + 1$

Ⓖ $f(x) = x^4 - x^3 + x^2 + 1$

Ⓗ $f(x) = 1 + x^2 - x^3 - x$

Ⓙ $f(x) = x^3 - x^4 + x - 1$

3. Which statement about the end behavior of $f(x) = -x^3 + x - 2$ is true?

Ⓐ $f(x)$ approaches $+\infty$ as x approaches $+\infty$.

Ⓑ $f(x)$ approaches $-\infty$ as x approaches $-\infty$.

Ⓒ $f(x)$ approaches $-\infty$ as x approaches $+\infty$.

Ⓓ $f(x)$ approaches $+\infty$ as x approaches 0.

4. What is the difference $(x^4 - 3x^2 + 4x + 7) - (x^4 - 6x^3 + 4x)$?

Ⓕ $3x^3 + 7$

Ⓖ $6x^3 - 3x^2 + 7$

Ⓗ $6x^3 - 3x^2 + 8x + 7$

Ⓙ $3x^3 + 8x + 7$

5. What is the product $(x + 5)(x^3 - 2x - 3)$?

Ⓐ $x^4 + 5x^3 - 2x^2 - 7x - 15$

Ⓑ $x^4 + 5x^3 - 2x^2 - 13x - 15$

Ⓒ $x^4 + 5x^3 - 2x^2 - 10x - 15$

Ⓓ $x^4 + 5x^3 - 2x^2 - 3x - 15$

6. What is the quotient of $(x^3 - 3x^2 + 4x - 6)$ and $(x - 2)$?

Ⓕ $x^2 - x + 2$

Ⓖ $x^2 - x + 3$

Ⓗ $x^2 - x + 2 + \dfrac{2}{x - 2}$

Ⓙ $x^2 - x + 2 - \dfrac{2}{x - 2}$

7. Which polynomial has the factorization $(x - 10)(x^2 + 10x + 100)$?

(A) $x^3 - 1000$ **(B)** $x^3 - 100$

(C) $x^3 + 100$ **(D)** $x^3 + 1000$

8. What are the solutions of $x^5 - 5x^3 = 36x$?

(F) $3, -3$ **(G)** $0, 3, -3, 2i, -2i$

(H) $0, 3, -3$ **(J)** $3, -3, 2i, -2i$

9. What are the solutions of $2x^3 + 4x^2 - 20x = 10x + 60$?

(A) $\sqrt{15}, -\sqrt{15}$ **(B)** $2, \sqrt{15}, -\sqrt{15}$

(C) $-2, \sqrt{15}, -\sqrt{15}$ **(D)** $2, \sqrt{15}$

10. How many turning points does the graph of $f(x) = x(x + 11)(x^2 - 8)$ have?

(F) 2   **(G)** 3   **(H)** 4   **(J)** 5

Gridded Response

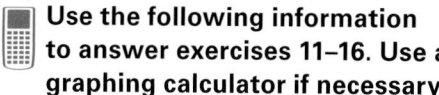 **Use the following information to answer exercises 11–16. Use a graphing calculator if necessary.**

The population p (in hundreds of people) of a town can be modeled by $p = 1.5x^3 - 9x^2 + 13.5x + 52$. The variable x is the number of years since 1998.

11. What is the leading coefficient of the model?

12. What is the degree of the model?

13. Graph the model for $0 \le x \le 6$. How many turning points does it have on this interval?

14. What is the local maximum on $0 \le x \le 3$?

15. What is the local mimimum on $0 \le x \le 4$?

16. What was the population of the town (in hundreds) in 2000?

17. The side length of a cube is 3 times greater than the side length of a smaller cube. How many times greater is the volume of the larger cube than the volume of the smaller cube?

18. How many distinct solutions are there to $x^3(x - 1)(x + 2) = 0$?

19. Approximate to two decimal places the real zero of $f(x) = -x^3 + 2x^2 + x + 5$.

Extended Response

20.  A window box has dimensions $(x + 14)$ inches, $(x - 2)$ inches, and $(x - 6)$ inches.

a. Write a function in standard form for the volume of the window box.

b. Use a graphing calculator to graph the function for $-20 \le x \le 10$.

c. Identify the local maximum and local minimum. Do these values represent possible maximum and minimum volumes of the window box? Explain your reasoning.

d. The volume of the window box is 768 cubic feet. Write and factor an equation in terms of x to find the dimensions of the window box.

e. How does the volume of the window box change if you double the width and height?

Simplify the expression. *(Lesson 1.3)*

1. $-3(-x)^2$ **2.** $3x + 5y + 2x - 3y$ **3.** $-4x + 3(x + 1)$

Solve the equation. *(Lessons 1.4, 4.4)*

4. $2x - 12 = 6$ **5.** $\frac{1}{2}x + 3 = 8$ **6.** $|x - 3| = 4$

7. **Average Temperature** The table gives the average temperature t in degrees Fahrenheit at the Bering Land Bridge National Preserve in Alaska for each month m from June through December. Find the mean, median, mode, and range of the temperatures to one decimal place. *(Lesson 1.7)*

m	6	7	8	9	10	11	12
t	51	51	50	42	22	10	4

Graph the linear equation. *(Lessons 2.1, 2.2, 2.4)*

8. $y = 3x - 3$ **9.** $y = -\frac{1}{2}x + 5$ **10.** $y = 7$

11. $x = -4.5$ **12.** $x - y = 8$ **13.** $2x + 2y = 5$

Find the slope of the line passing through the given points. *(Lesson 2.3)*

14. $(7, 9), (1, 3)$ **15.** $(3, -5), (-2, 5)$ **16.** $(4, 9), (-2, 4)$

Write an equation of the line with the given characteristics. *(Lesson 2.5)*

17. point: $(2, -1)$, slope: $\frac{1}{2}$ **18.** horizontal line through $(-3, 1)$

19. **Bering Land Bridge** Draw a scatter plot of the data in Exercise 7. Then tell whether the data have a *positive correlation*, *negative correlation*, or *relatively no correlation*. *(Lesson 2.7)*

Solve the system of linear equations. *(Lessons 3.1–3.3)*

20. $x + y = 3$ **21.** $3x - 5y = 3$ **22.** $2x - y = -3$
  $2x - y = 6$ $-3x + y = 5$ $-x + 3y = 9$

23. **Football** Tickets for your school's football game are \$2 for students and \$5 for adults. A total of 400 people attended the game. The total ticket sales were \$1250. How many students attended the game? How many adults attended the game? Use a verbal model and linear combinations to solve the linear system. *(Lesson 3.3)*

Graph the ordered triple or equation in a three-dimensional coordinate system. *(Lesson 3.4)*

24. $(-2, 0, 5)$ **25.** $x + 2y - z = 4$ **26.** $2x - 6y - 3z = 6$

Solve the system of linear equations. *(Lesson 3.5)*

27. $x + y + z = -9$ **28.** $x - y + 2z = 7$ **29.** $x + y - z = 2$
  $x - y - z = 5$ $2x + y + z = 2$ $2x - y + z = 4$
  $-x - y + z = -1$ $-x + 2y - z = -9$ $-x - y + 3z = -6$

Solve the inequality. Graph your solution on a real number line.
(Lessons 4.1, 4.5)

30. $2x - 7 \le -5$

31. $-11 < -2x + 5 < 7$

32. $3x < -9$ or $x - 8 \ge -1$

33. $|5x| \ge 30$

34. $|x + 3| < 6$

35. $|3x - 1| < -7$

36. Fruit Salad You want to buy mangoes and strawberries for a salad. A one-pound package of strawberries is $3 and mangoes are $1 each. You need at least 2 packages of strawberries and at least 4 mangoes. The most you can spend is $15. Write and graph a system of linear inequalities that shows the number of strawberry packages x and the number of mangoes y that you can afford. *(Lesson 4.3)*

Graph the absolute value function. *(Lessons 4.6)*

37. $y = 5|x|$

38. $y = -4|x|$

39. $y = \dfrac{3}{4}|x|$

40. $y = \dfrac{1}{3}|x|$

41. $y = -\dfrac{2}{5}|x| - 4$

42. $y = -1.5|x|$

Graph the function. *(Lessons 5.1, 6.2)*

43. $y = x^2 - 9x + 20$

44. $y = 3(x - 2)^2 - 4$

45. $y = -(x + 5)(x - 3)$

46. $y = -x^3 + 3x - 4$

47. $y = x^4 - 7$

48. $y = x^3 - 3x^2$

Write the expression as a complex number in standard form. *(Lesson 5.7)*

49. $(4 - 2i) - (9 - 5i)$

50. $(3i)(6 + 7i)$

51. $\dfrac{3 + i}{5 - i}$

Simplify the expression. *(Lesson 6.1)*

52. $(5x^6)^{-3}$

53. $\dfrac{x^{-11}}{x^5}$

54. $\dfrac{2x^6 y^{-1}}{10xy}$

Factor the expression. *(Lessons 5.3–5.5, 6.5, 6.6)*

55. $x^2 + 16x + 28$

56. $5x^2 + 12x + 7$

57. $x^4 - 144$

58. $x^3 + 13x^2 - 4x - 52$

59. $7x^4 + 56x$

60. $x^5 - 16x^3 + 63x$

Solve the equation. *(Lessons 5.3–5.9, 6.5, 6.6)*

61. $x^2 + 8x = 20$

62. $16x^2 + 24x + 9 = 0$

63. $3x^2 + 6 = 81$

64. $x^2 = -225$

65. $x^2 - 10x + 15 = 0$

66. $x^3 + 7x^2 = 8x + 56$

Perform the indicated operations. *(Lessons 6.3, 6.4)*

67. $(2x^3 - 5x + 1) - (x^2 - 4x + 3)$

68. $(3x^4 - 5x^2 + 7) + (x^4 + 8x^3 - 6)$

69. $(x - 4)(x - 1)(x + 8)$

70. $(2x^3 - x^2 + 5x + 1) \div (x - 3)$

71. Soccer A goalie kicks a soccer ball from a height of 2 feet. The ball is kicked with an initial velocity of 65 feet per second. About how long is the ball in the air? *(Lesson 5.9)*

72. Maximum Height Use a graphing calculator to graph the function in Exercise 71. Use the *Maximum* feature of the graphing calculator to estimate the maximum height of the soccer ball. *(Lesson 6.7)*

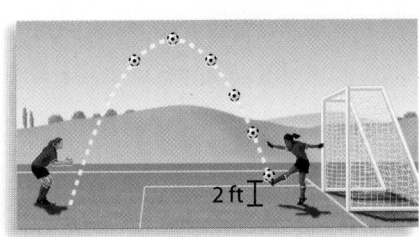

CHAPTER 7

Powers, Roots, and Radicals

▶ How does water pressure affect the water flow rate of a fire hose?

APPLICATION: Fire Fighting

The effect of water pressure on the water flow rate of a fire hose can be seen by comparing the graphs of two functions. The graph below shows the relationship between the diameter of a hose and its water flow rate for two different water pressures.

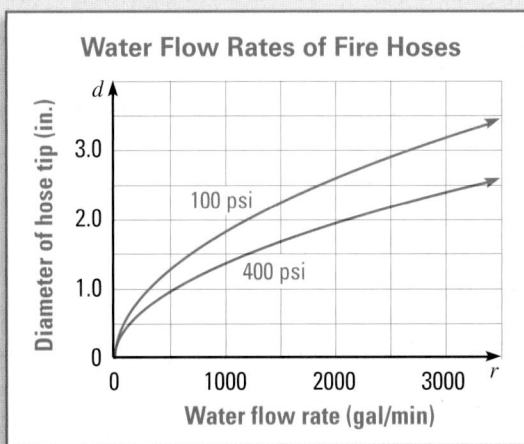

Water Flow Rates of Fire Hoses

Think & Discuss

Use the graph to answer the following questions.

1. What diameter hose tip do you need if you want a water flow rate of 1500 gallons per minute at 100 psi? What diameter hose tip do you need to have a water flow rate of 1500 gallons at 400 psi?

2. How does increasing the water pressure of a hose affect the water flow rate? Explain.

Learn More About It

You will graph a *square root function* to estimate the water flow rate of a hose with a water pressure of 150 pounds per square inch in Exercise 47 on page 393.

PREVIEW **What's the chapter about?**

• Evaluating *n*th roots of real numbers using radicals and rational exponents
• Solving equations containing radicals or rational exponents
• Finding inverse functions for both linear and nonlinear functions
• Graphing square root and cube root functions
• Finding and comparing standard deviations of data sets

Key Words

• *n*th root of a real number, *p. 353*
• index, *p. 353*
• simplest form of a radical, *p. 359*
• like radicals, *p. 360*
• radical equation, *p. 365*
• extraneous solution, *p. 366*

• composition of functions, *p. 374*
• inverse relation, *p. 380*
• inverse functions, *p. 380*
• radical function, *p. 389*
• standard deviation, *p. 395*

PREPARE **Chapter Readiness Quiz**

Take this quick quiz. If you are unsure of an answer, look back at the reference pages for help.

Vocabulary Check *(refer to p. 296)*

1. According to the product property of exponents, $(ab)^n = $ ___?___ .

(A) ab^n **(B)** $a^n b^n$ **(C)** $a^n b$ **(D)** $a^n + b^n$

2. According to the power of a power property of exponents, $(a^m)^n = $ ___?___ .

(F) a^{m+n} **(G)** $a^{m/n}$ **(H)** a^{mn} **(J)** a^{m-n}

Skill Check *(refer to p. 240)*

3. What is the solution of $2x^2 + 5 = 41$?

(A) $\sqrt{2}, -\sqrt{2}$ **(B)** 18 **(C)** $4\sqrt{2}, -4\sqrt{2}$ **(D)** $3\sqrt{2}, -3\sqrt{2}$

TAKE NOTES **Building on Skills**

As your knowledge of a topic grows, you may return and add to a section of your notes. You use the same steps to solve a radical equation as you would to solve any equation. Add the powers property of equality as another strategy you can use to solve an equation.

Steps for solving equations:

1) *Collect the variable terms on one side of the equation.*

2) *Use the same operation on each side of the equation to isolate the variable.*
   • *Add or subtract the same number.*
   • *Multiply or divide by the same number.*
   • *Raise each side to the same power.*

7.1 nth Roots and Rational Exponents

Key Words
- *n*th root of a real number
- index

GOAL Evaluate *n*th roots of real numbers.

Prerequisite Skills

Simplify the expression.

1. $\sqrt{49}$

2. $\sqrt{12}$

3. $\sqrt{2} \cdot \sqrt{32}$

4. $\sqrt{5} \cdot \sqrt{45}$

You know that to find the volume of a cube, you find the cube of the side length: $V = s^3$. If you know the volume, you can find the side length by taking the *cube root* of the volume: $s = \sqrt[3]{V}$. You can extend the concept of square roots to cube and other roots.

$V = 4096 \text{ mm}^3$, so
$s = \sqrt[3]{4096} = 16$ mm.

$$b \text{ is the } \textbf{square} \text{ root of } a \quad \text{if } b^2 = a$$
$$b \text{ is the } \textbf{cube} \text{ root of } a \quad \text{if } b^3 = a$$
$$b \text{ is the } \textbf{fourth} \text{ root of } a \quad \text{if } b^4 = a$$
$$b \text{ is the } \textbf{nth} \text{ root of } a \quad \text{if } b^n = a$$

You can write the **nth root of a** as $\sqrt[n]{a}$ where a is a real number and n is the **index** of the radical. The radical $\sqrt[n]{a}$ refers to the positive *n*th root of a. The radical $-\sqrt[n]{a}$ refers to the negative *n*th root of a.

Number of Real *n*th Roots

Let *n* be an integer greater than 1, and let *a* be a real number.

n	*a*	Number of real *n*th roots of *a*	Example(s)
odd	any real number	one	$\sqrt[3]{8} = 2$; $\sqrt[3]{-1} = -1$
even	greater than 0	two	$\sqrt[4]{16} = 2$; $-\sqrt[4]{16} = -2$
	0	one	$\sqrt{0} = 0$; $\sqrt[4]{0} = 0$
	less than 0	none	$\sqrt[4]{-20}$, no real root

EXAMPLE 1 Find *n*th Root(s)

Find the indicated *n*th root(s) of *a*.

a. $n = 3$, $a = -64$ **b.** $n = 4$, $a = 81$

Solution

a. Because *n* is odd, -64 has one real cube root. $\sqrt[3]{-64} = -4$

CHECK $(-4)^3 = (-4)(-4)(-4) = -64$ ✓

b. Because *n* is even and *a* is greater than 0, 81 has two real fourth roots.
$\sqrt[4]{81} = 3$ and $-\sqrt[4]{81} = -3$

CHECK $3^4 = 3 \cdot 3 \cdot 3 \cdot 3 = 81$ ✓ $(-3)^4 = (-3)(-3)(-3)(-3) = 81$ ✓

Solve an Equation To solve an equation involving x^n, isolate the power on one side of the equation, and then take the nth root of *each* side.

EXAMPLE 2 **Solve Equations Using *n*th Roots**

Solve the equation.

a. $2x^4 = 162$ **b.** $(x - 3)^3 = 8$

Solution

a.
$2x^4 = 162$	Write original equation.
$\dfrac{2x^4}{2} = \dfrac{162}{2}$	Divide each side by 2.
$x^4 = 81$	Simplify.
$\sqrt[4]{x^4} = \pm\sqrt[4]{81}$	Take fourth root of each side.
$x = \pm 3$	Simplify.

STUDENT HELP

AVOID ERRORS
When n is even and $a > 0$, be sure to consider both the positive and negative nth roots of a.

b.
$(x - 3)^3 = 8$	Write original equation.
$\sqrt[3]{(x - 3)^3} = \sqrt[3]{8}$	Take cube root of each side.
$x - 3 = 2$	Simplify.
$x = 5$	Add 3 to each side.

 **Find *n*th Roots and Solve Equations Using *n*th Roots**

Find the indicated *n*th root(s) of *a*.

1. $n = 2, a = 144$ **2.** $n = 3, a = 1000$ **3.** $n = 4, a = 256$

Solve the equation.

4. $x^3 = 64$ **5.** $\dfrac{1}{2}x^4 = 16$ **6.** $(x - 1)^3 = 27$

STUDENT HELP

WRITING ALGEBRA
When you write a square root, such as $\sqrt{3}$, you do not need to write "2" as the index. You do need to include the index for all other roots, such as $\sqrt[3]{7}$.

Rational Exponents You do not have to use a radical to write an nth root of a. You can write an nth root of a using a fraction as an exponent. Notice that the denominator of each rational exponent is equal to the index of the radical.

$$\sqrt{3} = 3^{1/2} \qquad\qquad \sqrt[3]{7} = 7^{1/3} \qquad\qquad \sqrt[n]{a} = a^{1/n}$$

EXAMPLE 3 **Evaluate Expressions with Rational Exponents**

Evaluate the expression.

a. $9^{1/2} = \sqrt{9} = 3$ **b.** $16^{1/4} = \sqrt[4]{16} = 2$

c. $64^{1/3} = \sqrt[3]{64} = 4$ **d.** $-32^{1/4} = \sqrt[4]{-32}$, no real solution

---

 **Evaluate Expressions**

Evaluate the expression.

7. $25^{1/2}$ **8.** $81^{1/2}$ **9.** $125^{1/3}$ **10.** $32^{1/5}$

Rational Exponents You can also use a fraction as an exponent to write a combination of a power and an nth root.

$$\left(\sqrt[3]{2}\right)^4 = (2^{1/3})^4 = 2^{4/3} \qquad\qquad \left(\sqrt[5]{9}\right)^7 = (9^{1/5})^7 = 9^{7/5}$$

Rational Exponents

Let $a^{1/n}$ be an nth root of a ($a > 0$ and $a \neq 1$), and let m be a positive integer.

$$a^{m/n} = \left(a^{1/n}\right)^m = \left(\sqrt[n]{a}\right)^m$$

$$a^{-m/n} = \frac{1}{a^{m/n}} = \frac{1}{\left(a^{1/n}\right)^m} = \frac{1}{\left(\sqrt[n]{a}\right)^m}$$

STUDENT HELP

KEYSTROKE HELP
To evaluate $5^{3/4}$ on your calculator, use the ⏶ key just as for other exponents. You will need to use parentheses when entering the fraction.

5 ⏶ (3 ÷ 4)

The result is about 3.344.

EXAMPLE **4** **Rewrite Expressions**

a. Rewrite $\left(\sqrt[4]{5}\right)^3$ using rational exponents. $\left(\sqrt[4]{5}\right)^3 = (5^{1/4})^3 = 5^{3/4}$

b. Rewrite $\dfrac{1}{\sqrt[6]{4}}$ using rational exponents. $\dfrac{1}{\sqrt[6]{4}} = \dfrac{1}{4^{1/6}} = 4^{-1/6}$

c. Rewrite $7^{2/5}$ using radicals. $7^{2/5} = (7^{1/5})^2 = \left(\sqrt[5]{7}\right)^2$

d. Rewrite $2^{-2/3}$ using radicals. $2^{-2/3} = \dfrac{1}{2^{2/3}} = \dfrac{1}{(2^{1/3})^2} = \dfrac{1}{\left(\sqrt[3]{2}\right)^2}$

EXAMPLE **5** **Evaluate Expressions with Rational Exponents**

Evaluate the expression.

a. $4^{3/2}$ **b.** $8^{-2/3}$

Solution

Use radicals to rewrite and evaluate each expression.

a. $4^{3/2} = \left(\sqrt{4}\right)^3 = 2^3 = 8$

b. $8^{-2/3} = \dfrac{1}{8^{2/3}} = \dfrac{1}{\left(\sqrt[3]{8}\right)^2} = \dfrac{1}{2^2} = \dfrac{1}{4}$

Checkpoint ✓ **Rewrite and Evaluate Expressions with Rational Exponents**

Rewrite the expression using rational exponents.

11. $\left(\sqrt[5]{2}\right)^2$ **12.** $\dfrac{1}{\sqrt[5]{3}}$ **13.** $\dfrac{1}{\sqrt[4]{13}}$

Rewrite the expression using radicals.

14. $15^{2/3}$ **15.** $11^{-1/3}$ **16.** $29^{-2/5}$

Evaluate the expression.

17. $25^{3/2}$ **18.** $16^{5/4}$ **19.** $8^{-5/3}$

Guided Practice

Vocabulary Check

1. Use radicals to express $a^{-m/n}$. Then state the index of the radical.

2. Copy and complete the statement: For an integer n greater than 1, if $b^n = a$, then b is a(n) __?__.

Skill Check

Find the indicated nth root(s) of a.

3. $n = 3, a = 0$ **4.** $n = 2, a = 64$ **5.** $n = 5, a = -32$

Solve the equation.

6. $4x^4 = 40,000$ **7.** $(x - 1)^3 = 125$ **8.** $(x + 4)^3 = -27$

Evaluate the expression.

9. $100^{1/2}$ **10.** $64^{1/2}$ **11.** $27^{1/3}$ **12.** $243^{1/5}$

Match equivalent expressions.

13. $\left(\sqrt[3]{5}\right)^4$ **14.** $\left(\sqrt[4]{5}\right)^3$ **15.** $\dfrac{1}{\sqrt[4]{5}}$ **16.** $\sqrt[4]{5}$

A. $5^{-1/4}$ **B.** $5^{4/3}$ **C.** $5^{1/4}$ **D.** $5^{3/4}$

Evaluate the expression.

17. $125^{2/3}$ **18.** $100^{3/2}$ **19.** $32^{-3/5}$ **20.** $81^{-4/3}$

Practice and Applications

STUDENT HELP

HOMEWORK HELP
Example 1: Exs. 21–26
Example 2: Exs. 27–35
Example 3: Exs. 36–51
Example 4: Exs. 52–75
Example 5: Exs. 76–83

Finding nth Roots **Find the indicated nth root(s) of a.**

21. $n = 3, a = 8$ **22.** $n = 5, a = 0$ **23.** $n = 2, a = 121$

24. $n = 4, a = -1$ **25.** $n = 3, a = -27$ **26.** $n = 7, a = -128$

Solving Equations **Solve the equation.**

27. $x^4 = 1$ **28.** $x^5 = 243$ **29.** $x^5 = -32$

30. $5x^3 = 135$ **31.** $2x^4 = 512$ **32.** $\dfrac{1}{2}x^4 = 8$

33. $\dfrac{1}{3}x^3 = -72$ **34.** $(x - 4)^3 = -64$ **35.** $(x + 3)^4 = 81$

Evaluating Expressions **Evaluate the expression.**

36. $\sqrt{16}$ **37.** $\sqrt[3]{125}$ **38.** $\sqrt[5]{0}$ **39.** $-\sqrt[4]{81}$

40. $\sqrt[3]{-8}$ **41.** $\sqrt[5]{-32}$ **42.** $\sqrt[3]{1000}$ **43.** $\sqrt[3]{-64}$

44. $144^{1/2}$ **45.** $196^{1/2}$ **46.** $64^{1/3}$ **47.** $1024^{1/5}$

48. $256^{1/4}$ **49.** $216^{1/3}$ **50.** $512^{1/3}$ **51.** $625^{1/4}$

Using Rational Exponents Rewrite the expression using rational exponents.

52. $\left(\sqrt[4]{2}\right)^3$ **53.** $\left(\sqrt[5]{3}\right)^2$ **54.** $\left(\sqrt[6]{6}\right)^5$ **55.** $\left(\sqrt[3]{9}\right)^4$

56. $\left(\sqrt[7]{x}\right)^8$ **57.** $\dfrac{1}{\sqrt{13}}$ **58.** $\dfrac{1}{\left(\sqrt[3]{11}\right)^4}$ **59.** $\dfrac{1}{\left(\sqrt[6]{10}\right)^5}$

60. $\dfrac{4}{\left(\sqrt{5^2}\right)^3}$ **61.** $\dfrac{1}{\left(\sqrt[3]{q}\right)^2}$ **62.** $\dfrac{1}{\left(\sqrt[5]{p}\right)^3}$ **63.** $\dfrac{1}{\left(\sqrt[4]{q}\right)^{10}}$

Using Radicals Rewrite the expression using radicals.

64. $3^{4/5}$ **65.** $16^{2/3}$ **66.** $23^{5/9}$ **67.** $20^{3/4}$

68. $10^{-2/7}$ **69.** $15^{-2/9}$ **70.** $12^{-5/6}$ **71.** $18^{-3/8}$

72. $x^{3/2}$ **73.** $b^{5/4}$ **74.** $t^{-2/9}$ **75.** $m^{-3/4}$

Evaluating Expressions Evaluate the expression.

76. $8^{4/3}$ **77.** $100^{5/2}$ **78.** $256^{3/4}$ **79.** $216^{5/3}$

80. $16^{-5/4}$ **81.** $64^{-2/3}$ **82.** $225^{-3/2}$ **83.** $1296^{-3/4}$

EXAMPLE   **Evaluating a Model with *n*th Roots**

Basketball The volume V of a sphere can be calculated using the formula $V = \dfrac{4}{3}\pi r^3$ where r is the radius of the sphere. A basketball has a volume of 434 cubic inches. Find the radius of the basketball to the nearest tenth of an inch.

Solution

$V = \dfrac{4}{3}\pi r^3$ Write the formula.

$434 = \dfrac{4}{3}\pi r^3$ Substitute 434 for *V*.

$\dfrac{3}{4\pi}(434) = r^3$ Solve for r^3.

$103.6 \approx r^3$ Evaluate using a calculator.

$4.7 \approx r$ Find the cube root of each side using a calculator.

ANSWER ▶ The radius of the basketball is about 4.7 inches.

---

84. Science Link The shape of Earth is nearly a sphere. The volume of Earth is approximately 1.083×10^{12} cubic kilometers. Use the formula for the volume of a sphere given in the example above. Find the radius of Earth. Round your answer to the nearest whole number.

85. Jewelry A jeweler is setting a stone cut in the shape of a regular octahedron. A regular octahedron is a solid with eight equilateral triangles as faces, as shown. The formula for the volume of the stone is $V = 0.47s^3$ where s is the side length of an edge of the stone. The volume of the stone is 161 cubic millimeters. Find the length of an edge of the stone to the nearest tenth of a millimeter.

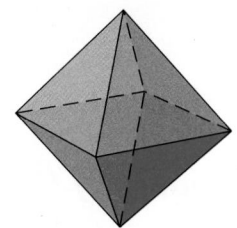

86. **Zoology** Zoologists can approximate a mammal's surface area S in square centimeters using the model $S = km^{2/3}$ where m is the mammal's mass in grams, and k is a constant that is related to the mammal. Use $k = 9.3$ to approximate the surface area of a marmot, shown at the right, whose mass is 3375 grams.

87. **Fans** The power p (in horsepower) used by a fan is given by $p = ks^3$ where s is the rotational speed of the fan in rotations per minute, and k is a constant that is related to the fan. A particular fan uses 1.2 horsepower. The value of k for the fan is 2.4×10^{-10}. Find the value of s for this fan.

88. **Challenge** Copy and complete the proof which shows that $\sqrt{3} = 3^{1/2}$.

Statements	Reasons
1. $\sqrt{3} \cdot \sqrt{3} = 3$	1. ___?___
2. $3^k \cdot 3^k = 3$	2. ___?___
3. $3^{2k} = 3^1$	3. ___?___
4. $2k = 1$	4. Set exponents equal when bases are equal.
5. $k = \dfrac{1}{2}$	5. ___?___

89. **Challenge** Use a proof like the one in Exercise 88 to show that $\sqrt[3]{7} = 7^{1/3}$.

90. **Multiple Choice** Rewrite $\dfrac{1}{\left(\sqrt[3]{5}\right)^2}$ using rational exponents.

   (**A**) $5^{2/3}$ (**B**) $3^{-2/5}$ (**C**) $5^{1/2}$ (**D**) $5^{-2/3}$

91. **Multiple Choice** What is the solution of $6x^5 = 192$?

   (**F**) ±2 (**G**) 2 (**H**) $4\sqrt{2}$ (**J**) 32

Mixed Review

Transforming Data **Find the slope of the line passing through the given points. Then tell whether the line *rises, falls, is horizontal*, or *is vertical*. (Lesson 4.8)**

92. $(0, 1), (4, 12)$ 93. $(-3, -2), (12, 4)$ 94. $(1, -2), (1, 4)$

Simplifying Algebraic Expressions **Simplify the expression. Tell which properties of exponents you used. (Lesson 6.1)**

95. $(x^2y^3)^2$ 96. $x^{-3}y^2$ 97. $\dfrac{x^{-4}}{x}$

Multiplying Polynomials **Find the product. (Lesson 6.4)**

98. $x(x^2 - 4x + 1)$ 99. $3x^2(2x + 5)$ 100. $(2x - 1)(3x + 4)$

101. $(x - 4)(x^2 - 3x - 5)$ 102. $(3x + 2)(4x^2 - 3x + 6)$ 103. $(2x^2 - 1)(x^2 - x + 5)$

Geometry Skills

Volume Given the volume of a cube, find its side length.

104. $V = 343$ in.^{3} 105. $V = 1331$ cm^3 106. $V = 216$ ft^3

7.2 Properties of Rational Exponents

Key Words
- simplest form of a radical
- like radicals

You learned the power of a product and the power of a quotient properties of exponents in Lesson 6.1. These properties can also be used with radicals.

Prerequisite Skills

Evaluate the expression.

1. $2^2 \cdot 2^3$
2. $(2^3)^2$
3. 3^{-2}
4. $\dfrac{4^5}{4^3}$

Product and Quotient Properties of Radicals

Product property $\sqrt[n]{a \cdot b} = \sqrt[n]{a} \cdot \sqrt[n]{b}$ **Quotient property** $\sqrt[n]{\dfrac{a}{b}} = \dfrac{\sqrt[n]{a}}{\sqrt[n]{b}}$

EXAMPLE 1 Use Properties of Radicals

a.
$$\sqrt[3]{3} \cdot \sqrt[3]{9} = \sqrt[3]{3 \cdot 9} \qquad \text{Product property of radicals}$$
$$= \sqrt[3]{3 \cdot 3 \cdot 3} \qquad \text{Factor.}$$
$$= 3 \qquad \text{Simplify.}$$

b.
$$\frac{\sqrt[4]{48}}{\sqrt[4]{3}} = \sqrt[4]{\frac{48}{3}} \qquad \text{Quotient property of radicals}$$
$$= \sqrt[4]{2 \cdot 2 \cdot 2 \cdot 2} \qquad \text{Divide and factor.}$$
$$= 2 \qquad \text{Simplify.}$$

STUDENT HELP

VOCABULARY
Recall that a *radicand* is the number, variable, or expression under the radical sign. The radicand of $4\sqrt[3]{2}$ is 2.

Simplifying Radicals A radical with index n is in **simplest form** if there are no perfect nth powers in the radicand, and there are no radicals in any denominators. To write a radical in simplest form, apply the properties of radicals, remove any perfect nth powers (other than 1), and rationalize any denominators.

EXAMPLE 2 Write Radicals in Simplest Form

a.
$$\sqrt[3]{40} = \sqrt[3]{8 \cdot 5} \qquad \text{Factor out a perfect cube.}$$
$$= \sqrt[3]{8} \cdot \sqrt[3]{5} \qquad \text{Product property of radicals}$$
$$= 2\sqrt[3]{5} \qquad \text{Simplify.}$$

b.
$$\sqrt[4]{\frac{1}{8}} = \sqrt[4]{\frac{1 \cdot 2}{8 \cdot 2}} \qquad \text{Make the denominator a perfect fourth power.}$$
$$= \sqrt[4]{\frac{2}{16}} \qquad \text{Multiply.}$$
$$= \frac{\sqrt[4]{2}}{\sqrt[4]{16}} \qquad \text{Quotient property of radicals}$$
$$= \frac{\sqrt[4]{2}}{2} \qquad \text{Simplify.}$$

Properties of Rational Exponents You studied the properties of integer exponents in Lesson 6.1. These properties are also true for rational exponents.

STUDENT HELP

LOOK BACK
These properties are the same as those listed on page 296, but now they apply to rational exponents, as shown.

Properties of Rational Exponents

Let a and b be positive real numbers. Let m and n be rational numbers.

PROPERTY	EXAMPLE
1. $a^m \cdot a^n = a^{m+n}$	$3^{1/2} \cdot 3^{3/2} = 3^{(1/2+3/2)} = 3^2 = 9$
2. $(a^m)^n = a^{mn}$	$(2^{3/2})^2 = 2^{(3/2 \cdot 2)} = 2^3 = 8$
3. $(ab)^m = a^m b^m$	$(9 \cdot 4)^{1/2} = 9^{1/2} \cdot 4^{1/2} = 3 \cdot 2 = 6$
4. $a^{-m} = \dfrac{1}{a^m},\ a \neq 0$	$16^{-1/2} = \dfrac{1}{16^{1/2}} = \dfrac{1}{4}$
5. $\dfrac{a^m}{a^n} = a^{m-n},\ a \neq 0$	$\dfrac{5^{3/2}}{5^{1/2}} = 5^{(3/2-1/2)} = 5^1 = 5$
6. $\left(\dfrac{a}{b}\right)^m = \dfrac{a^m}{b^m},\ b \neq 0$	$\left(\dfrac{8}{27}\right)^{1/3} = \dfrac{8^{1/3}}{27^{1/3}} = \dfrac{2}{3}$

EXAMPLE 3 Use Properties of Rational Exponents

a. $6^{2/3} \cdot 6^{1/3} = 6^{(2/3+1/3)} = 6^{3/3} = 6^1 = 6$

b. $(3^{3/4})^4 = 3^{(3/4 \cdot 4)} = 3^3 = 27$

c. $(16 \cdot 25)^{1/2} = 16^{1/2} \cdot 25^{1/2} = 4 \cdot 5 = 20$

d. $8^{-1/3} = \dfrac{1}{8^{1/3}} = \dfrac{1}{2}$

e. $\dfrac{7^{5/2}}{7^{1/2}} = 7^{(5/2-1/2)} = 7^{4/2} = 7^2 = 49$

Like Radicals Two radicals are **like radicals** if they have the same index and the same radicand. For example, $\sqrt[3]{2}$ and $4\sqrt[3]{2}$ are like radicals. To add or subtract like radicals, use the distributive property.

EXAMPLE 4 Add or Subtract Like Radicals

a. $4\sqrt[5]{3} + \sqrt[5]{3} = (4+1)\sqrt[5]{3}$
$= 5\sqrt[5]{3}$

b. $7(11^{1/3}) - 10(11^{1/3}) = (7-10)(11^{1/3})$
$= -3(11^{1/3})$

Checkpoint ✓ **Use Properties of Radicals and Rational Exponents**

Simplify the expression.

1. $\sqrt[3]{2} \cdot \sqrt[3]{4}$
2. $\sqrt[5]{4} \cdot \sqrt[5]{8}$
3. $\dfrac{\sqrt[3]{54}}{\sqrt[3]{2}}$
4. $\dfrac{\sqrt[3]{81}}{\sqrt[3]{3}}$

5. $9^{1/6} \cdot 9^{1/3}$
6. $\dfrac{81^{5/8}}{81^{3/8}}$
7. $(64 \cdot 49)^{1/2}$
8. $2^{1/2} + 5(2^{1/2})$

Chapter 7 *Powers, Roots, and Radicals*

Simplifying Variable Expressions You can apply the properties of radicals to expressions involving variables. When the value of a variable is negative, you may need to use absolute value to find an nth root.

$$\sqrt[n]{x^n} = x \text{ when } n \text{ is odd} \qquad \sqrt[n]{x^n} = |x| \text{ when } n \text{ is even}$$

Absolute value is not needed when all variables are assumed to be positive. In this lesson, assume that all variables are positive.

EXAMPLE 5 Simplify Expressions with Variables

Simplify the expression. Write your answer using positive exponents only. Assume all variables are positive.

a. $\sqrt{9x^6} = \sqrt{3^2(x^3)^2}$ Factor out perfect square factors.

$\qquad = 3x^3$ Simplify.

b. $(4y^6)^{1/2} = 4^{1/2}(y^6)^{1/2}$ Power of a product property

$\qquad\qquad = 4^{1/2}y^{(6\,\cdot\,1/2)}$ Power of a power property

$\qquad\qquad = 2y^3$ Simplify.

c. $\sqrt[3]{\dfrac{x^3}{y^6}} = \sqrt[3]{\dfrac{x^3}{(y^2)^3}}$ Factor out perfect cube factors.

$\qquad = \dfrac{x}{y^2}$ Simplify.

d. $\dfrac{3a^{1/2}c}{ac^{-2}} = 3a^{(1/2\,-\,1)}c^{[1\,-\,(-2)]}$ Quotient of powers property

$\qquad = 3a^{-1/2}c^3$ Simplify.

$\qquad = \dfrac{3c^3}{a^{1/2}}$ Write using positive exponents.

EXAMPLE 6 Add and Subtract Expressions with Variables

Simplify the expression. Assume all variables are positive.

a. $4\sqrt{x} - 3\sqrt{x} = (4 - 3)\sqrt{x}$ **b.** $5xy^{1/4} + 2xy^{1/4} = (5 + 2)xy^{1/4}$

$\qquad\qquad\qquad = \sqrt{x}$ $= 7xy^{1/4}$

Checkpoint ✓ **Simplify Expressions with Variables**

Simplify the expression. Write your answer using positive exponents only. Assume all variables are positive.

9. $\sqrt{25y^4}$ **10.** $\sqrt{\dfrac{x^6}{y^2}}$ **11.** $(8u^3v^9)^{1/3}$ **12.** $\dfrac{2x}{x^{1/3}z^{-3}}$

Simplify the expression. Assume all variables are positive.

13. $3\sqrt[3]{x} + \sqrt[3]{x}$ **14.** $8\sqrt[5]{r} - 4\sqrt[5]{r}$ **15.** $6a^{2/3} - 4a^{2/3}$

7.2 Exercises

Guided Practice

Vocabulary Check

1. Explain why $\dfrac{\sqrt[3]{3}}{\sqrt{7}}$ is *not* in simplest form.

2. Are $3\sqrt[4]{5}$ and $2\sqrt[4]{5}$ like radicals? Explain why or why not.

Skill Check

Simplify the expression.

3. $\sqrt[3]{5} \cdot \sqrt[3]{25}$ **4.** $\sqrt[4]{3} \cdot \sqrt[4]{27}$ **5.** $\dfrac{\sqrt{64}}{\sqrt{4}}$ **6.** $\dfrac{\sqrt[3]{256}}{\sqrt[3]{4}}$

Write the expression in simplest form.

7. $\sqrt[3]{40}$ **8.** $\sqrt[4]{32}$ **9.** $\sqrt[3]{\dfrac{1}{9}}$ **10.** $\sqrt[4]{\dfrac{1}{2}}$

Simplify the expression.

11. $8^{1/4} \cdot 8^{3/4}$ **12.** $(2^{2/5})^{10}$ **13.** $125^{-2/3}$ **14.** $\dfrac{16^{3/2}}{16^{1/2}}$

Simplify the expression. Write your answer using positive exponents only. Assume all variables are positive.

15. $(25x^6)^{1/2}$ **16.** $\sqrt[4]{8x^4y^8}$ **17.** $(36x^2y^6)^{1/2}$ **18.** $\dfrac{8ab}{2a^{2/3}b^{1/3}}$

19. Simplify the expression $11\sqrt[5]{t} - 7\sqrt[5]{t}$. Assume all variables are positive.

Practice and Applications

STUDENT HELP

HOMEWORK HELP
Example 1: Exs. 20–27
Example 2: Exs. 28–35
Example 3: Exs. 36–43
Example 4: Exs. 44–49
Example 5: Exs. 50–65
Example 6: Exs. 66–74

Using Properties of Radicals **Simplify the expression.**

20. $\sqrt[4]{4} \cdot \sqrt[4]{4}$ **21.** $\sqrt[5]{81} \cdot \sqrt[5]{3}$ **22.** $\sqrt[3]{-9} \cdot \sqrt[3]{3}$ **23.** $\sqrt[3]{25} \cdot \sqrt[3]{-5}$

24. $\dfrac{\sqrt{216}}{\sqrt{6}}$ **25.** $\dfrac{\sqrt[3]{28}}{\sqrt[3]{2}}$ **26.** $\dfrac{\sqrt[4]{324}}{\sqrt[4]{4}}$ **27.** $\dfrac{\sqrt[3]{250}}{\sqrt[3]{2}}$

Simplest Form **Write the expression in simplest form.**

28. $\sqrt[3]{72}$ **29.** $\sqrt[4]{162}$ **30.** $\sqrt[3]{32}$ **31.** $\sqrt[4]{25} \cdot \sqrt[4]{75}$

32. $\sqrt[5]{56} \cdot \sqrt[5]{12}$ **33.** $\dfrac{\sqrt[3]{54}}{\sqrt[3]{9}}$ **34.** $\sqrt[4]{\dfrac{4}{9}}$ **35.** $\dfrac{\sqrt[3]{56}}{\sqrt[3]{3}}$

Using Properties of Rational Exponents **Simplify the expression.**

36. $3^{5/3} \cdot 3^{4/3}$ **37.** $(7^{1/4})^{4/3}$ **38.** $8^{2/3} \cdot 8^{-1/3}$ **39.** $\dfrac{1}{16^{-1/2}}$

40. $\dfrac{11^{5/3}}{11^{2/3}}$ **41.** $5^{1/3} \cdot 25^{1/6}$ **42.** $(5^{1/6} \cdot 5^{1/3})^2$ **43.** $\left(\dfrac{3^4}{5^4}\right)^{-1/2}$

Adding and Subtracting Expressions **Simplify the expression.**

44. $\sqrt[3]{12} + 3\sqrt[3]{12}$ **45.** $4\sqrt[4]{2} - 5\sqrt[4]{2}$ **46.** $8\sqrt[3]{3} - 5\sqrt[3]{3}$

47. $-2(5^{1/4}) - 3(5^{1/4})$ **48.** $2(6^{1/3}) + 6^{1/3}$ **49.** $2(4^{1/4}) - 4(4^{1/4})$

Simplifying Expressions Simplify the expression. Write your answer using positive exponents only. Assume all variables are positive.

50. $(16x^6)^{1/2}$ **51.** $(64a^{12})^{1/3}$ **52.** $\sqrt[3]{27x^6}$ **53.** $\sqrt[4]{16x^4y^8}$

54. $\sqrt[5]{9x^5}$ **55.** $\sqrt[3]{32x^3y^9}$ **56.** $(27k^6)^{-1/3}$ **57.** $(32q^{10}r^{-3})^{-3/5}$

58. $\sqrt[4]{\dfrac{x^4}{y^3}}$ **59.** $\sqrt[5]{\dfrac{x^5}{32y^4}}$ **60.** $(64m^2n^{12})^{2/3}$ **61.** $(36c^6d^{12})^{3/2}$

62. $\dfrac{3st^2}{s^{1/3}t^{3/2}}$ **63.** $\dfrac{5g^{5/3}h^{3/2}}{g^{2/3}h^{1/2}}$ **64.** $\dfrac{6x^{2/5}y}{2x^{1/5}y^{2/3}}$ **65.** $\dfrac{a^{5/4}b^{7/3}c^{6/5}}{a^{1/4}b^{1/3}c^{1/5}}$

Adding and Subtracting Expressions Simplify the expression. Assume all variables are positive.

66. $7\sqrt{g} + 2\sqrt{g}$ **67.** $10\sqrt{st} - 6\sqrt{st}$ **68.** $5\sqrt{x^3y^2} - 9\sqrt{x^3y^2}$

69. $7xy^3 + 2xy^3$ **70.** $10m^{1/2}n^5 - 6m^{1/2}n^5$ **71.** $5p^2q^{2/3} - 9p^2q^{2/3}$

72. $10s^2t^{1/2} - (2st^{1/4})^2$ **73.** $(8gh^2)^{1/3} + 5g^{1/3}h^{2/3}$ **74.** $(27xy^9)^{1/3} + (x^{1/9}y)^3$

EXAMPLE   Evaluate a Model

Astronomy Astronomers calculate the time it takes a planet in our solar system to revolve around the sun using the model

$$T = (2 \times 10^{-10})d^{3/2}$$

where T is the number of days in one revolution and d is the average distance in kilometers from the planet to the sun. Find the number of days it takes Neptune to complete 1 revolution around the sun. Neptune is approximately 4.5×10^9 kilometers from the sun.

Solution

$T = (2 \times 10^{-10})d^{3/2}$	Write the model.
$= (2 \times 10^{-10}) \cdot (4.5 \times 10^9)^{3/2}$	Substitute 4.5×10^9 for d.
$= (2 \times 10^{-10}) \cdot 4.5^{3/2} \cdot (10^9)^{3/2}$	Power of a product property
$= 2 \cdot 10^{-10} \cdot 4.5^{3/2} \cdot 10^{27/2}$	Power of a power property
$= (2 \cdot 4.5^{3/2}) \cdot (10^{-10} \cdot 10^{27/2})$	Associative property of multiplication
$= 2 \cdot 4.5^{3/2} \cdot 10^{17/2}$	Product of powers property
$\approx 60{,}374$	Use a calculator.

ANSWER ▶ It takes Neptune approximately 60,374 days to complete 1 revolution around the sun.

Astronomy In Exercises 75 and 76, use the formula in the example above and the given distance to find the number of days it takes the given planet to complete 1 revolution around the sun.

75. Uranus is approximately 2.9×10^9 kilometers from the sun.

76. Jupiter is approximately 7.8×10^8 kilometers from the sun.

77. Pinhole Camera The optimum diameter d (in millimeters) of the hole in a pinhole camera can be modeled by $d = 1.9[(5.5 \times 10^{-4})\ell]^{1/2}$ where ℓ is the length of the camera box in millimeters. Determine the optimum diameter for a pinhole camera that has a length of 100 millimeters.

A photograph taken with a pinhole camera

78. 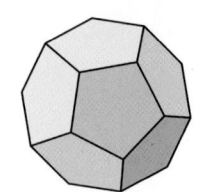 **Geometry Link** A regular dodecahedron is a solid with twelve regular pentagons as faces, as shown. You can approximate the volume V of a regular dodecahedron using the formula $V = 7.66a^3$ where a is the edge length of the dodecahedron. To the nearest cubic inch, find the volume of a dodecahedron with an edge length of $75^{1/2}$ inches.

79. **Challenge** The formula for the surface area S of a sphere is $S = (4\pi)^{1/3}(3V)^{2/3}$ where V is the volume of the sphere. The volume of a baseball is about 5.4 times the volume of a golf ball. By what factor is the surface area of the baseball greater than the surface area of the golf ball?

80. Multiple Choice What is $\dfrac{\sqrt[4]{125}}{\sqrt[4]{4}}$ written in simplest form?

(A) $5\sqrt[4]{5}$ (B) $\dfrac{5\sqrt[4]{10}}{2}$ (C) $\dfrac{\sqrt[4]{500}}{2}$ (D) 2

81. Multiple Choice What is $\sqrt[3]{\dfrac{27x^6}{4y^2}}$ written in simplest form?

(F) $\dfrac{3x^2\sqrt[3]{2y}}{2y}$ (G) $\dfrac{3x\sqrt[3]{2y}}{2}$ (H) $\dfrac{3x\sqrt[3]{2y^2}}{2y^2}$ (J) $\dfrac{3x\sqrt[3]{x^2y^2}}{2y^2}$

82. Multiple Choice Which expression is equivalent to $49^{1/3} \cdot 7^{2/3}$?

(A) $7^{1/3}$ (B) 7 (C) $49^{2/3}$ (D) $343^{2/9}$

Mixed Review

Simplifying Complex Numbers Write the expression as a complex number in standard form. *(Lesson 5.7)*

83. $3(4i)$ **84.** $(2i)(-5i)$ **85.** $\dfrac{10}{2+i}$ **86.** $\dfrac{6-i}{4+i}$

Identifying Polynomials Tell whether the function is a polynomial function. If it is, write the polynomial function in standard form. Then state its degree, type, and leading coefficient. *(Lesson 6.2)*

87. $f(x) = 3x^2 - 1 - 2x + 5x^4$ **88.** $f(x) = 2x^3 - 4x^{-1} - 7$

89. $f(x) = 2x + 5 - 3x^3$ **90.** $f(x) = 2x^4 - 4x^3 + 5x^2 - x - 2^x$

Geometry Skills

Right Triangles Find the values of x and y.

91.

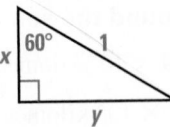

92.

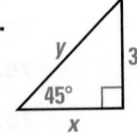

7.3 Solving Radical Equations

Key Words
- radical equation
- extraneous solution

Prerequisite Skills

Evaluate when $x = 2$.

1. $\sqrt{x + 2}$
2. $\sqrt[3]{10 - x}$
3. $\sqrt{18x}$
4. $\sqrt[3]{54 + 5x}$

GOAL Solve equations that contain radicals or rational exponents.

How old is an elephant?

In Exercise 60, you will solve a *radical equation* to estimate the age of an African elephant given its height.

A **radical equation** is an equation that contains radicals with the variable in the radicand. For example, $\sqrt{x + 6} = 5$ is a radical equation. To solve a radical equation, follow the steps below.

Solving Radical Equations

STEP 1 *Isolate* the radical on one side of the equation, if necessary.

STEP 2 *Raise* each side of the equation to the same power to eliminate the radical.

STEP 3 *Solve* the resulting equation using techniques that you learned in previous chapters.

STEP 4 *Check* your solution.

EXAMPLE 1 Solve a Radical Equation

Solve $\sqrt[3]{x} - 2 = 0$.

Solution

$\sqrt[3]{x} - 2 = 0$	Write original equation.
$\sqrt[3]{x} = 2$	Isolate the radical by adding 2 to each side.
$\left(\sqrt[3]{x}\right)^3 = 2^3$	Cube each side to eliminate the radical.
$x = 8$	Simplify.

ANSWER ▶ The solution is 8.

CHECK Check by substituting 8 for x in the original equation.

$\sqrt[3]{8} - 2 \stackrel{?}{=} 0$	Substitute 8 for x in the original equation.
$2 - 2 \stackrel{?}{=} 0$	Simplify.
$0 = 0 \checkmark$	Solution checks.

Checkpoint  **Solve Radical Equations**

1. Solve $\sqrt{x} - 4 = 0$.

2. Solve $\sqrt[3]{x} + 3 = 0$.

EXAMPLE 2 Solve a Radical Equation

Solve $3\sqrt{x + 4} - 1 = 8$.

Solution

$3\sqrt{x + 4} - 1 = 8$	Write original equation.
$3\sqrt{x + 4} = 9$	Add 1 to each side of the equation.
$\dfrac{3\sqrt{x + 4}}{3} = \dfrac{9}{3}$	Divide by 3 to isolate the radical.
$\sqrt{x + 4} = 3$	Simplify.
$\left(\sqrt{x + 4}\right)^2 = 3^2$	Square each side to eliminate the radical.
$x + 4 = 9$	Simplify.
$x = 5$	Subtract 4 from each side.

ANSWER ▶ The solution is 5. Check by substituting 5 for x in the original equation.

STUDENT HELP

SOLVING NOTE
In Example 2, notice how you eliminate the radical by raising each side of the equation to the power equal to the index of the radical.

Equations with Two Radicals To solve an equation with two radicals, first rewrite the equation so that each side has only one radical. Then raise each side of the equation to the same power.

EXAMPLE 3 Solve an Equation with Two Radicals

Solve $\sqrt{2x} - \sqrt{x + 1} = 0$.

Solution

$\sqrt{2x} - \sqrt{x + 1} = 0$	Write original equation.
$\sqrt{2x} = \sqrt{x + 1}$	Add $\sqrt{x + 1}$ to each side.
$\left(\sqrt{2x}\right)^2 = \left(\sqrt{x + 1}\right)^2$	Square each side to eliminate radicals.
$2x = x + 1$	Simplify.
$x = 1$	Solve for x.

ANSWER ▶ The solution is 1.

CHECK Check by substituting 1 for x in the original equation.

$\sqrt{2(1)} - \sqrt{1 + 1} \overset{?}{=} 0$	Substitute 1 for x in the original equation.
$\sqrt{2} - \sqrt{2} \overset{?}{=} 0$	Simplify.
$0 = 0 \checkmark$	Solution checks.

Checkpoint ✓ **Solve Equations with One or Two Radicals**

Solve the equation.

3. $\sqrt{x + 1} - 2 = 3$ **4.** $2\sqrt{x} = \sqrt{x + 3}$ **5.** $\sqrt{3x - 2} - \sqrt{x} = 0$

Extraneous Solutions Raising each side of an equation to the same power can lead to solutions that do *not* make the original equation true. An apparent solution that does not make the original equation true is called an **extraneous solution.** You must check each apparent solution in the original equation. Any solution that does not satisfy the original equation is extraneous.

EXAMPLE 4 Solve an Equation with an Extraneous Solution

Solve $x = \sqrt{x + 6}$. Check for extraneous solutions.

Solution

$x = \sqrt{x + 6}$	Write original equation.
$x^2 = \left(\sqrt{x + 6}\right)^2$	Square each side.
$x^2 = x + 6$	Simplify.
$x^2 - x - 6 = 0$	Write in standard form.
$(x + 2)(x - 3) = 0$	Factor the trinomial.
$x + 2 = 0$ or $x - 3 = 0$	Zero product property
$x = -2$ or $x = 3$	Solve for x.

STUDENT HELP

LOOK BACK
For help with factoring, see pages 234, 240, and 249.

CHECK Check by substituting -2 for x and 3 for x in the original equation.

$$-2 \overset{?}{=} \sqrt{-2 + 6} \qquad 3 \overset{?}{=} \sqrt{3 + 6}$$
$$-2 \overset{?}{=} \sqrt{4} \qquad 3 \overset{?}{=} \sqrt{9}$$
$$-2 \neq 2 \ \text{✗} \qquad 3 = 3 \ \checkmark$$

ANSWER ▶ Because -2 does not satisfy the original equation, the only solution is 3.

Rational Exponents When an equation contains a power with a rational exponent, you solve the equation the same way you would solve a radical equation. First, isolate the power on one side of the equation, then raise each side of the equation to the reciprocal of the rational exponent, and solve for the variable.

EXAMPLE 5 Solve an Equation with Rational Exponents

Solve $x^{3/2} - 2 = 25$. Check for extraneous solutions.

Solution

$x^{3/2} - 2 = 25$	Write original equation.
$x^{3/2} = 27$	Add 2 to each side.
$(x^{3/2})^{2/3} = 27^{2/3}$	Raise each side to the $\frac{2}{3}$ power.
$x = \left(\sqrt[3]{27}\right)^2$	Definition of rational exponents
$x = 9$	Simplify.

STUDENT HELP

SOLVING NOTE
Recall that multiplying a number by its reciprocal results in a product of 1. In Example 5, you want the exponent of x to be 1, so you raise x to the reciprocal of the power.

CHECK Check by substituting 9 for x in the original equation.

$$9^{3/2} - 2 \overset{?}{=} 25 \qquad \text{Substitute 9 for } x \text{ in the original equation.}$$
$$27 - 2 \overset{?}{=} 25 \qquad \text{Evaluate power.}$$
$$25 = 25 \ \checkmark \qquad \text{Solution checks.}$$

ANSWER ▶ The solution is 9.

 **Checkpoint** ✓ **Solve Radical Equations**

Solve the equation. Check for extraneous solutions.

6. $\sqrt{x + 2} = 0$ **7.** $x = \sqrt{x + 2}$ **8.** $x^{3/2} - 8 = 0$

Guided Practice

Vocabulary Check

1. Explain the steps you would take to solve $\sqrt{x} + 15 = 10$.

2. What is an extraneous solution?

Skill Check

Solve the equation. Check for extraneous solutions.

3. $\sqrt[3]{x} - 5 = 0$

4. $\sqrt{x} + 6 = 15$

5. $3\sqrt{x + 3} - 12 = 6$

6. $\sqrt{x - 2} = -1$

7. $\sqrt{x + 2} - \sqrt{2x + 1} = 0$

8. $2x^{1/3} = -6$

9. $x^{3/4} - 8 = 19$

10. $(4x + 1)^{1/2} = 7$

11. $4(x - 4)^{1/4} - 3 = 5$

Error Analysis **Describe and correct the error in solving the equation.**

12.
$$\sqrt[3]{3x - 8} = 4$$
$$\left(\sqrt[3]{3x - 8}\right)^3 = 4$$
$$3x - 8 = 4$$
$$3x = 12$$
$$x = 4 \quad \times$$

13.
$$8x^{3/2} = 1000$$
$$8(x^{3/2})^{2/3} = 1000^{2/3}$$
$$8x = 100$$
$$x = \frac{25}{2} \quad \times$$

Practice and Applications

STUDENT HELP

HOMEWORK HELP
Example 1: Exs. 18–26
Example 2: Exs. 18–26
Example 3: Exs. 27–35
Example 4: Exs. 36–44
Example 5: Exs. 45–53

Checking Solutions **Check whether the given value is a solution of the equation.**

14. $\sqrt[4]{x} + 3 = 5$; 16

15. $\sqrt{x + 5} - \sqrt{2x} = 0$; 5

16. $x^{2/3} - 8 = 1$; 9

17. $(x - 5)^{1/2} - 6 = -3$; 14

Solving Radical Equations **Solve the equation.**

18. $\sqrt{x + 4} = 0$

19. $\sqrt[3]{x} - 4 = 0$

20. $\sqrt{3x} - 9 = 0$

21. $\sqrt{2x} - 5 = 3$

22. $\sqrt[3]{4x} + 5 = 7$

23. $3\sqrt{x - 7} = 9$

24. $4\sqrt[4]{8x + 9} - 12 = 0$

25. $2\sqrt[3]{4x + 5} - 9 = 1$

26. $-2\sqrt{2x - 1} + 8 = -2$

Solving Equations with Two Radicals **Solve the equation. Check for extraneous solutions.**

27. $\sqrt{3x - 1} = \sqrt{2x + 4}$

28. $\sqrt{4x - 5} = \sqrt{x + 7}$

29. $\sqrt{x - 7} = \sqrt{2x + 3}$

30. $\sqrt{4x + 9} = \sqrt{7x - 12}$

31. $\sqrt[3]{x - 6} - \sqrt[3]{2x + 7} = 0$

32. $\sqrt[3]{4x} - \sqrt[3]{x + 5} = 0$

33. $\sqrt[4]{2x + 5} - \sqrt[4]{6x + 3} = 0$

34. $\sqrt[4]{3x} + \sqrt[4]{x - 7} = 0$

35. Challenge Without solving, explain why the equation $\sqrt{2x - 3} = -\sqrt{3x + 1}$ does not have a solution.

Solving Radical Equations Solve the equation. Check for extraneous solutions.

36. $x - 6 = \sqrt{3x}$

37. $x - 10 = \sqrt{9x}$

38. $x - \frac{1}{2} = \sqrt{\frac{1}{2}x}$

39. $x = \sqrt{16x + 225}$

40. $\sqrt{2x + 15} = x$

41. $\sqrt{x - 1} = x - 3$

42. $\sqrt{4x + 9} = x + 1$

43. $\sqrt{21x + 1} = x + 5$

44. $\sqrt{44 - 2x} = x - 10$

Solving Equations with Rational Exponents Solve the equation. Check for extraneous solutions.

45. $x^{5/3} = 32$

46. $x^{1/4} + 3 = 0$

47. $3x^{3/2} = 24$

48. $2x^{3/4} - 14 = 40$

49. $(x - 6)^{1/3} = -3$

50. $(3x + 5)^{3/2} = 125$

51. $3(2x + 7)^{1/4} = 6$

52. $\frac{1}{3}(10x - 7)^{4/5} = 27$

53. $(10x - 9)^{3/4} + 1 = 28$

EXAMPLE	**Use a Radical Equation**

Pendulum Clock The period of a pendulum is the time that it takes the pendulum to complete one cycle. The time t (in seconds) for a pendulum to complete one cycle is given by

$$t = 2\pi\sqrt{\frac{L}{32}}$$

where L is the length of the pendulum in feet. You have a clock whose pendulum has a period of 1.6 seconds. To the nearest tenth of a foot, how long is the pendulum?

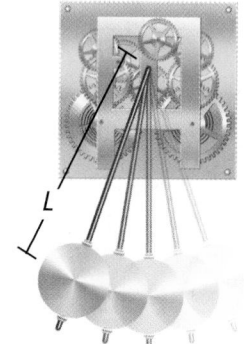

L

Solution

$t = 2\pi\sqrt{\dfrac{L}{32}}$	Write original equation.
$1.6 = 2\pi\sqrt{\dfrac{L}{32}}$	Substitute 1.6 for t.
$\dfrac{1.6}{2\pi} = \sqrt{\dfrac{L}{32}}$	Divide each side by 2π.
$\left(\dfrac{1.6}{2\pi}\right)^2 = \dfrac{L}{32}$	Square each side.
$32\left(\dfrac{1.6}{2\pi}\right)^2 = L$	Multiply each side by 32.
$2.1 \approx L$	Use a calculator.

ANSWER▶ The length of the pendulum is about 2.1 feet.

Link to

ARCHEOLOGY

STONE SPHERES
The Moeraki Boulders are stone spheres that were discovered along the coast of New Zealand. They have diameters of around 6 feet.

54. Pendulum Clock Suppose the clock in the example above has a period of 2 seconds. To the nearest tenth of a foot, how long is the pendulum?

55. Pendulum A pendulum on display at a museum has a period of about 11 seconds. To the nearest foot, how long is the pendulum?

56. Stone Spheres A formula for the radius r of a sphere is

$$r = \frac{1}{2}\sqrt{\frac{S}{\pi}}$$

where S is the surface area of the sphere. A stone sphere has a radius of about 6 feet. Find the surface area of the sphere to the nearest square foot.

57. Hang Time "Hang time" is the time you are suspended in the air during a jump. Hang time t (in seconds) is given by the function $t = 0.5\sqrt{h}$ where h is the height in feet to which you jump. Suppose a kangaroo and a snowboarder jump with the hang times shown. Find the heights to the nearest tenth of a foot that the kangaroo and the snowboarder jump.

$t = 0.81$ second

$t = 1.12$ seconds

58. Velocity The velocity v (in feet per second) of a free-falling object can be calculated using the formula

$$v = \sqrt{64h}$$

where h is the height in feet from which the object falls. A rock falls from a cliff and hits the ground below with a velocity of 50.6 feet per second. To the nearest foot, how far does the rock fall?

59. Product Pricing A company determines that the price p (in dollars) of a product can be modeled by

$$p = 70 - \sqrt{0.02x + 1}$$

where x is the number of units of the product demanded per day. If the price of the product is $67, what is the number of units demanded per day?

60. Elephants The shoulder height h (in centimeters) of a male African elephant can be modeled by

$$h = 62.5\sqrt[3]{t} + 75.8$$

where t is the elephant's age in years. Find the ages of two elephants, one with a shoulder height of 150 centimeters and the other with a shoulder height of 250 centimeters.

Standardized Test Practice

61. Multiple Choice What is the solution of $\sqrt{4x - 7} = 7$?

 (A) $\dfrac{7}{2}$ (B) 14   (C) 49   (D) no real solution

62. Multiple Choice What is the solution of $\sqrt{7x - 5} = x + 1$?

 (F) 2   (G) 2, 3   (H) 3   (J) no real solution

63. Multiple Choice What is the solution of $\sqrt[4]{2x - 3} = \sqrt[4]{x - 4}$?

 (A) −5   (B) −1   (C) 1   (D) no real solution

64. Multiple Choice What is the solution of $3(7x + 1)^{2/3} = 48$?

 (F) $\dfrac{15}{7}$ (G) 9   (H) 16   (J) no real solution

Mixed Review

Solving Linear Systems Solve the system using substitution. *(Lesson 3.2)*

65. $3x + y = 7$
$2x - y = -2$

66. $x + 2y = -1$
$2x + 3y = -3$

67. $3x + 4y = 0$
$2x + y = -5$

68. $x + 2y = 1$
$-x + y = -7$

69. $3x + y = 6$
$x - 2y = -12$

70. $x + 3y = -2$
$3x + 2y = 1$

Graphing Functions Graph the absolute value function. *(Lesson 4.6)*

71. $y = |x|$

72. $y = 2|x|$

73. $y = 4|x|$

Solving Equations Use the quadratic formula to solve the equation. *(Lesson 5.9)*

74. $2x^2 - 11x + 5 = 0$

75. $3x^2 - 4x - 6 = 0$

76. $2x^2 + x + 2 = 0$

77. $x^2 + 7x + 13 = 0$

78. $x^2 - 3x + 1 = 0$

79. $4x^2 + 10x - 9 = 0$

Geometry Skills

Pythagorean Theorem Find the unknown side length.

80.
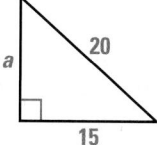

81.
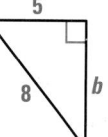

82.
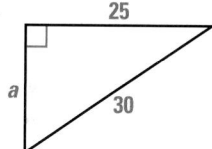

Quiz 1

Lesson 7.1 **Evaluate the expresion.**

1. $\sqrt[3]{729}$

2. $244^{1/2}$

3. $49^{3/2}$

Lesson 7.2 **Write the expression in simplest form. Assume all variables are positive.**

4. $\sqrt[3]{27x^6}$

5. $\sqrt[4]{x^8y^4}$

6. $\sqrt[3]{8x^3y^6}$

Lesson 7.2 **Simplify the expression. Write your answer using positive exponents only. Assume all variables are positive.**

7. $(8x^2)^{-1/3}$

8. $(x^8y^5)^{1/4}$

9. $(4x^4y^3)^{3/2}$

10. $\sqrt[3]{128y^9}$

11. $\sqrt[4]{\dfrac{32x^4}{y^8}}$

12. $\sqrt[2]{\dfrac{x^3}{8y^2}}$

13. $\dfrac{x}{x^{1/3}}$

14. $\left(\dfrac{x^3}{y^4}\right)^{-1/2}$

15. $\dfrac{x^2y^{1/3}}{x^{1/2}x^{2/3}}$

Lesson 7.3 **Solve the equation. Check for extraneous solutions.**

16. $\sqrt[4]{x} + 15 = 18$

17. $3\sqrt[3]{x - 5} - 4 = 2$

18. $\sqrt{x + 11} = x - 1$

19. $\sqrt{x - 3} = x - 3$

20. $\sqrt{3x - 1} = \sqrt{2x + 5}$

21. $2x^{1/2} - 5 = 59$

Lesson 7.3 **22. Tennis** You can find the volume V of a sphere with radius r using the formula $V = \dfrac{4}{3}\pi r^3$. You have a tennis ball that has a volume of 150 cubic centimeters. To the nearest tenth of a centimeter, find the radius of the ball.

You can use the *Intersect* feature of a graphing calculator to solve radical equations and check their solutions.

EXAMPLE 1

Solve $\sqrt{2x + 1} = x - 1$.

SOLUTION

1 In order to solve $\sqrt{2x + 1} = x - 1$, you can graph $y = \sqrt{2x + 1}$ and $y = x - 1$ and find the intersection of the graphs.

Enter $y = \sqrt{2x + 1}$ and $y = x - 1$ into a graphing calculator.

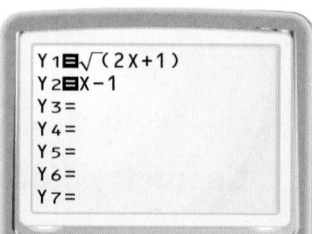

2 Graph the equations from Step 1. Then select the *Intersect* feature.

3 The intersection of the graphs is shown. The solution of $\sqrt{2x + 1} = x - 1$ is the *x*-coordinate of the point of intersection, or 4.

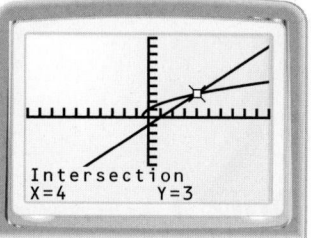

EXAMPLE 2

Tell whether 3 is a solution of the equation $\sqrt[3]{4 - 15x} = x + 8$.

SOLUTION

1 Enter $y = \sqrt[3]{4 - 15x}$ and $y = x + 8$ into the graphing calculator.

2 Graph the equations from Step 1. Then select the *Intersect* feature.

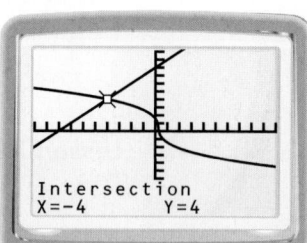

3 The intersection of the graphs is shown. You can see that the graphs do *not* intersect at 3, so 3 is *not* a solution of the equation. The solution is −4.

EXERCISES

Solve the equation using a graphing calculator.

1. $\sqrt{x + 3} = x + 1$ **2.** $\sqrt{x + 10} = x - 2$ **3.** $\sqrt{3x + 13} = x + 1$

4. $\sqrt[3]{x} = x - 3$ **5.** $\sqrt[3]{x + 4} = x + 1$ **6.** $\sqrt[3]{x - 5} = x + 2$

Use a graphing calculator to tell whether the given value is a solution of the equation.

7. $\sqrt[3]{7x - 5x} = x - 5$; 3   **8.** $\sqrt[3]{3x^2 + 9x} = x + 3$; −3.5

9. If you solve $\sqrt{2x + 1} = x - 1$ algebraically, the solutions are 0 and 4. Use the graph from Example 1 to explain how you know that 0 is an extraneous solution.

7.4 Function Operations and Composition of Functions

Key Words
- composition of functions

GOAL Perform operations with functions, including composition of functions.

How can you calculate the cost of your purchase at a hair salon?

In Example 5, you will use functions to calculate the amount of money that you will spend at a hair salon given various discounts.

In Chapter 6, you learned how to add, subtract, multiply, and divide polynomial functions. These operations can be defined for other types of functions as well.

Operations on Functions

Let $f(x)$ and $g(x)$ be any two functions. You can add, subtract, multiply, or divide $f(x)$ and $g(x)$ to form a new function $h(x)$.

Operation	Definition	Example Let $f(x) = 2x$ and $g(x) = x + 1$
Addition	$h(x) = f(x) + g(x)$	$h(x) = 2x + (x + 1) = 3x + 1$
Subtraction	$h(x) = f(x) - g(x)$	$h(x) = 2x - (x + 1) = x - 1$
Multiplication	$h(x) = f(x) \cdot g(x)$	$h(x) = (2x)(x + 1) = 2x^2 + 2x$
Division	$h(x) = \dfrac{f(x)}{g(x)}$	$h(x) = \dfrac{2x}{x + 1}, x \neq -1$

The domain of h consists of the x-values that are in the domains of both f and g. When h involves division, the domain does not include x-values for which the denominator is equal to zero.

EXAMPLE 1 Add and Subtract Functions

Let $f(x) = 4x^2$ and $g(x) = x + 1$. Find $h(x)$ and state its domain.

a. $h(x) = f(x) + g(x)$
b. $h(x) = f(x) - g(x)$

Solution

a. $h(x) = f(x) + g(x)$
$= 4x^2 + (x + 1)$
$= 4x^2 + x + 1$

b. $h(x) = f(x) - g(x)$
$= 4x^2 - (x + 1)$
$= 4x^2 - x - 1$

In both parts (*a*) and (*b*), the domains of f and g are all real numbers. So, the domain of h is all real numbers.

EXAMPLE 2 Multiply and Divide Functions

Let $f(x) = x^3$ and $g(x) = 2x$. Find $h(x)$ and state its domain.

a. $h(x) = f(x) \cdot g(x)$

b. $h(x) = \dfrac{f(x)}{g(x)}$

Solution

a. $f(x) \cdot g(x) = (x^3)(2x)$

$\qquad = 2x^{(3+1)}$

$\qquad = 2x^4$

The domains of both f and g are all real numbers. So, the domain of $h(x)$ is all real numbers.

b. $\dfrac{f(x)}{g(x)} = \dfrac{x^3}{2x}$

$\qquad = \dfrac{1}{2}x^{(3-1)}$

$\qquad = \dfrac{1}{2}x^2$

Because $g(0) = 0$, $\dfrac{f}{g}$ is undefined when $x = 0$. So, the domain of $h(x)$ is all real numbers except 0.

Checkpoint ✓ Perform Function Operations

Let $f(x) = 3x$ and $g(x) = x - 1$. Find $h(x)$ and state its domain.

1. $h(x) = f(x) + g(x)$ **2.** $h(x) = f(x) \cdot g(x)$ **3.** $h(x) = \dfrac{f(x)}{g(x)}$

STUDENT HELP

READING ALGEBRA
The composition $f(g(x))$ is read "f of g of x."

Composition of Functions Another operation that can be performed with two functions is **composition of functions**. You can form the composition of a function f with a function g by replacing each variable in f with the expression for g. The composition of f with g is written as $f(g(x))$.

For example, let $f(x) = 2x$ and $g(x) = 5x + 3$. The composition of f with g is:

$$f(g(x)) = f(5x + 3) = 2(5x + 3) = 10x + 6$$

The composition of g with f is:

$$g(f(x)) = g(2x) = 5(2x) + 3 = 10x + 3$$

Note that $f(g(x))$ does not mean the same thing as $g(f(x))$. As with subtraction and division of functions, you need to be alert to the order of functions when they are composed. In general, $f(g(x))$ is not equal to $g(f(x))$.

Composition of Functions

The composition of a function f with a function g is:

$$h(x) = f(g(x))$$

The domain of h is the set of all x-values where x is in the domain of g and $g(x)$ is in the domain of f.

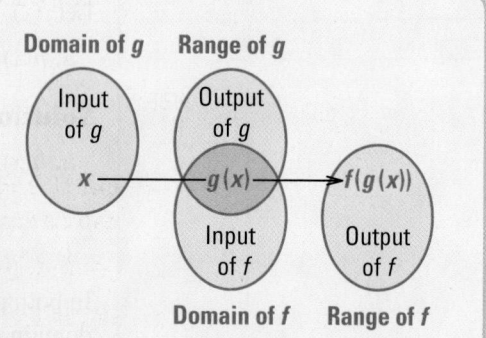

EXAMPLE 3 **Write a Composition of Functions**

Let $f(x) = x^2$ and $g(x) = 2x + 3$. Find the following.

a. $f(g(x))$ **b.** $g(f(x))$ **c.** the domain of each composition

Solution

To find the compositions, write the composition, substitute the expression for the inner function in the outer function, and simplify.

a. $f(g(x)) = f(2x + 3) = (2x + 3)^2 = 4x^2 + 12x + 9$

b. $g(f(x)) = g(x^2) = 2(x^2) + 3 = 2x^2 + 3$

c. The domain of each function is all real numbers, so the domain of each composition is all real numbers.

EXAMPLE 4 **Evaluate a Composition of Functions**

Let $f(x) = x^2 + 3$ and $g(x) = 5x$. Evaluate $f(g(2))$.

Solution

To evaluate $f(g(2))$, first find $g(2)$:

$$g(2) = 5(2) = 10$$

Then substitute $g(2) = 10$ into $f(g(2))$:

$$f(g(2)) = f(10) = 10^2 + 3 = 100 + 3 = 103$$

STUDENT HELP

READING ALGEBRA
Note that evaluating $f(g(2))$ is the same as finding the value of $f(g(x))$ when $x = 2$.

EXAMPLE 5 **Model a Real-World Situation**

Hair Salon You have a coupon for $10 off the cost of your purchase at a hair salon. The salon also offers a discount off your purchase, as shown.

Let x be the cost of your purchase. Then $f(x) = x - 10$ is the cost of the purchase using your coupon, and $g(x) = 0.85x$ is the cost of your purchase with the salon's discount. Find $g(f(x))$. Tell what it represents.

Solution

$$g(f(x)) = g(x - 10) = 0.85(x - 10) = 0.85x - 8.5$$

The composition $g(f(x))$ represents the cost of your purchase when the $10 coupon is applied before the 15% discount.

Checkpoint ✓ **Find and Evaluate Compositions of Functions**

Let $f(x) = x^2$ and $g(x) = x - 1$. Find the composition. Then evaluate the composition when $x = 2$.

4. $f(g(x))$ **5.** $g(f(x))$ **6.** $f(f(x))$ **7.** $g(g(x))$

8. In Example 5, find $f(g(x))$. Tell what it represents. Evaluate $f(g(x))$ if you spend $35 at the hair salon.

Guided Practice

Vocabulary Check

1. Let $f(x) = x$ and $g(x) = \sqrt{x}$. What is the domain of $f(x) + g(x)$?

2. Find the common meaning of the word "composition" in a dictionary. How can the common meaning help you remember the mathematical meaning?

Skill Check

Let $f(x) = 2x$ and $g(x) = x + 3$. Find $h(x)$ and state its domain.

3. $h(x) = f(x) + g(x)$ **4.** $h(x) = f(x) - g(x)$ **5.** $h(x) = f(x) \cdot g(x)$

6. $h(x) = \dfrac{f(x)}{g(x)}$ **7.** $h(x) = g(x) - f(x)$ **8.** $h(x) = \dfrac{g(x)}{f(x)}$

Let $f(x) = x^2 + x - 2$ and $g(x) = x + 1$. Find the composition.

9. $f(g(x))$ **10.** $g(f(x))$ **11.** $g(g(x))$

Let $f(x) = x^2 - 3$ and $g(x) = 4x$. Describe and correct the error in finding the composition.

12.

$f(g(x)) = f(4x)$
$= (x^2 - 3)(4x)$
$= 4x^3 - 12x$ ✗

13.

$f(g(x)) = f(4x)$
$= 4x^2 - 3$ ✗

Practice and Applications

STUDENT HELP

HOMEWORK HELP
Example 1: Exs. 14–19, 40–41
Example 2: Exs. 20–25, 42–44
Example 3: Exs. 26–31, 45–47
Example 4: Exs. 32–39
Example 5: Exs. 48–56

Adding and Subtracting Functions **Let $f(x) = 2x^2 + x - 3$ and $g(x) = x^2 + 1$. Find $h(x)$ and state its domain.**

14. $h(x) = f(x) + g(x)$ **15.** $h(x) = g(x) + f(x)$ **16.** $h(x) = f(x) + f(x)$

17. $h(x) = g(x) + g(x)$ **18.** $h(x) = f(x) - g(x)$ **19.** $h(x) = g(x) - f(x)$

Multiplying and Dividing Functions **Let $f(x) = 4x^2$ and $g(x) = 3x^3$. Find $h(x)$ and state its domain.**

20. $h(x) = f(x) \cdot g(x)$ **21.** $h(x) = g(x) \cdot f(x)$ **22.** $h(x) = f(x) \cdot f(x)$

23. $h(x) = g(x) \cdot g(x)$ **24.** $h(x) = \dfrac{f(x)}{g(x)}$ **25.** $h(x) = \dfrac{g(x)}{f(x)}$

Finding Compositions of Functions **Let $f(x) = x - 6$ and $g(x) = 4x^2$. Find the composition and the domain of the composition.**

26. $f(g(x))$ **27.** $g(f(x))$ **28.** $f(f(x))$

Finding Composition of Functions **Let $f(x) = \dfrac{1}{x + 5}$ and $g(x) = x^2$. Find the composition and the domain of the composition.**

29. $f(g(x))$ **30.** $g(f(x))$ **31.** $g(g(x))$

Evaluating Compositions Let $f(x) = x + 10$ and $g(x) = x - 2$. Evaluate the composition.

32. $f(g(1))$ **33.** $f(g(5))$ **34.** $g(f(4))$ **35.** $g(f(-2))$

Evaluating Compositions Let $f(x) = 3x + 4$ and $g(x) = 2x^2$. Evaluate the composition.

36. $f(g(2))$ **37.** $f(g(0))$ **38.** $g(f(-2))$ **39.** $g(f(1))$

Performing Function Operations Perform the operation using the given functions. Then state the domain of the resulting function.

40. Find $f + g$ given $f(x) = x + 5$ and $g(x) = 3x$.

41. Find $g - f$ given $f(x) = x^2 + 1$ and $g(x) = x^3 - x + 8$.

42. Find $f \cdot g$ given $f(x) = x + 1$ and $g(x) = 3x - 2$.

43. Find $\dfrac{f}{g}$ given $f(x) = 2x^5 - 4x$ and $g(x) = x^2$.

44. Find $\dfrac{f}{g}$ given $f(x) = x^2 - 1$ and $g(x) = x - 4$.

45. Find $f(g(x))$ given $f(x) = x + 1$ and $g(x) = 2x^2 - 5$.

46. Find $g(f(x))$ given $f(x) = \dfrac{1}{x^2}$ and $g(x) = x - 3$.

47. Find $f(f(x))$ given $f(x) = -5x - 10$.

48. Sales Bonus A salesperson at a car dealership is paid an annual salary plus a bonus of 5% of sales over \$300,000. Let x be the salesperson's total sales. Then $f(x) = x - 300{,}000$ is the amount of sales over \$300,000 and $g(x) = 0.05x$ is the amount of the salesperson's bonus of sales over \$300,000. So, the function $g(f(x))$ represents the salesperson's total earnings. Find $g(f(x))$ when the total sales are \$500,000.

Movies In Exercises 49–52, use the following information.

An online movie store is having a sale, as shown.

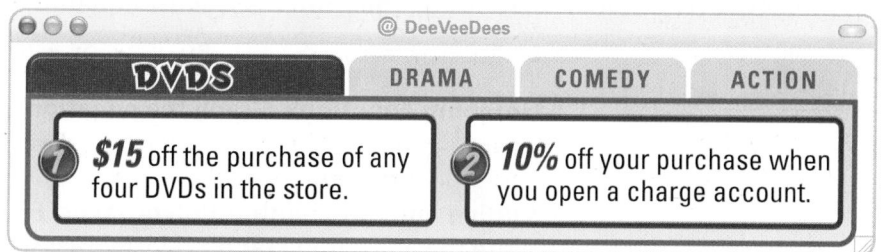

Let x be the total cost of the DVDs you buy. Then $f(x) = x - 15$ is the cost of your DVDs if you buy 4 DVDs, and $g(x) = 0.90x$ is the cost of your DVDs if you open a charge account. You open a charge account and buy 4 DVDs.

49. Find $f(g(x))$ and tell what it represents.

50. Find $g(f(x))$ and tell what it represents.

51. Evaluate $f(g(x))$ and $g(f(x))$ if you buy \$85 worth of DVDs.

52. Critical Thinking Is it better for the customers of the online movie store to apply the \$15 discount before or after the 10% discount? Explain.

ORNITHOMIMIDS were slender, light-framed, bird-like dinosaurs that reached lengths of over 20 feet.

Paleontology In Exercises 53 and 54, use the following information.

The height h (in centimeters) at the hip of an ornithomimid, a type of dinosaur, can be estimated by

$$h(\ell) = 3.5\ell$$

where ℓ is the length of the dinosaur's instep in centimeters. The length of the dinosaur's instep can be modeled by $\ell(f) = 1.5f$ where f is the length of the footprint in centimeters.

53. Find the composition $h(\ell(f))$.

54. Use the composition function from Exercise 53 to calculate the height at the hip of an ornithomimid with a footprint that is 30 centimeters long.

55. Product Prices The manufacturer of a plasma television offers an instant rebate of $500 off of the price of a plasma television. An electronics store offers a 10% discount off of the price of the plasma television. The price of the plasma television is p dollars. Consider the functions:

$$f(x) = p - 500 \text{ and } g(x) = 0.90p$$

If the electronics store applies the rebate before the discount, which composition, $f(g(x))$ or $g(f(x))$, represents the final price? Explain.

56. Critical Thinking Refer to the situation described in Exercise 55. Why would the electronics store apply the rebate before the discount?

Standardized Test Practice

57. Multiple Choice Let $f(x) = 3x - 1$ and $g(x) = x + 2$. What is $f \cdot g$?

Ⓐ $4x + 1$ Ⓑ $-2x + 3$

Ⓒ $3x^2 + 5x - 2$ Ⓓ $3x + 5$

58. Multiple Choice Let $f(x) = 4x + 3$ and $g(x) = x^2$. What is $g(f(x))$?

Ⓕ $x^2 + 4x + 3$ Ⓖ $16x^2 + 24x + 9$

Ⓗ $4x^2 + 3$ Ⓙ $x^2 - 4x - 3$

Mixed Review

Rewriting Equations Solve the equation for **y**. *(Lesson 1.5)*

59. $4x - 3y = -7$ **60.** $x = -5y + 6$ **61.** $x + y = -4$

Graphing Functions Graph the equation. *(Lesson 2.1)*

62. $y = 2x$ **63.** $y = x + 4$ **64.** $y = -2x + 5$

Adding and Subtracting Polynomials Find the sum or difference. Write the answer in standard form. *(Lesson 6.3)*

65. $(2x^2 + 3x - 4) + (-4x^2 + 7x + 10)$ **66.** $(x^3 + 3x^2 - 7x + 2) - (3x^2 + 2x - 5)$

67. $3(-2x^2 + 4x - 7) - (5x^2 + x - 3)$ **68.** $5(3x^3 + 4x + 7) - 2(-6x^3 + x - 12)$

Geometry Skills

Angles in Polygons Find the value of x given that the sum of the measures of the interior angles of a convex n-gon is $(n - 2) \cdot 180$.

69.

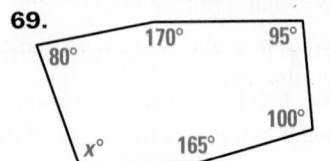

70.

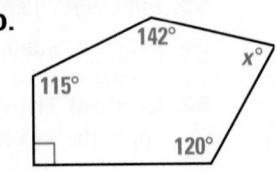

71.

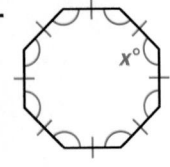

Goal

Find the inverse of a given linear function.

Materials

- graph paper
- straightedge

QUESTION

How are functions and their inverses related?

EXPLORE

1 Use the *work backward* strategy to solve the following problem. Then tell which operations you used and in which order.

> You go shopping and spend half of your money on a shirt. Then you spend $4 on lunch. You return home with $6. How much money did you have when you left home to go shopping?

2 Write a function $g(x)$ that gives the amount of money (in dollars) you had when you started shopping. Let x be the amount of money you had when you finished.

3 Write a different function $f(x)$ that gives the amount of money (in dollars) you had when you *finished* shopping. This time, let x be the amount of money you had when you *started* shopping.

4 Copy and complete the table for $f(x)$ and $g(f(x))$ for the given values of x. What do you notice about the results?

x	f(x)	g(f(x))
0	?	?
2	?	?
4	?	?
6	?	?

5 Graph $f(x)$ and $g(x)$ in the same coordinate plane. What do you notice about the graphs in relation to the line $y = x$?

THINK ABOUT IT

1. Find $f(g(x))$ and $g(f(x))$ for the functions in Steps 2 and 3. What do you notice about the results?

In Exercises 2–4, let $f(x) = 3x + 6$ and let $g(x) = \frac{1}{3}x - 2$.

2. Copy and complete the table. What do you notice about the results?

x	f(x)	g(f(x))
0	?	?
2	?	?
4	?	?

3. Find $f(g(x))$ and $g(f(x))$. What do you notice about the results?

4. Graph $f(x)$ and $g(x)$ in the same coordinate plane. What do you notice about the graphs in relation to the line $y = x$?

7.5 Inverse Functions

GOAL Find the inverses of linear and nonlinear functions.

Key Words
- inverse relation
- inverse functions

Prerequisite Skills

Solve for y.

1. $2y = 4x$
2. $3y - 6x = 9$
3. $y^3 = 5x$
4. $4y - 2x = 3$

In Lesson 2.1, you learned that a relation is a pairing of input and output values. For a given relation, an **inverse relation** switches input and output values. So, the domain of an inverse relation is the range of the original relation, and the range of an inverse relation is the domain of the original relation.

Original relation

Input x	−2	−1	0	1	2
Output y	−4	−2	0	2	4

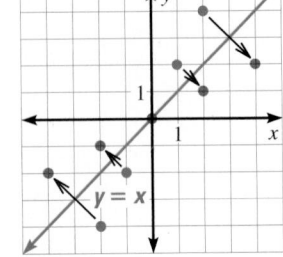

Inverse relation

Input x	−4	−2	0	2	4
Output y	−2	−1	0	1	2

Notice that the graph of an inverse relation is a *reflection* of the graph of the original relation. The line of reflection is $y = x$.

If both the original relation and the inverse relation are functions, then the two functions are called **inverse functions**.

Inverse Functions

Functions f and g are inverse functions if:
$$f(g(x)) = x \quad \text{and} \quad g(f(x)) = x$$
The inverse of f can be denoted by f^{-1}, which is read as "f inverse."

STUDENT HELP

READING ALGEBRA
When f^{-1} is used in function notation, it refers to the inverse of f, not the reciprocal of f. The −1 should not be interpreted as an exponent.

EXAMPLE 1 Verify Inverse Functions

Verify that $f(x) = x + 3$ and $g(x) = x - 3$ are inverse functions.

Solution

To verify $f(x)$ and $g(x)$ are inverse functions, show that $f(g(x)) = x$ and $g(f(x)) = x$.

$$f(g(x)) = f(x - 3) \qquad\qquad g(f(x)) = g(x + 3)$$
$$= (x - 3) + 3 \qquad\qquad = (x + 3) - 3$$
$$= x \checkmark \qquad\qquad\qquad = x \checkmark$$

Checkpoint ✓ **Verify Inverse Functions**

1. Verify that $f(x) = 3x - 5$ and $g(x) = \frac{1}{3}x + \frac{5}{3}$ are inverse functions.

Finding Inverse Functions

You can find the inverse of a function by following these steps.

STEP ❶ *Replace* $f(x)$ with y (if the function is written using function notation).

STEP ❷ *Switch* x and y.

STEP ❸ *Solve* for y.

STUDENT HELP

SOLVING NOTE
In Example 2, notice that both the original function and its inverse are linear. For any linear function $f(x) = mx + b$, where $m \neq 0$, the inverse of the function is also linear.

EXAMPLE 2 Find the Inverse of a Linear Function

Find the inverse of the function $f(x) = 2x + 4$.

Solution

$f(x) = 2x + 4$	Write original function.
$y = 2x + 4$	Replace $f(x)$ with y.
$x = 2y + 4$	Switch x and y.
$x - 4 = 2y$	Subtract 4 from each side.
$\frac{1}{2}x - 2 = y$	Divide each side by 2 to solve for y.

ANSWER ▶ The inverse function is $f^{-1}(x) = \frac{1}{2}x - 2$.

Checkpoint ✓ *Find Inverse Functions*

Find the inverse of the function.

2. $f(x) = 4x$ **3.** $f(x) = 3x - 1$ **4.** $f(x) = -x + 3$

Horizontal Line Test In Chapter 2, you learned that a relation is a function only if no vertical line intersects its graph more than once. You can use the horizontal line test to tell if the inverse of a function is also a function.

Horizontal Line Test

If no horizontal line intersects the graph of a function f more than once, then the inverse of f is also a function. Consider the examples below.

The inverse of f is a function.   **The inverse of g is *not* a function.**

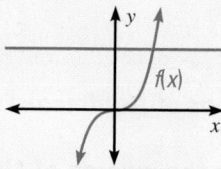   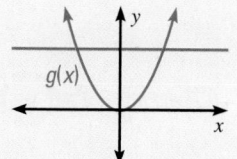

No horizontal line intersects the graph of f more than once.   **A horizontal line intersects the graph of g more than once.**

EXAMPLE **3** **Find the Inverse of a Nonlinear Function**

Determine whether the inverse of $f(x) = x^3 + 1$ is a function. Then find the inverse.

Solution

First, graph the function. Because no horizontal line intersects the graph more than once, the inverse of f is also a function.

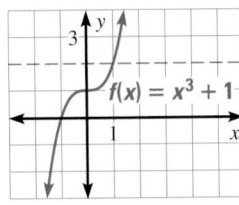

Next, find an equation for f^{-1}.

$f(x) = x^3 + 1$	Write original function.
$y = x^3 + 1$	Replace $f(x)$ with y.
$x = y^3 + 1$	Switch x and y.
$x - 1 = y^3$	Subtract 1 from each side.
$\sqrt[3]{x - 1} = y$	Take cube root of each side.

ANSWER ▶ The inverse function is $f^{-1}(x) = \sqrt[3]{x - 1}$.

Restricted Domains In the following example, a restriction is placed on the domain of the function f.

EXAMPLE **4** **Find the Inverse of a Nonlinear Function**

Determine whether the inverse of $f(x) = x^2$, where $x \geq 0$, is a function. Then find the inverse.

Solution

First, graph the function. Notice that the restriction on the domain of f results in the graph being only half of a parabola. Because no horizontal line intersects the graph more than once, the inverse of f is also a function.

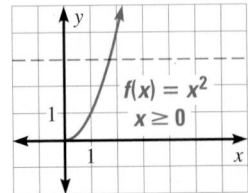

Next, find an equation for f^{-1}.

$f(x) = x^2$	Write original function.
$y = x^2$	Replace $f(x)$ with y.
$x = y^2$	Switch x and y ($y \geq 0$).
$\sqrt{x} = y$	Take square root of each side; x cannot be negative.

ANSWER ▶ The inverse function is $f^{-1}(x) = \sqrt{x}$, $x \geq 0$.

STUDENT HELP

SOLVING NOTE
When a function, such as $f(x) = x^2$, does not pass the horizontal line test, you may be able to restrict the domain to a portion of the graph that does pass the test.

Checkpoint ✔ **Find Inverse Functions of Nonlinear Functions**

Determine whether the inverse of f is a function. Then find the inverse.

5. $f(x) = x^3 - 2$ **6.** $f(x) = 9x^2, x \geq 0$ **7.** $f(x) = x^4, x \geq 0$

Guided Practice

Vocabulary Check

1. Copy and complete the statement: If $f(g(x)) = x$ and $g(f(x)) = x$, then the functions f and g are __?__ functions.

2. Explain how to use the horizontal line test to determine whether the inverse of a function is also a function.

3. Explain the steps in finding an inverse function.

Skill Check

Verify that f and g are inverse functions.

4. $f(x) = x - 6$, $g(x) = x + 6$

5. $f(x) = 2x - 5$, $g(x) = \frac{1}{2}x + \frac{5}{2}$

6. $f(x) = 4x^2$, $x \ge 0$; $g(x) = \frac{\sqrt{x}}{2}$

7. $f(x) = x^2 - 3$, $x \ge 0$; $g(x) = \sqrt{x + 3}$

Find the inverse of the function.

8. $f(x) = -x + 7$

9. $f(x) = 3x + 4$

10. $f(x) = 2x - 4$

Determine whether the inverse of f is a function. Then find the inverse.

11. $f(x) = \frac{1}{5}x^3$

12. $f(x) = x^3 - 5$

13. $f(x) = 3x^2$, $x \ge 0$

14. The graphs of the function $y = x^2$ and its reflection in $y = x$ are shown. Explain why the inverse of $y = x^2$ is *not* an inverse function.

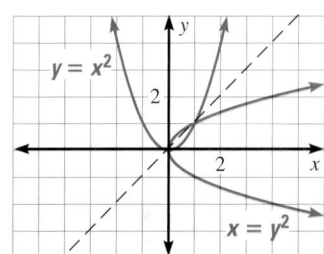

Practice and Applications

STUDENT HELP

HOMEWORK HELP
Example 1: Exs. 15–20
Example 2: Exs. 21–32
Example 3: Exs. 33–53
Example 4: Exs. 33–53

Verifying Inverses **Verify that f and g are inverse functions.**

15. $f(x) = x + 5$, $g(x) = x - 5$

16. $f(x) = 2x + 6$, $g(x) = \frac{1}{2}x - 3$

17. $f(x) = 4x - 3$, $g(x) = \frac{1}{4}x + \frac{3}{4}$

18. $f(x) = \frac{2}{5}x + 4$, $g(x) = \frac{5}{2}x - 10$

19. $f(x) = 16x^2$, $x \ge 0$; $g(x) = \frac{\sqrt{x}}{4}$

20. $f(x) = 3x^3 + 6$, $g(x) = \sqrt[3]{\frac{x - 6}{3}}$

Inverses of Linear Functions **Find the inverse of the function.**

21. $f(x) = x + 7$

22. $f(x) = -3x + 3$

23. $f(x) = 4x + 1$

24. $f(x) = 3x - 7$

25. $f(x) = 8x - 1$

26. $f(x) = -x - 5$

27. $f(x) = 4x + 10$

28. $f(x) = -5x + 25$

29. $f(x) = 12x - 54$

30. $f(x) = \frac{1}{4}x + 1$

31. $f(x) = -\frac{5}{7}x$

32. $f(x) = \frac{2}{3}x - \frac{4}{3}$

Inverses of Nonlinear Functions Determine whether the inverse of f is a function. Then find the inverse.

33. $f(x) = 8x^3$

34. $f(x) = -x^2 + 3$

35. $f(x) = x^3 + 4$

36. $f(x) = 9x^2, x \geq 0$

37. $f(x) = \frac{1}{4}x^2$

38. $f(x) = \frac{1}{5}x^5$

39. $f(x) = 2x^2 - 3$

40. $f(x) = x^4, x \geq 0$

41. $f(x) = 5 - x^3$

42. $f(x) = x^5 - 2$

43. $f(x) = x^5 + 1$

44. $f(x) = 3x^2 - 4$

45. $f(x) = 9x^2 + 7, x \geq 0$

46. $f(x) = \frac{1}{7}x^3 - 3$

47. $f(x) = 2x^3 + 2$

48. $f(x) = 2x^3 - 5$

49. $f(x) = -x^2, x \geq 0$

50. $f(x) = 16x^4 + 1, x \geq 0$

51. $f(x) = 8x^3 - 6$

52. $f(x) = 4x^2 - 1$

53. $f(x) = \frac{1}{2}x^4 - 1, x \geq 0$

EXAMPLE **Write an Inverse Model**

Fitness Elastic bands can be stretched when exercising to provide a range of resistance. A band's resistance R (in pounds) can be modeled by the function

$$R = \frac{3}{8}\ell - 5$$

where ℓ is the total length of the stretched band in inches.

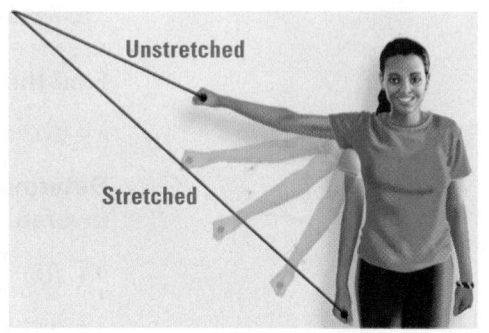

Unstretched

Stretched

a. Find the inverse of the function.

b. Use the inverse function to find the length at which the band will provide 19 pounds of resistance.

Solution

a.

$R = \frac{3}{8}\ell - 5$ Write original function.

$R + 5 = \frac{3}{8}\ell$ Add 5 to each side.

$\frac{8}{3}(R + 5) = \ell$ Multiply each side by $\frac{8}{3}$.

$\frac{8}{3}R + \frac{40}{3} = \ell$ Simplify.

STUDENT HELP

SOLVING NOTE

Notice that you do not switch the variables when you are finding inverses for models. This would be confusing, because the letters remind you of the real-world quantities they represent.

b. To find the length at which the band provides 19 pounds of resistance, substitute **19** for R in the inverse function.

$$\ell = \frac{8}{3}R + \frac{40}{3} = \frac{8}{3}(19) + \frac{40}{3} = \frac{152}{3} + \frac{40}{3} = \frac{192}{3} = 64$$

ANSWER ▶ The band provides 19 pounds of resistance when stretched 64 inches.

---

54. Bowling In bowling, a handicap is an adjustment to a bowler's score to even out differences in ability levels. You can find a bowler's handicap h in a particular bowling league using the formula

$$h = 0.9(200 - a)$$

where a is the bowler's average. Find the inverse of the function. Then find a bowler's average if the bowler's handicap is 45.

55. *Geometry Link* The volume V of a sphere can be found using the formula

$$V = \frac{4}{3}\pi r^3$$

where r is the radius of the sphere. Find the inverse of the function. Then find the radius of a sphere that has a volume of 382 cubic inches.

56. Converting Units The driving distance from a destination in Cleveland, Ohio, to a destination in Pittsburgh, Pennsylvania, is 114 miles. You can use the formula

$$m = 0.62k$$

to convert a distance in miles m to kilometers k. Find the inverse of the function. Then find the distance from Cleveland to Pittsburgh in kilometers.

57. Seagulls A seagull is flying at a height of 50 feet when it drops a clam. The height h (in feet) of the clam above the ground can be modeled by the function

$$h = -16t^2 + 50$$

where t is the time in seconds since the seagull dropped the clam. Find the inverse of the function. Then find the time when the clam is 15 feet above the ground.

50 feet

Logical Reasoning In Exercises 58 and 59, tell whether the statement is *true* or *false*. Explain your reasoning.

58. The inverse of the function $f(x) = ax^2 - bx + c$ is a function.

59. The inverse of the function $f(x) = mx + b$ is a function, provided $m \neq 0$.

Challenge In Exercises 60–63, you will explore functions that are their own inverses.

60. The functions $f(x) = x$ and $g(x) = -x + 1$ are their own inverses. Graph each function and explain why this is true.

61. Graph three other linear functions that are their own inverses.

62. Write the equations of the lines you graphed in Exercise 61.

63. Use your equations from Exercise 62 to find a general formula for a family of linear equations that are their own inverses.

Standardized Test Practice

64. Multiple Choice Which function is the inverse of $f(x) = 2x - 6$?

   A $f^{-1}(x) = -2x + 6$ **B** $f^{-1}(x) = \frac{1}{2}x - 3$

   C $f^{-1}(x) = \frac{1}{2}x + 3$ **D** $f^{-1}(x) = \frac{1}{2}x + 6$

65. Multiple Choice Which function is the inverse of $f(x) = 8x^3 + 6$?

   F $f^{-1}(x) = \dfrac{\sqrt[3]{x - 6}}{2}$ **G** $f^{-1}(x) = \dfrac{\sqrt[3]{x - 6}}{8}$

   H $f^{-1}(x) = \sqrt[3]{\dfrac{x - 6}{2}}$ **J** $f^{-1}(x) = -8x^3 - 6$

66. Multiple Choice Which two functions are *not* inverse functions?

Ⓐ $f(x) = 4x^2 - 5$, $x \geq 0$ and $f^{-1}(x) = \dfrac{\sqrt{x+5}}{2}$

Ⓑ $f(x) = 4x^2 - 5$, $x \geq 0$ and $f^{-1}(x) = \sqrt{\dfrac{x+5}{2}}$

Ⓒ $f(x) = 2x^2 - 5$, $x \geq 0$ and $f^{-1}(x) = \sqrt{\dfrac{x+5}{2}}$

Ⓓ $f(x) = 4x^2 + 5$, $x \geq 0$ and $f^{-1}(x) = \sqrt{\dfrac{x-5}{2}}$

Mixed Review

Quadratic Functions Graph the function. Label the vertex and axis of symmetry. *(Lesson 5.1)*

67. $y = x^2 + 3x - 4$ **68.** $y = x^2 + 8x + 15$ **69.** $y = (x + 1)^2 - 1$

Polynomial Functions Graph the polynomial function using the domain $x = -3, -2, -1, 0, 1, 2, 3$. *(Lesson 6.2)*

70. $f(x) = x^3 + 3$ **71.** $f(x) = -x^4 + 1$ **72.** $f(x) = x^5 - 1$

Radical Expressions Write the expression in simplest form. *(Lesson 7.2)*

73. $\sqrt[4]{80}$ **74.** $\sqrt[3]{25} \cdot \sqrt[3]{30}$ **75.** $\sqrt[5]{\dfrac{1}{16}}$

Geometry Skills

Transformations Tell whether the red triangle is a *translation*, a *reflection*, or a *rotation* of the blue triangle.

76. 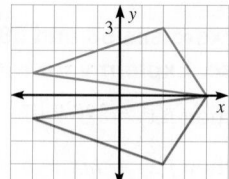   **77.** 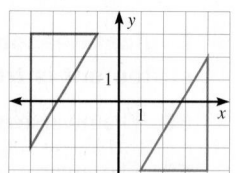   **78.**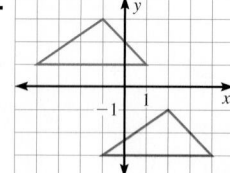

Quiz 2

Lesson 7.4   Let $f(x) = 4x$ and $g(x) = 2x + 5$. Perform the indicated operation and state the domain.

     1. $f(x) + g(x)$ **2.** $f(x) - g(x)$ **3.** $f(g(x))$ **4.** $g(f(x))$

Lesson 7.4   Let $f(x) = 2x^2$ and $g(x) = 3x - 2$. Perform the indicated operation and state the domain.

     5. $\dfrac{f(x)}{g(x)}$ **6.** $f(x) \cdot g(x)$ **7.** $f(f(x))$ **8.** $g(g(x))$

Lesson 7.5   Verify that f and g are inverse functions.

     9. $f(x) = x - 8$, $g(x) = x + 8$ **10.** $f(x) = 4x - 7$, $g(x) = \dfrac{1}{4}x + \dfrac{7}{4}$

Lesson 7.5   Find the inverse of the function.

     11. $f(x) = x + 6$ **12.** $f(x) = 4x - 2$ **13.** $f(x) = -2x + 3$

     14. $f(x) = x^3$ **15.** $f(x) = x^3 + 3$ **16.** $f(x) = 2x^2 - 1$, $x \geq 0$

You can use a graphing calculator to graph inverse functions.

EXAMPLE

Graph the inverse of $y = 3x - 4$.

SOLUTION

1 Graph the original function. Use the viewing
window $-10 \leq x \leq 10$ and $-10 \leq y \leq 10$.

The graph of $y = 3x - 4$ passes the horizontal
line test, so you know that the inverse of
$y = 3x - 4$ is also a function.

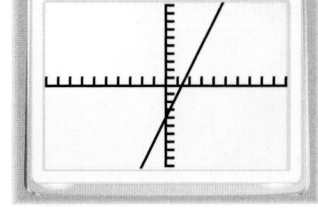

2 Use the *Draw Inverse* feature to graph
the inverse.

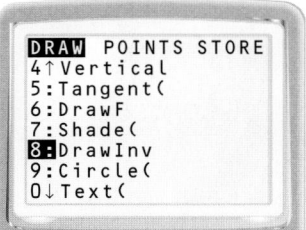

3 Display the graphs of the original function
and its inverse.

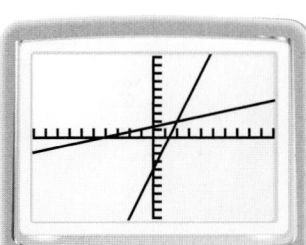

EXERCISES

**Graph the function on a graphing calculator. Determine whether the
inverse of the function is also a function. Then use the *Draw Inverse*
feature to graph the function's inverse in the same viewing window.**

1. $y = 2x + 5$

2. $y = 0.5x - 2$

3. $y = 0.4x + 1$

4. $y = -x + 3$

5. $y = x^2 + 1$

6. $y = 0.2x^2 - 2$

7. $y = x^2 - 7x + 10$

8. $y = x^2 - 4x$

9. $y = x^3 + 5$

10. $y = x^3 + 2x$

11. $y = x^3 - 2x^2 + 1$

12. $y = 2x^3 - x + 3$

13. $y = |x - 2|$

14. $y = |x + 4|$

15. $y = |x| + 3$

16. $y = |x| - 1$

17. $y = |x + 2| + 6$

18. $y = -|x + 1| + 5$

Goal

Compare graphs of functions of the form $y = a\sqrt{x}$ with the graph of $y = \sqrt{x}$ and determine how a affects the graph.

Materials

• graphing calculator or graph paper

QUESTION

How does the value of *a* affect the graph of $y = a\sqrt{x}$?

EXPLORE 1

1. Graph $y = \sqrt{x}$. The graph is shown to the right. If you use a graphing calculator, use the viewing window $-10 \le x \le 10$ and $-10 \le y \le 10$.

2. Graph $y = 2\sqrt{x}$ and $y = 3\sqrt{x}$.

3. Compare the graphs of $y = 2\sqrt{x}$ and $y = 3\sqrt{x}$ with the graph of $y = \sqrt{x}$. Are the graphs *vertical stretches*, *vertical shrinks*, or *reflections in the x-axis* of the graph of $y = \sqrt{x}$?

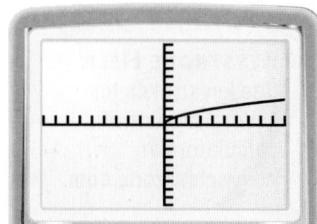

EXPLORE 2

1. Clear the graphs from Explore 1 from your calculator, but keep the graph of $y = \sqrt{x}$. Graph $y = \frac{1}{4}\sqrt{x}$ and $y = \frac{1}{2}\sqrt{x}$.

2. Compare the graphs of $y = \frac{1}{4}\sqrt{x}$ and $y = \frac{1}{2}\sqrt{x}$ with the graph of $y = \sqrt{x}$. Are the graphs *vertical stretches*, *vertical shrinks*, or *reflections in the x-axis* of the graph of $y = \sqrt{x}$?

EXPLORE 3

1. Clear the graphs from Explore 2 from your calculator, but keep the graph of $y = \sqrt{x}$. Graph $y = -2\sqrt{x}$ and $y = -3\sqrt{x}$.

2. Compare the graphs of $y = -2\sqrt{x}$ and $y = -3\sqrt{x}$ with the graph of $y = \sqrt{x}$. Are the graphs *vertical stretches*, *vertical shrinks*, or *reflections in the x-axis* of the graph of $y = \sqrt{x}$?

THINK ABOUT IT

1. Use your observations to copy and complete the table below.

Function	Value of a	How does a affect the graph of $y = a\sqrt{x}$?
$y = a\sqrt{x}$	$a > 1$	?
$y = a\sqrt{x}$	$0 < a < 1$	?
$y = a\sqrt{x}$	$a < 0$	?

Without graphing, tell whether the graph of the function would be a *vertical stretch*, *vertical shrink*, or *reflection in the x-axis* of the graph of $y = \sqrt{x}$.

2. $y = \frac{1}{3}\sqrt{x}$ 3. $y = -4\sqrt{x}$ 4. $y = 5\sqrt{x}$

Graphing Square Root and Cube Root Functions

Key Words

• radical function

Prerequisite Skills

Graph the functions in the same coordinate plane.

1. $y = x^2$, $y = x^2 + 3$

2. $y = x^3$, $y = x^3 - 2$

GOAL Graph square root and cube root functions.

How can you use skid marks to analyze the speed of a car?

In Example 5, you will use a square root function to find the speed of a car before an accident.

The square root function $y = \sqrt{x}$ is an example of a *radical function*. A **radical function** contains a radical with a variable in its radicand. The functions $y = \sqrt[3]{4x}$ and $y = \sqrt{x + 1}$ are also radical functions.

Graphs of Square Root and Cube Root Functions

The graphs of the square root function $y = a\sqrt{x}$ where $a > 0$ and the cube root function $y = a\sqrt[3]{x}$ where $a > 0$ are shown.

SQUARE ROOT FUNCTION

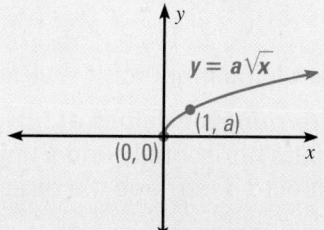

$y = a\sqrt{x}$
$(1, a)$
$(0, 0)$

CUBE ROOT FUNCTION

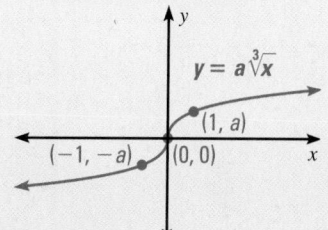

$y = a\sqrt[3]{x}$
$(1, a)$
$(-1, -a)$ $(0, 0)$

The domain of $y = a\sqrt{x}$ is $x \geq 0$. The range is $y \geq 0$ when $a > 0$.

The domain and range of $y = a\sqrt[3]{x}$ are all real numbers.

EXAMPLE 1 Graph a Square Root Function

Graph $y = \frac{1}{2}\sqrt{x}$. Then state its domain and range.

Solution

Make a table of values. Then plot the points from the table and connect them with a smooth curve.

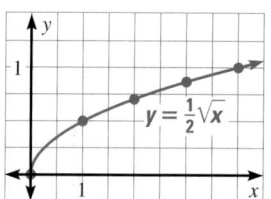

$y = \frac{1}{2}\sqrt{x}$

x	0	1	2	3	4
y	0	0.5	0.71	0.87	1

Because the radicand of a square root is always positive, the domain is $x \geq 0$.

You can see from the graph that the range is $y \geq 0$.

EXAMPLE **2** **Graph a Cube Root Function**

Graph $y = -3\sqrt[3]{x}$. Then state its domain and range.

Solution

Make a table of values and sketch the graph.

x	−2	−1	0	1	2
y	3.78	3	0	−3	−3.78

Because the radicand of a cube root can be any real number, the domain is all real numbers.

You can see from the graph that the range is all real numbers.

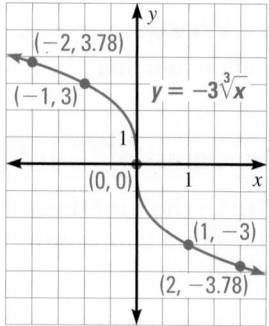

Checkpoint ✔ **Graph Square Root and Cube Root Functions**

Graph the function. Then state its domain and range.

1. $f(x) = 4\sqrt{x}$ **2.** $f(x) = 0.4\sqrt{x}$ **3.** $f(x) = 2\sqrt[3]{x}$

Graphs of Radical Functions

To graph $y = a\sqrt{x - h} + k$ or $y = a\sqrt[3]{x - h} + k$, follow these steps.

STEP ❶ **Sketch** the graph of $y = a\sqrt{x}$ or $y = a\sqrt[3]{x}$.

STEP ❷ **Determine** the values of h and k. Translate the graph h units horizontally and k units vertically. See the table below to determine the direction of the translation.

Value of h		Value of k	
Positive	**Negative**	**Positive**	**Negative**
translate right	translate left	translate up	translate down

EXAMPLE **3** **Graph a Square Root Function**

Graph $y = \sqrt{x} + 2$. Then state its domain and range.

Solution

❶ **Sketch** the graph of $y = \sqrt{x}$.

❷ **Determine** the values of h and k. Because $h = 0$, you don't translate the graph of $y = \sqrt{x}$ to the right or left. Because $k = 2$, you translate the graph 2 units up.

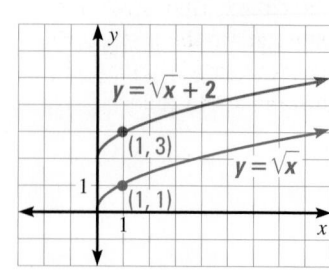

The domain is $x \geq 0$. The range is $y \geq 2$.

EXAMPLE ④ Graph a Cube Root Function

Graph $y = \sqrt[3]{x - 1} - 2$. Then state its domain and range.

Solution

① **Sketch** the graph of $y = \sqrt[3]{x}$.

② **Determine** the values of h and k. Because $h = 1$, you translate the graph of $y = \sqrt[3]{x}$ 1 unit to the right. Because $k = -2$, you shift the graph 2 units down.

The domain and range are all real numbers.

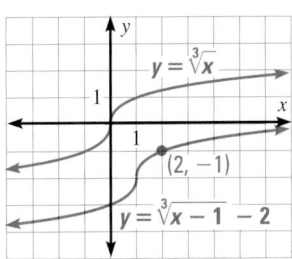

Checkpoint ✓ *Graph Square Root and Cube Root Functions*

Graph the function. Then state its domain and range.

4. $y = 2\sqrt{x} - 1$ **5.** $y = \sqrt{x - 1} + 1$ **6.** $y = \sqrt[3]{x + 2} - 1$

Radical Functions in the Real World When you use radical functions to model real-world situations, you must sometimes restrict the domain to values that make sense for the situation.

Link to
CAREERS

INVESTIGATORS attempt to recreate the conditions that occurred at the scene of an accident. They often use computers to reconstruct the accident using information gathered at the scene.

EXAMPLE ⑤ Model with a Square Root Function

Investigating Accidents An accident investigator determines how fast a car was traveling just prior to an accident in a parking lot using the model

$$s = 4\sqrt{d}$$

where s is the speed of the car in miles per hour and d is the length of the skid marks in feet.

a. Use a graphing calculator to graph the model. Then use the graph to estimate the length of the skid marks for a car that was traveling at the parking lot speed limit of 15 miles per hour.

b. The actual length of the skid marks is 20 feet. Was the car traveling faster than the speed limit of 15 miles per hour before the accident?

Solution

a. Graph $y = 4\sqrt{x}$ and $y = 15$.

Choose a window that shows the point where the graphs intersect. Use the *Intersect* feature to find the *x*-coordinate of the point.

The answer is $x \approx 14$. So, the length of the skid marks for a car traveling 15 miles per hour would be about 14 feet.

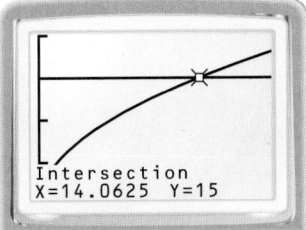

b. Because the actual length of the skid marks is 20 feet, the car was traveling faster than the parking lot speed limit of 15 miles per hour before the accident.

7.6 Exercises

Guided Practice

Vocabulary Check

1. Copy and complete the statement: $y = a\sqrt{x}$ and $y = a\sqrt[3]{x}$ are both examples of __?__ functions.

2. Copy and complete the statement: When graphing $y = a\sqrt[3]{x - h} + k$, translate the graph of $y = a\sqrt[3]{x}$ __?__ h units and __?__ k units.

Skill Check

3. **Error Analysis** Explain why the graph to the right is not the graph of $y = \sqrt[3]{x - 1} + 3$.

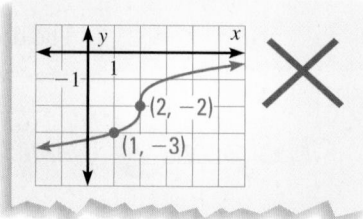

Graph the function. Then state its domain and range.

4. $y = 2\sqrt{x}$
5. $y = -2\sqrt{x}$
6. $y = -2\sqrt[3]{x}$

7. $y = \sqrt{x} + 5$
8. $y = 3\sqrt{x - 2}$
9. $y = \sqrt{x - 3} + 3$

10. $y = 3\sqrt[3]{x} + 1$
11. $y = \sqrt[3]{x - 4}$
12. $y = \sqrt[3]{x + 4} - 2$

13. **Writing** The functions $y = x^2$ and $y = \sqrt{x}$ are inverses. The functions $y = x^3$ and $y = \sqrt[3]{x}$ are inverses. How is the graph of $y = x^2$ related to the graph of $y = \sqrt{x}$? How is the graph of $y = \sqrt[3]{x}$ related to the graph of $y = x^3$?

14. **Investigating Accidents** Look back at Example 5 on page 391. Use a graphing calculator to graph the model. Then use the graph to estimate the length of the skid marks for a car traveling 20 miles per hour.

Practice and Applications

STUDENT HELP

HOMEWORK HELP
Example 1: Exs. 15–23
Example 2: Exs. 15–23
Example 3: Exs. 24–32
Example 4: Exs. 33–38
Example 5: Exs. 46–49

Graphing Radical Functions Graph the function. Then state its domain and range.

15. $y = 3\sqrt{x}$
16. $y = 4\sqrt{x}$
17. $y = 4\sqrt[3]{x}$

18. $y = -3\sqrt[3]{x}$
19. $y = \frac{1}{3}\sqrt{x}$
20. $y = \frac{1}{3}\sqrt[3]{x}$

21. $y = -3\sqrt[3]{x}$
22. $y = \frac{1}{5}\sqrt{x}$
23. $y = -\frac{1}{2}\sqrt[3]{x}$

Matching Graphs Match the function with its graph.

24. $y = \sqrt{x + 3}$
25. $y = \sqrt{x} + 3$
26. $y = \sqrt{x + 3} - 3$

A.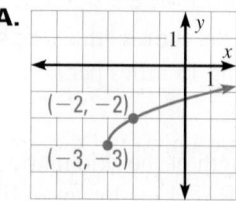

B.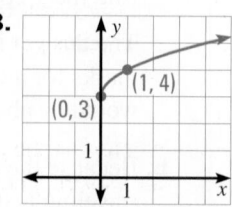

C.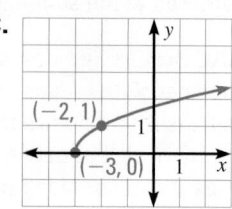

Graphing Square Root Functions Graph the function. Then state its domain and range.

27. $y = \sqrt{x} - 4$

28. $y = 2\sqrt{x+1}$

29. $y = \sqrt{x-5} - 3$

30. $y = \sqrt{x-4} - 6$

31. $y = \frac{1}{2}\sqrt{x+1}$

32. $y = -3\sqrt{x+2}$

Graphing Cube Root Functions Graph the function. Then state its domain and range.

33. $y = \sqrt[3]{x} - 5$

34. $y = \sqrt[3]{x} - 3$

35. $y = \sqrt[3]{x+2} - 4$

36. $y = \sqrt[3]{x-4} + 2$

37. $y = -\frac{3}{4}\sqrt[3]{x-1}$

38. $y = -2\sqrt[3]{x} + 5$

Logical Reasoning In Exercises 39–42, complete the statement with *sometimes*, *always*, or *never*.

39. The domain of the function $y = a\sqrt{x}$ is __?__ $x \geq 0$.

40. The range of the function $y = a\sqrt{x}$ is __?__ $y \geq 0$.

41. The domain and range of the function $y = \sqrt[3]{x-h} + k$ are __?__ all real numbers.

42. The domain of the function $y = \sqrt{(-x)}$ is __?__ $x \geq 0$.

Challenge The graph of $y = \sqrt{x}$ is the graph of $y = a\sqrt{x-h} + k$ with $a = 1$, $h = 0$, and $k = 0$. Predict how the graph of will change given the following condition.

43. $a = -1$

44. $a = -3$

45. $a = -\frac{1}{2}$

46. **Roller Coasters** You can approximate the speed v (in miles per hour) of a roller coaster car at the bottom of a hill on a track using the model

$$v = 5.5\sqrt{h}$$

where h is the height in feet from the top to the bottom of the hill. Use a graphing calculator to graph the model. Then use the graph to estimate the height of the hill when the speed of the roller coaster is 100 miles per hour.

47. **Fighting Fires** Fire fighters monitor the rate at which water flows from their hoses when fighting fires. You can determine the diameter d (in inches) of the tip of the hose using the model

$$d = \sqrt{\frac{r}{30\sqrt{P}}}$$

where r is the water flow rate in gallons per minute, and P is the water pressure in pounds per square inch at the nozzle. Use a graphing calculator to graph the model if the water pressure is 150 pounds per square inch. Then use the graph to estimate the water flow rate if the diameter of the tip of the hose is 2 inches.

48. **Car Racing** For a given total weight, the speed of a car at the end of a drag race is a function of the car's power. You can approximate the speed s (in miles per hour) of a car with a total weight of 3500 pounds using the model

$$s = 5.5\sqrt[3]{p}$$

where p is the power in horsepower of the car. Use a graphing calculator to graph the model. Then use the graph to estimate the power of the car if it reaches a speed of 200 miles per hour.

49. Geometry Link A square prism with a height that is eight times the length of the base b is given by the model

$$b = \frac{1}{2}\sqrt[3]{V}$$

where V is the volume of the prism. Use a graphing calculator to graph the model. Then use the graph to estimate the length of the base if the prism has a volume of 500 cubic centimeters.

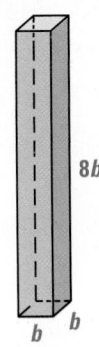

8b

b   b

50. Multiple Choice How do you obtain the graph of $g(x) = \sqrt[3]{x + 4} + 10$ from the graph of $f(x) = \sqrt[3]{x}$?

(A) Translate $f(x)$ 4 units to the right and 10 units up.

(B) Translate $f(x)$ 10 units to the left and 4 units up.

(C) Translate $f(x)$ 10 units to the right and 4 units down.

(D) Translate $f(x)$ 4 units to the left and 10 units up.

51. Multiple Choice What is the domain and range of $y = \sqrt[3]{x - 5} + 3$?

(F) domain: $x \geq 5$
range: $y \geq 3$

(G) domain: $x \leq 5$
range: $y \leq 3$

(H) domain: all real numbers
range: all real numbers

(J) domain: $x \geq 3$
range: $y \geq 5$

Mixed Review

Measures of Central Tendency Find the mean, median, and mode(s) of the data set. *(Lesson 1.7)*

52. 2, 3, 3, 6, 8, 10, 10

53. 5, 9, 9, 10, 11, 11

54. 15, 18, 25, 27, 38, 39, 41, 45

55. 55, 60, 65, 65, 75, 80, 85, 90, 100

56. 8, 15, 5, 2, 17, 10, 13, 11

57. 13, 28, 35, 11, 8, 38, 32, 25, 19, 22

Fitting a Line to Data Draw a scatter plot of the data. Then approximate the best-fitting line for the data. *(Lesson 2.7)*

58.

x	−1	0	0.5	1	2	2	1.5	2.5	3
y	−2	−1	0	−0.5	1	0.5	0	1.5	2

59.

x	−3	−2	−1	0	1	2	3	4	5	6
y	2.5	2.5	2	1.5	1.5	1	1	0.5	0.5	0

Geometry Skills

Dilations The red figure is the image of the blue figure after a dilation. Tell whether the dilation is a *reduction* or an *enlargement*. Then find the value of the variable.

60.

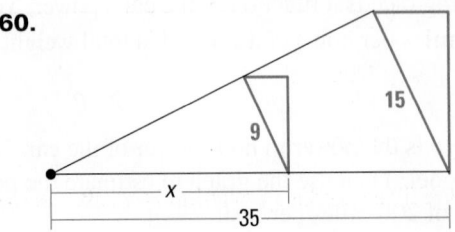

15

9

x

35

61.

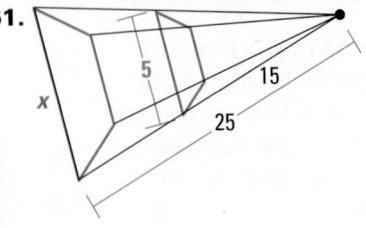

5

15

x

25

7.7 Standard Deviation

Key Words

• standard deviation

Prerequisite Skills

Find the mean of the data.

1. 20, 40, 60, 80, 100

2. 5, 10, 15, 20, 25, 30

3. 18, 24, 30, 50, 56, 62

4. 86, 91, 75, 88, 93

GOAL Use standard deviation to describe data sets.

How can you measure variation in attendance?

In September, a community theater ran a play for eight shows. The data set below gives the attendance at each of the eight shows:

| 250 | 300 | 290 | 240 |
| 200 | 230 | 210 | 280 |

In Lesson 1.7, you analyzed sets of data by finding measures of central tendency (mean, median, and mode) and measures of dispersion (range). Another measure of dispersion is *standard deviation*. **Standard deviation** describes the typical difference (or deviation) between the mean and any data value in a set.

STUDENT HELP

READING ALGEBRA
Using $\bar{x}$ to represent the mean of the data simplifies the written form of the expression for standard deviation.

Standard Deviation of a Set of Data

To find the standard deviation of a data set $x_1, x_2, \ldots, x_n$, follow these steps:

STEP ❶ *Find* the mean of the data set, $\bar{x}$ (read as "x bar").

STEP ❷ *Find* the standard deviation σ (read as "sigma").

$$\sigma = \sqrt{\frac{(x_1 - \bar{x})^2 + (x_2 - \bar{x})^2 + \cdots + (x_n - \bar{x})^2}{n}}$$

EXAMPLE ❶ Find Standard Deviation

Find the standard deviation of the attendance of the play in September.

Solution

❶ *Find* the mean.

$$\bar{x} = \frac{250 + 300 + \cdots + 280}{8} = 250$$

❷ *Find* the standard deviation.

$$\sigma = \sqrt{\frac{(250 - 250)^2 + (300 - 250)^2 + \cdots + (280 - 250)^2}{8}}$$

$$= \sqrt{\frac{9800}{8}}$$

$$= \sqrt{1200}$$

ANSWER ▶ The standard deviation is $\sqrt{1200}$, or about 35.

EXAMPLE 2 Compare Data After Adding a Constant

Suppose the theater runs the play for another eight shows in October. The attendance at each of the eight shows increases by 100 people, as shown below. The mean of the new data is 350.

| 350 | 400 | 390 | 340 | 300 | 330 | 310 | 380 |

a. Find the standard deviation of the attendance of the play in October.

b. Compare this standard deviation with the standard deviation of the attendance of the play in September.

c. Make a box-and-whisker plot of the data used in Example 1 and the new data above. What conclusions can you make about the two data sets?

Solution

a. $\sigma = \sqrt{\dfrac{(350-350)^2 + (400-350)^2 + \cdots + (380-350)^2}{8}} = \sqrt{\dfrac{9600}{8}} \approx 35$

b. The standard deviation is the same as in Example 1.

c. The two data sets have exactly the same shape. The graph for the new data is 100 units to the right of the graph for the data in Example 1.

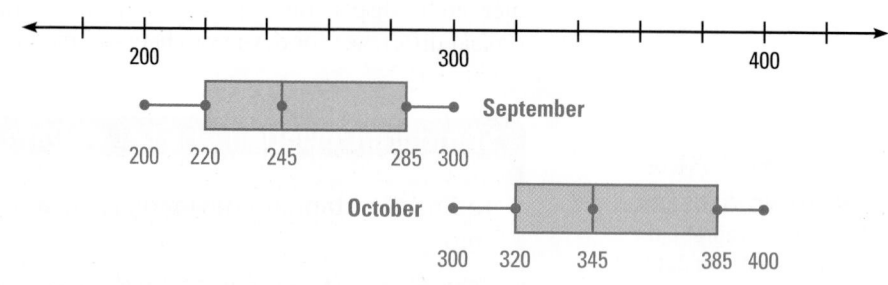

STUDENT HELP

LOOK BACK
Recall from Lesson 1.7 that the five key points for making a box-and-whisker plot are the upper and lower extremes, the upper and lower quartiles, and the median of the data set.

Checkpoint ✓ **Find and Compare Standard Deviations**

1. Find the standard deviation of the data set: 30, 1, 26, 19, 7, 30, 22. Round your answer to the nearest tenth.

2. Suppose you multiply each data value in Exercise 1 by 2, resulting in the data set 60, 2, 52, 38, 14, 60, 44. Find the standard deviation and compare it to the standard deviation in Exercise 1. What do you notice?

STUDENT HELP

READING ALGEBRA
Notice that you have to compare the standard deviation with the mean. For data with a mean of 12, a standard deviation of 25 is large. For data with a mean of 200, a standard deviation of 25 is small.

Comparing Data Sets The standard deviation of a data set can tell you whether the data values in a set are spread out or close together.

Set A
Standard Deviation: 14   Mean: 50
The standard deviation is small.
The data values are close together.

Set B
Standard Deviation: 37   Mean: 50
The standard deviation is large.
The data values are spread apart.

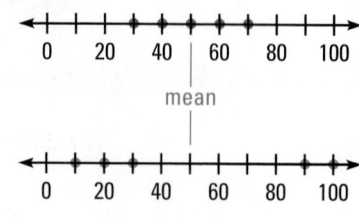

EXAMPLE 3 Compare Data Sets

Suppose the theater runs a different play for eight shows with the following attendance: 110, 113, 145, 170, 241, 217, 404, 600. The mean of the data is 250.

a. Find the standard deviation.

b. Compare the mean and standard deviation in this example with the mean and standard deviation found in Example 1.

c. What conclusions can you draw?

Solution

a. $\sigma = \sqrt{\dfrac{(110 - 250)^2 + (113 - 250)^2 + \cdots + (600 - 250)^2}{8}} = \sqrt{\dfrac{203{,}180}{8}} \approx 159$

b. The means of both data sets are the same, 250. The standard deviation for the new data is 159. The standard deviation in Example 1 is 39. So, the standard deviation of the new data set is greater.

c. Because the standard deviation for the new data set is greater than the standard deviation in Example 1, the new data values are more spread out.

Using Technology You can use a graphing calculator to find the standard deviation of a data set.

EXAMPLE 4 Find Standard Deviation

Use a graphing calculator to find the standard deviation of the data. Round to the nearest whole number.

299, 6338, 3006, 518, 1981, 2444, 475, 3065, 7057, 3132, 408, 1534, 2699

STUDENT HELP

READING ALGEBRA
On the calculator screen in Example 4, Σx represents the sum of the terms in the list, and Σx^2 represents the sum of the squares of the terms. The symbol Sx represents another measure of dispersion.

Solution

First, enter the data into a graphing calculator. Press **STAT** and select Edit. Enter the data into List 1 (L_1).

To calculate the standard deviation, press **STAT**. From the CALC menu select 1-Var Stats.

On this calculator screen, $\bar{x}$ stands for the mean, σx stands for the standard deviation, and n stands for the number of terms in the data set.

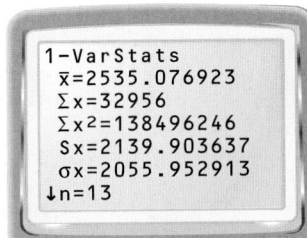

```
1-VarStats
x̄=2535.076923
Σx=32956
Σx²=138496246
Sx=2139.903637
σx=2055.952913
↓n=13
```

ANSWER ▶ The standard deviation is about 2056.

Checkpoint ✔ Find and Compare Standard Deviations

In Exercises 3 and 4, tell which data set is more spread out.

3. Set A: $\bar{x} = 24$, $\sigma = 8$
Set B: $\bar{x} = 24$, $\sigma = 3$

4. Set A: $\bar{x} = 30$, $\sigma = 15$
Set B: $\bar{x} = 300$, $\sigma = 15$

5. Use a graphing calculator to find the standard deviation of 110, 205, 322, 608, 1100, 240, 185, 552, 418, 300. Round to the nearest tenth.

7.7 Exercises

Guided Practice

Vocabulary Check

1. Is the *mean*, *median*, or *mode* used to compute standard deviation?

2. What can you use standard deviation to measure: the difference between the greatest and least values in a data set, whether values in a data set are spread out or close together, or the average of the values in a data set?

Skill Check **Find the mean, median, and quartiles of the data set.**

3. 16, 20, 15, 24, 17, 28

4. 20, 15, 16, 23, 18, 27, 31, 21

5. 69, 83, 104, 88, 93, 98

6. 234, 256, 211, 215, 198, 207

Find the standard deviation of the data set. Round your answer to the nearest tenth.

7. 3, 7, 10, 15, 26, 29

8. 12, 14, 15, 17, 19, 22, 23

9. 41, 44, 43, 39, 50, 54, 44, 46

10. 100, 94, 95, 89, 92, 83, 92

Practice and Applications

STUDENT HELP

HOMEWORK HELP
Example 1: Exs. 11–14
Example 2: Exs. 15–18
Example 3: Exs. 19–28
Example 4: Exs. 29–34

Measures of Central Tendency **Find the mean and the standard deviation of the data set. Round your answer to the nearest tenth.**

11. The number of mice born in 9 different litters: 5, 7, 6, 3, 8, 6, 4, 5, 4

12. The number of times at bat for each player on the 2004 U.S. women's Olympic softball team:

$$2, 6, 6, 16, 19, 20, 20, 21, 22, 25, 26, 30$$

13. The heights of nine pecan trees in feet:

$$72, 84, 81, 78, 80, 86, 70, 80, 88$$

14. Your weekly paychecks (in dollars) from your after school job:

$$44.50, 69, 50, 39.50, 28, 29, 26, 35, 42, 35.50, 25.50$$

Shoe Prices **In Exercises 15–18, use the following data set, which shows the prices (in dollars) of eight pairs of basketball shoes.**

$$65, 75, 40, 68, 80, 50, 56, 65$$

15. Find the standard deviation of the data set, to the nearest tenth.

16. The prices of these shoes increase by $10 per pair. What are the new prices? Find the standard deviation to the nearest tenth.

17. Compare the standard deviation of the original data set with the standard deviation of the new data set.

18. Make a box-and-whisker plot of the original data and the new data. What conclusions can you make about the two data sets?

Using Standard Deviation In Exercises 19–24, tell which data set is more spread out.

19. Set A: $\bar{x} = 14$, $\sigma = 2$
Set B: $\bar{x} = 14$, $\sigma = 7$

20. Set A: $\bar{x} = 110$, $\sigma = 25.5$
Set B: $\bar{x} = 110$, $\sigma = 16.5$

21. Set A: $\bar{x} = 164$, $\sigma = 57$
Set B: $\bar{x} = 258$, $\sigma = 57$

22. Set A: $\bar{x} = 70$, $\sigma = 35$
Set B: $\bar{x} = 125$, $\sigma = 35$

23. Set A: $\bar{x} = 13.25$, $\sigma = 2.25$
Set B: $\bar{x} = 18.45$, $\sigma = 2.25$

24. Set A: $\bar{x} = 0.02$, $\sigma = 0.00023$
Set B: $\bar{x} = 0.02$ $\sigma = 0.00023$

Test Scores In Exercises 25 and 26, use the following data sets which show test scores for two students.

Kayla: 79, 81, 95, 90, 82, 90, 82, 81, 85

Emily: 62, 80, 83, 99, 89, 85, 87, 94, 86

25. Find the standard deviation for each student to the nearest whole number.

26. Compare the mean and standard deviation for Kayla's scores with the mean and standard deviation for Emily's scores.

Waiting Times In Exercises 27 and 28, use the following data sets which show the waiting times (in minutes) of people at two bus stops.

Forest Hills: 2, 17, 8, 9, 11, 23, 14

Union: 10, 13, 18, 7, 5, 19, 12

27. Find the standard deviation for each stop to the nearest minute.

28. Compare the mean and standard deviation for the stop at Forest Hills with the mean and standard deviation for the stop at Union.

Finding Standard Deviation In Exercises 29–31, use a graphing calculator to find the standard deviation of the data. Round to the nearest tenth.

29. 66, 43, 9, 28, 7, 5, 90, 9, 78, 6, 69, 55, 28, 43, 10, 54, 13, 88, 21, 4

30. 3.5, 3.8, 4.1, 3.0, 3.8, 3.6, 3.3, 4.0, 3.8, 3.9, 3.2, 3.0, 3.3, 4.2, 3.0

31. 1002, 1540, 480, 290, 2663, 3800, 690, 1301, 1750, 2222, 4040, 800

Sports In Exercises 32–34, use a graphing calculator and the following data set.

The data show the attendance at each of eight county football tournament games.

1100, 1920, 1510, 1050,
2100, 1800, 1310, 1580

32. Find the standard deviation of the data set to the nearest whole number.

33. Suppose attendance increases by 10% next year. Find the attendance at each of the eight games. Then find the standard deviation to the nearest whole number.

34. Compare the standard deviation of the original data set with the standard deviation of the new data set.

35. Multiple Choice What is the standard deviation of the data set below?

$$14, 16, 17, 17, 19, 20, 22$$

(A) 42.9   (B) 17.9   (C) 6.12   (D) 2.47

36. Multiple Choice Which data set has a standard deviation of about 3.83?

(F) 12, 14, 17, 21, 26, 32   (G) 10, 15, 13, 18, 16, 21, 19

(H) 43, 42, 50, 40, 38, 45   (J) 20, 30, 25, 23, 40, 33, 36

37. Multiple Choice What is the standard deviation of the data set below?

$$20, 22, 18, 23, 17, 21, 19, 22$$

(A) 1.98   (B) 3.94   (C) 20.3   (D) 31.5

Mixed Review

Factoring **Factor the polynomial.** *(Lesson 6.6)*

38. $x^4 + x^3 - 2x^2$ **39.** $x^5 - 6x^4 + 8x^3$ **40.** $x^4 + 3x^2 + 2$

41. $x^4 - 8x^2 + 16$ **42.** $x^5 - 2x^3 - 8x$ **43.** $x^4 - 7x^2 + 10$

Finding Inverses **Find the inverse of the function.** *(Lesson 7.5)*

44. $f(x) = 2x - 7$ **45.** $f(x) = 3x + 2$ **46.** $f(x) = \frac{1}{9}x^2, x \geq 0$

47. $f(x) = 8x^3$ **48.** $f(x) = x^5 - 4$ **49.** $f(x) = x^4 + 1, x \geq 0$

Geometry Skills

Finding Angle Measures **Find the unknown angle measures of the isosceles trapezoid. The sum of the angle measures in an isosceles trapezoid is 360°. Additionally, pairs of base angles are congruent.**

50. 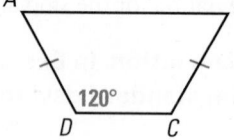   **51.** 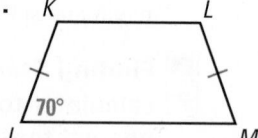   **52.**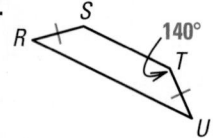

Quiz 3

Lesson 7.6   **Graph the function. Then state its domain and range.**

1. $y = \sqrt{x} + 2$ **2.** $y = 2\sqrt{x} - 3$ **3.** $y = -\sqrt{x + 1} - 4$

Lesson 7.6   **4.** Write the equation of the cube root function whose graph is shown below.

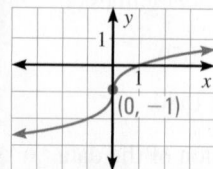

Lesson 7.7   **Tell which data set is more spread out.**

5. Set A: $\bar{x} = 256$, $\sigma = 21$ **6.** Set A: $\bar{x} = 41$, $\sigma = 25$
     Set B: $\bar{x} = 256$, $\sigma = 74$ Set B: $\bar{x} = 49$, $\sigma = 25$

Lesson 7.7   **Find the standard deviation of the data set. Round to the nearest tenth.**

7. 7, 19, 20, 14, 11, 12, 10   **8.** 91, 100, 97, 83, 85, 88, 90, 86

VOCABULARY

- *n*th root of a real number, *p. 353*
- index, *p. 353*
- simplest form of a radical, *p. 359*

- like radicals, *p. 360*
- radical equation, *p. 365*
- extraneous solution, *p. 366*
- composition of functions, *p. 374*

- inverse relation, *p. 380*
- inverse functions, *p. 380*
- radical function, *p. 389*
- standard deviation, *p. 395*

VOCABULARY EXERCISES

1. Copy and complete the statement: An equation that contains a radical with the variable in the radicand is called a(n) __?__ equation.

2. How do you write a radical in simplest form?

3. Provide three examples of pairs of like radicals.

4. How are the domain and range of a function and its inverse related?

7.1   NTH ROOTS AND RATIONAL EXPONENTS

Examples on pp. 353–355

EXAMPLE   To solve an equation involving x^n, take the *n*th root of *each* side.

REVIEW HELP

Exercises	Examples
5–8	2, p. 354
9, 10	3, p. 354
11, 12	5, p. 355

a. $(x + 5)^2 = 81$

$x + 5 = \pm\sqrt{81}$

$x + 5 = \pm 9$

$x = 4 \text{ or } x = -14$

b. $(x - 7)^3 = 125$

$x - 7 = \sqrt[3]{125}$

$x - 7 = 5$

$x = 12$

Solve the equation.

5. $x^2 = 169$

6. $4x^4 = 324$

7. $(x + 5)^3 = 27$

8. $(x - 10)^5 = 32$

EXAMPLE   You can use radicals to evaluate expressions involving rational exponents.

a. $49^{1/2} = \sqrt{49} = 7$

b. $8^{1/3} = \sqrt[3]{8} = 2$

c. $25^{3/2} = \left(\sqrt{25}\right)^3 = 125$

Evaluate the expression.

9. $1000^{1/3}$

10. $121^{1/2}$

11. $27^{2/3}$

12. $32^{-1/5}$

7.2 PROPERTIES OF RATIONAL EXPONENTS

Examples on
pp. 359–361

EXAMPLE You can use the properties of rational exponents to simplify an expression.

REVIEW HELP
Exercises Examples
13–20   **5,** p. 361
21–23   **6,** p. 361

a. $\sqrt{16x^6} = \sqrt{4^2(x^3)^2}$

$\qquad = 4x^3$

b. $\dfrac{5ac}{a^{1/2}c^{-2}} = 5a^{(1-1/2)}c^{[1-(-2)]}$

$\qquad = 5a^{1/2}c^3$

Simplify the expression. Write your answer using positive exponents only. Assume all variables are positive.

13. $(16x^{10})^{1/2}$ **14.** $(27m^9n^{15})^{1/3}$ **15.** $(81r^{12}s^6)^{1/4}$ **16.** $(64r^{10}s^5)^{1/5}$

17. $\dfrac{10w^2z^4}{2wz}$ **18.** $\dfrac{7a^3b^3}{ab^2}$ **19.** $\dfrac{16m^{3/5}n^{5/4}}{m^{2/5}n^{1/4}}$ **20.** $\dfrac{5x^{2/3}y^{3/4}}{35xy^{5/4}}$

Simplify the expression. Assume all variables are positive.

21. $4\sqrt[3]{x} + 6\sqrt[3]{x}$ **22.** $7ab^{4/5} - 16ab^{4/5}$ **23.** $64a^4b^2 + (16a^{16}b^8)^{1/4}$

7.3 SOLVING RADICAL EQUATIONS

Examples on
pp. 365–367

EXAMPLE To solve a radical equation, you isolate the radical or the expression with a rational exponent. Then raise each side of the equation to the same power.

REVIEW HELP
Exercises Examples
24   **1,** p. 365
25   **2,** p. 366
26, 27   **5,** p. 367
28–30   **3,** p. 366

a. $\sqrt[3]{x} - 4 = 0$

$\qquad \sqrt[3]{x} = 4$

$\qquad (\sqrt[3]{x})^3 = 4^3$

$\qquad x = 64$

b. $x^{2/3} - 9 = 0$

$\qquad x^{2/3} = 9$

$\qquad (x^{2/3})^{3/2} = 9^{3/2}$

$\qquad x = 27$

Solve the equation.

24. $\sqrt{x} - 4 = 0$ **25.** $\sqrt[3]{x-3} = 6$ **26.** $x^{1/3} - 8 = 0$ **27.** $(x-3)^{2/5} - 2 = 2$

EXAMPLE To solve an equation with two radicals, make sure that each side has only one radical. Then raise each side of the equation to the same power.

a. $\sqrt{5x} - \sqrt{x+8} = 0$

$\qquad \sqrt{5x} = \sqrt{x+8}$

$\qquad (\sqrt{5x})^2 = (\sqrt{x+8})^2$

$\qquad 5x = x + 8$

$\qquad x = 2$

b. $\sqrt[3]{3x} - \sqrt[3]{2x+4} = 0$

$\qquad \sqrt[3]{3x} = \sqrt[3]{2x+4}$

$\qquad (\sqrt[3]{3x})^3 = (\sqrt[3]{2x+4})^3$

$\qquad 3x = 2x + 4$

$\qquad x = 4$

Solve the equation.

28. $\sqrt{x-8} = \sqrt{3x+4}$ **29.** $\sqrt{5x+4} - \sqrt{3x} = 0$ **30.** $\sqrt[3]{10x-5} - \sqrt[3]{x+10} = 0$

EXAMPLE You can perform addition, subtraction, multiplication, division, or composition on any two functions.

Let $f(x) = 5x^4$ and $g(x) = x^3$. Find (a) the quotient $\frac{f}{g}$ and state its domain and (b) the composition $f(g(x))$ and state its domain.

a. $\dfrac{f(x)}{g(x)} = \dfrac{5x^4}{x^3}$ 　　　　　　**b.** $f(g(x)) = f(x^3)$

$\phantom{\dfrac{f(x)}{g(x)}} = 5x^{(4-3)}$ 　　　　　　　　$ = 5(x^3)^4$

$\phantom{\dfrac{f(x)}{g(x)}} = 5x$ 　　　　　　　　　　$ = 5x^{12}$

Domain: all real numbers, except 0 　　Domain: all real numbers

REVIEW HELP

Exercises	Examples
31–33	**1**, p. 373
34–36	**2**, p. 374
37	**5**, p. 375

Let $f(x) = 4x - 7$, and let $g(x) = 3x + 2$. Find $h(x)$ and state its domain.

31. $h(x) = f(x) + g(x)$ 　　**32.** $h(x) = f(x) - g(x)$ 　　**33.** $h(x) = g(x) - f(x)$

Let $f(x) = 2x^4$, and let $g(x) = 6x$. Find $h(x)$ and state its domain.

34. $h(x) = f(x) \cdot g(x)$ 　　**35.** $h(x) = \dfrac{f(x)}{g(x)}$ 　　**36.** $h(x) = \dfrac{g(x)}{f(x)}$

37. Let $f(x) = 2x + 3$ and $g(x) = 3x^2$. Find $f(g(x))$. Evaluate the composition when $x = 3$.

EXAMPLE You can find the inverse relation of a function by replacing $f(x)$ with y, switching x and y, and solving for y.

Find the inverse of the function.

a. 　　$f(x) = 5x + 7$ 　　　　　　**b.** 　　$f(x) = 3x^3 - 2$

$y = 5x + 7$ 　　　　　　　　　　$y = 3x^3 - 2$

$x = 5y + 7$ 　　　　　　　　　　$x = 3y^3 - 2$

$x - 7 = 5y$ 　　　　　　　　　　$x + 2 = 3y^3$

$\dfrac{1}{5}x - \dfrac{7}{5} = y$ 　　　　　　　　$\sqrt[3]{\dfrac{x+2}{3}} = y$

$f^{-1}(x) = \dfrac{1}{5}x - \dfrac{7}{5}$ 　　　　　　$f^{-1}(x) = \sqrt[3]{\dfrac{x+2}{3}}$

REVIEW HELP

Exercises	Example
38–46	**2**, p. 381

Find the inverse of the function.

38. $f(x) = 2x + 5$ 　　**39.** $f(x) = -3x$ 　　**40.** $f(x) = x - 9$

41. $f(x) = \dfrac{3}{4}x - 1$ 　　**42.** $f(x) = \dfrac{1}{3}x - \dfrac{2}{3}$ 　　**43.** $f(x) = 27x^3$

44. $f(x) = 36x^2$, when $x \geq 0$ 　　**45.** $f(x) = x^5 - 3$ 　　**46.** $f(x) = 64x^3 - 15$

7.6 GRAPHING SQUARE ROOT AND CUBE ROOT FUNCTIONS

Examples on pp. 389–391

EXAMPLE

You can use the graphs of $y = a\sqrt{x}$ and $y = a\sqrt[3]{x}$ to graph any function of the form $y = a\sqrt{x - h} + k$ or $y = a\sqrt[3]{x - h} + k$.

Graph $y = \sqrt{x - 2} + 4$. Then state its domain and range.

To graph the function, follow the steps below.

❶ Sketch the graph of $y = \sqrt{x}$.

❷ Determine the values of h and k.

Because $h = 2$, you translate the graph of $y = \sqrt{x}$ to the right 2 units. Because $k = 4$, you translate the graph 4 units up.

From the graph, you can see that the domain of $y = \sqrt{x - 2} + 4$ is $x \geq 2$. The range is $y \geq 4$.

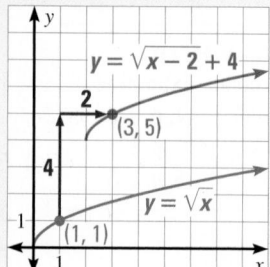

REVIEW HELP

Exercises	Examples
47, 48	**1**, p. 389
49	**2**, p. 390
50–52	**3**, p. 390
53–55	**4**, p. 391

Graph the function. Then state its domain and range.

47. $y = 5\sqrt{x}$

48. $y = \frac{1}{3}\sqrt{x}$

49. $y = 2\sqrt[3]{x}$

50. $y = \sqrt{x + 2}$

51. $y = 2\sqrt{x} + 1$

52. $y = \sqrt{x - 4} - 6$

53. $y = -\sqrt[3]{x - 1}$

54. $y = \sqrt[3]{x} + 4$

55. $y = \sqrt[3]{x + 3} - 1$

7.7 STANDARD DEVIATION

Examples on pp. 395–397

EXAMPLE

One measure of dispersion is standard deviation. It describes the typical difference (or deviation) between the mean and a data value.

The data set gives the daily attendance during 7 days at a school fair.

562	501	540	453	652	530	500

Mean: $\bar{x} = \dfrac{562 + 501 + \cdots + 500}{7} = 534$

Standard deviation: $\sigma = \sqrt{\dfrac{(562 - 534)^2 + (501 - 534)^2 + \cdots + (500 - 534)^2}{7}}$

$$= \sqrt{\frac{23566}{7}} \approx 58$$

REVIEW HELP

Exercises	Examples
56–61	**1**, p. 395
62	**4**, p. 397

Find the mean and standard deviation of the data set. Round your answer to the nearest tenth.

56. 9, 11, 12, 14, 15, 17

57. 18, 20, 20, 15, 16, 16, 22

58. 32, 35, 27, 31, 36, 39, 30

59. 10, 15, 12, 20, 22, 15

60. 45, 48, 41, 37, 55, 52, 42, 45

61. 70, 66, 62, 58, 71, 63, 65, 75

62. Use a graphing calculator to find the standard deviation of 1140, 1205, 3232, 2608, 1127, 1248, 1852, 5525, 2418, 1330. Round to the nearest tenth.

Write the expression in simplest form.

1. $\sqrt[3]{88}$ **2.** $\sqrt[4]{4} \cdot \sqrt[4]{12}$ **3.** $\sqrt[4]{\dfrac{1}{8}}$ **4.** $\sqrt[3]{\dfrac{8}{9}}$

Simplify the variable expression. Write your answer using positive exponents only. Assume all variables are positive.

5. $(9x^4)^{1/2}$ **6.** $(9x^2y)^{3/2}$ **7.** $\left(\dfrac{x^5}{y^4}\right)^{1/4}$ **8.** $\dfrac{x^2y^{1/4}}{x^{1/3}y^{3/4}}$

Solve the equation. Check for extraneous solutions.

9. $2\sqrt{x} + 3 = 11$ **10.** $\sqrt{3x + 7} = x + 1$

11. $7x^{1/2} - 3 = 17$ **12.** $2x^{3/2} + 5 = 21$

Let $f(x) = x - 7$ and $g(x) = 2x - 5$. Perform the indicated operation and state the domain of the resulting function.

13. $h(x) = f(x) + g(x)$ **14.** $h(x) = f(x) - g(x)$ **15.** $h(x) = g(x) - f(x)$

16. $h(x) = f(x) \cdot g(x)$ **17.** $f(g(x))$ **18.** $g(f(x))$

Find the inverse of the function.

19. $f(x) = 6x - 1$ **20.** $f(x) = 2x + 9$

21. $f(x) = \dfrac{1}{16}x^2,\ x \geq 0$ **22.** $f(x) = 4x^3 - 5$

23. Temperature Conversion The function $F = \dfrac{9}{5}C + 32$ can be used to convert temperatures from degrees Celsius to degrees Fahrenheit. Write the inverse of this function. The inverse can be used to convert temperatures from degrees Fahrenheit to degrees Celsius. Find the temperature in degrees Celsius that is equivalent to 86°F.

Graph the function. Then state its domain and range.

24. $y = \sqrt{x} - 3$ **25.** $y = -\sqrt{x} + 2$

26. Write the equation of the cube root function whose graph is shown below.

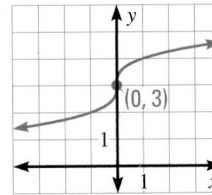

Find the standard deviation of the data set. Round your answer to the nearest tenth.

27. 26, 26, 27, 30, 31, 33   **28.** 67, 49, 61, 58, 55, 55, 59

Chapter Standardized Test

Test Tip   Work backward from the answer choices.

Ⓐ Ⓑ Ⓒ Ⓓ

EXAMPLE   What is the solution of $3\sqrt{3x + 1} = 12$?

Ⓐ 1   Ⓑ $\frac{8}{3}$ Ⓒ 5   Ⓓ $\frac{17}{3}$

Solution

Substitute the answer choices for x and simplify.

Choice A results in $6 \neq 12$.

Choice B results in $9 \neq 12$.

Choice C results in $12 = 12$, so C is the correct answer.

Multiple Choice

1. What is $\sqrt[3]{20} \cdot \sqrt[3]{6}$ in simplest form?

Ⓐ $\sqrt[3]{120}$ Ⓑ $2\sqrt{15}$

Ⓒ $8\sqrt[3]{15}$ Ⓓ $2\sqrt[3]{15}$

2. What is $\sqrt[3]{\dfrac{27}{25}}$ in simplest form?

Ⓕ $\dfrac{3\sqrt[3]{5}}{5}$ Ⓖ $\dfrac{3}{\sqrt[3]{25}}$

Ⓗ $\dfrac{\sqrt[3]{5}}{5}$ Ⓙ $\dfrac{3\sqrt{3}}{5}$

3. Simplify $(4x^4y)^{3/2}$. Assume all variables are positive.

Ⓐ $4x^6y^{3/2}$ Ⓑ $8x^6y^{3/2}$

Ⓒ $4x^4y^{3/2}$ Ⓓ $2x^6y^{3/2}$

4. Simplify $\dfrac{x^2y}{x^{3/4}y^{1/3}}$. Assume all variables are positive.

Ⓕ $x^{5/4}y^{2/3}$ Ⓖ $x^{11/4}y^{4/3}$

Ⓗ $x^{3/2}y^{1/3}$ Ⓙ $x^{1/2}y^{1/3}$

5. What is the solution of $5x^{2/3} - 7 = 13$?

Ⓐ -4 Ⓑ 4

Ⓒ 8   Ⓓ 20

6. What is $f - g$ if $f(x) = 3x + 2$ and $g(x) = 5 - 2x$?

Ⓕ $x + 7$ Ⓖ $5x - 3$

Ⓗ $x - 3$ Ⓙ $-2x + 4$

7. What is $f(g(x))$ if $f(x) = x^2 - 2$ and $g(x) = x + 4$?

Ⓐ $x^3 + 4x^2 - 2x - 8$ Ⓑ $x^2 + 8x + 16$

Ⓒ $x^2 + 8x + 14$ Ⓓ $x^2 + 2$

8. What is the inverse of the function $f(x) = 8x^3 - 7$?

Ⓕ $f^{-1}(x) = \dfrac{\sqrt[3]{x + 7}}{2}$ Ⓖ $f^{-1}(x) = \dfrac{\sqrt[3]{x + 7}}{8}$

Ⓗ $f^{-1}(x) = \sqrt[3]{\dfrac{x + 7}{2}}$ Ⓙ $f^{-1}(x) = -8x^3 + 7$

9. The graph of which function is shown?

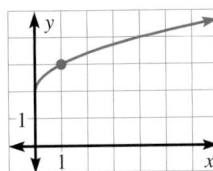

A $y = \sqrt{x} + 3$ **B** $y = \sqrt{x} - 3$

C $y = \sqrt{x} - 2$ **D** $y = \sqrt{x} + 2$

10. What is the domain of $f(x) = \sqrt[3]{x + 1} + 2$?

F $x \geq 1$ **G** $x \geq -1$

H $x \geq -9$ **J** all real numbers

11. What is the standard deviation of the data set?

13, 15, 16, 16, 19, 20, 21

A 17.1 **B** 7.3

C 2.9 **D** 2.7

12. What is the standard deviation of the data set?

45, 42, 44, 50, 51, 43

F 3.4 **G** 3.8

H 9.0 **J** 45.8

Gridded Response

13. Evaluate $\sqrt[4]{25} \cdot \sqrt[4]{25}$.

14. Evaluate $\sqrt[5]{\dfrac{96}{3}}$.

15. Evaluate $\sqrt[3]{\dfrac{108}{4}}$.

16. What is the solution of $\sqrt{x + 1} - 5 = 3$?

17. What is the solution of
$3\sqrt[3]{-3x - 2} - 7 = -13$?

18. What is the solution of $\sqrt{3x + 16} = x + 2$?

19. Evaluate $f(g(x))$ when $x = 3$, given
$f(x) = 4x - 3$ and $g(x) = 2x + 1$.

20. Evaluate $g(f(x))$ when $x = 2$, given
$f(x) = x - 3$ and $g(x) = x^2 + 1$.

21. Evaluate $f(g(x))$ when $x = -1$, given
$f(x) = \sqrt{x + 5}$ and $g(x) = \sqrt[3]{x}$.

Extended Response

Use the following data, which show the prices (in dollars) of six stereos at an electronics store.

95, 100, 210, 70, 80, 150

22. Find the standard deviation of the data set to the nearest tenth.

23. The store has a sale for 10% off all stereos. What are the new prices? Find the standard deviation of the new prices to the nearest tenth.

24. Compare the standard deviation of the original data set with the standard deviation of the new data set.

25. Make a box-and-whisker plot of the original data and the new data. What conclusions can you make about the two data sets?

CHAPTER 8

Exponential and Logarithmic Functions

▶ How can you describe a fractal?

APPLICATION: Fractals

The first four iterations of a fractal called the Sierpinski carpet are shown below. The number of shaded squares in the iterations can be expressed as powers with the same base.

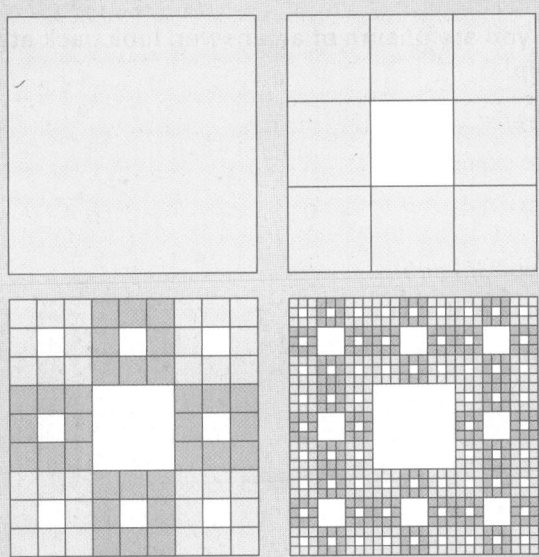

Think & Discuss

Use the diagrams to answer the following questions.

1. For each iteration of the Sierpinski carpet, find the number of shaded squares.

2. Write an expression for the number of shaded squares in the nth iteration.

Learn More About It

You will use exponential functions to describe the number of white squares and shaded squares in the Sierpinski carpet in Exercises 42–44 on page 416.

Study Guide

@HomeTutor
classzone.com
• Multi-Language Glossary
• Vocabulary practice

PREVIEW   What's the chapter about?

• Graphing and modeling exponential growth and exponential decay
• Evaluating and graphing logarithmic functions
• Solving exponential equations and logarithmic equations

> ### Key Words
> • exponential function, *p. 412*
> • exponential growth function, *p. 412*
> • asymptote, *p. 412*
> • exponential decay function, *p. 419*
>
> • growth factor, decay factor, *p. 426*
> • natural base *e*, *p. 429*
> • common logarithm, *p. 433*
> • logarithm of *y* with base *b*, *p. 433*

PREPARE   Chapter Readiness Quiz

Take this quick quiz. If you are unsure of an answer, look back at the reference pages for help.

Vocabulary Check *(refer to p. 9)*

1. What is the base of the expression 2^3?

  (**A**) 2   (**B**) 3   (**C**) 8   (**D**) 2^3

Skill Check *(refer to pp. 236, 306)*

2. What are the coordinates of the vertex of the graph of $y = 3(x - 4)^2 - 7$?

  (**F**) (4, 7)   (**G**) (4, −7)   (**H**) (−4, 7)   (**J**) (−4, −7)

3. What is the value of 5^{-3}?

  (**A**) −125   (**B**) −15   (**C**) $\dfrac{1}{125}$ (**D**) 2

4. What is the value of $(-4)^0$?

  (**F**) −4   (**G**) 0   (**H**) 1   (**J**) undefined

TAKE NOTES   Dictionary of Graphs

Make a dictionary of graphs in your notebook. When you learn about a new kind of function, you can add its graph to your dictionary.

EXPONENTIAL FUNCTIONS
The graph of $y = ab^x$ contains $(0, a)$.
When $b > 1$, the graph shows growth.
When $0 < b < 1$, the graph shows decay.

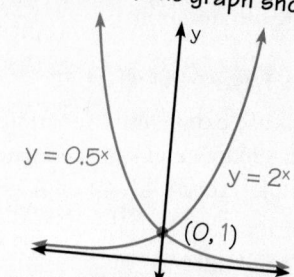

$y = 0.5^x$ $y = 2^x$

$(0, 1)$

ACTIVITY 8.1
Exponential Growth

Goal

Graph exponential functions of the form $y = ab^x$ and find how changing a affects the graphs.

Materials

- paper
- graph paper
- graphing calculator (optional)

QUESTION

How does the value of a affect the graph of $y = ab^x$?

EXPLORE

① Take **one sheet** of notebook paper. Fold it in half. Unfold the paper and count the number of rectangular regions formed. Then refold the paper and fold it in half again. Continue counting regions and folding in half many times.

Copy and complete a table like the first table shown below.

1 sheet of paper		3 sheets of paper		5 sheets of paper	
Folds, x	**Regions, y**	**Folds, x**	**Regions, y**	**Folds, x**	**Regions, y**
0	1	0	3	0	5
1	2	1	6	1	?
2	4	2	?	2	?
3	?	3	?	3	?
4	?	4	?	4	?

② Take **three sheets** of notebook paper and stack them. Repeat Step 1. Copy and complete a table like the second table shown above.

③ Take **five sheets** of notebook paper and stack them. Repeat Step 1. Copy and complete a table like the third table shown above.

④ Make three scatter plots of the data in the tables.

STUDENT HELP

READING GRAPHS
Use different scales on the x-axis and y-axis to include all the data in your scatter plots.

THINK ABOUT IT

1. The data in the paper-folding exploration are included in the graphs of these functions:

$$y = 2^x$$
$$y = 3 \cdot 2^x$$
$$y = 5 \cdot 2^x$$

Graph these three functions in one coordinate plane, or use a graphing calculator to graph them on one screen.

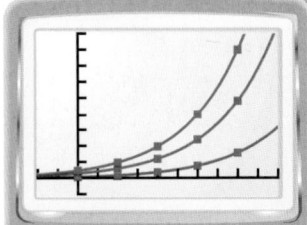

2. What is the y-intercept of each function?

3. What is the domain and range of each function?

4. All three functions are of the form $y = a \cdot 2^x$. When a is positive, how does changing the value of a affect the graph of the function?

8.1 Exponential Growth

GOAL Graph exponential growth functions.

Key Words

- exponential function
- exponential growth function
- asymptote

Prerequisite Skills

Evaluate the expression.

1. 5^3

2. 7^1

3. 6^{-2}

4. 12^0

An **exponential function** has the form $y = ab^x$ where $a \neq 0$ and the base b is a positive number other than 1. If $a > 0$ and $b > 1$, such a function is an **exponential growth function**, because the values of y grow as x increases.

To graph an exponential function, you can make a table of values and plot the corresponding points, as shown below.

EXAMPLE **1** Graph $y = ab^x$ when $a = 1$ and $b > 1$

Graph the function $y = 2^x$.

Solution

Make a table of values for the function.

x	−2	−1	0	1	2	3
y	$\frac{1}{4}$	$\frac{1}{2}$	1	2	4	8

Plot the points from the table.

Draw a curve that passes through the plotted points, as shown.

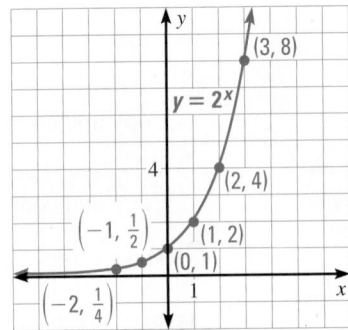

Exponential Growth Graphs

Here are some characteristics of the graph of $y = ab^x$ when $a > 0$ and $b > 1$.

- The graph *rises* from left to right.
- The graph passes through $(0, a)$ and $(1, ab)$.
- The domain is all real numbers.
- The range is $y > 0$.

$y = ab^x$

$(0, a)$ $(1, ab)$

$(b > 1)$

An **asymptote** is a line that a graph approaches more and more closely. The x-axis is an asymptote of the graph of $y = ab^x$.

The graph of $y = ab^x$ changes depending on the values of a and b.

EXAMPLE **2** **Graph $y = ab^x$ when $a \neq 1$ and $b > 1$**

a. Graph $y = 2 \cdot 3^x$.

b. Graph $y = \frac{1}{4} \cdot 2^x$.

Solution

a. Make a table of values. Then plot the points.

x	−3	−2	−1	0	1
y	$\frac{2}{27}$	$\frac{2}{9}$	$\frac{2}{3}$	2	6

Draw a curve that passes through the plotted points, as shown at the right.

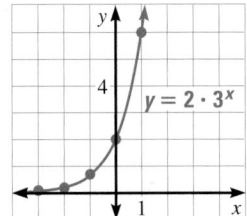

b. Make a table of values. Then plot the points.

x	−1	0	1	2	3
y	$\frac{1}{8}$	$\frac{1}{4}$	$\frac{1}{2}$	1	2

Draw a curve that passes through the plotted points, as shown at the right.

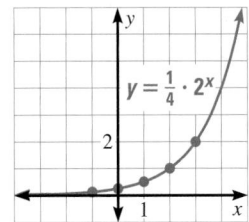

Checkpoint ✓ **Graph $y = ab^x$ when $b > 1$**

Graph the exponential function.

1. $y = 4^x$

2. $y = 5^x$

3. $y = 4 \cdot 3^x$

4. $y = 0.1 \cdot 2^x$

Translating Exponential Functions To graph the exponential function $y = ab^{x-h}$ or $y = ab^x + k$, sketch the graph of the function $y = ab^x$. Then translate the graph horizontally by h units or vertically by k units.

For example, the graphs of the functions $y = 2^{x-4}$ and $y = 2^x + 3$ shown below are translations of the graph of $y = 2^x$.

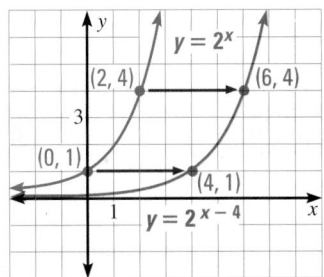

The graph approaches $y = 0$.

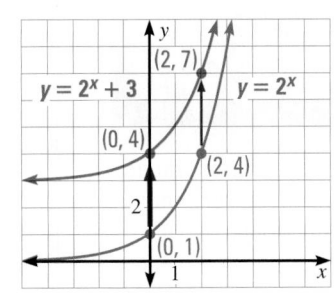

The graph approaches $y = 3$.

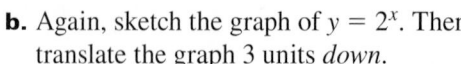

EXAMPLE 3 Graph an Exponential Function

Graph the function. Describe the horizontal asymptote. State the domain and range.

a. $y = 2^{x+3}$ **b.** $y = 2^x - 3$

Solution

a. Sketch the graph of $y = 2^x$, which passes through $(0, 1)$ and $(2, 4)$. Then translate the graph 3 units *to the left*.

The graph passes through $(-3, 1)$ and $(-1, 4)$.

The graph's asymptote is the x-axis.

The domain is all real numbers, and the range is $y > 0$.

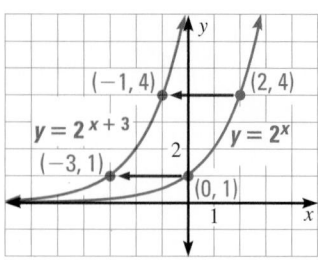

b. Again, sketch the graph of $y = 2^x$. Then translate the graph 3 units *down*.

The graph passes through $(0, -2)$ and $(2, 1)$.

The graph's asymptote is the line $y = -3$.

The domain is all real numbers, and the range is $y > -3$.

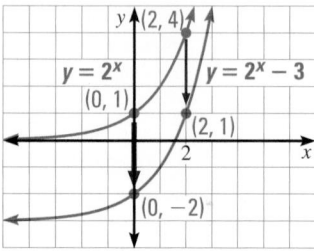

Checkpoint ✓ *Graph an Exponential Function*

Graph the function. Describe the horizontal asymptote. State the domain and range.

5. $y = 3^x + 2$ **6.** $y = 4^x - 5$ **7.** $y = 3^{x-4}$ **8.** $y = 2^{x+2}$

Link to
STOCK MARKET

The number of shares traded daily on the NYSE reached:
- 1 million in 1886
- 10 million in 1929
- 100 million in 1982
- 1000 million in 1997

EXAMPLE 4 Model Exponential Growth

Stock Market The annual number of shares S (in billions) traded on the New York Stock Exchange (NYSE) from 1990 to 2004 can be approximated by the model $S = 39(1.2)^x$ where x is the number of years since 1990. Graph the model. Then use the graph to estimate the number of shares traded in 1999.

Solution

Make a table of values or list of ordered pairs (x, S):

$(0, 39)$, $(2, 56)$, $(4, 81)$, $(6, 116)$, $(8, 168)$, $(10, 241)$, $(12, 348)$, $(14, 501)$

Plot the points. Draw a smooth curve through the points.

ANSWER ▶ Using the graph, you can estimate that about 200 billion shares were traded in 1999.

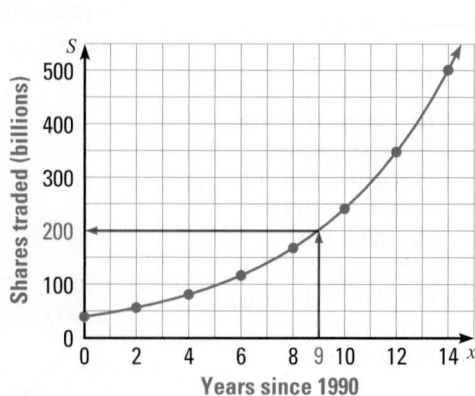

8.1 Exercises

Guided Practice

Vocabulary Check

1. Define the term *exponential function*.

2. What is the name of the horizontal line that the graph of an exponential growth function approaches?

3. For what values of a and b is the function $y = ab^x$ an exponential growth function?

Skill Check

Evaluate the expression for $x = -2$ and $x = 3$.

4. 3^x **5.** 5^x **6.** $8 \cdot 2^x$ **7.** $6 \cdot 3^x$

8. $3^x - 1$ **9.** $2^x + 5$ **10.** $2^x + 2$ **11.** $3^x - 3$

Graph the exponential function.

12. $f(x) = 7^x$ **13.** $f(x) = 3 \cdot 2^x$ **14.** $f(x) = 4^x + 1$ **15.** $f(x) = 3^{x-2}$

16. Stock Values The annual value of shares V (in trillions of dollars) traded on the New York Stock Exchange from 1990 to 2000 can be approximated by the model $V = 1.2 \cdot 1.25^x$ where $x = 0$ represents 1990. Graph the model. Then use the graph to estimate the value of shares in 1999.

Practice and Applications

STUDENT HELP

HOMEWORK HELP
Example 1: Exs. 17–33
Example 2: Exs. 17–33
Example 3: Exs. 34–39
Example 4: Exs. 40–44

Evaluating Expressions **Evaluate the expression for $x = -3$ and $x = 2$.**

17. 9^x **18.** 12^x **19.** $4 \cdot 7^x$ **20.** $5 \cdot 2^x$

21. $2^x + 3$ **22.** $4^x - 6$ **23.** $3^x - 2$ **24.** 10^{x+4}

Matching Graphs **Match the function with its graph.**

25. $y = 7^x - 5$ **26.** $y = \frac{1}{5} \cdot 7^x$ **27.** $y = 7^x$

A.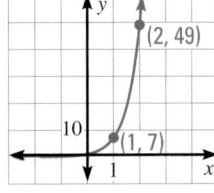

B.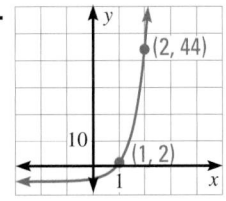

C.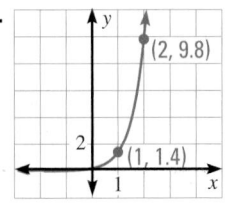

Graphing Functions **Graph the exponential function.**

28. $f(x) = 8^x$ **29.** $f(x) = 10^x$ **30.** $f(x) = 1.5^x$

31. $f(x) = 4 \cdot 2^x$ **32.** $f(x) = \frac{1}{8} \cdot 4^x$ **33.** $f(x) = \frac{1}{3} \cdot 3^x$

Translating Functions **Graph the exponential function. Describe the horizontal asymptote. State the domain and range.**

34. $y = 2^x - 5$ **35.** $y = 2^x + 5$ **36.** $y = 2^{x-2}$

37. $y = 3^x + 1$ **38.** $y = 3^x - 3$ **39.** $y = 4^{x-1}$

40. Aquatic Plants Duckweed is a small aquatic plant that floats in fresh water. The leaves of duckweed are called *fronds*. A researcher studying the growth of duckweed found that the number of fronds f observed could be modeled by the exponential function

$$f = 17.6 \cdot 1.35^d$$

where d is the number of days of growth under controlled conditions. Graph the function. Then use the graph to estimate after how many days the number of fronds was more than 100.

41. Blog Count The number of online blogs has increased rapidly. During a recent 24 month period, the number of blogs b (in millions) was modeled by the exponential function

$$b = 3(1.1225)^m$$

where m is the number of months since the beginning of the period. Graph the function. Between which two months did the number of blogs reach 10 million? reach 20 million?

Geometry Link **In Exercises 42–44, use the following information.**

The *Sierpinski carpet* is a fractal created by a process of iteration. Start with a square. In the first iteration, one square is removed from the center, leaving eight smaller squares. In the second iteration, a smaller square is removed from the center of each square in the first iteration. This process is repeated as shown below.

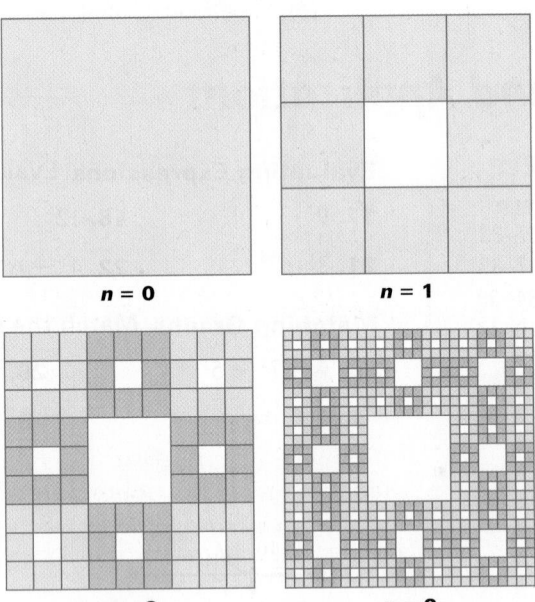

42. The total number of shaded squares in the nth iteration is given by the expression 8^n. How many shaded squares are in the third iteration? the fifth iteration? the seventh iteration?

43. The total number of white squares (of various sizes) in the nth iteration is given by the expression $\frac{1}{7} \cdot 8^n - \frac{1}{7}$. How many white squares are in the first iteration? the third iteration? the fifth iteration?

44. Graph $y = 8^x$ and $y = \frac{1}{7} \cdot 8^x - \frac{1}{7}$ in the same coordinate plane. Describe how the graphs are different.

Challenge Analyze the function as a horizontal and vertical translation of an exponential function of the form $y = ab^x$. Graph the function. Describe the horizontal asymptote. State the domain and range.

45. $y = 2^{x-4} - 3$ **46.** $y = 3^{x+5} - 1$ **47.** $y = 4^{x-1} + 2$

48. Logical Reasoning Graph $y = -2^x$ and $y = 2^x$ in the same coordinate plane. Graph $y = -3^x$ and $y = 3^x$ in the same coordinte plane. Using these graphs, what comparisons can you make between the graphs of $y = -b^x$ and $y = b^x$?

Standardized Test Practice

49. Multiple Choice What is the equation of the asymptote of the exponential growth function $y = 3^x - 7$?

   A $x = -7$ **B** $x = 7$ **C** $y = -7$ **D** $y = 7$

50. Multiple Choice Which exponential growth function is graphed below?

   F $y = 3^x - 2$

   G $y = 3^{x-2}$

   H $y = 3^{x+2}$

   J $y = 3^x + 2$

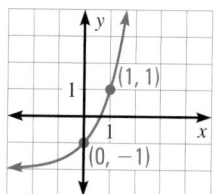

51. Multiple Choice What is the domain and range of $y = 2^x + 3$?

   A domain: $x > 3$;   **B** domain: $x < 3$;
      range: all real numbers   range: all real numbers

   C domain: all real numbers;   **D** domain: all real numbers;
      range: $y > 3$ range: $y < 3$

Mixed Review

Graphing Functions Graph the function. *(Lesson 2.1)*

52. $y = 6x$ **53.** $y = -5x$ **54.** $y = -x + 5$

55. $y = x - 8$ **56.** $y = 3x - \dfrac{1}{2}$ **57.** $y = -4x + 4$

Evaluating Expressions Evaluate the expression. *(Lesson 6.1)*

58. $\left(\dfrac{2}{5}\right)^1$ **59.** $\left(\dfrac{5}{6}\right)^0$ **60.** $\left(\dfrac{1}{3}\right)^4$ **61.** $\left(\dfrac{1}{2}\right)^5$

62. $\left(\dfrac{3}{4}\right)^2$ **63.** $\left(\dfrac{4}{5}\right)^3$ **64.** $9\left(\dfrac{2}{7}\right)^2$ **65.** $4\left(\dfrac{1}{8}\right)^3$

Describing End Behavior Identify the degree and the leading coefficient of the polynomial function. Then describe the end behavior of its graph. *(Lesson 6.2)*

66. $f(x) = 2x^4$ **67.** $f(x) = -5x^2 + 3$

68. $f(x) = -2 - x^3$ **69.** $f(x) = 8x^7 - 3x^6 - x$

70. $f(x) = 7x^2 - 4x^5$ **71.** $f(x) = x^4 - 8x + 4$

Geometry Skills

Finding Volume Find the volume of the hemisphere. The volume of a sphere is $V = \dfrac{4}{3}\pi r^3$.

72.
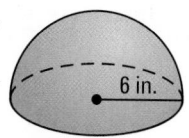
6 in.

73.
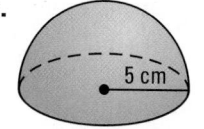
5 cm

74.

3 ft

Goal

Graph exponential decay functions of the form $y = a\left(\frac{1}{2}\right)^x$.

Materials

- 100 coins
- cup
- graph paper

QUESTION

How does the value of *a* affect the graph of $y = a\left(\frac{1}{2}\right)^x$?

EXPLORE

1 Place 100 coins in a cup and toss them onto a table. Record the toss number and the number of coins that land showing heads in a table like the one shown.

Toss number, *x*	1	2	3	4	5	6	7
Heads, *y*	?	?	?	?	?	?	?

2 Remove the coins that land showing tails and set them aside. Gather and toss the remaining coins again. Record the results.

3 Repeat Step 2 until only one coin remains.

4 Make a scatter plot of the data in the table, where *x* is the toss number and *y* is the number of coins that land showing heads.

5 Evaluate $y = 100\left(\frac{1}{2}\right)^x$ for each *x*-value in the table. Graph these points and connect them with a smooth curve.

6 Compare the graph of the function to the scatter plot.

THINK ABOUT IT

1. What part of the equation in Step 5 gives the number of coins you started with?

2. What function would you graph if you started with 50 coins? 200 coins?

3. Use a table of values to graph $y = a\left(\frac{1}{2}\right)^x$ for *a* = 3, 5, and 10.

4. What effect does the value of *a* have on the graph of the function?

5. Graph the exponential growth function $y = 3 \cdot 2^x$. How is this graph related to the graph of $y = 3\left(\frac{1}{2}\right)^x$?

Exponential Decay

Key Words

- exponential decay function

Prerequisite Skills

Evaluate the expression.

1. $\left(\frac{1}{2}\right)^3$

2. $\left(\frac{3}{4}\right)^{-3}$

3. $8\left(\frac{3}{7}\right)^0$

4. $5\left(\frac{2}{5}\right)^2$

GOAL Graph exponential decay functions.

What is the value of a used car?

In Example 5, you will estimate how the value of a used car changes using an *exponential decay function*.

An **exponential decay function** has the form $y = ab^x$ where $a > 0$ and $0 < b < 1$. Example 1 shows the basic shape of the graph of an exponential decay function.

EXAMPLE 1 Graph $y = b^x$ when $0 < b < 1$

Graph the function $y = \left(\frac{1}{2}\right)^x$.

Solution

Make a table of values for the function.

x	-3	-2	-1	0	1	2
y	8	4	2	1	$\frac{1}{2}$	$\frac{1}{4}$

Plot the points from the table.

Draw a curve that passes through the plotted points, as shown.

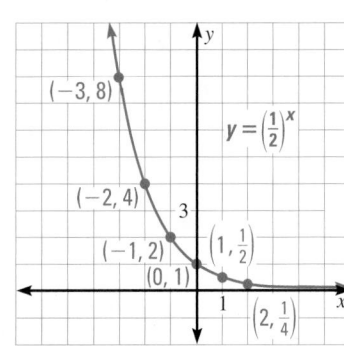

Exponential Decay Graphs

Here are some characteristics of the graph of $y = ab^x$ when $a > 0$ and $0 < b < 1$.

- The graph *falls* from left to right.
- The graph passes through $(0, a)$ and $(1, ab)$.
- The domain is all real numbers.
- The range is $y > 0$.

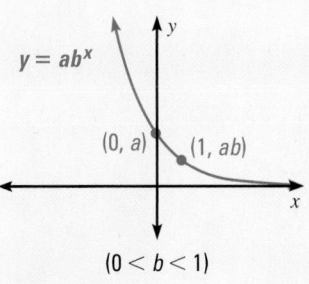

$y = ab^x$

$(0, a)$ $(1, ab)$

$(0 < b < 1)$

EXAMPLE 2 Graph $y = ab^x$ when $0 < b < 1$

Graph the function.

a. $y = 3\left(\dfrac{1}{2}\right)^x$
b. $y = \dfrac{1}{4}\left(\dfrac{2}{3}\right)^x$

Solution

a. *Make* a table of values.

x	−1	0	1	2	3
y	6	3	$\dfrac{3}{2}$	$\dfrac{3}{4}$	$\dfrac{3}{8}$

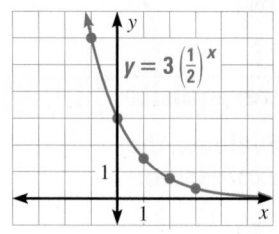

Plot the points.

Draw a curve that passes through the plotted points, as shown at the right.

b. *Make* a table of values.

x	−2	−1	0	1	2
y	$\dfrac{9}{16}$	$\dfrac{3}{8}$	$\dfrac{1}{4}$	$\dfrac{1}{6}$	$\dfrac{1}{9}$

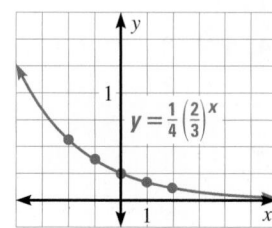

Plot the points.

Draw a curve that passes through the plotted points, as shown at the right.

Checkpoint ✓ **Graph $y = ab^x$ when $0 < b < 1$**

Graph the function.

1. $y = \left(\dfrac{1}{4}\right)^x$
2. $y = \left(\dfrac{2}{5}\right)^x$
3. $y = 2\left(\dfrac{1}{5}\right)^x$

4. $y = 10\left(\dfrac{1}{2}\right)^x$
5. $y = \dfrac{1}{2}\left(\dfrac{1}{3}\right)^x$
6. $y = \dfrac{2}{5}\left(\dfrac{4}{5}\right)^x$

EXAMPLE 3 **Graph an Exponential Function**

Graph $y = \left(\dfrac{1}{2}\right)^{x-2}$. Describe the horizontal asymptote. State the domain and range.

Solution

Sketch the graph of the function $y = \left(\dfrac{1}{2}\right)^x$. It passes through $(0, 1)$ and $(-2, 4)$.

Translate the graph 2 units to the right.

The graph's asymptote is the x-axis.

The domain is all real numbers, and the range is $y > 0$.

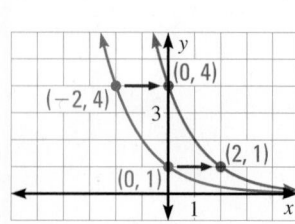

EXAMPLE 4 **Graph an Exponential Function**

Graph $y = \left(\frac{2}{3}\right)^x + 3$. Describe the horizontal asymptote. State the domain and range.

Solution

Sketch the graph of the function $y = \left(\frac{2}{3}\right)^x$.

It passes through $(0, 1)$ and $\left(-2, 2\frac{1}{4}\right)$.

Translate the graph 3 units up.

It passes through $(0, 4)$ and $\left(-2, 5\frac{1}{4}\right)$.

The graph's asymptote is the line $y = 3$.

The domain is all real numbers, and the range is $y > 3$.

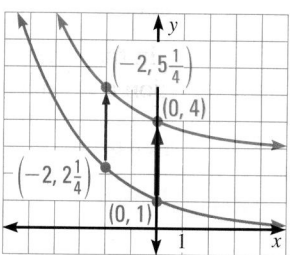

Checkpoint ✓ *Graph an Exponential Function*

Graph the function. Describe the horizontal asymptote. State the domain and range.

7. $y = \left(\frac{1}{2}\right)^{x + 3}$ **8.** $y = \left(\frac{3}{4}\right)^{x - 5}$ **9.** $y = \left(\frac{1}{4}\right)^x - 2$ **10.** $y = \left(\frac{1}{3}\right)^x + 3$

EXAMPLE 5 **Model Exponential Decay**

Depreciation The value of a used car y (in thousands of dollars) can be approximated by the model $y = 20(0.85)^x$ where x is the number of years since the car was new. Graph the model. Then use the graph to estimate when the value of the car will be $4000.

Solution

You can use a graphing calculator to make a graph. Enter the equation $y = 20(0.85)^x$.

Choose a suitable viewing window. For example, use $0 \le x \le 15$ and $0 \le y \le 25$.

The graph passes through $(0, 20)$, $(1, 17)$, $(2, 14.45)$, and so on. Use the *Trace* feature to determine that $y = 4$ when x is about 10.

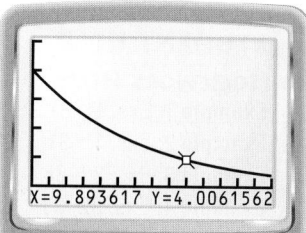

ANSWER ▶ The value of the car will be $4000 after nearly 10 years.

STUDENT HELP

AVOID ERRORS
When you evaluate an expression such as $20(0.85)^2$, follow the order of operations. Find the power first, and then multiply:
$20(0.85)^2 = 20 \cdot 0.7225$

Checkpoint ✓ *Model Exponential Decay*

11. The value of a van y (in thousands of dollars) can be approximated by the model $y = 24(0.9)^x$ where x represents the number of years since the van was new. Graph the model. Then use the graph to estimate when the value of the van will be $10,000.

Guided Practice

Vocabulary Check

1. Is the function $y = \left(\frac{4}{3}\right)^{x-1}$ an example of an exponential decay function? Explain why or why not.

2. What is the horizontal asymptote of the graph of the exponential decay function $y = ab^x + k$?

Skill Check

Classify the function as *exponential growth* or *exponential decay*.

3. $y = 3\left(\frac{2}{7}\right)^x$

4. $y = 8\left(\frac{5}{2}\right)^x$

5. $y = \frac{1}{4} \cdot 3^x$

6. $y = \frac{4}{3}\left(\frac{3}{5}\right)^x$

In Exercises 7–10, use the function $y = 2\left(\frac{1}{4}\right)^x$.

7. Copy and complete the table of values for the function.

x	−3	−2	−1	0	1	2	3
y	?	?	?	?	?	?	?

8. Graph the function by plotting the points from the table and connecting them with a smooth curve.

9. Describe the horizontal asymptote of the function.

10. State the domain and range of the function.

Practice and Applications

STUDENT HELP

HOMEWORK HELP
Example 1: Exs. 11–31
Example 2: Exs. 11–31
Example 3: Exs. 32–38
Example 4: Exs. 32–38
Example 5: Exs. 39–48

Classifying Functions Classify the function as *exponential growth* or *exponential decay*. Then match the function to its graph.

11. $y = \left(\frac{3}{4}\right)^x$

12. $y = \left(\frac{4}{3}\right)^x$

13. $y = \frac{1}{2}\left(\frac{3}{4}\right)^x$

A.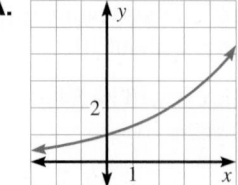

B.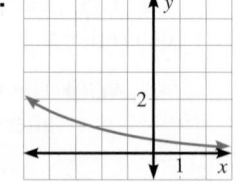

C.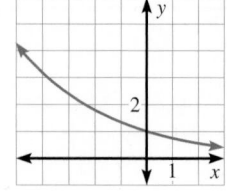

Evaluating Expressions Evaluate the exponential expression for $x = -5$ and $x = 2$.

14. $\left(\frac{1}{6}\right)^x$

15. $\left(\frac{3}{5}\right)^x$

16. $4\left(\frac{1}{2}\right)^x$

17. $6\left(\frac{1}{3}\right)^x$

18. 0.4^x

19. 0.7^x

20. $12(0.5)^x$

21. $5(0.3)^x$

PRINTING When the printed sheets are folded in half repeatedly, each sheet may create a group of 8 pages, 16 pages, or 32 pages.

22. Printing To make small pamphlets, large sheets of paper are printed and folded in half repeatedly. The area of a piece of paper decreases each time it is folded. For a 34 inch by 44 inch sheet, the area A (in square inches) can be modeled by the function

$$A = 1496(0.5)^n$$

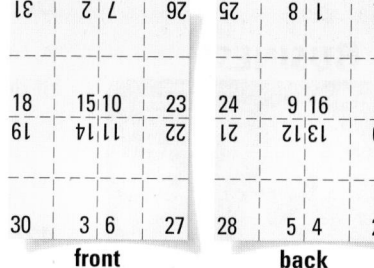

where n is the number of times the paper is folded. What is the area of the paper when it is folded 2 times? 3 times? 4 times?

23. Motorcycles You buy a new motorcycle for $18,000. The value V (in thousands of dollars) of the motorcycle can be modeled by the function

$$V = 18\left(\frac{9}{10}\right)^t$$

where t is the number of years since it was purchased. How much is the motorcycle worth 5 years after it was purchased?

Graphing Functions **Graph the exponential function.**

24. $y = \left(\frac{1}{5}\right)^x$ **25.** $y = \left(\frac{1}{10}\right)^x$ **26.** $y = 2\left(\frac{1}{2}\right)^x$ **27.** $y = 3\left(\frac{1}{4}\right)^x$

28. $y = 100\left(\frac{1}{8}\right)^x$ **29.** $y = 80\left(\frac{2}{5}\right)^x$ **30.** $y = 100(0.75)^x$ **31.** $y = 20(0.9)^x$

Matching **Match the function with its graph. State the domain and range of the function.**

32. $y = \left(\frac{1}{2}\right)^x + 4$ **33.** $y = \left(\frac{1}{2}\right)^{x+4}$ **34.** $y = \left(\frac{1}{2}\right)^{x-4}$

A. 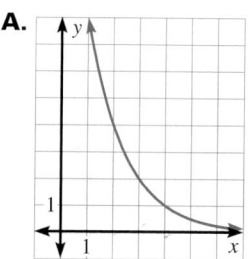 **B.** 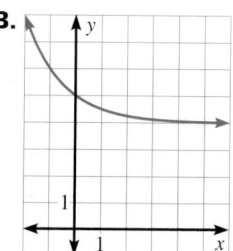 **C.**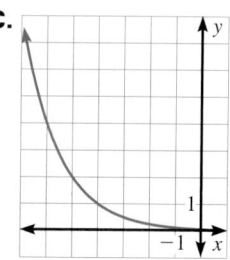

Graphing Functions **Graph the exponential function. Describe the horizontal asymptote. State the domain and range.**

35. $y = \left(\frac{1}{3}\right)^{x-5}$ **36.** $y = \left(\frac{1}{2}\right)^x - 1$ **37.** $y = \left(\frac{2}{3}\right)^x + 3$ **38.** $y = \left(\frac{4}{5}\right)^{x+3}$

Car Value **In Exercises 39–41, use the following information.**

You buy a new car for $24,000. The value y (in thousands of dollars) of the car can be approximated by the model $y = 24(0.82)^x$. The variable x represents the number of years since you bought the car.

39. Copy and complete the table of values for the function.

x	0	1	2	3	4
y	?	?	?	?	?

40. Use the table of values to graph the model.

41. Use the graph to estimate when the value of the car will be $6000.

Depreciation In Exercises 42–44, use the following information.

A small business owner buys equipment for $40,000. The value V (in thousands of dollars) of the equipment can be modeled by the function

$$V = 40(0.85)^x$$

where x is the number of years since the equipment was purchased.

42. Make a table of values for the function. Then graph the model.

43. Use the graph to estimate when the equipment will have a value of $11,000.

44. Will the value of the equipment ever be $0? Explain your reasoning.

Half-Life In Exercises 45 and 46, use the following information.

A 100-gram sample of radioactive lead-210 is stored in a container. The amount y (in grams) of lead-210 left in the sample can be modeled by the function

$$y = 100(0.97)^x$$

where x is the number of years that have elapsed.

45. Make a table of values. Use the x-values 10, 20, 30, 40, 50, 60, and 70. Round to the nearest tenth. Then graph the model.

46. Use the graph to estimate when only half of the lead-210 in the 100-gram sample will remain. This length of time is called the *half-life* of the material.

Pianos In Exercises 47 and 48, use the following information.

You purchase a new piano for $4000. The piano loses value over time. The value V (in dollars) of the piano can be modeled by the function

$$V = 4000(0.86)^x$$

where x is the number of years since the piano was purchased.

47. Make a table of values and graph the function.

48. After five years, a piano dealer offers to purchase the piano for $2000. Should you sell the piano at that price? Explain your reasoning.

49. Logical Reasoning The value of a financial investment A (in thousands of dollars) can be modeled by the function

$$A = 2(0.95)^x$$

where x is the time in years since the money was invested. According to the model, is the value of the investment increasing or decreasing? Explain your reasoning.

50. Challenge Graph $y = 0.5^x$ and $y = -0.5^x$ in the same coordinate plane. Then graph $y = 0.2^x$ and $y = -0.2^x$ in another coordinate plane. Use your results to describe how the graphs of $y = b^x$ and $y = -b^x$ are related.

Standardized Test Practice

51. Multiple Choice Which function's graph is shown below?

(A) $y = \left(\dfrac{4}{5}\right)^x$ (B) $y = \left(\dfrac{5}{4}\right)^x$

(C) $y = \left(\dfrac{4}{5}\right)^{x+2}$ (D) $y = \left(\dfrac{4}{5}\right)^x + 2$

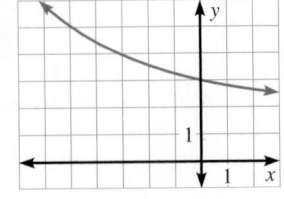

52. Multiple Choice An adult drinks a beverage containing 110 milligrams of caffeine. The amount c (in milligrams) of caffeine in the person's system can be modeled by the function

$$c = 110(0.89)^x$$

where x is the number of hours that have elapsed. About how much caffeine is in the person's system after 3 hours?

F 0 mg   **G** 55 mg   **H** 78 mg   **J** 110 mg

Mixed Review

Operations with Functions Let $f(x) = x + 4$, $g(x) = x + 2$, and $h(x) = x^2 - 4$. **Perform the indicated operation and state the domain.** *(Lesson 7.4)*

53. $f(x) \cdot g(x)$ **54.** $g(x) \cdot f(x)$ **55.** $f(x) \cdot f(x)$

56. $g(x) \cdot h(x)$ **57.** $h(x) \cdot h(x)$ **58.** $\dfrac{g(x)}{f(x)}$

59. $\dfrac{f(x)}{g(x)}$ **60.** $\dfrac{h(x)}{g(x)}$ **61.** $\dfrac{h(x)}{f(x)}$

Graphing Functions **Graph the exponential function. Describe the horizontal asymptote. State the domain and range.** *(Lesson 8.1)*

62. $y = 4^x - 3$ **63.** $y = 4^x + 3$ **64.** $y = 3^{x+2}$ **65.** $y = 3^{x-2}$

Geometry Skills

Inscribed Quadrilaterals **When a quadrilateral is inscribed in a circle, opposite angles are supplementary. Find the values of x and y.**

66.

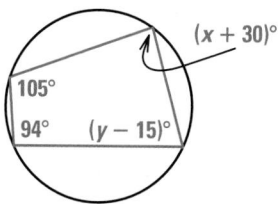

67.

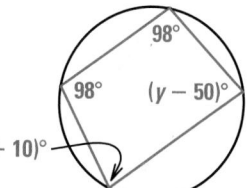

Quiz 1

Lessons 8.1 and 8.2

Evaluate the exponential expression for $x = -2$ and $x = 2$.

1. $\left(\dfrac{7}{2}\right)^x$ **2.** $\dfrac{1}{3} \cdot 6^x$ **3.** $\dfrac{1}{3}\left(\dfrac{1}{2}\right)^x$

Lesson 8.2

Classify the function as *exponential growth* or *exponential decay*.

4. $y = \dfrac{1}{5} \cdot 14^x$ **5.** $y = 8\left(\dfrac{1}{3}\right)^x$ **6.** $y = 15\left(\dfrac{1}{2}\right)^x$

Lessons 8.1 and 8.2

Graph the exponential function. Describe the horizontal asymptote. State the domain and range.

7. $y = 6^x$ **8.** $y = 2 \cdot 6^x$ **9.** $y = \left(\dfrac{1}{2}\right)^x$

10. $y = \left(\dfrac{1}{6}\right)^{x+4}$ **11.** $y = \left(\dfrac{3}{4}\right)^{x-5}$ **12.** $y = \left(\dfrac{3}{4}\right)^x + 3$

Lesson 8.1

13. Salaries The company you work for raises your salary 4% each year. Your salary S (in thousands of dollars) can be modeled by $S = 38(1.04)^t$ where t is the number of years since you started working. Make a table showing your salary for years 0 through 5. Then use the table to graph the function.

8.3 Modeling with Exponential Functions

Key Words
- growth factor
- decay factor
- natural base e

GOAL Write models for exponential growth and decay.

How can you predict the balance in a bank account after several years?

In Example 4, you will find the balance in a bank account after a given amount of time. You will use an exponential growth function to calculate the balance.

Some real-life quantities increase or decrease by a fixed percent each year (or other time period). The amount y of such a quantity after t years can be modeled by the equations shown below.

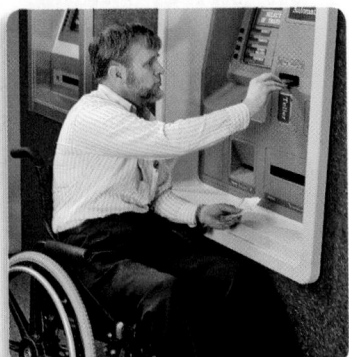

exponential growth	exponential decay
$y = a(1 + r)^t$	$y = a(1 - r)^t$

In these models, a is the initial amount, r is the percent increase or decrease written as a decimal, and t is the number of time periods. The quantity $(1 + r)$ is called the **growth factor**. The quantity $(1 - r)$ is called the **decay factor**.

EXAMPLE 1 Write and Use an Exponential Growth Model

Sales Figures One year, a clothing company had $1.5 million in sales. In later years, sales y (in millions of dollars) increased by about 25% each year.

a. Write an exponential growth model that represents the sales after t years.

b. Use the model to predict the sales after 8 years.

Solution

a. $y = a(1 + r)^t$ Write exponential growth model.

$= 1.5(1 + 0.25)^t$ Substitute 1.5 for a and 0.25 for r.

$= 1.5(1.25)^t$ Simplify.

ANSWER ▶ The model is $y = 1.5(1.25)^t$.

b. To predict the sales after 8 years, substitute 8 for t.

$y = 1.5(1.25)^8 \approx 8.9$

ANSWER ▶ The sales after 8 years will be about $8.9 million.

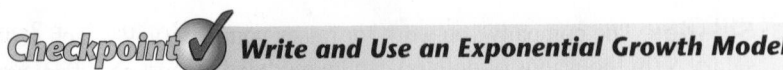

Checkpoint ✓ **Write and Use an Exponential Growth Model**

1. Redo Example 1 using a sales increase of 10% each year.

EXAMPLE 2 Write and Use an Exponential Decay Model

Computers You buy a new computer for $1500. The value y (in dollars) of the computer decreases by 40% each year.

a. Write an exponential decay model that represents the value of the computer.

b. Use the model from part (a) to estimate the value after 3 years.

Solution

a. Let t be the number of years since you bought the computer.

$y = a(1 - r)^t$ Write exponential decay model.

$= 1500(1 - 0.4)^t$ Substitute 1500 for a and 0.4 for r.

$= 1500(0.6)^t$ Simplify.

ANSWER ▶ The model is $y = 1500(0.6)^t$.

b. To estimate the value after 3 years, substitute 3 for t.

$y = 1500(0.6)^3 = 324$

ANSWER ▶ The value of the computer after 3 years is $324.

> **STUDENT HELP**
>
> **SOLVING NOTE**
> The computer's value decreases by 40% each year. So, its value is 60% of the prior year's value. This is the meaning of the 0.6 decay factor.

 **Write and Use an Exponential Decay Model**

2. Redo Example 2 using a new computer cost of $1200 and a value decrease of 35% each year.

Writing Exponential Functions Just as two points determine a line, two points also determine an exponential curve.

EXAMPLE 3 Write an Exponential Function

Write a function of the form $y = ab^x$ whose graph passes through (1, 6) and (2, 18).

Solution

Substitute the coordinates of the points into $y = ab^x$ to obtain two equations.

$6 = ab^1$ Substitute 6 for y and 1 for x, because (1, 6) is on the graph.

$18 = ab^2$ Substitute 18 for y and 2 for x, because (2, 18) is on the graph.

Solve the first equation for a to get $a = \dfrac{6}{b}$. Then substitute into the second equation.

$18 = \left(\dfrac{6}{b}\right)b^2$ Substitute $\dfrac{6}{b}$ for a.

$18 = 6b$ Quotient of powers property

$3 = b$ Divide each side by 6.

ANSWER ▶ Using $b = 3$, you find that $a = \dfrac{6}{b} = \dfrac{6}{3} = 2$. Because $a = 2$ and $b = 3$, $y = 2 \cdot 3^x$ is the exponential function whose graph passes through (1, 6) and (2, 18).

Compound Interest Compound interest is interest paid on an initial investment, called the *principal*, and on previously earned interest. Interest earned is expressed as an annual percent, but interest is usually compounded more than once per year.

Because interest is usually compounded more than once per year, the exponential growth model $y = a(1 + r)^t$ must be modified for compound interest problems.

Compound Interest

An initial principal P is deposited in an account that pays interest at an annual rate r (expressed as a decimal), compounded n times per year.

The amount A in the account after t years can be modeled by this formula:

$$A = P\left(1 + \frac{r}{n}\right)^{nt}$$

EXAMPLE 4 Find the Balance in an Account

Finance You deposit $2000 in an account that pays 2% annual interest. Find the balance after 10 years if the interest is compounded quarterly.

Solution

$A = P\left(1 + \frac{r}{n}\right)^{nt}$ Write compound interest formula.

$= 2000\left(1 + \frac{0.02}{4}\right)^{4 \,\cdot\, 10}$ Substitute 2000 for P, 0.02 for r, 4 for n, and 10 for t.

$= 2000(1.005)^{40}$ Simplify.

≈ 2441.59 Use a calculator.

ANSWER ▶ The balance after 10 years is about $2441.59.

STUDENT HELP

VOCABULARY
Here are some words that are used to describe how often interest is compounded:

yearly = 1 time/yr
quarterly = 4 times/yr
monthly = 12 times/yr
daily = 365 times/yr

CHECK You can check the solution by graphing the function $A = 2000(1.005)^t$.

Using the graph, you can see that after 40 compounding periods (10 years), the balance is between $2400 and $2500. ✓

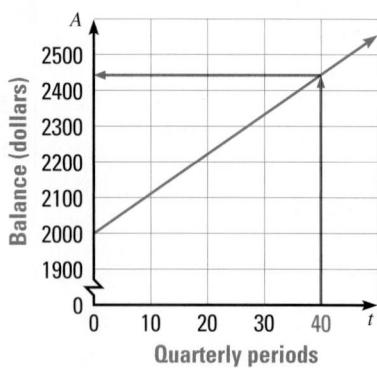

Checkpoint ✓ *Write and Use Exponential Functions*

Write an exponential function of the form $y = ab^x$ whose graph passes through the given points.

3. (2, 16), (3, 64)   **4.** (2, 3), (4, 12)   **5.** (1, 3), (3, 108)

6. You deposit $1500 in an account that pays 2% annual interest. Find the balance after 6 years if the interest is compounded monthly.

Continuous Compounding When interest is calculated as if an infinite number of compounding periods occur each year, it is called *continuously compounded*. The formula for continuously compounded interest contains the number *e*. Like π and *i*, the number *e* is denoted by a letter. The number is called the **natural base *e***, or the *Euler number*, after its discoverer, Leonhard Euler (1707–1783).

The Natural Base *e*

The natural base *e* is irrational. It is defined as follows:

As *n* approaches $+\infty$, $\left(1 + \dfrac{1}{n}\right)^n$ approaches $e \approx 2.71828$.

As *n* approaches positive infinity in the compound interest formula, it approximates the following formula for continuously compounded interest.

Compound Interest Formula		Continuously Compounded Interest Formula
$A = P\left(1 + \dfrac{r}{n}\right)^{nt}$	**approximates**	$A = Pe^{rt}$

EXAMPLE 5 Find the Balance in an Account

Finance You deposit $500 in an account that pays 4% annual interest compounded continuously.

a. Find the balance after one year.

b. Graph the continuously compounded interest model.

c. Use the graph to estimate how long it will take your money to grow to $700.

Solution

a. $A = Pe^{rt}$ Write continuously compounded interest formula.

$\quad = 500e^{0.04 \cdot 1}$ Substitute 500 for *P*, 0.04 for *r*, and 1 for *t*.

$\quad = 500e^{0.04}$ Simplify.

$\quad \approx 520.41$ Use a calculator.

ANSWER ▸ The balance after one year is about $520.41.

b. The graph of the model $y = 500e^{0.04x}$ is shown at the right.

c. Use the *Trace* feature to determine when the balance is $700. This happens when *x* is about 8.4. So, it will take about 8.4 years for your money to grow to $700.

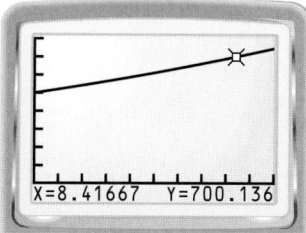

X=8.41667   Y=700.136

STUDENT HELP

KEYSTROKE HELP
To evaluate $500e^{0.04}$ in Example 5, use the following keystrokes:

500 **2nd** $[e^x]$ 0.04

The display should be 520.4053871.

 **Find the Balance in an Account**

7. You deposit $1000 in an account that pays 3% annual interest compounded continuously. Find the balance after 1 year, 3 years, and 5 years.

8.3 Exercises

Guided Practice

Vocabulary Check

1. In the equation $y = a(1 + r)^t$, what type of factor is $(1 + r)$?

2. Give an example of an exponential decay function.

3. Define the natural base e.

Skill Check

Determine whether the function shows *exponential growth* or *exponential decay*.

4. $y = 8(1 + 0.4)^t$

5. $y = 23(1 - 0.03)^t$

6. $y = 100(0.84)^t$

7. $y = 850(1.05)^t$

8. $y = 6(2.15)^t$

9. $y = 0.5(0.99)^t$

Write an exponential function of the form $y = ab^x$ whose graph passes through the given points.

10. $(1, 5)$, $(2, 25)$

11. $(1, 6)$, $(3, 24)$

12. $(2, 16)$, $(3, 32)$

13. **Growth or Decay?** The population p of a small town after x years can be modeled by the function $p = 6850(1.03)^x$. According to the model, will the population increase or decrease as time passes? Explain your reasoning.

Practice and Applications

STUDENT HELP

HOMEWORK HELP
Example 1: Exs. 14–32
Example 2: Exs. 14–32
Example 3: Exs. 33–43
Example 4: Exs. 44–50
Example 5: Exs. 51–53

Identifying Exponential Functions Determine whether the function shows *exponential growth* or *exponential decay*. Then identify the initial amount and the percent increase or decrease.

14. $y = 82(1 - 0.25)^t$

15. $y = 12(1 + 0.3)^t$

16. $y = 250(1.5)^t$

17. $y = 1500(1.05)^t$

18. $y = 150(0.5)^t$

19. $y = 2800(0.05)^t$

20. $y = 10(1.01)^t$

21. $y = 18(0.95)^t$

22. $y = 5(3.25)^t$

Gasoline Cost In Exercises 23–25, use the following information.

In January, the average cost of gasoline was $2.50 per gallon. During the year, the average cost c (in dollars) of gasoline increased about 1% each month.

23. Write an exponential growth model that represents the average cost of gasoline t months after January.

24. Graph the model.

25. Use the model to predict the cost of gasoline in December (when $t = 11$).

Simple Interest In Exercises 26–28, use the following information.

You deposit $900 into an account that pays simple interest. Each year the amount in the account increases by 2.5%.

26. Write an exponential growth model that represents the balance after t years.

27. Graph the model.

28. Use the model to estimate the balance after 5 years.

STOLEN BASES The current career record for most stolen bases in Major League Baseball is 1406, held by Rickey Henderson.

Writing Models In Exercises 29–32, write an exponential growth or decay model that describes the situation.

29. Stolen Bases One season, a baseball player stole 23 bases. During the player's next 4 seasons, the number of stolen bases b decreased by about 35% each season.

30. Car Value You purchase a car for $16,000. Each year, the value V of the car decreases by 15%.

31. Pocket Watch You purchase a pocket watch for $350. Each year, the value V of the pocket watch increases by 7%.

32. Cell Phone You purchase a cell phone for $120. Each year, the value V of the cell phone decreases by 45%.

Writing Exponential Functions Write an exponential function of the form $y = ab^x$ whose graph passes through the given points.

33. (1, 15), (2, 45) **34.** (1, 12), (2, 48) **35.** (1, 20), (2, 100)

36. (2, 28), (3, 56) **37.** (1, 3), (3, 27) **38.** (2, 8), (4, 32)

39. (1, 20), (2, 10) **40.** (3, 48), (4, 24) **41.** (1, 9), (3, 1)

42. Apartment Rent In 2000, the rent on an apartment was $800 per month. In 2002, the rent increased to $882 per month. Write an exponential function of the form $C = ab^t$ that models the cost C of rent t years after 2000.

43. Lawnmower Value In 2006, a lawnmower was worth $400. In 2007, the value decreased to $324. Write an exponential function of the form $V = ab^t$ that models the value V of the lawnmower t years after 2006. Predict the lawnmower's value in 2010.

Compound Interest In Exercises 44–46, use the following information.

You have $1400 to deposit and are comparing the offers of banks shown in the table below.

Bank	Interest rate	Compounding
X	2%	yearly
Y	3%	quarterly
Z	4%	monthly

44. Find the balance after 4 years if you deposit $1400 in an account at Bank X.

45. Find the balance after 4 years if you deposit $1400 in an account at Bank Y.

46. Find the balance after 4 years if you deposit $1400 in an account at Bank Z.

47. Logical Reasoning You have the choice of depositing $1000 into one of three bank accounts, described below.

• Account A pays 3% annual interest compounded quarterly

• Account B pays 3% annual interest compounded monthly

• Account C pays 3% annual interest compounded daily

Which account should you choose? Does your answer depend on the amount you have available to deposit? Explain your reasoning.

Reach Your Goal In Exercises 48–50, suppose your goal is to have at least $3000 in an account after 5 years.

48. You deposit $2400 in an account that pays 4.3% annual interest compounded annually. What is the balance after 5 years? Do you reach your goal?

49. You deposit $2500 in an account that pays 3.7% annual interest compounded monthly. What is the balance after 5 years? Do you reach your goal?

50. You deposit $2450 in an account that pays 4.1% annual interest compounded daily. What is the balance after 5 years? Do you reach your goal?

Continuous Compounding In Exercises 51–53, use the following information.

You deposit $1000 in an account that pays 3.5% annual interest compounded continuously.

51. Write an exponential growth model that represents the balance after t years.

52. Graph the model.

53. Use the graph to estimate how long it will take your money to grow to $1500.

Standardized Test Practice

54. Multi-Step Problem You have $3000 to put into an account. A teller at a bank tells you that an account pays 5% annual interest compounded quarterly.

a. Write an exponential model giving the balance A in the account after t years.

b. Does the model show *exponential growth* or *exponential decay*?

c. Evaluate the model when $t = 0$, $t = 5$, and $t = 10$.

d. An account at another bank yields a balance A after t years given by the model $A = 3000e^{0.0498t}$. What is the annual interest rate of this account? How is it compounded?

e. Evaluate the model in part (d) when $t = 0$, $t = 5$, and $t = 10$.

f. Critical Thinking Does the account with a greater interest rate or lesser interest rate yield a greater balance? Explain your answer.

Mixed Review

Evaluating Powers Evaluate the power. *(Lesson 1.2)*

55. 2^7

56. 13^2

57. -10^3

58. $(-10)^2$

Evaluating Expressions Evaluate the expression. Tell which properties of exponents you used. *(Lesson 6.1)*

59. $4^3 \cdot 4^2$

60. $(-2)^5 \cdot (-2)^3$

61. $(4^2)^{-2}$

62. $\left(\frac{1}{3}\right)^{-4}$

Graphing Functions Graph the exponential function. *(Lessons 8.1, 8.2)*

63. $f(x) = 7 \cdot 2^x$

64. $f(x) = 2^x - 1$

65. $f(x) = 2^{x-5}$

66. $y = 2\left(\frac{1}{3}\right)^x$

67. $y = 4^{x-2}$

68. $y = 10^x - 5$

Geometry Skills

Interior Angles Find the measure of an interior angle of the polygon.

69.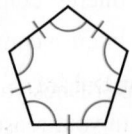

70.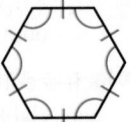

71.

8.4 Logarithms and Logarithmic Functions

Key Words

- common logarithm
- logarithm of y with base b

GOAL Evaluate and graph logarithmic functions.

Prerequisite Skills

Evaluate the expression.

1. 3^4

2. 9^0

3. 10^{-2}

4. $\left(\dfrac{1}{2}\right)^6$

You know that $3^2 = 9$ and $3^3 = 27$. However, for what value of x does $3^x = 18$? Because $3^2 < 18 < 3^3$, you would expect x to be between 2 and 3. To find the exact x-value, mathematicians defined *logarithms*.

$$x = \log_3 18 \approx 2.631 \text{ because } 3^{2.631} \approx 18$$

read as "log base 3 of 18"

The logarithm with base 10 is called the **common logarithm**. It is denoted by $\log_{10}$ or simply by log.

Definition of Logarithm with Base b

Let b and y be positive numbers such that $b \neq 1$.

The **logarithm of y with base b** is denoted by $\log_b y$ and is defined as follows:

$$\log_b y = x \text{ if and only if } b^x = y$$

This definition tells you that the equations $\log_b y = x$ and $b^x = y$ are equivalent. The first is in *logarithmic form* and the second is in *exponential form*. Given an equation in one of these forms, you can always rewrite it in the other form.

EXAMPLE 1 Rewrite Logarithmic Equations

LOGARITHMIC FORM	EXPONENTIAL FORM
a. $\log_2 16 = 4$	$2^4 = 16$
b. $\log_7 1 = 0$	$7^0 = 1$
c. $\log_5 5 = 1$	$5^1 = 5$
d. $\log 0.01 = -2$	$10^{-2} = 0.01$
e. $\log_{1/4} 4 = -1$	$\left(\dfrac{1}{4}\right)^{-1} = 4$

Checkpoint ✓ Rewrite Logarithmic Equations

Rewrite the equation in exponential form.

1. $\log_3 81 = 4$ 2. $\log_4 4 = 1$ 3. $\log_6 1 = 0$ 4. $\log_{1/2} 4 = -2$

> ## Special Logarithm Values
>
> Let b be a positive number such that $b \neq 1$.
>
> **LOGARITHM OF 1** $\log_b 1 = 0$ because $b^0 = 1$.
>
> **LOGARITHM OF BASE b** $\log_b b = 1$ because $b^1 = b$.

EXAMPLE 2 Evaluate Logarithmic Expressions

Evaluate the expression.

a. $\log_4 64$ **b.** $\log_4 2$ **c.** $\log_{1/3} 9$

Solution

To help you find the value of $\log_b y$, ask yourself what power of b gives you y.

a. $4^? = 64$ What power of 4 gives 64?

   $4^3 = 64$ Guess, check, and revise.

   $\log_4 64 = 3$ Definition of $\log_b y$

b. $4^? = 2$ What power of 4 gives 2?

   $4^{1/2} = 2$ Guess, check, and revise.

   $\log_4 2 = \dfrac{1}{2}$ Definition of $\log_b y$

c. $\left(\dfrac{1}{3}\right)^? = 9$ What power of $\dfrac{1}{3}$ gives 9?

   $\left(\dfrac{1}{3}\right)^{-2} = 9$ Guess, check, and revise.

   $\log_{1/3} 9 = -2$ Definition of $\log_b y$

Inverse Functions The logarithmic function $g(x) = \log_b x$ is the inverse of the exponential function $f(x) = b^x$. This means these statements are true:

$$g(f(x)) = \log_b b^x = x \qquad \text{and} \qquad f(g(x)) = b^{\log_b x} = x$$

EXAMPLE 3 Use Inverse Properties

a. Evaluate $10^{\log 6}$.   **b.** Simplify $\log_2 8^x$.

Solution

a. $10^{\log 6} = 10^{\log_{10} 6} = 6$ **b.** $\log_2 8^x = \log_2 (2^3)^x = \log_2 2^{3x} = 3x$

Checkpoint ✔ Evaluate and Simplify Logarithmic Expressions

5. Evaluate $\log_2 64$.   **6.** Evaluate $\log_4 \dfrac{1}{16}$.   **7.** Evaluate $\log_{16} 4$.

8. Simplify $7^{\log_7 x}$.   **9.** Simplify $\log_5 25^x$.   **10.** Simplify $\log_2 64^x$.

Because exponential functions and logarithmic functions are inverse functions, you can graph logarithmic functions using what you know about exponential graphs.

> ### Graphing Logarithmic Functions
>
> The graph of $y = \log_b x$ is shown where $b > 1$.
>
> - The graph of $y = \log_b x$ is the reflection of the graph of $y = b^x$ in the line $y = x$.
> - The graph of $y = \log_b x$ includes $(1, 0)$ and $(b, 1)$.
> - The y-axis is a vertical asymptote.
> - The domain is $x > 0$, and the range is all real numbers.
>
>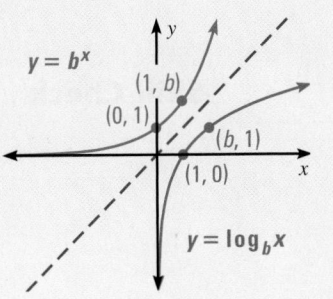

STUDENT HELP

READING GRAPHS
A positive value of h or k translates the graph to the right or up.
A negative value of h or k translates the graph to the left or down.

You can also graph translated logarithmic functions:

To graph $y = \log_b (x - h)$, translate the graph of $y = \log_b x$ horizontally h units.

To graph $y = \log_b x + k$, translate the graph of $y = \log_b x$ vertically k units.

EXAMPLE 4 Graph Logarithmic Functions

Graph the function. Describe the vertical asymptote. State the domain and range.

a. $y = \log_3 x$ **b.** $y = \log_3 (x - 2)$

Solution

For both graphs, find the two key points where $y = 0$ and where $y = 1$.

a. Let $x = 1$. Then $y = \log_3 1 = 0$, so $(1, 0)$ is on the graph.

Let $x = 3$. Then $y = \log_3 3 = 1$, so $(3, 1)$ is on the graph.

b. Let $x = 3$. Then $y = \log_3 (3 - 2) = 0$, so $(3, 0)$ is on the graph.

Let $x = 5$. Then $y = \log_3 (5 - 2) = 1$, so $(5, 1)$ is on the graph.

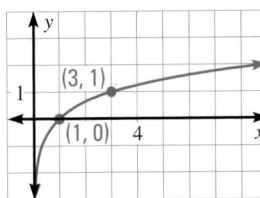

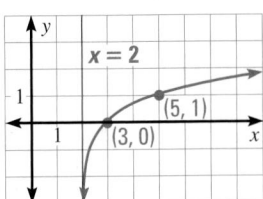

The vertical asymptote is the y-axis. The domain is $x > 0$, and the range is all real numbers.

The vertical asymptote is $x = 2$. The domain is $x > 2$, and the range is all real numbers.

Checkpoint ✓ *Graph Logarithmic Functions*

Graph the function. Describe the vertical asymptote. State the domain and range.

11. $y = \log_{10} x$ **12.** $y = \log_2 (x - 3)$ **13.** $y = \log_5 x + 3$

Guided Practice

Vocabulary Check

1. What are common logarithms?

2. Write an expression that represents the logarithm of y with base 4.

Skill Check **Rewrite the equation in exponential form.**

3. $\log_8 64 = 2$ **4.** $\log_7 1 = 0$ **5.** $\log_5 625 = 4$ **6.** $\log_3 27 = 3$

7. $\log_3 \frac{1}{9} = -2$ **8.** $\log \frac{1}{10} = -1$ **9.** $\log_{1/4} 16 = -2$ **10.** $\log_{1/2} \frac{1}{8} = 3$

Evaluate the expression.

11. $\log_3 9$ **12.** $\log_4 4$ **13.** $\log_9 1$ **14.** $\log 1000$

15. $\log_5 \frac{1}{25}$ **16.** $\log_{1/2} 16$ **17.** $\log_{1/6} 6$ **18.** $\log_8 2$

Simplify the expression.

19. $\log_6 6^x$ **20.** $\log_4 4^x$ **21.** $3^{\log_3 x}$ **22.** $5^{\log_5 2x}$

23. $3^{\log_3 6x}$ **24.** $7^{\log_7 10x}$ **25.** $\log_4 16^x$ **26.** $\log_3 81^x$

Error Analysis **Find and correct the error.**

27.

$\log_{1/3} 3 = 9$

because $\frac{1}{3} \cdot 9 = 3$ ✗

28.

$\log_3 27^x = \log_3 9 \cdot 3^x$

$= \log_3 3^2 \cdot 3^x$

$= \log_3 3^{2 + x}$

$= 2 + x$ ✗

Practice and Applications

STUDENT HELP

HOMEWORK HELP
Example 1: Exs. 29–44
Example 2: Exs. 45–60
Example 3: Exs. 61–68
Example 4: Exs. 69–80

Rewriting Logarithmic Equations **Rewrite the equation in exponential form.**

29. $\log_4 16 = 2$ **30.** $\log_3 3 = 1$ **31.** $\log_8 1 = 0$ **32.** $\log_5 125 = 3$

33. $\log_4 256 = 4$ **34.** $\log_{15} 1 = 0$ **35.** $\log_9 729 = 3$ **36.** $\log 100 = 2$

37. $\log_7 \frac{1}{7} = -1$ **38.** $\log_4 \frac{1}{64} = -3$ **39.** $\log \frac{1}{1000} = -3$ **40.** $\log_{1/4} \frac{1}{16} = 2$

41. $\log_{1/3} 27 = -3$ **42.** $\log_{1/6} 6 = -1$ **43.** $\log_{1/2} 32 = -5$ **44.** $\log_{1/5} 1 = 0$

Evaluating Logarithmic Expressions **Evaluate the expression.**

45. $\log_3 81$ **46.** $\log_5 5$ **47.** $\log_{12} 144$ **48.** $\log_2 128$

49. $\log_{19} 1$ **50.** $\log_6 36$ **51.** $\log 10,000$ **52.** $\log_7 343$

53. $\log_3 \frac{1}{9}$ **54.** $\log_2 \frac{1}{128}$ **55.** $\log_7 \frac{1}{49}$ **56.** $\log \frac{1}{10}$

57. $\log_{1/8} 1$ **58.** $\log_{1/5} 5$ **59.** $\log_{1/2} 64$ **60.** $\log_{1/3} 81$

Using Inverse Properties Simplify the expression.

61. $\log_2 2^x$ **62.** $\log_8 8^x$ **63.** $2^{\log_2 x}$ **64.** $4^{\log_4 x}$

65. $10^{\log 3x}$ **66.** $6^{\log_6 5x}$ **67.** $\log_3 9^x$ **68.** $\log_2 16^x$

Matching Match the function with its graph.

69. $y = \log_2 (x - 3)$ **70.** $y = \log_2 x + 3$ **71.** $y = \log_3 x + 2$

A. 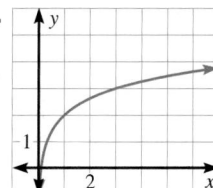 B. 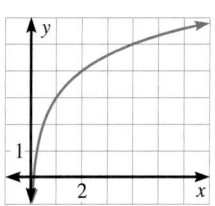 C.

Graphing Logarithmic Functions Graph the function. Describe the vertical asymptote. State the domain and range.

72. $y = \log_2 x$ **73.** $y = \log_4 x$ **74.** $y = \log_6 x$

75. $y = \log_2 (x - 5)$ **76.** $y = \log_4 (x - 3)$ **77.** $y = \log_6 (x + 1)$

78. $y = \log_2 x + 4$ **79.** $y = \log_4 x + 6$ **80.** $y = \log_6 x - 2$

81. Logical Reasoning Graph the functions $y = \log x$, $y = 5 \log x$, and $y = 10 \log x$ in the same coordinate plane. How are they similar? How are they different? How does changing k in the equation $y = k \log x$ affect the graph?

Common Logarithms In Exercises 82–85, use a calculator to evaluate the common log. Round your answers to the nearest hundredth.

82. $\log 5$ **83.** $\log 13$ **84.** $\log 150$ **85.** $\log 2010$

Natural Logarithms In Exercises 86–89, use the information below. Round your answers to the nearest hundredth.

The logarithm with base e is called the *natural logarithm*. It can be denoted by $\log_e$, but it is more often denoted by ln. Use the **LN** key on your calculator to evaluate the following expressions.

86. $\ln e$ **87.** $\ln 6$ **88.** $\ln 25$ **89.** $3 \ln 40$

Earthquakes In Exercises 90–93, use the following information.

The Richter magnitude R of an earthquake measured 100 km away from its epicenter can be approximated by the model $R = \log A + 3$ where A is the amplitude (in millimeters) of the greatest wave length recorded on a seismograph.

90. Determine the Richter magnitudes R of earthquakes with amplitudes A of 1 millimeter, 10 millimeters, and 100 millimeters.

91. Determine the Richter magnitudes R of earthquakes with amplitudes A of 2 millimeter, 20 millimeters, and 200 millimeters.

92. Determine the Richter magnitudes R of earthquakes with amplitudes A of 5 millimeter, 50 millimeters, and 500 millimeters.

93. Graph $y = \log x + 3$. Find the amplitudes associated with two different earthquakes whose magnitudes have a difference of 0.5. Then find the ratio of the amplitudes. Does the ratio depend on the specific magnitudes you choose?

SIEVES A geologist may use a series of sieves with increasing fineness. Larger particles are collected by the sieve and smaller particles pass through it.

Geology In Exercises 94–97, use the table and the following information.

Geologists have developed a system called the phi scale for describing sediment particle sizes. The size s of a particle in phi units is given by the model $s = -\log_2 d$ where d is the diameter of the particle in millimeters.

Particle	Diameter
Large boulder	1024 mm
Small boulder	256 mm
Small cobble	64 mm
Coarse gravel	16 mm
Fine gravel	4 mm
Very coarse sand	1 mm
Medium sand	0.25 mm
Very fine sand	0.0625 mm

94. Find the size of a small cobble particle in phi units.

95. Find the size of a fine gravel particle in phi units.

96. Find the size of a very fine sand particle in phi units.

97. Logical Reasoning Geologists use phi values to describe their sieves. A sieve with a given phi value collects all particles with a smaller phi value. What particles from the table does a sieve with a phi value of 2 collect?

98. Challenge Copy and complete the table below for the function $y = \log_{1/2} x$. Then graph the function in a coordinate plane.

x	?	?	?	1	?	?	?
$\log_{1/2} x$	3	2	1	0	−1	−2	−3

What are the characteristics of the graph of $y = \log_b x$ when b is between 0 and 1? Explain how the graph is related to the graph of $y = b^x$ when b is between 0 and 1.

Standardized Test Practice

99. Multiple Choice Which statement follows from the equation $7^3 = 343$?

Ⓐ $\log_3 7 = 343$ Ⓑ $\log_3 343 = 7$

Ⓒ $\log_7 343 = 3$ Ⓓ $\log_7 3 = 343$

100. Multiple Choice Evaluate the expression $\log_4 \frac{1}{2}$.

Ⓕ -2 Ⓖ $\frac{1}{2}$ Ⓗ $\frac{1}{2}$ Ⓙ 2

101. Multiple Choice Which of the following is equivalent to the expression $\log_2 16^x$?

Ⓐ x Ⓑ $2x$ Ⓒ $4x$ Ⓓ $8x$

102. Multiple Choice Which function's graph is shown below?

Ⓕ $y = \log_2 x$

Ⓖ $y = \log_3 x$

Ⓗ $y = \log_3 x - 1$

Ⓙ $y = \log_3 (x + 1)$

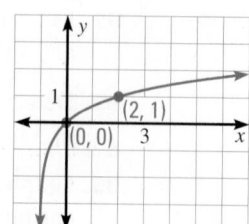

Mixed Review

Comparing Steepness Tell which line is steeper. *(Lesson 2.3)*

103. Line 1: through (5, 4) and (7, 4)
Line 2: through (5, 4) and (7, 8)

104. Line 1: through (0, 0) and (5, 10)
Line 2: through (0, 0) and (−5, 15)

Evaluating Numerical Expressions Evaluate the expression. Tell which properties of exponents you used. *(Lesson 6.1)*

105. $5^3 \cdot 5^2$

106. $(2^{-5})^{-1}$

107. $(6 \cdot 3)^2$

108. $2^{-4} \cdot 2^{-1}$

Writing Exponential Functions Write an exponential function of the form $y = ab^x$ whose graph passes through the given points. *(Lesson 8.3)*

109. (1, 20), (2, 40)

110. (1, 12), (2, 36)

111. (1, 2.5), (2, 12.5)

112. (0, 7), (2, 175)

Geometry Skills

Circles Find the circumference and the area of the circle with the given dimension. Round your answer to the nearest whole number.

113. 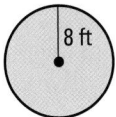 8 ft

114. 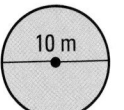 10 m

115. 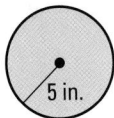 5 in.

Quiz 2

Lesson 8.3

Determine whether the function shows *exponential growth* or *exponential decay*. Then identify the initial amount and the percent increase or decrease.

1. $y = 60(1 - 0.2)^t$ **2.** $y = 4(1 + 0.05)^t$ **3.** $y = 7500(1.5)^t$

Lesson 8.3

Write an exponential growth or decay model that describes the situation.

4. Lathes A company purchases a lathe for $2500. Each year, the value V of the lathe decreases by 10%.

5. Souvenir You buy a souvenir T-shirt at a concert for $25. Each year, the value V of the T-shirt increases by 5%.

6. Savings Account You deposit $500 into an account. Each year, the amount A in the account increases by 2.5% compounded continuously.

Lesson 8.4

Evaluate the expression.

7. $\log_{11} 121$

8. $\log_6 216$

9. $\log 100{,}000$

10. $\log_9 \dfrac{1}{81}$

Lesson 8.4

Simplify the expression.

11. $\log_7 7^x$

12. $12^{\log_{12} x}$

13. $\log_5 25^x$

14. $\log_4 64^x$

Graphing Logarithmic Functions

To graph a logarithmic function having a base other than 10 on a calculator, you can use the following change-of-base formula to rewrite the function in terms of common logarithms.

Change-of-Base Formula

Let x, b, and c be positive numbers such that $b \neq 1$ and $c \neq 1$.

Then, $\log_b x = \dfrac{\log_c x}{\log_c b}$. In particular, $\log_b x = \dfrac{\log x}{\log b}$.

EXAMPLE Use a graphing calculator to graph $y = \log_2 x$.

SOLUTION

1 Use the change-of-base formula to rewrite the function.

$$y = \log_2 x = \frac{\log x}{\log 2}$$

2 Enter the function into a graphing calculator.

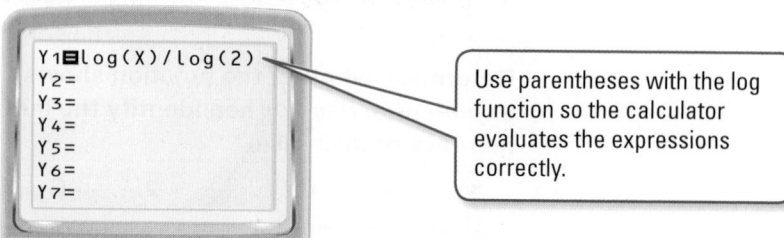

Use parentheses with the log function so the calculator evaluates the expressions correctly.

3 Graph the function.

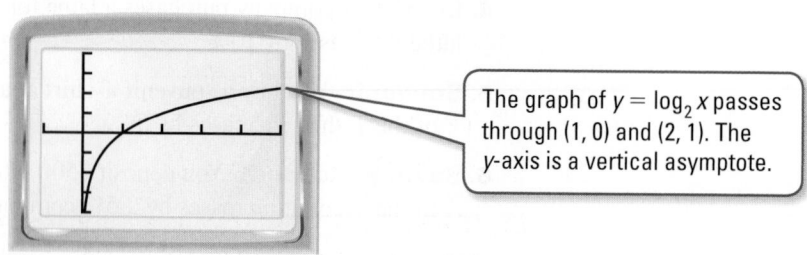

The graph of $y = \log_2 x$ passes through (1, 0) and (2, 1). The y-axis is a vertical asymptote.

EXERCISES

Graph the function. Give the coordinates of two points through which the graph passes, and describe the vertical asymptote of the graph.

1. $y = \log_6 x$

2. $y = \log_5 x$

3. $y = \log_3 (x - 1)$

4. $y = \log_3 (x + 1)$

5. $y = \log_3 x + 1$

6. $y = \log_4 (x + 1) + 2$

DEVELOPING CONCEPTS *(For use with Lesson 8.5)*

Logarithms of Products and Quotients

Goal

Discover the product and quotient properties of logarithms.

Materials

- pencil
- paper
- calculator

QUESTION

How are the logarithms of two numbers related to the logarithms of their products and quotients?

EXPLORE

1 Copy and complete the table one row at a time.

$\log_b m$	$\log_b n$	$\log_b mn$
$\log 100 = ?$	$\log 1000 = ?$	$\log 100{,}000 = ?$
$\log 10 = ?$	$\log 0.1 = ?$	$\log 1 = ?$
$\log_2 4 = ?$	$\log_2 2 = ?$	$\log_2 8 = ?$
$\log_4 64 = ?$	$\log_4 \dfrac{1}{16} = ?$	$\log_4 4 = ?$

2 Copy and complete the table one row at a time.

$\log_b m$	$\log_b n$	$\log_b \dfrac{m}{n}$
$\log 1000 = ?$	$\log 100 = ?$	$\log 10 = ?$
$\log 10 = ?$	$\log 0.01 = ?$	$\log 1000 = ?$
$\log_3 243 = ?$	$\log_3 27 = ?$	$\log_3 9 = ?$
$\log_5 125 = ?$	$\log_5 \dfrac{1}{5} = ?$	$\log_5 625 = ?$

THINK ABOUT IT

1. Use the first table to write a conjecture about the relationship among $\log_b m$, $\log_b n$, and $\log_b mn$.

2. Use the second table to write a conjecture about the relationship among $\log_b m$, $\log_b n$, and $\log_b \dfrac{m}{n}$.

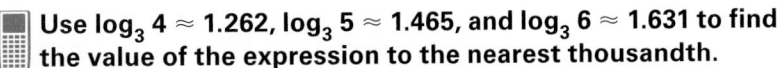 **Use $\log_3 4 \approx 1.262$, $\log_3 5 \approx 1.465$, and $\log_3 6 \approx 1.631$ to find the value of the expression to the nearest thousandth.**

3. $\log_3 20$ **4.** $\log_3 24$ **5.** $\log_3 30$

6. $\log_3 16$ **7.** $\log_3 25$ **8.** $\log_3 36$

9. $\log_3 \dfrac{4}{5}$ **10.** $\log_3 \dfrac{5}{6}$ **11.** $\log_3 \dfrac{2}{3}$

12. $\log_3 \dfrac{5}{4}$ **13.** $\log_3 \dfrac{6}{5}$ **14.** $\log_3 \dfrac{3}{2}$

Properties of Logarithms

Key Words

* logarithm, p. 433

Prerequisite Skills

Simplify.

1. $\log 100 + \log 1000$
2. $\log_4 64 - \log_4 16$
3. $\log_7 49^2$
4. $8 \log_3 27$

GOAL Use the properties of logarithms.

How much louder are two guitars than one?

In Example 4, you will use a logarithmic equation to explore this problem.

Because of the relationship between logarithms and exponents, logarithms have properties similar to the properties of exponents.

Properties of Logarithms

Let b, m, and n be positive numbers such that $b \neq 1$.

PRODUCT PROPERTY $\quad \log_b mn = \log_b m + \log_b n$

QUOTIENT PROPERTY $\quad \log_b \dfrac{m}{n} = \log_b m - \log_b n$

POWER PROPERTY $\quad \log_b m^n = n \log_b m$

EXAMPLE 1 Use Properties of Logarithms

Use $\log_7 2 \approx 0.356$ and $\log_7 5 \approx 0.827$ to find the value of the expression to the nearest thousandth.

a. $\log_7 \dfrac{2}{5}$ **b.** $\log_7 10$ **c.** $\log_7 25$

Solution

a. $\log_7 \dfrac{2}{5} = \log_7 2 - \log_7 5 \qquad$ Quotient property

$\phantom{\log_7 \dfrac{2}{5}} \approx 0.356 - 0.827 \qquad$ Use the given values of $\log_7 2$ and $\log_7 5$.

$\phantom{\log_7 \dfrac{2}{5}} = -0.471 \qquad$ Simplify.

b. $\log_7 10 = \log_7 (2 \cdot 5) \qquad$ Express 10 as a product.

$ = \log_7 2 + \log_7 5 \qquad$ Product property

$ \approx 0.356 + 0.827 \qquad$ Use the given values of $\log_7 2$ and $\log_7 5$.

$ = 1.183 \qquad$ Simplify.

c. $\log_7 25 = \log_7 5^2 \qquad$ Express 25 as a power.

$ = 2 \log_7 5 \qquad$ Power property

$ \approx 2(0.827) \qquad$ Use the given value of $\log_7 5$.

$ = 1.654 \qquad$ Simplify.

You can use the properties of logarithms to expand and condense logarithmic expressions. (An expanded expression is a sum or difference of logs; a condensed expression is a single log expression.) When you do this, assume all variables are positive.

EXAMPLE 2 Expand a Logarithmic Expression

Expand the expression. Assume all variables are positive.

a. $\log_4 5x^2$ **b.** $\log_7 \dfrac{3x}{y}$

Solution

a. $\log_4 5x^2 = \log_4 5 + \log_4 x^2$ Product property

           $= \log_4 5 + 2 \log_4 x$ Power property

b. $\log_7 \dfrac{3x}{y} = \log_7 3x - \log_7 y$ Quotient property

           $= \log_7 3 + \log_7 x - \log_7 y$ Product property

EXAMPLE 3 Condense a Logarithmic Expression

Condense the expression.

a. $\log 16 - 2 \log 2$ **b.** $3 \log 5 + \log 4$

Solution

a. $\log 16 - 2 \log 2 = \log 16 - \log 2^2$ Power property

           $= \log \dfrac{16}{2^2}$ Quotient property

           $= \log 4$ Simplify.

b. $3 \log 5 + \log 4 = \log 5^3 + \log 4$ Power property

           $= \log (5^3 \cdot 4)$ Product property

           $= \log 500$ Simplify.

Checkpoint ✓ Expand and Condense Logarithmic Expressions

Use $\log_5 3 \approx 0.683$ and $\log_5 7 \approx 1.209$ to find the value of the expression to the nearest thousandth.

1. $\log_5 21$ **2.** $\log_5 9$ **3.** $\log_5 49$ **4.** $\log_5 \dfrac{3}{7}$

Expand the expression. Assume all variables are positive.

5. $\log_2 5x$ **6.** $\log 2x^3$ **7.** $\log_3 \dfrac{5x}{7}$ **8.** $\log_6 \dfrac{4x^2}{y}$

Condense the expression.

9. $\log_5 12 - \log_5 4$ **10.** $\log_2 7 + \log_2 5$

11. $\log 4 + 2 \log 3$ **12.** $3 \log x - \log y$

CAREERS

SOUND TECHNICIANS
use equipment to amplify, enhance, record, mix, or reproduce sound. They may work in radio or television studios or at live performances.

EXAMPLE 4 Use Properties of Logarithms

Sound The loudness L of a sound (in decibels) is related to the intensity I of the sound (in watts per square meter) by the equation

$$L = 10 \log \frac{I}{I_0}$$

where I_0 is an intensity of 10^{-12} watt per square meter, roughly the faintest sound that can be heard by humans.

Decibel level	Example
130	Jackhammer
110	Dance club
90	Lawn mower
70	Television
50	Rainfall
30	Soft whisper
10	Rustling leaf

a. Two guitarists play their guitars at an intensity of 10^{-4} watt per square meter. How much louder is the sound than when only one is playing?

b. Generalize the result in part (a) by using I for the intensity of each guitar.

Solution

a. Let L_1 represent the loudness when one guitarist is playing. Let L_2 represent the loudness when both guitarists are playing.

The increase in loudness is $L_2 - L_1$.

$$L_2 - L_1 = 10 \log \frac{2 \cdot 10^{-4}}{10^{-12}} - 10 \log \frac{10^{-4}}{10^{-12}} \qquad \text{Substitute for } L_2 \text{ and } L_1.$$

$$= 10[\log (2 \cdot 10^8) - \log 10^8] \qquad \text{Simplify.}$$

$$= 10(\log 2 + \log 10^8 - \log 10^8) \qquad \text{Product property}$$

$$= 10 \log 2 \qquad \text{Simplify.}$$

$$\approx 3.01 \qquad \text{Use a calculator.}$$

ANSWER ▶ The music is about 3 decibels louder.

b. The increase in loudness is $L_2 - L_1$.

$$L_2 - L_1 = 10 \log \frac{2I}{10^{-12}} - 10 \log \frac{I}{10^{-12}}$$

$$= 10 \left(\log \frac{2I}{10^{-12}} - \log \frac{I}{10^{-12}} \right)$$

$$= 10 \left(\log 2 + \log \frac{I}{10^{-12}} - \log \frac{I}{10^{-12}} \right)$$

$$= 10 \log 2$$

$$\approx 3.01$$

ANSWER ▶ Again, the music is about 3 decibels louder. This result tells you that when the intensity of a sound doubles, the loudness increases by 3 decibels, regardless of the intensity of the original sound.

 **Checkpoint** ✓ *Use Properties of Logarithms*

13. Redo Example 4 to find the increase in loudness when four guitarists play instead of one.

8.5 Exercises

Guided Practice

Vocabulary Check

1. What is the base of a common logarithm?

2. The equation $\log_3 16 = 4 \log_3 2$ is an example of which property?

Skill Check

Use $\log_6 3 \approx 0.613$ and $\log_6 7 \approx 1.086$ to find the value of the expression to the nearest thousandth.

3. $\log_6 21$

4. $\log_6 \frac{3}{7}$

5. $\log_6 49$

6. $\log_6 \frac{1}{3}$

Expand the expression. Assume all variables are positive.

7. $\log 2x$

8. $\log x^5$

9. $\log_5 9x^2$

10. $\log_4 4x$

11. $\log \frac{x}{y}$

12. $\log \frac{2}{xy}$

13. $\log_4 \frac{x^2}{3y}$

14. $\log_3 \frac{2x}{y^5}$

Condense the expression. Assume all variables are positive.

15. $\log_8 3 + \log_8 7$

16. $6 \log 2 - \log 3$

17. $\log_4 7 + 3 \log_4 2$

18. $8 \log_3 x + \log_3 4$

19. $5 \log y - \log x$

20. $2 \log_5 10 - \log_5 x$

21. Error Analysis Find and correct the error in expanding the expression.

$$\log_4 \frac{x^2}{16y} = \log_4 16y - \log_4 x^2$$
$$= \log_4 16 + \log_4 y - \log_4 x^2$$
$$= 2 + \log_4 y - 2 \log_4 x \qquad \times$$

Practice and Applications

STUDENT HELP

HOMEWORK HELP
Example 1: Exs. 22–33
Example 2: Exs. 34–45
Example 3: Exs. 46–57
Example 4: Exs. 58–66

Matching Match the expression with its equivalent.

22. $\log 2 + \log 8$

23. $\log 8 - \log 2$

24. $8 \log 2$

25. $2 \log 8$

A. $\log 4$

B. $\log 16$

C. $\log 64$

D. $\log 256$

Approximating Expressions Use $\log_5 4 \approx 0.861$ and $\log_5 9 \approx 1.365$ to find the value of the expression to the nearest thousandth.

26. $\log_5 36$

27. $\log_5 81$

28. $\log_5 \frac{4}{9}$

29. $\log_5 \frac{9}{4}$

30. $\log_5 \frac{1}{4}$

31. $\log_5 \frac{1}{9}$

32. $\log_5 \frac{16}{9}$

33. $\log_5 \frac{81}{4}$

Expanding Expressions Expand the expression. Assume all variables are positive.

34. $\log x^3$

35. $\log 5x$

36. $\log_3 9x$

37. $\log_4 7x^4$

38. $\log_6 \frac{3x}{4}$

39. $\log xy$

40. $\log_4 x^2y$

41. $\log_6 7xy^4$

42. $\log_3 \frac{x}{y}$

43. $\log_4 \frac{x}{5y^2}$

44. $\log_5 \frac{x^3}{y}$

45. $\log_7 \frac{y^3}{20x^5}$

Condensing Expressions Condense the expression. Assume all variables are positive.

46. $\log_4 9 + \log_4 7$

47. $\log_5 2 - \log_5 3$

48. $3 \log 2 - \log 4$

49. $2 \log_2 5 + \log_2 3$

50. $3 \log_2 x + \log_2 6$

51. $2 \log_7 x - \log_7 2$

52. $7 \log y + 3 \log 4$

53. $4 \log_5 x - 5 \log_5 2$

54. $\log_2 y - 4 \log_2 x$

55. $6 \log_4 y + 8 \log_4 x$

56. $2 \log x - \log y$

57. $\log_2 x + 2 \log_2 y$

Acoustics In Exercises 58–62, use the following logarithmic equation from Example 4.

$$L = 10 \log \frac{I}{10^{-12}}$$

58. The intensity of the sound made by an alarm clock is about 10^{-4} watt per square meter. Find the decibel level of the alarm clock.

59. On parts of the Colorado River, boats must meet noise emission levels. A noise level above 86 decibels is illegal for any engine. The intensity of the sound emitted by a boat engine is 6.3×10^{-4} watt per square meter. Would the noise level of the engine be illegal?

60. Find the difference in the loudness of a sound with an intensity of 10^{-7} watt per square meter and a sound with an intensity of 10^{-9} watt per square meter.

61. Three subway trains leave a station at the same time. The intensity of the sound created by each train is 10^{-3} watt per square meter. How much louder is the train station when all three subway trains leave, compared to when just one subway train leaves?

62. Generalize the result in Exercise 61 by using I for the intensity of each subway train. Interpret the result.

Chemistry Link In Exercises 63–66, use the following information.

Lemon juice, vinegar, and cider are examples of liquids that are acidic. In chemistry, how acidic a substance is can be measured precisely as its pH.

The pH of a solution is defined by the equation

$$\text{pH} = -\log x$$

where x is the hydrogen ion concentration of the solution (in moles per liter).

63. Based on the table at the right, is a liquid with pH = 1.8 *more* or *less* acidic than a liquid with pH = 4.3?

64. Evaluate the pH of solutions where $x = 0.027$, $x = 4.3 \times 10^{-4}$, and $x = 1.2 \times 10^{-5}$.

65. Evaluate the pH of solutions where $x = 0.001$, $x = 1 \times 10^{-4.5}$, and $x = 1 \times 10^{-6.8}$.

66. When the hydrogen ion concentration of a solution can be written in the form 1×10^{-n}, what is the pH of the solution? Use the properties of logarithms to explain your answer.

pH	Example
1.2	sulfuric acid
2.0	stomach acid
2.3	lemon juice
2.9	vinegar
3.1	apple cider
6.5	milk
7.0	pure water

Challenge Use the given hint and properties of exponents to prove the property of logarithms.

67. PRODUCT PROPERTY: $\log_b mn = \log_b m + \log_b n$
(*Hint:* Let $x = \log_b m$ and let $y = \log_b n$. Then $m = b^x$ and $n = b^y$.)

68. QUOTIENT PROPERTY: $\log_b \frac{m}{n} = \log_b m - \log_b n$
(*Hint:* Let $x = \log_b m$ and let $y = \log_b n$. Then $m = b^x$ and $n = b^y$.)

69. POWER PROPERTY: $\log_b m^n = n \log_b m$
(*Hint:* Let $x = \log_b m$. Then $m = b^x$ and $m^n = b^{xn}$.)

70. Multiple Choice What is the approximate value of $\log_2 \frac{3}{5}$ given that $\log_2 3 \approx 1.585$ and $\log_2 5 \approx 2.322$?

ⓐ 3.907 ⓑ 0.737 ⓒ 0.683 ⓓ −0.737

71. Multiple Choice Which of the following is *not* equivalent to $\log_5 \frac{y^4}{3x}$?

ⓕ $4 \log_5 y - \log_5 3x$ ⓖ $4 \log_5 y - \log_5 3 + \log_5 x$

ⓗ $4 \log_5 y - \log_5 3 - \log_5 x$ ⓙ $\log_5 y^4 - \log_5 3 - \log_5 x$

72. Multiple Choice Which of the following equations is correct?

ⓐ $\log_7 x + 2 \log_7 y = \log_7 (x + y^2)$

ⓑ $9 \log x - 2 \log y = \log \frac{x^9}{y^2}$

ⓒ $5 \log_4 x + 7 \log_2 y = \log_6 x^5 y^7$

ⓓ $\log_9 x - 5 \log_9 y = \log_9 \frac{x}{5y}$

Mixed Review

Solving Equations Solve the linear equation. *(Lesson 1.4)*

73. $5 - x = 1$ **74.** $13y = 52$ **75.** $\frac{n}{3} + 1 = 10$

76. $5x = x + 24$ **77.** $7m + 33 = -4m$ **78.** $3x + 11 = 2x - 1$

79. $36 - 6u = 12u$ **80.** $\frac{1}{2}y - 1 = 8y - 1$ **81.** $\frac{1}{5}(x + 25) = 10$

Solving Equations Solve the quadratic equation. *(Lesson 5.7)*

82. $x^2 + 12x + 18 = 0$ **83.** $x^2 - 8x + 14 = 0$ **84.** $x^2 - 4x + 1 = 0$

85. $x^2 + 14x + 41 = 0$ **86.** $2x^2 + 12x + 6 = 0$ **87.** $3x^2 - 24x + 9 = 0$

Evaluating Logarithmic Expressions Evaluate the expression. *(Lesson 8.4)*

88. $\log_7 7$ **89.** $\log_5 25$ **90.** $\log_{13} 13$

91. $\log_8 1$ **92.** $\log_9 \frac{1}{81}$ **93.** $\log_2 \frac{1}{32}$

94. $\log_{27} 3$ **95.** $\log_{1/2} 128$ **96.** $\log_{1/7} 49$

Geometry Skills

Exterior Angles Find the measure of an exterior angle of the regular polygon. What kind of polygon is it?

97.
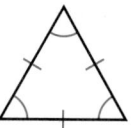

98.
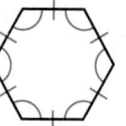

99.
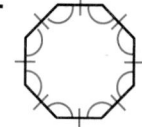

8.6 Solving Exponential and Logarithmic Equations

Key Words
- extraneous solutions, p. 366

GOAL Solve exponential and logarithmic equations.

To solve an *exponential equation* you can use the property that if two powers with the same base are equal, then their exponents must be equal.

Prerequisite Skills

Solve the equation.

1. $2x - 7 = 9$

2. $4x + 5 = x - 13$

3. $x + 7 = 15 - x$

4. $5x - 8 = x + 12$

Equal Powers Property

For $b > 0$ and $b \neq 1$, if $b^x = b^y$, then $x = y$.

EXAMPLE If $3^x = 3^5$, then $x = 5$.

EXAMPLE 1 Solve Using Equal Powers Property

Solve the equation.

a. $4^2 = 4^{9x - 5}$ **b.** $2^{3x} = 4^{x + 1}$

Solution

a.

$4^2 = 4^{9x - 5}$	Write original equation.
$2 = 9x - 5$	Equal powers property
$7 = 9x$	Add 5 to each side.
$\dfrac{7}{9} = x$	Divide each side by 9.

ANSWER ▶ The solution is $\dfrac{7}{9}$. Check this in the original equation.

b.

$2^{3x} = 4^{x + 1}$	Write original equation.
$2^{3x} = (2^2)^{x + 1}$	Rewrite 4 as 2^2 so powers have same base.
$2^{3x} = 2^{2(x + 1)}$	Power of a power property
$3x = 2(x + 1)$	Equal powers property
$3x = 2x + 2$	Distributive property
$x = 2$	Subtract $2x$ from each side.

ANSWER ▶ The solution is 2. Check this in the original equation.

Checkpoint ✓ Solve Using Equal Powers Property

Solve the equation.

1. $2^{7x - 4} = 2^3$

2. $3^{x - 2} = 3^{5x - 6}$

3. $5^{x + 3} = 5^{4x - 9}$

4. $2^{x + 2} = 16^{x - 4}$

5. $6^{4x + 1} = 36^{8x - 1}$

6. $10^{x - 3} = 100^{2x - 9}$

It may not be convenient to write each side of an exponential equation using the same base. You can still solve the equation by taking the common logarithm of each side.

EXAMPLE **2** **Take a Common Logarithm of Each Side**

Solve $3^x = 5$.

Solution

$$3^x = 5$$ Write original equation.

$$\log 3^x = \log 5$$ Take common logarithm of each side.

$$x \log 3 = \log 5$$ Power property of logarithms

$$x = \frac{\log 5}{\log 3}$$ Divide each side by log 3.

$$x \approx 1.465$$ Use a calculator.

ANSWER ▶ The solution is about 1.465. Check this in the original equation.

EXAMPLE **3** **Take a Common Logarithm of Each Side**

Solve $10^{3x - 1} = 19$.

Solution

$$10^{3x - 1} = 19$$ Write original equation.

$$\log 10^{3x - 1} = \log 19$$ Take common logarithm of each side.

$$3x - 1 = \log 19$$ $\log 10^x = x$

$$3x = 1 + \log 19$$ Add 1 to each side.

$$x = \frac{1 + \log 19}{3}$$ Divide each side by 3.

$$x \approx 0.760$$ Use a calculator.

CHECK You can check the solution by substituting it into the original equation. Or, you can check the solution graphically by graphing each side of the original equation as a function.

$$y_1 = 10^{3x - 1} \text{ and } y_2 = 19$$

The two graphs intersect when $x \approx 0.760$. ✓

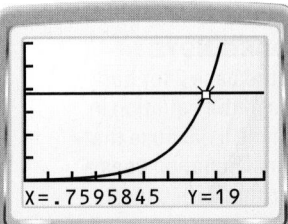

X=.7595845   Y=19

 **Take a Common Logarithm of Each Side**

Solve the equation.

7. $2^x = 9$

8. $4^x = 5$

9. $3^x = 40$

10. $10^{3x} = 5$

11. $10^{2x + 5} = 6$

12. $10^{-x} - 4 = 13$

Logarithmic Equations To solve a *logarithmic equation*, use the following property of logarithms with the same base.

> ### Equal Logarithms Property
>
> For positive numbers b, x, and y where $b \neq 1$:
>
> $$\log_b x = \log_b y \text{ if and only if } x = y$$

EXAMPLE 4 Solve a Logarithmic Equation

Solve $\log_7 (4x - 3) = \log_7 (x + 6)$.

Solution

$\log_7 (4x - 3) = \log_7 (x + 6)$	Write original equation.
$4x - 3 = x + 6$	Equal logarithms property
$4x = x + 9$	Add 3 to each side.
$3x = 9$	Subtract x from each side.
$x = 3$	Divide each side by 3.

ANSWER ▶ The solution is 3. Check this in the original equation.

Exponentiate Each Side of an Equation When only one side of an equation is a logarithmic expression, you can *exponentiate* each side of the equation, that is, use each side of the equation as an exponent in an expression with the same base.

> For $b > 0$ and $b \neq 1$, if $x = y$, then $b^x = b^y$.

EXAMPLE 5 Exponentiate Each Side

Solve $\log_2 (3x + 1) = 4$.

Solution

$\log_2 (3x + 1) = 4$	Write original equation.
$2^{\log_2(3x + 1)} = 2^4$	Exponentiate each side using base 2.
$3x + 1 = 16$	$b^{\log_b x} = x$
$3x = 15$	Subtract 1 from each side.
$x = 5$	Divide each side by 3.

ANSWER ▶ The solution is 5. Check this in the original equation.

STUDENT HELP

SOLVING NOTE
Use the base 2 for both sides of the equation in Example 5 because the original equation uses a logarithm with base 2.

 **Checkpoint** ✓ *Solve a Logarithmic Equation*

Solve the equation.

13. $\log_3 (x + 2) = \log_3 (2x - 5)$
14. $\log_5 (8x - 9) = \log_5 (3x + 1)$

15. $\log_4 (7x + 2) = 2$
16. $\log_3 (5x + 1) = 4$

EXAMPLE 6 Check for Extraneous Solutions

Solve $\log 10x + \log (x - 3) = 2$. Check for extraneous solutions.

Solution

$\log 10x + \log (x - 3) = 2$	Write original equation.
$\log [10x(x - 3)] = 2$	Product property of logarithms
$10^{\log [10x(x - 3)]} = 10^2$	Exponentiate each side using base 10.
$10x(x - 3) = 100$	$10^{\log x} = x$
$10x^2 - 30x = 100$	Simplify.
$10x^2 - 30x - 100 = 0$	Subtract 100 from each side.
$10(x - 5)(x + 2) = 0$	Factor.
$x = 5$ or $x = -2$	Zero product property

The solutions appear to be 5 and -2. However, when you check these in the original equation or use a graphic check as shown at the right, you can see that $x = 5$ is the only solution.

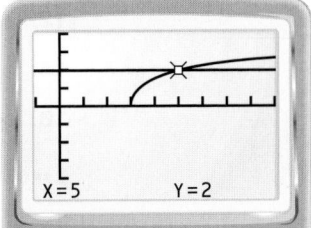

X = 5   Y = 2

ANSWER ▶ The solution is 5.

EXAMPLE 7 Use Logarithms with an Exponential Model

Radioactive Decay The exponential decay model for predicting the amount A of material left in a radioactive sample after t years is

$$A = A_0 \cdot 2^{-t/h}$$

where A_0 is the initial amount of the substance and h is the half-life of the substance.

Cesium is an element found in rocks and soil. A radioactive form of cesium, ^{137}Cs (read as "Cesium-137"), has a half-life of about 30.2 years. How long does it take for 32 grams of ^{137}Cs to decay to 4 grams?

Solution

$A = A_0 \cdot 2^{-t/h}$	Write radioactive decay model.
$4 = 32 \cdot 2^{-t/30.2}$	Substitute 4 for A, 32 for A_0, and 30.2 for h.
$\dfrac{1}{8} = 2^{-t/30.2}$	Divide each side by 32.
$\log_2 \dfrac{1}{2^3} = \log_2 2^{-t/30.2}$	Take logarithm of each side using base 2.
$-3 = \dfrac{-t}{30.2}$	$\log_b b^x = x$
$90.6 = t$	Multiply each side by -30.2.

ANSWER ▶ It takes about 90.6 years for 32 grams of ^{137}Cs to decay to 4 grams.

Guided Practice

Vocabulary Check

1. The equation $6^3 = 6^{9x}$ is an example of what kind of equation?

2. Explain the difference between taking the common logarithm of each side of an equation and exponentiating each side of an equation.

Skill Check

Solve the equation.

3. $8^3 = 8^{6x}$

4. $4^5 = 4^{2x-5}$

5. $3^{2x+1} = 3^{x-1}$

6. $7^{5x+3} = 49^x$

7. $2^{6x-7} = 16^{x-2}$

8. $5^x = 12$

9. $7^x = 50$

10. $10^{7x+3} = 3$

11. $10^{-x} + 4 = 15$

Solve the equation.

12. $\log_2 x = \log_2 (2x - 3)$

13. $\log_3 4x = \log_3 (2x + 5)$

14. $\log_5 (5x - 7) = \log_5 (2x + 3)$

15. $\log_2 5x = 3$

16. $\log_4 (7x + 1) = 3$

17. $\log_3 (6x - 3) = 4$

Error Analysis **Describe and correct the error.**

18.
$$6^{3x} = 36^{x-1}$$
$$6^{3x} = (6^2)^{x-1}$$
$$6^{3x} = 6^{2x-1}$$
$$3x = 2x - 1$$
$$x = -1 \qquad \times$$

19.
$$\log_3 (5x - 1) = 4$$
$$3^{\log_3 (5x-1)} = 4^3$$
$$5x - 1 = 64$$
$$5x = 65$$
$$x = 13 \qquad \times$$

Practice and Applications

STUDENT HELP

HOMEWORK HELP
Example 1: Exs. 20–25
Example 2: Exs. 26–35
Example 3: Exs. 26–35
Example 4: Exs. 36–41
Example 5: Exs. 42–48
Example 6: Exs. 49–54
Example 7: Exs. 55–57

Solving Exponential Equations **Use the equal powers property to solve the equation.**

20. $3^4 = 3^{3x+1}$

21. $6^{5x-7} = 6^{18}$

22. $7^{2x-4} = 7^x$

23. $5^{5x-6} = 25^x$

24. $4^{4x+3} = 64^{2x}$

25. $2^{6x-1} = 8^{x+1}$

Solving Exponential Equations **Take the common logarithm of each side to solve. Round your answer to the nearest thousandth.**

26. $2^x = 14$

27. $3^x = 7$

28. $8^x = 10$

29. $7^{3x} = 5$

30. $10^{5x} = 27$

31. $5^{4x} = 100$

32. $10^{2x+1} = 13$

33. $10^{-x} + 5 = 8$

34. $10^{4x-5} + 11 = 20$

35. **Population** The population of a county can be approximated by the model $P = 3762(0.964)^t$ where t is the number of years since 2000. According to this model, when will the population of the county be about 2800?

Solving Logarithmic Equations Use the equal logarithms property to solve the equation.

36. $\log x = \log (5x - 12)$

37. $\log (x + 7) = \log 2x$

38. $\log_3 4x = \log_3 (2x + 8)$

39. $\log_4 2x = \log_4 (3x - 2)$

40. $\log_5 (3x - 4) = \log_5 (x + 2)$

41. $\log_2 (3x - 1) = \log_2 (7x - 8)$

Solving Logarithmic Equations Exponentiate each side to solve the equation.

42. $\log_2 2x = 5$

43. $\log_5 10x = 2$

44. $\log_3 (4x - 1) = 3$

45. $\log_4 (7x + 11) = 1$

46. $\log_8 (2x - 3) = \frac{1}{3}$

47. $\log_9 (4 - x) = \frac{1}{2}$

48. Earthquakes The moment magnitude scale is a way to measure earthquakes. The moment magnitude M is defined by

$$M = \frac{2}{3}(\log s - 16)$$

where s is the seismic moment (in dyne-centimeters). The largest earthquake of the last century occurred in Chile in 1960. It had a moment magnitude M of about 9.5. Approximate the seismic moment s of the earthquake.

Extraneous Solutions Solve the equation. Check for extraneous solutions.

49. $\log 2x = \log (5x + 6)$

50. $\log (2x - 5) = \log (4x - 9)$

51. $\log x + \log (x + 30) = 3$

52. $\log 2x + \log (x - 5) = 2$

53. $\log (-x) + \log (x + 20) = 2$

54. $\log_4 (x + 12) + \log_4 x = 3$

Science Link In Exercises 55–57, use the formula for radioactive decay from Example 7.

55. The half-life of ^{210}Pb (lead-210) is 22.3 years. How long does it take for 64 grams of ^{210}Pb to decay to 2 grams?

56. The half-life of ^{226}Ra (radium-226) is 1600 years. How long does it take for 160 grams of ^{226}Ra to decay to 10 grams?

57. The half-life of ^{60}Co (cobalt-60) is 5.27 years. How long does it take for 50 grams of ^{60}Co to decay to 20 grams?

58. Challenge Suppose you know the half-life h of a radioactive substance. About how long, in terms of h, does it take for an amount of the substance to decay to less than $\frac{1}{1000}$ of its original amount? Explain your reasoning.

Standardized Test Practice

59. Multiple Choice What is the solution of $\left(\frac{1}{3}\right)^x = 243$?

(A) 5   (B) −4   (C) −5   (D) −6

60. Multiple Choice What is the solution of $\log_4 (7x - 3) = \log_4 (2x + 2)$?

(F) 4   (G) 1   (H) −1   (J) −4

61. Multiple Choice For what value(s) does $\log_4 8x + \log_4 (x - 2) = 3$?

(A) −2, 4   (B) −2   (C) 4   (D) no solution

Link to
CAREERS

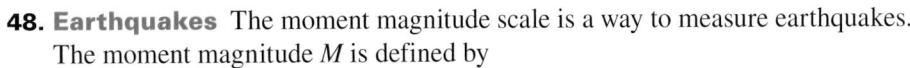

Mixed Review

Rewriting Equations **Solve the equation for *y*.** *(Lesson 1.5)*

62. $5x + y = 11$

63. $4x + 3y = -9$

64. $8x - y = 2$

65. $-2y + 6x = -3$

66. $2x + y = -5$

67. $\frac{1}{2}x - y = \frac{3}{2}$

Finding Equations **The variables *x* and *y* vary directly. Write an equation that relates the variables.** *(Lesson 2.6)*

68. $x = 1, y = 9$

69. $x = 38, y = 19$

70. $x = -10, y = -30$

71. $x = -7, y = 1$

72. $x = 6, y = -39$

73. $x = 1.5, y = 12$

Adding and Subtracting Functions **Let $f(x) = -x^2 + 3x - 1$ and let $g(x) = 2x^2 - x$. Perform the indicated operation.** *(Lesson 7.4)*

74. $f(x) + g(x)$

75. $g(x) + f(x)$

76. $f(x) + f(x)$

77. $g(x) + g(x)$

78. $f(x) - g(x)$

79. $g(x) - f(x)$

Geometry Skills

Surface Area **The area of the base is given. Find the surface area.**

80. $B = 78.5 \text{ cm}^2$

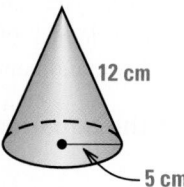
12 cm
5 cm

81. $B = 6.88 \text{ ft}^2$

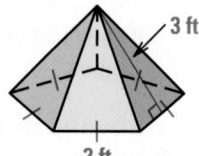
3 ft
2 ft

82. $B = 6 \text{ m}^2$

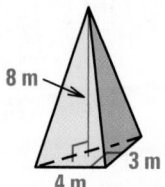
8 m
3 m
4 m

Quiz 3

Lesson 8.5

Expand the expression. Assume all variables are positive.

1. $\log_3 5x^7$

2. $\log_4 \frac{4}{7}$

3. $\log_2 xy^3$

Lesson 8.5

Condense the expression. Assume all variables are positive.

4. $2 \log 3 + 8 \log y$

5. $4 \log_6 y - 5 \log_6 x$

6. $3 \log_2 x - \log_2 5$

7. $6 \log_3 y + 4 \log_3 x$

Lesson 8.5

8. Air Horn An air horn emits sound with an intensity *I* of 1 watt per square meter. Find its decibel level *L* using the formula below.

$$L = 10 \log \frac{I}{10^{-12}}$$

How much louder is the sound of five air horns, compared to just one air horn?

Lesson 8.6

Solve the equation.

9. $8^{4x-3} = 8^{3x}$

10. $2^{2x+5} = 16^{x+1}$

11. $9^x = 100$

12. $7^{x-1} = 70$

Lesson 8.6

Solve the equation. Check for extraneous solutions.

13. $\log_2 5x = \log_2 (3x + 7)$

14. $\log_2 10x = 7$

15. $\log_7 (15x + 4) = 2$

16. $\log (x + 45) + \log x = 4$

Chapter Summary and Review

@HomeTutor
classzone.com
• Multi-Language Glossary
• Vocabulary practice

VOCABULARY

- exponential function, *p. 412*
- exponential growth function, *p. 412*
- asymptote, *p. 412*
- exponential decay function, *p. 419*
- growth factor, decay factor, *p. 426*
- natural base *e*, *p. 429*
- common logarithm, *p. 433*
- logarithm of *y* with base *b*, *p. 433*

VOCABULARY EXERCISES

1. How is the graph of an exponential growth function different from the graph of an exponential decay function?

2. Give a real-life example of a quantity that can be modeled as a function of time by an exponential decay function.

3. Which functions in this chapter have horizontal asymptotes? Which functions have vertical asymptotes?

4. The logarithm of *y* with base *b* is referred to as the common logarithm under what condition for *b*?

8.1 EXPONENTIAL GROWTH

Examples on pp. 412–414

EXAMPLE

An exponential growth function has the form $y = ab^x$ with $a > 0$ and $b > 1$. The graph of $y = 3^x$ is shown in blue below. It includes $(0, 1)$ and $(1, 3)$.

You can graph $y = 3^{x + 2}$. Sketch the graph of $y = 3^x$. Then translate it 2 units to the left. The graph passes through $(-2, 1)$ and $(-1, 3)$. It has the *x*-axis as an asymptote. The domain is all real numbers, and the range is $y > 0$.

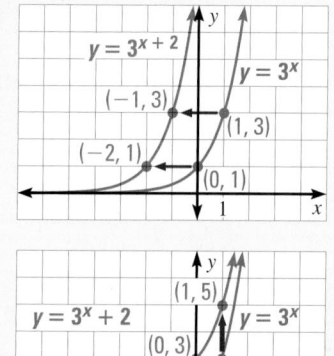

You can also graph $y = 3^x + 2$. Sketch the graph of $y = 3^x$. Then translate it 2 units up. The graph passes through $(0, 3)$ and $(1, 5)$. It has the line $y = 2$ as an asymptote. The domain is all real numbers, and the range is $y > 2$.

REVIEW HELP

Exercises	Examples
5	**1**, p. 412
6	**2**, p. 413
7, 8	**3**, p. 414

Graph the exponential function. Describe the horizontal asymptote. State the domain and range.

5. $y = 3^x$

6. $y = \dfrac{3}{2} \cdot 2^x$

7. $y = 3^{x + 4}$

8. $y = 2^x - 4$

8.2 EXPONENTIAL DECAY

Examples on
pp. 419–421

EXAMPLE An exponential decay function has the form $y = ab^x$ with $a > 0$ and $0 < b < 1$.

The graph of $y = \left(\frac{1}{3}\right)^x$ is shown in blue below. It passes through $(0, 1)$ and $(-1, 3)$.

You can graph $y = \left(\frac{1}{3}\right)^x - 2$. Sketch the graph of $y = \left(\frac{1}{3}\right)^x$.

Then translate it 2 units down. The graph passes through $(0, -1)$ and $(-1, 1)$. It has the line $y = -2$ as an asymptote. The domain is all real numbers, and the range is $y > -2$.

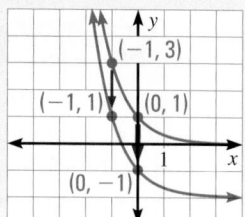

REVIEW HELP

Exercises	Examples
9	**1**, p. 419
10	**2**, p. 420
11	**3**, p. 420
12	**4**, p. 421

Graph the exponential function. Describe the horizontal asymptote. State the domain and range.

9. $y = \left(\frac{3}{5}\right)^x$ **10.** $y = 3\left(\frac{1}{5}\right)^x$ **11.** $y = \left(\frac{1}{5}\right)^{x+4}$ **12.** $y = \left(\frac{1}{5}\right)^x + 4$

8.3 MODELING WITH EXPONENTIAL FUNCTIONS

Examples on
pp. 426–429

EXAMPLE You can write an exponential function of the form $y = ab^x$ whose graph passes through two points, such as $(1, 21)$ and $(2, 63)$.

STEP ❶ Substitute the coordinates of the two points into $y = ab^x$ to obtain two equations in a and b.
$$21 = ab^1$$
$$63 = ab^2$$

STEP ❷ Solve the first equation for a.
$$a = \frac{21}{b}$$

STEP ❸ Substitute the expression for a into the second equation. Solve for b.
$$63 = \left(\frac{21}{b}\right)b^2$$
$$63 = 21b$$
$$3 = b$$

STEP ❹ You know $b = 3$, so you can solve for a.
$$a = \frac{21}{b} = \frac{21}{3} = 7$$

So, $y = 7 \cdot 3^x$ is the exponential function whose graph passes through $(1, 21)$ and $(2, 63)$.

REVIEW HELP

Exercises	Example
13–16	**3**, p. 427

Write an exponential function of the form $y = ab^x$ whose graph passes through the given points.

13. $(1, 16), (2, 128)$ **14.** $(2, 20), (3, 40)$ **15.** $(1, 2), (3, 18)$ **16.** $(2, 10), (3, 20)$

456 **Chapter 8** *Exponential and Logarithmic Functions*

8.4 LOGARITHMS AND LOGARITHMIC FUNCTIONS

Examples on pp. 433–435

EXAMPLE You can evaluate logarithmic expressions and graph logarithmic functions.

To evaluate $\log_{1/3} 81$, ask yourself what power of $\frac{1}{3}$ gives you 81.

$$\left(\frac{1}{3}\right)^? = 81 \qquad \text{What power of } \frac{1}{3} \text{ gives 81?}$$

$$\left(\frac{1}{3}\right)^{-4} = 81 \qquad 3^4 = 81 \text{ so use a negative exponent.}$$

$$\log_{1/3} 81 = -4 \qquad \text{Definition of } \log_b y$$

EXAMPLE To graph $y = \log_4 (x + 3)$, first sketch the graph of $y = \log_4 x$. Then translate the graph 3 units to the left.

The graph includes $(-2, 0)$ and $(1, 1)$. It has the line $x = -3$ as a vertical asymptote. The domain is $x > -3$, and the range is all real numbers.

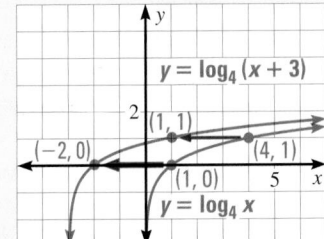

REVIEW HELP

Exercises	Examples
17–20	**2**, p. 434
21–24	**4**, p. 435

Evaluate the expression.

17. $\log_3 243$ **18.** $\log_5 \dfrac{1}{25}$ **19.** $\log_{1/4} 256$ **20.** $\log_{49} 7$

Graph the function. Describe the vertical asymptote. State the domain and range.

21. $y = \log_3 x + 5$ **22.** $y = \log_3 x - 5$ **23.** $y = \log_3 (x - 5)$ **24.** $y = \log_3 (x + 5)$

8.5 PROPERTIES OF LOGARITHMS

Examples on pp. 442–444

EXAMPLE You can use product, quotient, and power properties of logarithms to expand and condense logarithmic expressions. Assume all variables are positive.

Expand $\log_4 \dfrac{6y}{x} = \log_4 6y - \log_4 x$ **Quotient property**

$$= \log_4 6 + \log_4 y - \log_4 x \qquad \textbf{Product property}$$

Condense $\log_2 7 + \log_2 3 - 3 \log_2 y = \log_2 7 + \log_2 3 - \log_2 y^3$ **Power property**

$$= \log_2 21 - \log_2 y^3 \qquad \textbf{Product property}$$

$$= \log_2 \dfrac{21}{y^3} \qquad \textbf{Quotient property}$$

REVIEW HELP

Exercises	Examples
25–28	**2**, p. 443
29–32	**3**, p. 443

Expand the expression. Assume all variables are positive.

25. $\log_3 3x$ **26.** $\log xy^2$ **27.** $\log_5 \dfrac{9x}{y}$ **28.** $\log_2 \dfrac{x^4}{3y}$

Condense the expression. Assume all variables are positive.

29. $\log 4 + \log 12$ **30.** $2 \log 6 - \log 9$ **31.** $\log_3 4 + 3 \log_3 x$ **32.** $2 \log_2 x + \log_2 y$

EXAMPLE You can solve exponential equations by taking the common logarithm of each side.

$$4^x = 11$$ Write original equation.

$$\log 4^x = \log 11$$ Take common logarithm of each side.

$$x \log 4 = \log 11$$ Power property of logarithms

$$x = \frac{\log 11}{\log 4}$$ Divide each side by log 4.

$$x \approx 1.73$$ Use a calculator.

CHECK Check the solution algebraically by substituting into the original equation. The solution checks because $4^{1.73} \approx 11$. ✓

Use the equal powers property to solve the equation.

33. $7^{3x + 5} = 7^{11}$ **34.** $6^3 = 6^{2x + 5}$ **35.** $8^{4x - 9} = 8^x$

Take the common logarithm of each side to solve the equation. Round your answer to the nearest thousandth.

36. $7^x = 31$ **37.** $5^x = 80$ **38.** $2^x = 1000$

39. $10^{5x} = 45$ **40.** $10^{2x + 1} = 14$ **41.** $3^{x - 7} = 50$

EXAMPLE You can solve logarithmic equations by exponentiating each side of the equation.

$$\log_2 (5x - 1) = 6$$ Write original equation.

$$2^{\log_2 (5x - 1)} = 2^6$$ Exponentiate each side.

$$5x - 1 = 64$$ $b^{\log_b x} = x$

$$5x = 65$$ Add 1 to each side.

$$x = 13$$ Divide each side by 5.

CHECK Check the solution graphically by graphing both sides of the equation. The two graphs intersect at $x = 13$. ✓

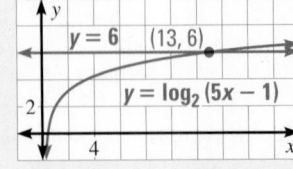

Solve the equation. Check for extraneous solutions.

42. $\log_6 (5x - 2) = \log_6 (2x + 7)$ **43.** $\log_4 (2x + 3) = \log_4 (x - 5)$

44. $\log_3 (4x + 1) = 4$ **45.** $\log_7 (2x - 3) = 2$

Graph the exponential function. Describe the horizontal asymptote. State the domain and range.

1. $y = 4^x$

2. $y = 3 \cdot 4^x$

3. $y = 3^x - 4$

4. $y = 5\left(\frac{1}{2}\right)^x$

Classify the function as *exponential growth* or *exponential decay*.

5. $y = 4\left(\frac{7}{6}\right)^x$

6. $y = 9\left(\frac{6}{7}\right)^x$

7. $y = \frac{3}{4}\left(\frac{2}{5}\right)^x$

8. $y = \frac{1}{3} \cdot 5^x$

9. Write an exponential function of the form $y = ab^x$ whose graph passes through the points $(1, 5)$ and $(3, 45)$.

10. What function is shown in the graph at the right?

  A. $y = 20^{x-1}$

  B. $y = 5^x - 5$

  C. $y = 5^x - 1$

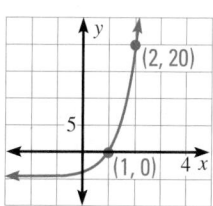

Evaluate the expression.

11. $\log_5 125$

12. $\log_3 1$

13. $\log_{1/2} 16$

Graph the function. Describe the vertical asymptote. State the domain and range.

14. $y = \log_4 x - 2$

15. $y = \log_2 x + 1$

16. $y = \log_4 (x - 2)$

17. Use $\log_6 3 \approx 0.613$ and $\log_6 8 \approx 1.161$ to find the value of $\log_6 24$ to the nearest thousandth.

Expand the expression. Assume all variables are positive.

18. $\log_5 6x^3$

19. $\log_3 \frac{x^2}{4}$

20. $\log_2 3x^4$

Condense the expression. Assume all variables are positive.

21. $\log_7 12 - \log_7 3$

22. $\log 3 + 2 \log 4$

23. $2 \log x - \log 4$

Solve the equation. Check for extraneous solutions.

24. $6^8 = 6^{3x-1}$

25. $10^{3x-1} = 5$

26. $\log (3x + 5) = \log (x - 9)$

27. Finance You deposit $800 in an account that pays 2.25% annual interest compounded continuously.

  a. Write an exponential growth model that represents the balance after t years.

  b. Graph the model.

  c. Use the graph to estimate the balance after 7 years.

28. Depreciation Your uncle buys a new truck for $35,000. The value y (in thousands of dollars) of the truck can be approximated by the model $y = 35(0.80)^x$ where x represents the number of years since he bought the truck. Graph the model. Use the graph to estimate when the truck will have a value of $5000.

Chapter Standardized Test

Test Tip   **Check your answer using a different method.**

Ⓐ Ⓑ Ⓒ Ⓓ

EXAMPLE   A construction company purchases a truck for $40,000. Each year, the value V of the truck decreases by 10%. How much will the truck be worth in two years?

   Ⓐ $26,244   **Ⓑ** $29,160   **Ⓒ** $32,400   **Ⓓ** $58,564

Solution

Write an exponential decay model describing the situation, using t for the number of years since the truck was purchased. Then substitute 2 for t and evaluate.

$$V = 40{,}000(1 - 0.1)^t = 40{,}000(0.9)^t = 40{,}000(0.9)^2 = 32{,}400$$

Choice C is the correct answer.

You can check your answer using a table. Calculate the value of the truck each year, as shown at the right.

Years since purchase	Value of truck (in dollars)
0	40,000
1	$40{,}000 - 40{,}000(0.1) = 36{,}000$
2	$36{,}000 - 36{,}000(0.1) = \mathbf{32{,}400}$

Multiple Choice

1. Evaluate the expression $3^{x + 2}$ when $x = -2$.

  Ⓐ $\dfrac{1}{3}$ **Ⓑ** 1

  Ⓒ 3   **Ⓓ** 81

2. Which function's graph is shown?

  Ⓕ $y = 6^x$

  Ⓖ $y = 2 \cdot 6^x$

  Ⓗ $y = \left(\dfrac{1}{6}\right)^x$

  Ⓙ $y = 2 \cdot \left(\dfrac{1}{6}\right)^x$

3. You purchase real estate for $85,000. Each year, the value of the real estate increases by 5%. To the nearest dollar, how much will the real estate be worth in two years?

  Ⓐ $76,713   **Ⓑ** $93,500

  Ⓒ $93,713   **Ⓓ** $98,398

4. Which function represents exponential decay?

  Ⓕ $f(x) = 2^x$ **Ⓖ** $f(x) = 8(0.9)^x$

  Ⓗ $f(x) = 6x^2$ **Ⓙ** $f(x) = 0.9 \cdot x$

5. Evaluate the expression $\log_7 343$.

  Ⓐ 1   **Ⓑ** 3

  Ⓒ 21   **Ⓓ** 49

6. Simplify the expression $\log 100^x$.

  Ⓕ 2   **Ⓖ** x

  Ⓗ $2x$ **Ⓙ** 2^x

7. Simplify the expression $4^{\log_4 16x}$.

  Ⓐ $2x$ **Ⓑ** $16x$

  Ⓒ 4^{2x} **Ⓓ** $\log 16x$

8. Which expression is equivalent to $\log \dfrac{3x^2}{y^4}$?

- **F** $2 \log 3x + 4 \log y$
- **G** $2 \log 3x - 4 \log y$
- **H** $\log 3 + 2 \log x + 4 \log y$
- **J** $\log 3 + 2 \log x - 4 \log y$

9. Which expression is equivalent to
$3 \log_4 x + \log_4 y - 4 \log_4 z$?

- **A** $\log_4 \dfrac{3xy}{4z}$
- **B** $\log_4 \dfrac{x^3 y}{z^4}$
- **C** $\log_4 x^3 y z^4$
- **D** $\log_4 x^3 + y - z^4$

10. What is the solution of $6^{x+1} = 6^{2x-3}$?

- **F** 0
- **G** 2
- **H** 4
- **J** no solution

11. What is the solution of $\log_5 (4x + 25) = 3$?

- **A** -5.5
- **B** 10
- **C** 25
- **D** 54.5

12. Solve $\log_2 2x + \log_2 (x + 2) = 4$.

- **F** -4
- **G** 2
- **H** $-4, 2$
- **J** no solution

Gridded Response

13. Evaluate 4^{x-1} when $x = 5$.

14. Evaluate $2(0.5)^x$ when $x = -2$.

15. Evaluate $\log_{256} 16$.

16. What is the solution of $2^{2x-1} = 16^{x-2}$?

17. What is the solution of $\log 5x = 2$?

18. Solve $\log_6 x + \log_6 (x + 1) = 1$.

In Exercises 19–21, use the following information.

The value A of an investment after t years can be modeled by the function $A = 1200(0.9)^t$.

19. What is the initial value of the investment?

20. Write the percent decrease each year as a decimal.

21. What is the value of the investment after two years?

Extended Response

22. The energy E (in kilocalories per gram-molecule) required to transport a substance from the outside of a cell to the inside can be approximated by

$$E = 1.4(\log C_2 - \log C_1)$$

where C_2 is the concentration of the substance inside the cell and C_1 is the concentration of the substance outside the cell.

a. Condense the expression for E.

b. The concentration of a substance inside a cell is 90%, and the concentration of the substance outside the cell is 50%. How much energy is required to transport the substance from the outside of the cell to the inside? Round your answer to the nearest hundredth.

c. The concentration of a substance inside a cell is ten times the concentration outside the cell. How much energy is required to transport the substance from the outside of the cell to the inside?

9

Rational Equations and Functions

▶ How does air temperature affect the speed at which sound travels?

462

Lightning and thunder occur at the same time, but thunder is usually heard after lightning is seen because light travels faster than sound. The air temperature during a lightning strike affects the speed at which sound of thunder travels.

Think & Discuss

The table below gives the time s (in seconds) it takes sound to travel 1 kilometer at temperature T (in degrees Celsius).

Temperature, $T(\degree C)$	Time, s (sec)
0	3.0211
3	2.9727
6	2.8361
9	2.6344
12	2.3958

1. Does sound travel faster at 38°C or at 128°C?

2. Based on the information in the table, would you expect sound to travel slower at 58°C or at 108°C?

3. Suppose you see lightning and then hear thunder about 12 seconds later. Temperature is 3°C. About how many kilometers are you from the lightning?

Learn More About It

You will approximate the air temperature during a lightning strike in Exercise 61 on page 477.

@HomeTutor
classzone.com
• Multi-Language Glossary
• Vocabulary practice

PREVIEW **What's the chapter about?**

• Writing and using inverse variation and joint variation models
• Graphing rational functions and identifying asymptotes
• Simplifying rational expressions
• Solving rational equations

Key Words

• inverse variation, *p. 466*
• constant of variation, *p. 466*
• joint variation, *p. 468*
• rational function, *p. 472*
• hyperbola, *p. 472*
• branch, *p. 472*

• rational expression, *p. 480*
• simplified form, *p. 480*
• complex fraction, *p. 488*
• least common denominator, *p. 494*
• rational equation, *p. 500*
• cross multiply, *p. 500*

PREPARE **Chapter Readiness Quiz**

Take this quick quiz. If you are unsure of an answer, look back at the reference pages for help.

Vocabulary Check *(refer to p. 412)*

1. Copy and complete the statement: A line that a graph approaches as the value of x increases is called a(n) __?__ of the graph.

  (A) asymptote   **(B)** axis   **(C)** parabola   **(D)** x-intercept

Skill Check *(refer to pp. 234, 16)*

2. Factor the expression $x^2 - 2x - 24$.

  (F) $(x - 3)(x + 8)$ **(G)** $(x + 3)(x - 8)$

  (H) $(x - 4)(x + 6)$ **(J)** $(x + 4)(x - 6)$

3. Simplify the expression $3x + 6 - (2x + 4)$.

  (A) $x + 10$ **(B)** $x + 2$ **(C)** $5x + 10$ **(D)** $x - 2$

TAKE NOTES **Write the Steps**

Write the steps for solving problems in your own words. Use an example, so you can see the steps when you do your homework.

Solving a rational equation is like solving a fraction equation.

$\dfrac{4}{x} + \dfrac{5}{2} = -\dfrac{11}{x}$ LCD is the product of denominators.

$2x\left(\dfrac{4}{x} + \dfrac{5}{2}\right) = 2x\left(-\dfrac{11}{x}\right)$ Multiply each side by the LCD.

$8 + 5x = -22$ Simplify.

$5x = -30$, so $x = -6$ Solve.

DEVELOPING CONCEPTS *(For use with Lesson 9.1)*
Investigating Inverse Variation

Goal

Measure a relationship between two distances that vary inversely.

Materials

- tape measure or meter stick
- centimeter ruler
- masking tape

QUESTION

What is the relationship between the distance you are standing from an object in the room and the apparent height of the object?

EXPLORE

1 Have your partner stand against a wall. Place the end of the tape measure against the wall at your partner's feet. Use tape to mark off each meter from 3 meters to 9 meters away from the wall in a straight line.

2 Stand facing your partner with your toes just touching the 3 meter mark. Hold a centimeter ruler at arm's length and line up the "0" end of the ruler with the top of your partner's head. Measure the apparent height of your partner to the nearest centimeter.

3 Record the height and the distance in a table like the one below. Repeat Step 2 for each of the marked distances. Then trade positions and record the measures in a new table.

Distance (m)	3	4	5	6	7	8	9
Apparent Height (cm)	?	?	?	?	?	?	?

THINK ABOUT IT

1. Does apparent height vary directly with distance? Justify your answer.

2. Multiply the paired values of distance and apparent height together. Do you notice any similarity in the results?

3. Based on your results from Exercise 2, write an equation you could use to find the apparent height if you are given a distance. Let d = distance and h = apparent height.

4. Use your equation from Exercise 3 to predict the apparent height of your partner from 5.5 meters. Test your prediction. How close was your prediction?

9.1 Inverse and Joint Variation

Key Words
- inverse variation
- constant of variation
- joint variation

GOAL Use inverse variation and joint variation models.

You have learned that two variables x and y show direct variation if $y = kx$ and $k \neq 0$. Another type of variation is *inverse variation*. Two variables x and y show **inverse variation** if:

$$y = \frac{k}{x}, \, k \neq 0 \qquad \text{Inverse Variation Equation}$$

The nonzero constant k is called the **constant of variation**. The variable y is said to *vary inversely* with x.

EXAMPLE 1 Classify Direct and Inverse Variation

Tell whether x and y show *direct variation*, *inverse variation*, or *neither*.

a. $xy = 2$ **b.** $\dfrac{y}{3} = x$ **c.** $y = x + 1$

GIVEN EQUATION	REWRITTEN EQUATION	TYPE OF VARIATION
a. $xy = 2$	$y = \frac{2}{x}$	Inverse
b. $\frac{y}{3} = x$	$y = 3x$	Direct
c. $y = x + 1$		Neither

 **Classify Direct and Inverse Variation**

Tell whether x and y show *direct variation*, *inverse variation*, or *neither*.

1. $y = 2x$ 2. $y = 5x + 6$ 3. $xy = 10$

4. $xy = \dfrac{1}{2}$ 5. $y = -7x$ 6. $x = 10 + 5y$

EXAMPLE 2 Write an Inverse Variation Equation

Write an equation that relates x and y such that x and y vary inversely and $y = 6$ when $x = 2$.

Solution

$y = \dfrac{k}{x}$ Write the inverse variation model.

$6 = \dfrac{k}{2}$ Substitute 2 for x and 6 for y.

$12 = k$ Solve for k.

ANSWER ▶ The inverse variation that relates x and y is $y = \dfrac{12}{x}$.

Link to
PHYSICS

FOUNTAINS
The Main Fountain Garden at Longwood Gardens can pump 2000 gallons per minute. This is equivalent to filling 400 bathtubs every 10 minutes.

EXAMPLE 3 Write an Inverse Variation Model

Pumping Rate The time required to empty a tank varies inversely with the pumping rate. The rate of a certain pump is 70 gallons per minute. It takes the pump 20 minutes to empty the tank.

a. Write an inverse variation model.

b. Describe the change in time to empty the tank as the pumping rate increases.

c. What does the value of k represent in the situation?

Solution

a. Write an inverse variation model relating the time t to empty the tank and the pumping rate r.

$$t = \frac{k}{r}$$ Model for inverse variation

$$20 = \frac{k}{70}$$ Substitute 20 for t and 70 for r.

$$1400 = k$$ Solve for k.

The model is $t = \frac{1400}{r}$.

b. As the pumping rate r increases, the time to empty the tank decreases.

c. The value of k is 1400 gallons, which is the volume of the tank being emptied.

Checkpoint ✓ **Write an Inverse Variation Equation**

The variables x and y vary inversely. Use the given values to write an equation relating x and y.

7. $x = 3, y = 4$ **8.** $x = 5, y = 2$ **9.** $x = 8, y = 6$

Rewriting Inverse Variation The equation for inverse variation can also be written as $xy = k$. So, a set of data pairs (x, y) shows inverse variation if the products xy are constant or approximately constant.

EXAMPLE 4 Check Data for Inverse Variation

Pressure and Volume The table compares the pressure (in atmospheres) to the volume of oxygen (in liters) at 0°C. Do these data show inverse variation? If so, find a model for the relationship between P and V.

P (atmospheres)	V (liters)
25	2.8
50	1.4
100	0.70
200	0.35

Solution

From the table you can see that PV is equal to 70. For example, $(25)(2.8) = 70$ and $(50)(1.4) = 70$. So, the data do show inverse variation. A model for the relationship between the pressure and the volume of oxygen at 0°C is $PV = 70$, or $P = \frac{70}{V}$.

Types of Variation **Joint variation** occurs when a quantity varies directly as the product of *two or more* other quantities. For example, if $z = kxy$ where $k \neq 0$, then z varies jointly with x and y. Other types of variation are also possible.

Types of Variation

In each equation, k is a constant and $k \neq 0$.

RELATIONSHIP	EQUATION
y varies directly with x.	$y = kx$
y varies inversely with x.	$y = \dfrac{k}{x}$
z varies jointly with x and y.	$z = kxy$
y varies inversely with the square of x.	$y = \dfrac{k}{x^2}$
z varies directly with y and inversely with x.	$z = \dfrac{ky}{x}$

Link to
MUSIC

CONCERTS Many musicians wear earplugs to protect their hearing. Over time, sounds louder than 80 decibels can damage hearing.

EXAMPLE 5 Write a Variation Model

Intensity of Sound The intensity y of a sound (in watts per square meter) varies inversely with the square of the distance d (in meters) from the source of the sound. At a distance of 1 meter from the stage, the intensity of the sound at a rock concert is about 10 watts per square meter, which is about 130 decibels.

a. Write an equation relating y and d.

b. You are 15 meters from the stage. What is the intensity of the sound you hear?

Solution

a. Choose the equation that shows that y varies inversely with the square of d.

$$y = \frac{k}{d^2} \qquad \text{Write equation.}$$

$$10 = \frac{k}{1^2} \qquad \text{Substitute 10 for } y \text{ and 1 for } d.$$

$$10 = k \qquad \text{Solve for } k.$$

ANSWER ▶ An equation relating y and d is $y = \dfrac{10}{d^2}$.

b. Substitute 15 for d and solve for y.

$$y = \frac{10}{15^2} = \frac{10}{225} \approx 0.044$$

ANSWER ▶ The intensity of the sound at 15 meters is 0.044 watts per square meter.

Checkpoint ✔ **Write a Variation Model**

10. Intensity of Sound In Example 5, suppose the intensity of the sound at a rock concert is about 15 watts per square meter when you are 1 meter from the stage. Write an equation relating y and d.

Guided Practice

Vocabulary Check

1. Copy and complete the statement: If x and y vary inversely, then the product xy is __?__.

Skill Check

Tell whether x and y show *direct variation*, *inverse variation*, or *neither*.

2. $y = \frac{1}{2}x$ **3.** $y = \frac{5}{x}$ **4.** $xy = 5$ **5.** $y = 2x - 1$

6. $\frac{y}{x} = 10$ **7.** $y = \frac{1}{x}$ **8.** $y = \frac{8}{x - 1}$ **9.** $xy = 7$

Tell whether x varies jointly with y and z.

10. $9yx = z$ **11.** $z = \frac{x}{3y}$ **12.** $xy = 0.3z$ **13.** $x = \frac{6z}{y}$

14. $x = y + z$ **15.** $4x = 5yz$ **16.** $\frac{3x}{z} = 2y$ **17.** $\frac{1}{xyz} = 3$

18. Interest The simple interest I on a bank account varies jointly with the time t (in years) and the principal P (in dollars). After one quarter (3 months) the interest on a principal of $6000 is $60.

   a. Find the value of k in $I = Ptk$. What does k represent in this situation?

   b. Find the interest earned on the account after two years.

Practice and Applications

STUDENT HELP

HOMEWORK HELP
Example 1: Exs. 19–26
Example 2: Exs. 27–36
Example 3: Exs. 35–36
Example 4: Exs. 37–39
Example 5: Exs. 40–45,
      50–54

Determining Variation Tell whether x and y show *direct variation*, *inverse variation*, or *neither*.

19. $xy = 12$ **20.** $y = \frac{2}{3}x$ **21.** $y = \frac{1}{x}$ **22.** $y - 3 = 2x$

23. $5y = 6x$ **24.** $y = \frac{3}{x + 15}$ **25.** $15 = \frac{x}{y}$ **26.** $x = \frac{4}{y}$

Inverse Variation Models The variables x and y vary inversely. Use the given values to write an equation relating x and y.

27. $x = 3, y = 1$ **28.** $x = 5, y = 6$ **29.** $x = 4, y = 9$

30. $x = -8, y = 3$ **31.** $x = \frac{1}{2}, y = 4$ **32.** $x = \frac{3}{4}, y = 12$

Direct Variation Models In Exercises 33 and 34, write a direct variation equation.

33. The variables t and r vary directly, and $r = 2$ when $t = 18$.

34. The variables p and q vary directly, and $p = -8$ when $q = 24$.

35. Traveling Time When driving in your car, the amount of time traveled varies inversely with the speed of the car. It takes you 1.5 hours to reach your destination driving 65 miles per hour. How long will it take if you drive 55 miles per hour? What does the value of k represent?

DIVING The deeper a diver is under water, the faster he or she uses air from the tank. So, a diver at 33 feet below sea level will use air faster than a diver at 15 feet below sea level.

36. Diving Scuba is a portable device that allows divers to breathe while under water. It consists of one or two tanks of compressed air connected by tubing to a mouthpiece. The pressure p inside the tank varies inversely with the volume v of the tank. The volume of the tank is 0.4 cubic feet of compressed air. The pressure inside a full tank is 3000 pounds per square inch. What is the equivalent volume of air at an atmospheric pressure of 15 pounds per square inch?

Interpreting Data Determine whether x and y show *direct variation*, *inverse variation*, or *neither*.

37.

x	y
7	35
11	55
15	75
20	100

38.

x	y
4	9
10	21
13	27
15	31

39.

x	y
5	6.4
8	4
10	3.2
20	1.6

Joint Variation Models The variable z varies jointly with x and y. Use the given values to write an equation relating x, y, and z.

40. $x = 2, y = 6, z = 24$

41. $x = 5, y = 3, z = 60$

42. $x = 8, y = 4, z = 16$

43. $x = 9, y = 6, z = 18$

44. $x = \frac{2}{5}, y = 5, z = 10$

45. $x = \frac{2}{3}, y = \frac{6}{5}, z = 8$

Writing Equations Write an equation for the given relationship.

46. z varies inversely with x and y, and $k = 4$.

47. y varies jointly with x and the square of z, and $k = \frac{1}{2}$.

48. w varies inversely with x and jointly with y and z, and $k = -3$.

49. Challenge The value of y varies directly with x and inversely with v. When $x = 45$ and $v = 12$, $y = 15$. Find the value of y when $x = 8$ and $v = 16$.

50. Levers You can use a simple lever to lift a 300-pound rock. The force F needed to lift the rock (in foot-pounds) is inversely related to the distance d from the pivot point of the lever (in feet). To lift the rock, you need 60 pounds of force applied to a lever with a distance of 10 feet from the pivot point. What force is needed when you increase the distance to 15 feet from the pivot point?

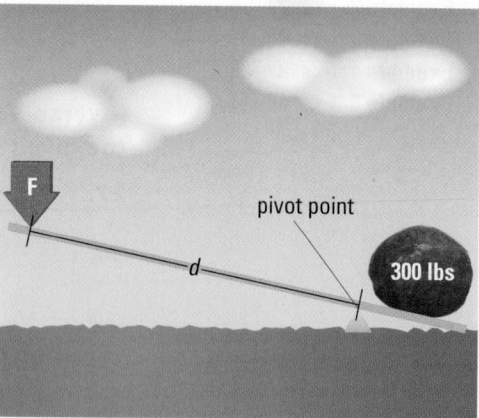
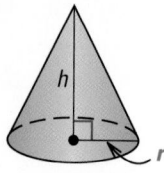

51. Geometry Link The volume V of a right circular cone varies jointly with the square of the radius r of the base and the height h of the cone. The volume of a right circular cone with a radius of 2 centimeters and a height of 4 centimeters is 16.76 cubic centimeters. Find the volume of a cone with $r = 3$ centimeters and $h = 7$ centimeters.

The load P (in pounds) that can be safely supported by a horizontal beam varies jointly with the product of the width W (in feet) of the beam and the square of the depth D (in feet) and inversely with the length L (in feet).

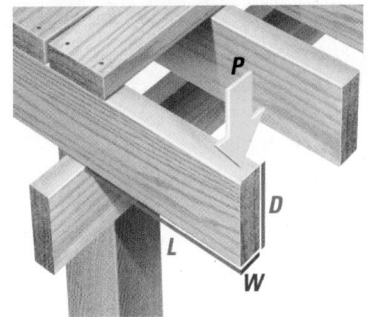

52. Write an equation relating P, W, D, L and a constant k.

53. How does P change when the length of the beam is doubled?

54. Challenge How does P change when the width is doubled and the depth of the beam is cut in half?

Standardized Test Practice

55. Multiple Choice The variables x and y vary inversely. Given the values $x = -5$ and $y = 15$, find the equation relating x and y.

  Ⓐ $y = \dfrac{1}{x}$ **Ⓑ** $y = -3x$ **Ⓒ** $y = \dfrac{-3}{x}$ **Ⓓ** $y = \dfrac{-75}{x}$

56. Multiple Choice The variable z varies directly with x and inversely with y. Given the values $x = \dfrac{3}{4}$, $y = \dfrac{5}{12}$, and $z = \dfrac{6}{25}$, find the equation relating x, y, and z.

  Ⓕ $z = \dfrac{96}{125}xy$ **Ⓖ** $z = \dfrac{2x}{15y}$ **Ⓗ** $z = \dfrac{96}{125xy}$ **Ⓙ** $z = \dfrac{54y}{125x}$

Mixed Review

Point-Slope Form Write an equation of the line that passes through the given point and has the given slope. *(Lesson 2.5)*

57. $(0, -1)$, $m = 4$ **58.** $(2, 1)$, $m = -1$ **59.** $(3, -2)$, $m = 2$

60. $(-2, 5)$, $m = 0$ **61.** $(5, -4)$, $m = \dfrac{2}{5}$ **62.** $(1, 3)$, $m = -\dfrac{1}{4}$

Simplest Form Simplify the variable expression. Assume all variables are positive. *(Lesson 7.2)*

63. $(49x^4)^{1/2}$ **64.** $(27a^{15})^{1/3}$ **65.** $(8m^{-3}n^{15})^{2/3}$

66. $(25c^8d^4)^{3/2}$ **67.** $(64k^9)^{-1/3}$ **68.** $(16x^5)^{-1/2}$

Graphing Functions Identify the asymptote of the function. Graph the function. Then state the domain and range. *(Lesson 7.6)*

69. $y = -\sqrt{x}$ **70.** $y = \sqrt{x} + 2$ **71.** $y = \sqrt[3]{x} + 4$

Geometry Skills

Triangle Similarity Determine whether the triangles are similar. If they are similar, name the triangle that is similar to $\triangle ABC$.

72.
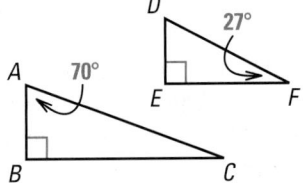

73.

9.2 Graphing Rational Functions

Key Words
- rational function
- hyperbola
- branches

Graph rational functions.

A **rational function** is a function of the form $f(x) = \dfrac{p(x)}{q(x)}$ where $p(x)$ and $q(x)$ are polynomials and $q(x) \neq 0$. Consider the parent functions and their graphs below.

Prerequisite Skills

Solve for *x*.

1. $x + 7 = 0$

2. $x^2 - 9 = 0$

Name the asymptote of the graph of the function.

3. $y = 2^{x+2}$

4. $y = 2^x - 6$

$y = \dfrac{1}{x}$

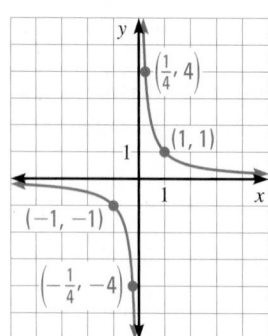

$y = \dfrac{-1}{x}$

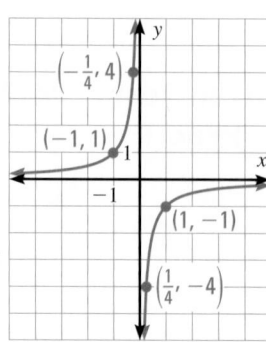

Each graph is a **hyperbola** with the following properties.

- The *x*-axis is a horizontal asymptote and the *y*-axis is a vertical asymptote.

- The domain and range are all nonzero real numbers.

- The graph has two symmetrical parts called **branches**.

- For each point (x, y) on one branch of $y = \dfrac{1}{x}$, the corresponding point $(-x, -y)$ is on the other branch.

EXAMPLE 1 Graph a Rational Function

Graph $y = \dfrac{-4}{x}$. State the domain and range.

Solution

Draw the asymptotes. The *y*-axis is the vertical asymptote and the *x*-axis is the horizontal asymptote.

Plot a few points on each side of the vertical asymptote.

$$(-1, 4), (-2, 2), (-4, 1)$$
$$(1, -4), (2, -2), (4, -1)$$

Draw the two branches of the hyperbola. Each branch approaches the asymptotes and passes through the plotted points.

ANSWER ▶ The domain and range are the same: all nonzero real numbers.

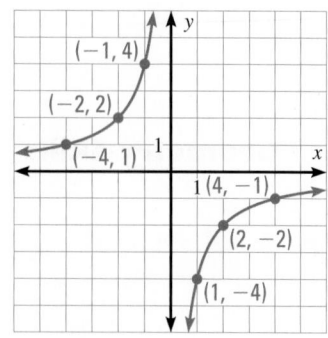

STUDENT HELP

READING GRAPHS
The hyperbola in Example 1 is symmetric about the origin. So, once you determine that $(-1, 4)$ is on one branch, you know that $(1, -4)$ is on the other.

For functions of the form $y = \frac{a}{x}$, the value of a tells you the shape of the graph.

- If $a > 0$, the branches of the hyperbola are in the first and third quadrants.
- If $a < 0$, the branches of the hyperbola are in the second and fourth quadrants.
- As $|a|$ increases, the branches of the hyperbola move farther from the axes.

Graphing Rational Functions of the Form $y = \frac{a}{x-h} + k$

The graph of a rational function of the form $y = \frac{a}{x-h} + k$ is a hyperbola with a vertical asymptote at $x = h$ and a horizontal asymptote at $y = k$.

To graph a rational function, use these steps.

STEP ❶ *Draw* the asymptotes $x = h$ and $y = k$.

STEP ❷ *Plot* points on each side of the the vertical asymptote $x = h$.

STEP ❸ *Draw* the two branches of the hyperbola that approach the asymptotes and pass through the plotted points.

EXAMPLE 2 Graph a Rational Function

Graph the function $y = \frac{10}{x+3}$. State the domain and range.

Solution

STUDENT HELP

GRAPHING NOTE
The branches of the graph are symmetric and the point of symmetry is the intersection of the asymptotes.

The function is in the form $y = \frac{a}{x-h} + k$. So, $a = 10$, $h = -3$, and $k = 0$.

❶ *Draw* the asymptotes $x = -3$ and $y = 0$.

❷ *Plot* a couple of points on each side of the vertical asymptote.

$(2, 2)$, $(-1, 5)$, $(-5, -5)$, and $(-8, -2)$

❸ *Draw* both branches of the hyperbola. Each branch approaches the asymptotes and passes through the plotted points.

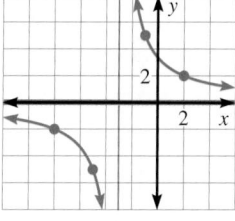

ANSWER ▶ The domain is all real numbers except -3. The range is all real numbers except 0.

Checkpoint ✓ Graph a Rational Function

Graph the function. State the domain and range.

1. $y = \frac{3}{x}$ **2.** $y = \frac{-2}{x}$ **3.** $y = \frac{1}{x+1} - 1$

4. Tickets In a radio contest, you win a certificate for $100 worth of concert tickets. The ticketing agency charges x dollars for each ticket plus a $2 processing fee. The function $y = \frac{100}{x+2}$ models the number of tickets y you can buy. State the domain and range in this situation.

Graphs of General Rational Functions

Let $p(x)$ and $q(x)$ be polynomials with no common factors other than ± 1. The graph of the rational function $f(x) = \dfrac{p(x)}{q(x)}$ has the following characteristics:

1. The x-intercepts of the graph of $f(x)$ are the real zeros of $p(x)$.

2. The graph of $f(x)$ has a vertical asymptote at each real zero of $q(x)$.

EXAMPLE The graph of $f(x) = \dfrac{x-3}{x^2 - 3x + 2}$ has an x-intercept of 3 and vertical asymptotes at $x = 2$ and $x = 1$.

To sketch the graph of a general rational function, use a graphing calculator.

EXAMPLE 3 Use a Calculator

Use a graphing calculator to sketch the graph of $y = \dfrac{x^2}{x^2 - 1}$.

Solution

Enter the function. Use parentheses as shown. Most graphing calculators have two graphing modes: *Connected* mode and *Dot* mode.

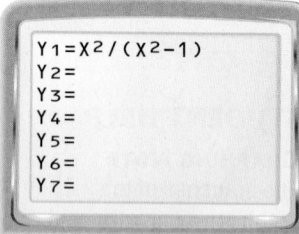

The graphs below show $y = \dfrac{x^2}{x^2 - 1}$ graphed in each mode.

CONNECTED MODE

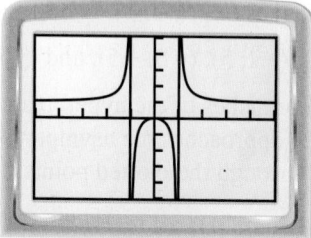

DOT MODE

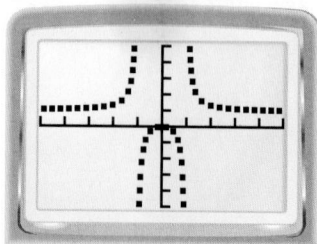

STUDENT HELP

GRAPHING NOTE
Be sure to choose a viewing window that shows all of the important characteristics of the graph, such as the branches and the intercepts.

Notice that the graph in connected mode has two vertical lines: $x = -1$ and $x = 1$. These lines are *not* part of the graph. They are the calculator's attempt to connect the three branches of the graph. These segments indicate the location of the asymptotes. The graph in dot mode eliminates the connecting lines. However, the graph is represented as a collection of dots instead of a smooth curve.

Checkpoint ✓ *Use a Calculator*

Graph the function. Identify the x-intercept(s) and the vertical asymptote(s).

5. $y = \dfrac{3}{x^2 + 1}$ **6.** $y = \dfrac{4x}{2x + 1}$ **7.** $y = \dfrac{2x^2}{x^2 - 4}$ **8.** $y = \dfrac{x^2 + 4}{x^2 - 4}$

474   **Chapter 9** *Rational Equations and Functions*

Exercises

Guided Practice

Vocabulary Check

1. Copy and complete the statement: The graph of a function of the form $y = \dfrac{a}{x - h}$ is called a(n) __?__.

Skill Check

Identify the vertical and horizontal asymptotes of the graph of the function.

2. $y = \dfrac{4}{x}$

3. $y = \dfrac{4}{x} - 4$

4. $y = \dfrac{2}{x - 3}$

5. $y = \dfrac{-1}{x + 2} + 2$

6. $y = \dfrac{-3}{x + 5} - 3$

7. $y = \dfrac{2}{x - 1} - 7$

8. You are creating a 100-point test. Each question will be worth y points. The value of y depends on the number of questions x. The function $y = \dfrac{100}{x}$ models the situation. Graph the function. State the domain and range in this situation.

Practice and Applications

STUDENT HELP

HOMEWORK HELP
Example 1: Exs. 9–25, 30–38
Example 2: Exs. 17–40
Example 3: Exs. 41–59

Properties of Graphs **Identify the vertical and horizontal asymptotes of the graph of the function. Then identify the points (1, _?_) and (−1, _?_) that are part of the graph.**

9. $y = \dfrac{4}{x}$

10. $y = \dfrac{-2}{x}$

11. $y = \dfrac{-7}{x}$

12. $y = \dfrac{3}{x}$

13. $y = \dfrac{5}{x}$

14. $y = \dfrac{-9}{x}$

15. $y = \dfrac{11}{x}$

16. $y = \dfrac{-16}{x}$

Identifying Asymptotes **Identify the vertical and horizontal asymptotes of the graph of the function. Then state the domain and range of the function.**

17. $y = \dfrac{2}{x} - 5$

18. $y = \dfrac{-5}{x} + 2$

19. $y = \dfrac{3}{x - 1}$

20. $y = \dfrac{4}{x - 2}$

21. $y = \dfrac{1}{x + 6} - 3$

22. $y = \dfrac{-3}{x + 4} + 1$

23. $y = \dfrac{2}{x + 5} - 1$

24. $y = \dfrac{-1}{x + 2} + 4$

25. $y = \dfrac{-4}{x - 7} + 3$

Matching Graphs **Match the function with its graph.**

26. $y = \dfrac{2}{x - 3} + 1$

27. $y = \dfrac{2}{x + 3} + 1$

28. $y = \dfrac{2}{x - 3} - 1$

A.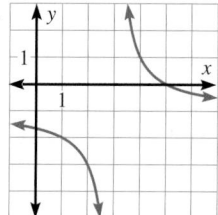

B.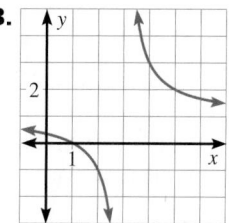

C.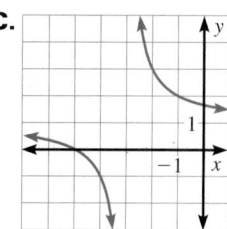

29. Error Analysis Explain why the graph shown is not the graph of

$$y = \frac{-1}{x - 4} - 2$$

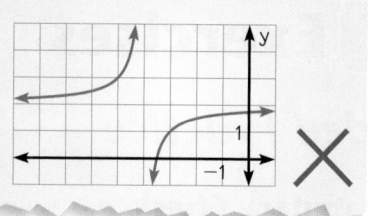

STUDENT HELP

GRAPHING NOTE
Use a different color to draw the asymptotes than you use to draw the graph. This shows that the asymptotes are not part of the graph of the function.

Graphing Functions Graph the function. State the domain and range.

30. $y = \dfrac{5}{x}$

31. $y = \dfrac{-2}{x}$

32. $y = \dfrac{1}{x + 2}$

33. $y = \dfrac{-2}{x + 1}$

34. $y = \dfrac{-3}{x + 5}$

35. $y = \dfrac{2}{x - 3}$

36. $y = \dfrac{4}{x + 2} + 6$

37. $y = \dfrac{-1}{x - 4} - 2$

38. $y = \dfrac{3}{x - 2} + 1$

Health Club **In Exercises 39 and 40, use the following information.**

You pay $200 for a membership to a health club. The price p per visit to the health club can be modeled by $p = \dfrac{200}{t}$ where t is the number of visits to the health club.

39. Graph the model. Identify the vertical and horizontal asymptotes of the graph of the function. Identify the part of the graph that models the situation.

40. Use the graph to determine how many visits to the health club are needed to have a price of $8 per visit.

Analyzing Graphs Identify the *x*-intercept(s) and vertical asymptote(s) of the graph of the function.

41. $y = \dfrac{x + 3}{x^2 - 4}$

42. $y = \dfrac{4x^2 - 1}{x + 1}$

43. $y = \dfrac{x^2 - 2x - 3}{2x + 3}$

44. $y = \dfrac{x - 1}{x^3}$

45. $y = \dfrac{x^2 + 2}{3x - 1}$

46. $y = \dfrac{x + 5}{x^2 - 9}$

Graphs **In Exercises 47–50, use a calculator to match the function with its graph.**

47. $y = \dfrac{x^2 + 3}{x - 1}$

48. $y = \dfrac{x - 4}{x^2}$

49. $y = \dfrac{x + 2}{x^3 - 8}$

50. $y = \dfrac{x - 2}{x^3 + 1}$

A.

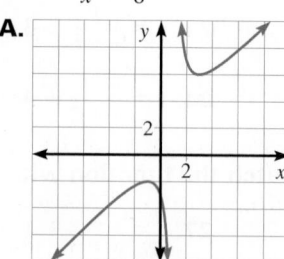

B.

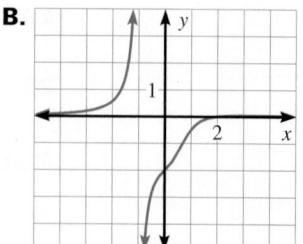

C.

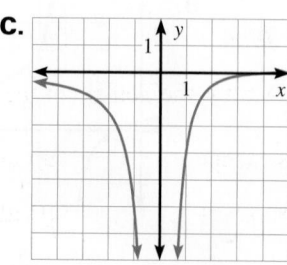

D.

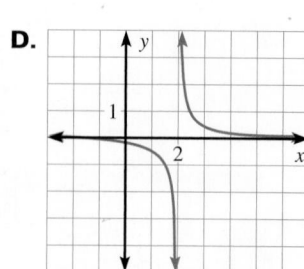

Graphing Functions In Exercises 51–59, use a calculator to graph the function.

51. $y = \dfrac{3}{x^2 - 1}$

52. $y = \dfrac{2x^2 + 1}{x}$

53. $y = \dfrac{x^2 - 4x - 3}{x - 4}$

54. $y = \dfrac{x - 3}{x^2 - 16}$

55. $y = \dfrac{x + 2}{x^3 + 9}$

56. $y = \dfrac{x^3}{x + 1}$

57. $y = \dfrac{x^2 - 1}{x^3 + 27}$

58. $y = \dfrac{2x + 5}{x^3 - 1}$

59. $y = \dfrac{x^3 + 8}{x^2 - 9}$

60. **School** Your school purchases a math software program. The program has an initial cost of $500 plus $20 for each student that uses the program. The price p per student can be modeled by

$$p = \frac{500 + 20s}{s}$$

where s is the number of students using the program. Use a calculator to graph the function. How many students need to use the program so that the price per student is $30?

61. **Lightning** The time it takes for sound to travel one kilometer can be modeled by

$$s = \frac{1000}{0.6T^2 + 331}$$

where s is time (in seconds) and T is temperature (in degrees Celsius). You are 1 kilometer from a lightning strike. You hear the thunder 2.9 seconds later. Use a graph to find the approximate air temperature. (*Hint:* Use tick marks that are 0.1 unit apart on the s-axis.)

62. **Reasoning** In what line(s) is the graph of $y = \dfrac{1}{x}$ symmetrical? What does this symmetry tell you about the inverse of the function $f(x) = \dfrac{1}{x}$?

63. **Challenge** The graph of the rational function f is a hyperbola. The asymptotes of the graph of f intersect at (3, 2). The point (2, 1) is on the graph. Find another point on the graph. Explain your reasoning.

Standardized Test Practice

64. Multiple Choice What is the vertical asymptote of the graph of the function?

$$y = \frac{2}{x + 4} + 7$$

(A) $x = -7$
(B) $x = -4$
(C) $x = 4$
(D) $x = 7$

65. Multiple Choice What are the x-intercept(s) of the graph of the function?

$$y = \frac{x - 4}{x^2 - 1}$$

(F) $1, -1$
(G) 4
(H) 1
(J) -4

66. Multiple Choice What is the domain of the function $y = \dfrac{x - 2}{x + 4}$?

(A) all real numbers except -2
(B) all real numbers except 4
(C) all real numbers except 2
(D) all real numbers except -4

Solving Equations Solve the equation. *(Lesson 1.4)*

67. $9x + 24 = 6$ **68.** $24 + 7n = -n$ **69.** $-4s + 2 = -7 - s$

70. $6r + 7 = 3r - 8$ **71.** $2(-2m + 10) = -2m$ **72.** $8(2x - 6) = 4x$

Simplifying Algebraic Expressions Simplify the expression. State which properties of exponents you used. *(Lesson 6.1)*

73. $(x^{-2}y^3)^2$ **74.** $(2x^3)^{-2}$ **75.** $\dfrac{x^{-4}}{x}$

76. $\dfrac{x^2y}{x^3y^{-2}}$ **77.** $\dfrac{6x^{-1}y^3}{2xy}$ **78.** $\dfrac{x^2y^{-5}}{x^{-4}y}$

Graphing Functions Graph the exponential function. *(Lesson 8.2)*

79. $y = 4\left(\dfrac{1}{2}\right)^x$ **80.** $y = 3\left(\dfrac{1}{4}\right)^x$ **81.** $y = -2\left(\dfrac{1}{3}\right)^x$

82. $y = -25\left(\dfrac{3}{4}\right)^x$ **83.** $y = 10\left(\dfrac{4}{5}\right)^x$ **84.** $y = -100(0.6)^x$

Volume of a Cone Find the volume of the cone. Round your answer to the nearest whole number.

85.

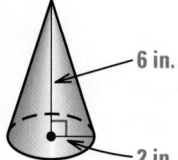

6 in.

2 in.

86.

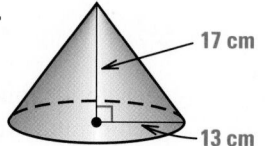

17 cm

13 cm

87.

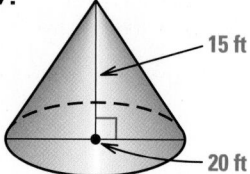

15 ft

20 ft

Quiz 1

Lesson 9.1 Tell whether *x* and *y* show *direct variation, inverse variation,* or *neither.*

1. $y = 4x$ **2.** $xy = 10$ **3.** $2x + 1 = y$

4. $y = \dfrac{2}{x}$ **5.** $x + 5 = 3y$ **6.** $8 = \dfrac{x}{y}$

Lesson 9.1 The variables *x* and *y* vary inversely. Use the given values to write an equation relating *x* and *y*.

7. $x = 4, y = 1$ **8.** $x = 2, y = -5$ **9.** $x = 3, y = 7$

10. $x = 2, y = -\dfrac{1}{4}$ **11.** $x = \dfrac{2}{3}, y = 9$ **12.** $x = 6, y = \dfrac{3}{4}$

Lesson 9.2 Identify the vertical and horizontal asymptotes of the graph of the function. Then state the domain and range.

13. $y = \dfrac{3}{x}$ **14.** $y = \dfrac{-2}{x} - 3$ **15.** $y = \dfrac{4}{x + 2} + 5$

16. $y = \dfrac{-1}{x + 1} - 1$ **17.** $y = \dfrac{3}{x - 3} + 71$ **18.** $y = \dfrac{2}{x - 4} - 6$

19. The volume V of a prism can be written as $V = Bh$, where B is the area of the base and h is the height. A prism has a volume of 64 cm^3. Graph all possible combinations of B and h for the prism.

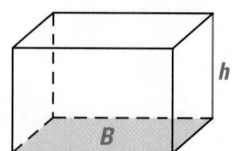

USING A GRAPHING CALCULATOR *(For use with Lesson 9.2)*
Horizontal Asymptotes

A rational function $f(x) = \dfrac{p(x)}{q(x)}$ has a horizontal asymptote when the degree of $p(x)$ is less than or equal to the degree of $q(x)$.

You can use the *Table* feature of a graphing calculator to find the horizontal asymptote of a rational function, if it exists.

EXAMPLE 1

Find the horizontal asymptote of $y = \dfrac{x + 3}{2x - 1}$, if it exists.

SOLUTION

❶ The degree of the numerator is equal to the degree of the denominator, so the function has a horizontal asymptote.

❷ Enter $y = \dfrac{x + 3}{2x - 1}$ into a graphing calculator. Use the *Table* feature to see the values of y as x increases and decreases without bound. In the Table Setup menu, change "indpnt" to "Ask" in order to enter values for x.

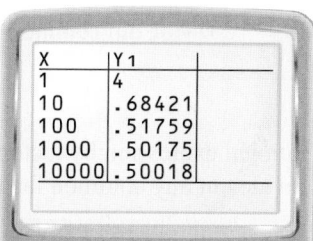

X	Y1
1	4
10	.68421
100	.51759
1000	.50175
10000	.50018

X	Y1
-1	-.66667
-10	.33333
-100	.48259
-1000	.49825
-10000	.49983

❸ You can use the tables to determine that the graph has a horizontal asymptote at $y = 0.5$ because the values of y become closer to 0.5 as x becomes increasingly large or small.

EXAMPLE 2

Find the horizontal asymptote of $y = \dfrac{x^2 + 1}{x - 4}$, if it exists.

SOLUTION

❶ The degree of the numerator is greater than the degree of the denominator, so the function $\dfrac{x^2 + 1}{x - 4}$ does not have a horizontal asymptote.

EXERCISES

Find the horizontal asymptote of the rational function, if it exists.

1. $y = \dfrac{3x - 1}{x + 2}$

2. $y = \dfrac{2x^2 - 1}{x}$

3. $y = \dfrac{3}{x^2 - 5}$

4. $y = \dfrac{x^2 - 4}{x + 1}$

5. $y = \dfrac{x^2}{4x^2 - 9}$

6. $y = \dfrac{2x + 3}{x^2 - 1}$

9.3 Simplifying and Multiplying Rational Expressions

Key Words
- rational expression
- simplified form

GOAL Simplify and multiply rational expressions.

Prerequisite Skills

Multiply.

1. $\dfrac{3}{4} \cdot \dfrac{8}{15}$

2. $\dfrac{2}{3} \cdot \dfrac{9}{10}$

Factor the expression.

3. $x^2 - x$

4. $2x + 4$

How do penguins adapt to very cold temperatures?

In Exercise 57, you will write a fraction to answer this question. A fraction whose numerator and denominator are nonzero polynomials is a **rational expression**. A rational expression is in **simplified form** when its numerator and denominator have no common factors (other than ± 1).

Simplifying Rational Expressions

Let a, b, and c be nonzero real numbers or variable expressions.

$$\dfrac{ac}{bc} = \dfrac{a \cdot c}{b \cdot c} = \dfrac{a}{b} \qquad \text{Divide out common factor } c.$$

You can simplify a rational expression by factoring the numerator and denominator. Then divide out any common factors, as shown in Example 1.

EXAMPLE 1 Simplify a Rational Expression

Simplify the rational expression, if possible.

a. $\dfrac{15x}{5} = \dfrac{3 \cdot 5 \cdot x}{5} = 3x$ Divide out the common factor 5 and simplify.

b. $\dfrac{x + 5}{x}$ This expression is already in simplest form.

c. $\dfrac{6x}{14x^2} = \dfrac{2 \cdot 3 \cdot x}{2 \cdot 7 \cdot x \cdot x} = \dfrac{3}{7x}$ Divide out the common factors 2 and x.

When you simplify rational expressions, you can divide out only *factors*, not *terms*. So in part (b) of Example 1 you cannot divide out x because it is not a factor of 5.

Checkpoint ✓ *Simplify a Rational Expression*

Simplify the expression, if possible.

1. $\dfrac{4x}{10}$ **2.** $\dfrac{8}{4x}$ **3.** $\dfrac{9x}{12(x + 1)}$ **4.** $\dfrac{1 - x}{x}$

EXAMPLE 2 Write in Simplest Form

Simplify the expression below, which gives the ratio of the volume of the solid to the volume of the hole.

$$\frac{\pi r^2 h - \pi(2)^2 h}{\pi(2)^2 h}$$

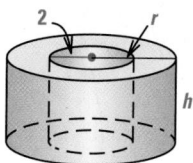

Solution

$$\frac{\pi r^2 h - \pi(2)^2 h}{\pi(2)^2 h} = \frac{\pi h(r^2 - 4)}{4\pi h}$$ Factor numerator and denominator.

$$= \frac{\pi \cancel{h}(r^2 - 4)}{4\pi \cancel{h}}$$ Divide out common factors π and h.

$$= \frac{r^2 - 4}{4}$$ Simplify.

In the simplified ratio in Example 2, the numerator has factors $(r + 2)$ and $(r - 2)$ and the numerator has factors 2 and 2. There are no common factors, so the ratio is in simplest form.

 **Write in Simplest Form**

Simplify the expression, if possible.

5. $\dfrac{2x + 1}{2x}$ **6.** $\dfrac{3x^2(x + 1)}{3x}$ **7.** $\dfrac{2x^2 + 8x}{12x}$ **8.** $\dfrac{x + 2}{3x + 6}$

Multiplying Rational Expressions Because the variables in a rational expression represent real numbers, the rules for multiplying rational expressions are the same as the rules for multiplying fractions.

Multiplying Rational Expressions

Let a, b, and c be nonzero variable expressions.

To multiply, multiply numerators and denominators.

$$\frac{a}{b} \cdot \frac{c}{d} = \frac{ac}{bd}$$

EXAMPLE 3 Multiply Rational Expressions

Multiply $\dfrac{4x^2}{3x} \cdot \dfrac{9x}{8x^5}$. Simplify the result.

Solution

$$\frac{4x^2}{3x} \cdot \frac{9x}{8x^5} = \frac{36x^3}{24x^6}$$ Multiply the numerators and denominators.

$$= \frac{\cancel{2} \cdot \cancel{2} \cdot \cancel{3} \cdot 3 \cdot \cancel{x} \cdot \cancel{x} \cdot \cancel{x}}{2 \cdot \cancel{2} \cdot \cancel{2} \cdot \cancel{3} \cdot \cancel{x} \cdot \cancel{x} \cdot \cancel{x} \cdot x \cdot x \cdot x}$$ Factor and divide out the common factors.

$$= \frac{3}{2x^3}$$ Simplify the expression.

STUDENT HELP

WRITING ALGEBRA
You do not need to write the prime factorizations of 36 and 24 if you recognize 12 as their greatest common factor.

EXAMPLE 4 Multiply Rational Expressions

Multiply $\dfrac{3x}{4x-12} \cdot \dfrac{x^2-9}{x}$. Simplify the result.

Solution

$$\frac{3x}{4x-12} \cdot \frac{x^2-9}{x} = \frac{3x}{4(x-3)} \cdot \frac{(x-3)(x+3)}{x}$$ Factor the numerators and denominators.

$$= \frac{3x(x-3)(x+3)}{4x(x-3)}$$ Multiply the numerators and denominators.

$$= \frac{3\cancel{x}(x\cancel{-3})(x+3)}{4\cancel{x}(x\cancel{-3})}$$ Divide out the common factors.

$$= \frac{3(x+3)}{4}$$ Simplify the expression.

CHECK You can check that your solution is correct by substituting the same value for x, such as 1, in the original expression and in your answer.

$$\frac{3x}{4x-12} \cdot \frac{x^2-9}{x} = \frac{3(1)}{4(1)-12} \cdot \frac{(1)^2-9}{(1)} = \frac{3}{-8} \cdot \frac{-8}{1} = 3$$

$$\frac{3(x+3)}{4} = \frac{3(1+3)}{4} = \frac{3 \cdot 4}{4} = 3 \checkmark$$

 **Multiply Rational Expressions**

Multiply the rational expressions. Simplify the result.

9. $\dfrac{3x}{14} \cdot \dfrac{7x}{6x^3}$ **10.** $\dfrac{2x}{3x-6} \cdot \dfrac{2x-4}{x^2}$ **11.** $\dfrac{4x+8}{x^3} \cdot \dfrac{6x}{x^2-4}$

EXAMPLE 5 Multiply by a Polynomial

Multiply $\dfrac{x}{x^2-5x+6} \cdot 3(2-x)$. Simplify the result.

Solution

$$\frac{x}{x^2-5x+6} \cdot 3(2-x) = \frac{x}{x^2-5x+6} \cdot \frac{3(2-x)}{1}$$ Write polynomial as a rational expression.

$$= \frac{x}{(x-2)(x-3)} \cdot \frac{-1 \cdot 3(x-2)}{1}$$ Factor -1 out of $(2-x)$.

$$= \frac{-3x(x\cancel{-2})}{(x\cancel{-2})(x-3)}$$ Multiply. Then divide out the common factor.

$$= \frac{-3x}{x-3}$$ Simplify.

STUDENT HELP

AVOID ERRORS
Look for terms that are common if you factor out -1 from one of them.
$(x-2) = -1(2-x)$

Multiply by a Polynomial

Multiply the expressions. Simplify the result.

12. $\dfrac{4}{x+3} \cdot (2x+6)$ **13.** $\dfrac{x}{3x+12} \cdot (x^2+4x)$ **14.** $\dfrac{3x}{x^2-x-2} \cdot (2-x)$

Guided Practice

Vocabulary Check

1. Explain how you know that a rational expression is in simplest form.

2. Copy and complete the statement: To multiply rational expressions, multiply the __?__ and the __?__.

Skill Check

Simplify the rational expression. If not possible, write *already in simplest form*.

3. $\dfrac{16x}{4}$ **4.** $\dfrac{24x^2}{8x}$ **5.** $\dfrac{48x}{16x^3}$

6. $\dfrac{6x+3}{12x^2-16}$ **7.** $\dfrac{5x^3+2x}{3x^2+x}$ **8.** $\dfrac{2x^4-6x^2}{4x^3+10x^2}$

Multiply the rational expressions. Simplify the result.

9. $\dfrac{8x^2}{3x} \cdot \dfrac{x^3}{2}$ **10.** $\dfrac{4x^4}{5x^2} \cdot \dfrac{10x}{6x}$ **11.** $\dfrac{x^5}{2x^3+4x^2} \cdot \dfrac{4x+8}{3x}$

12. $\dfrac{2x}{5x-20} \cdot \dfrac{x^2-16}{x^2}$ **13.** $\dfrac{x}{x^2-3x-10} \cdot (20-4x)$ **14.** $\dfrac{4x^2}{x+2} \cdot \dfrac{x^2-4x^2}{6-3x}$

15. Error Analysis Describe and correct the error in simplifying the rational expression shown.

$$\dfrac{8x^2}{8(x^2-4)} = \dfrac{\cancel{8} \cdot x^2}{\cancel{8}(x^2-4)} = \dfrac{x^2}{x^2-4} = \dfrac{\cancel{x} \cdot \cancel{x}}{\cancel{x} \cdot \cancel{x} - 4} = -\dfrac{1}{4} \quad \times$$

Practice and Applications

STUDENT HELP

HOMEWORK HELP
Example 1: Exs. 22–37
Example 2: Exs. 22–37
Example 3: Exs. 38–45
Example 4: Exs. 38–45
Example 5: Exs. 46–51

Common Factors Write the common factors of the expressions.

16. $24x,\ 8$ **17.** $72x^2,\ 18x$ **18.** $4x^2,\ 16x^2-12x$

19. $32x^5,\ 16x^4+56x^2$ **20.** $x^2-81,\ x^2-10x+9$ **21.** $x^2-9,\ x^2-4x-12$

Matching Match the expression with its simplified form.

22. $\dfrac{27x}{9x^2}$ **23.** $\dfrac{3x^2-6x^4}{x^3}$ **24.** $\dfrac{18x^6}{24x^7+6x^4}$ **25.** $\dfrac{15x^7+9x^3}{5x^5+3x}$

A. $3x^2$ **B.** $\dfrac{3x^2}{4x^3+1}$ **C.** $\dfrac{3}{x}$ **D.** $\dfrac{3(1-2x^2)}{x}$

Factoring and Simplifying Simplify the expression. If not possible, write *already in simplest form*.

26. $\dfrac{45x^2}{15x}$ **27.** $\dfrac{4x^2}{4(x+1)}$ **28.** $\dfrac{x^3}{x^2-4}$ **29.** $\dfrac{5x}{25x^3-35}$

30. $\dfrac{2x^4+1}{12x^3}$ **31.** $\dfrac{14x^2+21x}{42x^4}$ **32.** $\dfrac{3x^3+7x^2}{6x^5+9x^3}$ **33.** $\dfrac{4x^6+24x^3}{12x^2-30x^4}$

34. $\dfrac{x^2-4}{x+2}$ **35.** $\dfrac{x^2+9x+18}{4x+24}$ **36.** $\dfrac{x^2+6x-16}{x^2+10x-24}$ **37.** $\dfrac{x^3-x}{x^3-7x^2+6x}$

38. Error Analysis Describe and correct the error in multiplying the rational expressions shown.

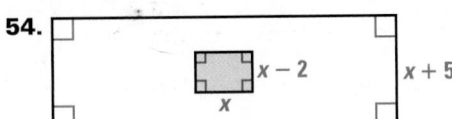

$$\frac{(x^2-9)}{(4-x)} \cdot \frac{x-4}{x+3} = \frac{(x-3)(x+3)}{x-4} \cdot \frac{x-4}{x+3} = \frac{(x-3)(x+3)(x-4)}{(x-4)(x+3)} = x-3 \qquad \times$$

Multiplying Rational Expressions **Multiply the rational expressions. Simplify the result.**

39. $\dfrac{5x}{2} \cdot \dfrac{1}{x}$

40. $\dfrac{7x^2}{3} \cdot \dfrac{6x}{4x^2}$

41. $\dfrac{6x^3}{4x} \cdot \dfrac{16}{2x^2}$

42. $\dfrac{-2}{x+3} \cdot \dfrac{x+3}{8(x-1)}$

43. $\dfrac{3x-4}{5} \cdot \dfrac{45}{8-6x}$

44. $\dfrac{x}{x^2-9} \cdot \dfrac{x+3}{4x^2}$

45. $\dfrac{x^3}{x+1} \cdot \dfrac{x^2+3x+2}{x+2}$

46. $\dfrac{5x+45}{x^2} \cdot \dfrac{3x^3}{x^2-81}$

47. $\dfrac{16x^4}{x+5} \cdot \dfrac{x^2+3x-10}{8x^6}$

Multiplying Polynomials **Multiply. Simplify the result.**

48. $\dfrac{x}{x+5} \cdot (6x+30)$

49. $\dfrac{16x^9}{(24x^6-8x^5)} \cdot (15x-5)$

50. $\dfrac{6x^2}{x^2-1} \cdot (3-3x)$

51. $\dfrac{5x+20}{x^2-x+20} \cdot (x^2-25)$

52. $\dfrac{2x^2}{4x^3-16x} \cdot (x^2+7x-9)$

53. $\dfrac{10x}{2x^2-4x-70} \cdot (x^2-49)$

Geometry Link In Exercises 54 and 55, find the ratio of the shaded region to the total area of the figure.

54.

A rectangle with outer dimensions $3x^2-12x$ (width) and $x+5$ (height), containing a small shaded rectangle of dimensions x by $x-2$.

55.

A right triangle with legs $2x$ and $2x$ (left side total) and base $4x+2$, containing a shaded smaller triangle with base $2x+1$.

Biology Link In Exercises 56–57, use the following information.

Animals that live in temperatures several degrees colder than their body temperatures must avoid losing heat to survive. Animals with a minimum amount of surface area exposed to the environment can better conserve body heat. As a result, animals with a similar body shape tend to be larger when they live in colder climates.

56. Find the surface area to volume ratio in simplest form for a cylindrical object.

57. To make an estimate of the ratio of a penguin's surface area to its volume, you can model a penguin with a cylinder. Find the ratio for each of the penguins described below. Based on the information above, which penguin lives in a colder climate? Explain your reasoning.

Emperor penguin: height = 31 inches, radius = 5 inches
Magellanic penguin: height = 18 inches, radius = 2.8 inches

58. Find the surface area-to-volume ratio in simplest form for a spherical object.

59. Reasoning For a spherical object, describe the relationship of the surface area to volume ratio and the radius of the sphere. What happens to the ratio as the radius increases?

60. Model Building You build a model for the construction of a new building. The dimensions are based on a value x that will be determined once the location is finalized. Write a model in terms of x for the total area of the base of the new building.

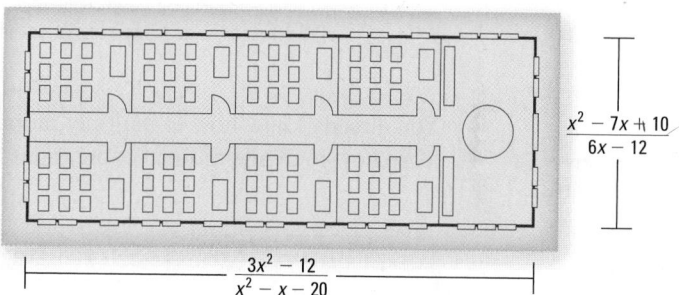

$$\dfrac{x^2 - 7x + 10}{6x - 12}$$

$$\dfrac{3x^2 - 12}{x^2 - x - 20}$$

Standardized Test Practice

61. Multiple Choice Write the expression in simplest form.

$$\dfrac{6x + 4}{3x^2 - 4x - 4}$$

A $\dfrac{2(3x - 2)^2}{3x^2 - 4x - 4}$ **B** $\dfrac{3x + 2}{x - 2}$ **C** $\dfrac{2}{x - 2}$ **D** $\dfrac{2(3x - 2)}{x - 2}$

62. Multiple Choice Multiply the expressions. Simplify the result.

$$\dfrac{x^3}{3x - 9} \cdot \dfrac{x^2 + 5x - 24}{x^3 + 8x^2}$$

F $\dfrac{1}{3}$ **G** $\dfrac{x^3(x + 8)}{x^3 + 8x^2}$ **H** $\dfrac{x(x - 8)}{3(x + 8)}$ **J** $\dfrac{x}{3}$

Mixed Review

Factoring Factor the polynomial. *(Lesson 6.5)*

63. $5x^3 - 20$ **64.** $125x^3 + 1$ **65.** $8x^3 - 64$

66. $5x^3 - 135$ **67.** $x(x - 9) - 6(x - 9)$ **68.** $x^3 - x^2 + x - 1$

Logarithmic Expressions Evaluate the expression. *(Lesson 8.4)*

69. $\log_9 81$ **70.** $\log_3 243$ **71.** $\log_5 125$ **72.** $\log_7 \dfrac{1}{49}$

73. $\log_{36} 6$ **74.** $\log_{11} 121$ **75.** $\log_{1/2} 64$ **76.** $\log_{1/4} 256$

Determining Variation Tell whether *x* and *y* show *direct variation*, *inverse variation*, or *neither*. *(Lesson 9.1)*

77. $y = -\dfrac{1}{x}$ **78.** $xy = 15$ **79.** $y - 4x + 10 = 0$ **80.** $y = \dfrac{1}{2}x$

81. $23 = \dfrac{x}{y}$ **82.** $3y = -7x$ **83.** $5y + 8 = x$ **84.** $x = \dfrac{12}{y}$

Geometry Skills

Identifying Parts of a Circle Give the coordinates of the part related to the circle.

85. center

86. endpoints of a diameter

87. point of tangency

88. endpoints of a radius

89. endpoints of a chord that is not a diameter

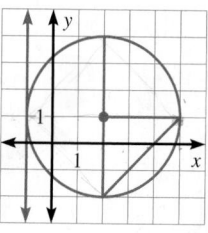

9.4 Dividing Rational Expressions

Key Words

• complex fraction

Prerequisite Skills

Divide.

1. $\dfrac{3}{4} \div \dfrac{8}{9}$

2. $\dfrac{7}{8} \div \dfrac{21}{32}$

Factor the expression.

3. $3x + 6$

4. $2x - 4$

GOAL Divide rational expressions and simplify complex fractions.

You already know how to multiply rational expressions. In this lesson, you will learn how to divide rational expressions.

Dividing Rational Expressions

Let a, b, c, and d be nonzero variable expressions. Use these steps to find the quotient $\dfrac{a}{b} \div \dfrac{c}{d}$.

STEP ❶ *Rewrite* the division as a product.

$$\frac{a}{b} \div \frac{c}{d} = \frac{a}{b} \cdot \frac{d}{c}$$

STEP ❷ *Multiply* the numerators and the denominators.

STEP ❸ *Factor* the numerator and denominator, if possible.

STEP ❹ *Divide* out the common factors.

STEP ❺ *Simplify*.

EXAMPLE 1 Divide Rational Expressions

Simplify $\dfrac{x}{10} \div \dfrac{x^2}{25}$.

Solution

$\dfrac{x}{10} \div \dfrac{x^2}{25} = \dfrac{x}{10} \cdot \dfrac{25}{x^2}$ Rewrite as a product. Use the reciprocal of the dividend.

$= \dfrac{25x}{10x^2}$ Multiply the numerators and the denominators.

$= \dfrac{5 \cdot 5 \cdot x}{2 \cdot 5 \cdot x \cdot x}$ Factor the numerators and the denominators.

$= \dfrac{5 \cdot \cancel{5} \cdot \cancel{x}}{2 \cdot \cancel{5} \cdot \cancel{x} \cdot x}$ Divide out the common factors x and 5.

$= \dfrac{5}{2x}$ Simplify the expression.

Checkpoint ✓ *Divide Rational Expressions*

Write the quotient in simplest form.

1. $\dfrac{x}{6} \div \dfrac{2x}{3}$ 2. $\dfrac{4}{x} \div \dfrac{8}{x^2}$ 3. $\dfrac{x^2}{2} \div \dfrac{2x}{5}$

EXAMPLE 2 Divide Rational Expressions

Simplify $\dfrac{1}{3x + 15} \div \dfrac{x}{2x + 10}$.

Solution

$$\frac{1}{3x + 15} \div \frac{x}{2x + 10} = \frac{1}{3x + 15} \cdot \frac{2x + 10}{x}$$
Rewrite as a product.

$$= \frac{2x + 10}{(3x + 15x)(x)}$$
Multiply the numerators and the denominators.

$$= \frac{2(x + 5)}{3(x + 5)(x)}$$
Factor the numerators and denominators.

$$= \frac{2\cancel{(x + 5)}}{3\cancel{(x + 5)}(x)}$$
Divide out the common factor $(x + 5)$.

$$= \frac{2}{3x}$$
Simplify the expression.

CHECK Check that the simplified expression is equivalent to the original expression by substituting a convenient value for x.

$$\frac{1}{3(1) + 15} \div \frac{1}{2(1) + 10} \overset{?}{=} \frac{2}{3(1)}$$
Substitute 1 for x.

$$\frac{1}{18} \cdot \frac{12}{1} \overset{?}{=} \frac{2}{3}$$
Simplify and rewrite as a product.

$$\frac{1}{\cancel{6} \cdot 3} \cdot \frac{\cancel{6} \cdot 2}{1} = \frac{2}{3} \checkmark$$
Solution checks.

> **STUDENT HELP**
>
> **AVOID ERRORS**
> When you multiply the numerators and the denominators, write the result as a product of factors. Then, in the next step, you are less likely to make a mistake when factoring.

EXAMPLE 3 Divide by a Polynomial

Simplify $\dfrac{6 - 3x}{5x^2} \div (x - 2)$.

Solution

$$\frac{6 - 3x}{5x^2} \div (x - 2) = \frac{6 - 3x}{5x^2} \cdot \frac{1}{(x - 2)}$$
Multiply by reciprocal.

$$= \frac{6 - 3x}{5x^2(x - 2)}$$
Multiply.

$$= \frac{-3(x - 2)}{5x^2(x - 2)}$$
Factor.

$$= \frac{-3\cancel{(x - 2)}}{5x^2\cancel{(x - 2)}}$$
Divide out common factor $(x - 2)$.

$$= -\frac{3}{5x^2}$$
Simplify the expression.

Checkpoint ✓ **Divide Expressions**

Write the quotient in simplest form.

4. $\dfrac{3}{x - 4} \div \dfrac{9}{x - 4}$

5. $\dfrac{x + 5}{3x} \div \dfrac{2x + 10}{6x^2}$

6. $\dfrac{9 - 3x}{x - 2} \div (x - 3)$

Complex Fractions A **complex fraction** is a fraction that has a fraction in its numerator or denominator, or both. To simplify a complex fraction, you can rewrite the fraction as a division expression. Then follow the steps for dividing fractions.

$$\frac{\dfrac{a}{b}}{\dfrac{c}{d}} = \frac{a}{b} \div \frac{c}{d} = \frac{a}{b} \cdot \frac{d}{c}$$

EXAMPLE 4 Simplify a Complex Fraction

Simplify $\dfrac{\dfrac{1}{x+1}}{\dfrac{2}{x}}$.

Solution

$$\frac{\dfrac{1}{x+1}}{\dfrac{2}{x}} = \frac{1}{x+1} \div \frac{2}{x} \qquad \text{Rewrite as a division expression.}$$

$$= \frac{1}{x+1} \cdot \frac{x}{2} \qquad \text{Multiply by reciprocal.}$$

$$= \frac{x}{2(x+1)} \qquad \text{Simplify.}$$

STUDENT HELP

ANOTHER WAY
You get the same result if you multiply the numerator and the denominator of the complex fraction by the reciprocal of the denominator.

$$\frac{\dfrac{1}{x+1} \cdot \dfrac{x}{2}}{\dfrac{2}{x} \cdot \dfrac{x}{2}} = \frac{\dfrac{1}{x+1} \cdot \dfrac{x}{2}}{1}$$

EXAMPLE 5 Simplify a Complex Fraction

Simplify $\dfrac{\dfrac{x+1}{x+5}}{\dfrac{x+1}{x+2}}$.

Solution

$$\frac{\dfrac{x+1}{x+5}}{\dfrac{x+1}{x+2}} = \frac{x+1}{x+5} \div \frac{x+1}{x+2} \qquad \text{Rewrite as a division expression.}$$

$$= \frac{x+1}{x+5} \cdot \frac{x+2}{x+1} \qquad \text{Multiply by reciprocal.}$$

$$= \frac{(x+1)(x+2)}{(x+5)(x+1)} \qquad \text{Divide out common factor } (x+1).$$

$$= \frac{x+2}{x+5} \qquad \text{Simplify.}$$

Checkpoint ✓ Simplify a Complex Fraction

Simplify the complex fraction.

7. $\dfrac{\dfrac{1}{x+2}}{\dfrac{1}{x}}$

8. $\dfrac{\dfrac{1}{2x}}{\dfrac{2}{x+1}}$

9. $\dfrac{\dfrac{x-1}{x+2}}{\dfrac{x-1}{x+3}}$

9.4 Exercises

Guided Practice

Vocabulary Check   **1.** What is a complex fraction?

Skill Check   **Write the quotient in simplest form.**

2. $\dfrac{5x}{7} \div \dfrac{3}{2x}$

3. $\dfrac{2x}{9} \div \dfrac{x}{3}$

4. $\dfrac{x}{4} \div x^2$

5. $\dfrac{4}{3x} \div \dfrac{8}{15x^3}$

6. $\dfrac{1}{x-5} \div \dfrac{2}{3x-15}$

7. $\dfrac{4x-6}{3x^2} \div \dfrac{2x-3}{2x^3}$

Simplify the complex fraction.

8. $\dfrac{\frac{1}{2}}{x}$

9. $\dfrac{\frac{x}{6}}{\frac{1}{3}}$

10. $\dfrac{\frac{1}{x-2}}{\frac{3}{x}}$

11. $\dfrac{\frac{x}{6}}{\frac{2}{x+1}}$

12. $\dfrac{\frac{4x}{x+2}}{\frac{x}{3}}$

13. $\dfrac{\frac{x+3}{x-1}}{\frac{x+3}{x+4}}$

14. $\dfrac{\frac{x-5}{x+8}}{\frac{7}{x+8}}$

15. $\dfrac{\frac{5x}{3x+9}}{\frac{x-4}{3}}$

Error Analysis Describe and correct the error.

16.

$$\dfrac{\frac{x+1}{x-3}}{\frac{x-3}{x+5}} = \dfrac{x+1}{x-3} \cdot \dfrac{x-3}{x+5} = \dfrac{x+1}{x+5} \quad \times$$

17.

$$\dfrac{x-4}{4-x} \div \dfrac{3}{x^2-16} = \dfrac{x-4}{4-x} \cdot \dfrac{(x-4)(x+4)}{3}$$

$$= \dfrac{(x-4)^2(x+4)}{3(4-x)} \quad \times$$

Practice and Applications

STUDENT HELP

HOMEWORK HELP
Example 1: Exs. 18–29
Example 2: Exs. 30–35
Example 3: Exs. 36–41
Example 4: Exs. 42–49
Example 5: Exs. 42–49

Dividing Rational Expressions Write the quotient in simplest form.

18. $\dfrac{x}{3} \div \dfrac{x^2}{6}$

19. $\dfrac{1}{2x} \div \dfrac{2}{4x}$

20. $\dfrac{x}{7} \div \dfrac{6}{x}$

21. $\dfrac{x}{8} \div \dfrac{9x}{4}$

22. $\dfrac{5}{x} \div \dfrac{3}{x^2}$

23. $\dfrac{2x}{3} \div \dfrac{x^2}{2}$

24. $\dfrac{x^2}{10} \div \dfrac{x}{5}$

25. $\dfrac{4x}{3} \div \dfrac{14x}{5}$

26. $\dfrac{5}{6x^3} \div \dfrac{1}{8x}$

27. $\dfrac{7x^2}{4} \div \dfrac{x^2}{7}$

28. $\dfrac{12}{x^3} \div \dfrac{4}{3x}$

29. $\dfrac{2x^3}{5} \div \dfrac{x^2}{2}$

Dividing Rational Expressions Write the quotient in simplest form. Check your answer.

30. $\dfrac{1}{x-4} \div \dfrac{x}{x-4}$

31. $\dfrac{4x}{x+3} \div \dfrac{3}{x+3}$

32. $\dfrac{2x+1}{6x} \div \dfrac{10x+5}{3x^2}$

33. $\dfrac{x+5}{x^2-9} \div \dfrac{3x+15}{x+3}$

34. $\dfrac{x^2-1}{x+7} \div \dfrac{1-x}{2}$

35. $\dfrac{x^2+4x-12}{x^2+3x-4} \div \dfrac{x+6}{2x-2}$

Divide by a Polynomial Write the quotient in simplest form.

36. $\dfrac{2x+6}{3x^2} \div (x+3)$

37. $\dfrac{4x-6}{4x} \div (2x-3)$

38. $\dfrac{x-9}{2x} \div (x^2-4x-45)$

39. $\dfrac{x-7}{4} \div (14-2x)$

40. $\dfrac{x^2-3x+10}{x-6} \div (20-4x)$

41. $\dfrac{x^2-25}{x+7} \div (x^2+2x-35)$

Complex Fractions Simplify the complex fraction.

42. $\dfrac{\frac{1}{x+4}}{\frac{1}{2x}}$

43. $\dfrac{\frac{1}{x-3}}{\frac{2}{x}}$

44. $\dfrac{\frac{1}{x+9}}{\frac{2}{x+9}}$

45. $\dfrac{\frac{2}{x}}{\frac{x+6}{x^2}}$

46. $\dfrac{\frac{x+1}{3}}{\frac{x-7}{6}}$

47. $\dfrac{\frac{x^2}{x+3}}{\frac{2x}{x+3}}$

48. $\dfrac{\frac{x+8}{x+3}}{\frac{x^2+4x-32}{x-4}}$

49. $\dfrac{\frac{x^2-6x+8}{4x-12}}{\frac{x^2+5x-14}{3-x}}$

50. Geometry Link Write a simplified expression for the ratio of the perimeter of the figure to its area.

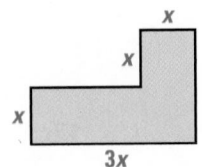

Efficiency Ratio In Exercises 51–53, use the following information.

The surface are S and the volume V of a cylindrical can are given by

$$S = 2\pi r^2 + 2\pi rh \qquad \text{and} \qquad V = \pi r^2 h$$

where r is the radius and h is the height.

	Radius, r	Height, h
Soup Can	3.4 cm	10.2 cm
Coffee Can	7.8 cm	15.9 cm
Paint Can	8.4 cm	19.4 cm

51. Write and simplify an expression for the efficiency ratio $\dfrac{S}{V}$.

52. Find the efficiency ratio for each can listed in the table above.

53. Rank the three cans in Exercise 52 according to efficiency. Explain your ranking.

Geometry Link Find the ratios $\dfrac{AB}{BC}$ and $\dfrac{AE}{ED}$. Explain how you know that *EB* is parallel to *DC*.

54.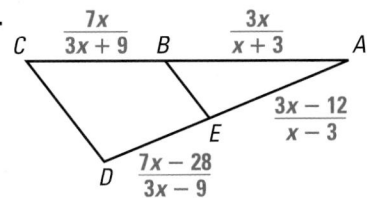

55.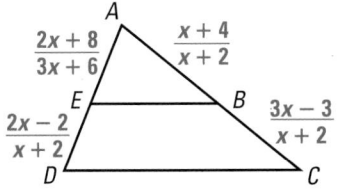

56. Geometry Link Use the Pythagorean theorem $a^2 + b^2 = c^2$ to find the ratio of the perimeter to the area of the triangle shown below.

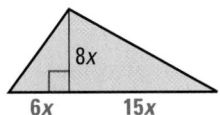

57. Challenge Write two rational functions $f(x)$ and $g(x)$ such that $\dfrac{f(x)}{g(x)} = \dfrac{x+3}{x-3}$.

Standardized Test Practice

58. Multiple Choice Which product represents $(x^2 - 5x - 6) \div \dfrac{3x^2 + 21x}{7}$?

(A) $\dfrac{1}{x^2 - 5x - 6} \cdot \dfrac{7}{3x^2 + 21x}$

(B) $\dfrac{7}{x^2 - 5x - 6} \cdot \dfrac{1}{3x^2 + 21x}$

(C) $\dfrac{x^2 - 5x - 6}{1} \cdot \dfrac{3x^2 + 21x}{7}$

(D) $\dfrac{x^2 - 5x - 6}{1} \cdot \dfrac{7}{3x^2 + 21x}$

59. Multiple Choice Which of the following represents $\dfrac{x+3}{x-5} \div \dfrac{x^2-9}{2x-10}$ in simplest form?

(F) $\dfrac{2}{x-3}$

(G) $\dfrac{2x-10}{(x-3)(x-5)}$

(H) $\dfrac{1}{x-3}$

(J) $\dfrac{(x+3)(x^2-9)}{2(x-5)^2}$

60. Multiple Choice Which of the following represents $\dfrac{x^2-16}{x-5} \div \dfrac{x-4}{x^2-25}$ in simplest form?

(A) $\dfrac{x+5}{x+4}$

(B) $(x+5)(x+4)$

(C) $\dfrac{x+4}{x+5}$

(D) $(x-5)(x-4)$

61. Multiple Choice Which of the following represents the complex fraction

$$\dfrac{\dfrac{x}{(x-2)^2}}{\dfrac{x^2-7x}{4x-8}}$$ in simplest form?

(F) $\dfrac{x-7}{4(x-2)}$

(G) $\dfrac{4x(x-2)}{x(x-2)^2(x-7)}$

(H) $\dfrac{4}{(x-2)(x-7)}$

(J) $\dfrac{x^2(x-7)}{4(x-2)^3}$

Linear Combinations Solve the system using the linear combinations method. *(Lesson 3.3)*

62. $3x + 5y = 8$
$6x - 2y = 40$

63. $2x + 3y = 13$
$x - 2y = 3$

64. $2x + 5y = 7$
$3x - y = -15$

Adding and Subtracting Polynomials Perform the indicated operation. Write the answer in standard form. *(Lesson 6.3)*

65. $(2x^2 - 3) + (x^2 + 2)$

66. $(3x^3 + 7) - (4 - x^3)$

67. $(x^3 + 4x^2 - 3x) - (-2x^3 + 3x^2 - 5)$

68. $(4x^3 - 5x + 4) + (x^3 + 3x^2 - 8)$

Multiplying Polynomials Find the product. *(Lesson 6.4)*

69. $x(x^2 + 2x - 3)$

70. $(3x + 2)(x + 5)$

71. $(x + 3)(x - 7)$

72. $(x + 2)(x^2 - x - 6)$

73. $(x + 4)(x^2 + 3x)$

74. $x(x - 5)(x^2 + 1)$

Geometry Skills

Exterior Angles Find the measure of $\angle 2$.

75.

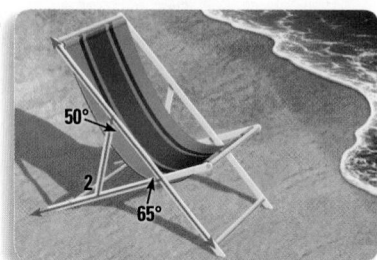

76.

Quiz 2

Lesson 9.3 **Simplify the expression, if possible.**

1. $\dfrac{2x^2}{6x^3 - 10x}$

2. $\dfrac{x^2 - x - 12}{x^2 - 6x + 8}$

3. $\dfrac{x^2 + 3x - 10}{x^2 + 5x + 6}$

Lesson 9.3 **Write the product in simplest form.**

4. $\dfrac{5x}{4} \cdot \dfrac{6}{15x^2}$

5. $\dfrac{4x - 8}{3x} \cdot \dfrac{5x^2}{2x - 4}$

6. $\dfrac{2x}{x^2 + 3x - 18} \cdot (x - 3)$

Lesson 9.3 **7.** Find the area of the rectangle.

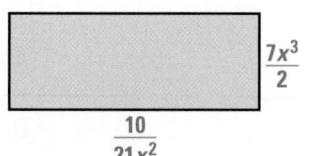

Lesson 9.4 **Write the quotient in simplest form.**

8. $\dfrac{2x^2}{3x + 3} \div \dfrac{x}{x + 1}$

9. $\dfrac{2x + 1}{4x^2} \div \dfrac{4x + 2}{x^2}$

10. $\dfrac{4x + 24}{x + 3} \div (x + 6)$

Lesson 9.4 **Simplify the complex fraction.**

11. $\dfrac{\dfrac{x - 1}{2}}{\dfrac{3x}{x + 2}}$

12. $\dfrac{\dfrac{x + 4}{x + 2}}{\dfrac{3x + 12}{x - 2}}$

13. $\dfrac{\dfrac{x - 4}{2x + 3}}{\dfrac{4x^2 - 16x}{6x + 9}}$

USING A GRAPHING CALCULATOR *(For use with Lesson 9.4)*
Simplifying Rational Expressions

You can use a graphing calculator to numerically and graphically check the results of operations on rational expressions.

EXAMPLE Use a graphing calculator to check that $\frac{x+3}{x-2}$ is the simplified form of $\frac{x^2 + 2x - 3}{x^2 - 3x + 2}$.

SOLUTION

① Enter the original expression as y_1 and the simplified result as y_2. Choose the *Path* style for y_2 by placing the cursor to the left of Y2 and pressing ENTER four times. Remember to use parentheses correctly.

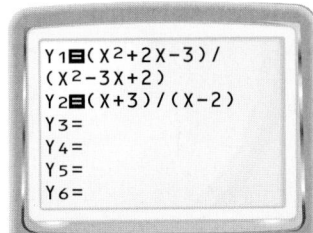

② **Check Numerically** Use the *Table* feature to view corresponding values of the two expressions.

Why is only y_1 undefined at $x = 1$?

The two expressions are equivalent if the values of y_1 and y_2 are the same *except where a common factor has been divided out.*

③ **Check Graphically** Put your calculator in *Connected* mode. Use the standard viewing window.

The *Path* style shows the graph of y_2 being drawn even though it coincides with the graph of y_1.

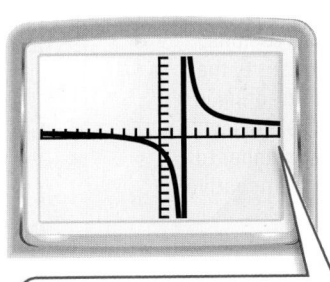

The two expressions are equivalent if the graphs of the two expressions coincide.

EXERCISES

Simplify the expression. Use a graphing calculator to verify the result numerically and graphically.

1. $\dfrac{2x^2 + 4x}{x^2 - x - 6}$

2. $\dfrac{x^2 + x}{x^2 + 5x + 4}$

3. $\dfrac{x^2 + x - 6}{x^2 + 8x + 15}$

Perform the indicated operation and simplify. Use a graphing calculator to verify the result numerically and graphically.

4. $\dfrac{x+4}{x-5} \cdot \dfrac{x-5}{x+3}$

5. $\dfrac{4x-12}{3x} \div \dfrac{x-3}{x^2}$

6. $\dfrac{x^2 - 4}{x^2 + x - 6} \cdot \dfrac{x+3}{x^2 - 2x - 8}$

Adding and Subtracting Rational Expressions

Key Words

- least common denominator (LCD)

Simplify.

1. $\dfrac{2}{5} + \dfrac{1}{5}$

2. $\dfrac{4}{7} - \dfrac{2}{7}$

3. $\dfrac{1}{3} + \dfrac{1}{6}$

4. $\dfrac{3}{4} - \dfrac{1}{2}$

GOAL Add and subtract rational expressions.

How long will a trip take?

In Example 5, you will add rational expressions to write a model for the total time it takes for a trip.

You can add and subtract rational expressions in the same way as fractions. So, if two rational expressions have a like denominator, add or subtract the numerators. Then write the result over the like denominator.

EXAMPLE 1 Add and Subtract with Like Denominators

Perform the indicated operation.

a. $\dfrac{3}{2x} + \dfrac{5}{2x}$

b. $\dfrac{x}{x+3} - \dfrac{2}{x+3}$

c. $\dfrac{6}{x-1} - \dfrac{x+6}{x-1}$

Solution

STUDENT HELP

AVOID ERRORS
When you subtract rational expressions, write the quantity that you are subtracting in parentheses. This will help you remember to distribute the negative factor.

a. $\dfrac{3}{2x} + \dfrac{5}{2x} = \dfrac{3+5}{2x} = \dfrac{8}{2x} = \dfrac{4}{x}$ Add numerators and simplify.

b. $\dfrac{x}{x+3} - \dfrac{2}{x+3} = \dfrac{x-2}{x+3}$ Subtract numerators.

c. $\dfrac{6}{x-1} - \dfrac{x+6}{x-1} = \dfrac{6-(x+6)}{x-1}$ Subtract numerators.

$= \dfrac{6-x-6}{x-1}$ Distribute the factor −1.

$= -\dfrac{x}{x-1}$ Simplify.

Checkpoint ✓ **Add and Subtract with Like Denominators**

Perform the indicated operation.

1. $\dfrac{2}{3x} + \dfrac{4}{3x}$

2. $\dfrac{2}{x-2} - \dfrac{x}{x-2}$

3. $\dfrac{2x}{x+4} - \dfrac{x-3}{x+4}$

Least Common Denominator To add or subtract rational expressions with *unlike* denominators, first rewrite each expression so that the expressions have *like* denominators. Use the least common multiple of the original denominators as the like denominator. It is called the **least common denominator** or **LCD.**

EXAMPLE 2 **Find the LCD of Rational Expressions**

Find the least common denominator.

a. $\dfrac{1}{6x}, \dfrac{1}{8x^3}$

b. $\dfrac{1}{2x-4}, \dfrac{1}{3x+9}$

Solution

a. The factors of $6x$ are **2**, **3**, and x and the factors of $8x^3$ are 2^3 and x^3. Use the greatest power of each factor in either denominator and multiply to find the LCD.

$$LCD = 2^3 \cdot 3 \cdot x^3 = 24x^3$$

b. The factors of $2x-4$ are **2** and $(x-2)$ and the factors of $3x+9$ are **3** and $(x+3)$. Use the greatest power of each factor in either denominator and multiply to find the LCD.

$$LCD = 2(x-2)(3)(x+3) = 6(x-2)(x+3)$$

Checkpoint ✓ **Find the LCD of Rational Expressions**

Find the least common denominator.

4. $\dfrac{2}{3x}, \dfrac{1}{9x^2}$

5. $\dfrac{3}{x-2}, \dfrac{x}{x^2-4}$

6. $\dfrac{x}{2x+1}, \dfrac{x-1}{x+1}$

EXAMPLE 3 **Add with Unlike Denominators**

Perform the indicated operation.

a. $\dfrac{3}{2x} + \dfrac{4}{x^2}$

b. $\dfrac{2x}{x-2} + \dfrac{3}{x+5}$

Solution

a. The LCD is $2x^2$. Rewrite the expression so they have like denominators.

$$\dfrac{3}{2x} + \dfrac{4}{x^2} = \dfrac{3}{2x} \cdot \dfrac{x}{x} + \dfrac{4}{x^2} \cdot \dfrac{2}{2} \quad \text{Rewrite using LCD.}$$

$$= \dfrac{3x}{2x^2} + \dfrac{8}{2x^2} \quad \text{Simplify each term.}$$

$$= \dfrac{3x+8}{2x^2} \quad \text{Add numerators.}$$

b. The LCD is $(x-2)(x+5)$.

STUDENT HELP

SOLVING NOTE
In part (b), neither denominator can be factored. The LCD is the product $(x-2)(x+5)$ because the LCD must contain both of these factors.

$$\dfrac{2x}{x-2} + \dfrac{3}{x+5} = \dfrac{2x(x+5)}{(x-2)(x+5)} + \dfrac{3(x-2)}{(x-2)(x+5)} \quad \text{Rewrite using LCD.}$$

$$= \dfrac{2x^2+10x}{(x-2)(x+5)} + \dfrac{3x-6}{(x-2)(x+5)} \quad \text{Simplify numerators.}$$

$$= \dfrac{2x^2+10x+3x-6}{(x-2)(x+5)} \quad \text{Add numerators.}$$

$$= \dfrac{2x^2+13x-6}{(x-2)(x+5)} \quad \text{Combine like terms.}$$

EXAMPLE 4 Subtract with Unlike Denominators

Subtract $\dfrac{1}{x^2 - x - 2} - \dfrac{2}{x^2 - 4}$.

Solution

The factors of $x^2 - x - 2$ are $(x - 2)$ and $(x + 1)$ and the factors of $x^2 - 4$ are $(x - 2)$ and $(x + 2)$. So, the LCD is $(x - 2)(x + 1)(x + 2)$.

$$\frac{1}{x^2 - x - 2} - \frac{2}{x^2 - 4} = \frac{1}{(x - 2)(x + 1)} - \frac{2}{(x - 2)(x + 2)} \qquad \text{Factor denominators.}$$

$$= \frac{(x + 2)}{(x - 2)(x + 1)(x + 2)} - \frac{2(x + 1)}{(x - 2)(x + 2)(x + 1)} \qquad \text{Rewrite using LCD.}$$

$$= \frac{x + 2 - 2(x + 1)}{(x - 2)(x + 1)(x + 2)} \qquad \text{Subtract numerators.}$$

$$= \frac{x + 2 - 2x - 2}{(x - 2)(x + 1)(x + 2)} \qquad \text{Distributive property}$$

$$= -\frac{x}{(x - 2)(x + 1)(x + 2)} \qquad \text{Combine like terms.}$$

STUDENT HELP

AVOID ERRORS
Sometimes the sum or difference will need to be simplified. Leave the denominator in factored form, and remember to check for common factors in the numerator.

Checkpoint ✓ *Add and Subtract with Unlike Denominators*

Perform the indicated operation.

7. $\dfrac{2}{x^2} + \dfrac{3}{2x}$

8. $\dfrac{3}{x - 1} + \dfrac{x}{x + 1}$

9. $\dfrac{1}{x^2 - 1} - \dfrac{1}{x + 1}$

EXAMPLE 5 Add Rational Expressions

Travel You are planning a trip for a group that will take a 40-mile bus ride and then ride a train. The entire trip is 140 miles. The average speed of the train is 30 miles per hour faster than the average speed of the bus. Let x equal the average speed of the bus. The time the bus travels is $y_1 = \dfrac{40}{x}$. The time the train travels is $y_2 = \dfrac{100}{x + 30}$. Write a model that shows the total time y it will take for the trip.

Solution

Add the time the bus travels to the time the train travels.

$$y = y_1 + y_2 \qquad \text{Write model for total time for the trip.}$$

$$= \frac{40}{x} + \frac{100}{x + 30} \qquad \text{Substitute.}$$

$$= \frac{40(x + 30)}{x(x + 30)} + \frac{100x}{x(x + 30)} \qquad \text{Rewrite using LCD.}$$

$$= \frac{40x + 1200 + 100x}{x(x + 30)} \qquad \text{Add fractions.}$$

$$= \frac{140x + 1200}{x(x + 30)} \qquad \text{Combine like terms.}$$

Link to
CAREERS

TRAVEL AGENTS often arrange all of the travel, meals, and hotels for groups of people traveling together.

Guided Practice

Vocabulary Check

1. Explain how adding and subtracting rational expressions is similar to adding and subtracting numerical fractions.

2. Why is $(x + 2)^3$ not the LCD of $\dfrac{1}{x + 2}$ and $\dfrac{1}{(x + 2)^2}$? What is the correct LCD?

Skill Check   **Find the least common denominator.**

3. $\dfrac{7}{8}, \dfrac{1}{x}$

4. $\dfrac{2}{x - 7}, \dfrac{3x}{x + 1}$

5. $\dfrac{x + 4}{x^2 - 9}, \dfrac{x}{x + 3}$

Perform the indicated operation and simplify.

6. $\dfrac{2}{5x} + \dfrac{4}{5x}$

7. $\dfrac{6}{5x} + \dfrac{2}{x^2}$

8. $\dfrac{x^2}{x - 2} - \dfrac{3x}{x + 3}$

9. Traveling by Canoe You take a 10-mile canoe trip on a river. You paddle upstream for 5 miles at a rate of $r - 3$ miles per hour. The second half of the trip you travel $r + 3$ miles per hour downstream. Write a model that shows the total time T it takes for the trip. Use the formula $\text{time} = \dfrac{\text{distance}}{\text{rate}}$.

Practice and Applications

STUDENT HELP

HOMEWORK HELP
Example 1: Exs. 10–15
Example 2: Exs. 16–24
Example 3: Exs. 27–42
Example 4: Exs. 27–42
Example 5: Exs. 43–48

Operations with like Denominators **Perform the indicated operation and simplify.**

10. $\dfrac{7}{8x} + \dfrac{5}{8x}$

11. $\dfrac{9}{2x^2} - \dfrac{3}{2x^2}$

12. $\dfrac{x}{x + 1} + \dfrac{3}{x + 1}$

13. $\dfrac{2}{x - 2} + \dfrac{3x - 8}{x - 2}$

14. $\dfrac{2x}{5x + 20} - \dfrac{x - 4}{5x + 20}$

15. $\dfrac{8x^2}{x^2 - 9} + \dfrac{24x}{x^2 - 9}$

Finding LCDs **Find the least common denominator.**

16. $\dfrac{5}{7x}, \dfrac{4}{3x}$

17. $\dfrac{10}{7x}, \dfrac{2}{x + 1}$

18. $\dfrac{x + 5}{x - 4}, \dfrac{x - 1}{x + 7}$

19. $\dfrac{3}{4x}, \dfrac{15}{2x^3}$

20. $\dfrac{x}{3(x - 5)}, \dfrac{5}{3x}$

21. $\dfrac{x}{(x + 2)(x - 2)}, \dfrac{x^2}{8(x - 2)}$

22. $\dfrac{2x}{x^2 - 36}, \dfrac{3}{x + 6}$

23. $\dfrac{x^3}{x - 8}, \dfrac{27}{x^2 + 3x - 40}$

24. $\dfrac{x + 1}{x^2 - 9x + 14}, \dfrac{x - 2}{x^2 - 6x - 7}$

Logical Reasoning **In Exercises 25 and 26, tell whether the statement is *always*, *sometimes*, or *never* true. Explain your reasoning.**

25. To obtain the LCD of two rational expressions, multiply the denominators.

26. The LCD of two rational expressions will have the greatest power of each factor in the denominators.

27. Error Analysis Describe and correct the error in adding the rational expressions.

$$\dfrac{2}{5x} + \dfrac{4}{x^2} = \dfrac{2 + 4}{5x + x^2} = \dfrac{6}{x(5 + x)} \quad \times$$

Operations with Unlike Denominators **Perform the indicated operation and simplify.**

28. $\dfrac{4}{x} + \dfrac{3}{5x}$

29. $\dfrac{10}{3x^2} - \dfrac{5}{x}$

30. $\dfrac{3}{6x^3} + \dfrac{1}{4x}$

31. $\dfrac{5}{x - 2} - \dfrac{x}{4}$

32. $\dfrac{x + 1}{x - 9} - \dfrac{x}{x - 1}$

33. $\dfrac{2}{x - 3} + \dfrac{4}{x + 5}$

34. $\dfrac{2x}{x + 2} + \dfrac{6}{x - 4}$

35. $\dfrac{7}{2x} + \dfrac{3x}{x - 3}$

36. $\dfrac{x + 8}{2x + 1} + \dfrac{x + 1}{x + 2}$

Adding and Subtracting **Simplify the expression.**

37. $\dfrac{5}{3x - 12} + \dfrac{x}{3}$

38. $\dfrac{x}{x + 9} - \dfrac{36}{x^2 + 14x + 45}$

39. $\dfrac{2x}{x^2 - 49} + \dfrac{x - 4}{x + 7}$

40. $\dfrac{4}{5(x + 2)} - \dfrac{2x}{x^2 - x - 6}$

41. $\dfrac{x - 5}{x^2 + 10x + 24} - \dfrac{4}{x^2 + 3x - 4}$

42. $\dfrac{2}{x + 1} + \dfrac{3}{x} + \dfrac{3}{x + 4}$

Triathlon **In Exercises 43–45, use the following information.**

You participate in a sprint triathlon that involves swimming, bicycling, and running. The table shows the distances (in miles) and your average speed for each portion of the race. Your average speed r for the swimming portion of the race in terms of your bicycling speed and your running speed.

	Distance (miles)	Speed (miles per hour)
Swimming	0.5	r
Bicycling	22	$15r$
Running	6	$r + 5$

43. Write an algebraic model for the total time (in hours) to complete the race.

Use the formula $\text{time} = \dfrac{\text{distance}}{\text{rate}}$.

44. Write your answer to Exercise 43 as a single rational expression.

45. Use your answer to Exercise 44 to find how long it would take you to complete the race if you can swim at an average speed of two miles per hour.

Washing Cars **In Exercises 46–48 use the following information.**

You are hired to wash the new cars in a dealership's parking lot with two other people, Sue and Tom. It takes you an average of 40 minutes to wash a car $\left(R_1 = \dfrac{1}{40} \text{ car per minute}\right)$. Sue can wash a car in x minutes. Tom can wash a car in $x + 10$ minutes.

46. Write an expression for the Sue's rate R_2 and Tom's rate R_3.

47. Write a single expression R for the combined rate of cars washed per minute by the group.

48. Evaluate your expression if Sue washes a car in 35 minutes. How many cars per hour does this represent? Explain your reasoning.

49. Geometry Link Find an expression for the surface area of the box.

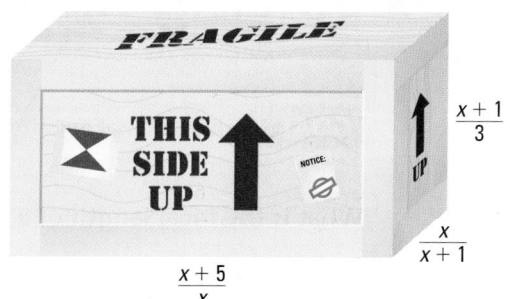

50. Multiple Choice Find the least common denominator of $\dfrac{x}{x^2 - 16}$ and $\dfrac{27}{x^2 - 7x + 12}$.

(A) $(x + 4)(x - 3)$ (B) $(x + 4)(x - 4)^2(x + 3)$

(C) $(x + 4)(x - 3)(x - 4)$ (D) $(x - 3)(x - 4)$

51. Multiple Choice What is the difference of $\dfrac{4x + 1}{x^2 + 3x}$ and $\dfrac{3x}{x^2 - 9}$ in simplest form?

(F) $\dfrac{-3x^2 + 4x + 1}{x(x - 3)}$ (G) $\dfrac{x^2 - 11x - 3}{x(x - 3)(x + 3)}$

(H) $\dfrac{x^2 + 13x + 3}{x(x + 3)(x - 3)}$ (J) $\dfrac{4x^2 + 9x + 1}{(x - 3)(x + 3)}$

Mixed Review

Solving Equations Solve the equation. *(Lesson 1.4)*

52. $x + 6 = -1$ **53.** $-3x + 25 = 7x - 35$ **54.** $5x + 13 = -4x - 6$

55. $-15x + 6 = -6x - 48$ **56.** $x = 10 + \dfrac{5}{6}x$ **57.** $2x + \dfrac{7}{8}x = 7$

Intercept Form Write the quadratic function in intercept form and give the zeros of the function. *(Lesson 5.4)*

58. $y = x^2 - 49$ **59.** $y = x^2 - 81$

60. $y = x^2 - 16x + 64$ **61.** $y = x^2 + 24x + 144$

62. $y = 9x^2 + 6x + 1$ **63.** $y = 100x^2 - 80x + 16$

Logarithmic Equations Solve the equation. *(Lesson 8.6)*

64. $\log_5 (x - 4) = \log_5 (4x + 1)$ **65.** $\log_4 (10x + 3) = \log_4 (4x - 9)$

66. $\log_2 (5x) = 5$ **67.** $\log_3 (4x - 1) = 3$

Geometry Skills

Transformations Tell whether the transformation that maps the red figure onto the blue figure is a *translation*, a *reflection*, or a *rotation*.

68. 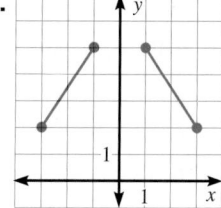 **69.** 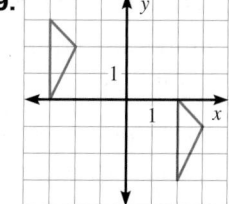 **70.**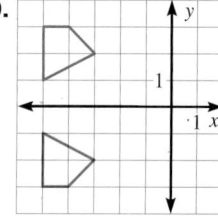

9.6 Solving Rational Equations

GOAL Solve rational equations.

What is the focal length of a camera?

In Example 5, you will solve a rational equation to find the focal length of a camera lens.

A **rational equation** is an equation that contains rational expressions. When each side of the equation is a single rational expression, you can **cross multiply** to solve.

$$\text{If } \frac{a}{b} = \frac{c}{d}, \text{ then } ad = bc.$$

For example, $\dfrac{2}{3} = \dfrac{6}{9}$, so $2 \cdot 9 = 3 \cdot 6 = 18$.

EXAMPLE 1 Solve an Equation by Cross Multiplying

Solve $\dfrac{4}{x+1} = \dfrac{3}{x}$.

Solution

$\dfrac{4}{x+1} = \dfrac{3}{x}$	Write the original equation.
$4x = 3(x+1)$	Cross multiply.
$4x = 3x + 3$	Use distributive property.
$x = 3$	Subtract $3x$ from each side.

ANSWER ▶ The solution is 3.

CHECK Substitute 3 for x into the original equation.

$\dfrac{4}{x+1} = \dfrac{3}{x}$	Write original equation.
$\dfrac{4}{3+1} \stackrel{?}{=} \dfrac{3}{3}$	Substitute 3 for x.
$1 = 1 \checkmark$	Simplify. Solution checks.

Checkpoint ✓ **Solve an Equation by Cross Multiplying**

Solve the equation. Check your solution.

1. $\dfrac{x}{3} = \dfrac{12}{18}$

2. $\dfrac{y}{4} = \dfrac{6}{7}$

3. $\dfrac{x}{9} = \dfrac{7}{15}$

4. $\dfrac{3}{m+2} = \dfrac{1}{5}$

5. $\dfrac{5}{y-1} = \dfrac{2}{y}$

6. $\dfrac{3}{2} = \dfrac{3}{x-4}$

Multiply by the LCD Another method for solving a rational equation is to multiply each term on each side of the equation by the least common denominator (LCD) of the terms. This method works for any rational equation.

EXAMPLE 2 Multiply by the LCD

Solve $\dfrac{2}{x} + \dfrac{3}{2} = \dfrac{5}{x}$.

Solution

The least common denominator is $2x$.

$$\dfrac{2}{x} + \dfrac{3}{2} = \dfrac{5}{x} \qquad \text{Write the original equation.}$$

$$\dfrac{2}{x} \cdot 2x + \dfrac{3}{2} \cdot 2x = \dfrac{5}{x} \cdot 2x \qquad \text{Multiply each term by the LCD } 2x.$$

$$4 + 3x = 10 \qquad \text{Simplify each side.}$$

$$3x = 6 \qquad \text{Subtract 4 from each side.}$$

$$x = 2 \qquad \text{Dividing each side by 3.}$$

ANSWER ▶ The solution is 2.

CHECK $\dfrac{2}{2} + \dfrac{3}{2} = \dfrac{5}{2}$ ✓

EXAMPLE 3 Solve an Equation with an Extraneous Solution

Solve $8 + \dfrac{2}{x-1} = \dfrac{2x}{x-1}$.

Solution

$$8 + \dfrac{2}{x-1} = \dfrac{2x}{x-1} \qquad \text{Write original equation.}$$

$$8 \cdot (x-1) + \dfrac{2}{x-1} \cdot (x-1) = \dfrac{2x}{x-1} \cdot (x-1) \qquad \text{Multiply by LCD } (x-1).$$

$$8(x-1) + 2 = 2x \qquad \text{Simplify.}$$

$$8x - 8 + 2 = 2x \qquad \text{Use distributive property.}$$

$$8x - 6 = 2x \qquad \text{Simplify.}$$

$$6x = 6 \qquad \text{Combine like terms.}$$

$$x = 1 \qquad \text{Divide each side by 6.}$$

ANSWER ▶ The solution 1 is extraneous because it leads to division by 0 in the original equation. So, the original equation has no solution.

$$8 + \dfrac{2}{1-1} \stackrel{?}{=} \dfrac{2(1)}{1-1} \ \text{✗}$$

STUDENT HELP

AVOID ERRORS
When solving rational equations, check your answers. If substituting a solution into the original equation results in division by 0, the solution is extraneous and must be rejected.

 **Solve Rational Equations**

Solve the equation. Check your solutions.

7. $\dfrac{2}{3} + \dfrac{1}{x} = \dfrac{3}{x}$

8. $\dfrac{1}{3x} + \dfrac{1}{2} = \dfrac{4}{3x}$

9. $\dfrac{1}{x+1} + 1 = \dfrac{x}{x+1}$

EXAMPLE 4 Solve an Equation with Two Solutions

Solve $\dfrac{2}{x-1} + \dfrac{3}{x} = 2$.

$$\dfrac{2}{x-1} + \dfrac{3}{x} = 2 \qquad \text{Write original equation.}$$

$$\dfrac{2}{x-1} \cdot x(x-1) + \dfrac{3}{x} \cdot x(x-1) = 2 \cdot x(x-1) \qquad \text{Multiply by LCD } x(x-1).$$

$$2x + 3(x-1) = 2x(x-1) \qquad \text{Simplify.}$$

$$2x + 3x - 3 = 2x^2 - 2x \qquad \text{Simplify each side.}$$

$$0 = 2x^2 - 7x + 3 \qquad \text{Write in standard form.}$$

$$0 = (2x-1)(x-3) \qquad \text{Factor.}$$

$$x = \dfrac{1}{2} \text{ or } x = 3 \qquad \text{Zero product property.}$$

ANSWER ▶ The solutions are $\dfrac{1}{2}$ and 3. Check these in the original equation.

Checkpoint ✔ **Solve Rational Equations**

Solve the equation. Check your solutions.

10. $1 - \dfrac{2}{x+2} = \dfrac{2}{x-2}$

11. $\dfrac{3}{x^2 + 2x + 1} + \dfrac{2}{x+1} = 1$

Link to
PHOTOGRAPHY

FOCAL LENGTH The focal length of a camera lens is the distance between the lens and the point where the light rays converge after passing through the lens.

EXAMPLE 5 Solve a Rational Equation

Photography The focal length f of a thin camera lens is given by

$$\dfrac{1}{f} = \dfrac{1}{p} + \dfrac{1}{q}$$

where p is the distance between an object being photographed and the lens and q is the distance between the lens and the film. Find the focal length when $p = 12$ centimeters and $q = 4$ centimeters.

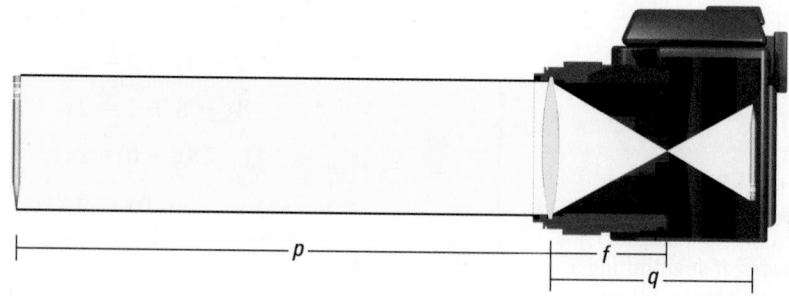

Solution

$$\dfrac{1}{f} = \dfrac{1}{12} + \dfrac{1}{4} \qquad \text{Substitute 12 for } p \text{ and 4 for } q \text{ in original equation.}$$

$$\dfrac{1}{f} \cdot 12f = \dfrac{1}{12} \cdot 12f + \dfrac{1}{4} \cdot 12f \qquad \text{Multiply each term by LCD } 12f.$$

$$12 = f + 3f \qquad \text{Simplify.}$$

$$12 = 4f \qquad \text{Combine like terms.}$$

$$3 = f \qquad \text{Divide each side by 4.}$$

ANSWER ▶ The focal length is 3 centimeters.

Exercises

Guided Practice

Vocabulary Check

1. How is a rational function different from a polynomial function?

2. Give an example of a rational equation that cannot be solved using cross multiplication. Explain your reasoning.

Skill Check

Solve the equation. Check your solutions.

3. $\dfrac{2}{x+4} = \dfrac{1}{x}$

4. $\dfrac{3}{x+1} = \dfrac{4}{x}$

5. $\dfrac{8}{x-1} = \dfrac{6}{x}$

6. $\dfrac{4}{x} = \dfrac{5}{x-3}$

7. $\dfrac{3}{x} + \dfrac{1}{3} = \dfrac{4}{x}$

8. $\dfrac{2}{x-1} + \dfrac{1}{4} = \dfrac{5}{x-1}$

9. $4 + \dfrac{2}{x+1} = \dfrac{x}{x+1}$

10. $\dfrac{3}{x-1} + 6 = \dfrac{3x}{x-1}$

11. $\dfrac{1}{x-2} + \dfrac{2}{x} = 1$

12. Use the fact that a segment parallel to a side of a triangle divides the side lengths proportionally to find the value of x and give the length of each labeled side.

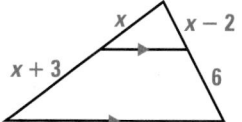

13. Describe and correct the error in identifying the solutions of the rational equation.

The solutions of $\dfrac{3}{x+1} = \dfrac{x}{2x+2}$ are $x = 6$ and $x = -1$. ✗

Practice and Applications

STUDENT HELP

HOMEWORK HELP
Example 1: Exs. 14–34
Example 2: Exs. 35–50
Example 3: Exs. 20–50
Example 4: Exs. 20–50
Example 5: Exs. 53–58

Checking Solutions **Determine whether the given value of x is a solution of the equation.**

14. $\dfrac{x}{x-3} = \dfrac{6}{x-3}, x = 6$

15. $\dfrac{2x}{x+1} = \dfrac{x}{x-1}, x = 3$

16. $\dfrac{x}{x+3} + \dfrac{1}{x} = 1, x = -3$

17. $\dfrac{3}{x} + \dfrac{x}{x-1} = 4, x = 1$

18. $\dfrac{2}{x+1} + \dfrac{x}{x+4} = 1, x = 2$

19. $\dfrac{3x}{x+2} + \dfrac{2}{x} = \dfrac{10}{x}, x = -4$

Cross Multiplying **Solve the equation. Check your solutions.**

20. $\dfrac{1}{4} = \dfrac{x}{7}$

21. $\dfrac{x}{5} = \dfrac{7}{10}$

22. $\dfrac{1}{x} = \dfrac{8}{9}$

23. $\dfrac{2}{3} = \dfrac{x}{x+3}$

24. $\dfrac{1}{x} = \dfrac{4}{x+5}$

25. $\dfrac{4}{x-1} = \dfrac{8}{x+2}$

26. $\dfrac{4}{x-6} = \dfrac{-2}{x+3}$

27. $\dfrac{3}{x+4} = \dfrac{9}{x+8}$

28. $\dfrac{6}{3x+2} = \dfrac{-3}{x-6}$

29. $\dfrac{x}{x-1} = \dfrac{2}{x-1}$

30. $\dfrac{2}{x-2} = \dfrac{x}{x-2}$

31. $\dfrac{2}{x} = \dfrac{2x}{x-1}$

32. $\dfrac{x}{x-3} = \dfrac{8}{x-2}$

33. $\dfrac{2x}{x+4} = \dfrac{-x}{x-8}$

34. $\dfrac{x-1}{x+6} = \dfrac{x}{5x+6}$

Least Common Denominator Solve the equation. Check your solutions.

35. $\frac{1}{3} + \frac{6}{x} = 1$

36. $\frac{1}{6} + \frac{x}{2} = 1$

37. $\frac{4}{x} - \frac{1}{3} = 1$

38. $\frac{3}{x} + \frac{1}{2} = \frac{5}{x}$

39. $\frac{5}{x+2} + \frac{1}{x} = \frac{5}{x}$

40. $\frac{3}{x-1} + \frac{1}{x} = \frac{5}{x-1}$

41. $\frac{x}{x+1} + \frac{1}{x-1} = \frac{5}{x+1}$

42. $\frac{1}{x-3} + \frac{1}{x} = \frac{2}{x-3}$

43. $\frac{x-1}{x+3} + \frac{x}{x-4} = \frac{-4}{x+3}$

44. $\frac{x-1}{x+5} + \frac{x+3}{x+4} = \frac{x+1}{x+4}$

Choosing a Method Solve the equation using any method. Check your solutions.

45. $\frac{5}{x+2} = \frac{x+4}{2x+1}$

46. $\frac{x-2}{x} = \frac{6}{x+8}$

47. $\frac{1}{x} + \frac{3}{x+2} = \frac{x+3}{x+2}$

48. $\frac{3}{x-4} + \frac{x+1}{x-2} = -1$

49. $\frac{x}{x-3} = \frac{x+5}{x-1}$

50. $\frac{x+2}{x} = \frac{x+6}{x+2}$

Logical Reasoning In Exercises 51 and 52, *a* is a nonzero real number. Tell whether the statement is *always*, *sometimes*, or *never* true. Explain your reasoning.

51. For the equation $\frac{1}{x-a} = \frac{x}{x-a}$, $x = a$ is an extraneous solution.

52. The equation $\frac{3}{x-a} = \frac{x}{x-a}$ has exactly one solution.

53. Park Maintenance You and a friend are cleaning a park. You can clean the park in two hours working alone. Your friend can clean the park in three hours working alone. Use the verbal model to determine how long it will take you to clean the park working together. Convert your answer to hours and minutes. There are 60 minutes in one hour.

$$\boxed{\frac{1}{\text{Your time}}} + \boxed{\frac{1}{\text{Your friend's time}}} = \boxed{\frac{1}{\text{Combined time}}}$$

54. Airplane Travel An airplane travels at a speed of 400 miles per hour in still air. The plane travels 920 miles with a tail wind in the same amount of time it takes to travel 680 miles into a head wind. The tail wind and the head wind are the same speed. Use the verbal model to find the speed of the wind.

$$\frac{\boxed{\begin{array}{c}\text{Distance traveled}\\\text{with tail wind}\end{array}}}{\boxed{\begin{array}{c}\text{Airplane speed}\\\text{with tail wind}\end{array}}} = \frac{\boxed{\begin{array}{c}\text{Distance traveled}\\\text{with head wind}\end{array}}}{\boxed{\begin{array}{c}\text{Airplane speed}\\\text{with head wind}\end{array}}}$$

55. Average Car Speeds Two cars start traveling at the same time. The first car travels 120 miles in the same time that the second car travels 108 miles. The average speed of the first car is 5 miles per hour greater than the average speed of the second car. What is the average speed of each car?

56. Volleyball You are playing in a volleyball match. So far, 37 of your 44 serves have remained in bounds. Solve the equation

$$\frac{90}{100} = \frac{37 + x}{44 + x}$$

to find the number of consecutive serves you need to have in bounds in order to raise your service percent to 90%.

Science Link In Exercises 57 and 58, use the model below. It shows how to calculate the acid concentration of a solution diluted in water.

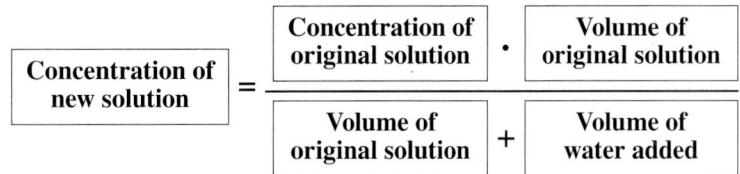

57. You have 0.5 liter of an acid solution whose acid concentration is 20 moles per liter. You want to dilute the solution with water so that its acid concentration is only 15 moles per liter. How much water should you add to the solution?

58. What would the acid concentration of the new solution be if you added 0.2 liter of water?

59. Choosing a Method Give an example of a rational equation that you would solve using cross multiplication. Then give an example of a rational equation that you would solve by multiplying each side by the LCD of the fractions.

60. Challenge From 1995 through 2003, the annual sales S (in billions of dollars) of entertainment software can be modeled by

$$S(t) = \frac{848t^2 + 3220}{115t^2 + 1000}, \; 0 \le t \le 8$$

where t is the number of years since 1995. For which year were the total sales S of entertainment software about $5.3 billion?

Standardized Test Practice

61. Multiple Choice Solve $\frac{2}{x - 1} = \frac{x}{x + 2}$.

  Ⓐ 4   Ⓑ −1   Ⓒ 4, −1   Ⓓ no solution

62. Multiple Choice Solve $\frac{1}{x} + 2 = \frac{x + 5}{x}$.

  Ⓕ 4   Ⓖ 2   Ⓗ 2, 4   Ⓙ no solution

63. Multiple Choice Solve $\frac{x - 1}{x + 4} = \frac{x}{x + 10}$.

  Ⓐ 2, 3   Ⓑ 2   Ⓒ 3   Ⓓ no solution

64. Multiple Choice Solve $2x - 2 = \frac{-2}{2x + 1}$.

  Ⓕ $\frac{1}{2}$, 0   Ⓖ $-\frac{1}{2}$, 0   Ⓗ $\frac{1}{2}$ Ⓙ no solution

Mixed Review

Multiplying Complex Numbers Write the expression as a complex number in standard form. *(Lesson 5.6)*

65. $(2i)(5i)$ **66.** $(2 + i)(1 - 2i)$ **67.** $(6 + 4i)(3 - 4i)$

Solving Radical Equations Solve the equation. Check for extraneous solutions. *(Lesson 7.3)*

68. $\sqrt{3x} + 5 = 8$ **69.** $\sqrt{x + 5} = 5$ **70.** $\sqrt[3]{5x + 4} + 7 = 11$

71. $\sqrt{2x + 19} = x + 2$ **72.** $\sqrt{2x + 6} = \sqrt{3x + 1}$ **73.** $\sqrt[3]{x + 8} = \sqrt[3]{4x + 5}$

Graphing Functions Graph the function. State the domain and range. *(Lesson 9.2)*

74. $y = \dfrac{4}{x} + 2$ **75.** $y = \dfrac{-2}{x + 1} - 3$ **76.** $y = \dfrac{2}{x - 4} + 5$

Geometry Skills

Parallelograms Find the value of *x* in the parallelogram.

77.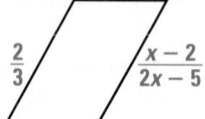

78.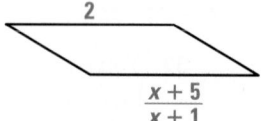

79.

Quiz 3

Lesson 9.5 **Find the least common denominator.**

1. $\dfrac{2}{3x}, \dfrac{3}{x + 2}$ **2.** $\dfrac{3}{8x^2}, \dfrac{5}{4x}$ **3.** $\dfrac{x}{2(x + 1)}, \dfrac{3}{2x^2}$

Lesson 9.5 **Simplify the expression.**

4. $\dfrac{3x}{x - 4} + \dfrac{2}{x - 4}$ **5.** $\dfrac{1}{x - 5} + \dfrac{3}{x - 3}$

6. $\dfrac{x + 4}{x + 5} - \dfrac{2x}{x - 2}$ **7.** $\dfrac{x}{x + 4} - \dfrac{3x}{x^2 + 8x + 16}$

Lesson 9.6 **Solve the equation. Check your solutions.**

8. $\dfrac{4}{x + 6} = \dfrac{2}{5}$ **9.** $\dfrac{6}{x + 3} = \dfrac{5}{2x - 1}$ **10.** $\dfrac{x}{x + 4} = \dfrac{2}{x + 9}$

11. $\dfrac{4}{x} + \dfrac{1}{2} = \dfrac{8}{x}$ **12.** $6 + \dfrac{4}{x - 2} = \dfrac{2x}{x - 2}$ **13.** $\dfrac{2}{x} + \dfrac{4}{x + 3} = \dfrac{4}{x}$

Lesson 9.6 **Perimeter and Area** For Exercises 14 and 15, use the rectangle below.

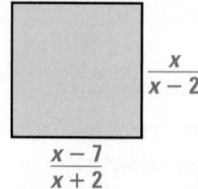

14. The perimeter of the rectangle is 3. Write a rational equation for the perimeter of the rectangle. Then solve the equation.

15. The area of the rectangle is 2. Write a rational equation for the area of the rectangle. Then solve the equation.

VOCABULARY

VOCABULARY

- inverse variation, *p. 466*
- constant of variation, *p. 466*
- joint variation, *p. 468*
- rational function, *p. 472*
- hyperbola, *p. 472*
- branch, *p. 472*
- rational expression, *p. 480*
- simplified form, *p. 480*
- complex fraction, *p. 488*
- least common denominator (LCD), *p. 494*
- rational equation, *p. 500*
- cross multiply, *p. 500*

VOCABULARY EXERCISES

1. How are two variables related if they show inverse variation?

2. Give an example of two rational expressions with like denominators. Give an example of two rational expressions with unlike denominators.

3. What does it mean for a rational expression to be in simplified form?

4. Name two methods that can be used to solve rational equations.

5. What is a complex fraction?

9.1 **INVERSE AND JOINT VARIATION**

Examples on pp. 466–468

EXAMPLE You can write an inverse or joint variation equation using a general equation for the variation and given values of the variables.

Inverse Variation $x = 3$, $y = 6$

$y = \dfrac{k}{x}$ *y varies inversely with x.*

$6 = \dfrac{k}{3}$ Substitute for *x* and *y.*

$18 = k$ Solve for *k.*

The inverse variation equation is $y = \dfrac{18}{x}$.

Joint Variation $x = 4$, $y = 9$, $z = 27$

$z = kxy$ *z varies jointly with x and y.*

$27 = k(4)(9)$ Substitute for *x, y* and *z.*

$27 = 36k$ Multiply.

$k = \dfrac{27}{36} = \dfrac{3}{4}$ Solve for *k.*

The joint variation equation is $z = \dfrac{3}{4}xy$.

REVIEW HELP

Exercises	Examples
6–8	**2,** p. 466
9–10	**5,** p. 468

In Exercises 6–8, the variables *x* and *y* vary inversely. Use the given values to write an equation relating *x* and *y*. Then find *y* when *x* = 3.

6. $x = 2$, $y = 6$

7. $x = 4$, $y = -3$

8. $x = \dfrac{1}{2}$, $y = 4$

9. Write an equation in which *z* varies inversely with *x* and *y* and *k* = 7.

10. Write an equation in which *z* varies jointly with *x* and inversely with *y* and *k* = −2.

9.2 GRAPHING RATIONAL FUNCTIONS

Examples on pp. 472–474

EXAMPLE Graph the function $y = \dfrac{-1}{x-3} + 2$.

The function is in the form $y = \dfrac{a}{x-h} + k$. So, $a = -1$, $h = 3$, and $k = 2$.

Draw the vertical asymptote $x = 3$ and the horizontal asymptote $y = 2$.

Plot a couple of points on each side of the vertical asymptote.

Draw the two branches of the hyperbola that approach the asymptotes and pass through the plotted points.

The domain is all real numbers except 3. The range is all real numbers except 2.

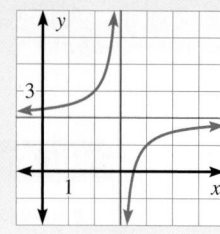

REVIEW HELP

Exercises	Examples
11–16	**1, 2**, p. 472

Graph the rational function.

11. $y = \dfrac{1}{x}$

12. $y = \dfrac{-3}{x}$

13. $y = \dfrac{5}{x+1} + 1$

14. $y = \dfrac{-1}{x+2} - 6$

15. $y = \dfrac{3}{x+5} - 4$

16. $y = \dfrac{-2}{x-4} - 4$

9.3 SIMPLIFYING AND MULTIPLYING RATIONAL EXPRESSIONS

Examples on pp. 480–482

EXAMPLES Simplify a rational expression by factoring the numerator and denominator and then dividing out any common factors.

$$\frac{7x^2}{14x(x^2+4)} = \frac{7 \cdot x \cdot x}{2 \cdot 7 \cdot x(x^2+4)} = \frac{x}{2(x^2+4)}$$

The rules for multiplying rational expressions are the same as the rules for multiplying fractions.

$$\frac{x+5}{x+4} \cdot \frac{x^2-16}{x^2+8x+15} = \frac{(x+5)(x^2-16)}{(x+4)(x^2+8x+15)}$$ Multiply numerators and denominators.

$$= \frac{(x+5)(x+4)(x-4)}{(x+4)(x+5)(x+3)}$$ Factor and divide out the common factors.

$$= \frac{x-4}{x+3}$$ Simplify.

REVIEW HELP

Exercises	Examples
17–19	**1, 2**, p. 480
20–22	**3, 4**, p. 481

Simplify the expression. If not possible, write *already in simplest form*.

17. $\dfrac{6x^2}{6x+12}$

18. $\dfrac{12x}{8x^2-24x}$

19. $\dfrac{x^2-7x+10}{5x+25}$

Multiply the rational expressions. Simplify the result.

20. $\dfrac{x+6}{x-2} \cdot \dfrac{x^2+x-6}{x^2+5x-6}$

21. $\dfrac{2x-2}{x-4} \cdot \dfrac{x^2-3x-4}{x^2-3x+2}$

22. $\dfrac{x^2+x-20}{x^2-4x-12} \cdot \dfrac{x^2+5x+6}{x^2+3x-28}$

9.4 DIVIDING RATIONAL EXPRESSIONS

Examples on pp. 486–488

EXAMPLES The rules for dividing rational expressions are the same as the rules for dividing fractions.

$$\frac{x^2 - 25}{x^2 + 2x - 3} \div \frac{x - 5}{2x^2 - 2} = \frac{x^2 - 25}{x^2 + 2x - 3} \cdot \frac{2x - 2}{x - 5}$$ Rewrite as a product. Use the reciprocal.

$$= \frac{(x - 5)(x + 5)(2)(x - 1)}{(x - 1)(x + 3)(x - 5)}$$ Multiply numerators and denominators.

$$= \frac{2(x + 5)}{x + 3}$$ Simplify.

To simplify a complex fraction, divide the numerator by the denominator.

$$\frac{\dfrac{x - 1}{x + 3}}{\dfrac{x + 1}{x + 3}} = \frac{x - 1}{x + 3} \div \frac{x + 1}{x + 3} = \frac{x - 1}{x + 3} \cdot \frac{x + 3}{x + 1} = \frac{x - 1}{x + 1}$$

REVIEW HELP

Exercises	Examples
23–25	**1, 2**, p. 486
26–28	**4, 5**, p. 488

Write the quotient in simplest form.

23. $\dfrac{2x + 3}{4x} \div \dfrac{4x + 10}{x}$

24. $\dfrac{x}{x - 1} \div \dfrac{x^2}{x^2 - 1}$

25. $\dfrac{x - 4}{x + 5} \div \dfrac{3x - 12}{(x + 5)^2}$

Simplify the complex fraction.

26. $\dfrac{\dfrac{x - 1}{x + 3}}{\dfrac{x + 1}{x + 3}}$

27. $\dfrac{\dfrac{x^2 - 4}{2x + 10}}{\dfrac{x + 2}{x + 5}}$

28. $\dfrac{\dfrac{x - 1}{x^2 - 9}}{\dfrac{x - 1}{x - 3}}$

9.5 ADDING AND SUBTRACTING RATIONAL EXPRESSIONS

Examples on pp. 494–496

EXAMPLE You can use the least common denominator (LCD) to add or subtract rational expressions with unlike denominators.

$$\frac{2}{x + 4} - \frac{5}{x - 1} = \frac{2(x - 1)}{(x + 4)(x - 1)} - \frac{5(x + 4)}{(x + 4)(x - 1)}$$ Rewrite with a common denominator.

$$= \frac{2(x - 1) - 5(x + 4)}{(x + 4)(x + 1)}$$ Subtract numerators.

$$= \frac{2x - 2 - 5x - 20}{(x + 4)(x - 1)}$$ Use the distributive property.

$$= \frac{-3x - 22}{(x + 4)(x - 1)}$$ Simplify.

REVIEW HELP

Exercises	Examples
29–34	**2, 3, 4**, p. 495

Simplify the expression.

29. $\dfrac{3}{x + 1} + \dfrac{4}{x - 5}$

30. $\dfrac{2}{x + 3} - \dfrac{6}{x + 2}$

31. $\dfrac{5}{x + 4} + \dfrac{2x}{x + 3}$

32. $\dfrac{x - 1}{x + 1} - \dfrac{x - 4}{x + 2}$

33. $\dfrac{x + 3}{x + 4} + \dfrac{x + 2}{x - 1}$

34. $\dfrac{x + 5}{x - 3} - \dfrac{x}{x + 6}$

EXAMPLES You can cross multiply to solve a rational equation when each side of the equation is a single rational expression.

$$\frac{6}{x+1} = \frac{3}{x-2}$$ Original equation

$$6(x-2) = 3(x+1)$$ Cross multiply.

$$6x - 12 = 3x + 3$$ Use distributive property.

$$3x = 15$$ Simplify.

$$x = 5$$ Divide each side by 3.

CHECK $$\frac{6}{5+1} \overset{?}{=} \frac{3}{5-2}$$ Substitute 5 for x in the original equation.

$$\frac{6}{6} = \frac{3}{3} \checkmark$$ Solution checks.

You can solve a rational equation by multiplying each term of the equation by the LCD of the terms. This method works for any rational equation.

$$\frac{3}{x} + \frac{2}{x-1} = \frac{6}{x}$$ Original equation

$$(x)(x-1)\frac{3}{x} + (x)(x-1)\frac{2}{x-1} = (x)(x-1)\frac{6}{x}$$ Multiply by the LCD $x(x-1)$.

$$3(x-1) + 2x = 6(x-1)$$ Simplify.

$$3x - 3 + 2x = 6x - 6$$ Use distributive property.

$$5x - 3 = 6x - 6$$ Simplify.

$$3 = x$$ Solve.

Always check solutions of rational equations to be sure they are not extraneous solutions.

REVIEW HELP

Exercises	Examples
35–40	**1, 3, 4**, p. 500
41–47	**2, 3, 4**, p. 501

Solve the equation. Check your solution(s).

35. $\dfrac{2}{x+4} = \dfrac{4}{x+6}$

36. $\dfrac{2}{x-2} = \dfrac{x}{x-2}$

37. $\dfrac{5}{x-3} = \dfrac{2x}{x-1}$

38. $\dfrac{x-4}{x-2} = \dfrac{x+2}{x-8}$

39. $\dfrac{x+3}{x+6} = \dfrac{2x+1}{3x+2}$

40. $\dfrac{x+1}{x-5} = \dfrac{x-4}{x+5}$

Solve the equation. Check your solution(s).

41. $\dfrac{4}{x} + \dfrac{1}{x+2} = \dfrac{9}{x+2}$

42. $\dfrac{2}{x-2} + \dfrac{1}{x+3} = \dfrac{5}{x+3}$

43. $\dfrac{4}{x+3} + \dfrac{2}{x} = \dfrac{7}{x+3}$

44. $\dfrac{x}{x+1} + \dfrac{1}{x-1} = \dfrac{x+2}{x-1}$

45. $\dfrac{x}{x+2} + \dfrac{3}{x+1} = \dfrac{6}{x+2}$

46. $\dfrac{x+1}{x-1} + \dfrac{x+1}{x+3} = \dfrac{2x-1}{x-1}$

47. Test Averages You have taken 5 quizzes in your history class. You have an average score of 83 points. If you can score 95 points on each of the rest of your quizzes, how many quizzes do you need to take to raise your average score to 90 points?

The variables *x* and *y* vary inversely. Use the given values to write an equation relating *x* and *y*. Then find *y* when *x* = 4.

1. $x = 6, y = 2$

2. $x = -2, y = 8$

3. $x = \frac{2}{3}, y = -1$

The variable *z* varies jointly with *x* and *y*. Use the given values to write an equation relating *x*, *y*, and *z*. Then find *z* when *x* = 2 and *y* = 6.

4. $x = 3, y = 5, z = 30$

5. $x = 6, y = 6, z = 9$

6. $x = \frac{1}{4}, y = \frac{2}{3}, z = \frac{1}{2}$

7. The graph of $y = \frac{a}{x-h} + k$ is shown at the right. Tell whether the value of each of the constants *a*, *h*, and *k* for this function is *positive*, *negative*, or *zero*.

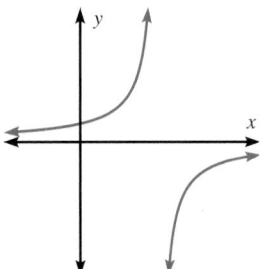

Graph the function. State the domain and range.

8. $y = \frac{2}{x}$

9. $y = \frac{4}{x} + 1$

10. $y = \frac{1}{x} - 1$

Simplify the expression. If not possible, write *already in simplest form*.

11. $\frac{36x^2}{16x}$

12. $\frac{x^2 + 3x - 28}{5x - 20}$

13. $\frac{x^2 - 14x - 48}{x^2 + 4x - 12}$

Multiply the rational expressions. Simplify the result.

14. $\frac{5x^4}{2} \cdot \frac{14x}{4x^3}$

15. $\frac{x}{x^2 - 25} \cdot \frac{4x + 20}{4x^3}$

16. $\frac{x^3}{x + 4} \cdot \frac{x^2 - 4x - 32}{x^2 - 8x}$

Write the quotient in simplest form.

17. $\frac{3x^3}{5} \div \frac{x^2}{6}$

18. $\frac{x + 9}{2x - 6} \div \frac{4x + 36}{x - 6}$

19. $\frac{x^2 - 9}{4x} \div \frac{x + 3}{10}$

20. Simplify the complex fraction $\dfrac{\frac{x - 8}{x + 5}}{\frac{4x - 32}{x - 5}}$.

Simplify the expression.

21. $\frac{3}{4x} + \frac{7}{2x^2}$

22. $\frac{3x}{x - 4} + \frac{6}{x - 4}$

23. $\frac{3x}{x + 6} - \frac{10}{x^2 - x - 42}$

Solve the equation. Check your solutions.

24. $\frac{2x + 3}{x - 4} = \frac{-3}{x - 4}$

25. $\frac{2}{x} + \frac{3}{2} = \frac{11}{x}$

26. $\frac{x - 2}{x} = \frac{6}{x + 8}$

27. Test Averages You have taken three math exams and have an average of 80 points. If you can score 100 points on each of the rest of your tests, how many tests do you need to raise your average to 90 points?

Chapter Standardized Test

EXAMPLE Which equation is graphed at the right?

Ⓐ $y = \dfrac{3}{x-1}$ Ⓑ $y = \dfrac{3}{x} + 2$

Ⓒ $y = \dfrac{1}{x-1} + 2$ Ⓓ $y = \dfrac{3}{x-1} + 2$

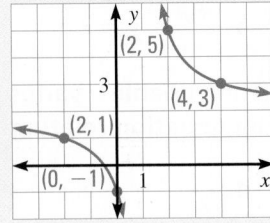

Solution

Pick point (2, 5) on the graph and substitute it in each equation.

Choice A results in $y = 3$, which is false.

Choice B results in $y = \dfrac{7}{2}$, which is false.

Choice C results in $y = 3$, which is false.

Choice D results in $y = 5$, which is the correct answer.

Multiple Choice

1. The variables x and y vary inversely. What is the value of k when $x = -9$ and $y = \dfrac{1}{3}$?

Ⓐ -27 Ⓑ -3

Ⓒ 3 Ⓓ 27

2. Which equation is graphed below?

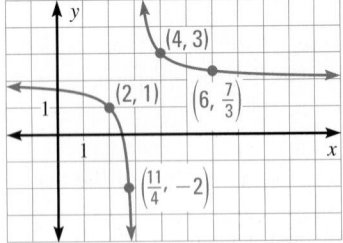

Ⓕ $y = \dfrac{1}{x}$ Ⓖ $y = \dfrac{1}{x-3} + 2$

Ⓗ $y = \dfrac{1}{x} + 2$ Ⓙ $y = \dfrac{1}{x-3}$

3. What are the common factor(s) of $5x^2 - 20$ and $6x^2 + 12x$?

Ⓐ $x + 2$ Ⓑ $3, (x + 2)$

Ⓒ $x, (x + 2), (x - 2)$ Ⓓ $2, 3, 5, x, x - 2$

4. Simplify the expression $\dfrac{5x^2 - 5x}{x^2 + 4x - 5}$.

Ⓕ $\dfrac{1}{2}$ Ⓖ $\dfrac{5x(x-1)}{(x+1)(x-5)}$

Ⓗ $\dfrac{x-1}{x+4}$ Ⓙ $\dfrac{5x}{x+5}$

5. Multiply $\dfrac{x+2}{x^2-4} \cdot \dfrac{x^2-3x}{4x^2}$. Simplify the result.

Ⓐ $\dfrac{x^2-3x}{4x^2(x-2)}$ Ⓑ $\dfrac{x-3}{4x(x^2-4)}$

Ⓒ $\dfrac{x-3}{4x(x-2)}$ Ⓓ $\dfrac{(x+2)(x+3)}{4x(x^2-4)}$

6. Write $\dfrac{x^2-9}{x^2+2x-15} \div \dfrac{x-1}{x+5}$ in simplest form.

Ⓕ $\dfrac{x+3}{x-1}$ Ⓖ $\dfrac{(x-3)(x-1)}{(x+5)^2}$

Ⓗ $\dfrac{x-1}{x+3}$ Ⓙ $\dfrac{x^2-9}{(x-3)(x-1)}$

7. The variable z varies jointly with x and y. What is the value of k when $x = 4$, $y = 1$, and $z = 4$?

Ⓐ -4 Ⓑ -1

Ⓒ 1 Ⓓ 4

8. Write $\dfrac{12x + 6}{x^2 - 9x - 36} + \dfrac{x + 1}{x + 3}$ in simplest form.

   (F) $\dfrac{x + 3}{x - 12}$ (G) $\dfrac{x^2 + x - 6}{(x - 12)(x + 3)}$

   (H) $\dfrac{x - 2}{x - 12}$ (J) $\dfrac{x^2 - 11x - 12}{(x - 12)(x + 3)}$

9. Solve $\dfrac{-3x}{x + 1} = \dfrac{-2}{x - 1}$.

   (A) $-1, 2$ (B) $-\dfrac{1}{3}, 2$

   (C) $\dfrac{1}{3}, -2$ (D) 2

10. Simplify $\dfrac{\dfrac{x^2 - x - 6}{3x - 3}}{\dfrac{3x + 6}{x^2 - 4x + 3}}$.

   (F) $\dfrac{(x - 3)^2}{9}$ (G) $\dfrac{x^2 - 9}{3}$

   (H) $\dfrac{(x + 2)^2}{(x - 1)^2}$ (J) $\dfrac{x^2 + 4}{x^2 - 1}$

11. Solve $\dfrac{8}{x + 4} + 1 = \dfrac{5x}{x^2 - 2x - 24}$.

   (A) $-5, 6$ (B) $5, -6$

   (C) $8, -9$ (D) $-8, 9$

Gridded Response

12. The variables x and y vary inversely. Find the value of k when $x = -3$ and $y = -5$.

13. The variables x and y vary inversely. Find the value of k when $x = \dfrac{4}{5}$ and $y = \dfrac{3}{2}$.

14. The variable z varies jointly with x and y. Find the value of k when $x = 3$, $y = 6$, and $z = 54$.

15. The graph of $y = \dfrac{-3}{x - 1} + 2$ has a horizontal asymptote at $y = k$. Find the value of k.

16. The graph of $y = \dfrac{-2}{x - 1} + 4$ has a vertical asymptote at $x = h$. Find the value of h.

17. Multiply $\dfrac{6x - 18}{2x - 8} \cdot \dfrac{x^2 - x - 12}{x^2 - 9}$.

18. Solve $\dfrac{5}{2} + \dfrac{15}{2x} = 4$.

19. Solve $\dfrac{12}{x + 5} + \dfrac{1}{2} = 2$.

20. Solve $\dfrac{3}{x - 2} + \dfrac{6}{2x} = \dfrac{7}{x}$.

Extended Response

21. A boat travels through still water at x miles per hour. The water in a river flows downstream at 4 miles per hour. The boat travels on the river 15 miles upstream and then returns downstream. The rate the boat travels upstream is $x - 4$ miles per hour because the boat moves against the flow of the water. The rate the boat travels downstream is $x + 4$ miles per hour because the boat moves with the flow of the water.

Speed of current: 4 miles per hour
Direction of current

a. Write a rational expression for the total time of the boat trip. Simplify the expression.

b. The total time for the trip is 2 hours. Find the speed of the boat.

Simplify the expression. *(Lesson 1.3)*

1. $3x + 6y - 2x + 2y$ **2.** $3x - 2(x + 4)$ **3.** $-4(-x)^2$

Find the slope of the line passing through the given points. *(Lesson 2.3)*

4. $(4, -2), (3, 1)$ **5.** $(-1, 3), (1, 7)$ **6.** $(3, -3), (6, -4)$

The variables *x* and *y* vary directly. Write an equation that relates the variables. *(Lesson 2.6)*

7. $x = 3, y = 18$ **8.** $x = 4, y = 10$ **9.** $x = 12, y = 9$

Solve the linear system. *(Lessons 3.1, 3.2, 3.3)*

10. $y = 3x - 7$
$5x - 2y = 12$

11. $3x - 2y = 9$
$x + 2y = 11$

12. $x - 2y = 4$
$3x + 2y = -20$

13. $-5x + 7y = 11$
$-5x + 3y = 19$

14. $3x + y = 1$
$-x + 2y = 16$

15. $2x + 3y = 9$
$3x - 4y = 5$

Solve the inequality. Then graph your solution on a real number line. *(Lesson 4.1)*

16. $2x - 1 \le 7$ **17.** $-5x - 6 \ge 19$ **18.** $2x + 4 \le 5$ or $x - 6 > -2$

Match the function with its graph. *(Lesson 4.6)*

19. $y = 3|x|$ **20.** $y = -3|x|$ **21.** $y = -\frac{1}{3}|x|$

A. 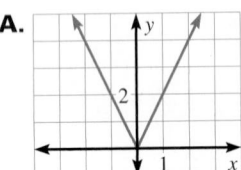   **B.** 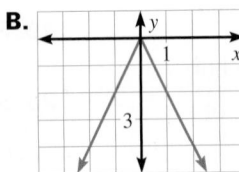   **C.**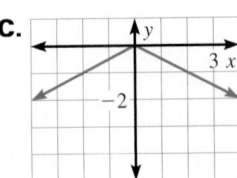

Solve the equation. *(Lessons 5.2–5.8)*

22. $x^2 + 3x - 10 = 0$ **23.** $2x^2 + 7x - 4 = 0$ **24.** $x^2 - 12x = -28$

Perform the indicated operation. *(Lessons 6.3, 6.4)*

25. $(x^2 + 3x + 9) - (2x^2 + 4x - 3)$ **26.** $(x - 1)(x + 3)(x + 1)$

27. $(x^3 + 5x^2 + 2x - 12) \div (x + 3)$ **28.** $(x^3 - 7x - 6) \div (x - 2)$

Solve the equation. Check for extraneous solutions. *(Lesson 7.3)*

29. $\sqrt{x} = 16$ **30.** $\sqrt{2x} + 9 = 13$ **31.** $\sqrt[3]{x - 1} - 6 = -3$

Perform the indicated operation and state the domain. *(Lesson 7.4)*

32. $f - g; f(x) = x - 5, g(x) = 3x - 2$ **33.** $f(g(x)); f(x) = x^2 + 1, g(x) = x - 7$

Find the inverse of the function. *(Lesson 7.5)*

34. $f(x) = 3x + 4$ **35.** $f(x) = 7x^5$ **36.** $f(x) = 2x^3 - 1$

Graph the function. *(Lessons 7.6, 8.1, 8.2)*

37. $y = \sqrt{x - 3} + 2$

38. $y = 2\sqrt[3]{x} + 4$

39. $y = \sqrt{x + 1} - 3$

40. $y = 3x - 1$

41. $y = 2x^{-1}$

42. $y = 4x^3 + 2$

43. $y = \left(\dfrac{1}{4}\right)^x$

44. $y = 2\left(\dfrac{1}{5}\right)^x$

45. $y = 10\left(\dfrac{2}{3}\right)^x$

Compound Interest In Exercises 46–48, use the following information.

You have $1200 to deposit and are comparing the bank offers shown in the table below. *(Lesson 8.3)*

Bank	Interest Rate	Compounding
X	3%	monthly
Y	4%	quarterly
Z	5%	yearly

46. Find the balance after 6 years if you deposit $1200 in an account at Bank X.

47. Find the balance after 6 years if you deposit $1200 in an account at Bank Y.

48. Find the balance after 6 years if you deposit $1200 in an account at Bank Z.

Evaluate the expression. *(Lesson 8.4)*

49. $\log_2 32$

50. $\log_{1/4} 16$

51. $\log_9 3$

Solve the equation. *(Lesson 8.6)*

52. $5^5 = 5^{2x + 1}$

53. $3^x = 11$

54. $\log_5 3x = \log_5 (5x + 3)$

Interpreting Data Determine whether x and y show *direct variation*, *inverse variation*, or *neither*. *(Lesson 9.1)*

55.

x	y
7	4
10	2.8
14	2
20	1.4

56.

x	y
8	20
10	25
12	30
14	35

57.

x	y
7	2.5
9	3
12	5
15	11

Perform the indicated operation and simplify. *(Lesson 9.3, 9.4, 9.5)*

58. $\dfrac{x + 5}{2x + 6} \cdot \dfrac{3x + 9}{x - 5}$

59. $\dfrac{x - 4}{x - 5} \div \dfrac{x + 3}{x^2 - 5x}$

60. $\dfrac{1}{x + 4} + \dfrac{x}{x + 2}$

Solve the equation. Check your solutions. *(Lesson 9.6)*

61. $\dfrac{4}{x + 2} = \dfrac{2}{x - 1}$

62. $\dfrac{x - 4}{x} = \dfrac{x - 3}{x + 5}$

63. $\dfrac{3}{x} + \dfrac{x + 4}{x + 2} = 3$

CHAPTER 10

Data Analysis and Probability

▶ How many ways can you choose dancers from a group?

APPLICATION: Dance Groups

Suppose that a choreographer is choosing groups from a dance company to perform different dances.

Think & Discuss

1. The partial list below shows possible groups of 2 dancers formed from the 6 dancers A, B, C, D, E, and F. Notice that repeated groups are crossed out. Copy and complete the list by adding 3 more rows.

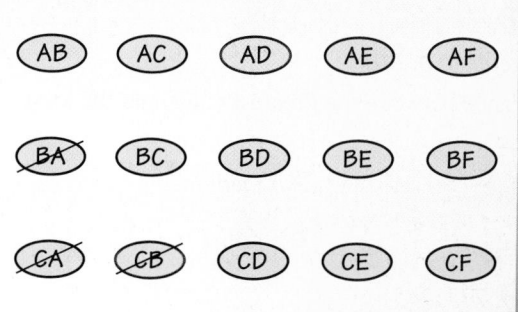

2. Make sure all repeated groups are crossed out in your list from Exercise 1. Then count the remaining groups. How many groups of 2 dancers are possible?

Learn More About It

You will use a formula to find a combination of dancers in a dance group in Exercise 22 on page 549.

PREVIEW

What's the chapter about?

• Identifying sources of bias in samples and survey questions
• Choosing random samples and finding the margin of error for a sample
• Using permutations and combinations to count the ways an event can happen
• Calculating and using probabilities

Key Words

• **population**, *p. 519*
• **unbiased, biased sample**, *p. 519*
• **random sample**, *p. 526*
• **margin of error**, *p. 528*
• **permutation**, *p. 540*
• **factorial**, *p. 540*
• **combination**, *p. 545*

• **geometric probability**, *p. 558*
• **compound event**, *p. 562*
• **overlapping, disjoint events**, *p. 562*
• **complement of an event**, *p. 564*
• **independent, dependent events**, *p. 569*
• **conditional probability**, *p. 570*

PREPARE

Chapter Readiness Quiz

Take this quick quiz. If you are unsure of an answer, look back at the reference pages for help.

Vocabulary Check *(refer to p. 46)*

1. In a data set, the difference between the greatest value and the least value is called the __?__ .

   A mean   **B** median

   C mode   **D** range

Skill Check *(refer to pp. 743, 745)*

2. Write the fraction $\frac{17}{50}$ as a percent.

   F 0.34%   **G** 1.7%   **H** 3.4%   **J** 34%

3. Simplify $\frac{17}{35} + \frac{2}{5} - \frac{1}{7}$. Round the answer to the nearest hundredth.

   A 0.51   **B** 0.63   **C** 0.69   **D** 0.74

TAKE NOTES

Compare and Contrast

Use your notes to compare formulas. Describe the differences in the formulas, and how the differences affect the outcomes.

PERMUTATIONS

$$_nP_r = \frac{n!}{(n-r)!}$$

• order is important
• greater than number of combinations

COMBINATIONS

$$_nC_r = \frac{n!}{(n-r)!\,r!}$$

• order not important
• fewer than number of permutations

10.1 Populations and Surveys

Key Words

- population
- sample
- unbiased sample
- biased sample

Prerequisite Skills

Solve.

1. What number is 25% of 124?

2. 52 is 20% of what number?

3. 162 is what percent of 180?

4. What number is 35% of 150?

GOAL Use unbiased samples and surveys to make predictions.

How can you use a survey to collect information?

A **population** is an entire group of people, animals, or objects that you want information about.

If you cannot collect information about every member of the population, you can study a smaller part, or **sample**, of the population.

EXAMPLE 1 Identify a Population and Sample

Market Research A company plans to open a new restaurant in a city. To study the preferences of people in the city, the company conducts a survey of 400 city residents. Identify the population and the sample for this situation.

Solution

The population consists of the residents of the city, who are the potential customers for the new restaurant. The sample is the 400 people from this population who are surveyed.

Checkpoint ✓ *Identify a Population and Sample*

1. Biologists studying the bluebirds nesting in a wildlife refuge count the numbers of eggs in 20 bluebird nests scattered throughout the refuge. Identify the population and the sample for this situation.

Samples and Bias An **unbiased sample** accurately represents a population. A **biased sample** overrepresents or underrepresents part of the population. The diagram below shows two samples of 12 out of a population of 96 students who were asked whether they prefer playing softball or tennis. Three fourths of the population, or 72 students, prefer softball.

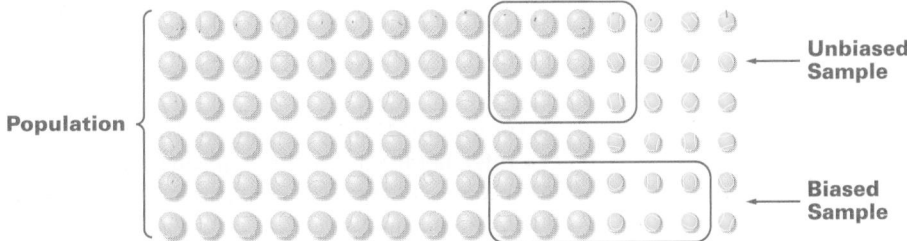

In the top sample, three fourths of the students prefer softball, the same as in the population. This sample accurately represents the population, so it is unbiased. In the bottom sample, only half of the students prefer softball. This sample does not accurately represent the population, so it is biased.

Eliminating Bias To obtain an unbiased sample of a population, you must be careful that the way you choose your sample does not introduce bias. Also, in general, a larger sample is more likely to be unbiased than a smaller sample chosen the same way.

EXAMPLE 2 Identify Potentially Biased Samples

Libraries A town wants to know if voters favor a tax increase for a new library. Tell whether the sample chosen is likely to be biased. Explain.

a. Survey 200 people from all town residents who have library cards.

b. Survey 20 people who come to town hall one afternoon.

c. Survey 175 people from all town residents who are registered voters.

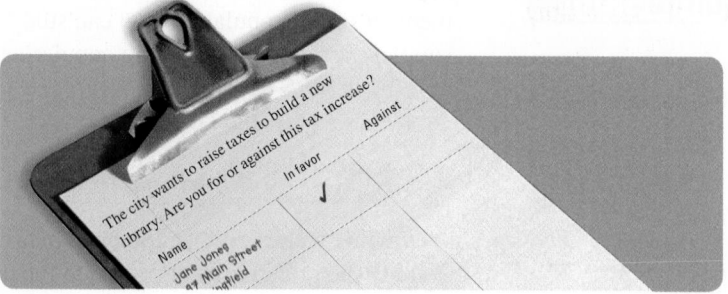

Solution

a. This sample is likely to be biased because those with library cards might be more likely than the whole population to support a new library.

b. This sample is likely to be biased because people who come to the town hall might not represent voters in general. Also, the sample size is very small.

c. This sample is less likely to be biased because the sample is large and is taken from those who are most likely to vote.

Checkpoint ✓ **Identify Potentially Biased Samples**

Tell whether the sample chosen is likely to be biased. Explain.

2. To choose the theme of an all-school dance, you survey all of the members of your drama class.

3. To study support for a proposed new cell phone tower, all the households within 200 yards of the proposed site are surveyed.

4. To find out if a new Web site is easy to use, the site's designer asks five people in the office to try it.

Survey Questions In a survey, not only must the people surveyed be chosen carefully, but the questions themselves must be worded carefully. Otherwise, the results may not reflect the true views of those surveyed even in a large, well-chosen sample.

A survey question must not hint that there is a preferred answer. A survey's setting or the questioner can also influence the results. For example, people asked in front of a news camera if they recycle might be more likely to answer "yes" than if they are asked to give an answer anonymously.

EXAMPLE **3** Identify Potentially Biased Survey Questions

Explain why the survey question may be biased. Then rewrite the question to remove the bias.

a. Would you like to see healthy food served in our cafeteria?

b. Do you plan to vote to replace the current mayor with a more effective one?

Solution

a. This question is biased because it suggests that the food now served is unhealthy, which encourages a response of *yes*. A more neutral wording might be "Do you think our cafeteria menu includes enough healthy food choices?"

b. This question is biased because it suggests that the current mayor is ineffective. A more neutral wording might be "If the mayoral election were held today, would you vote for the current mayor or the mayor's opponent?"

Checkpoint  *Identify Potentially Biased Survey Questions*

Explain why the survey question may be biased. Then rewrite the question to remove the bias.

5. Do you follow dentists' recommendations and floss daily?

6. Do you think the city should replace the outdated police cars it is using?

Making Predictions Samples that are carefully chosen to avoid giving biased results allow you to make predictions about a population.

EXAMPLE **4** **Make a Prediction from a Sample**

School Colors You want to find out if students at your school favor a proposed change in the school colors. Of the total of 960 students, you survey 40 who were chosen in an unbiased way. You find that 12 of the 40 favor the change. Predict how many students at your school favor the change.

Solution

You can predict that the ratio of students in the population who are in favor of the change will be about the same as the ratio in the sample who are in favor.

$$\frac{\text{Population number in favor}}{\text{Population size}} = \frac{\text{Sample number in favor}}{\text{Sample size}} \quad \text{Write a proportion.}$$

$$\frac{x}{960} = \frac{12}{40} \qquad \text{Substitute known values.}$$

$$40x = 11{,}520 \qquad \text{Cross product property}$$

$$x = 288 \qquad \text{Simplify.}$$

ANSWER ▶ You can predict that about 288 students favor the color change.

Checkpoint  *Make a Prediction from a Sample*

7. In Example 4, suppose that 18 of 50 students surveyed favor changing the colors. Predict how many of the 960 students favor the change.

Guided Practice

Vocabulary Check

1. Copy and complete the statement: A portion of a population that is studied in order to make predictions about the whole population is a(n) __?__.

2. Describe the difference between a biased sample and an unbiased sample. Give an example of each type of sample.

Skill Check

Identify the population and the sample for the situation.

3. The manager of a pet store plans to sell an additional brand of dog food. The manager asks all customers who purchase dog food or supplies at the store one day if they would like to indicate their choice of one of three possible new dog food brands on a card and put the card in a box.

4. A pecan grower brings in 60 sacks of pecans to sell. The buyer takes a handful of pecans from each of several bags, weighs the pecans before and after shelling them, and inspects the shelled pecans.

For a survey of student opinions about school subjects, you ask students which of several subjects they expect to be most useful to them as adults. Tell whether the given sampling method is likely to result in a biased sample. Explain.

5. You ask all of the students in each of your classes.

6. You ask 50 students whose names you draw without looking from a box containing all student names.

7. You ask all of the class officers for each grade.

Practice and Applications

STUDENT HELP

HOMEWORK HELP
Example 1: Exs. 8–9
Example 2: Exs. 10–16
Example 3: Exs. 17–20
Example 4: Exs. 21–26

Populations and Samples **In Exercises 8 and 9, identify the population and the sample for the situation.**

8. A television sports show wants to know which team its viewers predict will win the championship next week. During the show, viewers are asked to vote online. Of the 9 million people watching the show, 0.4 million vote.

9. A writer for the high school newspaper is conducting a survey to see who is the current leader in the race for senior class president. The writer hands out "ballots" to as many seniors as possible as they enter school, and asks them to vote for their favorite candidate and place the ballots in a box.

Representative Samples **A magazine wants to know which local ice cream shop residents think is the best. Tell whether the sample is likely to represent the population accurately. Explain.**

10. 20 customers surveyed at each one of the ice cream shops

11. newspaper readers who mail in a contest entry form that is included in the Sunday paper

12. 250 shoppers surveyed as they enter the town's only supermarket

Biased Samples Tell whether the described sample is likely to be biased. Explain.

13. A student investigating the most desired car color among students with driver's licenses at the school counts the numbers of cars of each color in the school parking lot.

14. A bus company researching riders' opinions of bus service surveys 200 people chosen by computer from all the riders who have a monthly bus pass.

15. Quality control workers at a shoe factory open and inspect 5 boxes of shoes from every shipment of 100 boxes.

16. A researcher at a large company needs to know the average number of televisions in U.S. households. The researcher surveys the households of all the company's employees.

Government A survey is conducted to find out opinions about new laws passed by a state's legislature. Explain why the survey question may be biased. Then rewrite the question to remove the bias.

17. Do you agree with the court's decision to overturn laws making public buildings and public transportation accessible to all?

18. Do you agree with the decision to slash state funding for the arts by nearly 25%?

19. Do you agree with the state's groundbreaking new program to extend health care to all citizens?

20. Do you think it was necessary for the state legislature to ban all dogs from ever being allowed off their leashes while in a state park?

Link to
GOVERNMENT

ACCESSIBILITY The Americans with Disabilities Act was passed July 26, 1990 to expand equal opportunity for people with disabilities.

Beaches In Exercises 21–24, use the following information.

The table shows results of an unbiased survey asking students at a school which of the four local beaches is their favorite.

Favorite Beach	Students
North Beach	24
Turtle Cove	40
Pirate's Point	12
South Beach	22

21. Suppose the school has 1250 students. Predict the number who prefer Turtle Cove and the number who prefer Pirate's Point.

22. Suppose the school has 2000 students. Predict the number who prefer North Beach and the number who prefer South Beach.

23. Suppose the school has 800 students. Predict the number who prefer a beach *other than* Pirate's Point.

24. Suppose the school has 100 teachers. Would you expect the survey results to predict teacher preferences accurately? Explain.

25. Consumer Electronics A company finds that 380 of 500 consumers it surveyed chose its new phone over the leading competitor's new phone. If the sample and survey question were unbiased, predict how many of 6.5 million potential customers are likely to choose the company's phone over the competitor's phone.

26. Jobs In a survey of teenagers, 23% said that teens should not have a paying job during the school year. If the sample and survey question were unbiased, predict how many in a group of 10,000 teenagers would say teens should not have a paying job during the school year.

27. Multiple Choice A manager of a restaurant is conducting a survey to find customers' opinions of service at the restaurant. Which sampling method is most likely to result in an unbiased sample?

(A) Personally ask 20 groups of diners each night for a week.

(B) Give customers who fill out a survey a free T-shirt.

(C) Hand all customers a survey card and ask them to place completed cards in a box as they leave.

(D) Survey all of the employees at the restaurant.

28. Multiple Choice In an unbiased survey of 400 households in a city, 320 said that they have a DVD player. If there are 45,000 households in the city, which is the best prediction of the total number of households with a DVD player?

(F) 20,000 households   (G) 25,000 households

(H) 36,000 households   (J) 56,250 households

29. Multiple Choice Which survey question is least likely to result in a biased sample?

(A) Would you prefer that we sell hats or these really cool glow-in-the-dark T-shirts for the fundraiser?

(B) Do you think that building additional parking at the stadium will affect attendance at the games?

(C) Are you willing to take public transportation to your job to help the environment?

(D) Do you think that increasing taxes in the city to upgrade the brand new civic center is a bad idea?

Mixed Review

Standard Deviation Find the standard deviation of the data set. Round your answer to the nearest tenth. *(Lesson 7.7)*

30. 40, 50, 20, 80, 10, 40   **31.** 13, 18, 17, 10, 12, 14

32. 20, 25, 25, 26, 30, 36, 34   **33.** 51, 65, 72, 58, 84, 90, 70

Rational Equations Solve the equation. Check your solutions. *(Lesson 9.6)*

34. $\dfrac{1}{x} = \dfrac{3}{2x + 4}$ **35.** $\dfrac{3}{x + 5} = \dfrac{x + 1}{5x - 3}$ **36.** $\dfrac{2x}{2x + 4} = \dfrac{3x}{x + 2}$

37. $\dfrac{3}{x} = \dfrac{5}{x} - \dfrac{1}{4}$ **38.** $\dfrac{3}{x} + 2 = \dfrac{4x}{x + 1}$ **39.** $1 + \dfrac{3}{x - 3} = \dfrac{4}{x^2 - 9}$

Geometry Skills

Chords If two chords intersect in the interior of a circle, then the product of the lengths of the segments of one chord equals the product of the lengths of the segments of the other chord. Find the value of x.

40.

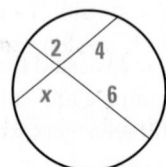

41.

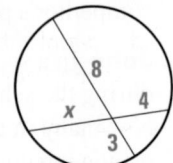

42.

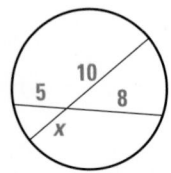

ACTIVITY 10.2

DEVELOPING CONCEPTS *(For use with Lesson 10.2)*
Investigating Samples

Goal

To model sampling from a population

Materials

- red beans
- pinto beans
- paper bag

QUESTION

How well do samples taken in different ways represent a situation?

EXPLORE

1 Drop 80 pinto beans into a container. Place 20 red beans directly on top of the pinto beans. Then out of 100 beans in the jar in all, twenty percent of the beans are red beans.

2 Without stirring, reach in and pull a handful of beans out of the jar. Count the number of red beans and the total number of beans in your handful. Record your results in a table like the one below. Return the beans to the jar.

3 Stir the jar thoroughly. Pull a handful of beans out of the jar. Record your results of this sample in your table. Return the beans to the jar.

4 Stir the jar thoroughly. Pull two handfuls of beans out of the jar. Record your results.

Sample	Number of red beans, b	Total number of beans, T	Percent that is red (b/T)
one handful, not stirred			
one handful, stirred			
two handfuls, stirred			

THINK ABOUT IT

1. Comparing Samples Compare the first two samples.

   a. How does stirring affect the results?

   b. Which sample seems to be more representative of the beans in the jar? Why do you think this occurred?

   c. How could you accomplish the same effect as stirring the beans when choosing a real-world sample for a survey or a study?

2. Comparing Samples Compare the last two samples. Which of these samples seemed to be more representative of the beans in the jar? Explain.

3. Drawing Conclusions You would like to perform a fourth trial. Which of the samples below do you think would produce the most representative sample? Explain your reasoning.

   A. 20 beans poured out, unstirred   **B.** two handfuls, stirred

   C. three handfuls, stirred   **D.** three handfuls, unstirred

10.2 Samples and Margin of Error

Classify sampling methods and find sampling error.

Key Words

- convenience sample
- self-selected sample
- systematic sample
- random sample
- margin of error

Prerequisite Skills

Evaluate. Round your answer to the nearest tenth of a percent.

1. $\dfrac{1}{\sqrt{10}}$

2. $\dfrac{1}{\sqrt{100}}$

3. $\dfrac{1}{\sqrt{500}}$

4. $\dfrac{1}{\sqrt{1000}}$

How can you select a sample?

You want to survey the families in your neighborhood to find out how the residents feel about a proposal to build a new superstore adjacent to the neighborhood.

What are some ways in which you can select your sample? Are there ways to increase the likelihood that your sample will be unbiased?

Some sample types are described below.

In a **convenience sample**, easy-to-reach members of a population are selected. For example, you could survey the households on your street plus those of two of your friends.

In a **self-selected sample**, members of a population volunteer to be included. For example, you could leave surveys at the doors of all the houses, then use those that are returned to you.

In a **systematic sample**, a rule or pattern is used to select members of a population. For example, you could survey every fourth household in the neighborhood.

In a **random sample**, each member of a population is equally likely to be chosen. For example, you could write each address on a slip of paper, and then draw slips from a bag.

Biased and Unbiased Samples In general, a random sample is least likely to be biased. In the situation above, the systematic sample is also unlikely to be biased. Convenience and self-selected samples are likely to be biased. Above, the convenience sample might overrepresent people very close to the new store, and the self-selected sample might overrepresent friends or people with strong feelings.

EXAMPLE 1 Classify a Sample

Health Employees who go to a company health fair are given survey cards that ask for opinions about new health-related programs. Those who fill in and return a card are given a coupon for a free "Healthy Habits" lunch at the company cafeteria.

a. Classify the sample as *convenience*, *self-selected*, *systematic*, or *random*. Explain your reasoning.

b. Tell whether this method is likely to result in a biased sample. Explain.

Solution

a. Employees must first choose to attend the fair, and then must choose to fill out the survey, so the sample is *self-selected*.

b. The survey is likely to be biased. Employees who attend may differ from those who don't, and those who choose to fill out cards may differ from those who don't. Offering a reward could also influence the results.

Checkpoint *Classify a Sample*

1. Suppose in Example 1 that every company employee whose employee number ends in a 3 is surveyed. Classify the sample. Then tell whether this method is likely to result in a biased sample.

EXAMPLE 2 Choose a Random Sample

Hobbies You plan to conduct a survey about the hobbies of students in your grade. You have a list of the names of all 240 students in your grade. Describe two ways you can choose a random sample of 30 students to survey.

Solution

METHOD 1 Number the list of students from 1 to 240. Open a phone book to a residential page. Treating the last three digits of each phone number as a number from 000 to 999, choose the first 30 different numbers from 001 to 240. Survey the 30 students corresponding to these numbers.

555-9047
555-3421
555-6218
555-7901
⋮

METHOD 2 Generate random numbers using a calculator. Use the first 30 different numbers that appear to select the 30 students.

This command creates a list of **40** random integers from **1** to **240**.

```
randInt(1,240,40)
{227 98 36 124...
```

STUDENT HELP

SOLVING NOTE
To make sure that you get at least 30 *different* numbers, set the *randInt* function to generate extra numbers.

Checkpoint *Choose a Random Sample*

2. Describe another way to choose a random sample in Example 2.

Sampling Error Even a random sample can give a biased result just by chance. The **margin of error** of a sample tells how close you can expect a measure in a population to be to a measure found using a random sample taken from the population.

STUDENT HELP

READING ALGEBRA
A margin of error is often stated as "plus or minus" a given percent. So, a survey might claim that "55% of those surveyed are against Proposal B, with a margin of error of plus or minus 3%."

Margin of Error Formula

If you take a random sample of size n from a large population, you can use the following formula to approximate the margin of error S.

$$\text{Margin of error} = \pm\frac{1}{\sqrt{n}}$$

This means that if $p\%$ of the sample responds a certain way, then it's likely that the interval from $p\% - S\%$ to $p\% + S\%$ contains the actual percent of the population that would respond the same way.

Notice in the margin of error formula that the sample size is in the denominator of the fraction. So, the *larger* the sample, the *smaller* the margin of error, and the more confident you can be that the sample represents the population.

Link to
TRANSPORTATION

COMMUTING TO WORK
In the United States, about 76% of workers drive to work alone, 12% carpool, 5% use public transportation, and 3% walk. Another 3% work at home.

EXAMPLE 3 Find and Interpret a Margin of Error

Commuting to Work In a random survey of 1600 workers in a city, 47.5% say that it takes them more than 30 minutes to get from home to work every day.

a. What is the margin of error for the survey?

b. Give an interval that is likely to contain the actual percent of all the city's workers who take more than 30 minutes to get to work.

Solution

a. Margin of error $= \pm\dfrac{1}{\sqrt{n}}$ Margin of error formula

   $= \pm\dfrac{1}{\sqrt{1600}}$ Substitute 1600 for n.

   $= \pm 0.025$, or $\pm 2.5\%$ Simplify.

   ANSWER ▶ The margin of error is $\pm 2.5\%$.

b. To find an interval that is likely to contain the actual population percent, subtract and add 2.5% to the sample result of 47.5%.

   $47.5\% - 2.5\% = 45\%$ Lower bound of interval

   $47.5\% + 2.5\% = 50\%$ Upper bound of interval

   ANSWER ▶ It's likely that it takes from 45% to 50% of the city's workers more than 30 minutes to get to work every day.

Checkpoint ✔ Find and Interpret a Margin of Error

3. In a survey of 6400 voters in a state, 51% favor a new tax law. What is the margin of error for the survey? Give an interval that is likely to contain the percent of all the voters in the state who favor the new tax law.

10.2 Exercises

Guided Practice

Vocabulary Check

Copy and complete the statement.

1. A sample in which each member of a population is equally likely to be selected is called a(n) __?__ .

2. The number that describes how close you can expect an actual population measure to be to a measure from a random sample is the __?__ .

Skill Check

Classify the sample as *convenience, self-selected, systematic,* or *random*. Explain your reasoning.

3. To assess customers' experience making purchases online, a rating company e-mails purchasers and asks that they click on a link and complete a survey.

4. To find out student opinions about the school dress code, you survey everyone in your algebra class.

Describe a way to choose a random sample from the population.

5. A company's human resources department wants to survey 50 of the company's 1200 employees to get opinions about a proposed benefits change.

6. A college wants to survey 100 of its 1600 soon-to-graduate seniors to find out how many have already found jobs in their field of study after graduation.

In Exercises 7–10, find the margin of error for a survey of a random sample of size *n* chosen from a large population. Round your answer to the nearest tenth of a percent.

7. $n = 25$ 8. $n = 80$ 9. $n = 225$ 10. $n = 840$

11. **Surveys** A survey of a random sample of adults in a state reports that 44% approve of the governor's performance, with a margin of error of $\pm 3\%$. What does the margin of error indicate about this result?

Practice and Applications

STUDENT HELP

HOMEWORK HELP
Example 1: Exs. 12–21
Example 2: Exs. 22–24
Example 3: Exs. 25–40

Classifying Samples **Classify the sample as *convenience, self-selected, systematic,* or *random*. Explain your reasoning.**

12. The owners of a chain of 260 convenience stores want to assess employee job satisfaction. All employees from 12 stores near the headquarters are surveyed.

13. As students enter a school assembly, they are asked to roll a six-sided die. Students who roll a 6 are given a survey question to answer before entering.

News Polls **In Exercises 14 and 15, use the following information.**

Each day, a television news show asks viewers to go online to tell whether they agree or disagree with a statement about national politics or events.

14. Classify the sampling method as *convenience, self-selected, systematic,* or *random*. Explain your reasoning.

15. Tell whether the sampling method is likely to give a biased sample. Explain.

Fairs **In Exercises 16–19, use the following information.**

You have a booth at a fair where you sell pottery. You want to find out how other booth holders feel about the booth locations they were given. Use the description and diagram to classify the sample as *convenience*, *self-selected*, *systematic*, or *random*.

16. Using a numbered diagram of the booths, you ask booth holders whose booth number is a multiple of 4. (Your booth is shaded dark.)

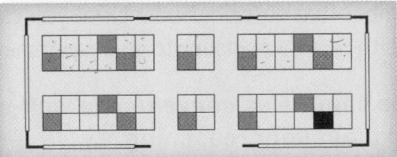

17. Using a diagram, you identify each booth and roll a 4-sided die for the booth. If you roll a 1 for the booth, you ask the booth holder.

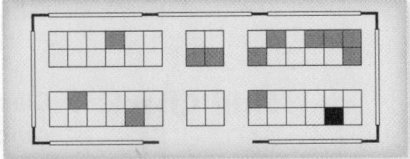

18. You give survey cards to all booth holders and ask for their return.

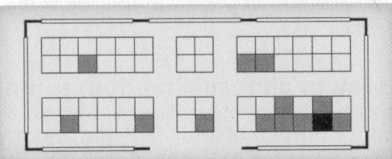

19. You ask all the other booth holders in your section.

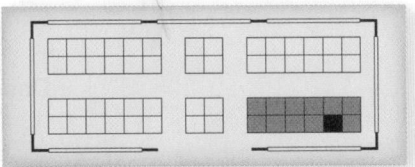

Elections **In Exercises 20 and 21, use the following information.**

A poll is conducted to predict the results of a statewide election in New Mexico before all the votes are counted. Fifty voters in each of the state's 33 counties are asked as they leave the voting place how they voted.

20. Classify the sample as *convenience*, *self-selected*, *systematic*, or *random*. Explain your reasoning.

21. **Critical Thinking** Explain how the diagram shows that the polling method could result in a biased sample.

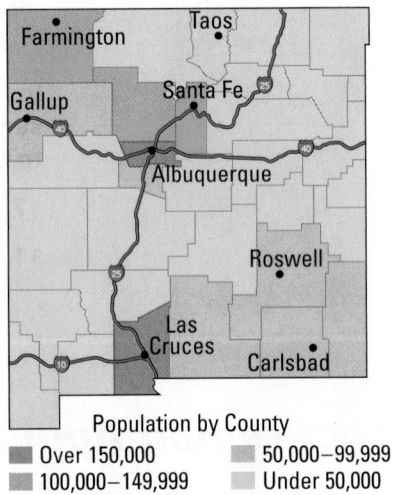

In Exercises 22–24, describe two ways you can choose a random sample of the given population.

22. **Messaging** A student newspaper wants to find out how many hours per week students spend instant messaging and text messaging.

23. **College Sports** A national college athletic association wants to survey 15 of the 120 head football coaches in a division about a proposed rules change.

24. **Car Sales** A car maker wants to survey customers who have purchased one of its cars in the past year. The company has a list of each customer's address.

25. **Retirement** In a random sample of 1000 U.S. adults from across the country, 20% said that saving for retirement was their most important financial goal. The margin of error is ±3.2%. Give an interval that is likely to contain the actual population percent for whom retirement was the most important financial goal.

Finding Margin of Error Find the margin of error for a survey of a random sample of size *n* chosen from a large population. Round your answer to the nearest tenth of a percent.

26. $n = 40$ **27.** $n = 75$ **28.** $n = 210$ **29.** $n = 3025$

30. $n = 1225$ **31.** $n = 600$ **32.** $n = 5000$ **33.** $n = 8000$

Nutrition In Exercises 34–37, a random sample of 500 high school students are asked how many servings of fruits and vegetables they ate on average last week. The results are shown.

	Daily Servings of Fruits and Vegetables			
	less than 1	1–2	3–5	more than 5
Female	8	86	101	46
Male	10	81	115	53

34. What is the margin of error for the survey?

35. From the table, 33.4% responded "1–2." Give an interval that is likely to contain the actual percent in the population who ate 1 to 2 servings a day.

36. If the females are considered as a separate sample, what is the margin of error?

37. Use your result from Exercise 36 to give an interval that is likely to contain the actual percent of females in the population who ate 3 to 5 servings a day.

Challenge In Exercises 38–40, use the following information.

You read that a survey of a random sample of a state's voters indicates that between 67.5% and 72.5% of the voters support a new law.

38. What is the margin of error for the sample?

39. Use the margin of error to find the size of the sample.

40. How many people would the sample have needed to include to reduce the margin of error to half of what you found in Exercise 38? What is the relationship of this sample size and the sample size from Exercise 39? Explain.

Standardized Test Practice

41. Multi-Step Problem A national chain of restaurants is studying the effects of a new company policy in its restaurants.

Effect	**Results**
Positive	80%
Negative	5%
None	15%

  a. Two restaurant managers from every state are surveyed. Classify the sample as *convenience*, *self-selected*, *systematic*, or *random*.

  b. Each store has a unique identification number. Describe a way to use this fact to select a random sample of managers.

  c. The table results shown are from a random sample. What is the margin of error for the sample?

  d. Give an interval that is likely to contain the actual percent of the chain's restaurant managers who would say that the effect of the change is "positive."

42. Multiple Choice A random sample of 2500 consumers reports that 61% prefer game A over game B. Which interval best represents the actual percent of people in the population likely to prefer game A over game B?

  A 60.5%–61.5%   **B** 60%–62%   **C** 59%–63%   **D** 56%–66%

Multiplying Rational Expressions **Multiply the expressions. Simplify the result.** *(Lesson 9.3)*

43. $\dfrac{12}{x} \cdot \dfrac{x}{4}$

44. $\dfrac{9x}{6} \cdot \dfrac{6x^2}{3x^4}$

45. $\dfrac{x^2}{x-2} \cdot \dfrac{x^2+x-6}{x+3}$

46. $\dfrac{x^5}{x+3} \cdot (4x+12)$

47. $\dfrac{3x}{x^2-4} \cdot (2x+4)$

48. $\dfrac{4x+8}{x^2-x-6} \cdot (x^2-9)$

Dividing Rational Expressions **Write the quotient in simplest form.** *(Lesson 9.4)*

49. $\dfrac{3x}{5} \div \dfrac{x}{15}$

50. $\dfrac{5x^3}{3} \div \dfrac{x}{4}$

51. $\dfrac{6}{4x^4} \div \dfrac{3}{10x^2}$

52. $\dfrac{x-3}{2x} \div \dfrac{x-3}{7}$

53. $\dfrac{3x+2}{2x} \div \dfrac{6x+4}{4x^3}$

54. $\dfrac{x^2-1}{x+2} \div \dfrac{x-1}{5x+10}$

Adding and Subtracting Rational Expressions **Perform the indicated operation and simplify.** *(Lesson 9.5)*

55. $\dfrac{x^2}{x-5} + \dfrac{7}{x-5}$

56. $\dfrac{5}{3x} - \dfrac{4}{3x}$

57. $\dfrac{2x}{7x-1} - \dfrac{1-5x}{7x-1}$

58. $\dfrac{3}{2x+8} + \dfrac{x}{2}$

59. $\dfrac{x}{x^2-64} + \dfrac{x-1}{x-8}$

60. $\dfrac{2}{x-1} - \dfrac{2}{x+1} - \dfrac{1}{x}$

Geometry Skills

Polygons **Use the formula** $S = (n-2) \cdot 180°$ **where** *n* **is the number of sides to find the sum of the angle measures in the polygon.**

61.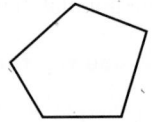

62.

63.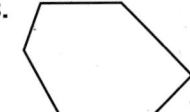

Quiz 1

Lesson 10.1

In Exercises 1–4, a governor wants to know if voters in the state support building a highway that will pass through a state forest. Tell whether the described sample is likely to be biased. Explain.

1. Survey members of a state wildlife conservation group.

2. Survey workers at random outside their offices near the state capitol building.

3. Survey residents whose property lies along the path of the highway.

4. Survey business owners in a town that is a destination of the highway.

Lesson 10.2

In Exercises 5–7, use the following information.

An unbiased survey of people with driver's licenses in a city asks whether they would favor paying an additional gasoline tax to expand public transportation. Of 150 people surveyed, 38 are in favor of the tax. There are 320,000 people with driver's licenses in the city.

5. Predict the number of people with driver's licenses in the city who are in favor of the new tax.

6. Find the margin of error.

7. Find an interval that is likely to contain the actual percent of the population who are in favor of the additional tax.

Transformations of Data

Key Words
- mean
- median
- mode
- range
- quartile

Prerequisite Skills

Find the indicated measure for the data set below.

16, 9, 11, 8, 10, 11, 6, 12

1. mean

2. median

3. mode

4. range

GOAL Find how statistical measures are affected by changes to data sets.

How does the average test score change when all students improve their scores?

In this lesson, you will examine how a data set's measures change when you increase or decrease the data values by a constant amount or when you multiply them by a constant factor.

In studying these transformations, you will look at *measures of central tendency*: mean, median, and mode; and at *measures of dispersion*: range and the difference between quartiles.

EXAMPLE 1 Compare Data After Adding a Constant

College Entrance Tests Ten students take a college entrance exam and receive the scores shown below as "First test." Suppose each student later takes the exam a second time and increases his or her score by 20 points, shown as "Second test."

First test: 870, 910, 970, 1050, 1080, 1120, 1200, 1210, 1210, 1340

Second test: 890, 930, 990, 1070, 1100, 1140, 1220, 1230, 1230, 1360

a. Compare the mean, median, and mode of the first test data and the second test data. What do you observe?

b. Compare the ranges and the differences between the upper and lower quartiles for the first test data and the second test data. What do you observe?

Solution

a.

	First test	**Second test**
Mean	$\dfrac{10{,}960}{10} = 1096$	$\dfrac{11{,}160}{10} = 1116$
Median	$\dfrac{1080 + 1120}{2} = 1100$	$\dfrac{1100 + 1140}{2} = 1120$
Mode	1210	1230

ANSWER ▶ The mean, median, and mode each increase by 20 points.

b. First test: Range = 1340 − 870 = **470**

Upper quartile − lower quartile = 1210 − 970 = **240**

Second test: Range = 1360 − 890 = **470**

Upper quartile − lower quartile = 1230 − 990 = **240**

ANSWER ▶ The range and the difference between the upper and lower quartiles remain the same.

STUDENT HELP

LOOK BACK
For help with mean, median, mode, range, and quartiles, see page 46.

EXAMPLE 2 **Compare Data After Multiplying by a Constant**

Suppose the students in Example 1 take the exam a third time and increase their scores by 10% from their original scores, giving the scores shown as "Third test."

First test: 870, 910, 970, 1050, 1080, 1120, 1200, 1210, 1210, 1340

Third test: 957, 1001, 1067, 1155, 1188, 1232, 1320, 1331, 1331, 1474

a. Compare the mean, median, and mode of the first test data and the third test data. What do you observe?

b. Compare the ranges and the differences between the upper and lower quartiles for the first test data and the third test data. What do you observe?

Solution

a.

	First test	Third test
Mean	$\dfrac{10,960}{10} = 1096$	$\dfrac{12,056}{10} = 1205.6$
Median	$\dfrac{1080 + 1120}{2} = 1100$	$\dfrac{1188 + 1232}{2} = 1210$
Mode	1210	1331

Find the percent increase in each measure:

Mean: $\dfrac{1205.6 - 1096}{1096} = 10\%$ Median: $\dfrac{1210 - 1100}{1100} = 10\%$

Similarly, you can show that the mode increases by 10%.

ANSWER ▶ The mean, median, and mode each increase by 10%.

b. First test: Range = 1340 − 870 = **470**

Upper quartile − lower quartile = 1210 − 970 = **240**

Third test: Range = 1474 − 957 = **517**

Upper quartile − lower quartile = 1331 − 1067 = **264**

Find the percent increase in each measure:

Range: $\dfrac{517 - 470}{470} = 10\%$ Difference: $\dfrac{264 - 240}{240} = 10\%$

ANSWER ▶ The range and the difference between the upper and lower quartiles each increase by 10%.

 **Compare Data**

Discounts Use the information below.

Regular prices of 9 jackets: $48, $40, $64, $72, $64, $80, $76, $80, $96

Prices after 25% discount: $36, $30, $48, $54, $48, $60, $57, $60, $72

1. Compare the mean, median, and mode of the set of original prices and the set of discounted prices. What do you observe?

2. Compare the ranges and the differences between the upper and lower quartiles for the original prices and the discounted prices. What do you observe?

EXAMPLE **3** Graph Data After Adding a Constant

Make a box-and-whisker plot of the first test data and the second test data from Example 1. How do the two graphs compare?

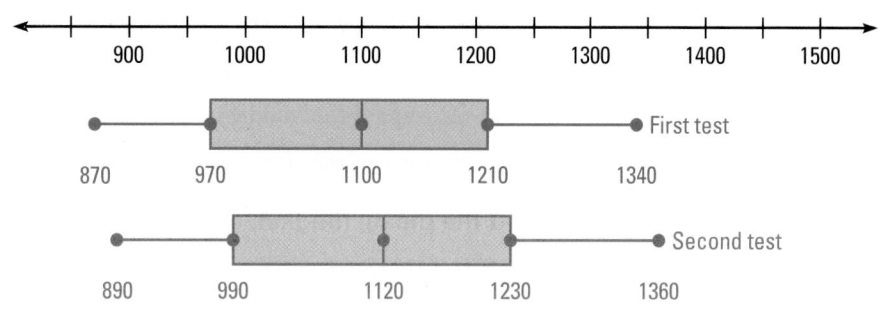

ANSWER ▶ The two box-and-whisker plots are the same shape, but the plot for the second test data is shifted 20 units to the right compared to the plot for the first test data.

In Example 3, adding a constant *shifts* the graph horizontally that number of units, but doesn't change the graph's shape. This corresponds to the data's middle (measures of central tendency) changing, but the spread (measures of dispersion) not changing.

EXAMPLE **4** Graph Data After Multiplying by a Constant

Make a box-and-whisker plot of the first test data and the third test data from Example 2. How do the two graphs compare?

Solution

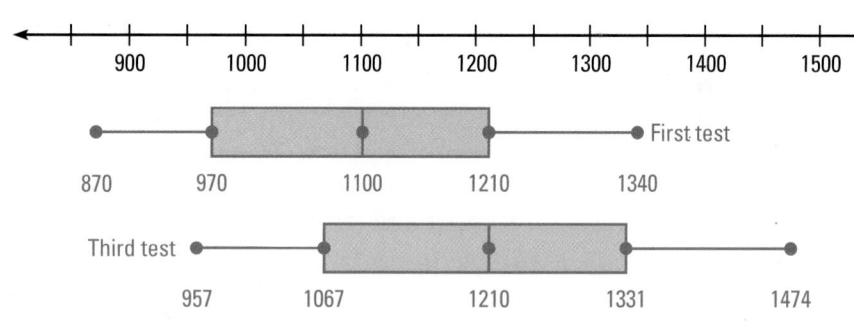

ANSWER ▶ The two plots are *not* the same shape. The plot for the third test is stretched out compared to the plot for the first. For example, the width of the box for the third test is 264, but for the first test the width is 240.

In Example 4, multiplying by a constant *stretches* the graph horizontally by the same factor. This both moves the data's middle and increases the data's spread.

Checkpoint ✓ **Graph Data**

3. Make a box-and-whisker plot of the two data sets from the Checkpoint at the bottom of page 534. How do the two graphs compare?

Guided Practice

Vocabulary Check   **Copy and complete the statement.**

   1. A measure of the middle of a set of data is a measure of __?__.

   2. A measure of the spread of a set of data is a measure of __?__.

Skill Check   **Find the mean, median, and mode(s) of the data set.**

   3. 0, 0, 1, 1, 4,   **4.** 2, 4, 5, 5, 5, 7,   **5.** 10, 10, 10, 15, 20,
   4, 4, 5, 5, 6   9, 10, 11, 12   25, 25, 30, 35

In Exercises 6–9, use the data set 2, 4, 6, 8, 10, 12, 14, 14, 20.

   6. Transform the data set by increasing each value by 50%.

   7. Compare the mean, median, and mode of the original data set and the new data set. What do you observe?

   8. Compare the ranges and the differences between the upper and lower quartiles for the original data set and the new data set. What do you observe?

   9. Make a box-and-whisker plot of the original data set and the new data set. How do the two graphs compare?

Practice and Applications

STUDENT HELP

HOMEWORK HELP
Example 1: Exs. 10–11,
   14–19, 23–31
Example 2: Exs. 12–13,
   20–31
Example 3: Exs. 16–19,
   29–31
Example 4: Exs. 20–22,
   29–31

Transforming Data Transform the data by adding −5 to each value. Compare the mean, median, mode, range, and difference between the upper and lower quartiles of the original data and the new data.

   10. 0, 1, 1, 2, 3, 4, 4, 4, 5, 5, 6, 6, 7, 7, 8   **11.** −4, −2, −2, −1, 0, 0, 1, 2, 2, 2, 3, 5

Transforming Data Transform the data by increasing each value by 25%. Compare the mean, median, mode, range, and difference between the upper and lower quartiles of the original data and the new data.

   12. 8, 8, 16, 24, 32, 40, 80, 100   **13.** 2, 4, 8, 10, 14, 20, 24, 32, 32, 38

Graphs of Transformations The box-and-whisker plot represents the daily high temperatures (°F) in June last year for a city.

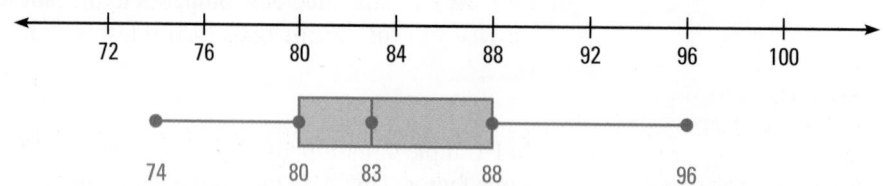

   14. You find out that last June's high temperatures in the city averaged 4° cooler than in a "normal" June. Use this fact and the plot above to predict the five measures on a box-and-whisker plot of the high temperatures for a normal June.

   15. What differences would you expect to see between the box-and-whisker plot above and a box-and-whisker plot for a normal June as described in Exercise 14?

Economics Link In Exercises 16–19, use the data set below. It shows the total state taxes (in cents per gallon) charged on gasoline for the 14 Atlantic Coast states in March, 2007.

37.0, 23.0, 32.6, 21.8, 28.3, 23.5, 23.5, 20.6, 14.5, 42.4, 30.2, 31.0, 16.8, 19.3

16. In addition to state taxes, consumers in all states pay a federal excise tax of 18.4 cents on each gallon of gasoline. Transform the original set of data to show the *total* state and federal tax on each gallon of gasoline.

17. Compare the mean, median, and mode of the original data set and the new data set. What can you conclude about each of these measures?

18. Compare the ranges and the differences between the upper and lower quartiles for the original data set and the new data set. What can you conclude about each of these measures?

19. What differences would you expect to see between a box-and-whisker plot of the original data and a box-and-whisker plot of the new data?

Energy Efficiency In Exercises 20–22, use the data set below. It shows the average daily electricity use (in kilowatt-hours, or kWh) for several families last year.

22, 26, 19, 31, 24, 16, 22

20. The families set a goal of reducing their electricity use by 10%. Transform the original data to show a 10% decrease in electricity use by each family.

21. Compare the mean, median, mode, range, and the difference between the upper and lower quartiles for the original data and for the transformed data.

22. What differences would you expect to see between a box-and-whisker plot of the original data and a box-and-whisker plot of the transformed data?

Logical Reasoning Complete the statement with *always, sometimes,* or *never*.

23. Transforming a set of data by adding a constant will __?__ change the range of the data set.

24. Transforming a set of data by multiplying by a positive constant will __?__ make the range of the new data set greater.

25. Transforming a set of data by multiplying by a positive constant will __?__ increase the mean, median, and mode of the data set.

Transformations and Calculation In Exercises 26–28, use the data set below. It shows the weights in kilograms of 6 male mule deer captured in a wildlife study.

83, 86, 89, 90, 91, 92

26. From examining the data, it appears that 89 might be a good estimate for the mean. Transform the data set by subtracting 89 from each value.

27. Find the mean of the transformed data set from Exercise 26. What does this mean represent?

28. Add the mean of the transformed data set to 89, the number used in the transformation. What does the result represent? Explain your reasoning, then verify your conclusion using the original data set.

Combining Transformations In Exercises 29 and 30, use the data set below. It shows the hourly wages of 8 retail workers.

$7.00, $7.40, $8.00, $8.00, $8.80, $9.60, $11.00, $13.00

29. The wages increase first by 5%, then by 25 cents per hour. Write an equation for the transformation where w is the original wage. Then transform the data.

30. What differences would you expect to see between a box-and-whisker plot of the original data and a box-and-whisker plot of the new data?

31. Challenge When multiplying a set of data by a positive constant c, what value(s) of c will make the range greater? What value(s) of c will make the range smaller? What value(s) of c will not change the range?

Standardized Test Practice

32. Multi-Step Problem Use the data set below. It shows the wholesale prices a department store pays per pair for various style of shoes.

$10, $20, $14, $8, $16, $18, $24, $34, $52, $30, $46, $40

a. Find the mean, median, range, and difference between the upper and lower quartiles for the wholesale prices.

b. Find the mean, median, range, and difference between the upper and lower quartiles for the retail prices if each pair is marked up $20 above wholesale.

c. Find the mean, median, range, and difference between the upper and lower quartiles for the retail prices if each pair is marked up 50% above wholesale.

d. What differences would you expect to see between the plots in a double box-and-whisker plot of the wholesale prices and the retail prices in part (b)?

e. What differences would you expect to see between the plots in a double box-and-whisker plot of the wholesale prices and the retail prices in part (c)?

Mixed Review

Substitution Method Solve the system using substitution. *(Lesson 3.5)*

33. $x + 2y - 3z = 1$
$x + z = 3$
$x - y = 1$

34. $y - 2z = 7$
$3x - y + z = -10$
$x + 2y = 0$

35. $x - 4z = -10$
$-2x + y + z = 3$
$3x - 2y - z = -2$

Graphing Inequalities Match the inequality with its graph. *(Lesson 4.2)*

36. $x + y < 1$

37. $y \geq x + 2$

38. $-x + y \leq -1$

A.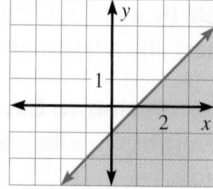

B.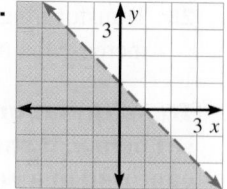

C.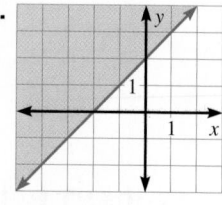

Geometry Skills

Translations Describe the translation from the blue triangle to the red triangle using coordinate notation.

39.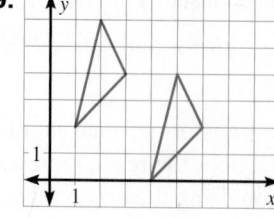

40.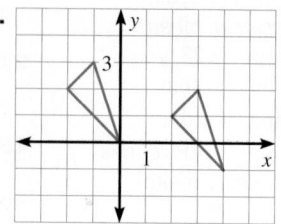

10.4 The Fundamental Counting Principle and Permutations

Key Words
- permutation
- factorial

Prerequisite Skills

Evaluate the expression.

1. $5 \times 4 \times 3 \times 2 \times 1$
2. $9 \times 8 \times 7 \times 6$
3. $\dfrac{4 \times 3 \times 2 \times 1}{3 \times 2 \times 1}$

GOAL Use the fundamental counting principle and permutations.

How can you find the number of meal possibilities at a cafeteria?

How many lunch specials can you choose from if you can choose chicken, pasta, or fish as a main dish and soup or salad as a side dish? One way to answer this question is to use a *tree diagram*, as shown below.

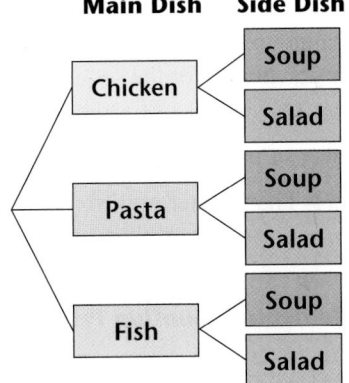

For each of the 3 main dishes, there are 2 possible side dishes, for a total of $3 \cdot 2 = 6$ different lunch special choices.

Fundamental Counting Principle

Two Events If one event can occur in *m* ways and another event can occur in *n* ways, then the number of ways that *both* events can occur is

$$m \cdot n$$

Three Events If one event can occur in *m* ways, a second event in *n* ways, and a third event in *p* ways, then the number of ways that *all three* events can occur is

$$m \cdot n \cdot p$$

The counting principle also extends to four or more events.

EXAMPLE 1 Use the Fundamental Counting Principle

Music You are ordering a case for your MP3 player. You can choose any of 30 colors for the main shell, any of 32 colors for the protective band, and any of 200 decals for the cover screen. How many different cases are possible?

Solution

Number of cases $= 30 \cdot 32 \cdot 200 = 192,000$

ANSWER ▶ There are 192,000 different cases.

EXAMPLE **2** **Use the Fundamental Counting Principle**

Passwords You are choosing a password that has 4 letters followed by 2 digits.

N C W J 3 7
4 letters   2 digits

a. How many passwords are possible if letters and digits can be repeated?

b. How many passwords are possible if letters and digits cannot be repeated?

Solution

a. There are **26** choices for each **letter** and **10** choices for each **digit**. Use the fundamental counting principle.

  Number of passwords = **26 • 26 • 26 • 26 • 10 • 10** = 45,697,600

  ANSWER ▶ The number of different passwords is 45,697,600.

b. If you cannot repeat letters and digits, there are 26 choices for the first letter, but only 25 choices for the second letter, 24 choices for the third letter, and so on. There are 10 choices for the first digit and 9 choices for the second digit.

  Number of passwords = **26 • 25 • 24 • 23 • 10 • 9** = 32,292,000

  ANSWER ▶ The number of different passwords is 32,292,000.

 **Use the Fundamental Counting Principle**

1. At the top of page 539, suppose that the lunch special also comes with your choice of 3 desserts. How many lunch specials are possible?

2. You are choosing a personal identification number (PIN) for your ATM card. The PIN has 4 digits. How many PINs are possible if digits can be repeated? if digits cannot be repeated?

Permutations An ordering of a set of objects is a **permutation** of the objects. By the fundamental counting principle, there are 3 • 2 • 1 = 6 permutations of 3 objects. For example, there are 6 permutations of the letters **A**, **B**, and **C**:

ABC   ACB   BAC   BCA   CAB   CBA

The expression 3 • 2 • 1 can also be written as 3!. The symbol ! is the **factorial** symbol, and 3! is read as "three factorial." In general, the number of permutations of *n* distinct objects is *n*!.

Permutations of *n* Objects

The number of permutations of *n* distinct objects is *n*!.

$$n! = n \cdot (n - 1) \cdot (n - 2) \cdot \cdots \cdot 3 \cdot 2 \cdot 1$$

EXAMPLES

4 Objects	5 Objects	6 Objects
4! = 4 • 3 • 2 • 1	5! = 5 • 4 • 3 • 2 • 1	6! = 6 • 5 • 4 • 3 • 2 • 1

EXAMPLE 3 Find the Number of Permutations

Link to
SPORTS

MOGULS skiing is one of two freestyle skiing events that are Olympic medal sports. Moguls skiing first became an Olympic medal sport at the 1992 Winter Olympics in Albertville, France.

Skiing Eight skiers are competing in a moguls (snow bumps) competition.

a. In how many different orders can the skiers finish the competition?

b. In how many different ways can 3 of the skiers finish first through third?

Solution

a. This is a permutation of 8 people. So, there are 8! different orders.

$$8! = 8 \cdot 7 \cdot 6 \cdot 5 \cdot 4 \cdot 3 \cdot 2 \cdot 1 = 40{,}320$$

ANSWER ▶ The skiers can finish in 40,320 different ways.

b. Any of the 8 skiers can finish first. Then one of 7 skiers can finish second. Then one of 6 skiers can finish third. The number of different orders is:

$$8 \cdot 7 \cdot 6 = 336$$

ANSWER ▶ The skiers can finish first through third in 336 different ways.

Using Factorial Notation In part (b) above, an ordered group of 3 skiers is taken from the group of 8 skiers. This is a permutation of **8 objects** taken **3 at a time**. It is denoted by $_8P_3$. This number can be expressed using factorial notation.

$$_8P_3 = 8 \cdot 7 \cdot 6 = \frac{8 \cdot 7 \cdot 6 \cdot 5 \cdot 4 \cdot 3 \cdot 2 \cdot 1}{5 \cdot 4 \cdot 3 \cdot 2 \cdot 1} = \frac{8!}{5!} = \frac{8!}{(8-3)!}$$

STUDENT HELP

AVOID ERRORS
The formula at the right suggests that if $r = n$,

$$_nP_n = \frac{n!}{(n-n)!} = \frac{n!}{0!}$$

In order for $_nP_n$ to be $n!$, the value of 0! must be 1. Zero factorial is defined this way:

$$0! = 1$$

Permutations of *n* Objects Taken *r* at a Time

The number of permutations of **n objects** taken **r at a time** is denoted by $_nP_r$ and is given by the following formula:

$$_nP_r = \frac{n!}{(n-r)!}$$

EXAMPLE 4 Permutations of *n* Objects Taken *r* at a Time

Text Messages You have 6 text messages on your cell phone. In how many orders can you reply to 4 of the messages? to all 6 of the messages?

Solution

Find the number of permutations of **6 objects** taken **4 at a time**.

$$_6P_4 = \frac{6!}{(6-4)!} = \frac{6!}{2!} = \frac{6 \cdot 5 \cdot 4 \cdot 3 \cdot 2 \cdot 1}{2 \cdot 1} = 6 \cdot 5 \cdot 4 \cdot 3 = 360$$

Find the number of permutations of **6 objects** taken **6 at a time**.

$$_6P_6 = \frac{6!}{(6-6)!} = \frac{6!}{0!} = \frac{6 \cdot 5 \cdot 4 \cdot 3 \cdot 2 \cdot 1}{1} = 720 \qquad \text{Remember: } 0! = 1.$$

Checkpoint ✓ Find Permutations

3. In how many different orders can 12 snowboarders finish a competition?

4. In how many orders can you respond to 5 of 8 text messages?

10.4 Exercises

Guided Practice

Vocabulary Check

1. Copy and complete the statement: An ordered arrangement of a set of objects is called a(n) __?__ of the set.

2. Describe how to evaluate $n!$ for a given nonnegative integer n.

Skill Check

3. Use the tree diagram to list all the possible outfits that you can make from the two pairs of jeans and 4 different T-shirts shown in the diagram.

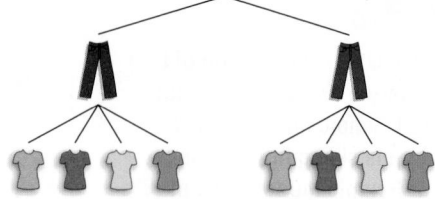

Evaluate the expression.

4. $4!$
5. $2!$
6. $\dfrac{7!}{6!}$
7. $\dfrac{5!}{3!}$

Find the number of permutations of n distinct objects.

8. $n = 3$
9. $n = 1$
10. $n = 5$
11. $n = 8$

Find the number of permutations of n objects taken r at a time.

12. $n = 5, r = 2$
13. $n = 5, r = 3$
14. $n = 5, r = 4$
15. $n = 5, r = 5$

16. **Passwords** You choose a password with 4 letters followed by 3 digits for your e-mail account. How many different passwords are possible (a) if letters and digits can be repeated, and (b) if letters and digits cannot be repeated?

Practice and Applications

STUDENT HELP

HOMEWORK HELP
Example 1: Exs. 17–24
Example 2: Exs. 25–30
Example 3: Exs. 31–42,
            55–60
Example 4: Exs. 43–60

Fundamental Counting Principle In Exercises 17–20, each event can occur in the given number of ways. Find the number of ways both or all of the events can occur.

17. Event A: 4 ways, Event B: 3 ways

18. Event A: 6 ways, Event B: 4 ways, Event C: 5 ways

19. Event A: 2 ways, Event B: 5 ways, Event C: 4 ways, Event D: 3 ways

20. Event A: 3 ways, Event B: 8 ways, Event C: 6 ways, Event D: 1 way

21. **Tree Diagram** Make a tree diagram to show all the possible combinations of class and time if you can take one of three sports classes (tennis, dance, or weight training) in one of first period, second period, or third period.

22. **Voting** There are 6 candidates for student council president, 3 candidates for vice-president, and 4 candidates for treasurer. In how many different ways can a president, vice-president, and treasurer be chosen?

23. **Pizza** You are ordering a pizza. You choose one of 3 sizes of pizza, one of 3 types of crust, one of 6 types of meat topping, and one of 5 types of vegetable topping. In how many different ways can you choose your pizza?

24. License Plates In some states you can choose a personalized license plate. Find how many different personalized license plates are possible (a) if the plate has 3 digits followed by 3 letters, and (b) if the plate has 2 digits followed by 4 letters.

Passwords Find how many different passwords are possible for the given configuration if (a) digits and letters can be repeated, and (b) digits and letters cannot be repeated.

25. 1 letter followed by 4 digits

26. 3 digits followed by 2 letters

27. 2 digits followed by 3 letters

28. 4 letters followed by 1 digit

Error Analysis Describe and correct the error.

29.

> Number of 3-digit numbers with only odd digits:
>
> total = 5 · 4 · 3
>
> = 60 ✗

30.

> Number of ways to arrange the letters C, O, D, E:
>
> total = 4 + 4 + 4 + 4
>
> = 16 ✗

Factorial Notation Evaluate the expression.

31. $5!$

32. $7!$

33. $0!$

34. $9!$

35. $\dfrac{5!}{2!}$

36. $\dfrac{8!}{3!}$

37. $\dfrac{6!}{4!}$

38. $\dfrac{10!}{8!}$

Permutations Find the number of permutations of *n* distinct objects.

39. $n = 2$

40. $n = 4$

41. $n = 6$

42. $n = 10$

Permutations Find the number of permutations of *n* objects taken *r* at a time.

43. $n = 6, r = 2$

44. $n = 7, r = 3$

45. $n = 8, r = 5$

46. $n = 9, r = 4$

Permutation Notation Find the number of permutations.

47. $_6P_3$

48. $_{10}P_4$

49. $_9P_9$

50. $_{14}P_2$

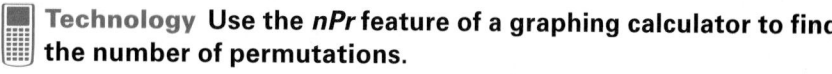 **Technology** Use the *nPr* feature of a graphing calculator to find the number of permutations.

51. $_{10}P_6$

52. $_{30}P_4$

53. $_{45}P_6$

54. $_{100}P_5$

Marathons Find how many different ways that the given number of runners can earn gold (first place), silver (second place), and bronze (third place) medals in a marathon race.

55. 10

56. 20

57. 30

58. 50

59. Movies You and a group of friends have a total of 45 movies. You decide to watch 3 of the movies together. Write and evaluate an expression that represents the number of ways you can select and watch 3 movies.

60. School A teacher selects 5 students from a class of 20 students to present their book reports next Monday. Write and evaluate an expression that represents the number of orders 5 students can be assigned to present their reports.

61. Reasoning Use the permutations formula to show that $_nP_1 = n$ for any positive integer n.

62. Challenge You are trying to remember a license plate number that consists of three letters followed by four digits. You remember the three letters, but can't remember what order they were in. You remember the first two digits in order, but can't remember the last two digits. Assuming letters and digits can repeat, how many possibilities are there for the license plate number?

Standardized Test Practice

63. Multiple Choice Your class is voting for class officers. There are 5 candidates for president, 3 for vice-president, and 6 for treasurer. How many different ways can a president, a vice-president, and a treasurer be chosen?

   A 14   **B** 60   **C** 90   **D** 846

64. Multiple Choice You are choosing a 5-digit password. The digits cannot be repeated. How many passwords are possible?

53931
not allowed

27805
allowed

   F 25   **G** 3125   **H** 5040   **J** 30,240

65. Multiple Choice How many permutations are there of 7 objects taken 3 at a time?

   A 21   **B** 210   **C** 343   **D** 2187

Mixed Review

Inequalities Tell whether the given number is a solution of the inequality. *(Lesson 4.5)*

66. $|x| \le 5; 3$

67. $\left|x + \dfrac{1}{4}\right| > 10; 0$

68. $|x - 10| \ge 5; 5$

69. $|3x + 6| \le 8; 1$

70. $|5x - 2| < 8; 2$

71. $\left|\dfrac{1}{2}x - 2\right| < 4; 10$

Solving Equations Using nth Roots Solve the equation. *(Lesson 7.1)*

72. $x^3 = 27$

73. $7x^3 = 189$

74. $\dfrac{1}{4}x^4 = 4$

75. $(x + 6)^4 = 16$

Geometry Skills

Surface Area of a Prism Find the indicated measurement for the rectangular prism shown below.

STUDENT HELP

SKILLS REVIEW
You can find the table of geometry formulas on page 798.

76. area of the base

77. perimeter of the base

78. Use the results from Exercises 76 and 77 to find the surface area of the prism.

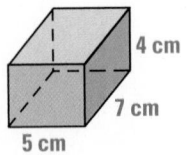
4 cm
7 cm
5 cm

Surface Area of a Cylinder Find the indicated measurement for the cylinder shown below. Use 3.14 for π. Round your answer to two decimal places.

79. area of the base

80. circumference of the base

81. Use the results from Exercises 79 and 80 to find the surface area of the cylinder.

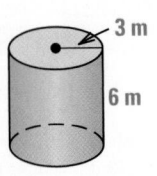
3 m
6 m

10.5 Combinations and Pascal's Triangle

Key Words
- combination
- Pascal's triangle

Prerequisite Skills

Find the number of permutations.

1. $_8P_3$

2. $_5P_5$

3. $_4P_2$

4. $_7P_4$

GOAL Use combinations and relate them to Pascal's triangle.

How many groups of 3 can be chosen from 4?

The number of orders in which 3 student volunteers can be chosen from 4 at a nonprofit organization's worksite is the number of permutations of 4 objects taken 3 at a time: $_4P_3 = 24$. But if the 3 students are all given the same task, the order in which they are chosen does not matter.

A **combination** is a selection of r objects from a group of n objects where the *order is not important*.

Combinations of n Objects Taken r at a Time

The number of combinations of n distinct objects taken r at a time is indicated by $_nC_r$, and is given by the formula:

$$_nC_r = \frac{_nP_r}{r!} = \frac{n!}{(n-r)! \cdot r!}$$

EXAMPLE 1 Find Combinations

STUDENT HELP

SOLVING NOTE
Choosing 3 of 4 students to be painters is the same as choosing 1 of the 4 *not* to be a painter. Notice:

$$_4C_1 = \frac{4!}{(4-1)! \cdot 1!} = \frac{4!}{3!} = 4$$

So, $_4C_1 = _4C_3$.
In general, $_nC_r = _nC_{n-r}$.

Volunteering Jamal, Kay, Li, and Max have volunteered to help a nonprofit organization build houses. Three of the 4 will be assigned to work as painters. How many choices are there for the 3 painters?

Solution

Use the combinations formula with $n = 4$ and $r = 3$.

$$_4C_3 = \frac{4!}{(4-3)! \cdot 3!} = \frac{4!}{1! \cdot 3!} = \frac{4!}{3!} = \frac{4 \cdot 3!}{3!} = 4$$

Notice: $4! = 4 \cdot 3 \cdot 2 \cdot 1$ and $3! = 3 \cdot 2 \cdot 1$, so $4! = 4 \cdot 3!$.

You can also list all the orders in which the three students can be chosen, then cross out any repeated listings of a group of the same three students.

JKL	~~JLK~~	~~KJL~~	~~KLJ~~	~~LJK~~	~~LKJ~~
JKM	~~JMK~~	~~KJM~~	~~KMJ~~	~~MJK~~	~~MKJ~~
JLM	~~JML~~	~~LJM~~	~~LMJ~~	~~MJL~~	~~MLJ~~
KLM	~~KML~~	~~LKM~~	~~LMK~~	~~MKL~~	~~MLK~~

Each row represents a single group of three students.

The list shows why the number of combinations is the number of permutations (24) divided by the number of ways of ordering each group of three students (6).

ANSWER There are 4 different groups of 3 painters that can be chosen from the 4 original volunteers.

 **Find Combinations**

1. In Example 1, suppose that the 3 painters are chosen from a group of 5 student volunteers. How many choices are there for the 3 painters?

EXAMPLE **2** **Distinguish Permutations and Combinations**

Tell whether the question can be answered using a *permutation* or a *combination*. Then find the answer.

a. For summer reading, you are asked to read 2 books from a list of 6 books. How many different pairs of books can you choose to read?

b. Twelve students enter a talent show. Awards are given for first place through fifth place. In how many ways can the students finish first through fifth?

Solution

 **STUDENT HELP**

AVOID ERRORS
You must perform the operation in parentheses first.
$(6 - 2)! \neq 6! - 2!$

a. The order in which you choose the books *is not* important. Use a combination to answer the question.

$$_6C_2 = \frac{6!}{(6-2)! \cdot 2!} = \frac{6!}{4! \cdot 2!} = \frac{6 \cdot 5 \cdot 4!}{4! \cdot 2} = 15 \text{ pairs of books}$$

b. The order in which the awards are given *is* important. Use a permutation to answer the question.

$$_{12}P_5 = \frac{12!}{(12-5)!} = \frac{12!}{7!} = \frac{12 \cdot 11 \cdot 10 \cdot 9 \cdot 8 \cdot 7!}{7!} = 95,040 \text{ ways}$$

 **Distinguish Permutations and Combinations**

Tell whether the question can be answered using a *permutation* or a *combination*. Then find the answer.

2. In how many ways can you play 3 of the 11 songs on a CD?

3. In how many ways can a soccer team choose 2 captains from 12 players?

Multiple Events From 5 students, you can choose $_5C_3 = 10$ groups of 3. But if the group of 5 consists of 3 girls and 2 boys, and you want to select a group of 3 with exactly 2 girls *and* 1 boy, then there are two events: choose the girls, and choose the boy. This is a *multiple event*.

1st event: Choose 2 of 3 girls. $_3C_2 = 3$ choices

2nd event: Choose 1 of 2 boys. $_2C_1 = 2$ choices

You can choose the girls in 3 ways and the boy in 2 ways, so use the fundamental counting principle. You can choose the group of 2 girls and 1 boy in $3 \cdot 2 = 6$ ways.

A deck of playing cards can help you to investigate combinations of simple events and of multiple events. A standard deck contains 52 cards, as shown.

There are 13 cards in each of the 4 *suits*: spades (♠), hearts (♥), diamonds (♦), and clubs (♣). In each suit there are cards numbered 2 through 10, an ace (A), and 3 face cards: the king (K), queen (Q), and jack (J).

K ♠	K ♥	K ♦	K ♣
Q ♠	Q ♥	Q ♦	Q ♣
J ♠	J ♥	J ♦	J ♣
10 ♠	10 ♥	10 ♦	10 ♣
9 ♠	9 ♥	9 ♦	9 ♣
8 ♠	8 ♥	8 ♦	8 ♣
7 ♠	7 ♥	7 ♦	7 ♣
6 ♠	6 ♥	6 ♦	6 ♣
5 ♠	5 ♥	5 ♦	5 ♣
4 ♠	4 ♥	4 ♦	4 ♣
3 ♠	3 ♥	3 ♦	3 ♣
2 ♠	2 ♥	2 ♦	2 ♣
A ♠	A ♥	A ♦	A ♣

EXAMPLE 3 Find Combinations of Multiple Events

Cards Consider a standard deck of 52 playing cards. The order in which the cards are dealt for a "hand" does not matter.

  a. How many different 5-card hands are possible?

  b. How many different 5-card hands have all 5 cards of a single suit?

Solution

STUDENT HELP

READING MATH
In part (b), the word "and" does not appear to indicate that this is a multiple event, but "a *single* suit" hints that you are making a choice from the 4 suits.

  a. This is a simple combination with $n = 52$ and $r = 5$. The number of hands is:

$$_{52}C_5 = \frac{52!}{47! \cdot 5!} = \frac{52 \cdot 51 \cdot 50 \cdot 49 \cdot 48 \cdot \cancel{47!}}{\cancel{47!} \cdot 5 \cdot 4 \cdot 3 \cdot 2 \cdot 1} = 2{,}598{,}960 \text{ hands}$$

  b. This is a multiple event: You must choose the suit *and* choose the cards within the suit. You can choose 1 suit from 4 in $_4C_1$ ways. You can choose 5 cards from the 13 in a suit in $_{13}C_5$ ways. Multiply to find the total number of hands.

$$_4C_1 \cdot {_{13}C_5} = \frac{4!}{3! \cdot 1!} \cdot \frac{13!}{8! \cdot 5!} = 4 \cdot \frac{13 \cdot 12 \cdot 11 \cdot 10 \cdot 9 \cdot \cancel{8!}}{\cancel{8!} \cdot 5 \cdot 4 \cdot 3 \cdot 2 \cdot 1} = 5148 \text{ hands}$$

Checkpoint ✔ Find Combinations of Multiple Events

  4. How many different 5-card hands have all 5 cards of a single color?

  5. How many ways can you choose 3 dogs and 2 cats from 5 dogs and 6 cats?

Pascal's Triangle If you arrange the values of $_nC_r$ in a triangular pattern in which each row corresponds to a value of n, you get a pattern called **Pascal's triangle**, shown below using both combinations notation and numbers.

$n = 0$ (0th row)	$_0C_0$	1
$n = 1$ (1st row)	$_1C_0 \quad _1C_1$	1 1
$n = 2$ (2nd row)	$_2C_0 \quad _2C_1 \quad _2C_2$	1 2 1
$n = 3$ (3rd row)	$_3C_0 \quad _3C_1 \quad _3C_2 \quad _3C_3$	1 3 3 1
$n = 4$ (4th row)	$_4C_0 \quad _4C_1 \quad _4C_2 \quad _4C_3 \quad _4C_4$	1 4 6 4 1
$n = 5$ (5th row)	$_5C_0 \quad _5C_1 \quad _5C_2 \quad _5C_3 \quad _5C_4 \quad _5C_5$	1 5 10 10 5 1

The first and last numbers in each row of Pascal's triangle are 1. Every other number is the sum of the two closest numbers in the row just above it.

EXAMPLE **4** Use Pascal's Triangle

Social Networking Use Pascal's triangle to find the number of groups of 4 of your friends you can choose from among 6 of your friends to post as "friends" on your profile on a social networking website.

Solution

The sixth row of Pascal's triangle represents combinations of 6 objects taken r at a time where r is from 0 to 6: $_6C_0$, $_6C_1$, $_6C_2$, $_6C_3$, $_6C_4$, $_6C_5$, $_6C_6$. You need to find $_6C_4$. Add entries from the fifth row to find the number corresponding to $_6C_4$.

$n = 5$ (5th row)   1   5   10   10   5   1

$n = 6$ (6th row) 1   6   15   20   15   6   1
                  $_6C_0$ $_6C_1$ $_6C_2$ $_6C_3$ $_6C_4$ $_6C_5$ $_6C_6$

ANSWER ▶ There are 15 different groups of 4 friends from a group of 6 friends.

Checkpoint ✓ **Use Pascal's Triangle**

6. Write the seventh row of Pascal's triangle using both combinations notation and numbers. Use your results to find the number of combinations of 5 fruits you can choose from among 7 fruits for a fruit salad.

10.5 Exercises

Guided Practice

Vocabulary Check

1. Describe the difference between a *combination* of n objects taken r at a time and a *permutation* of n objects taken r at a time. Give an example to illustrate the difference in the numerical result for specific values of n and r.

2. Describe the relationship between Pascal's triangle and combinations.

Skill Check

3. Use an ordered list to find all the combinations of 2 of the colors red, green, yellow, and blue that can be chosen as team colors.

Find the number of combinations of *n* objects taken *r* at a time.

4. $n = 5, r = 5$ **5.** $n = 5, r = 4$ **6.** $n = 5, r = 1$ **7.** $n = 5, r = 3$

In Exercises 8 and 9, tell whether the question can be answered using a *permutation* or a *combination*. Then find the answer.

8. Video Clips You are going to send 3 video clips to a friend as attachments to an e-mail. How many different groups of 3 video clips can you choose from 7 video clips?

9. Vacations You wanted to see 7 tourist sites on your vacation, but decide you have time to see only 4. In how many orders can you visit 4 of the 7 sites?

10. Movies How many different groups of 2 comedies and 1 drama can you select from 6 comedies and 5 dramas?

Practice and Applications

Pizza In Exercises 11–13, use the following information.

You are ordering pizza for a birthday party. You plan to choose 2 toppings from 5 available toppings: pepperoni (p), hamburger (h), mushrooms (m), olives (o), and roasted peppers (r).

11. Use an ordered list to find all possible pairs of toppings.

12. How many different choices of 2 toppings do you have?

13. When you place your order, you learn that extra cheese is also an available topping. How many different choices of 2 toppings do you have now?

Combinations Find the number of combinations.

14. $_6C_0$ **15.** $_4C_4$ **16.** $_8C_1$ **17.** $_6C_3$

18. $_7C_3$ **19.** $_8C_4$ **20.** $_{10}C_2$ **21.** $_9C_5$

22. Dance Groups A choreographer needs 4 dancers to perform a work. How many different combinations of 4 dancers can the choreographer choose from a dance company consisting of 9 dancers?

23. Entertainment A comedian begins a routine by choosing 4 people from the audience. How many different groups of 4 people can the comedian choose from an audience of 50 people?

Permutations and Combinations In Exercises 24–27, tell whether the question can be answered using a *permutation* or a *combination*. Then find the answer.

24. Track In a 4 by 100 meter relay race, a different runner runs each of the four successive 100 meter "legs" of the race. In how many ways can 4 from a group of 8 runners be assigned to run the legs of the race?

25. Basketball Each March, 64 teams complete the "bracket" in the Division 1 college basketball tournament. How many possibilities are there for the 4 teams that advance from these 64 to the semifinals, known as the "Final Four?"

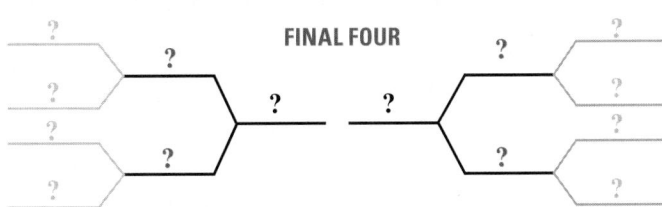

FINAL FOUR

26. Kentucky Derby Twenty horses competed in the 2006 Kentucky Derby. In how many ways could the horses have finished in first place through third place?

27. Work Groups Your teacher divides the class into groups of 5 for an activity. How many possibilities are there for the group that contains you if there are 25 students in the class in all? (*Hint:* How many remain to be chosen?)

28. Menus Planners for a company party will choose 2 of 4 vegetarian entrees and 3 of 6 meat entrees for the buffet. How many entree combinations are possible?

29. Government A *conference committee* is formed to reconcile different versions of a law passed by the U.S. Senate and U.S. House of Representatives. How many possible conference committees can be formed by choosing 3 out of a committee of 10 Senate members and 3 out of a committee of 16 House members?

Card Hands In Exercises 30–35, use the description of a standard 52-card deck given at the top of page 547 to find the number of possible 5-card hands that contain the specified cards.

30. 5 hearts

31. 2 twos and 3 threes

32. 5 face cards

33. 4 aces and 1 other card

34. 2 hearts and 3 diamonds

35. 4 cards of one number and an ace

36. Card Games When two people play the card game "Go Fish," each person begins the game with a 7-card hand. How many different 7-card hands contain 4 cards with the same value (four 2's, four 6's, four jacks, and so on)?

EXAMPLE **Adding Combinations**

Postcards You are on vacation and have a list of 12 friends that you want to send postcards. How many different sets of friends can you send postcards if:

a. you send postcards to at most 3 of them?

b. you send postcards to at least 10 of them?

Solution

a. You can choose 0 or 1 or 2 or 3. *Or* indicates addition. The total number is:

$$_{12}C_0 + {}_{12}C_1 + {}_{12}C_2 + {}_{12}C_3 = 1 + 12 + 66 + 220 = 299$$

b. You can choose 10 or 11 or 12. The total number is:

$$_{12}C_{10} + {}_{12}C_{11} + {}_{12}C_{12} = 66 + 12 + 1 = 79$$

Adding Combinations You've been given 9 extra-credit math problems. How many combinations of the given numbers of problems can you choose?

37. at least 8

38. at most 4

39. from 5 to 7

Pascal's Triangle Write the indicated row of Pascal's triangle using both combinations notation and numbers.

40. eighth row

41. ninth row

42. tenth row

43. Critical Thinking Which is larger, $_{50}C_9$ or $_{50}C_{41}$? Explain how you can tell without performing the calculations.

Challenge Show that the identity is true for any whole number *n*.

44. $_nC_0 = 1$

45. $_nC_n = 1$

46. $_nC_r = {}_nC_{n-r}$

Standardized Test Practice

47. Multiple Choice Which expression is equivalent to $_{11}C_7$?

(A) $\dfrac{7!}{(11-7)!}$ (B) $\dfrac{7!}{(11-7)! \cdot 7!}$ (C) $\dfrac{11!}{(11-7)!}$ (D) $\dfrac{11!}{(11-7)! \cdot 7!}$

48. Multiple Choice What is the value of $_8C_5$?

(F) 6720 (G) 336 (H) 56 (J) 40

49. Multiple Choice In how many ways can you choose 3 fish from 15?

(A) 0 (B) 220 (C) 455 (D) 2730

Mixed Review

50. Comparing Areas The radius of a circle is 7 times the radius of a smaller circle. How many times greater is the area of the larger circle than the area of the smaller circle? *(Lesson 6.1)*

51. Real Zeros How many real zeros does the function whose graph is shown have? Explain how you can tell immediately that the graph cannot be the graph of $y = x^3 - \frac{17}{4}x^2 + 1$. *(Lesson 6.6)*

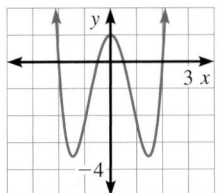

52. Permutations Ten bands are marching in a parade. In how many ways can you order (a) all 10 bands (b) the first 3 of the 10 bands? *(Lesson 10.4)*

Geometry Skills

Triangles Classify the triangle as *equilateral*, *isosceles*, or *scalene*.

53.

54.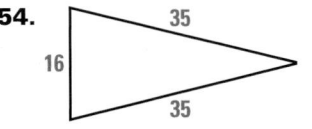

55.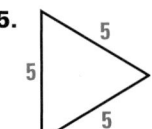

Quiz 2

Lesson 10.3

Sales Taxes **In Exercises 1 and 2, use the data showing the city sales tax rates for several Colorado locations in 2007.**

City/Town	Sales Tax	City/Town	Sales Tax
Alamosa	2%	Grand Junction	2.75%
Colorado Springs	2.5%	Pueblo	3.5%
Denver	3.62%	Winter Park	5%

1. In 2007, Colorado also had a 2.9% state sales tax. Transform the original data to show the combined city and state sales taxes charged in each location.

2. Without calculating, tell how the mean, median, mode, and range of the transformed data will compare to the same measures in the original data.

Lesson 10.4

Find the number of permutations.

3. $_5P_2$ **4.** $_8P_7$ **5.** $_{12}P_6$ **6.** $_{16}P_3$

Lesson 10.5

Find the number of combinations.

7. $_4C_2$ **8.** $_{10}C_8$ **9.** $_{13}C_7$ **10.** $_{14}C_{10}$

In Exercises 11–13, tell whether the number of possibilities can be found using a *permutation* or a *combination*. Then find the answer.

11. Amusement Parks An amusement park ride seats 4 people in a row. In how many ways can you and 3 friends be seated on the ride?

12. Concerts At an all-day concert, 12 bands are performing on the main stage. How many different possibilities are there of 4 of the bands that you can see?

13. Game Show A contestant on a game show has to choose 3 cases to open from 5 cases. How many possibilities are there for which cases to open?

In Lessons 10.4 and 10.5, you found permutations and combinations using
formulas. Some calculators have special keys or menu items designed for
evaluating permutations and combinations.

EXPLORE

Use a calculator to evaluate the expression.

a. $_{20}P_6$

b. $_{25}C_8$

Solution

a. Enter the expression $_{20}P_6$ into your
calculator. Notice that you enter
the value for n before accessing
the permutations command.

Keystrokes

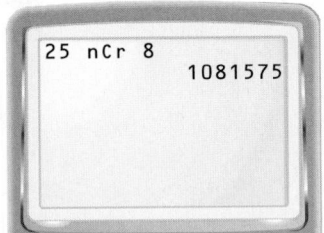

```
20 nPr 6
              27907200
```

b. Enter the expression $_{25}C_8$ into your
calculator. Notice that you enter
the value for n before accessing
the combinations command.

Keystrokes

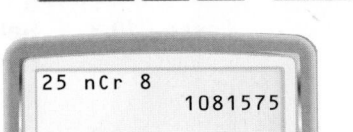

```
25 nCr 8
               1081575
```

EXERCISES

Permutations and Combinations **Use a calculator to evaluate the
permutation or combination.**

1. $_{12}P_9$

2. $_{20}P_4$

3. $_{16}P_5$

4. $_{80}P_3$

5. $_{80}P_5$

6. $_{80}P_{10}$

7. $_{11}C_6$

8. $_{14}C_9$

9. $_{22}C_{12}$

10. $_{24}C_4$

11. $_{38}C_{10}$

12. $_{30}C_{22}$

**Tell whether the number of possibilities can be found using a
permutation or a *combination*. Then answer the question.**

13. Employee Relations A 10 person employee advisory committee will be
selected from 180 workers at a business. How many possibilities are there for
the committee?

14. Lotteries In a lottery, six winning numbers are removed from a tumbler
containing balls with the numbers 1 through 40. How many possibilities are
there for the winning numbers?

15. Music You have room to place 30 of your 56 CDs on a rack. In how many
ways can you choose and place the CDs on the rack?

Pascal's Triangle and the Binomial Theorem

GOAL Relate Pascal's triangle to the terms of a binomial expansion.

In Lesson 10.5 you saw values of $_nC_r$ arranged in a triangular pattern to obtain *Pascal's triangle:*

$n = 0$ (0th row)	$_0C_0$	1
$n = 1$ (1st row)	$_1C_0 \quad _1C_1$	1 1
$n = 2$ (2nd row)	$_2C_0 \quad _2C_1 \quad _2C_2$	1 2 1
$n = 3$ (3rd row)	$_3C_0 \quad _3C_1 \quad _3C_2 \quad _3C_3$	1 3 3 1
$n = 4$ (4th row)	$_4C_0 \quad _4C_1 \quad _4C_2 \quad _4C_3 \quad _4C_4$	1 4 6 4 1
$n = 5$ (5th row)	$_5C_0 \quad _5C_1 \quad _5C_2 \quad _5C_3 \quad _5C_4 \quad _5C_5$	1 5 10 10 5 1

The numbers in Pascal's triangle have a very helpful algebraic connection. Recall the special product patterns for the square and cube of a binomial:

$$(a + b)^2 = a^2 + 2ab + b^2 = 1a^2 + 2ab + 1b^2 \quad \leftarrow \text{2nd row}$$
$$(a + b)^3 = a^3 + 3a^2b + 3ab^2 + b^3 = 1a^3 + 3a^2b + 3ab^2 + 1b^3 \quad \leftarrow \text{3rd row}$$

Notice the following about these expansions:

- The coefficients of the terms in the expansion of $(a + b)^n$ are the numbers in row n of Pascal's triangle.

- The powers of a decrease from n in the first term to 0 in the last term ($a^0 = 1$).

- The powers of b increase from 0 in the first term ($b^0 = 1$) to n in the last term.

EXAMPLE 1 Expand a Power of a Simple Binomial Sum

Expand $(a + b)^4$.

Solution

In $(a + b)^4$, the power is $n = 4$. So, the coefficients of the terms are the numbers in the 4th row of Pascal's Triangle.

Coefficients: 1, 4, 6, 4, 1

Powers of a: a^4, a^3, a^2, a^1, a^0

Powers of b: b^0, b^1, b^2, b^3, b^4

$$(a + b)^4 = 1a^4b^0 + 4a^3b^1 + 6a^2b^2 + 4a^1b^3 + 1a^0b^4$$
$$= a^4 + 4a^3b + 6a^2b^2 + 4ab^3 + b^4$$

Example 1 illustrates a more general result called the *binomial theorem*.

> ## The Binomial Theorem
>
> For any positive integer n, the expansion of $(a + b)^n$ is:
>
> $$(a + b)^n = {}_nC_0 a^n b^0 + {}_nC_1 a^{n-1} b^1 + {}_nC_2 a^{n-2} b^2 + \cdots + {}_nC_n a^0 b^n$$
>
> Note that each term has the form ${}_nC_r a^{n-r} b^r$ where r is an integer from 0 to n.

EXAMPLE 2 Expand a Power of a Binomial Sum

Expand $(x + 5)^3$.

Solution

Use the binomial theorem with $a = x$ and $b = 5$.

$$(x + 5)^3 = {}_3C_0 x^3 5^0 + {}_3C_1 x^2 5^1 + {}_3C_2 x^1 5^2 + {}_3C_3 x^0 5^3$$

$$= (1)(x^3)(1) + (3)(x^2)(5) + (3)(x^1)(25) + (1)(x^0)(125)$$

$$= x^3 + 15x^2 + 75x + 125$$

Note that in Example 2 you could have used the third row of Pascal's triangle to write the first step above as $(x + 5)^3 = 1x^3 5^0 + 3x^2 5^1 + 3x^1 5^2 + 1x^0 5^3$.

EXAMPLE 3 Expand a Power of a Binomial Difference

Expand $(2x - y)^4$.

Solution

First rewrite the difference as a sum: $(2x - y)^4 = [2x + (-y)]^4$.

Then use the binomial theorem with $a = 2x$ and $b = -y$.

$$[2x + (-y)]^4 = {}_4C_0(2x)^4(-y)^0 + {}_4C_1(2x)^3(-y)^1 + {}_4C_2(2x)^2(-y)^2 +$$
$$\qquad {}_4C_3(2x)^1(-y)^3 + {}_4C_4(2x)^0(-y)^4$$

$$= (1)(16x^4)(1) + (4)(8x^3)(-y) + (6)(4x^2)(y^2) +$$
$$\qquad (4)(2x)(-y^3) + (1)(1)(y^4)$$

$$= 16x^4 - 32x^3 y + 24x^2 y^2 - 8xy^3 + y^4$$

 **Checkpoint** ✔ *Expand a Power of a Binomial Sum or Difference*

Expand the power of the binomial sum or difference.

1. $(a + b)^5$ **2.** $(x + 2)^4$ **3.** $(3x + 5)^3$

4. $(p - 4)^3$ **5.** $(m - n)^4$ **6.** $(3s - t)^3$

Patterns When you examine the numbers in Pascal's triangle closely, you will discover many number patterns.

EXAMPLE 4 **Find Patterns in Pascal's Triangle**

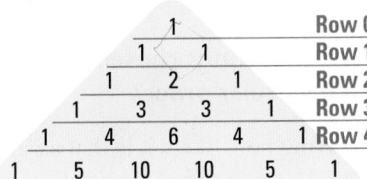

a. Find the sums of the entries in rows 0 through 4 of Pascal's triangle. Then predict the sum of the entries in row 11.

b. Find the sums of the entries along the diagonals indicated in the diagram. Then predict the next three sums.

Solution

a. The sums of rows 0 through 4 are 1, 2, 4, 8, and 16. Notice that these are the powers of 2: $2^0, 2^1, 2^2, 2^3, 2^4$. The sum of the entries in row 11 is $2^{11} = 2048$.

b. The sums are 1, 1, 2, 3, 5, 8. Each of these numbers after the first is the sum of the two numbers before it. (These are the *Fibonacci numbers*.) The next three sums will be $5 + 8 = 13$, $8 + 13 = 21$, and $13 + 21 = 34$.

Exercises

1. **Using Patterns** Copy rows 0 through 5 of Pascal's triangle from the top of this page. Then add rows for $n = 6, 7, 8,$ and 9.

Pascal's Triangle **Use the rows of Pascal's triangle from Exercise 1 to expand the power of the binomial.**

2. $(a + b)^6$ 3. $(x + y)^7$ 4. $(s + t)^9$

5. **Distributive Property** Verify the results of Example 1 by using the distributive property to expand $(a + b)^4$.

Binomial Theorem **Use the binomial theorem to expand the power of the binomial.**

6. $(a + 2)^5$ 7. $(2x + 1)^4$ 8. $(y + z)^5$

9. $(t - 5)^3$ 10. $(x - y)^5$ 11. $(3x - y)^4$

12. **Challenge** Use the binomial theorem to write the expansion of $(x^3 + 2y^2)^5$.

13. **Patterns** For rows 2 through 5 of Pascal's triangle, alternately subtract and add all the entries, as shown below.

$$1 - 2 + 1$$
$$1 - 3 + 3 - 1$$
$$1 - 4 + 6 - 4 + 1$$

What do you notice? Verify that this pattern continues for rows 6 through 9.

10.6 Introduction to Probability

Key Words

- outcome
- event
- probability
- theoretical probability
- experimental probability
- geometric probability

Prerequisite Skills

You are packing for a trip. You have 8 shirts and 6 pairs of pants.

1. How many different choices of 3 pairs of pants can you pack?

2. If you pack 5 shirts, in how many different ways can you choose 2 of them to wear on the first and second days?

GOAL Find theoretical and experimental probabilities.

How likely is it that songs chosen at random will play in a particular order?

Questions involving how likely it is that a particular thing will happen can be answered in terms of *probabilities*.

Consider a list of songs playing in random order. All the possible orders the songs can play in are *outcomes*. An *event* is a particular outcome or a group of outcomes. For example, your favorite song playing last is an event.

The **probability** of an event is a number from 0 to 1 that tells how likely it is to occur. If an event *must* occur, its probability is 1; if it *cannot* occur, its probability is 0. If an event is *equally likely* to occur or not, its probability is $\frac{1}{2}$.

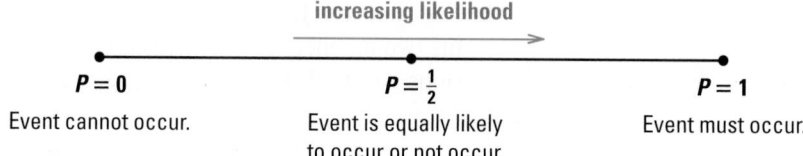

increasing likelihood

$P = 0$	$P = \frac{1}{2}$	$P = 1$
Event cannot occur.	Event is equally likely to occur or not occur.	Event must occur.

A probability can be expressed as a fraction, a decimal, or a percent.

Theoretical Probability of an Event

When all outcomes are equally likely, the **theoretical probability** that an event A will occur is:

$$P(A) = \frac{\text{Number of outcomes in event } A}{\text{Total number of outcomes}}$$

The theoretical probability of an event is often simply called its probability.

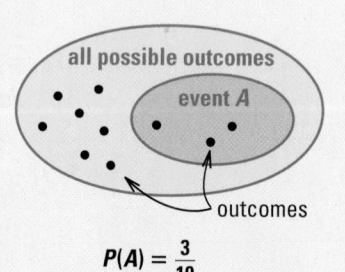

all possible outcomes

event A

outcomes

$P(A) = \frac{3}{10}$

EXAMPLE 1 Find the Probability of an Event

What is the probability that the spinner shown lands on red if it is equally likely to land on any section?

Solution

The 8 sections represent the 8 possible outcomes. Three outcomes correspond to the event "lands on red."

$$P(\text{red}) = \frac{\text{Number of outcomes in event}}{\text{Total number of outcomes}} = \frac{3}{8}$$

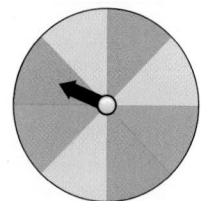

STUDENT HELP

READING ALGEBRA
In Example 1, you can alternately express the probability $\frac{3}{8}$ as 0.375 or $37\frac{1}{2}\%$.

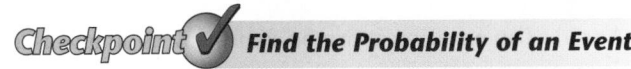 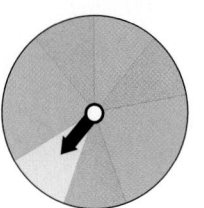

Checkpoint ✓ **Find the Probability of an Event**

Use the spinner shown to find the given probability.

1. lands on yellow
2. lands on green
3. lands on white
4. does not land on red

EXAMPLE 2 **Use Permutations or Combinations**

Music You have 8 songs on your workout songs MP3 playlist. You set your player to play all the songs on the list in random order without repeating any songs.

   a. What is the probability that the songs play in the exact opposite order they are listed in your playlist?

   b. Three of the songs on the playlist are by the same group. What is the probability that 2 of the songs by this group play first, in any order?

Solution

   a. Any ordering, or *permutation*, of the songs is a possible outcome. There are 8! permutations of the songs, but only 1 has the opposite order of your playlist.

$$P(\text{8 songs play in reverse order}) = \frac{1}{8!} = \frac{1}{40{,}320} \approx 0.000025$$

   b. The order in the group of 2 songs is not important. From the whole playlist, there are $_8C_2$ different *combinations* of 2 songs that can play as the first group of 2. From the 3 songs by the same group, there are $_3C_2$ combinations of 2.

$$P(\text{2 songs by the group play first}) = \frac{\text{combinations of 2 songs by the group}}{\text{total combinations of 2 songs}}$$

$$= \frac{_3C_2}{_8C_2}$$

$$= \frac{3}{28} \approx 0.11, \text{ or about } 11\%$$

Checkpoint ✓ **Use Permutations or Combinations**

5. Suppose in Example 2 that 4 of the songs on your playlist are jazz. What is the probability that these 4 songs play last, in any order?

Experimental Probability It's not always possible or convenient to find an event's theoretical probability. By conducting an experiment or survey or by looking at an event's history, you can find the *experimental probability* of an event.

Experimental Probability of an Event

For a given number of trials of an experiment, the **experimental probability** that an event A will occur is:

$$P(A) = \frac{\text{Number of trials where } A \text{ occurs}}{\text{Total number of trials}}$$

Experiments A trial of an experiment can be something as simple as a flip of a coin. A survey is an experiment where each response is a single trial.

EXAMPLE ③ Find Experimental Probabilities

Surveys The graph shows results of a survey asking students to name their favorite type of footwear. What is the experimental probability that a randomly chosen student prefers (a) sneakers or (b) shoes or boots?

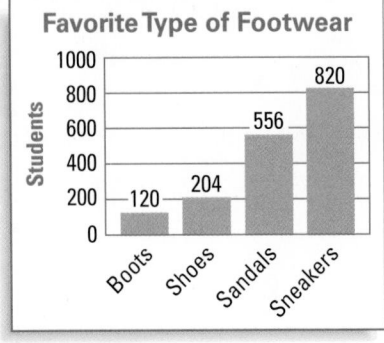

Favorite Type of Footwear

Solution

Find the total number of students surveyed.

$$820 + 556 + 204 + 120 = 1700$$

a. Of 1700 students, 820 prefer sneakers.

$$P(\text{prefers sneakers}) = \frac{\text{Number preferring sneakers}}{\text{Total number of students}} = \frac{820}{1700} \approx 0.48$$

b. Of 1700 students surveyed, $204 + 120 = 324$ prefer shoes or boots.

$$P(\text{prefers shoes or boots}) = \frac{\text{Number preferring shoes or boots}}{\text{Total number of students}} = \frac{324}{1700} \approx 0.19$$

STUDENT HELP

SOLVING NOTE
In a large, well-designed experiment or survey, an event's experimental probability should be a good approximation of its theoretical probability.

Geometric Probabilities You can find probabilities based on ratios of two lengths, areas, or volumes. These are called **geometric probabilities**.

EXAMPLE ④ Find a Geometric Probability

Archery You shoot an arrow at the target shown, whose diameter is 40 inches. The red bull's-eye is 8 inches in diameter. The rings have equal widths. If the arrow is equally likely to hit anywhere on the target, what is the probability it lands in the outermost ring?

Solution

The width of each of the rings is $(20 - 4) \div 4 = 4$ inches.

$$P(\text{outermost ring}) = \frac{\text{Area of the outermost ring}}{\text{Area of the entire target}}$$

$$= \frac{\pi \cdot 20^2 - \pi \cdot 16^2}{\pi \cdot 20^2}$$

$$= \frac{9}{25}, \text{ or } 36\%$$

 **Find Experimental and Geometric Probabilities**

6. Use the information in Example 3 to find the experimental probability that a randomly chosen student prefers (a) boots or (b) shoes or sandals.

7. In Example 4, what is the probability that the arrow lands in the bull's-eye?

10.6 Exercises

Guided Practice

Vocabulary Check

1. Copy and complete the statement: A probability found by calculating a ratio of two lengths, areas, or volumes is called a(n) __?__ probability.

2. Copy and complete the statement: To find a(n) __?__ probability, divide the number of trials in which an event occurs by the total number of trials.

Skill Check

A jar contains 3 red marbles, 2 blue marbles, and 2 green marbles. Find the probability of drawing the given type of marble at random.

3. a red marble

4. a blue marble

5. a red or a green marble

6. a blue or a green marble

Find the probability that a dart thrown at the target will hit the shaded region. Assume that the dart is equally likely to hit any point on the target.

7.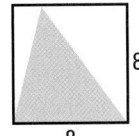

8.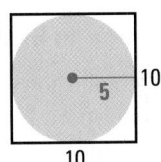

9.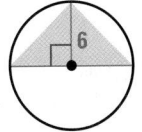

Practice and Applications

STUDENT HELP

HOMEWORK HELP
Example 1: Exs. 10–26
Example 2: Exs. 27–33
Example 3: Exs. 34–41
Example 4: Exs. 42–47

Logical Reasoning **Tell whether the statement is *always true*, *sometimes true*, or *never true*. Explain your reasoning.**

10. The probability of an event is greater than 1.

11. If there are exactly two possible outcomes, then the theoretical probability of either one occurring is 0.5.

12. An event is a single outcome.

Choosing Numbers **You have an equally likely chance of choosing any integer from 1 through 25. Find the probability of the given event.**

13. An even number is chosen.

14. A number less than 5 is chosen.

15. A number greater than 12 is chosen.

16. A perfect square is chosen.

17. A multiple of 4 is chosen.

18. A multiple of 2 or 3 is chosen.

19. A factor of 60 is chosen.

20. A number containing a 1 is chosen.

Choosing Cards **A card is drawn at random from a standard 52-card deck (see page 547). Find the probability of drawing the given card.**

21. the jack of hearts

22. a 7

23. a black card

24. a heart

25. a 2 or a 3

26. a card other than an ace

Ballots In Exercises 27–30, use the following information.

You are one of five people running for class treasurer. The names of the candidates will be listed in random order on the ballot.

27. What is the probability that your name will be last?

28. What is the probability that the names will be listed in alphabetical order?

29. What is the probability that the names of 2 of the 3 female candidates will be listed first?

30. Challenge What is the probability that the names of the 3 female and 2 male candidates will be listed girl-boy-girl-boy-girl?

Lotteries Find the probability of winning the lottery using the given rules. Assume that lottery numbers are selected at random.

31. You must correctly select 5 out of 40 numbers. The order is not important.

32. You must correctly select 6 out of 50 numbers. The order is not important.

33. You must correctly select 4 numbers, each an integer from 0 to 9. The order *is* important.

Surveys In Exercises 34–37, use the following information.

The graph shows the results of a survey asking high school students to name their favorite sport. For a high school student chosen at random, find the experimental probability of the event.

34. The student's favorite sport is football.

35. The student's favorite sport is baseball.

36. The student's favorite sport is football or basketball.

37. The student's favorite sport is *not* soccer.

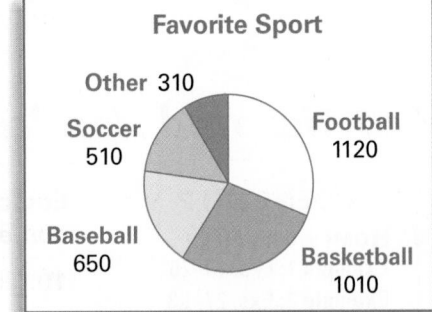

Favorite Sport

Other 310
Soccer 510
Football 1120
Baseball 650
Basketball 1010

38. Writing You ask 3 friends to each flip a penny 25 times, then report the probability the penny shows tails. Your friends report probabilities of 0.44, 0.48, and 0.60. You say the probability is 0.5. Can everyone be right? Explain.

Statistics Link In Exercises 39–41, use the following information.

The table shows the distribution of civilian workers by job category in the United States in 2005. Find the probability that a randomly selected worker was employed in the given job category.

39. sales/office

40. resources/construction/ maintenance

41. *not* managerial/professional

Job category	Number (millions)
Managerial/Professional	49.2
Sales/Office	36.0
Service	23.1
Production/Materials/ Transportation	18.0
Resources/Construction/ Maintenance	15.3

Geometry Link Find the probability that a dart thrown at the target will hit the given region(s) if it is equally likely to hit any point on the target.

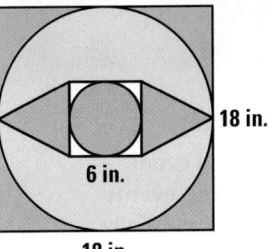

18 in.

6 in.

18 in.

42. the red region

43. the white region

44. either of the green regions

45. the yellow region

46. the yellow region or the blue region

47. **Challenge** A sphere fits exactly in a cube so that it touches each side. What is the probability a point chosen at random inside the cube is also inside the sphere?

48. **Multiple Choice** You are equally likely to choose any integer from 1 through 50. What is the probability that you choose a number that is divisible by 5?

(A) 0.25   (B) 0.2   (C) 0.15   (D) 0.1

49. **Multiple Choice** What is the probability of the spinner shown *not* landing on yellow?

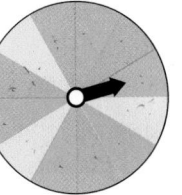

(F) $\frac{1}{4}$ (G) $\frac{2}{3}$

(H) $\frac{3}{4}$ (J) 1

50. **Multiple Choice** You draw 3 cards from a standard 52-card deck. Which expression represents the probability that all 3 of the cards are aces?

(A) $\frac{1}{_{52}C_3}$ (B) $\frac{_3C_3}{_{52}C_3}$ (C) $\frac{_4C_3}{_{52}C_3}$ (D) $\frac{_{13}C_3}{_{52}C_3}$

Mixed Review

Expanding Expressions Expand the expression. Assume all variables are positive. *(Lesson 8.5)*

51. $\log 6x$ 52. $\log_2 2x^2$ 53. $\log \frac{2}{3}$

54. $\log_3 81xy$ 55. $\log_5 \frac{x}{y}$ 56. $\log_3 \frac{8x^2}{y}$

Condensing Expressions Condense the expression. Assume all variables are positive. *(Lesson 8.5)*

57. $\log_4 5 + \log_4 x$ 58. $3 \log_6 x + \log_6 2$ 59. $\log_6 x - \log_6 y$

60. $4 \log_2 6 + 2 \log_2 15$ 61. $\log_{12} 40 - \log_{12} x$ 62. $5 \log_5 x - 4 \log_5 z$

Combinations Find the number of combinations. *(Lesson 10.5)*

63. $_5C_3$ 64. $_8C_2$ 65. $_{10}C_8$

66. $_7C_2$ 67. $_{12}C_{12}$ 68. $_8C_0$

Geometry Skills

Lines of Symmetry Determine the number of lines of symmetry in the figure. Then tell whether the figure has rotational symmetry. If it does, describe the rotations that map the figure onto itself.

69.    70.    71.

10.7 Probability of Compound Events

Key Words
- compound event
- overlapping events
- disjoint or mutually exclusive events
- complement of an event

GOAL Find probabilities of unions and intersections of events.

The *union* of two events A and B is all of the outcomes that are in either A or B. The *intersection* of A and B is all of the outcomes shared by both A and B. The union or intersection of two events is called a **compound event**.

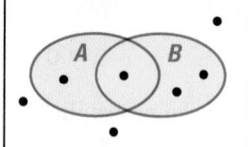

OVERLAPPING EVENTS

Union of *A* and *B*

Intersection of *A* and *B*

DISJOINT EVENTS

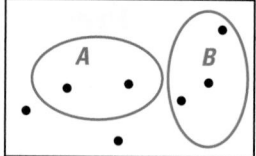

A and *B* do not intersect.

Two events that have outcomes in common are **overlapping events**. Two events that have no outcomes in common are **disjoint events**, or **mutually exclusive events**.

To find the probability of the union of two events, you need to know if the events share any outcomes.

Probability of Compound Events

Overlapping Events If A and B are overlapping events, then $P(A \text{ and } B) \neq 0$, and the probability of A or B is:

$$P(A \text{ or } B) = P(A) + P(B) - P(A \text{ and } B)$$

Disjoint Events If A and B are disjoint events, then $P(A \text{ and } B) = 0$, and the probability of A or B is:

$$P(A \text{ or } B) = P(A) + P(B)$$

EXAMPLE 1 Find *P(A or B)* for Disjoint Events

Cards A card is randomly selected from a standard deck of 52 cards. What is the probability that the card is a 10 *or* a face card (a jack, queen, or king)?

Solution

Let event A be selecting a 10 and let event B be selecting a face card. Event A has 4 outcomes and event B has 12 outcomes. Events A and B are disjoint events.

$$P(A \text{ or } B) = P(A) + P(B) = \frac{4}{52} + \frac{12}{52} = \frac{16}{52} = \frac{4}{13} \approx 0.308$$

ANSWER ▶ The probability is about 0.308, or about 31%.

EXAMPLE 2 Find *P(A or B)* for Overlapping Events

A card is randomly selected from a standard deck of 52 cards. What is the probability that the card is a face card *or* a spade?

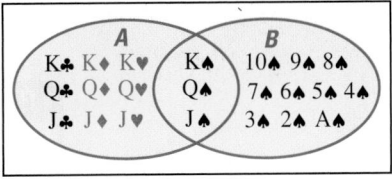

Solution

Let event *A* be selecting a face card. Let event *B* be selecting a spade. Event *A* has 12 outcomes, and event *B* has 13 outcomes. Three of the outcomes are common to both *A* and *B*.

$P(A \text{ or } B) = P(A) + P(B) - P(A \text{ and } B)$ Union of overlapping events

$\qquad\qquad = \dfrac{12}{52} + \dfrac{13}{52} - \dfrac{3}{52}$ Substitute probabilities.

$\qquad\qquad = \dfrac{22}{52}$, or about 0.42   Simplify.

ANSWER ▶ The probability is about 0.42, or 42%.

STUDENT HELP

AVOID ERRORS
Because *A* and *B* overlap, don't forget to subtract the probability of their intersection.

EXAMPLE 3 Find *P(A and B)* for Overlapping Events

College In a class of 20 seniors, 17 have applied to a state university and 11 have applied to a private university. In all, 19 of the 20 students have applied to a university. What is the probability that a class member chosen at random has applied to a state university *and* a private university?

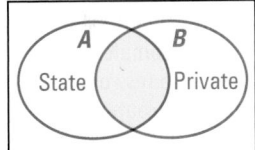

Solution

Let *A* represent the event "has applied to a state university." Let *B* represent the event "has applied to a private university." You need to find *P(A and B)*.

You are given: $P(A) = \dfrac{17}{20}$ $P(B) = \dfrac{11}{20}$ $P(A \text{ or } B) = \dfrac{19}{20}$

$P(A \text{ or } B) = P(A) + P(B) - P(A \text{ and } B)$ Write formula for *P(A or B)*.

$\dfrac{19}{20} = \dfrac{17}{20} + \dfrac{11}{20} - P(A \text{ and } B)$ Substitute probabilities.

$P(A \text{ and } B) = \dfrac{17}{20} + \dfrac{11}{20} - \dfrac{19}{20}$ Solve for *P(A and B)*.

$\qquad\qquad\quad = \dfrac{9}{20}$, or 0.45   Simplify.

ANSWER ▶ The probability is 0.45, or 45%.

Checkpoint ✔ *Find the Probability of a Compound Event*

In Exercises 1 and 2, a card is randomly selected from a standard deck of 52 cards. Find the probability of the given event.

1. The card is an ace *or* a jack.   **2.** The card is a heart *or* a 7.

3. Pets Of 25 students, 13 have a dog and 8 have a cat. In all, 16 of the 25 have a dog or a cat. What is the probability that any one of the 25 has a dog *and* a cat?

Complements The **complement of an event** consists of all outcomes that are not in the event. For example, if an integer from 1 to 10 is chosen at random, the complement of the event "the integer is even" is "the integer is odd."

> ### Probability of the Complement of an Event
>
> The sum of the probabilities of an event and its complement is 1.
>
> $$P(A) + P(\text{not } A) = 1, \text{ so } P(\text{not } A) = 1 - P(A).$$

EXAMPLE 4 Find Probabilities of Complements

Dice When two six-sided dice are rolled, 36 outcomes are possible, as shown. Find the probability of the given event.

a. The sum is not 2.

b. The sum is less than or equal to 10.

Solution

a. $P(\text{sum is not 2}) = 1 - P(\text{sum is 2}) = 1 - \dfrac{1}{36} = \dfrac{35}{36} \approx 0.972$

b. $P(\text{sum} \le 10) = 1 - P(\text{sum} > 10) = 1 - \dfrac{3}{36} = \dfrac{33}{36} = \dfrac{11}{12} \approx 0.917$

EXAMPLE 5 Find Probabilities of Complements

Birthdays A class has 23 students. What is the probability that at least 2 of the students share a birthday?

Solution

The complement of "at least 2 of the students share a birthday" is "each student has a different birthday." Because each student has a birthday on one of 365 days (ignoring leap year), there are 365^{23} possibilities for all the birthdays. The number of possibilities in which each of the 23 birthdays is different is:

$365 \cdot 364 \cdot 363 \cdot \cdots \cdot 345 \cdot 344 \cdot 343$	This is $_{365}P_{23}$.
$P(\text{at least 2 are the same}) = 1 - P(\text{all are different})$	Write the complement.
$= 1 - \dfrac{_{365}P_{23}}{365^{23}}$	Express the probability.
≈ 0.507	Use a calculator.

ANSWER ▸ There is about a 51% chance that at least two students share a birthday.

Checkpoint ✓ **Find Probabilities of Complements**

4. Use the information in Example 4 to find the probability that the sum is not 5.

5. What is the probability that at least 2 people in a family of 6 share a birthday?

Guided Practice

Vocabulary Check   **Copy and complete the statement.**

1. The __?__ of two events is all of the outcomes that are in either event.

2. The __?__ of two events is all of the outcomes that are in both events.

3. If two events have no outcomes in common, they are __?__ events.

Skill Check   **Events _A_ and _B_ are disjoint. Find _P(A or B)_.**

4. $P(A) = 0.3$
$P(B) = 0.3$

5. $P(A) = 0.4$
$P(B) = 0.6$

6. $P(A) = 0.11$
$P(B) = 0.19$

Events _A_ and _B_ are overlapping. Find _P(A or B)_.

7. $P(A) = 0.4$
$P(B) = 0.3$
$P(A \text{ and } B) = 0.2$

8. $P(A) = 0.5$
$P(B) = 0.5$
$P(A \text{ and } B) = 0.3$

A bag contains 10 pieces of paper numbered 1 through 10. You draw one piece of paper at random. Find _P(A or B)_ for the given events.

9. Event _A_: The number is at least 6.
Event _B_: The number is odd.

10. Event _A_: The number is even.
Event _B_: The number is prime.

Events _A_ and _B_ are overlapping. Find _P(A and B)_.

11. $P(A) = 0.2$
$P(B) = 0.6$
$P(A \text{ or } B) = 0.7$

12. $P(A) = 0.7$
$P(B) = 0.5$
$P(A \text{ or } B) = 0.9$

Given _P(A)_, find _P(not A)_.

13. $P(A) = 0.25$

14. $P(A) = 0.5$

15. $P(A) = 0.95$

Practice and Applications

STUDENT HELP

HOMEWORK HELP
Example 1: Exs. 16–24, 34–41
Example 2: Exs. 16–24, 27–29
Example 3: Exs. 22–29
Example 4: Exs. 30–41
Example 5: Exs. 42–43

Compound Events Tell whether events _A_ and _B_ are *disjoint* or *overlapping*. Then find _P(A or B)_.

16. $P(A) = 0.3$
$P(B) = 0.5$
$P(A \text{ and } B) = 0$

17. $P(A) = 0.7$
$P(B) = 0.4$
$P(A \text{ and } B) = 0.3$

18. $P(A) = 0.45$
$P(B) = 0.15$
$P(A \text{ and } B) = 0.1$

Compound Events In Exercises 19–21, the spinner is divided into 12 equal parts. Given events _A_ and _B_, find _P(A or B)_.

19. Event _A_: Spinner lands on the number 3.
Event _B_: Spinner lands on yellow.

20. Event _A_: Spinner lands on an even number.
Event _B_: Spinner lands on blue.

21. Event _A_: Spinner lands on a number less than or equal to 4.
Event _B_: Spinner lands on red.

Compound Events Find the indicated probability. Tell whether events *A* and *B* are *disjoint* or *overlapping*.

22. $P(A) = 0.2$
$P(B) = 0.5$
$P(A \text{ or } B) = 0.5$
$P(A \text{ and } B) = \underline{\ ?\ }$

23. $P(A) = 0.5$
$P(B) = 0.5$
$P(A \text{ or } B) = \underline{\ ?\ }$
$P(A \text{ and } B) = 0.2$

24. $P(A) = 0.1$
$P(B) = \underline{\ ?\ }$
$P(A \text{ or } B) = 0.9$
$P(A \text{ and } B) = 0$

Intersections In Exercises 25 and 26, a student at a high school is selected at random from the 10th, 11th, or 12th grades. The probabilities given represent $P(A)$, $P(B)$, and $P(A \text{ or } B)$. Find $P(A \text{ and } B)$.

25. $P(\text{male}) = 0.4$
$P(\text{11th grader}) = 0.3$
$P(\text{male or 11th grader}) = 0.66$

26. $P(\text{female}) = 0.6$
$P(\text{12th grader}) = 0.36$
$P(\text{female or 12th grader}) = 0.8$

27. Critical Thinking A high school has 1500 students, of which 725 are female. There are 900 students involved in after-school activities, of which 525 are female. Is it possible for the events "selecting a student involved in an after-school activity" and "selecting a female student" to be disjoint? Explain.

Link to
BIOLOGY

BLOOD TYPES determine what kinds of transfusions are allowed. People with blood type AB positive blood can receive blood of all types. People with blood type O can receive blood of type O only.

Biology Link In Exercises 28 and 29, use the following information.

A blood bank records the blood types, including positive or negative Rh-factor, during a blood drive. The table shows the number of donors with each type of blood.

		Blood Type				
		O	**A**	**B**	**AB**	**Total**
Rh-Factor	**Positive**	146	134	36	15	331
	Negative	26	26	11	6	69
	Total	172	160	47	21	400

28. Find the probability a donor chosen at random has type O or AB blood.

29. Find the probability a donor chosen at random has type A blood or is Rh-positive.

Finding Probabilities of Complements A meteorologist gives the following probabilities. If the probability is $P(A)$, find $P(\text{not } A)$.

30. $P(\text{rain today}) = 0.3$

31. $P(\text{snow tonight}) = 0.6$

32. $P(\text{sunny tomorrow}) = 0.9$

33. $P(\text{clear on weekend}) = 0.75$

Statistics Link In Exercises 34–37, use the following information.

The estimated percent age distribution of the U.S. population for 2010 is shown in the circle graph. Find the probability that a person chosen at random fits the description.

34. under 5 years old

35. not 65 or older

36. at least 15 years old

37. from 25 to 44 years old

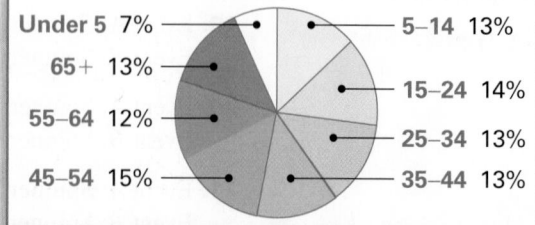

Under 5 7% 5–14 13%
65+ 13% 15–24 14%
55–64 12% 25–34 13%
45–54 15% 35–44 13%

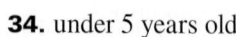

Using Complements **You roll two six-sided dice. Find the probability of the given event.**

38. The sum is not 4.

39. The sum is greater than or equal to 9.

40. The sum is neither 2 nor 12.

41. The sum is less than or equal to 9.

42. Home Electronics Five houses on a block have the same model of garage door opener. Each opener has one of 4096 possible codes. What is the probability that at least 2 of the houses have openers with the same code?

43. Testing A web-based test generator assigns 1 of 100 possible questions as the first question on a practice quiz. If 20 students take the quiz, what is the probability that at least 2 of the 20 are assigned the same first question?

44. Challenge Show that the following statement, an example of what is known as the *inclusion-exclusion principle*, is true.

$$P(A \text{ or } B \text{ or } C) = P(A) + P(B) + P(C) -$$
$$P(A \text{ and } B) - P(B \text{ and } C) -$$
$$P(C \text{ and } A) + P(A \text{ and } B \text{ and } C)$$

(*Hint:* Use probability notation to write expressions for each region of the Venn diagram shown.)

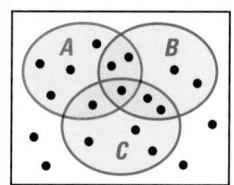

Standardized Test Practice

45. Multiple Choice You have a bag containing 10 red marbles, 15 blue marbles, and 5 green marbles. You choose a marble at random from the bag. What is the probability that you choose a blue marble or a green marble?

   A $\frac{1}{4}$ **B** $\frac{1}{3}$ **C** $\frac{1}{2}$ **D** $\frac{2}{3}$

46. Multiple Choice You roll a 12-sided die that has its faces numbered from 1 to 12. What is the probability that in a single roll you roll an even number or a multiple of 3?

   F $\frac{1}{4}$ **G** $\frac{1}{3}$ **H** $\frac{1}{2}$ **J** $\frac{2}{3}$

Mixed Review

Evaluating Expressions **Evaluate the expression.** *(Lesson 7.2)*

47. $9^{3/2}$ **48.** $81^{5/2}$ **49.** $64^{2/3}$ **50.** $256^{3/4}$

51. $27^{-1/3}$ **52.** $32^{-4/5}$ **53.** $169^{-3/2}$ **54.** $625^{-3/4}$

Identifying Exponential Functions **Tell whether the function shows *exponential growth* or *exponential decay*. Then identify the initial amount and the percent increase or decrease.** *(Lesson 8.3)*

55. $y = 54(1 + 0.2)^t$ **56.** $y = 16(1 + 0.65)^t$ **57.** $y = 125(1 - 0.4)^t$

58. $y = 750(1.5)^t$ **59.** $y = 1200(0.3)^t$ **60.** $y = 560(0.35)^t$

Using Inverse Properties **Simplify the expression.** *(Lesson 8.4)*

61. $\log_6 6^x$ **62.** $\log 10^x$ **63.** $5^{\log_5 x}$

64. $8^{\log_8 x}$ **65.** $10^{\log 6x}$ **66.** $\log_2 32^x$

Geometry Skills

Classifying Triangles **Use the converse of the Pythagorean theorem. Tell whether the triangle has a right angle.**

67.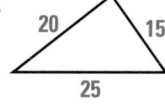

68.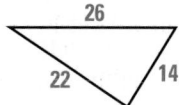

69.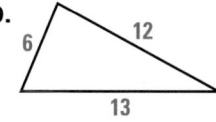

DEVELOPING CONCEPTS *(For use with Lesson 10.8)*

Simulating Probability Experiments

Goal

To use a simulation to find an experimental probability

Materials

• index cards

QUESTION

How can you explore probability using a simulation?

Often, you can make a model of a situation to help you find a probability. A *simulation* is an experiment performed to model a real life probability.

EXPLORE

Do a simulation to find an experimental probability that you and a friend are the 2 students randomly chosen from a group of 8 students.

1 Label eight index cards as shown. Use 1 to represent yourself, 2 to represent your friend, and the 3, 4, 5, 6, 7, and 8 to represent the other students.

| 1 | 2 | 3 | 4 |
| 5 | 6 | 7 | 8 |

2 Shuffle the cards. Randomly draw a card, and then another, without replacing the first. Record your results. Decide whether or not the results represent you and your friend being chosen. Replace the cards.

3 Repeat drawing a pair of cards. Draw a total of 10 pairs. For each pair of cards drawn, record the results. Use the ratio $\dfrac{\text{you and friend are chosen}}{\text{total number of pairs drawn}}$ to find the experimental probability that you and your friend are chosen.

Pair	Times Drawn
1, 4	I
7, 2	II
5, 8	I

THINK ABOUT IT

1. Use your results from the simulation above. Combine all the class results. Based on these results, what is the experimental probability that you and your friend are chosen?

2. The die at the right has 8 sides numbered 1–8. Each outcome is equally likely when the die is rolled. Describe how you can use this die to simulate the event above. Explain why each pair (n, n) must be disregarded.

3. Do you think *your results* or the *class results* are closer to the theoretical probability that you and your friend are chosen? Explain.

Probability of Independent and Dependent Events

Key Words
- independent events
- dependent events
- conditional probability

GOAL Find the probability of independent and dependent events.

Two events are **independent** if the occurrence of one event *does not* affect the occurrence of the other. Two events are **dependent** if the occurrence of one event *does* affect the occurrence of the other. The probability that both of two events occur depends on whether the events are independent or dependent.

Consider the probability of drawing a blue marble at random from a bag after first drawing a green marble. How does whether you replace the green marble affect the probability of drawing blue?

Prerequisite Skills

Evaluate.

1. $0.5 \cdot 0.5$

2. $0.25 \cdot 0.75$

3. $0.35 \div 0.5$

4. $0.075 \div 0.25$

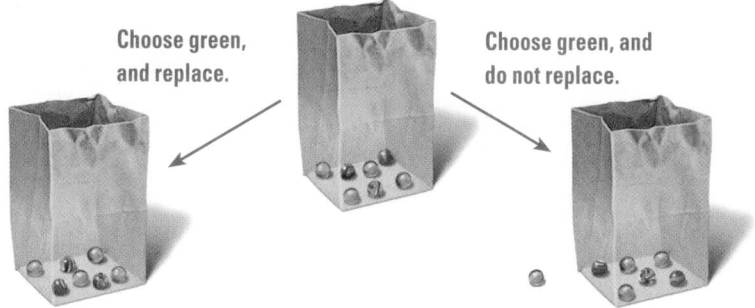

Choose green, and replace.

Choose green, and do not replace.

$P(\text{green}) = \dfrac{4}{7}; P(\text{blue}) = \dfrac{1}{7}$ $P(\text{green}) = \dfrac{4}{7}; P(\text{blue}) = \dfrac{1}{6}$

Independent Events
The probability of drawing blue is the *same* as it would have been if you had not chosen the first marble.

Dependent Events
The probability of drawing blue is *different* from what it would have been if you had not chosen the first marble.

EXAMPLE 1 Identify Events

Tell whether the events are *independent* or *dependent*. Explain.

a. Your teacher chooses students at random to present their projects. She chooses you first, and then chooses Kim from the remaining students.

b. You flip a coin, and it shows heads. You flip the coin again, and it shows tails.

c. One out of 25 of a model of digital camera has some random defect. You and a friend each buy one of the cameras. You each receive a defective camera.

Solution

a. Dependent; after you are chosen, there is one fewer student from which to make the second choice.

b. Independent; what happens the first flip has no effect on the second flip.

c. Independent; because the defects are random, whether one of you receives a defective camera has no effect on whether the other person does too.

Tell whether the events are *independent* or *dependent*. Explain.

1. You choose Alberto to be your lab partner. Then Tia chooses Shelby.

2. You spin a spinner for a board game, and then you roll a die.

Conditional Probability For two dependent events A and B, the probability that B will occur *given that A has occurred* is the **conditional probability** of B given A, written as $P(B|A)$.

EXAMPLE 2 Find Conditional Probabilities

Concerts A high school has a total of 850 students. The table shows the numbers of students by grade at the school who attended a concert.

a. What is the probability that a student at the school attended the concert?

b. What is the probability that a junior did *not* attend the concert?

Grade	Attended	Did not attend
Freshman	80	120
Sophomore	132	86
Junior	173	29
Senior	179	51

Solution

a. $P(\text{attended}) = \dfrac{\text{total who attended}}{\text{total students}} = \dfrac{80 + 132 + 173 + 179}{850} = \dfrac{564}{850} \approx 0.664$

b. $P(\text{did not attend}|\text{junior}) = \dfrac{\text{juniors who did not attend}}{\text{total juniors}}$

$$= \dfrac{29}{173 + 29} = \dfrac{29}{202} \approx 0.144$$

3. Use the table in Example 2 to find the probability that a student is a junior given that the student did not attend the concert.

Probability of Independent and Dependent Events

Independent Events If A and B are independent events, then the probability that both A and B occur is $P(A \text{ and } B) = P(A) \cdot P(B)$.

Dependent Events If A and B are dependent events, then the probability that both A and B occur is $P(A \text{ and } B) = P(A) \cdot P(B|A)$.

Notice that if events A and B are independent, then $P(B|A)$ is just $P(B)$, so the first formula in the box above is a special case of the second.

EXAMPLE 3 Independent and Dependent Events

Games A word game has 100 tiles, 98 of which are letters and two of which are blank. The numbers of tiles of each letter are shown in the diagram. Suppose you draw two tiles. Find the probability that both tiles are vowels in the situation described.

a. You replace the first tile before drawing the second tile.

b. You do *not* replace the first tile before drawing the second tile.

A	9	H	2	O	8	V	2
B	2	I	9	P	2	W	2
C	2	J	1	Q	1	X	1
D	4	K	1	R	6	Y	2
E	12	L	4	S	4	Z	1
F	2	M	2	T	6		2
G	3	N	6	U	4	Blank	

Solution

a. If you replace the first tile before selecting the second, the events are independent. Let A represent the first tile being a vowel and B represent the second tile being a vowel. Of 100 tiles, $9 + 12 + 9 + 8 + 4 = 42$ are vowels.

$$P(A \text{ and } B) = P(A) \cdot P(B) = \frac{42}{100} \cdot \frac{42}{100} = 0.1764$$

b. If you do *not* replace the first tile before selecting the second, the events are dependent. After removing the first vowel, 41 vowels remain out of 99 tiles.

$$P(A \text{ and } B) = P(A) \cdot P(B|A) = \frac{42}{100} \cdot \frac{41}{99} \approx 0.1739$$

Three or More Events You can extend the formulas for probabilities of independent and dependent events to three or more events. For example, for three independent events A, B, and C, $P(A \text{ and } B \text{ and } C) = P(A) \cdot P(B) \cdot P(C)$.

EXAMPLE 4 Probability of Three Independent Events

Forecasting The official weather forecast for an upcoming 3-day holiday weekend calls for a 30% chance of rain Saturday, a 40% chance of rain Sunday, and a 50% chance of rain Monday. Assuming these events are independent, what is the chance that it does not rain on any of the three days?

Solution

There is a $100\% - 30\% = 70\%$ chance it does *not* rain Saturday. Similarly, there is a 60% chance it doesn't rain Sunday and a 50% chance it doesn't rain Monday.

$P(\text{it does not rain any of the days}) = 70\% \cdot 60\% \cdot 50\% = 21\%$

ANSWER ▶ There is a 21% chance that it doesn't rain Saturday, Sunday, or Monday.

Checkpoint ✔ **Find Probabilities of Independent and Dependent Events**

4. In the game in Example 3, you draw two tiles. What is the probability that you draw a Q, then draw a Z if you first replace the Q? What is the probability that you draw both of the blank tiles (without replacement)?

5. Three sisters each order a phone that comes in 6 colors. If the sisters are equally likely to receive any of the colors, what is the probability that all three receive a red phone?

Guided Practice

Vocabulary Check

1. Copy and complete the statement: The probability that B will occur given that A has occurred is called the __?__ of B given A.

2. Copy and complete the statement: If the occurrence of one event affects the occurrence of another event, then the events are __?__ .

Skill Check

Events A and B are independent. Find the indicated probability.

3. $P(A) = 0.25$
$P(B) = 0.6$
$P(A \text{ and } B) = $ __?__

4. $P(A) = 0.8$
$P(B) = $ __?__
$P(A \text{ and } B) = 0.4$

5. $P(A) = $ __?__
$P(B) = 0.7$
$P(A \text{ and } B) = 0.21$

Events A and B are dependent. Find the indicated probability.

6. $P(A) = 0.2$
$P(B|A) = 0.9$
$P(A \text{ and } B) = $ __?__

7. $P(A) = 0.4$
$P(B|A) = $ __?__
$P(A \text{ and } B) = 0.12$

8. $P(A) = $ __?__
$P(B|A) = 0.6$
$P(A \text{ and } B) = 0.45$

Magazines In Exercises 9 and 10, eight magazines are stacked randomly. The stack has 5 news magazines and 3 sports magazines.

9. What is the probability that the second magazine in the stack is a sports magazine given that the top magazine in the stack is a sports magazine?

10. You pick up the top two magazines from the stack. What is the probability that they are both sports magazines?

Practice and Applications

Identifying Events Tell whether the events are *independent* or *dependent*. Explain.

11. You spin a spinner, then roll a die.

STUDENT HELP

HOMEWORK HELP
Example 1: Exs. 11–14
Example 2: Exs. 15–17
Example 3: Exs. 18–28
Example 4: Exs. 29–33

12. You draw a card at random, then draw another without replacing the first.

13. You choose one raffle ticket at random from each of two different bags.

14. You draw a name from a bag, return the name, shake the bag, and draw again.

History Link Use the table showing the numbers of members in the House of Representatives and Senate in the 110th U.S. Congress in 2007.

	Democrat	Republican	Independent	Other
House	233	201	0	0
Senate	49	49	1	1

15. What is the probability that a Congress member was a Democrat?

16. What is the probability that a Senate member was a Republican?

17. What is the probability that a Democrat was a member of the House?

Rolling a Number Cube In Exercises 18–20, you are playing a game that involves rolling a six-sided die. Find the indicated probability.

18. rolling an even number and then an odd number

19. rolling a number less than 3 and then a number greater than 3

20. rolling an odd number and then a 2

21. Marbles Refer to the diagram on page 569. Find the probability of drawing a green marble, then a blue one (a) with replacement and (b) without replacement.

Drawing Numbers You draw numbers at random without replacement from a hat holding 20 disks numbered 1 through 20. Find the probability.

22. drawing a 12 and then a 13

23. drawing an even number and then an odd number

24. drawing an odd number and then another odd number

Drawing Cards Find the probability of drawing the given cards at random from a standard 52-card deck (see page 547) under each condition: (a) with replacement and (b) without replacement.

25. a club, then a spade

26. an ace, then a queen

27. a face card (K, Q, or J), then a 4

28. a jack, then another jack

Drawing Cards A card is drawn at random from each of 3 standard 52-card decks. Find the probability that the given cards are chosen.

29. an ace, then a king, then a queen

30. a heart, then a diamond, then a club

Three Dependent Events In Exercises 31 and 32, use the fact that for 3 dependent events, $P(A \text{ and } B \text{ and } C) = P(A) \cdot P(B|A) \cdot P(C|A \text{ and } B)$.

31. Refer to Example 3 on page 571. You draw 3 tiles at random without replacement. What is the probability that you draw "E," then "G," then "G?"

32. A calculator generates random integers from 1 to 5. What is the probability that the first three integers generated are all different? (*Hint:* $P(A) = 1$.)

33. Challenge The diagram shows results of observations at one high school of seat belt use in cases where an adult drove a student to school. For example, there is a 31% chance the adult was not wearing a seat belt. If the adult was not wearing a seat belt, there is a 74% chance that the student wasn't either. Find the probability that a student driven by an adult was wearing a seat belt.

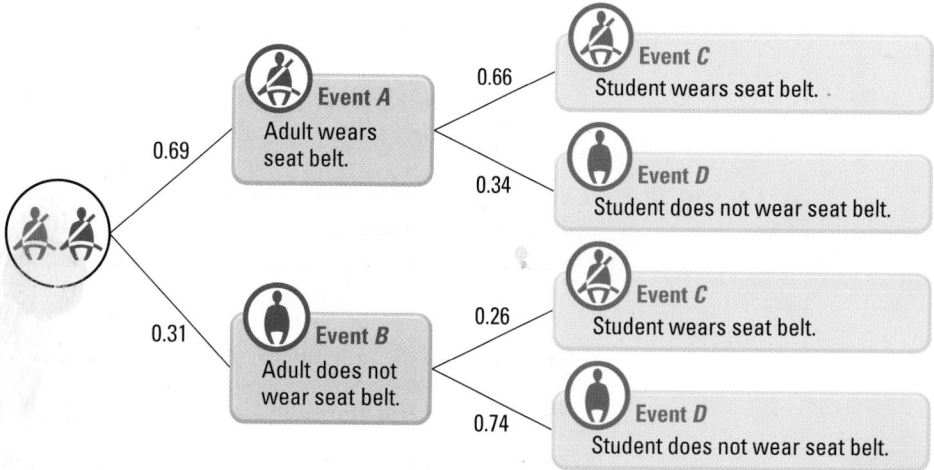

34. Multiple Choice The probability of event A occurring is $P(A) = 0.3$. The probability of event B occurring given that A has occurred is $P(B|A) = 0.4$. What is the probability that events A and B both occur?

   Ⓐ 0.4   Ⓑ 0.6   Ⓒ 0.7   Ⓓ 0.12

35. Multiple Choice What is the probability of drawing one heart and then another heart at random from a standard 52-card deck if you do not replace the first card after you draw it?

   Ⓕ 0.059   Ⓖ 0.0625   Ⓗ 0.500   Ⓙ 0.505

Mixed Review

Order of Operations Evaluate the expression. *(Lesson 1.2)*

36. $10 + 3 - 4$ **37.** $12 \div (4 - 2) \cdot 2$ **38.** $6 - 2(5 - 8)$

39. $2^4 \div 4 \cdot 2 + 5$ **40.** $(1 - 7 + 9 \div 3)^2$ **41.** $-(17 - 8)^2$

Quadratic Formula Use the quadratic formula to solve the equation. *(Lesson 5.8)*

42. $x^2 + 4x + 6 = 0$ **43.** $2x^2 + 8x + 1 = 0$ **44.** $3x^2 - 2x - 7 = 0$

45. $4x^2 - x + 3 = 0$ **46.** $x^2 + 10x - 6 = 0$ **47.** $2x^2 - 4x + 9 = 0$

Geometry Skills

Volume of a Cylinder Find the volume of the cylinder. Round your answer to the nearest whole number.

48. 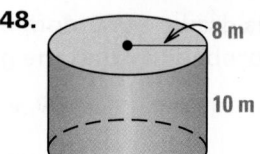 8 m, 10 m   **49.** 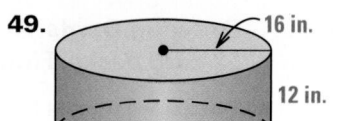 16 in., 12 in.   **50.** 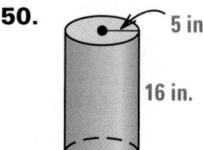 5 in., 16 in.

Quiz 3

Lesson 10.6   A card is drawn at random from a standard 52-card deck. Find the probability of drawing the given card.

   1. a 9   **2.** a club

   3. a face card (K, Q, or J)   **4.** a red card

Lesson 10.7   Find the indicated probability.

   5. $P(A) = 0.4$ **6.** $P(A) = 0.6$ **7.** $P(A) = 0.6$
       $P(B) = 0.2$ $P(B) = 0.3$ $P(\text{not } A) = \underline{\ ?\ }$
       $P(A \text{ or } B) = 0.5$ $P(A \text{ or } B) = \underline{\ ?\ }$
       $P(A \text{ and } B) = \underline{\ ?\ }$ $P(A \text{ and } B) = 0.2$

Lesson 10.8   You are drawing numbers at random from a hat. The hat contains 40 pieces of paper numbered 1 through 40. The numbers are not replaced after they are drawn. Find the indicated probability.

   8. You draw the number 10, then a number less than 5.

   9. You draw the number 10, then a multiple of 5.

   10. You draw a prime number greater than 2, then an odd number.

VOCABULARY

- **population,** *p. 519*
- **sample,** *p. 519*
- **unbiased sample,** *p. 519*
- **biased sample,** *p. 519*
- **convenience sample,** *p. 526*
- **self-selected sample,** *p. 526*
- **systematic sample,** *p. 526*
- **random sample,** *p. 526*
- **margin of error,** *p. 528*
- **permutation,** *p. 540*

- **factorial,** *p. 540*
- **combination,** *p. 545*
- **Pascal's triangle,** *p. 547*
- **probability,** *p. 556*
- **theoretical probability,** *p. 556*
- **experimental probability,** *p. 557*
- **geometric probability,** *p. 558*

- **compound event,** *p. 562*
- **overlapping events,** *p. 562*
- **disjoint or mutually exclusive events,** *p. 562*
- **complement of an event,** *p. 564*
- **independent events,** *p. 569*
- **dependent events,** *p. 569*
- **conditional probability,** *p. 570*

VOCABULARY EXERCISES

1. Why is it important to be careful that a sample taken from a population be unbiased instead of biased?

2. What is the margin of error of a sample? How is the margin of error related to the size of the sample?

3. What is the difference between a permutation of *n* objects taken *r* at a time and a combination of *n* objects taken *r* at a time?

4. What is the difference between the theoretical probability of an event and its experimental probability?

10.1 POPULATIONS AND SURVEYS

Examples on pp. 519–521

EXAMPLE You can use an unbiased sample to make predictions about a population.

In an unbiased survey of 50 of a school's 1500 students, 35 said that they favor changing the school's mascot. Predict the number of students at the school who favor changing the mascot.

$$\frac{\text{Population number who favor change}}{\text{Population size}} = \frac{\text{Sample number who favor change}}{\text{Sample size}}$$

$$\frac{x}{1500} = \frac{35}{50}$$

$$50x = 52{,}500$$

$$x = 1050 \text{ students}$$

REVIEW HELP
Exercises	Example
5	4, p. 521

5. Surveys In an unbiased survey of 75 of a high school's 1100 students, 55 say they participate in at least one after-school activity. Predict the number of students at the school who participate in at least one after-school activity.

EXAMPLE Some sample types are *convenience*, *self-selected*, *systematic*, and *random*. In general, a random sample is less likely to be biased. The margin of error of a random sample taken from a large population tells how close you can expect a population measure to be to a measure found from the sample.

Suppose that in a random sample of 800 phone company customers, 41.5% say they are dissatisfied with their service. Find the margin of error, and give an interval likely to contain the actual percent of the company's customers who are dissatisfied.

The margin of error S is approximated by $S \approx \pm\frac{1}{\sqrt{n}}$ where n is the sample size.

$$S \approx \pm\frac{1}{\sqrt{800}} \approx \pm 0.035$$

ANSWER ▶ The margin of error is about 3.5%. It is likely that between
41.5% − 3.5% = 38% and 41.5% + 3.5% = 45% of customers
are dissatisfied.

REVIEW HELP

Exercises	Examples
6	**1,** p. 527
7	**3,** p. 528

6. An electric company sends surveys to all its customers that they can fill out and return. Classify the sample, and tell whether it is likely to be biased. Explain.

7. Find the margin of error for a random sample of size n from a large population if (a) $n = 144$, (b) $n = 576$, and (c) $n = 2000$.

EXAMPLE You can find how the mean, median, and mode of a data set change when the data values are increased by or multiplied by a constant. Consider these prices:
$34, $36, $36, $39, $40, $44, $45, $48, $53, $55.

$10 increase: $44, $46, $46, $49, $50, $54, $55, $58, $63, $65

20% increase: $40.80, $43.20, $43.20, $46.80, $48, $52.80, $54, $57.60, $63.60, $66

	Original data set	New data set
Mean	$43	$53
Median	$42	$52
Mode	$36	$46

	Original data set	New data set
Mean	$43	$51.60
Median	$42	$50.40
Mode	$36	$43.20

REVIEW HELP

Exercises	Example
8–9	**2,** p. 535

When prices increase $10, the mean, median, and mode increase $10. When prices increase 20% (multiplication by 1.2), the mean, median, and mode increase 20%.

In Exercises 8 and 9, use this data set: 33, 39, 33, 42, 48, 45, 39, 33, 45.

8. Transform the set of data to show a $33\frac{1}{3}\%$ decrease in each data value.

9. Compare the mean, median, mode, range, and the difference between the upper and lower quartiles for the original data and for the transformed data. What can you conclude?

10.4 THE FUNDAMENTAL COUNTING PRINCIPLE AND PERMUTATIONS

Examples on pp. 539–541

EXAMPLE You can use the fundamental counting principle to count how many ways two or more events can occur, and to find the number of permutations of a set.

a. Find the number of meals possible from 2 soups, 6 entrées, and 5 side dishes.

By the fundamental counting principle, there are $2 \cdot 6 \cdot 5 = 60$ meals.

b. Find the number of orders that 4 members from a team of 10 can run a relay race.

$$_{10}P_4 = \frac{10!}{(10-4)!} = \frac{10!}{6!} = \frac{10 \cdot 9 \cdot 8 \cdot 7 \cdot \cancel{6} \cdot \cancel{5} \cdot \cancel{4} \cdot \cancel{3} \cdot \cancel{2} \cdot \cancel{1}}{\cancel{6} \cdot \cancel{5} \cdot \cancel{4} \cdot \cancel{3} \cdot \cancel{2} \cdot \cancel{1}} = 5040 \text{ ways}$$

REVIEW HELP

Exercises	Examples
10–11	**2**, p. 539
12–18	**4**, p. 541

10. A college student chooses 1 out of 3 math classes, 1 out of 11 arts classes, and 1 out of 8 science classes. How many possible choices are there for the 3 classes?

11. How many possible security codes can be made using 4 digits followed by 3 letters if (a) digits and letters can be repeated, and (b) digits and letters cannot be repeated?

Find the number of permutations of *n* objects taken *r* at a time.

12. $n = 4, r = 4$ **13.** $n = 8, r = 2$ **14.** $n = 8, r = 4$

Find the number of permutations.

15. $_7P_2$ **16.** $_9P_3$ **17.** $_{11}P_4$

18. In how many ways can the 40 contestants in a spelling bee finish first through third?

10.5 COMBINATIONS AND PASCAL'S TRIANGLE

Examples on pp. 545–548

EXAMPLE You can use combinations to count the number of ways an event can happen when order is not important.

a. You must read 3 books from a list of 15 books for a summer reading program. How many different choices do you have for the three books?

$$_{15}C_3 = \frac{15!}{(15-3!) \cdot 3!} = \frac{15!}{12! \cdot 3!} = \frac{\overset{5}{\cancel{15}} \cdot \overset{7}{\cancel{14}} \cdot 13}{\underset{1}{\cancel{3}} \cdot \underset{1}{\cancel{2}} \cdot 1} = 455 \text{ choices}$$

b. How many different 7-card hands dealt from a standard 52-card deck of playing cards have all 7 cards of the same color?

Choose 1 color from 2: $_2C_1$. Choose 7 cards from the 26 of a given color: $_{26}C_7$.

$$_2C_1 \cdot {_{26}C_7} = \frac{2!}{1!1!} \cdot \frac{26!}{19!7!} = 2 \cdot 657{,}800 = 1{,}315{,}600 \text{ hands}$$

REVIEW HELP

Exercises	Examples
19–24	**1**, p. 545
25	**3**, p. 547

Find the number of combinations of *n* objects taken *r* at a time.

19. $n = 9, r = 2$ **20.** $n = 8, r = 3$ **21.** $n = 10, r = 4$

Find the number of combinations.

22. $_6C_5$ **23.** $_8C_3$ **24.** $_{12}C_7$

25. How many groups containing 4 boys and 3 girls can you choose from a class that contains 12 boys and 9 girls?

> **EXAMPLE** You can find the probability that a simple or compound event will occur. Consider a card drawn from a standard 52-card deck.
>
> **a.** Find the probability that the card is a 7.
>
> $$P(7) = \frac{\text{Number of favorable outcomes}}{\text{Total number of outcomes}} = \frac{4}{52} = \frac{1}{13}$$
>
> **b.** Find the probability that the card is a 7 or a diamond.
>
> Let A represent the event that the card is a 7 and B represent the event that the card is a diamond. Then A and B are overlapping events.
>
> $$P(A \text{ or } B) = P(A) + P(B) - P(A \text{ and } B) = \frac{4}{52} + \frac{13}{52} - \frac{1}{52} = \frac{16}{52} = \frac{4}{13}$$

REVIEW HELP

Exercises	Examples
26–27	**1,** p. 556
28	**2,** p. 563
29	**3,** p. 563

In Exercises 26–28, a number is chosen at random from the numbers 1 through 50. Find the indicated probability.

26. The number is 10 or less.

27. The number is a multiple of 5.

28. The number is 10 or less *or* the number is a multiple of 5.

29. The probability that a student at a school participates in basketball is 8%. The probability that a student at the school participates in track and field is 10%. If the probability that a student participates in basketball *or* in track and field is 15%, what is the probability that a student participates in *both*?

> **EXAMPLE** To find the probability that both of two events will occur, you must know whether the events are dependent or independent.
>
> A hat contains pieces of paper numbered 1 through 15. You draw 2 numbers at random. What is the probability that the first number is odd and the second is even (a) with replacement and (b) without replacement.
>
> **a.** The events of drawing the two numbers are independent.
>
> $$P(\text{odd and even}) = P(\text{odd}) \cdot P(\text{even}) = \frac{8}{15} \cdot \frac{7}{15} = \frac{56}{225} \approx 0.25$$
>
> **b.** The events of drawing the two numbers are dependent. Find the probability that the second number is even *given that* an odd number has been removed.
>
> $$P(\text{odd and even}) = P(\text{odd}) \cdot P(\text{even}|\text{odd}) = \frac{8}{15} \cdot \frac{7}{14} = \frac{56}{210} = \frac{4}{15} \approx 0.27$$

REVIEW HELP

Exercises	Example
30–32	**3,** p. 571

Find the probability of drawing the given marbles at random from a bag of 3 red marbles, 5 blue marbles, and 2 green marbles.

30. drawing a blue marble, then a red marble (with replacement)

31. drawing a red marble, then a green marble (without replacement)

32. drawing a blue marble, then a green marble (without replacement)

1. **Vacations** In an unbiased survey of 40 of a company's employees, 25 responded that they considered it very important that the amount of vacation time be increased. The company has 825 employees. Predict how many employees at the company believe it very important that vacation time be increased.

2. **Marketing** A market research company surveys a randomly chosen sample of 7500 adults and finds that 62% prefer the taste of its energy drink over the taste of a competitor's energy drink. What is the margin of error?

Find the number of permutations.

3. $_7P_6$

4. $_8P_2$

5. $_{10}P_7$

Find the number of combinations.

6. $_7C_7$

7. $_{12}C_1$

8. $_{13}C_9$

9. **Food Choices** You are making a sandwich. You can choose from 5 types of cheese, 4 types of vegetables, 3 types of dressing, and 3 types of bread. How many different sandwiches can you make choosing one of each ingredient type?

10. **Insurance** An identification code on an insurance card has 3 letters followed by 3 digits followed by 2 letters. How many identification codes are there if letters and digits can be repeated?

11. **Security** In how many different ways can 6 family members line up to go through a metal detector at an airport?

12. **School Projects** How many different groups of 3 students can be chosen from a class of 17 to present the results of their term projects?

Use the spinner to find the probability.

13. landing on 4

14. landing on green or red

15. not landing on 2

16. landing on blue, and then landing on 2

Games You draw letter tiles at random from a bag of 100 tiles. Use the table to find the indicated probability.

17. drawing an A, replacing it, then drawing an E

18. drawing a G, replacing it, then drawing a G

19. drawing an A, then drawing a G

20. drawing an E, then drawing an A

21. drawing two letters at once that match

Letter	Number of tiles
A	5
E	8
G	3

Chapter Standardized Test

Test Tip **Make an organized list or table.**

Ⓐ Ⓑ Ⓒ Ⓓ

EXAMPLE A softball league division has 5 teams. If each team in the division plays every other team in the division exactly once during a season, how many games are there in all between division teams?

Ⓐ 5   Ⓑ 4   Ⓒ 10   Ⓓ 50

Solution

The number of games is the same as the number of combinations of 5 teams taken 2 at a time, or $_5C_2$.

You can list the possible outcomes by using an organized approach.

Name each of the teams: A, B, C, D, and E. Then ask yourself, "What games will Team A play? What games will Team B play?" and so on. There are ten possible games, so the correct answer is C.

Possible Games			
AB	BC	CD	DE
AC	BD	CE	
AD	BE		
AE			

Multiple Choice

1. You are conducting a survey of opinions about selecting a new school song. Which method is *least* likely to result in a biased sample?

   Ⓐ Survey 25 females in your grade.

   Ⓑ Survey 25 males in your grade.

   Ⓒ Survey each student in your music class.

   Ⓓ Survey 25 students chosen in a drawing.

2. You roll an 8-sided die, numbered from 1 to 8. What is the probability that you roll a 3 or a 7?

   Ⓕ $\frac{1}{4}$ Ⓖ $\frac{1}{8}$

   Ⓗ $\frac{1}{16}$ Ⓙ $\frac{1}{64}$

3. You roll a six-sided die. What is the probability of rolling a number less than 5?

   Ⓐ $\frac{5}{6}$ Ⓑ $\frac{3}{4}$

   Ⓒ $\frac{2}{3}$ Ⓓ $\frac{1}{3}$

4. A data set has a range of 33. If the data are transformed by multiplying each value by 10, what is the range of the transformed data?

   Ⓕ 3.3   Ⓖ 33

   Ⓗ 43   Ⓙ 330

5. How many different passwords are possible if a password has 2 letters followed by 3 digits, and letters and digits can be repeated?

   Ⓐ 1,757,600   Ⓑ 676,000

   Ⓒ 468,000   Ⓓ 67,600

6. In how many ways can a manager and an assistant manager be chosen from a group of 15 job candidates?

   Ⓕ 25   Ⓖ 30

   Ⓗ 105   Ⓙ 210

7. In how many ways can 3 cars be chosen from a group of 12 cars?

(A) 1320 (B) 220

(C) 36 (D) 4

8. Given $P(A) = 0.55$, what is $P(\text{not } A)$?

(F) 0 (G) 0.45

(H) 0.55 (J) 1

9. Events A and B are dependent, $P(A) = 0.2$, and $P(B\mid A) = 0.5$. What is $P(A \text{ and } B)$?

(A) 1 (B) 0.7

(C) 0.1 (D) 0.01

10. Events A and B are independent, $P(A) = 0.5$, and $P(B) = 0.4$. What is $P(A \text{ and } B)$?

(F) 0.02 (G) 0.1

(H) 0.2 (J) 0.9

Gridded Response

11. In an unbiased sample of 50 students in a school, 18 said that they own more than 10 movies. There are 1440 students at the school. Predict the number of students who own more than 10 movies.

12. To the nearest tenth of a percent, what is the margin of error in a random sample of 160 people chosen from a large population?

13. What is the value of $_8P_5$?

14. What is the value of $_8C_5$?

15. A number is drawn at random from a basket containing 50 balls numbered 1 to 50. What is the probability that the number contains the digit 5?

Assume that cards are drawn at random from a standard 52-card deck of playing cards. Give probabilities as decimals to three decimal places.

16. How many 2-card hands are possible?

17. If one card is drawn, what is the probability that it is not a diamond?

18. If one card is drawn, what is the probability that it is a black card *or* a face card?

19. If two cards are drawn without replacement, what is the probability that the first card is a king *and* the second card is a queen?

20. If two cards are drawn without replacement, what is the probability that both cards are aces?

Extended Response

21. The table shows the results of a survey asking adults in a town how they feel about the recent town square project. Assume that the survey was unbiased.

Opinion	Number
Satisfied	85
Dissatisfied	250
Indifferent	165

a. A town resident chosen at random is asked how she feels about the project. What is the experimental probability that she is *not indifferent* about the project?

b. Find the margin of error of the survey. What does this indicate about the actual percent of people in the town who are *dissatisfied* with the project?

CHAPTER 11
Discrete Mathematics

▶ How can you predict the future salary of a construction worker?

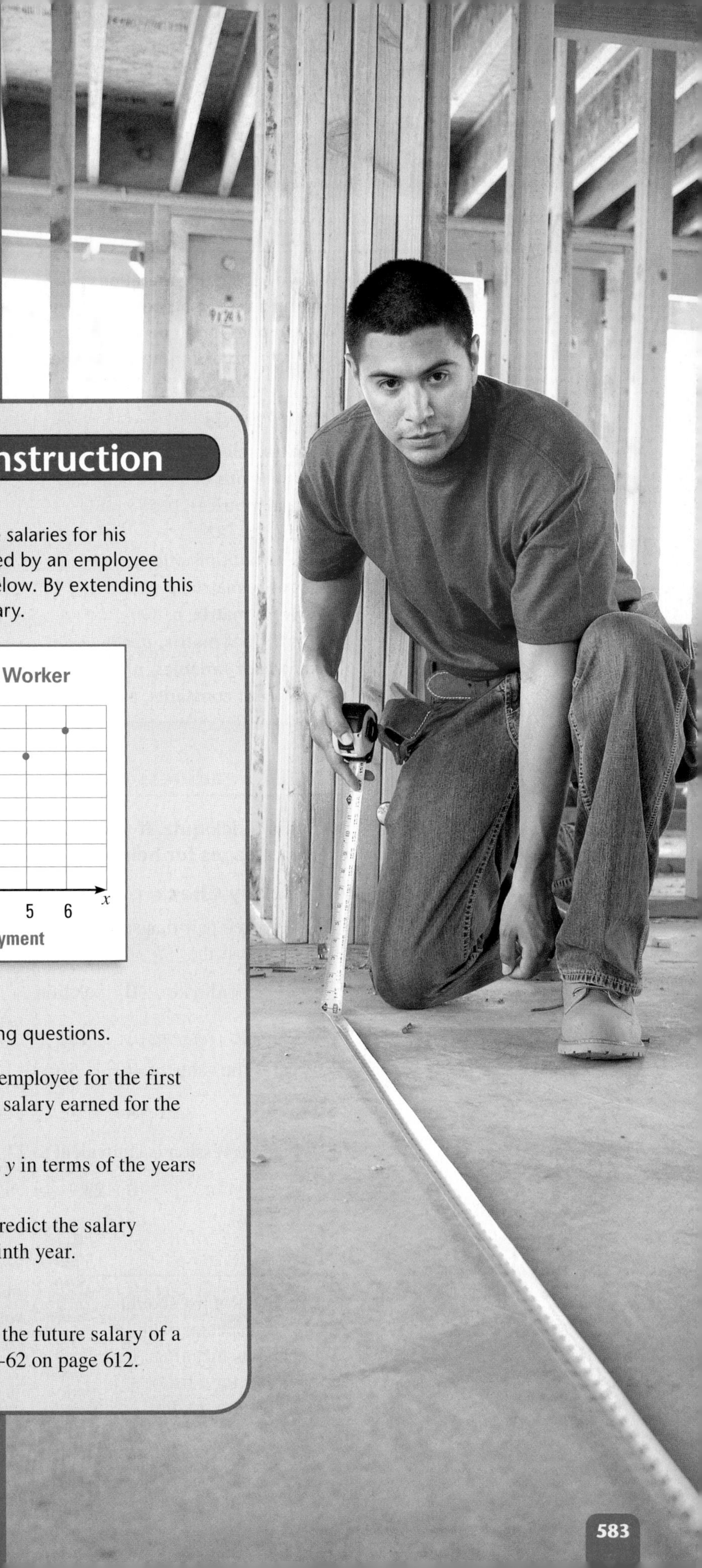

APPLICATION: Construction

▶ **A building contractor** sets the salaries for his employees. Suppose the salary earned by an employee forms a pattern seen in the graph below. By extending this pattern, you can predict a future salary.

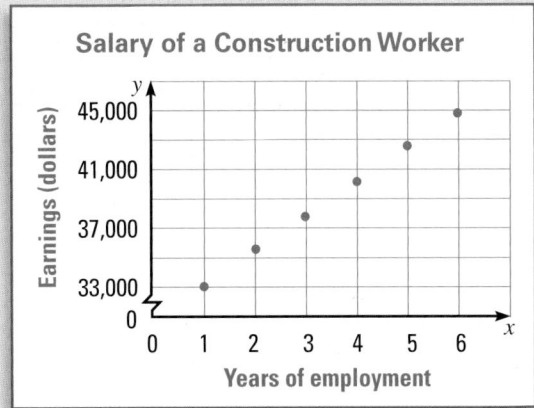

Salary of a Construction Worker

Think & Discuss

Use the graph to answer the following questions.

1. What is the salary earned by the employee for the first year of employment? What is the salary earned for the sixth year?

2. Write a rule for the salary earned y in terms of the years of employment x.

3. Use the rule from Exercise 2 to predict the salary earned by the employee for the ninth year.

Learn More About It

You will write a *sequence* to predict the future salary of a construction worker in Exercises 59–62 on page 612.

PREVIEW What's the chapter about?

• Performing matrix operations
• Finding inverse matrices and using them to solve linear systems
• Writing rules for sequences and finding sums of finite series
• Finding sums of infinite geometric series

Key Words

• matrix, element, *p. 585*
• dimensions of a matrix, *p. 585*
• equal matrices, *p. 585*
• scalar, *p. 587*
• scalar multiplication, *p. 587*
• identity matrix, *p. 600*
• inverse matrix, *p. 600*
• coefficient matrix, *p. 601*
• matrix of variables, *p. 601*
• matrix of constants, *p. 601*

• sequence, *p. 608*
• terms of a sequence, *p. 608*
• series, *p. 610*
• arithmetic sequence, *p. 615*
• common difference, *p. 615*
• arithmetic series, *p. 617*
• geometric sequence, *p. 621*
• common ratio, *p. 621*
• geometric series, *p. 623*

PREPARE Chapter Readiness Quiz

Take this quick quiz. If you are unsure of an answer, look back at the reference pages for help.

Vocabulary Check *(refer to p. 125)*

1. An ordered pair that satisfies both equations in a system of linear equations is the __?__ of the system.

   A *x*-coordinate   **B** solution   **C** graph   **D** slope

Skill Check *(refer to pp. 9, 16)*

2. What is the value of $4(3) - 5(6) + 1(3)$?

   F 15   **G** -15 **H** 45   **J** -21

3. Which expression is equivalent to $27 - 4(n - 1)$?

   A $26 - 4n$ **B** $23 - 4n$ **C** $27 - 3n$ **D** $31 - 4n$

TAKE NOTES Define Symbols

Your vocabulary list should include each special math symbol and its meaning. See page 794 for a list of symbols that are used in this book.

Matrix: a rectangular arrangement of numbers in horizontal rows and vertical columns. The dimensions of the matrix below are 3 × 4.

4 columns

3 rows $\begin{bmatrix} 1 & 4 & 3 & 0 \\ 5 & 8 & 2 & 4 \\ 5 & 2 & 8 & 0 \end{bmatrix}$

11.1 Matrix Operations

Key Words

- matrix
- element
- dimensions of a matrix
- equal matrices
- scalar
- scalar multiplication

GOAL Perform matrix addition, subtraction, and scalar multiplication.

The table shows the number of items sold during the first day of a class fundraiser.

Items	Large	Extra Large
T-shirts	10	15
Sweatshirts	8	12
Long sleeves	14	5

A *matrix* can help you organize data such as the fundraiser data. A **matrix** is a rectangular arrangement of numbers in horizontal rows and vertical columns. Each number in a matrix is called an **element**. The **dimensions of a matrix** with m rows and n columns are $m \times n$ (read "m by n").

Prerequisite Skills

Simplify.

1. $-10 + 12$
2. $-6 - 4$
3. $5 - (-1)$
4. $8 + (-2)$

A matrix for the fundraiser data is shown. Notice that the entries in the table above correspond to the elements in the matrix.

The matrix has 3 rows and 2 columns. So, the dimensions are 3×2. The element in the third row and second column is **5**.

$$\begin{matrix} & \text{Large} & \text{Extra Large} \\ \text{T-shirts} & \begin{bmatrix} 10 \\ \end{bmatrix} & \begin{bmatrix} 15 \\ \end{bmatrix} \\ \text{Sweatshirts} & 8 & 12 \\ \text{Long sleeves} & 14 & 5 \end{matrix} \right\} 3 \; rows$$

2 *columns*

Two matrices (the plural of *matrix*) are **equal** if their dimensions are the same and the elements in corresponding positions are equal.

EXAMPLE 1 Compare Matrices

STUDENT HELP

READING ALGEBRA
You can name a matrix using an uppercase letter such as *A*, *B*, or *C*.

Tell whether the matrix is equal to the fundraiser matrix. Explain.

a.
$$A = \begin{bmatrix} 10 & 15 \\ 8 & 6(2) \\ 14 & 5 \end{bmatrix}$$

The element 6(2) is equal to 12. So, matrix *A* is equal to the fundraiser matrix because all corresponding elements are equal.

b.
$$B = \begin{bmatrix} 10 & 15 \\ 16 & 6 \\ 14 & 5 \end{bmatrix}$$

Matrix *B* is *not* equal to the fundraiser matrix because the corresponding elements in the second row are not equal.

Checkpoint ✓ Compare Matrices

Tell whether the matrices are equal. Explain.

1. $\begin{bmatrix} 2 & 0 \\ 0 & -2 \end{bmatrix}, \begin{bmatrix} 2 & 0 \\ 0 & -2 \end{bmatrix}$

2. $\begin{bmatrix} 1 & -1 \\ 0 & \frac{4}{2} \end{bmatrix}, \begin{bmatrix} 1 & (4-5) \\ 0 & (3-1) \end{bmatrix}$

3. $\begin{bmatrix} 1 & 3 \end{bmatrix}, \begin{bmatrix} 1 \\ 3 \end{bmatrix}$

Matrix Operations You can add or subtract matrices only if they have the same dimensions. To add or subtract matrices, you add or subtract corresponding elements.

EXAMPLE 2 Add and Subtract Matrices

Add or subtract, if possible. If not possible, state the reason.

a. $\begin{bmatrix} 2 \\ 1 \\ 3 \end{bmatrix} + \begin{bmatrix} 4 \\ -1 \\ 5 \end{bmatrix} = \begin{bmatrix} 2+4 \\ 1+(-1) \\ 3+5 \end{bmatrix} = \begin{bmatrix} 6 \\ 0 \\ 8 \end{bmatrix}$

b. $\begin{bmatrix} 4 & -1 \\ 0 & 5 \end{bmatrix} - \begin{bmatrix} 1 & 2 \\ -2 & 3 \end{bmatrix} = \begin{bmatrix} 4-1 & -1-2 \\ 0-(-2) & 5-3 \end{bmatrix} = \begin{bmatrix} 3 & -3 \\ 2 & 2 \end{bmatrix}$

c. $\begin{bmatrix} 3 & -11 \\ 12 & -2 \end{bmatrix} - \begin{bmatrix} 1 \\ 15 \end{bmatrix}$

It is not possible to subtract the matrices. They have different dimensions.

EXAMPLE 3 Use a Matrix Operation

The number of items sold during the second day of the class fundraiser is shown.

a. Add the matrix for the second day of the fundraiser to the matrix for the first day of the fundraiser on page 585.

b. What is the total number of large, long sleeve shirts sold during the first two days of the fundraiser?

Second Day of Fundraiser

	Large	Extra Large
T-shirts	12	5
Sweatshirts	4	3
Long sleeves	5	6

Solution

a. Add corresponding elements in the matrices.

$\begin{bmatrix} 10 & 15 \\ 8 & 12 \\ 14 & 5 \end{bmatrix} + \begin{bmatrix} 12 & 5 \\ 4 & 3 \\ 5 & 6 \end{bmatrix} = \begin{bmatrix} 10+12 & 15+5 \\ 8+4 & 12+3 \\ 14+5 & 5+6 \end{bmatrix} = \begin{bmatrix} 22 & 20 \\ 12 & 15 \\ 19 & 11 \end{bmatrix}$

b. You need to find the element in the matrix from part (a) that corresponds to large, long sleeve shirts. The element in the third row and first column corresponds to large, long sleeve shirts. A total of **19** large, long sleeve shirts were sold.

	Large	Extra Large
T-shirts	22	20
Sweatshirts	12	15
Long sleeves	**19**	11

Checkpoint ✓ **Add and Subtract Matrices**

Add or subtract, if possible. If not possible, state the reason.

4. $\begin{bmatrix} 3 & 0 \\ 2 & 4 \end{bmatrix} + \begin{bmatrix} 1 & 3 \\ -2 & 2 \end{bmatrix}$

5. $\begin{bmatrix} 3 \\ 4 \\ 7 \end{bmatrix} + \begin{bmatrix} 5 & 2 \\ 6 & 4 \\ -3 & 6 \end{bmatrix}$

6. $\begin{bmatrix} 5 & 2 \\ 3 & 0 \end{bmatrix} - \begin{bmatrix} 4 & 3 \\ 1 & 2 \end{bmatrix}$

Scalar Multiplication In operations with matrices, a real number is often called a **scalar**. To multiply a matrix by a scalar, you multiply each entry in the matrix by the scalar. This process is called **scalar multiplication**.

EXAMPLE 4 Multiply a Matrix by a Scalar

a. $-1\begin{bmatrix} 3 & 0 \\ -2 & 1 \end{bmatrix} = \begin{bmatrix} -1(3) & -1(0) \\ -1(-2) & -1(1) \end{bmatrix} = \begin{bmatrix} -3 & 0 \\ 2 & -1 \end{bmatrix}$

b. $2\begin{bmatrix} -1 & 4 \\ 0 & 3 \end{bmatrix} = \begin{bmatrix} 2(-1) & 2(4) \\ 2(0) & 2(3) \end{bmatrix} = \begin{bmatrix} -2 & 8 \\ 0 & 6 \end{bmatrix}$

EXAMPLE 5 Perform Multiple Operations

A store sells small and large steel DVD racks with wooden bases. Each size is available in three types of wood: walnut, pine, and cherry. Sales of the racks for last month and this month are shown.

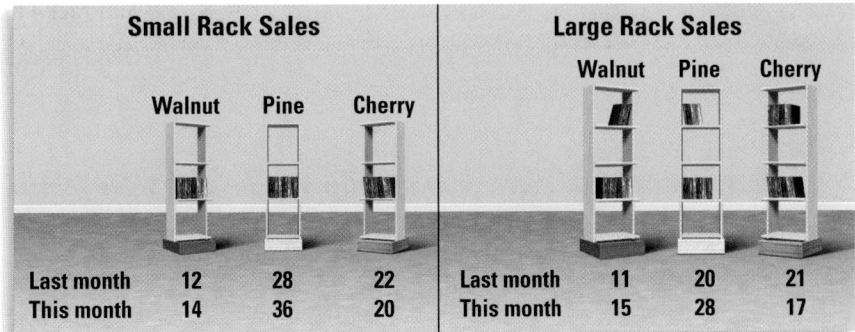

Small Rack Sales	Walnut	Pine	Cherry		Large Rack Sales	Walnut	Pine	Cherry
Last month	12	28	22		Last month	11	20	21
This month	14	36	20		This month	15	28	17

Use the matrices to find the average monthly sales for the two month period.

Last month (*A*)

	Small	Large
Walnut	12	11
Pine	28	20
Cherry	22	21

This month (*B*)

	Small	Large
Walnut	14	15
Pine	36	28
Cherry	20	17

Solution

You can find the average monthly sales for the two month period by adding matrices *A* and *B* together and multiplying the sum by $\frac{1}{2}$.

$\frac{1}{2}(A + B) = \frac{1}{2}\left(\begin{bmatrix} 12 & 11 \\ 28 & 20 \\ 22 & 21 \end{bmatrix} + \begin{bmatrix} 14 & 15 \\ 36 & 28 \\ 20 & 17 \end{bmatrix} \right)$ Write the average.

$= \frac{1}{2}\left(\begin{bmatrix} 26 & 26 \\ 64 & 48 \\ 42 & 38 \end{bmatrix} \right)$ Add matrices *A* and *B*.

$= \begin{bmatrix} 13 & 13 \\ 32 & 24 \\ 21 & 19 \end{bmatrix}$ Multiply each element by $\frac{1}{2}$.

STUDENT HELP

ANOTHER WAY
You can also evaluate $\frac{1}{2}(A + B)$ by first using the distributive property to write $\frac{1}{2}A + \frac{1}{2}B$, and then simplifying.

Solving Matrix Equations You can use what you know about matrix operations to solve an equation involving matrices.

EXAMPLE 6 Solve a Matrix Equation

Solve the matrix equation for x.
$$\begin{bmatrix} 2x & -1 \\ 3 & 0 \end{bmatrix} + \begin{bmatrix} 4 & -1 \\ 3 & 15 \end{bmatrix} = \begin{bmatrix} 12 & -2 \\ 6 & 15 \end{bmatrix}$$

Solution

To solve the matrix equation, add the matrices on the left side of the equation, equate the element involving x with its corresponding element, and solve for x.

$$\begin{bmatrix} 2x & -1 \\ 3 & 0 \end{bmatrix} + \begin{bmatrix} 4 & -1 \\ 3 & 15 \end{bmatrix} = \begin{bmatrix} 12 & -2 \\ 6 & 15 \end{bmatrix}$$ Write original equation.

$$\begin{bmatrix} 2x + 4 & -2 \\ 6 & 15 \end{bmatrix} = \begin{bmatrix} 12 & -2 \\ 6 & 15 \end{bmatrix}$$ Add corresponding matrix elements.

$2x + 4 = 12$ Equate corresponding elements $2x + 4$ and 12.

$2x = 8$ Subtract 4 from each side.

$x = 4$ Divide each side by 2.

Checkpoint ✓ *Perform Matrix Operations and Solve Matrix Equations*

Perform the indicated operation(s).

7. $2\begin{bmatrix} 1 & -2 \\ 3 & 5 \end{bmatrix}$

8. $5\left(\begin{bmatrix} -2 & 3 \\ 1 & 0 \end{bmatrix} + \begin{bmatrix} -1 & -2 \\ 4 & 7 \end{bmatrix}\right)$

Solve the matrix equation for x.

9. $\begin{bmatrix} x \\ 25 \\ -2 \end{bmatrix} + \begin{bmatrix} 24 \\ 5 \\ -10 \end{bmatrix} = \begin{bmatrix} 27 \\ 30 \\ -12 \end{bmatrix}$

10. $\begin{bmatrix} -1 & 3 \\ 3x & 7 \end{bmatrix} - \begin{bmatrix} -4 & 3 \\ 6 & 5 \end{bmatrix} = \begin{bmatrix} 3 & 0 \\ 18 & 2 \end{bmatrix}$

Matrix Operations The order of operations for matrix expressions is similar to that for real numbers. When multiplying one matrix by a scalar and adding the product to or subtracting the product from another matrix, perform the scalar multiplication first. Several properties of matrix operations are stated below.

Properties of Matrix Addition and Subtraction

Let A, B, and C be matrices with the same dimensions, and let k be a scalar.

Associative Property of Addition	$(A + B) + C = A + (B + C)$
Commutative Property of Addition	$A + B = B + A$
Distributive Property of Addition	$k(A + B) = kA + kB$
Distributive Property of Subtraction	$k(A - B) = kA - kB$

Guided Practice

Vocabulary Check

1. Copy and complete the statement: A 4×3 matrix has ___?___ columns.

2. Are $\begin{bmatrix} 1 & 3 \\ -4 & 2 \\ 6 & -7 \end{bmatrix}$ and $\begin{bmatrix} 1 & 3 \\ -4 & 2 \\ 6 & 7 \end{bmatrix}$ equal matrices? Explain.

3. Copy and complete the statement: You can add or subtract matrices only if the ___?___ are the same.

Skill Check

Add or subtract, if possible. If not possible, state the reason.

4. $\begin{bmatrix} 10 & 8 \\ -4 & 1 \end{bmatrix} + \begin{bmatrix} 5 & -2 \\ 12 & 3 \end{bmatrix}$

5. $\begin{bmatrix} 20 & 15 \\ 6 & 12 \end{bmatrix} - \begin{bmatrix} 16 & 13 \\ 1 & 5 \end{bmatrix}$

6. $\begin{bmatrix} -3 \\ 5 \\ 9 \end{bmatrix} + \begin{bmatrix} 4 & 0 \\ -14 & 12 \\ 11 & -20 \end{bmatrix}$

7. $\begin{bmatrix} -2 \\ 7 \\ -3 \end{bmatrix} - \begin{bmatrix} 3 \\ 15 \\ 4 \end{bmatrix}$

8. Inventory A department store has a clothing sale. The matrices show the number of items in stock before the sale and after the sale. Use the matrices to find the number of each item sold during the sale.

Before Sale

	Men's	Women's
T-shirts	100	125
Shorts	75	90
Hats	40	35

After Sale

	Men's	Women's
T-shirts	65	40
Shorts	50	53
Hats	15	20

Practice and Applications

STUDENT HELP

HOMEWORK HELP
Example 1: Exs. 9–12
Example 2: Exs. 13–20,
  30–35
Example 3: Exs. 21–23
Example 4: Exs. 24–35
Example 5: Exs. 36–37
Example 6: Exs. 38–43

Comparing Matrices **Tell whether the matrices are equal. Explain.**

9. $\begin{bmatrix} -1 & 9 \\ 7 & -2 \end{bmatrix}, \begin{bmatrix} -1 & 9 \\ 7 & -2 \end{bmatrix}$

10. $\begin{bmatrix} \frac{1}{2} & 4 & 20 \\ -3 & 7 & 11 \end{bmatrix}, \begin{bmatrix} \frac{1}{2} & -3 \\ 4 & 7 \\ 20 & 11 \end{bmatrix}$

11. $\begin{bmatrix} 6 & 10 & -3 \end{bmatrix}, \begin{bmatrix} 6 \\ (17-7) \\ (-9+6) \end{bmatrix}$

12. $\begin{bmatrix} 5 & -1 \\ 3(4) & 4 \end{bmatrix}, \begin{bmatrix} 5 & -1 \\ 12 & 6\left(\frac{2}{3}\right) \end{bmatrix}$

Error Analysis **Describe and correct the error.**

13. $\begin{bmatrix} 5 & -1 \\ 3 & 4 \end{bmatrix} + \begin{bmatrix} 7 \\ 3 \end{bmatrix} = \begin{bmatrix} 5 & -1 & 7 \\ 3 & 4 & 3 \end{bmatrix}$ ✗

14. $\begin{bmatrix} 9 & -2 \\ 10 & 5 \end{bmatrix} - \begin{bmatrix} -1 & 3 \\ 4 & 2 \end{bmatrix} = \begin{bmatrix} 8 & 1 \\ 14 & 7 \end{bmatrix}$ ✗

Adding and Subtracting Matrices Add or subtract, if possible. If not possible, state the reason.

15. $\begin{bmatrix} 6 \\ 1 \\ 3 \end{bmatrix} + \begin{bmatrix} 9 \\ -5 \\ -5 \end{bmatrix}$

16. $\begin{bmatrix} 4 & -6 \\ 5 & 3 \end{bmatrix} - \begin{bmatrix} -3 & 4 \\ 3 & 1 \end{bmatrix}$

17. $\begin{bmatrix} 1 & 7 \end{bmatrix} + \begin{bmatrix} 3 \\ 2 \end{bmatrix}$

18. $\begin{bmatrix} 3 & -5 \\ 2 & 7 \end{bmatrix} + \begin{bmatrix} 2 & -1 \\ 7 & -8 \end{bmatrix}$

19. $\begin{bmatrix} 10 & -2 \\ 4 & 1 \\ 9 & -5 \end{bmatrix} - \begin{bmatrix} 9 & -5 \\ 6 & 7 \\ 2 & 4 \end{bmatrix}$

20. $\begin{bmatrix} 6 & 2 \\ 1 & 9 \\ 7 & 5 \end{bmatrix} - \begin{bmatrix} 2 & 3 \\ 4 & 2 \end{bmatrix}$

21. Football The matrices below show the number of wins and losses for home and road games for four NFL teams during the 2006 season. Use matrix addition to write a matrix showing the total number of wins and losses for each team.

	Home Games Wins Losses	**Road Games** Wins Losses
Indianapolis	8 0	4 4
Tennessee	4 4	4 4
Jacksonville	6 2	2 6
Houston	4 4	2 6

22. Olympic Medals The matrices below show the number of gold, silver, and bronze medals won by three countries during the Winter Olympic Games in 2002 and 2006. Use matrix addition to write a matrix showing the total number of gold, silver, and bronze medals won by each country.

	2002 Gold Silver Bronze	**2006** Gold Silver Bronze
Finland	4 2 1	0 6 3
Australia	2 0 0	1 0 1
United States	10 13 11	9 9 7

23. College Costs The matrices below show the average yearly cost (in dollars) and the average room and board cost (in dollars) at colleges in the United States in 1993 and 2003. The total cost is the sum of the tuition cost and the room and board cost. Use matrix subtraction to write a matrix showing only the tuition cost for each type of college.

	Total Cost 1993 2003	**Room and Board** 1993 2003
Public 2-Year Colleges	3996 6020	2871 4319
Public 4-Year Colleges	6365 10,674	3829 6087
Private 2-Year Colleges	10,406 19,559	4037 8013
Private 4-Year Colleges	15,904 25,083	4951 7306

Multiplying by a Scalar Perform the indicated operation.

24. $3 \begin{bmatrix} 4 \\ -2 \end{bmatrix}$

25. $-4 \begin{bmatrix} -1 \\ 8 \\ -5 \end{bmatrix}$

26. $2 \begin{bmatrix} 3 & -1 \\ -4 & 7 \end{bmatrix}$

27. $5 \begin{bmatrix} 2 & 8 \\ -6 & 3 \end{bmatrix}$

28. $-1.5 \begin{bmatrix} -7 & 8 & 5 \\ 3 & -1 & 4 \end{bmatrix}$

29. $\frac{1}{4} \begin{bmatrix} 3 & 7 \\ -4 & 2 \\ -3 & 8 \end{bmatrix}$

Combining Matrix Operations Perform the indicated operations.

30. $3\begin{bmatrix} 1 \\ -3 \\ -4 \end{bmatrix} + \begin{bmatrix} 2 \\ 7 \\ 9 \end{bmatrix}$

31. $\begin{bmatrix} 0 & 4 \\ -5 & -6 \end{bmatrix} - 4\begin{bmatrix} 1 & -5 \\ 4 & 2 \end{bmatrix}$

32. $-6\left(\begin{bmatrix} 0 & -6 \\ -3 & 0 \end{bmatrix} + \begin{bmatrix} 5 & 4 \\ 5 & -6 \end{bmatrix} \right)$

33. $2\begin{bmatrix} 6 & -4 \\ 1 & -2 \\ 3 & -1 \end{bmatrix} - \begin{bmatrix} 10 & 3 \\ 5 & 6 \\ 12 & 9 \end{bmatrix}$

34. $\begin{bmatrix} 10 & -8 \\ -1 & 6 \\ 7 & 15 \end{bmatrix} - 5\begin{bmatrix} -3 & 5 \\ 2 & -1 \\ 1 & -4 \end{bmatrix}$

35. $4\left(\begin{bmatrix} 3 & 5 & 7 \\ 1 & 2 & 3 \end{bmatrix} - \begin{bmatrix} 1 & 3 & 6 \\ 0 & 2 & 6 \end{bmatrix} \right)$

Sales Bonus **In Exercises 36 and 37, use the following information.**

An insurance company is offering a reward plan for its sales staff. A salesperson receives a $100 bonus for each new policy and a $50 bonus for each policy renewal. The matrices below show the number of new policies, the number of policy renewals, and the base salary for three salespeople.

	New Policies (*N*)	Policy Renewals (*R*)	Base Salary (*B*)
Salesperson 1	$\begin{bmatrix} 20 \\ 15 \\ 25 \end{bmatrix}$	$\begin{bmatrix} 35 \\ 30 \\ 40 \end{bmatrix}$	$\begin{bmatrix} 35{,}000 \\ 40{,}000 \\ 30{,}000 \end{bmatrix}$
Salesperson 2			
Salesperson 3			

36. Use scalar multiplication and matrix addition to write an expression in terms of *N*, *R*, and *B* that you could use to determine the yearly earnings for each salesperson.

37. Evaluate the expression in Exercise 36 to write a matrix showing the yearly earnings for each salesperson.

Solving Matrix Equations **Solve the matrix equation for *x*.**

38. $\begin{bmatrix} x & 8 \\ 4 & 1 \end{bmatrix} = \begin{bmatrix} -4 & 8 \\ 4 & 1 \end{bmatrix}$

39. $\begin{bmatrix} 6 & 2x \\ -4 & 5 \end{bmatrix} = \begin{bmatrix} 6 & -12 \\ -4 & 5 \end{bmatrix}$

40. $\begin{bmatrix} 3 & 7 \\ 4 & -2 \end{bmatrix} + \begin{bmatrix} -9 & 8 \\ -7 & 2 \end{bmatrix} = \begin{bmatrix} 6x & 15 \\ -3 & 0 \end{bmatrix}$

41. $\begin{bmatrix} 4x \\ 28 \\ 10 \end{bmatrix} - \begin{bmatrix} 3 \\ -2 \\ 4 \end{bmatrix} = 3\begin{bmatrix} 5 \\ 10 \\ 2 \end{bmatrix}$

42. $2\begin{bmatrix} -1 & 3 & x \\ 3 & -8 & 1 \end{bmatrix} = \begin{bmatrix} -2 & 6 & 22 \\ 6 & -16 & 2 \end{bmatrix}$

43. $\begin{bmatrix} 2x & 3 \\ -4 & 1 \\ 6 & 7 \end{bmatrix} + \begin{bmatrix} 8 & 1 \\ 20 & 7 \\ 4 & 1 \end{bmatrix} = \begin{bmatrix} 6x & 4 \\ 16 & 8 \\ 10 & 8 \end{bmatrix}$

Challenge **Solve the matrix equation for *x* and *y*.**

44. $\begin{bmatrix} x & 6 \\ 3 & -1 \end{bmatrix} = \begin{bmatrix} -4 & 6 \\ y & -1 \end{bmatrix}$

45. $\begin{bmatrix} 4x \\ 2 \end{bmatrix} - \begin{bmatrix} 3 \\ -2 \end{bmatrix} = \begin{bmatrix} 13 \\ y \end{bmatrix}$

46. $3\begin{bmatrix} 4 & 3 & 3x \\ 1 & y & -1 \end{bmatrix} = \begin{bmatrix} 12 & 9 & -18 \\ 3 & -15 & -32 \end{bmatrix}$

47. $4\begin{bmatrix} 2x & 0 \\ 1 & 1 \end{bmatrix} + \begin{bmatrix} 8 & 1 \\ 7y & 2 \end{bmatrix} = \begin{bmatrix} -2x & 1 \\ 17 & 6 \end{bmatrix}$

48. Logical Reasoning Find two matrices *A* and *B* such that $A + B = \begin{bmatrix} 6 & 9 \\ 4 & 8 \end{bmatrix}$.

49. Multiple Choice Which matrix is equal to $\begin{bmatrix} 10 & 7 & -1 \\ 1 & -4 & 6 \end{bmatrix} - \begin{bmatrix} 4 & -1 & 9 \\ 5 & -6 & 2 \end{bmatrix}$?

(A) $\begin{bmatrix} 14 & 6 & 8 \\ 6 & -2 & 8 \end{bmatrix}$

(B) $\begin{bmatrix} 6 & 6 & -8 \\ -4 & -10 & 4 \end{bmatrix}$

(C) $\begin{bmatrix} 6 & -4 \\ 8 & 2 \\ -10 & 4 \end{bmatrix}$

(D) $\begin{bmatrix} 6 & 8 & -10 \\ -4 & 2 & 4 \end{bmatrix}$

50. Multiple Choice Which matrix is equal to $\begin{bmatrix} -10 & 5 \\ -9 & 3 \\ -5 & 20 \end{bmatrix} + 4\begin{bmatrix} 2 & 1 \\ 3 & -3 \\ 5 & -7 \end{bmatrix}$?

(F) $\begin{bmatrix} 2 & 3 & 15 \\ 9 & 9 & 8 \end{bmatrix}$
(G) $\begin{bmatrix} -8 & 6 \\ -6 & 0 \\ 0 & 13 \end{bmatrix}$
(H) $\begin{bmatrix} -18 & 1 \\ -21 & -9 \\ -25 & 48 \end{bmatrix}$
(J) $\begin{bmatrix} -2 & 9 \\ 3 & -9 \\ 15 & -8 \end{bmatrix}$

51. Multiple Choice Which value of x satisfies the following matrix equation?

$$\begin{bmatrix} -2 & 4x \\ 5 & 1 \end{bmatrix} + \begin{bmatrix} 5 & -3 \\ -14 & -7 \end{bmatrix} = \begin{bmatrix} 3 & -15 \\ -9 & -6 \end{bmatrix}$$

(A) -5 (B) -3 (C) $-\dfrac{15}{4}$ (D) $\dfrac{18}{4}$

Mixed Review

Simplifying Expressions Simplify the expression. Assume x is positive in Exercises 56 and 57. *(Lesson 8.5)*

52. $\log_4 5 + \log_4 6$

53. $\log_3 8 - \log_3 2$

54. $2 \log 6 - \log 12$

55. $2 \log_4 8 + \log_4 4$

56. $3 \log_2 x + \log_2 9$

57. $x \log_9 5 - \log_9 7$

Inverse Variation Models The variables *x* and *y* vary inversely. Use the given values to write an equation relating *x* and *y*. *(Lesson 9.1)*

58. $x = 6, y = 2$

59. $x = 4, y = 3$

60. $x = -2, y = 5$

61. $x = -7, y = 4$

62. $x = \dfrac{1}{4}, y = 8$

63. $x = 3, y = \dfrac{2}{3}$

Permutations Find the number of permutations. *(Lesson 10.4)*

64. $_6P_2$

65. $_8P_3$

66. $_5P_4$

67. $_9P_5$

68. $_{10}P_3$

69. $_{10}P_7$

Geometry Skills

Alternate Exterior Angles Find the measure of $\angle ABC$.

70.
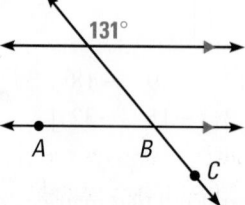

71.
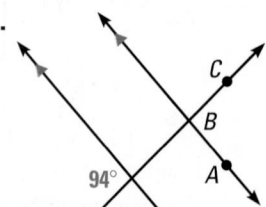

72.
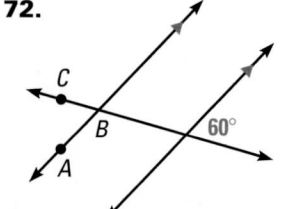

USING A GRAPHING CALCULATOR (For use with Lesson 11.1)
Using Matrix Operations

You can use a graphing calculator to perform matrix operations.

EXAMPLE

The matrices show movie sales (in thousands) for a video store chain during a two month period. The movie formats are DVD and VHS. The categories of movies are Comedy (C), Action (A), Children's (Ch), and Drama (D).

January

	C	A	Ch	D
DVD	32	21	12	19
VHS	24	15	30	18

a. Find the total sales for the two months.

b. Estimate the DVD sales of comedies in March if a 5% decrease from the February sales is expected.

February

	C	A	Ch	D
DVD	29	31	10	15
VHS	20	17	25	17

SOLUTION

STUDENT HELP

KEYSTROKE HELP
See keystrokes for several models of calculators at www.classzone.com.

a. Let matrix A represent January sales and matrix B represent February sales. Enter each matrix on a graphing calculator. Then find the sum of matrix A and matrix B.

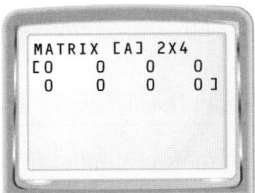

Enter the dimensions of each matrix.

Enter the elements in each matrix row by row.

Add the matrices to find the total cost.

STUDENT HELP

SOLVING NOTE
A 5% decrease from the February sales is expected for March sales, so to find the March sales, multiply the February sales by 100% − 5% = 95%, or 0.95.

b. To estimate the sales for March, multiply matrix B by the scalar 0.95. You can see that March sales for comedy DVDs are expected to be 27.55 thousand, or 27,550.

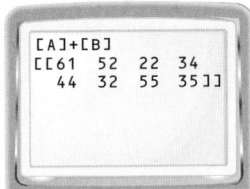

EXERCISES

Use a graphing calculator to perform the indicated operation(s).

1. $\begin{bmatrix} 97 & 83 \\ 42 & 58 \end{bmatrix} + \begin{bmatrix} 103 & 57 \\ 123 & 94 \end{bmatrix}$

2. $\begin{bmatrix} 578 & 601 & 492 \\ 529 & 501 & 592 \\ 495 & 612 & 534 \end{bmatrix} - \begin{bmatrix} 478 & 502 & 587 \\ 493 & 613 & 525 \\ 534 & 609 & 512 \end{bmatrix}$

3. $1.057 \begin{bmatrix} 6.3 & 7.9 \\ 3.2 & 12.8 \end{bmatrix}$

4. $2.45 \begin{bmatrix} 5.02 & 0.73 \\ 2.35 & 1.7 \end{bmatrix} + 0.13 \begin{bmatrix} 4.09 & 3.57 \\ 0.06 & 2.17 \end{bmatrix}$

5. Movies Write a matrix that gives the change in sales from January to February for the video store chain in the example. For which categories of DVD and VHS did sales increase? For which categories did sales decrease?

11.2 Multiplying Matrices

GOAL Multiply matrices.

Key Words
- dimensions of a matrix, p. 585

What is the cost of hockey equipment?

You will use matrix multiplication in Example 4 to find the cost of equipment for two hockey teams.

Prerequisite Skills

Simplify.

1. $2(3) + 1(-1)$
2. $3(-1) + 2(2)$
3. $5(1) + (-1)(-1) + 4(0)$
4. $2(-1) + (1)(-2) + 3(2)$

You can multiply two matrices A and B if the number of columns in A is equal to the number of rows in B. Otherwise, the product is not defined.

If the dimensions of A are $m \times n$, and the dimensions of B are $n \times p$, then the dimensions of the product AB are $m \times p$.

$$A \cdot B = AB$$
$$m \times n \quad n \times p \quad m \times p$$

equal

dimensions of AB

For example, you can multiply the two matrices $A = \begin{bmatrix} 2 & 0 \\ 1 & 1 \end{bmatrix}$ and $B = \begin{bmatrix} 1 \\ 2 \end{bmatrix}$ because there are two columns in A and two rows in B.

EXAMPLE 1 Describe Matrix Products

Given the dimensions of matrices A and B, tell whether the product AB is defined. If so, give the dimensions of AB.

a. A: 3×2, B: 2×1

b. A: 2×3, B: 2×2

Solution

a. Because A is a 3×2 matrix and B is a 2×1 matrix, the product AB is defined. The dimensions of AB are 3×1.

b. Because the number of columns in A (three) *does not* equal the number of rows in B (two), the product AB is *not* defined.

Matrix Multiplication

To find the product of two matrices, multiply the elements of each row of the first matrix by the elements of each column of the second matrix, and then add the products, as shown below.

ALGEBRA

$$\begin{bmatrix} a & b \\ c & d \end{bmatrix} \cdot \begin{bmatrix} e & f \\ g & h \end{bmatrix} = \begin{bmatrix} ae + bg & af + bh \\ ce + dg & cf + dh \end{bmatrix}$$

EXAMPLE

$$\begin{bmatrix} 2 & 3 \\ 5 & 0 \end{bmatrix} \begin{bmatrix} -1 & 4 \\ 1 & 3 \end{bmatrix} = \begin{bmatrix} 2(-1) + (3)(1) & 2(4) + (3)(3) \\ 5(-1) + (0)(1) & 5(4) + (0)(3) \end{bmatrix} = \begin{bmatrix} 1 & 17 \\ -5 & 20 \end{bmatrix}$$

EXAMPLE 2 Multiply Matrices

Find the product AB when $A = \begin{bmatrix} 1 & 4 \\ 3 & 2 \end{bmatrix}$ and $B = \begin{bmatrix} 5 & 0 \\ 9 & 6 \end{bmatrix}$.

Solution

Multiply the numbers in the first row of A by the numbers in the first column of B, add the products, and put the result in the first row, first column of AB.

$$\begin{bmatrix} 1 & 4 \\ 3 & 2 \end{bmatrix}\begin{bmatrix} 5 & 0 \\ 9 & 6 \end{bmatrix} = \begin{bmatrix} 1(5) + 4(9) & \\ & \end{bmatrix}$$

Multiply the numbers in the first row of A by the numbers in the second column of B, add the products, and put the result in the first row, second column of AB.

$$\begin{bmatrix} 1 & 4 \\ 3 & 2 \end{bmatrix}\begin{bmatrix} 5 & 0 \\ 9 & 6 \end{bmatrix} = \begin{bmatrix} 1(5) + 4(9) & 1(0) + 4(6) \\ & \end{bmatrix}$$

Multiply the numbers in the second row of A by the numbers in the first column of B, add the products, and put the result in the second row, first column of AB.

$$\begin{bmatrix} 1 & 4 \\ 3 & 2 \end{bmatrix}\begin{bmatrix} 5 & 0 \\ 9 & 6 \end{bmatrix} = \begin{bmatrix} 1(5) + 4(9) & 1(0) + 4(6) \\ 3(5) + 2(9) & \end{bmatrix}$$

Multiply the numbers in the second row of A by the numbers in the second column of B, add the products, and put the result in the second row, second column of AB.

$$\begin{bmatrix} 1 & 4 \\ 3 & 2 \end{bmatrix}\begin{bmatrix} 5 & 0 \\ 9 & 6 \end{bmatrix} = \begin{bmatrix} 1(5) + 4(9) & 1(0) + 4(6) \\ 3(5) + 2(9) & 3(0) + 2(6) \end{bmatrix}$$

Simplify the product matrix.

$$\begin{bmatrix} 1 & 4 \\ 3 & 2 \end{bmatrix}\begin{bmatrix} 5 & 0 \\ 9 & 6 \end{bmatrix} = \begin{bmatrix} 1(5) + 4(9) & 1(0) + 4(6) \\ 3(5) + 2(9) & 3(0) + 2(6) \end{bmatrix} = \begin{bmatrix} 41 & 24 \\ 33 & 12 \end{bmatrix}$$

In Example 2, you found the product AB. Notice that the product BA, shown below, is not the same as the product AB. In general, matrix multiplication is *not* commutative.

$$BA = \begin{bmatrix} 5 & 0 \\ 9 & 6 \end{bmatrix}\begin{bmatrix} 1 & 4 \\ 3 & 2 \end{bmatrix} = \begin{bmatrix} 5 & 20 \\ 27 & 48 \end{bmatrix} \neq AB$$

Checkpoint ✓ Multiply Matrices

Given the dimensions of the matrices *A* and *B*, tell whether the product *AB* is defined. If so, give the dimensions of *AB*.

1. $A: 2 \times 2, B: 2 \times 1$ **2.** $A: 2 \times 3, B: 3 \times 1$ **3.** $A: 3 \times 1, B: 2 \times 3$

Find the product. If it is not defined, state the reason.

4. $\begin{bmatrix} 2 & 1 \\ 1 & 3 \end{bmatrix}\begin{bmatrix} 0 \\ 1 \end{bmatrix}$ **5.** $\begin{bmatrix} 2 & 0 \\ -1 & 1 \end{bmatrix}\begin{bmatrix} 0 & -1 \\ 3 & 0 \end{bmatrix}$ **6.** $\begin{bmatrix} 1 & -1 \\ -1 & 0 \end{bmatrix}\begin{bmatrix} 1 & 3 \\ 2 & -1 \end{bmatrix}$

EXAMPLE 3 | Use a Property of Matrix Multiplication

Let $A = \begin{bmatrix} 2 & 1 \\ 0 & -1 \end{bmatrix}$, $B = \begin{bmatrix} 1 & 3 \\ 2 & -1 \end{bmatrix}$, and $C = \begin{bmatrix} 0 & -1 \\ 3 & 1 \end{bmatrix}$. Simplify $AB + AC$.

Solution

$$AB + AC = A(B + C) \qquad \text{Left Distributive Property}$$

$$= \begin{bmatrix} 2 & 1 \\ 0 & -1 \end{bmatrix} \left(\begin{bmatrix} 1 & 3 \\ 2 & -1 \end{bmatrix} + \begin{bmatrix} 0 & -1 \\ 3 & 1 \end{bmatrix} \right) \qquad \text{Substitute for } A, B, \text{ and } C.$$

$$= \begin{bmatrix} 2 & 1 \\ 0 & -1 \end{bmatrix} \left(\begin{bmatrix} 1 & 2 \\ 5 & 0 \end{bmatrix} \right) \qquad \text{Add } B \text{ and } C.$$

$$= \begin{bmatrix} 2(1) + 1(5) & 2(2) + 1(0) \\ 0(1) + (-1)(5) & 0(2) + (-1)(0) \end{bmatrix} \qquad \text{Multiply.}$$

$$= \begin{bmatrix} 7 & 4 \\ -5 & 0 \end{bmatrix} \qquad \text{Simplify.}$$

Link to
SPORTS

HOCKEY The Minnesota Golden Gophers celebrate scoring a goal during the final game of the Women's Frozen Four tournament.

EXAMPLE 4 | Use Matrix Multiplication

Hockey The matrices below show the equipment two hockey teams need and the price of each item. Use the matrices to find the total cost of the new equipment.

	Equipment				**Cost**
	Sticks	Pucks	Uniforms		Dollars
Women's Team	14	30	18	Sticks	60
Men's Team	16	25	20	Pucks	2
				Uniforms	35

Solution

Multiply the equipment matrix by the cost matrix to find each team's total cost.

$$\begin{bmatrix} 14 & 30 & 18 \\ 16 & 25 & 20 \end{bmatrix} \begin{bmatrix} 60 \\ 2 \\ 35 \end{bmatrix} = \begin{bmatrix} 14(60) + 30(2) + 18(35) \\ 16(60) + 25(2) + 20(35) \end{bmatrix} = \begin{bmatrix} 1530 \\ 1710 \end{bmatrix}$$

ANSWER ▶ The total cost is $1530 for the women's team and $1710 for the men's.

Checkpoint ✓ **Use Properties of Matrices**

7. Use the matrices in Example 3 to find $AB + AC$ without using the distributive property. Compare your answer to the solution in Example 3.

11.2 Exercises

Guided Practice

Vocabulary Check

1. Copy and complete the statement: The product of matrices A and B is defined when the number of __?__ in A is equal to the number of __?__ in B.

2. Let A, B, and C be 2×2 matrices. What property of matrix multiplication would you use to simplify $(A + B)C$?

Skill Check

Given the dimensions of A and B, tell whether the product AB is defined. If so, give the dimensions of AB.

3. A: 3×1, B: 3×1　　4. A: 5×5, B: 5×5　　5. A: 2×1, B: 1×2

Find the product.

6. $\begin{bmatrix} 1 & -2 \end{bmatrix} \begin{bmatrix} 3 & 4 \\ 0 & 1 \end{bmatrix}$

7. $\begin{bmatrix} 3 & 0 \\ 1 & -2 \\ 0 & 4 \end{bmatrix} \begin{bmatrix} -1 & 3 \\ 2 & 0 \end{bmatrix}$

8. $\begin{bmatrix} 1 & 2 \\ 0 & 1 \end{bmatrix} \begin{bmatrix} -3 & 0 \\ 1 & 3 \end{bmatrix}$

Practice and Applications

STUDENT HELP

HOMEWORK HELP
Example 1: Exs. 9–14
Example 2: Exs. 15–24
Example 3: Exs. 25–36
Example 4: Exs. 37–43

Describing Matrix Products Given the dimensions of A and B, tell whether the product AB is defined. If so, give the dimensions of AB.

9. A: 3×2, B: 1×2　　10. A: 3×4, B: 4×1　　11. A: 5×3, B: 3×4

12. A: 5×2, B: 4×2　　13. A: 4×1, B: 1×3　　14. A: 3×5, B: 5×2

Error Analysis Describe and correct the error in finding the element in the first row and first column of the matrix product.

15. $\begin{bmatrix} 3 & 1 \\ 6 & 2 \end{bmatrix} \begin{bmatrix} 7 & 0 \\ 1 & 6 \end{bmatrix} = \begin{bmatrix} 3(7) + 1(0) \end{bmatrix}$

$\times \qquad = \begin{bmatrix} 21 \end{bmatrix}$

16. $\begin{bmatrix} 2 & 5 \\ 1 & 7 \end{bmatrix} \begin{bmatrix} 1 & -1 \\ 3 & -1 \end{bmatrix} = \begin{bmatrix} 2(1) + 2(3) \end{bmatrix}$

$\times \qquad = \begin{bmatrix} 14 \end{bmatrix}$

Finding Products Find the product. If it is not defined, state the reason.

17. $\begin{bmatrix} 2 & 0 \\ 1 & -1 \end{bmatrix} \begin{bmatrix} 4 & -1 \\ 0 & 2 \end{bmatrix}$

18. $\begin{bmatrix} 4 & 2 \\ 0 & 1 \\ -2 & 0 \end{bmatrix} \begin{bmatrix} 2 \\ 1 \end{bmatrix}$

19. $\begin{bmatrix} 1 & 0 \\ 2 & -2 \end{bmatrix} \begin{bmatrix} -1 & 4 \end{bmatrix}$

20. $\begin{bmatrix} 2 & 0 & 1 \\ 0 & 1 & -2 \end{bmatrix} \begin{bmatrix} 4 & 1 \\ 0 & -2 \\ 1 & 0 \end{bmatrix}$

21. $\begin{bmatrix} 5 & 1 \\ 0 & -2 \end{bmatrix} \begin{bmatrix} 3 & 1 & 0 \\ 0 & 6 & -1 \end{bmatrix}$

22. $\begin{bmatrix} 8 & 0 \\ 1 & -2 \\ 0 & 3 \end{bmatrix} \begin{bmatrix} 2 & -1 \\ 0 & 4 \end{bmatrix}$

23. $\begin{bmatrix} 4 & 0 \\ 0 & 1 \\ 2 & -1 \end{bmatrix} \begin{bmatrix} 1 & 5 \\ -3 & 0 \\ 1 & 0 \end{bmatrix}$

24. $\begin{bmatrix} 0 & -1 & 0 \\ 2 & 1 & 0 \\ 3 & 0 & 7 \end{bmatrix} \begin{bmatrix} 1 & 2 & -1 \\ 0 & 2 & 0 \\ 1 & 5 & -2 \end{bmatrix}$

Simplifying Expressions Let $A = \begin{bmatrix} 3 & 1 \\ -2 & 0 \end{bmatrix}$, $B = \begin{bmatrix} 1 & -1 \\ 0 & -3 \end{bmatrix}$, and $C = \begin{bmatrix} 0 & 4 \\ -2 & 2 \end{bmatrix}$. Simplify the expression.

25. $3AB$

26. $-2(BC)$

27. $A(B + C)$

28. $(A + B)C$

29. $AB + BC$

30. $2AB + 3AC$

Simplifying Expressions Let $A = \begin{bmatrix} 6 & -8 \\ -11 & 10 \end{bmatrix}$, $B = \begin{bmatrix} -7 & -12 \\ 0 & -5 \end{bmatrix}$, and $C = \begin{bmatrix} 9 & 0 \\ -10 & 13 \end{bmatrix}$. Simplify the expression.

31. $-AB$

32. $-3(BC)$

33. $B(B + C)$

34. $(A + C)B$

35. $AB - BC$

36. $2A(B + 3C)$

Basketball In Exercises 37–39, use the following information.

The number of shots made by three players in a basketball game is shown in the matrix below. The three types of shots are 3 point field goals (3 PT), field goals (FG), and free throws (FT).

37. A player earns 3 points for a 3 point field goal, 2 points for a field goal, and 1 point for a free throw. Organize this information into a matrix B.

38. Find the product AB.

Matrix A

	3 PT	FG	FT
Player 1	1	2	4
Player 2	0	5	5
Player 3	3	2	1

39. Which player scored the most points? How many points did the player score?

Theater In Exercises 40–42, use the following information.

Your class is selling tickets to a play that will show for three nights. The numbers of student (S), adult (A), and senior citizen (SC) tickets are shown in the matrix below.

40. The tickets cost $2 for students, $5 for adults, and $3 for senior citizens. Organize this information into a matrix B.

41. Find the product AB.

Number of Tickets Sold

	S	A	SC
Night 1	120	75	40
Night 2	135	80	54
Night 3	100	72	52

42. On which night were the ticket sales highest? What was the amount earned from ticket sales on that night?

43. Art Supplies An art teacher buys supplies for two art classes. For class 1, the teacher buys 24 tubes of paint, 12 brushes, and 17 canvases. For class 2, the teacher buys 20 tubes of paint, 14 brushes, and 15 canvases. Each tube of paint costs $3.35, each brush costs $1.75, and each canvas costs $4.50. Write a matrix for the equipment and a matrix for the cost per item. Use matrix multiplication to find the total cost of the supplies for both classes.

Solving Matrix Equations In Exercises 44 and 45, solve for x and y.

44. $\begin{bmatrix} 3 & 1 & 2 \\ 0 & 2 & 0 \\ -1 & 0 & 1 \end{bmatrix} \begin{bmatrix} 1 \\ x \\ -1 \end{bmatrix} = \begin{bmatrix} 4 \\ 6 \\ y \end{bmatrix}$

45. $\begin{bmatrix} 1 & 4 & 0 \\ 0 & x & -3 \end{bmatrix} \begin{bmatrix} 0 & 1 \\ -1 & 2 \\ 3 & 0 \end{bmatrix} = \begin{bmatrix} y & 9 \\ -11 & 4 \end{bmatrix}$

Logical Reasoning In Exercises 46–48, A, B, and C are matrices. Tell whether or not the statement is *always* true. Explain your reasoning.

46. $AB = BA$

47. $(A + B)C = AC + BC$

48. $C(AB) = (CA)B$

Challenge In Exercises 49 and 50, use the matrices and graph below.

Matrix A is a transformation matrix. Matrix B gives the coordinates of the triangle's vertices shown in the graph.

$$A = \begin{bmatrix} 0 & -1 \\ 1 & 0 \end{bmatrix} \qquad B = \begin{bmatrix} 3 & 3 & 7 \\ 2 & 7 & 5 \end{bmatrix}$$

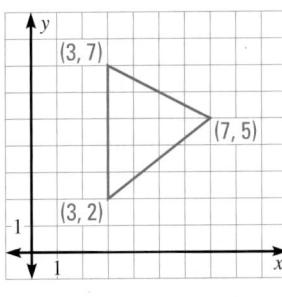

49. Calculate AB. Graph the coordinates of the vertices of the triangle given by AB. What transformation does AB represent in the graph?

50. Calculate $A(AB)$ and $A(A(AB))$. Graph the coordinates of the vertices of the triangle given by the products. What transformations do these products represent in the graph?

51. Multiple Choice A is a 2×3 matrix and B is a 3×4 matrix. What are the dimensions of the product AB?

(**A**) 3×3 (**B**) 4×2 (**C**) 2×4 (**D**) Not defined

52. Multiple Choice What is the product $\begin{bmatrix} 2 & 4 & 0 \\ 3 & 3 & 6 \end{bmatrix}\begin{bmatrix} 4 \\ 3 \end{bmatrix}$?

(**F**) $\begin{bmatrix} 8 & 16 & 0 \\ 9 & 9 & 18 \end{bmatrix}$ (**G**) $\begin{bmatrix} 17 & 25 & 18 \end{bmatrix}$ (**H**) $\begin{bmatrix} 24 \\ 36 \end{bmatrix}$ (**J**) Not defined

53. Multiple Choice What is the product $\begin{bmatrix} 1 & 0 & 3 \\ 2 & -1 & 0 \end{bmatrix}\begin{bmatrix} 3 & 1 \\ -2 & 0 \\ 0 & 3 \end{bmatrix}$?

(**A**) $\begin{bmatrix} 3 & 10 \\ 8 & 2 \end{bmatrix}$ (**B**) $\begin{bmatrix} 3 & 8 \\ 10 & 2 \end{bmatrix}$ (**C**) $\begin{bmatrix} 3 & 0 & 0 \\ 2 & 0 & 0 \end{bmatrix}$ (**D**) Not defined

Mixed Review

Solving Linear Systems Solve the system using the linear combinations method. *(Lesson 3.3)*

54. $3x - 2y = 7$
$2x + 3y = 9$

55. $2x + 3y = 1$
$4x + 5y = 7$

56. $5x + 7y = -6$
$2x - 3y = -14$

57. $2x - 5y = 4$
$7x + 2y = -25$

58. $5x + 4y = 4$
$7x + 2y = -25$

59. $7x + 6y = -4$
$3x + 4y = -1$

Multiplying by a Scalar Perform the indicated operation. *(Lesson 11.1)*

60. $2\begin{bmatrix} 2 & 0 \\ 3 & -1 \end{bmatrix}$

61. $-3\begin{bmatrix} 4 & -1 \\ 0 & 2 \\ 1 & 0 \end{bmatrix}$

62. $5\begin{bmatrix} 1 & 5 & -2 \end{bmatrix}$

63. $4\begin{bmatrix} 0 & 1 & 2 \\ -4 & 1 & 0 \\ 0 & -2 & 0 \end{bmatrix}$

64. $-2\begin{bmatrix} 0 & 2 & -1 \\ 5 & 1 & 1 \end{bmatrix}$

65. $10\begin{bmatrix} 5 & -2 \\ 0 & 3 \end{bmatrix}$

Geometry Skills

Surface Area Find the surface area of the sphere.

66.

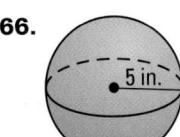

5 in.

67.

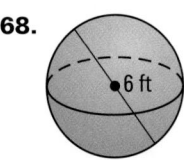

8 m

68.

6 ft

Solving Linear Systems Using Inverse Matrices

Key Words

- identity matrix
- inverse matrices
- coefficient matrix
- matrix of variables
- matrix of constants

GOAL Find inverse matrices and use them to solve linear systems.

Recall that the number 1 is the multiplicative identity for real numbers because $1 \cdot a = a \cdot 1 = a$. For matrices, the $n \times n$ **identity matrix** is a matrix that has 1's on the main diagonal and 0's elsewhere. If A is any $n \times n$ matrix and I is the $n \times n$ identity matrix, then $IA = AI = A$.

Prerequisite Skills

Find the product.

1. $\begin{bmatrix} 1 & 2 \\ 0 & 1 \end{bmatrix} \begin{bmatrix} 1 & -2 \\ 0 & 1 \end{bmatrix}$

2. $\begin{bmatrix} 2 & 1 \\ 3 & 2 \end{bmatrix} \begin{bmatrix} 2 & -1 \\ -3 & 2 \end{bmatrix}$

Solve the system of equations.

3. $x + y = 2$
$x + 2y = 5$

4. $2x - y = 4$
$x + 2y = 12$

2 × 2 Identity Matrix

$$I = \begin{bmatrix} 1 & 0 \\ 0 & 1 \end{bmatrix}$$

3 × 3 Identity Matrix

$$I = \begin{bmatrix} 1 & 0 & 0 \\ 0 & 1 & 0 \\ 0 & 0 & 1 \end{bmatrix}$$

Two $n \times n$ matrices are **inverse matrices** if their product (in both orders) is the $n \times n$ identity matrix. For example, consider the matrices below. The matrices are inverses of each other because $AB = BA = I$.

$$AB = \begin{bmatrix} 1 & 2 \\ 1 & 3 \end{bmatrix} \begin{bmatrix} 3 & -2 \\ -1 & 1 \end{bmatrix} = \begin{bmatrix} 1 & 0 \\ 0 & 1 \end{bmatrix} = I$$

$$BA = \begin{bmatrix} 3 & -2 \\ -1 & 1 \end{bmatrix} \begin{bmatrix} 1 & 2 \\ 1 & 3 \end{bmatrix} = \begin{bmatrix} 1 & 0 \\ 0 & 1 \end{bmatrix} = I$$

EXAMPLE 1 **Verify Inverse Matrices**

STUDENT HELP

AVOID ERRORS
Note that only square $n \times n$ matrices can have inverses.

Tell whether the matrices $A = \begin{bmatrix} 3 & -4 \\ 1 & -1 \end{bmatrix}$ and $B = \begin{bmatrix} -1 & 4 \\ -1 & 3 \end{bmatrix}$ are inverses.

Solution

You can show that A and B are inverses by showing that $AB = I$ and $BA = I$.

$$AB = \begin{bmatrix} 3 & -4 \\ 1 & -1 \end{bmatrix} \begin{bmatrix} -1 & 4 \\ -1 & 3 \end{bmatrix} = \begin{bmatrix} 3(-1) + (-4)(-1) & 3(4) + (-4)(3) \\ 1(-1) + (-1)(-1) & 1(4) + (-1)(3) \end{bmatrix} = \begin{bmatrix} 1 & 0 \\ 0 & 1 \end{bmatrix}$$

$$BA = \begin{bmatrix} -1 & 4 \\ -1 & 3 \end{bmatrix} \begin{bmatrix} 3 & -4 \\ 1 & -1 \end{bmatrix} = \begin{bmatrix} (-1)(3) + 4(1) & (-1)(-4) + 4(-1) \\ (-1)(3) + 3(1) & (-1)(-4) + 3(-1) \end{bmatrix} = \begin{bmatrix} 1 & 0 \\ 0 & 1 \end{bmatrix}$$

ANSWER ▶ Because both products AB and BA equal the 2 × 2 identity matrix, A and B are inverses.

Checkpoint ✓ Verify Inverse Matrices

Tell whether the matrices are inverses.

1. $\begin{bmatrix} 1 & 1 \\ -1 & 0 \end{bmatrix}, \begin{bmatrix} 0 & -1 \\ 1 & 1 \end{bmatrix}$ **2.** $\begin{bmatrix} 1 & 1 \\ 1 & 2 \end{bmatrix}, \begin{bmatrix} 2 & -1 \\ -1 & 1 \end{bmatrix}$ **3.** $\begin{bmatrix} 3 & 1 \\ -1 & 0 \end{bmatrix}, \begin{bmatrix} 0 & -1 \\ 1 & 3 \end{bmatrix}$

Finding Inverse Matrices To find the inverse of a matrix, you can use a graphing calculator. The symbol for the inverse of a matrix A is A^{-1}.

EXAMPLE 2 Find the Inverse of a Matrix

Use a graphing calculator to find the inverse of matrix A. Then use the calculator to verify that $AA^{-1} = I$ and $A^{-1}A = I$.

$$A = \begin{bmatrix} 1 & 0 & 0 \\ 3 & 1 & 0 \\ 2 & 5 & 1 \end{bmatrix}$$

Solution

Enter matrix A into the graphing calculator and calculate A^{-1}. Then find the products AA^{-1} and $A^{-1}A$ to verify that you obtain the 3×3 identity matrix.

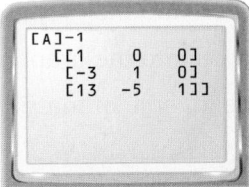

Find the inverse of A.

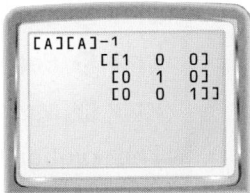

Verify $AA^{-1} = I$.

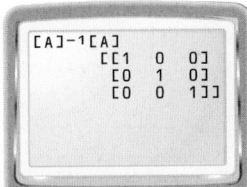

Verify $A^{-1}A = I$.

Checkpoint ✔ *Find Inverse Matrices*

Use a graphing calculator to find the inverse of matrix *A*. Then use the calculator to verify that $AA^{-1} = I$ and $A^{-1}A = I$.

4. $A = \begin{bmatrix} 3 & 5 \\ 1 & 2 \end{bmatrix}$

5. $A = \begin{bmatrix} 1 & 0 & 0 \\ -1 & 1 & 0 \\ 1 & 4 & 1 \end{bmatrix}$

6. $A = \begin{bmatrix} 2 & 3 & 1 \\ 2 & 1 & 0 \\ 1 & 3 & 1 \end{bmatrix}$

Writing a Matrix Equation A system of linear equations in standard form can be written as a matrix equation $AX = B$. The matrix A is the **coefficient matrix** of the system, X is the **matrix of variables**, and B is the **matrix of constants**.

EXAMPLE 3 Write a Matrix Equation

Write the system of linear equations as a matrix equation.

$x + 3y = 4$ Equation 1
$2x + 5y = 2$ Equation 2

Solution

You can write a matrix equation by finding the coefficient matrix A, the matrix of variables X, and the matrix of constants B. Then write the equation $AX = B$.

coefficient matrix (*A*)	matrix of variables (*X*)	matrix of constants (*B*)

$$\begin{bmatrix} 1 & 3 \\ 2 & 5 \end{bmatrix} \cdot \begin{bmatrix} x \\ y \end{bmatrix} = \begin{bmatrix} 4 \\ 2 \end{bmatrix}$$

Write the system of linear equations as a matrix equation.

7. $x - 4y = 5$
$4x + y = 3$

8. $2x - y = 4$
$3x - 2y = 8$

9. $3x - 2y = 2$
$4x - 3y = 1$

Solving a Matrix Equation Let $AX = B$ represent a system of linear equations. If A has an inverse, the linear system has exactly one solution: $X = A^{-1}B$.

Using an Inverse Matrix to Solve a Linear System

To find the solution of a linear system using a graphing calculator:

STEP ❶ Write the system as a matrix equation $AX = B$.

STEP ❷ Enter matrix A into the graphing calculator.

STEP ❸ Enter matrix B into the graphing calculator.

STEP ❹ Multiply the inverse of matrix A by matrix B.

The solution of $AX = B$ is $X = A^{-1}B$.

EXAMPLE 4 Solve a Linear System

Use an inverse matrix to solve the linear system.

$x + 2y = 4$ Equation 1
$2x + y = 2$ Equation 2

STUDENT HELP

SOLVING NOTE
Remember that you can use the method in Example 4 only if A has an inverse. If A does not have an inverse, then the system has either no solution or infinitely many solutions.

Solution

Write the linear system as a matrix equation: $\begin{bmatrix} 1 & 2 \\ 2 & 1 \end{bmatrix} \begin{bmatrix} x \\ y \end{bmatrix} = \begin{bmatrix} 4 \\ 2 \end{bmatrix}$.

Then use a graphing calculator to solve the system.

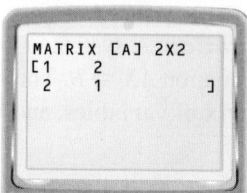   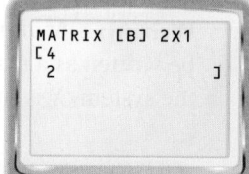   

Enter matrix A.   Enter matrix B.   Multiply A^{-1} by B.

So, $X = A^{-1}B = \begin{bmatrix} 0 \\ 2 \end{bmatrix}$, or $\begin{bmatrix} x \\ y \end{bmatrix} = \begin{bmatrix} 0 \\ 2 \end{bmatrix}$.

ANSWER ▶ The solution is $(0, 2)$. Check the solution in the original equations.

Use an inverse matrix to solve the linear system.

10. $x - 4y = 5$
$4x + y = 3$

11. $2x - y = 4$
$3x - 2y = 8$

12. $3x - 2y = 2$
$4x - 3y = 1$

11.3 Exercises

Guided Practice

Vocabulary Check

1. Identify the matrix of variables, the matrix of constants, and the coefficient matrix in the matrix equation $\begin{bmatrix} -4 & 5 \\ 1 & -7 \end{bmatrix} \begin{bmatrix} x \\ y \end{bmatrix} = \begin{bmatrix} -39 \\ 27 \end{bmatrix}$.

2. Provide an example of an $n \times n$ identity matrix.

Skill Check

Tell whether the matrices are inverses.

3. $\begin{bmatrix} 0 & 1 \\ 1 & -2 \end{bmatrix}, \begin{bmatrix} 2 & 1 \\ 1 & 0 \end{bmatrix}$

4. $\begin{bmatrix} 8 & -5 \\ -5 & 3 \end{bmatrix}, \begin{bmatrix} -3 & -5 \\ -5 & -8 \end{bmatrix}$

5. $\begin{bmatrix} 2 & 5 \\ 3 & 8 \end{bmatrix}, \begin{bmatrix} 8 & 5 \\ -3 & 2 \end{bmatrix}$

Use a graphing calculator to find the inverse of the matrix A. Then use the calculator to verify that $AA^{-1} = I$ and $A^{-1}A = I$.

6. $A = \begin{bmatrix} 9 & 4 \\ 4 & 2 \end{bmatrix}$

7. $A = \begin{bmatrix} 1 & -7 \\ 0 & 1 \end{bmatrix}$

8. $A = \begin{bmatrix} -1 & 3 \\ 2 & -7 \end{bmatrix}$

Write the system of linear equations as a matrix equation.

9. $5x + 2y = -14$
   $x + y = 0$

10. $4x - y = -14$
    $3x - 8y = -1$

11. $7x + 2y = -11$
    $2x - y = -10$

Practice and Applications

Identifying Inverses **Tell whether the matrices are inverses.**

12. $\begin{bmatrix} 3 & 1 \\ 1 & 0 \end{bmatrix}, \begin{bmatrix} 0 & 1 \\ 1 & -3 \end{bmatrix}$

13. $\begin{bmatrix} 0 & 2 \\ 1 & 0 \end{bmatrix}, \begin{bmatrix} 0 & 1 \\ 2 & 0 \end{bmatrix}$

14. $\begin{bmatrix} 1 & 1 \\ 2 & 1 \end{bmatrix}, \begin{bmatrix} -1 & -1 \\ 2 & -1 \end{bmatrix}$

15. $\begin{bmatrix} 4 & -1 \\ 1 & 0 \end{bmatrix}, \begin{bmatrix} 0 & 1 \\ -1 & 4 \end{bmatrix}$

16. $\begin{bmatrix} 1 & -2 \\ 1 & -1 \end{bmatrix}, \begin{bmatrix} -1 & 2 \\ -1 & 1 \end{bmatrix}$

17. $\begin{bmatrix} 2 & 1 \\ 0 & -1 \end{bmatrix}, \begin{bmatrix} 2 & 0 \\ 1 & -1 \end{bmatrix}$

18. $\begin{bmatrix} 1 & -1 & 0 \\ -1 & 1 & 1 \\ 0 & 1 & 1 \end{bmatrix}, \begin{bmatrix} 0 & -1 & 1 \\ -1 & -1 & 1 \\ 1 & 1 & 0 \end{bmatrix}$

19. $\begin{bmatrix} 0 & 2 & -2 \\ 1 & 0 & -1 \\ 0 & -4 & 0 \end{bmatrix}, \begin{bmatrix} -2 & 4 & -1 \\ 0 & 0 & -1 \\ -2 & 10 & -1 \end{bmatrix}$

Finding Inverses **Use a graphing calculator to find the inverse of matrix A. Then use the calculator to verify that $AA^{-1} = I$ and $A^{-1}A = I$.**

20. $A = \begin{bmatrix} 1 & 6 \\ 1 & 7 \end{bmatrix}$

21. $A = \begin{bmatrix} 3 & -4 \\ 2 & -3 \end{bmatrix}$

22. $A = \begin{bmatrix} -7 & 4 \\ -2 & 1 \end{bmatrix}$

23. $A = \begin{bmatrix} -1 & 0 \\ 6 & 4 \end{bmatrix}$

24. $A = \begin{bmatrix} -10 & -5 \\ 1 & 0 \end{bmatrix}$

25. $A = \begin{bmatrix} 7 & 4.1 \\ 5 & 3 \end{bmatrix}$

26. $A = \begin{bmatrix} 1 & -3 & 9 \\ 0 & 1 & 3 \\ 0 & 0 & 1 \end{bmatrix}$

27. $A = \begin{bmatrix} 1 & 0 & 0 \\ 8 & 1 & 0 \\ -6 & 5 & 1 \end{bmatrix}$

28. $A = \begin{bmatrix} 5 & 0 & 1 \\ -2 & 1 & 0 \\ 1 & 5 & 2 \end{bmatrix}$

Writing Matrix Equations Write the system of linear equations as a matrix equation.

29. $x + y = 3$
$\quad 2x - y = 12$

30. $8x + 5y = 39$
$\quad x + y = 6$

31. $x - y = 11$
$\quad -4x + 5y = -16$

32. $3x - y = -6$
$\quad 7x - 9y = -54$

33. $-2x - 4y = 14$
$\quad 6x = -42$

34. $9x + 8y = 0$
$\quad 2x + 14y = 2$

35. $6x - 7y - 3z = 17$
$\quad x + y - 5z = 17$
$\quad -4x - 2y + 7z = -30$

36. $8x + 3y - z = 23$
$\quad 2y + 5z = 23$
$\quad -5x - 2y = 14$

37. $x + 3y - 1.2z = 2.4$
$\quad 20.5y + 1.5z = -4.2$
$\quad -2.4x - 0.3y = 5.7$

Solving Systems Use an inverse matrix to solve the linear system.

38. $x + y = 26$
$\quad 12x + 3y = 0$

39. $x - 2y = 14$
$\quad 2x + 5y = -17$

40. $6x - y = 0$
$\quad -3x - 7y = 45$

41. $-4x + 8y = 24$
$\quad -x - 3y = -9$

42. $2x - 2y = -4$
$\quad 7x + y = 58$

43. $-5x + 4y = 25$
$\quad 2x = -10$

44. $x + y + z = 0$
$\quad 3x - 2y - z = 5$
$\quad 2x - 6y + 4z = 8$

45. $2x + y + 3z = 15$
$\quad -x - z = -3$
$\quad 5y - 2z = 10$

46. $y + 3z = -10$
$\quad -x + z = -4$
$\quad -2x - 6y = 4$

47. Interior Design An interior designer needs 9 square feet of tiles to decorate a wall in a kitchen. The designer is going to use blue and yellow tiles. The cost of a sheet of tiles that has an area of 1 square foot is $6 for blue tiles and $4 for yellow. The designer's budget for tiles is $40. Use matrices to solve the linear system below to find how many sheets of each color tile the designer should buy.

$$x + y = 9$$
$$6x + 4y = 40$$

48. Aviation A pilot has flown for 200 hours in single-engine airplanes and twin-engine airplanes. Renting a single-engine airplane costs $60 per hour, and renting a twin-engine airplane costs $240 per hour. The pilot has spent $21,000 on airplane rentals. Use matrices to solve the linear system below to find how many hours the pilot has flown each type of airplane.

$$x + y = 200$$
$$60x + 240y = 21,000$$

49. Math Exam A 100 point math exam consists of 32 problems. There are two types of problems. Type A problems are worth 5 points each and type B are worth 2 points. Write a system of linear equations to model the situation. Then use matrices to solve the system to find the number of each type of problem.

Challenge In Exercises 50–52, use the information below.

Below is the general expression for the inverse of a 2×2 matrix. A 2×2 matrix will not have an inverse if $ad - cb = 0$.

$$\text{If } A = \begin{bmatrix} a & b \\ c & d \end{bmatrix}, \text{ then } A^{-1} = \frac{1}{ad - cb} \begin{bmatrix} d & -b \\ -c & a \end{bmatrix}.$$

50. Write a 2×2 matrix that does not have an inverse.

51. Use the expression to find the inverse of the matrix $\begin{bmatrix} 1 & 6 \\ 1 & 7 \end{bmatrix}$.

52. Use the expression to show that $AA^{-1} = I$ and $A^{-1}A = I$ if $ad - cb \neq 0$.

53. Multiple Choice What is the inverse of $\begin{bmatrix} -5 & 7 \\ 2 & -3 \end{bmatrix}$?

(A) $\begin{bmatrix} 5 & -7 \\ -2 & 3 \end{bmatrix}$ (B) $\begin{bmatrix} -2 & 5 \\ -3 & 7 \end{bmatrix}$ (C) $\begin{bmatrix} -3 & 7 \\ -2 & 5 \end{bmatrix}$ (D) $\begin{bmatrix} -3 & -7 \\ -2 & -5 \end{bmatrix}$

54. Multiple Choice What is the solution of $\begin{bmatrix} 6 & -5 \\ -1 & 3 \end{bmatrix}\begin{bmatrix} x \\ y \end{bmatrix} = \begin{bmatrix} -27 \\ -2 \end{bmatrix}$?

(F) $(-152, 21)$ (G) $(-7, -3)$ (H) $(21, -152)$ (J) $(-3, -7)$

Mixed Review

55. Camping Your family rents an RV to go camping. The cost to use the RV is $.22 per mile, with 100 free miles per day. It costs $25 per night to stay at the campground. Write and simplify an expression that gives the total cost of traveling m miles per day, where $m > 100$. Find the total cost of traveling 550 miles in one day and staying two nights at the campground. *(Lesson 1.3)*

Factoring **Factor the trinomial.** *(Lesson 5.3)*

56. $x^2 - 14x - 72$ **57.** $3x^2 - 10x + 3$ **58.** $4x^2 + 12x + 5$

Finding Inverses **Find the inverse of the function.** *(Lesson 7.5)*

59. $f(x) = 2x + 1$ **60.** $f(x) = 3x - 6$ **61.** $f(x) = -x - 5$

Geometry Skills

Perpendicular Lines **Tell whether $\overleftrightarrow{AB}$ is perpendicular to $\overleftrightarrow{XY}$.**

62.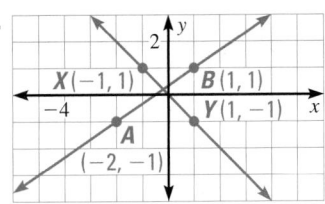

63.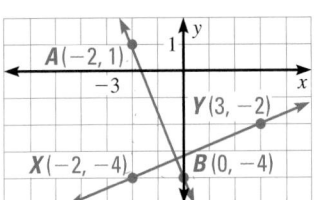

Quiz 1

Lesson 11.1   **Perform the indicated operation, if possible.**

1. $\begin{bmatrix} -8 & 8 \\ 10 & -4 \end{bmatrix} + \begin{bmatrix} 0 & -14 \\ -4 & 9 \end{bmatrix}$ **2.** $\begin{bmatrix} 18 & -7 \\ 5 & -12 \end{bmatrix} - \begin{bmatrix} 9 & 1 \\ -5 & -4 \end{bmatrix}$

3. $-3\begin{bmatrix} 8 & -9 \\ 5 & 6 \end{bmatrix}$ **4.** $\begin{bmatrix} 8 & -4 \\ 6 & 2 \end{bmatrix} - 2\begin{bmatrix} 3 & 0 \\ -1 & 4 \end{bmatrix}$

Lesson 11.2   **Let $A = \begin{bmatrix} 0 & -4 \\ 1 & 5 \end{bmatrix}$, $B = \begin{bmatrix} -1 & 0 \\ 6 & 8 \end{bmatrix}$, and $C = \begin{bmatrix} 3 & -7 \\ -5 & 3 \end{bmatrix}$. Simplify the expression.**

5. $2AB$ **6.** $(A - B)C$ **7.** $B(A + C)$

Lesson 11.3   **Use a graphing calculator to find the inverse of matrix A.**

8. $A = \begin{bmatrix} 0 & 1 \\ 1 & -6 \end{bmatrix}$ **9.** $A = \begin{bmatrix} -4 & 9 \\ 3 & -7 \end{bmatrix}$ **10.** $A = \begin{bmatrix} 2 & -10 \\ -4 & 21 \end{bmatrix}$

Lesson 11.3   **Use an inverse matrix to solve the linear system.**

11. $x - y = 27$
$3x + 2y = 4$

12. $-2x + y = -10$
$5x + 3y = 3$

13. $7x - 4y = -24$
$9x + 7y = 42$

Determinants and Cramer's Rule

GOAL Evaluate determinants and use Cramer's Rule to solve a linear system.

Associated with each square ($n \times n$) matrix is a real number called its **determinant**. The determinant of a matrix A is denoted by det A or by $|A|$.

The Determinant of a 2 × 2 Matrix

$$\det \begin{bmatrix} a & b \\ c & d \end{bmatrix} = \begin{vmatrix} a & b \\ c & d \end{vmatrix} = ad - cb$$

The determinant of a 2 × 2 matrix is the difference of the products of the elements on the diagonals.

EXAMPLE 1 Evaluate Determinants

Evaluate the determinant of the matrix $\begin{bmatrix} 2 & 1 \\ 3 & 5 \end{bmatrix}$.

Solution

Find the difference of the product of the elements on the diagonals.

$$\begin{vmatrix} 2 & 1 \\ 3 & 5 \end{vmatrix} = 2(5) - 3(1) = 10 - 3 = 7$$

Cramer's Rule You can use determinants to solve a system of equations. This method, called **Cramer's Rule**, uses the coefficient matrix of the linear system.

Cramer's Rule for a 2 × 2 System

Let A be the coefficient matrix of the linear system:

LINEAR SYSTEM	**COEFFICIENT MATRIX (A)**
$ax + by = e$	$\begin{bmatrix} a & b \\ c & d \end{bmatrix}$
$cx + dy = f$	

If det $A \neq 0$, then the system has exactly one solution. The solution is:

$$x = \frac{\begin{vmatrix} e & b \\ f & d \end{vmatrix}}{\det A} \quad \text{and} \quad y = \frac{\begin{vmatrix} a & e \\ c & f \end{vmatrix}}{\det A}.$$

Notice how the determinant in each numerator of the solution is formed in Cramer's Rule. For the numerator of x, you replace the coefficients of x in the first column of the coefficient matrix with the constants from the linear system. For the numerator of y, you replace the coefficients of y in the second column of the coefficient matrix with the constants from the linear system.

EXAMPLE **2** **Use Cramer's Rule for a 2 x 2 System**

Use Cramer's rule to solve the system.

$$2x + 7y = -3 \qquad \text{Equation 1}$$
$$3x - 8y = -23 \qquad \text{Equation 2}$$

Solution

Evaluate the determinant of the coefficient matrix.

$$\begin{vmatrix} 2 & 7 \\ 3 & -8 \end{vmatrix} = 2(-8) - 3(7) = -16 - 21 = -37$$

You can apply Cramer's Rule because the determinant is not 0.

$$x = \frac{\begin{vmatrix} -3 & 7 \\ -23 & -8 \end{vmatrix}}{-37} = \frac{24 - (-161)}{-37} = \frac{185}{-37} = -5$$

$$y = \frac{\begin{vmatrix} 2 & -3 \\ 3 & -23 \end{vmatrix}}{-37} = \frac{-46 - (-9)}{-37} = \frac{-37}{-37} = 1$$

ANSWER ▶ The solution is $(-5, 1)$.

CHECK Check $x = -5$ and $y = 1$ in the original equations.

$$2x + 7y = -3 \qquad\qquad 3x - 8y = -23$$
$$2(-5) + 7(1) \stackrel{?}{=} -3 \qquad\qquad 3(-5) - 8(1) \stackrel{?}{=} -23$$
$$-3 = -3 \checkmark \qquad\qquad -23 = -23 \checkmark$$

Exercises

Evaluating Determinants **Evaluate the determinant of the matrix.**

1. $\begin{bmatrix} -2 & 3 \\ 1 & 6 \end{bmatrix}$

2. $\begin{bmatrix} -3 & 5 \\ -2 & 1 \end{bmatrix}$

3. $\begin{bmatrix} 10 & 12 \\ 5 & 2 \end{bmatrix}$

4. $\begin{bmatrix} -7 & 11 \\ -7 & 2 \end{bmatrix}$

5. $\begin{bmatrix} 8 & 0 \\ -1 & 3 \end{bmatrix}$

6. $\begin{bmatrix} 1 & 8 \\ 5 & 9 \end{bmatrix}$

7. $\begin{bmatrix} 0 & 3 \\ 8 & 10 \end{bmatrix}$

8. $\begin{bmatrix} -3 & -6 \\ -1 & 3 \end{bmatrix}$

9. $\begin{bmatrix} -12 & 6 \\ -9 & -4 \end{bmatrix}$

Using Cramer's Rule **Use Cramer's Rule to solve the system.**

10. $2x + y = 3$
$5x + 6y = 4$

11. $9x + 2y = 8$
$4x - 3y = 42$

12. $-x - 12y = 44$
$12x - 15y = -51$

13. $7x - 5y = 11$
$3x + 10y = -56$

14. $4x - 5y = 13$
$2x - 7y = 24$

15. $3x + 10y = 50$
$12x + 15y = 64$

16. **Challenge** The attendance at a rock concert was 6700 people. The tickets cost \$40 for floor seats and \$25 for all other seats. The total ticket sales were \$185,500. Write a linear system that models this situation. Use Cramer's Rule to solve the system.

11.4 An Introduction to Sequences and Series

Key Words

• sequence
• terms of a sequence
• series

GOAL Use and write sequences and series.

When a collection of objects is listed *in sequence*, the collection is ordered so that it has a first item, a second item, a third item, and so on. Some familiar examples of objects listed in sequence are days of the week or months of the year.

In algebra, you can think of a **sequence** as a function whose domain is a set of consecutive integers. If the domain is not specified, it is understood that the domain starts with 1. The values in the range of the function are called the **terms** of the sequence.

Domain:	1	2	3	4 . . . n	Relative position of each term
Range:	a_1	a_2	a_3	a_4 . . . a_n	Terms of the sequence

The first term of a sequence, a_1, is read "a sub one." The next term is read "a sub two," and so on. A finite sequence has a limited number of terms. An infinite sequence continues without stopping.

Finite sequence: $2, 4, 6, 8$ **Infinite sequence:** $2, 4, 6, 8, . . .$

EXAMPLE 1 Write the Terms of a Sequence

Write the first six terms of the sequence.

a. $a_n = 2n + 1$ **b.** $a_n = (-1)^n$

Solution

To find a term of a sequence given the rule for the sequence, substitute the position of the term into the rule.

a. $a_1 = 2(1) + 1 = 3$	1st term	**b.** $a_1 = (-1)^1 = -1$	1st term
$a_2 = 2(2) + 1 = 5$	2nd term	$a_2 = (-1)^2 = 1$	2nd term
$a_3 = 2(3) + 1 = 7$	3rd term	$a_3 = (-1)^3 = -1$	3rd term
$a_4 = 2(4) + 1 = 9$	4th term	$a_4 = (-1)^4 = 1$	4th term
$a_5 = 2(5) + 1 = 11$	5th term	$a_5 = (-1)^5 = -1$	5th term
$a_6 = 2(6) + 1 = 13$	6th term	$a_6 = (-1)^6 = 1$	6th term

Prerequisite Skills

Find *f*(2) for the function.

1. $f(x) = x + 3$

2. $f(x) = 3x$

State the range of the function for the given domain.

3. $f(x) = x + 1$; domain: positive integers less than 6

4. $f(x) = 2x$; domain: positive integers less than 5

STUDENT HELP

READING ALGEBRA
In part (b) of Example 1, notice how a negative number raised to a power causes the terms to have alternating signs.

Checkpoint ✓ Write the Terms of a Sequence

Write the first five terms of the sequence.

1. $a_n = n + 3$ **2.** $a_n = 3n$ **3.** $a_n = 2n - 1$

4. $a_n = 3^n$ **5.** $a_n = n^2 + 3$ **6.** $a_n = (-3)^n$

Writing Rules for Sequences The terms of a sequence may have a recognizable pattern. If so, you may be able to write a rule for the nth term of the sequence. Some common patterns are:

- A particular value is added to each consecutive term of the sequence.
- Each term is multiplied by a constant.
- Each term is raised to a particular power.

STUDENT HELP

WRITING ALGEBRA
The general rule for a sequence can also be written using function notation. For instance, you can write the rule for part (a) of Example 2 as $f(n) = n + 2$.

EXAMPLE 2 Write a Rule for a Sequence

For the given sequence, describe the pattern, write the next term, and write a rule for the nth term.

a. 3, 4, 5, 6, . . .   **b.** $-2, 4, -8, 16, . . .$

Solution

First, find the pattern in the sequence, use the pattern to write the next term, then write the rule.

a. You can write the terms as $a_1 = 1 + 2$, $a_2 = 2 + 2$, $a_3 = 3 + 2$, $a_4 = 4 + 2$, and so on. So, 2 is being added to each term.

The next term is $a_5 = 5 + 2 = 7$. A rule for the nth term is $a_n = n + 2$.

b. You can write the terms as $a_1 = (-2)^1$, $a_2 = (-2)^2$, $a_3 = (-2)^3$, $a_4 = (-2)^4$, and so on. So, -2 is being raised to consecutive integer powers.

The next term is $a_5 = (-2)^5 = -32$. A rule for the nth term is $a_n = (-2)^n$.

 **Write Rules for Sequences**

For the given sequence, describe the pattern, write the next term, and write a rule for the nth term.

7. 2, 3, 4, 5, . . .   **8.** 3, 6, 9, 12, . . .   **9.** 4, 8, 12, 16, . . .

Graphing a Sequence You can graph a sequence by letting the horizontal axis represent the position numbers (the domain) and the vertical axis represent the terms (the range).

EXAMPLE 3 Graph a Sequence

Graph the sequence 3, 5, 7, 9, 11, 13.

Solution

Make a table of values.

n	1	2	3	4	5	6
a_n	3	5	7	9	11	13

Plot the points. Do not connect the points with a line. The sequence is defined only for integer values of n.

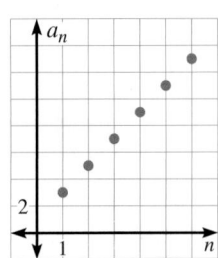

Graph the sequence.

10. 2, 4, 6, 8, 10   **11.** 2, 3, 4, 5, 6   **12.** 1, 3, 4, 7, 9

Finding the Sum of a Series When the terms of a sequence are added, the resulting expression is a **series**. A series can be finite or infinite.

Finite Sequence	Finite Series
2, 4, 6, 8, 10	2 + 4 + 6 + 8 + 10

Infinite Sequence	Infinite Series
2, 4, 6, 8, 10, . . .	2 + 4 + 6 + 8 + 10 + · · ·

The sum of a finite series can be found by adding the terms.

EXAMPLE **4** **Find the Sum of a Series**

Find the sum of the series.

a. 3 + 5 + 7 + 9   **b.** 3 + 4 + 5 + 6

Solution

a. 3 + 5 + 7 + 9 = 24   **b.** 3 + 4 + 5 + 6 = 18

Sequences with Many Terms For sequences with many terms, adding the terms can be tedious. You can use the formulas given below to find the sums of the terms of three special types of series.

Formulas for Special Series

Sum of n 1's

$$\underbrace{1 + 1 + 1 + 1 + 1 + \cdots + 1}_{n \text{ terms}} = n$$

Sum of the first n positive integers

$$1 + 2 + 3 + 4 + 5 + \cdots + n = \frac{n(n + 1)}{2}$$

Sum of the squares of the first n positive integers

$$1^2 + 2^2 + 3^2 + 4^2 + 5^2 + \cdots + n^2 = \frac{n(n + 1)(2n + 1)}{6}$$

Find the sum of the series.

13. 4 + 5 + 6 + 7 + 8 + 9 + 10 + 11   **14.** 4 + 8 + 12 + 16 + 20 + 24 + 28

15. sum of sixteen 1's   **16.** sum of the first 12 positive integers

Guided Practice

Vocabulary Check

1. Copy and complete the statement: For a sequence of numbers, the numbers in the sequence are called __?__.

2. The __?__ term of a sequence is a_n.

Skill Check   **Write the first six terms of the sequence.**

3. $a_n = 3n$ **4.** $a_n = 2n - 1$ **5.** $a_n = n + 4$ **6.** $f(n) = n + 3$

Write the next term in the sequence. Then write a rule for the nth term.

7. 2, 4, 6, 8, 10, . . .   **8.** 16, 12, 8, 4, 0, . . .   **9.** 1, 4, 9, 16, 25, . . .

Find the sum of the series.

10. $1 + 2 + 3 + 4$ **11.** $1 + (-1) + (-3) + (-5)$ **12.** $5 + 7 + 9 + 11$

Practice and Applications

STUDENT HELP

HOMEWORK HELP
Example 1: Exs. 13–24
Example 2: Exs. 25–33
Example 3: Exs. 34–39
Example 4: Exs. 40–49

Writing Terms **Write the first six terms of the sequence.**

13. $a_n = n + 2$ **14.** $a_n = 1 - n$ **15.** $a_n = 4n - 1$

16. $a_n = 2n^2$ **17.** $a_n = 3n^2$ **18.** $a_n = n^3 - 1$

19. $a_n = n^2 + 1$ **20.** $a_n = (n + 2)^2$ **21.** $f(n) = 3n + 2$

22. $f(n) = n^2 - 5$ **23.** $f(n) = \dfrac{n + 1}{n}$ **24.** $f(n) = \dfrac{n^2}{2n + 1}$

Writing Rules **Write the next term in the sequence. Then write a rule for the nth term.**

25. 1, 3, 5, 7, . . .   **26.** 2, 1, 0, −1, . . .   **27.** 1, 4, 7, 10, . . .

28. 5, 10, 15, 20, . . .   **29.** 4, 7, 12, 19, . . .   **30.** 16, 25, 36, 49, . . .

31. 2, 8, 18, 32, . . .   **32.** $\dfrac{1}{3}, \dfrac{2}{4}, \dfrac{3}{5}, \dfrac{4}{6}, \ldots$ **33.** $\dfrac{2}{2}, \dfrac{4}{3}, \dfrac{6}{4}, \dfrac{8}{5}, \ldots$

Graphing Sequences **Graph the sequence.**

34. 3, 7, 11, 15, 19, 23   **35.** −1, 1, 3, 5, 7, 9, 11   **36.** 1, 4, 9, 16, 25, 36

37. 4, 8, 12, 16, 20, 24   **38.** −2, −5, −8, −11, −14   **39.** −2, 1, 6, 13, 22, 33

Finding Sums of Series **Find the sum of the series.**

40. $3 + 5 + 7 + 9 + 11 + 13 + 15$ **41.** $1 + 5 + 9 + 13 + 17$

42. $6 + 12 + 18 + 24 + 30 + 36$ **43.** $1 + 4 + 9 + 16 + 25$

44. $0 + 3 + 8 + 15 + 24 + 35$ **45.** $6 + 11 + 16 + 21 + 26 + 31$

46. $3 + 0 - 5 - 12 - 21 - 32$ **47.** $2 + 8 + 18 + 32 + 50$

48. $\dfrac{1}{2} + \dfrac{3}{2} + \dfrac{5}{2} + \dfrac{7}{2} + \dfrac{9}{2}$ **49.** $\dfrac{1}{1} + \dfrac{1}{2} + \dfrac{1}{3} + \dfrac{1}{4}$

Using Formulas Use the formulas for special series to find the sum of the series.

50. $1 + 1 + 1 + 1 + 1 + 1$

51. $1 + 1 + 1 + 1 + 1 + 1 + 1 + 1$

52. $1 + 2 + 3 + 4 + 5 + 6 + 7$

53. $1 + 2 + 3 + 4 + 5 + 6 + 7 + 8$

54. $1 + 2 + 3 + 4 + 5 + 6 + 7 + 8 + 9$

55. $1 + 4 + 9 + 16 + 25$

56. $1 + 4 + 9 + 16 + 25 + 36$

57. $1 + 4 + 9 + 16 + 25 + 36 + 49$

58. *Geometry Link* The measurement of each angle at the tips of the six stars shown below is given by $d_n = \dfrac{180(n-4)}{n}$, where n is the number of points on the star and $n \geq 5$. Write the first six terms of the sequence of angle measurements.

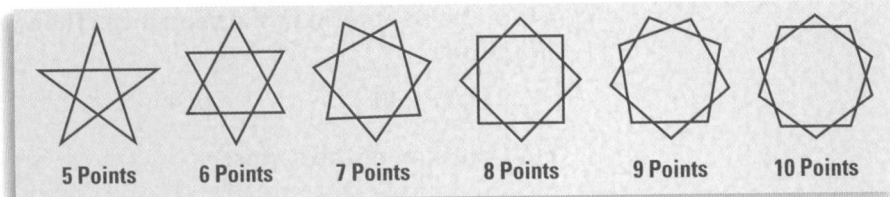

| 5 Points | 6 Points | 7 Points | 8 Points | 9 Points | 10 Points |

Salary In Exercises 59–62, use the following information.

An employee at a construction company earns $33,000 for the first year of employment. Employees at the company receive raises of $2400 each year.

59. What will the employee's salary be for each of the first five years?

60. Write a rule to determine the employee's salary for the nth year.

61. Use the rule from Exercise 60 to determine the employee's salary for the seventh year.

62. Find the total amount of money the employee will earn working for the company for six years.

Retail Displays In Exercises 63–65, use the following information.

You work at a grocery store. You are stacking apples in the shape of a square pyramid. A side of each layer has one more apple than the layer above it, as shown. The first layer has one apple. You make the pyramid seven layers high.

63. Write a rule to determine the number of apples in the nth layer.

← First layer

64. How many apples are in the sixth layer?

65. How many apples are used to make the display?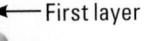

Savings In Exercises 66–68, use the following information.

You want to save $500 for a school trip. You begin by saving a penny on the first day. You plan to save an additional penny each day after that. For example, you will save 2 pennies on the second day, 3 pennies on the third day, and so on.

66. How much money will you have saved after 100 days?

67. How many days must you save in order to save $500?

68. Explain how you used a series to find your answer to Exercise 67.

69. Exercise Program You are in an exercise program. The first week you do 25 push ups. Each week you do 10 more push ups than the previous week. How many push ups will you do the ninth week? Explain how you found your answer.

70. Writing Explain the difference between a sequence and a series.

71. Multiple Choice What is the next term in the sequence?

$$2, 5, 8, 11, 14, 17, \ldots$$

  (A) 18   (B) 19   (C) 20   (D) 21

72. Multiple Choice What is the rule for the nth term of the sequence?

$$5, 11, 17, 23, 29, \ldots$$

  (F) $a_n = n + 1$ (G) $a_n = 6n - 1$

  (H) $a_n = 5n + 1$ (J) $a_n = 6(n - 1)$

73. Multiple Choice What is the next term in the sequence?

$$1, 3, 9, 27, 81, \ldots$$

  (A) 121   (B) 162   (C) 243   (D) 729

74. Multiple Choice What is the sum of the series?

$$3 + 7 + 11 + 15 + 19$$

  (F) 23   (G) 50   (H) 52   (J) 55

Mixed Review

Simplifying Expressions Simplify the expression. *(Lesson 1.3)*

75. $12 + 4n - 4$ **76.** $2n + 3n - 11$ **77.** $10 - 2(n - 1)$

78. $16n - 5(n - 6)$ **79.** $-7(2n - 3) + 4n$ **80.** $3n + 4 + 6(n - 5)$

Slope-Intercept Form Write an equation of the line that has the given slope and y-intercept. *(Lesson 2.5)*

81. $m = -1, b = 5$ **82.** $m = 3, b = -2$ **83.** $m = \dfrac{2}{3}, b = 1$

84. $m = 2\dfrac{1}{2}, b = -4$ **85.** $m = -4, b = 2\dfrac{3}{4}$ **86.** $m = \dfrac{5}{2}, b = \dfrac{3}{4}$

Graphing Functions Graph the function. State the domain and range. *(Lesson 9.2)*

87. $y = \dfrac{2}{x + 6} + 1$ **88.** $y = \dfrac{4}{x + 1} + 2$ **89.** $y = \dfrac{3}{x + 8} - 2$

90. $y = \dfrac{-2}{x - 5} + 5$ **91.** $y = \dfrac{1}{x - 7} - 3$ **92.** $y = \dfrac{-1}{x + 4} - 7$

Geometry Skills

Arc Measures Find the measure of the blue intercepted arc.

93.
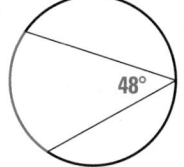

94.
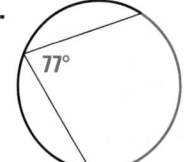

95.
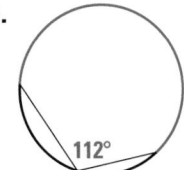

USING A GRAPHING CALCULATOR *(For use with Lesson 11.4)*
Working with Sequences

You can use a graphing calculator to find the terms of a sequence, graph a sequence, and find the sum of a series.

EXAMPLE

Use a graphing calculator to:

• find the first eight terms of the sequence $a_n = 4n - 3$.

• graph the sequence.

• find the sum of the first eight terms of the sequence.

SOLUTION

① Be sure that the graphing calculator is in *Sequence* mode and *Dot* mode. Enter the sequence. Note that the calculator uses $u(n)$ rather than a_n.

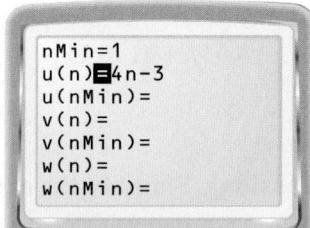

② Use the *Table* feature to view the terms of the sequence. The first eight terms are 1, 5, 9, 13, 17, 21, 25, and 29.

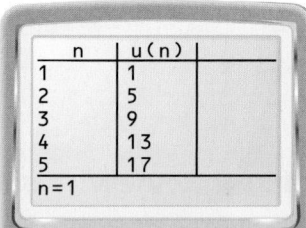

③ Set the viewing window so that $1 \leq n \leq 8$, $1 \leq x \leq 8$, and $0 \leq y \leq 30$. Graph the sequence. You can use the *Trace* feature to view the terms of the sequence.

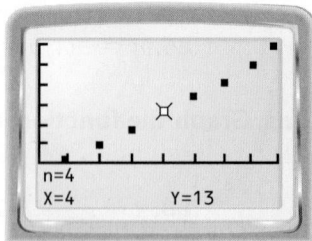

④ Use the *Summation* feature to find the sum of the first eight terms of the sequence. The screen shows that the sum is 120.

```
sum(seq(4n-3,n,1,
8,1))
                    120
```

EXERCISES

Use a graphing calculator to find the first ten terms of the sequence, graph the sequence, and find the sum of the first ten terms.

1. $a_n = 4n - 1$ **2.** $a_n = 2n + 6$ **3.** $a_n = 20 - 3n$

4. $a_n = 5(n - 1)$ **5.** $a_n = n^2$ **6.** $a_n = 2n^2$

7. $a_n = 3n^2 + 1$ **8.** $a_n = n^2 - 5$ **9.** $a_n = \dfrac{1}{n + 1}$

11.5 Arithmetic Sequences and Series

Key Words
- arithmetic sequence
- common difference
- arithmetic series

GOAL Write rules for arithmetic sequences and find sums of arithmetic series.

How many cards are in a house of cards?

In Example 4, you will see how to find the number of cards in a house of cards. The first three rows of a house of cards are shown. There are 3 cards in the first row, 6 cards in the second row, 9 cards in the third row, and so on. The sequence below represents the number of cards in each of the first five rows.

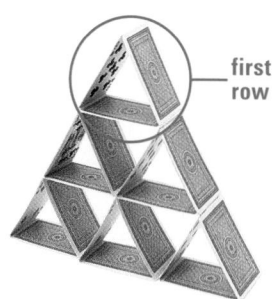

first row

$$3, 6, 9, 12, 15$$

This is an example of an *arithmetic sequence*. In an **arithmetic sequence**, the difference between consecutive terms is constant. This constant difference is called the **common difference** and is denoted by d.

For example, the number of cards in each row of the house of cards has a common difference of 3.

$$a_2 - a_1 = 6 - 3 = 3 \qquad a_3 - a_2 = 9 - 6 = 3$$
$$a_4 - a_3 = 12 - 9 = 3 \qquad a_5 - a_4 = 15 - 12 = 3$$

EXAMPLE 1 Identify Arithmetic Sequences

Tell whether the sequence is arithmetic.

a. 0, 7, 14, 21, 28

b. 1, 3, 6, 10, 15

Solution

To tell whether a sequence is arithmetic, find the differences of consecutive terms.

a. $a_2 - a_1 = 7 - 0 = 7$

$a_3 - a_2 = 14 - 7 = 7$

$a_4 - a_3 = 21 - 14 = 7$

$a_5 - a_4 = 28 - 21 = 7$

Each difference is 7, so the sequence is arithmetic.

b. $a_2 - a_1 = 3 - 1 = 2$

$a_3 - a_2 = 6 - 3 = 3$

$a_4 - a_3 = 10 - 6 = 4$

$a_5 - a_4 = 15 - 10 = 5$

The differences are not constant, so the sequence is not arithmetic.

 **Identify Arithmetic Sequences**

Tell whether the sequence is arithmetic.

1. 1, 8, 27, 64, 125

2. 0, 2, 4, 6, 8

3. 1, 4, 7, 10, 13

Rule for an Arithmetic Sequence

The nth term of an arithmetic sequence with first term a_1 and common difference d can be found using the following rule.

$$a_n = a_1 + (n - 1)d$$

EXAMPLE 2 Write a Rule for a Sequence

Write a rule for the nth term of the arithmetic sequence 20, 18, 16, 14, ...
Then find a_9.

Solution

The sequence is arithmetic with first term $a_1 = 20$. The common difference is $d = 18 - 20 = -2$. So, a rule for the nth term is as follows.

$a_n = a_1 + (n - 1)d$	Write general rule.
$= 20 + (n - 1)(-2)$	Substitute 20 for a_1 and -2 for d.
$= 20 - 2n + 2$	Use distributive property.
$= 22 - 2n$	Simplify.

You can find the 9th term by substituting 9 for n in the rule $a_n = 22 - 2n$.
The 9th term is $a_9 = 22 - 2(9) = 22 - 18 = 4$.

EXAMPLE 3 Graph a Sequence

One term of an arithmetic sequence is $a_{11} = 24$. The common difference is $d = 2$.

   a. Write a rule for the nth term.   **b.** Graph the sequence.

Solution

  a. Find the first term.

$a_n = a_1 + (n - 1)d$	Write general rule.
$a_{11} = a_1 + (11 - 1)d$	Substitute 11 for n.
$24 = a_1 + 10(2)$	Substitute 24 for a_{11} and 2 for d.
$24 = a_1 + 20$	Multiply.
$4 = a_1$	Subtract 20 from each side.

     Write a rule for the nth term.

$a_n = a_1 + (n - 1)d$	Write general rule.
$= 4 + (n - 1)2$	Substitute.
$= 4 + 2n - 2$	Distributive property
$= 2 + 2n$	Simplify.

  b. Make a table of values and plot the points.

n	1	2	3	4	5	6
a_n	4	6	8	10	12	14

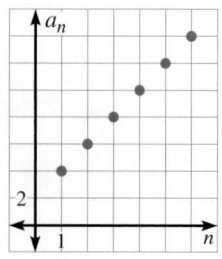

STUDENT HELP

READING GRAPHS
For the graph in part (b) of Example 3, notice that the points lie on a line. This is true for *any* arithmetic sequence.

4. Write a rule for the *n*th term of the sequence 3, 5, 7, 9, ... Then find a_{12}.

5. Write a rule for the *n*th term of the sequence where $a_4 = 10$ and $d = -3$. Then graph the sequence.

Arithmetic Series The expression formed by adding the terms of an arithmetic sequence is called an **arithmetic series**. The sum of the first *n* terms of an arithmetic series is denoted by S_n and can be found using the following formula.

STUDENT HELP

WRITING ALGEBRA
To help remember the rule for the sum of the first *n* terms of an arithmetic series, write the meaning in words.

The Sum of a Finite Arithmetic Series

The sum of the first *n* terms of an arithmetic series is given by the following formula.

$$S_n = n\left(\frac{a_1 + a_n}{2}\right)$$

In words, the sum of the first *n* terms of an arithmetic series, S_n, is the mean of the first and *n*th terms, multiplied by the number of terms.

EXAMPLE 4 Find the Sum of an Arithmetic Series

Find the number of cards in the first 20 rows of the house of cards on page 615.

Solution

Notice that the first term is $a_1 = 3$. The common difference is $d = 6 - 3 = 3$. You need to write a rule for the *n*th term so that you can find the 20th term.

$a_n = a_1 + (n - 1)d$	Write general rule.
$\quad = 3 + (n - 1)3$	Substitute 3 for a_1 and 3 for *d*.
$\quad = 3n$	Simplify.

Find the 20th term. The 20th term is $a_{20} = 3(20) = 60$.

Find the sum of the first 20 terms.

$S_{20} = 20\left(\dfrac{a_1 + a_{20}}{2}\right)$	Write rule for S_{20}.
$\quad = 20\left(\dfrac{3 + 60}{2}\right)$	Substitute 3 for a_1 and 60 for a_{20}.
$\quad = 630$	Simplify.

ANSWER ▸ There are 630 cards in the first 20 rows of the house of cards.

Find the sum of the first 10 terms of the arithmetic series.

6. $2 + 5 + 8 + 11 + 14 + 17 + \cdots$ **7.** $5 + 6 + 7 + 8 + 9 + 10 + \cdots$

8. $-4 + 0 + 4 + 8 + 12 + 16 + \cdots$ **9.** $(-9) + (-2) + 5 + 12 + 19 + \cdots$

Guided Practice

Vocabulary Check

1. Copy and complete the statement: The expression formed by adding the terms of an arithmetic sequence is called a(n) __?__ .

2. Is the sequence 2, 5, 8, 11, 14 an arithmetic sequence? Explain why or why not.

Skill Check

Write a rule for the *n*th term of the arithmetic sequence. Then find a_{15}.

3. 13, 18, 23, 28, 33, . . .   **4.** 36, 32, 28, 24, 20, . . .   **5.** 9, 21, 33, 45, 57, . . .

Write a rule for the *n*th term of the arithmetic sequence.

6. $d = 7, a_3 = 21$ **7.** $d = 23, a_5 = 29$ **8.** $d = \frac{1}{3}, a_4 = \frac{11}{3}$

Find the sum of the first 10 terms of the arithmetic series.

9. $3 + 8 + 13 + 18 + 23 + \cdots$ **10.** $\frac{1}{2} + 1 + \frac{3}{2} + 2 + \frac{5}{2} + \cdots$

Practice and Applications

STUDENT HELP

HOMEWORK HELP
Example 1: Exs. 11–14
Example 2: Exs. 15–20
Example 3: Exs. 21–35
Example 4: Exs. 36–47

Identifying Arithmetic Sequences **Tell whether the sequence is arithmetic. Explain why or why not.**

11. 1, 5, 7, 12, 14, . . .   **12.** 48, 43, 38, 33, 28, . . .

13. $-3, -1, -\frac{1}{3}, -\frac{1}{9}, -\frac{1}{27}, \ldots$ **14.** $-\frac{7}{3}, -\frac{5}{3}, -1, -\frac{1}{3}, \frac{1}{3}, \ldots$

Writing Terms **Write a rule for the *n*th term of the arithmetic sequence. Then find a_{12}.**

15. 32, 30, 28, 26, 24, . . .   **16.** 17, 22, 27, 32, 37, . . .

17. 47, 54, 61, 68, 75, . . .   **18.** 51, 45, 39, 33, 27, . . .

19. $\frac{4}{5}, 1, \frac{6}{5}, \frac{7}{5}, \frac{8}{5}, \ldots$ **20.** 9.8, 9.5, 9.2, 8.9, 8.6, . . .

Writing Rules **Write a rule for the *n*th term of the arithmetic sequence.**

21. $d = 9, a_6 = 66$ **22.** $d = -4, a_5 = 89$ **23.** $d = 8, a_7 = 7$

24. $d = 5, a_9 = 11$ **25.** $d = \frac{1}{3}, a_1 = \frac{5}{6}$ **26.** $d = -0.3, a_8 = -5$

Matching **Match the graph with the appropriate sequence.**

27. $a_n = 8 - 3n$ **28.** $a_n = 3 + 8n$ **29.** $a_n = 8 + 3n$

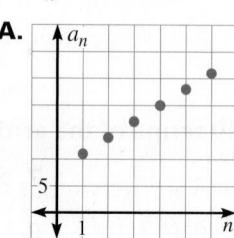

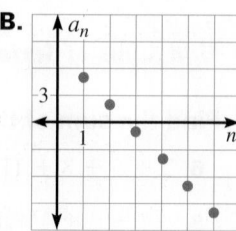

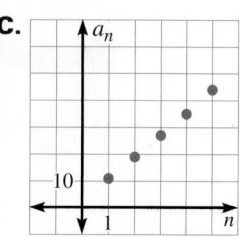

Graphing Sequences Graph the first six terms of the arithmetic sequence.

30. $a_n = 11 + 4n$ **31.** $a_n = 3 + 6n$ **32.** $a_n = 9 + 2n$

33. $a_n = 13 - n$ **34.** $a_n = 27 - 4n$ **35.** $a_n = 9.1 - 0.5n$

Finding Sums Find the sum of the first 12 terms of the arithmetic series.

36. $3 + 6 + 9 + 12 + 15 + \cdots$ **37.** $2 + 11 + 20 + 29 + 38 + \cdots$

38. $8 + 8\frac{1}{2} + 9 + 9\frac{1}{2} + 10 + \cdots$ **39.** $12 + \frac{25}{2} + 13 + \frac{27}{2} + 14 + \cdots$

40. $56 + 54 + 52 + 50 + 48 + \cdots$ **41.** $93 + 88 + 83 + 78 + 73 + \cdots$

Finding Sums Find the sum of the first 18 terms of the arithmetic series.

42. $5 + 13 + 21 + 29 + 37 + \cdots$ **43.** $21 + 27 + 33 + 39 + 45 + \cdots$

44. $1.6 + 2.3 + 3 + 3.7 + 4.4 + \cdots$ **45.** $\frac{5}{3} + 2 + \frac{7}{3} + \frac{8}{3} + 3 + \cdots$

46. $144 + 137 + 130 + 123 + 116 + \cdots$ **47.** $108 + 105 + 102 + 99 + 96 + \cdots$

48. Quilting A quilting pattern is shown. The innermost layer has 8 blocks. Each layer in the pattern has 16 more blocks than the layer before it, as shown in the diagram. Write a rule for the number of blocks in the nth layer where $n = 1$ represents the first layer.

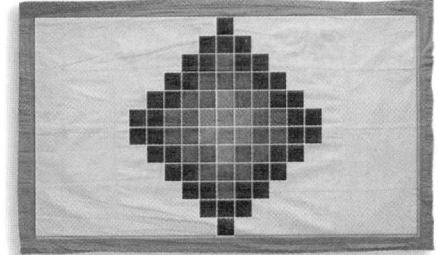

49. Car Payments You buy a used car. The down payment is $500. The monthly payment is $250. The sequence showing your total payment after n months is 750, 1000, 1250, 1500, and so on. Write a rule for the nth term of the sequence.

Honeycombs In Exercises 50 and 51, use the information below.

Domestic bees start with a single hexagonal cell to make their honeycombs. Then they form ring after ring of hexagonal cells around the initial cell, as shown. The numbers of cells in successive rings form an arithmetic sequence.

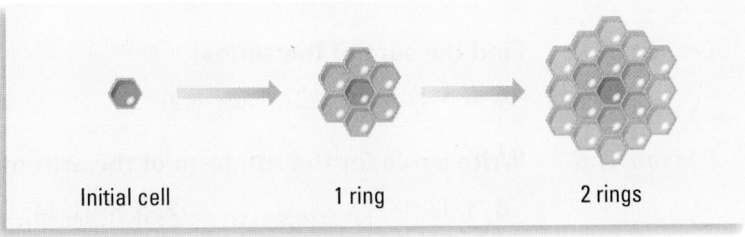

Initial cell   1 ring   2 rings

50. Write a rule for the number of cells in the nth ring.

51. Find a_8. What is the total number of cells in the honeycomb after the eighth ring is formed?

52. Earnings Suppose you earn 25 cents on the first day of the month, 50 cents on the second day, 75 cents on the third day, and so on. Write an arithmetic sequence for this situation. Then write a rule for the nth term. Find the total amount you earn during a 30-day month.

53. Multiple Choice What is a rule for the *n*th term of the arithmetic sequence?

$$9, 16, 23, 30, 37, \ldots$$

(**A**) $a_n = 2 + 7n$ (**B**) $a_n = 9 + 7n$

(**C**) $a_n = -2 - 7n$ (**D**) $a_n = 7n - 2$

54. Multiple Choice What is the sum of the first 25 terms of the arithmetic series?

$$14 + 34 + 54 + 74 + 94 + \cdots$$

(**F**) 494   (**G**) 506   (**H**) 6350   (**J**) 6500

Mixed Review

Joint Variation **The variable *z* varies jointly with *x* and *y*. Use the given values to write an equation relating *x*, *y*, and *z*.** *(Lesson 9.1)*

55. $x = 1, y = 6, z = 30$ **56.** $x = 8, y = 4, z = 96$ **57.** $x = 2, y = 7, z = 12$

Combinations **Find the number of combinations.** *(Lesson 10.5)*

58. $_5C_3$ **59.** $_7C_4$ **60.** $_{11}C_9$

Graphing Sequences **Graph the sequence.** *(Lesson 11.4)*

61. 13, 21, 29, 37, 45, 53   **62.** 16, 19, 22, 25, 28, 31   **63.** 0.76, 1.16, 1.56, 1.96

Geometry Skills

Finding Angle Measures ***ABCD* is a parallelogram. Find the unknown angle measures.**

64.
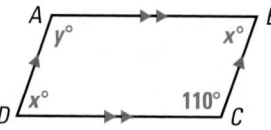

65.
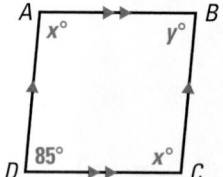

Quiz 2

Lesson 11.4

Write the next term in the sequence. Then write a rule for the *n*th term.

1. 5, 9, 13, 17, ...   **2.** −3, −5, −7, −9, ...   **3.** 3, 9, 27, 81, ...

Lesson 11.4

Find the sum of the series.

4. 6 + 11 + 16 + 21 + 26 + 31   **5.** 4 + (−16) + 64 + (−256) + 1024

Lesson 11.5

Write a rule for the *n*th term of the arithmetic sequence.

6. 8, 13, 18, 23, 28, ...   **7.** 5, 8, 11, 14, 17, ...   **8.** 10, 6, 2, −2, −6, ...

9. $d = 2, a_1 = 2$ **10.** $d = -4, a_6 = 15$ **11.** $d = \frac{2}{5}, a_8 = \frac{18}{5}$

Lesson 11.5

12. Find the sum of the first 22 terms of the arithmetic series.

$$11 + 17 + 23 + 29 + 35 + \cdots$$

Lesson 11.5

13. Boxes You are stacking boxes in a warehouse. The bottom row (row 1) has 47 boxes and the top row (row 6) has 42 boxes. Each row has one less box than the row below it. How many boxes are in the stack?

11.6 Geometric Sequences and Series

Key Words

- geometric sequence
- common ratio
- geometric series

GOAL Write rules for geometric sequences and find sums of geometric series.

The diagram below shows a snowflake curve at each of the first three stages.

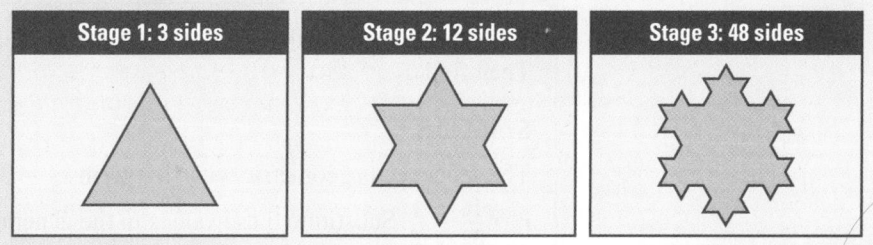

| Stage 1: 3 sides | Stage 2: 12 sides | Stage 3: 48 sides |

The sequence 3, 12, 48, 192, 768 represents the number of sides in the snowflake curve at each of the first five stages. This is an example of a *geometric sequence*.

In a **geometric sequence**, the ratio of any term to the previous term is constant. This constant ratio is called the **common ratio** and is denoted by r. For example, the sequence of the number of sides in the snowflake curve shown above has a common ratio of 4.

$$\frac{a_2}{a_1} = \frac{12}{3} = 4 \qquad \frac{a_3}{a_2} = \frac{48}{12} = 4 \qquad \frac{a_4}{a_3} = \frac{192}{48} = 4 \qquad \frac{a_5}{a_4} = \frac{768}{192} = 4$$

EXAMPLE 1 **Identify Geometric Sequences**

Tell whether the sequence is geometric.

a. 32, 16, 8, 4, 2, . . .   **b.** 1, 2, 6, 24, 120, . . .

Solution

To tell whether a sequence is geometric, find the ratios of consecutive terms. If the ratios are the same, the sequence is geometric.

a. $\frac{a_2}{a_1} = \frac{16}{32} = \frac{1}{2} \qquad \frac{a_3}{a_2} = \frac{8}{16} = \frac{1}{2} \qquad \frac{a_4}{a_3} = \frac{4}{8} = \frac{1}{2} \qquad \frac{a_5}{a_4} = \frac{2}{4} = \frac{1}{2}$

Because the ratios are the same, the sequence is geometric.

b. $\frac{a_2}{a_1} = \frac{2}{1} = 2 \qquad \frac{a_3}{a_2} = \frac{6}{2} = 3 \qquad \frac{a_4}{a_3} = \frac{24}{6} = 4 \qquad \frac{a_5}{a_4} = \frac{120}{24} = 5$

Because the ratios are different, the sequence is *not* geometric.

Checkpoint ✓ **Identify Geometric Sequences**

Tell whether the sequence is geometric.

1. 1, 3, 9, 27, 81   **2.** 1, 4, 7, 10, 13   **3.** 4, 2, 1, $\frac{1}{2}, \frac{1}{4}$

Prerequisite Skills

Write the fraction in simplest form.

1. $\frac{10}{2}$

2. $\frac{24}{12}$

3. $\frac{4}{6}$

Rule for a Geometric Sequence

The nth term of a geometric sequence with first term a_1 and common ratio r can be found using the following rule.

$$a_n = a_1 r^{n-1}$$

EXAMPLE **2** **Write a Rule for the nth Term**

Write a rule for the nth term of the geometric sequence 32, 16, 8, 4, 2, ... Then find a_8.

Solution

The sequence is geometric with first term $a_1 = 32$. The common ratio is $r = \frac{16}{32} = \frac{1}{2}$. Substitute these values in the general rule.

$$a_n = a_1 r^{n-1} \qquad \text{Write general rule.}$$
$$a_n = 32\left(\frac{1}{2}\right)^{n-1} \qquad \text{Substitute 32 for } a_1 \text{ and } \frac{1}{2} \text{ for } r.$$

A rule for the nth term is $a_n = 32\left(\frac{1}{2}\right)^{n-1}$. To find the 8th term of the sequence, substitute 8 for n. The 8th term is $a_8 = 32\left(\frac{1}{2}\right)^{8-1} = 32\left(\frac{1}{2}\right)^{7} = 32\left(\frac{1}{128}\right) = \frac{1}{4}$.

EXAMPLE **3** **Write a Rule for the nth Term**

One term of a geometric sequence is $a_4 = 54$. The common ratio is $r = 3$.

a. Write a rule for the nth term. **b.** Graph the sequence.

Solution

a. Find the first term.

$$a_n = a_1 r^{n-1} \qquad \text{Write general rule.}$$
$$a_4 = a_1 r^{4-1} \qquad \text{Substitute 4 for } n.$$
$$54 = a_1 (3)^3 \qquad \text{Substitute 54 for } a_4 \text{ and 3 for } r.$$
$$54 = a_1 (27) \qquad \text{Evaluate power.}$$
$$2 = a_1 \qquad \text{Divide each side by 27.}$$

Write a rule for the nth term with $a_1 = 2$ and $r = 3$.

$$a_n = a_1 r^{n-1} \qquad \text{Write general rule.}$$
$$a_n = 2(3)^{n-1} \qquad \text{Substitute for } a_1 \text{ and } r.$$

STUDENT HELP

READING GRAPHS
In part (b) of Example 3, notice the points lie on an exponential curve. This is true for *any* geometric sequence with $r > 0$.

b. Make a table of values and plot the points.

n	1	2	3	4	5	6
a_n	2	6	18	54	162	486

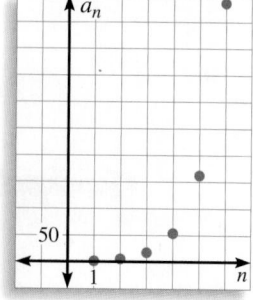

Write a rule for the *n*th term of the geometric sequence.

4. 5, 20, 80, 320, . . .   **5.** $a_4 = 32, r = 2$ **6.** $a_3 = 96, r = 4$

7. The third term of a geometric sequence is $a_3 = 40$. The common ratio is $r = 2$. Write a rule for the *n*th term. Then graph the sequence.

Geometric Series The expression formed by adding the terms of a geometric sequence is called a **geometric series**. The sum of the first *n* terms of a geometric series is denoted by S_n and can be found using the following formula.

The Sum of a Finite Geometric Series

The sum of the first *n* terms of a geometric series with common ratio r ($r \neq 1$) is given by the following formula.

$$S_n = a_1\left(\frac{1 - r^n}{1 - r}\right)$$

EXAMPLE 4 Find the Sum of a Geometric Series

Find the sum of the first 10 terms of the geometric series.

$$5 + 10 + 20 + 40 + \cdots$$

Solution

Notice that the first term is $a_1 = 5$. The common ratio is $r = \dfrac{10}{5} = 2$.

$S_n = a_1\left(\dfrac{1 - r^n}{1 - r}\right)$	Write general rule.
$S_{10} = a_1\left(\dfrac{1 - r^{10}}{1 - r}\right)$	Substitute 10 for *n*.
$= 5\left(\dfrac{1 - 2^{10}}{1 - 2}\right)$	Substitute 5 for a_1 and 2 for *r*.
$= 5\left(\dfrac{1 - 1024}{1 - 2}\right)$	Evaluate power.
$= 5\left(\dfrac{-1023}{-1}\right)$	Subtract.
$= 5115$	Multiply.

ANSWER ▶ The sum of the first 10 terms, S_{10}, is 5115.

Find the sum of the first 10 terms of the geometric series.

8. $3 + 9 + 27 + 81 + \cdots$ **9.** $20 + 10 + 5 + \dfrac{5}{2} + \cdots$

11.6 Exercises

Guided Practice

Vocabulary Check

1. What is the difference between a geometric sequence and an arithmetic sequence?

2. Copy and complete the statement: The expression formed by adding the terms of a geometric sequence is called a(n) __?__.

Skill Check

Find the common ratio of the geometric sequence.

3. $2, 6, 18, 54, \ldots$ **4.** $1, 4, 16, 64, \ldots$ **5.** $-1, -4, -16, -64, \ldots$

6. $-1, -2, -4, -8, \ldots$ **7.** $80, 40, 20, 10, \ldots$ **8.** $-27, -9, -3, -1, \ldots$

Tell whether the sequence is geometric. Explain why or why not.

9. $1, 2, 3, 4, 5, \ldots$ **10.** $1, 2, 4, 8, 16, \ldots$ **11.** $16, 8, 4, 2, 1, \ldots$

12. $1.5, 3, 4.5, 6, 7.5, \ldots$ **13.** $\frac{1}{3}, \frac{1}{9}, \frac{1}{27}, \frac{1}{81}, \frac{1}{243}, \ldots$ **14.** $\frac{3}{2}, \frac{3}{4}, \frac{3}{8}, \frac{3}{16}, \frac{3}{32}, \ldots$

15. $-3, -6, 12, 24, 48, \ldots$ **16.** $1, -3, 9, -27, 81, \ldots$ **17.** $\frac{1}{2}, 1, \frac{3}{2}, 2, \frac{5}{2}, \ldots$

Write a rule for the _n_th term of the geometric sequence.

18. $54, 18, 6, 2, \ldots$ **19.** $8, 16, 32, 64, \ldots$ **20.** $-5, -10, -20, -40, \ldots$

Practice and Applications

STUDENT HELP

HOMEWORK HELP
Example 1: Exs. 21–33, 49
Example 2: Exs. 34–48, 50–51
Example 3: Exs. 52–66
Example 4: Exs. 67–75

Classifying Sequences **Tell whether the sequence is _arithmetic_, _geometric_, or _neither_. Explain your answer.**

21. $2, 5, 8, 11, \ldots$ **22.** $4, 8, 16, 32, \ldots$ **23.** $3, 12, 48, 192, \ldots$

24. $7, 8, 10, 14, \ldots$ **25.** $1, 4, 8, 13, \ldots$ **26.** $2, 1, \frac{1}{2}, \frac{1}{4}, \ldots$

27. $0, -6, -12, -18, \ldots$ **28.** $-2, 2, 6, 10, \ldots$ **29.** $-4, -6, -9, -13, \ldots$

30. $-16, -8, -4, -2, \ldots$ **31.** $2, -4, 8, -16, \ldots$ **32.** $-\frac{1}{9}, \frac{1}{3}, -1, 3, \ldots$

33. Error Analysis Describe and correct the error in finding the common ratio of the following sequence.

$$540, 180, 60, 20, \ldots$$

$\frac{540}{180} = 3$ $\frac{180}{60} = 3$ $\frac{60}{20} = 3$

The geometric sequence has a common ratio of 3.

Writing Rules **Write a rule for the _n_th term of the geometric sequence.**

34. $4, 16, 64, 256, \ldots$ **35.** $13.5, 9, 6, 4, \ldots$ **36.** $\frac{1}{16}, \frac{1}{8}, \frac{1}{4}, \frac{1}{2}, \ldots$

37. $-8, -12, -18, -27, \ldots$ **38.** $-3, 6, -12, 24, \ldots$ **39.** $1, -\frac{1}{3}, \frac{1}{9}, -\frac{1}{27}, \ldots$

Writing Terms Write a rule for the *n*th term of the geometric sequence. Then find a_6.

40. 24, 12, 6, 3, . . .

41. 1, 10, 100, 1000, . . .

42. −1, −5, −25, −125, . . .

43. −1, 3, −9, 27, . . .

44. 4, 2, 1, 0.5, . . .

45. $2, \frac{3}{2}, \frac{9}{8}, \frac{27}{32}, \ldots$

46. $-\frac{1}{6}, 1, -6, 36, \ldots$

47. $\frac{1}{2}, \frac{1}{6}, \frac{1}{18}, \frac{1}{54}, \ldots$

48. −0.3, 0.6, −1.2, 2.4, . . .

Chemistry Link In Exercises 49–51, use the following information.

A scientist begins an experiment with 120 grams of Tungsten-187 and records the amount of Tungsten-187 left each day. The sequence 120, 60, 30, 15, . . . represents the number of grams the scientist records each day.

49. Tell whether the sequence is *arithmetic*, *geometric*, or *neither*. If the sequence is geometric, find the common ratio.

50. Write a rule for the *n*th term of the sequence.

51. Find a_6. What is the meaning of this value?

Writing Rules Write a rule for the *n*th term of the geometric sequence given one term and the common ratio.

52. $a_1 = 4, r = 2$

53. $a_1 = 44, r = \frac{1}{2}$

54. $a_3 = 48, r = 4$

55. $a_1 = -4, r = 3$

56. $a_3 = -8, r = 4$

57. $a_2 = 6, r = -3$

58. $a_2 = -24, r = -3$

59. $a_2 = 7, r = \frac{1}{7}$

60. $a_3 = 16, r = \frac{1}{2}$

Graphing Sequences Graph the geometric sequence.

61. $a_n = (2)^{n-1}$

62. $a_n = 3(2)^{n-1}$

63. $a_n = 4(3)^{n-1}$

64. $a_n = 2(4)^{n-1}$

65. $a_n = \left(\frac{1}{2}\right)^{n-1}$

66. $a_n = 27\left(\frac{1}{3}\right)^{n-1}$

Finding Sums Find the sum of the first 8 terms of the geometric series.

67. $1 + 2 + 4 + 8 + \cdots$

68. $54 + 18 + 6 + 2 + \cdots$

69. $100 + 20 + 4 + \frac{4}{5} + \cdots$

70. $\frac{9}{2} + 9 + 18 + 36 + \cdots$

71. $128 + (-64) + 32 + (-16) + \cdots$

72. $-1 + (-6) + (-36) + (-216) + \cdots$

Basketball In Exercises 73 and 74, use the following information.

The number of basketball games played in round *n* of the women's NCAA basketball tournament is given by $a_n = 32\left(\frac{1}{2}\right)^{n-1}$.

73. Find the sum of the first 6 terms of the geometric series.

74. If there are 6 rounds in the tournament, what does your answer to Exercise 73 mean in the context of the situation?

75. **Skydiving** In a skydiving formation, skydivers form rings by holding on to each other. The first ring is made up of 5 skydivers, and each ring after the first has twice as many skydivers as the preceding ring. A rule for the number of skydivers in the *n*th ring is $a_n = 5(2)^{n-1}$. Find the sum of the first three terms and state the meaning of its value.

Logical Reasoning Complete the statement with *sometimes,
always,* or *never*. Explain your reasoning.

76. A geometric sequence __?__ has a zero as one of its terms.

77. A geometric sequence containing negative terms __?__ has a negative
common ratio.

78. A geometric sequence with alternating negative terms __?__ has a negative
common ratio.

Challenge Write a rule for the *n*th term of the geometric sequence
that has the two given terms.

79. $a_3 = 10, a_6 = 270$ **80.** $a_2 = 40, a_4 = 10$ **81.** $a_2 = -24, a_5 = 1536$

82. Multiple Choice Which of the following is a geometric sequence?

   (**A**) 1, 11, 22, 34, . . .   (**B**) $\frac{1}{11}$, 1, 11, 121, . . .

   (**C**) 36, 18, 0, −18, . . .   (**D**) 16, 12, 9, 7, . . .

83. Multiple Choice Which of the following is a rule for the *n*th term of the
geometric sequence where $a_3 = 1$ and $r = \frac{1}{4}$?

   (**F**) $a_n = \frac{1}{4}(16)^{n-1}$ (**G**) $a_n = 16\left(\frac{1}{4}\right)^{n-1}$

   (**H**) $a_n = \frac{1}{4}(4)^{n-1}$ (**J**) $a_n = 4\left(\frac{1}{4}\right)^{n-1}$

84. Multiple Choice Which geometric sequence is shown by
the graph at the right?

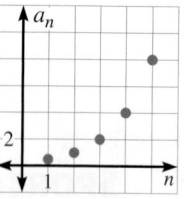

   (**A**) $a_n = \frac{1}{4}(2)^{n-1}$ (**B**) $a_n = 2\left(\frac{1}{2}\right)^{n-1}$

   (**C**) $a_n = \frac{1}{2}(2)^{n-1}$ (**D**) $a_n = 2\left(\frac{1}{4}\right)^{n-1}$

Describing Graphs Tell whether the graph of the function opens *up*
or *down*. Then tell whether the graph is *wider* or *narrower* than the
graph of $y = |x|$. *(Lesson 4.6)*

85. $y = -3|x|$ **86.** $y = 6|x|$ **87.** $y = \frac{3}{5}|x|$

Graphing Radical Functions Graph the function. Then state its
domain and range. *(Lesson 7.6)*

88. $y = 6\sqrt{x}$ **89.** $y = 2.5\sqrt{x}$ **90.** $y = \frac{3}{2}\sqrt[3]{x}$

91. $y = \sqrt{x} - 8$ **92.** $y = 3\sqrt{x+1}$ **93.** $y = \sqrt{x-5} - 2$

Finding Sums Find the sum of the first 11 terms of the arithmetic
series. *(Lesson 11.5)*

94. $4 + 8 + 12 + 16 + 20 + \cdots$ **95.** $20 + 19 + 18 + 17 + 16 + \cdots$

96. $0.4 + 1.2 + 2 + 2.8 + 3.6 + \cdots$ **97.** $\frac{1}{2} + 2 + \frac{7}{2} + 5 + \frac{13}{2} + \cdots$

98. Comparing Areas The radius of Circle *A* is 1 centimeter, the radius of
Circle *B* is 2 centimeters, and the radius of Circle *C* is 3 centimeters. Find the
area of each circle. Use a ratio to compare the area of Circle *B* to the area of
Circle *A* and the area of Circle *C* to the area of Circle *A*.

Goal

Find the sum of an infinite geometric series.

Materials

• scissors
• piece of paper

QUESTION

What is the sum of an infinite geometric series?

EXPLORE

You can illustrate an infinite geometric series by cutting a piece of paper into smaller and smaller pieces. Start with a rectangular piece of paper. Define the area of the paper to be 1 square unit.

 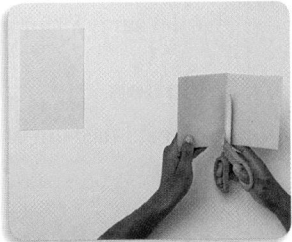 

1 Fold the piece of paper in half and cut along the fold. Place one half on a desktop and hold the remaining half.

2 Fold the piece of paper you are holding in half. Cut along the fold. Place one half on the desktop. Hold the remaining half.

3 Repeat Steps 1 and 2 until you find it too difficult to fold and cut the piece of paper you are holding.

4 The first piece of paper you placed on the desktop has an area of $\frac{1}{2}$ square unit. The second piece of paper has an area of $\frac{1}{4}$ square unit. Find the areas of the next three pieces of paper. Explain why these areas form a geometric sequence.

5 Copy and complete the table by recording the number of pieces of paper on the desktop and the combined area of the pieces at each step.

Number of pieces of paper	1	2	3	4	5	...
Combined area	$\frac{1}{2}$	$\frac{1}{2} + \frac{1}{4} = ?$	?	?	?	...

THINK ABOUT IT

1. Based on your table, what number does the combined area of the pieces of paper appear to be approaching?

2. The formula for the combined area after n cuts is $A_n = \frac{1}{2}\left(\dfrac{1 - \left(\frac{1}{2}\right)^n}{1 - \frac{1}{2}}\right)$. What happens to the formula as n approaches infinity? (*Hint:* The only term with n in it, $\left(\frac{1}{2}\right)^n$, approaches 0 as n gets larger. Use this to evaluate the formula.)

Infinite Geometric Series

Key Words

- geometric series, p. 623

Prerequisite Skills

Find the sum of the first 9 terms of the geometric series.

1. $1 + 2 + 4 + 8 + \ldots$

2. $54 + 18 + 6 + 2 + \ldots$

3. $32 + 16 + 8 + 4 + \ldots$

GOAL Find sums of infinite geometric series.

You can find the *partial sum*, S_n, of the first n terms of an infinite geometric series by adding the terms. The partial sums may approach a certain value.

EXAMPLE 1 Find Partial Sums

Consider the geometric series $\frac{1}{2} + \frac{1}{4} + \frac{1}{8} + \frac{1}{16} + \frac{1}{32} + \cdots$. Find and graph the partial sums S_n for $n = 1, 2, 3, 4, 5$. Describe what happens to S_n as n increases.

Solution

Compute the sum of the first n terms for the given values of n. Then graph the sums.

$S_1 = \frac{1}{2} = 0.5$

$S_2 = \frac{1}{2} + \frac{1}{4} = 0.75$

$S_3 = \frac{1}{2} + \frac{1}{4} + \frac{1}{8} \approx 0.88$

$S_4 = \frac{1}{2} + \frac{1}{4} + \frac{1}{8} + \frac{1}{16} \approx 0.94$

$S_5 = \frac{1}{2} + \frac{1}{4} + \frac{1}{8} + \frac{1}{16} + \frac{1}{32} \approx 0.97$

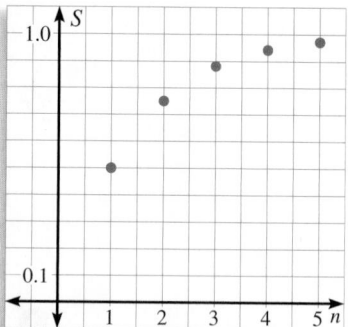

You can see from the graph and from the partial sums that the sum appears to be approaching 1 as n increases.

Sums of Infinite Series To see why S_n appears to be approaching 1 as n increases, consider the rule for S_n with $a_1 = \frac{1}{2}$ and $r = \frac{1}{2}$.

$$S_n = a_1\left(\frac{1 - r^n}{1 - r}\right) = \frac{1}{2}\left(\frac{1 - \left(\frac{1}{2}\right)^n}{1 - \frac{1}{2}}\right) = \frac{1}{2}\left(\frac{1 - \left(\frac{1}{2}\right)^n}{\frac{1}{2}}\right) = 1 - \left(\frac{1}{2}\right)^n$$

As n increases, $\left(\frac{1}{2}\right)^n$ gets closer to 0, which means S_n gets closer to 1. The sum of any infinite geometric series with $-1 < r < 1$ is given by the following formula.

STUDENT HELP

SOLVING NOTE
For the series
$\frac{1}{2} + \frac{1}{4} + \frac{1}{8} + \frac{1}{16} + \cdots$,
the sum is $S = \dfrac{\frac{1}{2}}{1 - \frac{1}{2}} = 1$,
as expected.

The Sum of an Infinite Geometric Series

The sum of an infinite geometric series with first term a_1 and common ratio r is given by

$$S = \frac{a_1}{1 - r}$$

where $|r| < 1$. If $|r| \geq 1$, the series has no sum.

EXAMPLE 2 Find Sums of Infinite Geometric Series

Find the sum of the infinite geometric series, if it exists.

a. $a_1 = 1, r = -\dfrac{1}{2}$

b. $2 + \dfrac{2}{3} + \dfrac{2}{9} + \dfrac{2}{27} + \cdots$

Solution

Identify the first terms and common ratio. Then substitute the values into the formula for the sum of an infinite geometric series.

a. Here, $a_1 = 1$ and $r = -\dfrac{1}{2}$.

$$S = \frac{a_1}{1 - r} = \frac{1}{1 - \left(-\dfrac{1}{2}\right)} = \frac{1}{\dfrac{3}{2}} = \frac{2}{3}$$

b. Here, $a_1 = 2$ and $r = \dfrac{1}{3}$.

$$S = \frac{a_1}{1 - r} = \frac{2}{1 - \dfrac{1}{3}} = \frac{2}{\dfrac{2}{3}} = 3$$

Checkpoint ✔ *Find Sums of Infinite Geometric Series*

1. Consider the series $\dfrac{2}{5} + \dfrac{4}{25} + \dfrac{8}{125} + \dfrac{16}{625} + \dfrac{32}{3125} + \cdots$. Find and graph the partial sums S_n for $n = 1, 2, 3, 4, 5$. Describe what happens to S_n as n increases.

Find the sum of the infinite geometric series, if it exists.

2. $a_1 = 5, r = 2$

3. $a_1 = 3, r = \dfrac{5}{4}$

4. $3 - \dfrac{3}{4} + \dfrac{3}{16} - \dfrac{3}{64} + \cdots$

EXAMPLE 3 Find the Common Ratio

What is the common ratio of the infinite geometric series with sum $S = 8$ and first term $a_1 = 3$?

Solution

$S = \dfrac{a_1}{1 - r}$	Write rule for sum.
$8 = \dfrac{3}{1 - r}$	Substitute 8 for S and 3 for a_1.
$8(1 - r) = 3$	Multiply each side by $1 - r$.
$1 - r = \dfrac{3}{8}$	Divide each side by 8.
$-r = \dfrac{3}{8} - 1$	Subtract 1 from each side.
$r = \dfrac{5}{8}$	Solve for r.

ANSWER ▶ The common ratio is $\dfrac{5}{8}$.

Checkpoint ✔ *Find Common Ratios*

Find the common ratio of the infinite geometric series with the given sum and first term.

5. $S = 3, a_1 = 1$

6. $S = 10, a_1 = 1$

7. $S = 6, a_1 = 2$

Repeating Decimals To write a repeating decimal as a fraction, write the decimal as a sum and use the rule for the sum of an infinite geometric series.

EXAMPLE **4** **Write a Repeating Decimal as a Fraction**

Write 0.171717. . . as a fraction.

Solution

Rewrite the repeating decimal as a sum.

$$0.171717\ldots = 0.17 + 0.0017 + 0.000017 + \cdots \qquad \text{Write as a sum.}$$

$$= 17(0.01) + 17(0.01)^2 + 17(0.01)^3 + \cdots \qquad \text{Rewrite sum.}$$

$$= \frac{a_1}{1 - r} \qquad \text{Write rule for sum.}$$

$$= \frac{17(0.01)}{1 - 0.01} \qquad \text{Substitute } 17(0.01) \text{ for } a_1 \text{ and } 0.01 \text{ for } r.$$

$$= \frac{17}{99} \qquad \text{Write as a quotient of integers.}$$

ANSWER ▶ The repeating decimal 0.171717. . . is $\frac{17}{99}$ written as a fraction.

STUDENT HELP

SOLVING NOTE
You can check the result in Example 4 by dividing 17 by 99 on a calculator.

 **Write Repeating Decimals as Fractions**

Write the repeating decimal as a fraction.

8. 0.222. . .   **9.** 0.454545. . .   **10.** 0.357357357. . .

EXAMPLE **5** **Use an Infinite Series as a Model**

Pendulum A pendulum is released to swing freely. On the first swing, the pendulum travels a distance of 18 inches. On each successive swing, the pendulum travels 80% of the distance of the previous swing, as shown. What is the total distance *d* the pendulum travels?

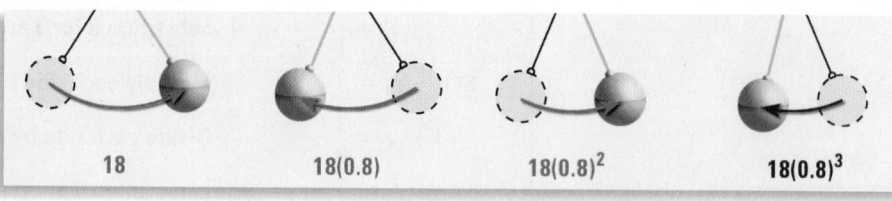

18   18(0.8)   18(0.8)²   18(0.8)³

Solution

The total distance *d* that the pendulum travels is given by an infinite geometric series with $a_1 = 18$ and $r = 0.8$.

$$d = 18 + 18(0.8) + 18(0.8)^2 + 18(0.8)^3 + \cdots$$

$$d = \frac{a_1}{1 - r} \qquad \text{Write rule for the sum of an infinite geometric series.}$$

$$= \frac{18}{1 - 0.8} \qquad \text{Substitute 18 for } a_1 \text{ and 0.8 for } r.$$

$$= 90 \qquad \text{Simplify.}$$

ANSWER ▶ The total distance the pendulum travels is 90 inches.

Guided Practice

Vocabulary Check

1. Copy and complete the statement: An infinite geometric series has a sum if its __?__ is between -1 and 1.

2. What two things do you need to know in order to find the sum of an infinite geometric series?

Skill Check

Consider the geometric series. Find and graph the partial sums S_n for $n = 1, 2, 3, 4$, and 5. Describe what happens to S_n as n increases.

3. $1 + \frac{3}{2} + \frac{9}{4} + \frac{27}{8} + \frac{81}{16} + \cdots$

4. $\frac{1}{2} + \frac{1}{6} + \frac{1}{18} + \frac{1}{54} + \frac{1}{162} + \cdots$

5. $2 + \frac{2}{6} + \frac{2}{36} + \frac{2}{216} + \frac{2}{1296} + \cdots$

6. $4 + \frac{12}{5} + \frac{36}{25} + \frac{108}{125} + \frac{324}{625} + \cdots$

Find the sum of the infinite geometric series, if it exists.

7. $a_1 = 3, r = \frac{1}{3}$

8. $1 + \frac{4}{3} + \frac{16}{9} + \frac{64}{27} + \cdots$

9. $a_1 = \frac{2}{3}, r = \frac{1}{2}$

Find the common ratio of the infinite geometric series with the given sum and first term.

10. $S = 4, a_1 = 2$

11. $S = 8, a_1 = 3$

12. $S = -12, a_1 = -5$

Write the repeating decimal as a fraction or mixed number.

13. $0.151515\ldots$

14. $0.333\ldots$

15. $25.2525\ldots$

Practice and Applications

STUDENT HELP

HOMEWORK HELP
Example 1: Exs. 16–19
Example 2: Exs. 20–38
Example 3: Exs. 39–47
Example 4: Exs. 48–56
Example 5: Exs. 57–63

Finding Partial Sums **Consider the geometric series. Find and graph the partial sums S_n for $n = 1, 2, 3, 4$, and 5. Describe what happens to S_n as n increases.**

16. $1 + \frac{1}{3} + \frac{1}{9} + \frac{1}{27} + \frac{1}{81} + \cdots$

17. $1 + \frac{1}{5} + \frac{1}{25} + \frac{1}{125} + \frac{1}{625} + \cdots$

18. $3 + \frac{3}{4} + \frac{3}{16} + \frac{3}{64} + \frac{3}{256} + \cdots$

19. $5 + \frac{10}{3} + \frac{20}{9} + \frac{40}{27} + \frac{80}{81} + \cdots$

Determining if a Sum Exists **Given the first term and common ratio, tell whether the infinite geometric series has a sum. Explain.**

20. $a_1 = 4, r = -5$

21. $a_1 = 2, r = \frac{3}{7}$

22. $a_1 = 5, r = \frac{3}{10}$

23. $a_1 = 3, r = -\frac{7}{2}$

24. $a_1 = \frac{1}{2}, r = 1.2$

25. $a_1 = -1.5, r = \frac{6}{5}$

26. Error Analysis Describe and correct the error in finding the sum of the geometric series where $a_1 = 1$ and $r = \frac{3}{2}$.

$$S = \frac{a_1}{1 - r} = \frac{1}{1 - \frac{3}{2}} = -2 \qquad \times$$

Finding Sums Find the sum of the infinite geometric series, if it exists.

27. $5 - \dfrac{4}{3} + \dfrac{16}{45} - \dfrac{64}{675} + \cdots$

28. $3 + \dfrac{15}{4} + \dfrac{75}{16} + \dfrac{375}{64} + \cdots$

29. $1 + \dfrac{5}{4} + \dfrac{25}{16} + \dfrac{125}{64} + \cdots$

30. $1 + \dfrac{1}{4} + \dfrac{1}{16} + \dfrac{1}{64} + \cdots$

31. $1 + \dfrac{2}{3} + \dfrac{4}{9} + \dfrac{8}{27} + \cdots$

32. $10 - \dfrac{5}{3} + \dfrac{5}{18} - \dfrac{5}{108} + \cdots$

33. $5 - \dfrac{5}{2} + \dfrac{5}{4} - \dfrac{5}{8} + \cdots$

34. $7 + \dfrac{21}{10} + \dfrac{63}{100} + \dfrac{189}{1000} + \cdots$

35. $6 - 15 + \dfrac{75}{2} - \dfrac{375}{4} + \cdots$

36. $3 - \dfrac{12}{5} + \dfrac{48}{25} - \dfrac{192}{125} + \cdots$

37. $4 - \dfrac{8}{7} + \dfrac{16}{49} - \dfrac{32}{343} + \cdots$

38. $2 + \dfrac{10}{3} + \dfrac{50}{9} + \dfrac{250}{27} + \cdots$

Finding Common Ratios Find the common ratio of the infinite geometric series with the given sum and first term.

39. $S = 3,\ a_1 = 1$

40. $S = 7,\ a_1 = 2$

41. $S = 5,\ a_1 = 4$

42. $S = 12,\ a_1 = 3$

43. $S = -12,\ a_1 = -6$

44. $S = \dfrac{24}{5},\ a_1 = 3$

45. $S = \dfrac{3}{2},\ a_1 = 2$

46. $S = \dfrac{2}{3},\ a_1 = \dfrac{1}{2}$

47. $S = \dfrac{5}{2},\ a_1 = \dfrac{5}{3}$

Writing Repeating Decimals Write the repeating decimal as a fraction or mixed number.

48. $0.111\ldots$

49. $0.999\ldots$

50. $0.121212\ldots$

51. $0.505050\ldots$

52. $0.353535\ldots$

53. $0.848484\ldots$

54. $27.272727\ldots$

55. $7.777\ldots$

56. $61.616161\ldots$

Geometry Link In Exercises 57–59, use the following information.

A square has sides that are 12 inches long. You can form a new square by connecting the midpoints of the sides of the square. The figure below shows this process for four new squares. You can continue this process to create an infinite geometric series. The area of each new square is half the area of the previous square.

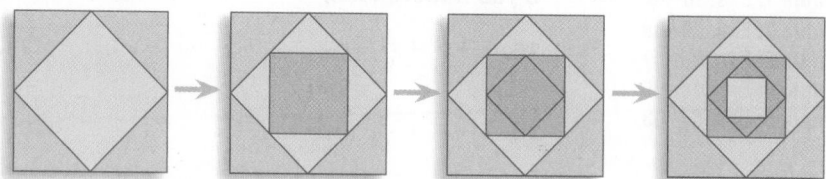

57. Find a_1, the area of the initial square.

58. Find the common ratio r of the infinite geometric series.

59. Find the sum of the infinite geometric series and state what it represents.

60. Contest Winners A radio station has a daily contest in which a random listener is asked a trivia question. On the first day, the station gives $500 to the listener who answers correctly. On each successive day, the winner receives 90% of the previous day's winnings. The contest continues until no money is left. How much total prize money does the radio station give away during the contest?

Ball Bouncing In Exercises 61–63, use the following information.

You drop a ball from a height of 20 feet. Each time the ball hits the ground, it bounces to 75% of its previous height.

61. The following series represents the distances that the ball bounces down. Find the sum of the series.

$$20 + 20(0.75)^1 + 20(0.75)^2 + 20(0.75)^3 + \cdots$$

62. The following series represents the distances the ball bounces up. Find the sum of the series.

$$15 + 15(0.75)^1 + 15(0.75)^2 + 15(0.75)^3 + \cdots$$

63. Use your answers to Exercises 61 and 62 to find the total distance traveled by the ball.

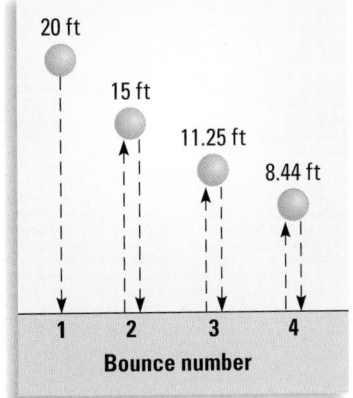

Challenge In Exercises 64–65, use the following information.

The Chamber of Commerce announced that a new advertising campaign helped to increase summer tourism this year. On average, each tourist spent an additional $10 on goods or services. Also, 80% of every $1 a tourist spends on goods or services is re-spent, creating a "multiplier" effect.

The total spending for every $1 spent on goods or services is represented by the following infinite geometric series.

$$\$1 + \$1(0.8) + \$1(0.8)^2 + \$1(0.8)^3 + \cdots$$

64. Find the total spending that was generated for every $1 spent on goods or services.

65. Find the total spending that would be generated by the average tourist during the summer months.

66. Multiple Choice What is the sum of the following infinite geometric series?

$$4 + \frac{8}{3} + \frac{16}{9} + \frac{32}{27} + \cdots$$

(A) 6   (B) 12   (C) $-\frac{12}{5}$ (D) No sum

67. Multiple Choice What is the sum of the following infinite geometric series?

$$2 - \frac{14}{5} + \frac{98}{25} - \frac{686}{125} + \cdots$$

(F) $-\frac{7}{5}$ (G) $-\frac{5}{6}$ (H) $-\frac{10}{7}$ (J) No sum

68. Multiple Choice What is the common ratio of the infinite geometric series with $S = 10$ and $a_1 = 6$?

(A) 5   (B) $\frac{3}{5}$ (C) $\frac{2}{5}$ (D) 2

69. Multiple Choice Which fraction is equal to the repeating decimal 36.3636. . . ?

(F) $\frac{9}{10}$ (G) $\frac{36}{99}$ (H) $\frac{73}{2}$ (J) $\frac{400}{11}$

Biased Samples In Exercises 70–72, use the following information.

You are conducting a survey to determine the public's opinion on increasing the retirement age to 70. Tell whether the method could result in a biased sample. *(Lesson 10.1)*

70. Survey high school freshmen.

71. Survey every tenth person in the phone book.

72. Survey the first 50 employees walking into an office building.

Finding Probabilities **A card is drawn randomly from a standard deck of cards. Find the probability of drawing the given card.** *(Lesson 10.6)*

73. the queen of diamonds

74. a red card

75. a 5 or 7

76. a spade

Finding Matrix Products **Find the product. If it is not defined, state the reason.** *(Lesson 11.2)*

77. $\begin{bmatrix} 3 & 1 \\ 2 & -1 \end{bmatrix}\begin{bmatrix} 5 & 0 \\ 0 & -1 \end{bmatrix}$

78. $\begin{bmatrix} -2 & 4 \\ -3 & 0 \\ 0 & 1 \end{bmatrix}\begin{bmatrix} -1 \\ 1 \end{bmatrix}$

79. $\begin{bmatrix} 5 \\ -2 \end{bmatrix}\begin{bmatrix} 3 & -1 \end{bmatrix}$

Geometry Skills

Volume of a Pyramid **Find the volume of the pyramid.**

80.
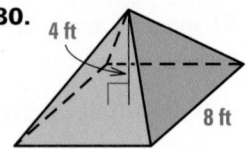
4 ft
8 ft
6 ft

81.

3 ft
3 ft
5 ft

82.
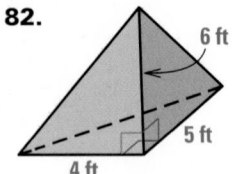
6 ft
5 ft
4 ft

Quiz 3

Lesson 11.6

Write a rule for the *n*th term of the geometric sequence.

1. $a_1 = 5, r = 3$

2. $a_1 = 32, r = \frac{1}{4}$

3. $a_1 = -10, r = \frac{5}{3}$

Lesson 11.6

Find the sum of the first 6 terms of the geometric series.

4. $1 + 3 + 9 + 27 + \cdots$

5. $120 + 60 + 30 + 15 + \cdots$

6. $150 + 30 + 6 + \frac{6}{5} + \cdots$

7. $\frac{15}{4} + 15 + 60 + 240 + \cdots$

Lesson 11.7

Find the sum of the infinite geometric series, if it exists.

8. $1 + \frac{1}{5} + \frac{1}{25} + \frac{1}{125} + \cdots$

9. $1 - \frac{3}{4} + \frac{9}{16} - \frac{27}{64} + \cdots$

10. $3 + \frac{6}{7} + \frac{12}{49} + \frac{24}{343} + \cdots$

11. $5 + \frac{20}{9} + \frac{80}{81} + \frac{320}{729} + \cdots$

Lesson 11.7

Write the repeating decimal as a fraction.

12. $0.444\ldots$

13. $0.2424\ldots$

14. $0.0606\ldots$

VOCABULARY

• matrix, *p. 585*
• element, *p. 585*
• dimensions of a matrix, *p. 585*
• equal matrices, *p. 585*
• scalar, *p. 587*
• scalar multiplication, *p. 587*

• identity matrix, *p. 600*
• inverse matrix, *p. 600*
• coefficient matrix, *p. 601*
• matrix of variables, *p. 601*
• matrix of constants, *p. 601*
• sequence, *p. 608*
• terms of a sequence, *p. 608*

• series, *p. 610*
• arithmetic sequence, *p. 615*
• common difference, *p. 615*
• arithmetic series, *p. 617*
• geometric sequence, *p. 621*
• common ratio, *p. 621*
• geometric series, *p. 623*

VOCABULARY EXERCISES

1. What are the dimensions of the matrix $\begin{bmatrix} 3 & -7 & 0 \\ 7 & 5 & -2 \end{bmatrix}$?

2. What is an identity matrix? Give an example of an identity matrix.

3. Explain the difference between a sequence and a series.

4. Copy and complete the statement: The common __?__ of the arithmetic sequence 1, 9, 17, 25, 33, . . . is 8.

11.1 MATRIX OPERATIONS

Examples on pp. 585–588

EXAMPLE You can add or subtract matrices that have the same dimension by adding or subtracting corresponding elements.

$$\begin{bmatrix} 4 & 0 \\ 1 & -2 \end{bmatrix} + \begin{bmatrix} -3 & 6 \\ 4 & 5 \end{bmatrix} = \begin{bmatrix} 4+(-3) & 0+6 \\ 1+4 & -2+5 \end{bmatrix} = \begin{bmatrix} 1 & 6 \\ 5 & 3 \end{bmatrix}$$

To perform scalar multiplication, multiply each element by the scalar.

$$-2\begin{bmatrix} 1 & 4 & -5 \\ 0 & -2 & 6 \end{bmatrix} = \begin{bmatrix} -2(1) & -2(4) & -2(-5) \\ -2(0) & -2(-2) & -2(6) \end{bmatrix} = \begin{bmatrix} -2 & -8 & 10 \\ 0 & 4 & -12 \end{bmatrix}$$

REVIEW HELP

Exercises	Examples
5–7	**2**, p. 586
8–10	**4**, p. 587

Add or subtract, if possible. If not possible, state the reason.

5. $\begin{bmatrix} 4 & -1 \\ 7 & 3 \end{bmatrix} - \begin{bmatrix} 3 & -1 \\ 2 & 6 \end{bmatrix}$

6. $\begin{bmatrix} 8 & 6 \\ 3 & 0 \\ -1 & 5 \end{bmatrix} - \begin{bmatrix} 7 & 5 \\ 9 & -4 \\ 0 & 2 \end{bmatrix}$

7. $\begin{bmatrix} 5 & -1 & 2 \\ 7 & 0 & -3 \end{bmatrix} + \begin{bmatrix} 1 & -4 \\ 1 & 6 \end{bmatrix}$

Perform the indicated operation(s).

8. $4\begin{bmatrix} -1 \\ 2 \\ 5 \end{bmatrix}$

9. $-3\begin{bmatrix} 0 & 2 & 1 \\ 6 & 2 & -4 \\ -3 & -5 & 0 \end{bmatrix}$

10. $\begin{bmatrix} 4 & 6 \\ 1 & 8 \end{bmatrix} + 3\begin{bmatrix} -7 & 0 \\ -2 & 1 \end{bmatrix}$

11.2 MULTIPLYING MATRICES

Examples on pp. 594–596

EXAMPLE You can multiply two matrices if the number of columns in the first matrix equals the number of rows in the second matrix.

REVIEW HELP
Exercises	Examples
11–16	**2**, p. 595
17	**3**, p. 596

$$\begin{bmatrix} 3 & -5 \\ 2 & 1 \\ 7 & 0 \end{bmatrix}\begin{bmatrix} 2 & 0 \\ -3 & 4 \end{bmatrix} = \begin{bmatrix} 3(2) + (-5)(-3) & 3(0) + (-5)(4) \\ 2(2) + 1(-3) & 2(0) + 1(4) \\ 7(2) + 0(-3) & 7(0) + 0(4) \end{bmatrix} = \begin{bmatrix} 21 & -20 \\ 1 & 4 \\ 14 & 0 \end{bmatrix}$$

In Exercises 11–16, find the product. If it is not defined, state the reason.

11. $\begin{bmatrix} 3 & 0 \\ -4 & 2 \\ 1 & 4 \end{bmatrix}\begin{bmatrix} 6 & -3 \\ 0 & 1 \\ 3 & 0 \end{bmatrix}$

12. $\begin{bmatrix} 1 \\ -2 \end{bmatrix}\begin{bmatrix} 2 & -3 & 1 \end{bmatrix}$

13. $\begin{bmatrix} 2 & 0 & 1 \end{bmatrix}\begin{bmatrix} -1 \\ 6 \\ 3 \end{bmatrix}$

14. $\begin{bmatrix} 1 & 3 \end{bmatrix}\begin{bmatrix} -1 & 3 & 3 \end{bmatrix}$

15. $\begin{bmatrix} -4 & 0 \\ 1 & 5 \end{bmatrix}\begin{bmatrix} 1 \\ -3 \end{bmatrix}$

16. $\begin{bmatrix} 2 & -2 \\ 5 & -3 \end{bmatrix}\begin{bmatrix} -3 & 0 \\ 4 & 1 \end{bmatrix}$

17. Let $A = \begin{bmatrix} 5 & -1 \\ 1 & 0 \end{bmatrix}$, $B = \begin{bmatrix} -4 & 1 \\ 1 & 2 \end{bmatrix}$, and $C = \begin{bmatrix} 0 & -3 \\ 6 & 1 \end{bmatrix}$. Simplify $AB + AC$.

11.3 SOLVING LINEAR SYSTEMS USING INVERSE MATRICES

Examples on pp. 600–602

EXAMPLE You can use inverse matrices to solve systems of linear equations.

Write the system in matrix form $AX = B$.

$$\begin{aligned} 3x + 2y &= 2 \\ 6x + 5y &= -1 \end{aligned} \quad\Longrightarrow\quad \begin{bmatrix} 3 & 2 \\ 6 & 5 \end{bmatrix}\begin{bmatrix} x \\ y \end{bmatrix} = \begin{bmatrix} 2 \\ -1 \end{bmatrix}$$

Use a graphing calculator to solve the system.

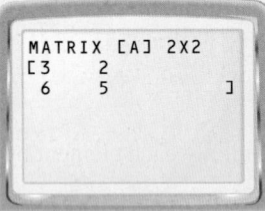

Enter matrix A.

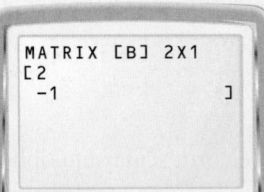

Enter matrix B.

Multiply A^{-1} by B.

REVIEW HELP
Exercises	Example
18–23	**4**, p. 602

Because $X = A^{-1}B = \begin{bmatrix} 4 \\ -5 \end{bmatrix}$, you know that $\begin{bmatrix} x \\ y \end{bmatrix} = \begin{bmatrix} 4 \\ -5 \end{bmatrix}$.

The solution is $(4, -5)$.

Use an inverse matrix to solve the linear system.

18. $\begin{aligned} 4x - y &= 9 \\ 2x + y &= 15 \end{aligned}$

19. $\begin{aligned} 3x + 2y &= 9 \\ 7x + y &= -1 \end{aligned}$

20. $\begin{aligned} 2x + y &= 12 \\ 3x - 5y &= 5 \end{aligned}$

21. $\begin{aligned} 3x - y &= -3 \\ -x + 2y &= -9 \end{aligned}$

22. $\begin{aligned} 2x + y &= -4 \\ 3x - 2y &= 22 \end{aligned}$

23. $\begin{aligned} 5x + 4y &= -6 \\ 2x - 3y &= -7 \end{aligned}$

11.4 AN INTRODUCTION TO SEQUENCES AND SERIES

Examples on pp. 608–610

EXAMPLE You can write the first six terms of the sequence $a_n = 3n - 4$.

$$a_1 = 3(1) - 4 = -1 \quad \text{1st term}$$
$$a_2 = 3(2) - 4 = 2 \quad \text{2nd term}$$
$$a_3 = 3(3) - 4 = 5 \quad \text{3rd term}$$
$$a_4 = 3(4) - 4 = 8 \quad \text{4th term}$$
$$a_5 = 3(5) - 4 = 11 \quad \text{5th term}$$
$$a_6 = 3(6) - 4 = 14 \quad \text{6th term}$$

You can find the sum of the terms of a finite sequence. The resulting expression is called a series.

$$-1 + 2 + 5 + 8 + 11 + 14 = 39$$

REVIEW HELP

Exercises	Examples
24–27	**1**, p. 608
28–30	**2**, p. 609
31–34	**4**, p. 610

Write the first six terms of the sequence.

24. $a_n = 2n + 5$ **25.** $a_n = 8 - 3n$ **26.** $a_n = 3n^2$ **27.** $a_n = n^2 - 1$

Write the next term in the sequence. Then write a rule for the *n*th term.

28. $1, 6, 11, 16, 21, \ldots$ **29.** $4, 7, 10, 13, 16, 19, \ldots$ **30.** $1, -3, 9, -27, 81, \ldots$

Find the sum of the series.

31. $3 + 7 + 11 + 15 + 19 + 23 + 27$ **32.** $1 + 2 + 3 + 4 + 5 + 6 + 7 + 8 + 9 + 10 + 11$

33. $3 + 1 - 1 - 3 - 5 - 7 - 9$ **34.** $1 + 4 + 9 + 16 + 25 + 36 + 49$

11.5 ARITHMETIC SEQUENCES AND SERIES

Examples on pp. 615–617

EXAMPLE You can tell if a sequence is an arithmetic sequence by determining whether the difference between consecutive terms is constant. To tell whether the sequence $8, 14, 20, 26, 32, \ldots$ is arithmetic, find the differences between terms.

$$14 - 8 = 6 \qquad 20 - 14 = 6 \qquad 26 - 20 = 6 \qquad 32 - 26 = 6$$

There is a common difference of 6, so the sequence is arithmetic.

You can write a rule for the sequence by substituting the values of d and a_1 into the formula $a_n = a_1 + (n - 1)d$. A rule for the *n*th term of the arithmetic sequence above is shown below.

$$a_n = a_1 + (n - 1)d = 8 + (n - 1)6 = 2 + 6n$$

REVIEW HELP

Exercises	Examples
35–37	**2**, p. 616
38–40	**3**, p. 616
41–42	**4**, p. 617

Write a rule for the *n*th term of the arithmetic sequence.

35. $3, 7, 11, 15, 19, 23, \ldots$ **36.** $5, 11, 17, 23, 29, 35, \ldots$ **37.** $8, 11, 14, 17, 20, 23, \ldots$

38. $d = 2, a_1 = 7$ **39.** $d = 7, a_1 = 3$ **40.** $d = 4, a_1 = 16$

Find the sum of the first 12 terms of the arithmetic series.

41. $7 + 13 + 19 + 25 + 31 + \cdots$ **42.** $-9 + (-3) + 3 + 9 + 15 + \cdots$

11.6 GEOMETRIC SEQUENCES AND SERIES

Examples on pp. 621–623

EXAMPLE You can tell if a sequence is geometric by determining whether the ratio between consecutive terms is constant. To tell whether the sequence 2, 8, 32, 128, 512, . . . is geometric, find the ratio of each term to the previous term.

$$\frac{8}{2} = 4 \qquad \frac{32}{8} = 4 \qquad \frac{128}{32} = 4 \qquad \frac{512}{128} = 4$$

There is a common ratio of 4, so the sequence is geometric.

You can write a rule for the sequence by substituting the values of r and a_1 into the formula $a_n = a_1 r^{n-1}$. A rule for the nth term of the geometric sequence above is shown below.

$$a_n = a_1 r^{n-1} = 2(4)^{n-1}$$

REVIEW HELP

Exercises	Examples
43–45	**2,** p. 622
46–48	**3,** p. 622
49–52	**4,** p. 623

Write a rule for the *n*th term of the geometric sequence.

43. 12, 24, 48, 96, 192, . . . **44.** 2, 10, 50, 250, 1250, . . . **45.** 972, 324, 108, 36, 12, . . .

46. $a_1 = 7, r = 3$ **47.** $a_1 = 3, r = -2$ **48.** $a_1 = 60, r = \frac{1}{5}$

Find the sum of the first 10 terms of the geometric series.

49. $6 + 18 + 54 + 162 + \cdots$ **50.** $9 + 18 + 36 + 72 + \cdots$

51. $600 + 60 + 6 + 0.6 + \cdots$ **52.** $50 + 10 + 2 + \frac{2}{5} + \cdots$

11.7 INFINITE GEOMETRIC SERIES

Examples on pp. 628–630

EXAMPLES You can find the sum of the infinite geometric series $1 + \frac{1}{3} + \frac{1}{9} + \frac{1}{27} + \frac{1}{81} + \cdots$ using the formula for S with $r = \frac{1}{3}$ and $a = 1$.

REVIEW HELP

Exercises	Examples
53–55	**1,** p. 628
56–61	**2,** p. 629
62–65	**3,** p. 629

$$S = \frac{a_1}{1 - r} = \frac{1}{1 - \frac{1}{3}} = \frac{3}{2}$$

The infinite geometric series $2 + 10 + 50 + 250 + \cdots$ has no sum because $|r| = 5$, which is greater than 1.

Find the sum of the infinite geometric series, if it exists.

53. $2 + \frac{2}{5} + \frac{2}{25} + \frac{2}{125} + \cdots$ **54.** $16 + 8 + 4 + 2 + \cdots$ **55.** $\frac{3}{2} + \frac{3}{4} + \frac{3}{8} + \frac{3}{16} + \cdots$

Find the common ratio of the infinite geometric series with the given sum and first term.

56. $S = 9, a_1 = 3$ **57.** $S = 5, a_1 = 4$ **58.** $S = 5, a_1 = 8$

59. $S = 25, a_1 = 5$ **60.** $S = -8, a_1 = -2$ **61.** $S = \frac{8}{9}, a_1 = 1$

Write the repeating decimal as a fraction or mixed number.

62. 0.6666. . . **63.** 0.3232. . . **64.** 0.050505. . . **65.** 12.1212. . .

638 Chapter 11 *Discrete Mathematics*

Add or subtract, if possible. If not possible, state the reason.

1. $\begin{bmatrix} -5 & 2 \\ 1 & -2 \end{bmatrix} + \begin{bmatrix} 5 \\ 3 \end{bmatrix}$

2. $\begin{bmatrix} 5 & 1 \\ 4 & 2 \\ -3 & 1 \end{bmatrix} + \begin{bmatrix} -2 & -5 \\ 3 & -8 \\ -7 & -1 \end{bmatrix}$

3. $\begin{bmatrix} 10 & 5 & -7 \\ -1 & 9 & 3 \end{bmatrix} - \begin{bmatrix} 4 & 9 & -2 \\ 3 & 1 & 7 \end{bmatrix}$

Find the product. If it is not defined, state the reason.

4. $\begin{bmatrix} 1 & -2 \end{bmatrix} \begin{bmatrix} 5 & 2 \\ -1 & 0 \end{bmatrix}$

5. $\begin{bmatrix} 2 & 0 \\ 5 & -1 \\ 0 & 3 \end{bmatrix} \begin{bmatrix} 3 \\ -2 \end{bmatrix}$

6. $\begin{bmatrix} 3 & 4 \\ -2 & 0 \end{bmatrix} \begin{bmatrix} 2 & -5 \\ 0 & 1 \\ 3 & 1 \end{bmatrix}$

Let $A = \begin{bmatrix} 2 & -1 \\ 4 & 0 \end{bmatrix}$, $B = \begin{bmatrix} -1 & 0 \\ 3 & 1 \end{bmatrix}$, **and** $C = \begin{bmatrix} 0 & 5 \\ 1 & -2 \end{bmatrix}$. **Simplify the expression.**

7. $2AB$

8. $A(B + C)$

9. $2A + 2B$

Use a graphing calculator to find the inverse of the matrix A. Then use the calculator to verify that $AA^{-1} = I$ and $A^{-1}A = I$.

10. $A = \begin{bmatrix} 7 & 2 \\ 3 & 1 \end{bmatrix}$

11. $A = \begin{bmatrix} 3 & -2 \\ -2 & 2 \end{bmatrix}$

12. $A = \begin{bmatrix} 3 & 4 & 5 \\ -2 & 5 & 0 \\ 1 & 2 & 2 \end{bmatrix}$

Use an inverse matrix to solve the linear system.

13. $2x + y = 3$
$5x + 6y = 4$

14. $9x + 2y = 7$
$4x - 3y = 42$

15. $4x + y + 6z = 7$
$3x + 3y + 2z = 17$
$-x - y + z = -9$

Write a rule for the nth term of the sequence. Then find a_{10}.

16. $62, 57, 52, 47, 42, \ldots$

17. $-3, 6, -12, 24, \ldots$

18. $r = \frac{1}{8}, a_1 = 4$

Find the sum of the first 12 terms of the series.

19. $4 + 10 + 16 + 22 + 28 + \cdots$

20. $5 - 15 + 45 - 135 + \cdots$

Find the sum of the infinite geometric series, if it exists.

21. $1 + \frac{4}{5} + \frac{16}{25} + \frac{64}{125} + \cdots$

22. $2 + \frac{14}{3} + \frac{98}{9} + \frac{686}{27} + \cdots$

Write the repeating decimal as a fraction or mixed number.

23. $0.0404\ldots$

24. $0.2626\ldots$

25. $8.888\ldots$

26. Snack Mix A grocer wants to mix two kinds of nuts to obtain a mixture that costs $51.00. The price per pound of each type of nut is shown in the table. The grocer wants twice as many almonds in the mixture as cashews. Write a system of equations to describe the situation. Use matrices to determine how many pounds of each type of nut the grocer should use.

Nut	Cashews	Almonds
Price	$5.00	$6.00

Chapter Standardized Test

EXAMPLE What is the rule for the nth term of the sequence $4, 1, \frac{1}{4}, \frac{1}{16}, \ldots$?

Ⓐ $a_n = 7 - 3n$ Ⓑ $a_n = 4\left(\frac{1}{4}\right)^{n-1}$

Ⓒ $a_n = \frac{7}{4} - \frac{3}{4}n$ Ⓓ $a_n = \frac{1}{4}(4)^{n-1}$

Solution

The sequence is a geometric sequence with $a_1 = 4$ and $r = \frac{1}{4}$.

Choices A and C are rules for arithmetic sequences.

Choice D incorrectly substitutes a_1 and r in the general rule for a geometric sequence.

So, Choice B is the correct answer.

Multiple Choice

1. Evaluate $\begin{bmatrix} -4 & 7 \\ 3 & -1 \end{bmatrix} + \begin{bmatrix} 5 & 3 \\ -6 & -4 \end{bmatrix}$.

Ⓐ $\begin{bmatrix} -1 & 4 \\ 3 & -5 \end{bmatrix}$ Ⓑ $\begin{bmatrix} -1 & -4 \\ 3 & 5 \end{bmatrix}$

Ⓒ $\begin{bmatrix} 1 & 10 \\ -3 & -5 \end{bmatrix}$ Ⓓ Not defined

2. Evaluate $\begin{bmatrix} 10 & -1 & 5 \\ -4 & 12 & 3 \end{bmatrix} - \begin{bmatrix} 3 & 6 & 2 \\ -3 & -1 & 9 \end{bmatrix}$.

Ⓕ $\begin{bmatrix} 13 & 5 & 7 \\ -7 & 11 & 12 \end{bmatrix}$ Ⓖ $\begin{bmatrix} 7 & -7 & 3 \\ -1 & 13 & -6 \end{bmatrix}$

Ⓗ $\begin{bmatrix} 7 & 7 & 7 \\ -7 & -7 & -7 \end{bmatrix}$ Ⓙ Not defined

3. Evaluate $2\begin{bmatrix} 1 & -2 \\ 4 & -1 \end{bmatrix} - \begin{bmatrix} 3 & -1 \\ 5 & -6 \end{bmatrix}$.

Ⓐ $\begin{bmatrix} -4 & -2 \\ -2 & 10 \end{bmatrix}$ Ⓑ $\begin{bmatrix} -1 & -3 \\ 3 & 4 \end{bmatrix}$

Ⓒ $\begin{bmatrix} 5 & -5 \\ 13 & -8 \end{bmatrix}$ Ⓓ Not defined

4. Evaluate $\begin{bmatrix} 2 & -2 & 0 \\ 3 & 4 & 1 \end{bmatrix}\begin{bmatrix} 1 & -2 \\ 0 & 3 \end{bmatrix}$.

Ⓕ $\begin{bmatrix} 2 & 2 & 0 \\ 0 & 12 & 1 \end{bmatrix}$ Ⓖ $\begin{bmatrix} 2 & -7 \\ 3 & 6 \end{bmatrix}$

Ⓗ $\begin{bmatrix} -1 & 2 \\ 4 & -5 \end{bmatrix}$ Ⓙ Not defined

5. Which matrix is equal to $AC + BC$ if
$A = \begin{bmatrix} -2 & 0 \\ 1 & 1 \end{bmatrix}, B = \begin{bmatrix} 1 & 2 \\ 1 & 0 \end{bmatrix}$, and $C = \begin{bmatrix} 1 & 2 \\ 0 & 4 \end{bmatrix}$?

Ⓐ $\begin{bmatrix} 3 & 8 \\ 4 & 4 \end{bmatrix}$ Ⓑ $\begin{bmatrix} -1 & 6 \\ 2 & 8 \end{bmatrix}$

Ⓒ $\begin{bmatrix} 1 & 2 \\ 6 & 8 \end{bmatrix}$ Ⓓ $\begin{bmatrix} -1 & 4 \\ 0 & 4 \end{bmatrix}$

6. Use an inverse matrix to solve the linear system.
$$x + 4y = -2$$
$$3x - 2y = -13$$

Ⓕ $\left(-4, \frac{1}{2}\right)$ Ⓖ $\left(\frac{1}{2}, -4\right)$

Ⓗ $(-54, 20)$ Ⓙ $(-4, 2)$

7. What is the rule for the nth term of the sequence 50, 42, 34, 26, 18, . . . ?

A $a_n = 18 - 2n$ **B** $a_n = 50 - 4n$

C $a_n = 58 - 8n$ **D** $a_n = 50(8)^{n-1}$

8. What is the rule for the nth term of the sequence $-2, -16, -128, -1024, . . .$?

F $a_n = -2 - 8n$ **G** $a_n = -2(8)^{n-1}$

H $a_n = -8(2)^{n-1}$ **J** $a_n = 2(-8)^{n-1}$

9. What is the sum of the first 12 terms of the series $-6 - 2 + 2 + 6 + \cdots$?

A 384 **B** 192

C 48 **D** 12

10. What is the sum of the first six terms of the series with $r = 3$ and $a_3 = 36$?

F 972 **G** 1456

H 2928 **J** 13,104

Gridded Response

11. Solve the matrix equation for x.
$$\begin{bmatrix} 5 & -4 \\ 8 & 2 \end{bmatrix} + \begin{bmatrix} x & -2 \\ -4 & 6 \end{bmatrix} = \begin{bmatrix} 12 & -6 \\ 4 & 8 \end{bmatrix}$$

12. Solve the matrix equation for x.
$$\begin{bmatrix} 9 & -4 \\ 6 & 3 \\ -2 & 5 \end{bmatrix} - \begin{bmatrix} 6 & -2 \\ -2 & x \\ 1 & -3 \end{bmatrix} = \begin{bmatrix} 3 & -2 \\ 8 & -9 \\ -3 & 8 \end{bmatrix}$$

13. Solve the matrix equation for x.
$$\begin{bmatrix} -5 & -7 \\ -9 & 1 \end{bmatrix} + 3\begin{bmatrix} -1 & 4 \\ x & 0 \end{bmatrix} = \begin{bmatrix} -8 & 5 \\ 15 & 1 \end{bmatrix}$$

14. Use your calculator to find the value of x.
$$\begin{bmatrix} 4 & -1 \\ -3 & 1 \end{bmatrix}^{-1} = \begin{bmatrix} 1 & 1 \\ x & 4 \end{bmatrix}$$

15. Find a_{15} of the following sequence.
5, 12, 19, 26, 33, . . .

16. Find the sum of the first 8 terms of the series.
$9 + 17 + 25 + 33 + 41 + \cdots$

17. Find a_9 of the following sequence.
6, 12, 24, 48, 96, . . .

18. Find the sum of the first 9 terms of the series.
$5 - 10 + 20 - 40 + \cdots$

19. Find the sum of the infinite geometric series.
$4 + \dfrac{12}{7} + \dfrac{36}{49} + \dfrac{108}{343} + \cdots$

20. Find the common ratio of the infinite geometric series where $S = 6$ and $a_1 = 2$.

21. Write 0.555. . . as a fraction.

Extended Response

22. An accounting firm has a job opening with a salary of $40,000 for the first year. During the next 39 years, there is a 5% raise each year.

 a. Write a rule to determine the salary for the nth year.

 b. What is the salary for the 39th year?

 c. Find the total amount of money the accounting firm will have paid at the end of the 39th year.

 d. If the pattern in the series of salaries continued forever, would the associated infinite geometric series have a sum? Explain your answer.

CHAPTER 12

Introduction to Trigonometry

▶ How can you find the distance traveled by a seaplane?

APPLICATION: Seaplanes

The distance traveled by a seaplane during its landing can be found using a diagram and the Pythagorean theorem. In Chapter 12, you will learn how to find the distance traveled by a seaplane during landing using just the angle of descent and the starting height.

Think & Discuss

The diagram below shows the landing of a seaplane from a starting height of 1000 feet and descending at an angle of 15°.

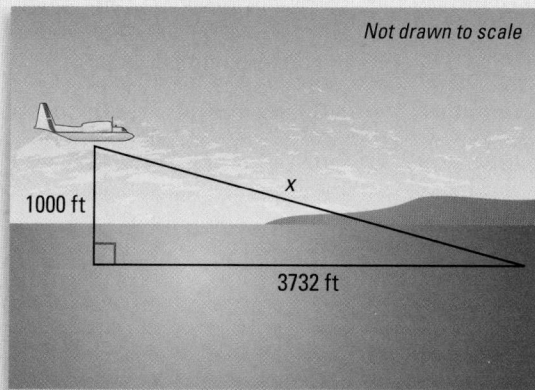

Not drawn to scale

1000 ft

x

3732 ft

1. Find the distance x traveled by the seaplane during its landing. Round your answer to the nearest foot.

2. Find the ratio of distance traveled to starting height.

3. When the seaplane is at a height of 600 feet, it has 2318 feet to travel until landing. Find the ratio of distance to height. What do you notice?

Learn More About It

You will use a trigonometric function to find a distance flown by a seaplane in Example 4 on page 647.

PREVIEW **What's the chapter about?**

• Evaluating trigonometric ratios
• Graphing trigonometric functions
• Finding side lengths and angle measures of triangles

Key Words

• **sine**, *p. 645*
• **cosine**, *p. 645*
• **tangent**, *p. 645*
• **cosecant**, *p. 645*
• **secant**, *p. 645*
• **cotangent**, *p. 645*
• **initial side**, *p. 652*
• **terminal side**, *p. 652*

• **standard position**, *p. 652*
• **coterminal**, *p. 653*
• **quadrantal angle**, *p. 654*
• **periodic**, *p. 660*
• **cycle**, *p. 660*
• **period**, *p. 660*
• **law of sines**, *p. 668*
• **law of cosines**, *p. 675*

PREPARE **Chapter Readiness Quiz**

Take this quick quiz. If you are unsure of an answer, look back at the reference pages for help.

Vocabulary Check *(refer to p. 5)*

1. Complete the statement: The ___?___ of any nonzero number a is $\frac{1}{a}$.

    A opposite   **B** product   **C** reciprocal   **D** quotient

Skill Check *(refer to pp. 255, 747)*

2. Simplify the expression $\sqrt{96}$.

    F $4\sqrt{3}$ **G** $4\sqrt{6}$ **H** $4\sqrt{12}$ **J** $16\sqrt{6}$

3. Solve the equation $\frac{9}{4} = \frac{x}{2}$.

    A $\frac{2}{9}$ **B** $\frac{9}{2}$ **C** 18   **D** 72

TAKE NOTES **Organize a Topic**

A *concept map* is a diagram that highlights connections between ideas. Drawing a concept map can help you organize important topics.

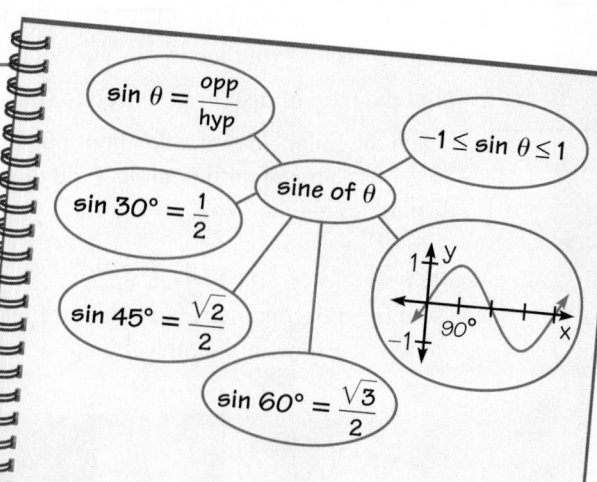

12.1 Right Triangle Trigonometry

Key Words
- sine
- cosine
- tangent
- cosecant
- secant
- cotangent

Prerequisite Skills

Solve the proportion.

1. $\dfrac{3}{4} = \dfrac{x}{16}$

2. $\dfrac{5}{8} = \dfrac{40}{x}$

3. $\dfrac{2}{x} = \dfrac{12}{66}$

4. $\dfrac{x}{42} = \dfrac{2}{7}$

STUDENT HELP

VOCABULARY
Trigonometry is used to find measures in triangles.

   trigono-metry
   triangle measure

GOAL Evaluate trigonometric functions of acute angles.

How can you find an airplane's distance from a landing spot?

In Example 4, you will use an airplane's height and angle of descent to find this distance.

Each of the six possible ratios of the three sides of a right triangle is used to define a **trigonometric function**.

sine (sin)   **cosecant** (csc)

cosine (cos)   **secant** (sec)

tangent (tan)   **cotangent** (cot)

Right Triangle Definition of Trigonometric Functions

Let θ be an acute angle of a right triangle. The six trigonometric functions of θ are defined as follows:

$$\sin \theta = \frac{\text{opp}}{\text{hyp}} \qquad \csc \theta = \frac{\text{hyp}}{\text{opp}}$$

$$\cos \theta = \frac{\text{adj}}{\text{hyp}} \qquad \sec \theta = \frac{\text{hyp}}{\text{adj}}$$

$$\tan \theta = \frac{\text{opp}}{\text{adj}} \qquad \cot \theta = \frac{\text{adj}}{\text{opp}}$$

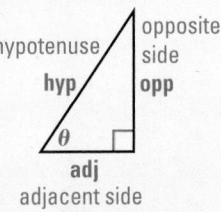

Notice that the ratios in the second column are the reciprocals of the ratios in the first column.

$$\csc \theta = \frac{1}{\sin \theta} \qquad \sec \theta = \frac{1}{\cos \theta} \qquad \cot \theta = \frac{1}{\tan \theta}$$

EXAMPLE 1 Evaluate Trigonometric Functions

Evaluate the six trigonometric functions of the angle θ shown in the triangle.

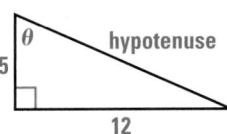

Solution

From the Pythagorean theorem, the length of the hypotenuse is

$$\sqrt{5^2 + 12^2} = \sqrt{169} = 13.$$

Using **adj** $= 5$, **opp** $= 12$, and **hyp** $= 13$, you can write the following.

$$\sin \theta = \frac{\text{opp}}{\text{hyp}} = \frac{12}{13} \qquad \cos \theta = \frac{\text{adj}}{\text{hyp}} = \frac{5}{13} \qquad \tan \theta = \frac{\text{opp}}{\text{adj}} = \frac{12}{5}$$

$$\csc \theta = \frac{\text{hyp}}{\text{opp}} = \frac{13}{12} \qquad \sec \theta = \frac{\text{hyp}}{\text{adj}} = \frac{13}{5} \qquad \cot \theta = \frac{\text{adj}}{\text{opp}} = \frac{5}{12}$$

1. Evaluate the six trigonometric functions of the angle θ shown in the triangle.

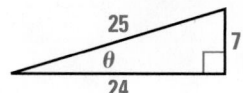

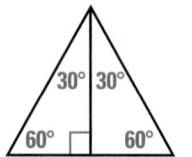
Special Right Triangles If you cut an equilateral triangle in half, the measures of the acute angles of the resulting triangles are 30° and 60°. The measures of the acute angles in an isosceles right triangle are both 45°. These angles are common, so you should know their trigonometric ratios. You can remember the side lengths or memorize the table.

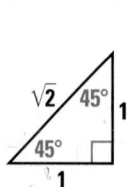

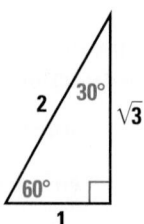

θ	sin θ	cos θ	tan θ
30°	$\dfrac{1}{2}$	$\dfrac{\sqrt{3}}{2}$	$\dfrac{\sqrt{3}}{3}$
60°	$\dfrac{\sqrt{3}}{2}$	$\dfrac{1}{2}$	$\sqrt{3}$
45°	$\dfrac{\sqrt{2}}{2}$	$\dfrac{\sqrt{2}}{2}$	1

You can use trigonometric functions to find a missing side length or angle measure of a right triangle.

EXAMPLE 2 **Find a Missing Side Length**

Find the value of *x* for the right triangle shown.

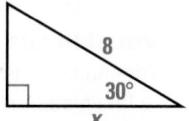

Solution

Write an equation using a trigonometric function that involves the ratio of *x* and 8. Then solve the equation for *x*.

$$\cos 30° = \frac{adj}{hyp}$$ Write trigonometric equation.

$$\cos 30° = \frac{x}{8}$$ Substitute.

$$\frac{\sqrt{3}}{2} = \frac{x}{8}$$ Use table to find cos 30°.

$$4\sqrt{3} = x$$ Multiply each side by 8.

ANSWER ▶ The length of the longer leg is $4\sqrt{3} \approx 6.93$.

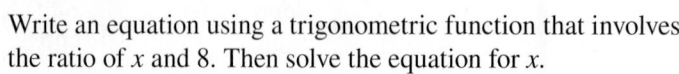

Find the value of *x* for the right triangle.

2.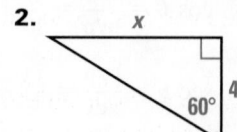

3.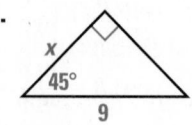

4.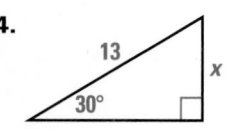

Technology You can use a calculator to evaluate trigonometric functions of any angle, not just 30°, 45°, and 60°. Use the keys [SIN], [COS], and [TAN] for sine, cosine, and tangent. Use these keys and the reciprocal key for cosecant, secant, and cotangent. Before using the calculator, be sure it is set in degree mode.

EXAMPLE 3 Use a Calculator

Find the value of x for the right triangle.

a.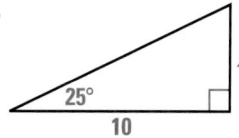

b.

Solution

a.
$$\tan \theta = \frac{\text{opp}}{\text{adj}}$$

$$\tan 25° = \frac{x}{10}$$

$$10(\tan 25°) = x$$

$$4.7 \approx x$$

b.
$$\cos \theta = \frac{\text{adj}}{\text{hyp}}$$

$$\cos 63° = \frac{3}{x}$$

$$x(\cos 63°) = 3$$

$$x = \frac{3}{\cos 63°}$$

$$x \approx 6.6$$

STUDENT HELP

ANOTHER WAY
You can also use the secant function to find the unknown length in part (b).

$$\sec 63° = \frac{x}{3}$$

EXAMPLE 4 Use Trigonometry in Real-life

Planes How far is the plane from the landing spot?

Solution

Write an equation using a trigonometric function that involves the ratio of x and 800. Then solve the equation for x.

$$\csc \theta = \frac{\text{hyp}}{\text{opp}}$$ Write trigonometric equation.

$$\csc 15° = \frac{x}{800}$$ Substitute.

$$\frac{1}{\sin 15°} = \frac{x}{800}$$ Use the reciprocal of csc 15°.

$$3091 \approx x$$ Multiply each side by 800.

ANSWER ▶ The plane is about 3091 feet from the landing spot.

 **Use Trigonometric Equations**

5. Write a trigonometric equation to find the length of the hypotenuse in part (a) of Example 3.

6. In Example 4, how far is the plane from the landing spot if the plane is flying at a height of 650 feet and is heading toward the landing spot at an angle of 20°?

Guided Practice

Vocabulary Check

1. What do the abbreviations *opp*, *adj*, and *hyp* represent? Include a diagram in your answer.

2. What is a reciprocal?

Skill Check

3. Sketch and label a right triangle with adj = 6, opp = 3, and hyp = $3\sqrt{5}$. Evaluate the six trigonometric functions of the angle θ.

Evaluate the six trigonometric functions of the angle θ.

4.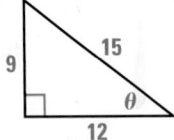

5.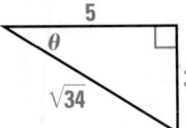

Find the value of *x* for the right triangle.

6.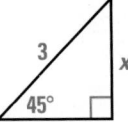

7.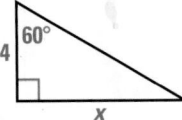

Sketch and label a triangle. Use a calculator to solve for *x*.

8. $\cos 35° = \dfrac{x}{9}$

9. $\sec 54° = \dfrac{x}{3}$

10. $\cot 26° = \dfrac{x}{20}$

Practice and Applications

STUDENT HELP

HOMEWORK HELP
Example 1: Exs. 11–17, 38
Example 2: Exs. 18–23
Example 3: Exs. 24–37
Example 4: Exs. 40–44

Evaluating Functions Evaluate the six trigonometric functions of the angle θ.

11.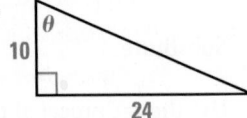

12.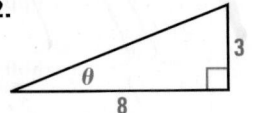

13.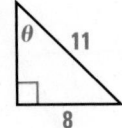

14.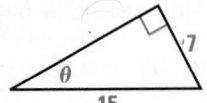

15.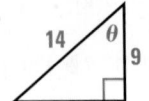

16.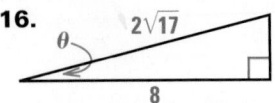

17. Error Analysis Describe and correct the error in finding sin θ.

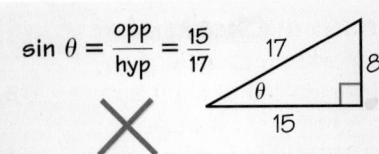

Finding Side Lengths Find the value of *x* for the right triangle.

18.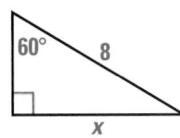

19.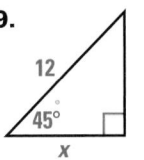

20.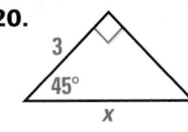

21.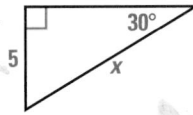

22.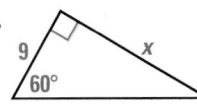

23.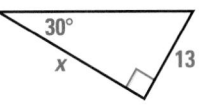

Evaluating Functions Use a calculator to evaluate the trigonometric function. Round your answer to four decimal places.

24. $\sin 23°$ **25.** $\tan 56°$ **26.** $\cos 42°$ **27.** $\cos 34°$

28. $\cot 15°$ **29.** $\sec 67°$ **30.** $\csc 71°$ **31.** $\sec 12°$

Finding Side Lengths Find the value of *x* for the right triangle. Round your answer to two decimal places.

32.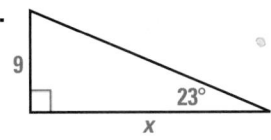

33.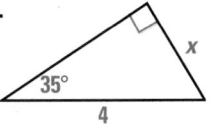

34.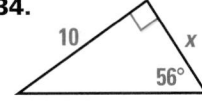

35.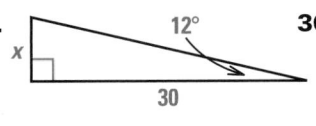

36.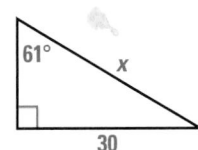

37.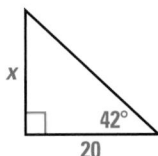

38. Visual Thinking The lengths of the sides of a right triangle are 4 inches, 8 inches, and $4\sqrt{5}$ inches. Sketch and label the triangle. Let θ represent the angle that is opposite the side that has a length of 8 inches. Evaluate the six trigonometric functions of the angle θ.

39. Challenge Find the value of *x* in Exercise 33 using the cosecant ratio.

Mount Rushmore In Exercises 40 and 41, suppose you are standing on the Grand View Terrace viewing platform at Mount Rushmore 550 feet from the base of the monument.

40. You look up at the top of Mount Rushmore at an angle of 39°. How high is the top of the monument from where you are standing?

41. The elevation of the Grand View Terrace is 5280 feet. Use your answer to Exercise 40 to find the elevation of the top of Mount Rushmore.

MOUNT RUSHMORE was sculpted by Gutzen Borglum. During the course of the six and a half years of work, 450,000 tons of granite were removed from the moutain.

Not drawn to scale

42. Flagpole A flagpole casts a shadow 10 feet long. A person standing at the end of the shadow looks up at the top of the flagpole at an angle of 63°. Sketch a diagram that represents this situation. What is the height of the flagpole?

43. Plane A plane is heading toward an airport runway at an angle of 20°. The plane is 25,000 feet from the airport runway. Sketch a diagram that represents this situation. How high is the plane flying?

44. Skateboard Ramp A skateboard ramp has an angle of elevation of 12°. The height of the ramp is 2 feet. Sketch a diagram that represents this situation. What is the length of the ramp?

Standardized Test Practice

45. Multiple Choice Find the value of x for the right triangle.

   Ⓐ 4

   Ⓑ $4\sqrt{2}$

   Ⓒ $4\sqrt{3}$

   Ⓓ $8\sqrt{2}$

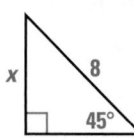

46. Multiple Choice Find the approximate value of x for the right triangle.

   Ⓕ 3.75

   Ⓖ 4.04

   Ⓗ 4.40

   Ⓙ 9.27

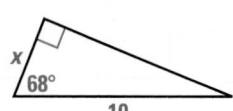

Mixed Review

Inequalities Match the system of linear inequalities with its graph. *(Lesson 4.3)*

47. $y \le 1$
    $y < x - 3$

48. $x \le 1$
    $y - x < -3$

49. $y < 1$
    $-3y < -3x + 9$

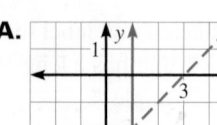

A.
B.
C.

Inequalities Tell whether the given point is a solution of the system of linear inequalities. *(Lesson 4.3)*

50. (3, 5);
    $y + x \ge 4$
    $x < 3$

51. (0, 0);
    $x < 1$
    $2y + \frac{1}{2} < 0$

52. (4, 1);
    $2x - y > 6$
    $y > -x + 3$

53. (2, 4);
    $3x + y > 5$
    $y < 5$

54. (6, 7);
    $x - y \ge 4$
    $x > y - 8$

55. (0, 3);
    $x < 2$
    $y \ge x + 5$

Geometry Skills

Surface Area Use the diagram of the regular pyramid to find the indicated measurement.

56. area of the base

57. area of one triangular face

58. total surface area of the pyramid

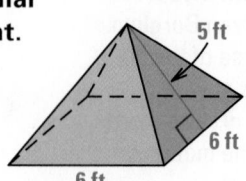

DEVELOPING CONCEPTS *(For use with Lesson 12.2)*

Functions of Any Angle

Goal

Relate the definitions of the trigonometric functions to the coordinates of a point on the terminal side of an angle in standard position.

Materials

- pencil
- graph paper
- compass
- straightedge
- calculator
- protractor

QUESTION

How do you evaluate the trigonometric functions of any angle?

EXPLORE

① Draw a coordinate plane on a piece of graph paper with the x-axis near the bottom edge of the paper. Label the origin O. Draw an 8-inch line segment on the x-axis, centered at O.

② Use a compass to draw a half circle with center at O and radius of 4 inches.

③ Mark and label point A on the half circle. Draw radius $\overline{AO}$. Draw a segment through A that is perpendicular to $\overline{PQ}$. Label the points as shown. Measure ∠AOQ, and record the values of r, x, and y in a table like the one below.

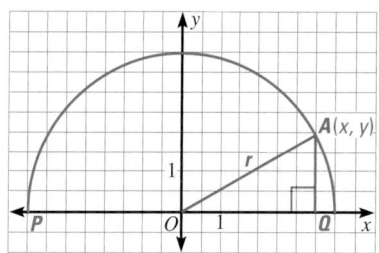

θ	$m\angle\theta$	x	y	r	$\dfrac{y}{r}$	$\dfrac{x}{r}$	$\dfrac{y}{x}$
AOQ	29	3.5	2	4	0.5	0.875	0.571
BOQ	?	?	?	?	?	?	?
COQ	?	?	?	?	?	?	?
DOQ	?	?	?	?	?	?	?
EOQ	?	?	?	?	?	?	?

④ Repeat Step 3 four more times. Try to place points B, C, D, and E at the intersection of two grid lines. Complete the table.

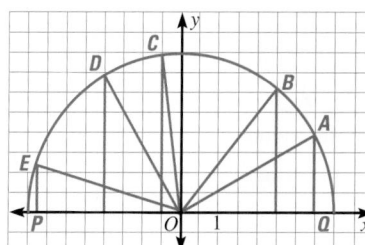

THINK ABOUT IT

1. Use a calculator to find the value of sin θ, cos θ, and tan θ for each angle.

2. a. Compare the value of $\dfrac{y}{r}$ and sin θ. What do you notice?

   b. Compare the value of $\dfrac{x}{r}$ and cos θ. What do you notice?

   c. Compare the value of $\dfrac{y}{x}$ and tan θ. What do you notice?

3. Logical Reasoning Use your answers to Exercise 2 to develop general definitions for csc θ, sec θ, and cot θ.

12.2 Functions of Any Angle

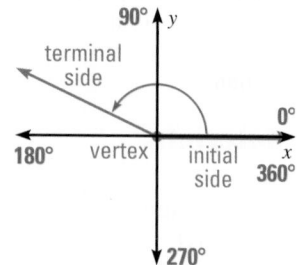

GOAL Evaluate the trigonometric functions of any angle.

Key Words
- initial side
- terminal side
- standard position
- coterminal
- quadrantal angle

Prerequisite Skills

Simplify.

1. $475° - 360°$

2. $65° - 360°$

3. $120° - 360°$

4. $-30° - 360°$

In Lesson 12.1, you worked only with acute angles in right triangles. In this lesson, you will study angles with measures greater than 90°.

An angle is formed by two rays that have a common endpoint, called the vertex. To generate any angle, fix one ray, called the **initial side**. Then rotate the other ray, called the **terminal side**, about the vertex.

In a coordinate plane, an angle whose vertex is at the origin and whose initial side is the positive *x*-axis is in **standard position**.

Angle Measure The angle measure is *positive* if the rotation of its terminal side is *counterclockwise*, and the measure is *negative* if the rotation is *clockwise*.

EXAMPLE 1 Draw Angles in Standard Position

Draw an angle with the given measure in standard position.

   a. 215°   **b.** 410°   **c.** −60°

Solution

a. Because 215° is 35° more than 180°, the terminal side is 35° counterclockwise past the negative *x*-axis.

b. Because 410° is 50° more than 360°, the terminal side makes one whole revolution counterclockwise plus 50° more.

c. Because −60° is negative, the terminal side is 60° clockwise from the positive *x*-axis.

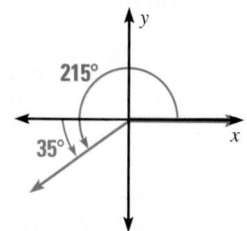

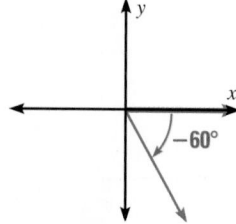

STUDENT HELP

AVOID ERRORS
Picture a clock to determine the direction an angle rotates.

clockwise

counterclockwise

Checkpoint ✓ *Draw Angles in Standard Position*

Draw an angle with the given measure in standard position.

   1. −30°   **2.** 460°   **3.** 230°

   4. Draw an angle with measure 90° in standard position. On a different coordinate grid, draw an angle with measure 90° not in standard position.

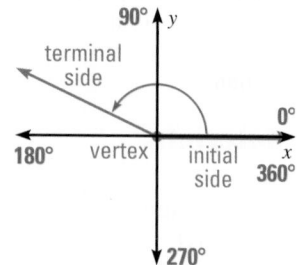

Coterminal Angles In part (b) of Example 1, the angles 410° and 50° are **coterminal** because their terminal sides coincide. An angle coterminal with a given angle can be found by adding or subtracting multiples of 360°.

EXAMPLE **2** **Find Coterminal Angles**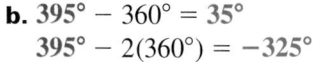

Find one positive angle and one negative angle that are coterminal with the given angle.

  a. −45°   **b.** 395°

Solution

There are many correct answers. Choose a multiple of 360° to add or subtract.

  a. −45° + 360° = 315°   **b.** 395° − 360° = 35°
    −45° − 360° = −405°   395° − 2(360°) = −325°

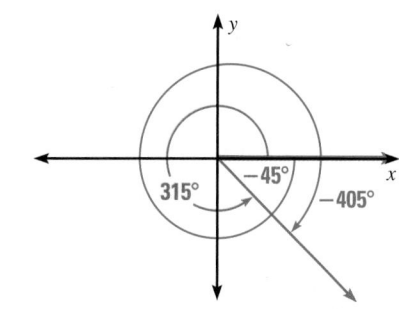 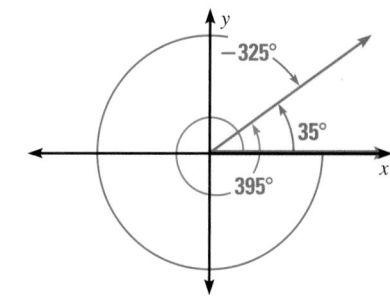

Checkpoint ✔ **Find Coterminal Angles**

Find one positive angle and one negative angle that are coterminal with the given angle.

  5. 50°   **6.** 375°   **7.** −70°

Trigonometric Functions of Any Angle In Lesson 12.1, you evaluated trigonometric functions of acute angles. Now, you will evaluate trigonometric functions of any angle.

General Definition of Trigonometric Functions

Let θ be an angle in standard position and (x, y) be any point (except the origin) on the terminal side of θ. The six trigonometric functions of θ are defined as follows.

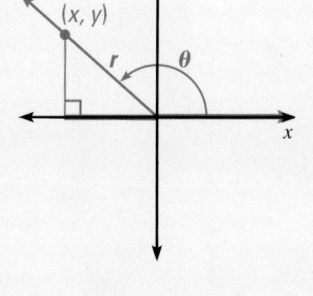

$$\sin \theta = \frac{y}{r} \qquad\qquad \csc \theta = \frac{r}{y} \;\; (y \neq 0)$$

$$\cos \theta = \frac{x}{r} \qquad\qquad \sec \theta = \frac{r}{x} \;\; (x \neq 0)$$

$$\tan \theta = \frac{y}{x} \;\; (x \neq 0) \qquad \cot \theta = \frac{x}{y} \;\; (y \neq 0)$$

For acute angles, these definitions give the same values as those given by the definitions in Lesson 12.1.

STUDENT HELP

SOLVING NOTE
Use the Pythagorean theorem to solve for r if you know x and y.
$$r = \sqrt{x^2 + y^2}$$

EXAMPLE 3 Evaluate Trigonometric Functions Given a Point

Let $(4, -3)$ be a point on the terminal side of an angle θ in standard position. Evaluate the sine, cosine, and tangent functions of θ.

Solution

Use the Pythagorean theorem to find the value of r.

$$r = \sqrt{x^2 + y^2} = \sqrt{4^2 + (-3)^2} = \sqrt{25} = 5$$

Find the value of each function using $x = 4$, $y = -3$, and $r = 5$.

$$\sin \theta = \frac{y}{r} = -\frac{3}{5} \qquad \cos \theta = \frac{x}{r} = \frac{4}{5} \qquad \tan \theta = \frac{y}{x} = -\frac{3}{4}$$

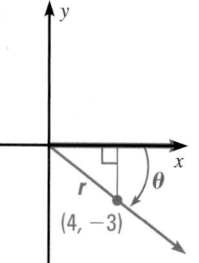

Checkpoint ✓ **Evaluate Trigonometric Functions Given a Point**

Use the given point on the terminal side of an angle θ in standard position. Evaluate the sine, cosine, and tangent functions of θ.

8. $(-3, 4)$ **9.** $(6, 8)$ **10.** $(-8, 15)$

Quadrantal Angles If the terminal side of θ lies on an axis, then θ is a **quadrantal angle**. The diagrams below show the values of x and y for the quadrantal angles 0°, 90°, 180°, and 270°.

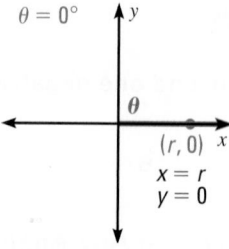

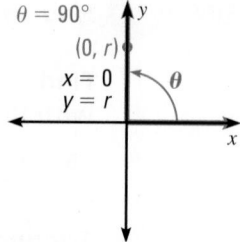

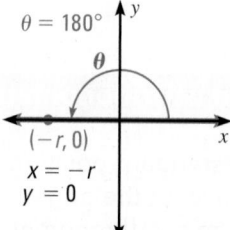

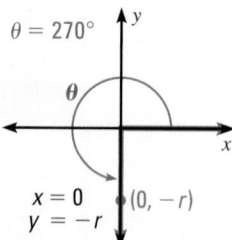

EXAMPLE 4 Trigonometric Functions of a Quadrantal Angle

Evaluate the sine, cosine, and tangent functions of $\theta = 180°$.

Solution

When $\theta = 180°$, you know that $x = -r$ and $y = 0$.

$$\sin \theta = \frac{y}{r} = \frac{0}{r} = 0 \qquad \cos \theta = \frac{x}{r} = \frac{-r}{r} = -1 \qquad \tan \theta = \frac{y}{x} = \frac{0}{-r} = 0$$

Signs of Trigonometric Functions

The signs of the trigonometric function values in the four quadrants can be determined from the function definitions.

For example, because $\sin \theta = \dfrac{y}{r}$ and r is always positive, it follows that $\sin \theta$ is positive whenever $y > 0$, which is in Quadrants I and II. The signs of the sine, cosine, and tangent functions are shown in the coordinate plane at the right.

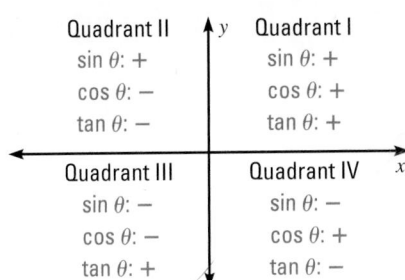

Quadrant II
sin θ: +
cos θ: −
tan θ: −

Quadrant I
sin θ: +
cos θ: +
tan θ: +

Quadrant III
sin θ: −
cos θ: −
tan θ: +

Quadrant IV
sin θ: −
cos θ: +
tan θ: −

EXAMPLE 5 | Positive and Negative Trigonometric Functions

Determine whether the sine, cosine, and tangent functions of the given angle are positive or negative.

a.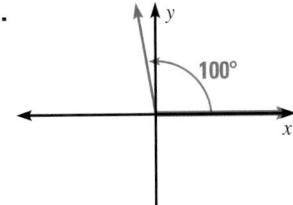

b.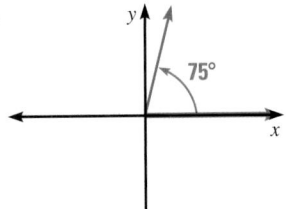

c.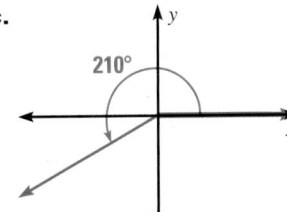

d.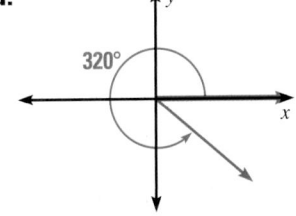

STUDENT HELP

ANOTHER WAY
You can use a calculator to check the answers in Example 5.

Solution

a. Because the terminal side lies in Quadrant II, sin 100° is positive, cos 100° is negative, and tan 100° is negative.

b. Because the terminal side lies in Quadrant I, sin 75° is positive, cos 75° is positive, and tan 75° is positive.

c. Because the terminal side lies in Quadrant III, sin 210° is negative, cos 210° is negative, and tan 210° is positive.

d. Because the terminal side lies in Quadrant IV, sin 320° is negative, cos 320° is positive, and tan 320° is negative.

Checkpoint ✓ *Positive and Negative Trigonometric Functions*

11. Evaluate the sine, cosine, and tangent functions of $\theta = 90°$.

Determine whether the sine, cosine, and tangent functions of the angle are positive or negative.

12. 40° **13.** 150° **14.** 225°

Guided Practice

Vocabulary Check

1. Copy and complete the statement: When an angle is in standard position, its vertex is at __?__ .

2. Copy and complete the statement: Two angles in standard position are coterminal if their __?__ coincide.

Skill Check

Draw an angle with the given measure in standard position.

3. 150°   **4.** 480°   **5.** −45°   **6.** −330°

Find one positive angle and one negative angle that are coterminal with the given angle.

7. 20°   **8.** 390°   **9.** −75°   **10.** 170°

Determine whether the trigonometric function of the angle is positive or negative.

11. sin 230°   **12.** tan 140°   **13.** cos 310°   **14.** sin 70°

15. Let $(3, -4)$ be a point on the terminal side of an angle θ in standard position. Evaluate the sine, cosine, and tangent functions of θ.

Practice and Applications

STUDENT HELP

HOMEWORK HELP
Example 1: Exs. 16–27
Example 2: Exs. 28–36
Example 3: Exs. 37–48
Example 4: Exs. 49–51
Example 5: Exs. 52–60

Visual Thinking Match the angle measure with the angle.

16. 510°   **17.** −330°   **18.** −405°

A. 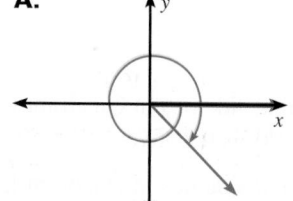   **B.** 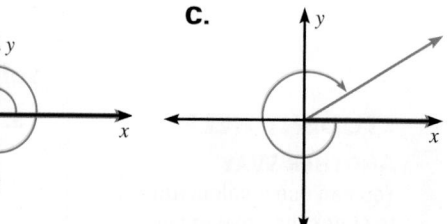   **C.**

Drawing Angles Draw an angle with the given measure in standard position.

19. −50°   **20.** 200°   **21.** 390°

22. −240°   **23.** −570°   **24.** 805°

25. 1000°   **26.** −750°   **27.** −500°

Finding Coterminal Angles Find one positive angle and one negative angle that are coterminal with the given angle.

28. 35°   **29.** −80°   **30.** 225°

31. 350°   **32.** −130°   **33.** 420°

34. −380°   **35.** −400°   **36.** 660°

Using a Point Use the given point on the terminal side of an angle θ in standard position to evaluate the sine, cosine, and tangent functions of θ.

37.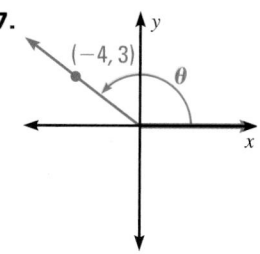

38.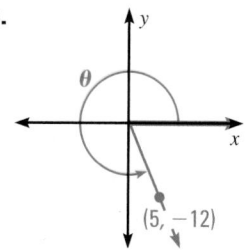

39.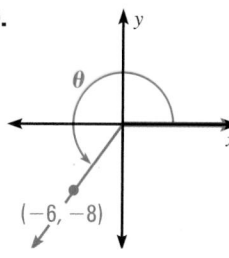

40. $(-12, -9)$ **41.** $(8, -15)$ **42.** $(-10, 24)$ **43.** $(7, 24)$

44. $(1, -2)$ **45.** $(-1, -1)$ **46.** $(3, 1)$ **47.** $(-2, 3)$

48. Error Analysis Let $(-3, 2)$ be a point on the terminal side of an angle θ in standard position. Describe and correct the error in finding tan θ.

$$\tan \theta = \frac{x}{y} = -\frac{3}{2}$$

Quadrantal Angles Evaluate the sine, cosine, and tangent functions of θ.

49. $\theta = 0°$ **50.** $\theta = 270°$ **51.** $\theta = 540°$

Positive or Negative Values Determine whether the trigonometric function of the angle is positive or negative.

52. $\sin 55°$ **53.** $\tan 127°$ **54.** $\tan 245°$

55. $\cos 340°$ **56.** $\cos 160°$ **57.** $\sin 300°$

58. $\tan 300°$ **59.** $\sin 220°$ **60.** $\cos 265°$

Using a Calculator Use a calculator to evaluate the function. Round your answer to four decimal places.

61. $\sin (-35°)$ **62.** $\tan 224°$ **63.** $\cos 290°$

64. $\cos 140°$ **65.** $\sin 190°$ **66.** $\tan (-20°)$

67. Challenge Explain how to determine the sign of csc θ, sec θ, and cot θ given the quadrant in which the terminal side of θ lies.

68. Writing Explain how an angle's direction of rotation determines its sign.

69. Volleyball The horizontal distance d (in feet) traveled by a projectile with an initial speed v (in feet per second) is given by $d = \frac{v^2}{32} \sin 2\theta$ where θ is the angle at which the projectile is launched.

Estimate the horizontal distance traveled by a volleyball that is hit at an angle of 60° with an initial speed of 40 feet per second.

70. Marching Band Your school's marching band is performing at halftime during a football game. In the last formation, the band members form a circle 100 feet wide in the center of the field. You start at a point on the circle 100 feet from the goal line, march 300° around the circle, and then walk toward the goal line to exit the field. How far from the goal line are you at the point where you leave the circle?

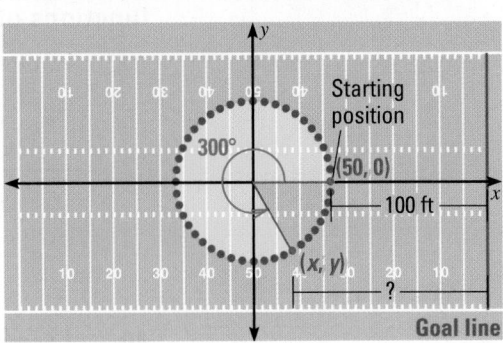

71. Multiple Choice Which angle is coterminal with 60°?

(A) −300°   (B) 300°   (C) 480°   (D) −60°

72. Multiple Choice Let (−15, 20) be a point on the terminal side of an angle θ in standard position. What is the value of the cosine function of θ?

(F) $-\frac{4}{5}$ (G) $-\frac{4}{3}$ (H) $-\frac{3}{5}$ (J) $\frac{4}{5}$

73. Multiple Choice Let (−15, −8) be a point on the terminal side of an angle θ in standard position. What is the value of the tangent function of θ?

(A) $\frac{15}{8}$ (B) $\frac{8}{15}$ (C) $-\frac{8}{15}$ (D) $-\frac{15}{8}$

Rational Equations Solve the equation. Check your solutions.
(Lesson 9.6)

74. $\frac{x}{x+1} = \frac{5}{x+1}$ **75.** $\frac{3}{x+4} = \frac{x+2}{x+4}$ **76.** $\frac{2}{x-1} = \frac{1}{x-4}$

77. $\frac{1}{x-3} = \frac{-7}{x+5}$ **78.** $\frac{3}{x} = \frac{x+2}{x+4}$ **79.** $\frac{x+2}{3x+2} = \frac{x-1}{x}$

Adding and Subtracting Matrices Perform the indicated operation.
(Lesson 11.1)

80. $\begin{bmatrix} 2 & -1 & 3 \end{bmatrix} + \begin{bmatrix} 1 & 5 & 2 \end{bmatrix}$ **81.** $\begin{bmatrix} 3 & 1 \\ 0 & 5 \end{bmatrix} + \begin{bmatrix} 4 & -2 \\ 0 & 5 \end{bmatrix}$

82. $\begin{bmatrix} 5 & 0 & 1 \\ -4 & -3 & 2 \\ 1 & 7 & -3 \end{bmatrix} + \begin{bmatrix} -1 & 3 & -4 \\ 2 & -5 & 9 \\ -4 & 3 & 1 \end{bmatrix}$ **83.** $\begin{bmatrix} -3 & 3 \\ 0 & 6 \\ 9 & 2 \end{bmatrix} - \begin{bmatrix} 1 & -4 \\ 3 & 2 \\ -2 & 1 \end{bmatrix}$

Writing Rules Write a rule for the *n*th term of the arithmetic sequence. *(Lesson 11.5)*

84. $d = 3, a_1 = 8$ **85.** $d = 4, a_5 = 21$ **86.** $d = 7, a_6 = 45$

87. $d = -2, a_8 = -10$ **88.** $d = -0.3, a_7 = 2$ **89.** $d = 1.4, a_{10} = 20$

Finding Angles Determine the angle θ in the regular polygon.

90.

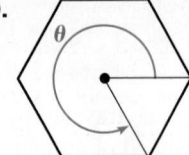

91.

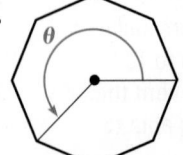

DEVELOPING CONCEPTS *(For use with Lesson 12.3)*

Graphing the Sine Function

Goal

Use the common angles to sketch a graph of $y = \sin \theta$.

Materials

- pencil
- paper
- graph paper
- calculator

QUESTION

How do you graph the sine function?

EXPLORE

1 Use a calculator to copy and complete the table.

θ	$y = \sin \theta$
0°	0
45°	0.707
90°	?
135°	?
180°	?
225°	?
270°	?
315°	?
360°	?

2 Use what you know about coterminal angles to complete the table below.

θ	$y = \sin \theta$
360°	?
405°	?
450°	?
495°	?
540°	?
585°	?
630°	?
675°	?
720°	?

3 Use the values from the tables to sketch a graph of $y = \sin \theta$.

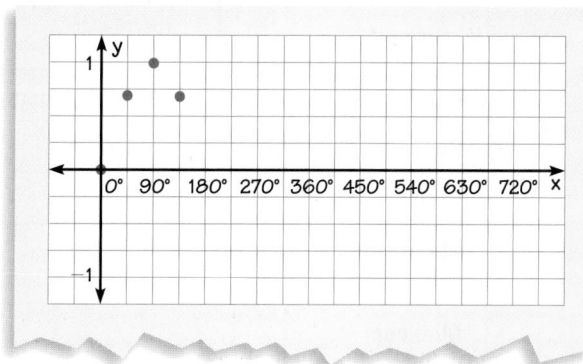

THINK ABOUT IT

1. What are the domain and range of the function $y = \sin \theta$?

2. What is the maximum value of $y = \sin \theta$?

3. Copy and complete: The graph of $y = \sin \theta$ repeats itself every __?__ degrees.

4. Choose the correct phrase that completes the statement: The value of $\sin \theta$ will always be (*less than*, *greater than*, *equal to*) the value of $\sin (\theta + 360°)$.

12.3 Graphing the Trigonometric Functions

Key Words
- periodic
- cycle
- period

GOAL Graph the sine, cosine, and tangent functions.

What is the height of a hot air balloon?

In Exercise 55, you will graph the height of a hot air balloon as it rises after taking off.

In Exercise 55, you will graph the height of a hot air balloon as it rises after taking off.

In this lesson, you will learn to graph functions of the form $y = a \sin bx$ and $y = a \cos bx$, where a and b are positive constants and x is measured in degrees.

Prerequisite Skills

Evaluate the function.

1. $\cos 30°$
2. $\sin 60°$
3. $\sin 45°$
4. $\cos 0°$

Each function is **periodic**, which means that its graph has a repeating pattern that continues indefinitely. The shortest repeating portion is called a **cycle**. The horizontal length of each cycle is called the **period**.

The graphs of all sine and cosine functions are related to the graphs of $y = \sin x$ and $y = \cos x$, which are shown below.

	$y = \sin x$	$y = \cos x$
Graph	period: 360°	period: 360°
Domain	All real numbers	All real numbers
Range	$-1 \leq y \leq 1$	$-1 \leq y \leq 1$
Period	360°	360°
Maximum value	1	1
Minimum value	-1	-1

From the graph of $y = \sin x$ above, you can see that a maximum value of $y = \sin x$ occurs when $x = 90°$ and a minimum value occurs when $x = 270°$. Because the sine function has a period of 360°, the maximum and minimum values occur every 360°. For example, maximum values occur when $x = 450°$, 810°, 1170°, . . . and minimum values occur when $x = 630°$, 990°, 1350°, ...

Similarly, maximum values of $y = \cos x$ occur when $x = 0°$, 360°, 720°, 1080°, . . . and minimum values occur when $x = 180°$, 540°, 900°, 1260°, ...

Graphing the Sine and Cosine Functions

To graph $y = a \sin bx$ and $y = a \cos bx$ when $a > 0$ and $b > 0$, you can use the characteristics below. The period is $\dfrac{360°}{b}$.

Characteristic	$y = a \sin bx$	$y = a \cos bx$
Intercepts	$(0°, 0), \left(\dfrac{180°}{b}, 0\right), \left(\dfrac{360°}{b}, 0\right)$	$\left(\dfrac{90°}{b}, 0\right), \left(\dfrac{270°}{b}, 0\right)$
Maximum(s)	$\left(\dfrac{90°}{b}, a\right)$	$(0°, a), \left(\dfrac{360°}{b}, a\right)$
Minimum	$\left(\dfrac{270°}{b}, -a\right)$	$\left(\dfrac{180°}{b}, -a\right)$

EXAMPLE 1 Graph a Sine Function

Graph $y = \sin 180x$.

Find the characteristics of the graph using $a = 1$ and $b = 180$. There is one intercept at $(0°, 0)$ and the period is $\dfrac{360°}{180} = 2°$.

Find the intercepts.

$$\left(\frac{180°}{b}, 0\right) = \left(\frac{180°}{180}, 0\right) = (1°, 0)$$

$$\left(\frac{360°}{b}, 0\right) = \left(\frac{360°}{180}, 1\right) = (2°, 0)$$

Find the maximum and minimum.

$$\left(\frac{90°}{b}, a\right) = \left(\frac{90°}{180}, 1\right) = (0.5°, 1)$$

$$\left(\frac{270°}{b}, -a\right) = \left(\frac{270°}{180}, -1\right) = (1.5°, -1)$$

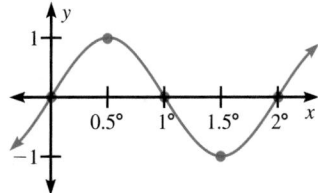

EXAMPLE 2 Graph a Cosine Function

Graph $y = 2 \cos x$.

Find the characteristics using $a = 2$ and $b = 1$. Because $b = 1$, you can see that the intercepts are at $(90°, 0)$ and $(270°, 0)$, and the period is $360°$.

The maximums are at $(0°, a) = (0°, 2)$

and $\left(\dfrac{360°}{b}, a\right) = (360°, 2)$.

The minimum is at $\left(\dfrac{180°}{b}, -a\right) = (180°, -2)$.

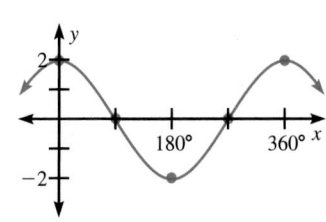

Graphing Tangent Functions The domain of the graph of $y = \tan x$ is all real numbers except odd multiples of $90°$. At odd multiples of $90°$, the graph has vertical asymptotes. The range of the function is all real numbers and its period is $180°$.

For the graph of $y = a \tan bx$, the following are true when $a > 0$ and $b > 0$.

1. The period is $\dfrac{180°}{b}$.

2. There are vertical asymptotes at odd multiples of $\dfrac{90°}{b}$.

Graphing the Tangent Function

Use these steps to graph $y = a \tan bx$ on the interval $-\dfrac{90°}{b} < x < \dfrac{90°}{b}$.

STEP ① *Plot* the x-intercept at $(0°, 0)$.

STEP ② *Draw* the vertical asymptotes at $x = -\dfrac{90°}{b}$ and $x = \dfrac{90°}{b}$.

STEP ③ *Plot* the points that occur halfway between the x-intercept at $(0°, 0)$ and the asymptotes, $\left(-\dfrac{45°}{b}, -a\right)$ and $\left(\dfrac{45°}{b}, a\right)$.

EXAMPLE 3 Graph a Tangent Function

Graph $y = \tan 2x$.

Solution

Use $a = 1$ and $b = 2$ to find the key points on the interval $-\dfrac{90°}{2} < x < \dfrac{90°}{2}$, or $-45° < x < 45°$.

① *Plot* the x-intercept at $(0°, 0)$.

② *Draw* the vertical asmptotes.

$$x = -\frac{90°}{b} = -\frac{90°}{2} = -45°$$

$$x = \frac{90°}{b} = \frac{90°}{2} = 45°$$

③ *Plot* the halfway points.

$$\left(-\frac{45°}{b}, -a\right) = \left(-\frac{45°}{2}, -1\right) = (-22.5°, -1)$$

$$\left(\frac{45°}{b}, a\right) = \left(\frac{45°}{2}, 1\right) = (22.5°, 1)$$

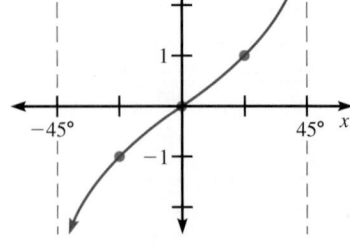

Notice that the period of $y = \tan 2x$ is $\dfrac{180°}{b} = \dfrac{180°}{2} = 90°$. So, one period is shown.

 **Graphing Sine, Cosine, and Tangent Functions**

Graph the function.

1. $y = 2 \sin x$ **2.** $y = \cos 360x$ **3.** $y = 3 \tan x$

12.3 Exercises

Guided Practice

Vocabulary Check **Copy and complete the statement.**

1. The cycle is the shortest repeating portion of a(n) __?__ function.

2. The horizontal length of each cycle is called the __?__.

Skill Check **Find the maximum(s), the minimum, and the intercepts of the function on the interval $0° \leq x \leq \dfrac{360°}{b}$.**

3. $y = 5 \sin x$

4. $y = 3 \cos 60x$

5. $y = \frac{1}{2} \sin 180x$

Graph the function.

6. $y = 2 \sin 180x$

7. $y = 4 \cos x$

8. $y = 5 \cos 45x$

Find the intercept, the vertical asymptotes, and the halfway points of the function on the interval $0° \leq x \leq \dfrac{360°}{b}$.

9. $y = \tan 3x$

10. $y = 2 \tan 5x$

11. $y = 4 \tan 45x$

Graph the function.

12. $y = \tan 45x$

13. $y = 5 \tan x$

14. $y = 3 \tan 15x$

15. Error Analysis Describe and correct the error in finding the minimum of $y = 2 \sin 30x$.

$$\text{Minimum} = \left(\frac{90°}{b}, a\right) = \left(\frac{90°}{30}, 2\right)$$
$$= (3°, 2) \quad \times$$

Practice and Applications

Matching Graphs Match the function with its graph.

16. $y = 2 \sin 2x$

17. $y = 2 \cos 2x$

18. $y = 2 \sin \frac{1}{2}x$

19. $y = 2 \tan \frac{1}{2}x$

20. $y = 2 \cos \frac{1}{2}x$

21. $y = 2 \tan 2x$

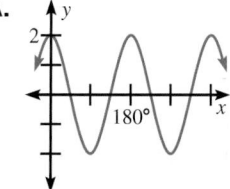
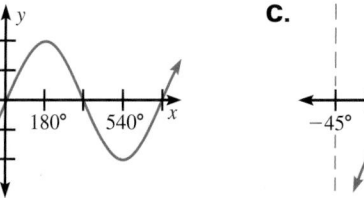
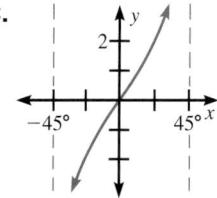
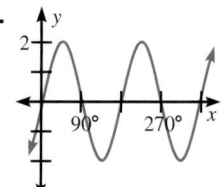
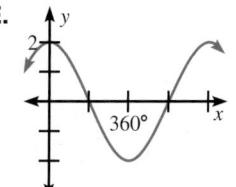
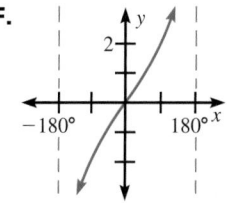

Analyzing Functions In Exercises 22–27, find the maximum(s), the minimum, and the intercepts of the function on the interval $0° \le x \le \dfrac{360°}{b}$.

22.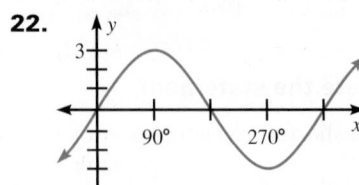

23.

24. $y = 4 \cos 135x$

25. $y = 2 \sin 180x$

26. $y = \dfrac{1}{2} \sin 45x$

27. $y = \dfrac{1}{3} \cos 720x$

Graphing Graph the function.

28. $y = 3 \sin x$

29. $y = 4 \sin x$

30. $y = 5 \cos x$

31. $y = \cos 3x$

32. $y = \sin 90x$

33. $y = \cos 180x$

34. $y = 3 \sin 6x$

35. $y = 2 \cos 90x$

36. $y = 4 \sin 360x$

Writing Equations Write an equation of the form $y = a \sin bx$, where $a > 0$ and $b > 0$, so the graph has the given maximum or minimum value, and period.

37. Maximum: 1
   Period: 45°

38. Maximum: 10
   Period: 180°

39. Minimum: −4
   Period: 3°

Analyzing Functions In Exercises 40–43, find the intercept, the vertical asymptotes, and the halfway points of the function.

40.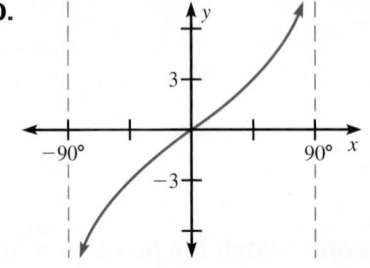

41.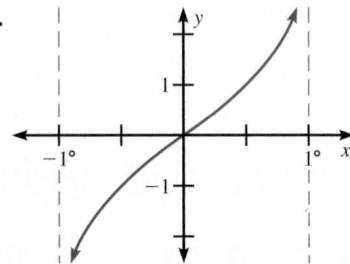

42. $y = 4 \tan 5x$

43. $y = 3 \tan 180x$

Graphing Graph the function.

44. $y = \tan 9x$

45. $y = 6 \tan x$

46. $y = 3 \tan x$

47. $y = 2 \tan 135x$

48. $y = 5 \tan 270x$

49. $y = \dfrac{1}{2} \tan 45x$

50. Physics The motion of a tire swing can be modeled by

$$d = 3 \cos 90t$$

where d is the swing's horizontal displacement (in feet) relative to its position at rest and t is the time (in seconds).

a. Graph the displacement.

b. What is the maximum displacement of the swing?

51. Tides Tides are the alternating rise and fall of sea level with respect to land. In one location, the change in sea level h (in feet) can be modeled by $h = 2 \sin 30t$ where t is the time (in hours). Graph the change in sea level. What is the maximum and minimum height of sea level? What is the period?

Pendulum In Exercises 52 and 53, use the following information.

You make a pendulum by hanging a funnel and filling it with sand. You place a piece of paper under the pendulum and set the pendulum in motion. As you slide the paper out at a steady rate in the plane perpendicular to the pendulum's motion, the sand traces a curve as shown.

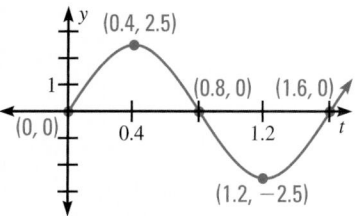

52. Write a model for the curve traced by the sand, where y is measured in inches and t is measured in seconds.

53. Find the coordinates of the next minimum point of the curve.

54. Radar An airplane flies at an altitude of 5 miles directly over a radar antenna. The horizontal distance d is the distance (in miles) from the airplane to a point directly above the antenna (d is positive as the airplane moves away from the radar antenna). Let x represent the angle the airplane makes as it passes over the radar antenna. Write an equation for the distance d in terms of the angle x. Graph the distance on the interval $0° \leq x < 90°$.

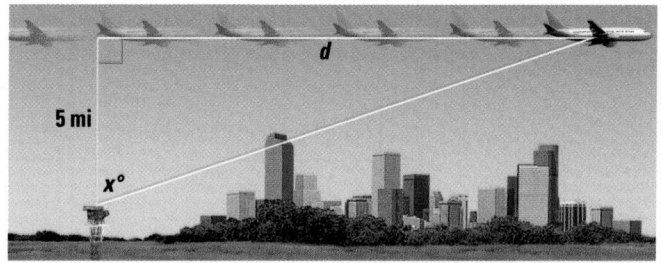

55. Challenge You are standing 100 feet from a hot-air balloon ride launch site. The angle between the ground and balloon increases 3° per second. Write an equation for the height h (in feet) of the hot air balloon in terms of the time t. Graph the height of the hot air balloon on the interval $0 \leq t < 20$.

Standardized Test Practice

56. Multiple Choice Which function is shown in the graph?

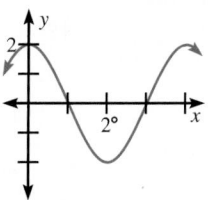

Ⓐ $y = 2 \cos x$

Ⓑ $y = 2 \cos 90x$

Ⓒ $y = \cos 90x$

Ⓓ $y = \sin 90x$

57. Multiple Choice What is the minimum value of $y = 4 \sin 540x$?

Ⓕ -540 Ⓖ -4 Ⓗ 4 Ⓙ 540

58. Multiple Choice What are the vertical asymptotes of $y = 4 \tan 45x$?

Ⓐ $x = -45°$ and $x = 45°$ Ⓑ $x = -2°$ and $x = 2°$

Ⓒ $x = -1°$ and $x = 1°$ Ⓓ $x = -90°$ and $x = 90°$

Mixed Review

Probability A puppy is randomly chosen from a litter of 4 black males, 3 black females, 2 brown males, and 2 brown females. Find the indicated probability. *(Lesson 10.6)*

59. $P(\text{male or brown})$

60. $P(\text{female or black})$

Finding Probabilities of Complements A ball is randomly chosen from a bag of 10 balls numbered 1, 1, 2, 3, 4, 4, 4, 5, 6, and 6. Find the indicated probability. *(Lesson 10.6)*

61. $P(\text{number is less than } 6)$

62. $P(\text{number is not } 4)$

Identifying Inverses Tell whether the matrices are inverses of each other. *(Lesson 11.3)*

63. $\begin{bmatrix} 1 & 4 \\ -1 & -3 \end{bmatrix}$ and $\begin{bmatrix} -3 & -4 \\ 1 & 1 \end{bmatrix}$

64. $\begin{bmatrix} 1 & -1 \\ 2 & -1 \end{bmatrix}$ and $\begin{bmatrix} -1 & 1 \\ -2 & 1 \end{bmatrix}$

65. $\begin{bmatrix} 1 & 1 \\ 2 & 1 \end{bmatrix}$ and $\begin{bmatrix} -1 & -1 \\ 2 & -1 \end{bmatrix}$

66. $\begin{bmatrix} 2 & 3 \\ 1 & 4 \end{bmatrix}$ and $\begin{bmatrix} 4 & -3 \\ 2 & -1 \end{bmatrix}$

Sequences Write the next term in the sequence. Then write a rule for the *n*th term. *(Lesson 11.4)*

67. 3, 5, 7, 9, . . .

68. 6, 13, 20, 27, . . .

69. 5, 8, 11, 14, . . .

70. 10, 4, −2, −8, . . .

71. −2, −8, −18, −32, . . .

72. 0, 3, 8, 15, . . .

Geometry Skills

Bisectors Find the value of *x*.

73.
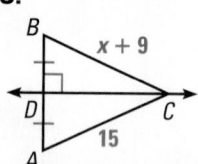

74.
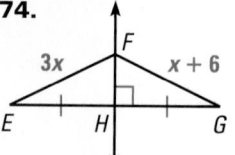

75.
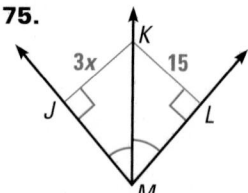

Quiz 1

Lesson 12.1 Find the value of *x* for the right triangle. Round the result to two decimal places.

1.
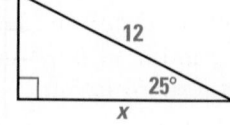

2.
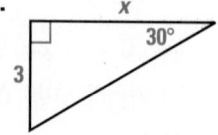

3.
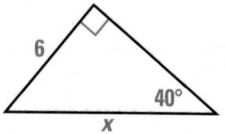

Lesson 12.2 Use the given point on the terminal side of an angle θ in standard position. Evaluate the sine, cosine, and tangent functions of θ.

4. $(-6, 8)$

5. $(-5, 6)$

6. $(-3, -3)$

7. $(3, 9)$

Lesson 12.3 Graph the function.

8. $y = 5 \sin 60x$

9. $y = 3 \cos 450x$

10. $y = 2 \tan 270x$

USING A GRAPHING CALCULATOR *(For use with Lesson 12.3)*
Graphing Trigonometric Functions

You can use a graphing calculator to graph the trigonometric functions $y = a \sin bx$ and $y = a \cos bx$ and observe the effects of changing the values of a and b.

EXAMPLE

Graph $y = 2 \sin x$ and $y = \sin 2x$.

SOLUTION

❶ Enter the functions into the graphing calculator. Be sure that your calculator is in degree mode.

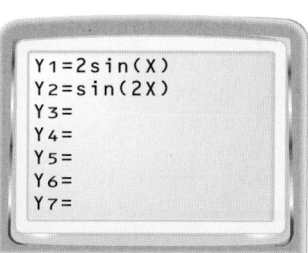

❷ Use the viewing window shown. Note: Depending on the values of a and b, you may need to change the viewing window.

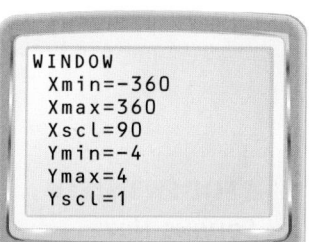

❸ Use the *Maximum*, *Minimum*, and *Zero* features to find the maximum value, the minimum value, and the period of each function.

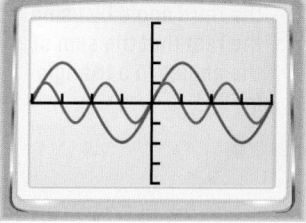

$y = 2 \sin x$	$y = \sin 2x$
Maximum value = 2	Maximum value = 1
Minimum value = -2	Minimum value = -1
Period = 360°	Period = 180°

EXERCISES

Use a graphing calculator to graph the function for the given values of a or b in $y = a \sin bx$. Find the maximum value, the minimum value, and the period of each function.

1. $y = 3 \sin x$ **2.** $y = \frac{1}{2} \sin x$ **3.** $y = \frac{1}{4} \sin x$ **4.** $y = 4 \sin x$

5. $y = \sin 3x$ **6.** $y = \sin \frac{1}{3}x$ **7.** $y = \sin \frac{1}{2}x$ **8.** $y = \sin 5x$

9. $y = \sin 4x$ **10.** $y = 5 \sin x$ **11.** $y = \frac{1}{3} \sin x$ **12.** $y = \sin \frac{1}{4}x$

13. Describe the effect of a on the graph of $y = a \sin x$ where $a > 0$.

14. Describe the effect of b on the graph of $y = \sin bx$ where $b > 0$.

12.4 The Law of Sines

GOAL Use the law of sines to find the sides and angles of a triangle.

Key Words
• law of sines

Prerequisite Skills

Use a calculator to solve for x.

1. $\dfrac{x}{\sin 40°} = 4$

2. $\dfrac{x}{\sin 100°} = 7$

3. $\dfrac{\sin 25°}{x} = 5$

4. $\dfrac{\sin 130°}{x} = 10$

How far from a path is an eagle's nest?

In Example 6, you will use the *law of sines* to find a distance.

Law of Sines To find the side lengths and angle measures of a triangle with no right angle, you need to know the measure of at least one side and any two other parts of the triangle. This gives four possible cases.

1. Two angles and any side (AAS or ASA)

2. Two sides and an angle opposite one of them (SSA)

3. Three sides (SSS)

4. Two sides and their included angle (SAS)

The first two cases can be solved using the **law of sines**. The last two cases can be solved using the law of cosines, which you will study in the next lesson.

STUDENT HELP

SOLVING NOTE
If you know two angles in a triangle, you can find the third angle by using the fact that the sum of the angles in a triangle is 180°.

Law of Sines

If $\triangle ABC$ has sides of length a, b, and c, then:

$$\frac{\sin A}{a} = \frac{\sin B}{b} = \frac{\sin C}{c}.$$

Also, $\dfrac{a}{\sin A} = \dfrac{b}{\sin B} = \dfrac{c}{\sin C}.$

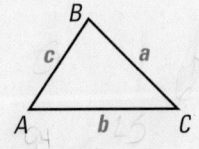

EXAMPLE 1 Solve for a Side (AAS)

Find the length c given that $A = 32°$, $a = 10$, and $C = 105°$.

Solution

You are given values for A, a, and C and are trying to find c, so use $\dfrac{a}{\sin A} = \dfrac{c}{\sin C}$.

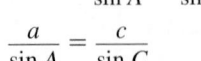

$\dfrac{a}{\sin A} = \dfrac{c}{\sin C}$ Write law of sines.

$\dfrac{10}{\sin 32°} = \dfrac{c}{\sin 105°}$ Substitute for A, a, and C.

$\dfrac{10 \sin 105°}{\sin 32°} = c$ Solve for the variable.

$18.2 \approx c$ Simplify using a calculator.

Inverse Trigonometric Functions You have used angles to find lengths of sides. You can also use ratios of side lengths to find angles. For a positive value of sin θ, there may be *two* angles between 0° and 180° for which the value of sin θ is the same. You can find θ by using inverse sine (sin⁻¹). For example, if sin θ = 0.5, then θ = sin⁻¹(0.5) = 30° and θ = 180° − 30° = 150°.

STUDENT HELP

KEYSTROKE HELP
On most calculators, you can evaluate inverse trigonometric functions using the keys `2nd` `SIN` for inverse sine, `2nd` `COS` for inverse cosine, and `2nd` `TAN` for inverse tangent.

EXAMPLE 2 Find Two Angle Measures

Find two values of θ between 0° and 180° that satisfy sin θ = 0.6428.

Solution

Use the inverse sine function on your calculator to find the angle between 0° and 90°.

$$\theta = \sin^{-1}(0.6428) \approx 40°$$

To find the second angle, subtract 40° from 180°.

$$180° - 40° = 140°$$

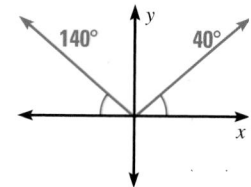

ANSWER ▶ So, sin θ = 0.6428 when θ = 40° and when θ = 140°.

Checkpoint ✓ Solve for Sides and Angles

1. In △ABC, a = 20, B = 25°, and C = 40°. Find the value of b.

2. Find two values of θ between 0° and 180° that satisfy sin θ = 0.5736.

SSA Two angles and one side (AAS or ASA) determine exactly one triangle. Two sides and an angle opposite one of the sides (SSA) may determine no triangle, one triangle, or two triangles.

Possible Triangles in SSA Case

Consider a triangle in which you are given *a*, *b*, and *A*. By fixing side *b* and angle *A*, you can sketch the possible positions of side *a* to figure out how many triangles can be formed. In the diagrams below, note that *h* = *b* sin *A*.

A is obtuse.

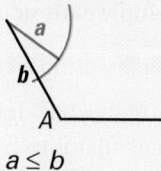

a ≤ *b*
No triangle

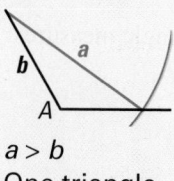

a > *b*
One triangle

A is acute.

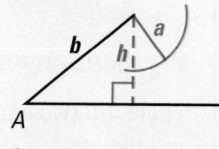

h > *a*
No triangle

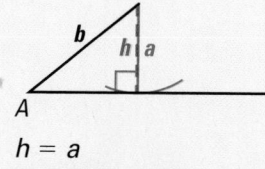

h = *a*
One triangle

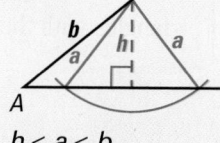

h < *a* < *b*
Two triangles

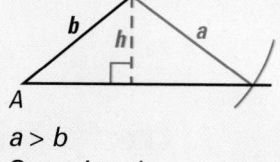

a > *b*
One triangle

EXAMPLE 3 Solve for an Angle (SSA)

Find the measure of angle C given that A = 120°, a = 9, and c = 7.

First make a sketch. Because A is obtuse and $a > c$, you know that only one triangle can be formed.

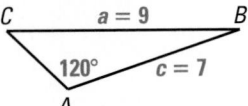

$\dfrac{\sin C}{c} = \dfrac{\sin A}{a}$	Write law of sines.
$\dfrac{\sin C}{7} = \dfrac{\sin 120°}{9}$	Subsitute for c, A, and a.
$\sin C = \dfrac{7 \sin 120°}{9}$	Multiply each side by 7.
$\sin C \approx 0.6736$	Simplify using a calculator.
$C \approx \sin^{-1}(0.6736)$	Use inverse sine function.
$\approx 42.3°$	Simplify.

ANSWER ▶ The measure of angle C is about 42.3°.

EXAMPLE 4 Solve for an Angle (SSA)

Find the measure of angle B given that A = 40°, a = 13, and b = 16.

First make a sketch. Because A is acute, and $a < b$, you need to find h.

$$h = b \sin A = 16 \sin 40° \approx 10.3$$

Because $h < a$ and $a < b$, two triangles can be formed.

STUDENT HELP

AVOID ERRORS
If you were given the triangle shown below for Example 4, because angle B is clearly obtuse, you would know that $B = 127.7°$ and not 52.3°.

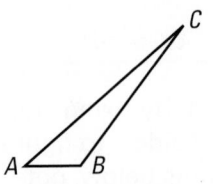

Triangle 1 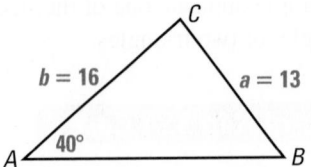 **Triangle 2**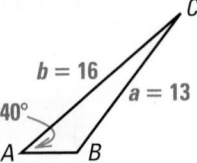

Use the law of sines to find the possible measures of B.

$\dfrac{\sin B}{b} = \dfrac{\sin A}{a}$	Write law of sines.
$\dfrac{\sin B}{16} = \dfrac{\sin 40°}{13}$	Substitute for b, A, and a.
$\sin B = \dfrac{16 \sin 40°}{13}$	Multiply each side by 16.
$\sin B \approx 0.7911$	Simplify using a calculator.

There are two angles between 0° and 180° for which $\sin B \approx 0.7911$. One is acute and the other is obtuse. Use a calculator to find the acute angle:

$$B = \sin^{-1}(0.7911) \approx 52.3°.$$

The second angle is $B = 180° - 52.3° = 127.7°$. So, there are two possible triangles with the following angle measures: 40°, 52.3°, 87.7° and 40°, 127.7°, 12.3°.

Checkpoint ✓ **Solve for an Angle**

3. Find the measure of angle B given that $A = 40°$, $a = 6$, and $b = 9$.

EXAMPLE 5 Recognize an Impossible Triangle

Find the measure of angle A given that $a = 7$, $b = 3$, and $B = 50°$.

Solution

Using the law of sines, you can write the following.

$$\frac{\sin A}{7} = \frac{\sin 50°}{3} \qquad \text{Write law of sines.}$$

$$\sin A = \frac{7 \sin 50°}{3} \qquad \text{Multiply each side by 7.}$$

$$\sin A \approx 1.7874 \qquad \text{Simplify using a calculator.}$$

Because the value of $\sin \theta$ is always between -1 and 1, there is no angle that satisfies the equation. So, it is not possible to draw the indicated triangle.

STUDENT HELP

LOOK BACK
For help with the maximum and minimum values of the sine function, see page 661.

EXAMPLE 6 Use the Law of Sines

Hiking Two hikers want to find the distance from a hiking path to an eagle's nest. One hiker is standing on the path at C and determines that her angle to the nest is 50°. The other hiker is standing 200 feet from the first hiker and determines that his angle to the nest is 40°. Find the length a, the distance from the path to the nest.

Not drawn to scale

Solution

First, find the measures of angles B and C of $\triangle ABC$.

$$C = 180° - 50° = 130° \qquad B = 180° - 130° - 40° = 10°$$

Then, use the law of sines.

$$\frac{a}{\sin A} = \frac{b}{\sin B} \qquad \text{Write law of sines.}$$

$$\frac{a}{\sin 40°} = \frac{200}{\sin 10°} \qquad \text{Substitute for } A, B, \text{ and } b.$$

$$a = \frac{200 \sin 40°}{\sin 10°} \qquad \text{Solve for the variable.}$$

$$a \approx 740 \qquad \text{Simplify using a calculator.}$$

ANSWER ▶ The distance from the path to the nest is about 740 feet.

Checkpoint ✓ *Use the Law of Sines*

4. Explain how you could change one measurement in Example 5 so that the triangle is possible to draw.

5. Find the measure of angle A given that $a = 8$, $b = 5$, and $B = 60°$.

6. Use the information in Example 6 and the law of sines to find the length c, the distance from the other hiker to the nest.

12.4 Exercises

Guided Practice

Vocabulary Check

1. What information do you need in order to use the law of sines?

2. Suppose *a*, *b*, and *A* are given for △*ABC* where *A* < 90°. Under what conditions would you have no triangle? one triangle? two triangles?

Skill Check

Find the indicated side length of the triangle.

3. Find *a*.

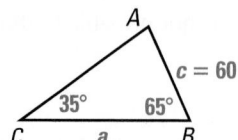

4. Find *b*.

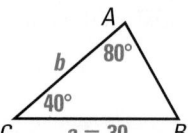

5. Find *c*.

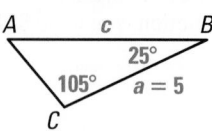

Find two angle measures between 0° and 180° that have the given value.

6. sin *θ* = 0.8192

7. sin *θ* = 0.1736

8. sin *θ* = 0.9063

Find the value of *x*.

9.

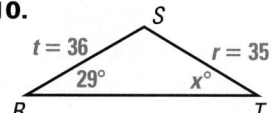

10.

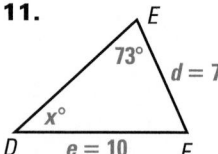

11.

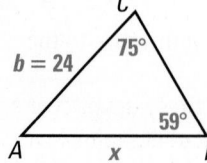

Sketch △*ABC*, then find the measure of angle *A*. If the triangle is impossible, explain why.

12. *a* = 5 inches
  b = 11 inches
  B = 105°

13. *a* = 5 inches
  c = 6 inches
  C = 46°

14. *a* = 20 inches
  b = 5 inches
  B = 25°

Practice and Applications

STUDENT HELP

HOMEWORK HELP
Example 1: Exs. 15–20,
    34–41
Example 2: Exs. 21–26
Example 3: Exs. 27–41
Example 4: Exs. 28–41
Example 5: Exs. 34–41
Example 6: Exs. 42–46

Solving for a Side Find the value of *x*.

15.

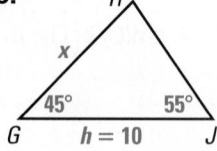

16.

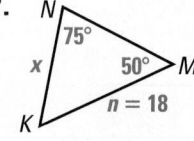

17.

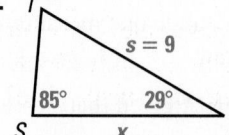

18.

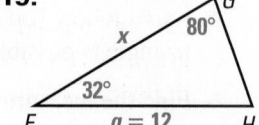

19.

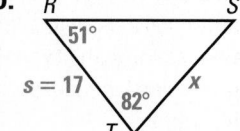

20.

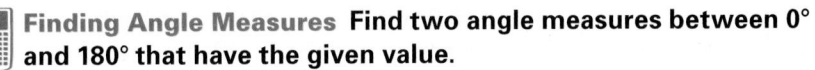

Finding Angle Measures Find two angle measures between 0°
and 180° that have the given value.

21. $\sin \theta = 0.5$

22. $\sin \theta = 0.7071$

23. $\sin \theta = 0.8860$

24. $\sin \theta = 0.4226$

25. $\sin \theta = 0.9848$

26. $\sin \theta = 0.3333$

27. Reasoning Refer to Example 3 on page 670. Can another triangle be formed
with the given measurements and $C = 137.7°$? Explain.

Solving for an Angle Find the measure(s) of the indicated angle(s).

28.

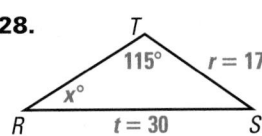

29.

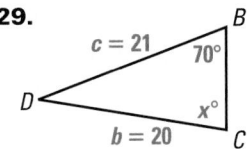

30.

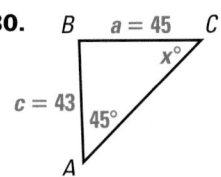

31.

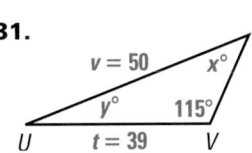

32.

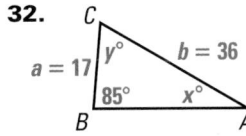

33.

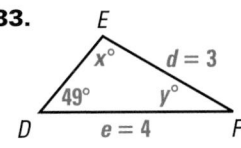

Finding Side Lengths Sketch $\triangle ABC$, then find the length of side b. If
the triangle is impossible, explain why.

34. $A = 105°, B = 20°, a = 20$

35. $A = 135°, a = 5, c = 12$

36. $C = 132°, c = 25, a = 6$

37. $B = 20°, C = 40°, a = 20$

Solving Triangles Sketch $\triangle ABC$, then find all of the angle measures
and side lengths. If the triangle is impossible, explain why.

38. $A = 55°, B = 85°, b = 10$

39. $C = 118°, b = 9, c = 11$

40. $A = 105°, C = 30°, b = 5$

41. $A = 35°, a = 9, b = 15$

42. Critical Thinking You are asked to build a triangular sign for a design class.
The specifications state that the side lengths for the sign need to be 10 feet,
6 feet, and 4 feet. The angle opposite the 6-foot side needs to be 115°. Make a
sketch of the sign. Can you build this sign? Explain your answer.

SAILING Triangular race
courses are used in sailing to
test a sailor's ability to deal
with winds from different
directions.

43. Boat Race In the first leg of a race, the boats
travel from point A to point B. The second leg
of the race continues from point B to point C.
In the final leg of the race, the boats return to
point A. The boats travel 4 miles in the first leg
of the race. What is the distance d (in miles)
for the final leg of the race?

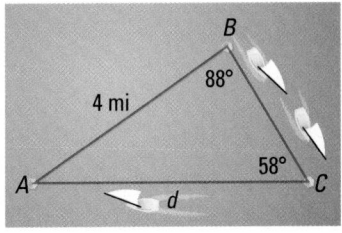

44. Baseball On a baseball field, the pitcher's
mound at P is 60.5 feet from home plate at
H and 95 feet from an arc where the outfield
grass begins. A ball is hit 25° to the right of the
pitcher's mound and travels to the edge of the
grass. What distance d must an outfielder at G
throw the ball to make an out at home plate?

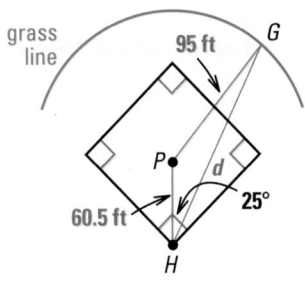

45. Koi Pond You are constructing a triangular koi pond in your backyard. You are given the following measurements, $a = 5$ ft, $A = 65°$, and $B = 40°$. What are the other side lengths of the pond?

46. Challenge A reservoir supplies water through an aqueduct to Springfield, which is 15 miles from the reservoir at 25° south of east. A pumping station at Springfield pumps water 7.5 miles to Centerville, which is due east from the reservoir. Plans have been made to build an aqueduct directly from the reservoir to Centerville. How long will the aqueduct be?

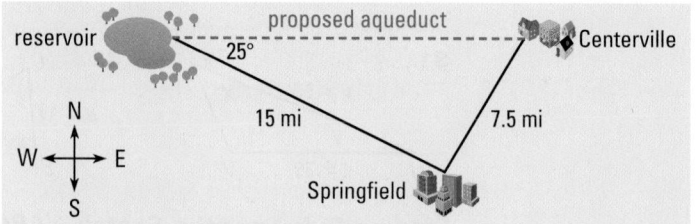

47. Multiple Choice What is the value of a?

    A 8.22   **B** 10

    C 13.47   **D** impossible triangle

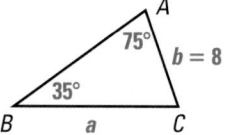

48. Multiple Choice In $\triangle ABC$, $A = 120°$, $a = 16$, and $c = 7$. What is the measure of angle C?

    F 22.26°   **G** 37.74°   **H** 52.5°   **J** 102°

Finding Side Lengths Find the value of *x* for the right triangle. Round your answer to two decimal places, if necessary. *(Lesson 12.1)*

49.
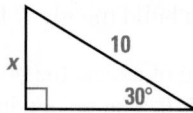

50.
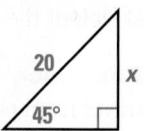

51.
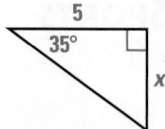

Writing Terms Write a rule for the *n*th term of the geometric sequence. Then find a_8. *(Lesson 11.6)*

52. 2, 4, 8, 16, . . .   **53.** −1, −4, −16, −64, . . .   **54.** 108, 36, 12, 4, . . .

55. 2, −6, 18, −54, . . .   **56.** −1, 5, −25, 125, . . .   **57.** $\frac{1}{4}, \frac{1}{8}, \frac{1}{16}, \frac{1}{32}, \ldots$

Area of a Sector Given the area *A* of the circle, find the area of the blue sector.

58. $A = 64$ square meters   **59.** $A = 72$ square inches   **60.** $A = 45$ square feet

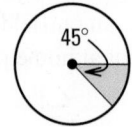
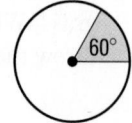
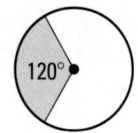

The Law of Cosines

Key Words

- law of cosines

Prerequisite Skills

Use the law of sines to find the measure of angle *C*.

1. $B = 60°, b = 7, c = 4$
2. $A = 20°, a = 5, c = 9$

How far is the pitcher's mound from first base?

In Exercise 45, you will use the law of cosines to find this distance.

Law of Cosines Suppose you have a triangle for which two sides and an included angle (SAS) or three sides (SSS) are given. To find the missing side lengths and angle measures, you can use the **law of cosines**.

Law of Cosines

If $\triangle ABC$ has sides of length *a*, *b*, and *c* as shown, then:

$$a^2 = b^2 + c^2 - 2bc \cos A$$
$$b^2 = a^2 + c^2 - 2ac \cos B$$
$$c^2 = a^2 + b^2 - 2ab \cos C$$

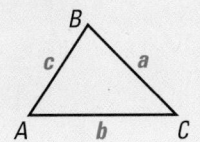

EXAMPLE **1** **Solve for a Side (SAS)**

Find the length *b* given that $a = 7$, $c = 12$, and $B = 41°$.

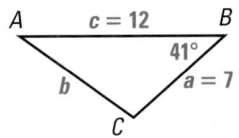

Solution

Use the law of cosines to find the length *b*. You need to find *b*, so use $b^2 = a^2 + c^2 - 2ac \cos B$.

$b^2 = a^2 + c^2 - 2ac \cos B$	Write law of cosines.
$b^2 = 7^2 + 12^2 - 2(7)(12) \cos 41°$	Substitute for *a*, *c*, and *B*.
$b^2 = 49 + 144 - 168 \cos 41°$	Evaluate powers and multiply.
$b^2 \approx 66.2$	Simplify.
$b \approx \sqrt{66.2} \approx 8.1$	Take positive square root.

Checkpoint  *Solving for a Side*

Find the unknown side length of the triangle to the nearest tenth.

1. *T*   *s* = 4   *R*   35°   *r* = 6   *t*   *S*

2. *F*   *e* = 10   *d*   50°   *D*   *f* = 13   *E*

3. *A*   *c* = 7   *B*   78°   *b* = 6   *a*   *C*

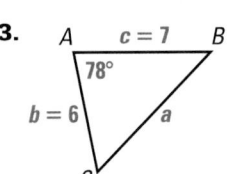

EXAMPLE 2 Solve for an Angle (SSS)

Find the measure of angle *B*.

Use the law of cosines to find the measure of angle *B*.

$$b^2 = a^2 + c^2 - 2ac \cos B \qquad \text{Write law of cosines.}$$

$$\cos B = \frac{a^2 + c^2 - b^2}{2ac} \qquad \text{Rewrite formula, by solving for cos } B.$$

$$\cos B = \frac{5^2 + 8^2 - 11^2}{2(5)(8)} \qquad \text{Substitute for } a, b, \text{ and } c.$$

$$\cos B = -0.4 \qquad \text{Simplify using a calculator.}$$

Use the inverse cosine function to find the angle measure.

$$B = \cos^{-1}(-0.4) \approx 113.6°$$

A *c* = 8 *B*

b = 11 *a* = 5

C

 **Checkpoint** ✓ *Solving for an Angle*

4. Find the measure of angle *C* given that *a* = 3, *b* = 7, and *c* = 9. Sketch the triangle.

5. Find the measure of angle *A* given that *a* = 4, *b* = 8, and *c* = 6. Sketch the triangle.

Choosing a Method

Method	Given information
Law of sines	2 angles and 1 side (AAS or ASA)
	2 sides and the angle opposite one of them (SSA)
Law of cosines	3 sides (SSS)
	2 sides and their included angle (SAS)

EXAMPLE 3 Choose a Method

Find the length *a* given that *b* = 5, *B* = 28°, and *C* = 110°.

You know two angles and one side. Use the law of sines. Use the fact that the sum of the angle measures is 180° to find *A*.

$$A = 180° - 110° - 28° = 42°$$

$$\frac{a}{\sin A} = \frac{b}{\sin B} \qquad \text{Write law of sines.}$$

$$\frac{a}{\sin 42°} = \frac{5}{\sin 28°} \qquad \text{Substitute for } A, B, \text{ and } b.$$

$$a = \frac{5 \sin 42°}{\sin 28°} \qquad \text{Solve for the variable.}$$

$$a \approx 7.1 \qquad \text{Simplify using a calculator.}$$

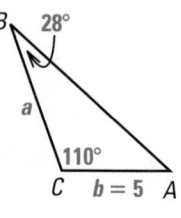

B 28°

a

110°

C *b* = 5 *A*

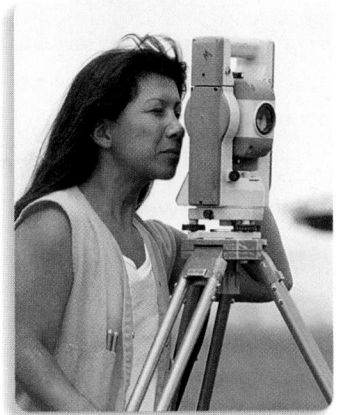
EXAMPLE 4 Use the Law of Sines and the Law of Cosines

Surveyor A bridge is being built across a river. A surveyor needs to measure the distance from point A to point B. The surveyor is at point C and measures an angle of 44°. The surveyor measures the distances from point C to points A and B and finds the distances to be 140 feet and 125 feet.

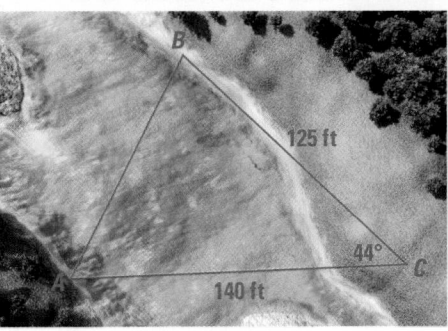

a. What is the distance from A to B?

b. Find the measures of the angles in the triangle.

Solution

a. You know the lengths of two sides and their included angle. So, use the law of cosines.

$c^2 = a^2 + b^2 - 2ab \cos C$	Write law of cosines.
$c^2 = 125^2 + 140^2 - 2(125)(140) \cos 44°$	Substitute for a, b and C.
$c^2 = 15{,}625 + 19{,}600 - 35{,}000 \cos 44°$	Evaluate powers.
$c^2 \approx 10{,}048.1$	Simplify.
$c \approx \sqrt{10{,}048.1} \approx 100.2$	Take positive square root.

ANSWER ▶ The distance from A to B is about 100 feet.

b. To find the measures of the angles in the triangle, use the law of sines.

$\dfrac{\sin A}{a} = \dfrac{\sin C}{c}$	Write law of sines.
$\dfrac{\sin A}{125} = \dfrac{\sin 44°}{100}$	Substitute for a, c, and C.
$\sin A = \dfrac{125 \sin 44°}{100}$	Multiply each side by 125.
$\sin A \approx 0.8683$	Simplify using a calculator.

Use the inverse sine function to find the angle measure.

$$A = \sin^{-1}(0.8683) \approx 60.3°$$

You then know that $B \approx 180° - 44° - 60.3° = 75.7°$.

ANSWER ▶ The measure of angle A is about 60.3° and the measure of angle B is about 75.7°.

Checkpoint ✓ *Use the Law of Sines and the Law of Cosines*

Use any method to find the unknown angle measures and side lengths.

6.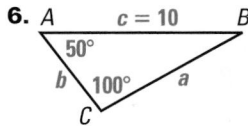

7.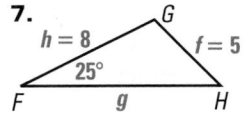

8.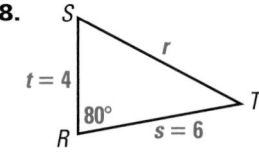

Guided Practice

Vocabulary Check

1. What information about a triangle do you need to know in order to use the law of cosines?

Skill Check

Find the unknown side length of the triangle. Round your answer to the nearest tenth.

2.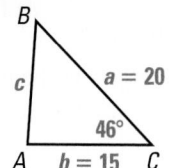

3.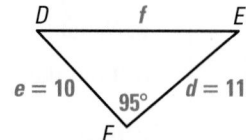

4.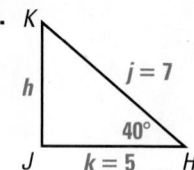

Find the value of *x*. Round your answer to the nearest tenth.

5.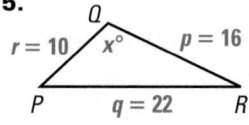

6.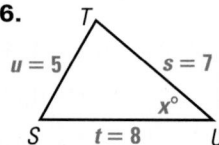

7.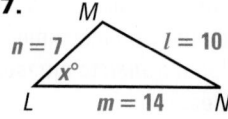

Practice and Applications

STUDENT HELP

HOMEWORK HELP
Example 1: Exs. 8–16,
  24–37
Example 2: Exs. 17–37
Example 3: Exs. 38–43
Example 4: Exs. 44–48

Finding Sides Find the unknown side length of the triangle. Round your answer to the nearest tenth.

8.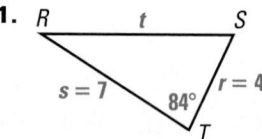

9.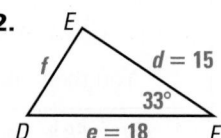

10.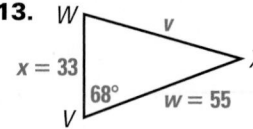

11.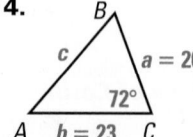

12.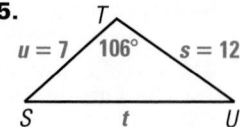

13.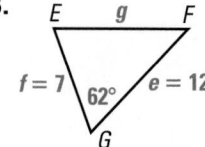

14.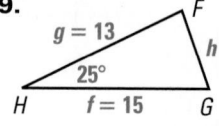

15.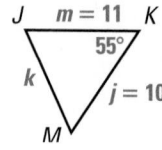

16.

17. Error Analysis Describe and correct the error in finding the measure of angle *A* in $\triangle ABC$ if $a = 18$, $b = 15$, and $c = 10$.

$$\cos A = \frac{15^2 + 10^2 - 18^2}{2(18)(15)} \approx 0.0019$$

$$A \approx \cos^{-1}(0.0019) \approx 89.9°$$

×

Finding Angle Measures Find the value of *x*. Round your answer to the nearest tenth.

18.

Triangle with vertices U, T, V. $v = 22$, $t = 25$, $u = 28$, angle $x°$ at V.

19.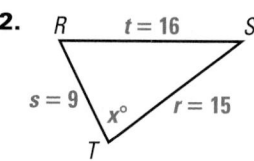

Triangle M, N, P. $p = 20$, $n = 18$, $m = 14$, angle $x°$ at P.

20.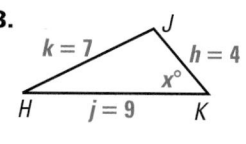

Triangle A, B, C. $c = 23$, angle $x°$ at B, $a = 30$, $b = 45$.

21.

Triangle F, G, H. $h = 23$, angle $x°$ at F, $f = 14$, $g = 25$.

22.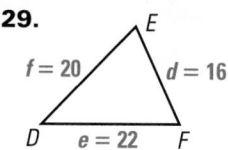

Triangle R, S, T. $t = 16$, $s = 9$, $r = 15$, angle $x°$ at T.

23.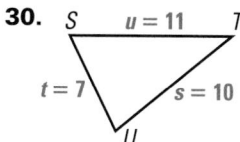

Triangle H, J, K. $k = 7$, $h = 4$, $j = 9$, angle $x°$ at K.

Finding Angles or Sides Sketch △*ABC*, then find the indicated angle measure or side length.

24. $C = 52°$, $a = 17$, $b = 22$, $c = \underline{\ ?\ }$

25. $A = 131°$, $b = 12$, $c = 15$, $a = \underline{\ ?\ }$

26. $a = 30$, $b = 38$, $c = 21$, $A = \underline{\ ?\ }$

27. $a = 20$, $b = 24$, $c = 25$, $B = \underline{\ ?\ }$

Finding All Angles Find the measures of all of the angles of the triangle. Round your answers to the nearest tenth.

28.

Triangle X, Y, Z. $z = 9$, $x = 8$, $y = 15$.

29.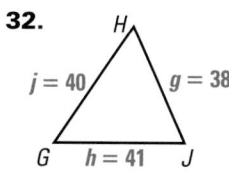

Triangle D, E, F. $f = 20$, $d = 16$, $e = 22$.

30.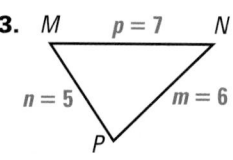

Triangle S, T, U. $u = 11$, $t = 7$, $s = 10$.

31.

Triangle A, B, C. $b = 20$, $c = 32$, $a = 22$.

32.

Triangle G, H, J. $j = 40$, $g = 38$, $h = 41$.

33.

Triangle M, N, P. $p = 7$, $n = 5$, $m = 6$.

Solving Triangles Sketch △*ABC*, then find all of the angle measures and side lengths.

34. $a = 50$, $b = 45$, $c = 40$

35. $a = 100$, $b = 110$, $c = 90$

36. $A = 84°$, $b = 24$, $c = 20$

37. $a = 43$, $b = 58$, $c = 48$

Choosing a Method Sketch △*ABC*, then use the law of sines or the law of cosines to find all of the angle measures and side lengths.

38. $A = 46°$, $B = 68°$, $a = 14$

39. $A = 32°$, $C = 102°$, $c = 24$

40. $a = 30$, $b = 22$, $c = 28$

41. $A = 110°$, $b = 12$, $c = 15$

42. $A = 98°$, $a = 18$, $b = 15$

43. $a = 15$, $b = 22$, $c = 25$

44. Trapeze Artists The diagram shows the paths of two trapeze artists who are both 5 feet long when hanging by their knees. The "flyer" on the left bar is preparing to make hand-to-hand contact with the "catcher" on the right bar. At what angle θ will the two meet?

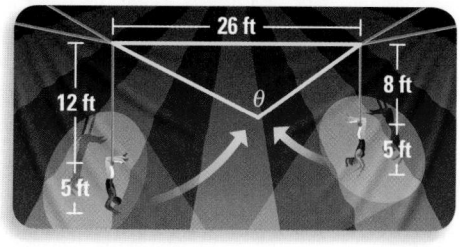

45. Baseball The pitcher's mound on a baseball field is 60.5 feet from home plate. The distance between the bases is 90 feet. How far is the pitcher's mound from first base?

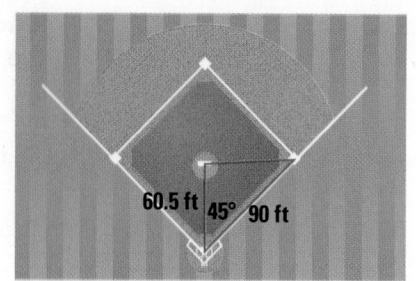
60.5 ft 45° 90 ft

46. Distances The three cities, Pittsburgh, Buffalo, and Cleveland form a triangle on a map. The distance from Pittsburgh to Buffalo is 177 miles, the distance from Buffalo to Cleveland is 170 miles, and the included angle is 39°. Sketch a triangle to represent the relationship between the three cities. What is the distance from Cleveland to Pittsburgh? What are the measures of all of the angles in the triangle you sketched?

Golf A golfer hits a drive 260 yards on a hole that is 400 yards long. The shot is 15° off target.

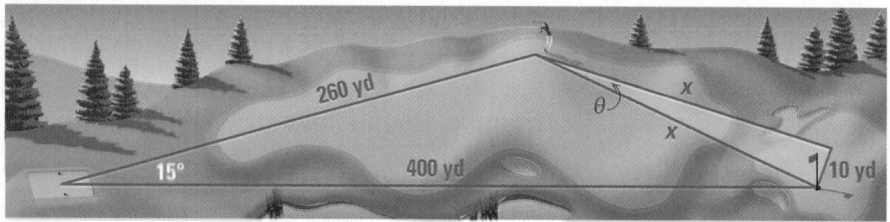
260 yd   θ   x   x
15°   400 yd   10 yd

47. What is the distance x from the golfer's ball to the hole?

48. Challenge Assume the golfer is able to hit the ball precisely the distance found in Exercise 47. What is the maximum angle θ by which the ball can be off target in order to land no more than 10 yards from the hole?

49. Critical Thinking Explain why the Pythagorean theorem is a special case of the law of cosines.

50. Multiple Choice What is the value of a?

Ⓐ 7.1   Ⓑ 8.5
Ⓒ 11.3   Ⓓ 13.6

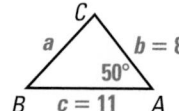
C
a $b = 8$
50°
B $c = 11$ A

51. Multiple Choice In $\triangle ABC$, $C = 95°$, $a = 24$, and $b = 32$. Find c.

Ⓕ 8.4   Ⓖ 40   Ⓗ 40.8   Ⓙ 41.6

52. Multiple Choice In $\triangle ABC$, $a = 14$, $b = 18$, and $c = 15$. Find B.

Ⓐ 13.4°   Ⓑ 49.2°   Ⓒ 54.2°   Ⓓ 76.6°

53. Multiple Choice In $\triangle ABC$, $a = 33$, $b = 40$, and $c = 42$. Find A.

Ⓕ 42.6°   Ⓖ 47.4°   Ⓗ 63.1°   Ⓙ 69.5°

Mixed Review

Perpendicular Lines Write an equation of the line that passes through the given point and is perpendicular to the given line. *(Lesson 2.5)*

54. $(2, -4)$, $y = 2x - 6$ **55.** $(1, 5)$, $y = -x + 3$ **56.** $(-3, -7)$, $y = x + 2$

57. $(2, 2)$, $y = -2x - 1$ **58.** $(-5, 2)$, $y = x - 2$ **59.** $(4, -1)$, $y = -x + 2$

Properties of Square Roots Simplify the expression. *(Lesson 5.5)*

60. $\sqrt{80}$

61. $\sqrt{63}$

62. $\sqrt{50}$

63. $\sqrt{\dfrac{16}{24}}$

64. $\sqrt{\dfrac{44}{18}}$

65. $\sqrt{\dfrac{72}{50}}$

Geometric Series Find the sum of the infinite geometric series. *(Lesson 11.7)*

66. $1 + \dfrac{2}{5} + \dfrac{4}{25} + \dfrac{8}{125} + \cdots$

67. $3 + \dfrac{3}{4} + \dfrac{3}{16} + \dfrac{3}{64} + \cdots$

68. $12 + 9 + \dfrac{27}{4} + \dfrac{81}{16} + \cdots$

69. $20 + 2 + 0.2 + 0.02 + 0.002 + \cdots$

Geometry Skills

Determining Parallelograms Tell whether the quadrilateral is a parallelogram. Explain your reasoning.

70.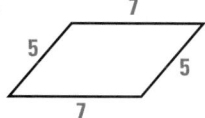

71.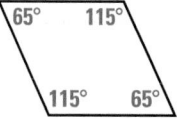

72.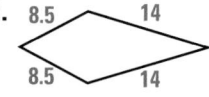

Quiz 2

Lesson 12.4 **Find the indicated side length of the triangle.**

1.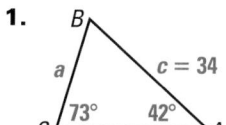

2.

3.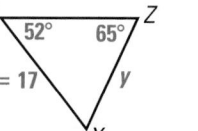

Lesson 12.4 **Use a calculator to find two angle measures between 0° and 180° that have the given value.**

4. $\sin \theta = 0.4067$

5. $\sin \theta = 0.9848$

6. $\sin \theta = 0.8746$

Lesson 12.4 **Sketch $\triangle ABC$, then find the indicated angle measure or side length. If the triangle is impossible, explain why.**

7. $B = 38°, C = 71°, b = 15, c = \underline{\ ?\ }$

8. $A = 62°, B = 41°, c = 7, a = \underline{\ ?\ }$

9. $A = 28°, a = 11, c = 11, B = \underline{\ ?\ }$

10. $B = 100°, a = 5, b = 14, A = \underline{\ ?\ }$

Lesson 12.5 **Find the unknown side length of the triangle. Round your answer to the nearest tenth.**

11.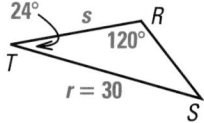

12.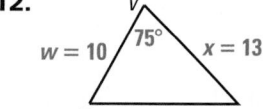

13.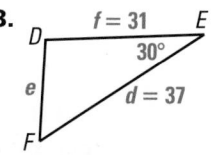

Lesson 12.5 **Sketch $\triangle ABC$, then find the indicated angle measure or side length.**

14. $B = 76°, a = 42, c = 33, b = \underline{\ ?\ }$

15. $C = 33°, a = 22, b = 28, c = \underline{\ ?\ }$

16. $a = 23, b = 24, c = 19, A = \underline{\ ?\ }$

17. $a = 35, b = 36, c = 27, C = \underline{\ ?\ }$

VOCABULARY

- sine, *p. 645*
- cosine, *p. 645*
- tangent, *p. 645*
- cosecant, *p. 645*
- secant, *p. 645*
- cotangent, *p. 645*

- initial side, *p. 652*
- terminal side, *p. 652*
- standard position, *p. 652*
- coterminal, *p. 653*
- quadrantal angle, *p. 654*

- periodic, *p. 660*
- cycle, *p. 660*
- period, *p. 660*
- law of sines, *p. 668*
- law of cosines, *p. 675*

VOCABULARY EXERCISES

1. Explain what it means for an angle to be in standard position.

2. What is the relationship between the sine function and the cosecant function?

3. Copy and complete: An angle in standard position whose terminal side lies on an axis is called a(n) __?__ .

4. Explain what it means for two angles to be coterminal.

12.1 RIGHT TRIANGLE TRIGONOMETRY

Examples on
pp. 645–647

EXAMPLE You can evaluate the six trigonometric functions of the angle θ shown.

Find the length of the hypotenuse: $\sqrt{8^2 + 15^2} = \sqrt{289} = 17$.

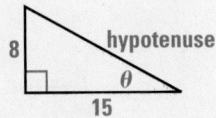

$\sin \theta = \dfrac{\text{opp}}{\text{hyp}} = \dfrac{8}{17}$ $\cos \theta = \dfrac{\text{adj}}{\text{hyp}} = \dfrac{15}{17}$ $\tan \theta = \dfrac{\text{opp}}{\text{adj}} = \dfrac{8}{15}$

$\csc \theta = \dfrac{\text{hyp}}{\text{opp}} = \dfrac{17}{8}$ $\sec \theta = \dfrac{\text{hyp}}{\text{adj}} = \dfrac{17}{15}$ $\cot \theta = \dfrac{\text{adj}}{\text{opp}} = \dfrac{15}{8}$

REVIEW HELP

Exercises	Examples
5–7	**1**, p. 645
8–10	**3**, p. 647

Evaluate the six trigonometric functions of the angle θ.

5.

6.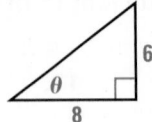

7.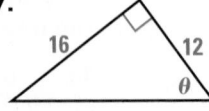

Find the value of *x* for the right triangle. Round the result to two decimal places.

8.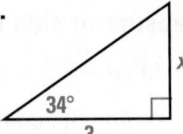

9.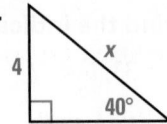

10.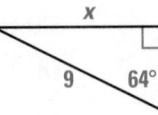

12.2 FUNCTIONS OF ANY ANGLE

Examples on pp. 652–655

EXAMPLE You can draw an angle with a measure of 500° in standard position. Because 500° is 140° more than 360°, the terminal side makes one whole revolution counterclockwise plus 140° more.

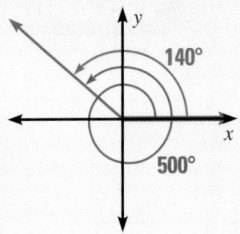

EXAMPLE You can evaluate the sine, cosine, and tangent functions of an angle θ, given a point on the terminal side of the angle in standard position.

Given the point $(6, -8)$, you can use the Pythagorean theorem to find the value of r.

$$r = \sqrt{x^2 + y^2} = \sqrt{6^2 + (-8)^2} = \sqrt{100} = 10$$

Using $x = 6$, $y = -8$, and $r = 10$, you can write the following.

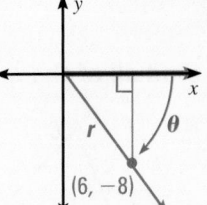

$$\sin \theta = \frac{y}{r} = -\frac{8}{10} = -\frac{4}{5} \qquad \cos \theta = \frac{x}{r} = \frac{6}{10} = \frac{3}{5} \qquad \tan \theta = \frac{y}{x} = -\frac{8}{6} = -\frac{4}{3}$$

REVIEW HELP

Exercises	Examples
11–14	**1**, p. 652
15–18	**3**, p. 654

Draw an angle with the given measure in standard position. Then tell in which quadrant the terminal side lies.

11. 330° **12.** $-150°$ **13.** $-300°$ **14.** 420°

Use the given point on the terminal side of an angle θ in standard position to evaluate the sine, cosine, and tangent functions of θ.

15. $(-12, 5)$ **16.** $(8, 6)$ **17.** $(-8, -15)$ **18.** $(-1, 1)$

12.3 GRAPHING THE TRIGONOMETRIC FUNCTIONS

Examples on pp. 660–662

EXAMPLE You can graph the function $y = 3 \sin x$. Notice that $a = 3$ and $b = 1$.
There is one intercept at $(0°, 0)$ and the period is $\frac{360°}{1} = 360°$.
Find the intercepts.

$$\left(\frac{180°}{b}, 0 \right) = \left(\frac{180°}{1}, 0 \right) = (180°, 0)$$

$$\left(\frac{360°}{b}, 0 \right) = \left(\frac{360°}{1}, 0 \right) = (360°, 0)$$

Find the maximum and minimum.

$$\left(\frac{90°}{b}, a \right) = \left(\frac{90°}{1}, 3 \right) = (90°, 3)$$

$$\left(\frac{270°}{b}, -a \right) = \left(\frac{270°}{1}, -3 \right) = (270°, -3)$$

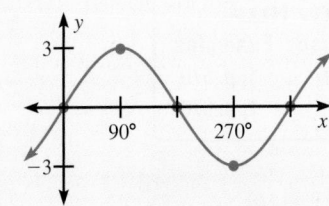

REVIEW HELP

Exercises	Examples
19	**1**, p. 661
20, 21	**2**, p. 661
22	**3**, p. 662

Graph the function.

19. $y = 5 \sin x$ **20.** $y = 3 \cos x$ **21.** $y = 2 \cos 3x$ **22.** $y = 4 \tan x$

12.4 THE LAW OF SINES

Examples on pp. 668–671

EXAMPLE You can use the law of sines to find missing angle measures and side lengths of triangles in which you know the values of two angles and any side (AAS or ASA), or two sides and an angle opposite one of them (SSA).

The measure of angle A is: $180° - 85° - 40° = 55°$.

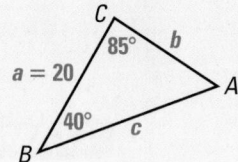

$$\frac{b}{\sin 40°} = \frac{20}{\sin 55°} \qquad \frac{c}{\sin 85°} = \frac{20}{\sin 55°}$$

$$b = \frac{20 \sin 40°}{\sin 55°} \qquad c = \frac{20 \sin 85°}{\sin 55°}$$

$$b \approx 15.7 \qquad c \approx 24.3$$

REVIEW HELP

Exercises	Example
23–25	**1**, p. 668

Find all of the angle measures and side lengths of △ABC.

23.
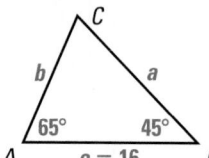

24.
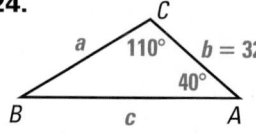

25.
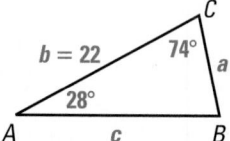

12.5 THE LAW OF COSINES

Examples on pp. 675–677

EXAMPLE You can use the law of cosines to find missing angle measures and side lengths of triangles in which you know the values of two sides and an included angle (SAS), or three sides (SSS).

Law of cosines: $b^2 = a^2 + c^2 - 2ac \cos B$

$$b^2 = 22^2 + 15^2 - 2(22)(15) \cos 66°$$

$$b^2 = 484 + 225 - 660 \cos 66°$$

$$b^2 \approx 441$$

$$b \approx \sqrt{441} \approx 21$$

Law of sines: $\dfrac{\sin C}{15} = \dfrac{\sin 66°}{21}$

$$\sin C = \frac{15 \sin 66°}{21} \approx 0.6525$$

$$C = \sin^{-1}(0.6525) \approx 40.7°$$

$$A \approx 180° - 66° - 40.7° \approx 73.3°$$

REVIEW HELP

Exercises	Examples
26, 27	**1**, p. 675
28	**2**, p. 676

Find all of the angle measures and side lengths of △ABC.

26.
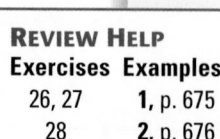

27.
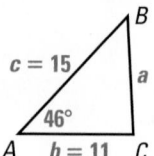

28.
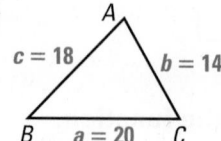

Evaluate the six trigonometric functions of the angle θ.

1.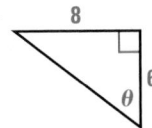

2.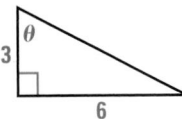

3.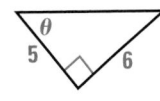

4. Use a calculator to evaluate sin 65°. Round your answer to four decimal places.

Draw an angle with the given measure in standard position.

5. 220°   **6.** −135°   **7.** 405°   **8.** −440°

Use the given point on the terminal side of an angle θ in standard position to evaluate the sine, cosine, and tangent functions of θ.

9. (5, 12)   **10.** (−3, −4)   **11.** (−3, 1)   **12.** (15, −8)

Find the maximum(s), minimum, and intercepts of the function on the interval $0° \le x \le \dfrac{360°}{b}$.

13. $y = 6 \cos 9x$ **14.** $y = 5 \sin 30x$ **15.** $y = \dfrac{1}{2} \cos 360x$

Graph the function.

16. $y = 2 \sin 4x$ **17.** $y = 3 \cos 180x$ **18.** $y = \tan 3x$

Find two angle measures between 0° and 180° that have the given value.

19. $\sin \theta = 0.5299$ **20.** $\sin \theta = 0.8192$ **21.** $\sin \theta = 0.2492$

Sketch △ABC, then find the indicated angle measure or side length.

22. $a = 18, A = 32°, c = 12, C = \underline{\ ?\ }$ **23.** $b = 24, B = 128°, C = 42°, a = \underline{\ ?\ }$

Find all of the angle measures and side lengths of △ABC.

24.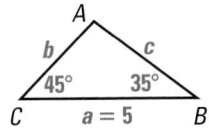

25.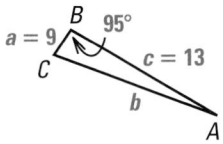

26.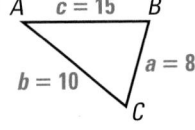

27. Escalator An escalator rises at an angle of 30°. The length of the escalator is 152 feet. Sketch the situation. What is the height of the escalator?

28. Navigation A boat travels 40 miles due west before turning 20° and traveling an additional 25 miles.

    a. Copy and label the triangle shown to represent this situation.

    b. How far is the boat from its point of departure?

Chapter Standardized Test

EXAMPLE Which is a possible value of the angle θ?

(A) $-405°$ (B) $-45°$

(C) $45°$ (D) $405°$

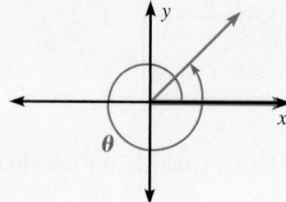

Solution

The rotation of the angle is counterclockwise, so the angle must be positive. Choices A and B are incorrect.

The terminal side of the angle makes more than 1 complete rotation, so the angle must be greater than 360°. Choice C is incorrect.

Choice D is the correct answer.

Multiple Choice

1. Which of the following has a positive value?

(A) $\cos 120°$ (B) $\tan 255°$

(C) $\sin 315°$ (D) $\tan 150°$

2. What is an approximate value of θ between 0° and 90° that satisfies $\sin \theta = 0.7862$?

(F) $61.2°$ (G) $51.8°$

(H) $-51.8°$ (J) $128.2°$

3. What is the approximate value of B?

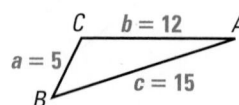

(A) $30°$ (B) $45°$

(C) $52°$ (D) $78°$

4. What is the period of $y = 10 \sin 4x$?

(F) $4°$ (G) $10°$

(H) $90°$ (J) $180°$

5. Which angle is coterminal with 60°?

(A) $-60°$ (B) $90°$

(C) $120°$ (D) $420°$

6. What is the maximum value of $y = 5 \cos 2x$?

(F) 2   (G) 5

(H) 90   (J) 180

7. Which is the horizontal length of a cycle?

(A) domain   (B) period

(C) range   (D) maximum

8. What is the approximate value of c?

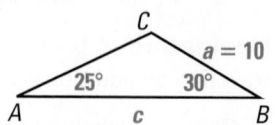

(F) 0.05   (G) 125

(H) 19.38   (J) 46.55

9. What is the value of x in the triangle shown below?

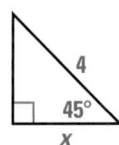

(A) $\dfrac{\sqrt{2}}{8}$ (B) $\sqrt{2}$

(C) 2 (D) $2\sqrt{2}$

10. Which is a possible value of the angle θ?

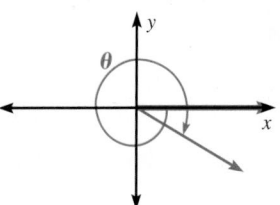

(F) $-390°$ (G) $-30°$

(H) $30°$ (J) $390°$

Gridded Response

For Exercises 11 and 12, find the value of x. Approximate your answer to the nearest hundredth.

11.

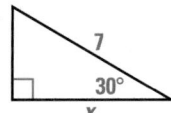

12.

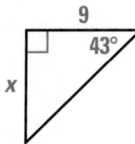

13. To the nearest tenth, find a value of θ between $90°$ and $180°$ for which $\sin \theta = 0.8862$.

For Exercises 14 and 15, find the value of b. Approximate your answer to the nearest hundredth.

14.

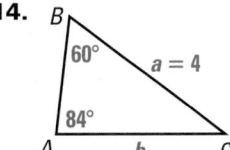

15.

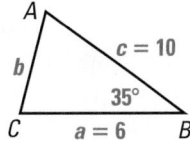

Extended Response

16. Use the graph shown to answer the following questions.

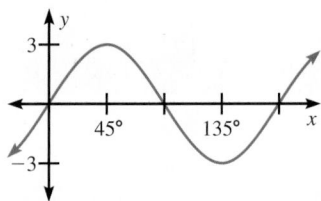

    a. Find the maximum, minimum, and period of the function.

    b. Write an equation of the form $y = a \sin bx$, where $a > 0$ and $b > 0$, for the graph.

    c. Compare the graph above to the graph of $y = \sin x$.

CHAPTER 13

Conic Sections

▶ What does the cross section of a parabolic reflector look like?

APPLICATION: Solar Energy

A parabolic reflector collects solar energy. The cross sections of a parabolic reflector are parabolas and can be modeled by quadratic equations. The diagram below shows one cross section of a parabolic reflector.

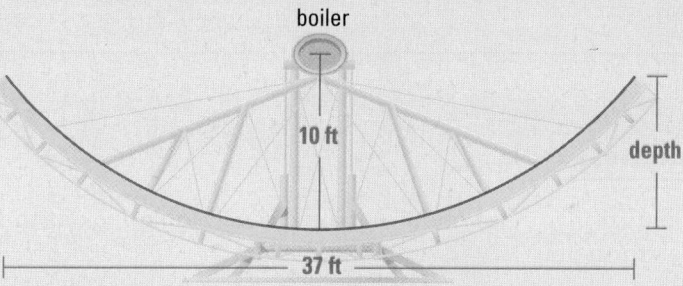

boiler

10 ft

depth

37 ft

In Lesson 13.2 you will write an equation of a parabola using information given in the graph.

Think & Discuss

Use the diagram to answer the following questions.

1. If the vertex of the parabola is at (0, 0), what is the axis of symmetry?

2. If the equation of the parabola is $y = ax^2 + bx + c$, which statement is true about the values of a, b, and c?

   A. $a > 0$, $b = 0$, and $c = 0$

   B. $a < 0$, $b = 0$, and $c = 0$

   C. $a > 0$, $b \neq 0$, and $c \neq 0$

Learn More About It

You will write an equation for the cross section of a parabolic reflector using the distance from the vertex to the boiler in Example 3 on page 699.

@HomeTutor
classzone.com
• Multi-Language Glossary
• Vocabulary practice

PREVIEW **What's the chapter about?**

• Finding the distance between two points
• Finding the midpoint of the line segment joining two points
• Graphing equations of parabolas, circles, ellipses, and hyperbolas
• Writing equations of parabolas, circles, ellipses, and hyperbolas

Key Words

• distance formula, *p. 691*
• midpoint formula, *p. 692*
• focus, foci, *pp. 697, 710, 717*
• directrix, *p. 697*
• circle, *p. 703*
• center, *pp. 703, 710, 717*
• radius, *p. 703*
• ellipse, *p. 710*

• vertices, *pp. 710, 717*
• major axis, *p. 710*
• co-vertices, *p. 710*
• minor axis, *p. 710*
• hyperbola, *p. 717*
• transverse axis, *p. 717*
• conic sections, *p. 724*
• discriminant, *p. 726*

PREPARE **Chapter Readiness Quiz**

Take this quick quiz. If you are unsure of an answer, look back at the reference pages for help.

Vocabulary Check *(refer to p. 222)*

1. Complete the statement: The lowest or highest point on the graph of a quadratic function is called the ___?___.

(**A**) origin   (**B**) *x*-intercept   (**C**) vertex   (**D**) axis

Skill Check *(refer to pp. 228, 255)*

2. Simplify the expression $\sqrt{72}$.

(**F**) $36\sqrt{2}$ (**G**) $2\sqrt{6}$ (**H**) $6\sqrt{12}$ (**J**) $6\sqrt{2}$

3. What is the vertex of the graph of $y = 2(x + 4)^2 + 7$?

(**A**) $(4, 7)$ (**B**) $(-4, 7)$ (**C**) $(4, -7)$ (**D**) $(-4, -7)$

TAKE NOTES **Summarize in Your Notes**

Write down definitions, equations, diagrams, or hints that will help you prepare for a test. Even if your teacher does not allow you to use your study sheet during the test, you will benefit from having summarized in your notes.

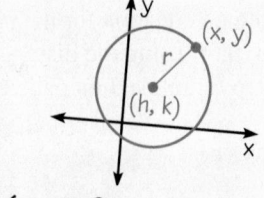

Circle with center at (h, k) and radius r

$(x - h)^2 + (y - k)^2 = r^2$

13.1 Distance and Midpoint Formulas

Key Words
- distance formula
- midpoint formula

GOAL Find the distance between and midpoint of two points.

Prerequisite Skills

Find the unknown side length of a right triangle with legs *a* and *b*, and hypotenuse *c*.

1. $a = 8, b = 15$

2. $b = 12, c = 20$

3. $a = 12, c = 13$

4. $b = 10, c = 26$

To find a general formula for the distance between points $A(x_1, y_1)$ and $B(x_2, y_2)$, apply the Pythagorean theorem to triangle ABC shown.

$$(AB)^2 = (AC)^2 + (BC)^2$$
$$d^2 = (x_2 - x_1)^2 + (y_2 - y_1)^2$$
$$d = \sqrt{(x_2 - x_1)^2 + (y_2 - y_1)^2}$$

The result is called the **distance formula**.

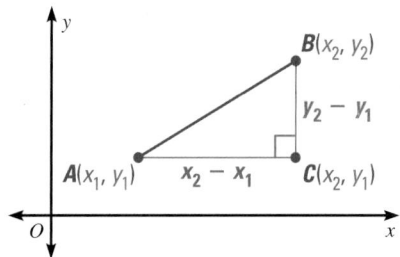

The Distance Formula

The distance formula gives the distance d between two points (x_1, y_1) and (x_2, y_2).

$$d = \sqrt{(x_2 - x_1)^2 + (y_2 - y_1)^2}$$

EXAMPLE 1 Find the Distance Between Two Points

Find the distance between $(-3, 1)$ and $(5, -2)$.

Solution

Let $(x_1, y_1) = (-3, 1)$ and $(x_2, y_2) = (5, -2)$.

$$d = \sqrt{(x_2 - x_1)^2 + (y_2 - y_1)^2} \qquad \text{Write the distance formula.}$$

$$= \sqrt{(5 - (-3))^2 + (-2 - 1)^2} \qquad \text{Substitute values.}$$

$$= \sqrt{8^2 + (-3)^2} \qquad \text{Subtract in parentheses.}$$

$$= \sqrt{64 + 9} \qquad \text{Evaluate powers.}$$

$$= \sqrt{73} \qquad \text{Simplify.}$$

$$\approx 8.54 \qquad \text{Use a calculator.}$$

Checkpoint ✓ *Find the Distance Between Two Points*

Find the distance between the two points.

1. $(0, 0), (-3, 4)$ 2. $(-1, 2), (5, 3)$ 3. $(-2, -4), (1, -4)$

4. $(4, -1), (-3, 5)$ 5. $(-1, 5), (3, -3)$ 6. $(-4, 4), (5, -4)$

EXAMPLE **2** **Classify a Triangle Using the Distance Formula**

Classify $\triangle ABC$ as *scalene*, *isosceles*, or *equilateral*.

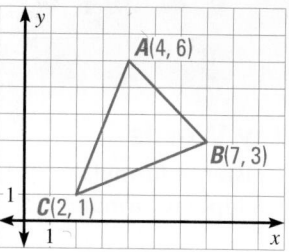

Solution

Find the distances between the vertices.

$$AB = \sqrt{(7-4)^2 + (3-6)^2} = \sqrt{18} = 3\sqrt{2}$$

$$BC = \sqrt{(2-7)^2 + (1-3)^2} = \sqrt{25+4} = \sqrt{29}$$

$$AC = \sqrt{(2-4)^2 + (1-6)^2} = \sqrt{4+25} = \sqrt{29}$$

ANSWER ▶ Because $BC = AC$, $\triangle ABC$ is isosceles.

Midpoint Formula The midpoint of a line segment is the point on the segment that is equidistant from the two endpoints. You can use the **midpoint formula** to find the coordinates of the midpoint of a line segment.

The Midpoint Formula

The midpoint formula gives the midpoint M of the line segment joining $A(x_1, y_1)$ and $B(x_2, y_2)$.

$$\text{Midpoint} = M\left(\frac{x_1 + x_2}{2}, \frac{y_1 + y_2}{2}\right)$$

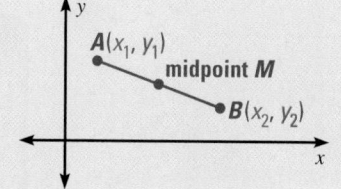

EXAMPLE **3** **Find the Midpoint of a Line Segment**

Find the midpoint of the line segment joining $(-5, 1)$ and $(-1, 6)$.

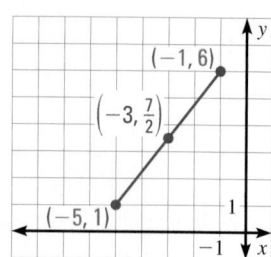

Solution

Let $(x_1, y_1) = (-5, 1)$ and $(x_2, y_2) = (-1, 6)$.

$$\left(\frac{x_1 + x_2}{2}, \frac{y_1 + y_2}{2}\right) = \left(\frac{-5 + (-1)}{2}, \frac{1 + 6}{2}\right) \quad \text{Substitute values into the midpoint formula.}$$

$$= \left(-\frac{6}{2}, \frac{7}{2}\right) = \left(-3, \frac{7}{2}\right) \quad \text{Simplify.}$$

 **Classify a Triangle and Find Midpoints**

7. The vertices of a triangle are $(1, 4)$, $(6, 5)$, and $(3, 0)$. Classify the triangle as *scalene*, *isosceles*, or *equilateral*.

Find the midpoint of the line segment joining the two points.

8. $(0, 0)$, $(-4, 6)$ **9.** $(0, 5)$, $(8, -3)$ **10.** $(-8, 1)$, $(3, -3)$

EXAMPLE 4 Find a Perpendicular Bisector

Write an equation for the perpendicular bisector of the line segment joining $A(-3, 4)$ and $B(5, 6)$.

Solution

❶ **Find** the midpoint of the line segment.
$$\left(\frac{x_1 + x_2}{2}, \frac{y_1 + y_2}{2}\right) = \left(\frac{-3 + 5}{2}, \frac{4 + 6}{2}\right) = (1, 5)$$

❷ **Calculate** the slope of the line segment.
$$m = \frac{y_2 - y_1}{x_2 - x_1} = \frac{6 - 4}{5 - (-3)} = \frac{2}{8} = \frac{1}{4}$$

❸ **Find** the slope of the perpendicular bisector. Its slope is the negative reciprocal of $\frac{1}{4}$, or -4.

❹ **Write** the equation. Use point-slope form.
$$y - y_1 = m(x - x_1)$$
$$y - 5 = -4(x - 1)$$
$$y = -4x + 9$$

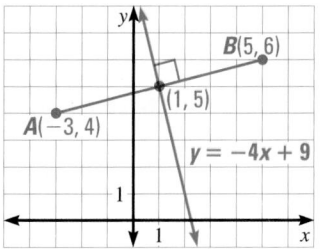

Link to ARCHAEOLOGY

POTTERY Archaeologists use pieces of pottery, like the Native American pottery shown, found on sites of ancient cities and villages, to learn about civilizations.

EXAMPLE 5 Use Formulas in Real Life

Archaeology A piece of a circular broken dish is placed on a coordinate plane and three points on the edge are labeled. You can find equations for the perpendicular bisectors of $\overline{AO}$ and $\overline{OB}$. The perpendicular bisectors will intersect at the center of the dish.

$$y = 2x + 5 \quad \text{Perpendicular bisector of } \overline{AO}$$
$$y = -\frac{3}{2}x + \frac{13}{2} \quad \text{Perpendicular bisector of } \overline{OB}$$

a. Find the center of the original dish.

b. Find the radius of the dish (in inches).

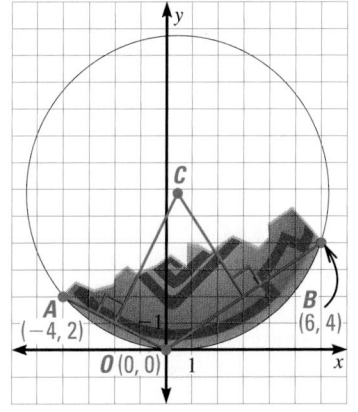

Solution

a. Both perpendicular bisectors pass through the center. So, the center is the solution of the system formed by their equations.
$$2x + 5 = -\frac{3}{2}x + \frac{13}{2} \quad \text{Substitute for } y.$$
$$x = \frac{3}{7} \quad \text{Solve for } x.$$
Substitute $\frac{3}{7}$ for x in original equation and solve for y. The center is $\left(\frac{3}{7}, \frac{41}{7}\right)$.

b. The radius is the distance between the center and a point on the circle.
$$OC = \sqrt{\left(\frac{3}{7} - 0\right)^2 + \left(\frac{41}{7} - 0\right)^2} = \sqrt{\frac{1690}{49}} \approx 5.87 \text{ inches}$$

Checkpoint ✓ Find a Perpendicular Bisector

11. Write an equation for the perpendicular bisector of the line segment joining $(-2, 0)$ and $(6, 4)$.

Guided Practice

Vocabulary Check   **1.** What is the distance formula?

2. How is an isosceles triangle different from an equilateral triangle?

Skill Check   **Find the distance between the two points.**

3. $(0, 0)$, $(3, 4)$

4. $(-2, 3)$, $(0, 0)$

5. $(0, 2)$, $(6, 4)$

6. $(-3, 0)$, $(-1, 4)$

7. $(1, 6)$, $(5, 3)$

8. $(2, -1)$, $(-3, 2)$

Classify the triangle as *scalene, isosceles,* or *equilateral*. Use the distance formula.

9.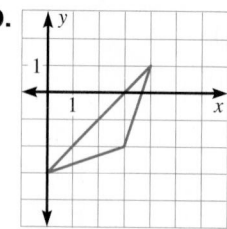

10.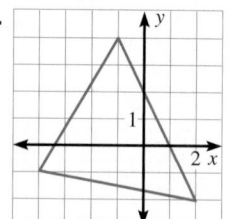

11.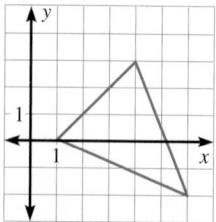

Find the midpoint of the line segment joining the two points.

12. $(0, 0)$, $(6, -2)$

13. $(-8, -6)$, $(0, 0)$

14. $(4, 0)$, $(-2, -2)$

15. $(3, 1)$, $(-1, 7)$

16. $(-2, -3)$, $(6, -2)$

17. $(2, -5)$, $(-1, 6)$

Practice and Applications

STUDENT HELP

HOMEWORK HELP
Example 1: Exs. 18–31, 47–52
Example 2: Exs. 32–40
Example 3: Exs. 18–29
Example 4: Exs. 41–46
Example 5: Exs. 53–55

Using Formulas **Find the distance between the two points. Then find the midpoint of the line segment joining the two points.**

18. $(0, 0)$, $(-6, 8)$

19. $(4, -2)$, $(0, 0)$

20. $(0, -2)$, $(6, 0)$

21. $(0, -2)$, $(-1, 3)$

22. $(3, 0)$, $(-1, -6)$

23. $(-2, 1)$, $(-6, 4)$

24. $(8, 3)$, $(2, -1)$

25. $(1, 3)$, $(3, 11)$

26. $(-1, 7)$, $(7, -1)$

27. $(-3, -1)$, $(7, 4)$

28. $(10, -2)$, $(3, 2)$

29. $(-1, 5)$, $(-8, -6)$

Error Analysis **Describe and correct the error in finding the distance between the two points.**

30. $(5, -1)$, $(2, 6)$

31. $(-4, 3)$, $(2, 8)$

$$d = \sqrt{(2 - 5)^2 + (6 - 1)^2}$$
$$d = \sqrt{(-3)^2 + (5)^2}$$
$$d = \sqrt{9 + 25}$$
$$d = \sqrt{34}$$

$$d = \sqrt{(2 - (-4)^2 - (8 - 3)^2}$$
$$d = \sqrt{(36 - 25)}$$
$$d = \sqrt{11}$$

Classify Triangles Classify the triangle as *scalene, isosceles,* or *equilateral*. Use the distance formula.

32.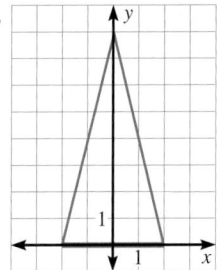

33.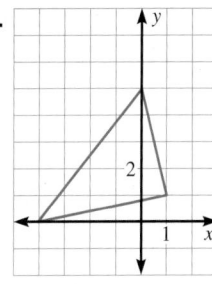

34.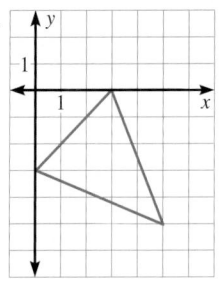

Classify Triangles The vertices of a triangle are given. Classify the triangle as *scalene, isosceles,* or *equilateral*.

35. $(0, 0), (4, -5), (8, 0)$

36. $(-3, 0), (0, 2), (5, -1)$

37. $(5, -1), (-4, 0), (3, 5)$

38. $(0, -3), (3, 5), (-5, 2)$

39. $(2, 4), (3, -2), (-1, 1)$

40. $(-1, -6), (-4, 2), (4, 2)$

Writing Equations Write an equation for the perpendicular bisector of the line segment joining the two points.

41. $(0, 0), (2, -6)$

42. $(0, -3), (2, 5)$

43. $(-4, 2), (2, -4)$

44. $(3, -7), (-3, 1)$

45. $(-3, 0), (1, -6)$

46. $(-2, -3), (5, 1)$

47. Soccer Half of a standard soccer field is shown at the right. Use the information in the diagram to draw the field on a coordinate plane. Give coordinates for the corner of the penalty area P and the corner of the goal area G. Then find the distance from P to G.

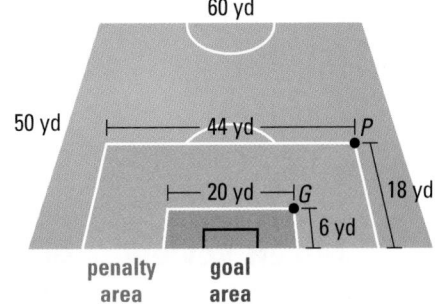

48. Robots A robot can be instructed to move by entering coordinates on a control panel. If the robot is instructed to move from $(6, 11)$ straight to $(-2, 26)$, how far does the robot move? Assume the coordinates are in meters.

49. Commuting To get from her home to her office, Lori must drive around a lake. If she drives 2 miles north, then 5 miles east, and then 4 miles south, what is the straight-line distance between Lori's home and her office?

Hiking In Exercises 50–52, use the following information.

The diagram shows part of a trail system at a nature preserve. Each unit represents 0.1 mile. Suppose that you walk from the visitor center V to the observation stand S, and then take a break at M, halfway between S and P.

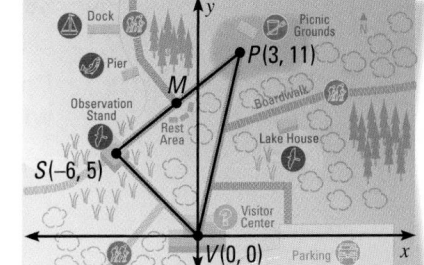

50. What are the coordinates of M?

51. What is the total distance that you walk from V to M?

52. What is the distance from M back to V through P?

Asteroid Crater In Exercises 53–55, use the following information.

Many scientists believe that an asteroid hit the Earth about 65 million years ago on what is now Mexico's Yucatan peninsula, creating an enormous crater that is now deeply buried by sediment.

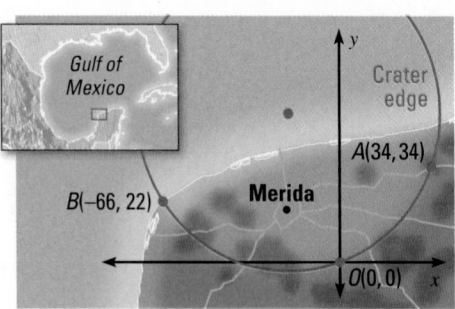

53. Write equations of the perpendicular bisectors of $\overline{AO}$ and $\overline{OB}$.

54. Find the radius of the circular crater.

55. Estimate the diameter of the circular crater. Each unit in the coordinate plane represents 1 mile.

Standardized Test Practice

56. Multiple Choice What is the distance between the points (1, 2) and (−2, 4)?

   (A) $\sqrt{5}$
       (B) $\sqrt{13}$

   (C) 4
       (D) 13

57. Multiple Choice What is the midpoint of the line segment joining the points (−4, 1) and (5, −2)?

   (F) $\left(\frac{9}{2}, -\frac{3}{2}\right)$
       (G) $\left(\frac{1}{2}, -\frac{1}{2}\right)$

   (H) (1, −1)
       (J) (2, −2)

58. Multiple Choice What is an equation for the perpendicular bisector of the line segment joining (3, −1) and (−1, 5)?

   (A) $y = -\frac{3}{2}x + \frac{7}{2}$
       (B) $y = -\frac{4}{3}x + \frac{2}{3}$

   (C) $y = \frac{2}{3}x + \frac{4}{3}$
       (D) $y = -x + \frac{4}{3}$

Mixed Review

Graphing Parabolas Graph the quadratic function. Label the vertex and the axis of symmetry. *(Lesson 5.1)*

59. $y = x^2$
     60. $y = 3x^2$
     61. $y = -2x^2$

62. $y = \frac{1}{2}x^2$
     63. $y = \frac{2}{3}x^2$
     64. $y = -\frac{1}{4}x^2$

Finding Coterminal Angles Find one positive angle and one negative angle that are coterminal with the given angle. *(Lesson 12.2)*

65. 25°
     66. 165°
     67. −75°

68. 225°
     69. −150°
     70. 405°

Geometry Skills

Congruent Triangles Determine if the triangles are congruent. If so, write a congruence statement.

71.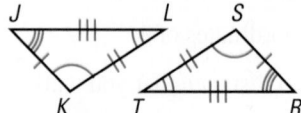
     72.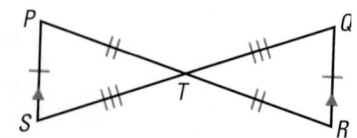

13.2 Parabolas

Key Words
- focus
- directrix

GOAL Graph and write equations of parabolas.

In Chapter 5, you saw that the graph of $y = ax^2$ is a parabola opening up or down with vertex $(0, 0)$ and vertical axis of symmetry $x = 0$. Each point on a parabola is equidistant from a point called the **focus** and a line called the **directrix**.

Prerequisite Skills

Tell whether the graph of the equation is a parabola.

1. $y = 2x^2 - x + 1$

2. $y = 5 + 2x$

3. $y^2 = 4x^2$

4. $x^2 + y = 3$

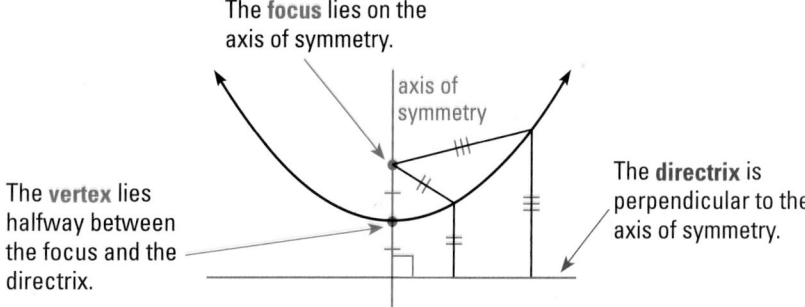

The **focus** lies on the axis of symmetry.

The **vertex** lies halfway between the focus and the directrix.

The **directrix** is perpendicular to the axis of symmetry.

The equation of a parabola opening up or down with vertex $(0, 0)$ can also be written in the form $x^2 = 4py$. Parabolas opening to the left or right with vertex $(0, 0)$ have equations of the form $y^2 = 4px$. In the four cases shown below, the focus and the directrix each lie $|p|$ units from the vertex.

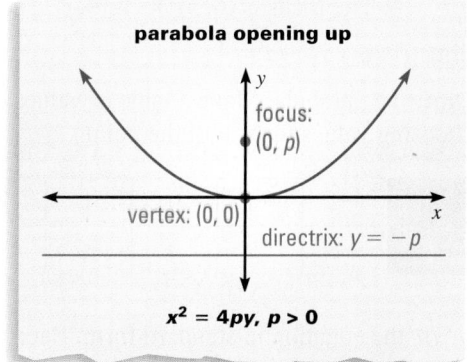

parabola opening up

focus: $(0, p)$

vertex: $(0, 0)$

directrix: $y = -p$

$x^2 = 4py, p > 0$

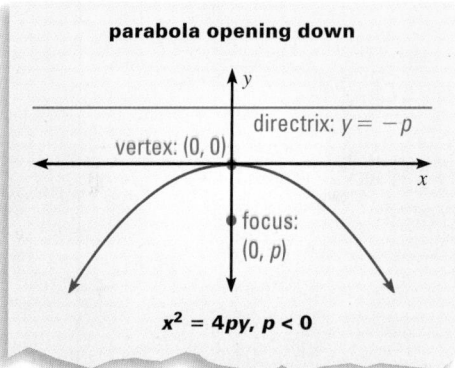

parabola opening down

directrix: $y = -p$

vertex: $(0, 0)$

focus: $(0, p)$

$x^2 = 4py, p < 0$

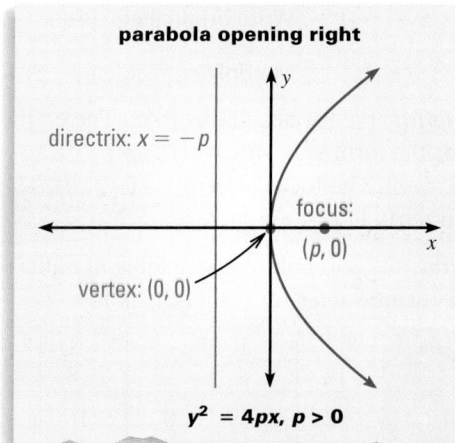

parabola opening right

directrix: $x = -p$

focus: $(p, 0)$

vertex: $(0, 0)$

$y^2 = 4px, p > 0$

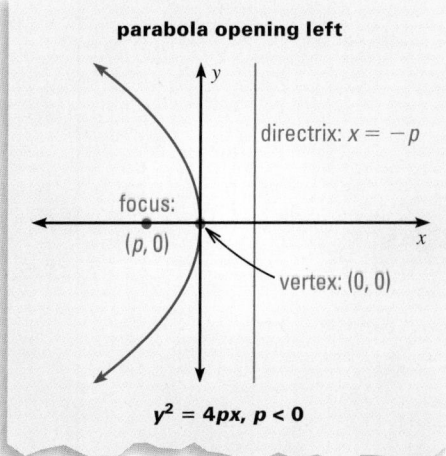

parabola opening left

directrix: $x = -p$

focus: $(p, 0)$

vertex: $(0, 0)$

$y^2 = 4px, p < 0$

Standard Equation of a Parabola with Vertex at (0, 0)

The standard form of the equation of a parabola with vertex at (0, 0) is as follows:

EQUATION	FOCUS	DIRECTRIX	AXIS OF SYMMETRY
$x^2 = 4py$	$(0, p)$	$y = -p$	Vertical ($x = 0$)
$y^2 = 4px$	$(p, 0)$	$x = -p$	Horizontal ($y = 0$)

EXAMPLE 1 Graph Equations of Parabolas

Graph the equation. Identify the focus, directrix, and axis of symmetry.

a. $y = -2x^2$

b. $x = -\dfrac{1}{8}y^2$

Solution

a. ❶ **Write** the equation in standard form. Because the variable x is squared, the axis of symmetry is the y-axis.

$y = -2x^2$ Write original equation.

$-\dfrac{1}{2}y = x^2$ Multiply each side by $-\dfrac{1}{2}$.

❷ **Identify** the focus and directrix. The equation has the form $x^2 = 4py$ where $4p = -\dfrac{1}{2}$, so $p = -\dfrac{1}{8}$. The focus is $(0, p) = \left(0, -\dfrac{1}{8}\right)$. The directrix is $y = -p = \dfrac{1}{8}$.

❸ **Draw** the parabola. Make a table of values by choosing values for x. Plot the points.

x	−2	−1	0	1	2
y	−8	−2	0	−2	−8

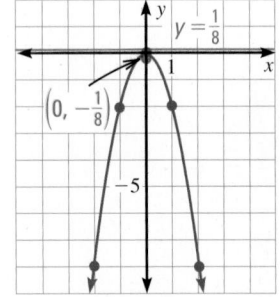

b. ❶ **Write** the equation in standard form. Because the variable y is squared, the axis of symmetry is the x-axis.

$x = -\dfrac{1}{8}y^2$ Write original equation.

$-8x = y^2$ Multiply each side by -8.

❷ **Identify** the focus and directrix. The equation has the form $y^2 = 4px$ where $4p = -8$ so $p = -2$. The focus is $(p, 0) = (-2, 0)$. The directrix is $x = -p = 2$.

❸ **Draw** the parabola. Make a table of values by choosing values for y. Plot the points.

x	$-\dfrac{1}{2}$	$-\dfrac{1}{8}$	0	$-\dfrac{1}{8}$	$-\dfrac{1}{2}$
y	−2	−1	0	1	2

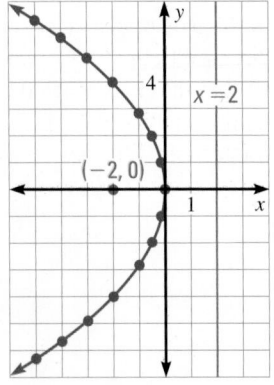

EXAMPLE 2 Write an Equation of a Parabola

Write an equation of the parabola.

Solution

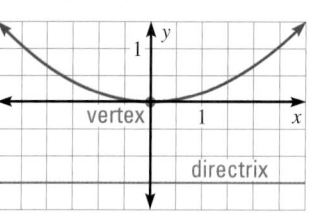

The directrix is $y = -p = -\frac{3}{2}$. Use the equation for a parabola with a vertical axis of symmetry.

$x^2 = 4py$ **Standard equation**

$x^2 = 4\left(\frac{3}{2}\right)y$ **Substitute $\frac{3}{2}$ for p.**

$x^2 = 6y$ **Simplify.**

Checkpoint ✓ Graph and Write Equations of Parabolas

1. Graph $x = -\frac{1}{4}y^2$. Identify the focus, directrix, and axis of symmetry.

2. Write the standard form of the equation of the parabola with vertex at $(0, 0)$ and directrix at $x = 4$.

Link to
SCIENCE

PARABOLIC REFLECTORS
Sound or light that hits a parabolic reflector parallel to the axis of symmetry is directed to the focus. Sound or light that comes from the focus and hits the parabolic reflector is directed parallel to the axis of symmetry.

EXAMPLE 3 Model a Parabola

Solar Energy A parabolic reflector collects solar energy. The sun's rays are reflected from the mirrors toward two boilers at the focus of the parabola. When heated, the boilers produce steam that leads to energy production. Write an equation for the parabola. How deep is the parabola?

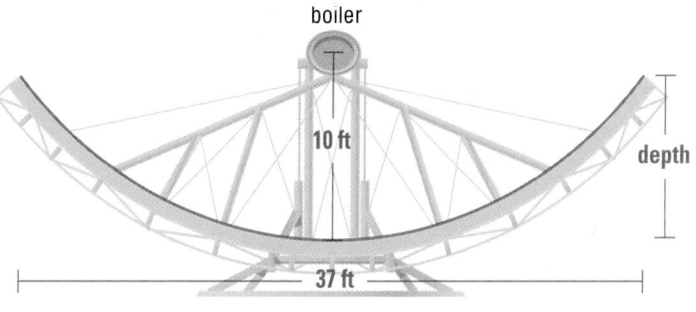

Solution

The parabola's vertex is at $(0, 0)$. The focus, or the boiler, is at $(0, p) = (0, 10)$.

$x^2 = 4py$ **Equation for a parabola with vertical axis of symmetry**

$x^2 = 4(\mathbf{10})y$ **Substitute 10 for p.**

$x^2 = 40y$ **Simplify.**

The reflector extends $37 \div 2 = 18.5$ feet on either side of $(0, 0)$. To find the depth of the reflector, substitute 18.5 for x in the equation.

$x^2 = 40y$ **Equation from above**

$(\mathbf{18.5})^2 = 40y$ **Substitute 18.5 for x.**

$y \approx 8.6$ **Solve for y.**

ANSWER ▶ An equation is $x^2 = 40y$. The dish is about 8.6 feet deep.

Guided Practice

Vocabulary Check

1. Copy and complete the statement: A parabola is the set of points equidistant from a point called the __?__ and a line called the __?__ .

Skill Check

Graph the equation. Identify the focus, directrix, and axis of symmetry of the parabola.

2. $x^2 = 2y$ **3.** $y = 2x^2$ **4.** $-8x = y^2$

5. $x = -4y^2$ **6.** $4y = x^2$ **7.** $2x = y^2$

Write the standard form of the equation of the parabola.

8.
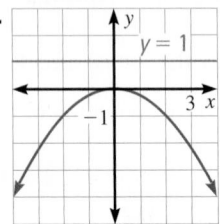

9.
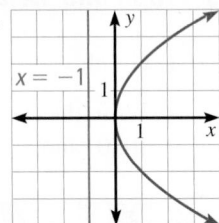

10.
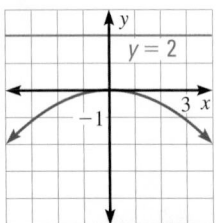

Practice and Applications

STUDENT HELP

HOMEWORK HELP
Example 1: Exs. 11–35
Example 2: Exs. 36–47
Example 3: Exs. 48–52

Matching **Match the equation with its graph.**

11. $x^2 = -2y$ **12.** $y^2 = \frac{1}{2}x$ **13.** $x^2 = \frac{1}{2}y$

A.
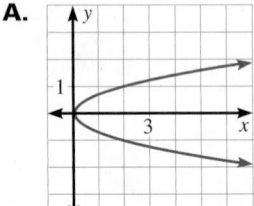

B.
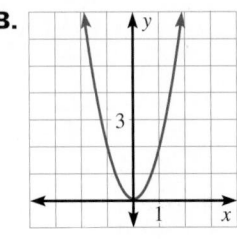

C.
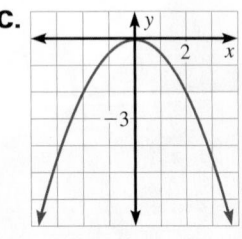

Focus and Directrix **Identify the focus and directrix of the parabola.**

14. $3y^2 = x$ **15.** $x^2 = y$ **16.** $-6x = y^2$

17. $4x^2 = -y$ **18.** $y^2 = 20x$ **19.** $5x^2 = y$

20. $-y^2 = 6x$ **21.** $x^2 = -24x$ **22.** $3x^2 = 2y$

Graphing **Graph the equation. Identify the focus, directrix, and axis of symmetry of the parabola.**

23. $x^2 = -12y$ **24.** $y^2 = 8x$ **25.** $x^2 = -4y$

26. $y^2 = -16x$ **27.** $y^2 = 4x$ **28.** $x^2 = -14y$

29. $x^2 = 6y$ **30.** $y^2 = -20x$ **31.** $x^2 = 10y$

32. $x^2 = -3y$ **33.** $y^2 = x$ **34.** $x^2 = 5y$

35. Error Analysis Describe and correct the error in graphing the parabola.

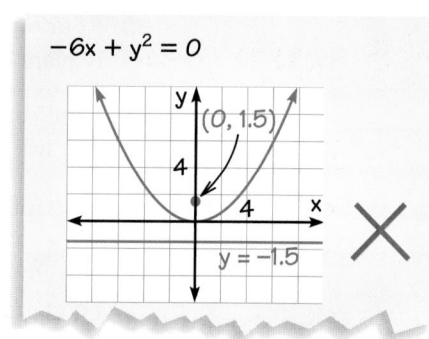

$-6x + y^2 = 0$

(0, 1.5)

4

4   x

$y = -1.5$

Writing Equations Write the standard form of the equation of the parabola with vertex at (0, 0) and the given focus or directrix.

36. Directrix: $x = \dfrac{1}{2}$

37. Directrix: $y = -1$

38. Directrix: $y = 2$

39. Directrix: $x = -2$

40. Directrix: $x = 2$

41. Directrix: $y = -3$

42. Focus: $(0, 3)$

43. Focus: $\left(\dfrac{3}{2}, 0\right)$

44. Focus: $(5, 0)$

45. Focus: $(0, 4)$

46. Focus: $(-3, 0)$

47. Focus: $\left(0, -\dfrac{3}{4}\right)$

Solar Energy In Exercises 48 and 49, use the following information.

A solar dish provides electricity in remote areas using a parabolic reflector to concentrate sunlight onto a high-efficiency engine, where it heats helium to 650°C to power the engine. The engine is located at the focus of the reflector.

48. Write an equation for the cross section of the dish with its vertex at the origin.

49. How deep is the dish?

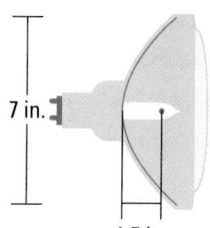

8.5 m

4.5 m

Automotive Engineering In Exercises 50 and 51, use the following information.

The filament of a light bulb is a thin wire that glows when electricity passes through it. The filament of a car headlight is at the focus of a parabolic reflector, which sends light out in a straight beam. The filament is 1.5 inches from the vertex.

50. Write an equation for the cross section.

51. How deep is the reflector?

7 in.

1.5 in.

52. Solar Cooking You can make a solar hot dog cooker by shaping foil-lined cardboard into a parabolic trough and passing a wire through the focus of each end piece. For the trough shown, how far from the bottom, to the nearest tenth of an inch, should the wire be placed?

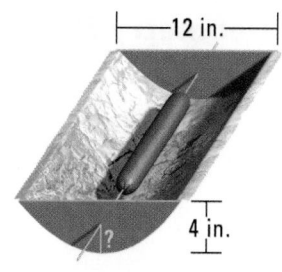

12 in.

4 in.

?

53. Reasoning Suppose that $x^2 = 4py$ and $y = ax^2$ represent the same parabola. Explain how a and p are related.

54. Challenge For an equation of the form $y = ax^2$, describe what effect increasing $|a|$ has on the focus and directrix of the parabola.

55. Multiple Choice In which direction does the parabola $x^2 = -4y$ open?

    (A) up   **(B)** down

    (C) left   **(D)** right

56. Multiple Choice What is the focus of the parabola $y^2 = 10x$?

    (F) $(0, 10)$ **(G)** $(10, 0)$

    (H) $\left(\frac{5}{2}, 0\right)$ **(J)** $\left(0, \frac{5}{2}\right)$

57. Multiple Choice What is the directrix of the parabola $x^2 = -12y$?

    (A) $x = 3$ **(B)** $x = -3$

    (C) $y = 3$ **(D)** $y = -3$

58. Multiple Choice What is the directrix of the parabola $15y + 3x^2 = 0$?

    (F) $x = -5$ **(G)** $x = -1.25$

    (H) $y = 1.25$ **(J)** $y = -1.25$

Mixed Review

Solving Equations Solve the equation by completing the square. *(Lesson 5.7)*

59. $x^2 - 4x = 7$ **60.** $x^2 + 8x = -2$ **61.** $x^2 + 12x = -18$

62. $2x^2 - 16x = 2$ **63.** $x^2 + 5x = 7$ **64.** $x^2 - 9x = -24$

Combinations Find the number of combinations given by the expression. *(Lesson 10.4)*

65. $_5C_2$ **66.** $_6C_3$ **67.** $_4C_2$

68. $_8C_7$ **69.** $_6C_4$ **70.** $_5C_3$

71. $_8C_6$ **72.** $_6C_2$ **73.** $_5C_4$

Evaluating Functions Evaluate the six trigonometric functions of the angle θ. *(Lesson 12.1)*

74. 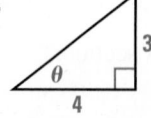   **75.** 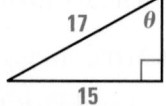   **76.**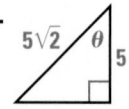

Geometry Skills

Spheres Find the volume of the sphere. Round your answer to two decimal places.

77. 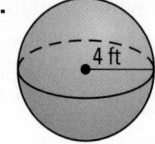   **78.** 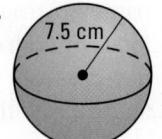   **79.**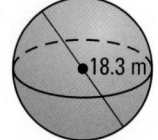

13.3 Circles

GOAL Graph and write equations of circles.

Key Words
- circle
- center
- radius

Can you see the beam from a lighthouse?

You will use a model for a circle in Example 4 to describe the beam from a lighthouse.

A **circle** is the set of all points P in a plane that are equidistant from a fixed point, called the **center** of the circle. The distance between the center and any point on the circle is the **radius**.

Prerequisite Skills

Simplify.

1. $\sqrt{28}$

2. $\sqrt{150}$

Evaluate.

3. $\left(\sqrt{5}\right)^2$

4. $\left(\sqrt{17}\right)^2$

Standard Equation of a Circle with Center at (0, 0)

The standard form of the equation of a circle with center at (0, 0) and radius r is as follows:

$$x^2 + y^2 = r^2$$

EXAMPLE A circle with center at (0, 0) and radius 2 has this equation:

$$x^2 + y^2 = 4$$

EXAMPLE ① Graph an Equation of a Circle

Graph $x^2 = -y^2 + 36$.

Solution

❶ **Write** the equation in standard form.

$$x^2 = -y^2 + 36 \qquad \text{Write original equation.}$$
$$x^2 + y^2 = 36 \qquad \text{Add } y^2 \text{ to each side.}$$

❷ **Identify** the center and the radius. In this form you can see that the graph is a circle with center at the origin and with radius $r = \sqrt{36} = 6$.

❸ **Plot** several points that are 6 units from the origin. The points (0, 6), (6, 0), (0, −6), and (−6, 0) are most convenient.

❹ **Draw** a circle that passes through the four points.

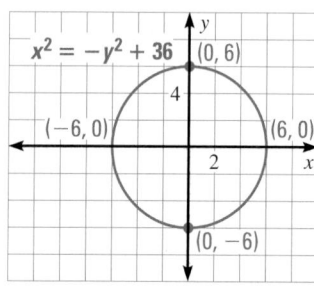

Checkpoint ✓ *Graph an Equation of a Circle*

Graph the equation. Identify the radius of the circle.

1. $x^2 + y^2 = 64$

2. $x^2 = 1 - y^2$

3. $x^2 - 18 = -y^2$

EXAMPLE 2 Write an Equation of a Circle

The point (3, 1) lies on a circle with center at the origin. Write the standard form of the equation of the circle.

Solution

Because the point (3, 1) is on the circle, the radius of the circle must be the distance between the center (0, 0) and the point (3, 1).

$$r = \sqrt{(x_2 - x_1)^2 + (y_2 - y_1)^2}$$ Use the distance formula.

$$= \sqrt{(3 - 0)^2 + (1 - 0)^2}$$ Substitute values.

$$= \sqrt{10}$$ Simplify. The radius is $\sqrt{10}$.

Use the standard form with $r = \sqrt{10}$ to write an equation of the circle.

$$x^2 + y^2 = r^2$$ Standard form

$$x^2 + y^2 = \left(\sqrt{10}\right)^2$$ Substitute $\sqrt{10}$ for r.

$$x^2 + y^2 = 10$$ Simplify.

Tangent Lines to Circles A theorem in geometry states that a line is perpendicular to a circle's radius if and only if it is tangent to the circle at its endpoint on the circle.

As shown in the diagram, $\overleftrightarrow{AB}$ is perpendicular to $\overline{BC}$, so $\overleftrightarrow{AB}$ is tangent to the circle at B.

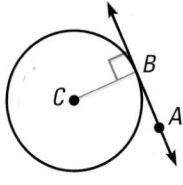

EXAMPLE 3 Write an Equation of a Tangent Line

Write an equation of the line that is tangent to the circle $x^2 + y^2 = 13$ at $(-3, 2)$.

Solution

A line is tangent to the circle at $(-3, 2)$ if it is perpendicular to the radius of the circle at $(-3, 2)$.

❶ *Calculate* the slope of the radius through $(-3, 2)$ and center $(0, 0)$.

$$m = \frac{2 - 0}{-3 - 0} = -\frac{2}{3}$$

❷ *Find* the slope of the tangent line at $(-3, 2)$. Because the tangent line at $(-3, 2)$ is perpendicular to this radius, its slope is the negative reciprocal of $-\frac{2}{3}$, or $\frac{3}{2}$.

❸ *Write* an equation. Use point-slope form.

$$y - y_1 = m(x - x_1)$$ Point-slope form

$$y - 2 = \frac{3}{2}[x - (-3)]$$ Substitute $(-3, 2)$ for (x_1, y_1) and $\frac{3}{2}$ for m.

$$y = \frac{3}{2}x + \frac{13}{2}$$ Solve for y.

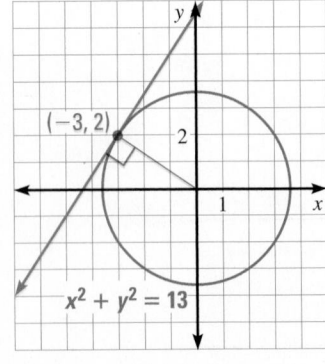

Write the standard form of the equation of the circle that passes through the given point with center at the origin.

4. $(4, 3)$

5. $(-2, 1)$

Write an equation of the line that is tangent to the given circle at the given point.

6. $x^2 + y^2 = 10$; $(1, 3)$

7. $x^2 + y^2 = 17$; $(4, -1)$

EXAMPLE **4** **Use a Circle as a Model**

Lighthouse The beam of a light from a lighthouse can be seen for up to 20 miles from the lighthouse.

a. Write an inequality to describe the region in which the lighthouse beam is visible. Assume that the lighthouse is at the origin.

b. You are on a ship that is 10 miles east and 16 miles north of the lighthouse. Can you see the lighthouse beam from your ship?

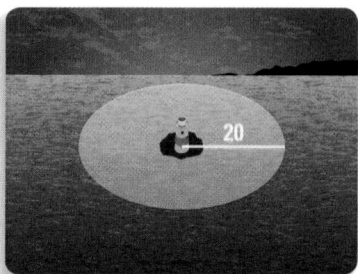

Solution

a. The region in which the lighthouse beam is visible is a circle, with a radius of 20 miles. Because you can see the lighthouse beam from any point within the boundary of the circle with a radius of 20 miles, the region where the beam is visible is best described with an inequality.

$x^2 + y^2 < r^2$ Standard form of a circle inequality

$x^2 + y^2 < 20^2$ Substitute 20 for r.

$x^2 + y^2 < 400$ Simplify.

b. To determine whether or not you can see the lighthouse beam, substitute the coordinates of your ship into the inequality from part (a).

$x^2 + y^2 < 400$ Inequality from part (a)

$(10)^2 + (16)^2 \overset{?}{<} 400$ Substitute 10 for x and 16 for y.

$100 + 256 \overset{?}{<} 400$ Simplify.

$356 < 400$ The inequality is true.

ANSWER ▶ Because the inequality is true for the coordinates of your ship, you can see the lighthouse beam.

Checkpoint ✓ **Use a Circular Model**

8. In Example 4, suppose your ship is located 16 miles north and 16 miles west of the lighthouse. Can you see the lighthouse beam from your ship?

Guided Practice

Vocabulary Check

1. Copy and complete the statement: The set of all points in a plane that are equidistant from a fixed point is a(n) __?__.

2. Copy and complete the statement: The distance between the center of a circle and any point on the circle is the __?__.

3. How are the slope of a line tangent to a circle and the slope of the radius at the point of tangency related?

Skill Check

Write the standard form of the equation of the circle with the given radius and center at (0, 0).

4. 3   **5.** 5   **6.** 6

7. $\sqrt{2}$ **8.** $\sqrt{3}$ **9.** $5\sqrt{2}$

Graph the equation. Identify the radius of the circle.

10. $x^2 + y^2 = 49$ **11.** $x^2 + y^2 = 121$ **12.** $x^2 + y^2 = 81$

13. $y^2 = 169 - x^2$ **14.** $5x^2 + 5y^2 = 500$ **15.** $2x^2 + 2y^2 = 32$

16. Swimming Pool A community swimming pool for very young children is circular with a diameter of 38 feet. Write the standard form of the equation of the boundary of the swimming pool if the center is at the origin.

Practice and Applications

STUDENT HELP

HOMEWORK HELP
Example 1: Exs. 17–31, 49–54
Example 2: Exs. 32–48
Example 3: Exs. 55–60
Example 4: Exs. 61–67

Matching Graphs **Match the equation with its graph.**

17. $x^2 + y^2 = 9$ **18.** $x^2 + y^2 = 36$ **19.** $x^2 + y^2 = 4$

20. $x^2 + y^2 = 6$ **21.** $x^2 + y^2 = 16$ **22.** $x^2 + y^2 = 3$

A. 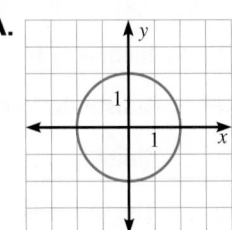   **B.** 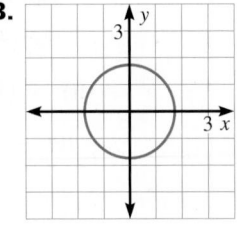   **C.**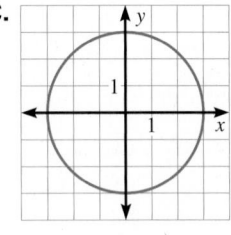

D. 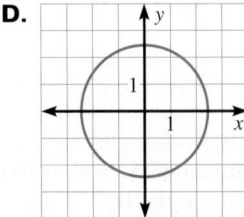   **E.** 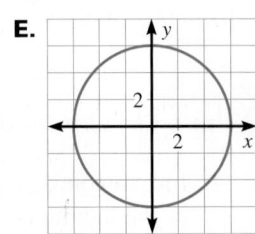   **F.**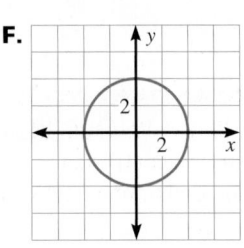

Graphing Graph the equation. Identify the radius of the circle.

23. $x^2 + y^2 = 1$ **24.** $x^2 + y^2 = 49$ **25.** $x^2 + y^2 = 121$

26. $y^2 = 196 - x^2$ **27.** $x^2 = 400 - y^2$ **28.** $10x^2 + 10y^2 = 250$

29. $4x^2 + 4y^2 = 64$ **30.** $8y^2 = 72 - 8x^2$ **31.** $16x^2 + 16y^2 = 32$

Writing Equations Write the standard form of the equation of the circle with the given radius and center at (0, 0).

32. 6   **33.** 15   **34.** $\sqrt{7}$ **35.** $\sqrt{19}$

36. $\sqrt{30}$ **37.** $4\sqrt{3}$ **38.** $5\sqrt{6}$ **39.** $2\sqrt{10}$

40. Error Analysis Describe and correct the error in writing an equation of the circle with radius 9 and center (0, 0).

$$x^2 + y^2 = 9 \quad \times$$

Writing Equations Write the standard form of the equation of the circle that passes through the given point with center at (0, 0).

41. (3, 0)   **42.** (0, −8)   **43.** (6, −8)   **44.** (3, −1)

45. (−4, −5)   **46.** (−3, 3)   **47.** (4, 6)   **48.** (−5, 10)

Graphing Tell whether the graph of the equation is a circle or a parabola. Then graph the equation.

49. $5x^2 + 5y^2 = 5$ **50.** $x^2 + y = 0$ **51.** $x^2 + y^2 = 225$

52. $4x^2 + y = 0$ **53.** $9x^2 + 9y^2 = 81$ **54.** $2x - y^2 = 0$

Tangent Lines Write an equation of the line that is tangent to the given circle at the given point.

55. $x^2 + y^2 = 32;\ (4, -4)$ **56.** $x^2 + y^2 = 5;\ (2, -1)$

57. $x^2 + y^2 = 40;\ (2, -6)$ **58.** $x^2 + y^2 = 13;\ (-3, 2)$

59. $x^2 + y^2 = 26;\ (-1, 5)$ **60.** $x^2 + y^2 = 89;\ (-5, 8)$

Park Security In Exercises 61 and 62, use the following information.

Security lights are placed along the circular boundary of a recreation park. The center of the park is located at the origin. One security light is located at (−5, 3).

61. What is the radius of the circular recreation park?

62. Write an equation that represents the boundary of the recreation park.

Commuter Trains In Exercises 63 and 64, use the following information.

A city's commuter train system has several stations that are within the downtown zone. The downtown zone has a radius of 3 miles. Suppose the center of the downtown zone is located at the origin.

63. Write an inequality that describes the downtown zone of the commuter train system.

64. The North Station is 2 miles north and 2 miles west of the center of the downtown zone. Is the North Station in the downtown zone?

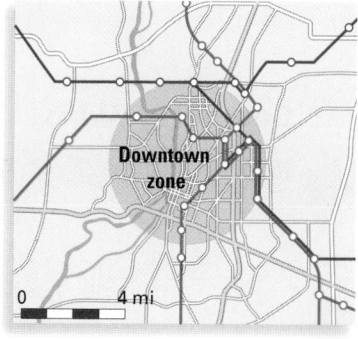

Survey In Exercises 65–67, use the following information.

A market research company would like to survey people who live and work within 15 miles of a stadium. In order to better define the survey region, the research company uses a coordinate plane with the location of the stadium at the origin.

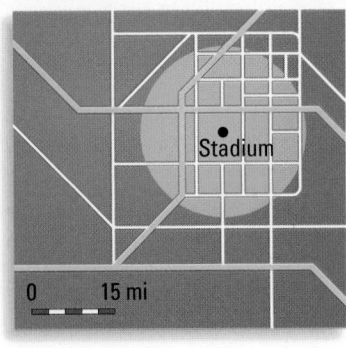

65. Write an inequality that describes the region in which the survey was conducted.

66. Your house is located 8 miles east and 11 miles north of the stadium. Do you live in the company's survey region?

67. Your friend's house is located 10 miles east and 11 miles south of the stadium. Does your friend live in the company's survey region?

Standardized Test Practice

68. **Multiple Choice** What is the standard form of the equation of a circle with a radius of $3\sqrt{6}$ and center at the origin?

(**A**) $x^2 + y^2 = 9$ (**B**) $2x^2 + 2y^2 = 54$

(**C**) $x^2 + y^2 = 54$ (**D**) $x^2 + y^2 = 6$

69. **Multiple Choice** What is the standard form of the equation of a circle that passes through $(-5, 1)$ with center at the origin?

(**F**) $3x^2 + 3y^2 = 75$ (**G**) $x^2 + y^2 = 26$

(**H**) $x^2 + y^2 = 1$ (**J**) $x^2 + y^2 = -26$

70. **Multiple Choice** What is the radius of the circle $3x^2 + 3y^2 = 54$?

(**A**) $3\sqrt{2}$ (**B**) $3\sqrt{6}$

(**C**) 18   (**D**) 54

Mixed Review

Types of Samples Classify the sample as *random*, *convenience*, *self-selected*, or *systematic*. Explain your reasoning. *(Lesson 10.2)*

71. The owners of a fast food chain want to measure employee job satisfaction. Every employee from one location is given a survey.

72. A newspaper publisher has an alphabetical listing of newspaper subscribers. The publisher asks every fifth person on the list whether he or she is satisfied with the delivery service.

Graphing Graph one cycle of the function. *(Lesson 12.3)*

73. $y = \sin x$ **74.** $y = 3 \cos x$ **75.** $y = 5 \sin x$

76. $y = \sin 180x$ **77.** $y = \cos 90x$ **78.** $y = 2 \cos 270x$

Geometry Skills

Congruent Arcs Tell whether the red arcs are congruent. Explain why or why not.

79.
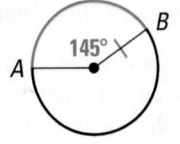
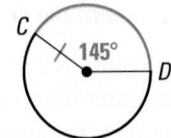

80.
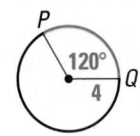

TECHNOLOGY 13.3

Graphing Circles

EXAMPLE

Use a graphing calculator to graph $x^2 + y^2 = 25$.

SOLUTION

1 Solve the equation for y.

$$x^2 + y^2 = 25$$
$$y^2 = 25 - x^2$$
$$y = \pm\sqrt{25 - x^2}$$

Together the functions $y = \sqrt{25 - x^2}$ and $y = -\sqrt{25 - x^2}$ represent the circle.

2 Enter the two functions into the graphing calculator as y_1 and y_2. You can enter the second equation as as $-y_1$.

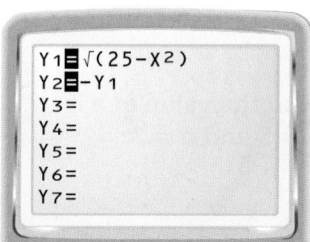

3 The graphs are shown in the standard viewing window. Because the calculator screen is not square, a horizontal distance of 1 unit is longer than a vertical distance of 1 unit, and the circle is stretched into an oval.

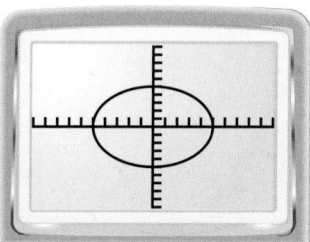

4 Set the viewing window so that the axes have the same scale. Press **ZOOM** and select ZSquare from the menu. Some calculators may not connect the ends of the two graphs.

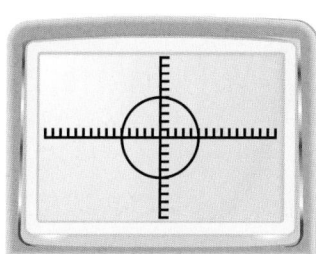

EXERCISES

Use a graphing calculator to graph the equation. Use a viewing window with axes that have the same scale.

1. $x^2 + y^2 = 25$ **2.** $x^2 + y^2 = 49$ **3.** $x^2 + y^2 = 36$

4. $4x^2 + 4y^2 = 144$ **5.** $3x^2 + 3y^2 = 30$ **6.** $6x^2 + 6y^2 = 6$

7. $y^2 = 64 - x^2$ **8.** $x^2 = 4 - y^2$ **9.** $5y^2 = 25 - 5x^2$

13.4 Ellipses

Key Words
- ellipse
- foci
- vertices
- major axis
- center
- co-vertices
- minor axis

GOAL Graph and write equations of ellipses.

An **ellipse** is the set of all points P in a plane such that the sum of the distances between P and two fixed points, called the **foci**, is a constant.

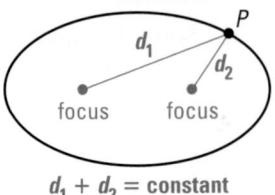

$d_1 + d_2 = $ constant

Prerequisite Skills

Find the value of c if $a = 4$ and $b = 2$.

1. $c^2 = a^2 + b^2$

2. $c^2 = a^2 - b^2$

Find the value of a if $c = 5$ and $b = 3$.

3. $c^2 = a^2 + b^2$

4. $c^2 = a^2 - b^2$

The line through the foci intersects the ellipse at the two **vertices**. The **major axis** joins the vertices. Its midpoint is the **center** of the ellipse. The line perpendicular to the major axis at the center intersects the ellipse at the two **co-vertices**. The **minor axis** joins the co-vertices. In this lesson, you will study ellipses that have a horizontal or vertical major axis.

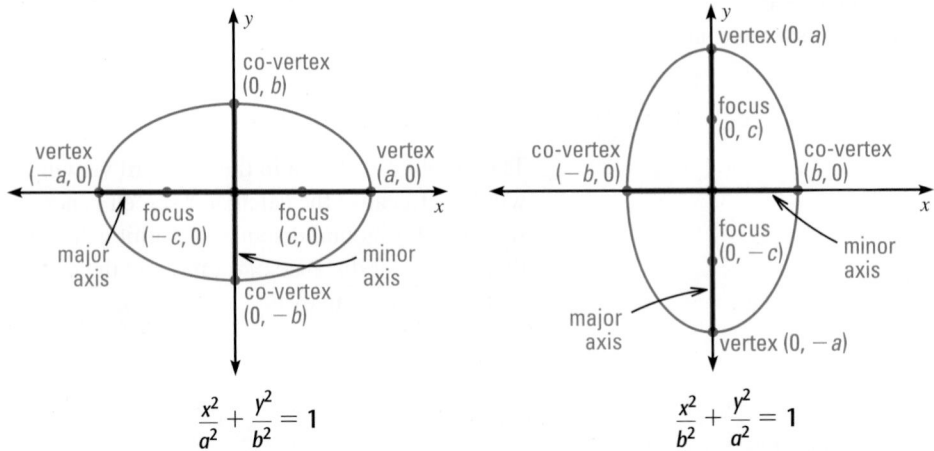

Ellipse with horizontal major axis

$$\frac{x^2}{a^2} + \frac{y^2}{b^2} = 1$$

Ellipse with vertical major axis

$$\frac{x^2}{b^2} + \frac{y^2}{a^2} = 1$$

The Standard Equation of an Ellipse with Center at (0, 0)

The standard form of the equation of an ellipse with center at (0, 0) is as follows:

EQUATION	MAJOR AXIS	VERTICES	CO-VERTICES
$\dfrac{x^2}{a^2} + \dfrac{y^2}{b^2} = 1$	Horizontal	$(\pm a, 0)$	$(0, \pm b)$
$\dfrac{x^2}{b^2} + \dfrac{y^2}{a^2} = 1$	Vertical	$(0, \pm a)$	$(\pm b, 0)$

The major and minor axes are of lengths $2a$ and $2b$, respectively, where $a > b > 0$.

The foci of the ellipse lie on the major axis, c units from the center where $c^2 = a^2 - b^2$.

EXAMPLE 1 Graph an Equation of an Ellipse

Graph $4x^2 + 25y^2 = 100$. Identify the vertices, co-vertices, and foci of the ellipse.

Solution

❶ **Write** the equation in standard form.

$$4x^2 + 25y^2 = 100$$ Write the original equation.

$$\frac{4x^2}{100} + \frac{25y^2}{100} = \frac{100}{100}$$ Divide each side by 100 to make the right-hand side equal to 1.

$$\frac{x^2}{25} + \frac{y^2}{4} = 1$$ Simplify.

❷ **Identify** the vertices, co-vertices, and foci. Note that $a^2 = 25$, so $a = 5$. Also $b^2 = 4$, so $b = 2$. Because the denominator of the x^2-term is greater than the denominator of the y^2-term, the major axis is horizontal.

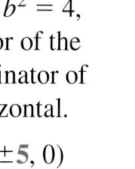

So, the vertices are at $(\pm a, 0) = (\pm 5, 0)$ and the co-vertices are at $(0, \pm b) = (0, \pm 2)$. Next, find the foci.

$$c^2 = a^2 - b^2 = 5^2 - 2^2 = 25 - 4 = 21, \text{ so } c = \pm\sqrt{21}$$

❸ **Draw** the ellipse that passes through each vertex and co-vertex.

Checkpoint ✓ **Graph an Equation of an Ellipse**

1. Graph $4x^2 + y^2 = 4$. Identify the vertices, co-vertices, and foci of the ellipse.

EXAMPLE 2 Write an Equation of an Ellipse

Write an equation of the ellipse that has a vertex at $(0, 4)$, a co-vertex at $(-3, 0)$, and a center at $(0, 0)$.

Solution

❶ **Sketch** the ellipse. By symmetry you know the ellipse has a vertex at $(0, -4)$ and a co-vertex at $(3, 0)$.

❷ **Identify** the values of a and b. Because the vertex is on the y-axis, the major axis is vertical with $a = 4$. The minor axis is horizontal with $b = 3$.

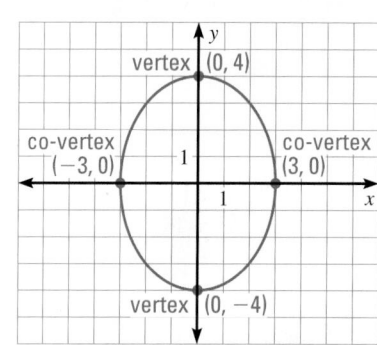

❸ **Write** an equation.

$$\frac{x^2}{b^2} + \frac{y^2}{a^2} = 1$$ Equation for an ellipse with a vertical major axis

$$\frac{x^2}{3^2} + \frac{y^2}{4^2} = 1$$ Substitute 4 for a and 3 for b.

$$\frac{x^2}{9} + \frac{y^2}{16} = 1$$ Simplify.

EXAMPLE 3 · Write an Equation of an Ellipse

Write an equation of the ellipse that has a vertex at (−8, 0), a focus at (4, 0), and center at (0, 0).

① **Sketch** the ellipse. By symmetry you know the ellipse has a vertex at (8, 0) and a focus at (−4, 0).

② **Identify** the values of a and b. The major axis is horizontal with $a = 8$ and $c = 4$.

$$c^2 = a^2 - b^2$$
$$4^2 = 8^2 - b^2$$
$$b^2 = 48$$
$$b = \sqrt{48} \text{ or } 4\sqrt{3}$$

③ **Write** an equation.

$$\frac{x^2}{a^2} + \frac{y^2}{b^2} = 1 \qquad \text{Equation for an ellipse with a horizontal major axis}$$

$$\frac{x^2}{8^2} + \frac{y^2}{(4\sqrt{3})^2} = 1 \qquad \text{Substitute 8 for } a \text{ and } 4\sqrt{3} \text{ for } b.$$

$$\frac{x^2}{64} + \frac{y^2}{48} = 1 \qquad \text{Simplify.}$$

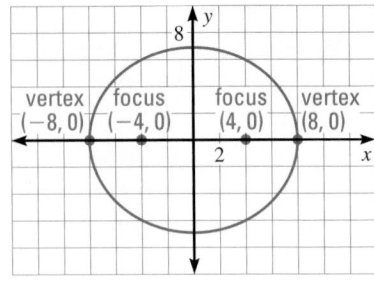

vertex (−8, 0) focus (−4, 0) focus (4, 0) vertex (8, 0)

 **Write an Equation of an Ellipse**

2. Write an equation of an ellipse that has a vertex at (4, 0), a co-vertex at (0, 2), and a center at (0, 0).

MARS ROVER The image shown is an artist's version of the landing of the Mars rover Spirit.

EXAMPLE 4 · Find the Area of an Ellipse

Mars On January 3, 2004, the Mars rover Spirit bounced on its air bags to land within Gusev crater. Scientists estimated that there was a 99% chance the rover would land inside an ellipse with a major axis 81 kilometers long and a minor axis 12 kilometers long. Write an equation of the ellipse. Then find its area using the formula for the area of an ellipse, $A = \pi ab$.

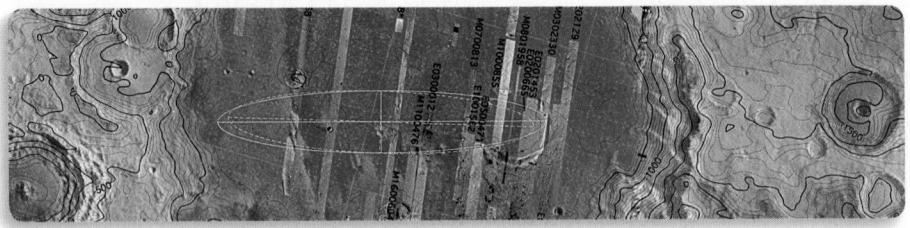

Solution

The major axis is horizontal, with $a = \frac{81}{2} = 40.5$ and $b = \frac{12}{2} = 6$.

An equation is $\frac{x^2}{40.5^2} + \frac{y^2}{6^2} = 1$, or $\frac{x^2}{1640.25} + \frac{y^2}{36} = 1$.

The area is $A = \pi(40.5)(6) = 243\pi \approx 763.41$ square kilometers.

13.4 Exercises

Guided Practice

Vocabulary Check

1. Copy and complete the statement: The line that joins the co-vertices of an ellipse is called the __?__.

2. Copy and complete the statement: The midpoint of the major axis of an ellipse is called the __?__ of the ellipse.

Skill Check

Graph the equation. Identify the vertices, co-vertices, and foci of the ellipse.

3. $\frac{x^2}{9} + \frac{y^2}{25} = 1$

4. $\frac{x^2}{16} + \frac{y^2}{4} = 1$

5. $\frac{x^2}{49} + \frac{y^2}{36} = 1$

Find the coordinates of the foci of the ellipse with the given characteristics and center at (0, 0).

6. Vertices: $(-5, 0)$, $(5, 0)$
   Co-vertices: $(0, -4)$, $(0, 4)$

7. Vertices: $(0, -10)$, $(0, 10)$
   Co-vertices: $(-8, 0)$, $(8, 0)$

Write an equation of the ellipse with the given characteristics and center at (0, 0).

8. Vertex: $(0, 3)$
   Co-vertex: $(-2, 0)$

9. Vertex: $(-10, 0)$
   Co-vertex: $(0, 5)$

10. Vertex: $(5, 0)$
    Focus: $\left(\sqrt{21}, 0\right)$

11. Vertex: $(0, -8)$
    Focus: $(0, 7)$

12. Co-vertex: $(5, 0)$
    Focus: $\left(0, -\sqrt{11}\right)$

13. Co-vertex: $(0, -3)$
    Focus: $(2, 0)$

Practice and Applications

STUDENT HELP

HOMEWORK HELP
Example 1: Exs. 14–39,
  50–48
Example 2: Exs. 40–49,
  65–67
Example 3: Exs. 44–49,
  65–67
Example 4: Exs. 59–64

Matching Match the equation with its graph.

14. $\frac{x^2}{36} + \frac{y^2}{9} = 1$

15. $\frac{x^2}{49} + \frac{y^2}{16} = 1$

16. $\frac{x^2}{9} + \frac{y^2}{25} = 1$

17. $\frac{x^2}{16} + \frac{y^2}{16} = 1$

18. $\frac{x^2}{64} + \frac{y^2}{100} = 1$

19. $\frac{x^2}{16} + \frac{y^2}{49} = 1$

A.

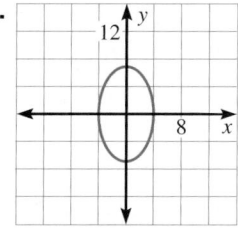

B.
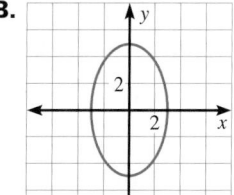

C.
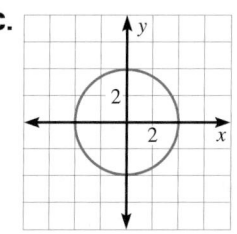

D.
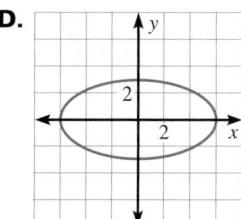

E.
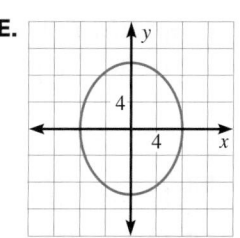

F.
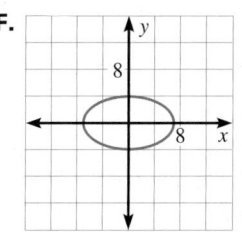

Identifying Parts Use the equation to identify the vertices, co-vertices, and foci of the ellipse.

20. $\dfrac{x^2}{121} + \dfrac{y^2}{25} = 1$

21. $\dfrac{x^2}{64} + \dfrac{y^2}{81} = 1$

22. $\dfrac{x^2}{9} + \dfrac{y^2}{4} = 1$

23. $\dfrac{x^2}{36} + \dfrac{y^2}{16} = 1$

24. $\dfrac{x^2}{100} + \dfrac{y^2}{75} = 1$

25. $\dfrac{x^2}{49} + \dfrac{y^2}{53} = 1$

26. $x^2 + 9y^2 = 9$

27. $25x^2 + 16y^2 = 400$

28. $50x^2 + 9y^2 = 450$

Graphing Ellipses Graph the equation. Identify the vertices, co-vertices, and foci of the ellipse.

29. $\dfrac{x^2}{36} + \dfrac{y^2}{49} = 1$

30. $\dfrac{x^2}{81} + \dfrac{y^2}{9} = 1$

31. $\dfrac{x^2}{144} + \dfrac{y^2}{25} = 1$

32. $\dfrac{x^2}{49} + \dfrac{y^2}{100} = 1$

33. $\dfrac{x^2}{1} + \dfrac{y^2}{9} = 1$

34. $\dfrac{x^2}{64} + \dfrac{y^2}{169} = 1$

35. $4x^2 + y^2 = 36$

36. $9x^2 + 16y^2 = 144$

37. $25x^2 + 49y^2 = 1225$

Error Analysis Describe and correct the error in graphing the ellipse.

38.

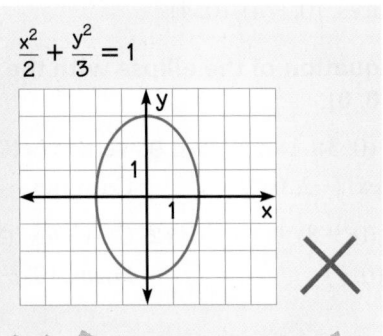

$\dfrac{x^2}{2} + \dfrac{y^2}{3} = 1$

39.

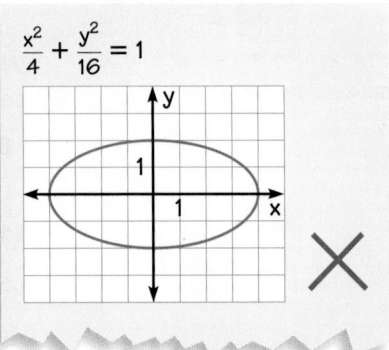

$\dfrac{x^2}{4} + \dfrac{y^2}{16} = 1$

Identifying Foci Find the coordinates of the foci of the ellipse with the given characteristics and center at **(0, 0)**.

40. Vertices: $(0, -7), (0, 7)$
Co-vertices: $(-5, 0), (5, 0)$

41. Vertices: $(-11, 0), (11, 0)$
Co-vertices: $(0, -4), (0, 4)$

42. Vertices: $(-9, 0), (9, 0)$
Co-vertices: $(0, -7), (0, 7)$

43. Vertices: $(0, -8), (0, 8)$
Co-vertices: $(-6, 0), (6, 0)$

Writing Equations Write an equation of the ellipse with the given characteristics and center at **(0, 0)**.

44. Vertex: $(0, 4)$
Co-vertex: $(-1, 0)$

45. Vertex: $(-8, 0)$
Co-vertex: $(0, 6)$

46. Vertex: $(0, -6)$
Focus: $(0, 3)$

47. Vertex: $(0, 9)$
Focus: $\left(0, 4\sqrt{2}\right)$

48. Co-vertex: $(4, 0)$
Focus: $(0, -3)$

49. Co-vertex: $(0, 6)$
Focus: $\left(-\sqrt{13}, 0\right)$

Graphing Tell whether the graph of the equation is a *parabola*, *circle*, or *ellipse*. Then graph the equation.

50. $x^2 + y^2 = 64$

51. $12x + y^2 = 0$

52. $\dfrac{x^2}{25} + \dfrac{y^2}{64} = 1$

53. $2x^2 - y = 0$

54. $\dfrac{x^2}{9} + \dfrac{y^2}{49} = 1$

55. $3x^2 + 3x^2 = 48$

56. $81x^2 + 100y^2 = 8100$

57. $6x^2 + 6y^2 = 150$

58. $16x + 4y^2 = 0$

WHITE HOUSE The Ellipse is the southern part of President's Park. It is used for large gatherings, including concerts in the summer and political demonstrations.

The Ellipse In Exercises 59–61, use the following information and the diagram shown.

A portion of the White House lawn is called the Ellipse. It is 1060 feet long and 890 feet wide.

59. Write an equation of the Ellipse.

60. How far from the center of the Ellipse are its foci?

61. Find the area of the Ellipse using the formula for the area of an ellipse, $A = \pi ab$.

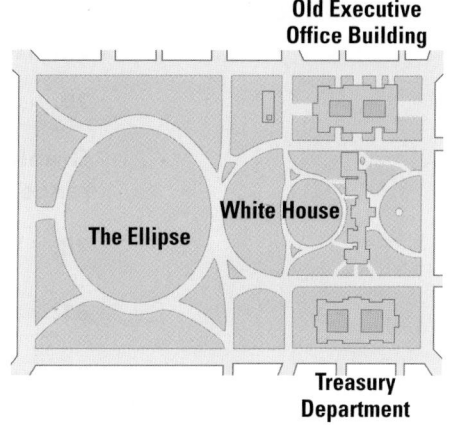

Reflecting Pool In Exercises 62–64, use the following information.

A reflecting pool in a city park is shaped like an ellipse. The pool is 72 feet long and 44 feet wide. The pool has two fountains that are located at the foci of the ellipse.

62. Write an equation of the reflecting pool.

63. How far from the center of the pool are the fountains?

64. Find the area of the pool using the formula for the area of an ellipse, $A = \pi ab$.

Mercury In Exercises 65–67, use the following information.

Mercury has an elliptical orbit. In this orbit, Mercury ranges from 29 million miles to 44 million miles from the sun, which is at one focus of the orbit.

65. Draw a sketch of the situation.

66. Find the values of a and c.

67. Write an equation of Mercury's orbit.

Standardized Test Practice

68. Multiple Choice Which point is a vertex of the ellipse $\dfrac{x^2}{16} + \dfrac{y^2}{144} = 1$?

  (A) $(12, 0)$ **(B)** $(4, 0)$ **(C)** $(0, 4)$ **(D)** $(0, 12)$

69. Multiple Choice Which point is a focus of the ellipse $\dfrac{x^2}{36} + \dfrac{y^2}{25} = 1$?

  (F) $(0, 11)$ **(G)** $(-11, 0)$ **(H)** $(0, -\sqrt{11})$ **(J)** $(\sqrt{11}, 0)$

70. Multiple Choice What is an equation of an ellipse with a vertex at $(8, 0)$ and a co-vertex at $(0, -5)$?

  (A) $\dfrac{x^2}{64} + \dfrac{y^2}{25} = 1$ **(B)** $\dfrac{x^2}{25} + \dfrac{y^2}{64} = 1$

  (C) $\dfrac{x^2}{8} + \dfrac{y^2}{5} = 1$ **(D)** $\dfrac{x^2}{5} + \dfrac{y^2}{8} = 1$

71. Multiple Choice What is an equation of an ellipse with a vertex at $(0, -7)$ and a focus at $(0, 6)$?

  (F) $\dfrac{x^2}{36} + \dfrac{y^2}{49} = 1$ **(G)** $\dfrac{x^2}{13} + \dfrac{y^2}{49} = 1$

  (H) $\dfrac{x^2}{49} + \dfrac{y^2}{36} = 1$ **(J)** $\dfrac{x^2}{49} + \dfrac{y^2}{13} = 1$

Inverses of Functions Find the inverse of the function. *(Lesson 7.5)*

72. $f(x) = 4x - 7$ **73.** $f(x) = 2x + 6$ **74.** $f(x) = 8x^3$

75. $f(x) = 9x^2, x \geq 0$ **76.** $f(x) = 2x^3 - 9$ **77.** $f(x) = 3x^5 + 4$

Graphing Functions Graph the function. State the domain and range of the function. *(Lesson 9.2)*

78. $y = \dfrac{3}{x + 5}$ **79.** $y = \dfrac{2}{x - 7} + 3$ **80.** $y = \dfrac{-1}{x + 4} + 4$

81. $y = \dfrac{2}{x - 4} - 6$ **82.** $y = \dfrac{4}{x + 1} - 5$ **83.** $y = \dfrac{-3}{x - 5} + 6$

Distance and Midpoint Find the distance between the two points. Then find the midpoint of the line segment joining the two points. *(Lesson 13.1)*

84. $(4, 2), (6, -4)$ **85.** $(-5, 2), (1, 6)$ **86.** $(-4, -4), (1, -3)$

87. $(3, 4), (8, 10)$ **88.** $(-1, 5), (7, 2)$ **89.** $(3, -1), (8, -6)$

Geometry Skills

Arc Length Use the following information to find the length of $\overset{\frown}{AB}$.

A proportion that relates arc length and central angle measure in a circle is given by $\dfrac{\text{length of } \overset{\frown}{AB}}{2\pi r} = \dfrac{m\overset{\frown}{AB}}{360}$ where $m\overset{\frown}{AB}$ is the measure of the arc and r is the radius of the circle.

90.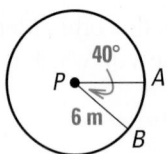

91.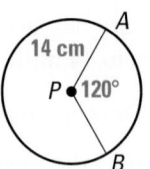

92.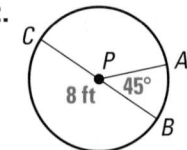

Quiz 1

Lesson 13.1   Find the distance between the two points. Then find the midpoint of the line segment joining the two points.

1. $(6, 3), (10, 7)$ **2.** $(3, -3), (8, 1)$ **3.** $(-5, 4), (3, -4)$

4. $(1, 0), (7, -4)$ **5.** $(-2, -6), (3, 4)$ **6.** $(1, 6), (9, -3)$

Lesson 13.2   Graph the equation. Identify the focus, directrix, and axis of symmetry of the parabola.

7. $x^2 = -24y$ **8.** $y^2 = 12x$ **9.** $x^2 = -10y$

10. Write the standard form of the equation of the parabola with a focus at $(-6, 0)$ and vertex at $(0, 0)$.

Lesson 13.3   Graph the equation. Identify the radius of the circle.

11. $x^2 + y^2 = 36$ **12.** $x^2 + y^2 = 81$ **13.** $x^2 = 100 - y^2$

Lesson 13.4   Graph the equation. Identify the vertices, co-vertices, and foci of the ellipse.

14. $\dfrac{x^2}{16} + \dfrac{y^2}{25} = 1$ **15.** $\dfrac{x^2}{81} + \dfrac{y^2}{64} = 1$ **16.** $\dfrac{x^2}{36} + \dfrac{y^2}{9} = 1$

13.5 Hyperbolas

Key Words

- hyperbola
- foci
- vertices
- transverse axis
- center

Prerequisite Skills

Tell whether the major axis of the ellipse is *vertical* or *horizontal*.

1. $\dfrac{x^2}{4} + \dfrac{y^2}{16} = 1$

2. $\dfrac{x^2}{9} + y^2 = 1$

3. $\dfrac{x^2}{25} + \dfrac{y^2}{20} = 1$

4. $\dfrac{x^2}{100} + \dfrac{y^2}{9} = 1$

GOAL Graph and write equations of hyperbolas.

A **hyperbola** is the set of all points P such that the difference of the distances from P to the two **foci** is a constant.

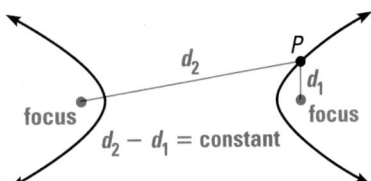

The line through the foci intersects the hyperbola at the two **vertices**. The **transverse axis** joins the vertices. Its midpoint is the **center** of the hyperbola.

A hyperbola has two *branches* and two *asymptotes*. The asymptotes contain the diagonals of a rectangle centered at the hyperbola's center, as shown.

Hyperbola with horizontal transverse axis

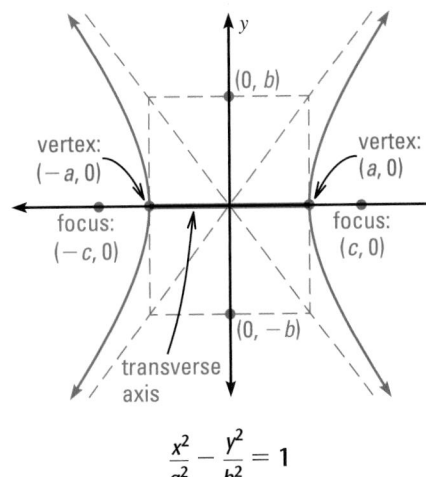

$$\frac{x^2}{a^2} - \frac{y^2}{b^2} = 1$$

Hyperbola with vertical transverse axis

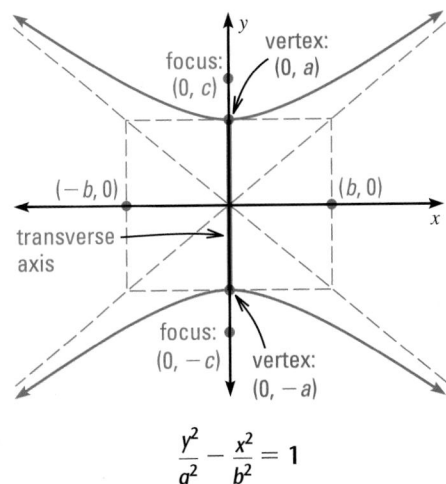

$$\frac{y^2}{a^2} - \frac{x^2}{b^2} = 1$$

STUDENT HELP

AVOID ERRORS

The equations of hyperbolas and ellipses are very similar. Notice that the equation of a hyperbola includes a difference while the equation of an ellipse includes a sum.

Standard Equation of a Hyperbola with Center at (0, 0)

The standard form of the equation of a hyperbola with center at (0, 0) is as follows:

EQUATION	TRANSVERSE AXIS	ASYMPTOTES	VERTICES
$\dfrac{x^2}{a^2} - \dfrac{y^2}{b^2} = 1$	horizontal	$y = \pm\dfrac{b}{a}x$	$(\pm a, 0)$
$\dfrac{y^2}{a^2} - \dfrac{x^2}{b^2} = 1$	vertical	$y = \pm\dfrac{a}{b}x$	$(0, \pm a)$

The foci of the hyperbola lie on the transverse axis, c units from the center where $c^2 = a^2 + b^2$.

EXAMPLE **1** **Graph an Equation of a Hyperbola**

Graph $25y^2 - 4x^2 = 100$. Identify the vertices, foci, and asymptotes.

Solution

1 ***Write*** the equation in standard form.

$$25y^2 - 4x^2 = 100 \qquad \text{Write original equation.}$$

$$\frac{y^2}{4} - \frac{x^2}{25} = 1 \qquad \text{Divide each side by 100 and simplify.}$$

2 ***Identify*** the vertices, foci, and asymptotes. Note that $a^2 = 4$, so $a = 2$. Also $b^2 = 25$, so $b = 5$. The y^2-term is positive, so the transverse axis is vertical and the vertices are at $(0, \pm 2)$.

$$c^2 = a^2 + b^2$$

$$c^2 = a^2 + b^2$$

$$= 2^2 + 5^2$$

$$= 29, \text{ so } c = \pm\sqrt{29}$$

The foci are $\left(0, \pm\sqrt{29}\right)$, and the asymptotes are $y = \pm\frac{a}{b}x$, or $y = \pm\frac{2}{5}x$.

3 ***Draw*** the hyperbola. Draw a rectangle centered at the origin that is $2a = 2(2) = 4$ units high and $2b = 2(5) = 10$ units wide. The asymptotes are the diagonals of the rectangle.

Draw the branches of the hyperbola passing through the vertices and approaching the asymptotes.

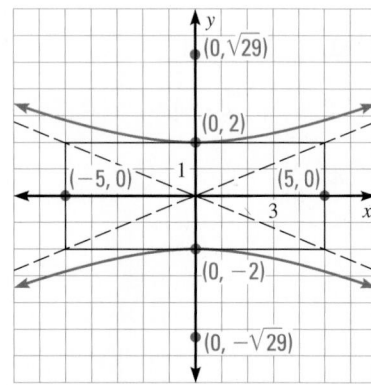

EXAMPLE **2** **Write an Equation of a Hyperbola**

Write an equation of the hyperbola with foci at $(-4, 0)$ and $(4, 0)$ and vertices at $(-3, 0)$ and $(3, 0)$.

Solution

The foci and vertices lie on the x-axis, so the transverse axis is horizontal. The foci are each 4 units from the center, so $c = 4$. The vertices are each 3 units from the center, so $a = 3$. Find the value of b.

$$c^2 = a^2 + b^2$$

$$(4)^2 = (3)^2 + b^2$$

$$b^2 = 7$$

Write an equation of the hyperbola.

$$\frac{x^2}{a^2} - \frac{y^2}{b^2} = 1 \qquad \text{Standard equation for hyperbola with horizontal axis}$$

$$\frac{x^2}{9} - \frac{y^2}{7} = 1 \qquad \text{Substitute } 3^2 = 9 \text{ for } a^2 \text{ and 7 for } b^2.$$

EXAMPLE **3** **Write a Hyperbolic Model**

Photography A hyperbolic mirror is used to take panoramic photographs. Light rays aimed at the focus behind the mirror are reflected to a camera positioned at the other focus. Computers can fix the distorted image to create a 360° view.

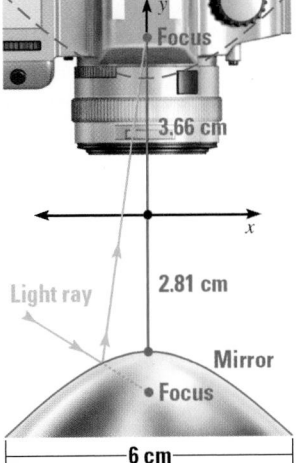

a. Write an equation for the cross section of the mirror shown.

b. The mirror is 6 centimeters wide. How tall is the mirror?

Solution

a. The diagram shows that $a = 2.81$ and $c = 3.66$. Find the value of b.

$$c^2 = a^2 + b^2$$

$$(3.66)^2 = (2.81)^2 + b^2$$

$$b \approx \sqrt{5.50}$$

Because the transverse axis is vertical, use the standard equation of a hyperbola with a vertical transverse axis.

$$\frac{y^2}{a^2} - \frac{x^2}{b^2} = 1 \qquad \text{Standard equation for hyperbola with vertical transverse axis}$$

$$\frac{y^2}{(2.81)^2} - \frac{x^2}{(\sqrt{5.50})^2} = 1 \qquad \text{Substitute 2.81 for } a \text{ and } \sqrt{5.50} \text{ for } b.$$

$$\frac{y^2}{7.90} - \frac{x^2}{5.50} = 1 \qquad \text{Simplify.}$$

b. To find how tall the mirror is, find the y-coordinate at the mirror's bottom edge. Because the mirror is 6 centimeters wide, substitute 3 for x in the equation and solve for y.

$$\frac{y^2}{7.90} - \frac{x^2}{5.50} = 1 \qquad \text{Write equation from part (a).}$$

$$\frac{y^2}{7.90} - \frac{3^2}{5.50} = 1 \qquad \text{Substitute 3 for } x.$$

$$y^2 \approx 20.83 \qquad \text{Solve for } y^2.$$

$$y \approx \pm 4.56 \qquad \text{Solve for } y.$$

ANSWER▶ The mirror is $-2.81 - (-4.56) = 1.75$ centimeters tall.

Checkpoint ✓ **Graph and Write Equations of Hyperbolas**

1. Graph $4x^2 - y^2 = 4$. Identify the vertices, foci, and asymptotes.

Write an equation of the hyperbola with the given foci and vertices.

2. Foci: $(-3, 0)$ and $(3, 0)$
Vertices: $(-2, 0)$ and $(2, 0)$

3. Foci: $(-6, 0)$ and $(6, 0)$
Vertices: $(-3, 0)$ and $(3, 0)$

Guided Practice

Vocabulary Check

Copy and complete the statement.

1. The line segment joining the vertices of a hyperbola is the __?__ .

2. A hyperbola is the set of all points P such that the __?__ of the distances between P and the foci is a constant.

Skill Check

Graph the equation. Identify the vertices, foci, and asymptotes of the hyperbola.

3. $\dfrac{x^2}{25} - \dfrac{y^2}{9} = 1$

4. $\dfrac{y^2}{16} - \dfrac{x^2}{36} = 1$

5. $\dfrac{y^2}{100} - \dfrac{x^2}{64} = 1$

6. $\dfrac{x^2}{6} - \dfrac{y^2}{16} = 1$

Write an equation of the hyperbola with the given foci and vertices.

7. Foci: $(-5, 0), (5, 0)$
Vertices: $(-3, 0), (3, 0)$

8. Foci: $(0, -9), (0, 9)$
Vertices: $(0, -6), (0, 6)$

9. Foci: $(-\sqrt{41}, 0), (\sqrt{41}, 0)$
Vertices: $(-4, 0), (4, 0)$

10. Foci: $(0, -8), (0, 8)$
Vertices: $(0, -\sqrt{55}), (0, \sqrt{55})$

Practice and Applications

Matching Match the equation with its graph.

11. $\dfrac{y^2}{16} - \dfrac{x^2}{9} = 1$

12. $\dfrac{x^2}{16} - \dfrac{y^2}{9} = 1$

13. $\dfrac{y^2}{9} - \dfrac{x^2}{16} = 1$

14. $\dfrac{x^2}{9} - \dfrac{y^2}{16} = 1$

15. $\dfrac{x^2}{25} - \dfrac{y^2}{49} = 1$

16. $\dfrac{y^2}{25} - \dfrac{x^2}{49} = 1$

A.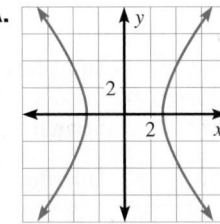

B.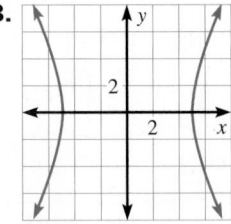

C.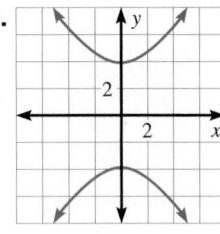

D.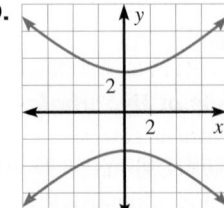

E.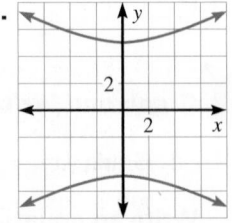

F.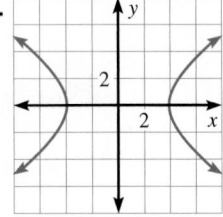

Identifying Foci Identify the foci of the hyperbola.

17. $x^2 - \dfrac{y^2}{4} = 1$

18. $\dfrac{x^2}{36} - \dfrac{y^2}{13} = 1$

19. $\dfrac{y^2}{16} - \dfrac{x^2}{20} = 1$

Hyperbolas Identify the vertices, foci, and asymptotes of the graph.

20. $\dfrac{y^2}{64} - \dfrac{x^2}{25} = 1$

21. $\dfrac{x^2}{16} - \dfrac{y^2}{49} = 1$

22. $\dfrac{y^2}{49} - \dfrac{x^2}{36} = 1$

23. $\dfrac{x^2}{27} - \dfrac{y^2}{9} = 1$

24. $49y^2 - 9x^2 = 441$

25. $4x^2 - 81y^2 = 324$

Graphing Graph the equation. Identify the vertices, foci, and asymptotes of the hyperbola.

26. $\dfrac{y^2}{4} - \dfrac{x^2}{9} = 1$

27. $\dfrac{y^2}{36} - \dfrac{x^2}{16} = 1$

28. $\dfrac{x^2}{49} - \dfrac{y^2}{81} = 1$

29. $\dfrac{x^2}{64} - \dfrac{y^2}{100} = 1$

30. $\dfrac{y^2}{25} - \dfrac{x^2}{49} = 1$

31. $\dfrac{x^2}{81} - \dfrac{y^2}{36} = 1$

32. $25x^2 - 16y^2 = 400$

33. $y^2 - 16x^2 = 16$

34. $4x^2 - 9y^2 = 36$

Error Analysis Describe and correct the error in graphing the equation.

35.

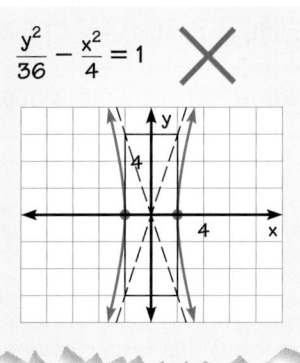

$\dfrac{y^2}{36} - \dfrac{x^2}{4} = 1$

36.

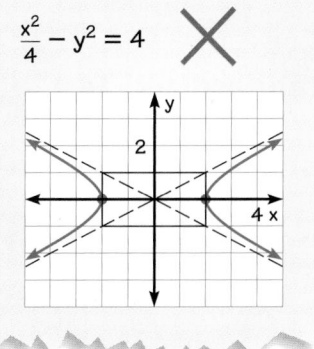

$\dfrac{x^2}{4} - y^2 = 4$

Writing Equations Write an equation of the hyperbola with the given foci and vertices.

37. Foci: $(0, -4), (0, 4)$
Vertices: $(0, -2), (0, 2)$

38. Foci: $(0, -10), (0, 10)$
Vertices: $(0, -6), (0, 6)$

39. Foci: $(-6, 0), (6, 0)$
Vertices: $(-3, 0), (3, 0)$

40. Foci: $(0, -12), (0, 12)$
Vertices: $(0, -7), (0, 7)$

41. Foci: $(0, -3), (0, 3)$
Vertices: $(0, -1), (0, 1)$

42. Foci: $\left(0, -2\sqrt{13}\right), \left(0, 2\sqrt{13}\right)$
Vertices: $(0, -6), (0, 6)$

Graphing Tell whether the graph of the equation is a *parabola*, *circle*, *ellipse*, or *hyperbola*. Then graph the equation.

43. $x^2 + y^2 = 49$

44. $\dfrac{x^2}{49} - \dfrac{y^2}{64} = 1$

45. $\dfrac{x^2}{25} + \dfrac{y^2}{9} = 1$

46. $x^2 + 16y = 0$

47. $15x^2 + 15y^2 = 60$

48. $\dfrac{x^2}{16} + \dfrac{y^2}{36} = 1$

49. Spinning Cube The outline of a cube spinning around an axis through a pair of opposite corners contains part of a hyperbola, as shown. The coordinates given represent a vertex and a focus of the hyperbola for a cube that measures 1 unit on each edge. Write an equation that models this hyperbola.

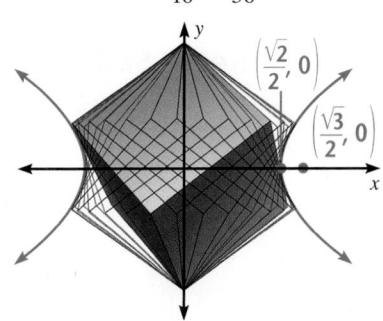

$\left(\dfrac{\sqrt{2}}{2}, 0\right)$

$\left(\dfrac{\sqrt{3}}{2}, 0\right)$

Science Link In Exercises 50 and 51, use the following information.

Each day, except at the fall and spring equinoxes, the tip of the shadow of a vertical pole traces a branch of a hyperbola across the ground. The diagram shows shadow paths for a 20 meter tall flagpole in a particular location.

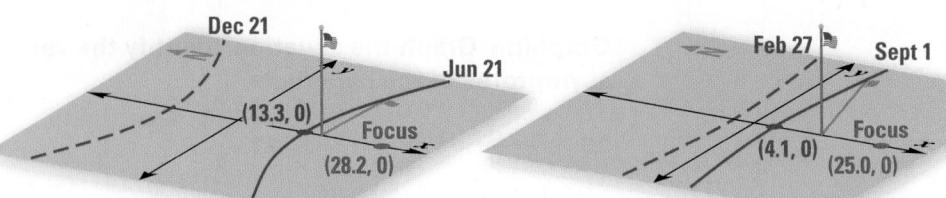

50. Write an equation of the hyperbola with center at the origin that models the June 21 path, given that $a = 13.3$ meters and $c = 28.2$ meters.

51. Write an equation of the hyperbola with center at the origin that models the September 1 path, given that $a = 4.1$ meters and $c = 25.0$ meters.

Standardized Test Practice

52. Multiple Choice What are the asymptotes of the hyperbola $\dfrac{y^2}{64} - \dfrac{x^2}{36} = 1$?

  A $y = \pm\dfrac{4}{3}x$ **B** $y = \pm\dfrac{3}{4}x$ **C** $y = \pm\dfrac{16}{9}x$ **D** $y = \pm\dfrac{9}{16}x$

53. Multiple Choice Which point is a focus of the hyperbola $\dfrac{x^2}{25} - \dfrac{y^2}{64} = 1$?

  F $(5, 0)$ **G** $(25, 0)$ **H** $(8, 0)$ **J** $\left(\sqrt{89}, 0\right)$

54. Multiple Choice What is an equation of the hyperbola with foci at $\left(0, -6\sqrt{3}\right)$ and $\left(0, 6\sqrt{3}\right)$ and with vertices at $(0, -8)$ and $(0, 8)$?

  A $\dfrac{x^2}{64} - \dfrac{y^2}{108} = 1$ **B** $\dfrac{x^2}{44} - \dfrac{y^2}{68} = 1$

  C $\dfrac{y^2}{64} - \dfrac{x^2}{44} = 1$ **D** $\dfrac{y^2}{108} - \dfrac{x^2}{64} = 1$

Mixed Review

Finding Matrix Products Find the product. If it is not defined, state the reason. *(Lesson 11.2)*

55. $\begin{bmatrix} -1 & 3 \end{bmatrix} \begin{bmatrix} 1 & 4 \\ 5 & -2 \end{bmatrix}$ **56.** $\begin{bmatrix} 2 & 3 \end{bmatrix} \begin{bmatrix} 6 & 0 \\ -1 & 3 \end{bmatrix}$

57. $\begin{bmatrix} 9 & -3 \\ 0 & 2 \end{bmatrix} \begin{bmatrix} 0 & 1 \\ 4 & -2 \end{bmatrix}$ **58.** $\begin{bmatrix} 5 & 0 \\ -4 & 1 \end{bmatrix} \begin{bmatrix} -3 & 2 \\ 6 & 2 \end{bmatrix}$

Solving Triangles Sketch $\triangle ABC$, then find all of the angle measures and side lengths. *(Lesson 12.5)*

59. $B = 68°, a = 17, c = 24$ **60.** $C = 104°, a = 21, b = 18$

61. $a = 11, b = 14, c = 9$ **62.** $a = 28, b = 20, c = 25$

Geometry Skills

Surface Area Find the surface area of the cone. Round your answer to the nearest whole number.

63.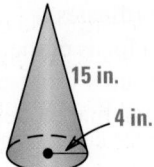

64.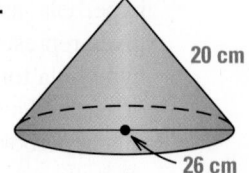

65.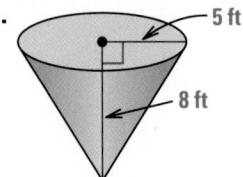

DEVELOPING CONCEPTS *(For use with Lesson 13.6)*

Exploring Conic Sections

Goal

Explore the intersection of a plane and a double cone.

Materials

- **graph paper**
- **flashlight**
- **tape**

QUESTION

How do a plane and a double cone intersect to form different conic sections?

The reason that parabolas, circles, ellipses, and hyperbolas are called *conics* or *conic sections* is that each can be formed by the intersection of a plane and a double cone, as shown below.

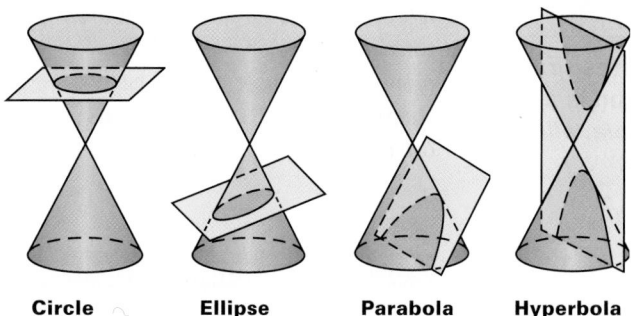

| Circle | Ellipse | Parabola | Hyperbola |

The beam of light from a flashlight is a cone. When the light hits a flat surface such as a wall, the edge of the beam of light forms a conic section.

EXPLORE

1 Work in a group. On a piece of graph paper, draw *x*- and *y*-axes to make a coordinate plane. Tape the paper to a wall.

2 Aim a flashlight so that the beam of light is perpendicular to the paper and forms a circle centered at the origin.

3 Trace the circle on the graph paper. Find the radius of the circle and use it to write the standard form of the equation of the circle.

4 Tilt the flashlight and aim it at the graph paper to form an ellipse with a vertical major axis and center at the origin. Trace the ellipse. Write the standard form of the equation of the ellipse.

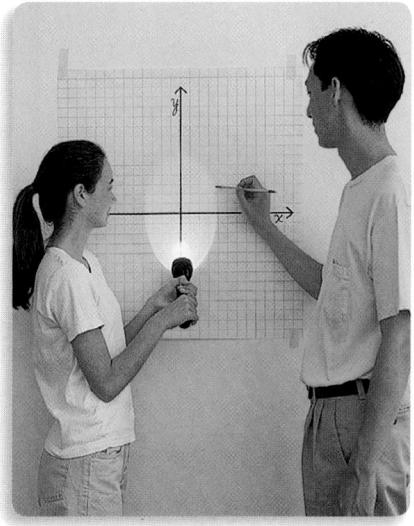

THINK ABOUT IT

1. Compare the equations of your circle and of your ellipse with the equations written by other groups. Are your equations the same? Why or why not?

2. Tilt the flashlight and aim it at the graph paper to form an ellipse with a horizontal major axis and center at the origin. Trace the ellipse. Write the standard form of the equation of the ellipse.

13.6 Graphing and Classifying Conics

Key Words

- conic sections (conics)
- general second-degree equation
- discriminant

GOAL Translate and graph conic sections.

What is an equation of a hyperbolic mirror?

In Exercise 45, you will write an equation of a hyperbolic mirror.

Parabolas, circles, ellipses, and hyperbolas are all curves that are formed by the intersection of a plane and a double cone. These shapes are called **conic sections** or simply **conics**.

Prerequisite Skills

Tell whether the graph of the equation is a *circle, parabola, ellipse,* or *hyperbola*.

1. $x^2 = 6 - y^2$

2. $\dfrac{x^2}{16} - \dfrac{y^2}{36} = 1$

3. $\dfrac{x^2}{25} + y^2 = 1$

4. $x = 6y^2$

Standard Equations of Translated Conics

In the following equations the point (h, k) is the *vertex* of the parabola and the *center* of the other conics.

Circle　　$(x - h)^2 + (y - k)^2 = r^2$

	HORIZONTAL AXIS	**VERTICAL AXIS**
Parabola	$(y - k)^2 = 4p(x - h)$	$(x - h)^2 = 4p(y - k)$
Ellipse	$\dfrac{(x - h)^2}{a^2} + \dfrac{(y - k)^2}{b^2} = 1$	$\dfrac{(x - h)^2}{b^2} + \dfrac{(y - k)^2}{a^2} = 1$
Hyperbola	$\dfrac{(x - h)^2}{a^2} - \dfrac{(y - k)^2}{b^2} = 1$	$\dfrac{(y - k)^2}{a^2} - \dfrac{(x - h)^2}{b^2} = 1$

EXAMPLE 1 Graph a Translated Circle

Graph $(x - 2)^2 + (y + 3)^2 = 9$.

❶ *Compare* the given equation to the standard form of the equation of a circle, $(x - h)^2 + (y - k)^2 = r^2$. The graph is a circle with center at $(h, k) = (2, -3)$ and radius $r = \sqrt{9} = 3$. Plot the center.

❷ *Plot* several points that are each **3** units from the center.

First plot two points 3 units to the left and right of the center, $(-1, -3)$ and $(5, -3)$.

Then plot two points 3 units above and below the center, $(2, 0)$ and $(2, -6)$.

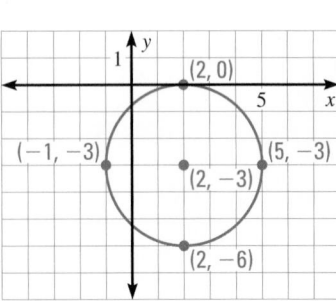

❸ *Draw* a circle that passes through the four points.

EXAMPLE 2 **Graph a Translated Hyperbola**

Graph $\dfrac{(y-3)^2}{4} - \dfrac{(x+1)^2}{9} = 1.$

Solution

❶ **Compare** the equation to the standard equations of translated conics. The form of the equation tells you that its graph is a hyperbola. The y^2-term is positive, so the transverse axis is vertical with center at $(h, k) = (-1, 3)$. You know $a^2 = 4$ so $a = 2$ and $b^2 = 9$ so $b = 3$.

❷ **Plot** the vertices $a = 2$ units above and below the center, at $(-1, 3 + 2) = (-1, 5)$ and $(-1, 3 - 2) = (-1, 1)$.

❸ **Identify** the foci using $c^2 = a^2 + b^2$. Substitute values and solve for c. The foci are $c = \sqrt{13} \approx 3.6$ units above and below the center at $(-1, 3 + 3.6) = (-1, 6.6)$ and $(-1, 3 - 3.6) = (-1, -0.6)$.

❹ **Draw** a rectangle centered at $(-1, 3)$ that is $2a = 4$ units high and $2b = 6$ units wide. The asymptotes of the hyperbola are the diagonals of the rectangle. Draw the hyperbola so that it passes through the vertices and approaches the asymptotes.

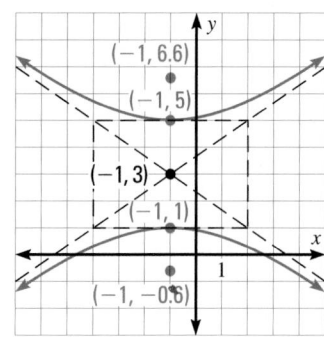

Checkpoint ✓ **Graph Equations of Translated Conics**

Graph the equation. Identify the important characteristics of the graph.

1. $(x + 1)^2 + (y - 2)^2 = 4$

2. $(x + 3)^2 - \dfrac{(y-4)^2}{4} = 1$

EXAMPLE 3 **Write an Equation of a Translated Parabola**

Write an equation of the parabola with vertex at $(-2, 3)$ and focus at $(-4, 3)$.

Solution

❶ **Plot** the given points. Sketch the parabola. The parabola opens left, so its equation has the form $(y - k)^2 = 4p(x - h)$ where $p < 0$.

❷ **Find** the values of h and k. The vertex is at $(h, k) = (-2, 3)$, so $h = -2$ and $k = 3$.

❸ **Find** the value of p. The vertex $(-2, 3)$ and focus $(-4, 3)$ both lie on the line $y = 3$. The distance between them is $|p| = |-4 - (-2)| = 2$. Because $p < 0$, $p = -2$, and $4p = -8$.

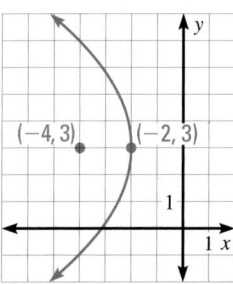

❹ **Write** the equation.

$(y - k)^2 = 4p(x - h)$ Standard form

$(y - 3)^2 = -8(x + 2)$ Substitute 3 for k, -8 for $4p$, and -2 for h.

EXAMPLE 4 **Write an Equation of a Translated Ellipse**

Write an equation of the ellipse with foci at (1, 2) and (7, 2) and co-vertices at (4, 0) and (4, 4).

❶ *Plot* the given points and make a rough sketch of the ellipse. Notice the foci lie on the major axis. The axis is horizontal, so the equation has this form:

$$\frac{(x - h)^2}{a^2} + \frac{(y - k)^2}{b^2} = 1$$

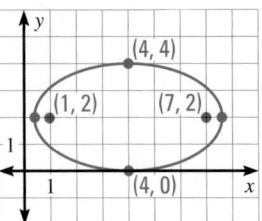

❷ *Find* the values of h and k. The center (h, k) is halfway between the foci.

$$(h, k) = \left(\frac{1 + 7}{2}, \frac{2 + 2}{2}\right) = (4, 2)$$

❸ *Find* the value of b, the distance between one co-vertex and the center $(4, 2)$. Also, find the value of c, the distance between one focus and the center $(4, 2)$. Use the co-vertex $(4, 4)$ and the focus $(1, 2)$.

$$b = |4 - 2| = 2 \quad \text{and} \quad c = |1 - 4| = 3$$

❹ *Find* the value of a. Because the equation is for an ellipse, use $a^2 = b^2 + c^2$.

$$a^2 = b^2 + c^2 = 2^2 + 3^2 = 13, \text{ so } a = \sqrt{13}$$

The standard form of the equation is $\dfrac{(x - 4)^2}{13} + \dfrac{(y - 2)^2}{4} = 1$.

 **Write an Equation of a Translated Conic**

Write an equation of the conic section.

3. Parabola with vertex at $(3, -1)$ and focus at $(3, 2)$

4. Hyperbola with vertices at $(-7, 3)$ and $(-1, 3)$ and foci at $(-9, 3)$

Classifying Conics The equation of any conic can be written in the form

$$Ax^2 + Bxy + Cy^2 + Dx + Ey + F = 0$$

which is called a **general second-degree equation** in x and y. The expression $B^2 - 4AC$ is called the **discriminant** of the equation. You can use the determinant to determine which type of conic an equation represents.

Classifying Conic Sections

If the graph of $Ax^2 + Bxy + Cy^2 + Dx + Ey + F = 0$ is a conic, then the type of conic can be determined by the following characteristics.

DISCRIMINANT	TYPE OF CONIC
$B^2 - 4AC < 0$, $B = 0$, and $A = C$	Circle
$B^2 - 4AC < 0$ and either $B \neq 0$ or $A \neq C$	Ellipse
$B^2 - 4AC = 0$	Parabola
$B^2 - 4AC > 0$	Hyperbola

EXAMPLE 5 Use the Discriminant

Classify the conic section given by $4x^2 + y^2 - 8x - 8 = 0$.

Solution

The equation is written in the form $Ax^2 + Bxy + Cy^2 + Dx + Ey + F = 0$ where $A = 4$, $B = 0$, and $C = 1$. Find the discriminant.

$$B^2 - 4AC = 0^2 - 4(4)(1)$$
$$= 0 - 16 = -16$$

ANSWER ▶ Because $B^2 - 4AC < 0$ and $A \neq C$, the conic is an ellipse.

EXAMPLE 6 Use the Equation of a Translated Conic

Physical Science In a lab experiment, you record images of a steel ball rolling past a magnet. The equation $16x^2 - 9y^2 - 96x + 36y - 36 = 0$ models the path of the ball.

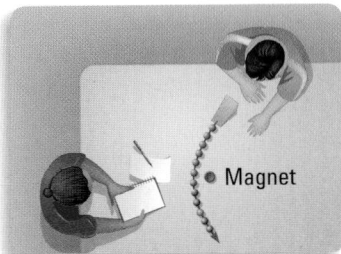

● Magnet

a. What is the shape of the path?

b. Write an equation for the path in standard form.

Solution

a. The equation of the path is a general second-degree equation, with the form $Ax^2 + Bxy + Cy^2 + Dx + Ey + F = 0$ where $A = 16$, $B = 0$, and $C = -9$. Find the discriminant.

$$B^2 - 4AC = 0^2 - 4(16)(-9)$$
$$= 576$$

Because $B^2 - 4AC > 0$, the shape of the path is a branch of a hyperbola.

b. To write an equation of the hyperbola in standard form, complete the square in both x and y at the same time.

$$16x^2 - 9y^2 - 96x + 36y - 36 = 0$$
$$(16x^2 - 96x) - (9y^2 - 36y) = 36$$
$$16(x^2 - 6x + \,?\,) - 9(y^2 - 4y + \,?\,) = 36 + 16(?) - 9(?)$$
$$16(x^2 - 6x + \mathbf{9}) - 9(y^2 - 4y + \mathbf{4}) = 36 + 16(\mathbf{9}) - 9(\mathbf{4})$$
$$16(x - 3)^2 - 9(y - 2)^2 = 144$$
$$\frac{(x - 3)^2}{9} - \frac{(y - 2)^2}{16} = 1$$

STUDENT HELP

LOOK BACK
For help with completing the square, see page 268.

Checkpoint ✓ Classifying a Conic

Use the discriminant to classify the conic section.

5. $y^2 - 12y + 4x + 4 = 0$

6. $x^2 - y^2 - 8y + 2x + 3 = 0$

7. $x^2 + y^2 - 2x + 4y + 1 = 0$

8. $2x^2 + y^2 - 4x - 4 = 0$

Guided Practice

Vocabulary Check

1. Copy and complete the statement: All curves that are formed by the intersection of a plane and a double cone are called __?__.

2. Copy and complete the statement: The expression $B^2 - 4AC$ is called the __?__ of a general second-degree equation.

Skills Check

Write an equation of the conic section.

3. Circle with center $(1, 3)$ and radius 3

4. Circle with center $(-2, 4)$ and radius 5

5. Ellipse with foci at $(0, 1)$ and $(4, 1)$ and vertices at $(-4, 1)$ and $(8, 1)$

6. Hyperbola with foci at $(5, 2)$ and $(5, -6)$ and vertices at $(5, 0)$ and $(5, -4)$

Use the discriminant to classify the conic section.

7. $x^2 + y^2 - 6x + 2y - 4 = 0$

8. $y^2 + 3x - 3y + 3 = 0$

9. $-2x^2 - 3y^2 + x - 2y + 1 = 0$

10. $5x^2 - 2y^2 + 3x - y + 2 = 0$

Practice and Applications

STUDENT HELP

HOMEWORK HELP
Example 1: Exs. 11–18
Example 2: Exs. 11–18
Example 3: Exs. 19–28,
    45–49, 52, 53
Example 4: Exs. 19–28,
    45–49, 52, 53
Example 5: Exs. 29–36,
    50, 51, 54–56
Example 6: Exs. 37–44,
    57, 58

Graphing **Graph the equation. Identify the important characteristics of the graph.**

11. $(x - 1)^2 + y^2 = 9$

12. $\dfrac{(y - 1)^2}{4} - (x + 2)^2 = 1$

13. $\dfrac{x^2}{4} + \dfrac{(y + 6)^2}{16} = 1$

14. $(x - 2)^2 + (y + 3)^2 = 25$

15. $\dfrac{(x + 2)^2}{4} + \dfrac{(y + 6)^2}{16} = 1$

16. $3(x + 4)^2 + 3(y + 1)^2 = 48$

17. $\dfrac{x^2}{64} - \dfrac{(y - 3)^2}{9} = 1$

18. $\dfrac{(x + 1)^2}{81} + \dfrac{(y + 4)^2}{36} = 1$

Writing Equations **Write an equation for the conic section.**

19. Circle with center at $(2, 5)$ and radius 2

20. Circle with center at $(-3, 1)$ and radius 3

21. Circle with center at $(-6, -3)$ and radius 6

22. Ellipse with vertices at $(-9, 3)$ and $(1, 3)$ and foci at $(-7, 3)$ and $(-1, 3)$

23. Ellipse with vertices at $(-5, 1)$ and $(2, 1)$ and co-vertices at $(-2, 0)$ and $(-2, 2)$

24. Hyperbola with foci at $(-3, -2)$ and $(9, -2)$ and vertices at $(-1, -2)$ and $(7, -2)$

25. Hyperbola with foci at $(2, -4)$ and $(2, 8)$ and vertices at $(-2, -2)$ and $(2, 6)$

26. Parabola with vertex at $(-4, -3)$ and focus at $(1, -3)$

27. Parabola with vertex at $(5, 3)$ and directrix at $y = 6$

28. Error Analysis Describe and correct the error in writing an equation of the ellipse with vertices at $(-7, 3)$ and $(3, 3)$ and co-vertices at $(-2, 6)$ and $(-2, 0)$.

> Axis is horizontal; $(h, k) = (-2, 3)$;
> $a = |-7 - (-2)| = 5; b = |6 - 3| = 3;$
> Equation: $\dfrac{(x-2)^2}{25} + \dfrac{(y+3)^2}{9} = 1$ ✗

Classifying Conics Use the discriminant to classify the conic section.

29. $x^2 + y^2 - 12x - 6y - 4 = 0$

30. $x^2 - 3y^2 + 4x - 2y + 30 = 0$

31. $y^2 - 8x - 2y + 9 = 0$

32. $3x^2 + 4y^2 - 6x + 10y - 10 = 0$

33. $16y^2 - x^2 + 2x + 32y + 50 = 0$

34. $9x^2 + 16y^2 + 9x - 96y + 32 = 0$

35. $x^2 - 4x + 20y - 15 = 0$

36. $4x^2 + 4y^2 - 24x + 16y - 40 = 0$

Classifying and Graphing Classify the conic section and write its equation in standard form. Then graph the equation.

37. $x^2 + y^2 + 10x + 21 = 0$

38. $x^2 - 4y^2 - 8x + 12 = 0$

39. $36x^2 + y^2 + 6y - 27 = 0$

40. $4x^2 + y^2 + 10y + 9 = 0$

41. $4x^2 - 9y^2 - 8x - 132 = 0$

42. $9y^2 - 25x^2 - 50x - 275 = 0$

43. $5x^2 + 5y^2 + 10x - 20y - 20 = 0$

44. $x^2 + 16y^2 - 4x + 128y + 256 = 0$

45. Hyperbolic Mirror A hyperbolic mirror reflects light directed toward one focus to the other focus. The hyperbolic mirror has foci at $(13, 2)$ and $(-11, 2)$ and vertices at $(9, 2)$ and $(-7, 2)$. Write an equation of the mirror.

46. Ferris Wheels An engineer draws the design of a Ferris wheel on a coordinate plane. The wheel is centered at $(20, 120)$ with a diameter of 200 feet. Write an equation of the circular Ferris wheel.

47. Australian Football Australian football is played on an elliptical field. On a coordinate plane, a field has vertices $(67.5, 165)$ and $(67.5, 0)$ and co-vertices $(0, 82.5)$ and $(135, 82.5)$. Write an equation of the field.

Water Surface In Exercises 48 and 49, use the following information.

A cylindrical glass of water has a 1.5 inch radius. If the glass is tilted 60°, the water's surface meets the glass in an ellipse with minor axis 3 inches long and major axis 6 inches long.

48. Write an equation that model the water's surface with the glass upright. Assume that the center of the water's surface is at the origin.

49. Write an equation that models the water's surface with the glass tilted. One focus of the ellipse is the origin and the other has a positive x-coordinate.

Conic Sections In Exercises 50 and 51, refer to the diagram. Tell what conic section is formed in the situation described.

50. To use a new tube of caulk for the first time, you cut the cone-shaped tip diagonally.

51. When you sharpen a pencil with flat sides, each side intersects the cone-shaped tip.

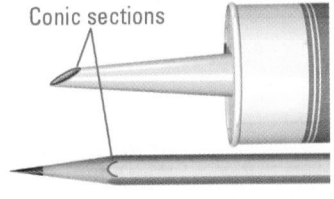

Conic sections

Link to HISTORY

FERRIS WHEEL The first Ferris wheel was designed and built by George W. G. Ferris, an engineer from Galesburg, Ill., for the World's Columbian Exposition held in Chicago in 1892.

Link to
SPORTS

Ice Skating **In Exercises 52 and 53, use the following information.**

A figure skater practices skating figure eights, which are formed by tracing two externally tangent circles in the ice. Each circle in the figure eight is 8 feet in diameter, and the circles intersect at the origin. The centers of the circles are on the *y*-axis.

52. Sketch a graph of the situation described.

53. Write equations for the circles in the figure eight.

Telescopes **In Exercises 54 and 55, use the following diagram of the mirrors in a Cassegrain telescope.**

54. The equation of mirror A is $y^2 - 72x - 450 = 0$. Is the mirror shaped like a *parabola*, an *ellipse*, or a *hyperbola*?

55. The equation of mirror B is $88.4x^2 - 49.7y^2 - 4390 = 0$. Is the mirror shaped like a *parabola*, an *ellipse*, or a *hyperbola*?

eyepiece

mirror B

★ star

mirror A

56. **Reasoning** What does the discriminant tell you about the graph of an equation that has the form $Ax^2 + Bxy + Cy^2 + Dx + Ey + F = 0$?

Swimming Pool **In Exercises 57 and 58, use the following information.**

A new swimming pool will have a boundary represented by the equation $4x^2 + y^2 - 40x - 20y + 100 = 0$ where *x* and *y* are measured in yards.

57. What is the shape of the swimming pool?

58. Write an equation of the swimming pool in standard form.

Standardized Test Practice

59. Multiple Choice What is an equation of an ellipse with vertices at $(-1, 4)$ and $(5, 4)$ and foci at $(0, 4)$ and $(4, 4)$?

Ⓐ $\dfrac{(x-4)^2}{5} + \dfrac{(y-2)^2}{9} = 1$

Ⓑ $\dfrac{(y-2)^2}{9} - \dfrac{(x-4)^2}{5} = 1$

Ⓒ $\dfrac{(x-2)^2}{9} + \dfrac{(y-4)^2}{4} = 1$

Ⓓ $\dfrac{(x-2)^2}{9} + \dfrac{(y-4)^2}{5} = 1$

60. Multiple Choice What are the coordinates of the co-vertices of the ellipse with equation $\dfrac{(x-4)^2}{16} + \dfrac{(y-1)^2}{4} = 1$?

Ⓕ $(0, 1), (8, 1)$

Ⓖ $(-8, 1), (0, 1)$

Ⓗ $(4, 3), (4, -1)$

Ⓙ $(-4, 3), (-4, 1)$

61. Multiple Choice Which equation represents a hyperbola?

Ⓐ $x^2 - 3y + 4x - 15 = 0$

Ⓑ $x^2 + y^2 + 4x - 18y - 15 = 0$

Ⓒ $x^2 - y^2 + 4x - 18y - 15 = 0$

Ⓓ $-2x^2 - y^2 + 4x - 18y - 15 = 0$

62. Multiple Choice The equation $25x^2 + y^2 - 100x - 2y + 76 = 0$ represents which conic section?

Ⓕ parabola   Ⓖ circle   Ⓗ ellipse   Ⓙ hyperbola

63. Multiple Choice The graph of $16x^2 - 25y^2 + 5x - 6y + 15 = 0$ is a __?__?

Ⓐ parabola   Ⓑ circle   Ⓒ ellipse   Ⓓ hyperbola

Mixed Review

Solving Systems Use matrices to solve the linear system. *(Lesson 11.3)*

64. $x + y = -3$
$3x - 2y = 13$

65. $2x + y = 9$
$-3x + y = -1$

66. $x + 2y = 1$
$5x - 4y = -23$

67. $2x + 5y = -4$
$3x - y = 11$

68. $4x - 5y = 0$
$2x - 5y = -10$

69. $4x + 7y = -1$
$-3x - 10y = -4$

Finding Angles or Sides Sketch $\triangle ABC$, then find the indicated angle measure or side length. (*Hint:* Some of the triangles have no solution and some have two solutions.) *(Lesson 12.4)*

70. $A = 35°, B = 65°, a = 5, b = $ __?__

71. $A = 50°, C = 70°, c = 15, a = $ __?__

72. $C = 135°, c = 10, b = 4, B = $ __?__

73. $B = 115°, b = 6, a = 15, A = $ __?__

74. $C = 105°, c = 20, b = 13, B = $ __?__

75. $A = 30°, a = 8, b = 12, B = $ __?__

Geometry Skills

Using Angle Bisectors Find the value of x.

76.

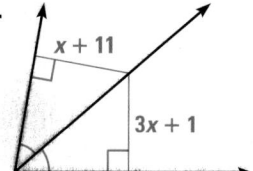

$x + 11$
$3x + 1$

77.

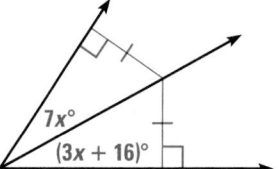

$7x°$
$(3x + 16)°$

Quiz 2

Lesson 13.5

Write an equation of the hyperbola with the given foci and vertices.

1. Foci: $(-5, 0), (5, 0)$
Vertices: $(-4, 0), (4, 0)$

2. Foci: $(0, -3), (0, 3)$
Vertices: $(0, -1), (0, 1)$

3. Foci: $(-4, 0), (4, 0)$
Vertices: $(-3, 0), (3, 0)$

4. Foci: $(-7, 0), (7, 0)$
Vertices: $(-2, 0), (2, 0)$

Lesson 13.6

Graph the equation. Identify the important characteristics of the graph.

5. $(x - 2)^2 + (y + 3)^2 = 16$

6. $x^2 + \dfrac{(y - 1)^2}{4} = 1$

7. $\dfrac{(x - 2)^2}{4} - \dfrac{(y - 4)^2}{9} = 1$

8. $\dfrac{(x - 3)^2}{16} + \dfrac{(y - 4)^2}{25} = 1$

Lesson 13.6

Classify the conic section and write its equation in standard form. Then graph the equation.

9. $9x^2 + 4y^2 + 18x + 8y - 41 = 0$

10. $x^2 - 6y^2 + 5x - 7y + 25 = 0$

11. $x^2 - 4x - 14y + 20 = 0$

12. $3x^2 + 3y^2 - 6x + 30y - 4 = 0$

13. $x^2 + y^2 - 14x + 4y - 11 = 0$

12. $y^2 + 14y + 16x + 33 = 0$

USING A GRAPHING CALCULATOR *(For use with Lesson 13.6)*
Solving Quadratic Systems

EXAMPLE

Use a graphing calculator to find the points of intersection of the graphs of
$x^2 + (y - 1)^2 = 10$ and $y = x^2 + 3$.

SOLUTION

1 Begin by solving the first equation for y.

$$x^2 + (y - 1)^2 = 10$$
$$(y - 1)^2 = 10 - x^2$$
$$y - 1 = \pm \sqrt{10 - x^2}$$
$$y = 1 \pm \sqrt{10 - x^2}$$

2 Enter the three equations into the graphing calculator. Use parentheses to identify the radicands.

3 Graph the equations. Use the *Intersect* feature to find the points of intersection. The points of intersection are $(1, 4)$ and $(-1, 4)$.

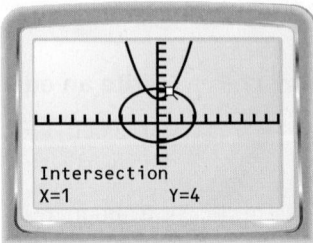

EXERCISES

Use a graphing calculator to find the points of intersection, if any, of the graphs in the system.

1. $y = x^2 + 2$ and $y = 2$

2. $y = (x - 3)^2 + 1$ and $y = -x$

3. $x^2 + y^2 = 20$ and $y = 2x$

4. $(x - 3)^2 + y^2 = 9$ and $y = 3x - 6$

5. $y = (x - 1)^2 + 3$ and $(x - 1)^2 + y^2 = 9$

6. $x^2 + y^2 = 16$ and $y - 2x = 1$

Sketch examples to illustrate the different numbers of points of intersection that the graphs can have.

7. Circle and parabola

8. Ellipse and hyperbola

9. Circle and ellipse

10. Hyperbola and line

VOCABULARY

- distance formula, *p. 691*
- midpoint formula, *p. 692*
- focus, foci, *pp. 697, 710, 717*
- directrix, *p. 697*
- circle, *p. 703*
- center, *pp. 703, 710, 717*
- radius, *p. 703*

- ellipse, *p. 710*
- vertices, *pp. 710, 717*
- major axis, *p. 710*
- co-vertices, *p. 710*
- minor axis, *p. 710*
- hyperbola, *p. 717*

- transverse axis, *p. 717*
- conic sections, *p. 724*
- conics, *p. 724*
- general second-degree equation, *p. 726*
- discriminant, *p. 726*

VOCABULARY EXERCISES

1. Copy and complete the statement: The vertices of an ellipse are joined by a line called the __?__.

2. What is the midpoint formula?

3. Compare the definitions of an ellipse and a hyperbola.

13.1 DISTANCE AND MIDPOINT FORMULAS

Examples on pp. 691–693

EXAMPLE You can use formulas to find the distance between points $(-4, 2)$ and $(3, -4)$ and the midpoint of the line segment joining the two points.

$$d = \sqrt{(x_2 - x_1)^2 + (y_2 - y_1)^2}$$ Use the distance formula.

$$= \sqrt{(3 - (-4))^2 + (-4 - 2)^2}$$ Substitute values.

$$= \sqrt{49 + 36}$$ Simplify.

$$= \sqrt{85}$$ Simplify.

$$\approx 9.22$$ Use a calculator.

$$\text{Midpoint} = M\left(\frac{x_1 + x_2}{2}, \frac{y_1 + y_2}{2}\right)$$ Use the midpoint formula.

$$= \left(\frac{-4 + 3}{2}, \frac{2 + (-4)}{2}\right)$$ Substitute values.

$$= \left(-\frac{1}{2}, -1\right)$$ Simplify.

REVIEW HELP

Exercises	Examples
4–9	**1**, p. 691
4–9	**3**, p. 692

Find the distance between the two points. Then find the midpoint of the line segment joining the two points.

4. $(-3, 4), (0, 6)$

5. $(-4, -2), (5, 8)$

6. $(2, -1), (4, -7)$

7. $(5, 9), (8, 3)$

8. $(-6, 5), (-1, 0)$

9. $(1, 4), (5, -6)$

13.2 PARABOLAS

Examples on pp. 697–699

EXAMPLE You can graph a parabola by using its equation to identify the important characteristics of the graph.

Graph $y^2 = 12x$

The equation has the form $y^2 = 4py$ where $4p = 12$, so $p = 3$. The focus is $(p, 0) = (3, 0)$. The directrix is $x = -p = -3$.

Make a table of values by choosing values for y.

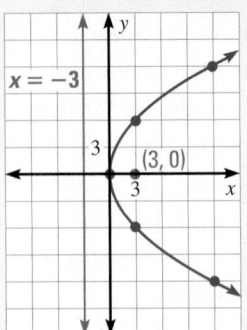

REVIEW HELP

Exercises	Examples
10–12	**1**, p. 698
13–15	**2**, p.

x	12	3	3	12
y	−12	−6	6	12

Plot the points and draw the parabola through them.

Graph the equation. Identify the focus, directrix, and axis of symmetry of the parabola.

10. $x^2 = 4y$ **11.** $2y^2 = x$ **12.** $-y^2 = 12x$

Write the standard form of the equation for the parabola with vertex at (0, 0) and the given focus or directrix.

13. Focus: $(-5, 0)$ **14.** Focus: $(0, 3)$ **15.** Directrix: $x = -6$

13.3 CIRCLES

Examples on pp. 703–705

EXAMPLE You can graph a circle by using its equation to identify the important characteristics of the graph.

Graph $x^2 + y^2 = 64$.

The graph is a circle with center at the origin and radius $r = \sqrt{64} = 8$.

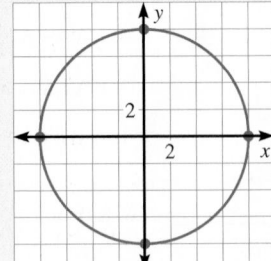

699Review Help

Exercises	Examples
16–18	**1**, p. 703
19–22	**2**, p. 704

Plot four points that are 8 units from $(0, 0)$. The points $(8, 0)$, $(-8, 0)$, $(0, 8)$, and $(0, -8)$ are most convenient.

Draw a circle through the points.

Graph the equation. Identify the radius of the circle.

16. $x^2 + y^2 = 4$ **17.** $x^2 + y^2 = 36$ **18.** $x^2 + y^2 = 49$

Write the standard form of the equation of the circle with the given radius and center at the origin.

19. 11   **20.** 9   **21.** $\sqrt{20}$

EXAMPLE You can graph an ellipse by using its equation to identify the important characteristics of the graph.

Graph $\dfrac{x^2}{4} + \dfrac{y^2}{16} = 1$.

The equation has the form $\dfrac{x^2}{b^2} + \dfrac{y^2}{a^2} = 1$ where $b = 2$ and $a = 4$.

Because the denominator of the x^2-term is less than the denominator of the y^2-term, the major axis is vertical. The vertices are at $(\pm b, 0) = (\pm 2, 0)$ and $(0, \pm a) = (0, \pm 4)$.

Find the foci using the equation $c^2 = a^2 - b^2$.

$$c^2 = 4^2 - 2^2 = 12, \text{ so } c = \pm\sqrt{12} = \pm 2\sqrt{3}$$

The foci are at $\left(0, 2\sqrt{3}\right)$ and $\left(0, -2\sqrt{3}\right)$.

Draw the ellipse that passes through the vertices and co-vertices.

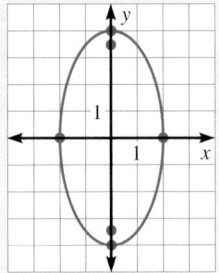

REVIEW HELP

Exercises	Examples
22–24	**1**, p. 711
25–27	**3**, p. 712

Graph the equation. Identify the vertices, co-vertices, and foci of the ellipse.

22. $\dfrac{x^2}{9} + \dfrac{y^2}{36} = 1$

23. $\dfrac{x^2}{25} + \dfrac{y^2}{16} = 1$

24. $25x^2 + 36y^2 = 900$

Write an equation of the ellipse with the given characteristics and center at (0, 0).

25. Vertex: $(6, 0)$
Co-vertex: $(0, -4)$

26. Vertex: $(-5, 0)$
Co-vertex: $(0, 2)$

27. Vertex: $(0, 7)$
Focus: $(0, -5)$

EXAMPLE You can graph a hyperbola by using its equation to identify the important characteristics of the graph.

Graph $\dfrac{x^2}{9} - \dfrac{y^2}{4} = 36$.

The equation has the form $\dfrac{x^2}{a^2} - \dfrac{y^2}{b^2} = 1$ where $a = 3$ and $b = 2$.

Because the x^2-term is positive, the transverse axis is horizontal and the vertices are $(\pm a, 0) = (\pm 3, 0)$.

Find the foci using the equation $c^2 = a^2 + b^2$.

$$c^2 = 3^2 + 2^2 = 13, \text{ so } c = \pm\sqrt{13}.$$

The foci are at $\left(\sqrt{13}, 0\right)$ and $\left(-\sqrt{13}, 0\right)$.

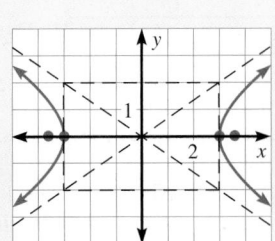

Draw a rectangle centered at the origin that is $2a = 2(3) = 6$ units high and $2b = 2(2) = 4$ units wide. The asymptotes are the diagonals of the rectangle. Draw the hyperbola.

REVIEW HELP

Exercises	Example
28–30	**1**, p. 718

Graph the equation. Identify the foci and asymptotes.

28. $\dfrac{x^2}{36} - \dfrac{y^2}{4} = 1$

29. $\dfrac{y^2}{25} - \dfrac{x^2}{36} = 1$

30. $36x^2 - 25y^2 = 900$

13.6 GRAPHING AND CLASSIFYING CONICS

Examples on pp. 724–727

> **EXAMPLE** You can graph a translated conic by using its equation to identify the important characteristics of the graph.
>
> Graph $\dfrac{(y-6)^2}{4} - (x-4)^2 = 1$.
>
> The form of the equation is $\dfrac{(y-k)^2}{a^2} + \dfrac{(x-h)^2}{b^2} = 1$. This tells you that its graph is a hyperbola with vertical transverse axis and center at $(h, k) = (4, 6)$. Because $a^2 = 4$, $a = 2$. Also, because $b^2 = 1$, $b = 1$.
>
> Use the equation $c^2 = a^2 + b^2$ to find the foci.
> The foci are $c = \sqrt{5} \approx 2.2$ units above and below the center. So, the foci are at $(4, 6 + 2.2) = (4, 8.2)$ and $(4, 6 - 2.2) = (4, 3.8)$.
>
> Draw a rectangle centered at $(4, 6)$ that is $2a = 8$ units high and $2b = 6$ units wide. The asymptotes of the hyperbola are the diagonals of the rectangle.
>
> Draw the diagonals of the rectangle. Then draw the branches of the hyperbola passing through the vertices and approaching the asymptotes.

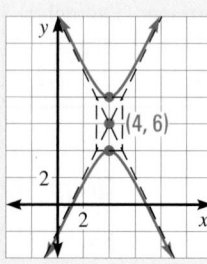

REVIEW HELP

Exercises	Examples
31–36	**1,** p. 724
31–36	**2,** p. 725

Graph the equation. Identify the important characteristics of the graph.

31. $(x + 2)^2 + (y - 3)^2 = 16$

32. $\dfrac{(x-4)^2}{16} - (y - 3)^2 = 1$

33. $\dfrac{(x+3)^2}{25} + \dfrac{(y+2)^2}{9} = 1$

34. $4(y-2)^2 - 16(x+1)^2 = 64$

35. $5(x+4)^2 + 5(y-2)^2 = 125$

36. $(x-5)^2 + \dfrac{(y-6)^2}{9} = 1$

> **EXAMPLE** You can classify a conic section whose equation is written in the form $Ax^2 + Bxy + Cy^2 + Dx + Ey + F = 0$ by using the discriminant.
>
> Classify the conic section given by the equation $4x^2 + 9y^2 + 40x + 72y + 208 = 0$.
>
> In the equation, $A = 4$, $B = 0$, and $C = 9$. Find the discriminant.
>
> $B^2 - 4AC = 0^2 - 4(4)(9)$ Substitute values into the formula for the discriminant.
>
> $= 144$ Evaluate.
>
> Because $B^2 - 4AC > 0$, the conic section is a hyperbola.

REVIEW HELP

Exercises	Examples
37–40	**5,** p. 727

Use the discriminant to classify the conic section.

37. $x^2 - 2y^2 + 6x + 4y + 5 = 0$

38. $3x^2 + 2y^2 - 12x + 8 = 0$

39. $4x^2 + 4y^2 - 2x + 10y + 4 = 0$

40. $5x^2 - 3x + 4y - 7 = 0$

Find the distance between the two points. Then find the midpoint of the line segment joining the two points.

1.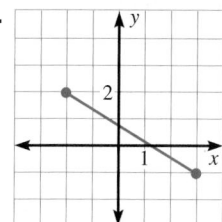

2.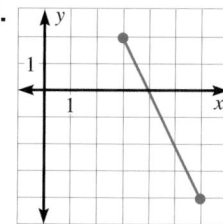

3.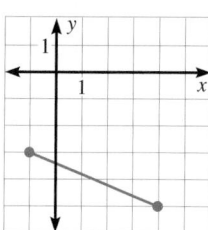

Graph the equation. Identify the important characteristics of the graph.

4. $x^2 = -12y$

5. $x^2 + y^2 = 25$

6. $4x^2 - y^2 = 36$

7. $9x^2 + 25y^2 = 225$

8. $y^2 = -10x$

9. $\dfrac{x^2}{4} + \dfrac{(y-3)^2}{16} = 1$

10. $\dfrac{(y-4)^2}{9} - x^2 = 1$

11. $\dfrac{(x-2)^2}{36} + \dfrac{(y-6)^2}{25} = 1$

12. $7(x+5)^2 + 7y^2 = 343$

Write the equation for the conic section with the given characteristics.

13. Parabola with vertex at $(0, 0)$ and directrix $y = -2$

14. Parabola with vertex at $(0, 0)$ and directrix $x = -6$

15. Circle with center at $(0, 0)$ and passing through $(-2, 6)$

16. Circle with center at $(-4, 7)$ and radius 7

17. Ellipse with vertices at $(0, 6)$ and $(0, -6)$ and co-vertices at $(-2, 0)$ and $(2, 0)$

18. Ellipse with vertices at $(-5, -2)$ and $(1, -2)$ and foci at $(-3, -2)$ and $(-1, -2)$

19. Hyperbola with foci at $(-4, 0)$ and $(4, 0)$ and vertices at $(-2, 0)$ and $(2, 0)$

20. Hyperbola with foci at $(3, 4)$ and $(3, -2)$ and vertices at $(3, 2)$ and $(3, 0)$

Classify the conic section and write its equation in standard form. Then graph the equation.

21. $x^2 + 4y^2 - 2x - 3 = 0$

22. $x^2 + y^2 - 12y + 16 = 0$

23. $4x^2 - y^2 - 16x - 24 = 0$

24. $3x^2 + 5y^2 + 18x - 30y - 3 = 0$

25. $y^2 - 4x^2 - 24x - 2y - 51 = 0$

26. $6x^2 + 6y^2 - 36x - 48y - 66 = 0$

Exercise In Exercises 27 and 28, use the following information.

Each day you run through the city park along the path given by the equation $x^2 + 4y^2 - 4x - 32y - 9932 = 0$, where x and y are measured in meters.

27. What is the shape of the path?

28. Write the equation of the path in standard form.

Chapter Standardized Test

EXAMPLE   Find the length of the major axis of the ellipse whose equation is $\dfrac{(x-4)^2}{49} + \dfrac{(y+1)^2}{25} = 1$.

(A) 49   **(B)** 14

(C) 7   **(D)** 5

Solution

From the equation, you can see that $a^2 = 49$, so $a = 7$. Do not choose answer C. The question asks for the length of the major axis. The length of the major axis is $2a = 2(7) = 14$. So, B is the correct answer.

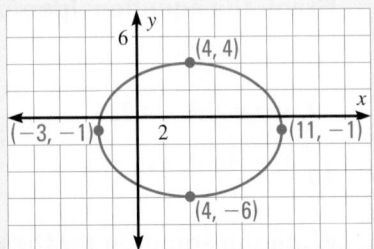

Multiple Choice

1. What is the distance between $(-4, 3)$ and $(2, -1)$?

(A) 52   **(B)** $2\sqrt{13}$

(C) $4\sqrt{2}$ **(D)** $2\sqrt{5}$

2. What is the midpoint of the segment joining $(-3, 4)$ and $(-5, 2)$?

(F) $(3, -4)$ **(G)** $(-4, 3)$

(H) $(-8, 6)$ **(J)** $(4, -3)$

3. What is an equation for the perpendicular bisector of the line segment joining $(-2, 5)$ and $(4, -1)$?

(A) $y = -\dfrac{1}{2}x + 3$

(B) $y = x + 1$

(C) $y = 2x + 4$

(D) $y = -x + 3$

4. What is the focus of the parabola $x^2 = -18y$?

(F) $\left(-\dfrac{9}{2}, 0\right)$ **(G)** $\left(-\dfrac{9}{2}, -\dfrac{9}{2}\right)$

(H) $(0, -18)$ **(J)** $\left(0, -\dfrac{9}{2}\right)$

5. What is an equation of a circle that passes through $(-4, -2)$ and whose center is the origin?

(A) $x^2 + y^2 = \sqrt{20}$ **(B)** $x^2 + y^2 = 5$

(C) $x^2 + y^2 = 20$ **(D)** $x^2 - y^2 = \sqrt{4}$

6. What are the foci of the ellipse given by $\dfrac{x^2}{36} + \dfrac{y^2}{11} = 1$?

(F) $(-5, 0)$ and $(5, 0)$

(G) $(0, -5)$ and $(0, 5)$

(H) $(0, -\sqrt{11})$ and $(0, \sqrt{11})$

(J) $(6, 0)$ and $(-6, 0)$

7. What are the asymptotes of the hyperbola given by the equation $\dfrac{x^2}{36} - \dfrac{y^2}{16} = 1$?

(A) $y = -\dfrac{2}{3}x$ and $y = \dfrac{2}{3}x$

(B) $y = -6x$ and $y = 6x$

(C) $y = -4x$ and $y = 4x$

(D) $y = -\dfrac{3}{2}x$ and $y = \dfrac{3}{2}x$

8. What is the center of the circle with equation $(x - 9)^2 + (y + 6)^2 = 25$?

(F) $(0, 0)$ (G) $(9, -6)$

(H) $(-6, 9)$ (J) $(-9, 6)$

9. What is an equation of the ellipse with vertices $(-4, -5)$ and $(6, -5)$ and foci $(-1, -5)$ and $(3, -5)$?

(A) $\dfrac{x^2}{25} + \dfrac{y^2}{21} = 1$

(B) $\dfrac{(x - 1)^2}{25} + \dfrac{(y + 5)^2}{4} = 1$

(C) $\dfrac{(x - 1)^2}{25} + \dfrac{(y + 5)^2}{21} = 1$

(D) $\dfrac{(x + 1)^2}{4} + \dfrac{(y - 5)^2}{25} = 1$

10. The graph of the equation $16y^2 - x^2 + 16x - 128 = 0$ is a __?__ .

(F) parabola   (G) circle

(H) ellipse   (J) hyperbola

Gridded Response

11. Find the distance between $(-5, -1)$ and $(1, -4)$.

12. What is the y-coordinate of the midpoint of the segment joining $(6, -2)$ and $(-3, 7)$?

13. For the parabola $3y^2 = x$, the focus is $(p, 0)$. Find the value of p.

14. What is the radius of the circle $x^2 = 900 - y^2$?

15. For the ellipse $x^2 + \dfrac{y^2}{16} = 1$, the vertices are $(0, -j)$ and $(0, j)$. Find the value of j.

16. For the ellipse $\dfrac{x^2}{100} + \dfrac{y^2}{64} = 1$, the foci are $(-k, 0)$ and $(k, 0)$. Find the value of k.

17. For the hyperbola $\dfrac{y^2}{4} - \dfrac{x^2}{16} = 1$, the asymptotes are $y = -mx$ and $y = mx$. Find the value of m.

18. What is the value of the discriminant of $8x^2 - 16y^2 - 10x - 18y + 4 = 0$?

19. What is the x-coordinate of the center of the circle $x^2 + y^2 - 6x + 4y - 36 = 0$?

Extended Response

20. The beam from a lighthouse is visible along a path given by the equation $x^2 + y^2 + 6x - 10y - 366 = 0$ where x and y are measured in miles.

   a. What is the shape of the path of the lighthouse beam?

   b. Write the equation of the path of the lighthouse beam in standard form.

   c. What are the coordinates of the lighthouse?

   d. How far from the lighthouse is the beam visible?

Solve the equation. *(Lessons 1.4, 5.2, and 5.3)*

1. $\frac{1}{2}x + 4 = 4x - 1$

2. $10(x + 2) = 4(1 - 2x)$

3. $x^2 - 18x + 72 = 0$

4. $x^2 - 2x = 63$

5. $3x^2 - 7x - 10 = 0$

6. $12x^2 - 2x = -24$

Evaluate the expression without using a calculator. *(Lessons 7.2, 8.4)*

7. $256^{3/4}$

8. $125^{-2/3}$

9. $\log 0.01$

Find the number of permutations or combinations. *(Lessons 10.3, 10.4)*

10. $_6P_2$

11. $_{10}P_4$

12. $_8C_3$

Tell whether events *A* and *B* are *disjoint* or *overlapping*. Find *P(A or B)*. *(Lesson 10.7)*

13. $P(A) = 0.5$,
$P(B) = 0.3$
$P(A \text{ and } B) = 0$

14. $P(A) = 0.7$,
$P(B) = 0.4$
$P(A \text{ and } B) = 0.2$

15. $P(A) = 0.8$,
$P(B) = 0.5$
$P(A \text{ and } B) = 0$

You are playing a game that involves spinning the spinner shown. Find the probability of spinning the given colors. *(Lesson 10.8)*

16. green, then blue

17. blue, then red

18. yellow, then green

19. blue, then green, then red

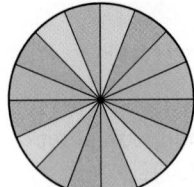

Perform the indicated operation, if possible. If not possible, state the reason. *(Lessons 11.1, 11.2)*

20. $\begin{bmatrix} 5 & -3 \\ 10 & -1 \end{bmatrix} + \begin{bmatrix} 4 & -2 \\ -3 & 8 \end{bmatrix}$

21. $\begin{bmatrix} 4 & -2 \\ 3 & -5 \end{bmatrix} + 2\begin{bmatrix} -1 & 3 \\ -6 & 4 \end{bmatrix}$

22. $\begin{bmatrix} 2 & 0 \\ -1 & 4 \end{bmatrix}\begin{bmatrix} 0 & 1 \\ -3 & 2 \end{bmatrix}$

23. $\begin{bmatrix} -1 & 2 \\ 4 & 0 \\ 1 & 3 \end{bmatrix}\begin{bmatrix} 1 & -3 \\ 0 & -2 \end{bmatrix}$

Use matrices to solve the linear system. *(Lesson 11.3)*

24. $2x - y = -10$
$3x + 2y = -1$

25. $3x + 4y = -2$
$5x + 3y = 4$

26. $3x + 6y = 5$
$6x + 14y = 11$

Write a rule for the *n*th term of the sequence. Then find a_{15}. *(Lessons 11.4–11.6)*

27. 4, 7, 10, 13, 16, . . .

28. 5, 20, 80, 320, . . .

29. $a_5 = 25, d = -5$

30. **Salary** You accept a job as a chemist that pays an annual salary of \$39,000 the first year. During the next 39 years, you will receive a 5% raise each year. What will be your total amount of money earned over the 40-year period? *(Lessons 8.1)*

Find the sum of the infinite geometric series. If it does not have a sum, write
no sum. *(Lesson 11.7)*

31. $7 + \dfrac{7}{3} + \dfrac{7}{9} + \dfrac{7}{27} + \ldots$

32. $2 - \dfrac{6}{5} + \dfrac{18}{25} - \dfrac{54}{125} + \ldots$

33. $1 - \dfrac{4}{3} + \dfrac{16}{9} - \dfrac{64}{27} + \ldots$

34. $3 + \dfrac{1}{2} + \dfrac{1}{12} + \dfrac{1}{72} + \ldots$

**Find the value of *x* for the given right triangle. Round the result to two decimal
places.** *(Lesson 12.1)*

35.
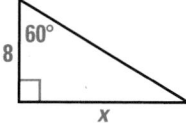

36.

37.
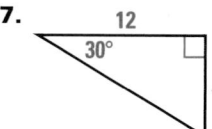

**Determine whether the trigonometric function of the angle is positive or
negative.** *(Lesson 12.2)*

38. $\sin 70°$

39. $\cos 315°$

40. $\tan 228°$

Graph the function. *(Lesson 12.3)*

41. $y = \sin 90x$

42. $y = \cos 3x$

43. $y = \tan 45x$

Sketch $\triangle ABC$. Then find the missing angle measures and side lengths.
(*Hint:* Some of the triangles have no solution and some have two solutions.)
(Lessons 12.4, 12.5)

44. $A = 110°, B = 34°, b = 14$

45. $B = 65°, a = 45, c = 28$

**Find the distance between the two points. Then find the midpoint of the
segment joining the two points.** *(Lesson 13.1)*

46. $(0, 0), (-2, -6)$

47. $(-1, 3), (-5, -2)$

48. $(6, -3), (2, 4)$

Graph the conic section. *(Lessons 13.2–13.5)*

49. $4x^2 + 4y^2 = 100$

50. $\dfrac{1}{20}x^2 = y$

51. $\dfrac{x^2}{36} - \dfrac{y^2}{16} = 1$

Write the equation of the conic section. *(Lessons 13.2–13.5)*

52. Parabola with vertex at $(0, 0)$ and directrix $x = 2$

53. Circle with center at $(0, 0)$ and passing through $(7, -2)$

54. Ellipse with vertices at $(-4, 0)$ and $(4, 0)$ and co-vertices at $(0, 3)$ and $(0, -3)$

55. Hyperbola with foci at $(0, 4)$ and $(0, -4)$ and vertices at $(0, 2)$ and $(0, -2)$

Classify the conic section. Then write its equation in standard form.
(Lesson 13.6)

56. $25x^2 + 4y^2 - 24y - 64 = 0$

57. $y^2 - 9x^2 - 72x - 153 = 0$

58. $3x^2 + 3y^2 + 12x - 63 = 0$

59. $x^2 - 4y^2 + 8x - 24y - 24 = 0$

Contents of Student Resources

Skills Review Handbook

Fractions, Decimals, and Percents

A percent is a ratio with a denominator of 100. The symbol for percent is %.
For example, 67% is $\frac{67}{100}$ or 67 divided by 100.

To write a percent as a decimal, move the decimal point two places to the *left* and
remove the percent symbol.

EXAMPLE Write the percent as a decimal.

a. $75\% = 75\% = 0.75$ **b.** $8\% = 08\% = 0.08$ **c.** $336\% = 336\% = 3.36$

To write a percent as a fraction in lowest terms, first write the percent as a fraction with
a denominator of 100. Then simplify if possible.

EXAMPLE Write the percent as a fraction.

a. $53\% = \frac{53}{100}$ **b.** $20\% = \frac{20}{100} = \frac{1}{5}$ **c.** $175\% = \frac{175}{100} = \frac{7}{4} = 1\frac{3}{4}$

To write a fraction as a percent, rewrite the fraction as a decimal. Once in decimal form,
move the decimal two places to the *right* and insert the percent symbol.

EXAMPLE Write the fraction as a percent.

a. $\frac{18}{25} = 0.72 = 72\%$ **b.** $\frac{1}{10} = \frac{10}{100} = 10\%$ **c.** $\frac{1}{9} = 0.1111\ldots \approx 0.111 = 11.1\%$

Practice

Write the percent as a decimal.

1. 22%   **2.** 89%   **3.** 6%   **4.** 9%

5. 258%   **6.** 105%   **7.** 35.5%   **8.** 40.8%

**Write the fraction as a decimal and as a percent. Round the percent to the
nearest whole number.**

9. $\frac{1}{4}$ **10.** $\frac{5}{8}$ **11.** $\frac{12}{25}$ **12.** $\frac{13}{16}$

13. $\frac{56}{125}$ **14.** $\frac{17}{20}$ **15.** $\frac{5}{9}$ **16.** $\frac{54}{96}$

Write the decimal as a percent and as a fraction in simplest form.

17. 0.45   **18.** 0.62   **19.** 0.8   **20.** 0.07

21. 1.36   **22.** 3.64   **23.** 0.375   **24.** 0.9375

Calculating Percents

You can use equations to calculate with percents. Replace the words with symbols as shown in the table to the right.

Word	what	of	is
Symbol	n	$\times$	$=$

EXAMPLE Answer the question.

a. What is 25% of 280?

$n = 0.25 \times 280$

$n = 70$

70 is 25% of 280.

b. What percent of 15 is 3?

$n \times 15 = 3$

$n = \dfrac{3}{15} = 0.2 = 20\%$

20% of 15 is 3.

c. 60% of what number is 3?

$0.60 \times n = 3$

$n = \dfrac{3}{0.60} = 5$

60% of **5** is 3.

$$\text{Percent of change} = \frac{\text{Amount of increase or decrease}}{\text{Original amount}}$$

EXAMPLE Find the percent of change.

A pair of jeans is marked down from $20 to $12. Find the percent of change.

Solution

$$\text{Percent change in price} = \frac{\text{New price} - \text{Original price}}{\text{Original price}} = \frac{12 - 20}{20} = \frac{-8}{20} = -0.4 = -40\%$$

The negative sign indicates that the percent of change is a decrease. So, the price of the pair of jeans decreased 40%.

Practice

Answer the question.

1. What is 15% of 60?

2. What is 10% of 2?

3. What is 40% of 80?

4. What is 1% of 29?

5. What is 24% of 75?

6. What is 100% of 93?

7. What is 50% of $\dfrac{1}{2}$?

8. What is 65% of $\dfrac{1}{10}$?

9. What is 125% of 84?

10. What percent of 18 is 9?

11. What percent of 8 is 2?

12. What percent of 7 is 7?

13. What percent of 10 is 1?

14. What percent of 100 is 150?

15. What percent of 40 is 18?

16. What percent of 12 is 4?

17. What percent of 90 is 117?

18. What percent of 50 is 70?

19. 25% of what number is 3?

20. 45% of what number is 9?

21. 65% of what number is 26?

22. 30% of what number is 6?

23. 68% of what number is 17?

24. 74% of what number is 37?

25. 95% of what number is 38?

26. 160% of what number is 24?

27. 200% of what number is 13?

Find the percent of change. Round to the nearest percent if necessary.

28. 80 votes increased to 140 votes

29. $192 decreased to $160

30. 5 dogs increased to 10 dogs

31. $240 increased to $348

32. 36 students decreased to 28 students

33. 20 ounces increased to 32 ounces

Factors and Multiples

Factors are numbers or variable expressions that are multiplied together. A **prime number** is a whole number greater than 1 that has exactly two factors. To write the **prime factorization** of a number, write the number as a product of prime numbers.

Prime numbers less than 100
2, 3, 5, 7, 11, 13, 17, 19, 23, 29, 31, 37, 41, 43, 47, 53, 59, 61, 67, 71, 73, 79, 83, 89, 97

EXAMPLE   **Write the prime factorization of 84.**

Solution   Use a tree diagram to factor the number until all factors are prime numbers.

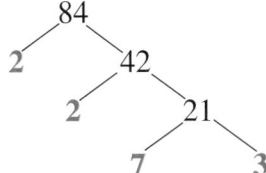

ANSWER ▶ The prime factorization of 84 is $2 \cdot 2 \cdot 3 \cdot 7$. This may also be written as $2^2 \cdot 3 \cdot 7$.

A **common factor** of two whole numbers is a whole number that is a factor of each number. The **greatest common factor (GCF)** of two whole numbers is the greatest whole number that is a factor of each number.

EXAMPLE   **What is the greatest common factor of 36 and 40?**

Solution   First write the prime factorization of each number. Multiply the common prime factors to find the greatest common factor.

$$36 = 2 \cdot 2 \cdot 3 \cdot 3$$
$$40 = 2 \cdot 2 \cdot 2 \cdot 5$$

ANSWER ▶ The greatest common factor is $2 \cdot 2 = 4$.

A **multiple** of a whole number is the product of the number and any nonzero whole number. The **least common multiple (LCM)** of two whole numbers is the smallest whole number (other than zero) that is a multiple of each number.

EXAMPLE   **What is the least common multiple of 16 and 24?**

Solution   First write the prime factorization of each number using exponents. The LCM of the two numbers is the product of the highest power of each prime number that appears in the factorization of either number.

$$16 = 2^4$$
$$24 = 2^3 \cdot 3$$

ANSWER ▶ The least common multiple is $2^4 \cdot 3 = 48$.

The **least common denominator (LCD)** of two fractions is the least common multiple of the denominators. To add or subtract two fractions with unlike denominators, first write equivalent fractions using the LCD, then add or subtract the numerators.

EXAMPLE Add: $\dfrac{7}{16} + \dfrac{11}{24}$

Solution The least common multiple of 16 and 24 is 48. So, the least common denominator (LCD) of the fractions is 48.

Rewrite the fractions using the LCD.

$$\frac{7}{16} = \frac{7 \cdot 3}{16 \cdot 3} = \frac{21}{48} \qquad \frac{11}{24} = \frac{11 \cdot 2}{24 \cdot 2} = \frac{22}{48}$$

Add the rewritten fractions.

$$\frac{21}{48} + \frac{22}{48} = \frac{43}{48}$$

Practice

Write the prime factorization of the number. If the number is prime, write *prime*.

1. 12   **2.** 27   **3.** 17   **4.** 30   **5.** 63

6. 16   **7.** 28   **8.** 73   **9.** 15   **10.** 42

11. 57   **12.** 86   **13.** 56   **14.** 34   **15.** 100

Give the greatest common factor (GCF) and least common multiple (LCM) of the pair of numbers.

16. 4, 6   **17.** 21, 9   **18.** 15, 30   **19.** 1, 17   **20.** 24, 36

21. 30, 42   **22.** 45, 63   **23.** 10, 18   **24.** 9, 24   **25.** 16, 28

26. 13, 7   **27.** 33, 21   **28.** 39, 54   **29.** 100, 40   **30.** 26, 49

Find the least common denominator.

31. $\dfrac{4}{7}, \dfrac{1}{6}$ **32.** $\dfrac{3}{5}, \dfrac{3}{4}$ **33.** $\dfrac{1}{12}, \dfrac{5}{8}$ **34.** $\dfrac{16}{21}, \dfrac{2}{3}$ **35.** $\dfrac{13}{15}, \dfrac{7}{10}$

36. $\dfrac{11}{16}, \dfrac{19}{24}$ **37.** $\dfrac{1}{2}, \dfrac{4}{11}$ **38.** $\dfrac{4}{5}, \dfrac{6}{7}$ **39.** $\dfrac{15}{26}, \dfrac{10}{13}$ **40.** $\dfrac{5}{6}, \dfrac{13}{20}$

41. $\dfrac{1}{2}, \dfrac{5}{6}, \dfrac{7}{8}$ **42.** $\dfrac{1}{3}, \dfrac{3}{5}, \dfrac{11}{15}$ **43.** $\dfrac{7}{9}, \dfrac{5}{12}, \dfrac{1}{6}$ **44.** $\dfrac{3}{5}, \dfrac{2}{9}, \dfrac{1}{3}$ **45.** $\dfrac{17}{20}, \dfrac{7}{8}, \dfrac{9}{10}$

Perform the indicated operation(s). Simplify the result.

46. $\dfrac{7}{8} - \dfrac{1}{4}$ **47.** $\dfrac{3}{4} + \dfrac{13}{18}$ **48.** $\dfrac{3}{10} + \dfrac{1}{6}$ **49.** $\dfrac{2}{3} - \dfrac{9}{10}$

50. $-\dfrac{7}{12} + \dfrac{4}{15}$ **51.** $\dfrac{11}{15} - \dfrac{5}{6}$ **52.** $-\dfrac{17}{10} - \dfrac{16}{25}$ **53.** $\dfrac{8}{11} + \dfrac{11}{8}$

54. $\dfrac{1}{4} + \dfrac{3}{14} - \dfrac{6}{7}$ **55.** $\dfrac{25}{64} + \dfrac{17}{8} - \dfrac{9}{16}$ **56.** $\dfrac{4}{3} - \dfrac{2}{9} - \dfrac{5}{6}$ **57.** $\dfrac{13}{9} + \dfrac{5}{3} - \dfrac{1}{2}$

Writing Ratios and Proportions

A **ratio** compares two quantities using division. If a and b are two quantities measured in the same units, then the ratio of a to b can be written as a to b, $\frac{a}{b}$, or $a : b$. Ratios should be written in simplest form.

EXAMPLE   Write the ratio 10 to 35 in three ways.

Solution   First write the ratio as a fraction in simplest form:

$$\frac{10}{35} = \frac{10 \div 5}{35 \div 5} = \frac{2}{7}$$

The three ways to write the ratio 10 to 35 are 2 to 7, $\frac{2}{7}$, and 2 : 7.

A **proportion** is an equation stating that two ratios are equivalent. You can use cross multiplication to solve a proportion.

Using Cross Multiplication to Solve Proportions

If $\frac{a}{b} = \frac{c}{d}$, where $b \neq 0$ and $d \neq 0$, then $ad = bc$.

EXAMPLE   Solve the proportion $\frac{4}{11} = \frac{8}{x}$.

Solution
$$\frac{4}{11} = \frac{8}{x} \qquad \text{Rewrite the proportion.}$$
$$4 \cdot x = 11 \cdot 8 \qquad \text{Cross multiply.}$$
$$4x = 88 \qquad \text{Simplify.}$$
$$x = 22 \qquad \text{Solve for } x.$$

Practice

Write the ratio in simplest form. Express the answer in three ways.

1. 5 to 15

2. 3 : 9

3. $\frac{9}{27}$

4. 2 : 4

5. 3 to 6

6. $\frac{2}{12}$

7. 8 to 28

8. $\frac{12}{4}$

9. 13 : 26

10. 15 to 6

11. $\frac{38}{32}$

12. 7 : 49

Solve the proportion.

13. $\frac{4}{6} = \frac{12}{x}$

14. $\frac{c}{5} = \frac{8}{2}$

15. $\frac{4}{y} = \frac{72}{18}$

16. $\frac{40}{32} = \frac{w}{4}$

17. $\frac{3}{q} = \frac{2}{26}$

18. $\frac{6}{7} = \frac{42}{k}$

19. $\frac{3}{8} = \frac{p}{32}$

20. $\frac{r}{11} = \frac{9}{3}$

21. $\frac{2}{7} = \frac{w}{21}$

22. $\frac{39}{u} = \frac{6}{2}$

23. $\frac{8}{18} = \frac{4}{m}$

24. $\frac{v}{50} = \frac{10}{25}$

Operations with Positive and Negative Numbers

To add positive and negative numbers, you can use a number line.

To subtract any number, add its opposite.

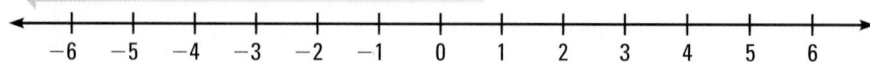

To add a positive number, move to the right.

To add a negative number, move to the left.

EXAMPLE Add or subtract.

a. $1 + (-5)$

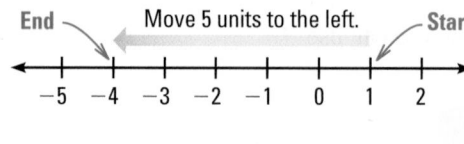

$1 + (-5) = -4$

b. $-2 - (-5) = -2 + 5$

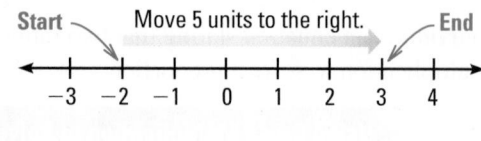

$-2 - (-5) = 3$

To multiply or divide positive and negative numbers, use the following rules.

- The product or quotient of two numbers with the same sign is *positive*.

- The product or quotient of two numbers with *different* signs is *negative*.

EXAMPLE Multiply or divide.

a. $3 \cdot 7 = 21$

c. $18 \div 2 = 9$

e. $-3(7) = -21$

g. $-18 \div 2 = -9$

b. $-3(-7) = 21$

d. $-18 \div (-1) = 9$

f. $3(-7) = -21$

h. $18 \div (-2) = -9$

Practice

Perform the indicated operation.

1. $2 + (-8)$ **2.** $5 - 12$ **3.** $-6(10)$ **4.** $-30 \div (-2)$ **5.** $-4 + 6$

6. $7(-5)$ **7.** $18 - 10$ **8.** $-7 + (-12)$ **9.** $11(4)$ **10.** $81 \div (-9)$

11. $-12 \div 3$ **12.** $-9(-8)$ **13.** $-1 + 13$ **14.** $45 \div (-9)$ **15.** $-6(12)$

16. $14 - (-9)$ **17.** $-32 \div 16$ **18.** $-23 + (-5)$ **19.** $28 - (25)$ **20.** $17 - (-18)$

21. $-9(-1)$ **22.** $-3 - (-11)$ **23.** $-18 \div (-3)$ **24.** $14 + (-7)$ **25.** $5(-3)$

26. $21 + (-8)$ **27.** $-2 - 10$ **28.** $-9 + 26$ **29.** $-20 \div (-4)$ **30.** $22 \div (-2)$

31. $-7(-6)$ **32.** $1 - 24$ **33.** $-15 - 2$ **34.** $0 + (-4)$ **35.** $16 \div 8$

36. $5(-6)$ **37.** $-17 + 1$ **38.** $-10 - 18$ **39.** $-10 \div (-2)$ **40.** $13(-3)$

Significant Digits

Significant digits indicate how precisely a number or quantity is known. The following can be used to round a number to the appropriate number of significant digits.

- All nonzero digits are significant.
- All zeros that appear between two nonzero digits are significant.
- For a decimal, all zeros that appear after the last nonzero digit are significant. For an integer, you cannot tell whether any zeros after the last nonzero digit are significant, so you should assume that they are not significant (unless you know otherwise).

Sometimes calculations involve measurements that have different numbers of significant digits. When this occurs, a good rule of thumb is to carry all digits through the calculation and then round the result to the same number of significant digits as the measurement with the *fewest* number of significant digits.

EXAMPLE Perform the indicated operation. Write your answer with the appropriate number of significant digits.

a.

63.498	5 significant digits
+ 32	2 significant digits
95.498	The sum has 2 significant digits.
95	Round to 2 significant digits.

b.

5605	4 significant digits
× 0.134	3 significant digits
751.204	The product has 3 significant digits.
751	Round to 3 significant digits.

EXAMPLE Multiply: 0.9000 · 20 · 13.526

Solution Of the three numbers, 20 has the fewest significant digits. Multiply all three numbers, then round the product to one significant digit.

$$0.9000 \cdot 20 \cdot 13.526 = 243.468$$
$$\approx 200$$

Note that some units, such as number of people, cannot be divided into fractional parts. In that case, use the significant digits of the other numbers to round the answer.

EXAMPLE A bill of $46.92 is divided among 3 people. How much does each person pay?

Solution The number of people is exact, so the fact that it is a one-digit number is irrelevant. Use the 4 significant digits of the bill, 46.92.

$46.92 \div 3 = \$15.64$

Each person should pay $15.64.

Practice

Simplify the expression. Write your answer with the appropriate number of significant digits.

1. $1569 + 98$

2. $1.0035 \cdot 9.5$

3. $-65 - 2.30$

4. $20 \div 29.6003$

5. $1984 - 1730$

6. $0.5 \div 0.0023$

7. $800 + 8$

8. $0.962 \cdot 0.1$

9. $1000 \cdot 0.30002$

10. $48.032 - 0.0009$

11. $0.05 \div 0.006$

12. $90 + 710$

13. $586 - 95 - 5$

14. $42.365 + 0.1008 + 3000$

15. $8888 \div 11 \div 4$

16. $4 \cdot 16 \cdot 1.023$

17. $2012 - 12 - 0.39561$

18. $4 + 1.32 + 1.0003$

19. $0.001 \div 1000 \div 0.02$

20. $981 \cdot 2003 \cdot 32.12$

21. $0.0222 - 0.2022 - 0.2200$

22. $645 + 10 \cdot 84$

23. $2 - 30 \cdot 6.09$

24. $84 \div 312 \cdot 0.3187$

25. $19.36 + 0.006 - 12$

26. $0.30020 \cdot 90 \div 27$

27. $(94{,}158.36 - 0.36) + 865$

28. $(0.32056 + 0.7944) \cdot 1.001$

29. $40.6 + 0.36 - 0.6512$

30. $(2 + 3.01) - (3 + 2.02)$

Perform the calculation. Write your answer with the appropriate number of significant digits.

31. \$22.50 per plant • 3 plants

32. \$56.80 per meal ÷ 4 customers

33. \$15.88 per shirt • 5 shirts

34. 36 miles ÷ 7.2 gallons

35. 40 tires • \$10.01 per tire

36. 3 cups per batch • 2 cups

37. 1532 dozens of donuts ÷ 11 donut shops

38. 32 math students • 3.25 bonus points per math student

39. 1.875 inches + 16.25 inches + 101 inches − 36.251 inches

40. 1.5 pounds of tomatoes + 3.25 pounds of tomatoes + 4.05 pounds of tomatoes

41. 0.025 tons of topsoil − 1.230 tons of topsoil + 7.90 tons of topsoil

42. 64.18 pounds of groceries ÷ 9 pounds of groceries per bag

43. \$1.25 per bottle of water • 12 bottles of water

44. 0.85 pound of apples + 2.79 pounds of apples

45. 16.27 ounces of tea ÷ 4 ounces of tea per bag

46. 800 square feet + 230 square feet + 405 square feet

47. (593.16 liters of solution + 276.03 liters of solution) • 4.1 moles of salt per liter of solution

48. 500 kilograms of paint + 6500 kilograms of paint + 3000 kilograms of paint + 625 kilograms of paint

49. 25.50 milligrams of aspirin + 400 milligrams of aspirin − 350 milligrams of aspirin

50. 0.007 micrograms of selenium + 0.0126 micrograms of potassium + 0.050438 micrograms of magnesium

51. (51 miles + 36 miles + 103 miles) ÷ 45 runners

Scientific Notation

Scientific notation is a way to write numbers using powers of 10. Numbers written in **scientific notation** have the form $c \times 10^n$ where $1 \le c < 10$ and n is an integer. Recall that $10^0 = 1$.

EXAMPLE   **Write each number in scientific notation.**

a. 93,000,000   Standard form

93,000,000   Move the decimal 7 places to the left.

9.3×10^7 Use 7 as an exponent of 10.

b. 0.002031   Standard form

0.002031   Move the decimal 5 places to the right.

2.031×10^{-5} Use −5 as an exponent of 10.

EXAMPLE   **Write each number in standard form.**

a. 4.26×10^{-5} The exponent of 10 is −5.

0.0000426   Move the decimal 5 places to the left.

0.0000426   Standard form

b. 8.309×10^4 The exponent of 10 is 4.

83,090   Move the decimal 4 places to the right.

83,090   Standard form

Practice

Write the number in scientific notation.

1. 3200

2. 4.1

3. 86,905

4. 0.000030351

5. 8.62

6. 791,000

7. 4.903

8. 6

9. 0.0042

10. 7651

11. 625,000,000

12. 12.4513802

13. 0.0090090

14. 49.52

15. 217

16. 0.10

17. 324

18. 134,028,501,000

19. 0.51000

20. 0.0000003

21. 16,020

22. 0.042603

23. 805.3090

24. 3.057000

25. 987,654,321

26. 0.0001897

27. 0.30258

28. 476.154283

Write the number in standard form.

29. 5×10^5

30. 3.01×10^{-8}

31. 1.25×10^3

32. 7.021×10^{-2}

33. 8.51×10^0

34. 9×10^{-4}

35. 7.35×10^6

36. 4.2×10^2

37. 1.89×10^{-2}

38. 2.004×10^3

39. 9.514×10^{-1}

40. 3.21005×10^9

41. 2.459×10^{-7}

42. 1.16×10^6

43. 2.17×10^2

44. 5.5661×10^{-1}

45. 4.57×10^4

46. 1.0010010×10^{-5}

47. 9.3502×10^{10}

48. 3.6054000×10^0

49. 6.42×10^{-2}

50. 5.6102×10^{-1}

51. 8.059030×10^2

52. 1.60003×10^{11}

53. 3.7×10^4

54. 8.6092×10^{-3}

55. 2.809075×10^9

56. 9.7014561×10^5

Points in the Coordinate Plane

A **coordinate plane** is formed by the intersection of a horizontal number line called the **x-axis** and a vertical number line called the **y-axis**. The axes meet at a point called the **origin** and divide the coordinate plane into four **quadrants**, numbered I, II, III, and IV.

Each point in a coordinate plane corresponds to an **ordered pair**, (x, y), of real numbers. The first number in an ordered pair is the **x-coordinate**, and the second number is the **y-coordinate**.

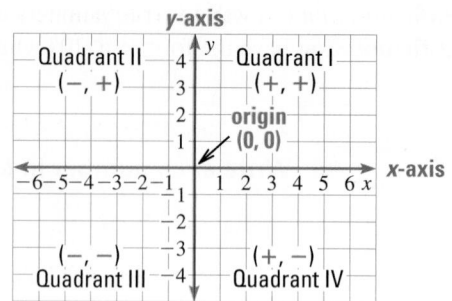

You can tell which quadrant a point is in by looking at the signs of its coordinates.

EXAMPLE   **Tell which quadrant the point is in. Then plot the point.**

A(3, 2)   The coordinates are positive, so the point is in Quadrant I. Start at the origin. The x-coordinate is 3, so move right 3 units. The y-coordinate is 2, so move up 2 units. Draw a point at (3, 2) and label it A.

B(0, −4)   The x-coordinate is zero, so the point is on the x-axis. Start at the origin. The x-coordinate is 0, so move left 0 units. The y-coordinate is −4, so move down 4 units. Draw a point at (0, −4) and label it B.

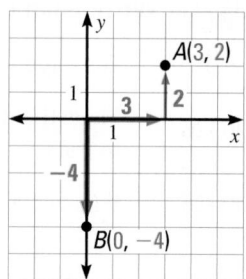

Practice

Write the ordered pairs that correspond to the points labeled *A*, *B*, *C*, and *D* in the coordinate plane.

1.
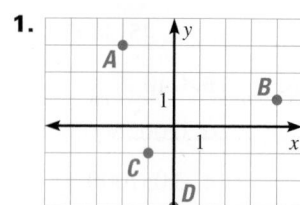

2.
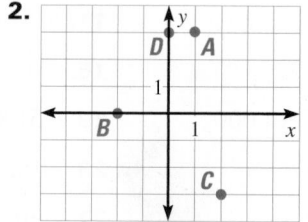

3.
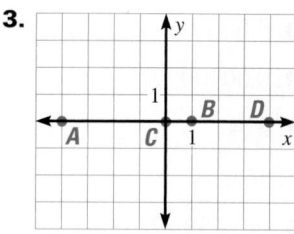

Plot and label the ordered pairs in a coordinate plane.

4. $A(1, 3), B(4, -2), C(-3, 0)$

5. $A(0, 1), B(-1, -2), C(5, 4)$

6. $A(-4, 0), B(3, 5), C(0, 2)$

7. $A(2, -2), B(5, -5), C(-4, 4)$

8. $A(1, -1), B(0, 0), C(-1, -1)$

9. $A(5, 2), B(5, -2), C(5, 0)$

Without plotting the point, tell whether it is in Quadrant I, Quadrant II, Quadrant III, or Quadrant IV.

10. $(-1, -10)$

11. $(-0.25, 0.125)$

12. $(8, -9)$

13. $(9, -8)$

14. $(7, -17)$

15. $(61, 34)$

16. $(3, -0.3)$

17. $(-4, -2)$

Perimeter and Circumference

The **perimeter** P of a figure is the distance around the figure, or the sum of the lengths of the edges.

> **EXAMPLE** Find the perimeter of the figure.
>
> **a.**
>
>
> **b.**
>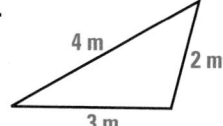
>
> **Solution**   **a.** $P = 4 + 8 + 1 + 5 = 18$ in.   **b.** $P = 3 + 2 + 4 = 9$ m

A **circle** consists of all points in a plane that are the same distance from a fixed point called the **center**. The distance between the center and any point on the circle is the **radius**. The distance across the circle through the center is the **diameter**. The diameter is twice the radius.

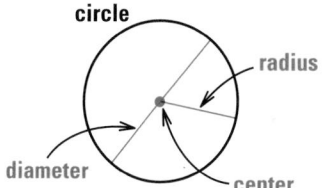

The **circumference** of a circle is the distance around the circle, or the perimeter of the circle. To find the circumference C of a circle, use the formula $C = 2\pi r$ where r is the radius.

> **EXAMPLE** Find the circumference of a circle with a radius of 10 feet.
>
> **Solution** $C = 2\pi r = 2\pi(10) = 20\pi \approx 20(3.14) = 62.8$
>
>   The circumference is 20π feet or about 62.8 feet.

Practice

Find the perimeter or circumference of the figure.

1.
2 ft, 4 ft, 4 ft, 2 ft

2.
3 m

3.
6 mm, 6 mm, 9 mm

4.

5 in., 3 in., 2 in., 3 in., 7 in.

5.
hexagon, 1.21 cm

6.
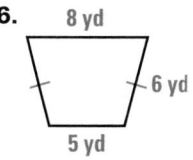
8 yd, 6 yd, 5 yd

7. a rectangle with length 5 ft and width 1 ft

8. a triangle with sides 3 m, 7 m, and 1 m

9. a circle with radius 8 miles

10. a semicircle with a diameter of 3 inches

11. a square with sides of 2.3 inches

12. a triangle with sides of 9 cm, 4 cm, 6 cm

13. a trapezoid with sides 4 m, 1 m, 7 m, and 1 m

14. a circle with a diameter of 3.71 ft

15. a triangle with sides 15 cm, 4 cm, and 15 cm

16. a rectangle with length 30.42 m and width 2 m

Area

The **area** of a two-dimensional figure is the number of square units enclosed by the figure.

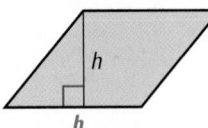

Area of a triangle: $A = \frac{1}{2}bh$

Area of a square: $A = s^2$

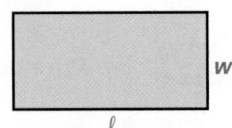

Area of a rectangle: $A = \ell w$

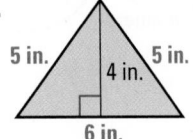

Area of a parallelogram: $A = bh$

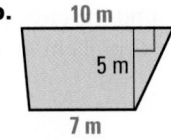

Area of a trapezoid: $A = \frac{1}{2}(b_1 + b_2)h$

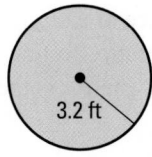

Area of a circle: $A = \pi r^2$

EXAMPLE Find the area of the figure.

a.

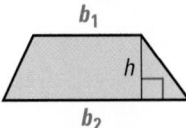

5 in.   5 in.   4 in.   6 in.

b.

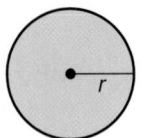

10 m   5 m   7 m

c.

3.2 ft

Solution

a. $A = \frac{1}{2}bh$

$= \frac{1}{2}(6)(4)$

$= 12$ square inches

b. $A = \frac{1}{2}(b_1 + b_2)h$

$= \frac{1}{2}(10 + 7)(5)$

$= 42.5$ square meters

c. $A = \pi r^2$

$= \pi(3.2)^2$

≈ 32 square feet

Practice

Find the area of the figure.

1.

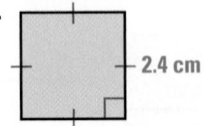

2.4 cm

2.

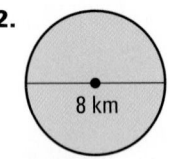

8 km

3.

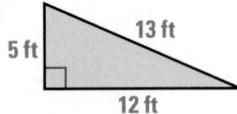

13 ft   5 ft   12 ft

4.

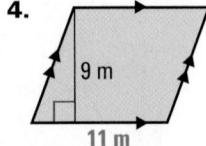

9 m   11 m

5. a parallelogram with height 4 m and base 9 m

6. a 3 mi by 8.4 mi rectangle

7. a trapezoid with bases 1 ft and 2.3 ft and height 9 ft

8. a circle with radius 5.98 in.

9. a triangle with base 7 cm and height 1 cm

10. a square with sides of length 13 mm

11. a 6 yd by 3.28 yd rectangle

12. a circle with a diameter of 1.5 ft

13. a triangle with base 34 m and height 9 m

14. a square with sides of length 46.5 yd

15. a parallelogram with height 6 cm and base 8 cm

16. a circle with radius 4.7 in.

Volume

The **volume** V of a solid is the amount of three-dimensional space in its interior. Volume is measured in cubic units, such as cubic meters (m^3). The volume of a solid can be found by multiplying the area of its base by its height.

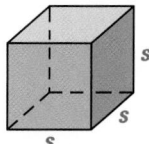

Volume of a cube: $V = s^3$

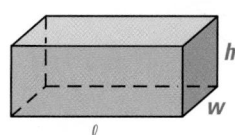

Volume of a box: $V = \ell wh$

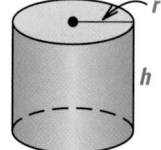

Volume of a cylinder: $V = \pi r^2 h$

EXAMPLE   Find the volume of the solid.

Solution

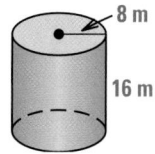

$V = \pi r^2 h$	Volume of a cylinder
$= \pi(8)^2(16)$	Substitute know values.
$= 1024\pi$	Multiply.
≈ 3215 cubic meters (m^3)	

EXAMPLE   Find the volume of a box with length 12 inches, width 7 inches, and height 2 inches.

Solution

$$V = \ell wh = (12)(7)(2) = 168$$

The volume is 168 cubic inches.

Practice

Find the volume of the solid

1.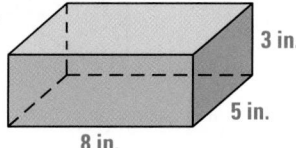
3 in.
5 in.
8 in.

2.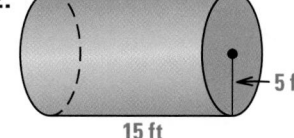
5 ft
15 ft

3.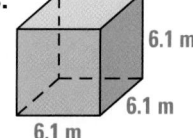
6.1 m
6.1 m
6.1 m

4. a cylinder with diameter 4.2 m and height 1 m

5. a cube with sides of length 1.01 cm

6. a cubic shipping box with sides of length 3 ft

7. a cube with sides of length 0.2 ft

8. a box with length 6 m, width 6 m, and height 8 m

9. a cube with sides of length 5 m

10. a cylinder with radius 0.05 ft and height 110 ft

11. a cube with sides of length 60 mm

12. a car battery with length 18 in., width 6 in., and height 8 in.

13. a cylindrical metal rod with diameter 0.3 m and length 15 m

Triangle Relationships

The sum of the measures of the angles of a triangle is 180°.

EXAMPLE   **Find the value of *x*.**

Solution

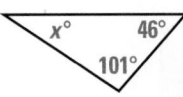

$$180° = 101° + 46° - x$$

$$x = 33°$$

The **triangle inequality theorem** states that the sum of the lengths of any two sides of a triangle is greater than the length of the third side.

$$AB + BC > AC$$

$$AC + BC > AB$$

$$AB + AC > BC$$

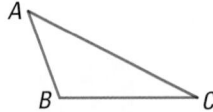

EXAMPLE   **Can the side lengths form a triangle? Explain.**

   a. 3, 5, 8   **b.** 4, 7, 10   **c.** 2, 6, 9

Solution

  a. No, because
     3 + 5 = 8.

  b. Yes, because
     4 + 7 > 10
     4 + 10 > 7, and
     7 + 10 > 4.

  c. No, because
     2 + 6 < 9.

Practice

Find the value of *x*.

1.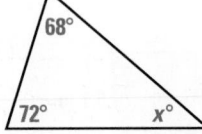

2.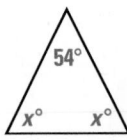

3.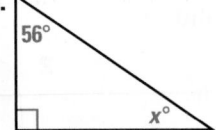

4.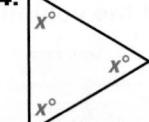

5. a triangle with angles $x°$, 32°, and 28°   **6.** a triangle with angles $x°$, 110°, and 67°

Can a triangle have the given angle measures? Explain.

  7. 150°, 25°, 75°   **8.** 12°, 133°, 5°   **9.** 59°, 60°, 61°   **10.** 17°, 4°, 159°

11. 78°, 22°, 100°   **12.** 54°, 66°, 71°   **13.** 1°, 10°, 169°   **14.** 20°, 40°, 80°

Can the given side lengths form a triangle? Explain.

15. 8, 10, 12   **16.** 13, 5, 19   **17.** 23, 64, 41   **18.** 45, 46, 47

19. 1, 2, 3   **20.** 5, 10, 20   **21.** 3, 8, 10   **22.** 0.5, 0.75, 0.77

Right Triangle Relationships

The **Pythagorean theorem** states that the sum of the squares of the lengths of the legs equals the square of the length of the hypotenuse.

$$a^2 + b^2 = c^2$$

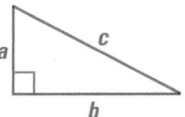

EXAMPLE   Find the value of *x*.

a.

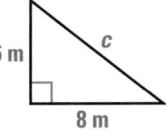

b.

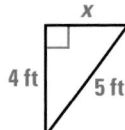

Solution

a. $6^2 + 8^2 = c^2$

$36 + 64 = c^2$

$100 = c^2$

$10 = c$

b. $x^2 + 4^2 = 5^2$

$x^2 + 16 = 25$

$x^2 = 9$

$x = 3$

A right triangle with angle measures of 45°, 45°, and 90° is called a **45°-45°-90° triangle**. In a 45°-45°-90° triangle, the length of the hypotenuse is the length of a leg times √2. Notice that a 45°-45°-90° is an isosceles triangle.

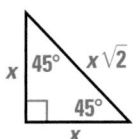

In a **30°-60°-90° triangle,** the hypotenuse is twice as long as the shorter leg, and the longer leg is the length of the shorter leg times √3.

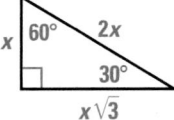

Practice

Find the value of *x*. Give your answer in simplest radical form.

1.

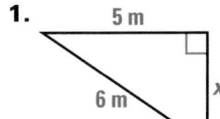

2.

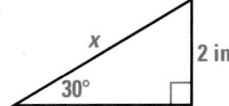

3.

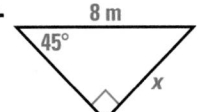

4.

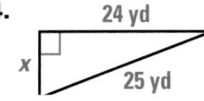

5.

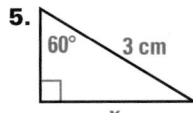

6.

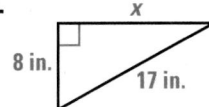

7.

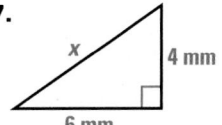

8.

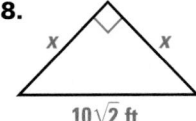

9.

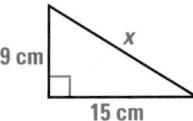

10.

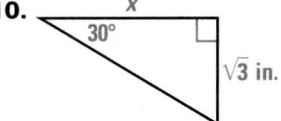

11.

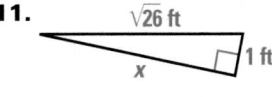

12.

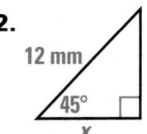

Symmetry

A figure has **line symmetry** if it can be divided by a line into two equal parts, each of which is the mirror image of the other. The line that divides the figure into two parts is called the **line of symmetry**.

EXAMPLE   Identify the line(s) of symmetry in the figure.

a.

b.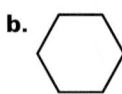

c.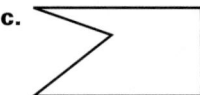

Solution

a. This figure has a horizontal line of symmetry and a vertical line of symmetry.

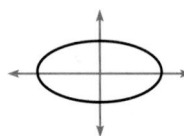

b. This figure has six lines of symmetry.

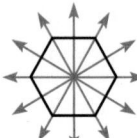

c. This figure is not symmetric. It has no line of symmetry.

A figure has **rotational symmetry** if it coincides with itself after rotating 180° or less, either clockwise or counterclockwise, about a point. The point of rotation is usually the center of the figure.

EXAMPLE   Identify any rotational symmetry in the figure.

a.

b.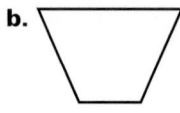

c.

Solution

a. This figure has rotational symmetry. It will coincide with itself after being rotated 90° or 180° in either direction. Note that the point of rotation is located at the center of the figure.

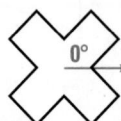      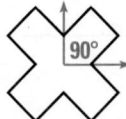

b. This figure has no rotational symmetry.

c. This figure has rotational symmetry. It will coincide with itself after being rotated 120° in either direction.

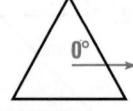   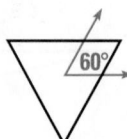   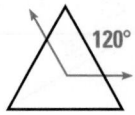

Practice

Identify any lines of symmetry.

1.

2.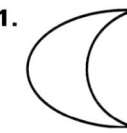

3.

4.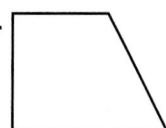

5.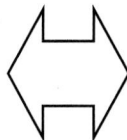

6.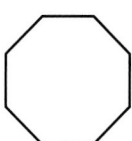

7.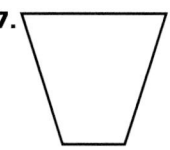

8.

9.

10.

11. **8**

12.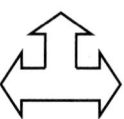

13.

14.

15. **WOW**

16.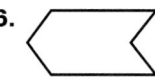

Identify any rotational symmetry.

17.

18.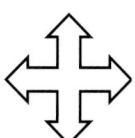

19.

20.

21.

22.

23.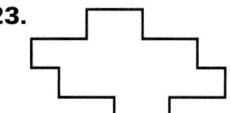

24. **I**

25.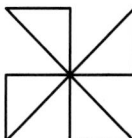

26.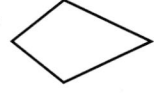

27.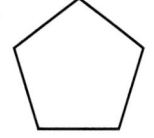

28.

29.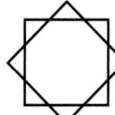

30.

31. **906**

32.

Transformations

A **transformation** is a change made to the size or position of a figure. The new figure after a transformation is called the **image**.

A **translation** is a transformation that slides every point of a figure the same distance in the same direction. A figure and its translated image are congruent.

> **EXAMPLE** Translate $\overline{AB}$ right 4 units and down 1 unit.
>
> **Solution**
>
> To shift $\overline{AB}$ right 4 units, add 4 to each x-coordinate. To shift $\overline{AB}$ down 1 unit, subtract 1 from each y-coordinate. You can describe this transformation as $\overline{AB}$ *is mapped onto* $\overline{A'B'}$. This is written symbolically as $\overline{AB} \rightarrow \overline{A'B'}$.
>
> $$A(-1, 4) \rightarrow A'(-1 + 4, 4 + (-1)) = A'(3, 3)$$
> $$B(0, 0) \rightarrow B'(0 + 4, 0 + (-1)) = B'(4, -1)$$

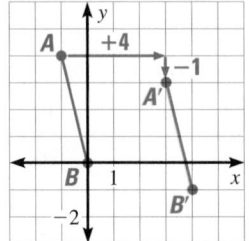

A **reflection** is a transformation that creates a mirror image of the figure. The original figure is reflected in a line that is called the **line of reflection**. A figure and its reflected image are congruent.

> **EXAMPLE** Reflect the figure as described.
>
> **a.** Reflect the blue figure in the y-axis. **b.** Reflect the blue trapezoid in the x-axis.
>
> **Solution**
>
> **a.** Use $(x, y) \rightarrow (-x, y)$ with each vertex. **b.** Use $(x, y) \rightarrow (x, -y)$ with each vertex.
>
> Change the sign of each x-coordinate.
>
> Change the sign of each y-coordinate.

A **rotation** is a transformation in which a figure is turned about a fixed point, called the **center of rotation**. The direction can be clockwise or counterclockwise.

Rotation About the Origin	
180° either direction	$(x, y) \rightarrow (-x, -y)$
90° clockwise	$(x, y) \rightarrow (y, -x)$
90° counterclockwise	$(x, y) \rightarrow (-y, x)$

EXAMPLE Rotate *RSTV* 180° about the origin.

Solution

Use $(x, y) \rightarrow (-x, -y)$ with each vertex.

$R(0, 3) \rightarrow R'(0, -3)$
$S(4, 3) \rightarrow S'(-4, -3)$
$T(4, 1) \rightarrow T'(-4, -1)$
$V(1, 1) \rightarrow V'(-1, -1)$

Change every coordinate to its opposite.

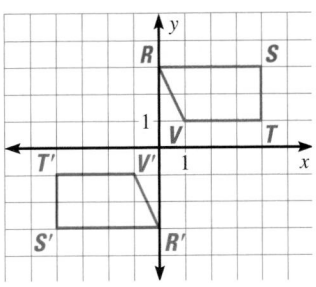

Graph the new vertices. Then draw the image.

A **dilation** is a transformation in which every point of a figure is multiplied by a **scale factor**, k, to create a similar image (see page 762). A figure *stretches* if $k > 1$ and *shrinks* if $0 < k < 1$. A figure and its dilated image are similar.

EXAMPLE Dilate $\overline{AB}$ by a scale factor of 3.

Solution

Multiply the coordinates of A and B by the scale factor 3.

Use $(x, y) \rightarrow (3x, 3y)$ with each vertex.

$A(2, 0) \rightarrow A'(3 \cdot 2, 3 \cdot 0) = A'(6, 0)$
$B(5, 4) \rightarrow B'(3 \cdot 5, 3 \cdot 4) = B'(15, 12)$

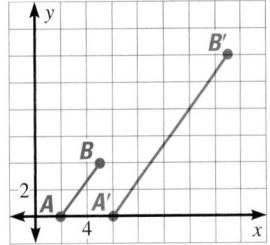

Graph the new vertices. Then draw the image.

Practice

Give the coordinates of $A(-5, 3)$ after the transformation. For rotations, rotate about the origin.

1. Translate 2 units down.

2. Reflect in the x-axis.

3. Dilate by $\frac{5}{9}$.

4. Dilate by 20.

5. Translate 4 units right.

6. Rotate 90° clockwise.

7. Reflect in the y-axis.

8. Rotate 180°.

9. Dilate by 4.

10. Translate 8 units left and 4 units up.

11. Translate 2 units left and 3 units down.

12. Translate 5 units right and 9 units up.

13. Reflect in the x-axis and the y-axis.

Transform *EFGH*. Graph the result. For rotations, rotate about the origin.

14. Reflect in the y-axis.

15. Rotate 90° clockwise.

16. Translate 1 unit down.

17. Dilate by $\frac{5}{2}$.

18. Translate 7 units left.

19. Reflect in the x-axis.

20. Rotate 180°.

21. Dilate by $\frac{1}{4}$.

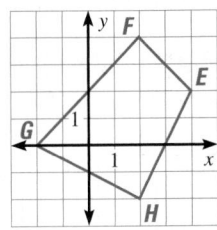

Similar Figures

Two figures are *congruent* if they have the same shape and the same size. If two figures are congruent, then corresponding angles are congruent and corresponding sides are congruent. Congruent angles are represented by matching arcs, and congruent sides are represented by matching tick marks.

Two figures are **similar** if they have the same shape but not necessarily the same size. If two figures are similar, then corresponding angles are congruent and the ratios of the lengths of corresponding sides are equal. The triangles shown are similar.

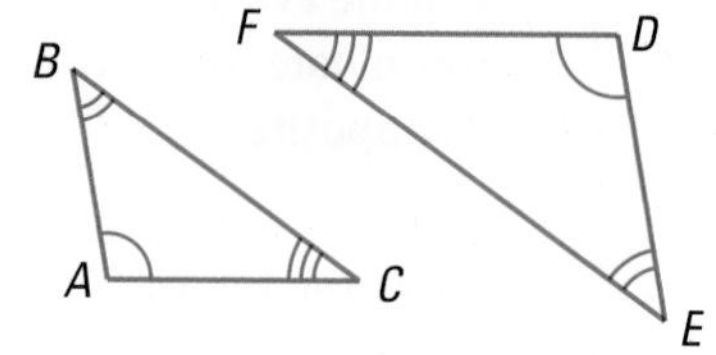

$m\angle A \cong m\angle D$ $\quad m\angle B \cong m\angle E$ $\quad m\angle C \cong m\angle F$ $\quad \frac{AB}{DE} = \frac{AC}{DF} = \frac{BC}{EF}$

EXAMPLE **The two polygons are similar. Find the values of *x* and *y*.**

Solution

Write and solve a proportion to find each unknown length.

$$\frac{AB}{EF} = \frac{BC}{FG} \qquad \frac{AD}{EH} = \frac{CD}{GH}$$

$$\frac{3}{3.75} = \frac{6}{x} \qquad \frac{y}{12.5} = \frac{11}{13.75}$$

$$3x = 22.5 \qquad 13.75y = 137.5$$

$$x = 7.5 \qquad y = 10$$

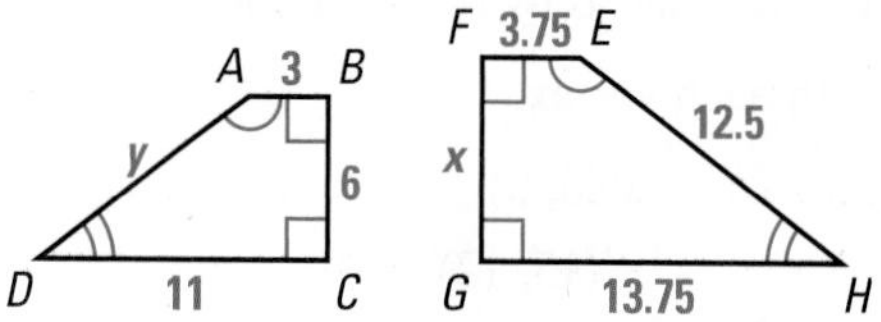

Practice

The two polygons are similar. Find the values of *x* and *y*.

1.

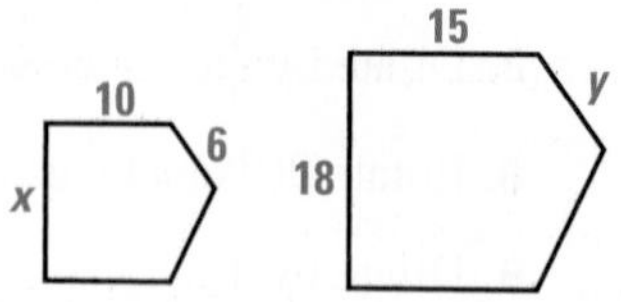

2.

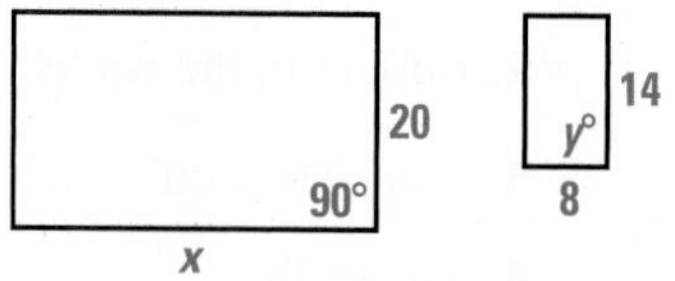

3.

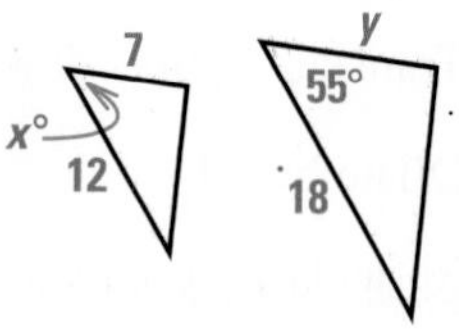

4.

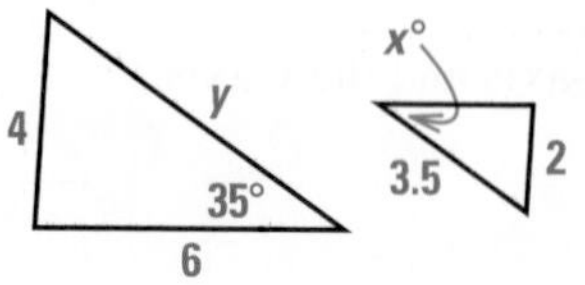

5.

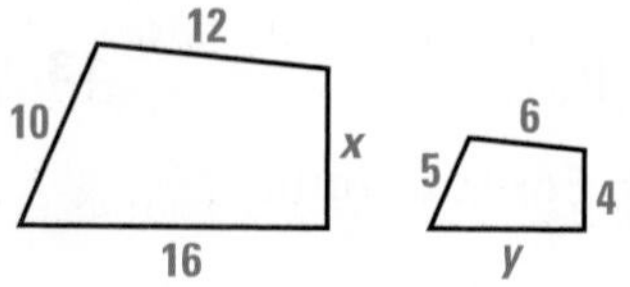

6.

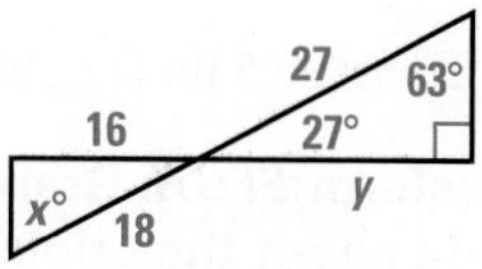

7.

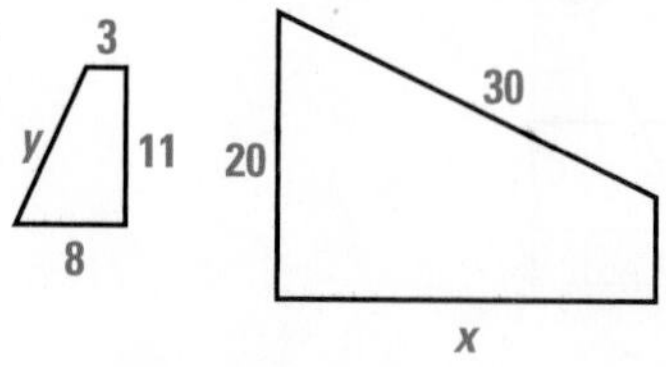

8.

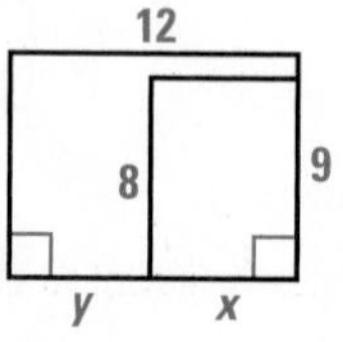

9.

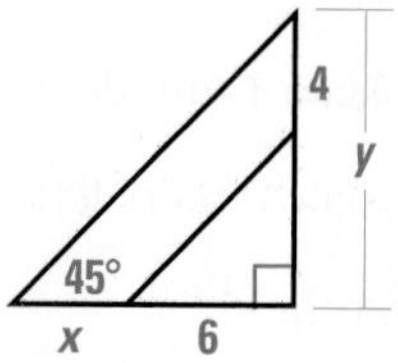

Logical Argument

A logical argument has two given statements, called **premises**, and a statement that follows them, called a **conclusion**.

If a figure is a square, then it is a quadrilateral.	Premise 1
ABCD is a square.	Premise 2
Therefore, ABCD is a quadrilateral.	Conclusion

There are five types of logical arguments that can be made using these statements. Arguments that use these patterns correctly will have a **valid conclusion**. Arguments that use these patterns incorrectly will have an **invalid conclusion**.

The letters *p*, *q* and *r* are often used to write an argument symbolically. In the examples below, *p*, *q* and *r* are given the following meanings.

p: a figure is a square

q: a figure is a quadrilateral

r: a figure is a parallelogram

Type of Argument	Pattern	Example
Direct Argument	If *p* is true, then *q* is true. *p* is true. Therefore, *q* is true.	If *ABCD* is a square, then it is a quadrilateral. *ABCD* is a square. Therefore, *ABCD* is a quadrilateral.
Indirect Argument	If *p* is true, then *q* is true. *q* is not true. Therefore, *p* is not true.	If *ABCD* is a square, then it is a quadrilateral. *ABCD* is not a quadrilateral. Therefore, *ABCD* is not a square.
Chain Rule	If *p* is true, then *q* is true. If *q* is true, then *r* is true. Therefore, if *p*, then *r*.	If *ABCD* is a square, then it is a quadrilateral. If *ABCD* is a quadrilateral, then it is a polygon. If *ABCD* is a square, then it is a polygon.
Or **Rule**	*p* is true or *q* is true. *p* is not true. Therefore, *q* is true.	*ABCD* is a square or a quadrilateral. *ABCD* is not a square. Therefore, *ABCD* is a quadrilateral.
And **Rule**	*p* and *q* are not both true. But *q* is true. Therefore, *p* is not true.	*ABCD* is not both a square and a quadrilateral. *ABCD* is a quadrilateral. Therefore, *ABCD* is not a square.

EXAMPLE State whether the conclusion is *valid* or *invalid*. If the conclusion is valid, name the type of logical argument used.

a. If you play drums, then you are a musician. You are a musician. Therefore, you play drums.

b. If $3x + 2 = 5$, then $x = 1$. $x \neq 1$. Therefore, $3x + 2 \neq 5$.

Solution

a. The conclusion is invalid.

b. The conclusion is valid. This is an example of an indirect argument.

A compound statement has two or more parts joined by *or* or *and*. For an *and* statement to be true, each part must be true. For an *or* statement to be true, at least one part must be true.

EXAMPLE Tell whether the compound statement is *true* or *false*. Explain.

a. $2 + 3 = 5$ and $2 \cdot 3 = 6$

b. $2 + 3 = 6$ and $2 \cdot 3 = 6$

c. $2 + 3 = 6$ or $2 \cdot 3 = 6$

d. $2 + 3 = 6$ or $2 \cdot 3 = 5$

Solution

a. True; both parts are true.

b. False; only one part is true, but both must be true for an *and* statement.

c. True; at least one part is true, as required for an *or* statement.

d. False; no part is true.

Practice

Use logical reasoning to decide whether the conclusion is *valid* or *invalid*. If the conclusion is valid, name the type of argument used.

1. Bill is at the game or Bill is at work.
   Bill is not at the game.
   Therefore, Bill is at work.

2. If $x = 3$, then $y = 9$.
   If $y = 9$, then $z = 81$.
   Therefore, if $z = 81$, then $x = 3$.

3. If Jack writes books, Jack is an author.
   Jack is not an author.
   Therefore, Jack writes books.

4. A whale is not both a fish and a mammal.
   A whale is not a fish.
   Therefore, a whale is not a mammal.

5. If $x = 4$, then $2x - 8 = 0$.
   $x = 4$.
   Therefore, $2x - 8 = 0$.

6. Mike wins the race or Sam wins the race.
   Sam loses the race.
   Therefore, Mike wins the race.

7. If Al is from Paris, he is from France.
   If Al is from France, he is from Europe.
   Therefore, if Al is from Paris, he is from Europe.

8. $\angle ABC$ is not both acute and obtuse.
   $\angle ABC$ is obtuse.
   Therefore, $\angle ABC$ is acute.

9. The car is blue or the car is purple.
   The car is not blue.
   Therefore, the car is purple.

10. If that tree is tall, Paul is a short.
    Paul is a short.
    Therefore, that tree is tall.

State whether each compound statement is *true* or *false*.

11. $3 < 5$ or $8 > 9$

12. $4 \geq -4$ and $1 > 1$

13. $3 \cdot 0.3 < 1$ or $3 \cdot 0.3 > 1$

14. $1 + 1 = 2$ or $1 - 1 = -2$

15. $6 > 7$ or $7 < 6$

16. $1 \cdot 1 = 1$ and $-1 \cdot -1 = -1$

17. $1 \cdot 1 = 1$ and $-1 \div -1 = 1$

18. $4 \geq 4$ and $4 = 4$ and $4 \leq 4$

19. $164 < 165$ and $164 \leq 165$ and $164 > 165$

20. $101 = 102$ or $101 < 201$ or $101 \geq 101$

If-Then Statements and Counterexamples

The **if-then statement** "if p, then q" has two parts. The "if" part contains the **hypothesis** and the "then" part contains the **conclusion**.

SKILLS REVIEW HANDBOOK

EXAMPLE Identify the hypothesis and conclusion.

a. Things get wet when it rains.   **b.** Great Danes are big dogs.

Solution

Rewrite the statement as an if-then statement.

a. If it rains, then things get wet.   **b.** If a dog is a Great Dane, then the dog is big.
Hypothesis: it rains   Hypothesis: a dog is a Great Dane
Conclusion: things get wet   Conclusion: the dog is big

The **converse** of a conditional statement is formed by switching the hypothesis and the conclusion. The converse of a true statement is not necessarily true.

EXAMPLE Write the converse of the conditional statement. Then tell whether the converse is *true* or *false*.

a. If $x < 5$, then $x < 7$.   **b.** If $x + 5 = 12$, then $x = 7$.

Solution
a. Converse: If $x < 7$, then $x < 5$. False

b. Converse: If $x = 7$, then $x + 5 = 12$. True

A **biconditional statement** is a statement that has the words "if and only if". You can write a conditional statement and its converse together as a biconditional statement. A biconditional statement is true only when the conditional statement and its converse are both true.

EXAMPLE Tell whether the biconditional statement is *true* or *false*. Explain.

a. A triangle is isosceles if and only if it has two equal sides.

b. An angle measures 45° if and only if it is an acute angle.

Solution
a. Conditional: If a triangle is isosceles, then it has two equal sides. True

Converse: If a triangle has two equal sides, then it is isosceles. True

The biconditional statement is true because the conditional and its converse are both true.

b. Conditional: If the measure of an angle is 45°, then it is an acute angle. True

Converse: If an angle is acute, then its measure is 45°. False

The biconditional is false because the converse is not true.

A **counterexample** is an example that shows that a statement is false.

> **EXAMPLE** Tell whether the statement is true or false. If it is false, give a counterexample.
>
> **a.** If a and b are real numbers, then $|a + b| = |a| + |b|$
>   False. A counterexample is $a = 1$ and $b = -2$, because $|1 + (-2)| = 1$
>   and $|1| + |-2| = 3$.
>
> **b.** If $x^2 = 9$, then $x = 3$.
>   False. A counterexample is $x = -3$, because $(-3)^2 = 9$.

Practice

Rewrite the statement as an if-then statement.

1. You can go to the movies if you take your brother.

2. $5x = 10$ when $x = 2$.

3. A hexagon has 6 sides.

4. The area of a circle is $A = \pi r^2$.

5. Janet does very well on math tests.

6. Alternate interior angles are congruent.

7. The equation of the unit circle is $x^2 + y^2 = 1$.

8. The volume of a cube is $V = s^3$.

Write the converse of the conditional statement. Then tell whether the converse is *true* or *false*.

9. If two lines intersect, their intersection is a point.

10. If it snows tonight, the roads will be icy tomorrow.

11. If a triangle has two equal angles, the triangle has two equal sides.

12. If $x = 5$, then $x^2 + 5 = 30$.

13. If $5x + 13 < 23$, then $x < 2$.

14. If Marquisa moves out-of-town, then her phone number will change.

Tell whether the biconditional statement is *true* or *false*. Explain.

15. A polygon is a hexagon if and only if it has 6 sides.

16. $x^2 = 25$ if and only if $x = 5$.

17. A quadrilateral is a rectangle if and only if it has four right angles.

18. $x^2 > 1$ if and only if $x > 1$.

19. A number is divisible by 3 if and only if the sum of the digits of a number is divisible by 3.

20. Two lines are parallel if and only if they never intersect.

Determine whether the statement is *true* or *false*. If it is false, give a counterexample.

21. All birds fly.

22. If $\sqrt{x} = 2$, then $x = 4$.

23. If $x^2 = 144$, then $x = 12$.

24. All musicians play the piano.

Justify Reasoning

Algebraic reasoning can be justified using the properties of equality.

Property	Statement of Property	Example
Addition Property of Equality	*Add* the same number to each side.	If $a = b$, then $a + c = b + c$.
Subtraction Property of Equality	*Subtract* the same number from each side.	If $a = b$, then $a - c = b - c$.
Multiplication Property of Equality	*Multiply* each side by the same nonzero number.	If $a = b$ and $c \neq 0$, then $a \cdot c = b \cdot c$.
Division Property of Equality	*Divide* each side by the same nonzero number.	If $a = b$ and $c \neq 0$, then $a \div c = b \div c$
Distributive Property	The product of a number and a sum (or difference) is equal to the sum (or difference) of the products.	$a(b + c) = ab + ac$ $a(b - c) = ab - ac$

You may also use algebraic definitions, such as the definition of raising to a power, to justify algebraic reasoning.

EXAMPLE Solve the equation $x^2 + 4 = 40$. Justify each step.

Solution

$x^2 + 4 = 40$	Given
$x^2 = 36$	Subtraction property of equality
$x = \pm 6$	Find square roots.

Practice

Name the property that justifies the statement.

1. If $6(x - 2) = 3$, then $6x - 12 = 3$.

2. If $x - 5 = 6$, then $x = 11$.

3. If $4x = 12$, then $x = 3$.

4. If $\frac{4x}{7} = 8$, then $4x = 56$.

5. If $2x + 4 = 8$, then $2(x + 2) = 8$.

6. If $7x = 5$, then $7x + 5 = 10$.

7. If $\sqrt{x} = 5$, then $x = 25$.

8. If $x = 8$, then $2x - 4 = 12$.

9. If $5x - 3 = 0$, then $8(5x - 3) = 0$.

10. If $3x = 27$, then $x = 9$.

Solve the equation for *x*. Justify each step.

11. $-x = 5$

12. $7 - x = 14$

13. $9x = 45$

14. $\frac{8x}{3} = 72$

15. $x + 8 = 22$

16. $4(1 - x) = 10$

17. $-2x - 5 = -4$

18. $4 + 12x = 24$

19. $-\frac{5}{2}(-6 - 2x) = 15$

20. $3x + 6 = 18$

21. $x^2 = 36$

22. $x^3 + 3 = 30$

Use an Equation or Formula

Some situations require you to use a specific formula to solve the problem.

EXAMPLE You drive at an average of 45 miles per hour for 20 minutes. How far do you drive?

Solution

The formula for distance is $d = rt$ where d is the distance (in miles), r is the rate (in miles per hour), and t is the time (in hours).

Convert 20 minutes to hours.

$$20 \text{ min} \cdot \frac{1 \text{ hour}}{60 \text{ min}} = \frac{20}{60} \text{ hour} = \frac{1}{3} \text{ hour}$$

$\quad d = rt$ Write formula for distance.

$\quad = 45 \cdot \dfrac{1}{3}$ Substitute $r = 45$ and $t = \dfrac{1}{3}$.

$\quad = 15$ Simplify.

You drive 15 miles.

Practice

Use an equation or formula to solve the problem. See page 798 for a table of geometry formulas.

1. You jog 5 miles in 60 minutes. Find the rate at which you jog.

2. The perimeter of a rectangle is 40 cm. The length is 3 times the width. Find the length and width of the rectangle.

3. A farmer wants to fence a rectangular pen. The area of the pen is 36 square yards. The width of the pen is 3 yards. What is the total length of fencing the farmer will need?

4. You bike at an average of 12 miles an hour for 45 minutes. How far do you bike?

5. A rectangular pool has length 15 feet, width 10 feet, and depth 10 feet. How much water will the pool hold?

6. How many small cubes with side length 1 centimeter does it take to fill a larger cube with side length 5 centimeters?

7. How long does it take you to drive 200 miles at an average of 50 miles per hour?

8. The midpoint of the line segment formed by the points (x_1, y_1) and (x_2, y_2) is given by the formula $M\left(\dfrac{x_1 + x_2}{2}, \dfrac{y_1 + y_2}{2}\right)$. In a coordinate plane, what is the midpoint of the line segment formed by the points $(-2, 3)$ and $(4, 2)$?

9. The slope m of a line through points (x_1, y_1) and (x_2, y_2) is given by the formula $m = \dfrac{y_2 - y_1}{x_2 - x_1}$. Use this formula to find the slope of the line through $(5, 3)$ and $(8, 12)$.

Draw a Diagram

When a problem is not illustrated, you may find it helpful to draw a diagram that summarizes the information you are given.

EXAMPLE A transversal intersects two parallel lines. One pair of alternate interior angles measures 62°. Find the measures of the other two alternate interior angles.

Solution

From the diagram, you can see that the unknown angle and the 62° angle form a straight line. So, the angles are complementary.

$$62 + x = 180$$
$$x = 180 - 62$$
$$x = 118$$

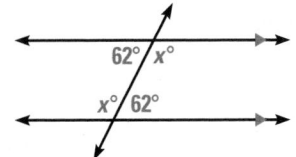

Practice

Use a diagram to solve the problem.

1. Ken runs halfway around a circle with a circumference of 31.4 meters. He then runs in a straight line back to his starting point. What is the length of this line segment?

2. Consider the square $ABCD$ in the coordinate plane with vertices $(0, 0)$, $(3, 0)$, $(3, 3)$, and $(0, 3)$. Reflect $ABCD$ about the x-axis, then translate 2 units down and 1 unit right.

3. The area of a rectangular garden is 72 square yards. The length of the garden is 9 yards. Copy and label the rectangle shown to represent this situation. What is the width of the garden?

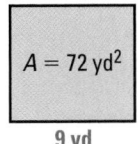

$A = 72 \text{ yd}^2$

9 yd

4. You build a pyramid in which each layer is one inch shorter than the previous layer. The first layer is 13 inches tall. There are 10 layers. How tall is the pyramid?

5. A rectangular stage 12 meters wide is built on a hill. A support is needed at the front of the stage to make it level. The distance from the back of the stage to the bottom of the support at the front of the stage is 13 meters. Copy and label the diagram shown to represent this situation. How tall is the support at the front of the stage?

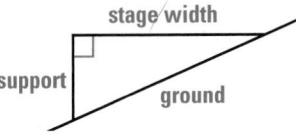

6. Justin wants to frame a picture that measures 5 inches by 3 inches. He plans to use a framing mat that is 1 inch wide on all sides. Find the total area of the picture and the mat.

7. Nicole cuts a rectangular pizza into pieces that measure 8 square centimeters. The pizza is 4 pieces wide and 12 pieces long. What is the area of the pizza?

8. Dale cuts a round cake into equally sized wedges that measure 5 inches from tip to outside edge. What is the circumference of the cake?

Make a Table or List

When a problem contains many different possibilities, it is often helpful to make a table or list of all of the possibilities.

EXAMPLE A car dealership offers a new model car in blue, black, or red, with 2 doors, 4 doors, or a hatchback. How many different ways could you choose a car?

Solution

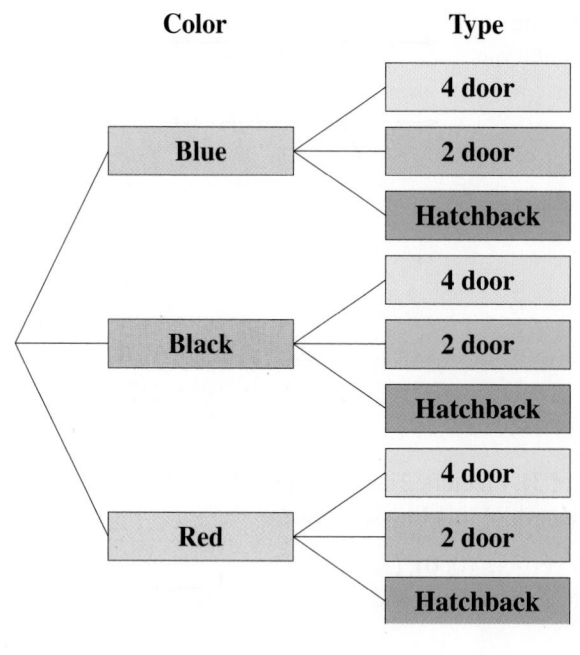

Color	Type	Possible Combinations
Blue	4 door	Blue with 4 doors
	2 door	Blue with 2 doors
	Hatchback	Blue with a hatchback
Black	4 door	Black with 4 doors
	2 door	Black with 2 doors
	Hatchback	Black with a hatchback
Red	4 door	Red with 4 doors
	2 door	Red with 2 doors
	Hatchback	Red with a hatchback

Practice

Use a table or list to solve the problem.

1. Alexandra forgot the code to unlock her bicycle lock. The code is a four-digit number composed of zeros and ones. How many different possibilities are there?

2. An ice cream shop offers sundaes with vanilla, chocolate, or strawberry ice cream and fudge, chocolate syrup, strawberry syrup, or butterscotch as toppings. How many different ways could you choose a sundae?

3. Walter is packing for a camping trip and wants to bring 2 pairs of shoes, 3 pairs of shorts, and 5 different t-shirts. How many different outfits will he have?

4. You can choose from red, pink, or white roses. How many different ways can you choose 3 roses?

5. A restaurant offers a dinner special. You can choose from 3 kinds of meat and 5 side dishes. How many different ways can you choose a meal?

6. Five runners are competing in a track race. How many different ways can they finish in first, second, and third place?

Solve a Simpler Problem

When solving a problem, it is often easier to solve a similar problem with simpler numbers. Then you can use what you learned from solving the simpler problem to solve the orginal problem.

EXAMPLE Evaluate $(1001)^2$ without using a calculator.

Solution

Notice that $(1001)^2$ can be written as $(x + 1)^2$ when $x = 1000$.

$$(x + 1)^2 = x^2 + 2x + 1$$
$$= (1000)^2 + 2(1000) + 1$$
$$= 1,000,000 + 2000 + 1$$
$$= 1,002,001$$

EXAMPLE What is the last digit of $(234,720)^9$?

Solution

Notice that $(234,720)^9$ can be written as $(23,472 \cdot 10)^9 = (23,472)^9(10)^9$. Recall that any number that is a multiple of 10 ends in a zero. So the last digit of $(234,720)^9$ is 0.

Practice

Solve the problem by first solving simpler problems.

1. If $253x^2 - 506x + 253 = 0$, what must x equal?

2. Gloria works 35 hours a week and 52 weeks a year. She earns an income of $24,115 per year. How much does she make in one hour?

3. How many diagonals does a convex polygon with 18 sides have?

4. Evaluate $(0.000000011)^{11}$ without using a calculator.

5. You deposit $840 in an account that pays 4.5% annual interest compounded yearly. What is the account balance after 9 years?

6. Mike takes a walk where each step is twice as long as the first. If the first step he takes is 1 inch long, how many feet will he have walked after 5 steps?

7. Find the sum of the integers from 1 to 100 without using a calculator.

8. Evaluate 2^{16} without using a calculator.

9. Evaluate 16^2 without using a calculator.

10. If a particle moving at 1 kilometer per second were to triple its speed every five minutes, how long will it take to reach a speed of 59,049 km/s?

11. A round cake is cut in half through the center. How many cuts through the center are needed to divide the cake into 12 equal pieces?

Break into Simpler Parts

You may want to break a difficult problem into more easily managed parts or cases. Be sure the parts or cases are *mutually exclusive* (that is, they do not overlap) and *collectively exhaustive* (that is, they cover all the possibilities).

EXAMPLE   **Find the area of the figure shown below.**

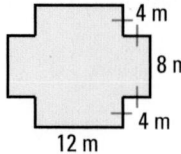

Solution

Break the figure into 3 rectangles as shown at the right.

Total Area = **Area of big rectangle + Area of small rectangles**

$$= (12)[4 + 8 + 4] + 2[(8)(4)]$$

$$= (12)(16) + 64$$

$$= 192 + 64$$

$$= 256$$

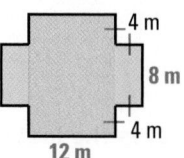

The area of the figure is 256 square meters.

Practice

Solve the problem by breaking it into simpler parts or cases.

1. A maintenance worker is putting numbers on school lockers starting with 0001. There are 4000 lockers. How many times will the last digit be 3?

2. In a best-of-seven series, the first team to win four games wins the series. How many ways are there for a team to lose a best-of-seven series?

3. You run west 5 miles, north 5.6 miles, west 2 miles, and north 3 miles. You then run straight back to your starting point. How far do you run?

4. Find the sum of the even integers between 0 and 100. Then find the sum of the odd integers between 0 and 100. Subtract the sums. What is the final result?

Find the area of the shaded region.

5.
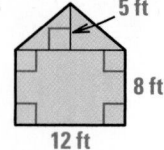

6.
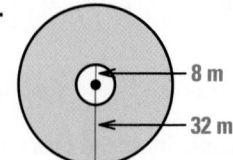

7.
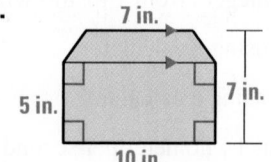

8.
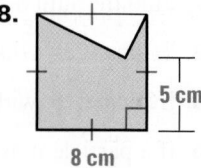

Guess, Check, and Revise

Some problems can be solved by choosing a reasonable guess for the answer, then checking whether the guess is correct. If the guess is not correct, you can revise the guess and try again.

EXAMPLE You are saving money for a new bike that costs $275. You already have $80. You are able to save $15 a week. How long will it take you to save enough money for the bike?

Solution

Guess: Try 10 weeks.

Check: After 10 weeks, you will have saved $80 + 10($15) = $230, which is less than the cost of the bike.

Revise: Try a larger number of weeks.

Guess: Try 14 weeks.

Check: After 14 weeks you will have saved $80 + 14($15) = $290, which is greater than the cost of the bike.

Revise: Try a smaller number of weeks.

Guess: Try 13 weeks.

Check: After 13 weeks, you will have saved $80 + 13($15) = $275, which is equal to the cost of the bike.

ANSWER ▶ It will take you 13 weeks to save enough money for the bike.

Practice

Use the strategy *guess*, *check*, and *revise* to solve the problem.

1. You borrowed $132 from your grandparents. You have repaid $20 and plan to pay your grandparents $7 a week. How long will it take you to repay your grandparents?

2. The sum of three consecutive integers is 129. What are the integers?

3. A tree farm sold 17 spruce trees for $940. The tree farm sold white spruce trees for $50 each and blue spruce trees for $65 each. How many of each type of tree were sold?

4. A store sells small fans for $12 each and large fans for $35 each. The store sells 14 fans for $375. How many of each type of fan are sold?

5. The floor of a classroom is a square with an area of 676 square feet. What is the length of the floor?

6. The volume of a cube is 29,791 cubic centimeters. What is the length of an edge of the cube?

7. You are working on a project in woodshop. You have a wooden rod that is 72 inches long. You need to cut the rod so that one piece is 6 inches longer than the other piece. How long should each piece be?

Translating Words into Symbols

To solve a problem algebraically, you often must translate words into symbols.

EXAMPLE   Write the given phrase as an algebraic expression.

a. 5 less than a number   **b.** twice a number   **c.** the quotient of x and y

Solution

a. "Less than" indicates subtraction:

$$x - 5$$

b. "Twice" indicates multiplication by 2:

$$2x$$

c. "Quotient of" indicates division:

$$\frac{x}{y}$$

EXAMPLE   Write an algebraic expression to answer the question.

a. You bike at x miles per hour for 2.5 hours. How far do you travel?

b. You have x dollars more than your friend. Your friend has 3 dollars. How much do you have?

Solution

a. The distance you travel is the product of the number of hours you travel and your speed: $2.5x$

b. The amount of money you have is the sum of x and the amount your friend has: $x + 3$

Practice

Write the phrase as an algebraic expression.

1. 6 more than a number

2. 5 times a number

3. 10 less than a number

4. 16 minus a number

5. the quotient of x and 9

6. one eighth of a number

7. $\frac{9}{10}$ less than a number

8. 10 more than a number

9. 13% of a number

10. the square of a number

11. the quotient of a number and 1

12. a number multiplied by 2

13. twice the sum of a number and 25

14. the cube root of 1 more than a number

15. the difference of 21 and twice a number

16. 5 times the sum of two equal numbers

Write an algebraic expression to answer the question.

17. Aubrey spends $20 to fill her gas tank just before a trip that will use x full tanks of gas. How much money will she spend on the trip?

18. Jamal purchases an item that is on sale for $16 off its original price x. How much does Jamal pay for the item?

19. You want to buy two 3-pound bags of carrots. The carrots cost x dollars per pound. How much do you spend?

Combining Like Terms

A **monomial** is a number, a variable, or the product of a number and a variable. The number multiplied by the variable is called the **coefficient** of the variable.

$$-x + 10y^3$$

−1 is the coefficient of *x*. ⟶   ⟵ 10 is the coefficient of y^3.

Like terms are terms in an expression that have the same variable raised to the same power. In the expression below, $4t$ and $-9t$ are like terms, but $-9t$ and t^2 are not like terms. The **constant terms** 12 and 7 are also like terms.

$$t^2 - 9t + 12 + 4t + 7$$

The distributive property allows you to *combine like terms* that have variables by adding the coefficients.

EXAMPLE   Simplify by combining like terms.

a. $25x + 2x = (25 + 2)x$ Distributive property
$$= 27x$$ Combine like terms.

b. $8y^2 - 3 + 2.3y^2 = 8y^2 + 2.3y^2 - 3$ Group like terms.
$$= 10.3y^2 - 3$$ Combine like terms.

c. $5(3 - x) + 1 = (5)(3) + (5)(-x) + 1$ Distributive property
$$= 15 - 5x + 1$$ Simplify.
$$= 15 + 1 - 5x$$ Group like terms.
$$= 16 - 5x$$ Combine like terms.

Practice

Simplify the expression by combining like terms.

1. $x + 2 - 7x + 1$

2. $5 - y + 8$

3. $x^2 + 5 + 2x - 4x^2$

4. $9(-3 + t^3) - t^3$

5. $2.9 + 2.9r + 1.8$

6. $y(1 + y) - 2y^2 - y$

7. $6 + 2r - 12 + r$

8. $14(3t - 5) - 18$

9. $32x^{12} + 16x - 48x^{11}(2x)$

10. $y(4y + 3) - 2y^2$

11. $-25x - 15 - 5(x - 3)$

12. $9.8 + 7.1v - v^2 + 2$

13. $13 - 19n + 36 - 2n$

14. $72t^{31} + 64t^{30} - 191t^{31}$

15. $4.9(1.7 + r^2) - 2.3(1 - r^2)$

16. $x^4(6x - 3x^2) + 2x^3 - x^6$

17. $-0.12(n^2 + 3.1n) - 4.6n$

18. $2y^{100} - y^4 + 4.1y^{99}(2y)$

19. $21y^{15} - y^3(2y + 47y^{12})$

20. $t(19t^2 - t^4) - 2t^2$

21. $-(38 - u^{23}) + 13.6$

22. $182 - 281t^{13} + 15(3t^{13})$

Multiplying Polynomials and Simplifying Rational Expressions

When you multiply two polynomials, you apply the distributive property to all terms in the expression.

When you multiply two binomials, you can remember the results of the distributive property using the **FOIL** method. Add the products of the **F**irst terms, **O**uter terms, **I**nner terms, and **L**ast terms.

EXAMPLE Find the product $(x - 4)(x + 8)$.

Solution

Product of First Terms	Product of Outer Terms	Product of Inner Terms	Product of Last Terms
x^2	$8x$	$-4x$	-32

$(x - 4)(x + 8) = $

$= x^2 + 4x - 32$

The distributive property can also be used to factor polynomials and simplify rational expressions. A **rational expression** is a fraction whose numerator and denominator are nonzero polynomials.

EXAMPLE Simplify $\dfrac{2x + 8}{4}$.

Solution

$\dfrac{2x + 8}{4} = \dfrac{2(x + 4)}{4}$ Factor a common monomial.

$= \dfrac{(x + 4)}{2}$ Simplify.

Practice

Find the product.

1. $(x + 3)(x - 3)$ **2.** $(x - 5)(x + 2)$ **3.** $(x + 3)(9 - x)$

4. $(4 + x)(x - 5)$ **5.** $(y - 7)(y - 1)$ **6.** $(1 + s)(s + 3)$

7. $(5 - a)(a - 6)$ **8.** $(t + 10)(t - 11)$ **9.** $(t - 8)(t + 5)$

Simplify the expression.

10. $\dfrac{3x + 9}{3}$ **11.** $\dfrac{5x}{25}$ **12.** $\dfrac{7x + 42}{14}$ **13.** $\dfrac{8x}{24}$

14. $\dfrac{6x - 3}{18}$ **15.** $\dfrac{4x + 16}{12}$ **16.** $\dfrac{12x + 36}{6}$ **17.** $\dfrac{9x - 45}{27}$

18. $\dfrac{20x + 35}{10}$ **19.** $\dfrac{14x + 28}{35}$ **20.** $\dfrac{3x + 24}{6}$ **21.** $\dfrac{4x + 40}{16}$

SKILLS REVIEW HANDBOOK

Solving Linear Equations

A **linear equation** in one variable is an equation that can be written in the form $ax = b$ where a and b are constants and $a \neq 0$. A number is a **solution** of an equation if the statement is true when the number is substituted for the variable. Two equations are **equivalent** if they have the same solution(s).

EXAMPLE Solve $\frac{9}{7}x - 13 = 50$.

Solution

Isolate the variable on one side of the equation by combining like terms.

$$\frac{9}{7}x - 13 = 50 \qquad \text{Write original equation.}$$

$$\frac{9}{7}x - 13 + 13 = 50 + 13 \qquad \text{Add 13 to each side.}$$

$$\frac{9}{7}x = 63 \qquad \text{Simplify.}$$

$$\frac{7}{9} \cdot \frac{9}{7}x = 63\left(\frac{7}{9}\right) \qquad \text{Multiply each side by } \frac{7}{9}.$$

$$x = 63\left(\frac{7}{9}\right) \qquad \text{Simplify.}$$

$$x = 49 \qquad \text{Simplify.}$$

EXAMPLE Solve $4x + 1 = 7x - 5$.

Solution

$$4x + 1 = 7x - 5 \qquad \text{Write original equation.}$$

$$4x + 1 - 1 = 7x - 5 - 1 \qquad \text{Subtract 1 from each side.}$$

$$4x = 7x - 6 \qquad \text{Simplify.}$$

$$4x - 7x = 7x - 7x - 6 \qquad \text{Subtract } 7x \text{ from each side.}$$

$$-3x = -6 \qquad \text{Simplify.}$$

$$x = 2 \qquad \text{Divide each side by } -3.$$

Practice

Solve the equation.

1. $10r + 3 = 2$

2. $13t - 10 = 5$

3. $4.4 - 5.1x = -0.7$

4. $4 - 7.4y = 0.3$

5. $18m - 9 = 0$

6. $7s + 16 = -5$

7. $8x - 7 = 9$

8. $5a + 12 = -3$

9. $12n - 11 = 25$

10. $6.3v + 0.7 = 1.4$

11. $7.3 + 24n = 4.3$

12. $0.75 - 15k = -0.25$

13. $5x + 9 = 6 - 9x$

14. $u - 1 = 2.5u + 0.5$

15. $2.13 - w = 6 + 2w$

16. $9.1 - 7v = 2.1 - 14v$

17. $-(x + 6) - 15 = 16(3 - x)$

18. $15(4 - 3r) = 60r$

Extra Practice

Chapter 1

Graph the numbers on a number line. Then write the numbers in order from least to greatest. *(Lesson 1.1)*

1. $-2, 6, -4, 1, -7$

2. $\sqrt{7}, 1, -3, -\frac{5}{2}, 3$

3. $1.6, \frac{2}{3}, \sqrt{2}, -1\frac{2}{3}, -0.6$

Identify the property shown. *(Lesson 1.1)*

4. $3(4 + 2) = 3 \cdot 4 + 3 \cdot 2$

5. $(-2 \cdot 5) \cdot 6 = -2 \cdot (5 \cdot 6)$

6. $(-7) + 0 = -7$

Evaluate the power. *(Lesson 1.2)*

7. 3^4

8. 5^5

9. $(-6)^3$

10. -7^4

Evaluate the expression. *(Lesson 1.2)*

11. $3 \cdot 6 \div 2$

12. $9 + 5 \cdot 3 - 7$

13. $11 + 5 \cdot 8 \div 10$

14. $18 \div (7 - 4) \cdot 5$

Simplify the expression. *(Lesson 1.3)*

15. $7x - 5y + 3x - 2y$

16. $3 + 2(x - 1)$

17. $3(x - 3) + 5(x - 10)$

18. $8 - 3(2 + x)$

19. $-3(2x + 4) - (x + 5)$

20. $5(y - 2) - 3y$

21. $3b - 5a + \frac{1}{2}b - a$

22. $22 - 4(n - 5)$

Solve the equation. Check your solution. *(Lesson 1.4)*

23. $a - 14 = -4$

24. $7x = -21$

25. $\frac{b}{4} = 7$

26. $7s + 3 = 24$

27. $-5c + 6 = 36$

28. $3x - 4 = 2x$

29. $3(2x - 1) - 4x = -7$

30. $5y - 3 = 2y + 9$

Solve the formula for the indicated variable. *(Lesson 1.5)*

31. Investment at simple interest
Solve for r: $A = P + Prt$

32. Perimeter of a rectangle
Solve for w: $P = 2\ell + 2w$

33. **Simple Interest** You invest $1000 in an account that collects simple interest. After one year, the balance of your account is $1050. Use the formula $A = P + Prt$ to find the rate. *(Lesson 1.5)*

34. **Groceries** Granola bars cost $3 per pack. Yogurts cost $3.50 per pack. You pay $13 to buy g packs of granola bars and y packs of yogurt. How many packs of each do you buy? *(Lesson 1.6)*

35. **Woodshop** You are working on a project in woodshop. You have a wooden rod that is 60 inches long. You need to cut the rod so that one piece is 8 inches longer than the other piece. Draw a diagram and write an algebraic model to find how long each piece should be. *(Lesson 1.6)*

36. Find the mean, median, mode, and range of the numbers 2, 5, 6, 7, 8, 8, and 13. *(Lesson 1.7)*

37. Draw a box-and-whisker plot for the data set 3, 9, 11, 13, 22, 34, 35, 41, 44, 44, 44, 45, 45, 47, 48, and 50. *(Lesson 1.7)*

38. Make a frequency distribution of the data set 1, 2, 2, 3, 3, 3, 4, 5, 6, 7, 7, 9, 10, 12, 12, 12, and 12. Use four intervals beginning with 1–3. Then draw a histogram. *(Lesson 1.8)*

Chapter 2

Identify the domain and range. Then tell whether the relation is a function. *(Lesson 2.1)*

1. Input Output

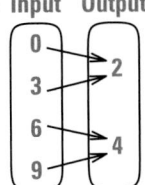

2.

Input	Output
-2	4
0	2
0	0

3.

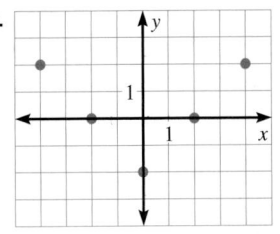

Tell whether the function is linear. Then evaluate the function when $x = -4$. *(Lesson 2.2)*

4. $h(x) = 6x$

5. $f(x) = -100$

6. $r(x) = -x + \dfrac{4}{5}$

7. $v(x) = 3x^2 - 4x + 1$

8. $g(x) = 12 - \dfrac{1}{4}x$

9. $c(x) = -8x^3 + 20x$

Find the slope of the line passing through the given points. Then tell whether the line *rises, falls, is horizontal,* or *is vertical.* *(Lesson 2.3)*

10. $(3, 8), (1, 7)$

11. $(-5, -1), (-5, 0)$

12. $(0, 4), (8, 4)$

Tell which line is steeper. *(Lesson 2.3)*

13. Line 1: through $(4, 4)$ and $(-2, -3)$
  Line 2: through $(3, 6)$ and $(-4, 0)$

14. Line 1: through $(-1, 9)$ and $(5, 2)$
  Line 2: through $(-6, -6)$ and $(7, 7)$

Find the slope and *y*-intercept of the line. Then graph the equation. *(Lesson 2.4)*

15. $y = 2x + 1$

16. $y = \dfrac{2}{3}x + 5$

17. $y = -\dfrac{4}{3}x - 4$

Graph the equation. Label the intercepts. *(Lesson 2.4)*

18. $-3x + y = 0$

19. $4x - 2y = 8$

20. $6x + 10y = 7$

Write an equation of the line with the given characteristics. *(Lesson 2.5)*

21. passes through $(0, -1)$ and has slope $m = -2$

22. passes through $(-6, 5)$ and has slope $m = -\dfrac{5}{2}$

23. passes through $(7, -4)$ and is parallel to the line $y = -3x - 1$

24. passes through $(4, -16)$ and is perpendicular to the line $y = -\dfrac{2}{3}x + 8$

25. passes through $(-11, 2)$ and $(-18, -12)$

The variables *x* and *y* vary directly. Write an equation that relates the variables. Then find the value of *y* when $x = 6$. *(Lesson 2.6)*

26. $x = 5, y = 20$

27. $x = -\dfrac{1}{2}, y = 10$

28. $x = -27, y = -3$

Draw a scatter plot of the data. Then approximate the best-fitting line, and predict the value of *y* when $x = 5$. *(Lesson 2.7)*

29.

x	-3	-2	-1	0	0	1	2	3	3
y	0	1	1	2	3	3	4	4	5

Chapter 3

Solve the system by graphing. Then check your solution. *(Lesson 3.1)*

1. $y = \frac{4}{3}x + 1$

$y = 2x - 17$

2. $5x - 6y = -3$

$x + y = -5$

3. $x + 7y = 15$

$-2x + 5y = -11$

Graph the linear system and tell how many solutions it has. If it has exactly one solution, find and check the solution. *(Lesson 3.1)*

4. $y = -5x + 11$

$y = \frac{1}{2}x - 13$

5. $-3x + 4y = 12$

$6x - 8y = -12$

6. $x - 3y = 7$

$-2x + 6y = -14$

Solve the system using substitution. Tell which equation you chose to solve and use for the substitution. Explain. *(Lesson 3.2)*

7. $-3x + 2y = 7$

$y = -2x$

8. $x = 3y$

$-3x + 5y = 8$

9. $-x + y = 0$

$4x + 5y = 27$

10. $4x - y = 10$

$x + 2y = -2$

11. $-3x + 4y = 50$

$4x + y = 3$

12. $-4x + 5y = 11$

$-2x - y = 2$

13. Fitness For 30 minutes you do a combination of walking and jogging. At the end of your workout your pedometer displays a total of 2.5 miles. You know that you walk 0.05 mile per minute and jog 0.1 mile per minute. Use a verbal model to write and solve a system of linear equations. For how many minutes did you walk? For how many minutes did you jog? *(Lesson 3.2)*

Solve the system using the linear combination method. Then check your solution. *(Lesson 3.3)*

14. $3x - y = 10$

$x + y = 6$

15. $x + 3y = -3$

$-x + 2y = 8$

16. $2x + y = -13$

$5x - 3y = 6$

17. $3x - 2y = 4$

$6x - 4y = 8$

18. Fundraising Your soccer team sells frozen yogurt at a fair to raise money for new uniforms. The team makes \$565 and uses 250 cones. A single-scoop cone costs \$2 and a double-scoop cone costs \$2.50. How many of each type of cone did the team sell? *(Lesson 3.3)*

Plot the ordered triple in a three-dimensional coordinate system. *(Lesson 3.4)*

19. $(2, 4, 0)$

20. $(3, 2, 5)$

21. $(4, -1, 5)$

22. $(-3, 2, -2)$

Sketch the graph of the equation. Label the points where the graph crosses the *x*-, *y*-, and *z*-axes. *(Lesson 3.4)*

23. $x + y + z = 5$

24. $3x + 4y + 2z = 12$

25. $6x + 12y + 8z = 24$

Solve the system using any algebraic method. *(Lesson 3.5)*

26. $-2x + y + 3z = 8$

$x + 3y - z = -9$

$x - 4y - 2z = 1$

27. $x - 2y = -3$

$2x + y + z = 7$

$2x + 2y - 3z = -3$

28. $3x - 2y + z = -8$

$x + y - 4z = 11$

$x + 2y + 4z = -2$

29. Geometry In $\triangle ABC$, the measure of angle C is 6° more than twice the measure of angle A. The measure of angle B is three times the measure of angle A. Sketch the triangle. Find the measure of the three angles. *(Lesson 3.5)*

Chapter 4

Solve the inequality. Then graph your solution. *(Lesson 4.1)*

1. $4x - 5 < 3$

2. $-2x - 6 \geq -9$

3. $-3 < 2x - 1 < 5$

4. $-1 \leq -2x - 4 \leq 8$

5. $2x + 3 < -9$ or $x - 7 \geq -3$

6. $-5x - 4 \leq 6$ or $-x - 9 \geq 1$

7. Temperature Mars has a maximum temperature of $-7°C$ at the equator and a minimum temperature of $-133°C$ at the winter pole. Write and solve a compound inequality that describes the possible temperatures on Mars. Graph your solution and identify three possible temperatures on Mars. *(Lesson 4.1)*

Match the inequality with its graph. *(Lesson 4.2)*

8. $x + y \geq -3$

9. $x - y \leq 3$

10. $x - y \geq -3$

A.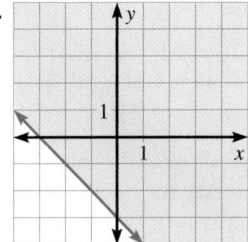

B.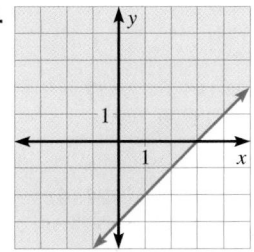

C.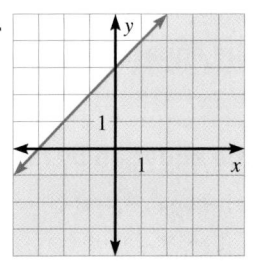

Graph the inequality in a coordinate plane. *(Lesson 4.2)*

11. $y > x + 4$

12. $y \leq -5x - 1$

13. $2x + 2y < 7$

Graph the system of linear inequalities. *(Lesson 4.3)*

14. $x \leq 5$
$y \geq -4$

15. $y > 0$
$x + y < 4$

16. $y < -2x + 1$
$x - 2y \leq 5$

17. $y \leq 2$
$x \geq 0$
$y > -4$

18. $x < 0$
$y \leq 5$
$x + y > 1$

19. $x > -1$
$y \leq x + 2$
$x + y > 1$

Solve the absolute value equation and check your solutions. *(Lesson 4.4)*

20. $|x + 4| = 1$

21. $|2x - 5| = 3$

22. $|7 - 2x| = 5$

23. $|3x + 1| = 1$

24. $|-4x - 3| = 9$

25. $\left|8 + \frac{1}{2}x\right| = 3$

Solve the inequality. Then graph and check the solution. *(Lesson 4.5)*

26. $|x| < 4$

27. $|x - 2| > 8$

28. $|x + 4| > 3$

29. $|2x - 5| > 11$

30. $|3x - 6| < 21$

31. $|8x + 7| < -9$

Evaluate the function for $x = -5$ and $x = 4$. *(Lesson 4.6)*

32. $f(x) = |x| + 3$

33. $g(x) = 3|x| - 10$

34. $q(x) = |x - 5|$

35. $h(x) = \frac{1}{2}|x - 3|$

36. $p(x) = |x + 4| + 1$

37. $r(x) = 2|x - 1| - 1$

Graph the function. *(Lesson 4.6)*

38. $y = 5|x|$

39. $y = -\frac{1}{5}|x|$

40. $y = |x| - 2$

Chapter 5

Graph the function. Label the vertex and axis of symmetry. *(Lesson 5.1)*

1. $y = x^2 - 5$ **2.** $y = -x^2$ **3.** $y = -2x^2 + x + 5$ **4.** $y = x^2 + 3x - 4$

Write the function in standard form. *(Lesson 5.1)*

5. $y = (x + 5)(x + 7)$ **6.** $y = -(x + 2)(x - 1)$ **7.** $y = -3(x + 3)^2 - 4$ **8.** $y = (x - 6)^2 + 2$

Graph the function. Label the vertex and axis of symmetry. *(Lesson 5.2)*

9. $y = 2(x + 4)^2 + 3$ **10.** $y = \frac{1}{2}(x - 4)^2 + 2$ **11.** $y = (x + 3)^2 - 4$

Graph the function. Label the vertex and *x*-intercepts. *(Lesson 5.2)*

12. $y = (x + 1)(x - 4)$ **13.** $y = -\frac{1}{3}(x + 2)(x - 1)$ **14.** $y = 2(x + 4)(x + 2)$

Solve the equation by factoring. *(Lesson 5.3)*

15. $x^2 + 2x - 15 = 0$ **16.** $x^2 + 5x - 14 = 0$ **17.** $x^2 - 2x - 24 = 0$ **18.** $x^2 + 56 = 15x$

Solve the equation by factoring. *(Lesson 5.4)*

19. $4x^2 + 11x - 3 = 0$ **20.** $3x^2 - 16x + 5 = 0$ **21.** $4x^2 - 5x + 1 = 0$ **22.** $6x^2 - 11x = 10$

Factor the expression. *(Lesson 5.5)*

23. $x^2 - 25$ **24.** $9x^2 - 144$ **25.** $x^2 - 14x + 49$ **26.** $4x^2 + 12x + 9$

Solve the equation by taking square roots. *(Lesson 5.6)*

27. $x^2 = 49$ **28.** $x^2 - 15 = 9$ **29.** $2(x + 5)^2 = 40$ **30.** $4(x - 7)^2 = 72$

Solve the equation by taking square roots. *(Lesson 5.7)*

31. $x^2 = -81$ **32.** $x^2 = -24$ **33.** $x^2 - 4 = -12$ **34.** $2x^2 + 5 = -20$

Write the expression as a complex number in standard form. *(Lesson 5.7)*

35. $(8 + 3i) + (7 + 2i)$ **36.** $(2 + 4i) - (5 + i)$ **37.** $(9 + 5i)(1 + 8i)$ **38.** $\dfrac{6 + 7i}{4 + 2i}$

Solve the equation by completing the square. *(Lesson 5.8)*

39. $x^2 + 4x - 7 = 0$ **40.** $x^2 - 12x = -24$ **41.** $2x^2 + 16x - 48 = 0$ **42.** $3x^2 - 18x = 33$

Write the quadratic function in vertex form. Then identify the vertex. *(Lesson 5.8)*

43. $y = x^2 - 14x + 28$ **44.** $y = x^2 + 10x + 26$ **45.** $y = x^2 + 8x - 1$ **46.** $y = x^2 - 6x + 8$

Use the quadratic formula to solve the equation. *(Lesson 5.9)*

47. $3x^2 - 8x + 10 = 0$ **48.** $x^2 + 3x - 9 = 0$ **49.** $2x^2 - 4x = 13$ **50.** $4x^2 + 2 = x$

Find the discriminant of the quadratic equation and give the number and type of solutions of the equation. *(Lesson 5.9)*

51. $x^2 - 12x + 36 = 0$ **52.** $2x^2 + x + 17 = 0$ **53.** $2x^2 + 9x - 5 = 0$ **54.** $3x^2 - 7x + 10 = 0$

55. Stopping Distance On a road covered with dry, packed snow, the distance d (in feet) needed for a car to stop is given by $d = 0.08s^2 + 1.1s$, where s is the car's speed (in miles per hour). What speed is a car traveling if it needs 125 feet to come to a stop? *(Lesson 5.9)*

Chapter 6

Evaluate the expression. Tell which properties of exponents you used.
(Lesson 6.1)

1. $2^4 \cdot 2^2$ **·** **2.** $(2^4)^2$ **3.** $(2 \cdot 5)^3$ **4.** $\left(\dfrac{3}{4}\right)^{-3}$ **5.** $7^0 \cdot 7^{-6}$

Simplify the expression. Tell which properties of exponents you used.
(Lesson 6.1)

6. $x^4 \cdot \dfrac{5}{x^4}$ **7.** $(3x^2 \cdot x^3)^{-2}$ **8.** $\dfrac{x^2}{x^{-3}}$ **9.** $(2x^{-3}y^{-2})^{-7}$ **10.** $\dfrac{x^5 y^{-3}}{x^{-4}y}$

Write the polynomial function in standard form. Then state its degree, type, and leading coefficient. *(Lesson 6.2)*

11. $f(x) = 7 - x^3$ **12.** $f(x) = -5x^4 + 5x^2 - 5$ **13.** $f(x) = 13x^2 - x^5 + 2$

Graph the function using the domain $x = -3, -2, -1, 0, 1, 2, 3$. Then describe the end behavior of the graph. *(Lesson 6.2)*

14. $f(x) = -2x^3$ **15.** $f(x) = x^2 + 6$ **16.** $f(x) = -x^4 + 5x - 5$ **17.** $f(x) = x^5 + x^3 - 4$

Simplify the expression. *(Lesson 6.3)*

18. $(3x^3 + 2) - (4 - x^3)$ **19.** $(3x^4 - 2x^2 + 1) - (2x^3 - 2x^2 + 5)$

20. $(x^5 + 2x^3) + (2x^5 + x^4 - 3x^3 - 9)$ **21.** $3(4x^3 - 2x^2 + x) + x(5x^2 + 7x - 2)$

Simplify the expression. *(Lesson 6.4)*

22. $(x + 9)(x - 9)$ **23.** $(x + 6)^3$ **24.** $(2x - y)^2$

25. $(x - 7)(2x^2 - 3x - 11)$ **26.** $(3x^2 + 8x - 1)(2x + 1)$ **27.** $(x - 2)(x - 5)(x - 2)$

28. $(3x^2 + 8x - 6) \div (x + 3)$ **29.** $(x^2 + 2x - 35) \div (x - 5)$ **30.** $(4x^3 + x + 9) \div (2x + 3)$

31. Volleyball The volleyball court in the diagram has a width of $(5x - 1)$ meters and a length of $(4x + 10)$ meters. Write the area of the volleyball court as a polynomial expression in standard form. *(Lesson 6.4)*

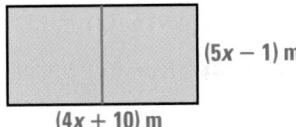

$(5x - 1)$ m

$(4x + 10)$ m

Factor the polynomial. *(Lessons 6.5)*

32. $8x^3 - 8$ **33.** $27x^3 + 64$ **34.** $125x^3 + 216$

35. $27x^3 - 1$ **36.** $x(x - 1) + 3(x - 1)$ **37.** $x(x - 7) + 6(x - 7)$

38. $x^3 - 2x^2 + 10x - 20$ **39.** $x^3 + 7x^2 - 4x - 28$ **40.** $2x^3 - 4x^2 + x - 2$

Factor the polynomial. *(Lessons 6.6)*

41. $x^4 - 121$ **42.** $25x^4 - 16$ **43.** $x^4 + 4x^2 - 5$

44. $x^4 - 216x$ **45.** $72x^5 - 2x$ **46.** $3x^5 - 81x^2$

47. $x^4 + 11x^2 + 18$ **48.** $3x^4 + 4x^2 - 7$ **49.** $3x^5 + 24x^3 + 45x$

Graph the function. Identify the x-intercepts and the coordinates where the local maximums and local minimums occur. *(Lesson 6.7)*

50. $f(x) = x^3 - 6x + 5$ **51.** $f(x) = 2x^4 - 4x^2$ **52.** $f(x) = x^5 - x^3 - 2x$ **53.** $f(x) = x^4 - 8x^2 + 15$

Chapter 7

Solve the equation. *(Lesson 7.1)*

1. $x^3 = -64$ **2.** $x^4 = 625$ **3.** $4x^3 = -108$ **4.** $(x + 1)^3 = -8$ **5.** $3x^4 = 48$

Rewrite the expression using either rational exponents or radicals.
(Lesson 7.1)

6. $\left(\sqrt[5]{3}\right)^4$ **7.** $\left(\sqrt[3]{7}\right)^2$ **8.** $\dfrac{1}{\left(\sqrt[4]{12}\right)^3}$ **9.** $5^{3/5}$ **10.** $16^{11/4}$

Write the expression in simplest form. *(Lesson 7.2)*

11. $\sqrt[5]{24} \cdot \sqrt[5]{4}$ **12.** $\sqrt[3]{15} \cdot \sqrt[3]{18}$ **13.** $\sqrt[4]{\dfrac{80}{90}}$ **14.** $\dfrac{\sqrt[3]{36}}{\sqrt[3]{24}}$ **15.** $\sqrt[5]{\dfrac{8}{81}}$

Simplify the variable expression. Write your answer using positive exponents only. Assume all variables are positive. *(Lesson 7.2)*

16. $(36x^8)^{1/2}$ **17.** $(32m^{10}n^4)^{3/5}$ **18.** $\dfrac{25c^{12}d^5}{5c^9d^4}$ **19.** $\dfrac{4a^4b^5}{5a^9b^3}$

Simplify the expression. Assume all variables are positive. *(Lesson 7.2)*

20. $4x^2y + 5x^2y$ **21.** $8p^3q^{5/2} - 5p^3q^{5/2}$ **22.** $16m^{4/3}n^{1/2} - 9m^{4/3}n^{1/2}$ **23.** $15s^4t^{3/2} - (3s^2t^{3/4})^2$

Solve the equation. Check for extraneous solutions. *(Lesson 7.3)*

24. $\sqrt{5x} - 7 = 3$ **25.** $\sqrt[4]{2x} + 8 = 10$ **26.** $\sqrt[3]{9x} + 6 = 9$

27. $\sqrt{3x - 13} = 8$ **28.** $\sqrt[3]{4x - 6} = \sqrt[3]{x - 3}$ **29.** $\sqrt[4]{4x + 1} = \sqrt[4]{7x + 8}$

30. $x^{2/3} = 25$ **31.** $x^{1/3} + 10 = 8$ **32.** $(5x - 2)^{2/3} = 4$

Perform the indicated operation using the given functions. Then state the domain of the resulting function. *(Lesson 7.4)*

33. Find $f + g$ given $f(x) = x + 3$ and $g(x) = 7x$.

34. Find $f - g$ given $f(x) = x^2 - 5x$ and $g(x) = x - 4$.

35. Find $f \cdot g$ given $f(x) = \dfrac{1}{x^2}$ and $g(x) = 2x^3 + 7x$.

36. Find $\dfrac{f}{g}$ given $f(x) = x^5 - 3x^2$ and $g(x) = x^3$.

37. Find $f(g(x))$ given $f(x) = 3x + 10$ and $g(x) = x^2 - 2$

38. Find $g(f(x))$; given $f(x) = 2x^2 - 12$ and $g(x) = 3x$.

Determine whether the inverse of f is a function. Then find the inverse.
(Lesson 7.5)

39. $f(x) = 5x - 1$ **40.** $f(x) = -x + 4$ **41.** $f(x) = x^2, x \geq 0$ **42.** $f(x) = -8x^3$

43. $f(x) = 4x + 3$ **44.** $f(x) = x^5$ **45.** $f(x) = x^2 + 8, x \geq 0$ **46.** $f(x) = 2x^3 + 1$

Graph the function. Then state its domain and range. *(Lesson 7.6)*

47. $y = \sqrt{x} - 1$ **48.** $y = \sqrt{x - 1} + 2$ **49.** $y = \sqrt[3]{x - 1}$ **50.** $y = \sqrt[3]{x + 3} - 5$

Find the standard deviation of the data set. Round your answer to the nearest tenth. *(Lesson 7.7)*

51. 16, 19, 20, 23, 24, 24, 27 **52.** 24, 26, 28, 29, 33, 33, 34 **53.** 65, 66, 58, 63, 71, 69, 64

Chapter 8

Graph the exponential function. State the domain and range. *(Lesson 8.1)*

1. $y = 5^x$ **2.** $y = 8 \cdot 2^x$ **3.** $y = 2^x - 7$ **4.** $y = 3^{x+1}$

5. The graph of which function is shown?

    Ⓐ $f(x) = 2(1.5^x) - 1$

    Ⓑ $f(x) = 2(1.5^x) + 1$

    Ⓒ $f(x) = 3(1.5^x) - 1$

    Ⓓ $f(x) = 3(1.5^x) + 1$

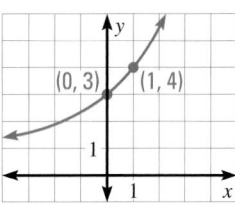

Graph the exponential function. State the domain and range. *(Lesson 8.2)*

6. $y = \left(\dfrac{1}{4}\right)^x$ **7.** $y = 3\left(\dfrac{1}{10}\right)^x$ **8.** $y = \left(\dfrac{2}{5}\right)^x + 5$ **9.** $y = \left(\dfrac{1}{2}\right)^{x-1}$

10. Depreciation You buy a car for \$20,000. The value y (in thousands of dollars) of the car can be approximated by the model $y = 20(0.75)^x$. The variable x represents the number of years since you bought the car. *(Lesson 8.2)*

    a. Make a table of values for the function.

    b. Use the table of values to graph the model.

    c. Use the graph to estimate when the value of the car will be \$2000.

Write an exponential function of the form $y = ab^x$ whose graph passes through the given points. *(Lesson 8.3)*

11. $(1, 7), (2, 49)$ **12.** $(1, 30), (2, 150)$ **13.** $(2, 12), (3, 144)$ **14.** $(3, 12), (4, 6)$

Evaluate the expression. *(Lesson 8.4)*

15. $\log_{13} 169$ **16.** $\log_{1/2} 64$ **17.** $\log 100{,}000$ **18.** $\log_4 64$

Simplify the expression. *(Lesson 8.4)*

19. $\log_5 5^{3x}$ **20.** $4^{\log_4 x}$ **21.** $\log_6 36^x$ **22.** $\log_2 16^x$

Graph the function. Describe the vertical asymptote. State the domain and range. *(Lesson 8.4)*

23. $y = \log_3 x$ **24.** $y = \log_2 (x + 1)$ **25.** $y = \log_6 x - 10$ **26.** $y = \log (x - 4)$

Expand the expression. Assume all variables are positive. *(Lesson 8.5)*

27. $\log_4 x^9$ **28.** $\log_5 3y^3$ **29.** $\log_2 \dfrac{64x}{y}$ **30.** $\log_5 \dfrac{x^2 y}{25}$

Condense the expression. Assume all variables are positive. *(Lesson 8.5)*

31. $\log_3 14 + \log_3 2$ **32.** $3 \log 4 - \log 5$ **33.** $6 \log_3 x - \log_3 3$

Solve the equation. Check for extraneous solutions. *(Lesson 8.6)*

34. $8^3 = 8^{4x-1}$ **35.** $2^x = 4^{3x-2}$

36. $4^x = 60$ **37.** $7^x = 150$

38. $\log_2 (9x - 11) = \log_2 (4x + 9)$ **39.** $\log_3 (2x - 7) = \log_3 (4x + 3)$

40. $\log_8 (6x + 4) = 2$ **41.** $\log (30x - 500) = 3$

Chapter 9

The variables x and y vary inversely. Use the given values to write an equation relating x and y. Then find y when $x = 4$. *(Lesson 9.1)*

1. $x = -2, y = 8$ **2.** $x = 6, y = -3$ **3.** $x = -5, y = -7$ **4.** $x = \dfrac{2}{3}, y = \dfrac{1}{4}$

5. Carpentry The cost of constructing a wooden box with a square base varies jointly with the height h (in inches) of the box and the square of the width w (in inches) of the box. A box of height 16 inches and of width 6 inches costs $28.80. Find the cost of a box with $h = 14$ inches and $w = 8$ inches. *(Lesson 9.1)*

Graph the function. State the domain and range. *(Lesson 9.2)*

6. $y = \dfrac{1}{x} + 4$ **7.** $y = \dfrac{2}{x - 3} + 1$ **8.** $y = \dfrac{3}{x + 2} - 5$ **9.** $y = \dfrac{-1}{x + 3} + 2$

Simplify the expression. If not possible, write *already in simplest form*. *(Lesson 9.3)*

10. $\dfrac{50x^3}{10x}$ **11.** $\dfrac{x^4}{x^3 - 8}$ **12.** $\dfrac{3x + 6}{x^2 + 6x + 8}$ **13.** $\dfrac{x^2 + 3x - 28}{x^2 - 14x + 40}$

Multiply the rational expressions. Simplify the result. *(Lesson 9.3)*

14. $\dfrac{5x^2}{2} \cdot \dfrac{8x}{10x^2}$ **15.** $\dfrac{x^2}{x^2 - 16} \cdot \dfrac{x + 4}{3x^3}$

16. $\dfrac{10x}{x^2 + 4x} \cdot (9x + 36)$ **17.** $\dfrac{x^2 - 9}{x^2 + 2x + 1} \cdot \dfrac{x + 1}{x - 3}$

18. $\dfrac{x^2 - 4}{x^2 + 12x + 36} \cdot \dfrac{x^2 + 2x - 24}{x^2 + 2x - 8}$ **19.** $\dfrac{x^2 - 11x + 28}{x^2 - 9x + 18} \cdot \dfrac{x^2 + 4x - 21}{x^2 - 6x - 7}$

Write the quotient in simplest form. *(Lesson 9.4)*

20. $\dfrac{2x}{x + 4} \div \dfrac{4x^2}{3x + 12}$ **21.** $\dfrac{3x - 6}{4x^3} \div \dfrac{x - 2}{6x^2}$ **22.** $\dfrac{7x^2 - 14x}{x^3} \div \dfrac{5x - 10}{x^5}$

23. $\dfrac{4x - 2}{x + 7} \div \dfrac{2x^2 - x}{3x + 21}$ **24.** $\dfrac{4x + 10}{x - 10} \div (6x + 15)$ **25.** $\dfrac{x^2 + 2x - 35}{x^2} \div \dfrac{x - 5}{3x^2 - 12x}$

Simplify the complex fraction. *(Lesson 9.4)*

26. $\dfrac{\dfrac{2}{3x}}{\dfrac{1}{x + 4}}$ **27.** $\dfrac{\dfrac{2x}{x - 1}}{\dfrac{3x^2}{x + 1}}$ **28.** $\dfrac{\dfrac{3}{x + 4}}{\dfrac{6}{x + 4}}$ **29.** $\dfrac{\dfrac{x + 4}{x - 4}}{\dfrac{x + 2}{x - 4}}$ **30.** $\dfrac{\dfrac{x - 3}{x + 6}}{\dfrac{x - 3}{x + 1}}$

Perform the indicated operation and simplify. *(Lesson 9.5)*

31. $\dfrac{2}{3x} + \dfrac{5}{3x}$ **32.** $\dfrac{x}{x + 2} - \dfrac{7}{x - 2}$ **33.** $\dfrac{12}{3x + 15} - \dfrac{x}{x + 5}$ **34.** $\dfrac{3}{2(x - 1)} + \dfrac{x + 1}{4}$

35. $\dfrac{x + 10}{3x + 1} + \dfrac{x + 4}{x + 1}$ **36.** $\dfrac{4 - 9x}{x + 5} - \dfrac{1}{2x - 1}$ **37.** $\dfrac{x - 9}{x^2 - 25} + \dfrac{x^2}{x + 5}$ **38.** $\dfrac{8x - 1}{x^2 + x - 6} - \dfrac{4}{x - 2}$

Solve the equation. Check your solutions. *(Lesson 9.6)*

39. $\dfrac{2}{x + 4} = \dfrac{1}{x}$ **40.** $\dfrac{x}{x + 3} = \dfrac{-3}{x + 3}$ **41.** $\dfrac{4}{x} = \dfrac{3x + 5}{x + 1}$

42. $\dfrac{1}{x} + \dfrac{1}{x + 2} = \dfrac{2}{x}$ **43.** $2 - \dfrac{4}{x + 2} = \dfrac{2}{x}$ **44.** $\dfrac{4}{x - 2} + \dfrac{6x^2}{x^2 - 4} = \dfrac{3x}{x + 2}$

Chapter 10

1. **Cell Phones** In a random survey of 300 students in your school, 195 said they have a cell phone. The total population of your school is about 2000. Assume the sample is representative of the entire school. Predict how many students in your school have a cell phone. *(Lesson 10.1)*

In Exercises 2 and 3, classify the sample as *convenience*, *self-selected*, *systematic*, or *random*. Explain your reasoning. *(Lesson 10.2)*

2. A small company wants to measure how employees feel about their computers. Five employees are randomly selected to complete a survey.

3. You want to determine an average for how much new brakes would cost. You go to the 5 closest repair shops and ask for an estimate of the total cost.

Smokejumpers The data set below gives the weights (in pounds) of eight smokejumpers with their equipment. *(Lesson 10.3)*

$$287, 265, 273, 275, 295, 280, 290, 280$$

4. The equipment each smokejumper carries weighs about 115 pounds. Transform the original set of data to show the weights without the equipment.

5. Compare the mean, median, mode, ranges, and differences between upper and lower quartiles for the original data set and the new data set. What can you conclude about each of these measures?

In Exercises 6–8, tell whether the number of possibilities can be found using a permutation or a combination. Then find the answer. *(Lessons 10.4 and 10.5)*

6. An employee at a pet store needs to catch 5 tetras in an aquarium containing 27 tetras. In how many groupings can the employee capture 5 tetras?

7. Fifty-two athletes are competing in a bicycle race. In how many orders can three of the bicyclists finish in first, second, and third?

8. Sixteen people are competing in a pie baking contest. In how many orders can two of the people place first and second?

9. You plan to visit four stores to shop. In how many orders can you visit these stores?

You have an equally likely chance of choosing any integer from 1 through 20. Find the probability of the given event. *(Lesson 10.6)*

10. An odd number is chosen.

11. A multiple of 3 is chosen.

12. A factor of 24 is chosen.

13. A number less than 7 is chosen.

A student is chosen randomly from the 10th, 11th, or 12th grades. Given the probabilities for events A and B, find $P(A \text{ and } B)$. *(Lesson 10.7)*

14. $P(\text{person is a male student}) = 0.48$
    $P(\text{person is a } 11^{th} \text{ grader}) = 0.35$
    $P(\text{male or } 11^{th} \text{ grader}) = 0.52$

15. $P(\text{person is a female student}) = 0.56$
    $P(\text{person is a } 12^{th} \text{ grader}) = 0.22$
    $P(\text{female or } 12^{th} \text{ grader}) = 0.65$

Find the probability of drawing the given cards from a standard 52-card deck (a) with replacement and (b) without replacement. *(Lesson 10.8)*

16. a heart, then a club

17. a face card (K, Q, or J), then a 7

18. an ace, then a 2, then a 3

Chapter 11

Add or subtract, if possible. If not possible, state the reason. *(Lesson 11.1)*

1. $\begin{bmatrix} 3 \\ 8 \\ -4 \end{bmatrix} + \begin{bmatrix} 4 \\ 2 \\ -3 \end{bmatrix}$

2. $\begin{bmatrix} 10 & -3 \\ 1 & 6 \end{bmatrix} - \begin{bmatrix} 7 & 3 \\ -2 & 5 \end{bmatrix}$

3. $\begin{bmatrix} 4 & -10 \\ 7 & -8 \end{bmatrix} + \begin{bmatrix} -2 & 0 \\ 4 & 12 \\ 19 & -2 \end{bmatrix}$

Find the product. If it is not defined, state the reason. *(Lesson 11.2)*

4. $\begin{bmatrix} 4 & 1 \\ -3 & 0 \end{bmatrix}\begin{bmatrix} -2 \\ 2 \end{bmatrix}$

5. $\begin{bmatrix} 1 & 5 & -2 \\ 0 & 2 & 1 \\ 3 & 0 & 1 \end{bmatrix}\begin{bmatrix} -1 & 0 \\ 3 & 5 \\ 1 & -2 \end{bmatrix}$

6. $\begin{bmatrix} 6 & 0 & 1 \\ -1 & 0 & 3 \\ 2 & 4 & 0 \end{bmatrix}\begin{bmatrix} 1 & 4 & 0 \\ 2 & 1 & 3 \\ -1 & 0 & -2 \end{bmatrix}$

Use a graphing calculator to find the inverse of matrix A. Then use the calculator to verify that $AA^{21} = I$ and $A^{21}A = I$. *(Lesson 11.3)*

7. $A = \begin{bmatrix} 8 & 7 \\ 7 & 6 \end{bmatrix}$

8. $A = \begin{bmatrix} 5 & -2 \\ -13 & 5 \end{bmatrix}$

9. $A = \begin{bmatrix} -2 & 3 \\ 8 & -11 \end{bmatrix}$

Use an inverse matrix to solve the linear system. *(Lesson 11.3)*

10. $x - y = -8$
$\quad -x - y = 3$

11. $3x - 4y = 7$
$\quad -2x + y = 9$

12. $7x + 6y = -18$
$\quad 5x - 11y = 3$

Write the next term in the sequence. Then write a rule for the *n*th term.
(Lesson 11.4)

13. 4, 9, 14, 19, 24, …

14. 7, 8, 9, 10, 11, …

15. 9, 16, 25, 36, 49, 64, …

Use the formulas for special series to find the sum of the series.
(Lesson 11.4)

16. $1 + 1 + 1 + 1 + 1 + 1 + 1$

17. $1 + 2 + 3 + 4 + 5 + 6$

18. $1 + 4 + 9 + 16$

Write a rule for the *n*th term of the arithmetic sequence. *(Lesson 11.5)*

19. $d = 6, a_3 = 19$

20. $d = 10, a_2 = -3$

21. $d = 3, a_4 = -7$

Find the sum of the first 10 terms of the arithmetic series. *(Lesson 11.5)*

22. $22 + 19 + 16 + 13 + 10 + \cdots$

23. $1.7 + 2.1 + 2.5 + 2.9 + 3.3 + \cdots$

Tell whether the sequence is *arithmetic*, *geometric*, or *neither*. Explain your answer. *(Lesson 11.6)*

24. 15, 20, 25, 30, . . .

25. $-1, 1, 3, 5, . . .$

26. 12, 24, 48, 96, . . .

27. $\frac{1}{5}, -1, 5, -25, . . .$

28. 0, 1, 3, 6, . . .

29. $-9, -3, 3, 9, . . .$

Write a rule for the *n*th term of the geometric sequence. *(Lesson 11.6)*

30. $r = 2, a_1 = 9$

31. $r = \frac{1}{3}, a_1 = 81$

32. $r = -2, a_2 = 10$

Find the sum of the infinite geometric series, if it exists. *(Lesson 11.7)*

33. $1 + \frac{1}{6} + \frac{1}{36} + \frac{1}{216} + \cdots$

34. $2 - \frac{8}{7} + \frac{32}{49} - \frac{128}{343} + \cdots$

35. $3 + 2 + \frac{4}{3} + \frac{8}{9} + \cdots$

Write the repeating decimal as a fraction or mixed number. *(Lesson 11.7)*

36. $0.444. . .$

37. $0.6262. . .$

38. $50.5050. . .$

Chapter 12

1. Evaluate the six trigonometric functions of the angle θ shown in the triangle. *(Lesson 12.1)*

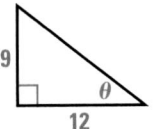

Find the value of *x* for the right triangle. Round your answer to two decimal places. *(Lesson 12.1)*

2.
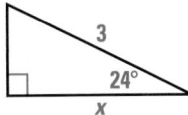

3.
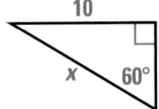

4.

5.

Draw an angle with the given measure in standard position. Tell in which quadrant the terminal side lies. *(Lesson 12.2)*

6. $225°$

7. $-240°$

8. $510°$

9. $-440°$

Use the given point on the terminal side of an angle θ in standard position. Evaluate the sine, cosine, and tangent functions of θ. *(Lesson 12.2)*

10. $(1, 2)$

11. $(-3, 5)$

12. $(-6, -4)$

13. $(4, -7)$

Find the maximum(s), the minimum, and the intercepts of the function on the interval $0° \le x \le \dfrac{360°}{b}$. Graph one cycle of the function. *(Lesson 12.3)*

14. $y = 3 \sin x$

15. $y = 2 \cos 6x$

16. $y = \sin 225x$

17. $y = 5 \cos 270x$

Find the intercept, the vertical asymptotes, and the halfway points of the function on the interval $0° \le x \le \dfrac{360}{b}°$. Graph one cycle of the function. *(Lesson 12.3)*

18. $y = \tan 90x$

19. $y = 2 \tan x$

20. $y = 4 \tan 135x$

21. $y = 5 \tan 5x$

Sketch $\triangle ABC$, then find all of the angle measures and side lengths. If the triangle is impossible, explain why. *(Lesson 12.4)*

22. $A = 20°, B = 85°, a = 7$

23. $A = 25°, a = 6, c = 20$

24. $C = 18°, c = 16, b = 10$

Find the unknown side length in the triangle. Round your answer to the nearest tenth. *(Lesson 12.5)*

25.
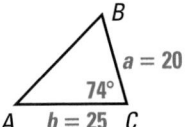

26.
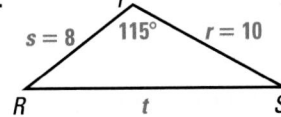

27.
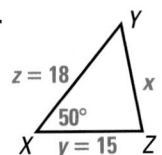

Sketch $\triangle ABC$, then find all of the angle measures and side lengths. *(Lesson 12.5)*

28. $a = 10, b = 16, c = 15$

29. $a = 17, b = 15, c = 20$

30. $A = 44°, b = 10, c = 6$

Chapter 13

Find the distance between the two points. Then find the midpoint of the line segment joining the two points. *(Lesson 13.1)*

1. $(0, 0)$, $(-4, 3)$ **2.** $(0, 0)$, $(5, -1)$ **3.** $(-2, -6)$, $(6, -3)$ **4.** $(0, 3)$, $(-2, 0)$

Write an equation for the perpendicular bisector of the line segment joining the two points. *(Lesson 13.1)*

5. $(0, 0)$, $(-2, -4)$ **6.** $(1, -1)$, $(-3, 6)$ **7.** $(-4, -6)$, $(3, -5)$ **8.** $(-5, -1)$, $(1, 5)$

Graph the equation. Identify the focus, directrix, and axis of symmetry of the parabola. *(Lesson 13.2)*

9. $4x^2 = y$ **10.** $-8x = y^2$ **11.** $2y = -x^2$ **12.** $16y = x^2$

Graph the equation. Identify the radius of the circle. *(Lesson 13.3)*

13. $6x^2 + 6y^2 = 24$ **14.** $8x^2 + 8y^2 = 72$ **15.** $12x^2 = 432 - 12y^2$ **16.** $5x^2 + 5y^2 = 500$

Write the standard form of the equation of the circle that passes through the given point and whose center is (0, 0). *(Lesson 13.3)*

17. $(-5, 0)$ **18.** $(-3, 2)$ **19.** $(-4, 4)$ **20.** $(7, -2)$

Write an equation of the line that is tangent to the given circle at the given point. *(Lesson 13.3)*

21. $x^2 + y^2 = 8$; $(2, -2)$ **22.** $x^2 + y^2 = 90$; $(-3, 9)$ **23.** $x^2 + y^2 = 25$; $(4, -3)$

Graph the equation. Identify the vertices, co-vertices, and foci of the ellipse. *(Lesson 13.4)*

24. $\dfrac{x^2}{4} + \dfrac{y^2}{25} = 1$ **25.** $\dfrac{x^2}{64} + \dfrac{y^2}{25} = 1$ **26.** $\dfrac{x^2}{16} + \dfrac{y^2}{9} = 1$ **27.** $\dfrac{x^2}{36} + \dfrac{y^2}{64} = 1$

Write an equation of the ellipse with the given characteristics and center at (0, 0). *(Lesson 13.4)*

28. Vertex: $(0, 6)$ **29.** Vertex: $(-7, 0)$ **30.** Vertex: $(6, 0)$ **31.** Vertex: $(0, -10)$
     Co-vertex: $(-4, 0)$ Co-vertex: $(0, 5)$ Focus: $(-1, 0)$ Focus: $(0, \sqrt{19})$

Graph the equation. Identify the vertices, foci, and asymptotes of the hyperbola. *(Lesson 13.5)*

32. $\dfrac{y^2}{16} - \dfrac{x^2}{36} = 1$ **33.** $\dfrac{x^2}{64} - \dfrac{y^2}{100} = 1$ **34.** $\dfrac{x^2}{36} - y^2 = 1$ **35.** $\dfrac{y^2}{121} - \dfrac{x^2}{64} = 1$

Write an equation of the hyperbola with the given foci and vertices. *(Lesson 13.5)*

36. Foci: $(-7, 0)$, $(7, 0)$ **37.** Foci: $(-\sqrt{61}+, 0)$, $(\sqrt{61}, 0)$ **38.** Foci: $(0, -10)$, $(0, 10)$
     Vertices: $(-2, 0)$, $(2, 0)$ Vertices: $(-5, 0)$, $(5, 0)$ Vertices: $(0, -8)$, $(0, 8)$

Classify the conic section and write its equation in standard form. Then graph the equation. *(Lesson 13.6)*

39. $6x^2 + 6y^2 - 72x - 72y - 24 = 0$ **40.** $y^2 - 8x - 2y + 9 = 0$

41. $10x^2 - 9y^2 + 40x - 18y - 59 = 0$ **42.** $5x^2 + 8y^2 - 10x - 48y - 3 = 0$

43. $x^2 - 4x + 12y + 28 = 0$ **44.** $12x^2 + 5y^2 + 24x - 60y - 48 = 0$

End-of-Course Test

ALGEBRAIC EXPRESSIONS AND LINEAR EQUATIONS

Simplify the expression.

1. $5x - 3y + 2x - 8y$

2. $-2(3x - 5) - 6$

3. $3(x - 1) - 2(x + 7)$

Solve the equation.

4. $4y - 7 = 9$

5. $5n - 2(n + 1) = 6$

6. $8a + 3 = 2a - 15$

Write an equation of the line with the given characteristics.

7. slope: -5; y-intercept: 9

8. slope: $-\frac{5}{6}$; point: $(-6, -4)$

9. slope: $\frac{2}{3}$; point: $(-3, 3)$

SYSTEMS OF EQUATIONS

Solve the system.

10. $y = x - 5$
$2x - 3y = -9$

11. $x + y = 4$
$2x + 4y = 4$

12. $3x - 4y = 12$
$5x - 2y = 6$

13. $5x + 8y = 6$
$2x + 5y = 15$

14. $2x - y = 4$
$x + y - 3z = 2$
$3x - 2y + 4z = 1$

15. $x + y - z = 3$
$x - 2y + 2z = -3$
$3x + y - z = 5$

INEQUALITIES AND ABSOLUTE VALUE

Solve the inequality. Then graph your solution.

16. $-3x + 1 > 16$

17. $0 \leq x + 5 < 7$

18. $2x - 7 < 5$

Graph the inequality or function in a coordinate plane.

19. $4x - 5 \geq y$

20. $2x + 5y < 6$

21. $f(x) = -x + 7 - 1$

QUADRATIC FUNCTIONS AND COMPLEX NUMBERS

Factor the expression.

22. $x^2 + 4x - 21$

23. $x^2 + 8x + 16$

24. $12x^2 - 26x + 10$

Solve the equation.

25. $x^2 - 6 = 250$

26. $12x^2 + 16x + 5 = 0$

27. $0 = 4x^2 - 8x - 5$

28. $x^2 - 5 = -41$

29. $x^2 - 4x - 50 = 0$

30. $x^2 + 9 = 6x$

Write the expression as a complex number in standard form.

31. $(4 + 3i) - (6 - 7i)$

32. $(5 + 8i)(3 - 2i)$

33. $\dfrac{2 + i}{9 - 6i}$

34. The height h in feet of a golf ball t seconds after being struck is $h = -16t^2 + 96t$. How long is the golf ball in the air?

POLYNOMIALS AND POLYNOMIAL FUNCTIONS

Simplify the expression.

35. $3(2x^4 + 5) - (3x^4 - 7)$

36. $(2x^3 + 7x^2 + x - 25) \div (x + 4)$

37. $(3x - 4)^3$

Estimate the coordinates of each local maximum, local minimum, and real zero. Tell the least degree the function represented by the graph can have.

38.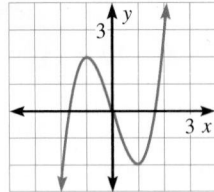

39.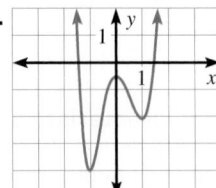

40.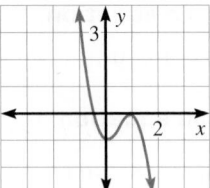

RADICAL, EXPONENTIAL, AND LOGARITHMIC EQUATIONS AND FUNCTIONS

Simplify the expression. Write your answer using positive exponents only. Assume all variables are positive.

41. $(49x^4)^{1/2}$

42. $(8x^{12}y^3)^{2/3}$

43. $6n^{1/2}m^{3/4} - (9nm^{3/2})^{1/2}$

44. $\dfrac{3a^{3/5}b^{4/3}}{9a^{2/5}b^{2/3}}$

Solve the equation. Check for extraneous solutions.

45. $\sqrt[3]{8x - 5} = 3$

46. $\sqrt{x - 2} = x - 4$

47. $x^{2/3} + 5 = 9$

48. $(2x - 1)^{1/3} = 5$

Graph the function. Then state its domain and range.

49. $y = \sqrt{x + 2}$

50. $y = \sqrt[3]{x + 4}$

51. $y = 3^x - 1$

52. $y = \log_2 (x - 1)$

Solve the equation. Check for extraneous solutions.

53. $5^{4x - 1} = 25x$

54. $10^{3x - 2} = 23$

55. $\log_5 x = \log_5 (2x - 1)$

56. $\log_8 (x - 4) = \dfrac{1}{3}$

RATIONAL EQUATIONS AND FUNCTIONS

Simplify the expression.

57. $\dfrac{6x^2 - 7x - 3}{3x + 1}$

58. $\dfrac{3}{x} \div \dfrac{x + 5}{x^3}$

59. $\dfrac{x + 3}{x^2 - 49} \cdot \dfrac{x + 7}{x^2 + x - 6}$

60. $\dfrac{\dfrac{x^2}{x - 2}}{\dfrac{4x}{x - 2}}$

Identify the vertical and horizontal asymptotes of the graph of the function. Then state the domain and range.

61. $y = \dfrac{5}{x}$

62. $y = \dfrac{5}{x} + 2$

63. $y = \dfrac{3x - 2}{x^2 - 9}$

64. $y = \dfrac{x^3}{x^2 - 1}$

Solve the equation. Check your solutions.

65. $\dfrac{8}{x} = \dfrac{12}{7}$

66. $\dfrac{6}{x - 4} = \dfrac{x}{x + 4}$

67. $\dfrac{2}{x + 3} + \dfrac{3x}{x^2 - 9} = \dfrac{x^2}{x - 3}$

68. $\dfrac{3}{x} + \dfrac{2}{x + 5} = \dfrac{4}{x}$

69. The time a car trip takes varies inversely with the speed of the car. It takes 2 hours to reach a destination at 55 miles per hour. How long would it take at 60 miles per hour?

DATA ANALYSIS

Find the number of permutations or combinations.

70. $_6P_4$

71. $_7P_3$

72. $_7C_2$

73. $_9C_4$

Find the probability of drawing the given cards at random from a standard 52-card deck (a) with replacement and (b) without replacement.

74. an ace, then another ace

75. a 5, then a king

76. a diamond, then a heart

DISCRETE MATHEMATICS

Perform the matrix operation, if possible. If not possible, state the reason.

77. $\begin{bmatrix} 5 & -2 \\ 0 & 3 \end{bmatrix} + \begin{bmatrix} 1 & 4 \\ -2 & 5 \end{bmatrix}$

78. $\begin{bmatrix} 4 & 0 \\ 2 & -8 \end{bmatrix} + \begin{bmatrix} 5 & 2 \\ -1 & -4 \\ 0 & 8 \end{bmatrix}$

79. $\begin{bmatrix} 3 & 2 \\ 2 & 5 \end{bmatrix}\begin{bmatrix} 0 \\ 4 \end{bmatrix}$

Tell whether the sequence is *arithmetic*, *geometric*, or *neither*. Write a rule for the nth term of the sequence, then find the sum of the first 12 terms.

80. 1, 4, 16, 64, 256, . . .

81. 4, 7, 10, 13, 16, . . .

82. 1, −2, 4, −8, 16, . . .

TRIGONOMETRY

Find the value of x for the right triangle. Round your answer to two decimal places.

83.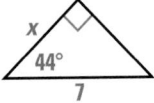

84.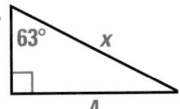

85.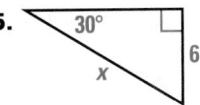

Evaluate the sine, cosine, and tangent functions of θ.

86. $\theta = 0°$

87. $\theta = 180°$

88. $\theta = 450°$

89. $\theta = 990°$

Sketch ABC, then find all of the angle measures and side lengths. If the triangle is impossible, explain why.

90. $A = 110°, b = 9, c = 6$

91. $a = 5, b = 3, c = 7$

92. $A = 60°, B = 40°, c = 12$

CONIC SECTIONS

Write the equation of the conic section with the given characteristics.

93. Parabola with vertex at $(0, 0)$ and directrix $x = -2$

94. Circle with center at $(-3, 2)$ with radius 6

95. Ellipse with center at $(0, 0)$, a vertex at $(0, 5)$, and a co-vertex at $(-3, 0)$

96. Hyperbola with center at $(0, 0)$, foci at $(\pm 2\sqrt{5}, 0)$, and vertices at $(\pm 2, 0)$

Tables

Symbols

Symbol	Meaning	Page
. . .	and so on	3
$\approx$	is approximately equal to	3
$\cdot$	multiplication, times	5
$-a$	opposite of a	5
$\dfrac{1}{a}$	reciprocal of a, $a \neq 0$	5
b_1	b sub 1	33
π	pi; irrational number ≈ 3.14	33
(x, y)	ordered pair	68
$f(x)$	f of x, or the value of f at x	73
m	slope	79
(x, y, z)	ordered triple	147
$>$	is greater than	172
$\leq$	is less than or equal to	172
$\geq$	is greater than or equal to	172
$<$	is less than	173
$|x|$	absolute value of x	192
$\sqrt{a}$	the nonnegative square root of a	255
i	imaginary unit equal to $\sqrt{-1}$	261
$+\infty$	positive infinity	303
$-\infty$	negative infinity	303
$\sqrt[n]{a}$	nth root of a	353
$\neq$	not equal to	367
f^{-1}	inverse of function f	380
$\bar{x}$	x-bar; the mean of a data set	395
σ	sigma; the standard deviation of a data set	395

Symbol	Meaning	Page
e	irrational number ≈ 2.718	429
$\log_b y$	log base b of y	433
$\log x$	log base 10 of x	433
$\ln x$	log base e of x	437
$n!$	n factorial; number of permutations of n objects	540
$_nP_r$	number of permutations of n distinct objects taken r at a time	541
$_nC_r$	number of combinations of n distinct objects taken r at a time	545
$P(A)$	probability of event A	556
$P(B\,|\,A)$	conditional probability	570
$\begin{bmatrix} 1 & 0 \\ 0 & 1 \end{bmatrix}$	matrix	585
A^{-1}	inverse of matrix A	601
$|A|$	determinant of matrix A	606
S_n	sum of the first n terms of an arithmetic or geometric series	617
θ	theta, name of an angle, or measure of an angle	645
sin	sine	645
cos	cosine	645
tan	tangent	645
csc	cosecant	645
sec	secant	645
cot	cotangent	645
$\sin^{-1}$	inverse sine	669

Measures

Time

60 seconds (sec) = 1 minute (min)
60 minutes = 1 hour (h)
24 hours = 1 day
7 days = 1 week
4 weeks (approx.) = 1 month

$\left.\begin{array}{l}\text{365 days} \\ \text{52 weeks (approx.)} \\ \text{12 months}\end{array}\right\}$ = 1 year

10 years = 1 decade
100 years = 1 century

Metric

Length

10 millimeters (mm) = 1 centimeter (cm)

$\left.\begin{array}{l}\text{100 cm} \\ \text{1000 mm}\end{array}\right\}$ = 1 meter (m)

1000 m = 1 kilometer (km)

Area

100 square millimeters = 1 square centimeter
(mm^2) (cm^2)
$10{,}000\ cm^2$ = 1 square meter (m^2)
$10{,}000\ m^2$ = 1 hectare (ha)

Volume

1000 cubic millimeters = 1 cubic centimeter
(mm^3) (cm^3)
$1{,}000{,}000\ cm^3$ = 1 cubic meter (m^3)

Liquid Capacity

$\left.\begin{array}{l}\text{1000 milliliters (mL)} \\ \text{1000 cubic centimeters } (cm^3)\end{array}\right\}$ = 1 liter (L)

1000 L = 1 kiloliter (kL)

Mass

1000 milligrams (mg) = 1 gram (g)
1000 g = 1 kilogram (kg)
1000 kg = 1 metric ton (t)

Temperature   Degrees Celsius (°C)

0°C = freezing point of water
37°C = normal body temperature
100°C = boiling point of water

United States Customary

Length

12 inches (in.) = 1 foot (ft)

$\left.\begin{array}{l}\text{36 in.} \\ \text{3 ft}\end{array}\right\}$ = 1 yard (yd)

$\left.\begin{array}{l}\text{5280 ft} \\ \text{1760 yd}\end{array}\right\}$ = 1 mile (mi)

Area

144 square inches $(in.^2)$ = 1 square foot (ft^2)
$9\ ft^2$ = 1 square yard (yd^2)

$\left.\begin{array}{l}43{,}560\ ft^2 \\ 4840\ yd^2\end{array}\right\}$ = 1 acre (A)

Volume

1728 cubic inches $(in.^3)$ = 1 cubic foot (ft^3)
$27\ ft^3$ = 1 cubic yard (yd^3)

Liquid Capacity

8 fluid ounces (fl oz) = 1 cup (c)
2 c = 1 pint (pt)
2 pt = 1 quart (qt)
4 qt = 1 gallon (gal)

Weight

16 ounces (oz) = 1 pound (lb)
2000 lb = 1 ton

Temperature   Degrees Fahrenheit (°F)

32°F = freezing point of water
98.6°F = normal body temperature
212°F = boiling point of water

TABLES

Formulas and Properties

Formulas from Coordinate Geometry

Slope of a line (p. 79)	$m = \dfrac{y_2 - y_1}{x_2 - x_1}$ is the slope m of the nonvertical line through points (x_1, y_1) and (x_2, y_2).
Distance formula (p. 691)	$d = \sqrt{(x_2 - x_1)^2 + (y_2 - y_1)^2}$ is the distance d between points (x_1, y_1) and (x_2, y_2).
Midpoint formula (p. 692)	$M\left(\dfrac{x_1 + x_2}{2}, \dfrac{y_1 + y_2}{2}\right)$ is the midpoint of the line segment joining points (x_1, y_1) and (x_2, y_2).

Formulas and Theorems from Algebra

Quadratic formula (p. 274)	The solutions of $ax^2 + bx + c = 0$ are $$x = \frac{-b \pm \sqrt{b^2 - 4ac}}{2a}$$ where a, b, and c are real numbers such that $a \neq 0$.
Discriminant of a quadratic equation (p. 276)	The expression $b^2 - 4ac$ is called the discriminant of the associated equation $ax^2 + bx + c = 0$. The value of the discriminant can be positive, zero, or negative, which corresponds to an equation having two real solutions, one real solution, or two imaginary solutions, respectively.
Special product patterns (p. 316)	**Sum and difference:** $\quad (a + b)(a - b) = a^2 - b^2$ **Square of a binomial:** $\quad (a + b)^2 = a^2 + 2ab + b^2$ $\quad\quad\quad\quad\quad\quad\quad\quad\quad (a - b)^2 = a^2 - 2ab + b^2$ **Cube of a binomial:** $\quad (a + b)^3 = a^3 + 3a^2b + 3ab^2 + b^3$ $\quad\quad\quad\quad\quad\quad\quad\quad\quad (a - b)^3 = a^3 - 3a^2b + 3ab^2 - b^3$
Special factoring patterns (p. 323)	**Sum of two cubes:** $\quad\quad a^3 + b^3 = (a + b)(a^2 - ab + b^2)$ **Difference of two cubes:** $\quad a^3 - b^3 = (a - b)(a^2 + ab + b^2)$
Fundamental theorem of algebra (p. 331)	If $f(x)$ is a polynomial of degree n where $n > 0$, then the equation $f(x) = 0$ has at least one root in the set of complex numbers.
Corollary to the fundamental theorem of algebra (p. 331)	If $f(x)$ is a polynomial of degree n where $n > 0$, then the equation $f(x) = 0$ has exactly n solutions provided each repeated solution is counted individually.
Discriminant of a general second-degree equation (p. 726)	If the graph of $Ax^2 + Bxy + Cy^2 + Dx + Ey + F = 0$ is a conic, then the type of conic can be determined by the following characteristics. **Discriminant** — **Type of Conic** $B^2 - 4AC < 0$, $B = 0$, and $A = C$ — Circle $B^2 - 4AC < 0$, and either $B \neq 0$ or $A \neq C$ — Ellipse $B^2 - 4AC = 0$ — Parabola $B^2 - 4AC > 0$ — Hyperbola

Formulas from Discrete Mathematics

Fundamental counting principle (p. 539)	If one event can occur in m ways and another event can occur in n ways, then the number of ways that both events can occur is $m \cdot n$.
Permutations of n objects taken r at a time (p. 541)	The number of permutations of n distinct objects taken r at a time is denoted by ${}_nP_r$ and is given by: $${}_nP_r = \frac{n!}{(n-r)!}$$
Combinations of n objects taken r at a time (p. 545)	The number of combinations of n distinct objects taken r at a time is denoted by ${}_nC_r$ and is given by: $${}_nC_r = \frac{n!}{(n-r)! \cdot r!}$$

Formulas from Probability

Theoretical probability of an event (p. 556)	When all outcomes are equally likely, the theoretical probability that an event A will occur is: $$P(A) = \frac{\text{Number of outcomes in event } A}{\text{Total number of outcomes}}$$
Experimental probability of an event (p. 557)	For a given number of trials of an experiment, the experimental probability that an event A will occur is: $$P(A) = \frac{\text{Number of trials where event } A \text{ occurs}}{\text{Total number of trials}}$$
Probability of compound events (p. 562)	If A and B are overlapping events, $P(A \text{ and } B) \neq 0$, the probability of A or B is: $$P(A \text{ or } B) = P(A) + P(B) - P(A \text{ and } B)$$ If A and B are disjoint events, then $P(A \text{ and } B) = 0$, and the probability of A or B is: $$P(A \text{ or } B) = P(A) + P(B)$$
Probability of the complement of an event (p. 564)	The probability of the complement of A is: $$P(\text{not } A) = 1 - P(A)$$
Probability of independent events (p. 570)	If A and B are independent events, then the probability that both A and B occur is: $$P(A \text{ and } B) = P(A) \cdot P(B)$$
Probability of dependent events (p. 570)	If A and B are dependent events, then the probability that both A and B occur is: $$P(A \text{ and } B) = P(A) \cdot P(B \mid A)$$

Formulas from Statistics

Standard deviation of a data set (p. 395)	$\sigma = \sqrt{\dfrac{(x_1 - \bar{x})^2 + (x_2 - \bar{x})^2 + \ldots + (x_n - \bar{x})^2}{n}}$ where σ (read "sigma") is the standard deviation of the data $x_1, x_2, \ldots, x_n$

Geometric Formulas

Pythagorean Theorem (p. 757)

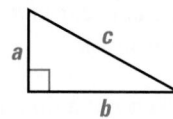

In a right triangle, $a^2 + b^2 = c^2$ where a and b are the lengths of the legs and c is the length of the hypotenuse.

Square (pp. 753, 754)

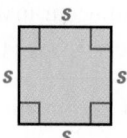

Area
$A = s^2$

Perimeter
$P = 4s$

Rectangle (pp. 753, 754)

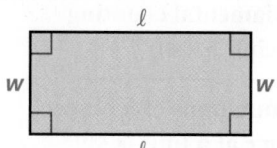

Area
$A = \ell w$

Perimeter
$P = 2\ell + 2w$

Parallelogram (p. 754)

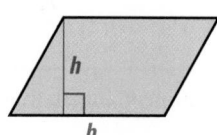

Area
$A = bh$

Triangle (p. 754)

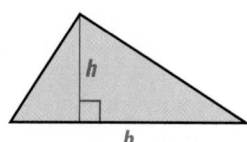

Area
$A = \dfrac{1}{2}bh$

Trapezoid (p. 754)

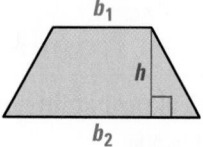

Area
$A = \dfrac{1}{2}(b_1 + b_2)h$

Circle (pp. 753, 754)

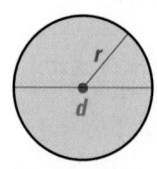

Circumference
$C = \pi d$ or
$C = 2\pi r$

Area
$A = \pi r^2$

Prism

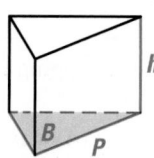

Surface Area
$S = 2B + Ph$

Volume
$V = Bh$

Cylinder (p. 755)

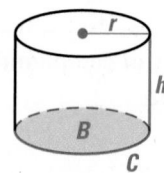

Surface Area
$S = 2B + Ch$
$= 2\pi r^2 + 2\pi rh$

Volume
$V = Bh$
$= \pi r^2 h$

Pyramid

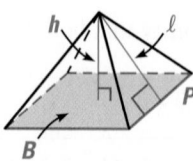

Surface Area
$S = B + \dfrac{1}{2}P\ell$

Volume
$V = \dfrac{1}{3}Bh$

Cone

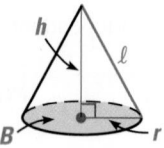

Surface Area
$S = B + \pi r\ell$
$= \pi r^2 + \pi r\ell$

Volume
$V = \dfrac{1}{3}Bh$
$= \dfrac{1}{3}\pi r^2 h$

Sphere

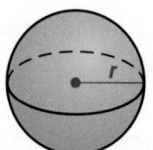

Surface Area
$S = 4\pi r^2$

Volume
$V = \dfrac{4}{3}\pi r^3$

Formulas and Identities from Trigonometry

Definition of trigonometric functions (pp. 645, 653)	Let θ be an angle in standard position and (x, y) be any point (except the origin) on the terminal side of θ. Let $r = \sqrt{x^2 + y^2}$. $\sin \theta = \dfrac{y}{r}$ $\quad$ $\cos \theta = \dfrac{x}{r}$ $\quad$ $\tan \theta = \dfrac{y}{x}, x \neq 0$ $\csc \theta = \dfrac{r}{y}, y \neq 0$ $\quad$ $\sec \theta = \dfrac{r}{x}, x \neq 0$ $\quad$ $\cot \theta = \dfrac{x}{y}, y \neq 0$
Reciprocal identities (p. 645)	$\csc \theta = \dfrac{1}{\sin \theta}$ $\qquad$ $\sec \theta = \dfrac{1}{\cos \theta}$ $\qquad$ $\cot \theta = \dfrac{1}{\tan \theta}$
Law of sines (p. 668)	If $\triangle ABC$ has sides of length a, b, and c, then: $$\frac{\sin A}{a} = \frac{\sin B}{b} = \frac{\sin C}{c}$$
Law of cosines (p. 675)	If $\triangle ABC$ has sides of length a, b, and c, then: $$a^2 = b^2 + c^2 - 2bc \cos A$$ $$b^2 = a^2 + c^2 - 2ac \cos B$$ $$c^2 = a^2 + b^2 - 2ab \cos C$$

Properties of Real Numbers

Let a, b, and c be real numbers.

	Addition	**Multiplication**
Closure Property	$a + b$ is a real number.	ab is a real number.
Commutative Property (p. 5)	$a + b = b + a$	$ab = ba$
Associative Property (p. 5)	$(a + b) + c = a + (b + c)$	$(ab)c = a(bc)$
Identity Property (p. 5)	$a + 0 = a, 0 + a = a$	$a \cdot 1 = a, 1 \cdot a = a$
Inverse Property (p. 5)	$a + (-a) = 0$	$a \cdot \dfrac{1}{a} = 1, a \neq 0$
Distributive Property (p. 5)	The distributive property involves both addition and multiplication: $a(b + c) = ab + ac$	
Zero Product Property (p. 235)	Let A and B be real numbers or algebraic expressions. If $AB = 0$, then $A = 0$ or $B = 0$.	

Properties of Exponents

Let a and b be real numbers, and let m and n be integers.

Product of Powers Property (p. 296)	$a^m \cdot a^n = a^{m+n}$
Power of a Power Property (p. 296)	$(a^m)^n = a^{mn}$
Power of a Product Property (p. 296)	$(ab)^m = a^m b^m$
Negative Exponent Property (p. 296)	$a^{-m} = \dfrac{1}{a^m}, a \neq 0$
Zero Exponent Property (p. 296)	$a^0 = 1, a \neq 0$
Quotient of Powers Property (p. 296)	$\dfrac{a^m}{a^n} = a^{m-n}, a \neq 0$
Power of a Quotient Property (p. 296)	$\left(\dfrac{a}{b}\right)^m = \dfrac{a^m}{b^m}, b \neq 0$

Properties of Radicals and Rational Exponents

Number of Real nth Roots (p. 353)	Let n be an integer greater than 1, and let a be a real number. • If n is odd, then a has one real nth root: $\sqrt[n]{a} = a^{1/n}$ • If n is even and $a > 0$, then a has two real nth roots: $\pm\sqrt[n]{a} = \pm a^{1/n}$ • If n is even and $a = 0$, then a has one nth root: $\sqrt[n]{0} = 0^{1/n} = 0$ • If n is even and $a < 0$, then a has no real nth roots.
Radicals and Rational Exponents (p. 355)	Let $a^{1/n}$ be an nth root of a, and let m be a positive integer. • $a^{m/n} = \left(a^{1/n}\right)^m = \left(\sqrt[n]{a}\right)^m$ • $a^{-m/n} = \dfrac{1}{a^{m/n}} = \dfrac{1}{\left(a^{1/n}\right)^m} = \dfrac{1}{\left(\sqrt[n]{a}\right)^m},\ a \neq 0$
Product and Quotient Properties of Radicals (p. 359)	Let n be an integer greater than 1, and let a and b be positive real numbers. Then $\sqrt[n]{a \cdot b} = \sqrt[n]{a} \cdot \sqrt[n]{b}$ and $\sqrt[n]{\dfrac{a}{b}} = \dfrac{\sqrt[n]{a}}{\sqrt[n]{b}}$.
Properties of Rational Exponents (p. 360)	All of the properties of exponents listed on the previous page apply to rational exponents as well as integer exponents.

Properties of Logarithms

	Let $a, b, c, m, n, x,$ and y be positive real numbers such that $b \neq 1$ and $c \neq 1$.
Logarithms and Exponents (p. 433)	$\log_b y = x$ if and only if $b^x = y$
Common Logarithm (p. 433)	$\log_{10} x = \log x$
Special Logarithm Values (p. 434)	$\log_b 1 = 0$ because $b^0 = 1$ and $\log_b b = 1$ because $b^1 = b$
Product Property of Logarithms (p. 442)	$\log_b mn = \log_b m + \log_b n$
Quotient Property of Logarithms (p. 442)	$\log_b \dfrac{m}{n} = \log_b m - \log_b n$
Power Property of Logarithms (p. 442)	$\log_b m^n = n \log_b m$

Properties of Functions

Operations on Functions (pp. 373, 374)	Let $f(x)$ and $g(x)$ be any two functions. A new function $h(x)$ can be defined using any of the following operations. **Addition:** $\quad h(x) = f(x) + g(x)$ $\qquad$ **Division:** $\quad h(x) = \dfrac{f(x)}{g(x)}$ **Subtraction:** $\quad h(x) = f(x) - g(x)$ $\qquad$ **Composition:** $\quad h(x) = f(g(x))$ **Multiplication:** $\quad h(x) = f(x) \cdot g(x)$ For addition, subtraction, multiplication, and division, the domain of h consists of the x-values that are in the domains of both f and g. Additionally, the domain of the quotient does not include x-values for which $g(x) = 0$. For composition, the domain of h is the set of all x-values where x is in the domain of g and $g(x)$ is in the domain of f.
Inverse Functions (p. 380)	Functions f and g are inverse functions if: $f(g(x)) = x$ and $g(f(x)) = x$

Squares and Square Roots

No.	Square	Sq. Root	No.	Square	Sq. Root	No.	Square	Sq. Root
1	1	1.000	51	2601	7.141	101	10,201	10.050
2	4	1.414	52	2704	7.211	102	10,404	10.100
3	9	1.732	53	2809	7.280	103	10,609	10.149
4	16	2.000	54	2916	7.348	104	10,816	10.198
5	25	2.236	55	3025	7.416	105	11,025	10.247
6	36	2.449	56	3136	7.483	106	11,236	10.296
7	49	2.646	57	3249	7.550	107	11,449	10.344
8	64	2.828	58	3364	7.616	108	11,664	10.392
9	81	3.000	59	3481	7.681	109	11,881	10.440
10	100	3.162	60	3600	7.746	110	12,100	10.488
11	121	3.317	61	3721	7.810	111	12,321	10.536
12	144	3.464	62	3844	7.874	112	12,544	10.583
13	169	3.606	63	3969	7.937	113	12,769	10.630
14	196	3.742	64	4096	8.000	114	12,996	10.677
15	225	3.873	65	4225	8.062	115	13,225	10.724
16	256	4.000	66	4356	8.124	116	13,456	10.770
17	289	4.123	67	4489	8.185	117	13,689	10.817
18	324	4.243	68	4624	8.246	118	13,924	10.863
19	361	4.359	69	4761	8.307	119	14,161	10.909
20	400	4.472	70	4900	8.367	120	14,400	10.954
21	441	4.583	71	5041	8.426	121	14,641	11.000
22	484	4.690	72	5184	8.485	122	14,884	11.045
23	529	4.796	73	5329	8.544	123	15,129	11.091
24	576	4.899	74	5476	8.602	124	15,376	11.136
25	625	5.000	75	5625	8.660	125	15,625	11.180
26	676	5.099	76	5776	8.718	126	15,876	11.225
27	729	5.196	77	5929	8.775	127	16,129	11.269
28	784	5.292	78	6084	8.832	128	16,384	11.314
29	841	5.385	79	6241	8.888	129	16,641	11.358
30	900	5.477	80	6400	8.944	130	16,900	11.402
31	961	5.568	81	6561	9.000	131	17,161	11.446
32	1024	5.657	82	6724	9.055	132	17,424	11.489
33	1089	5.745	83	6889	9.110	133	17,689	11.533
34	1156	5.831	84	7056	9.165	134	17,956	11.576
35	1225	5.916	85	7225	9.220	135	18,225	11.619
36	1296	6.000	86	7396	9.274	136	18,496	11.662
37	1369	6.083	87	7569	9.327	137	18,769	11.705
38	1444	6.164	88	7744	9.381	138	19,044	11.747
39	1521	6.245	89	7921	9.434	139	19,321	11.790
40	1600	6.325	90	8100	9.487	140	19,600	11.832
41	1681	6.403	91	8281	9.539	141	19,881	11.874
42	1764	6.481	92	8464	9.592	142	20,164	11.916
43	1849	6.557	93	8649	9.644	143	20,449	11.958
44	1936	6.633	94	8836	9.695	144	20,736	12.000
45	2025	6.708	95	9025	9.747	145	21,025	12.042
46	2116	6.782	96	9216	9.798	146	21,316	12.083
47	2209	6.856	97	9409	9.849	147	21,609	12.124
48	2304	6.928	98	9604	9.899	148	21,904	12.166
49	2401	7.000	99	9801	9.950	149	22,201	12.207
50	2500	7.071	100	10,000	10.000	150	22,500	12.247

TABLES

Trigonometric Ratios

Angle	Sine	Cosine	Tangent
1°	.0175	.9998	.0175
2°	.0349	.9994	.0349
3°	.0523	.9986	.0524
4°	.0698	.9976	.0699
5°	.0872	.9962	.0875
6°	.1045	.9945	.1051
7°	.1219	.9925	.1228
8°	.1392	.9903	.1405
9°	.1564	.9877	.1584
10°	.1736	.9848	.1763
11°	.1908	.9816	.1944
12°	.2079	.9781	.2126
13°	.2250	.9744	.2309
14°	.2419	.9703	.2493
15°	.2588	.9659	.2679
16°	.2756	.9613	.2867
17°	.2924	.9563	.3057
18°	.3090	.9511	.3249
19°	.3256	.9455	.3443
20°	.3420	.9397	.3640
21°	.3584	.9336	.3839
22°	.3746	.9272	.4040
23°	.3907	.9205	.4245
24°	.4067	.9135	.4452
25°	.4226	.9063	.4663
26°	.4384	.8988	.4877
27°	.4540	.8910	.5095
28°	.4695	.8829	.5317
29°	.4848	.8746	.5543
30°	.5000	.8660	.5774
31°	.5150	.8572	.6009
32°	.5299	.8480	.6249
33°	.5446	.8387	.6494
34°	.5592	.8290	.6745
35°	.5736	.8192	.7002
36°	.5878	.8090	.7265
37°	.6018	.7986	.7536
38°	.6157	.7880	.7813
39°	.6293	.7771	.8098
40°	.6428	.7660	.8391
41°	.6561	.7547	.8693
42°	.6691	.7431	.9004
43°	.6820	.7314	.9325
44°	.6947	.7193	.9657
45°	.7071	.7071	1.0000

Angle	Sine	Cosine	Tangent
46°	.7193	.6947	1.0355
47°	.7314	.6820	1.0724
48°	.7431	.6691	1.1106
49°	.7547	.6561	1.1504
50°	.7660	.6428	1.1918
51°	.7771	.6293	1.2349
52°	.7880	.6157	1.2799
53°	.7986	.6018	1.3270
54°	.8090	.5878	1.3764
55°	.8192	.5736	1.4281
56°	.8290	.5592	1.4826
57°	.8387	.5446	1.5399
58°	.8480	.5299	1.6003
59°	.8572	.5150	1.6643
60°	.8660	.5000	1.7321
61°	.8746	.4848	1.8040
62°	.8829	.4695	1.8807
63°	.8910	.4540	1.9626
64°	.8988	.4384	2.0503
65°	.9063	.4226	2.1445
66°	.9135	.4067	2.2460
67°	.9205	.3907	2.3559
68°	.9272	.3746	2.4751
69°	.9336	.3584	2.6051
70°	.9397	.3420	2.7475
71°	.9455	.3256	2.9042
72°	.9511	.3090	0.0777
73°	.9563	.2924	3.2709
74°	.9613	.2756	3.4874
75°	.9659	.2588	3.7321
76°	.9703	.2419	4.0108
77°	.9744	.2250	4.3315
78°	.9781	.2079	4.7046
79°	.9816	.1908	5.1446
80°	.9848	.1736	5.6713
81°	.9877	.1564	6.3138
82°	.9903	.1392	7.1154
83°	.9925	.1219	8.1443
84°	.9945	.1045	9.5144
85°	.9962	.0872	11.4301
86°	.9976	.0698	14.3007
87°	.9986	.0523	19.0811
88°	.9994	.0349	28.6363
89°	.9998	.0175	52.2900

English-Spanish Glossary

A

absolute value (p. 192) The absolute value of a number x, represented by the symbol $|x|$, is the distance the number is from 0 on a number line.

valor absoluto (pág. 192) El valor absoluto de un número x, representado por el símbolo $|x|$, es la distancia a la que está el número de 0 en una recta numérica.

$\left|\frac{2}{3}\right| = \frac{2}{3}$, $|-4.3| = 4.3$, and $|0| = 0$.

$\left|\frac{2}{3}\right| = \frac{2}{3}$, $|-4.3| = 4.3$ y $|0| = 0$.

---

absolute value equation (p. 192) An equation that contains an absolute value expression.

ecuación con valor absoluto (pág. 192) Una ecuación que contiene una expresión con valor absoluto.

$|x + 2| = 3$ is an absolute value equation.

$|x + 2| = 3$ es una ecuación con valor absoluto.

---

absolute value function (p. 204) A function that contains an absolute value expression.

función de valor absoluto (pág. 204) Función que contiene una expresión de valor absoluto.

$y = |x|$, $y = |x - 3|$, and $y = 4|x + 8| - 9$ are absolute value functions.

$y = |x|$, $y = |x - 3|$ e $y = 4|x + 8| - 9$ son funciones de valor absoluto.

---

absolute value inequality (p. 198) An inequality that has one of the following forms:

$|ax + b| < c$, $|ax + b| \le c$, $|ax + b| > c$, or $|ax + b| \ge c$.

desigualdad con valor absoluto (p. 198) Una desigualdad que tiene una de las expresiones siguientes:

$|ax + b| < c$, $|ax + b| \le c$, $|ax + b| > c$, o $|ax + b| \ge c$.

$|2x + 1| \ge 5$ is an absolute value inequality.

$|2x + 1| \ge 5$ es una desigualdad con valor absoluto.

---

algebraic expression (p. 10) An expression involving variables. Also called variable expression.

expresión algebraica (pág. 10) Una expresión que incluye variables. También se le denomina expresión variable.

$\frac{2}{3}p$, $\frac{8}{7 - r}$, $k - 5$, and $n^2 + 2n$ are algebraic expressions.

$\frac{2}{3}p$, $\frac{8}{7 - r}$, $k - 5$ y $n^2 + 2n$ son expresiones algebraicas.

---

algebraic model (p. 40) A mathematical statement that represents a real-life problem.

modelo algebraico (pág. 40) Un enunciado matemático que representa un problema de la vida real.

The algebraic model $130 = 65t$ can be used to find the time t it takes a car to travel 130 miles at a speed of 65 miles per hour.

El modelo algebraico $130 = 65t$ puede usarse para determinar el tiempo t que tarda un coche para recorrer 130 millas a una velocidad de 65 millas por hora.

---

arithmetic sequence (p. 615) A sequence in which the difference of consecutive terms is constant.

progresión aritmética (pág. 615) Progresión en la que la diferencia entre los términos consecutivos es constante.

$-4, 1, 6, 11, 16, \ldots$ is an arithmetic sequence with common difference 5.

$-4, 1, 6, 11, 16, \ldots$ es una progresión aritmética con una diferencia común de 5.

arithmetic series (p. 617) The expression formed by adding the terms of an arithmetic sequence. **serie aritmética** (pág. 617) La expresión formada al sumar los términos de una progresión aritmética.	$2 + 4 + 6 + 8 + 10 + \ldots$
asymptote (p. 412) A line that a graph approaches more and more closely. **asíntota** (pág. 412) Recta a la que se aproxima una gráfica cada vez más.	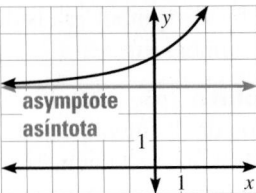 The asymptote for the graph shown is the line $y = 3$. La asíntota para la gráfica que se muestra es la recta $y = 3$.
axis of symmetry of a parabola (pp. 222, 697) The line perpendicular to the parabola's directrix and passing through its focus. The axis of symmetry divides the parabola into mirror images. **eje de simetría de una parábola** (págs. 222, 697) La recta perpendicular a la directriz de la parábola y que pasa por su foco y su vértice. El eje de simetría divide a la parábola en dos partes que son imágenes reflejas entre sí.	*See* parabola. *Ver* parábola.

base of a power (p. 9) The number or expression that is used as a factor in a repeated multiplication. **base de una potencia** (pág. 9) El número o la expresión que se usa como factor en la multiplicación repetida.	In the power 2^5, the base is 2. En la potencia 2^5, la base es 2.
best-fitting line (p. 108) The line that lies as close as possible to all the data points in a scatter plot. **mejor recta de regresión** (pág. 108) La recta que se ajusta lo más posible a todos los puntos de datos de un diagrama de dispersión.	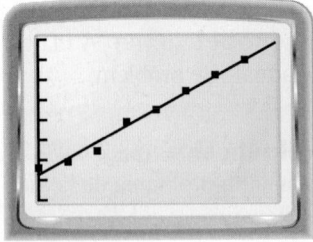

best-fitting quadratic model (p. 283) The model given by using quadratic regression on a set of paired data.

modelo cuadrático con mejor ajuste (pág. 283) El modelo dado al realizar una regresión cuadrática sobre un conjunto de pares de datos.

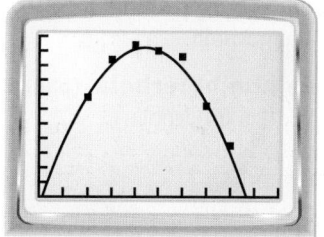

biased question (p. 521) A question that elicits responses that do not accurately reflect the opinions or actions of the people surveyed.

pregunta capciosa (pág. 521) Pregunta que induce a respuestas que no reflejan con exactitud las opiniones o acciones de los encuestados.

"Would you rather see an exciting laser show or a boring movie?" is a biased question.

"¿Preferirías ver un emocionante espectáculo de láser o una película aburrida?" es una pregunta capciosa.

biased sample (p. 519) A sample that overrepresents or underrepresents part of a population.

muestra sesgada (pág. 519) Muestra que representa de forma excesiva o insuficiente a parte de una población.

The members of a school's basketball team would form a biased sample for a survey about whether to build a new gym.

Los miembros del equipo de baloncesto de una escuela formarían una muestra sesgada si participaran en una encuesta sobre si quieren que se construya un nuevo gimnasio.

binomial (p. 224) The sum of two monomials.

binomio (pág. 224) La suma de dos monomios.

$3x - 1$ and $t^3 - 4t$ are binomials.

$3x - 1$ y $t^3 - 4t$ son binomios.

binomial theorem (p. 554) The binomial expansion of $(a + b)^n$ for any positive integer n:

$(a + b)^n = {}_nC_0a^nb^0 + {}_nC_1a^{n-1}b^1 + {}_nC_2a^{n-2}b^2 + \cdots + {}_nC_na^0b^n$.

teorema binomial (pág. 554) La expansión binomial de $(a + b)^n$ para cualquier número entero positivo n:

$(a + b)^n = {}_nC_0a^nb^0 + {}_nC_1a^{n-1}b^1 + {}_nC_2a^{n-2}b^2 + \cdots + {}_nC_na^0b^n$.

$(x^2 + y)^3$

$= {}_3C_0(x^2)^3y^0 + {}_3C_1(x^2)^2y^1 + {}_3C_2(x^2)^1y^2 + {}_3C_3(x^2)^0y^3$

$= (1)(x^6)(1) + (3)(x^4)(y) + (3)(x^2)(y^2) + (1)(1)(y^3)$

$= x^6 + 3x^4y + 3x^2y^2 + y^3$

box-and-whisker plot (p. 47) A type of statistical graph in which a "box" encloses the middle half of the data set and "whiskers" extend to the minimum and maximum data values.

diagrama de líneas y bloques (pág. 47) Un tipo de gráfica estadística en la que un "bloque" encierra la mitad de en medio de un conjunto de datos y las "líneas" se extienden hacia los valores mínimos y máximos.

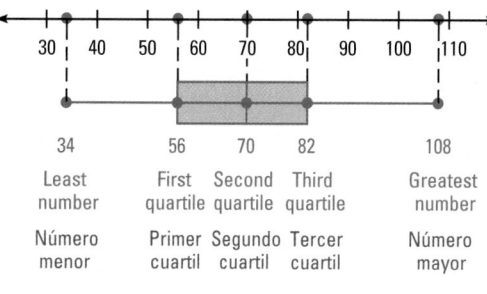

branches of a hyperbola (p. 472) The two symmetrical parts of a hyperbola.

See hyperbola.

ramas de una hipérbola (pág. 472) Las dos partes simétricas de la hipérbola.

Ver hipérbola.

C

center of a circle (p. 703) *See* circle.

The circle with equation $(x - 3)^2 + (y + 5)^2 = 36$ has its center at $(3, -5)$.

centro de un círculo (pág. 703) *Ver* círculo.

El círculo con la ecuación $(x - 3)^2 + (y + 5)^2 = 36$ tiene el centro en $(3, -5)$.

center of a hyperbola (p. 717) The midpoint of the transverse axis of a hyperbola.

See hyperbola.

centro de una hipérbola (pág. 717) El punto medio del eje transverso de una hipérbola.

Ver hipérbola.

center of an ellipse (p. 710) The midpoint of the major axis of an ellipse.

See ellipse.

centro de una elipse (pág. 710) El punto medio del eje mayor de una elipse.

Ver elipse.

circle (p. 703) The set of all points P in a plane that are of distance r from a fixed point, called the center C of the circle.

círculo (pág.703) El conjunto de todos los puntos P de un plano que están a una distancia r de un punto fijo, llamado centro C del círculo.

center
centro

(x, y)

r

circle
círculo

$x^2 + y^2 = r^2$

coefficient (p. 16) When a term is the product of a number and a power of a variable, the number is the coefficient of the power.

In the algebraic expression $2x^2 + (-4x) + (-1)$, the coefficient of $2x^2$ is 2 and the coefficient of $-4x$ is -4.

coeficiente (pág. 16) Cuando un término es el producto de un número y una potencia de una variable, el número es el coeficiente de la potencia.

En la expresión algebraica $2x^2 + (-4x) + (-1)$, el coeficiente de $2x^2$ es 2 y el coeficiente de $-4x$ es -4.

coefficient matrix (p. 601) The matrix A when a system of linear equations is written as a matrix equation $AX = B$.

matriz coeficiente (pág. 601) La matriz A cuando un sistema de ecuaciones lineales se escribe como una ecuación de matriz $AX = B$.

$$9x + 4y = -6$$
$$3x - 5y = -21$$

coefficient matrix:
matriz coeficiente: $\begin{bmatrix} 9 & 4 \\ 3 & -5 \end{bmatrix}$

matrix of constants:
matriz de constantes: $\begin{bmatrix} -6 \\ -21 \end{bmatrix}$

matrix of variables:
matriz de variables: $\begin{bmatrix} x \\ y \end{bmatrix}$

---

combination (p. 545) A selection of r objects from a group of n objects where the order is not important, denoted $_nC_r$ where $_nC_r = \dfrac{n!}{(n-r)! \cdot r!}$.

combinación (pág. 545) Selección de r objetos de un grupo de n objetos en el que el orden no importa, denotado $_nC_r$, donde $_nC_r = \dfrac{n!}{(n-r)! \cdot r!}$.

There are 6 combinations of the $n = 4$ letters A, B, C, and D selected $r = 2$ at a time: AB, AC, AD, BC, BD, and CD.

Hay 6 combinaciones de las letras $n = 4$ A, B, C y D seleccionadas $r = 2$ cada vez: AB, AC, AD, BC, BD y CD.

---

common difference (p. 615) The constant difference of consecutive terms of an arithmetic sequence.

diferencia común (pág. 615) La diferencia constante entre los términos consecutivos de una progresión aritmética.

See arithmetic sequence.

Ver progresión aritmética.

---

common logarithm (p. 433) A logarithm with base 10. It is denoted by $\log_{10}$ or simply by log.

logaritmo común (pág. 433) Logaritmo con base 10. Se denota por $\log_{10}$ ó simplemente por log.

$\log_{10} 100 = \log 100 = 2$ because $10^2 = 100$.

$\log_{10} 100 = \log 100 = 2$ ya que $10^2 = 100$.

---

common ratio (p. 621) The constant ratio of consecutive terms of a geometric sequence.

razón común (pág. 621) La razón constante entre los términos consecutivos de una progresión geométrica.

See geometric sequence.

Ver progresión geométrica.

complement of an event (p. 564) The complement of event A consists of all outcomes that are not in A.	A card is randomly selected from a standard deck of 52 cards. The probability that the card is not an ace is: $$P \text{ (not an ace)} = 1 - P \text{ (ace)}$$ $$= 1 - \frac{1}{13}$$ $$= \frac{12}{13} \approx 0.923$$
complemento de un evento (pág. 564) El complemento de un evento A consiste en todos los resultados del espacio muestral que no están incluidos en A.	Una carta se selecciona de modo aleatorio de un paquete estándar de 52 cartas. La probabilidad de que la carta no sea un as es de: $$P \text{ (de que la carta no sea as)} = 1 - P \text{ (as)}$$ $$= 1 - \frac{1}{13}$$ $$= \frac{12}{13} \approx 0.923$$
completing the square (p. 268) The process of adding a term to a quadratic expression of the form $x^2 + bx$ to make it a perfect square trinomial.	To complete the square for $x^2 + 16x$, add $\left(\frac{16}{2}\right)^2 = 64: x^2 + 16x + 64 = (x + 8)^2$.
completar el cuadrado (pág. 268) El proceso de sumar un término a una expresión cuadrática de la forma $x^2 + bx$, de modo que sea un trinomio cuadrado perfecto.	Para completar el cuadrado para $x^2 + 16x$, suma $\left(\frac{16}{2}\right)^2 = 64: x^2 + 16x + 64 = (x + 8)^2$.
complex conjugates (p. 263) Two complex numbers of the form $a + bi$ and $a - bi$. **números complejos conjugados** (pág. 263) Dos números complejos de la forma $a + bi$ y $a - bi$.	$2 + 4i, 2 - 4i$
complex fraction (p. 488) A fraction that contains a fraction in its numerator, denominator, or both. **fracción compleja** (pág. 488) Fracción que tiene una fracción en su numerador o en su denominador.	$\dfrac{\frac{5}{x + 4}}{\frac{6x}{3x^2}}, \dfrac{1}{\frac{1}{p} + \frac{1}{q}}$
complex number (p. 262) A number $a + bi$ where a and b are real numbers and i is the imaginary unit. **número complejo** (pág. 262) Un número $a + bi$, donde a y b son números reales e i es la unidad imaginaria.	$0, 2.5, \sqrt{3}, \pi, 5i, 2 - i$

complex plane (p. 265) A coordinate plane in which each point (a, b) represents a complex number $a + bi$. The horizontal axis is the real axis and the vertical axis is the imaginary axis.

plano complejo (pág. 265) Plano de coordenadas en el que cada punto (a, b) representa un número complejo $a + bi$. El eje horizontal es el eje real, y el eje vertical es el eje imaginario.

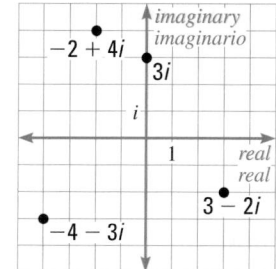

composition of functions (p. 374) The composition of a function f with a function g is found by replacing each variable in f with the expression for g. The composition of f with g is written as $f(g(x))$.

composición de funciones (pág. 374) La composición de una función f con una función g se determina si se substituye cada variable de f con la expresión de g. La composición de f con g se escribe de la siguiente manera $f(g(x))$.

$$f(x) = 5x - 2, \ g(x) = 4x^{-1}$$
$$g(f(x)) = g(5x - 2)$$
$$= 4(5x - 2)^{-1}$$
$$= \frac{4}{5x - 2}, x \neq \frac{2}{5}$$

compound event (p. 562) The union or intersection of two events.

suceso compuesto (pág. 562) La unión o la intersección de dos sucesos.

When you roll a six-sided die, the event "roll a 2 or an odd number" is a compound event.

Cuando lanzas un cubo numerado de seis lados, el suceso "salir el 2 ó un número impar" es un suceso compuesto.

compound inequality (p. 174) Two simple inequalities joined by "and" or "or."

desigualdad compuesta (pág. 174) Dos desigualdades simples unidas por "y" u "o".

$2x > 0$ or $x + 4 < -1$ is a compound inequality.

$2x > 0$ ó $x + 4 < -1$ es una desigualdad compuesta.

conditional probability (p. 570) The conditional probability of B given A, written $P(B|A)$, is the probability that event B will occur given that event A has occurred.

probabilidad condicional (pág. 570) La probabilidad condicional de B dado A, escrito $P(B|A)$, es la probabilidad de que ocurra el suceso B dado que ha ocurrido el suceso A.

Two cards are randomly selected from a standard deck of 52 cards. Let event A be "the first card is a club" and let event B be "the second card is a club." Then
$P(B|A) = \frac{12}{51} = \frac{4}{17}$ because there are 12 (out of 13) clubs left among the remaining 51 cards.

Dos cartas se seleccionan al azar de un paquete normal de 52 cartas. Sea el suceso A "la primera carta es de tréboles" y sea el suceso B "la segunda carta es de tréboles". Entonces $P(B|A) = \frac{12}{51} = \frac{4}{17}$ ya que quedan 12 (del total de 13) cartas de tréboles entre las 51 cartas restantes.

conic (p. 724) *See* conic section.	*See* **conic section.**
cónica (pág. 724) *Ver* sección cónica.	*Ver* **sección cónica.**
conic section (p. 724) A curve formed by the intersection of a plane and a double-napped cone. Conic sections are also called conics.	*See* **circle, ellipse, hyperbola,** *and* **parabola.**
sección cónica (pág. 724) Una curva formada por la intersección de un plano y un cono doble. Las secciones cónicas también se llaman cónicas.	*Ver* **círculo, elipse, hipérbola** *y* **parábola.**
constant of variation (pp. 101, 466) The nonzero constant k in a direct variation equation $y = kx$, an inverse variation equation $y = \dfrac{k}{x}$, or a joint variation equation $z = kxy$.	In the direct variation equation $y = -\dfrac{5}{2}x$, the constant of variation is $-\dfrac{5}{2}$.
constante de variación (págs. 101, 466) La constante distinta de cero a de una ecuación de variación directa $y = kx$, de una ecuación de variación inversa $y = \dfrac{k}{x}$ o de una ecuación de variación conjunta $z = kxy$.	En la ecuación de variación directa $y = -\dfrac{5}{2}x$, la constante de variación es $-\dfrac{5}{2}$.
constant term (pp. 16, 302) A term that has a number part but no variable part.	The constant term of the algebraic expression $3x^2 + 5x + (-7)$ is -7.
término constante (págs. 16, 302) Término que tiene una parte numérica pero sin variable.	El término constante de la expresión algebraica $3x^2 + 5x + (-7)$ es -7.
convenience sample (p. 526) A sample in which only members of a population who are easy to reach are selected.	You can select a convenience sample of a school's student population by choosing only students who are in your classes.
muestra de conveniencia (pág. 526) Un muestreo de conveniencia se logra si se eligen los elementos que están al alcance inmediato.	Puedes crear una muestra de conveniencia de la población estudiantil si eliges sólo estudiantes que están en tu clase.
coordinate (p. 3) The number that corresponds to a point on a number line.	*See* **graph of a real number.**
coordenada (pág. 3) El número que corresponde a un punto en una recta numérica.	*Ver* **gráfica de número real.**
cosecant function (p. 645) If θ is an acute angle of a right triangle, the cosecant of θ is the length of the hypotenuse divided by the length of the side opposite θ.	*See* **sine function.**
función cosecante (pág. 645) Si θ es un ángulo agudo de un triángulo rectángulo, la cosecante de θ es la longitud de la hipotenusa dividida por la longitud del lado opuesto a θ.	*Ver* **función seno.**

cosine function (p. 645) If θ is an acute angle of a right triangle, the cosine of θ is the length of the side adjacent to θ divided by the length of the hypotenuse.

función coseno (pág. 645) Si θ es un ángulo agudo de un triángulo rectángulo, el coseno de θ es la longitud del lado adyacente a θ dividida por la longitud de la hipotenusa.

See **sine function.**

Ver **función seno.**

---

cotangent function (p. 645) If θ is an acute angle of a right triangle, the cotangent of θ is the length of the side adjacent to θ divided by the length of the side opposite θ.

función cotangente (pág. 645) Si θ es un ángulo agudo de un triángulo rectángulo, la cotangente de θ es la longitud del lado adyacente a θ dividida por la longitud del lado opuesto a θ.

See **sine function.**

Ver **función seno.**

---

coterminal angles (p. 653) Angles in standard position with terminal sides that coincide.

ángulos coterminales (pág. 653) Ángulos en posición normal cuyos lados terminales coinciden.

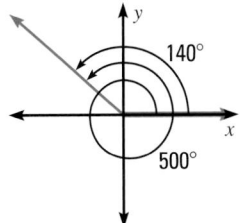

The angles with measures 500° and 140° are coterminal.

Los ángulos que miden 500° y 140° son coterminales.

---

co-vertices of an ellipse (p. 710) The points of intersection of an ellipse and the line perpendicular to the major axis at the center.

puntos extremos del eje menor de una elipse (pág. 710) Los puntos de intersección de una elipse y la recta perpendicular al eje mayor en el centro.

See **ellipse.**

Ver **elipse.**

Cramer's rule (p. 606) A method for solving a system of linear equations using determinants: For the linear system $ax + by = e$, $cx + dy = f$, let A be the coefficient matrix. If $\det A \neq 0$, the solution of the system is as follows:

$$x = \frac{\begin{vmatrix} e & b \\ f & d \end{vmatrix}}{\det A}, \quad y = \frac{\begin{vmatrix} a & e \\ c & f \end{vmatrix}}{\det A}$$

regla de Cramer (pág. 606) Método para resolver un sistema de ecuaciones lineales usando determinantes: Para el sistema lineal $ax + by = e$, $cx + dy = f$, sea A la matriz coeficiente. Si $\det A \neq 0$, la solución del sistema es la siguiente:

$$x = \frac{\begin{vmatrix} e & b \\ f & d \end{vmatrix}}{\det A}, \quad y = \frac{\begin{vmatrix} a & e \\ c & f \end{vmatrix}}{\det A}$$

$$9x + 4y = -6$$
$$3x - 5y = -21; \quad \begin{vmatrix} 9 & 4 \\ 3 & -5 \end{vmatrix} = -57$$

Applying Cramer's rule gives the following:

Al aplicar la regla de Cramer se obtiene lo siguiente:

$$x = \frac{\begin{vmatrix} -6 & 4 \\ -21 & -5 \end{vmatrix}}{-57} = \frac{114}{-57} = -2$$

$$y = \frac{\begin{vmatrix} 9 & -6 \\ 3 & -21 \end{vmatrix}}{-57} = \frac{-171}{-57} = 3$$

ENGLISH-SPANISH GLOSSARY

cross multiplying (p. 500) A method for solving a simple rational equation for which each side of the equation is a single rational expression. **multiplicar en cruz** (pág. 500) Método para resolver una ecuación racional simple en la que cada lado es una sola expresión racional.	To solve $\dfrac{3}{x+1} = \dfrac{9}{4x+5}$, cross multiply. Para resolver $\dfrac{3}{x+1} = \dfrac{9}{4x+5}$, multiplica en cruz. $$3(4x+5) = 9(x+1)$$ $$12x + 15 = 9x + 9$$ $$3x = -6$$ $$x = -2$$
cycle (p. 660) The shortest repeating portion of the graph of a periodic function. **ciclo** (pág. 660) En una función periódica, la parte más corta de la gráfica que se repite.	*See* periodic function. *Ver* función periódica.

D

decay factor (p. 426) The expression $1 - r$ in the exponential decay model $y = a(1-r)^t$. **factor de decrecimiento** (pág. 426) La expresión $1 - r$ en el modelo de decrecimiento exponencial $y = a(1-r)^t$.	**In the exponential decay model $y = 3.2(0.65)^t$, the decay factor is 0.65.** **El factor de decrecimiento de la función $y = 3.2(0.65)^t$ es 0.65.**
degree of a polynomial (p. 302) The exponent in the term of a polynomial where the variable is raised to the greatest power. **grado de un polinomio** (pág. 302) En un polinomio, el exponente del término donde la variable se eleva a la mayor potencia.	**The polynominal $2x^2 + x - 5$ has a degree of 2.** **El polinomio $2x^2 + x - 5$ es de grado 2.**
dependent events (p. 569) Two events such that the occurrence of one event affects the occurrence of the other event. **sucesos dependientes** (pág. 569) Dos sucesos tales que la ocurrencia de uno de ellos afecta a la ocurrencia del otro.	**Two cards are drawn from a deck without replacement. The events "the first is a 3" and "the second is a 3" are dependent.** **Se sacan dos cartas de una baraja y no se reemplazan. Los sucesos "la primera es un 3" y "la segunda es un 3" son dependientes.**
dependent variable (p. 69) The output variable in an equation in two variables. **variable dependiente** (pág. 69) La variable de salida de una ecuación con dos variables.	*See* independent variable. *Ver* variable independiente.
determinant (p. 606) A real number associated with any square matrix A, denoted by det A or $|A|$. **determinante** (pág. 606) Número real asociado a toda matriz cuadrada A, denotada por det A o $|A|$.	$$\det \begin{bmatrix} a & b \\ c & d \end{bmatrix} = ad - cb$$ $$\det \begin{bmatrix} 5 & 4 \\ 3 & 1 \end{bmatrix} = 5(1) - 3(4) = -7$$

dimensions of a matrix (p. 585) The dimensions of a matrix with m rows and n columns are $m \times n$.	A matrix with 2 rows and 3 columns has the dimensions 2×3 (read "2 by 3").
dimensiones de una matriz (pág. 585) Las dimensiones de una matriz con m filas y n columnas son $m \times n$.	Una matriz con 2 filas y 3 columnas tiene por dimensiones 2×3 (leído "2 por 3").
directrix of a parabola (p. 697) *See* parabola.	*See* parabola.
directriz de una parábola (pág. 697) *Ver* parábola.	*Ver* parábola.
direct variation (p. 101) Two variables x and y show direct variation provided that $y = kx$ where k is a nonzero constant.	The equation $5x + 2y = 0$ represents direct variation because it is equivalent to the equation $y = -\frac{5}{2}x$.
variación directa (pág. 101) Dos variables x e y indican una variación directa siempre que $y = kx$, donde k es una constante distinta de cero.	La ecuación $5x + 2y = 0$ representa una variación directa ya que es equivalente a la ecuación $y = -\frac{5}{2}x$.
discriminant of a general second-degree equation (p. 726) The expression $B^2 - 4AC$ for the equation $Ax^2 + Bxy + Cy^2 + Dx + Ey + F = 0$. Used to identify which type of conic the equation represents.	For the equation $4x^2 + y^2 - 8x - 8 = 0$, $A = 4$, $B = 0$, and $C = 1$. $$B^2 - 4AC = 0^2 - 4(4)(1) = -16$$ Because $B^2 - 4AC < 0$, $B = 0$, and $A \neq C$, the conic is an ellipse.
discriminante de una ecuación general de segundo grado (pág. 726) La expresión $B^2 - 4AC$ para la ecuación $Ax^2 + Bxy + Cy^2 + Dx + Ey + F = 0$. Se usa para identificar qué tipo de cónica representa la ecuación.	Para la ecuación $4x^2 + y^2 - 8x - 8 = 0$, $A = 4$, $B = 0$ y $C = 1$. $$B^2 - 4AC = 0^2 - 4(4)(1) = -16$$ Debido a que $B^2 - 4AC < 0$, $B = 0$ y $A \neq C$, la cónica es un elipse.
discriminant of a quadratic equation (p. 276) The expression $b^2 - 4ac$ for the quadratic equation $ax^2 + bx + c = 0$; also the expression under the radical sign in the quadratic formula.	The value of the discriminant of $2x^2 - 3x - 7 = 0$ is $b^2 - 4ac = (-3)^2 - 4(2)(-7) = 65$.
discriminante de una ecuación cuadrática (pág. 276) La expresión $b^2 - 4ac$ para la ecuación cuadrática $ax^2 + bx + c = 0$; es también la expresión situada bajo el signo radical de la fórmula cuadrática.	El valor del discriminante de $2x^2 - 3x - 7 = 0$ es $b^2 - 4ac = (-3)^2 - 4(2)(-7) = 65$.
disjoint events (p. 562) Events A and B are disjoint if they have no outcomes in common; also called mutually exclusive events.	When you randomly select a card from a standard deck of 52 cards, selecting a club and selecting a heart are disjoint events.
sucesos disjuntos (pág. 562) Los sucesos A y B son disjuntos si no tienen casos en común; también se llaman sucesos mutuamente excluyentes.	Al seleccionar al azar una carta de paquete normal de 52 cartas, sacar una de tréboles y sacar una de corazones son sucesos disjuntos.

distance formula (p. 691) The distance d between any two points (x_1, y_1) and (x_2, y_2) is $d = \sqrt{(x_2 - x_1)^2 + (y_2 - y_1)^2}$.

fórmula de la distancia (pág. 691) La distancia d entre dos puntos cualesquiera (x_1, y_1) y (x_2, y_2) es $d = \sqrt{(x_2 - x_1)^2 + (y_2 - y_1)^2}$.

The distance between $(-3, 5)$ and $(4, -1)$ is $\sqrt{(4 - (-3))^2 + (-1 - 5)^2} = \sqrt{49 + 36} = \sqrt{85}$.

La distancia entre $(-3, 5)$ y $(4, -1)$ es $\sqrt{(4 - (-3))^2 + (-1 - 5)^2} = \sqrt{49 + 36} = \sqrt{85}$.

---

domain (p. 67) The set of input values of a relation.

dominio (pág. 67) El conjunto de los valores de entrada de una relación.

See **relation.**

Ver **relación.**

E

---

element of a matrix (p. 585) Each number in a matrix.

elemento de una matriz (pág. 585) Cada número de una matriz.

See **matrix.**

Ver **matriz.**

---

ellipse (p. 710) The set of all points P in a plane such that the sum of the distances between P and two fixed points, called the foci, is a constant.

elipse (pág. 710) El conjunto de todos los puntos P de un plano tales que la suma de las distancias entre P y dos puntos fijos, llamados focos, es una constante.

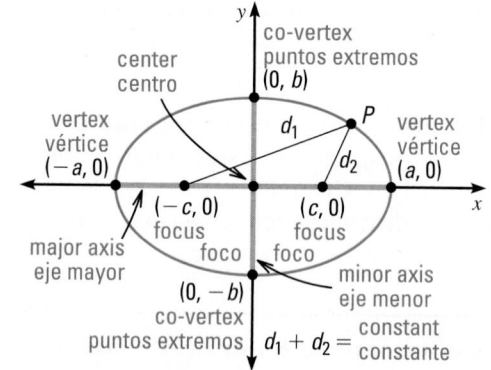

---

end behavior (p. 303) The behavior of the graph of a function $f(x)$ as x gets very large or very small.

comportamiento (pág. 303) El comportamiento de la gráfica de una función $f(x)$ cuando x se agranda o se acorta.

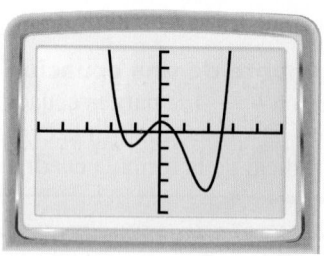

$f(x) \to +\infty$ as $x \to -\infty$ or as $x \to +\infty$.

$f(x) \to +\infty$ según $x \to -\infty$ o según $x \to +\infty$.

---

equal matrices (p. 585) Matrices that have the same dimensions and equal elements in corresponding positions.

matrices iguales (pág. 585) Matrices que tienen las mismas dimensiones y elementos iguales en posiciones correspondientes.

$$\begin{bmatrix} 6 & 0 \\ -\dfrac{4}{4} & \dfrac{3}{4} \end{bmatrix} = \begin{bmatrix} 3 \cdot 2 & -1 + 1 \\ -1 & 0.75 \end{bmatrix}$$

---

equation (p. 26) A statement that two expressions are equal. **ecuación** (pág. 26) Enunciado que establece la igualdad de dos expresiones.	$2x - 3 = 7, 2x^2 = 4x$
equation in two variables (p. 68) An equation that contains two variables. **ecuación con dos variables** (pág. 68) Ecuación que tiene dos variables.	$y = 3x - 5, d = -16t^2 + 64$
equivalent equations (p. 26) Equations that have the same solution(s). **ecuaciones equivalentes** (pág. 26) Ecuaciones que tienen la misma solución o soluciones.	$x + 8 = 3$ and $4x = -20$ are equivalent because both have the solution -5. $x + 8 = 3$ y $4x = -20$ son equivalentes porque tienen ambas la solución -5.
equivalent expressions (p. 17) Two algebraic expressions that have the same value for all values of their variable(s). **expresiones equivalentes** (pág. 17) Dos expresiones algebraicas que tienen el mismo valor para todos los valores de la variable o variables.	$8x + 3x$ and $11x$ are equivalent expressions, as are $2(x - 3)$ and $2x - 6$. $8x + 3x$ y $11x$ son expresiones equivalentes, como también lo son $2(x - 3)$ y $2x - 6$.
equivalent inequalities (p. 172) Inequalities that have the same solution. **desigualdades equivalentes** (pág. 172) Desigualdades que tienen la misma solución.	$3n - 1 \leq 8$ and $n + 1.5 \leq 4.5$ are equivalent inequalities because the solution of both inequalities is all numbers less than or equal to 3. $3n - 1 \leq 8$ y $n + 1.5 \leq 4.5$ son desigualdades equivalentes ya que la solución de ambas son todos los números menores o iguales a 3.
experimental probability (p. 557) A probability based on performing an experiment, conducting a survey, or looking at the history of an event. **probabilidad experimental** (pág. 557) Probabilidad basada en la realización de un experimento o una encuesta o en el estudio de la historia de un suceso.	You roll a six-sided die 100 times and get a 4 nineteen times. The experimental probability of rolling a 4 with the dice is $\frac{19}{100} = 0.19$. Lanzas 100 veces un dado de seis caras y sale diecinueve veces el 4. La probabilidad experimental de que salga el 4 al lanzar el dado es $\frac{19}{100} = 0.19$.
exponent (p. 9) The number or variable that represents the number of times the base of a power is used as a factor. **exponente** (pág. 9) El número o la variable que representa la cantidad de veces que la base de una potencia se usa como factor.	In the power 2^5, the exponent is 5. En la potencia 2^5, el exponente es 5.

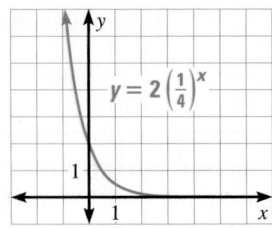

exponential decay function (p. 419) If $a > 0$ and $0 < b < 1$, then the function $y = ab^x$ is an exponential decay function.

función de decrecimiento exponencial (pág. 419) Si $a > 0$ y $0 < b < 1$, entonces la función $y = ab^x$ es una función de decrecimiento exponencial.

$$y = 2\left(\frac{1}{4}\right)^x$$

---

exponential function (p. 412) A function of the form $y = ab^x$, where $a \neq 0$, $b > 0$, and $b \neq 1$.

función exponencial (pág. 412) Función de la forma $y = ab^x$, donde $a \neq 0$, $b > 0$ y $b \neq 1$.

See exponential growth function *and* exponential decay function.

Ver función de crecimiento exponencial y función de decrecimiento exponencial.

---

exponential growth function (p. 412) If $a > 0$ and $b > 1$, then the function $y = ab^x$ is an exponential growth function .

función de crecimiento exponencial (pág. 412) Si $a > 0$ y $b > 1$, entonces la función $y = ab^x$ es una función de crecimiento exponencial.

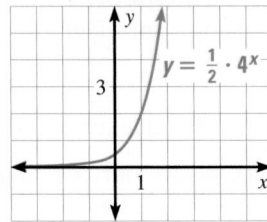

$$y = \frac{1}{2} \cdot 4^x$$

---

extraneous solution (p. 366) An apparent solution that must be rejected because it does not satisfy the original equation.

solución extraña (pág. 366) Solución aparente que debe rechazarse ya que no satisface la ecuación original.

When you square both sides of the radical equation $\sqrt{6 - x} = x$, the resulting equation has two solutions, 2 and -3, but -3 is an extraneous solution because it does not satisfy the original equation $\sqrt{6 - x} = x$.

Cuando se saca la raíz cuadrada de los dos lados de la ecuación radical $\sqrt{6 - x} = x$, la ecuación resultante tiene dos soluciones, 2 y -3, pero -3 es una solución extraña porque no resuelve la ecuación original $\sqrt{6 - x} = x$.

F

factor by grouping (p. 324) To factor a polynomial with four terms by grouping, factor common monomials from pairs of terms, and then look for a common binomial factor.

factorizar por grupos (pág. 324) Para factorizar por grupos un polinomio con cuatro términos, factoriza unos monomios comunes a partir de los pares de términos y luego busca un factor binómico común.

$$x^3 - 3x^2 - 16x + 48$$
$$= x^2(x - 3) - 16(x - 3)$$
$$= (x^2 - 16)(x - 3)$$
$$= (x + 4)(x - 4)(x - 3)$$

factorial (p. 540) For any positive integer n, the expression $n!$, read "n factorial," is the product of all the integers from 1 to n. Also, 0! is defined to be 1.

factorial (pág. 540) Para cualquier número entero positivo n, la expresión $n!$, leída "factorial de n", es el producto de todos los números enteros entre 1 y n. También, 0! se define como 1.

$$6! = 6 \cdot 5 \cdot 4 \cdot 3 \cdot 2 \cdot 1 = 720$$

---

finite sequence (p. 608) A sequence with a limited number of terms.

secuencia finita (pág. 608) Una secuencia con un número limitado de términos.

The sequence 3, 6, 9, 12 is a finite sequence.

La secuencia 3, 6, 9, 12 es una secuencia finita.

---

foci of a hyperbola (p. 717) *See* hyperbola.

focos de una hipérbola (pág. 717) *Ver* hipérbola.

See hyperbola.

Ver hipérbola.

---

foci of an ellipse (p. 710) *See* ellipse.

focos de una elipse (pág. 710) *Ver* elipse.

See ellipse.

Ver elipse.

---

focus of a parabola (p. 697) *See* parabola.

foco de una parábola (pág. 697) *Ver* parábola.

See parabola.

Ver parábola.

---

formula (p. 33) An equation that relates two or more quantities, usually represented by variables.

fórmula (pág. 33) Ecuación que relaciona dos o más cantidades que generalmente se representan por variables.

The formula $P = 2\ell + 2w$ relates the length and width of a rectangle to its perimeter.

La fórmula $P = 2\ell + 2w$ relaciona el largo y el ancho de un rectángulo con su perímetro.

---

frequency distribution (p. 52) A table that shows how many times the numbers in each interval occur in the data.

distribución de frecuencias (pág. 52) Una tabla que muestra la cantidad de veces que los números ocurren en cada intervalo de datos.

Price of sandwiches Precios de los sándwiches		
Interval Intervalo	Tally Cuenta	Frequency Frecuencia
$4.00–4.49	IIII	4
$4.50–4.99	II	2
$5.00–5.49		0
$5.50–5.99	IIII	4

function (p. 67) A relation for which each input has exactly one output.

The relation $(-4, 6)$, $(3, -9)$, and $(7, -9)$ is a function. The relation $(0, 3)$, $(0, 6)$, and $(10, 8)$ is not a function because the input 0 is mapped onto both 3 and 6.

función (pág. 67) Relación para la que cada entrada tiene exactamente una salida.

La relación $(-4, 6)$, $(3, -9)$ y $(7, -9)$ es una función. La relación $(0, 3)$, $(0, 6)$ y $(10, 8)$ no es una función ya que la entrada 0 se hace corresponder tanto con 3 como con 6.

function notation (p. 73) Using $f(x)$ (or a similar symbol such as $g(x)$ or $h(x)$) to represent the dependent variable of a function.

The linear function $y = mx + b$ can be written using function notation as $f(x) = mx + b$.

notación de función (pág. 73) Usar $f(x)$ (o un símbolo semejante como $g(x)$ o $h(x)$) para representar la variable dependiente de una función.

La función lineal $y = mx + b$ escrita en notación de función es $f(x) = mx + b$.

G

general second-degree equation in x and y (p. 726) The form $Ax^2 + Bxy + Cy^2 + Dx + Ey + F = 0$.

$16x^2 - 9y^2 - 96x + 36y - 36 = 0$ and $4x^2 + y^2 - 8x - 8 = 0$ are second-degree equations in x and y.

ecuación general de segundo grado en x e y (pág. 726) La forma $Ax^2 + Bxy + Cy^2 + Dx + Ey + F = 0$.

$16x^2 - 9y^2 - 96x + 36y - 36 = 0$ y $4x^2 + y^2 - 8x - 8 = 0$ son ecuaciones de segundo grado en x e y.

geometric probability (p. 558) A probability found by calculating a ratio of two lengths, areas, or volumes.

probabilidad geométrica (pág. 558) Probabilidad hallada al calcular una razón entre dos longitudes, áreas o volúmenes.

The probability that a dart that hits the square at random lands inside the circle is $\dfrac{\pi \cdot 7^2}{14^2} \approx 0.785$.

La probabilidad de que un dardo que da con el blanco cuadrado, dé al azar en el interior del círculo es $\dfrac{\pi \cdot 7^2}{14^2} \approx 0.785$.

geometric sequence (p. 621) A sequence in which the ratio of any term to the previous term is constant.

$-19, 38, -76, 152$ is a geometric sequence with common ratio -2.

progresión geométrica (pág. 621) Progresión en la que la razón entre cualquier término y el término precedente es constante.

$-19, 38, -76, 152$ es una progresión geométrica con una razón común de -2.

geometric series (p. 623) The expression formed by adding the terms of a geometric sequence.

serie geométrica (pág. 623) La expresión formada al sumar los términos de una progresión geométrica.

$$4 + 12 + 36 + 108 + 324 + ...$$

---

graph of a linear inequality in two variables (p. 179) The set of all points in a coordinate plane that represent solutions of the inequality.

gráfica de una desigualdad lineal con dos variables (pág. 179) El conjunto de todos los puntos de un plano de coordenadas que representan las soluciones de la desigualdad.

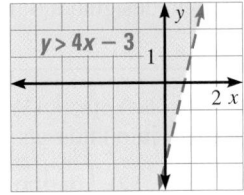

---

graph of an equation in two variables (p. 69) The set of all points (x, y) that represent solutions of the equation.

gráfica de una ecuación con dos variables (pág. 69) El conjunto de todos los puntos (x, y) que representan soluciones de la ecuación.

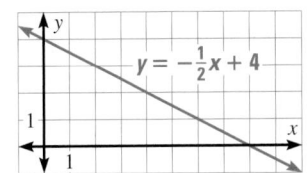

---

graph of an inequality in one variable (p. 173) All points on a real number line that are solutions of the inequality.

gráfica de una desigualdad con una variable (pág. 173) Todos los puntos de una recta numérica que representan soluciones de la desigualdad.

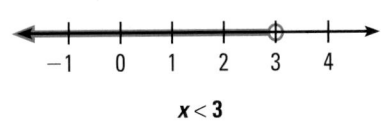

---

graph of a real number (p. 3) The point on a number line that corresponds to a real number called the coordinate of the point. The graph of -2 is shown at the right.

gráfica de un número real (pág. 3) El punto en una recta numérica que corresponde a un número real denominado punto de coordenada. A la derecha se muestra la gráfica de -2.

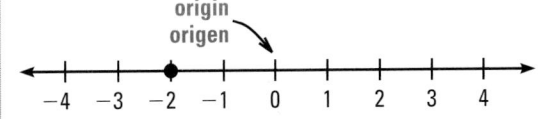

---

graph of a system of linear inequalities (p. 185) The graph of all solutions of the system.

gráfica de un sistema de desigualdades lineales (pág. 185) La gráfica de todas las soluciones del sistema.

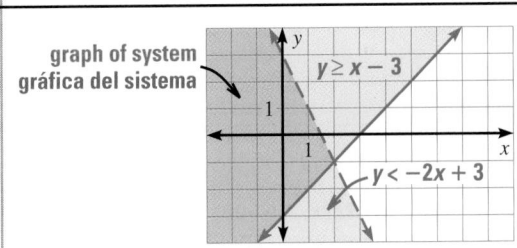

---

growth factor (p. 426) The expression $1 + r$ in the exponential growth model $y = a(1 + r)^t$.

factor de crecimiento (pág. 426) La expresión $1 + r$ en el modelo exponencial de crecimiento $y = a(1 + r)^t$.

In the exponential growth model $y = 2(1.75)^t$, the growth factor is 1.75.

En el modelo exponencial de crecimiento $y = 2(1.75)^t$, el factor de crecimiento es 1.75.

ENGLISH-SPANISH GLOSSARY

half-planes (p. 179) The two regions into which the boundary line of a linear inequality divides the coordinate plane.

semiplanos (pág. 179) Las dos regiones en que la recta límite de una desigualdad lineal divide al plano de coordenadas.

The solution of $y < 3$ is the half-plane consisting of all the points below the line $y = 3$.

La solución de $y < 3$ es el semi-plano que consta de todos los puntos que se encuentran debajo de la recta $y = 3$.

---

histogram (p. 52) A special type of bar graph in which data values are grouped into intervals of the same size.

histograma (pág. 52) Un tipo de gráfica de barras en el que los valores de los datos se agrupan en intervalos del mismo tamaño.

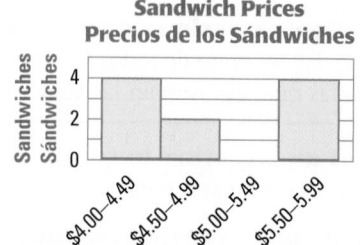

---

hyperbola (pp. 472, 717) The set of all points P in a plane such that the difference of the distances from P to two fixed points, called the foci, is constant.

hipérbola (págs. 472, 717) El conjunto de todos los puntos P de un plano tales que la diferencia de distancias entre P y dos puntos fijos, llamados focos, es constante.

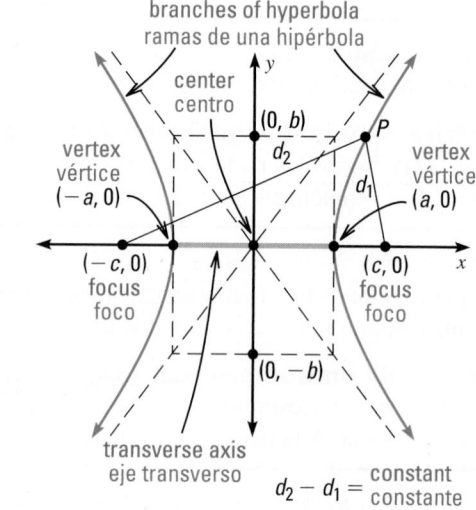

I

identity matrix (p. 600) The $n \times n$ matrix that has 1's on the main diagonal and 0's elsewhere.

matriz identidad (pág. 600) La matriz $n \times n$ que tiene los 1 en la diagonal principal y los 0 en las otras posiciones.

The 2×2 identity matrix is $\begin{bmatrix} 1 & 0 \\ 0 & 1 \end{bmatrix}$.

La matriz identidad 2×2 es $\begin{bmatrix} 1 & 0 \\ 0 & 1 \end{bmatrix}$.

---

imaginary number (p. 262) A complex number $a + bi$ where $b \neq 0$.

número imaginario (pág. 262) Un número complejo $a + bi$, donde $b \neq 0$.

$5i$ and $2 - i$ are imaginary numbers.

$5i$ y $2 - i$ son números imaginarios.

imaginary unit *i* (p. 261) $i = \sqrt{-1}$, so $i^2 = -1$. **unidad imaginaria *i*** (pág. 261) $i = \sqrt{-1}$, por lo que $i^2 = -1$.	$$\sqrt{-3} = i\sqrt{3}$$
independent events (p. 569) Two events such that the occurrence of one event has no effect on the occurrence of the other event. **sucesos independientes** (pág. 569) Dos sucesos tales que la ocurrencia de uno de ellos no afecta a la ocurrencia del otro.	If a coin is tossed twice, the outcome of the first toss (heads or tails) and the outcome of the second toss are independent events. Al lanzar una moneda dos veces, el resultado del primer lanzamiento (cara o cruz) y el resultado del segundo lanzamiento son sucesos independientes.
independent variable (p. 69) The input variable in an equation in two variables. **variable independiente** (pág. 69) La variable de entrada de una ecuación con dos variables.	In $y = 3x - 5$, the independent variable is x. The dependent variable is y because the value of y depends on the value of x. En $y = 3x - 5$, la variable independiente es x. La variable dependiente es y ya que el valor de y depende del valor de x.
index of a radical (p. 353) The integer n, greater than 1, in the expression $\sqrt[n]{a}$. **índice de un radical** (pág. 353) El número entero n, que es mayor que 1 y aparece en la expresión $\sqrt[n]{a}$.	The index of $\sqrt[3]{-216}$ is 3. El índice de $\sqrt[3]{-216}$ es 3.
infinite sequence (p. 608) A sequence that continues without stopping. **secuencia infinita** (pág. 608) Una secuencia que continúa sin detenerse.	The sequence 3, 6, 9, 12, . . . is an infinite sequence. La secuencia 3, 6, 9, 12, . . . es una secuencia infinita.
initial side of an angle (p. 652) *See* terminal side of an angle. **lado inicial de un ángulo** (pág. 652) *Ver* lado terminal de un ángulo.	*See* standard position of an angle. *Ver* posición normal de un ángulo.
intercept form of a quadratic function (p. 229) The form $y = a(x - p)(x - q)$, where the x-intercepts of the graph are p and q. **forma de intercepto de una función cuadrática** (pág. 229) La forma $y = a(x - p)(x - q)$, donde los interceptos en x de la gráfica son p y q.	The function $y = 2(x + 3)(x - 1)$ is in intercept form. La función $y = 2(x + 3)(x - 1)$ está en la forma de intercepto.

inverse functions (p. 380) If a relation and its inverse are functions, then the two functions are inverse functions. Functions f and g are inverse functions provided that $f(g(x)) = x$ and $g(f(x)) = x$.

función inversa (pág. 380) Si una relación y su inversa son funciones, entonces las dos son funciones inversas. Las funciones f y g son funciones inversas siempre y cuando $f(g(x)) = x$ and $g(f(x)) = x$.

$$f(x) = x + 5; g(x) = x - 5$$
$$f(g(x)) = (x - 5) + 5 = x$$
$$g(f(x)) = (x + 5) - 5 = x$$

So, f and g are inverse functions.

Entonces, f y g son funciones inversas.

---

inverse matrices (p. 600) Two $n \times n$ matrices are inverses of each other if their product (in both orders) is the $n \times n$ identity matrix. *See also* identity matrix.

matrices inversas (pág. 600) Dos matrices $n \times n$ son inversas entre sí si su producto (de ambos órdenes) es la matriz identidad $n \times n$. *Ver también* matriz identidad.

$$\begin{bmatrix} -5 & 8 \\ 2 & -3 \end{bmatrix}^{-1} = \begin{bmatrix} 3 & 8 \\ 2 & 5 \end{bmatrix} \text{ because }$$
$$\begin{bmatrix} -5 & 8 \\ 2 & -3 \end{bmatrix}\begin{bmatrix} 3 & 8 \\ 2 & 5 \end{bmatrix} = \begin{bmatrix} 1 & 0 \\ 0 & 1 \end{bmatrix} \text{ and }$$
$$\begin{bmatrix} 3 & 8 \\ 2 & 5 \end{bmatrix}\begin{bmatrix} -5 & 8 \\ 2 & -3 \end{bmatrix} = \begin{bmatrix} 1 & 0 \\ 0 & 1 \end{bmatrix}$$

---

inverse relation (p. 380) A relation that switches the input and output values of the original relation. The graph of an inverse relation is a reflection of the graph of the original relation, with $y = x$ as the line of reflection.

relación inversa (pág. 380) Relación en la que se cambian los valores de entrada y de salida de la relación original. La gráfica de una relación inversa es una reflexión de la gráfica de la relación original, con $y = x$ como eje de reflexión.

To find the inverse of $y = 3x - 5$, switch x and y to obtain $x = 3y - 5$. Then solve for y to obtain the inverse relation $y = \frac{1}{3}x + \frac{5}{3}$.

Para hallar la inversa de $y = 3x - 5$, intercambia x e y para obtener $x = 3y - 5$. Luego resuelve para y para obtener la relación inversa $y = \frac{1}{3}x + \frac{5}{3}$.

---

inverse variation (p. 466) The relationship of two variables x and y if there is a nonzero number k such that $y = \frac{k}{x}$.

variación inversa (pág. 466) La relación entre dos variables x e y si hay un número k distinto de cero tal que $y = \frac{k}{x}$.

The equations $xy = 7$ and $y = -\frac{3}{x}$ represent inverse variation.

Las ecuaciones $xy = 7$ e $y = -\frac{3}{x}$ representan la variación inversa.

---

joint variation (p. 468) A relationship that occurs when a quantity varies directly with the product of two or more other quantities.

variación conjunta (pág. 468) Relación producida cuando una cantidad varía directamente con el producto de dos o más otras cantidades.

The equation $z = 5xy$ represents joint variation.

La ecuación $z = 5xy$ representa la variación conjunta.

law of cosines (p. 675) If $\triangle ABC$ has sides of length a, b, and c as shown, then $a^2 = b^2 + c^2 - 2bc \cos A$, $b^2 = a^2 + c^2 - 2ac \cos B$, and $c^2 = a^2 + b^2 - 2ab \cos C$.

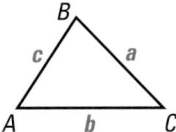

ley de los cosenos (pág. 675) Si $\triangle ABC$ tiene lados de longitud a, b y c como se indica, entonces $a^2 = b^2 + c^2 - 2bc \cos A$, $b^2 = a^2 + c^2 - 2ac \cos B$ y $c^2 = a^2 + b^2 - 2ab \cos C$.

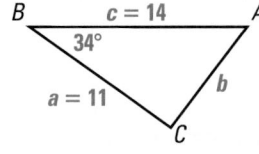

$b^2 = a^2 + c^2 - 2ac \cos B$
$b^2 = 11^2 + 14^2 - 2(11)(14) \cos 34°$
$b^2 \approx 61.7$
$b \approx 7.85$

---

law of sines (p. 668) If $\triangle ABC$ has sides of length a, b, and c as shown, then $\dfrac{\sin A}{a} = \dfrac{\sin B}{b} = \dfrac{\sin C}{c}$.

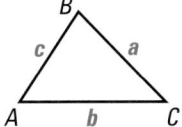

ley de los senos (pág. 668) Si $\triangle ABC$ tiene lados de longitud a, b y c como se indica, entonces $\dfrac{\operatorname{sen} A}{a} = \dfrac{\operatorname{sen} B}{b} = \dfrac{\operatorname{sen} C}{c}$.

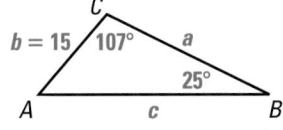

$\dfrac{\sin 25°}{15} = \dfrac{\sin 107°}{c} \to c \approx 33.9$

$\dfrac{\operatorname{sen} 25°}{15} = \dfrac{\operatorname{sen} 107°}{c} \to c \approx 33.9$

---

leading coefficient (p. 302) The coefficient in the term of a polynomial function that has the greatest exponent.

coeficiente inicial (pág. 302) En una función polinómica, el coeficiente del término con el mayor exponente.

The leading coefficient of the polynomial $2x^3 - x^2 - 5x + 12$ is 2.

El coeficiente inicial del polinomio $2x^3 - x^2 - 5x + 12$ is 2.

---

least common denominator (LCD) of rational expressions (p. 494) The least common multiple of the denominators of the rational expressions.

mínimo común denominador (m. c. d.) de expresiones racionales (pág. 494) El mínimo común múltiplo de los denominadores de las expresiones racionales.

The LCD of $\dfrac{5}{(x-3)^2}$ and $\dfrac{3x+4}{(x-3)(x+2)}$ is $(x-3)^2(x+2)$.

El m. c. d. of $\dfrac{5}{(x-3)^2}$ and $\dfrac{3x+4}{(x-3)(x+2)}$ es $(x-3)^2(x+2)$

---

like radicals (p. 360) Radical expressions with the same index and radicand.

radicales semejantes (pág. 360) Expresiones radicales con el mismo índice y el mismo radicando.

$\sqrt[4]{10}$ and $7\sqrt[4]{10}$ are like radicals.

$\sqrt[4]{10}$ y $7\sqrt[4]{10}$ son radicales semejantes.

---

like terms (p. 16) Terms that have the same variable parts. Constant terms are also like terms.

términos semejantes (pág. 16) Términos que tienen las mismas variables. Los términos constantes también son términos semejantes.

In the algebraic expression
$$5x^2 + (-3x) + 7 + 4x + (-2),$$
$-3x$ and $4x$ are like terms, and 7 and -2 are like terms.

En la expresión algebraica
$$5x^2 + (-3x) + 7 + 4x + (-2),$$
$-3x$ y $4x$ son términos semejantes, y 7 y -2 también lo son.

linear combination method (p. 139) A method of solving a system of equations by multiplying equations by constants, then adding the revised equations to eliminate a variable.

método de combinación lineal (pág. 139) Un método de resolución de sistemas de ecuaciones en el que se multiplican las ecuaciones por las constantes y luego se agrega la ecuación revisada para eliminar una variable.

To use the linear combination method to solve the system with equations $3x - 7y = 10$ and $6x - 8y = 8$, multiply the first equation by -2 and add the equations to eliminate x.

Uso del método de combinación lineal para resolver el sistema de ecuaciones $3x - 7y = 10$ y $6x - 8y = 8$. Multiplicar la primera ecuación por -2 y luego agregar las ecuaciones para eliminar x.

linear equation in one variable (p. 26) An equation that can be written in the form $ax = b$ where a and b are constants and $a \neq 0$.

ecuación lineal con una variable (pág. 26) Ecuación que puede escribirse en la forma $ax = b$, donde a y b son constantes y $a \neq 0$.

The equation $\frac{4}{5}x + 8 = 0$ is a linear equation in one variable.

La ecuación $\frac{4}{5}x + 8 = 0$ es una ecuación lineal con una variable.

linear equation in three variables (p. 148) An equation of the form $Ax + By + Cz = D$ where A, B, and C are not all zero.

ecuación lineal con tres variables (pág. 148) Ecuación de la forma $Ax + By + Cz = D$, donde A, B y C no son todos cero.

$2x + y - z = 5$ is a linear equation in three variables.

$2x + y - z = 5$ es una ecuación lineal con tres variables.

linear function (p. 73) A function that can be written in the form $y = mx + b$ where m and b are constants.

función lineal (pág. 73) Función que puede escribirse en la forma $y = mx + b$, donde m y b son constantes.

The function $y = -2x - 1$ is a linear function with $m = -2$ and $b = -1$.

La función $y = -2x - 1$ es una función lineal con $m = -2$ y $b = -1$.

linear inequality in one variable (p. 172) An inequality that can be written in one of the following forms, where a and b are real numbers and $a \neq 0$:
$ax + b < 0$, $ax + b \leq 0$, $ax + b > 0$, or $ax + b \geq 0$.

desigualdad lineal con una variable (pág. 172) Desigualdad que puede escribirse de una de las siguientes formas, donde a y b son números reales y $a \neq 0$:
$ax + b < 0$, $ax + b \leq 0$, $ax + b > 0$ ó $ax + b \geq 0$.

$5x + 2 > 0$ is a linear inequality in one variable.

$5x + 2 > 0$ es una desigualdad lineal con una variable.

linear inequality in two variables (p. 179) An inequality that can be written in one of the following forms:
$Ax + By < C$, $Ax + By \leq C$, $Ax + By > C$, or $Ax + By \geq C$.

desigualdad lineal con dos variables (pág. 179) Desigualdad que puede escribirse de una de las siguientes formas:
$Ax + By < C$, $Ax + By \leq C$, $Ax + By > C$ o $Ax + By \geq C$.

$5x - 2y \geq -4$ is a linear inequality in two variables.

$5x - 2y \geq -4$ es una desigualdad lineal con dos variables.

local maximum (p. 335) The y-coordinate of a turning point of a function if the point is higher than all nearby points.

máximo local (pág. 335) La coordenada y de un punto crítico de una función si el punto está situado más alto que todos los puntos cercanos.

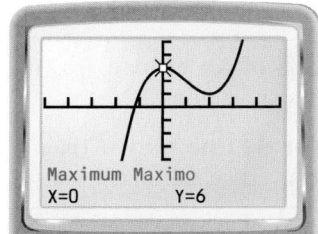

Maximum Maximo
X=0   Y=6

The function $f(x) = x^3 - 3x^2 + 6$ has a local maximum of $y = 6$ when $x = 0$.

La función $f(x) = x^3 - 3x^2 + 6$ tiene un máximo local de $y = 6$ cuando $x = 0$.

---

local minimum (p. 335) The y-coordinate of a turning point of a function if the point is lower than all nearby points.

mínimo local (pág. 335) La coordenada y de un punto crítico de una función si el punto está situado más bajo que todos los puntos cercanos.

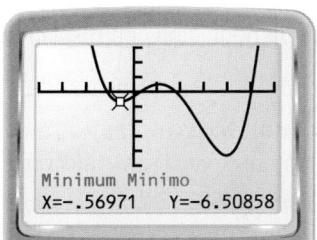

Minimum Minimo
X=-.56971   Y=-6.50858

The function $f(x) = x^4 - 6x^3 + 3x^2 + 10x - 3$ has a local minimum of $y < 26.51$ when $x < 20.57$.

La función $f(x) = x^4 - 6x^3 + 3x^2 + 10x - 3$ tiene un mínimo local de $y < 26.51$ cuando $x < 20.57$.

---

logarithmic equation (p. 450) An equation that involves a logarithm of a variable expression.

ecuación logarítmica (pág. 450) Ecuación en la que aparece el logaritmo de una expresión algebraica.

$\log_5 (4x - 7) = \log_5 (x + 5)$ is a logarithmic equation.

$\log_5 (4x - 7) = \log_5 (x + 5)$ es una ecuación logarítmica.

---

logarithm of y with base b (p. 433) Let b and y be positive numbers with $b \neq 1$. The logarithm of y with base b, denoted $\log_b y$ and read "log base b of y," is defined as follows: $\log_b y = x$ if and only if $b^x = y$.

logaritmo de y con base b (pág. 433) Sean b e y números positivos, con $b \neq 1$. El logaritmo de y con base b, denotado por $\log_b y$ y leído "log base b de y", se define de esta manera: $\log_b y = x$ si y sólo si $b^x = y$.

$\log_2 8 = 3$ because $2^3 = 8$.

$\log_{1/4} 4 = -1$ because $\left(\frac{1}{4}\right)^{-1} = 4$.

$\log_2 8 = 3$ ya que $2^3 = 8$.

$\log_{1/4} 4 = -1$ ya que $\left(\frac{1}{4}\right)^{-1} = 4$.

---

lower quartile (p. 47) The median of the lower half of a data set.

cuartil inferior (pág. 47) En un conjunto de datos, la mediana de la mitad inferior del conjunto.

See **box-and-whisker plot.**

Ver **diagramas de líneas y bloques.**

major axis of an ellipse (p. 710) The line segment joining the vertices of an ellipse.

See ellipse.

eje mayor de una elipse (pág. 710) El segmento de recta que une los vértices de una elipse.

Ver elipse.

---

margin of error (p. 528) The margin of error gives how close you can expect an actual population measure to be to a result from a random sample.

If **40%** of the people in a poll prefer candidate A, and the margin of error is ±4%, then it is expected that between **36%** and **44%** of the entire population prefer candidate A.

margen de error (pág. 528) El margen de error da una idea sobre la aproximación que se puede suponer que tendrá la medida de la población con respecto a la muestra aleatoria.

Si el **40%** de los encuestados prefiere al candidato A y el margen de error es ±4%, entonces se prevé que entre el **36%** y el **44%** de la población total prefiere al candidato A.

---

matrix, matrices (p. 585) A rectangular arrangement of numbers in horizontal rows and vertical columns. Each number in a matrix is an element.

$$A = \begin{bmatrix} 4 & -1 & 5 \\ 0 & 6 & 3 \end{bmatrix}$$

Matrix A has 2 rows and 3 columns. The element in the second row and first column is 0.

matriz, matrices (pág. 585) Disposición rectangular de números colocados en filas horizontales y columnas verticales. Cada número de la matriz es un elemento.

La matriz A tiene 2 filas y 3 columnas. El elemento en la segunda fila y en la primera columna es 0.

---

matrix of constants (p. 601) The matrix B when a system of linear equations is written as a matrix equation $AX = B$.

See coefficient matrix.

matriz de constantes (pág. 601) La matriz B cuando un sistema de ecuaciones lineales se escribe como una ecuación de matriz $AX = B$.

Ver matriz coeficiente.

---

matrix of variables (p. 601) The matrix X when a system of linear equations is written as a matrix equation $AX = B$.

See coefficient matrix.

matriz de variables (pág. 601) La matriz X cuando un sistema de ecuaciones lineales se escribe como una ecuación de matriz $AX = B$.

Ver matriz coeficiente.

---

maximum value of a quadratic function (p. 230) The y-coordinate of the vertex for $y = ax^2 + bx + c$ when $a < 0$.

valor máximo de una función cuadrática (pág. 230) La coordenada y del vértice para $y = ax^2 + bx + c$ cuando $a < 0$.

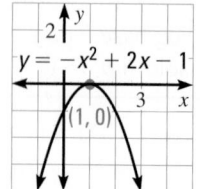

The maximum value of $y = -x^2 + 2x^2 - 1$ is 0.

El valor máximo de $y = -x^2 + 2x^2 - 1$ es 0.

mean (p. 46) For the data set $x_1, x_2, \ldots, x_n$, the mean is $\bar{x} = \dfrac{x_1 + x_2 + \cdots + x_n}{n}$. Also called average.

media (pág. 46) Para el conjunto de datos $x_1, x_2, \ldots, x_n$, la media es $\bar{x} = \dfrac{x_1 + x_2 + \cdots + x_n}{n}$. También se llama promedio.

See measure of central tendency.

Ver medida de tendencia central.

---

measure of central tendency (p. 46) A number used to represent the center or middle of a set of data values. Mean, median, and mode are three measures of central tendency.

medida de tendencia central (pág. 46) Número usado para representar el centro o la posición central de un conjunto de valores de datos. La media, la mediana y la moda son tres medidas de tendencia central.

14, 17, 18, 19, 20, 24, 24, 30, 32

The mean is $\dfrac{14 + 17 + 18 + \cdots + 32}{9} = \dfrac{198}{9} = 22.$

The median is the middle number, 20.
The mode is 24 because 24 occurs the most frequently.

La media es $\dfrac{14 + 17 + 18 + \cdots + 32}{9} = \dfrac{198}{9} = 22.$

La mediana es el número central, 20.
La moda es 24 ya que 24 ocurre más veces.

---

measure of dispersion (p. 47) A statistic that tells you how dispersed, or spread out, data values are. Range and standard deviation are measures of dispersion.

medida de dispersión (pág. 47) Estadística que te indica cómo se dispersan, o distribuyen, los valores de datos. El rango y la desviación típica son medidas de dispersión.

See range *and* standard deviation.

Ver rango *y* desviación típica.

---

median (p. 46) The median of n numbers is the middle number when the numbers are written in numerical order. If n is even, the median is the mean of the two middle numbers.

mediana (pág. 46) La mediana de n números es el número central cuando los números se escriben en orden numérico. Si n es par, la mediana es la media de los dos números centrales.

See measure of central tendency.

Ver medida de tendencia central.

---

midpoint formula (p. 692) The midpoint M of the line segment joining $A(x_1, y_1)$ and $B(x_2, y_2)$ is $M\left(\dfrac{x_1 + x_2}{2}, \dfrac{y_1 + y_2}{2}\right)$.

fórmula del punto medio (pág. 692) El punto medio M del segmento de recta que une $A(x_1, y_1)$ y $B(x_2, y_2)$ es $M\left(\dfrac{x_1 + x_2}{2}, \dfrac{y_1 + y_2}{2}\right)$.

The midpoint of the line segment joining $(-2, 3)$ and $(8, 6)$ is $\left(\dfrac{-2 + 8}{2}, \dfrac{3 + 6}{2}\right) = \left(3, \dfrac{9}{2}\right)$.

El punto medio del segmento de recta que une $(-2, 3)$ y $(8, 6)$ es $\left(\dfrac{-2 + 8}{2}, \dfrac{3 + 6}{2}\right) = \left(3, \dfrac{9}{2}\right)$.

minimum value of a quadratic function (p. 230) The y-coordinate of the vertex for $y = ax^2 + bx + c$ when $a > 0$.

valor mínimo de una función cuadrática (pág. 230) La coordenada y del vértice para $y = ax^2 + bx + c$ cuando $a > 0$.

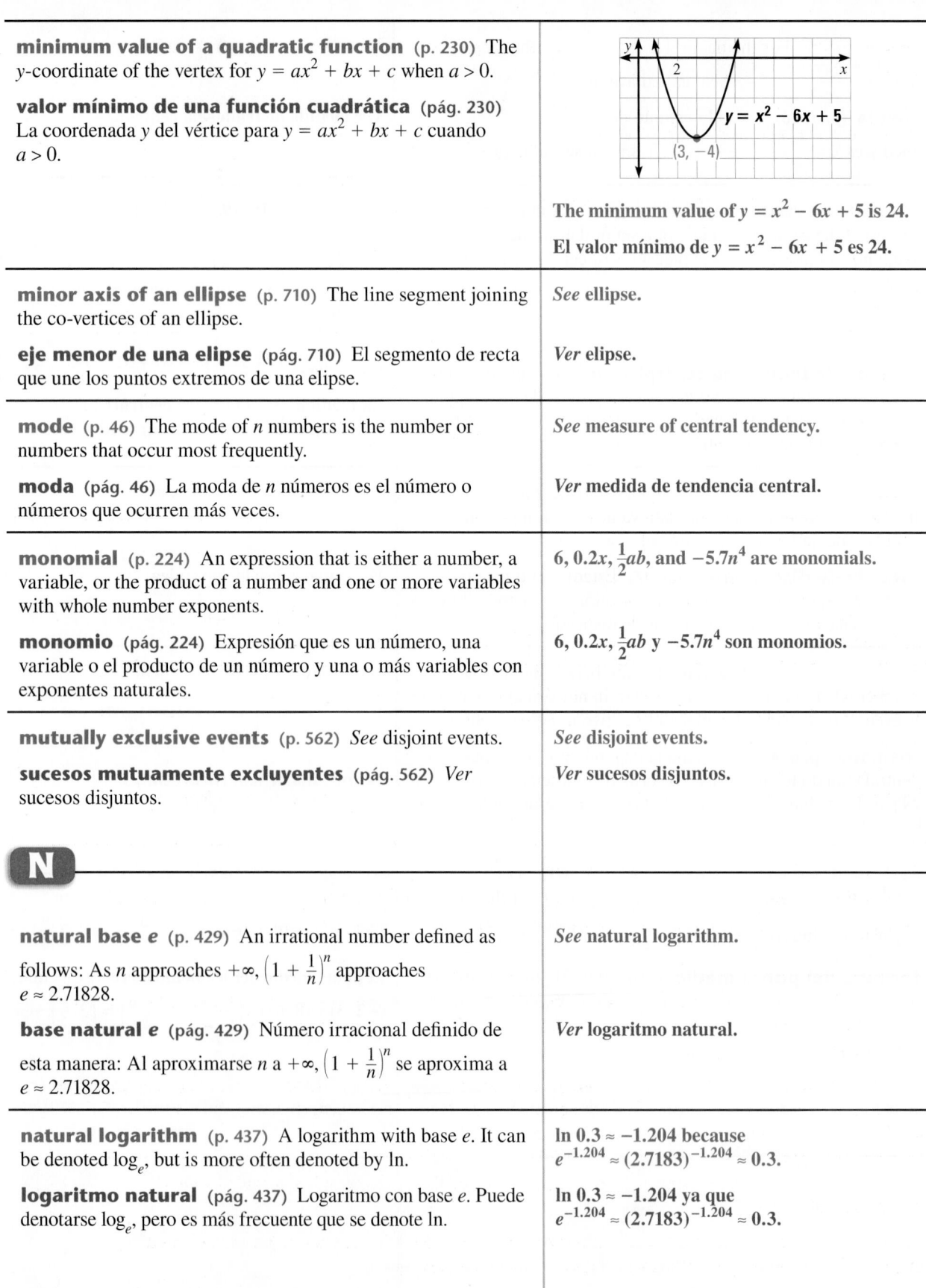

The minimum value of $y = x^2 - 6x + 5$ is 24.

El valor mínimo de $y = x^2 - 6x + 5$ es 24.

---

minor axis of an ellipse (p. 710) The line segment joining the co-vertices of an ellipse.

eje menor de una elipse (pág. 710) El segmento de recta que une los puntos extremos de una elipse.

See **ellipse.**

Ver **elipse.**

---

mode (p. 46) The mode of n numbers is the number or numbers that occur most frequently.

moda (pág. 46) La moda de n números es el número o números que ocurren más veces.

See **measure of central tendency.**

Ver **medida de tendencia central.**

---

monomial (p. 224) An expression that is either a number, a variable, or the product of a number and one or more variables with whole number exponents.

monomio (pág. 224) Expresión que es un número, una variable o el producto de un número y una o más variables con exponentes naturales.

$6, 0.2x, \frac{1}{2}ab$, and $-5.7n^4$ are monomials.

$6, 0.2x, \frac{1}{2}ab$ y $-5.7n^4$ son monomios.

---

mutually exclusive events (p. 562) *See* disjoint events.

sucesos mutuamente excluyentes (pág. 562) *Ver* sucesos disjuntos.

See **disjoint events.**

Ver **sucesos disjuntos.**

N

natural base e (p. 429) An irrational number defined as follows: As n approaches $+\infty$, $\left(1 + \frac{1}{n}\right)^n$ approaches $e \approx 2.71828$.

base natural e (pág. 429) Número irracional definido de esta manera: Al aproximarse n a $+\infty$, $\left(1 + \frac{1}{n}\right)^n$ se aproxima a $e \approx 2.71828$.

See **natural logarithm.**

Ver **logaritmo natural.**

---

natural logarithm (p. 437) A logarithm with base e. It can be denoted $\log_e$, but is more often denoted by ln.

logaritmo natural (pág. 437) Logaritmo con base e. Puede denotarse $\log_e$, pero es más frecuente que se denote ln.

$\ln 0.3 \approx -1.204$ because $e^{-1.204} \approx (2.7183)^{-1.204} \approx 0.3$.

$\ln 0.3 \approx -1.204$ ya que $e^{-1.204} \approx (2.7183)^{-1.204} \approx 0.3$.

negative correlation (p. 107) The paired data (x, y) have a negative correlation if y tends to decrease as x increases.

correlación negativa (pág. 107) Los pares de datos (x, y) presentan una correlación negativa si y tiende a disminuir al aumentar x.

nth root of a (p. 353) For an integer n greater than 1, if $b^n = a$, then b is an nth root of a. Written as $\sqrt[n]{a}$.

raíz enésima de a (pág. 353) Para un número entero n mayor que 1, si $b^n = a$, entonces b es una raíz enésima de a. Se escribe $\sqrt[n]{a}$.

$\sqrt[3]{-216} = -6$ because $(-6)^3 = -216$.

$\sqrt[3]{-216} = -6$ ya que $(-6)^3 = -216$.

numerical expression (p. 9) An expression that consists of numbers, operations, and grouping symbols.

expresión numérica (pág. 9) Expresión formada por números, operaciones y signos de agrupación.

$-4(-3)^2 - 6(-3) + 11$ is a numerical expression.

$-4(-3)^2 - 6(-3) + 11$ es una expresión numérica.

O

octants (p. 147) *See* three-dimensional coordinate system.

octantes (pág. 147) *Ver* sistema de coordenadas tridimensionales.

See **three-dimensional coordinate system.**

Ver **sistema de coordenadas tridimensionales.**

operations on functions (p. 373) The addition, subtraction, multiplication, or division of two functions, $f(x)$ and $g(x)$, to form a new function, $h(x)$.

operación de funciones (pág. 373) La suma, resta, multiplicación o división de dos funciones, $f(x)$ y $g(x)$ para formar una nueva funcion: $h(x)$.

Let $f(x) = 3x$, $g(x) = 2x + 1$, and $h(x) = f(x) + g(x)$. Then $h(x) = 3x + (2x + 1) = 5x + 1$.

Si $f(x) = 3x$, $g(x) = 2x + 1$, y $h(x) = f(x) + g(x)$. Entonces $h(x) = 3x + (2x + 1) = 5x + 1$.

opposite (p. 5) The opposite, or additive inverse, of any number a is $-a$.

opuesto (pág. 5) El opuesto, o inverso aditivo, de cualquier número a es $-a$.

6.2 and -6.2 are opposites.

6.2 y -6.2 son opuestos.

ordered triple (p. 147) A set of three numbers of the form (x, y, z) that represents a point in space. *See also* three-dimensional coordinate system.

terna ordenada (pág. 147) Un conjunto de tres números de la forma (x, y, z) que representa un punto en el espacio. *Ver también* sistema de coordenadas tridimensionales.

The ordered triple $(2, 1, -3)$ is a solution of the equation $4x + 2y + 3z = 1$.

La terna ordenada $(2, 1, -3)$ es una solución de la ecuación $4x + 2y + 3z = 1$.

origin of a real number line (p. 3) The point labeled 0 on a real number line.

origen de la recta numérica de números reales (pág. 3) El punto marcado con 0 en una recta numérica de números reales.

See **graph of a real number.**

Ver **gráfica de un número real.**

overlapping events (p. 562) Events that have at least one common outcome.

eventos solapados (pág. 562) Eventos que tienen, al menos, un resultado en común.

When you roll a number cube, "roll a 3" and "roll an odd number" are overlapping events.

Es un evento solapado cuando se arroja un cubo numerado y se obtiene "un 3" y "un número impar".

P

parabola (pp. 222, 697) The set of all points equidistant from a point called the focus and a line called the directrix. The graph of a quadratic function $y = ax^2 + bx + c$ is a parabola.

parábola (págs. 222, 697) El conjunto de todos los puntos equidistantes de un punto, llamado foco, y de una recta, llamada directriz. La gráfica de una función cuadrática $y = ax^2 + bx + c$ es una parábola.

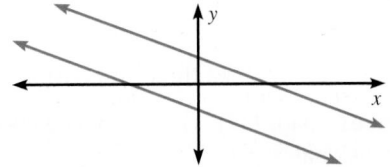

axis of symmetry
eje de simetría
focus
foco
vertex
vértice
directrix
directriz

parallel lines (p. 89) Two lines in the same plane that do not intersect.

rectas paralelas (pág. 89) Dos rectas del mismo plano que no se cortan.

partial sum (p. 628) The sum S_n of the first n terms of an infinite series.

suma parcial (pág. 628) La suma S_n de los n primeros términos de una serie infinita.

$$\frac{1}{2} + \frac{1}{4} + \frac{1}{8} + \frac{1}{16} + \frac{1}{32} + \cdots$$

The series above has the partial sums
$S_1 = 0.5, S_2 = 0.75, S_3 \approx 0.88, S_4 \approx 0.94, \ldots.$

La serie de arriba tiene las sumas parciales
$S_1 = 0.5, S_2 = 0.75, S_3 \approx 0.88, S_4 \approx 0.94, \ldots.$

Pascal's triangle (p. 547) An arrangement of the values of $_nC_r$ in a triangular pattern in which each row corresponds to a value of n.

triángulo de Pascal (pág. 547) Disposición de los valores de $_nC_r$ en un patrón triangular en el que cada fila corresponde a un valor de n.

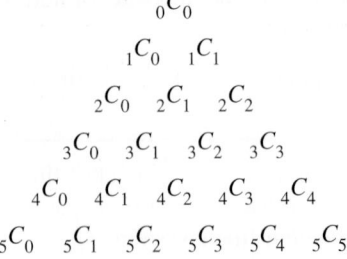

$_0C_0$

$_1C_0 \quad _1C_1$

$_2C_0 \quad _2C_1 \quad _2C_2$

$_3C_0 \quad _3C_1 \quad _3C_2 \quad _3C_3$

$_4C_0 \quad _4C_1 \quad _4C_2 \quad _4C_3 \quad _4C_4$

$_5C_0 \quad _5C_1 \quad _5C_2 \quad _5C_3 \quad _5C_4 \quad _5C_5$

period (p. 660) The horizontal length of each cycle of a periodic function.

período (pág. 660) La longitud horizontal de cada ciclo de una función periódica.

See periodic function.

Ver función periódica.

periodic function (p. 660) A function whose graph has a repeating pattern that continues indefinitely.

función periódica (pág. 660) Función cuya gráfica tiene un patrón que se repite y que continúa indefinidamente.

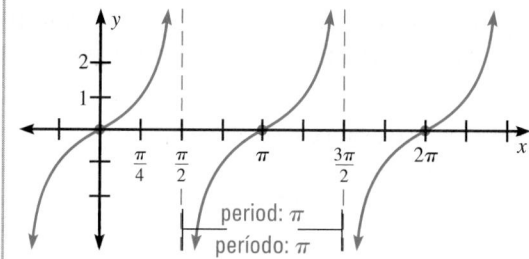

period: π
período: π

The graph shows 3 cycles of $y = \tan x$, a periodic function with a period of π.

La gráfica muestra 3 ciclos de $y = \tan x$, función periódica con período π.

---

permutation (p. 540) An ordering of objects. The number of permutations of n objects taken r at a time is denoted ${}_nP_r$ where ${}_nP_r = \dfrac{n!}{(n-r)!}$.

permutación (pág. 540) Ordenación de objetos. Al número de permutaciones de n objetos tomados r veces se le denomina ${}_nP_r$, donde ${}_nP_r = \dfrac{n!}{(n-r)!}$.

There are 6 permutations of the $n = 3$ letters A, B, and C taken $r = 3$ at a time: ABC, ACB, BAC, BCA, CAB, and CBA.

Hay 6 permutaciones de las letras $n = 3$ A, B y C tomadas $r = 3$ veces: ABC, ACB, BAC, BCA, CAB y CBA.

---

perpendicular lines (p. 89) Two lines in the same plane that intersect to form a right angle.

rectas perpendiculares (pág. 89) Dos rectas del mismo plano que al cortarse forman un ángulo recto.

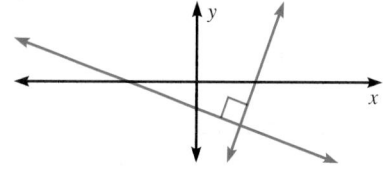

---

point-slope form (p. 94) An equation of a line written in the form $y - y_1 = m(x - x_1)$ where the line passes through the point (x_1, y_1) and has a slope of m.

forma punto-pendiente (pág. 94) Ecuación de una recta escrita en la forma $y - y_1 = m(x - x_1)$, donde la recta pasa por el punto (x_1, y_1) y tiene pendiente m.

The equation $y + 2 = -4(x - 5)$ is in point-slope form.

La ecuación $y + 2 = -4(x - 5)$ está en la forma punto-pendiente.

---

polynomial (p. 302) A monomial or a sum of monomials with real number coefficients. *See also* monomial.

polinomio (pág. 302) Monomio o suma de monomios con coeficientes de números reales. *Ver también* monomio.

$-14, x^4 - \frac{1}{4}x^2 + 3$, and $7b - \sqrt{3} + \pi b^2$ are polynomials.

$-14, x^4 - \frac{1}{4}x^2 + 3$ y $7b - \sqrt{3} + \pi b^2$ son polinomios.

---

polynomial function (p. 302) A function of the form $f(x) = a_n x^n + a_{n-1} x^{n-1} + \cdots + a_1 x + a_0$ where $a_n \neq 0$, the exponents are all whole numbers, and the coefficients are all real numbers.

función polinómica (pág. 302) Función de la forma $f(x) = a_n x^n + a_{n-1} x^{n-1} + \cdots + a_1 x + a_0$ donde $a_n \neq 0$, los exponentes son todos números enteros y los coeficientes son todos números reales.

$f(x) = 11x^5 - 0.4x^2 + 16x - 7$ is a polynomial function. The degree of $f(x)$ is 5, the leading coefficient is 11, and the constant term is -7.

$f(x) = 11x^5 - 0.4x^2 + 16x - 7$ es una función polinómica. El grado de $f(x)$ es 5, el coeficiente inicial es 11 y el término constante es -7.

polynomial long division (p. 317) A method used to divide polynomials similar to the way you divide whole numbers.

división desarrollada polinómica (pág. 317) Método utilizado para dividir polinomios semejante a la manera en que divides números enteros.

$$
\begin{array}{r}
x^2 + 7x + 7 \\
x - 2 \overline{\smash{\big)}\, x^3 + 5x^2 - 7x + 2} \\
\underline{x^3 - 2x^2} \\
7x^2 - 7x \\
\underline{7x^2 - 14x} \\
7x + 2 \\
\underline{7x - 14} \\
16
\end{array}
$$

$$
\frac{x^3 + 5x^2 - 7x + 2}{x - 2} = x^2 + 7x + 7 + \frac{16}{x - 2}
$$

population (p. 519) A group of people, animals, or objects that you want information about.

población (pág. 519) Grupo de personas, animales u objetos acerca del cual deseas informarte.

A sportswriter randomly selects 5% of college baseball coaches for a survey. The population is all college baseball coaches. The 5% of coaches selected is the sample.

Un periodista deportiva selecciona al azar al 5% de los entrenadores universitarios de béisbol para que participe en una encuesta. La población son todos los entrenadores universitarios de béisbol. El 5% de los entrenadores que resultó seleccionado es la muestra.

positive correlation (p. 107) The paired data (x, y) have a positive correlation if y tends to increase as x increases.

correlacion positiva (pág. 107) Los pares de datos (x, y) presentan una correlación positiva si y tiende a aumentar al aumentar x.

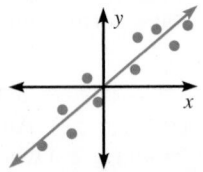

power (p. 9) An expression that represents repeated multiplication of the same factor.

potencia (pág. 9) Expresión que representa la multiplicación repetida del mismo factor.

32 is the fifth power of 2 because $32 = 2 \cdot 2 \cdot 2 \cdot 2 \cdot 2 = 2^5$.

32 es la quinta potencia de 2 ya que $32 = 2 \cdot 2 \cdot 2 \cdot 2 \cdot 2 = 2^5$.

probability of an event (p. 556) A number from 0 to 1 that tells how likely the event is to occur.

probabilidad de un suceso (pág. 556) Número entre 0 y 1 que indica que tan probable es que ocurra el suceso.

See experimental probability, geometric probability, *and* theoretical probability.

Ver probabilidad experimental, probabilidad geométrica *y* probabilidad teórica.

quadrantal angle (p. 654) An angle in standard position whose terminal side lies on an axis.

ángulo cuadrantal (pág. 654) Ángulo en posición normal cuyo lado terminal se encuentra en un eje.

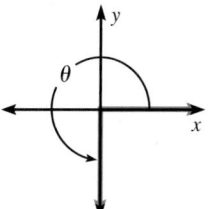

quadratic equation in one variable (p. 235) An equation that can be written in the form $ax^2 + bx + c = 0$ where $a \neq 0$.

ecuación cuadrática con una variable (pág. 235) Ecuación que puede escribirse en la forma $ax^2 + bx + c = 0$, donde $a \neq 0$.

The equation $x^2 - 5x = 36$ is a quadratic equation in one variable because it can be written in the form $x^2 - 5x - 36 = 0$.

La ecuación $x^2 - 5x = 36$ es una ecuación cuadrática con una variable ya que puede escribirse en la forma $x^2 - 5x - 36 = 0$.

quadratic form (p. 329) The form $au^2 + bu + c$, where u is any expression in x.

forma cuadrática (pág. 329) La forma $au^2 + bu + c$, donde u es cualquier expresión en x.

The expression $16x^4 - 8x^2 - 8$ is in quadratic form because it can be written as $u^2 - 2u - 8$ where $u = 4x^2$.

La expresión $16x^4 - 8x^2 - 8$ está en la forma cuadrática ya que puede escribirse $u^2 - 2u - 8$, donde $u = 4x^2$.

quadratic formula (p. 274) The formula $x = \dfrac{-b \pm \sqrt{b^2 - 4ac}}{2a}$ used to find the solutions of the quadratic equation $ax^2 + bx + c = 0$ when a, b, and c are real numbers and $a \neq 0$.

fórmula cuadrática (pág. 274) La fórmula $x = \dfrac{-b \pm \sqrt{b^2 - 4ac}}{2a}$ que se usa para hallar las soluciones de la ecuación cuadrática $ax^2 + bx + c = 0$ cuando a, b y c son números reales y $a \neq 0$.

To solve $3x^2 + 6x + 2 = 0$, substitute 3 for a, 6 for b, and 2 for c in the quadratic formula.

Para resolver $3x^2 + 6x + 2 = 0$, sustituye a por 3, b por 6 y c por 2 en la fórmula cuadrática.

$$x = \frac{-6 \pm \sqrt{6^2 - 4(3)(2)}}{2(3)} = \frac{-3 \pm \sqrt{3}}{3}$$

quadratic function (p. 222) A function that can be written in the standard form $y = ax^2 + bx + c$ where $a \neq 0$.

función cuadrática (pág. 222) Función que puede escribirse en la forma estándar $y = ax^2 + bx + c$, donde $a \neq 0$.

The functions $y = 3x^2 - 5$ and $y = x^2 - 4x + 6$ are quadratic functions.

Las funciones $y = 3x^2 - 5$ e $y = x^2 - 4x + 6$ son funciones cuadráticas.

radical (p. 255) An expression of the form $\sqrt{a}$ or $\sqrt[n]{a}$, where a is a number or an expression.

radical (pág. 255) Expresión de la forma $\sqrt{a}$ o $\sqrt[n]{a}$, donde a es un número o una expresión.

$$\sqrt{5}, \ \sqrt[3]{2x + 1}$$

radical equation (p. 365) An equation with one or more radicals that have variables in their radicands. **ecuación radical** (pág. 365) Ecuación con uno o más radicales en cuyo radicando aparecen variables.	$\sqrt[3]{2x + 7} = 3$
radical function (p. 389) A function that contains a radical with a variable in its radicand. **función radical** (pág. 389) Función que tiene un radical con una variable en su radicando.	$f(x) = \frac{1}{2}\sqrt{x}, g(x) = -3\sqrt[3]{x + 5}$
radicand (p. 255) The number or expression beneath a radical sign. **radicando** (pág. 255) El número o la expresión que aparece bajo el signo radical.	The radicand of $\sqrt{5}$ is 5, and the radicand of $\sqrt{8y^2}$ is $8y^2$. El radicando de $\sqrt{5}$ es 5, y el radicando de $\sqrt{8y^2}$ es $8y^2$.
radius of a circle (p. 703) The distance from the center of a circle to a point on the circle. Also, a line segment that connects the center of a circle to a point on the circle. *See also* circle. **radio de un círculo** (pág. 703) La distancia desde el centro de un círculo hasta un punto del círculo. También, es un segmento de recta que une el centro de un círculo con un punto del círculo. *Ver también* círculo.	The circle with equation $(x - 3)^2 + (y + 5)^2 = 36$ has radius $\sqrt{36} = 6$. El círculo con la ecuación $(x - 3)^2 + (y + 5)^2 = 36$ tiene el radio $\sqrt{36} = 6$.
random sample (p. 526) A sample in which every member of the population has an equal chance of being selected. **muestra aleatoria** (pág. 526) Una muestra seleccionada de tal manera en la que cada miembro de la población tiene la misma probabilidad de ser seleccionado.	You can select a random sample of a school's student population by having a computer randomly choose 100 student identification numbers. Puedes crear una muestra aleatoria de la población estudiantil si haces que una computadora seleccione 100 números de estudiantes.
range of a relation (p. 67) The set of output values of a relation. **rango de una relación** (pág. 67) El conjunto de los valores de salida de una relación.	*See* relation. *Ver* relación.
range of data values (p. 47) A measure of dispersion equal to the difference between the greatest and least data values. **rango de valores de datos** (pág. 47) Medida de dispersión igual a la diferencia entre el valor máximo y el valor mínimo de los datos.	**14, 17, 18, 19, 20, 24, 24, 30, 32** The range of the data set above is $32 - 14 = 18$. El rango del conjunto de datos de arriba es $32 - 14 = 18$.

rate of change (p. 81) A comparison of how much one quantity changes, on average, relative to the change in another quantity.

relación de cambio (pág. 81) Comparación entre el cambio producido, por término medio, en una cantidad y el cambio producido en otra cantidad.

The temperature rises from 75°F at 8 A.M. to 91°F at 12 P.M. The average rate of change in temperature is $\dfrac{91°F - 75°F}{12\ \text{P.M.} - 8\ \text{A.M.}} = \dfrac{16°F}{4\ h} = 4°/h$.

La temperatura sube de 75°F a las 8 de la mañana a 91°F a las 12 del mediodía. La relación de cambio media en la temperatura es $\dfrac{91°F - 75°F}{12\ \text{P.M.} - 8\ \text{A.M.}} = \dfrac{16°F}{4\ h} = 4°/h$.

---

rational equation (p. 500) An equation that contains one or more rational expressions.

ecuación racional (pág. 500) Una ecuación que contiene una expresión racional o más.

The equations $\dfrac{6}{x+4} = \dfrac{x}{2}$ and $\dfrac{x}{x-2} + \dfrac{1}{5} = \dfrac{2}{x-2}$ are rational equations.

Las ecuaciones $\dfrac{6}{x+4} = \dfrac{x}{2}$ y $\dfrac{x}{x-2} + \dfrac{1}{5} = \dfrac{2}{x-2}$ son ecuaciones racionales.

---

rational exponent (p. 354) An exponent written as a fraction. The *n*th root of *a* can be written using a rational exponent: $\sqrt[n]{a} = a^{1/n}$

exponente racional (pág. 354) Un exponente que se representa como fracción. La raíz enésima de *a* se puede representar con un exponente racional: $\sqrt[n]{a} = a^{1/n}$

The expression $\dfrac{1}{\sqrt[2]{9^3}}$ can be rewritten using the rational exponent $-\dfrac{3}{2}$: $\dfrac{1}{\sqrt[2]{9^3}} = \dfrac{1}{9^{3/2}} = 9^{-3/2}$

La expresión $\dfrac{1}{\sqrt[2]{9^3}}$ se puede representar también con el exponente racional $-\dfrac{3}{2}$:

$\dfrac{1}{\sqrt[2]{9^3}} = \dfrac{1}{9^{3/2}} = 9^{-3/2}$

---

rational expression (p. 480) A fraction whose numerator and denominator are nonzero polynomials.

expresión racional (pág. 480) Una fracción cuyo numerador y denominador son polinomios distintos de cero.

$\dfrac{x+8}{10x}$ and $\dfrac{5}{x^2} - 1$ are rational expressions.

$\dfrac{x+8}{10x}$ y $\dfrac{5}{x^2} - 1$ son expresiones racionales.

---

rational function (p. 472) A function of the form $f(x) = \dfrac{p(x)}{q(x)}$, where $p(x)$ and $q(x)$ are polynomials and $q(x) \neq 0$.

función racional (pág. 472) Función de la forma $f(x) = \dfrac{p(x)}{q(x)}$, donde $p(x)$ y $q(x)$ son polinomios y $q(x) \neq 0$.

The functions $y = \dfrac{6}{x}$ and $y = \dfrac{2x+1}{x-3}$ are rational functions.

Las funciones $y = \dfrac{6}{x}$ e $y = \dfrac{2x+1}{x-3}$ son funciones racionales.

---

rationalizing the denominator (p. 256) The process of eliminating a radical expression in the denominator of a fraction by multiplying both the numerator and denominator by an appropriate radical expression.

racionalizar el denominador (pág. 256) El proceso de eliminar una expresión radical del denominador de una fracción al multiplicar tanto el numerador como el denominador por una expresión radical adecuada.

To rationalize the denominator of $\dfrac{\sqrt{5}}{\sqrt{2}}$, multiply the numerator and denominator by $\sqrt{2}$.

Para racionalizar el denominador de $\dfrac{\sqrt{5}}{\sqrt{2}}$, multiplica el numerador y el denominador por $\sqrt{2}$.

reciprocal (p. 5) The reciprocal, or multiplicative inverse, of any nonzero number a is $\frac{1}{a}$. **recíproco** (pág. 5) El recíproco, o inverso multiplicativo, de cualquier número a distinto de cero es $\frac{1}{a}$.	-2 and $\frac{1}{-2} = -\frac{1}{2}$ are reciprocals. -2 y $\frac{1}{-2} = -\frac{1}{2}$ son recíprocos.
relation (p. 67) A mapping, or pairing, of input values with output values. **relación** (pág. 67) Correspondencia entre los valores de entrada y los valores de salida.	The ordered pairs $(-2, -2)$, $(-2, 2)$, $(0, 1)$, and $(3, 1)$ represent the relation with inputs (domain) of $-2, 0,$ and 3 and outputs (range) of $-2, 1,$ and 2. Los pares ordenados $(-2, -2)$, $(-2, 2)$, $(0, 1)$ y $(3, 1)$ representan la relación con entradas (dominio) de $-2, 0$ y 3 y salidas (rango) de $-2, 1$ y 2.
relatively no correlation (p. 107) The paired data (x, y) have relatively no correlation when there is no obvious pattern between x and y. **correlación nula** (pág. 107) Los datos (x, y) tienen una correlación nula porque no existe una relación obvia entre x e y.	
repeated solution (p. 331) A solution of a polynomial equation that appears more than once. **solución repetida** (pág. 331) Una solución de una ecuación polinómica que aparece más de una vez.	-1 is a repeated solution of the equation $(x + 1)^2 (x - 2) = 0$. -1 es una solución repetida de la ecuación $(x + 1)^2 (x - 2) = 0$.

S

sample (p. 519) A part of a population. **muestra** (pág. 519) Parte de una población.	*See* population. *Ver* población.
scalar (p. 587) A real number by which you multiply a matrix. **escalar** (pág. 587) Número real por el que se multiplica una matriz.	*See* scalar multiplication. *Ver* multiplicación escalar.
scalar multiplication (p. 587) Multiplication of each element of a matrix by a real number, called a scalar. **multiplicación escalar** (pág. 587) Multiplicación de cada elemento de una matriz por un número real llamado escalar.	$-2\begin{bmatrix} 4 & 1 \\ 1 & -0 \\ 2 & 7 \end{bmatrix} = \begin{bmatrix} -8 & 2 \\ -2 & 0 \\ -4 & -14 \end{bmatrix}$

scatter plot (p. 107) A graph of a set of data pairs (x, y) used to determine whether there is a relationship between the variables x and y.

diagrama de dispersión (pág. 107) Gráfica de un conjunto de pares de datos (x, y) que sirve para determinar si hay una relación entre las variables x e y.

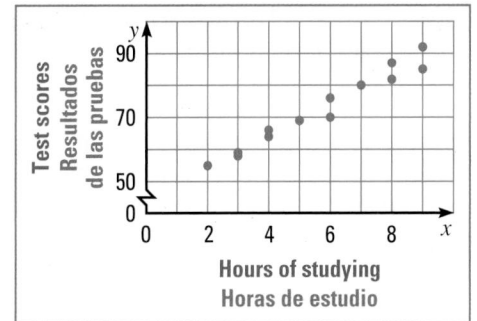

scientific notation (p. 298) The representation of a number in the form $c \times 10^n$ where $1 \le c < 10$ and n is an integer.

notación científica (pág. 298) La representación de un número de la forma $c \times 10^n$, donde $1 \le c < 10$ y n es un número entero.

0.693 is written in scientific notation as 6.93×10^{-1}.

0.693 escrito en notación científica es 6.93×10^{-1}.

secant function (p. 645) If θ is an acute angle of a right triangle, the secant of θ is the length of the hypotenuse divided by the length of the side adjacent to θ.

función secante (pág. 645) Si θ es un ángulo agudo de un triángulo rectángulo, la secante de θ es la longitud de la hipotenusa dividida por la longitud del lado adyacente a θ.

See sine function.

Ver función seno.

self-selected sample (p. 526) A sample in which members of the population select themselves by volunteering.

muestra autoseleccionada (pág. 526) Una muestra en la que los miembros de la población se seleccionan a sí mismos porque se ofrecen como voluntarios.

You can obtain a self-selected sample of a school's student population by asking students to return surveys to a collection box.

Puedes obtener una muestra autoseleccionada de la población de una escuela si pides a los estudiantes que completen una encuesta y la depositen en un buzón.

sequence (p. 608) A function whose domain is a set of consecutive integers. The domain gives the relative position of each term of the sequence. The range gives the terms of the sequence.

progresión (pág. 608) Función cuyo dominio es un conjunto de números enteros consecutivos. El dominio da la posición relativa de cada término de la secuencia. El rango da los términos de la secuencia.

For the domain $n = 1, 2, 3,$ and 4, the sequence defined by $a_n = 2n$ has the terms 2, 4, 6, and 8.

Para el dominio $n = 1, 2, 3$ y 4, la secuencia definida por $a_n = 2n$ tiene los términos 2, 4, 6 y 8.

series (p. 610) The expression formed by adding the terms of a sequence. A series can be finite or infinite.

serie (pág. 610) La expresión formada al sumar los términos de una progresión. La serie puede ser finita o infinita.

Finite series: $2 + 4 + 6 + 8$
Infinite series: $2 + 4 + 6 + 8 + \cdots$

Serie finita: $2 + 4 + 6 + 8$
Serie infinita: $2 + 4 + 6 + 8 + \cdots$

simplest form of a radical (p. 359) A radical with index *n* is in simplest form if there are no perfect *n*th powers in the radicand, and there are no radicals in any denominators.

forma más simple de un radical (pág. 359) Un radical con índice *n* está escrito en la forma más simple si no hay ninguna potencia enésima perfecta en el radicando y si no hay radicales en ningun denominador.

$\sqrt[3]{135}$ in simplest form is $3\sqrt[3]{5}$.
$\dfrac{\sqrt[5]{7}}{\sqrt[5]{8}}$ in simplest form is $\dfrac{\sqrt[5]{28}}{2}$.

$\sqrt[3]{135}$ en la forma más simple es $3\sqrt[3]{5}$.
$\dfrac{\sqrt[5]{7}}{\sqrt[5]{8}}$ en la forma más simple es $\dfrac{\sqrt[5]{28}}{2}$.

---

simplified expression (p. 17) An expression in which all grouping symbols have been removed and all like terms have been combined.

expresión simplificada (pág. 17) Una expresión de la que se han quitado los símbolos de agrupamiento y todos los términos semejantes se han combinado.

$$2x + 8(3 - x) = 2x + 24 - 8x = -6x + 24$$
$$\uparrow$$
simplified expression
expresión simplificada

---

simplified form of a rational expression (p. 480) A rational expression in which the numerator and denominator have no common factors other than ±1.

forma simplificada de una expresión racional (pág. 480) Expresión racional en la que el numerador y el denominador no tienen factores comunes además de ±1.

$$\frac{x^2 - 2x - 15}{x^2 - 9} = \frac{(x + 3)(x - 5)}{(x + 3)(x - 3)} = \frac{x - 5}{x - 3}$$
$$\uparrow$$
simplified form
forma simplificada

---

sine function (p. 645) If θ is an acute angle of a right triangle, the sine of θ is the length of the side opposite θ divided by the length of the hypotenuse.

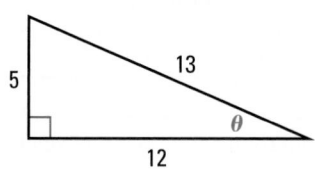

$$\sin \theta = \frac{\text{opp}}{\text{hyp}} = \frac{5}{13} \qquad \csc \theta = \frac{\text{hyp}}{\text{opp}} = \frac{13}{5}$$
$$\cos \theta = \frac{\text{adj}}{\text{hyp}} = \frac{12}{13} \qquad \sec \theta = \frac{\text{hyp}}{\text{adj}} = \frac{13}{12}$$
$$\tan \theta = \frac{\text{opp}}{\text{adj}} = \frac{5}{12} \qquad \cot \theta = \frac{\text{adj}}{\text{opp}} = \frac{12}{5}$$

función seno (pág. 645) Si θ es un ángulo agudo de un triángulo rectángulo, el seno de θ es la longitud del lado opuesto a θ dividida por la longitud de la hipotenusa.

$$\text{sen } \theta = \frac{\text{op}}{\text{hip}} = \frac{5}{13} \qquad \text{cosec } \theta = \frac{\text{hip}}{\text{op}} = \frac{13}{5}$$
$$\cos \theta = \frac{\text{ady}}{\text{hip}} = \frac{12}{13} \qquad \sec \theta = \frac{\text{hip}}{\text{ady}} = \frac{13}{12}$$
$$\tan \theta = \frac{\text{op}}{\text{ady}} = \frac{5}{12} \qquad \cot \theta = \frac{\text{ady}}{\text{op}} = \frac{12}{5}$$

slope (p. 79) The ratio of vertical change (the rise) to horizontal change (the run) for a nonvertical line. For a nonvertical line passing through the points (x_1, y_1) and (x_2, y_2), the slope is $m = \dfrac{y_2 - y_1}{x_2 - x_1}$.

pendiente (pág. 79) Para una recta no vertical, la razón entre el cambio vertical (distancia vertical) y el cambio horizontal (distancia horizontal). Para una recta no vertical que pasa por los puntos (x_1, y_1) y (x_2, y_2), la pendiente es $m = \dfrac{y_2 - y_1}{x_2 - x_1}$.

The slope of the line that passes through the points $(-3, 0)$ and $(3, 4)$ is:

La pendiente de la recta que pasa por los puntos $(-3, 0)$ y $(3, 4)$ es:

$$m = \frac{y_2 - y_1}{x_2 - x_1} = \frac{4 - 0}{3 - (-3)} = \frac{4}{6} = \frac{2}{3}$$

---

slope-intercept form (p. 87) A linear equation written in the form $y = mx + b$ where m is the slope and b is the y-intercept of the equation's graph.

forma pendiente-intercepto (pág. 87) Ecuación lineal escrita en la forma $y = mx + b$, donde m es la pendiente y b es el intercepto en y de la gráfica de la ecuación.

The equation $y = -\dfrac{2}{3}x - 1$ is in slope-intercept form.

La ecuación $y = -\dfrac{2}{3}x - 1$ está en la forma pendiente-intercepto.

---

solution of a linear inequality in two variables (p. 179) An ordered pair (x, y) that produces a true statement when the values of x and y are substituted into the inequality.

solución de una desigualdad lineal con dos variables (pág. 179) Par ordenado (x, y) que produce un enunciado verdadero cuando x e y se sustituyen por sus valores en la desigualdad.

The ordered pair $(1, 2)$ is a solution of $3x + 4y > 8$ because $3(1) + 4(2) = 11$, and $11 > 8$.

El par ordenado $(1, 2)$ es una solución de $3x + 4y > 8$ ya que $3(1) + 4(2) = 11$, y $11 > 8$.

---

solution of an equation in one variable (p. 26) A number that produces a true statement when substituted for the variable in the equation.

solución de una ecuación con una variable (pág. 26) Número que produce un enunciado verdadero al sustituir la variable por él en la ecuación.

The solution of the equation $\dfrac{4}{5}x + 8 = 20$ is 15.

La solución de la ecuación $\dfrac{4}{5}x + 8 = 20$ es 15.

---

solution of an equation in two variables (p. 68) An ordered pair (x, y) that produces a true statement when the values of x and y are substituted in the equation.

solución de una ecuación con dos variables (pág. 68) Par ordenado (x, y) que produce un enunciado verdadero al sustituir x e y por sus valores en la ecuación.

$(-2, 3)$ is a solution of $y = -2x - 1$.

$(-2, 3)$ es una solución de $y = -2x - 1$.

---

solution of an inequality in one variable (p. 172) A number that produces a true statement when substituted for the variable in the inequality.

solución de una desigualdad con una variable (pág. 172) Número que produce un enunciado verdadero al sustituir la variable por él en la desigualdad.

-1 is a solution of the inequality $5x + 2 > 7x - 4$.

-1 es una solución de la desigualdad $5x + 2 > 7x - 4$.

solution of a system of linear equations in three variables (p. 153) An ordered triple (x, y, z) whose coordinates make each equation in the system true.

solución de un sistema de ecuaciones lineales en tres variables (pág. 153) Terna ordenada (x, y, z) cuyas coordenadas hacen que cada ecuación del sistema sea verdadera.

$$4x + 2y + 3z = 1$$
$$2x - 3y + 5z = -14$$
$$6x - y + 4z = -1$$

$(2, 1, -3)$ is the solution of the system above.

$(2, 1, -3)$ es la solución del sistema de arriba.

---

solution of a system of linear equations in two variables (p. 125) An ordered pair (x, y) that satisfies each equation of the system.

solución de un sistema de ecuaciones lineales en dos variables (pág. 125) Par ordenado (x, y) que satisface cada ecuación del sistema.

$$4x + y = 8$$
$$2x - 3y = 18$$

$(3, -4)$ is the solution of the system above.

$(3, -4)$ es la solución del sistema de arriba.

---

solution of a system of linear inequalities in two variables (p. 185) An ordered pair (x, y) that is a solution of each inequality in the system.

solución de un sistema de desigualdades lineales en dos variables (pág. 185) Par ordenado (x, y) que es una solución de cada desigualdad del sistema.

$$y > -2x - 5$$
$$y \leq x + 3$$

$(-1, 1)$ is a solution of the system above.

$(-1, 1)$ es una solución del sistema de arriba.

---

solve for a variable (p. 33) Rewrite an equation as an equivalent equation in which the variable is on one side and does not appear on the other side.

resolver para una variable (pág. 33) Escribir una ecuación como ecuación equivalente que tenga la variable en uno de sus lados pero no en el otro.

When you solve the circumference formula $C = 2\pi r$ for r, the result is $r = \dfrac{C}{2\pi}$.

Al resolver para r la fórmula de circunferencia $C = 2\pi r$, el resultado es $r = \dfrac{C}{2\pi}$.

---

square root (p. 255) If $b^2 = a$, then b is a square root of a. The radical symbol $\sqrt{\ }$ represents a nonnegative square root.

raíz cuadrada (pág. 255) Si $b^2 = a$, entonces b es una raíz cuadrada de a. El signo radical $\sqrt{\ }$ representa una raíz cuadrada no negativa.

The square roots of 9 are 3 and -3 because $3^2 = 9$ and $(-3)^2 = 9$. So, $\sqrt{9} = 3$ and $-\sqrt{9} = -3$.

Las raíces cuadradas de 9 son 3 y -3 ya que $3^2 = 9$ y $(-3)^2 = 9$. Así pues, $\sqrt{9} = 3$ y $-\sqrt{9} = -3$.

---

standard deviation (p. 395) The typical difference (or deviation) between a data value and the mean. The standard deviation σ of a numerical data set $x_1, x_2, \ldots, x_n$ is given by the following formula:

$$\sigma = \sqrt{\frac{(x_1 - \bar{x})^2 + (x_2 - \bar{x})^2 + \cdots + (x_n - \bar{x})^2}{n}}$$

desviación típica (pág. 395) La diferencia (o desviación) más común entre un valor de los datos y la media. La desviación típica σ de un conjunto de datos numéricos $x_1, x_2, \ldots, x_n$ viene dada por la siguiente fórmula:

$$\sigma = \sqrt{\frac{(x_1 - \bar{x})^2 + (x_2 - \bar{x})^2 + \cdots + (x_n - \bar{x})^2}{n}}$$

14, 17, 18, 19, 20, 24, 24, 30, 32

Because the mean of the data set is 22, the standard deviation is:

Como la media del conjunto de datos es 22, la desviación típica es:

$$\sigma = \sqrt{\frac{(14 - 22)^2 + (17 - 22)^2 + \ldots + (32 - 22)^2}{9}}$$

$$= \sqrt{\frac{290}{9}}$$

$$\approx 5.7$$

---

standard form of a complex number (p. 262)
The form $a + bi$ where a and b are real numbers and i is the imaginary unit.

forma general de un número complejo (pág. 262)
La forma $a + bi$, donde a y b son números reales e i es la unidad imaginaria.

The standard form of the complex number $i(1 + i)$ is $-1 + i$.

La forma general del número complejo $i(1 + i)$ es $-1 + i$.

---

standard form of a linear equation (p. 88) A linear equation written in the form $Ax + By = C$ where A and B are not both zero.

forma general de una ecuación lineal (pág. 88) Ecuación lineal escrita en la forma $Ax + By = C$, donde A y B no son ambos cero.

The linear equation $y = -3x + 4$ can be written in standard form as $3x + y = 4$.

La ecuación lineal $y = -3x + 4$ escrita en la forma general es $3x + y = 4$.

---

standard form of a polynomial function (p. 302)
The form of a polynomial function that has terms written in descending order of exponents from left to right.

forma general de una función polinómica (pág. 302) La forma de una función polinómica en la que los términos se ordenan de tal modo que los exponentes disminuyen de izquierda a derecha.

The function $g(x) = 7x - \sqrt{3} + \pi x^2$ can be written in standard form as $g(x) = \pi x^2 + 7x - \sqrt{3}$.

La función $g(x) = 7x - \sqrt{3} + \pi x^2$ escrita en la forma general es $g(x) = \pi x^2 + 7x - \sqrt{3}$.

---

standard form of a quadratic equation in one variable (p. 235) The form $ax^2 + bx + c = 0$ where $a \neq 0$.

forma general de una ecuación cuadrática con una variable (pág. 235) La forma $ax^2 + bx + c = 0$, donde $a \neq 0$.

The quadratic equation $x^2 - 5x = 36$ can be written in standard form as $x^2 - 5x - 36 = 0$.

La ecuación cuadrática $x^2 - 5x = 36$ escrita en la forma general es $x^2 - 5x - 36 = 0$.

---

standard form of a quadratic function (p. 222)
The form $y = ax^2 + bx + c$ where $a \neq 0$.

forma general de una función cuadrática (pág. 222) La forma $y = ax^2 + bx + c$, donde $a \neq 0$.

The quadratic function $y = 2(x + 3)(x - 1)$ can be written in standard form as $y = 2x^2 + 4x - 6$.

La función cuadrática $y = 2(x + 3)(x - 1)$ escrita en la forma general es $y = 2x^2 + 4x - 6$.

---

standard position of an angle (p. 652) In a coordinate plane, the position of an angle whose vertex is at the origin and whose initial side lies on the positive x-axis.

posición normal de un ángulo (pág. 652) En un plano de coordenadas, la posición de un ángulo cuyo vértice está en el origen y cuyo lado inicial se sitúa en el eje de x positivo.

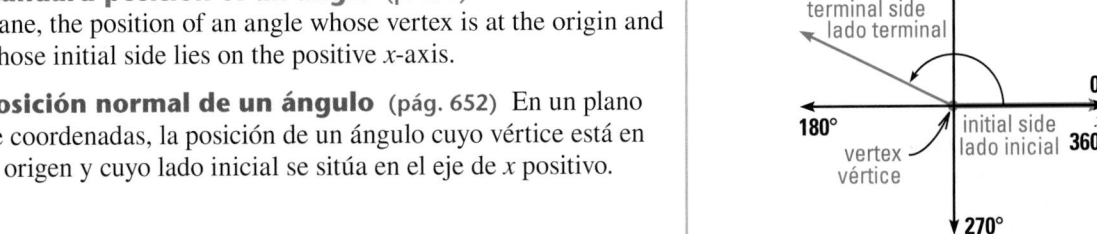

substitution method (p. 132) A method of solving a system of equations by solving one of the equations for one of the variables and then substituting the resulting expression in the other equation(s). **método de sustitución** (pág. 132) Método para resolver un sistema de ecuaciones mediante la resolución de una de las ecuaciones para una de las variables seguida de la sustitución de la expresión resultante en la(s) otra(s) ecuación (ecuaciones).	$$2x + 5y = -5$$ $$x + 3y = 3$$ Solve equation 2 for x: $x = -3y + 3$. Substitute the expression for x in equation 1 and solve for y: $y = 11$. Use the value of y to find the value of x: $x = -30$. Resuelve la ecuación 2 para x: $x = -3y + 3$. Sustituye la expresión para x en la ecuación 1 y resuelve para y: $y = 11$. Usa el valor de y para hallar el valor de x: $x = -30$.
systematic sample (p. 526) A sample in which a rule or pattern is used to select members of the population. **muestra sistemática** (pág. 526) Muestra en la cual se usa una regla o patrón para seleccionar los miembros de una población.	You can select a systematic sample of a school's student population by choosing every tenth student on an alphabetical list of all students at the school. Puedes optener una muestra sistemática de la población estudiantil de una escuela eligiendo uno de cada diez estudiantes de una lista alfabética de todos los estudiantes de la escuela.
system of linear inequalities in two variables (p. 185) A system consisting of two or more linear inequalities in the same variables. *See also* linear inequality in two variables. **sistema de desigualdades lineales con dos variables** (pág. 185) Sistema que consiste de dos o más desigualdades lineales con la misma variables. *Ver también* desigualdad lineal con dos variables.	$$x + y \leq 8$$ $$4x - y > 6$$
system of three linear equations in three variables (p. 153) A system consisting of three linear equations in three variables. *See also* linear equation in three variables. **sistema de tres ecuaciones lineales en tres variables** (pág. 153) Sistema formado por tres ecuaciones lineales con tres variables. *Ver también* ecuación lineal con tres variables.	$$2x + y - z = 5$$ $$3x - 2y + z = 16$$ $$4x + 3y - 5z = 3$$
system of two linear equations in two variables (p. 125) A system consisting of two linear equations in two variables. **sistema de dos ecuaciones lineales con dos variables** (pág. 125) Un sistema que consiste en dos ecuaciones lineales con dos variables.	$$4x + y = 8$$ $$2x - 3y = 18$$

tangent function (p. 645) If θ is an acute angle of a right triangle, the tangent of θ is the length of the side opposite θ divided by the length of the side adjacent to θ.

función tangente (pág. 645) Si θ es un ángulo agudo de un triángulo rectángulo, la tangente de θ es la longitud del lado opuesto a θ dividida por la longitud del lado adyacente a θ.

See sine function.

Ver función seno.

---

terminal side of an angle (p. 652) In a coordinate plane, an angle can be formed by fixing one ray, called the initial side, and rotating the other ray, called the terminal side, about the vertex.

lado terminal de un ángulo (pág. 652) En un plano de coordenadas, un ángulo puede formarse al fijar un rayo, llamado lado inicial, y al girar el otro rayo, llamado lado terminal, en torno al vértice.

See standard position of an angle.

Ver posición normal de un ángulo.

---

terms of an expression (p. 16) The parts of an expression that are added together.

términos de una expresión (pág. 16) Las partes de una expresión que se suman.

The terms of the algebraic expression $3x^2 + 5x + (-7)$ are $3x^2$, $5x$, and -7.

Los términos de la expresión algebraica $3x^2 + 5x + (-7)$ son $3x^2$, $5x$ y -7.

---

terms of a sequence (p. 608) The values in the range of a sequence.

términos de una progresión (pág. 608) Los valores del rango de una progresión.

The first 4 terms of the sequence $1, -3, 9, -27, 81, -243, \ldots$ are $1, -3, 9$, and -27.

Los 4 primeros términos de la progresión $1, -3, 9, -27, 81, -243, \ldots$ son $1, -3, 9$ y -27.

---

theoretical probability (p. 556) When all outcomes are equally likely, the theoretical probability that an event A will occur is $P(A) = \dfrac{\text{Number of outcomes in event } A}{\text{Total number of outcomes}}$.

probabilidad teórica (pág. 556) Cuando todos los casos son igualmente posibles, la probabilidad teórica de que ocurra un suceso A es $P(A) = \dfrac{\text{Número de casos del suceso } A}{\text{Número total de casos}}$.

The theoretical probability of rolling an even number using a standard six-sided die is $\dfrac{3}{6} = \dfrac{1}{2}$ because 3 outcomes correspond to rolling an even number out of 6 total outcomes.

La probabilidad teórica de sacar un número par al lanzar un dado normal de seis caras es $\dfrac{3}{6} = \dfrac{1}{2}$ ya que 3 casos corresponden a un número par del total de 6 casos.

three-dimensional coordinate system (p. 147) A coordinate system formed by the x-, y-, and z-axes. The three axes, taken two at a time, determine three coordinate planes that divide space into eight octants. A point in space is represented by an ordered triple of the form (x, y, z).

Sistema de coordenadas tridimensional (pág. 147) Un sistema de coordenadas que se conforma por los ejes x, y, y z. Los tres ejes, que se toman dos a la vez, determinan tres planos de coordenadas que dividen el espacio en ocho octantes. Un punto en el espacio se representa por el triple ordenado (x, y, z).

transverse axis of a hyperbola (p. 717) The line segment joining the vertices of a hyperbola.

See hyperbola.

eje transverso de una hipérbola (pág. 717) El segmento de recta que une los vértices de una hipérbola.

Ver hipérbola.

trinomial (p. 234) The sum of three monomials.

$4x^2 + 3x - 1$ is a trinomial.

trinomio (pág. 234) La suma de tres monomios.

$4x^2 + 3x - 1$ es un trinomio.

U

unbiased sample (p. 519) A sample that is representative of the population you want information about.

You want to poll members of the senior class about where to hold the prom. If every senior has an equal chance of being polled, then the sample is unbiased.

muestra no sesgada (pág. 519) Muestra que es representativa de la población acerca de la cual deseas informarte.

Quieres encuestar a algunos estudiantes de último curso sobre el lugar donde organizar el baile de fin de año. Si cada estudiante de último curso tiene iguales posibilidades de ser encuestado, entonces es una muestra no sesgada.

upper quartile (p. 47) The median of the upper half of a data set.

See box-and-whisker plot.

cuartil superior (pág. 47) En un conjunto de datos, la mediana de la mitad superior del conjunto.

Ver diagrama de líneas y bloques.

V

variable (p. 10) A letter that is used to represent one or more numbers.

In the expressions $6x$, $3x^2 + 1$, and $12 - 5x$, the letter x is the variable.

variable (pág. 10) Letra utilizada para representar uno o más números.

En las expresiones $6x$, $3x^2 + 1$ y $12 - 5x$, la letra x es la variable.

verbal model (p. 40) A word equation that represents a real-life problem.

modelo verbal (pág. 40) Ecuación expresada mediante palabras que representa un problema de la vida real.

Distance	=	Rate	·	Time
(miles)		(miles/hour)		(hours)

Distancia	=	Velocidad	·	Tiempo
(millas)		(millas/hora)		(horas)

---

vertex form of a quadratic function (p. 228) The form $y = a(x - h)^2 + k$, where the vertex of the graph is (h, k) and the axis of symmetry is $x = h$.

forma de vértice de una función cuadrática (pág. 228) La forma $y = a(x - h)^2 + k$, donde el vértice de la gráfica es (h, k) y el eje de simetría es $x = h$.

The quadratic function $y = -\frac{1}{4}(x + 2)^2 + 5$ is in vertex form.

La función cuadrática $y = -\frac{1}{4}(x + 2)^2 + 5$ está en la forma de vértice.

---

vertex of an absolute value graph (p. 204) The common endpoint of the two rays in the graph of an absolute value function.

vértice de una gráfica de valor absoluto (pág. 204) El punto común de las dos rectas en una gráfica de función de valor absoluto.

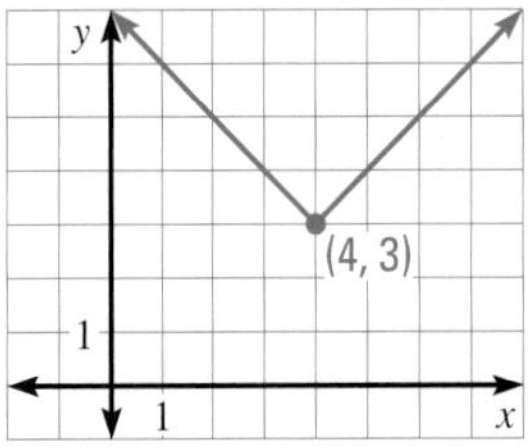

The vertex of the graph of $y = |x - 4| + 3$ is the point (**4, 3**).

El vértice de la gráfica de $y = |x - 4| + 3$ es el punto (**4, 3**).

---

vertex of a parabola (pp. 222, 697) The lowest or highest point on a parabola. The vertex lies on the axis of symmetry.

vértice de una parábola (págs. 222, 697) El punto de una parábola más bajo o más alto. El vértice se encuentra en el eje de simetría.

See **parabola.**

Ver **parábola.**

---

vertices of a hyperbola (p. 717) The points of intersection of a hyperbola and the line through the foci of the hyperbola.

vértices de una hipérbola (pág. 717) Los puntos de intersección de una hipérbola y la recta que pasa por los focos de la hipérbola.

See **hyperbola.**

Ver **hipérbola.**

---

vertices of an ellipse (p. 710) The points of intersection of an ellipse and the line through the foci of the ellipse.

vértices de una elipse (pág. 710) Los puntos de intersección de una elipse y la recta que pasa por los focos de la elipse.

See **ellipse.**

Ver **elipse.**

X

x-intercept (p. 88) The x-coordinate of a point where a graph intersects the x-axis.

intercepto en x (pág. 88) La coordenada x de un punto donde una gráfica corta al eje de x.

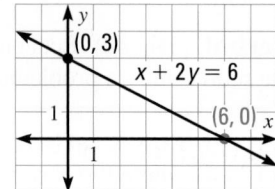

The x-intercept is 6.

El intercepto en x es 6.

Y

y-intercept (p. 87) The y-coordinate of a point where a graph intersects the y-axis.

intercepto en y (pág. 87) La coordenada y de un punto donde una gráfica corta al eje de y.

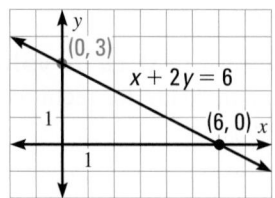

The y-intercept is 3.

El intercepto en y es 3.

Z

z-axis (p. 147) A vertical line through the origin and perpendicular to the xy-coordinate plane in a three-dimensional coordinate system.

eje Z (pág. 147) Una línea vertical que atraviesa el origen y que es perpendicular al plano de coordenadas xy en un sistema de coordenadas tridimensional.

See **three-dimensional coordinate system.**

Ver **sistema de coordenadas tridimensional.**

zero of a function (p. 242) An x-value for which $f(x) = 0$.

cero de una función (pág. 242) Un valor x para el cual $f(x) = 0$.

The zeros of the function $f(x) = 2(x + 3)(x - 1)$ are −3 and 1.

Los ceros de la función $f(x) = 2(x + 3)(x - 1)$ are −3 and 1.

Index

A

population, 13, 300, 314, 347, 430, 452, 566
recreation, 69, 77, 92, 176, 188, 208, 255, 384, 497, 527, 558, 605, 625, 671, 730
running, 187, 543, 549, 768, 769, 770, 772
shopping, 49, 190, 284
soccer, 319, 349, 695
space missions, 55, 104, 712
structures, 41, 137, 208, 230, 259, 348, 650, 674, 703, 705, 706, 715, 730
student activities, 35, 82, 129, 477, 510, 511, 522, 542, 543, 546, 549, 560, 566, 577, 580
taxes, 92, 104, 551
temperature, 4, 195, 202, 207, 283, 333, 348
theater, 129, 395, 396, 397, 769
transportation, 129, 151, 206, 298, 528
travel, 43, 50, 61, 125, 127, 207, 385, 469, 496, 504, 513, 685, 695, 707, 768
vacations, 125, 127, 151, 548
vehicles, 313, 393, 423, 660, 673
volleyball, 279, 505, 657
volunteering, 190, 545
weather, 3, 82, 84, 111, 339, 566, 571
wildlife, 94, 96, 99, 370, 385, 480, 537
winter sports, 40, 119, 370, 541
wrestling, 203
Approximation, *See also* Estimation; Prediction
of the area of an ellipse, 712, 715
of best-fitting line, 106
of best-fitting quadratic model, 283–284
of local maximums and minimums, 336–338
of *n*th roots, 357
to plot real numbers on a number line, 4
of real zeros, 331, 333
of *x*-intercepts, 336–338
Area, *See also* Formulas; Geometry Skills, 754, 795
of a circle, 33, 754, 798
of an ellipse, 712, 715
of a parallelogram, 754, 798

of a rectangle, 33, 754, 798
of a square, 754, 798
of a trapezoid, 33, 39, 754, 798
of a triangle, 33, 39, 754, 798
Arithmetic sequence(s), 615–620, 637
common difference of, 615
graphing, 616, 618
rule for finding *n*th term of, 616
writing a rule for, 616, 618–620, 637
Arithmetic series, 617
sum of the terms of, 617–620, 637
Assessment, *See also* Review(s)
Chapter Readiness Quiz, 2, 66, 124, 170, 220, 294, 352, 410, 464, 518, 584, 644, 690
Chapter Standardized Test, 62–63, 120–121, 164–165, 216–217, 290–291, 346–347, 406–407, 460–461, 512–513, 580–581, 640–641, 686–687, 738–739
Chapter Test, 61, 119, 163, 215, 289, 345, 405, 459, 511, 579, 639, 685, 737
Cumulative Practice, 166–167, 348–349, 514–515, 740–741
End-of-Course Test, 791–793
Pre-Course Practice, xxiv–xxvii
Pre-Course Test, xxii–xxiii
Quiz, 15, 39, 56, 85, 100, 113, 144, 159, 191, 210, 247, 266, 281, 308, 321, 340, 371, 386, 400, 425, 439, 478, 492, 532, 551, 574, 605, 620, 634, 666, 681, 716, 731
Associative property, 5–8
for matrix operations, 588, 596
Assumed mean, 537
Asymptote(s), 412
of an exponential decay function, 420–421
of an exponential growth function, 412
horizontal, 472
of a hyperbola, 717
of a logarithmic function, 435
of a rational function, 472–477
of a tangent function, 662–664
vertical, 472, 474
@Home Tutor, *Throughout. See for example* 2, 57, 66, 115, 124, 160, 170, 212, 220, 285, 294,

341, 352
Axis (Axes)
of a coordinate plane, 752
of an ellipse, 710
imaginary, 265
of a three-dimensional coordinate system, 147
Axis of symmetry
of a parabola, 697
identifying, 698–702
of a quadratic function, 222

B

Base
of an exponential function, 412
of a logarithm, 433
of a power, 9
Best-fitting line, 106, 108
approximating, 106, 108–112, 118
on a graphing calculator, 114
writing an equation for, 108–112, 118
Best-fitting quadratic model, 283–284
Biased sample, 519
identifying, 519–520, 522–523, 576
Biased survey question, 521, 523–524
Biconditional statement, 765–766
Binomial(s), *See also* Polynomial(s)
cube of, 316, 318–320
expansion, 553–555
multiplying, 224–227, 776
square of, 316, 318–320
Binomial theorem, 554
Pascal's triangle and, 553–555
Boundary line, of an inequality, 179
Box-and-whisker plot, 46–50, 60
data transformation and, 535–538
steps for drawing, 48
Branches
of a graph of a rational function, 472
of a hyperbola, 717
Break a problem into simpler parts, problem solving strategy, 772

C

Calculator, *See also* Graphing

calculator; Scientific
calculator

exercises, *Throughout. See for
example* 31, 49, 92, 232,
280, 307, 327, 333, 334,
338

Capacity, units of, 795

Careers
accident investigator, 391
air traffic controller, 504
astronomer, 363
caterer, 141
chef, 102
conductor, 158
contractor, 270
high school coach, 48
make-up artist, 598
mason, 190
meteorologist, 4
museum curator, 134
musician, 174
nutritionist, 521
pilot, 333
retail salesperson, 377
seismologist, 453
smokejumper, 257
sound technician, 444
surveyor, 677
tiling contractor, 604
travel agent, 496
veterinary technician, 30
volcanologist, 81
zoologist, 358

Center
of a circle, 703, 753
of an ellipse, 710
of a hyperbola, 717
of rotation, 760

Central tendency, measures of,
46–50, 533–538

Chain rule, 763

Challenge, exercises, *Throughout.
See for example* 8, 14, 30,
38, 45, 92, 104, 137, 177, 184,
190, 208

Change
percent of, 744
rate of, 80–83, 116

Change of base formula, 440

Chapter Standardized Test, *See*
Assessment

Chapter Summary and Review,
57–60, 115–118, 160–162,

212–214, 285–288, 341–344,
401–404, 455–458, 507–510,
575–578, 635–638, 682–684,
733–736

Chapter Test, *See* Assessment

Checking solutions
using a calculator, 133, 630, 655
using a different method, 460, 493
by graphing, 95, 133, 164, 242,
277, 428, 449, 451, 458, 493
using inverse operations, 234–235,
317, 353
using substitution, *Throughout.
See for example* 26, 27, 28,
59, 74, 125, 127, 132, 133,
139, 140, 145, 146
using unit analysis, 11, 40

Checkpoints, *Throughout. See for
example* 4, 5, 9, 10, 11, 16, 17,
18, 27, 28, 34, 35

Choose a method
exercises, 146, 184, 504, 679
to solve for an angle, 676
to solve a linear system, 145–146

Circle, *See also* Geometry Skills,
703, 753
area of, 33, 754, 798
center of, 703, 753
circumference of, 753, 798
as conic section, 724, 726–731
diameter of, 753
equation of
graphing, 703, 706–707, 709,
734
standard form, 703
translated, 724, 726–731
writing, 704–708, 734
radius of, 703, 753
tangent line to, 704
writing an equation of, 704–705,
707

Circular model, 705, 707–708

Circumference, *See also* Geometry
Skills, 33, 753, 798

Classifying
conic sections, 724, 726–727,
729–730, 736
exponential functions, 422
lines using slope, 80, 82, 83
polynomial functions, 302–303,
305–306
samples, 526–527, 529–531, 576
triangles using the distance

formula, 692, 694, 695
types of variation, 466–469

Coefficient, 775
of an algebraic expression, 16
identifying, 16, 19
matrix, 601

Combinations, 545
adding, 550
distinguishing from permutations,
546, 548, 549
finding, 545–550, 577
on a graphing calculator, 552
multiple events and, 546–550
of n objects taken r at a time, 545,
797
Pascal's triangle and, 547–550, 577
probability and, 557–561

Common constant, factoring out,
241–246, 250–253

Common difference, of an
arithmetic sequence, 615

Common factor, 745
greatest, 745–746

Common logarithm, *See also*
Logarithm(s), 433

Common monomial, factoring out,
323–328, 329–334

Common ratio
of a geometric sequence, 621
of an infinite geometric series, 629

Communication, *See also* Writing
describing in words, *Throughout.
See for example* 7, 12, 29,
136, 142, 189, 197, 225, 226,
232, 237, 238

Commutative property, 5–8
for matrix operations, 588

Comparing
data
after transformation, 533–538,
576
using standard deviation,
396–399
graphs of quadratic functions, 221
matrices, 585, 589
real numbers, 4, 6–8
on a number line, 4, 6–8
samples, 525
steepness of lines, 81–83

Complement of an event, 564
probability of, 564–567, 797

Completing the square, 268
modeling, 267, 268

INDEX

on a graphing calculator, 421

for matrix operations, 588

Origin

in a coordinate plane, 752

on a number line, 3

in a three-dimensional coordinate system, 147

Or **rule,** 763

Outcome(s), of an event, 556

Overlapping events, 562

probability of, 562–563, 565–567

P

Parabola

axis of symmetry of, 697

as conic section, 724–731

directrix of, 697

equation of, 697–702, 734

graphing, 698–702, 734

standard form, 698

translated, 725–728

writing, 699–701, 734

focus of, 697

graphs of quadratic functions and, 221–227, 282–284

vertex of, 697

Parallel lines

equations of, 96–99

slope of, 89, 91

Parallelogram, area of, 754

Pascal's triangle, 547

binomial theorem and, 553–555

combinations and, 547–555, 577

patterns in, 555

Pattern(s), *See also* Sequence(s)

best-fitting line and, 106

differences of two squares, 249, 253–254, 287

difference of two cubes, 323

finding to solve problems, 40, 43–45

Pascal's triangle, 547, 555

perfect square trinomial, 250–253, 287

product of powers, 295

quotient of powers, 295

special product, polynomial, 316, 318–320

sum of two cubes, 323

Percent, 743

calculating, 744

of change, 744

fractions, decimals and, 743

Perfect square trinomial, 250

completing the square and, 268–273

factoring, 250–253, 287

Perimeter, *See also* Geometry Skills, 33, 753, 798

Period

of a cosine function, 660

of a function, 660

of a sine function, 660

Periodic function, *See also* Cosine function; Sine function, 660

Permutation(s), 540

distinguishing from combinations, 546, 548, 549

formula, 518, 540

fundamental counting principle and, 540–544, 577

on a graphing calculator, 552

of *n* objects, 540–544, 577

of *n* objects taken *r* at a time, 541–544, 577, 797

probability and, 557, 559–560

Perpendicular bisector, writing an equation for, 693, 695–696

Perpendicular lines

equations of, 96–99

slope of, 89, 91

Plotting a point

on a number line, 3

in a three-dimensional coordinate system, 147, 150

Point-slope form, 94

writing equations in, 94–99

Polynomial(s), 302

adding, 310–314, 342

cubic, factoring, 322, 323–328, 343

degree of, 302

of degrees greater than three, 329–334, 344

dividing, 317–320, 343

dividing rational expressions by, 487–491

leading coefficient of, 302

multiplying, 315–316, 318–321, 343, 776

multiplying rational expressions by, 482–485

in quadratic form, factoring, 329–334

special product patterns, 316

using, 316, 318–321

standard form of, 302

subtracting, 310–314, 342

Polynomial equation(s)

fundamental theorem of algebra and, 331, 333

solving, 330–334

Polynomial function(s), 302

approximating zeros of, 331, 333

end behavior for, 303–307

graphing, 303–307, 335–339, 342, 344

on a graphing calculator, 309, 336–339, 344

identifying, 302–303, 305–306, 342

local maximum of, 335

local minimum of, 335

modeling with, 335–339

standard form of, 302

turning points of, 335

finding, 335–339

types of, 302

Polynomial long division, 317

using, 317–320

Polynomial model, 337–339

maximizing, 337, 339

Population, 519

identifying, 519, 522

Positive correlation, 107

Positive slope, 80

Power(s), 9

evaluating, 9–14

scientific notation and, 298–301, 751

Power of a power property, 296

using, 296–301

Power of a product property, 296

of radicals, 359

using, 359–364

using, 296–301

Power property

of logarithms, 442, 800

using, 442–447

Power of a quotient property, 296

of radicals, 359

using, 359–364

using, 296–301

Pre-Course Practice, xxiv–xxvii

Pre-Course Test, xxii–xxiii

Prediction, *See also* Approximation

from an equation, 106, 109

using exponential models,

426–432
from a graph, 86, 211
from samples, 521, 523–524, 575
Premise, of a logical argument, 763
Prerequisite skills, *See also* Skills
Review Handbook
Throughout. See for example 3,
9, 16, 26, 33, 40, 46, 52, 67,
73, 79
Prime factorization, 745–746
Prime number, 745
Prism, surface area and volume of,
798
Probability, 556
combinations and, 557–561
of the complement of an event,
564–567
of compound events, 562–567, 578,
797
disjoint, 562, 565–567
mutually exclusive, 562,
565–567
overlapping, 562–563, 565–567
conditional, 570–574
of dependent events, 569–574, 578
event, 556
experimental, 557–560
geometric, 558–561
inclusion-exclusion principle and,
567
of independent events, 569–573,
578
likelihood of an event, 556
outcome, 556
permutations and, 557–560
simulating experiments, 568
theoretical, 556–561
of three or more events, 571, 573
Venn diagrams and, 562–563
Problem solving plan, 40
flow chart of, 40
Problem solving strategies, *See also*
Modeling
use an algebraic model, 40–45
break a problem into simpler parts,
772
draw a diagram, 42–45, 769
use an equation or formula, 768
guess, check, and revise, 773
look for a pattern, 40, 43–45
make an organized list, 545, 770
make a table, 770
solve a simpler problem, 771

work backward, 379, 406
write and use a formula,
40, 43–45
Product of powers, pattern, 295
Product of powers property, 296
using, 296–301
Product property
of logarithms, 442, 800
using, 442–447
of square roots, 255
using, 255–260
Properties
of addition, 5, 26, 767
using, 5–8, 26–30
of division, 26, 767
of equality, 26, 767
using to justify algebraic
reasoning, 767
using to solve linear equations,
26–30, 59
equal powers, 448
using, 448–449, 451–453
of exponents, 296, 799
using to evaluate expressions,
296–301, 341
of inequalities, 172
to solve linear inequalities,
172–177, 212
inverse, 5
of logarithms, 441, 442, 800
using, 442–447, 457
matrix
of addition, 588
of multiplication, 596
of subtraction, 588
of multiplication, 5, 26, 767
using, 5–8, 26–31
of radicals, 359, 800
using, 359–364
of rational exponents, 360, 800
using, 360–364, 402
of square roots, 255
using to solve quadratic
equations, 256–260, 287
of subtraction, 26, 767
table of, 799–800
zero product, 235
Proportion, 747
cross multiplication and, 747
Pyramid, surface area and volume
of, 798
Pure imaginary number, 262
Pythagorean theorem, 159, 757, 798

Q

Quadrant(s), in a coordinate plane,
752
Quadrantal angle, 654
trigonometric functions of,
654–658
Quadratic equation(s), *See also*
Factoring; Polynomial(s), 235
with complex solutions, 261, 264
discriminant of, 276, 796
solutions and, 276, 278, 279,
288
using to maximize, 243, 245–246
solving
by completing the square,
268–273, 288
by factoring, 235–239, 286
by finding square roots,
255–260, 287
using properties of square roots,
256–260
using the quadratic formula,
274–275, 277–280, 288
using special patterns, 251–253,
287
standard form of, 235, 302
vertical motion, 276–277, 279–280
writing
in vertex form, 270–273
for vertical motion, 277,
279–280
zero product property and, 235
Quadratic form, 329
factoring polynomials in, 329–334
Quadratic formula, 274, 796
using to solve quadratic equations,
274–275, 277–280, 288
Quadratic function(s), 222
axis of symmetry of, 222
graphing
in intercept form, 229–233, 286
in standard form, 221–227, 285
in vertex form, 228–233, 286
intercept form of, 229
maximum value of, 230, 242
finding, 230–233, 243, 245–246
minimum value of, 230, 242
finding, 230–233, 243, 245–246
parabola and, 222
vertex form of, 228, 270
vertex of, 222, 230
writing
in intercept form, 282, 284

in standard form, 224, 226
in vertex form, 270–273, 282, 284
zeros of, 242
finding, 242–247

Quadratic regression, 283
best-fitting quadratic model and, 283–284

Quadratic system, solving, using a graphing calculator, 732

Quartile(s), 47–50, 533–538

Quiz, *See* Assessment

Quotient of powers, pattern, 295

Quotient of powers property, 296
using, 296–301

Quotient property
of logarithms, 442, 800
using, 442–447
of square roots, 255
using, 255–259

R

Radical(s), *See also* Exponent(s); Root(s), 255
index of, 353
like, 360
adding and subtracting, 360–363
*n*th root of *a*, 353
properties of, 359
using, 359–364
rewriting expressions using, 355, 357
simplest form, 359
simplifying, 359–364

Radical equation(s), 365
extraneous solutions of, 366
solving, 365–370, 402
using a graphing calculator, 372
steps for solving, 365

Radical function, graphing, 388–394

Radical sign, 255

Radicand, 255, 359

Radius, of a circle, 703, 753

Random sample, 526
choosing, 527, 529–531
classifying, 526–527, 529–530

Range, 47–50
of a cosine function, 660
data transformation and, 533–538
interquartile, 50

of a relation, 67
of a sequence, 608
of a sine function, 660

Rate of change, slope and, 81–85, 116

Ratio(s), 747
common, of a geometric sequence, 621
constant, of a geometric sequence, 621
direct variation, 102, 104
percent, 743
slope, 79
trigonometric, 645, 802
writing, 747

Rational equation(s), 500
cross multiplication and, 500, 503–505
extraneous solutions and, 501
multiplying by the LCD and, 501–505
solving, 500–505, 510

Rational exponent(s), 355
evaluating expressions with, 354–358, 401
properties of, 360
using, 360–364, 402

Rational expression(s), 480, 776
adding and subtracting, 494–499, 509
dividing, 486–491, 509
finding least common denominator for, 494–499, 509
multiplying, 481–485, 508
by a polynomial, 482–485
simplified form of, 480
simplifying, 480–485, 508, 776

Rational function(s), 472
general, 474–477
graphing, 472–477, 508
on a graphing calculator, 474
to find horizontal asymptotes, 479

Rationalizing the denominator, 256, 258

Rational number, 3

Readiness, chapter, 2, 66, 124, 170, 220, 294, 352, 410, 464, 518, 584, 644, 690

Reading algebra, *See* Student Help

Real axis, 265

Real number(s), 3
comparing, 4, 6–8
on a number line, 4, 6–8

graphing on a number line, 3, 4
graph of, 3
operations with, 5–8
ordering, 4, 6–8
on a number line, 6–8
Venn diagram of, 3

Real number line, 3

Real zeros, approximating, 331, 333

Reciprocal(s), 5

Rectangle
area of, 33, 236, 754
perimeter of, 33

Rectangular solid
surface area of, 38
volume of, 755

Reflection, 761–762
as graph of an inverse function, 380
line of, 760

Relation(s), 67
domain of, 67
identifying as a function, 67–68, 70–71
inverse, 380
mapping diagrams and, 67, 70, 71, 72
range of, 67
vertical line test and, 68, 71

Relatively no correlation, 107

Repeated solution, 331

Repeating decimal, writing as a fraction, 630–632, 638

Restricted domain, 382

Review(s), *See also* Assessment; Pre-Course Practice; Pre-Course Test; Skill Check; Skills Review Handbook
Chapter Summary and Review, 57–60, 115–118, 160–162, 212–214, 285–288, 341–344, 401–404, 455–458, 507–510, 575–578, 635–638, 682–684, 733–736
Cumulative Practice, 166–167, 348–349, 514–515, 740–741
Mixed Review, *Throughout. See for example* 8, 15, 21, 31, 38, 45, 51, 56, 72, 78, 85, 92
Prerequisite Skills, *Throughout. See for example* 3, 9, 16, 26, 33, 40, 46, 52, 67, 73, 79
Skills Review Handbook, 743–777

Review Help, *Throughout. See for*

operations, with positive and negative numbers, 748

problem solving strategies

break a problem into simpler parts, 772

draw a diagram, 769

use an equation or formula, 768

guess, check, and revise, 773

make a table or list, 770

solve a simpler problem, 771

Slope, 79

classifying lines by, 80, 82, 83

finding, 79, 82–84, 116

formula, 79, 796

of a horizontal line, 80

negative, 80

of parallel lines, 89, 91

of perpendicular lines, 89, 91

positive, 80

rate of change and, 81–85, 116

steepness of lines and, 80–83, 116

undefined, 80

of a vertical line, 80

zero, 80

Slope-intercept form, 87

to graph linear equations, 87–93, 117

on a graphing calculator, 93

investigating, 86

writing equations in, 94–99

Solution

of a linear equation, 26, 777

in three variables, 148

of a linear inequality

in one variable, 172

in two variables, 179

repeated, 331

of a system

of linear inequalities, 185

of three linear equations, 153

of two linear equations, 125

Solve a simpler problem, problem solving strategy, 771

Sphere, surface area and volume of, 798

Square, area of, 754, 798, 801

Square of a binomial, 316, 318–320, 796

Square root(s), 255

evaluating, on a graphing calculator, 23

finding to solve quadratic equations, 256–260, 287

of a negative number, 261

of −1, 261

properties of, 255

using, 255–260, 287

radical sign and, 255

radicand and, 255

simplifying, 255

table of, 801

Square root function(s), graphing, 388–394, 404

Standard deviation, 395, 797

using to describe data sets, 395–399, 404

Standard form

of a complex number, 262

of a cubic function, 302

of the equation of a circle, 703, 724

of the equation of an ellipse, 710, 724

of the equation of a hyperbola, 717, 724

of the equation of a parabola, 698, 724

of a linear equation, 88

graphing linear equations in, 88–93, 117

of a linear function, 302

of a number, 751

of a polynomial, 302

of a polynomial function, 302

of a quadratic equation, 235

of a quadratic function, 222, 302

graphing quadratic functions in, 221–227, 285

Standardized test practice, *See also* Assessment; Test Tips

extended response, 63, 121, 165, 217, 291, 347, 407, 461, 513, 581, 641, 687, 739

gridded response, 63, 121, 165, 217, 291, 347, 407, 461, 513, 581, 641, 687, 739

multiple choice, *Throughout. See for example* 8, 14, 21, 51, 55, 62–63, 72, 77–78, 84

multi-step problem, *Throughout. See for example* 31, 38, 45, 84, 112, 184, 197, 314, 339, 432, 531, 538

Standard position, for an angle, 652

Statistics, *See also* Data; Probability

best-fitting line, 106, 108–112, 118

best-fitting quadratic model, 283–284

frequency distribution, 52–55

identifying bias, 519–523

linear regression, 114

margin of error, 528–531, 576

measures of central tendency, 46–50, 533–538

measures of dispersion, 47–50, 533–538

positive and negative correlation, 107

sampling methods, 525–531

standard deviation, 395, 395–399, 404

survey questions, 521, 523–524

Student Help, *See also* Review(s); Skill Check; Skills Review Handbook; Test Tips

another way, 98, 114, 140, 194, 488, 571, 587, 655

avoid errors, *Throughout. See for example* 17, 27, 40, 41, 73, 74, 79, 80, 95, 157, 173, 180, 185, 189, 192, 199

geometry note, 692

graphing note, 473, 474, 476

homework help, *Throughout. See for example* 6, 12, 19, 29, 36, 43, 49, 54, 70, 76, 82, 90

keystroke help, *Throughout. See for example* 22, 32, 93, 114, 131, 178, 211, 248, 309, 355, 372, 387

look back, 86, 296, 304, 310, 360, 367, 396, 533, 535, 671

reading algebra, *Throughout. See for example* 3, 9, 46, 69, 174, 261, 274, 361, 374, 380, 396

reading diagrams, 322

reading graphs, *Throughout. See for example* 53, 106, 148, 180, 186, 283, 309, 336, 411, 413, 435, 472

reasoning, 32

skills review, 28, 68, 204

solving note, *Throughout. See for example* 5, 28, 35, 41, 47, 102, 108, 133, 145, 148, 155

vocabulary note, 47, 69, 89, 229, 359, 428, 645

writing algebra, 22, 354, 481, 609, 617

INDEX

Credits

Photographs

See copyright page for cover and frontmatter credits.

1 © Bryan and Cherry Alexander Photography/Alamy; **3** © Gerald L. Kooyman/Animals Animals/Earth Scenes; **4** © Ann Hawthorne/Arctic Photo; **7** © David Bergman/Corbis; **11** © Creatas/age fotostock; **13** © Chase Jarvis/Getty Images; **14** © Creatas Images/Jupiter Images; **16** © Omni Photo Communications Inc./Index Stock Imagery; **18** © Carolyne Pehora/Shutterstock; **20** © Ted Soqui/Corbis; **26** © Philippe Poulet/Mission/Getty Images; **30** © Skip Nall/Getty Images; **35** © Bob Daemmrich/The Image Works; **37** © Scott Camazine/Photo Researchers, Inc.; **40** © Jonathan Nourok/PhotoEdit; **42** The Granger Collection; New York; **43** © Lee Snider/Photo Images/Corbis; **44** © Myrleen Ferguson Cate/PhotoEdit; **46** © Icon SMI/Corbis; **48** © Dennis Degnan/Corbis; **52** © The Image Bank/Getty Images; **55** NASA; **64** NOAA/NESDIS; **65** © Don Farrall/PhotoDisc Green/Getty Images; **67** © Phil Schermeister/Corbis; **72** © Eitan Simanor/Alamy; **73** © Bob Daemmrich/The Image Works; **75** © David Sacks/Getty Images; **77** © Wayne Conradie/epa/Corbis; **78** © Reuters/Corbis; **79** © Sean Justice/Getty Images; **81** © G. Brad Lewis/Photo Resource Hawaii; **84** © Geoff Gourley; **92** © Alaska Stock LLC/Alamy; **94** © blickwinkel/Alamy; **96** © Joel Wolfson; **99** © Norbert Rosing/Getty Images; **101** Ken O'Donoghue/McDougal Littell/Houghton Mifflin Company; **102** © BananaStock/Alamy; **104** NASA/Johnson; **106** *both* McDougal Littell/Houghton Mifflin Company; **109** © SW Productions/Getty Images; **111** NOAA; **113** *center left* © Stepán Jezek/Shutterstock, *center* © Mark Bolton/Corbis, *center right* © Royalty-Free/Corbis; **122** © Paul J. Sutton/Duomo/Corbis; **123** © Tim Kiusalaas/Corbis; **125** © Chuck Place/Alamy; **127** © Esbin-Anderson/The Image Works; **129** © John A. Rizzo/Getty Images; **132** Jim West/NewsCom/ZUMA Press; **134** © Stephen McBrady/PhotoEdit; **137** © Izzet Keribar/Lonely Planet Images/Getty Images; **141** © Syracuse Newspapers/Gloria Wright/The Image Works; **144** *center left* © Yanik Chauvin/Shutterstock, *center* © adv/Shutterstock, *center right* © Jozsef Szasz-Fabian/Shutterstock; **149** © Graca Victoria/Shutterstock; **151** © Jim West/Alamy; **153** © Dennis MacDonald/PhotoEdit; **158** © David Bacon/NewsCom; **168** © Purestock/Getty Images; **169** © 2006 Cedar Fair, L.P.; **172** © Hill Street Studios/Blend Images/Getty Images; **174** © PhotoDisc/Getty Images; **176** © Carsten Peter/National Geographic/Getty Images; **181** © Jerry Young/DK Limited/Corbis; **183** © Ethan Miller/NewsCom/Getty Images; **187** © James Dickens; **190** © Masterfile (Royalty-Free Div.); **192** © Mark Richards/PhotoEdit; **198** © Matthias Kulka/zefa/Corbis; **200** © McConnell & McNamara; **203** © Empics/SportsChrome; **218** Henny Wiggers/AP Images; **219** © Johner Images/Getty Images; **227** © Art Vandalay/Getty Images; **228** © Dennis MacDonald/PhotoEdit; **234** © Yadid Levy/Alamy; **240** © Robert Benson www.robertbenson.com; **243** © Rick Doyle/Corbis; **245** © David Young-Wolff/PhotoEdit; **246** © John Warden/SuperStock; **249** *inset* © Daniel Barillot/Masterfile, *background* © Image Ideas Inc./Index Stock Imagery; **255** © Alan Thornton/Getty Images; **257** © Mike McMillan/Spotfire Images; **259** © Bettmann/Corbis; **267** *all* McDougal Littell/Houghton Mifflin Company; **268** © Scott Tysick/Masterfile; **270** © Zigy Kaluzny/Stone/Getty Images; **274** © Brad Wilson/Getty Images; **279** © Masterfile (Royalty-Free Div.); **280** © Royalty-Free/Corbis; **292** © Thinkstock/Alamy; **293** © Ryan McVay/PhotoDisc Green/Getty Images; **298** Purdue University Bands Archives; **300** © Yapanchintsev Yevgeny/ITAR-TASS/Corbis; **304** © David Papazian/Corbis; **306** © Dennis MacDonald/Alamy; **307** © Craig Aurness/Corbis; **310** AP Images; **313** © Tony Campbell/Shutterstock; **319** © Tony Freeman/PhotoEdit; **323** © Jason Hawkes/Corbis; **324** © Royalty-Free/Corbis; **327** © Tom Neiman/Stock Montage, Inc./Alamy; **329** © Justin Kase/Alamy; **333** © Royalty-Free/Corbis; **339** © PhotoCreate/Shutterstock; **350** © TAOLMOR/Shutterstock; **351** © James R. Hearn/Shutterstock; **353** © Lev Mel/Shutterstock; **357** © Andres Rodriguez/Shutterstock; **358** *top left* © Wolfgang Kaehler/Corbis, *top right* © Tom Brakefield/Corbis; **363** © James King-Holmes/Photo Researchers, Inc.; **364** *top left* © Florida Images/Alamy, *top right* © Peter Casolino/Alamy; **365** © Royalty-Free/Corbis; **369** © Kevin Schafer/Corbis; **370** *top left* © John W. Banagan/Getty Images, *top right* © Mikael Utterström/Alamy, *center right* © OSF/Colbeck; M./Animals Animals/Earth Scenes; **373** © Frances Roberts/Alamy; **377** © Gabe Palmer/Corbis; **378** © Royal Tyrrell Museum/Alberta Community Development; **389** © Tony Freeman/PhotoEdit; **391** © David Frazier/PhotoEdit; **393** © George Hall/Corbis; **395** © Bonnie Kamin/PhotoEdit; **399** © Tom Carter/PhotoEdit; **408** © Paola Kathuria/Alamy; **409** © Larry Keenan Associates/Getty Images; **414** © John Henshall/Alamy; **416** © David Davis Photoproductions/Alamy; **418** *both* Jay Penni Photography/McDougal Littell/Houghton Mifflin Co.; **419** © Myrleen Ferguson Cate/PhotoEdit; **423** © TNT MAGAZINE/Alamy; **424** © Richard Ransier/Corbis; **426** © Steve Dunwell/Index Stock Imagery; **431** © Michael Zito/SportsChrome; **438** © Jim West/Alamy; **442** © Royalty-Free/Corbis; **444** © Michael Newman/PhotoEdit; **446** © LeighSmithImages/Alamy; **453** © MAST IRHAM/epa/Corbis; **462** © Jim Reed/Corbis; **463** © Pete Turner/The Image Bank/Getty Images; **465** *both* RMIP/Richard Haynes/McDougal Littell; **467** © Wm. Baker/GhostWorx Images/Alamy; **468** John Russell/AP Images; **470** © K. Thorsen/Shutterstock; **477** © James "BO" Insogna/Shutterstock;

CREDITS

480 © David Tipling/Stone/Getty Images; 484 © Gerry Ellis/Science Faction/Getty Images;494 © Kelly-Mooney/Corbis; 496 © Virgo Productions/zefa/Corbis; 498 © Elizabeth Kreutz/NewSport/Corbis; 500 © Phillippe Caron/Sygma/Corbis; 502 © Robert Sarosiek/Shutterstock; 504 © David Tejada/Stone/Getty Images; 516, 517 © Bonnie Kamin/PhotoEdit; 519 © Jeff Greenberg/PhotoEdit; 520 © PhotoDisc; 521 © IMAGEMORE Co; Ltd/Getty Images; 522 © PhotoDisc; 523 © Amy Etra/PhotoEdit; 526 all © Thinkstock/Corbis; 528 © Peter Bennett/Alamy; 533 © Jose Luis Pelaez; Inc./Corbis; 537 © Spencer Grant/PhotoEdit; 541 © POPPERFOTO/Alamy; 545 © Kayye M. Deioma/PhotoEdit; 546 girls, black shirt, white jacket © RubberBall Productions, all others © PhotoObjects/Jupiter Images; 549 © Daniel Dempster Photography/Alamy; 556 © David Young-Wolff/PhotoEdit; 558 © Terry Husebye/Getty Images; 566 © ArtPix/Alamy; 582 © Lester Lefkowitz/The Image Bank/Getty Images; 583 © John Lund/Drew Kelly/Blend Images/Getty Images; 590 © POPPERFOTO/Alamy; 594 © William Sallaz/Duomo/Corbis; 596 © David Stluka/Getty Images; 598 © Spencer Grant/PhotoEdit; 604 © David Young-Wolff/PhotoEdit; 615 © Stockbyte/PictureQuest;

619 © Mark Karrass/Corbis; 625 © Rick Buenham/Icon SMI/Corbis; 627 all Jay Penni Photography/McDougal Littell, Houghton Mifflin Co.; 642 © Hermann Erber/LOOK/Getty Images; 643 © Chip Porter/The Image Bank/Getty Images; 645 © George D. Lepp/Corbis; 649 © PhotoDisc; 657 © David Young-Wolff/PhotoEdit; 660 © Pascal Rondeau/Allsport Concepts/Getty Images; 664 © Ryan McVay/Photodisc Green/Getty Images; 668 © David Young-Wolff/PhotoEdit; 673 © John Foxx/Stockbyte Silver/Getty Images; 675 © Brian Bailey/Corbis; 677 © Steve Smith/Getty Images; 688 © Stephen Coburn/Shutterstock; 689 © Manuel Fernandes/Shutterstock; 693 © Dewitt Jones/Corbis; 699 © Louie Psihoyos/Corbis; 703 © Kerry Muzzey/Shutterstock; 707 © Brian Pieters/Masterfile; 712 bottom left © Detlev Van Ravenswaay/SPL/Photo Researchers, Inc., bottom right NASA/ARC; 715 © Cameron Davidson/Photographer's Choice/Gettty Images; 723 RMIP/Richard Haynes/McDougal Littell; 724 © Paul A. Souders/Corbis; 729 © North Wind Picture Archive/Alamy; 730 © Nathan Bilow/Allsport Concepts/Getty Images.

Illustrations

76 Dan Stuckenschneider; 77 Carol Zuber-Mallison; 84 bottom Steve Cowden; 104 Matt Zang/American Artists; 232 Dan Stuckenschneider; 233 Steve Cowden; 238 Patrick Gnan/Deborah Wolfe; 272 Patrick Gnan/Deborah Wolfe; 277 all Doug Stevens; 300 Carol Zuber-Mallison; 347 Dan Stuckenschneider; 349 Steve McEntee; 369 Mark Schroeder; 384 Steve Cowden; 385 Stephen Durke; 471 Dan Stuckenschneider; 492 all Dan Stuckenschneider; 502 Patrick Gnan/Deborah Wolfe; 513 John Francis; 569 Dan Stuckenschneider; 585 Dan Stuckenschneider; 587 Dan Stuckenschneider; 612 Dan Stuckenschneider; 619 center right Dan Stuckenschneider, bottom center Stephen Durke; 630 Patrick Gnan/Deborah Wolfe; 643 Patrick Gnan/Deborah Wolfe; 647 Patrick Gnan/Deborah Wolfe; 649 Dan Stuckenschneider; 657 Steve McEntee; 665 Dan Stuckenschneider; 671 Stephen Durke; 674 top right Dan Stuckenschneider, center School Division, Houghton Mifflin Company; 677 Patrick Gnan/Deborah Wolfe; 679 Steve McEntee; 680 center Steve McEntee; 695 bottom right Carol Zuber-Mallison; 696 Carol Zuber-Mallison; 701 center right Stephen Durke; bottom right Patrick Gnan/Deborah Wolfe; 719 Patrick Gnan/Deborah Wolfe; 721 Argosy; 727 Argosy; 729 Patrick Gnan/Deborah Wolfe.

All other illustrations by McDougal Littell/Houghton Mifflin Company.

Selected Answers

Pre-Course Practice

Fractions, Decimals, and Percents (p. xxiv)
1. 0.55 **3.** 1.2 **5.** 0.225, 23% **7.** 0.903, 90% **9.** 60%, $\frac{3}{5}$
11. 87.5%, $\frac{7}{8}$ **13.** 16.1 **15.** 26.5% **17.** $\frac{13}{28}$ **19.** $\frac{11}{12}$

Writing Ratios and Proportions (p. xxiv) **1.** 3 to 2,
3:2, $\frac{3}{2}$ **3.** 7 to 12, 7:12, $\frac{7}{12}$ **5.** 68 **7.** 30.8

**Integers, Significant Digits, and Scientific
Notation** (p. xxiv) **1.** 13 **3.** 0 **5.** 160 **7.** 5 **9.** 6.31×10^2
11. 5.2×10^7

The Coordinate Plane (p. xxv) **1.** $(-2, 0)$ **3.** $(6, 0)$
5. $(5, -5)$ **7.** $(0, 4)$

Perimeter, Circumference, Area, and Volume
(p. xxv) **1.** 23 m **3.** $3.8\pi \approx 11.9$ cm **5.** $121\pi \approx 379.9$ in.^{2}
7. 18 ft^2 **9.** 680 in.^{3}

Triangle Relationships (p. xxv) **1.** yes **3.** yes **5.** yes
7. yes **9.** $2\sqrt{13}$

**Symmetry, Transformations, and Similar
Figures** (p. xxvi) **1.**

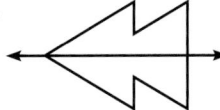

3. none **5.** $A'(-3, -8)$, $B'(0, 1)$ **7.** 2.5 **9.** 9

Logical Argument (p. xxvi) **1.** invalid

**If-Then Statements, Counterexamples, and
Justify Reasoning** (p. xxvi) **1.** false; 0 **3.** False;
A, B, and C could form a triangle. **5.** division property
of equality **7.** subtraction property of equality
9. multiplication property of equality **11.** 8 **13.** -4
15. -14 **17.** -1

Problem Solving Strategies (p. xxvii) **1.** AB, AC,
AD, AE, BC, BD, BE, CD, CE, DE so 10 possibilities
3. $4.5^2 + 6^2 = x^2$, $x = 7.5$ mi **5.** $2000^5 = 2^5 \times 10^{15} =$
$3.2 \times 10^{15} = 3,200,000,000,000,000$ **7.** *Sample answer:*
  Guess: 10 t-shirts
  Check: $25 + 10(8) = 25 + 80 = 105$
  Revise: Try smaller number.
  Guess: 9 t-shirts
  Check: $25 + 9(8) = 25 + 72 = 97$
  You can buy 9 t-shirts.

Translating Words into Symbols (p. xxvii) **1.** $x - 15$
3. $2x$ **5.** $1 + \frac{1}{2}x$

**Combining Like Terms and Multiplying
Polynomials** (p. xxvii) **1.** $7a - 9$ **3.** $4x^2 - 4x$
5. $x^4 + 8x^2 - 6x$ **7.** $x^3 + 2x^2 - 7x + 4$

Solving Linear Equations (p. xxvii) **1.** $\frac{19}{3}$ **3.** -9 **5.** 6
7. -3 **9.** 2 **11.** $\frac{3}{8}$

Chapter 1

1.1 Guided Practice (p. 6) **1.** A rational number can
be written as the quotient of two integers, but irrational
numbers cannot be written this way. The decimal form
of a rational number terminates or repeats, but the
decimal form of an irrational number neither terminates
nor repeats. **3.** Write 298 as $300 - 2$. Then $4 \cdot 298 =$
$4(300 - 2) = 4(300) - 4(2) = 1200 - 8 = 1192$.
5. always **7.** sometimes

9.

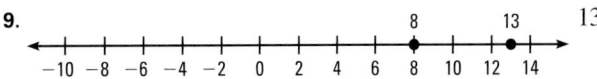

11. inverse property of addition **13.** commutative property
of multiplication

1.1 Practice and Applications (pp. 6–8)

15.

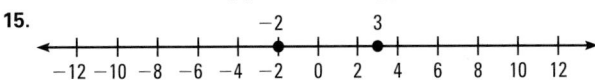

21.

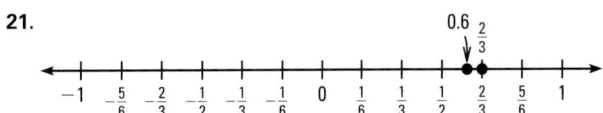

25. $-2.36 < -1.04$

27. $\frac{2}{5} > \frac{1}{6}$

33. $-3.6, -2, \frac{3}{2}, 3.2, 8$

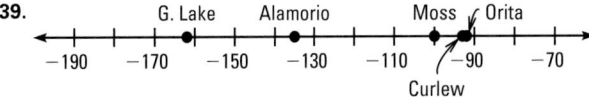

37. Karrie Webb, Michelle Wie, Se Ri Pak, Annika
Sorenstam, Angela Standford, Meg Mallon

39.

41. Alamorio and Gieselmann Lake **43.** associative
property of addition **45.** distributive property **47.** 2090
49. 9 should have been distributed to 600 and to 3;
$9(600 + 3) = 9(600) + 9(3) = 5400 + 27 = 5427$.
51. $-8 + 25 = 17$ **53.** $-15 \div \left(-\frac{5}{3}\right) = 9$ **55.** $-6 \cdot 0 = 0$
57. $-10 - (-1) = -9$

1.2 Guided Practice (p. 12) **1.** base $\rightarrow 7^5 \leftarrow$ exponent;
the base, 7, is the factor to be multiplied by itself and

the exponent, 5, is the number of times that the base, 7, is to be used as a factor. **3.** 3; 7 **5.** 8 **7.** 36 **9.** 3 **11.** -6 **13.** The first step should be simplifying the product in the parentheses; $3 + (2 \cdot 5)^2 = 3 + 10^2 = 3 + 100 = 103$.

1.2 Practice and Applications (pp. 12–14) **15.** 9^4
17. n^6 **19.** 7^6 **21.** 32 **23.** 256 **25.** 81 **27.** -49 **29.** -64
31. -1 **33.** 18 **35.** 17 **37.** 20 **39.** 18 **41.** -54 **43.** 375
45. 10 **47.** 9 **49.** 17 **51.** 32 **53.** 24 **55.** 20 **57.** 13 **59.** 12
61. 9 **63.** 17,354,000 people **65.** $1.42t + 67.8$
67. $5.50n - 35$ **71.** $67,150 + 12,500t$; 117,150 mi

1.3 Guided Practice (p. 19) **1.** No; $-3x$ is a term.
3. like terms **5.** equivalent expressions **7.** $-5y$, 3 **9.** $13p$
11. $6s^2 - 2s$ **13.** $2x + 4$ **15.** $-2r + 10$ **17.** $4185t +$
155,000; 171,740 physical therapy jobs

1.3 Practice and Applications (pp. 19–20) **19.** $11f$,
-3 **21.** $8m$, $-12n$ **23.** 9, $-3w$, $2w^2$, 12 **25.** coefficients:
5, -10; like terms: $5b^2$ and $-10b^2$ **27.** coefficients: 2, 3;
like terms: $2m$ and $3m$, 1 and 3 **29.** coefficients: 13, -5,
6, -2; like terms: $13x^2$ and $-2x^2$, $-5x$ and $6x$ **31.** $-y$
33. $-h + 8$ **35.** $-10n + 3$ **37.** $3p^2 + 2p$ **39.** $m + 4$
41. $2z - 2$ **43.** $-3b - 17$ **45.** $2h^2 + 11h$ **47.** $2g - 4$
49. $-3w - 11$ **51.** $43.49 + 3.99(m - 3)$ **53.** $63.44
55. $0.35m - 105$

1.3 Technology Activity (pp. 22–23) **1.** $(-4)^2 - 3$; 13
3. 146 **5.** 72 **7.** 2.667 **9.** $\dfrac{5}{-3 - 7}$; -0.5 **11.** 72
13. 5912.099 **15.** 26 **17.** -0.875 **19.** 0.18
21. $(4 + \sqrt{289}) \times 3$; 24 **23.** 169.312 **25.** -658.220
27. -179.741 **29.** 16.154

1.4 Guided Practice (p. 29) **1.** a statement of the
equality of two expressions **3.** It has the form $ax = b$
where a and b are constants and $a \neq 0$. **5.** 13 **7.** 75 **9.** -2
11. 2 **13.** In the second step, $2x$ should be subtracted from
both sides; $x + 5 = 0$, $x = -5$. **15.** $8

1.4 Practice and Applications (pp. 29–30)
17. subtraction property **19.** multiplication property
21. addition property and multiplication property **23.** 31
25. 28 **27.** -4 **29.** -63 **31.** 30 **33.** -3 **35.** -20 **37.** -3
39. 3 **41.** 8 **43.** 3 **45.** 5 **47.** 20 yr **49.** 18 **51.** -68 **53.** 1
55. 3 **57.** 8 incorrect answers **59.** 11 h

1.4 Technology Activity (p. 32) **1.** False; $y_1 = y_2$ when
$x = -2$, not when $x = 1$. **3.** 2 **5.** -1 **7.** -7

1.5 Guided Practice (p. 36) **1.** formula
3. $y = -\dfrac{2}{3}x + 3$; 1 **5.** $y = \dfrac{3}{5}x + \dfrac{1}{5}$; 2 **7.** $y = -\dfrac{1}{4}x + \dfrac{15}{4}$; 3
9. $w = \dfrac{P - 4\ell}{3}$ **11.** $A = \dfrac{8\ell(25 - \ell)}{3}$
1.5 Practice and Applications (pp. 36–38) **13.** $m = \dfrac{E}{c^2}$
15. $h = \dfrac{V}{\ell w}$ **17.** $v_0 = \dfrac{h + 16t^2 - h_0}{t}$ **19.** $r = \dfrac{I}{Pt}$ **21.** $35;
$1035 **23.** 4 **25.** -2 **27.** 1 **29.** 6 **31.** -7 **33.** -4
35. $L = \dfrac{D + 21m}{m}$ **39.** $m = 10T + 75$

1.6 Guided Practice (p. 43) **1.** an equation written in
words **3.** Number of minutes **5.** $400 = 3.8f$

1.6 Practice and Applications (pp. 43–45) **7.** A: no;
B: yes; C: yes **9.** $108 = 8t$ **11.** 13.5 h **13.** $80t = 160(4)$
15. Monthly car expenses = Monthly car payment +
Insurance payment ÷ Number of months per payment
17. $D = 252 + 684 \div 6$ **19.** Total Calories = Calories/
gram of protein • Number of grams of protein +
Calories/gram of carbohydrate • Number of grams of
carbohydrate + Calories/gram of fat • Number of grams
of fat **21.** $T = 4p + 4c + 9f$ **23.** *Sample answer: dw =*
529, where d = dollars/wk and w = number of wk; 27 wk
25. Puppy's weight = w (lb); Weight at 3 months =
5.5 (lb); Monthly weight gain = 2.5 (lb); Number of
additional months = m (months); $w = 5.5 + 2.5m$
27. $x + 6$; $x + (x + 6) = 72$; 33 in. and 39 in.

1.7 Guided Practice (p. 49) **1.** The mean is the average,
calculated by dividing the sum of the numbers by n, the
number of numbers. The median is the middle number
when the numbers are written in order. If n is even, the
median is the mean of the two middle numbers. The mode
is the number or numbers that occur most frequently. The
range is the difference between the greatest and least
numbers in the data set. **3.** 6 **5.** 2 and 5 **7.** 2

9.

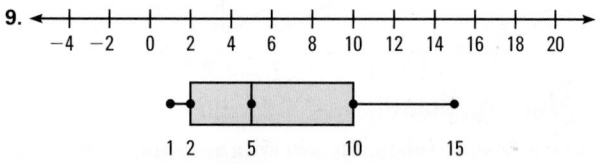

1.7 Practice and Applications (pp. 49–50) **11.** mean:
$8\dfrac{1}{3}$; median: 9; mode: 9 **13.** mean: 80; median: 80; mode:
75 **15.** mean: 28; median: 31.5; mode: 33 **17.** mean: 550;
median: 500; no mode **19.** 57 **21.** 124 **23.** 5.4 **25.** mean:
$9546.67; median: $9760; mode: $10,400 **27.** *Sample
answer:* The mean increases by more than $1500; the
median increases by just $40. **29.** 4; 10 **31.** 48.5; 52
33. 211; 335 **35.** 10.1; 10.8

39.

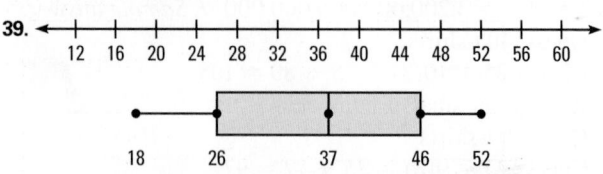

43. 9 min **45.** school B **47.** 31

1.8 Guided Practice (p. 54) **1.** A bar graph displays
separate categories while a histogram displays data
grouped into intervals. Also, the bars of a bar graph have
spaces between them, while the bars of a histogram do
not. **3.** 150–179, 180–209, 210–239, 240–269, 270–299

5.

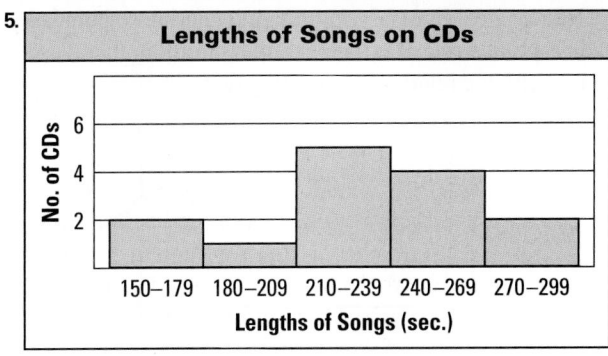

Lengths of Songs on CDs

1.8 Practice and Applications (p. 54–55) **7.** 42–44, 45–47, 48–50, 51–53, 54–56, 57–59, 60–62 **9.** 121–125, 126–130, 131–135, 136–140, 141–145, 146–150, 151–155, 156–160

11.

Interval	Tally	Frequency
42–44	I	1
45–47		0
48–50	II	2
51–53	IIII	4
54–56	II	2
57–59	I	1
60–62	II	2

17.

Minutes on Math Homework		
Interval	Tally	Frequency
10–19	ℍℍ	5
20–29	ℍℍ	5
30–39	ℍℍ II	7
40–49	II	2
50–59	I	1

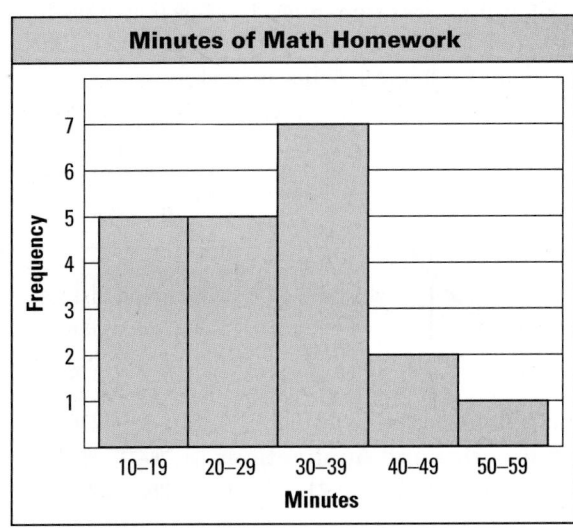

Minutes of Math Homework

19. 6 missions **21.** 6 missions

23.

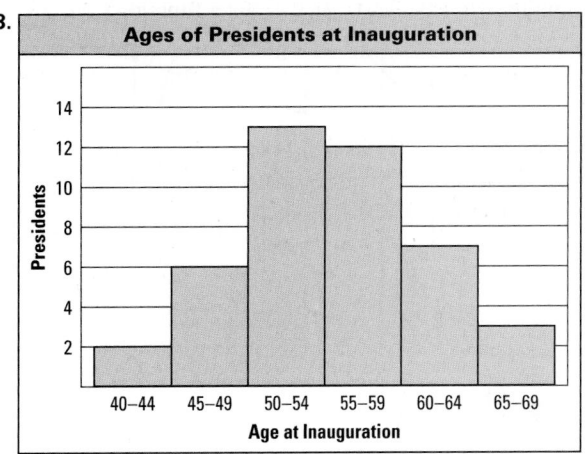

Ages of Presidents at Inauguration

Chapter Review (pp. 57–60) **1.** *Sample answer:* Whole number, 7; integer, -3; rational number, 1.4; irrational number, $\sqrt{52}$ **3.** An expression is simplified if it has no grouping symbols and if all the like terms have been combined. *Sample answer:* $3x + y$, $n^2 + 4n$
5. $-7, -4, -1, 1, 3, 5$

7. $-5, -1.6, -0.5, 0.8, \frac{5}{3}, \frac{11}{4}, 4$

9. 2376 **11.** 10 **13.** -7 **15.** -12 **17.** 8 **19.** 45 **21.** 24 **23.** $2x$ **25.** $12x^2 - 10x$ **27.** $6x + 1$ **29.** $C = 9.95 + 1.25(t - 2)$; $11.20; $13.70 **31.** 2 **33.** 10 **35.** 4 **37.** -30 **39.** $a = P - b - c$ **41.** $y = -\frac{3}{2}x + 3$ **43.** $y = \frac{3}{5}x - 3$ **45.** 0 **47.** 10 mi

49.

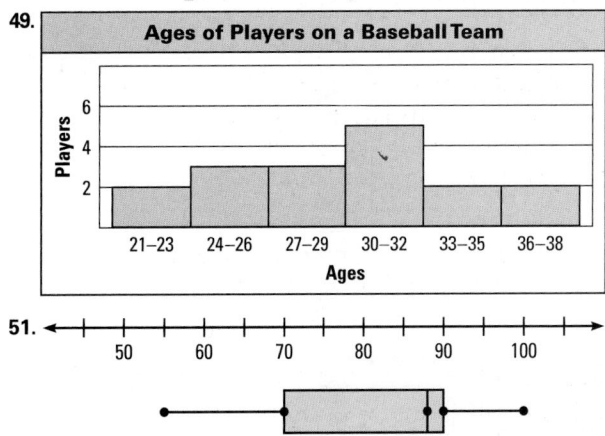

Ages of Players on a Baseball Team

51.

Chapter 2

2.1 Guided Practice (p. 70) **1.** relation **3.** The domain consists of inputs: 10, 20, 30, 40, the range consists of outputs: 100, 200, 300, 400; function. **5.** The domain consists of inputs: $-10, -6, -1, 6$, the range consists of outputs: $-4, -3, -2, 0, 2, 3, 4$; not a function.

7. 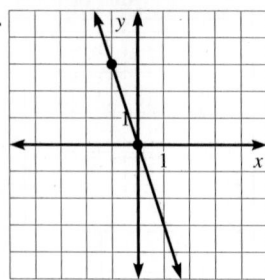 **9.**

13.

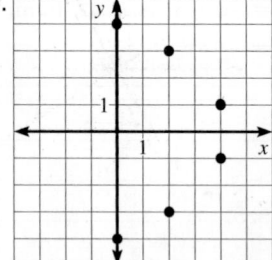

35. If a vertical line passes through two or more points on the graph of a relation, then an input has more than one output and the relation is not a function.

41. 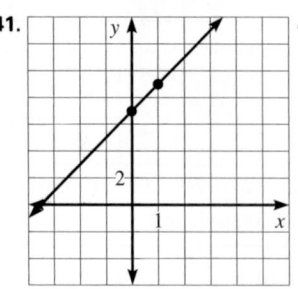 **47.**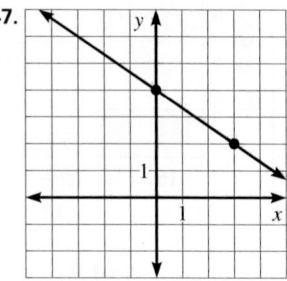

49.

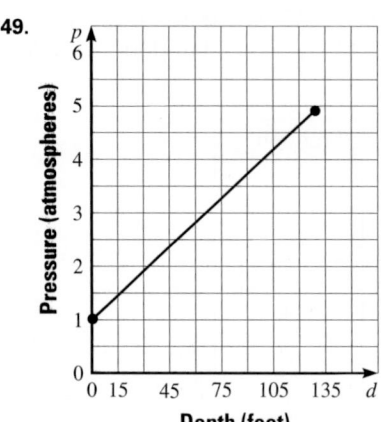

51.

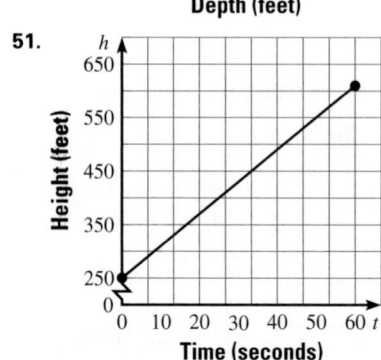

2.1 Practice and Applications (pp. 70–72)

25. $\{(4, 2), (4, 3), (4, 5), (4, 6)\}$

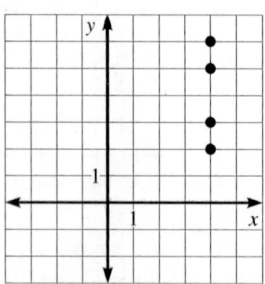

27. not a function

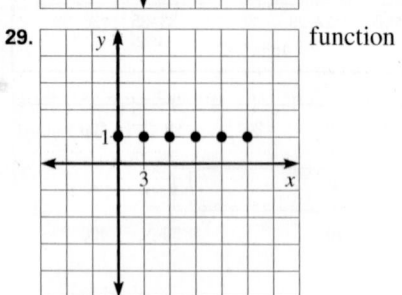

29. function

31. sometimes **33.** always

2.2 Guided Practice (p. 76) **1.** A function of the form $y = mx + b$, where m and b are constants, is a linear function. **3.** not linear **5.** linear **7.** 11

9. 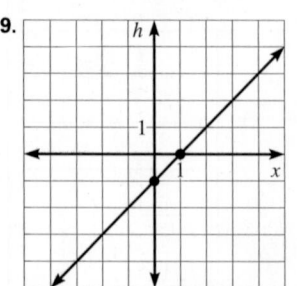 **11.**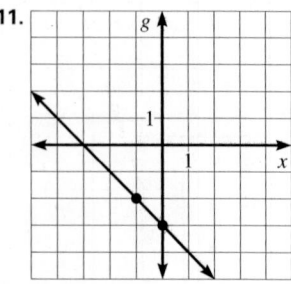

13. $120

2.2 Practice and Applications (pp. 76–77) **15.** linear **17.** not linear **19.** linear **21.** -1 **23.** -1 **25.** 1 **27.** -5

29. 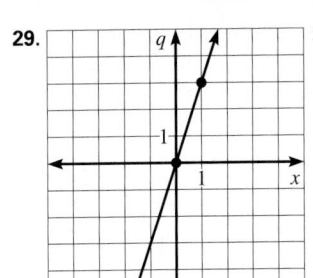 **33.**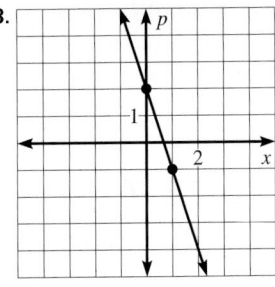

39. 2550 mi

41. 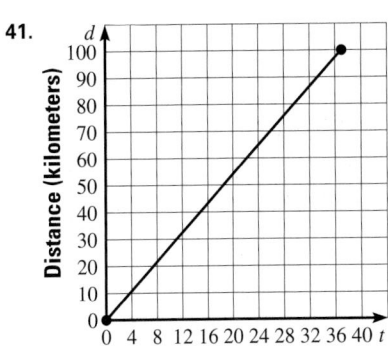 **45.** $4800

2.3 Guided Practice (p. 82) **1.** slope **3.** vertical **5.** −1; falls **7.** 0; is horizontal **9.** $\frac{1}{2}$; rises **11.** line 2 **13.** 26.25 pages per h

2.3 Practice and Applications (pp. 82–84) **15.** −1 **17.** $\frac{1}{12}$ **19.** $\overline{AB}$: positive, $\overline{BC}$: negative, $\overline{AC}$: positive

21. −5; falls **23.** 1; rises **25.** −2; falls **27.** $\frac{1}{6}$; rises **29.** $-\frac{1}{4}$; falls **31.** b **33.** d **35.** line 2 **37.** line 1 **39.** 2 mi per h **41.** 3 in. per day **43.** −2°F per h **45.** c **47.** a and b **49.** yes; $\frac{5}{15} = \frac{1}{3}$ **51.** $-\frac{1}{200}$ ° per ft **53.** 11.5 MB per min

2.4 Guided Practice (p. 90) **1.** $y = mx + b$, $Ax + By = C$ **3.** 7; parallel lines have the same slope. **5.** −2, −7 **7.** 9, 9 **9.** 6, −9

2.4 Practice and Applications (pp. 90–92) **11.** $-\frac{3}{2}$ **13.** −3 **15.** B

17. 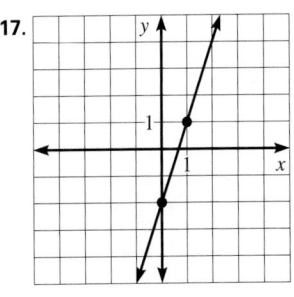 **21.**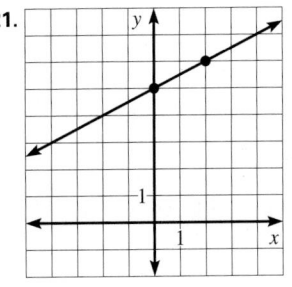

23. 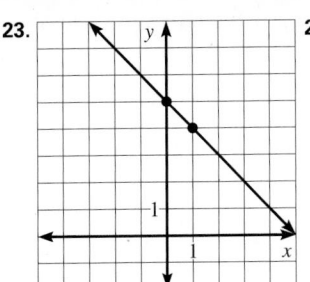 **27.**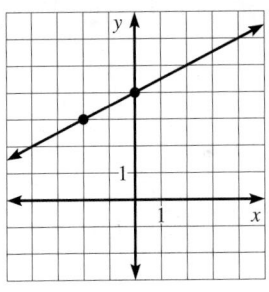

29. B **31.** A

33.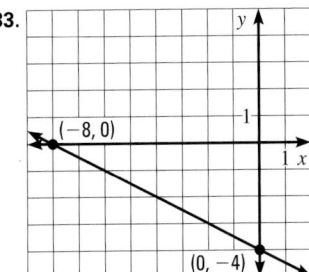

35.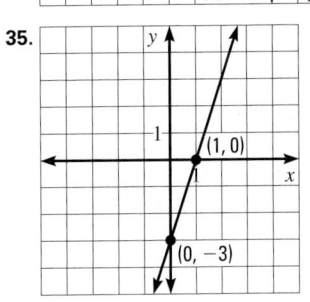

39. neither **41.** perpendicular **43.** perpendicular

45. 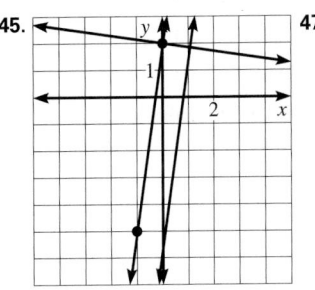 **47.**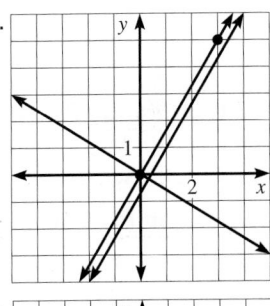

51. 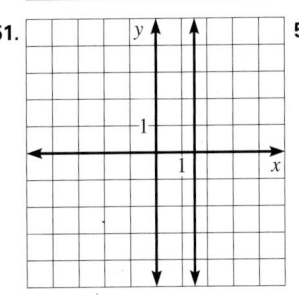 **53.**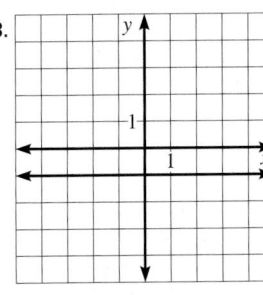

57. 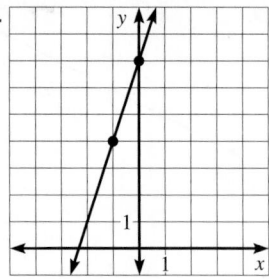 **59.**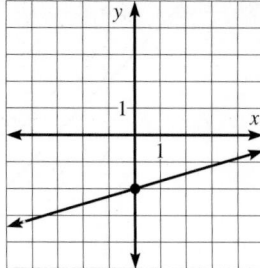

63.

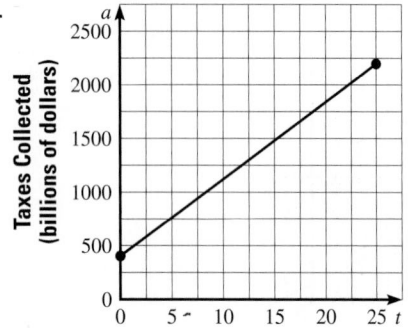

Years (since 1980)

65. 2.5, 35

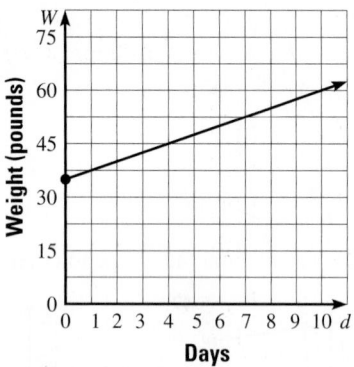

Days

2.4 Technology Activity (p. 93) **7.** *Sample answer:*
Xmin = −10, Xmax = 30, Xscl = 2, Ymin = −10,
Ymax = 20, Yscl = 1

2.5 Guided Practice (p. 97) **3.** $y = 2x − 3$

5. $y = \frac{2}{5}x + 1$ **7.** $y = 2x + 7$ **9.** $y = 2x − 14$ **11.** −$2200
per yr; $V(t) = −2200t + 19{,}000$

2.5 Practice and Applications (pp. 97–99) **13.** $\frac{3}{2}$, −4

15. $y = x + 3$ **17.** $y = 5$ **19.** $y = \frac{3}{2}x − 3$ **21.** $y = 3x − 4$

23. $y = −\frac{3}{2}x − 2$ **25.** $y = 3x + 2$ **27.** $y = −2$

29. $y = −5x − 20$ **31.** $y = −\frac{2}{3}x + 8$ **33.** $y = \frac{6}{7}x + \frac{78}{7}$

35. $y = \frac{1}{2}x − \frac{1}{2}$ **37.** $y = 2x + 1$ **39.** $y = \frac{1}{2}x + 6$

41. $y = \frac{3}{4}x − 4$ **43.** $c = −8h + 76$; 76 candy bars

45. $y = −2x − 1$ **47.** $y = \frac{3}{2}x + 2$ **49.** $y = −9$

51. $x = 6$ **53.** $b = \frac{36}{25}t + 13$ **55.** $y = 2x + 17$

2.6 Guided Practice (p. 103) **1.** direct variation

3. 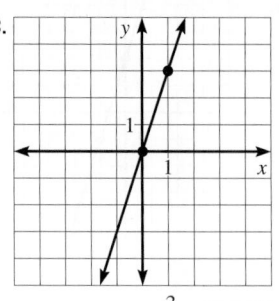 **5.**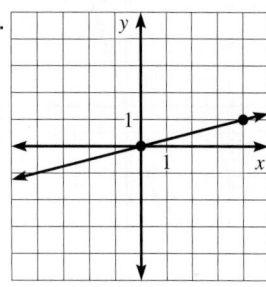

7. $y = 4x$ **9.** $y = \frac{3}{4}x$,

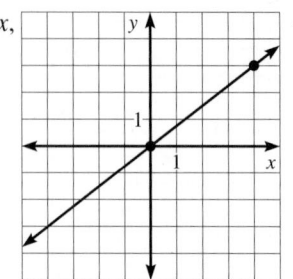

$\frac{3}{2}$

2.6 Practice and Applications (pp. 103–105) **11.** Yes;
the curve is a line containing the origin.

15. 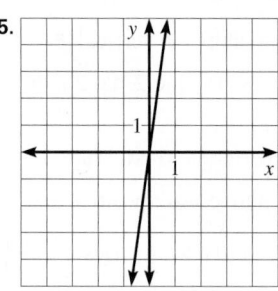 **17.**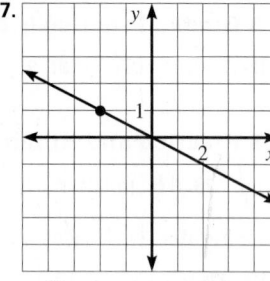

19. always **21.** never **23.** −9 **25.** $−\frac{2}{21}$ **27.** $y = 8x$; 72

29. $y = −8x$; −72 **31.** $y = \frac{1}{2}x$; $\frac{9}{2}$ **33.** $y = −\frac{1}{9}x$; −1

35. $y = 4x$; 36 **37.** $t = 0.06p$; $15 **39.** $d = 0.6p$; $108, $72
43. no **45.** $c = 2.54n$, 19.05 cm **47.** $k = 1.61m$, about
3.11 mi

2.7 Guided Practice (p. 110) **5.** *Sample answer:* $y = 12x + 123$

2.7 Practice and Applications (pp. 110–112)
7. relatively no correlation **9.** negative correlation

11. positive correlation
13. negative correlation
15. positive correlation
17. relatively no
correlation **19.** *Sample
answer:* $y = −x + 3$.

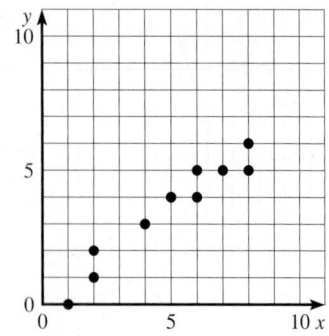

23.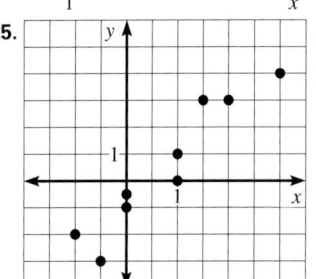

Sample answer:
$y = \dfrac{8}{11}x + \dfrac{6}{11}, \dfrac{78}{11}$

25.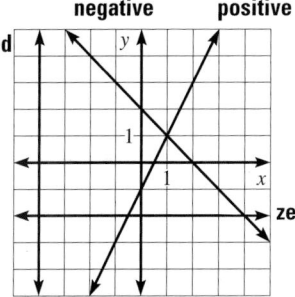

Sample answer:
$y = 2x - 1, 17$

27. *Sample answer:* $y = 0.2x + 67.7$

Chapter Review (pp. 115–118)

3.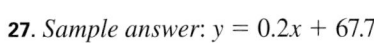

the line whose slope is undefined

5. The domain consists of inputs: $-3, -1, 0, 1, 3$, the range consists of outputs: $-3, -1, 0, 2$; the relation is a function. **7.** linear; 6 **9.** not linear; -11

11. 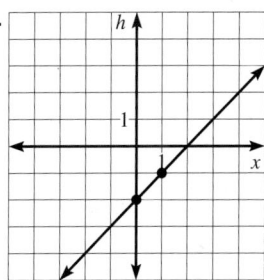 **13.**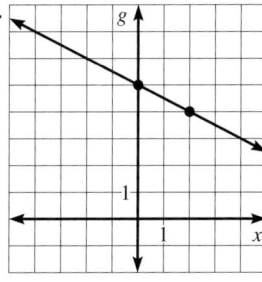

15. 1; rises **17.** -2; falls **19.** $-\dfrac{1}{3}$; falls **21.** line 2

23. 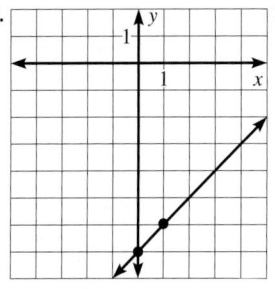 **25.**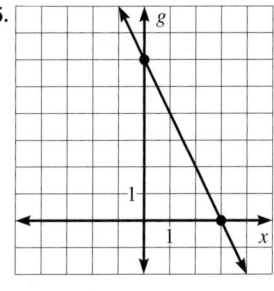

27.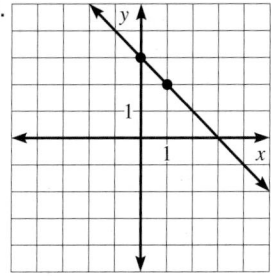

31. $y = -2x + 8$ **33.** $y = -3x - 1$ **35.** $y = 3x - 9$
37. $y = 2x$ **39.** $y = -\dfrac{1}{5}x$ **41.** yes; $y = -3x$

43. 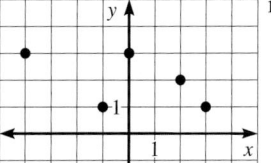 relatively no correlation

Chapter 3

3.1 Guided Practice (p. 128) **1.** solution **3.** yes

5. 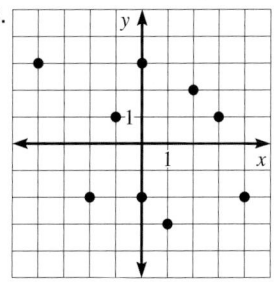 1

7. 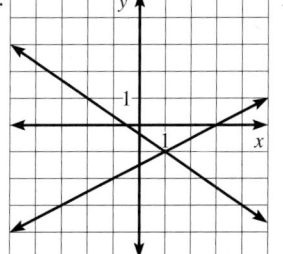 infinitely many

3.1 Practice and Applications (pp. 128–130) **9.** yes
11. no **13.** no **15.** $(3, -4)$ **17.** $(3, 7)$ **19.** $(-1, 3)$ **21.** $(7, 1)$
23. B; infinitely many **25.** C; 1

27. 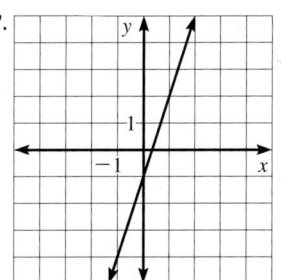 infinitely many

29.

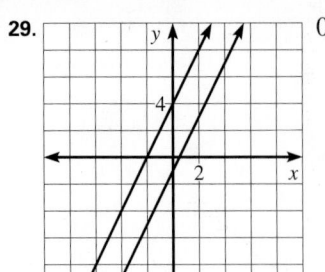

0

31.

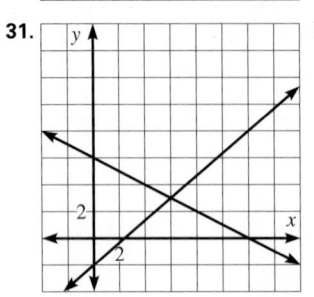

1; (6, 3)

35. $x = 2y$, $2x + 3y = 21$; 6 two-point shots and 3 three-point shots **37.** $x = y + 25$; $x + 4y = 75$; 35 balloons and 10 lanterns **39.** $y = x + 30$, $y = 2.5x$; 20 rides

3.1 Technology Activity (p. 131) **1.** $(-1, 3)$ **3.** $(2, -2)$
5. $(-3, -4)$

3.2 Guided Practice (p. 135) **1.** *Sample answer:* Look for an equation that has a variable with a coefficient of 1 or -1 and solve for that variable. **3.** Solve for y in Equation 2 since the coefficient of y is -1. This makes it easy to solve for y. **5.** $4x + 7y = -3$; $4x + 7(3x - 4) = -3$; $25x - 28 = -3$; $25x = 25$; $x = 1$

3.2 Practice and Applications (pp. 135–136)
11–15. Sample answers are given. **11.** Equation 1; it is already solved for y **13.** Equation 2; d has a coefficient of -1 **15.** Equation 2, a has a coefficient of 1 and b has a coefficient of -1 **17.** $(7, 21)$ **19.** $(4, -4)$

21. $(1, -1)$ **23.** $(-2, -2)$ **25.** $(0, 5)$ **27.** $\left(\frac{3}{2}, \frac{1}{2}\right)$ **29.** The distributive property was used incorrectly; substituting $5y - 1$ for x in Equation 1 yields $2(5y - 1) - y = 7$; $9y - 2 = 7$; $9y = 9$; $y = 1$; $x = 5(1) - 1 = 4$; $(4, 1)$.
31. 560 Class-A shares and 240 Class-B shares
33. Bedroom 1: 185 ft²; Bedroom 2: 135 ft²

3.3 Guided Practice (p. 142) **1.** When you add the revised equations, one of the variables is eliminated. Then you can solve for the other variable. **3.** Adding the revised equations yields $7x = 21$, not $-x = 5$. So, $x = 3$ and $2(3) - y = 4$, and so $y = 2$. The solution is $(3, 2)$.
7. 20 quarters; 27 dimes

3.3 Practice and Applications (pp. 142–143) **9.** $(4, -3)$
11. $(7, 2)$ **13.** $(8, 3)$ **15.** $(-2, -6)$ **17.** $(5, 1)$ **19.** $(3, 9)$
21. $(21, -18)$ **23.** $(3, 7)$ **25.** $(9, 0)$ **27.** infinitely many solutions **29.** no solution **31.** one solution **33.** 35 min of inline skating and 25 min of swimming **35.** 4 birdhouses and 13 bird feeders **37.** 4 packs of 24 light bulbs and 1 pack of 12 light bulbs

Extension (p. 146) **1.** *Sample answer:* Substitution method; the coefficient of x is -1. **3.** *Sample answer:* Linear combination method; no variable has a coefficient of 1 or -1. **5.** $(1, 3)$ **7.** $(3, -7)$ **9.** $(6, 3)$ **11.** $(-4, 5)$
13. 180 baseball cards

3.4 Guided Practice (p. 150) **1.** ordered triple
3. $ax + by + cz = d$

5.

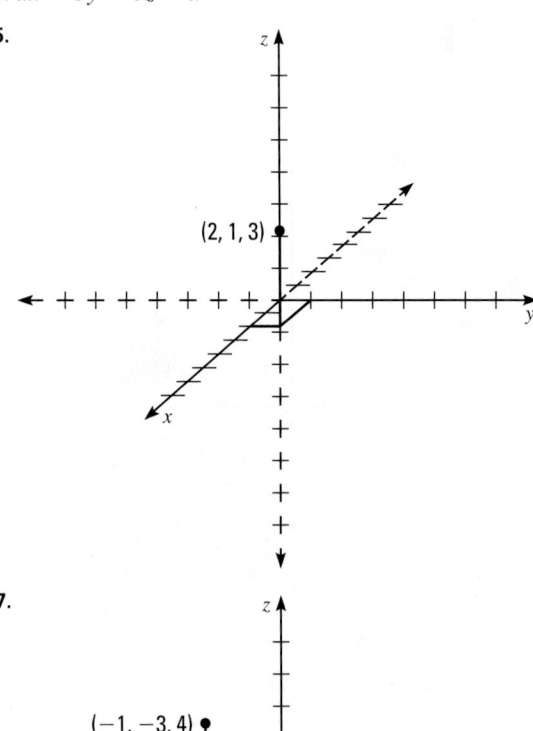

7.

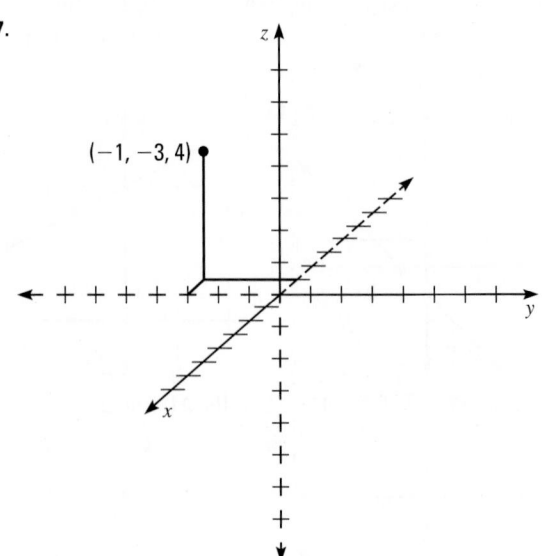

9.

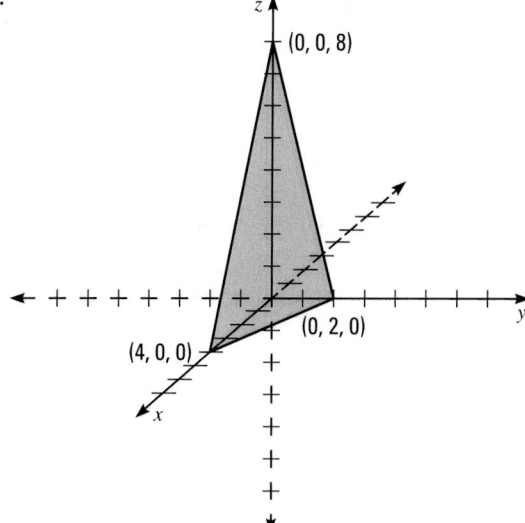

13.

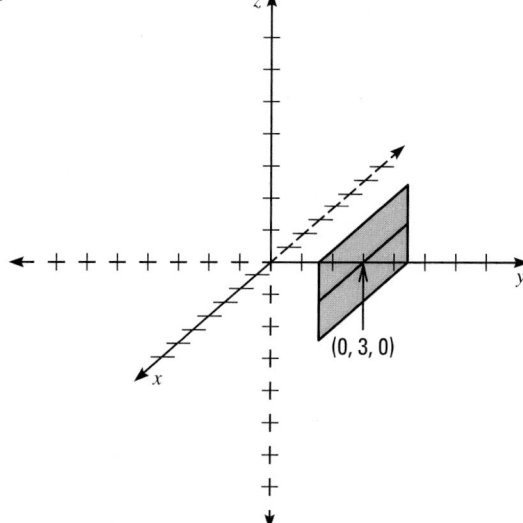

3.4 Practice and Applications (pp. 150–151)

15.

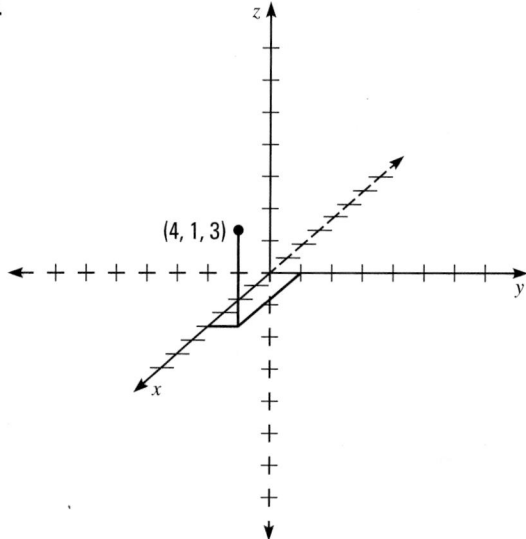

19.

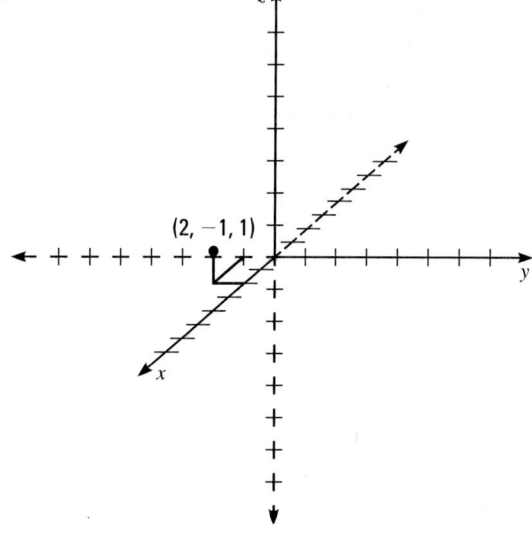

23.

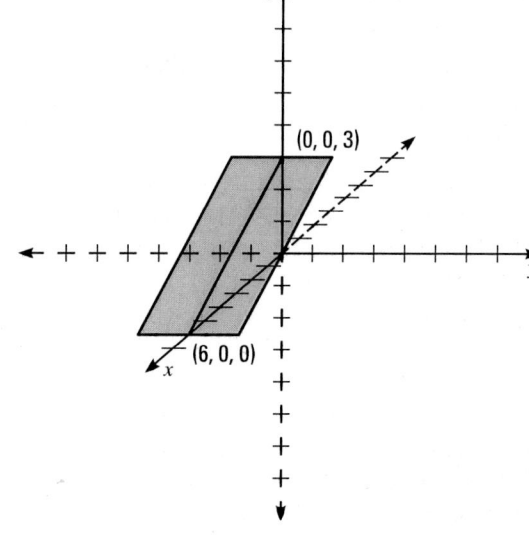

25.

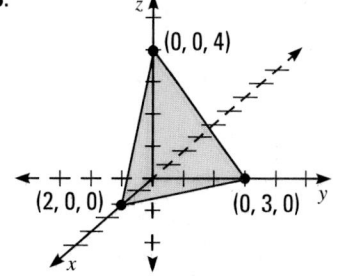

35. $J(0, -2, 2)$, $K(0, 0, 2)$, $L(3, 0, 0)$, $M(3, -2, 0)$ **37.** 12 cubic units **39.** Weekly earnings = Number of cashier hours • Hourly cashier pay + Number of lifeguard hours • Hourly lifeguard pay + Weekly allowance; $T = 6c + 8\ell + 15$ **41.** $T = 0.75b + 0.5s + 30$

43. $C = 10x + 13y + 30$. *Sample answer:*

		y (large shirts)		
		30	50	40
x (medium shirts)	40	$820	$1080	$950
	50	$920	$1180	$1050
	60	$1020	$1280	$1150

3.5 Guided Practice (p. 156)

1. *Sample answer:* $x + 3z = 5$, $y - z = 3$, $x + y + z = 6$
3. no **5.** yes **7.** $(2, -3, 3)$ **9.** $(2, 3, 5)$ **11.** 0

3.5 Practice and Applications (pp. 156–158)

13. no **15.** yes **17.** $(2, 1, -1)$ **19.** $(3, 1, 1)$ **21.** $\left(\frac{2}{3}, 9\frac{1}{3}, 3\frac{2}{3}\right)$
23. infinitely many solutions **25.** $(3, 1, 1)$ **27.** $(5, 10, -2)$
29. $(1, 0, -3)$ **31.** jeans: $20; shorts: $12; shirts: $8
33. $m\angle A = 60°$, $m\angle B = 44°$, $m\angle C = 76°$

Chapter Review (pp. 160–162)

1. Graph both equations on the same coordinate axes. If the lines are parallel, then they do not intersect and the system has no solution. **3.** The graphs are three planes that intersect in exactly one point.

5.
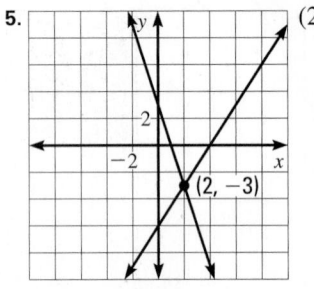
$(2, -3)$

7.
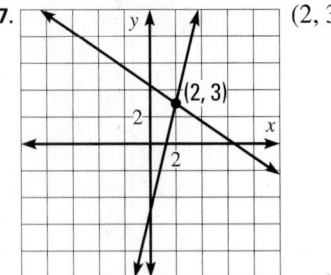
$(2, 3)$

9. $(-3, 1)$ **11.** $(-3, -7)$ **13.** $(4, 8)$ **15.** $(6, -5)$

17.
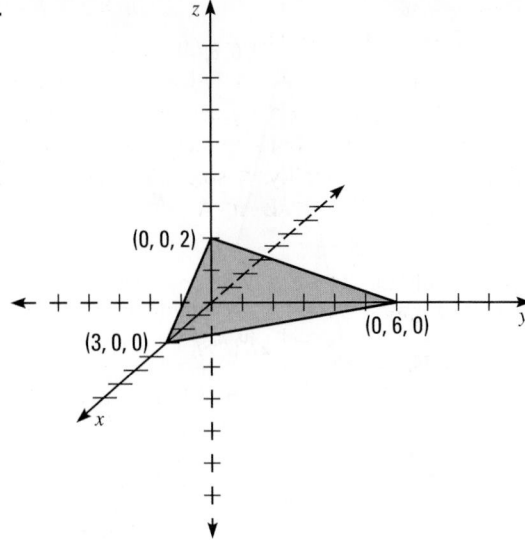

19. $(1, -3, 2)$ **21.** $(3, 2, -4)$

Chapter 4

4.1 Guided Practice (p. 175) **1.** *Sample answer:* The solution of the equation is the number 1, while the solution of the inequality is all real numbers that are less than 1.
7. $x \le 6$

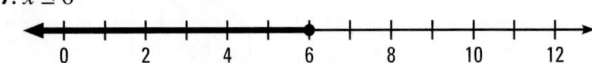

9. $x > 5$

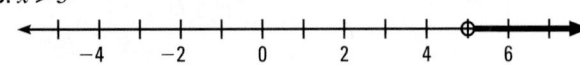

11.

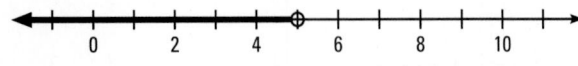

13. a. $6 + s > 8$, $6 + 8 > s$, $s + 8 > 6$ **b.** $2 < s < 14$
4.1 Practice and Applications (pp. 175–177) **15.** not a solution **17.** solution **19.** solution **21.** not a solution **23.** C
25. A **27.** B
31. $x < 5$

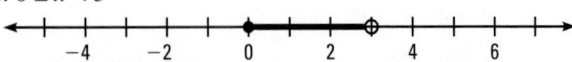

33. $x \ge 2$

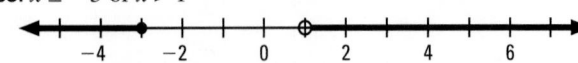

39. $0.16s + 0.2 \le 4$, $s \le 23.75$; 23 sheets or fewer
41. $x < -7$ or $x > 4$ **43.** $158 \le s \le 206$ **47.** $-40 \le t < 5$
51. $0 \le x < 3$

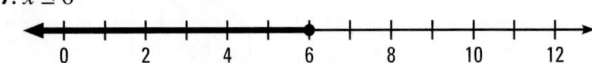

53. $x \le -3$ or $x > 1$

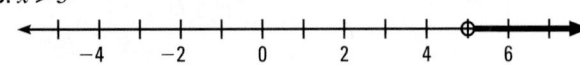

4.1 Technology Activity (p. 178) **1.** $x \le 4$ **3.** $x > 3$
5. $x \le -6$ **7.** $x < 1$ **9.** $x < 6$ **11.** $x < -3$

4.2 Guided Practice (p. 182) **1.** False; for any point on
the line, $x + y$ is equal to 4, not greater than 4. **3.** True;
the symbol $\ge$ means that points on the boundary line
are solutions of the inequality. **5.** solution **7.** solution
9. solution **11.** solid line **13.** B **15.** A

4.2 Practice and Applications (pp. 182–184)
17. solution; solution **19.** not a solution; solution
21. solution; solution **23.** solution; solution

25. 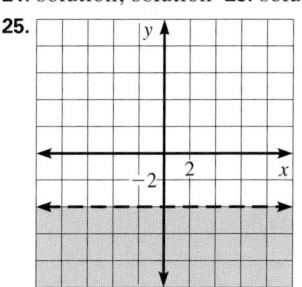 **27.**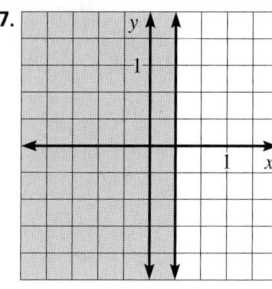

31. The graph consists of all the points below the dashed
horizontal line $y = c$. **33.** A

35. 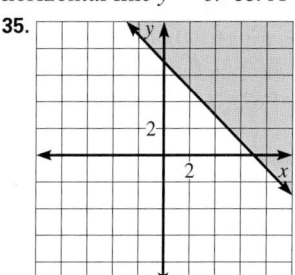 **41.**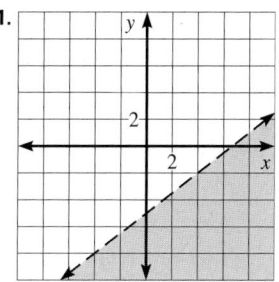

47. $300m + 275y \ge 1300$ **49.** *Sample answer:* 4 cups
of skim milk and 1 cup of yogurt, 2.5 cups of milk and
2 cups of yogurt, 3 cups of milk and 1.5 cups of yogurt

51.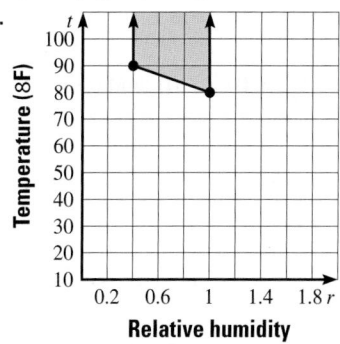

53. $1.4x + 6.2y \le 100$ **55.** *Sample answer:* 50 photographs
and 3 video clips, 40 photographs and 7 video clips,
25 photographs and 10 video clips

4.3 Guided Practice (p. 188) **1.** system **3.** solution
5. not a solution

7.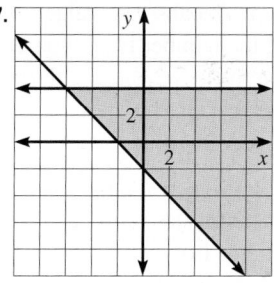

9. $12 \le \ell \le 16, w \ge 2.25$

4.3 Practice and Applications (pp. 188–190) **11.** not
a solution **13.** solution **15.** not a solution **17–21.** Sample
answers are given. **17.** $(2, 1)$ **19.** $(1, 4)$ **21.** $(-3, 10)$ **23.** C
25. D **27.** F

29. 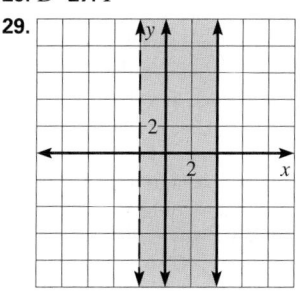 **33.**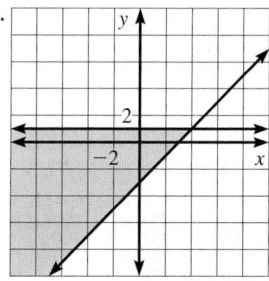

37. 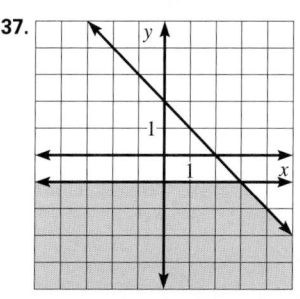 **41.**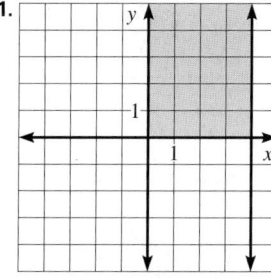

45. 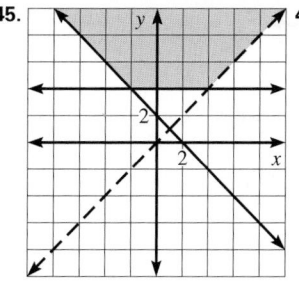 **47.**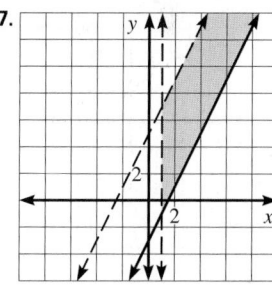

51. $x \ge 5, y \ge 2, 6x + 10y \le 70$ **53.** yes

55.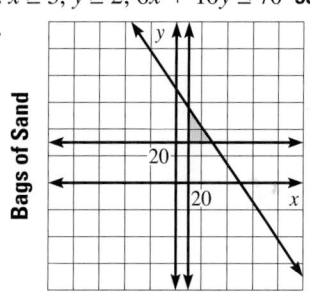

57. $x \ge 0, y \ge 0, y \le 12, 12x + 15y \ge 300$ **59.** yes

4.4 Guided Practice (p. 195)
1. The absolute value of a number x is the distance of the number from 0 on a number line. **3.** $x - 9 = 5$ or $x - 9 = -5$ **5.** $2x + 2 = 4$ or $2x + 2 = -4$ **7.** $x - 3 = 5$ or $x - 3 = -5$ **9.** $|x - 3| = 2$ **11.** $|x - 3| = 5$

4.4 Practice and Applications (pp. 195–197)
13. solution **15.** not a solution **17.** not a solution **19.** $x + 3 = 2$ or $x + 3 = -2$ **21.** $4x - 2 = 1$ or $4x - 2 = -1$ **23.** $3 + 2x = 1$ or $3 + 2x = -1$ **25.** $9, -5$ **27.** $-1, -3$ **29.** -0.5 **31.** $2, -1$ **33.** $-1, 4$ **35.** $2.5, -2$ **37.** $105°F$, $-5°F$ **39.** C **41.** A **43.** $|x - 4| = 4$ **45.** $|x + 1| = 6$ **47.** $|x + 6| = 3$ **49.** $|x - 32.5| = 14.5$ **51.** 149.6 million km; 111.4 million km **53.** true **55.** false

4.5 Guided Practice (p. 201)
3. The graph consists of two rays, one pointing to the left with an open dot at $x = -c + b$ and the other pointing to the right with an open dot at $x = c + b$. **5.** not a solution **7.** solution **9.** $-3 \le x \le 2$

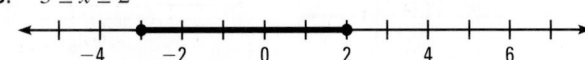

4.5 Practice and Applications (pp. 201–203)
11. $-9 < x - 7 < 9$ **13.** $-10 < x + 8 < 10$ **15.** $2x + 7 \le -11$ or $2x + 7 \ge 11$ **17.** B **19.** A **21.** $-3 < x < 3$

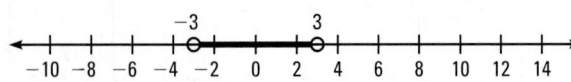

27. $x \le -28$ or $x \ge 28$

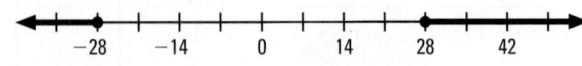

31. never **33.** sometimes **35.** $-4 \le x \le 2$

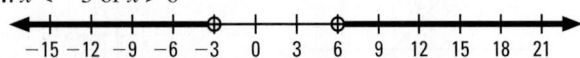

41. $x < -3$ or $x > 6$

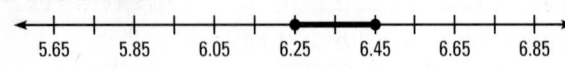

47. $|x - 580| \le 200$ **49.** 97.8°F to 99°F, inclusive **51.** $|x - 6.35| \le 0.1$

52. $6.25 \le x \le 6.45$

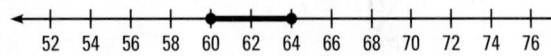

53. $60 \le w \le 64$

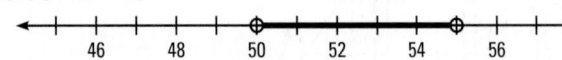

55. $50 < w < 55$

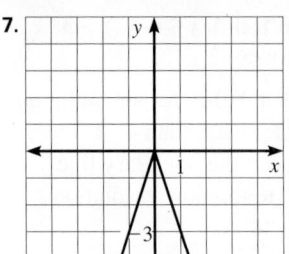

4.6 Guided Practice (p. 207)
1. the common endpoint of the rays that form the absolute value graph **3.** 3 **5.** -4

7.

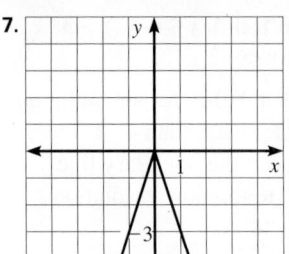

9.

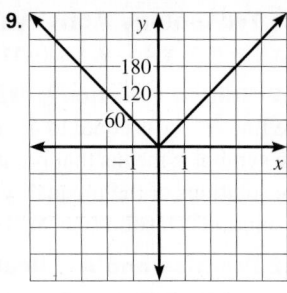

4.6 Practice and Applications (pp. 207–208)
11. -5; -15 **13.** 3; 1 **15.** 4; 0 **17.** 10; 2 **19.** 76°F **21.** up; narrower **23.** up; narrower **25.** down; wider **27.** B **29.** A **31.** $(2, 20)$ **33.** $(-3, -9)$ **35.** $(-6, 9)$

37.

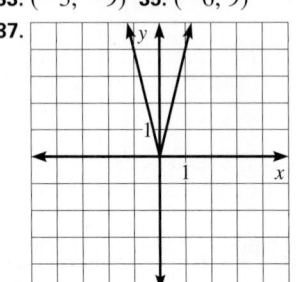

41.

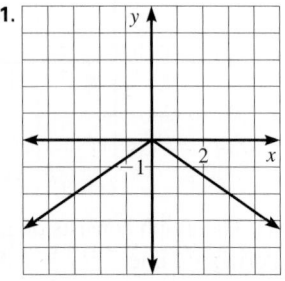

45. Yes. *Sample answer:* The points $(0, 0)$, $(-3, -6)$, and $(3, -6)$ all lie on the graph of the function $y = -2|x|$.
47. $y = 3|t|$ **49.** $y = -2|x|$

4.6 Technology Activity (p. 211)
1.

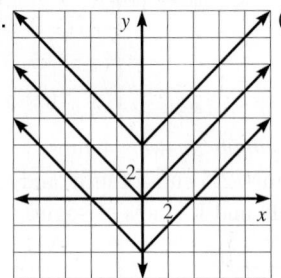

$(0, -4)$, $(0, 0)$, and $(0, 4)$

3.

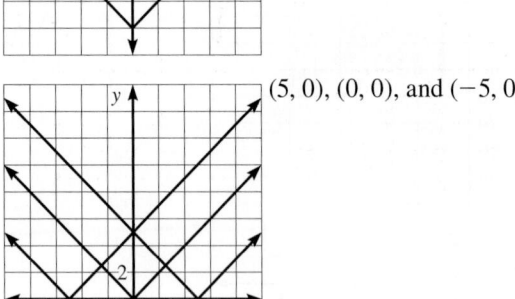

$(5, 0)$, $(0, 0)$, and $(-5, 0)$

5. $(5, 4)$

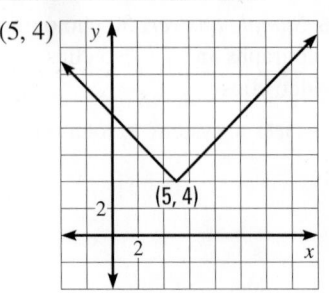

7. $(-5, 4)$

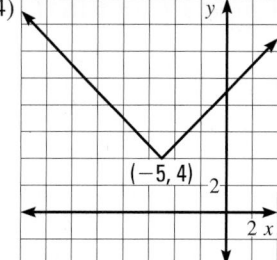

Chapter Review (pp. 212–214) **1.** The graph of a linear inequality in one variable is displayed on a number line, while the graph of a linear inequality in two variables is displayed on a coordinate plane. **3.** $|p - q|$ or $|q - p|$
5. $x > 5$

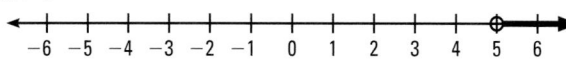

7. $-1 < x \le 4$

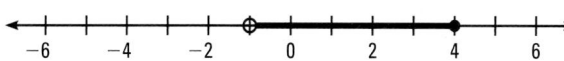

9. $x \le -2$ or $x \ge 2$

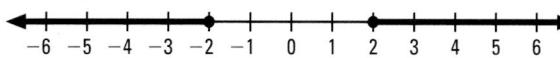

11. 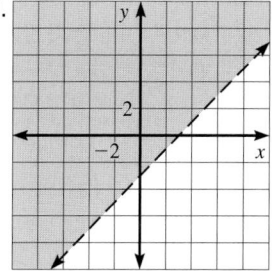 **13.**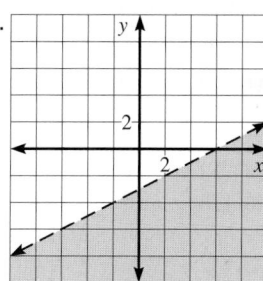

15. 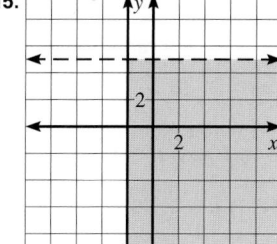 **17.**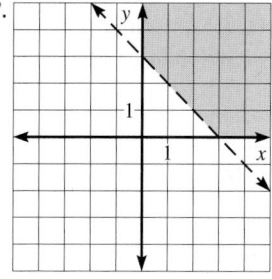

19. 6, 2 **21.** 5, 1
25. $-2 \le x \le 7$

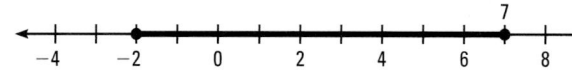

27. $x < -8$ or $x > 2$

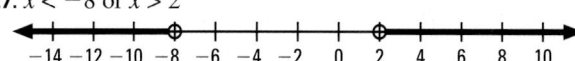

29. 6 **31.** -2

33.

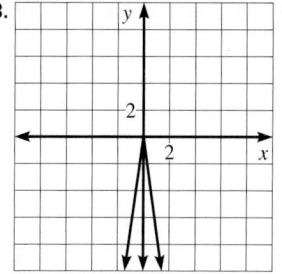

Chapter 5

5.1 Guided Practice (p. 225) **1.** parabola

3. 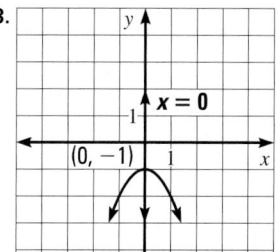 **7.**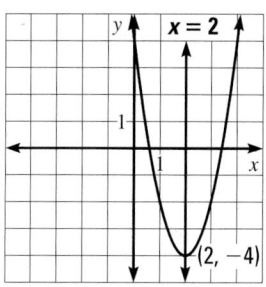

9. In step 2, -4 and -3 should have been multiplied instead of added; $x^2 - 3x - 4x + 12$; $x^2 - 7x + 12$.
11. $y = -3x^2 + 6x + 24$ **13.** $y = -x^2 + 10x - 22$
15. $y = \frac{3}{4}x^2 + \frac{3}{2}x - 6$

5.1 Practice and Applications (pp. 225–227) **17.** 17, 5, 1, 5, 17 **19.** 10, 4, 2, 4, 10 **21.** 1, 3, 0 **23.** (0, 0) **25.** $(-1, 0)$
27. $(-4, 7)$ **29.** In step 2, the formula should use the opposite of b; $x = \frac{-b}{2a} = \frac{-16}{8} = -2$. **31.** C

33. 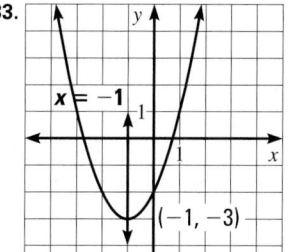 **39.**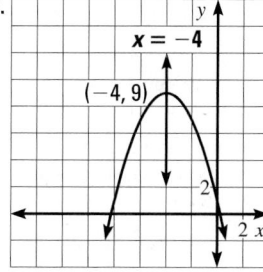

45. $x^2 + 3x + 2$ **47.** $n^2 - 6n + 5$ **49.** $a^2 - 10a + 24$
51. $2x^2 - 11x + 12$ **53.** $10y^2 - 13y - 3$ **55.** $4x^2 + 31x + 21$ **57.** $y = x^2 + x - 6$ **59.** $y = 2x^2 - 6x - 20$
61. $y = -x^2 - 4x + 1$ **63.** $y = 2x^2 - 16x + 31$
65. $y = \frac{2}{3}x^2 - 4x + 12$ **67.** $\left(\frac{13}{2}, \frac{169}{24}\right), x = \frac{13}{2}$

69.

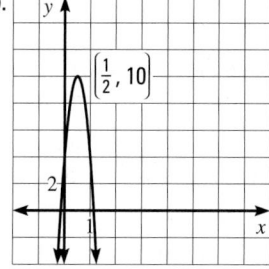

5.2 Guided Practice (p. 231) 1. false 3. intercept form

5.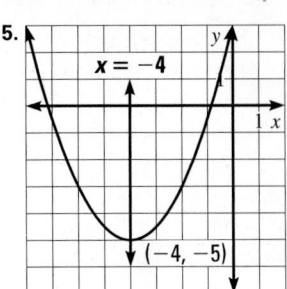

7.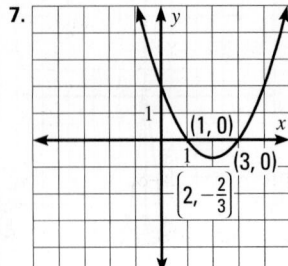

9. 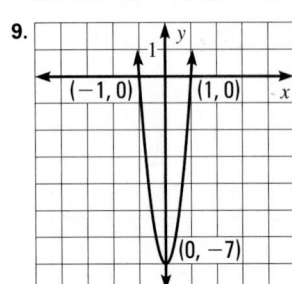   **11.** maximum; −1

5.2 Practice and Applications (pp. 231–233)

13. intercept form; $x = 1$ **15.** vertex form; $x = 1$
17. intercept form; $x = -3$ **19.** standard form; $x = 4$
21. vertex form; $x = 4$ **23.** $(-2, -5)$ **25.** $(2, 4)$ **27.** $(-4, 0)$
29. $-6, 4$ **31.** A **33.** B

35. 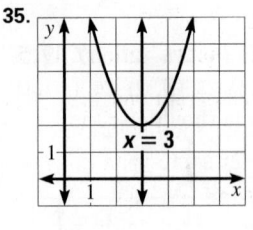   **39.**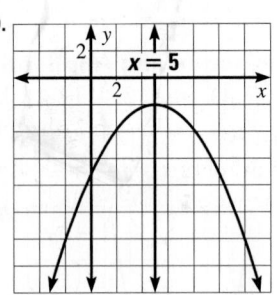

45. 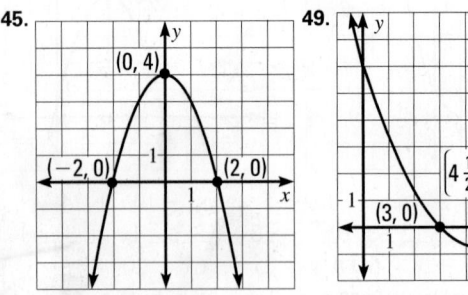   **49.**

53. When you set $-3x$ equal to 0 and solve for x, $x = 0$ not -3. The x-intercepts are 0 and 2.

55. $\left(\dfrac{13}{15}, -\dfrac{49}{90}\right)$;

57. minimum; 2 **59.** maximum; 1 **61.** minimum; −4

---

63. minimum; 7 **65.** $(14, 6)$ **67.** 6 ft **69.** 6 ft **71.** intercept form **73.** 13.754 ft

5.3 Guided Practice (p. 237) 1. trinomial 3. C 5. B
7. $(y + 9)(y + 2)$ **9.** $(x - 2)(x - 7)$ **11.** $(t - 12)(t + 2)$
13. $-7, 4$

5.3 Practice and Applications (pp. 237–238) 15. B
17. B **19.** $(x + 12)(x + 2)$ **21.** $(x + 7)(x + 8)$
23. $(x - 6)(x - 3)$ **25.** $(x + 10)(x - 1)$ **27.** $(x - 8)(x + 2)$
29. $(v + 9)(v - 3)$ **31.** $(y + 12)(y - 8)$ **33.** The sum of the
numbers in the factors should be -2, not 2, so the signs
are reversed; $(x - 4)(x + 2)$. **35.** $5, -1$ **37.** -3 **39.** $-11, 2$
41. $-9, 5$ **43.** $11, -3$ **45.** $-12, 6$ **47.** 4 **49.** 2000 yd^2
51. $(40 + x)(50 + x) = 3000$ **53.** $(30 + x)(20 + x) =$
1064 **55.** $x^2 + 5x + 6$

57.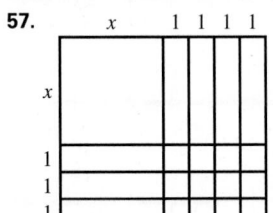

5.4 Guided Practice (p. 244) 3. C 5. B
7. $(3w + 1)(w + 7)$ **9.** $(3x + 4)(2x - 3)$
11. $3(3y + 1)(2y + 3)$ **13.** $-\dfrac{1}{3}, -\dfrac{7}{2}$ **15.** $\dfrac{3}{5}, \dfrac{5}{2}$ **17.** $\dfrac{3}{5}, -\dfrac{1}{4}$

5.4 Practice and Applications (pp. 244–246) 19. A
21. $(5y + 3)(y + 1)$ **23.** $(3x - 1)(x - 5)$
25. $(7h + 3)(h + 1)$ **27.** $3(x + 2)(x + 1)$
29. $5(z + 7)(z - 2)$ **31.** $(3b + 2)(b - 2)$
33. $(4x - 3)(x - 3)$ **35.** $(6t - 5)(3t - 5)$
37. $3(2x + 1)(2x - 3)$ **39.** $4(3r + 2)(r + 3)$
41. $2(3s - 2)(3s - 7)$ **43.** $-6(s - 5)(s - 1)$
45. In the third step, $6x^2 - 7x - 3$ is factored wrong;
$2(2x - 3)(3x + 1)$. **47.** $\dfrac{3}{2}, -7$ **49.** $\dfrac{1}{3}, \dfrac{2}{3}$ **51.** $-\dfrac{9}{2}, 3$ **53.** $\dfrac{3}{7}, -2$
55. The trinomial $16x^2 - 2x - 5$ is not factored
correctly. Step 3 should be $0 = (8x - 5)(2x + 1)$
and the zeros are $\dfrac{5}{8}$ and $-\dfrac{1}{2}$. **57.** $-4, -\dfrac{2}{9}$ **59.** $\dfrac{4}{3}, \dfrac{5}{3}$
61. $-\dfrac{11}{7}, 1$ **63.** $\dfrac{1}{7}, -\dfrac{2}{3}$ **65.** $-\dfrac{7}{2}, -\dfrac{4}{3}$ **67.** $-\dfrac{3}{5}, \dfrac{9}{2}$ **69.** 18
71. 6.25 **73.** 180 **75.** -50 **77.** -27 **79.** -4.5 **81.** 3
83. 2 ft **85.** 0.5 ft **87.** 100, -60 **89.** $25,600$ **91.** $5.75;
$1983.75

5.4 Technology Activity (p. 248) 1. $-1.53, 1.53$
3. $-2.27, 1.77$ **5.** $-0.22, 2.22$ **7.** -5

5.5 Guided Practice (p. 252) 1. Difference of two
squares pattern and perfect square trinomial pattern.
Sample answer: $x^2 - 9 = (x + 3)(x - 3)$ and $x^2 +$
$10x + 25 = (x + 5)^2$ **3.** $(x + 4)(x - 4)$ **5.** $(z + 7)(z - 7)$
7. $(x + 11)^2$ **9.** $(9x - 1)^2$ **11.** $3(s + 5)(s - 5)$ **13.** $11, -11$
15. 7 **17.** 3

5.5 Practice and Applications (pp. 252–254)

19. $(x + 2)(x - 2)$ **21.** $(x + 4)^2$ **23.** $(m + 6)^2$
25. $(2k + 7)(2k - 7)$ **27.** $(w - 15)^2$ **29.** $(x + 15)(x - 15)$
31. $\left(\frac{1}{3}x - 8\right)\left(\frac{1}{3}x + 8\right)$ **33.** $(4x - 1)^2$ **35.** $(7x - 9)(7x + 9)$
37. In step 2, the sign of $12x$ should be negative;
$-6(4x^2 - 12x + 9)$; $-6(2x - 3)^2$. **39.** $2(n + 8)(n - 8)$
41. $5(r + 5)^2$ **43.** $2(4x - 3)^2$ **45.** $11(3z + 2)(3z - 2)$
49. $11(y + 2)(y - 2)$ **51.** $-\frac{1}{3}$ **53.** $-6, 6$ **55.** $-\frac{7}{3}$ **57.** $\frac{3}{2}$
59. $5, -5$ **61.** $9, -9$ **63.** $-\frac{5}{2}$ **65.** 3 **67.** 0.95 in.
69. $\ell = 16 - w$ **71.** $0, 16$ **73.** 64 ft^2 **75.** 12 ft, 9 ft
77. 24 m, 9 m

5.6 Guided Practice (p. 258)

1. radicand **3.** 6 **5.** $3\sqrt{7}$
7. $\frac{3}{4}$ **9.** $\frac{2\sqrt{5}}{5}$ **11.** The square root of 9 is 3, not 9; $3\sqrt{3}$.
13. $6, -6$ **15.** $2\sqrt{3}, -2\sqrt{3}$ **17.** $3\sqrt{2}, -3\sqrt{2}$

5.6 Practice and Applications (pp. 258–259)

19. $4\sqrt{2}$
21. $5\sqrt{3}$ **23.** $3\sqrt{11}$ **25.** 10 **27.** 12 **29.** $50\sqrt{3}$ **31.** $\frac{3}{8}$ **33.** $\frac{6}{5}$
35. $\frac{\sqrt{13}}{5}$ **37.** $\frac{\sqrt{7}}{6}$ **39.** $\frac{7\sqrt{13}}{13}$ **41.** $\frac{\sqrt{42}}{6}$ **43.** $\frac{\sqrt{91}}{14}$ **45.** $\frac{2\sqrt{42}}{21}$
47. yes **49.** no **51.** $4, -4$ **53.** $3\sqrt{6}, -3\sqrt{6}$ **55.** $\sqrt{5}, -\sqrt{5}$
57. $2\sqrt{7}, -2\sqrt{7}$ **59.** $8, 2$ **61.** $7, 1$ **63.** $7 - 3\sqrt{2}, 7 + 3\sqrt{2}$
65. $4 + \frac{2\sqrt{2}}{3}, 4 - \frac{2\sqrt{2}}{3}$ **67.** $-6 + 2\sqrt{14}, -6 - 2\sqrt{14}$
69. $h = -16t^2 + 220$ **71.** $h = -16t^2 + 80$; $\sqrt{5} \approx 2.24$ sec
73. 3.23 sec

5.7 Guided Practice (p. 264)

1. The real part is 4 and the imaginary part is $-7i$. **3.** $i\sqrt{14}, -i\sqrt{14}$
5. $2i\sqrt{6}, -2i\sqrt{6}$ **7.** $2i\sqrt{3}, -2i\sqrt{3}$ **9.** $7 + 7i$ **11.** $5 - 14i$
13. $-2 + 11i$

5.7 Practice and Applications (pp. 264–265)

15. $6i, -6i$ **17.** $i\sqrt{13}, -i\sqrt{13}$ **19.** $3i\sqrt{2}, -3i\sqrt{2}$
21. $\sqrt{10}, -\sqrt{10}$ **23.** $i\sqrt{14}, -i\sqrt{14}$ **25.** $i\sqrt{22}, -i\sqrt{22}$
27. $7 + 7i$ **29.** $-2 - 5i$ **31.** $8 - 5i$ **33.** $-2 + 3i$ **35.** $2 + 7i$
37. $-3 + i$ **39.** $30i$ **41.** 20 **43.** $14 + 6i$ **45.** $27 + 11i$
47. $28 - 4i$ **49.** 85 **51.** $-4i$ **53.** $\frac{23}{17} + \frac{10}{17}i$ **55.** $-\frac{1}{5} + \frac{11}{15}i$
57. $-\frac{5}{3} + \frac{2}{3}i$ **59.** always **61.** sometimes **63.** sometimes

5.8 Guided Practice (p. 271)

3. $9, 1$ **5.** $8, -2$ **7.** $-8, -6$
9. $16; (x + 4)^2$ **11.** $49; (v - 7)^2$ **13.** $\frac{49}{4}; \left(x - \frac{7}{2}\right)^2$
15. $y = (x - 2)^2 + 3; (2, 3)$ **17.** $y = (x + 6)^2 - 11;$
$(-6, -11)$ **19.** $y = (x + 5)^2 + 5; (-5, 5)$

5.8 Practice and Applications (pp. 271–272)

21. $9, -1$
23. $22, 2$ **25.** $9 \pm \sqrt{5}$ **27.** $-\frac{1}{2} \pm \frac{5\sqrt{3}}{2}$ **29.** $25; (x + 5)^2$
31. $100; (x + 10)^2$ **33.** $9; (x - 3)^2$ **35.** $\frac{25}{4}; \left(z - \frac{5}{2}\right)^2$
37. $\frac{169}{4}; \left(w + \frac{13}{2}\right)^2$ **39.** $-3 \pm \sqrt{6}$ **41.** $-3 \pm \sqrt{15}$
43. $-\frac{9}{2} \pm \frac{\sqrt{85}}{2}$ **45.** $-9 \pm i\sqrt{19}$ **47.** $-\frac{11}{2} \pm \frac{\sqrt{145}}{2}$

49. $4 \pm \sqrt{21}$ **51.** $2 \pm i\sqrt{5}$ **53.** $\frac{3}{2} \pm \frac{\sqrt{33}}{2}$ **55.** $-6, 1$ **57.** In step 5, the negative square root of 13 was left out;
$(x + 3)^2 = 13$ or $(x + 3)^2 = -13; x = -3 + \sqrt{13} \approx 0.61$
or $x = -3 - \sqrt{13} \approx -6.61$. **59.** $y = (x + 5)^2 + 3; (-5, 3)$
61. $y = (x - 3)^2 - 11; (3, -11)$ **63.** $y = (x + 4)^2 - 12;$
$(-4, -12)$ **65.** $y = \left(x + \frac{3}{2}\right)^2 - \frac{13}{4}; \left(-\frac{3}{2}, -\frac{13}{4}\right)$
67. $-3 + \sqrt{57} \approx 4.55$ **69.** *Sample answer:* width x, length
$40 - 2x; 40x - 2x^2 = 80$ **71.** $120x - 2x^2 = 1512$

5.9 Guided Practice (p. 278)

1. discriminant **3.** $5, 2$
5. $-2 \pm i\sqrt{5}$ **7.** $\frac{3 + \sqrt{7}}{2} \approx 2.82, \frac{3 - \sqrt{7}}{2} \approx 0.18$ **9.** $0,$
1 real solution **11.** -71, 2 imaginary solutions **13.** $0,$
1 real solution **15.** In step 2, $4bc$ was used rather than
$4ac; (-8)^2 - 4(1)(16) = 0$.

5.9 Practice and Applications (pp. 278–280)

17. $4x^2 + x - 3 = 0; 4, 1, -3$ **19.** $3x^2 - 4x + 1 =$
$0; 3, -4, 1$ **21.** $2x^2 - 3x + 7 = 0; 2, -3, 7$ **23.** $3x^2 +$
$x = 0; 3, 1, 0$ **25.** $\frac{1 \pm i\sqrt{47}}{2}$ **27.** $-1 \pm \frac{\sqrt{14}}{2}$ **29.** $\frac{-7 \pm \sqrt{29}}{10}$
31. $-1 \pm i\sqrt{5}$ **33.** $\frac{1 \pm \sqrt{2}}{2}$ **35.** $\frac{-9 \pm \sqrt{33}}{4}$ **37.** $-5 \pm \sqrt{14}$
39. $\frac{-3 \pm \sqrt{57}}{4}$ **41.** $\frac{7 \pm i\sqrt{35}}{6}$ **43.** $\frac{11 \pm i\sqrt{39}}{4}$ **45.** $\frac{5 \pm 3\sqrt{5}}{8}$
47. $-8 \pm i$ **49.** Inside the square root in step 3, the
subtraction of a negative should be addition;
$x = \frac{3 \pm \sqrt{9 + 8}}{2} = \frac{3 \pm \sqrt{17}}{2}$. **51.** 9, 2 real solutions **53.** $0,$
1 real solution **55.** -24, 2 imaginary solutions **57.** -87, 2
imaginary solutions **59.** -35, 2 imaginary solutions **61.** $0,$
1 real solution **63.** Launched model; there is an initial
velocity. **65.** 1.56 sec **67.** 0.21 sec **69.** 5.66 sec
71. 2.57 sec **73.** $h = -16t^2 + 75$

Extension (p. 284)

1. $y = (x - 3)^2 + 2$
3. $y = \frac{1}{2}(x + 1)^2 - 3$ **5.** $y = \frac{1}{3}(x + 4)^2 + 6$
7. $y = -\frac{1}{2}(x + 1)(x - 4)$ **9.** $y = \frac{1}{2}(x + 3)(x - 3)$
11. $y = \frac{2}{3}(x + 2)(x - 2)$ **13.** $y = 2.44x^2 - 87.36x + 853.34$

Chapter Review (pp. 285–288)

1. vertex

5.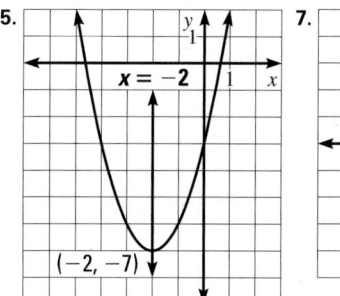

7.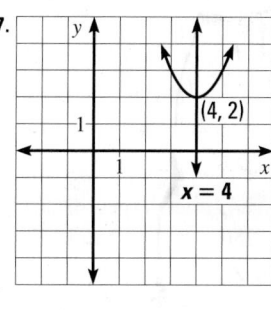

9.

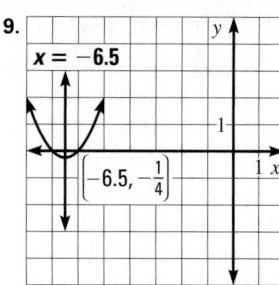

$x = -6.5$

$\left(-6.5, -\dfrac{1}{4}\right)$

11. $-6, 5$ **13.** $-1, \dfrac{5}{2}$ **15.** $-\dfrac{5}{7}, \dfrac{3}{4}$ **17.** $(2x + 7)(2x - 7)$

19. $(x - 10)^2$ **21.** $9, -9$ **23.** $\sqrt{66}, -\sqrt{66}$ **25.** $-3 + i$

27. $-22 - 34i$ **29.** $\dfrac{7}{5} - \dfrac{16}{5}i$ **31.** $3 \pm \sqrt{11}$ **33.** $10, 2$

35. $\dfrac{1 \pm i\sqrt{14}}{5}$ **37.** $220, 2$ real solutions

Chapter 6

6.1 Guided Practice (p. 299) **1.** product of powers **3.** 81

5. $\dfrac{16}{9}$ **7.** x **9.** x^5 **11.** 25 times greater

6.1 Practice and Applications (pp. 299–301) **13.** 64;

power of a power **15.** 729; product of powers **17.** $\dfrac{1}{625}$;

product of powers, negative exponent **19.** $\dfrac{8}{125}$; power of

a quotient **21.** 8; quotient of powers **23.** $\dfrac{1}{81}$; product of

powers, negative exponent **25.** $\dfrac{1}{9x^6}$; power of a product,

power of a power, negative exponent **27.** $\dfrac{1}{x^7}$; quotient

of powers, negative exponent **29.** $\dfrac{y^{10}}{x^{20}}$; power of a power,

negative exponent **31.** $\dfrac{y^7}{x^3}$; quotient of powers, negative

exponent **33.** $\dfrac{x^{20}y^{30}}{243}$; power of a power, negative exponent

35. $4x^5$; quotient of powers, zero exponent

37. 6.873×10^{-13} **39.** about 2.3×10^{-12} **41.** $4\pi x^3$

43.

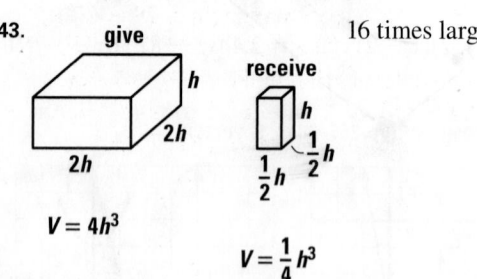

give

receive

16 times larger

$2h$ h $2h$

h $\dfrac{1}{2}h$ $\dfrac{1}{2}h$

$V = 4h^3$

$V = \dfrac{1}{4}h^3$

45. 3.4 times larger **47.** 7.78×10 **49.** 8.28×10

51. 250 grains of sand

6.2 Guided Practice (p. 305) **1.** standard form **3.** 3, -1;

$f(x)$ approaches $+\infty$ as x approaches $-\infty$ and

$f(x)$ approaches $-\infty$ as x approaches $+\infty$. **5.** 4, 1;

$f(x)$ approaches $+\infty$ as x approaches $+\infty$ or $-\infty$.

6.2 Practice and Applications (pp. 305–307) **13.** D

15. B **17.** $f(x) = -x^3 + 8$; 3, cubic, -1 **19.** $f(x) = -x^4 + x^2 + 4$; 4, quartic, -1 **21.** $f(x) = -6x^4 + x^3 - 6x$; 4,

quartic, -6 **23.** -15 **25.** 1 **27.** 6 **29.** 3, 1; $f(x)$ approaches

$-\infty$ as x approaches $-\infty$ and $f(x)$ approaches $+\infty$ as

x approaches $+\infty$. **31.** 1, 3; $f(x)$ approaches $-\infty$ as x

approaches $-\infty$ and $f(x)$ approaches $+\infty$ as x approaches

$+\infty$. **33.** 2, -3; $f(x)$ approaches $-\infty$ as x approaches $+\infty$

or $-\infty$. **35.** 5, 1; $f(x)$ approaches $-\infty$ as x approaches $-\infty$

and $f(x)$ approaches $+\infty$ as x approaches $+\infty$. **37.** 3, 7;

$f(x)$ approaches $-\infty$ as x approaches $-\infty$ and $f(x)$

approaches $+\infty$ as x approaches $+\infty$. **39.** A

41.

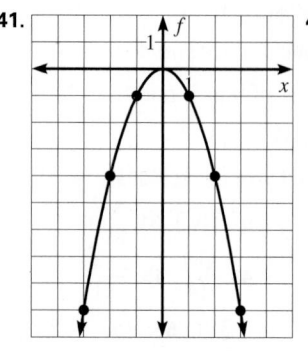

45.

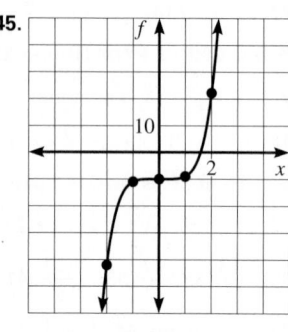

49. A

51.

Salary

46,000
45,000
44,000
43,000
42,000
41,000
40,000
39,000
38,000
37,000
0

0 1 2 3 4 5 6 7 8 9 10 t

Years (since 1990)

6.2 Technology Activity (p. 309) **1.** $f(x)$ approaches

$+\infty$ as x approaches $-\infty$ and $f(x)$ approaches $-\infty$ as x

approaches $+\infty$. **3–7.** Sample answers are given.

3. $X\mathrm{min} = -10$, $X\mathrm{max} = 10$, $X\mathrm{scl} = 1$, $Y\mathrm{min} = -10$,

$Y\mathrm{max} = 30$, $Y\mathrm{scl} = 1$ **5.** $X\mathrm{min} = -10$, $X\mathrm{max} = 10$,

$X\mathrm{scl} = 1$, $Y\mathrm{min} = -20$, $Y\mathrm{max} = 10$, $Y\mathrm{scl} = 1$

7. $X\mathrm{min} = -10$, $X\mathrm{max} = 10$, $X\mathrm{scl} = 1$, $Y\mathrm{min} = -100$,

$Y\mathrm{max} = 100$, $Y\mathrm{scl} = 10$

6.3 Guided Practice (p. 312) **1.** coefficients **3.** $2x^2 - x$

5. $x^3 - 3x + 2$ **7.** $-x^5 + 2x^3 - 4x^2 - 8$ **9.** $3x^2 - 3$

11. $22x^2 + 12x$

6.3 Practice and Applications (pp. 312–313) **13.** $6x^2$

and x^2, $11xy$ and $-3xy$, -1 and -4 **15.** $-6x$ and $-3x$, 2

and -8 **17.** $2x^5 + x^4 + x - 3$ **19.** $8x^2 + 9x - 25$

21. $3x^2y + xy^2 - 5x + 9$ **23.** $3x - 2$ **25.** $-7x + 14$

27. $x^2 + xy - x - y$ **29.** $x^3 + 4x^2 + 2x - 18$

31. $x^6 - 2x^4 + x^2$ **33.** $-x^2 + x - 1$ **35.** $12\pi x^2 + 20\pi x$

37. a. $2x^2 + 12x$ b. $8x + 12$ 39. about 53 nesting pairs
41. About 1651; there were 1,651,000 more trucks sold than cars in 2003.

6.4 Guided Practice (p. 318) 1. $x + 2, x + 4, -11$
3. $5x^2 - 3x$ 5. $4x^3 - 11x^2 + 7x - 2$ 7. $x^2 - 121y^2$
9. $x - 9 + \dfrac{30}{x+4}$ 11. $8x^2 + 2x - 3$

6.4 Practice and Applications (pp. 318–320)
13. $3x^2 + 5x$ 15. $-x^3 + 10x^2 + 12x + 1$ 17. $2x^3 - 11x^2 - 3x + 4$ 19. $12x^2 - 2x$ 21. $x^3 + 5x^2 + 5x - 2$
23. $x^3 + 3x^2 - x + 12$ 25. $12x^4 - 8x^3 - 3x^2 + 2x$
27. $x^3 + 11x^2 + 36x + 36$ 29. $x^3 + 2x^2 - 36x - 72$
31. $x^2 + 12x + 36$ 33. $9x^2 + 24x + 16$ 35. $x^3 + 30x^2 + 300x + 1000$ 37. $x^3 + 12x^2 + 48x + 64$ 39. $27x^3 + 135x^2 + 225x + 125$ 41. $x^2 - 9$ 43. $4x^2 - 16$ 45. $36x^2 - 64$ 47. $y^2 - 6y + 9$ 49. $27x^3 - 108x^2 + 144x - 64$
51. $16x^2 - 8xy + y^2$ 53. sometimes 55. $x^3 + 9x^2 + 23x + 15$ 57. $-x^3 + x^2 + 28x - 10$ 59. $x^3 + 24x^2 + 192x + 512$ 61. $64x^3 - 144x^2 + 108x - 27$ 63. $4x^2 - 25y^2$ 65. $36x^2 + 10x - 200$ 69. 300 ft² 71. 1500 ft³
73. $15\frac{1}{3}$ 75. $359\frac{1}{7}$ 77. $179\frac{19}{26}$ 79. $4x - 9 + \dfrac{17}{x+2}$
81. $x - 3 + \dfrac{-33}{3x+11}$ 83. $-x^2 + 11x + 5$ 85. $2x + 4$

6.5 Guided Practice (p. 326) 3. $(x-2)(x^2+2x+4)$
5. $x(x+8)(x-1)$ 7. $(x+5)(x-7)$ 9. $2, 5, -5$
11. $-1, 1, 3$ 13. The factor x needs to be considered when solving the equation; $x = -3, x = 0,$ and $x = 2.$

6.5 Practice and Applications (pp. 326–328) 15. 3
17. $7x$ 19. $3x$ 21. C 23. D 25. $(x-1)(x^2+x+1)$
27. $(3x+1)(9x^2-3x+1)$ 29. $(2x+3)(4x^2-6x+9)$
31. $(x-y)(x^2+xy+y^2)$ 33. $(x-2)(x+3)$
35. $(x-1)(x^2+1)$ 37. $(x-4)(2x^2+1)$ 39. $-1, 0, 7$
41. $\pm\frac{1}{2}, 0$ 43. $\pm\sqrt{3}, 6$ 45. B 47. A 49. $-2.41, -1, 0.41$
51. -3.15 53. 3 in., 3 in., 58 in. 55. a. $9x^3 - 27x^2 + 14x = 42$ b. 3; 3 in., 7 in., 2 in.

6.6 Guided Practice (p. 332) 1. quadratic form 3. x^2
5. $2x$ 7. $(2x^2 - 3)(2x^2 + 3)$ 9. $\pm 2\sqrt{3}, \pm 2i\sqrt{3}$
11. $0, \pm 2i, \pm i$

6.6 Practice and Applications (pp. 332–333) 13. x^2
15. $4x$ 17. x^2 19. $2x^2$ 21. C 23. B 25. E
27. $(x^2 - 7)(x^2 + 7)$ 29. $(x-1)(x+1)(x^2-3)$
31. $3x(x-2)(x+2)(x^2+4)$ 35. $4x(x^2+5)(x^2-2)$
37. $\pm\sqrt{3}, \pm\sqrt{2}$ 39. $\pm\dfrac{i\sqrt{10}}{2}, \pm\dfrac{\sqrt{10}}{2}$ 41. $\pm 2, \pm i\sqrt{7}$
43. $-\frac{1}{2}, 0, 8$ 45. C 47. B 49. $-1.95, 1.95$
51. $-1.62, -0.73, 0.62, 2.73$ 53. $-1.71, 0.13, 1.65$ 55. 1.15

6.7 Guided Practice (p. 338) 7. 3; maximum 9. 3; maximum 11. local maximum (2.67, 6.48), local minimum (0, -3) 13. local maximum (0.16, -0.92), local minimum (-1, -3) and (1.59, -4.62)

6.7 Practice and Applications (pp. 338–339) 15. 2;

exact 17. 3; maximum 19. 3; maximum 21. 3; maximum
23. B 25. C 27. $(-1, 0), (0.5, 5), (2, 0)$; local minimum, local maximum, local minimum; $-1, 2; 4$ 29. $-3, 1,$ local maximum $(-1, 4)$, local minimum $(1, 0)$ 31. $-1, 1,$ local maximum $(0, 1)$ 33. $-2, -1, 0, 1, 2,$ local maximum $(-0.54, 1.42), (1.64, 3.63)$, local minimum $(-1.64, -3.63), (0.54, -1.42)$ 35. *Sample answer:* The number of days per month with precipitation of 0.01 inch or more increases through February, March, and April. The peak number of days is reached in April. After that the number of days per month with precipitation of 0.01 inch or more begins to decrease. 37. local maximum (3.28, 3.35), local minimum (0.85, 1.48)

Chapter Review (pp. 341–344) 5. 32; product of powers 7. 262,144; quotient of powers, power of a power 9. 64; power of a product, power of a power, product of powers, zero exponent 11. $64x^{11}$; power of a product, power of a power, product of powers 13. not a polynomial function

15. 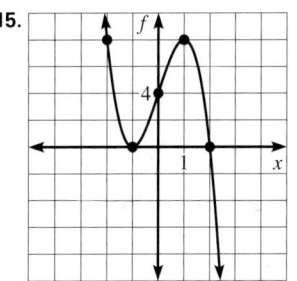 17.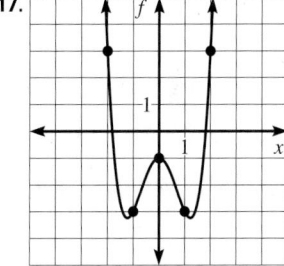

19. $4x^2 + 7x - 4$ 21. $x^4 - 3x^3 - x^2 + 4x - 5$ 23. $-x^3 + x^2 + 7x$ 25. $x^4 + 3x^3 - 3x^2 + 6x - 10$ 27. $16x^2 - 9$
29. $8x^3 + 36x^2 + 54x + 27$ 31. $x^2 + 3x - 6 + \dfrac{7}{x+2}$
33. $(x-5)(x^2+5x+25)$ 35. $(3x+2)(9x^2-6x+4)$
37. $2x(x-5)(x+4)$ 39. $(x-4)(x^2-7)$
41. $(x+5)(x-3)(x+3)$ 43. $-5, -1, 1$
45. $5x^2(x-2)(x^2+2x+4)$ 47. $(3x-2)(3x+2)(9x^2+4)$
49. $5x^2(x+1)(x-1)(x^2-5)$ 51. $0, \pm\sqrt{2}, \pm\sqrt{7}$ 53. $0, \pm\sqrt{2}, \pm i\sqrt{2}$ 55. -2.86; local maximum (1.29, -4.70), local minimum (-1.29, -13.30) 57. $-2.11, 2.11$; local maximum (0, -2), local minimum (-1.41, -6), (1.41, -6) 59. $-2.24, -1, 0, 1, 2.24$; local maximum (-0.55, 1.80), (1.82, 7.10), local minimum (-1.82, 7.10), (0.55, -1.80)

Chapter 7

7.1 Guided Practice (p. 356) 1. $\dfrac{1}{\sqrt[n]{a^m}}$; n 3. 0 5. -2 7. 6
9. 10 11. 3 13. B 15. A 17. 25 19. $\dfrac{1}{8}$

7.1 Practice and Applications (pp. 356–358) 21. 2
23. 11 25. -3 27. ± 1 29. -2 31. ± 4 33. -6 35. 0 37. 5
39. -3 41. -2 43. -4 45. 14 47. 4 49. 6 51. 5 53. $3^{2/5}$
55. $9^{4/3}$ 57. $13^{-1/2}$ 59. $10^{-5/6}$ 61. $q^{-2/3}$ 63. $q^{-5/2}$
65. $(\sqrt[3]{16})^2$ 67. $(\sqrt[4]{20})^3$ 69. $\dfrac{1}{(\sqrt[9]{15})^2}$ 71. $\dfrac{1}{(\sqrt[8]{18})^3}$ 73. $(\sqrt[4]{b})^5$

75. $\dfrac{1}{(\sqrt[4]{m})^3}$ **77.** 100,000 **79.** 7776 **81.** $\dfrac{1}{16}$ **83.** $\dfrac{1}{216}$

85. 7.0 mm **87.** 1710 rotations per min

7.2 Guided Practice (p. 362) **3.** 5 **5.** 4 **7.** $2\sqrt[3]{5}$ **9.** $\dfrac{\sqrt[3]{3}}{3}$
11. 8 **13.** $\dfrac{1}{25}$ **15.** $5x^3$ **17.** $6xy^3$ **19.** $4\sqrt[5]{t}$

7.2 Practice and Applications (pp. 362–364) **21.** 3
23. −5 **25.** $\sqrt[3]{14}$ **27.** 5 **29.** $3\sqrt[4]{2}$ **31.** $5\sqrt[4]{3}$ **33.** $\sqrt[3]{6}$
35. $\dfrac{2\sqrt[3]{63}}{3}$ **37.** $7^{1/3}$ **39.** 4 **41.** $5^{2/3}$ **43.** $\dfrac{25}{9}$ **45.** $-\sqrt[4]{2}$
47. $-5\left(5^{1/4}\right)$ **49.** $-2\left(2^{1/2}\right)$ **51.** $4a^4$ **53.** $2xy^2$
57. $\dfrac{r^{9/5}}{8q^6}$ **61.** $216c^9d^{18}$ **63.** $5gh$ **65.** ab^2c **67.** $4\sqrt{st}$
69. $9xy^3$ **71.** $-4p^2q^{2/3}$ **73.** $7g^{1/3}h^{2/3}$ **75.** 31,234 days
77. 0.45 mm

7.3 Guided Practice (p. 368) **3.** 125 **5.** 33 **7.** 1 **9.** 81
11. 20 **13.** *Sample answer:* In step 2, the student should
have taken all of both sides to the $\dfrac{2}{3}$ power; $\left(8(x^{3/2})\right)^{2/3} =$
$1000^{2/3}$, $4x = 100$, $x = 25$.

7.3 Practice and Applications (pp. 368–370) **15.** yes
17. yes **19.** 64 **21.** 32 **23.** 16 **25.** 30 **27.** 5 **29.** No real
solution because $x = -10$ is not in the domain. **31.** −13
33. $\dfrac{1}{2}$ **37.** 25 **39.** 25 **41.** 5 **43.** 3, 8 **45.** 8 **47.** 4 **49.** −21
51. $\dfrac{9}{2}$ **53.** 9 **55.** 98.1 ft **57.** snowboarder: 5.0 ft, kangaroo:
2.6 ft **59.** 400 units

7.3 Technology Activity (p. 372) **1.** 1 **3.** 4 **5.** 0.67
7. not a solution

7.4 Guided Practice (p. 376) **1.** $x \geq 0$ **3.** $3x + 3$, all real
numbers **5.** $2x^2 + 6x$, all real numbers **7.** $-x + 3$, all real
numbers **9.** $x^2 + 3x$ **11.** $x + 2$ **13.** Parentheses should be
used around all of $4x$; $(4x)^2 - 3 = 16x^2 - 3$.

7.4 Practice and Applications (pp. 376–378) **15.** $3x^2 +$
$x - 2$, all real numbers **17.** $2x^2 + 2$, all real numbers
19. $-x^2 - x + 4$, all real numbers **21.** $12x^5$, all real
numbers **23.** $9x^6$, all real numbers **25.** $\dfrac{3x}{4}$, $x \neq 0$
27. $4x^2 - 48x + 144$, all real numbers **29.** $\dfrac{1}{x^2 + 5}$, all real
numbers **31.** x^4, all real numbers **33.** 13 **35.** 6 **37.** 4
39. 98 **41.** $x^3 - x^2 - x + 7$; all real numbers **43.** $\dfrac{2x^4 - 4}{x}$,
$x \neq 0$ **45.** $2x^2 - 4$; all real numbers **47.** $25x + 40$; all
real numbers **49.** $f(g(x)) = 0.90x - 15$; this represents
taking the 10% discount off the original price and then
subtracting an additional \$15. **51.** $f(g(85)) = \$61.50$ and
$g(f(85)) = \$63$ **53.** $h(\ell(f)) = 5.25f$

7.5 Guided Practice (p. 383) **1.** inverse **5.** $f(g(x)) =$
$f\left(\dfrac{1}{2}x + \dfrac{5}{2}\right) = 2\left(\dfrac{1}{2}x + \dfrac{5}{2}\right) - 5 = x + 5 - 5 = x$, $g(f(x)) =$
$g(2x - 5) = \dfrac{1}{2}(2x - 5) + \dfrac{5}{2} = x - \dfrac{5}{2} + \dfrac{5}{2} = x$
7. $f(g(x)) = f\left(\sqrt{x + 3}\right) = \left(\sqrt{x + 3}\right)^2 - 3 = x + 3 - 3 =$

x, $g(f(x)) = g(x^2 - 3) = \sqrt{x^2 - 3 + 3} = \sqrt{x^2} = x$
9. $f^{-1}(x) = \dfrac{x - 4}{3}$ **11.** yes; $f^{-1}(x) = \sqrt[3]{5x}$ **13.** yes;
$f^{-1}(x) = \dfrac{\sqrt{3x}}{3}$, $x \geq 0$

7.5 Practice and Applications (pp. 383–385)
15. $f(g(x)) = f(x - 5) = (x - 5) + 5 = x$, $g(f(x)) =$
$g(x + 5) = (x + 5) - 5 = x$ **17.** $f(g(x)) = f\left(\dfrac{1}{4}x + \dfrac{3}{4}\right) =$
$4\left(\dfrac{1}{4}x + \dfrac{3}{4}\right) - 3 = x + 3 - 3 = x$, $g(f(x)) = \dfrac{1}{4}(4x - 3) +$
$\dfrac{3}{4} = x - \dfrac{3}{4} + \dfrac{3}{4} = x$ **19.** $f(g(x)) = f\left(\dfrac{\sqrt{x}}{4}\right) = 16\left(\dfrac{\sqrt{x}}{4}\right)^2 =$
$16\left(\dfrac{x}{16}\right) = x$, $g(f(x)) = g(16x^2) = \dfrac{\sqrt{16x^2}}{4} = \dfrac{4x}{4} = x$
21. $x - 7$ **23.** $\dfrac{x - 1}{4}$ **25.** $\dfrac{x + 1}{8}$ **27.** $\dfrac{x - 10}{4}$ **29.** $\dfrac{x + 54}{12}$
31. $-\dfrac{7}{5}x$ **33.** yes; $f^{-1}(x) = \dfrac{\sqrt[3]{x}}{2}$ **35.** yes; $f^{-1}(x) = \sqrt[3]{x - 4}$
37. no **39.** no **41.** yes; $f^{-1}(x) = \sqrt[5]{5 - x}$ **43.** yes; $f^{-1}(x) =$
$\sqrt[5]{x - 1}$ **45.** yes; $f^{-1}(x) = \dfrac{\sqrt{x - 7}}{3}$, $x \geq 7$ **47.** yes; $f^{-1}(x) =$
$\dfrac{\sqrt[3]{4x - 8}}{2}$ **49.** yes; $f^{-1}(x) = \sqrt{-x}$, $x \leq 0$ **51.** yes; $f^{-1}(x) =$
$\dfrac{\sqrt[3]{x + 6}}{2}$ **53.** yes; $f^{-1}(x) = \sqrt[4]{2x + 2}$ **55.** $r = \sqrt[3]{\dfrac{3}{4\pi}V}$;
4.5 in. **57.** $t = \dfrac{\sqrt{50 - h}}{4}$; 1.5 sec

7.5 Technology Activity (p. 387)

1.

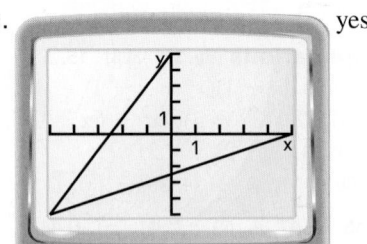

yes

5.

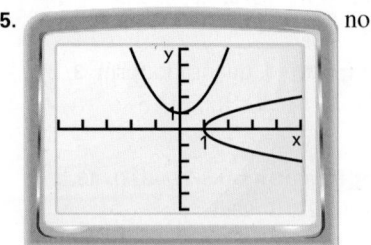

no

7.6 Guided Practice (p. 392) **1.** radical **3.** It was shifted
down three units instead of up three units.

7.

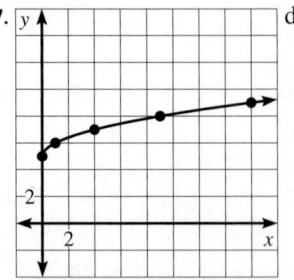

domain $x \geq 0$, range $y \geq 5$

11. 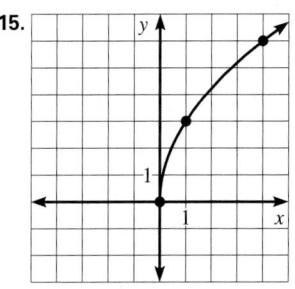 domain and range are both all real numbers

13. The graphs are reflections of each other across the line $y = x$.

7.6 Practice and Applications (pp. 392–394)

15. 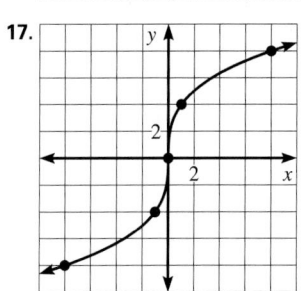 domain $x \geq 0$, range $y \geq 0$

17. 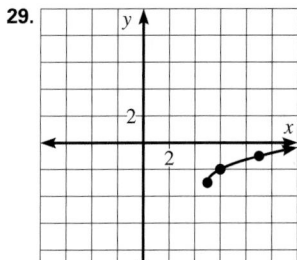 domain and range are both all real numbers

25. B

29. 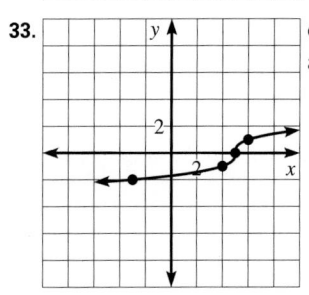 domain $x \geq 5$, range $y \geq -3$

33. 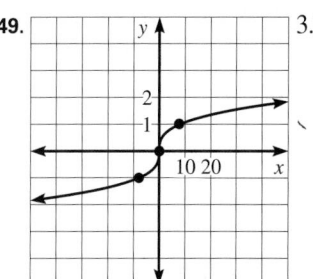 domain and range are both all real numbers

39. always **41.** always **43.** reflect over the x-axis
45. reflect over the x-axis and vertical shrink

47. 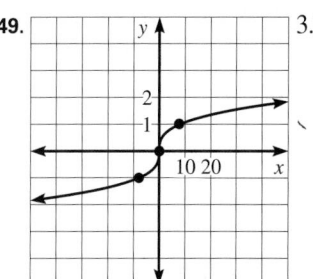 1470 gal per min

49. 3.97 cm

7.7 Guided Practice (p. 398) **1.** mean **3.** 20, 18.5, 16, 24
5. 89.2, 90.5, 83, 98 **7.** 9.6 **9.** 4.6

7.7 Practice and Applications (pp. 398–399) **11.** 5.3,
1.5 **13.** 79.9, 5.6 **17.** The standard deviations are the same. **19.** set B **21.** set A **23.** set A **25.** Kayla 5, Emily 10
27. Forest Hills 6, Union 5 **29.** 29.1 **31.** 1192.5 **33.** 1210,
2112, 1666, 1155, 2310, 1980, 1441, 1738; 392

Chapter Review (pp. 401–404) **1.** radical **3.** *Sample answer:* $2\sqrt{2}$ and $3\sqrt{2}$, $4\sqrt[3]{2}$ and $\sqrt[3]{16}$, $13\sqrt[5]{x}$ and $10\sqrt[5]{x}$
5. ± 13 **7.** -2 **9.** 10 **11.** 9 **13.** $4x^5$ **15.** $3r^3s^{3/2}$ **17.** $5wz^3$
19. $16m^{1/5}n$ **21.** $10\sqrt[3]{x}$ **23.** $66a^4b^2$ **25.** 219 **27.** 35 **29.** no real solution in the domain **31.** $7x - 5$ **33.** $-x + 9$
35. $\dfrac{x^3}{3}$, $x \neq 0$ **37.** $f(g(x)) = 6x^2 + 3$; 57 **39.** $f^{-1}(x) = -\dfrac{x}{3}$
41. $f^{-1}(x) = \dfrac{4}{3}x + \dfrac{4}{3}$ **43.** $f^{-1}(x) = \dfrac{\sqrt[3]{x}}{3}$ **45.** $f^{-1}(x) = \sqrt[5]{x + 3}$

47. 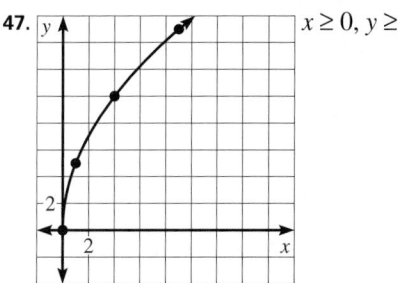 $x \geq 0$, $y \geq 0$

49. 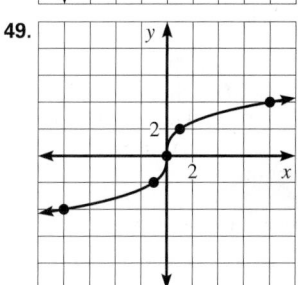 domain and range are both all real numbers

57. 18.1, 2.4 **59.** 15.7, 4.2 **61.** 66.3, 5.1

Chapter 8

8.1 Guided Practice (p. 415) **1.** *Sample answer:* An exponential function is a function that can be written in the form ab^x where $a \neq 0$, $b > 0$, and $b \neq 1$. **3.** $a > 0$ and $b > 1$ **5.** $\frac{1}{25}$, 125 **7.** $\frac{2}{3}$, 162 **9.** $\frac{21}{4}$, 13 **11.** $-\frac{26}{9}$, 24

13. 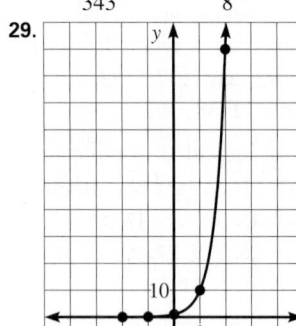 **15.**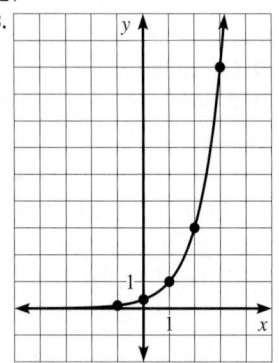

8.1 Practice and Applications (pp. 415–416) **17.** $\frac{1}{729}$, 81 **19.** $\frac{4}{343}$, 196 **21.** $\frac{25}{8}$, 7 **23.** $-\frac{53}{27}$, 7 **25.** B **27.** A

29. 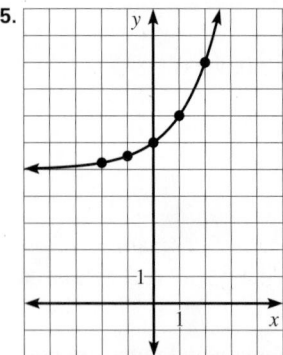 **33.**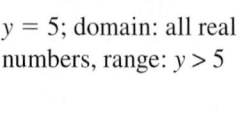

35. 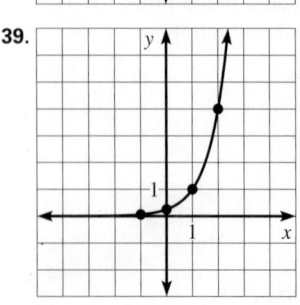 $y = 5$; domain: all real numbers, range: $y > 5$

39. 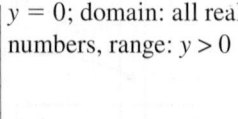 $y = 0$; domain: all real numbers, range: $y > 0$

41. 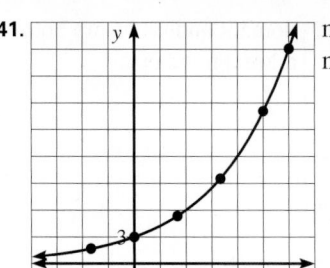 months 10 and 11; months 16 and 17

43. 1 white square; 73 white squares; 4681 white squares

8.2 Guided Practice (p. 422) **3.** decay **5.** growth

7.

x	-3	-2	-1	0	1	2	3
y	128	32	8	2	$\frac{1}{2}$	$\frac{1}{8}$	$\frac{1}{32}$

9. $y = 0$

8.2 Practice and Applications (pp. 422–424)

11. decay; C **13.** decay; B **15.** $\frac{3125}{243}$, $\frac{9}{25}$ **17.** 1458, $\frac{2}{3}$ **19.** $\frac{100,000}{16,807}$, $\frac{49}{100}$ **21.** $\frac{500,000}{243}$, $\frac{9}{20}$ **23.** \$10,628.82

25. 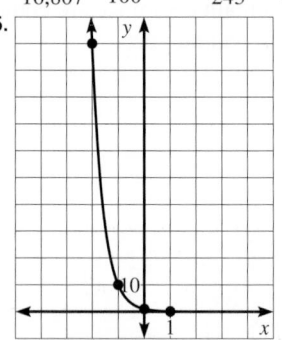 **27.**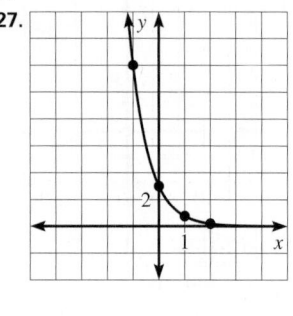

33. C; domain: all real numbers, range: $y > 4$

35. 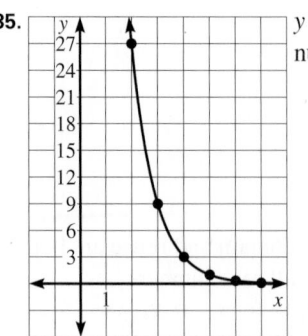 $y = 0$; domain: all real numbers, range: $y > 0$

37.

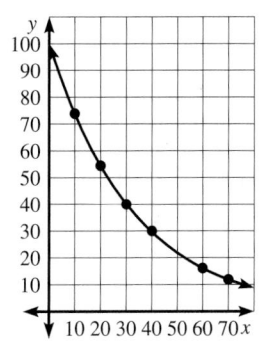

$y = 3$; domain: all real numbers, range: $y > 3$

39.

x	0	1	2	3	4
y	24	19.68	16.14	13.23	10.85

41. 7 yr **43.** 8 yr

45.

x	10	20	30	40	50	60	70
y	73.7	54.4	40.1	29.6	21.8	16.1	11.9

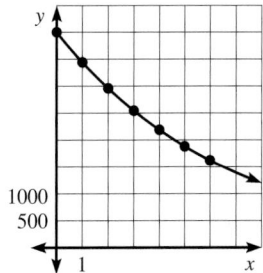

47.

x	0	1	2	3	4	5	6
y	4000	3440	2958	2544	2188	1882	1618

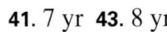

8.3 Guided Practice (p. 430) **1.** exponential growth factor **3.** *Sample answer:* The natural base e is an irrational number that is approximately equal to 2.71828. **5.** decay **7.** growth **9.** decay **11.** $y = 3 \cdot 2^x$

8.3 Practice and Applications (pp. 430–432)
15. growth; $a = 12$, 30% increase **17.** growth; $a = 1500$, 5% increase **19.** decay; $a = 2800$, 95% decrease **21.** decay; $a = 18$, 5% decrease **23.** $c = 2.5(1.01)^t$
25. $2.79

27.

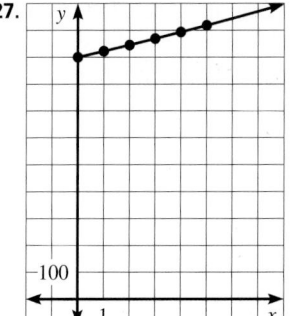

29. $y = 23(0.65)^t$, $0 < t < 4$ **31.** $V = 350(1.07)^t$, $t \geq 0$
33. $y = 5 \cdot 3^x$ **35.** $y = 4 \cdot 5^x$ **37.** $y = 3^x$ **39.** $y = 40\left(\frac{1}{2}\right)^x$
41. $y = 27\left(\frac{1}{3}\right)^x$ **43.** $V = 400(0.81)^t$; $172 **45.** $1577.79
49. $3007.19; yes **51.** $A = 1000e^{0.035t}$ **53.** between 11 and 12 yr

8.4 Guided Practice (p. 436) **1.** Common logarithms have base 10. **3.** $8^2 = 64$ **5.** $5^4 = 625$ **7.** $3^{-2} = \frac{1}{9}$
9. $\left(\frac{1}{4}\right)^{-2} = 16$ **11.** 2 **13.** 0 **15.** -2 **17.** -1 **19.** x **21.** x
23. $6x$ **25.** $2x$ **27.** $\log_{1/3} 3 = -1$ because $\left(\frac{1}{3}\right)^{-1}$

8.4 Practice and Applications (pp. 436–438) **29.** $4^2 = 16$ **31.** $8^0 = 1$ **33.** $4^4 = 256$ **35.** $9^3 = 729$ **37.** $7^{-1} = \frac{1}{7}$
39. $10^{-3} = \frac{1}{1000}$ **41.** $\left(\frac{1}{3}\right)^{-3} = 27$ **43.** $\left(\frac{1}{2}\right)^{-5} = 32$ **45.** 4
47. 2 **49.** 0 **51.** 4 **53.** -2 **55.** -2 **57.** 0 **59.** -6 **61.** x **63.** x
65. $3x$ **67.** $2x$ **69.** C **71.** A

73.

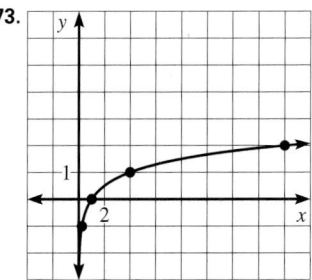

$x = 0$; domain: $x > 0$, range: all real numbers

75.

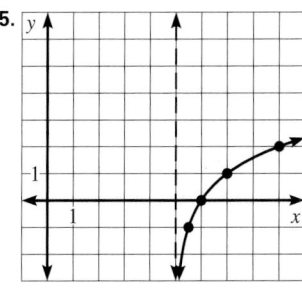

$x = 5$; domain: $x > 5$, range: all real numbers

81.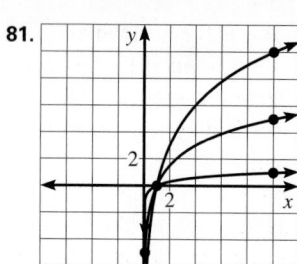

All graphs include the point $(1, 0)$ and have the same basic shape; the graphs are stretched as k increases.

83. 1.11 **85.** 3.30 **87.** 1.79 **89.** 11.07 **91.** $3.3, 4.3, 5.3$

93.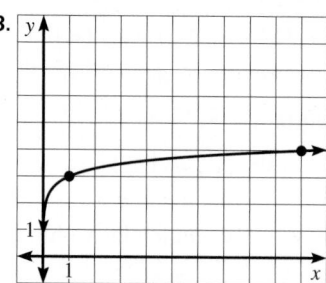

Sample answer: $A = 0.01$ and $A = 0.03$; ratio is 3 to 1; yes

95. -2 phi units **97.** very coarse sand, fine gravel, coarse gravel, small cobble, small boulder, and large boulder

8.4 Technology Activity (p. 440)

1.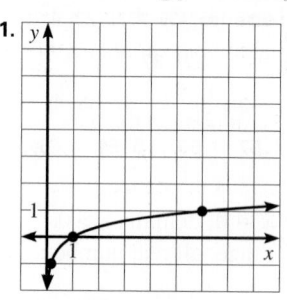

Sample answer: $(1, 0)$, $(6, 1)$, $x = 0$

3.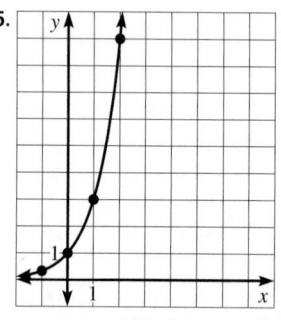

Sample answer: $(2, 0)$, $(4, 1)$, $x = 1$

8.5 Guided Practice (p. 445)
1. 10 **3.** 1.699 **5.** 2.172
7. $\log 2 + \log x$ **9.** $\log_5 9 + 2 \log_5 x$ **11.** $\log x - \log y$
13. $2 \log_4 x - \log_4 3 - \log_4 y$ **15.** $\log_8 21$ **17.** $\log_4 56$
19. $\log \dfrac{y^5}{x}$ **21.** $\log_4 x^2 - \log_4 16y = 2 \log_4 x - \log_4 16 - \log_4 y = 2 \log_4 x - 2 - \log_4 y$

8.5 Practice and Applications (pp. 445–446) **23.** A
25. C **27.** 2.73 **29.** 0.504 **31.** -1.365 **33.** 1.869 **35.** $\log 5 + \log x$ **37.** $\log_4 7 + 4 \log_4 x$ **39.** $\log x + \log y$ **41.** $\log_6 7 + \log_6 x + 4 \log_6 y$ **43.** $\log_4 x - \log_4 5 - 2 \log_4 y$
45. $3 \log_7 y - \log_7 20 - 5 \log_7 x$ **47.** $\log_5 \dfrac{2}{3}$ **49.** $\log_2 75$

51. $\log_7 \dfrac{x^2}{2}$ **53.** $\log_5 \dfrac{x^4}{32}$ **55.** $\log_4 x^8 y^6$ **57.** $\log_2 xy^2$ **59.** yes
61. 4.8 decibels louder **63.** more acidic **65.** $3, 4.5, 6.8$

8.6 Guided Practice (p. 452) **1.** exponential equation
3. $\dfrac{1}{2}$ **5.** -2 **7.** $-\dfrac{1}{2}$ **9.** 2.010 **11.** -1.041 **13.** $\dfrac{5}{2}$ **15.** $\dfrac{8}{5}$ **17.** 14
19. Sample answer: Both sides of the original equation should be in the exponent. So, it should have 3^4 instead of 4^3; $5x - 1 = 81$, and $x = \dfrac{82}{5}$.

8.6 Practice and Applications (pp. 452–453) **21.** 5
23. 2 **25.** $\dfrac{4}{3}$ **27.** 1.771 **29.** 0.276 **31.** 0.715 **33.** -0.477
35. 2008 **37.** 7 **39.** 2 **41.** $\dfrac{7}{4}$ **43.** $\dfrac{5}{2}$ **45.** -1 **47.** 1 **49.** no solution **51.** 20 **53.** -10 **55.** 111.5 yr **57.** 6.97 yr

Chapter Review (pp. 455–458) **1.** Sample answer:
The graph of a growth function increases from left to right, and the graph of a decay function decreases from left to right. **3.** Exponential functions have horizontal asymptotes; logarithmic functions have vertical asymptotes.

5.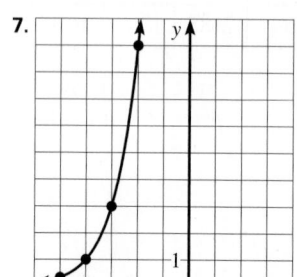

$y = 0$; domain: all real numbers, range: $y > 0$

7.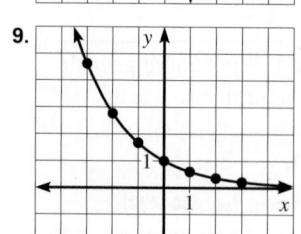

$y = 0$; domain: all real numbers, range: $y > 0$

9.

$y = 0$; domain: all real numbers, range: $y > 0$

11. 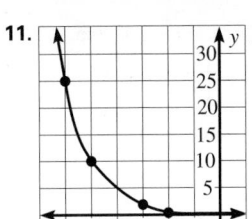 $y = 0$; domain: all real numbers, range: $y > 0$

13. $y = 2 \cdot 8^x$ **15.** $y = \frac{2}{3} \cdot 3^x$ **17.** 5 **19.** -4

21. 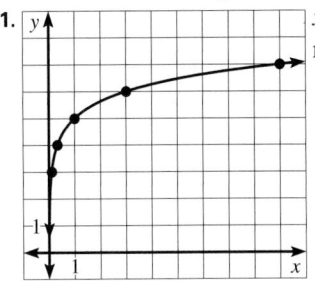 $x = 0$; domain $x > 0$, range: all real numbers

23. 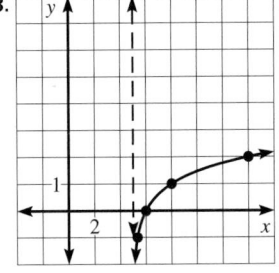 $x = 5$; domain $x > 5$, range: all real numbers

25. $1 + \log_3 x$ **27.** $\log_5 9 + \log_5 x - \log_5 y$ **29.** $\log 48$
31. $\log_3 4x^3$ **33.** 2 **35.** 3 **37.** 2.723 **39.** 0.331 **41.** 10.561
43. no solution **45.** 26

Chapter 9

9.1 Guided Practice (p. 469) **1.** constant **3.** inverse
5. neither **7.** inverse **9.** inverse **11.** jointly **13.** not jointly
15. jointly **17.** not jointly

9.1 Practice and Applications (pp. 469–471)
19. inverse **21.** inverse **23.** direct **25.** direct **27.** $y = \frac{3}{x}$
29. $y = \frac{36}{x}$ **31.** $y = \frac{2}{x}$ **33.** $t = 9r$ **35.** about 1.8 h; distance
37. direct **39.** inverse **41.** $z = 4xy$ **43.** $z = \frac{1}{3}xy$
45. $z = 10xy$ **47.** $y = \frac{1}{2}xz^2$ **49.** 2 **51.** about 66 cm^3
53. The load the beam can safely support is cut in half.

9.2 Guided Practice (p. 475) **1.** hyperbola **3.** The y-axis
is the vertical asymptote and the line with equation $y = -4$ is the horizontal asymptote **5.** The line with equation $x = -2$ is the vertical asymptote and the line with equation $y = 2$ is the horizontal asymptote. **7.** The line with equation $x = 1$ is the vertical asymptote and the line with equation $y = -7$ is the horizontal asymptote.

9.2 Practice and Applications (pp. 475–477) **9.** The y-axis is the vertical asymptote and x-axis is the horizontal asymptote; $(1, 4)$, $(-1, -4)$. **11.** The y-axis

is the vertical asymptote and x-axis is the horizontal asymptote; $(1, -7)$, $(-1, 7)$. **13.** The y-axis is the vertical asymptote and x-axis is the horizontal asymptote; $(1, 5)$, $(-1, -5)$. **15.** The y-axis is the vertical asymptote and x-axis is the horizontal asymptote; $(1, 11)$, $(-1, -11)$.
17. The y-axis is the vertical asymptote and the line with equation $y = -5$ is the horizontal asymptote; the domain is the set of nonzero real numbers and the range is all real numbers except -5. **19.** The line with equation $x = 1$ is the vertical asymptote and the x-axis is the horizontal asymptote; the domain is all real numbers except 1 and the range is all nonzero real numbers. **21.** The line with equation $x = -6$ is the vertical asymptote and the line with equation $y = -3$ is the horizontal asymptote; the domain is all real numbers except -6 and the range is all real numbers except -3. **23.** The line with equation $x = -5$ is the vertical asymptote and the line with equation $y = -1$ is the horizontal asymptote; the domain is all real numbers except -5 and the range is all real numbers except -1. **25.** The line with equation $x = 7$ is the vertical asymptote and the line with equation $y = 3$ is the horizontal asymptote; the domain is all real numbers except 7 and the range is all real numbers except 3.
27. C **29.** The vertical asymptote should be the line with equation $x = 4$ and horizontal asymptote should be the line with equation $y = -2$.

33. 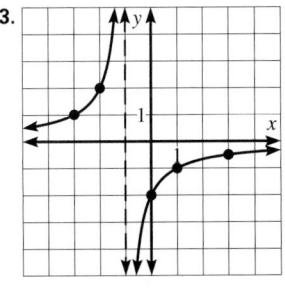 The domain is the real numbers except -1 and the range is the nonzero real numbers.

37. 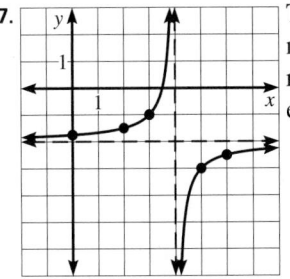 The domain is the real numbers except 4 and the range is the real numbers except -2.

39. 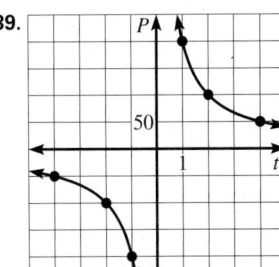 The y-axis is the vertical asymptote and the x-axis is the horizontal asymptote; that part of the graph found in quadrant I models the situation.

41. $(-3, 0)$, $x = \pm 2$ **43.** $(-2.24, 0)$, $x = -\dfrac{3}{2}$ **45.** no
x-intercept, $x = \dfrac{1}{3}$ **47.** A **49.** D

51.

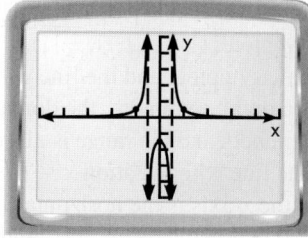

55.

61. $4.8°C$

9.2 Technology Activity (p. 479) **1.** $y = 3$ **3.** $y = 0$
5. $y = \dfrac{1}{4}$

9.3 Guided Practice (p. 483) **3.** $4x$ **5.** $\dfrac{3}{x^2}$ **7.** $\dfrac{5x^2 + 2}{3x + 1}$

9. $\dfrac{4x^4}{3}$ **11.** $\dfrac{2x^2}{3}$ **13.** $\dfrac{-4x}{x + 2}$ **15.** $\dfrac{x^2}{x^2 - 4}$ does not equal $-\dfrac{1}{4}$. It is
already in simplest form.

9.3 Practice and Applications (pp. 483–484) **17.** $18x$
19. $8x^2$ **21.** ± 1 **23.** D **25.** A **27.** $\dfrac{x^2}{x + 1}$ **29.** $\dfrac{x}{5x^3 - 7}$
31. $\dfrac{2x + 3}{6x^3}$ **33.** $\dfrac{2x(x^3 + 6)}{3(2 - 5x^2)}$ **35.** $\dfrac{x + 3}{4}$ **37.** $\dfrac{x + 1}{x - 6}$ **39.** $\dfrac{5}{2}$ **41.** 12
43. $-\dfrac{9}{2}$ **45.** x^3 **47.** $\dfrac{2(x - 2)}{x^2}$ **49.** $10x^4$ **53.** $\dfrac{5x(x + 7)}{x + 5}$ **55.** $\dfrac{1}{4}$
57. Emperor Penguin: about 0.46, Magellan Penguin:
about 0.83; Emperor Penguin; the ratio of surface area to
volume is smaller. **59.** *Sample answer:* $\dfrac{4\pi r^2}{\frac{4}{3}\pi r^3} = \dfrac{3}{4}$; the
ratio decreases.

9.4 Guided Practice (p. 489) **1.** A complex fraction is a
fraction that contains a fraction in its numerator or
denominator. **3.** $\dfrac{2}{3}$ **5.** $\dfrac{5x^2}{2}$ **7.** $\dfrac{4x}{3}$ **9.** $\dfrac{x}{2}$ **11.** $\dfrac{x(x + 1)}{12}$ **13.** $\dfrac{x + 4}{x - 1}$
15. $\dfrac{5x}{(x + 3)(x - 4)}$ **17.** The factor $4 - x$ can be written as
$-1(x - 4)$ which leads to a reduced rational expression.
The correct answer is $\dfrac{-(x - 4)(x + 4)}{3}$.

9.4 Practice and Applications (pp. 489–490) **19.** 1
21. $\dfrac{1}{18}$ **23.** $\dfrac{4}{3x}$ **25.** $\dfrac{10}{21}$ **27.** $\dfrac{49}{4}$ **29.** $\dfrac{4x}{5}$ **31.** $\dfrac{4x}{3}$ **33.** $\dfrac{1}{3(x - 3)}$
35. $\dfrac{2(x - 2)}{x + 4}$ **37.** $\dfrac{1}{2x}$ **39.** $-\dfrac{1}{8}$ **41.** $\dfrac{x + 5}{(x + 7)^2}$ **43.** $\dfrac{x}{2(x - 3)}$
45. $\dfrac{2x}{x + 6}$ **47.** $\dfrac{x}{2}$ **49.** $\dfrac{-(x - 4)}{4(x + 7)}$ **51.** $\dfrac{2r + 2h}{rh}$

9.4 Technology Activity (p. 493) **1.** $\dfrac{2x}{x - 3}$; $x \neq 3$,
$x \neq -2$ **3.** $\dfrac{x - 2}{x + 5}$; $x \neq -3$, $x \neq -5$ **5.** $\dfrac{4}{3}x$; $x \neq 0$, $x \neq 3$

9.5 Guided Practice (p. 497) **3.** $8x$ **5.** $(x - 3)(x + 3)$
7. $\dfrac{6x + 10}{5x^2}$ **9.** $\dfrac{10r}{(r - 3)(r + 3)}$

9.5 Practice and Applications (pp. 497–499) **11.** $\dfrac{3}{x^2}$
13. 3 **15.** $\dfrac{8x}{x - 3}$ **17.** $7x(x + 1)$ **19.** $4x^3$ **21.** $8(x + 2)(x - 2)$
23. $(x + 8)(x - 8)(x - 5)$ **25.** sometimes **27.** When
adding rational expressions common denominators are
necessary. The correct answer is $\dfrac{2x + 20}{5x^2}$. **29.** $\dfrac{10 - 15x}{3x^2}$
31. $\dfrac{-x^2 + 2x + 20}{4(x - 2)}$ **33.** $\dfrac{6x - 2}{(x - 3)(x + 5)}$ **35.** $\dfrac{6x^2 + 7x - 21}{2x(x - 3)}$
37. $\dfrac{x^2 - 4x + 5}{3(x - 4)}$ **39.** $\dfrac{x^2 - 9x + 28}{(x - 7)(x + 7)}$ **41.** $\dfrac{x^2 - 10x - 19}{(x + 6)(x + 4)(x - 1)}$
43. $\dfrac{0.5}{r} + \dfrac{22}{15r} + \dfrac{6}{r + 5}$ **45.** about 1.85 h **47.** $\dfrac{x^2 + 18x + 40}{4x(x + 10)}$
49. $\dfrac{4x^3 + 22x^2 + 52x + 10}{3x(x + 1)}$

9.6 Guided Practice (p. 503) **1.** A rational function has
a polynomial in both its numerator and denominator. **3.** 4
5. -3 **7.** 3 **9.** -2 **11.** 1, 4 **13.** $\dfrac{3}{x + 1}$ is undefined if x is
replaced by -1. The correct answer is 6.

9.6 Practice and Applications (pp. 503–505)
15. solution **17.** not a solution **19.** not a solution **21.** $\dfrac{7}{2}$
23. 6 **25.** 4 **27.** -2 **29.** 2 **33.** 0, 4 **35.** 9 **37.** 3 **39.** 8 **41.** 2, 3
43. 2 **45.** 1, 3 **47.** -1, 2 **49.** 5 **51.** always **53.** 1 h 12 min
55. first car: 50 mph, second car: 45 mph **57.** $\dfrac{1}{6}$ L

Chapter Review (pp. 507–510) **1.** Two variables x and y
show inverse variation if $y = \dfrac{k}{x}$, k a nonzero constant.
3. A rational expression is in simplified form when its
numerator and denominator have no common factors
(other than ± 1). **5.** A complex fraction is a fraction that
contains a fraction in its numerator or denominator.
7. $y = -\dfrac{12}{x}$; -4 **9.** $z = \dfrac{7}{xy}$

11. 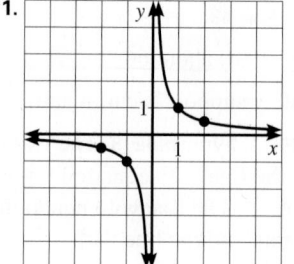 **13.**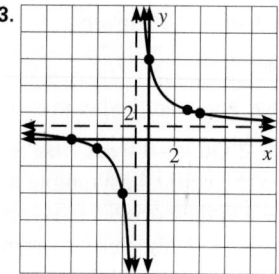

17. $\dfrac{x^2}{x + 2}$ **21.** $\dfrac{2(x + 1)}{x - 2}$ **23.** $\dfrac{2x + 3}{8(2x + 5)}$ **25.** $\dfrac{x + 5}{3}$ **27.** $\dfrac{x - 2}{2}$
29. $\dfrac{7x - 11}{(x + 1)(x - 5)}$ **31.** $\dfrac{(2x + 3)(x + 5)}{(x + 4)(x + 3)}$ **33.** $\dfrac{2x^2 + 8x + 15}{(x + 4)(x - 1)}$
35. -2 **37.** $\dfrac{1}{2}$, 5 **39.** 2, 0 **41.** 2 **43.** 6 **45.** 0, 2 **47.** 7

Chapter 10

10.1 Guided Practice (p. 522) **1.** sample **3.** customers; customers who purchased dog food or supplies on one day

10.1 Practice and Applications (pp. 522–523)
9. seniors at school; seniors she sees entering school
17. *Sample answer:* Should accessibility of public buildings and public transportation be increased?
19. *Sample answer:* Should the state extend health care to all citizens? **21.** 510 students, 153 students
23. 702 students **25.** 4,940,000 customers

10.2 Guided Practice (p. 529) **1.** random sample
5. *Sample answer:* Write names of employees on slips of paper and draw names. **7.** ±20% **9.** ±6.7% **11.** The actual percent that approves is between 41% and 47%.

10.2 Practice and Applications (pp. 529–532)
17. random **19.** convenience **23.** *Sample answer:* Throw an 8-sided die for each. If it lands on 1 survey the coach. Use a random number generator to select the coaches.
25. 16.8%–23.2% **27.** ±11.5% **29.** ±1.8% **31.** ±4.1%
33. ±1.1% **35.** 28.9%–37.9% **37.** 35.5%–48.3%

10.3 Guided Practice (p. 536) **1.** central tendency **3.** 3, 4, 4 **5.** 20, 20, 10 **7.** Original: 10.22, 10, none; new: 15.33, 15, none; mean and median are 50% higher, mode is unchanged.

9.

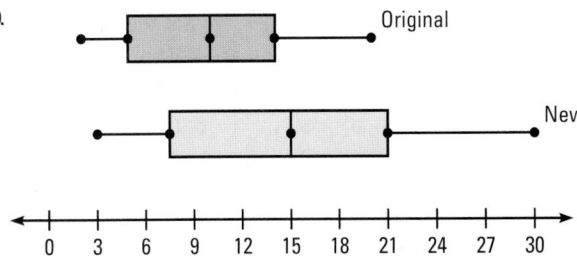

Sample answer: The new plot is 50% larger.

10.3 Practice and Applications (pp. 536–538)
11. −10, −9, −7, −7, −6, −5, −5, −4, −3, −3, −2, −2, 0, 1, 5, 7; original mean 1.875, median 1.5, mode −2, 0, 2, 3, range 17, quartile difference 5.5; new mean −3.125, median −3.5, mode −7, −5, −3, −2, range 17, quartile difference 5.5; mean, median, mode decreased by 5, range and quartile difference remain the same. **13.** 2.5, 5, 10, 12.5, 17.5, 25, 30, 37.5, 40, 47.5; original mean 15.2, median 12, mode none, range 38, quartile difference 20; new mean 19, median 15, mode none, range 47.5, quartile difference 25; all increased by 25% except modes which do not exist. **15.** The entire box plot would shift left 4.
17. Original mean 27.06, median 23.5, mode 23.5; new mean 45.46, median 38.5, mode 38.5; all increased by 18.4. **19.** It will move right but have the same shape.
21. Original mean 22.86, median 22, mode 22, range 15, quartile difference 7; new mean 20.57, median 19.8, mode 19.8, range 13.5, quartile difference 6.3; all are 10% less.

23. never **25.** sometimes **27.** −0.5; 89 less than the real mean **29.** $n = 1.05w + 0.25$; 7.60, 8.02, 8.65, 8.65, 9.49, 10.33, 11.80, 13.90

10.4 Guided Practice (p. 542) **1.** permutation **3.** blue, orange; blue, red; blue, yellow; blue, green; black, orange; black, red; black, yellow; black, green **5.** 2 **7.** 20 **9.** 1
11. 40,320 **13.** 60 **15.** 120

10.4 Practice and Applications (pp. 542–544) **17.** 12 ways **19.** 120 ways

21.

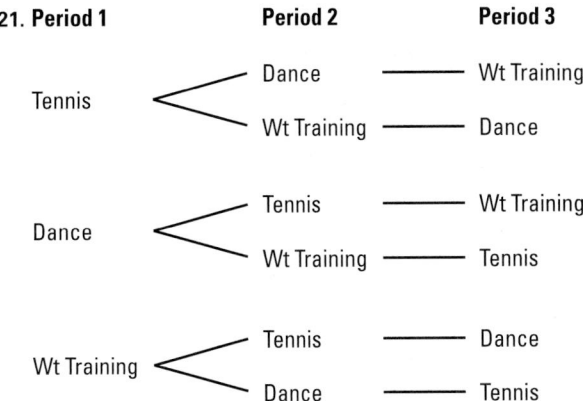

23. 270 ways **25. a.** 260,000 passwords **b.** 131,040 passwords **27. a.** 1,757,600 passwords **b.** 140,400 passwords **29.** A digit can be repeated; $5 \cdot 5 \cdot 5 = 125$.
31. 120 **33.** 1 **35.** 60 **37.** 30 **39.** 2 **41.** 720 **43.** 30 **45.** 6720
47. 120 **49.** 362,880 **51.** 151,200 **53.** 5,864,443,200

55. 720 **57.** 24,360 **59.** 85,140 ways **61.** $_nP_1 =$
$$\frac{n!}{1!(n-1)!} = \frac{n!}{(n-1)!} = \frac{1 \cdot 2 \cdot 3 \cdot \cdots \cdot (n-1) \cdot n}{1 \cdot 2 \cdot 3 \cdot \cdots \cdot (n-1)} = n$$

10.5 Guided Practice (p. 548) **1.** *Sample answer:* In a combination order does not matter. In a permutation order matters. Given a, b, and c, $_3C_2$ is ab, ac, bc = 3 while $_3P_2$ is ab, ba, ac, ca, bc, cb = 6. **3.** red, green; red, yellow; red, blue; green, yellow; green, blue; yellow, blue **5.** 5
7. 10 **9.** permutation; 24 orders

10.5 Practice and Applications (pp. 549–550)
11. ph, pm, po, pr, hm, ho, hr, mo, mr, or **13.** 15 choices **15.** 1 **17.** 20 **19.** 70 **21.** 126 **23.** 230,300 groups
25. combination; 677,040 possibilities **27.** combination; 10,626 possibilities **29.** 67,200 committees **31.** 24 hands
33. 48 hands **35.** 48 hands **37.** 10 sets **39.** 246 sets
41. $_9C_0$, $_9C_1$, $_9C_2$, $_9C_3$, $_9C_4$, $_9C_5$, $_9C_6$, $_9C_7$, $_9C_8$, $_9C_9$, 1, 9, 36, 84, 126, 126, 84, 36, 9, 1

10.5 Technology Activity (p. 552) **1.** 79,833,600
3. 524,160 **5.** 2,884,801,920 **7.** 462 **9.** 646,646
11. 472,733,756 **13.** $7.628275985 \times 10^{15}$ possibilities
15. $1.762989441 \times 10^{48}$ ways

Extension (p. 555)

1.

$$
\begin{array}{ccccccccccccccccc}
 & & & & & & & & 1 & & & & & & & & \\
 & & & & & & & 1 & & 1 & & & & & & & \\
 & & & & & & 1 & & 2 & & 1 & & & & & & \\
 & & & & & 1 & & 3 & & 3 & & 1 & & & & & \\
 & & & & 1 & & 4 & & 6 & & 4 & & 1 & & & & \\
 & & & 1 & & 5 & & 10 & & 10 & & 5 & & 1 & & & \\
 & & 1 & & 6 & & 15 & & 20 & & 15 & & 6 & & 1 & & \\
 & 1 & & 7 & & 21 & & 35 & & 35 & & 21 & & 7 & & 1 & \\
1 & & 8 & & 28 & & 56 & & 70 & & 56 & & 28 & & 8 & & 1
\end{array}
$$

3. $x^7 + 7x^6y + 21x^5y^2 + 35x^4y^3 + 35x^3y^4 + 21x^2y^5 + 7xy^6 + y^7$ **7.** $16x^4 + 32x^3 + 24x^2 + 8x + 1$
9. $t^3 - 15t^2 + 75t - 125$ **11.** $81x^4 - 108x^3y + 54x^2y^2 - 12xy^3 + y^4$

10.6 Guided Practice (p. 559) **1.** geometric **3.** $\frac{3}{7} \approx 0.43$
5. $\frac{5}{7} \approx 0.71$ **7.** $\frac{1}{2} = 0.5$ **9.** $\frac{1}{\pi} \approx 0.32$

10.6 Practice and Applications (pp. 559–561)
11. Sometimes true; if they are equally likely to occur each will have probability 0.5. **13.** $\frac{12}{25} = 0.48$ **15.** $\frac{13}{25} = 0.52$ **17.** $\frac{6}{25} = 0.24$ **19.** $\frac{8}{25} = 0.32$ **21.** $\frac{1}{52} \approx 0.02$ **23.** $\frac{1}{2} = 0.5$ **25.** $\frac{2}{13} \approx 0.15$ **27.** $\frac{1}{5} = 0.2$ **29.** $\frac{3}{10} = 0.3$ **31.** $\frac{1}{658,008} \approx 0.00000152$ **33.** $\frac{1}{5040} \approx 0.0002$ **35.** $\frac{13}{72} \approx 18.1\%$
37. $\frac{103}{120} \approx 85.8\%$ **39.** $\frac{1}{4} = 0.25$ **41.** $\frac{79}{120} \approx 65.8\%$
43. $\frac{4-\pi}{36} \approx 0.024$ **45.** $\frac{9\pi-8}{36} \approx 0.56$

10.7 Guided Practice (p. 565) **1.** union **3.** disjoint
5. 1.0 **7.** 0.5 **9.** $\frac{4}{5} = 0.8$ **11.** 0.1 **13.** 0.75 **15.** 0.05

10.7 Practice and Applications (pp. 565–567)
17. overlapping; 0.8 **19.** $\frac{7}{12}$ **21.** $\frac{3}{4}$ **23.** overlapping; 0.8
25. 0.04 **29.** $\frac{9}{10} = 0.9$ **31.** 0.4 **33.** 0.25 **35.** 0.87 **37.** 0.26
39. $\frac{5}{18} \approx 0.28$ **41.** $\frac{5}{6} \approx 0.83$ **43.** 0.87

10.8 Guided Practice (p. 572) **1.** conditional
probability **3.** 0.15 **5.** 0.3 **7.** 0.3 **9.** $\frac{2}{7} \approx 0.29$

10.8 Practice and Applications (pp. 572–573)
11. independent **13.** independent **15.** $\frac{282}{532} \approx 0.53$
17. $\frac{233}{282} \approx 0.83$ **19.** $\frac{1}{6} \approx 0.17$ **21. a.** $\frac{4}{49} \approx 0.08$ **b.** $\frac{2}{21} \approx 0.095$ **23.** $\frac{5}{19} \approx 0.26$ **25. a.** $\frac{1}{16} \approx 0.063$ **b.** $\frac{13}{204} \approx 0.064$
27. a. $\frac{3}{169} \approx 0.018$ **b.** $\frac{4}{221} \approx 0.018$ **29.** $\frac{1}{2197} \approx 0.0005$
31. 0.0000742

Chapter Review (pp. 575–578) **1.** *Sample answer:* A sample should be unbiased so the results will be meaningful and not skewed. **3.** *Sample answer:* A permutation is an arrangement in order while a combination is an arrangement where order does not matter. **5.** 807 students **7. a.** $\pm\frac{1}{12} \approx \pm8.3\%$ **b.** $\pm\frac{1}{24} \approx \pm4.2\%$ **c.** $\pm\frac{\sqrt{5}}{100} \approx \pm2.2\%$ **9.** original mean 39.7, median 39, mode 33, range 15, quartile difference 12; transformed mean 52.8, median 52, mode 44, range 20, quartile difference 16; all increased by $33\frac{1}{3}\%$ **11. a.** 175,760,000 security codes **b.** 78,624,000 security codes **13.** 56 **15.** 42 **17.** 7920 **19.** 36 **21.** 210 **23.** 56
25. 41,580 groups **27.** $\frac{1}{5} = 0.2$ **29.** 3% **31.** $\frac{1}{15} \approx 0.067$

Chapter 11

11.1 Guided Practice (p. 589) **1.** 3 **3.** dimensions
5. $\begin{bmatrix} 4 & 2 \\ 5 & 7 \end{bmatrix}$ **7.** $\begin{bmatrix} -5 \\ -8 \\ -7 \end{bmatrix}$

11.1 Practice and Applications (pp. 589–591) **13.** Not possible; their dimensions are not the same. **15.** $\begin{bmatrix} 15 \\ -4 \\ -2 \end{bmatrix}$
17. Not possible; their dimensions are not the same.
19. $\begin{bmatrix} 1 & 3 \\ -2 & -6 \\ 7 & -9 \end{bmatrix}$ **21.** $\begin{bmatrix} 12 & 4 \\ 8 & 8 \\ 8 & 8 \\ 6 & 10 \end{bmatrix}$ **23.** $\begin{bmatrix} 1125 & 1701 \\ 2536 & 4587 \\ 6369 & 11,546 \\ 10,953 & 17,777 \end{bmatrix}$
25. $\begin{bmatrix} 4 \\ -32 \\ 20 \end{bmatrix}$ **27.** $\begin{bmatrix} 10 & 40 \\ -30 & 15 \end{bmatrix}$ **29.** $\begin{bmatrix} \frac{3}{4} & \frac{7}{4} \\ -1 & \frac{1}{2} \\ \frac{-3}{4} & 2 \end{bmatrix}$ **31.** $\begin{bmatrix} -4 & 24 \\ -21 & -14 \end{bmatrix}$
33. $\begin{bmatrix} 2 & -11 \\ -3 & -10 \\ -6 & -11 \end{bmatrix}$ **35.** $\begin{bmatrix} 8 & 8 & 4 \\ 4 & 0 & -12 \end{bmatrix}$ **37.** $\begin{bmatrix} 38,750 \\ 43,000 \\ 34,500 \end{bmatrix}$ **39.** -6
41. 4.5 **43.** 2

11.1 Technology Activity (p. 593) **1.** $\begin{bmatrix} 200 & 140 \\ 165 & 152 \end{bmatrix}$
3. $\begin{bmatrix} 6.6591 & 8.3503 \\ 3.3824 & 13.5296 \end{bmatrix}$ **5.** DVD: A, VHS: C; DVD and VHS: C, Ch, D

11.2 Guided Practice (p. 597) **1.** columns, rows **3.** not defined **5.** defined; 2×2 **7.** $\begin{bmatrix} -3 & 9 \\ -5 & 3 \\ 8 & 0 \end{bmatrix}$

11.2 Practice and Applications (pp. 597–598) **9.** not defined **11.** defined; 5×4 **13.** defined; 4×3 **15.** The elements in row 1 in the first matrix should be multiplied by the elements in column 1 in the second matrix;

$$\begin{bmatrix} 3(7) + 1(1) & \\ & \end{bmatrix} = \begin{bmatrix} 22 & \\ & \end{bmatrix}.$$ **17.** $\begin{bmatrix} 8 & -2 \\ 4 & -3 \end{bmatrix}$ **19.** The

number of columns in the first matrix does not match the number of rows in the second matrix.

21. $\begin{bmatrix} 15 & 11 & -1 \\ 0 & -12 & 2 \end{bmatrix}$ **23.** The number of columns in the first matrix does not match the number of rows in the

second matrix. **25.** $\begin{bmatrix} 9 & -18 \\ -6 & 6 \end{bmatrix}$ **27.** $\begin{bmatrix} 1 & 8 \\ -2 & -6 \end{bmatrix}$

29. $\begin{bmatrix} 5 & -4 \\ 4 & -4 \end{bmatrix}$ **31.** $\begin{bmatrix} 42 & 32 \\ -77 & -82 \end{bmatrix}$ **33.** $\begin{bmatrix} 106 & -12 \\ 50 & -40 \end{bmatrix}$

35. $\begin{bmatrix} -99 & 124 \\ 27 & 147 \end{bmatrix}$ **37.** $\begin{bmatrix} 3 \\ 2 \\ 1 \end{bmatrix}$ **39.** Player 2; 15 points

41. $\begin{bmatrix} 735 \\ 832 \\ 716 \end{bmatrix}$ **43.** $\begin{bmatrix} 24 & 12 & 17 \\ 20 & 14 & 15 \end{bmatrix}, \begin{bmatrix} 3.35 \\ 1.75 \\ 4.50 \end{bmatrix}; \begin{bmatrix} 177.90 \\ 159 \end{bmatrix}$

45. $x = 2, y = -4$

11.3 Guided Practice (p. 603)

1. $\begin{bmatrix} x \\ y \end{bmatrix}, \begin{bmatrix} -39 \\ 27 \end{bmatrix}, \begin{bmatrix} -4 & 5 \\ 1 & -7 \end{bmatrix}$ **3.** inverses **5.** not inverses

7. $\begin{bmatrix} 1 & 7 \\ 0 & 1 \end{bmatrix}$ **9.** $\begin{bmatrix} 5 & 2 \\ 1 & 1 \end{bmatrix} \cdot \begin{bmatrix} x \\ y \end{bmatrix} = \begin{bmatrix} -14 \\ 0 \end{bmatrix}$

11. $\begin{bmatrix} 7 & 2 \\ 2 & -1 \end{bmatrix} \cdot \begin{bmatrix} x \\ y \end{bmatrix} = \begin{bmatrix} -11 \\ -10 \end{bmatrix}$

11.3 Practice and Applications (pp. 603–604) **13.** not inverses **15.** inverses **17.** not inverses **19.** not inverses

21. $\begin{bmatrix} 3 & -4 \\ 2 & -3 \end{bmatrix}$ **23.** $\begin{bmatrix} -1 & 0 \\ 1.5 & 0.25 \end{bmatrix}$ **25.** $\begin{bmatrix} 6 & -8.2 \\ -10 & 14 \end{bmatrix}$

27. $\begin{bmatrix} 1 & 0 & 0 \\ -8 & 1 & 0 \\ 46 & -5 & 1 \end{bmatrix}$ **29.** $\begin{bmatrix} 1 & 1 \\ 2 & -1 \end{bmatrix} \cdot \begin{bmatrix} x \\ y \end{bmatrix} = \begin{bmatrix} 3 \\ 12 \end{bmatrix}$

31. $\begin{bmatrix} 1 & -1 \\ -4 & 5 \end{bmatrix} \cdot \begin{bmatrix} x \\ y \end{bmatrix} = \begin{bmatrix} 11 \\ -16 \end{bmatrix}$

33. $\begin{bmatrix} -2 & -4 \\ 6 & 0 \end{bmatrix} \cdot \begin{bmatrix} x \\ y \end{bmatrix} = \begin{bmatrix} 14 \\ -42 \end{bmatrix}$

35. $\begin{bmatrix} 6 & -7 & -3 \\ 1 & 1 & -5 \\ -4 & -2 & 7 \end{bmatrix} \cdot \begin{bmatrix} x \\ y \\ z \end{bmatrix} = \begin{bmatrix} 17 \\ 17 \\ -30 \end{bmatrix}$

37. $\begin{bmatrix} 1 & 3 & -1.2 \\ 0 & 20.5 & 1.5 \\ -2.4 & -0.3 & 0 \end{bmatrix} \cdot \begin{bmatrix} x \\ y \\ z \end{bmatrix} = \begin{bmatrix} 2.4 \\ -4.2 \\ 5.7 \end{bmatrix}$ **39.** $(4, -5)$

41. $(0, 3)$ **43.** $(-5, 0)$ **45.** $(-2, 4, 5)$ **47.** 2 blue sheets,

7 yellow sheets **49.** $A + B = 32, 5A + 2B = 100$; 12 A problems and 20 B problems

Extension (p. 607) **1.** -15 **3.** -40 **5.** 24 **7.** -24 **9.** 102

11. $\left(\dfrac{108}{35}, -\dfrac{346}{35}\right)$ **13.** $(-2, -5)$ **15.** $\left(-\dfrac{22}{15}, \dfrac{136}{25}\right)$

11.4 Guided Practice (p. 611) **1.** terms **3.** 3, 6, 9, 12, 15, 18 **5.** 5, 6, 7, 8, 9, 10 **7.** 12; $a_n = 2n$ **9.** 36; $a_n = n^2$

11. -8

11.4 Practice and Applications (pp. 611–613) **13.** 3, 4, 5, 6, 7, 8 **15.** 3, 7, 11, 15, 19, 23 **17.** 2, 8, 18, 32, 50, 72

19. 2, 5, 10, 17, 26, 37 **21.** 5, 8, 11, 14, 17, 20 **23.** 2, $\dfrac{3}{2}, \dfrac{4}{3}, \dfrac{5}{4},$

$\dfrac{6}{5}, \dfrac{7}{6}$ **25.** 9; $a_n = 2n - 1$ **27.** 13; $a_n = = 3n - 2$ **29.** 28;

$a_n = n^2 + 3$ **31.** 50; $a_n = 2n^2$ **33.** $\dfrac{10}{6}$; $a_n = \dfrac{2n}{n + 1}$

35.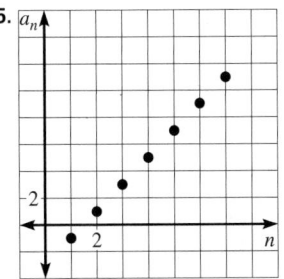

41. 45 **43.** 55 **45.** 111 **47.** 110 **49.** $\dfrac{25}{12}$ **51.** 8 **53.** 36 **55.** 55

57. 140 **59.** $33,000; $35,400; $37,800; $40,200; $42,600

61. $47,400 **63.** $a_n = n^2$ **65.** 140 **67.** 316

11.4 Technology Activity (p. 614)

1. 3, 7, 11, 15, 19, 23, 27, 31, 35, 39, 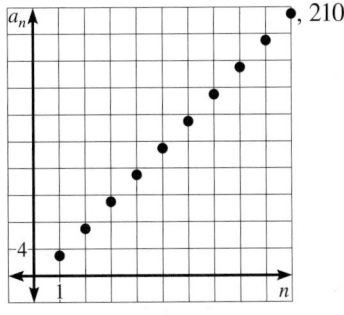, 210

3. 17, 14, 11, 8, 5, 2, -1, -4, -7, -10, 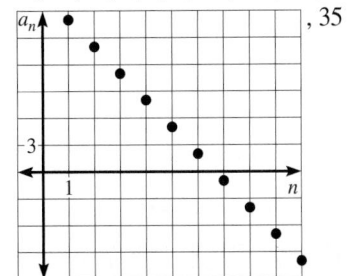, 35

11.5 Guided Practice (p. 618) **1.** arithmetic series

3. $a_n = 5n + 8$; 83 **5.** $a_n = 12n - 3$; 177

7. $a_n = 23n - 86$ **9.** 255

11.5 Practice and Applications (pp. 618–619) **11.** No; the difference between consecutive terms is not constant. **13.** No; the difference between consecutive terms is not constant. **15.** $a_n = -2n + 34$; 10 **17.** $a_n = 7n + 40$; 124 **19.** $a_n = \frac{1}{5}n + \frac{3}{5}$; 3 **21.** $a_n = 9n + 12$ **23.** $a_n = 8n - 49$ **25.** $a_n = \frac{1}{3}n + \frac{1}{2}$ **27.** B **29.** A

33.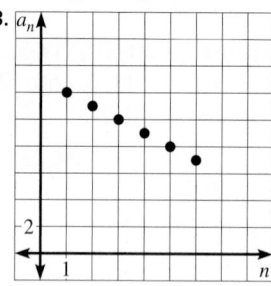

37. 618 **39.** 177 **41.** 786 **43.** 864 **45.** 66 **47.** 1485 **49.** $a_n = 250n + 250$ **51.** 48; 217

11.6 Guided Practice (p. 624) **1.** In an arithmetic sequence the difference between consecutive terms is constant whereas in a geometric sequence the ratio of any term to the previous term is constant. **3.** 3 **5.** 4 **7.** $\frac{1}{2}$ **19.** $a_n = 8(2)^{n-1}$

11.6 Practice and Applications (pp. 624–626) **33.** The ratios should be any term divided by the previous term; $\frac{1}{3}$.

35. $a_n = 13.5\left(\frac{2}{3}\right)^{n-1}$ **37.** $a_n = -8\left(\frac{3}{2}\right)^{n-1}$ **39.** $a_n = \left(-\frac{1}{3}\right)^{n-1}$ **41.** $a_n = (10)^{n-1}$; 100,000 **43.** $a_n = -(-3)^{n-1}$; 243 **45.** $a_n = 2\left(\frac{3}{4}\right)^{n-1}$; $\frac{243}{512}$ **47.** $a_n = \frac{1}{2}\left(\frac{1}{3}\right)^{n-1}$; $\frac{1}{486}$ **49.** geometric; $\frac{1}{2}$ **51.** 3.75; how much Tungsten-187 is left on day 6 **53.** $a_n = 44\left(\frac{1}{2}\right)^{n-1}$ **55.** $a_n = -4(3)^{n-1}$ **57.** $a_n = -2(-3)^{n-1}$ **59.** $a_n = 49\left(\frac{1}{7}\right)^{n-1}$

61. 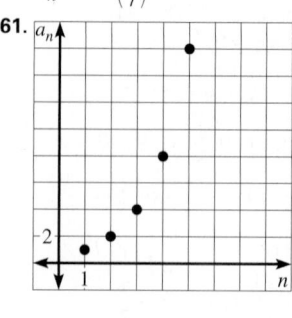 **65.**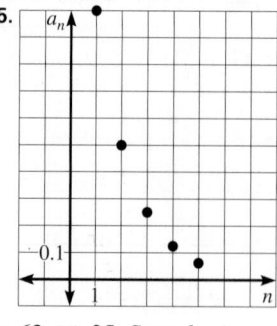

67. 255 **69.** about 125 **71.** 85 **73.** 63 **75.** 35. *Sample answer:* It takes 35 skydivers to form 3 rings. **77.** sometimes

11.7 Guided Practice (p. 631) **1.** common ratio **3.** $1, \frac{5}{2}, \frac{19}{4}, \frac{65}{8}, \frac{211}{16}$

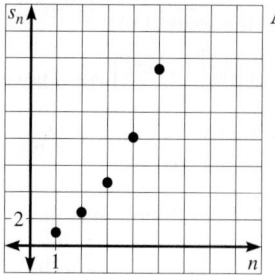 As n increase S_n increases.

5. $2, \frac{14}{6}, \frac{86}{36}, \frac{518}{216}, \frac{3110}{1296}$

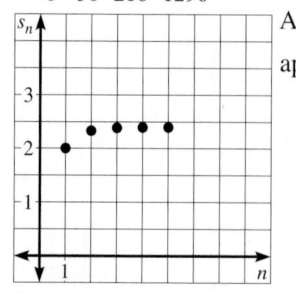 As n increase S_n approaches $\frac{12}{5}$.

7. $\frac{9}{2}$ **9.** $\frac{4}{3}$ **11.** $\frac{5}{8}$ **13.** $\frac{5}{33}$ **15.** $\frac{2500}{99}$

11.7 Practice and Applications (pp. 631–633) **17.** $1, \frac{6}{5}, \frac{31}{25}, \frac{156}{125}, \frac{781}{625}$

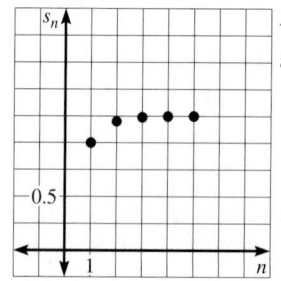 As n increase S_n approaches $\frac{5}{4}$.

19. $5, \frac{25}{3}, \frac{95}{9}, \frac{325}{27}, \frac{1055}{81}$

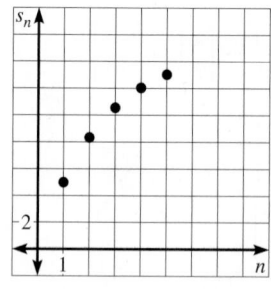 As n increase S_n approaches 15.

21. Sum; r is between -1 and 1. **23.** No sum; r is not between -1 and 1. **25.** No sum; r is not between -1 and 1. **27.** $\frac{75}{19}$ **29.** no sum **31.** 3 **33.** $\frac{10}{3}$ **35.** no sum **37.** $\frac{28}{9}$ **39.** $\frac{2}{3}$ **41.** $\frac{1}{5}$ **43.** $\frac{1}{2}$ **45.** $-\frac{5}{3}$ **47.** $\frac{1}{3}$ **49.** 1 **51.** $\frac{50}{99}$ **53.** $\frac{28}{33}$ **55.** $\frac{70}{9}$ **57.** 144 in.^{2} **59.** 288 in.^{2} *Sample answer:* It represents the sum of the areas of the infinite number of squares. **61.** 80 ft **63.** 140 ft

Chapter Review (pp. 635–638) **1.** 2×3 **5.** $\begin{bmatrix} 1 & 0 \\ 5 & -3 \end{bmatrix}$

7. No solution; the number of columns in the first matrix does not match the number of rows in the second matrix.

9. $\begin{bmatrix} 0 & -6 & -3 \\ -18 & -6 & 12 \\ 9 & 15 & 0 \end{bmatrix}$ **11.** No solution; the number of columns in the first matrix does not match the number of rows in the second matrix. **13.** [1] **15.** $\begin{bmatrix} -4 \\ -14 \end{bmatrix}$

17. $\begin{bmatrix} -27 & -13 \\ -4 & -2 \end{bmatrix}$ **19.** $(-1, 6)$ **21.** $(-3, -6)$ **23.** $(-2, 1)$
25. $5, 2, -1, -4, -7, -10$ **27.** $0, 3, 8, 15, 24, 35$ **29.** 22;
$a_n = 3n + 1$ **31.** 105 **33.** -21 **35.** $a_n = 4n - 1$
37. $a_n = 3n + 5$ **39.** $a_n = 7n - 4$ **41.** 480 **43.** $a_n = 12(2)^{n-1}$ **45.** $a_n = 972\left(\frac{1}{3}\right)^{n-1}$ **47.** $a_n = 3(-2)^{n-1}$

49. 177,144 **51.** 666.666 **53.** $\frac{5}{2}$ **55.** 3 **57.** $\frac{1}{5}$ **59.** $\frac{4}{5}$ **61.** $-\frac{1}{8}$

63. $\frac{32}{99}$ **65.** $\frac{400}{33}$

Chapter 12

12.1 Guided Practice (p. 648) **1.** opposite side, adjacent side, hypotenuse

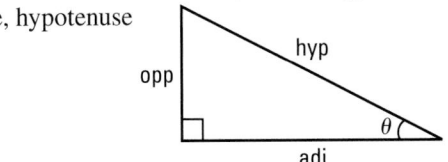

3.

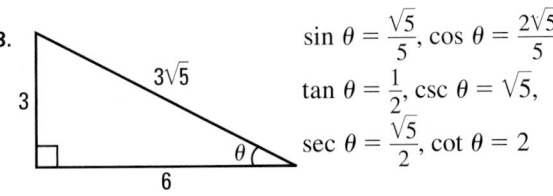

$\sin \theta = \frac{\sqrt{5}}{5}$, $\cos \theta = \frac{2\sqrt{5}}{5}$,
$\tan \theta = \frac{1}{2}$, $\csc \theta = \sqrt{5}$,
$\sec \theta = \frac{\sqrt{5}}{2}$, $\cot \theta = 2$

5. $\sin \theta = \frac{3\sqrt{34}}{34}$, $\cos \theta = \frac{5\sqrt{34}}{34}$, $\tan \theta = \frac{3}{5}$, $\csc \theta = \frac{\sqrt{34}}{3}$,
$\sec \theta = \frac{\sqrt{34}}{5}$, $\cot \theta = \frac{5}{3}$ **7.** $4\sqrt{3}$ **9.** 5.1

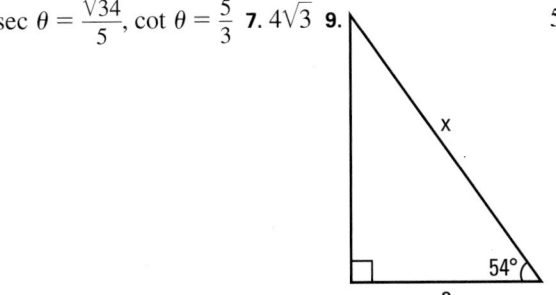

12.1 Practice and Applications (pp. 648–650)

11. $\sin \theta = \frac{12}{13}$, $\cos \theta = \frac{5}{13}$, $\tan \theta = \frac{12}{5}$, $\csc \theta = \frac{13}{12}$,
$\sec \theta = \frac{13}{5}$, $\cot \theta = \frac{5}{12}$ **13.** $\sin \theta = \frac{8}{11}$, $\cos \theta = \frac{\sqrt{57}}{11}$,
$\tan \theta = \frac{8\sqrt{57}}{57}$, $\csc \theta = \frac{11}{8}$, $\sec \theta = \frac{11\sqrt{57}}{57}$, $\cot \theta = \frac{\sqrt{57}}{8}$

15. $\sin \theta = \frac{\sqrt{115}}{14}$, $\cos \theta = \frac{9}{14}$, $\tan \theta = \frac{\sqrt{115}}{9}$, $\csc \theta = \frac{14\sqrt{115}}{115}$, $\sec \theta = \frac{14}{9}$, $\cot \theta = \frac{9\sqrt{115}}{115}$ **17.** The side opposite the angle is 8 not 15; $\sin \theta = \frac{\text{opp}}{\text{hyp}} = \frac{8}{17}$. **19.** $6\sqrt{2}$ **21.** 10
23. $13\sqrt{3}$ **25.** 1.4826 **27.** 0.8290 **29.** 2.5593 **31.** 1.0223
33. 2.29 **35.** 6.38 **37.** 18 **41.** 5725 ft

43.

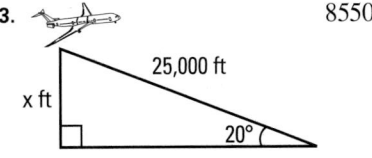
8550.5 ft

12.2 Guided Practice (p. 656) **1.** the origin

3. **5.**

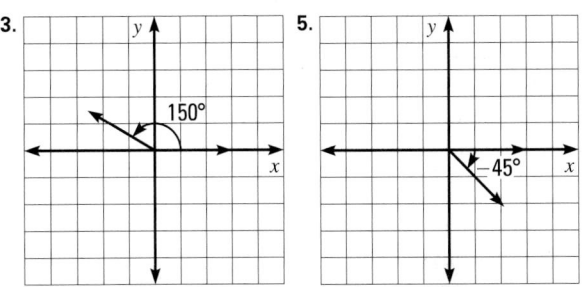

7. *Sample answer:* $380°$, $-340°$ **9.** *Sample answer:* $285°$, $-435°$ **11.** negative **13.** positive **15.** $\sin \theta = -\frac{4}{5}$, $\cos \theta = \frac{3}{5}$, $\tan \theta = -\frac{4}{3}$

12.2 Practice and Applications (pp. 656–658) **17.** C

19. **21.**

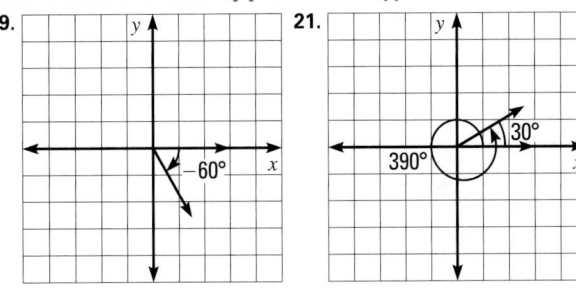

29–35. Sample answers are given. **29.** $280°$, $-440°$
31. $710°$, $-10°$ **33.** $60°$, $-300°$ **35.** $320°$,
$-40°$ **37.** $\sin \theta = \frac{3}{5}$, $\cos \theta = -\frac{4}{5}$, $\tan \theta = -\frac{3}{4}$
39. $\sin \theta = -\frac{4}{5}$, $\cos \theta = -\frac{3}{5}$, $\tan \theta = \frac{4}{3}$ **41.** $\sin \theta = -\frac{15}{17}$,
$\cos \theta = \frac{8}{17}$, $\tan \theta = -\frac{15}{8}$ **43.** $\sin \theta = \frac{24}{25}$, $\cos \theta = \frac{7}{25}$,
$\tan \theta = \frac{24}{7}$ **45.** $\sin \theta = -\frac{\sqrt{2}}{2}$, $\cos \theta = -\frac{\sqrt{2}}{2}$, $\tan \theta = 1$
47. $\sin \theta = \frac{3\sqrt{13}}{13}$, $\cos \theta = -\frac{2\sqrt{13}}{13}$, $\tan \theta = -\frac{3}{2}$
49. $\sin 0° = 0$, $\cos 0° = 1$, $\tan 0° = 0$ **51.** $\sin 540° = 0$,
$\cos 540° = -1$, $\tan 540° = 0$ **53.** negative **55.** positive
57. negative **59.** negative **61.** -0.5736 **63.** 0.3420
65. -0.1736 **69.** $25\sqrt{3}$ ft ≈ 43.3 ft

12.3 Guided Practice (p. 663) **1.** periodic **3.** 5, −5, (0°, 0), (180°, 0), (360°, 0) **5.** $\frac{1}{2}$, $-\frac{1}{2}$, (0°, 0), (1°, 0), (2°, 0)

7.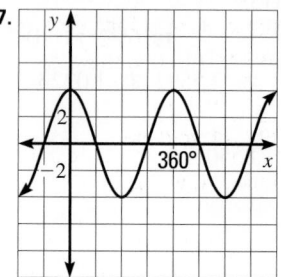

9. (0°, 0), (60°, 0), (120°, 0), $x = 30°$, $x = 90°$, (15°, 1), (45°, −1), (75°, 1), (105°, −1) **11.** (0°, 0), (4°, 0), (8°, 0), $x = 2°$, $x = 6°$, (1°, 4), (3°, −4), (5°, 4), (7°, −4)

13.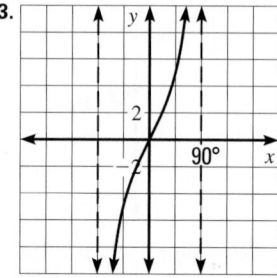

15. The formula for the maximum was used instead of the minimum; minimum = $\left(\frac{270°}{b}, -a\right) = \left(\frac{270°}{30}, -2\right) = (9°, -2)$.

12.3 Practice and Applications (pp. 663–665) **17.** A **19.** F **21.** C **23.** 3, −3, (1°, 0), (3°, 0) **25.** 2, −2, (0°, 0), (1°, 0), (2°, 0) **27.** $\frac{1}{3}$, $-\frac{1}{3}$, (0.125°, 0), (0.375°, 0)

29. 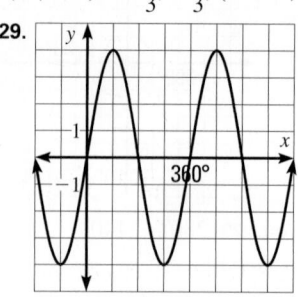 **33.**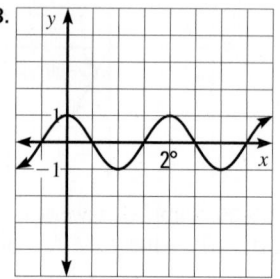

37. $y = \sin 8x$ **39.** $y = 4 \sin 120x$ **41.** (0°, 0), $x = -1°$, $x = 1°$, (−0.5°, −1), (0.5°, 1) **43.** (0°, 0), $x = -0.5°$, $x = 0.5°$, (−0.25°, −3), (0.25°, 3)

45. 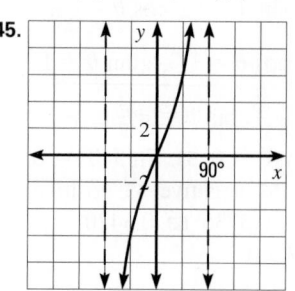 **47.**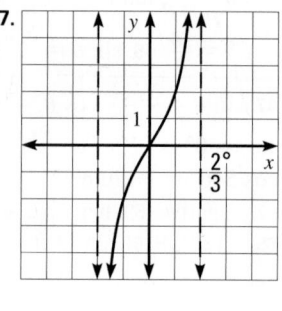

51. 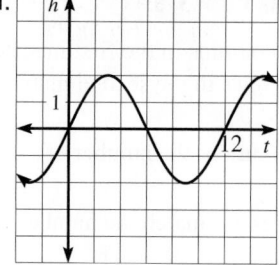 2 ft, −2 ft; 12 h

53. (2.8, −2.5)

12.4 Guided Practice (p. 672) **1.** two angles and a side or two sides and a non-included angle **3.** 103.02 **5.** 6.3 **7.** 10°, 170° **9.** 45.6° or 134.4° **11.** 42°

13. 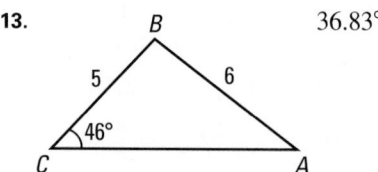 36.83°

12.4 Practice and Applications (pp. 672–674) **15.** 27.05 **17.** 14.28 **19.** 11.3 **21.** 30°, 150° **23.** 62°, 118° **25.** 80°, 100° **29.** $x = 80.6$ **31.** $x = 45$, $y = 20$ **33.** no triangle

37. 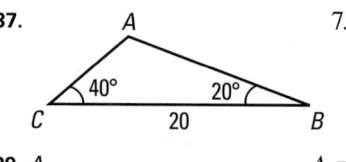 7.9

39. 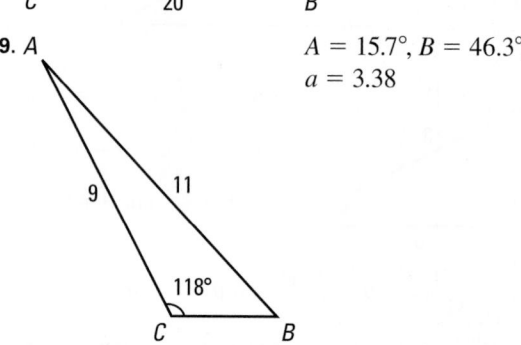 $A = 15.7°$, $B = 46.3°$, $a = 3.38$

43. 4.71 mi **45.** $b = 3.55$ ft, $c = 5.33$ ft

12.5 Guided Practice (p. 678) **1.** two sides and the included angle or three sides **3.** 15.5 **5.** 113.61 **7.** 42.3

12.5 Practice and Applications (pp. 678–681) **9.** 6.4 **11.** 7.7 **13.** 52.5 **15.** 15.5 **17.** The denominator should contain c not a. Also, the −1 should be an exponent. $\cos A = \frac{15^2 + 10^2 - 18^2}{2(15)(10)} \approx 0.0033$, $A \approx \cos^{-1}(0.0033) \approx 89.8°$ **19.** 76.2 **21.** 33.6 **23.** 48.2

25. 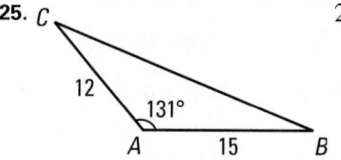 24.6

29. $D = 44.5°$, $E = 74.4°$, $F = 61.1°$ **31.** $A = 42.7°$, $B = 38.1°$, $C = 99.2°$ **33.** $M = 57.1°$, $N = 44.4°$, $P = 78.5°$

35.

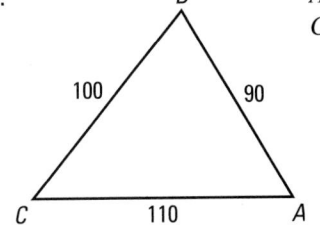

$A = 59°$, $B = 70.5°$, $C = 50.5°$

39.

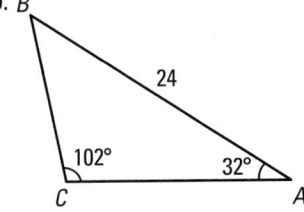

$B = 46°$, $a = 13$, $b = 17.65$

Chapter Review (pp. 682–684) **3.** quadrantal angle

5. $\sin \theta = \frac{24}{25}$, $\cos \theta = \frac{7}{25}$, $\tan \theta = \frac{24}{7}$, $\csc \theta = \frac{25}{24}$, $\sec \theta = \frac{25}{7}$, $\cot \theta = \frac{7}{24}$ **7.** $\sin \theta = \frac{4}{5}$, $\cos \theta = \frac{3}{5}$, $\tan \theta = \frac{4}{3}$, $\csc \theta = \frac{5}{4}$, $\sec \theta = \frac{5}{3}$, $\cot \theta = \frac{3}{4}$ **9.** 6.22

11.

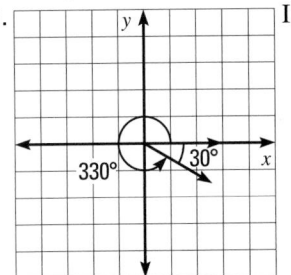

IV

13.

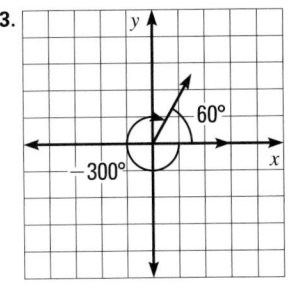

I

15. $\sin \theta = \frac{5}{13}$, $\cos \theta = -\frac{12}{13}$, $\tan \theta = -\frac{5}{12}$

17. $\sin \theta = -\frac{15}{17}$, $\cos \theta = -\frac{8}{17}$, $\tan \theta = \frac{15}{8}$

23. $C = 70°$, $a = 15.43$, $b = 12.04$ **25.** $B = 78°$, $a = 10.56$, $c = 21.62$ **27.** $a = 33.5$, $B = 45.1°$, $C = 52.9°$

Chapter 13

13.1 Guided Practice (p. 694)

1. $d = \sqrt{(x_2 - x_1)^2 + (y_2 - y_1)^2}$ **3.** 5 **5.** $2\sqrt{10}$ **7.** 5
9. isosceles **11.** isosceles **13.** $(-4, -3)$ **15.** $(1, 4)$
17. $(0.5, 0.5)$

13.1 Practice and Applications (pp. 694–696)
19. $2\sqrt{5}$; $(2, -1)$ **21.** $\sqrt{26}$; $(-0.5, 0.5)$ **23.** 5; $(-4, 2.5)$
25. $2\sqrt{17}$; $(2, 7)$ **27.** $5\sqrt{5}$; $(2, 1.5)$ **29.** $\sqrt{170}$; $(-4.5, -0.5)$ **31.** One part of the parentheses is missing, and the squared terms are subtracted instead of added, making the correct solution $\sqrt{(2 - (-4))^2 + (8 - 3)^2} = \sqrt{(6)^2 + (5)^2} = \sqrt{36 + 25} = \sqrt{61}$. **33.** scalene

35. isosceles **37.** scalene **39.** scalene **41.** $y = \frac{1}{3}x - \frac{10}{3}$

43. $y = x$ **45.** $y = \frac{2}{3}x - \frac{7}{3}$ **47.** 25 yd **49.** 5.4 mi

51. 0.81 mi **53.** *Sample answer:* About 125 mi **55.** $\sqrt{3170}$ or about 56.3 mi

13.2 Guided Practice (p. 700) **1.** focus; directrix

3.

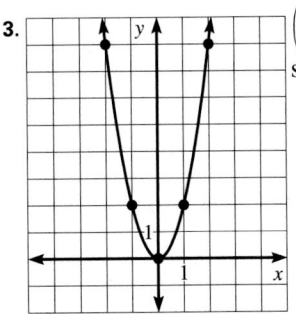

$\left(0, \frac{1}{8}\right)$, $y = -\frac{1}{8}$, axis of symmetry $x = 0$

5.

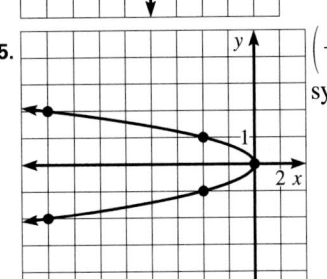

$\left(-\frac{1}{16}, 0\right)$, $x = \frac{1}{16}$, axis of symmetry $y = 0$

9. $y^2 = 4x$

13.2 Practice and Applications (pp. 700–701) **11.** C
13. B **15.** $\left(0, \frac{1}{4}\right)$, $y = -\frac{1}{4}$ **17.** $\left(0, -\frac{1}{16}\right)$, $y = \frac{1}{16}$ **19.** $\left(0, \frac{1}{20}\right)$, $y = -\frac{1}{20}$ **21.** $(0, -6)$, $y = 6$

23.

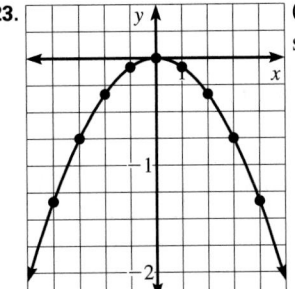

$(0, -3)$, $y = 3$, axis of symmetry $x = 0$

27. 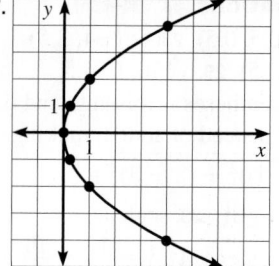 $(1, 0)$, $x = -1$, axis of symmetry $y = 0$

35. The parabola should open to the right instead of up.

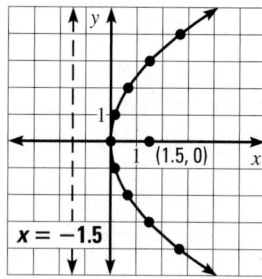

37. $x^2 = 4y$ **39.** $y^2 = 8x$ **41.** $x^2 = 12y$ **43.** $y^2 = 6x$
45. $x^2 = 16y$ **47.** $x^2 = -3y$ **49.** about 1 m **51.** 1.5 in.

13.3 Guided Practice (p. 706) **1.** circle **3.** *Sample answer:* The slopes are opposite reciprocals because the lines are perpendicular. **5.** $x^2 + y^2 = 25$ **7.** $x^2 + y^2 = 2$
9. $x^2 + y^2 = 50$

11. 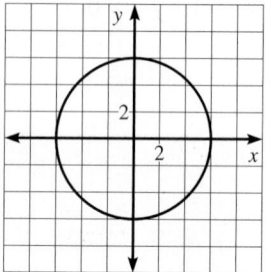 $r = 6$

15. 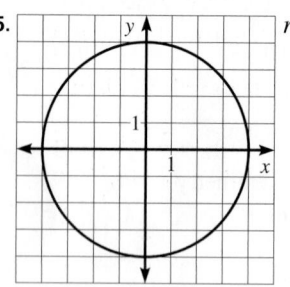 $r = 4$

13.3 Practice and Applications (pp. 706–708) **17.** C
19. A **21.** F

25. 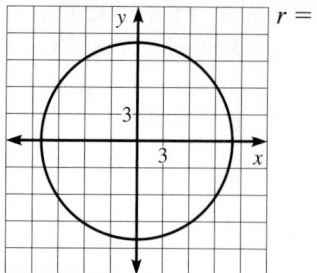 $r = 11$

29. 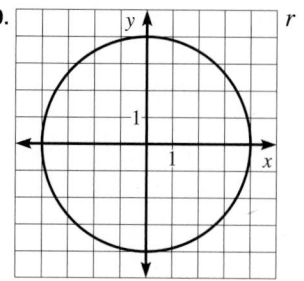 $r = 4$

33. $x^2 + y^2 = 225$ **35.** $x^2 + y^2 = 19$ **37.** $x^2 + y^2 = 48$
39. $x^2 + y^2 = 40$ **41.** $x^2 + y^2 = 9$ **43.** $x^2 + y^2 = 100$
45. $x^2 + y^2 = 41$ **47.** $x^2 + y^2 = 52$

49. circle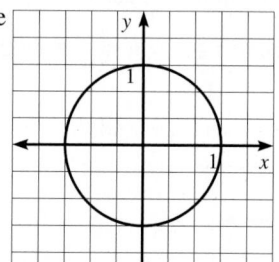

55. $y = x$ **57.** $y = \frac{1}{3}x - \frac{20}{3}$ **59.** $y = \frac{1}{5}x + \frac{26}{5}$ **61.** $\sqrt{34} \approx$ 5.8 **63.** $x^2 + y^2 \leq 9$ **65.** $x^2 + y^2 \leq 225$ **67.** yes

13.3 Technology Activity (p. 709)

1.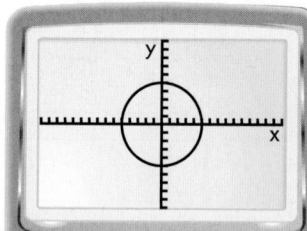

5.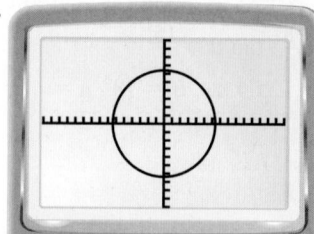

13.4 Guided Practice (p. 713) **1.** minor axis

3. 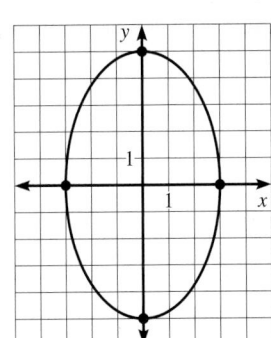 vertices $(0, 5)$ and $(0, -5)$, co-vertices $(-3, 0)$ and $(3, 0)$, foci $(0, 4)$ and $(0, -4)$

5. 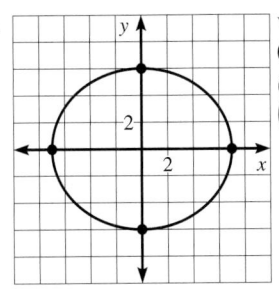 vertices $(-7, 0)$ and $(7, 0)$, co-vertices $(0, 6)$ and $(0, -6)$, foci $\left(\sqrt{13}, 0\right)$ and $\left(-\sqrt{13}, 0\right)$

7. $(0, 6)$ and $(0, -6)$

9. $\dfrac{x^2}{100} + \dfrac{y^2}{25} = 1$ **11.** $\dfrac{x^2}{15} + \dfrac{y^2}{64} = 1$ **13.** $\dfrac{x^2}{13} + \dfrac{y^2}{9} = 1$

13.4 Practice and Applications (pp. 713–716)

15. F **17.** C **19.** A **21.** vertices $(0, 9)$ and $(0, -9)$, co-vertices $(-8, 0)$ and $(8, 0)$, foci $\left(0, \sqrt{17}\right)$ and $\left(0, -\sqrt{17}\right)$
23. vertices $(6, 0)$ and $(-6, 0)$, co-vertices $(0, -4)$ and $(0, 4)$, foci $(2\sqrt{5}, 0)$ and $(-2\sqrt{5}, 0)$ **25.** vertices $\left(0, \sqrt{53}\right)$ and $\left(0, -\sqrt{53}\right)$, co-vertices $(-7, 0)$ and $(7, 0)$, foci $(0, 2)$ and $(0, -2)$ **27.** vertices $(0, 5)$ and $(0, -5)$, co-vertices $(-4, 0)$ and $(4, 0)$, foci $(0, 3)$ and $(0, -3)$

39. The major axis should be along the y-axis, not the x-axis.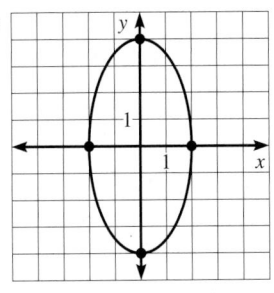

41. $\left(\sqrt{105}, 0\right), \left(-\sqrt{105}, 0\right)$ **43.** $\left(0, 2\sqrt{7}\right), \left(0, -2\sqrt{7}\right)$
45. $\dfrac{x^2}{64} + \dfrac{y^2}{36} = 1$ **47.** $\dfrac{x^2}{49} + \dfrac{y^2}{81} = 1$ **49.** $\dfrac{x^2}{49} + \dfrac{y^2}{36} = 1$
51. parabola

53. parabola **55.** circle **57.** circle **59.** $\dfrac{x^2}{198,025} + \dfrac{y^2}{280,900} = 1$ **61.** 740,945 ft^2 **63.** 28.5 ft

65. *Sample answer:*

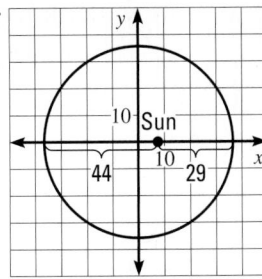

67. *Sample answer:* $\dfrac{x^2}{1332} + \dfrac{y^2}{1274} = 1$

13.5 Guided Practice (p. 720) **1.** transverse axis

3. 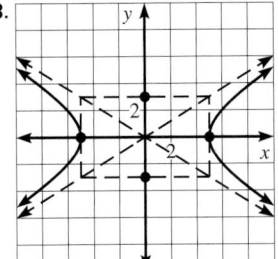 vertices $(-5, 0)$ $(5, 0)$, foci $\left(-\sqrt{34}, 0\right)\left(\sqrt{34}, 0\right)$, asymptotes $y = \pm\dfrac{3}{5}x$

5. 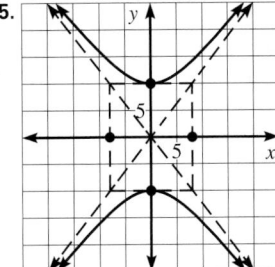 vertices $(0, -10)$ $(0, 10)$, foci $\left(0, -2\sqrt{41}\right)\left(0, 2\sqrt{41}\right)$, asymptotes $y = \pm\dfrac{5}{4}x$

7. $\dfrac{x^2}{9} - \dfrac{y^2}{16} = 1$ **9.** $\dfrac{x^2}{16} - \dfrac{y^2}{25} = 1$

13.5 Practice and Applications (pp. 720–722) **11.** C
13. D **15.** B **17.** $(\pm\sqrt{5}, 0)$ **19.** $(0, \pm6)$ **21.** vertices $(-4, 0)$ $(4, 0)$, foci $\left(-\sqrt{65}, 0\right)\left(\sqrt{65}, 0\right)$, asymptotes $y = \pm\dfrac{7}{4}x$
23. vertices $\left(-3\sqrt{3}, 0\right)\left(3\sqrt{3}, 0\right)$, foci $(-6, 0)$ $(6, 0)$, asymptotes $y = \pm\dfrac{\sqrt{3}}{3}x$ **25.** vertices $(-9, 0)$ $(9, 0)$, foci $\left(-\sqrt{85}, 0\right)\left(\sqrt{85}, 0\right)$, asymptotes $y = \pm\dfrac{2}{9}x$

27. 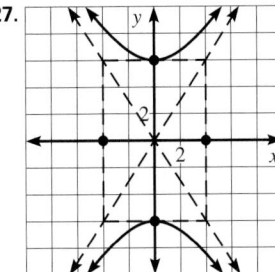 vertices $(0, -6)$ $(0, 6)$, foci $\left(0, -2\sqrt{13}\right)\left(0, 2\sqrt{13}\right)$, asymptotes $y = \pm\dfrac{3}{2}x$

29. 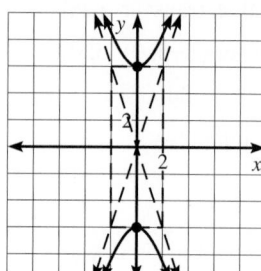 vertices $(-8, 0)$ $(8, 0)$, foci $\left(-2\sqrt{41}, 0\right)\left(2\sqrt{41}, 0\right)$, asymptotes $y = \pm\frac{5}{4}x$

35. Since the term with a positive coefficient is y^2, the transverse axis should be vertical, not horizontal.

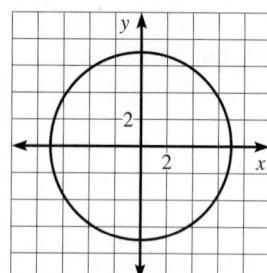

37. $\frac{y^2}{4} - \frac{x^2}{12} = 1$ **39.** $\frac{x^2}{9} - \frac{y^2}{27} = 1$ **41.** $y^2 - \frac{x^2}{8} = 1$

43. circle

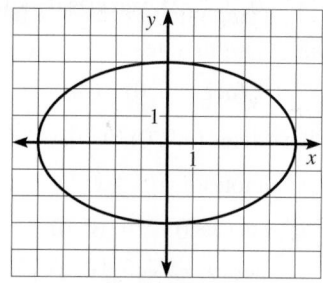

45. ellipse

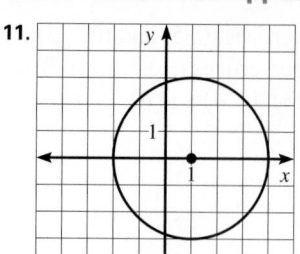

49. $2x^2 - 4y^2 = 1$ **51.** $\frac{x^2}{16.8} - \frac{y^2}{608.2} = 1$

13.6 Guided Practice (p. 728) **1.** conic sections
3. $(x - 1)^2 + (y - 3)^2 = 9$ **5.** $\frac{(x - 2)^2}{36} + \frac{(y - 1)^2}{32} = 1$
7. circle **9.** ellipse

---

11. 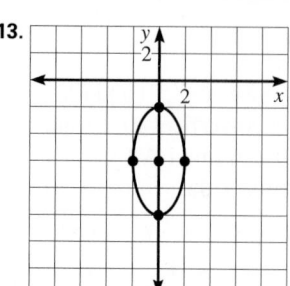 circle with center $(1, 0)$ and radius 3

13. 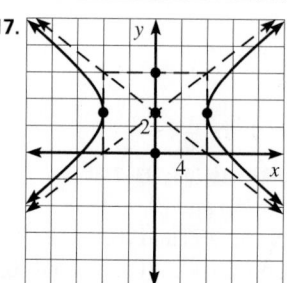 ellipse centered at $(0, -6)$ with vertices $(0, -2)$ and $(0, -10)$ and co-vertices $(-2, -6)$ and $(2, -6)$

17. 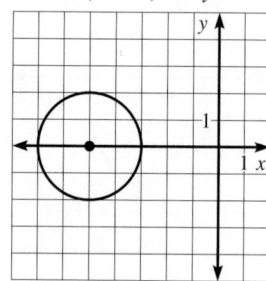 hyperbola with center $(0, 3)$, vertices $(8, 3)$ and $(-8, 3)$, foci $\left(\sqrt{73}, 3\right)$ and $\left(-\sqrt{73}, 3\right)$, and asymptotes $y = \frac{8}{3}x + 3$

19. $(x - 2)^2 + (y - 5)^2 = 4$ **21.** $(x + 6)^2 + (y + 3)^2 = 36$
23. $\frac{(x + 1.5)^2}{12.25} + (y - 1)^2 = 1$ **25.** $\frac{(y - 2)^2}{16} - \frac{(x - 2)^2}{20} = 1$
27. $(x - 5)^2 = -12(y - 3)$ **29.** circle **31.** parabola
33. hyperbola **35.** parabola

37. circle; $(x + 5)^2 + y^2 = 4$

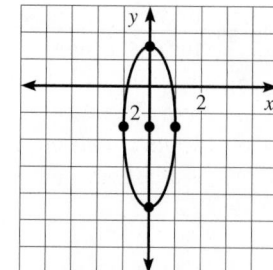

39. ellipse; $x^2 + \frac{(y + 3)^2}{36} = 1$

---

41. hyperbola; $\dfrac{(x-1)^2}{34} - \dfrac{y^2}{\frac{136}{9}} = 1$

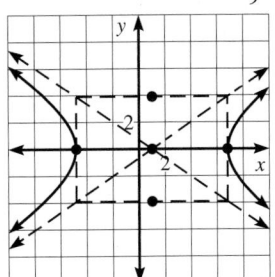

45. $\dfrac{(x-1)^2}{64} - \dfrac{(y-2)^2}{80} = 1$

47. $\dfrac{(x-67.5)^2}{67.5^2} + \dfrac{(y-82.5)^2}{82.5^2} = 1$

49. $\dfrac{(x-3)^2}{9} + \dfrac{y^2}{2.25} = 1$ **51.** parabola **53.** $x^2 + (y-4)^2 = 16$ and $x^2 + (y+4)^2 = 16$ **55.** hyperbola **57.** ellipse

13.6 Technology Activity (p. 732) **1.** (0, 2) **3.** (2, 4) and (−2, −4) **5.** (1, 0)

7. between 0 and 2 intersection points

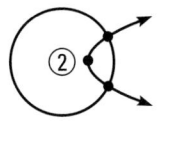 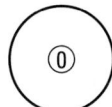

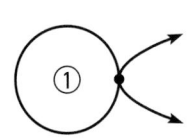 

9. between 0 and 4 intersection points

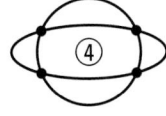 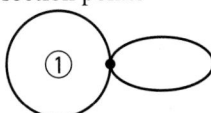

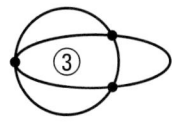 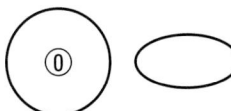

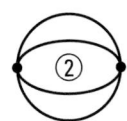

Chapter Review (pp. 733–736) **1.** major axis **3.** An ellipse is the set of all points P in a plane such that the *sum* of the distances between P and two fixed points, called the foci, is constant. A hyperbola is the set of all points P in a plane such that the *difference* of the distances between P and two fixed points, called the foci, is constant.
5. $\sqrt{181}$; (0.5, 3) **7.** $3\sqrt{5}$; (6.5, 6) **9.** $2\sqrt{29}$; (3, −1)

11.

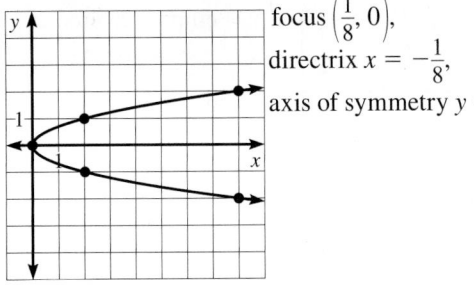

focus $\left(\dfrac{1}{8}, 0\right)$, directrix $x = -\dfrac{1}{8}$, axis of symmetry $y = 0$

13. $y^2 = -20x$ **15.** $y^2 = 24x$

17.

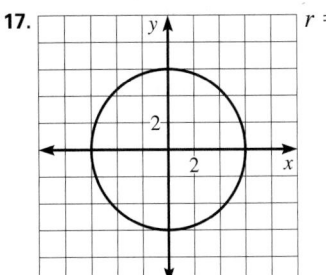

$r = 6$

19. $x^2 + y^2 = 121$ **21.** $x^2 + y^2 = 20$

23.

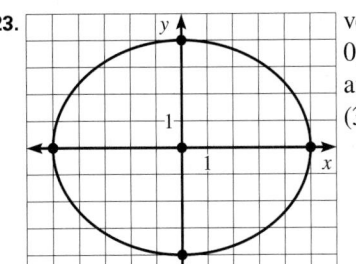

vertices (5, 0) and (−5, 0), co-vertices (0, 4) and (0, −4), and foci (3, 0) and (−3, 0)

25. $\dfrac{x^2}{36} + \dfrac{y^2}{16} = 1$ **27.** $\dfrac{x^2}{25} + \dfrac{y^2}{49} = 1$

29.

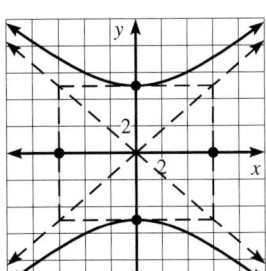

foci $\left(0, \sqrt{61}\right)\left(0, -\sqrt{61}\right)$, asymptotes $y = \pm\dfrac{5}{6}x$

31.

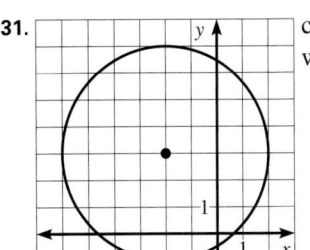

circle centered at (−2, 3) with radius 4

33. 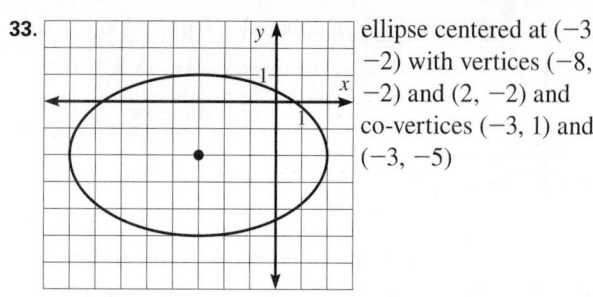 ellipse centered at $(-3, -2)$ with vertices $(-8, -2)$ and $(2, -2)$ and co-vertices $(-3, 1)$ and $(-3, -5)$

37. hyperbola **39.** circle

Skills Review Handbook

Fractions, Decimals, and Percents (p. 743) **1.** 0.22
3. 0.06 **5.** 2.58 **7.** 0.355 **9.** 0.25, 25% **11.** 0.48, 48%
13. 0.448, 45% **15.** $0.\overline{5}$, 56% **17.** 45%, $\frac{9}{20}$ **19.** 80%, $\frac{4}{5}$
21. 136%, $1\frac{9}{25}$ **23.** 37.5%, $\frac{3}{8}$

Calculating Percents (p. 744) **1.** 9 **3.** 32 **5.** 18 **7.** $\frac{1}{4}$
9. 105 **11.** 25% **13.** 10% **15.** 45% **17.** 130% **19.** 12
21. 30.7692. . . **23.** 25 **25.** 40 **27.** 6.5 **29.** 17% **31.** 45%
33. 60%

Factors and Multiples (p. 746) **1.** $2^2 \cdot 3$ **3.** prime
5. $3^2 \cdot 7$ **7.** $2^2 \cdot 7$ **9.** $3 \cdot 5$ **11.** $3 \cdot 19$ **13.** $2^3 \cdot 7$ **15.** $2^2 \cdot 5^2$
17. 3, 63 **19.** 1, 17 **21.** 6, 210 **23.** 2, 90 **25.** 4, 112 **27.** 3,
231 **29.** 20, 200 **31.** 42 **33.** 24 **35.** 30 **37.** 22 **39.** 26 **41.** 24
43. 36 **45.** 40 **47.** $\frac{53}{36}$ **49.** $-\frac{7}{30}$ **51.** $-\frac{1}{10}$ **53.** $\frac{185}{88}$ **55.** $\frac{125}{64}$
57. $\frac{47}{18}$

Writing Ratios and Proportions (p. 747) **1.** 1 to 3,
1:3, $\frac{1}{3}$ **3.** 1 to 3, 1:3, $\frac{1}{3}$ **5.** 1 to 2, 1:2, $\frac{1}{2}$ **7.** 2 to 7, 2:7, $\frac{2}{7}$
9. 1 to 2, 1:2, $\frac{1}{2}$ **11.** 19 to 16, 19:16, $\frac{19}{16}$ **13.** 18 **15.** 1 **17.** 39
19. 12 **21.** 6 **23.** 9

Operations with Positive and Negative Numbers
(p. 748) **1.** -6 **3.** -60 **5.** 2 **7.** 8 **9.** 44 **11.** -4 **13.** 12
15. -72 **17.** -2 **19.** 3 **21.** 9 **23.** 6 **25.** -15 **27.** -12 **29.** 5
31. 42 **33.** -17 **35.** 2 **37.** -16 **39.** 5

Significant Digits (p. 750) **1.** 1700 **3.** -67 **5.** 254
7. 800 **9.** 300.0 **11.** 8.3 **13.** 500 **15.** 200 **17.** 2000
19. 0 **21.** -0.4000 **23.** -200 **25.** 7.4 **27.** 95,000 **29.** 40
31. $67.50 **33.** $79.40 **35.** $400.40 **37.** 140 **39.** 82.9
41. 6.70 **43.** $15.00 **45.** 4 **47.** 3600 **49.** 80 **51.** 4.2

Scientific Notation (p. 751) **1.** 3.2×10^3
3. 8.6905×10^4 **5.** 8.62×10^0 **7.** 4.903×10^0
9. 4.2×10^{-3} **11.** 6.25×10^8 **13.** 9.0090×10^{-3}
15. 2.17×10^2 **17.** 3.24×10^2 **19.** 5.1×10^{-1}
21. 1.602×10^4 **23.** 8.05309×10^2
25. 9.87654321×10^8 **27.** 3.0258×10^{-1} **29.** 500,000
31. 1250 **33.** 8.51 **35.** 7,350,000 **37.** 0.0189 **39.** 0.9514
41. 0.0000002459 **43.** 217 **45.** 45,700 **47.** 93,502,000,000
49. 0.0642 **51.** 805.903 **53.** 37,000 **55.** 2,809,075,000

Points in the Coordinate Plane (p. 752)
1. $A(-2, 3)$, $B(4, 1)$, $C(-1, -1)$, $D(0, -3)$
3. $A(-4, 0)$, $B(1, 0)$, $C(0, 0)$, $D(4, 0)$

5.
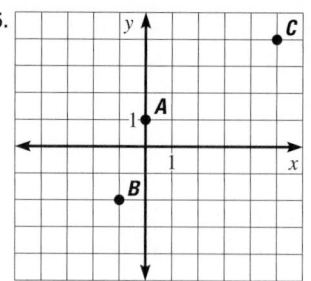

7.
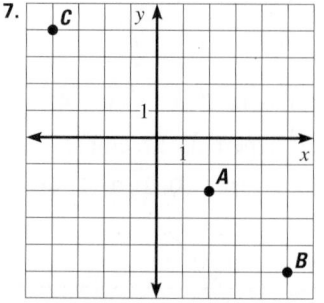

11. II **13.** IV **15.** I **17.** III

Perimeter and Circumference (p. 753) **1.** 12 ft
3. 21 mm **5.** 7.26 cm **7.** 12 ft **9.** $16\pi \approx 50.2$ mi **11.** 9.2 in.
13. 13 m **15.** 34 cm

Area (p. 754) **1.** 5.76 cm^2 **3.** 30 ft^2 **5.** 36 m^2 **7.** 14.85 ft^2
9. 3.5 cm^2 **11.** 19.68 yd^2 **13.** 153 m^2 **15.** 48 cm^2

Volume (p. 755) **1.** 120 m^3 **3.** 226.981 cm^3
5. 1.030301 cm^3 **7.** 0.008 ft^3 **9.** 125 m^3 **11.** 216,000 mm^3
13. $0.3375\pi \approx 1.06$ m^3

Triangle Relationships (p. 756) **1.** 40 **3.** 34 **5.** 120
7. no; $150 + 25 + 75 = 250$ **9.** yes; $59 + 60 + 61 = 180$
11. no; $78 + 22 + 100 = 200$
13. yes; $1 + 10 + 169 = 180$ **15.** yes; $8 + 10 > 12, 8 + 12 > 10, 10 + 12 > 8$ **17.** no; $23 + 41 = 64$ **19.** no; $1 + 2 = 3$ **21.** yes; $3 + 8 > 10, 3 + 10 > 8, 8 + 10 > 3$

Right Triangle Relationships (p. 757) **1.** $\sqrt{11}$ m
3. $4\sqrt{2}$ m **5.** $1.5\sqrt{3}$ cm **7.** $2\sqrt{13}$ mm **9.** $3\sqrt{34}$ cm **11.** 5 ft

Symmetry (p. 759)
1.
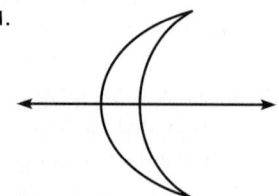

3. none

5.

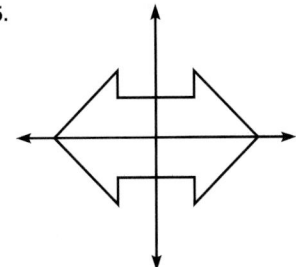

13. none **17.** 180° either direction **19.** 180° either direction
21. none **23.** 180° either direction **25.** 90° or 180° either
direction **27.** 72° or 144° either direction **29.** 45°, 90°,
135°, or 180° either direction **31.** 180° either direction

Transformations (p. 761) **1.** $(-5, 1)$ **3.** $\left(-\dfrac{25}{9}, \dfrac{5}{3}\right)$
5. $(-1, 3)$ **7.** $(5, 3)$ **9.** $(-20, 12)$ **11.** $(-7, 0)$ **13.** $(5, -3)$

15. 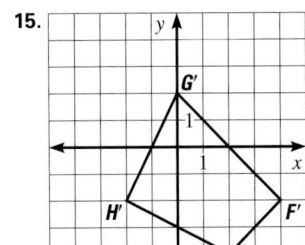 **17.**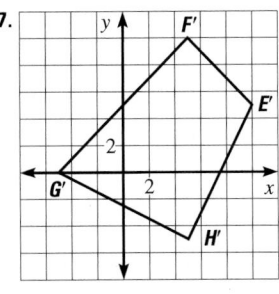

Similar Figures (p. 762) **1.** $x = 12, y = 9$ **3.** $x = 55°$,
$y = 10.5$ **5.** $x = 8, y = 8$ **7.** $x = 27.5, y = 12$ **9.** $x = 4$,
$y = 10$

Logical Argument (p. 764) **1.** valid; *Or* Rule **3.** invalid
5. valid; Direct Argument **7.** valid; Chain Rule **9.** valid;
Or Rule **11.** true **13.** true **15.** false **17.** true **19.** false

If-Then Statements and Counterexamples (p. 766)
1. If you take your brother, then you can go to the movies.
3. If a figure is a hexagon, then it has 6 sides. **5.** If Janet
takes a math test, then she does very well. **7.** If a circle
is a unit circle, then its equation is $x^2 + y^2 = 1$. **9.** If the
intersection of two lines is a point, then the two lines
intersect; true. **11.** If a triangle has two equal sides, then
it has two equal angles; true. **13.** If $x < 2$, then $5x + 13 <$
23; true. **15.** True; if a polygon is a hexagon, then it has
6 sides; true; if a polygon has 6 sides, then it is a hexagon;
true. **17.** True; if a quadrilateral is a rectangle, then it has
four right angles; true; if a quadrilateral has four right
angles, then it is a rectangle; true. **19.** True; if a number
is divisible by 3, then the sum of the digits of the number
is divisible by 3; true; if the sum of the digits of a number
is divisible by 3, then the number is divisible by 3; true.
21. False; penguins do not fly. **23.** False; x could also be
-12.

Justify Reasoning (p. 767) **1.** distributive property
3. division property of equality **5.** distributive property
7. definition of raising to a power (square both sides)
9. multiplication property of equality **11.** $-x = 5$, given;

$x = -5$, multiplication property of equality **13.** $9x = 45$,
given; $x = 5$, division property of equality **15.** $x + 8 =$
22, given; $x = 14$, subtraction property of equality
17. $-2x - 5 = -4$, given; $-2x = 1$, addition property of
equality; $x = -\dfrac{1}{2}$, division property of equality
19. $-\dfrac{5}{2}(-6 - 2x) = 15$, given; $15 + 5x = 15$, distributive
property; $5x = 0$, subtraction property of equality; $x = 0$,
division property of equality **21.** $x^2 = 36$, given; $x = 6$ or
$x = -6$, square root property

Use an Equation or Formula (p. 768) **1.** $5 = 60x$;
$\dfrac{1}{12}$ mi per min or 5 mi per h **3.** $3x = 36; x = 12$; 12 yd
5. $V = 15 \cdot 10 \cdot 10; V = 1500$; 1500 ft³ **7.** $200 = 50t$;
$t = 4$; 4 h **9.** $m = \dfrac{12 - 3}{8 - 5} = \dfrac{9}{3} = 3$

Draw a Diagram (p. 769)

1. 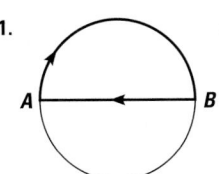 $31.4 = 3.14d; d = 10, AB = 10$ m

3. 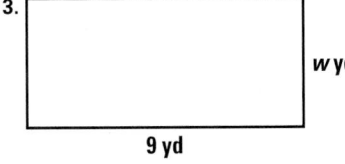 $9w = 72; w = 8$; 8 yd

5. 5 m **7.** 384 cm²

Make a Table or List (p. 770)

1. 16;

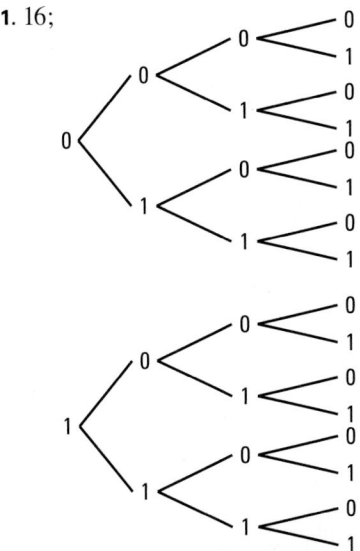

3. 30 outfits **5.** 15 ways

Solve a Simpler Problem (p. 771) **1.** $x^2 - 2x + 1 = 0$;
$(x - 1)^2 = 0; x = 1$; so $x = 253$ **3.** 4 sides has
2 diagonals; 5 sides has 5 diagonals; 6 sides has
9 diagonals; so 18 sides has 126 diagonals

5. $840(1.045)^9 = 840(1.48609514) = \$1248.32$ **7.** $1 + 2 + 3 + \cdots + 98 + 99 + 100 = 50(101) = 5050$
9. $16^2 = (20 - 4)^2 = 20^2 - 2(20)(4) + 4^2 = 400 - 160 + 16 = 256$

Break into Simpler Parts (p. 772) **1.** 0003, 0013, 0023, . . ., 0093 = 10; 0103, 0113, . . . 0193 = 10; 0203, . . . 0293 = 10; same for 3, 4, 5, 6, 7, 8, and 9 so $10 \cdot 10 \cdot 10 \cdot 1$ or 1000 times.

3.

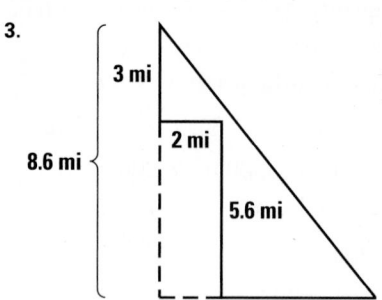

$8.6^2 + 7^2 = x^2$, $x \approx 11.09$; $5 + 5.6 + 2 + 3 + 11.09 = 26.69$ mi

5. $12(8) + \dfrac{12 \cdot 5}{2} = 96 + 30 = 126$ ft^2

7. $10(5) + \dfrac{(10 + 7)2}{2} = 50 + 17 = 67$ in.^{2}

Guess, Check, and Revise (p. 773) **1–7.** Sample answers are given.

1. Guess: 3 weeks
Check: $20 + 7(3) = 20 + 21 = 41$
Revise: Try a larger number of weeks.

Guess: 15 weeks
Check: $20 + 15(7) = 20 + 105 = 125$
Revise: Try a slightly larger number of weeks.

Guess: 16 weeks
Check: $20 + 16(7) = 20 + 112 = 132$
16 weeks

3. Guess: 10 white, 7 blue
Check: $10(50) + 7(65) = 955$
Revise: Try smaller number of blue.

Guess: 11 white, 6 blue
Check: $11(50) + 6(65) = 940$
11 white spruce and 6 blue spruce were sold.

5. Guess: 20
Check: $20(20) = 400$
Revise: Try larger number.

Guess: 30
Check: $30(30) = 900$
Revise: Try smaller number.

Guess: 26
Check: $26(26) = 676$
The length of the floor is 26 feet.

7. Guess: 30, 42
Check: $42 - 30 = 12$
Revise: Try numbers closer together.

Guess: 32, 40
Check: $40 - 32 = 8$
Revise: Try numbers even closer together.

Guess: 33, 39
Check: $39 - 33 = 6$

The lengths of the pieces should be 33 in. and 39 in.

Translating Words into Symbols (p. 774) **1.** $6 + x$
3. $x - 10$ **5.** $\dfrac{x}{9}$ **7.** $x - \dfrac{9}{10}$ **9.** $0.13x$ **11.** $\dfrac{x}{1}$ **13.** $2(x + 25)$
15. $21 - 2x$ **17.** $20x$ **19.** $6x$

Combining Like Terms (p. 775) **1.** $-6x + 3$ **3.** $-3x^2 + 2x + 5$ **5.** $2.9r + 4.7$ **7.** $3r - 6$ **9.** $-64x^{12} + 16x$
11. $-30x$ **13.** $-21n + 49$ **15.** $7.2r^2 + 6.03$ **17.** $-0.12n^2 - 4.972n$ **19.** $-26y^{15} - 2y^4$ **21.** $u^{23} - 24.4$

Multiplying Polynomials and Simplifying Rational Expressions (p. 776) **1.** $x^2 - 9$ **3.** $-x^2 + 6x + 27$ **5.** $y^2 - 8y + 7$ **7.** $-a^2 + 11a - 30$ **9.** $t^2 - 3t - 40$
11. $\dfrac{x}{5}$ **13.** $\dfrac{x}{3}$ **15.** $\dfrac{x + 4}{3}$ **17.** $\dfrac{x - 5}{3}$ **19.** $\dfrac{2x + 4}{5}$ **21.** $\dfrac{x + 10}{4}$

Solving Linear Equations (p. 777) **1.** $-\dfrac{1}{10}$ **3.** $\dfrac{55}{51}$ **5.** $\dfrac{1}{2}$
7. 2 **9.** 3 **11.** $-\dfrac{1}{8}$ **13.** $-\dfrac{3}{14}$ **15.** -1.29 **17.** $\dfrac{23}{5}$

Extra Practice

Chapter 1 (p. 778)

1.

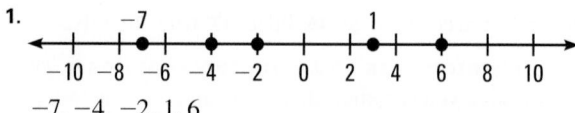

$-7, -4, -2, 1, 6$

3.

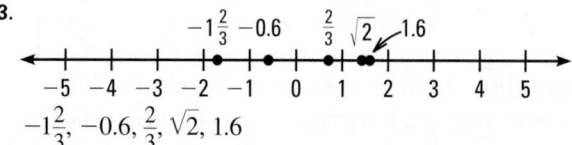

$-1\dfrac{2}{3}, -0.6, \dfrac{2}{3}, \sqrt{2}, 1.6$

5. associative property of multiplication **7.** 81 **9.** -216
11. 9 **13.** 15 **15.** $10x - 7y$ **17.** $8x - 59$ **19.** $-7x - 17$
21. $-6a + 3\dfrac{1}{2}b$ **23.** 10; $10 - 14 = -4$ **25.** 28; $\dfrac{28}{4} = 7$
27. -6; $-5(-6) + 6 = 36$, $30 + 6 = 36$ **29.** -2;
$3(2(-2) - 1) - 4(-2) = -7$, $3(-4 - 1) + 8 = -7$,
$3(-5) + 8 = -7$, $-15 + 8 = -7$ **31.** $r = \dfrac{A - P}{Pt}$ **33.** 5%

35.

x	*x + 8*

60 in

$x + x + 8 = 60$; 26 in., 34 in.

37.

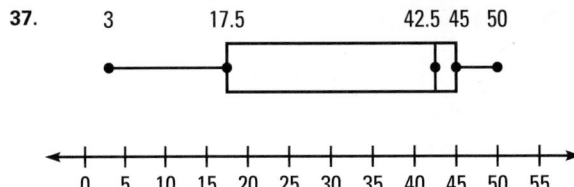

Chapter 2 (p. 779) **1.** domain {0, 3, 6, 9}, range {2, 4}, function **3.** domain {−4, −2, 0, 2, 4}, range {−2, 0, 2}, function **5.** linear; −100 **7.** not linear; 65 **9.** not linear; 432 **11.** undefined; is vertical **13.** Line 1

15. 2, 1;

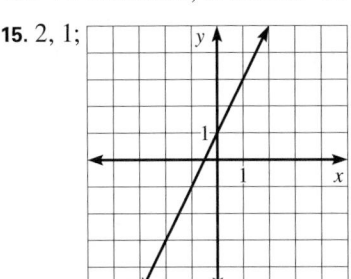

17. $-\frac{4}{3}$, −4;

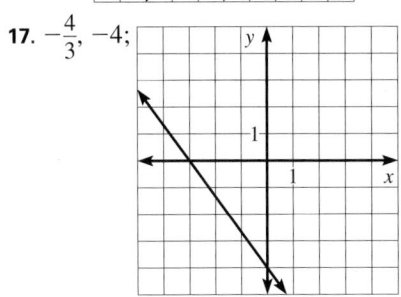

19.

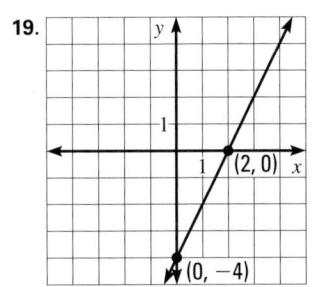

21. $y = -2x - 1$ **23.** $y = -3x + 17$ **25.** $y = 2x + 24$
27. $y = -20x$; −120

29.

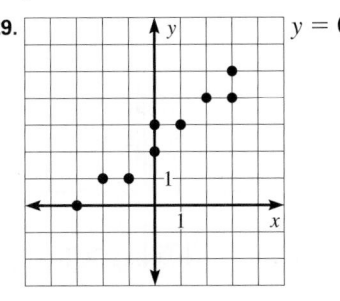 $y = 0.8x + 2.3$; 6.3

Chapter 3 (p. 780) **1.** (27, 37); $37 = \frac{4}{3}(27) + 1$, $37 = 37$; $37 = 2(27) - 17$, $37 = 37$ **3.** (8, 1); $8 + 7 = 15$, $15 = 15$; $-2(8) + 5(1) = -11$, $-11 = -11$

5.

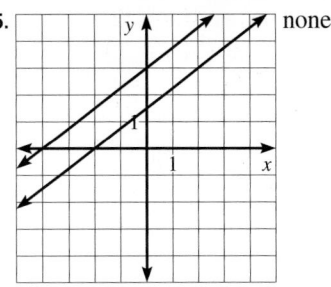 none

7. (−1, 2); the second equation is solved for y so it is ready to substitute. **9.** (3, 3); solve the first equation for y because it is easier. **11.** (−2, 11); solve the second equation for y because the coefficient is 1. **13.** $x + y = 30$, $0.05x + 0.1y = 2.5$; 10 minutes walking and 20 minutes jogging **15.** (−6, 1); $-6 + 3(1) = -6 + 3 = -3$; $-1(-6) + 2(1) = 6 + 2 = 8$ **17.** infinitely many solutions

19.

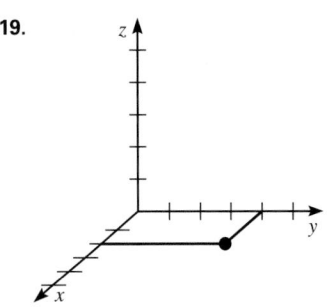

21.

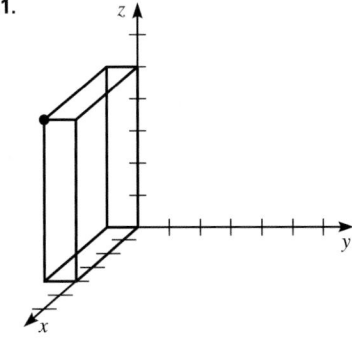

23.

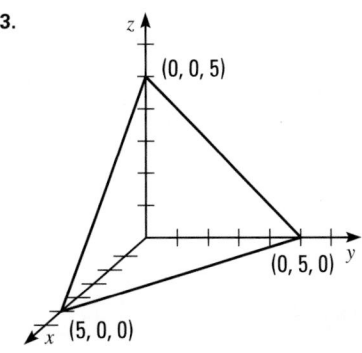

25.

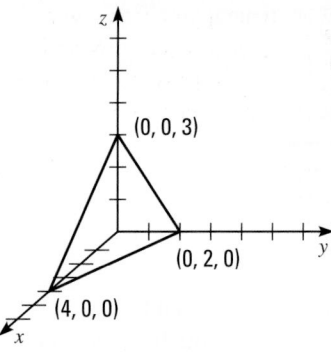

27. $(1, 2, 3)$

29.

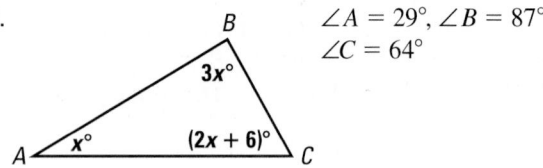

$\angle A = 29°$, $\angle B = 87°$, $\angle C = 64°$

Chapter 4 (p. 781)

1. $x < 2$

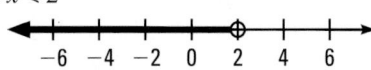

3. $-1 < x < 3$

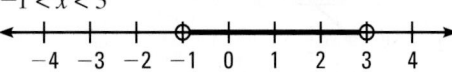

5. $x < -6$ or $x \geq 4$

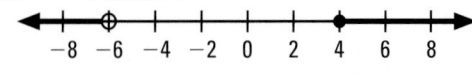

7. $-133 \leq t \leq -7$

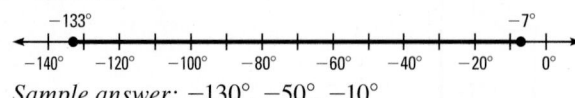

Sample answer: $-130°, -50°, -10°$

9. B

11.

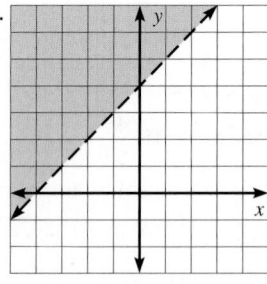

13.

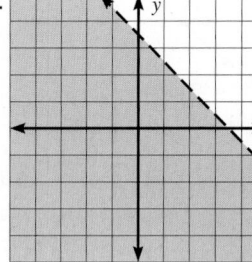

15.

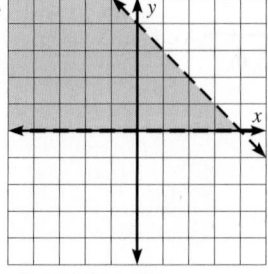

17.

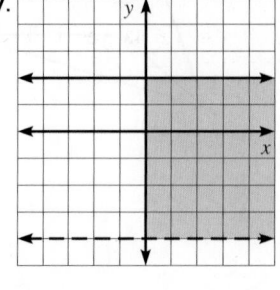

19.

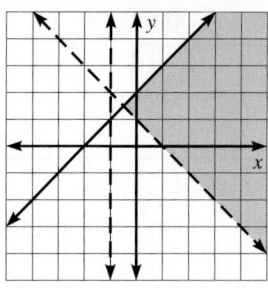

21. 4, 1; $\left|2(4) - 5\right| = \left|3\right| = 3$, $\left|2(1) - 5\right| = \left|-3\right| = 3$

23. 0, $-\frac{2}{3}$; $\left|3(0) + 1\right| = \left|1\right| = 1$, $\left|3\left(-\frac{2}{3}\right) + 1\right| = \left|-1\right| = 1$ **25.** −10, −22; $\left|8 + \frac{1}{2}(-10)\right| = \left|3\right| = 3$, $\left|8 + \frac{1}{2}(-22)\right| = \left|-3\right| = 3$

27. $x < -6$ or $x > 10$;

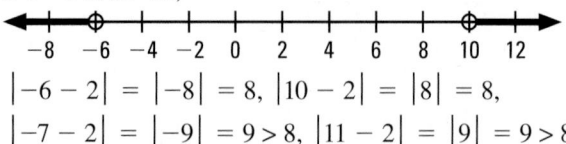

$\left|-6 - 2\right| = \left|-8\right| = 8$, $\left|10 - 2\right| = \left|8\right| = 8$, $\left|-7 - 2\right| = \left|-9\right| = 9 > 8$, $\left|11 - 2\right| = \left|9\right| = 9 > 8$

29. $x < -3$ or $x > 8$;

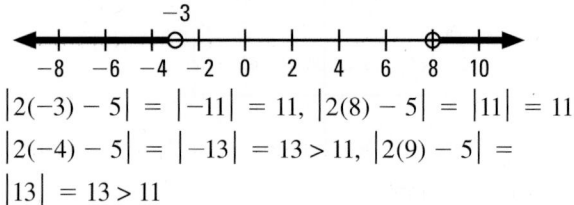

$\left|2(-3) - 5\right| = \left|-11\right| = 11$, $\left|2(8) - 5\right| = \left|11\right| = 11$, $\left|2(-4) - 5\right| = \left|-13\right| = 13 > 11$, $\left|2(9) - 5\right| = \left|13\right| = 13 > 11$

31. no solution **33.** 5, 2 **35.** 4, $\frac{1}{2}$ **37.** 11, 5

39.

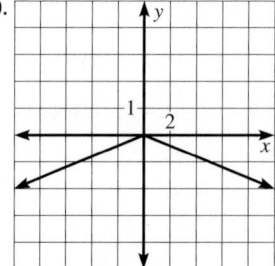

Chapter 5 (p. 782)

1.

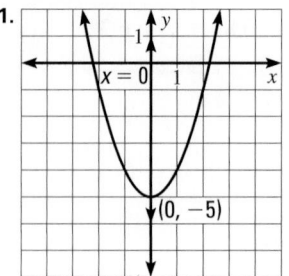

3.

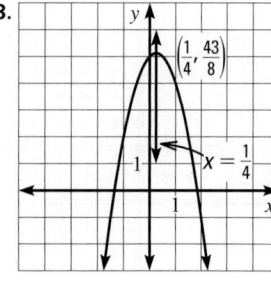

5. $y = x^2 + 12x + 35$ **7.** $y = -3x^2 - 18x - 31$

9. 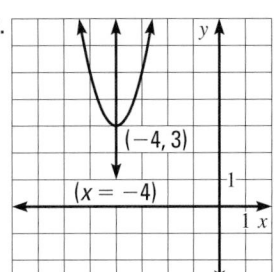 **11.**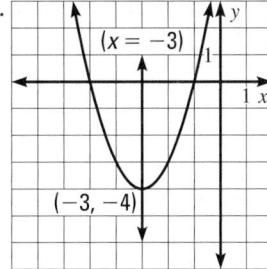

13.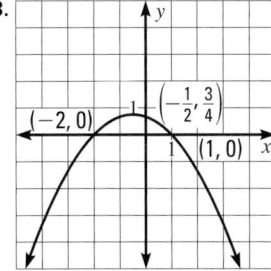

15. $-5, 3$ **17.** no solution **19.** $\dfrac{1}{4}, -3$ **21.** $\dfrac{1}{4}, 1$

23. $(x + 5)(x - 5)$ **25.** $(x - 7)^2$ **27.** $7, -7$ **29.** $-5 \pm 2\sqrt{5}$

31. $9i, -9i$ **33.** $\pm 2i\sqrt{2}$ **35.** $15 + 5i$ **37.** $-31 + 77i$

39. $-2 \pm \sqrt{11}$ **41.** $-4 \pm 2\sqrt{10}$ **43.** $y = (x - 7)^2 - 21$;

$(7, -21)$ **45.** $y = (x + 4)^2 - 17$; $(-4, -17)$ **47.** $\dfrac{4 \pm i\sqrt{14}}{3}$

49. $\dfrac{2 \pm \sqrt{30}}{2}$ **51.** 0, 1 real solution **53.** 121, 2 real solutions

55. about 33.25 mph

Chapter 6 (p. 783) **1.** 64; product of powers **3.** 1000;

power of a product **5.** $\dfrac{1}{117,649}$; zero power, negative

exponent **7.** $\dfrac{1}{9x^{10}}$; product of powers, power of product,

power of powers, negative exponent **9.** $\dfrac{x^{21}y^{14}}{128}$; power of

product, power of power, negative exponent

11. $f(x) = -x^3 + 7$; 3, cubic, -1 **13.** $f(x) = -x^5 + 13x^2 + 2$; 5, quintic, -1

15. 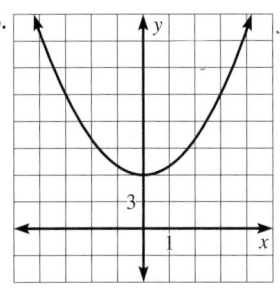 $f(x)$ approaches $+\infty$ as x approaches $+\infty$ or $-\infty$.

17. 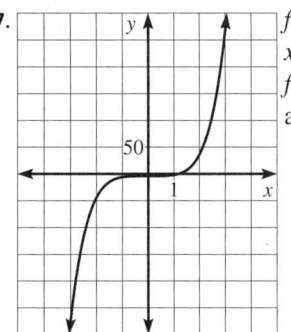 $f(x)$ approaches $-\infty$ as x approaches $-\infty$ and $f(x)$ approaches $+\infty$ as x approaches $+\infty$.

19. $3x^4 - 2x^3 - 4$ **21.** $17x^3 + x^2 + x$ **23.** $x^3 + 18x^2 + 108x + 216$ **25.** $2x^3 - 17x^2 + 10x + 77$ **27.** $x^3 - 9x^2 + 24x - 20$ **29.** $x + 7$ **31.** $20x^2 + 46x - 10$

33. $(3x + 4)(9x^2 - 12x + 16)$ **35.** $(3x - 1)(9x^2 + 3x + 1)$

37. $(x - 7)(x + 6)$ **39.** $(x + 7)(x + 2)(x - 2)$

41. $(x^2 + 11)(x^2 - 11)$ **43.** $(x^2 + 5)(x + 1)(x - 1)$

45. $2x(6x^2 + 1)(6x^2 - 1)$ **47.** $(x^2 + 9)(x^2 + 2)$

49. $3x(x^2 + 3)(x^2 + 5)$

51. 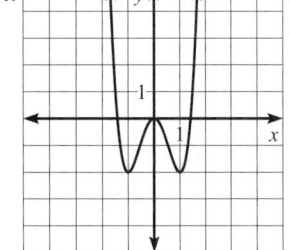 $(0, 0), \left(\pm\sqrt{2}, 0\right), (-1, -2),$ $(1, -2)$

53. 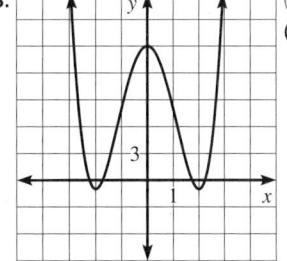 $\left(\pm\sqrt{5}, 0\right)\left(\pm\sqrt{3}, 0\right), (-2, -1),$ $(2, -1), (0, 15)$

Chapter 7 (p. 784) **1.** -4 **3.** -3 **5.** $2, -2$ **7.** $7^{2/3}$ **9.** $\left(\sqrt[5]{5}\right)^3$

11. $2\sqrt[5]{3}$ **13.** $\dfrac{\sqrt[4]{72}}{3}$ **15.** $\dfrac{\sqrt[5]{24}}{3}$ **17.** $8m^6n^{12/5}$ **19.** $\dfrac{4b^2}{5a^5}$

21. $3p^3q^{5/2}$ **23.** $6s^4t^{3/2}$ **25.** 8 **27.** $\dfrac{77}{3}$ **29.** no solution **31.** -8

33. $8x + 3$; all real numbers **35.** $2x + \dfrac{7}{x}$ **37.** $3x^2 + 4$; all

real numbers **39.** yes; $f^{-1}(x) = \dfrac{x + 1}{5}$ **41.** yes;

$f^{-1}(x) = \sqrt{x}$ **43.** yes; $f^{-1}(x) = \dfrac{x - 3}{4}$ **45.** yes; $f^{-1}(x) = \sqrt{x - 8}$

47. 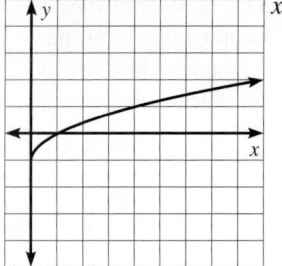 $x \geq 0, y \geq -1$

49. 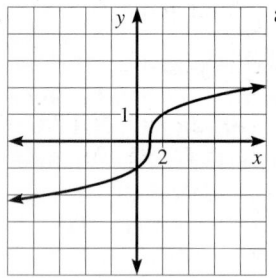 all reals, all reals

51. 3.4 **53.** 3.9

Chapter 8 (p. 785)

1. 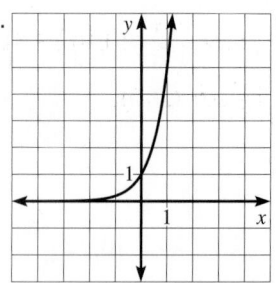 all real numbers, $y > 0$

3. 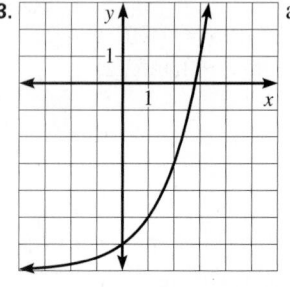 all real numbers, $y > -7$

5. B

7. 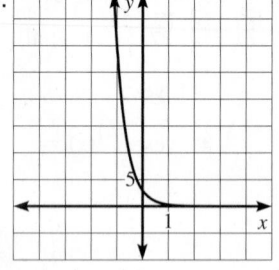 all real numbers, $y > 0$

9. 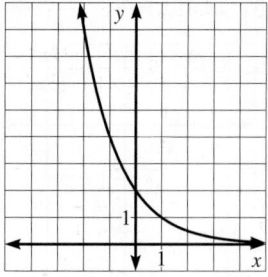 all real numbers, $y > 0$

11. $y = 7^x$ **13.** $y = \dfrac{1}{12} \cdot 12^x$ **15.** 2 **17.** 5 **19.** $3x$ **21.** $2x$

23. 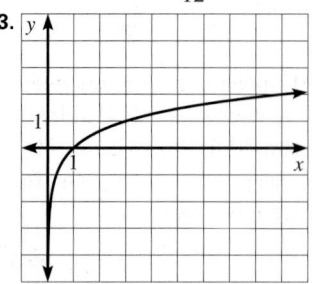 $x = 0; x > 0$, all real numbers

25. 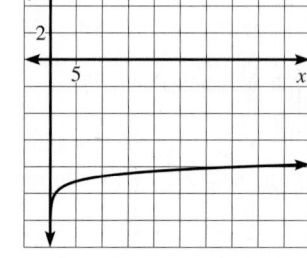 $x = 0; x > 0$, all real numbers

27. $9 \log_4 x$ **29.** $\log_2 64x - \log_2 y$ **31.** $\log_3 28$
33. $\log_3 x^6 - 1$ **35.** $\dfrac{4}{5}$ **37.** 2.57 **39.** no solution **41.** 50

Chapter 9 (p. 786) **1.** $y = \dfrac{-16}{x}; -4$ **3.** $y = \dfrac{35}{x}; \dfrac{35}{4}$
5. \$44.80

7. 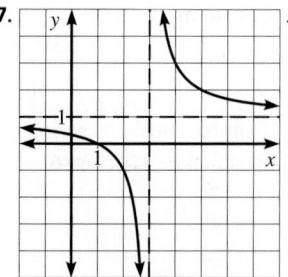 $x \neq 3, y \neq 1$

9. 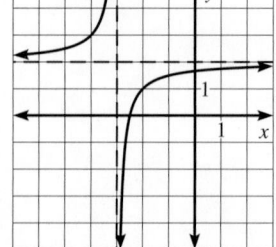 $x \neq -3, y \neq 2$

11. already in simplest form **13.** $\dfrac{x + 7}{x - 10}$ **15.** $\dfrac{1}{3x(x - 4)}$

17. $\dfrac{x+3}{x+1}$ **19.** $\dfrac{(x-4)(x+7)}{(x-6)(x+1)}$ **21.** $\dfrac{9}{2x}$ **23.** $\dfrac{6}{x}$ **25.** $\dfrac{3(x+7)(x-4)}{x}$

27. $\dfrac{2(x+1)}{3x(x-1)}$ **29.** $\dfrac{x+4}{x+2}$ **31.** $\dfrac{7}{3x}$ **33.** $\dfrac{4-x}{x+5}$ **35.** $\dfrac{4x^2+24x+14}{(x+1)(3x+1)}$

37. $\dfrac{x^3-5x^2+x-9}{x^2-25}$ **39.** $4;\ \dfrac{2}{4+4}=\dfrac{2}{8}=\dfrac{1}{4}$

41. $\dfrac{-4}{3},\ 1;\ \dfrac{4}{1}=\dfrac{3(1)+5}{1+1}=\dfrac{8}{2}=\dfrac{4}{1},\quad \dfrac{4}{-\frac{4}{3}}=\dfrac{3\left(-\frac{4}{3}\right)+5}{-\frac{4}{3}+1}=$

$\dfrac{-4+5}{-\frac{1}{3}}=\dfrac{1}{-\frac{1}{3}}=-3$ **43.** $2,\ -1;\ 2-\dfrac{4}{2+2}=2-\dfrac{4}{4}=2-$

$1=1=\dfrac{2}{2},\ 2-\dfrac{4}{-1+2}=2-\dfrac{4}{1}=-2=\dfrac{2}{-1}$

Chapter 10 (p. 787) **1.** 1300 students **3.** Convenience; they were chosen because they were close. **5.** Original 280.625, 280, 280, 30, 14.5; new 165.625, 165, 165, 30, 14.5; all are reduced by 115 except for the range and the quartile difference which stayed the same.

7. permutation; 132,600 **9.** permutation; 24 **11.** $\dfrac{3}{10}$ **13.** $\dfrac{3}{10}$

15. 0.13 **17a.** $\dfrac{3}{169}\approx1.8\%$ **b.** $\dfrac{4}{221}\approx1.8\%$

Chapter 11 (p. 788) **1.** $\begin{bmatrix}7\\10\\-7\end{bmatrix}$ **3.** Not possible. The

dimensions are not the same. **5.** $\begin{bmatrix}12&29\\7&8\\-2&-2\end{bmatrix}$

7. $\begin{bmatrix}-6&7\\7&-8\end{bmatrix}$ **9.** $\begin{bmatrix}\frac{11}{2}&\frac{3}{2}\\4&1\end{bmatrix}$ **11.** $\left(-\dfrac{43}{5},\ -\dfrac{41}{5}\right)$

13. $29;\ a_n=5n-1$ **15.** $81;\ a_n=(n+2)^2$ **17.** 21
19. $a_n=6n+1$ **21.** $a_n=3n-19$ **23.** 35 **25.** Arithmetic; terms increase by 2. **27.** Geometric; terms are multiplied by -5. **29.** Arithmetic; terms increase by

6. **31.** $a_n=81\left(\dfrac{1}{3}\right)^{n-1}$ **33.** $\dfrac{6}{5}$ **35.** 9 **37.** $\dfrac{62}{99}$

Chapter 12 (p. 789) **1.** $\sin\theta=\dfrac{3}{5},\ \cos\theta=\dfrac{4}{5},\ \tan\theta=\dfrac{3}{4},$

$\csc\theta=\dfrac{5}{3},\ \sec\theta=\dfrac{5}{4},\ \cot\theta=\dfrac{4}{3}$ **3.** $\dfrac{20\sqrt{3}}{3}\approx11.55$ **5.** 6

7. 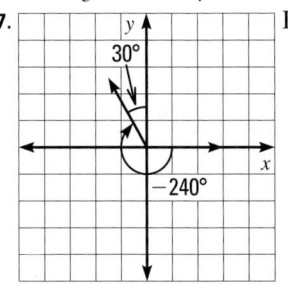 II

9. 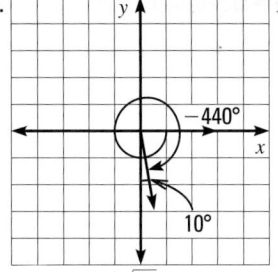 IV

11. $\sin\theta=\dfrac{5\sqrt{34}}{34},\ \cos\theta=-\dfrac{3\sqrt{34}}{34},\ \tan\theta=-\dfrac{5}{3}$

13. $\sin\theta=-\dfrac{7\sqrt{65}}{65},\ \cos\theta=\dfrac{4\sqrt{65}}{65},\ \tan\theta=-\dfrac{7}{4}$

15. 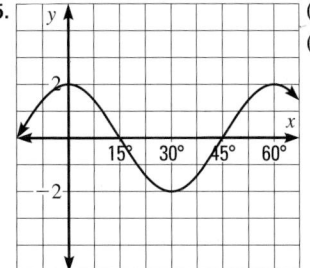 $(0°, 2), (60°, 2), (30°, -2), (15°, 0), (45°, 0)$

17. 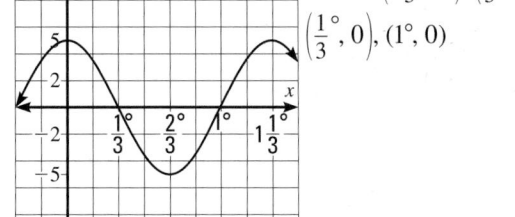 $(0°, 5),\left(1\frac{1}{3}°, 5\right),\left(\frac{2}{3}°, -5\right),$ $\left(\frac{1}{3}°, 0\right), (1°, 0)$

19. 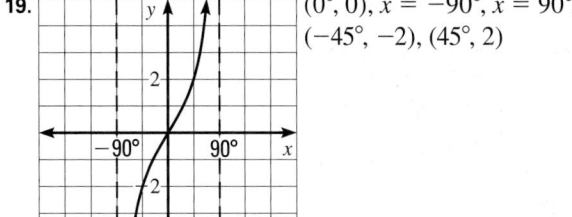 $(0°, 0), x=-90°, x=90°,$ $(-45°, -2), (45°, 2)$

21. 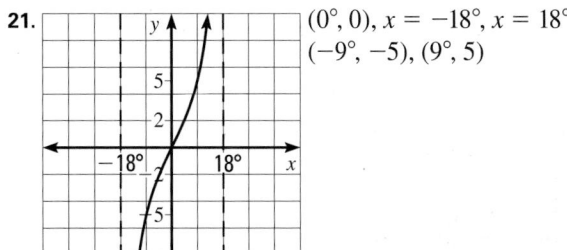 $(0°, 0), x=-18°, x=18°,$ $(-9°, -5), (9°, 5)$

23. No triangle because the height is about 8.5 and a is less than the height. **25.** 28.1 **27.** 14.2

29. 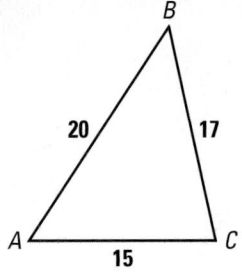 $\angle A = 55.9°, \angle B = 47.0°,$
$\angle C = 77.1°$

Chapter 13 (p. 790) **1.** $5; \left(-2, \dfrac{3}{2}\right)$ **3.** $\sqrt{73}; \left(2, -\dfrac{9}{2}\right)$

5. $y = -\dfrac{1}{2}x - \dfrac{5}{2}$ **7.** $y = -7x - 9$

9. 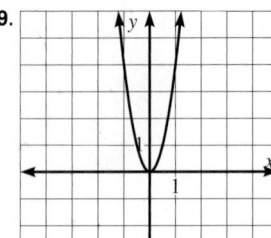 $\left(0, \dfrac{1}{16}\right), y = -\dfrac{1}{16}, x = 0$

11. 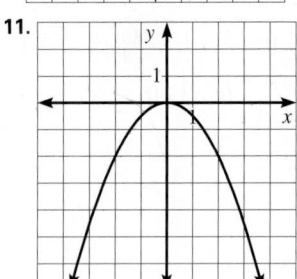 $\left(0, -\dfrac{1}{2}\right), y = \dfrac{1}{2}, x = 0$

13. 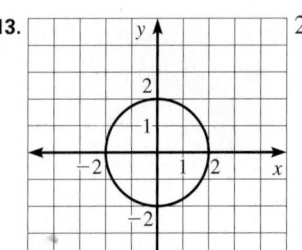 2

15. 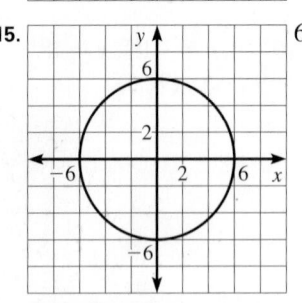 6

17. $x^2 + y^2 = 25$ **19.** $x^2 + y^2 = 32$ **21.** $y = x - 4$

23. $y = \dfrac{4}{3}x - \dfrac{25}{3}$

25. 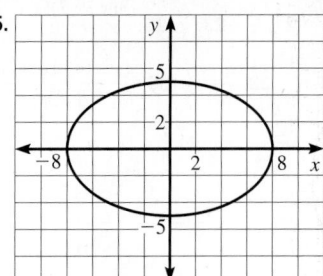 $(8, 0), (-8, 0), (0, 5),$
$(0, -5), \left(\sqrt{39}, 0\right),$
$\left(-\sqrt{39}, 0\right)$

27. 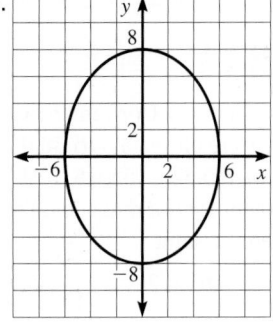 $(0, 8), (0, -8), (6, 0),$
$(-6, 0), \left(0, 2\sqrt{7}\right), \left(0, -2\sqrt{7}\right)$

29. $\dfrac{x^2}{49} + \dfrac{y^2}{25} = 1$ **31.** $\dfrac{x^2}{81} + \dfrac{y^2}{100} = 1$

33. 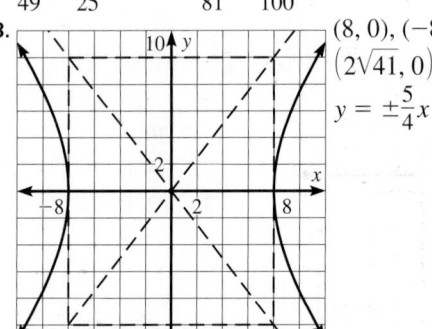 $(8, 0), (-8, 0),$
$\left(2\sqrt{41}, 0\right), \left(-2\sqrt{41}, 0\right),$
$y = \pm\dfrac{5}{4}x$

35. 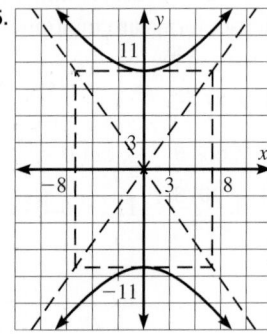 $(0, 11), (0, -11), \left(0, \sqrt{185}\right),$
$\left(0, -\sqrt{185}\right), y = \pm\dfrac{11}{8}x$

37. $\dfrac{x^2}{25} - \dfrac{y^2}{36} = 1$

39. circle, $(x - 6)^2 + (y - 6)^2 = 76$

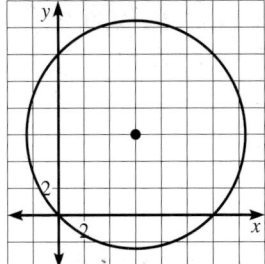

41. hyperbola, $\dfrac{(x + 2)^2}{9} - \dfrac{(y + 1)^2}{10} = 1$

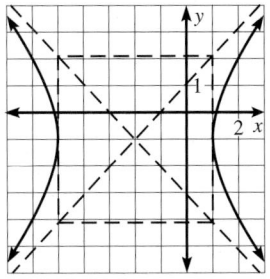

43. parabola, $(x - 2)^2 = -12\left(y + \dfrac{7}{6}\right)$

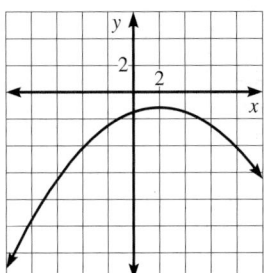